Weiss Ratings' Guide to Closed-End Mutual Funds

A Quarterly Compilation of Investment Ratings and Analyses Covering Closed-End Mutual Funds

Summer 2005

P.O. Box 689608
Jupiter, FL 33468-9608
(561) 627-3300

www.WeissRatings.com

Our customer hotline is here to serve you.
Don't hesitate to call us at

(800) 289-9222

ISSN: 1544-9327
ISBN: 1-58773-229-7

Edition No. 9, Summer 2005

Data Source: Thomson Wealth Management
1455 Research Boulevard
Rockville, MD 20850

Date of data analyzed: June 30, 2005

Contents

Terms and Conditions

Welcome to Weiss Ratings'
Guide to Closed-End Mutual Funds

With the growing popularity of mutual fund investing, consumers need a reliable source to help them track and evaluate the performance of their mutual fund holdings. Plus, they need a way of identifying and monitoring other funds as potential new investments. Unfortunately, the hundreds of performance and risk measures available – multiplied by the vast number of mutual fund investments on the market today – can make this a daunting task for even the most sophisticated investor.

The Weiss Investment Ratings simplify the evaluation process. We condense all of the available mutual fund data into a single composite opinion of each fund's risk-adjusted performance. This allows you to instantly identify those funds that have historically done well and those that have underperformed the market. While there is no guarantee of future performance, the Weiss Investment Ratings provide a solid framework for making informed investment decisions.

Weiss Ratings' Mission Statement

Weiss Ratings' mission is to empower consumers, professionals, and institutions with high quality advisory information for selecting or monitoring a financial services company or financial investment.

In doing so, Weiss Ratings will adhere to the highest ethical standards by maintaining our independent, unbiased outlook and approach to advising our customers.

Why rely on Weiss?

For more than 30 years, Weiss has been recognized as a leader in helping consumers manage their finances. To that end, we provide risk ratings evaluating the financial stability of insurance companies and banks in addition to the Weiss Investment Ratings. Our goal is to provide fair, objective information to help professionals and consumers alike make educated purchasing decisions.

At Weiss, objectivity and total independence are never compromised. We never take a penny from rated companies for issuing our ratings, and we publish them without regard for the companies' preferences. Weiss' ratings are more frequently reviewed and updated than any other ratings, so you can be sure that the information you receive is accurate and current.

Weiss' rating scale, from A to E, is easy to understand as follows:

	Rating	Description
Top 10% of closed-end mutual funds	A	Excellent
Next 20% of closed-end mutual funds	B	Good
Middle 40% of closed-end mutual funds	C	Fair
Next 20% of closed-end mutual funds	D	Weak
Bottom 10% of closed-end mutual funds	E	Very Weak

In addition, a plus or minus sign designates that a fund is in the top third or bottom third of funds with the same letter grade.

Thank you for your trust and purchase of this Guide. If you have any comments, or wish to review other products from Weiss Ratings, please call 1-800-289-9222 or visit www.WeissRatings.com. We look forward to hearing from you.

How Others View Weiss Ratings

"Correctly identified"

"Weiss' ratings…correctly identified some of the worst-performing stocks."

L.A. Times

"The first to see the danger"

"Weiss was the first to see the danger and to say so unambiguously."

The New York Times

"A glowing tribute"

"The U.S. General Accounting Office's report is a glowing tribute to Weiss"

Barron's

"Free of any possible conflict of interest"

"The only company [that] provides financial grades free of any possible conflict of interest."

Esquire

"Tougher"

"A tougher service"

Louis Rukeyser, host of CNBC's Wall Street

"So good...[you] need look no further"

"Weiss' record ... is so good compared with that of his competitors...[you] need look no further."

Worth

How to Use This Guide

The purpose of the *Guide to Closed-End Mutual Funds* is to provide investors with a reliable source of investment ratings and analyses on a timely basis. We realize that past performance is an important factor to consider when making the decision to purchase shares in a mutual fund. The ratings and analyses in this Guide can make that evaluation easier when you are considering closed-end:

- growth funds
- sector or international funds
- municipal bond funds
- corporate bond funds
- or other closed-end funds

However, this Guide does not include open-end mutual funds since they represent a whole separate class of investments with unique risk profiles and performance expectations. For information on open-end equity funds, refer to *Weiss Ratings' Guide to Stock Mutual Funds.* And if you are interested in open-end bond or money market funds, refer to *Weiss Ratings' Guide to Bond and Money Market Mutual Funds.*

The rating for a particular fund indicates our opinion regarding that fund's past risk-adjusted performance. When evaluating a specific mutual fund, we recommend you follow these steps:

Step 1 **Confirm the fund name and ticker symbol.** To ensure you evaluate the correct mutual fund, verify the fund's exact name and ticker symbol as it was given to you in its prospectus or appears on your account statement. Many funds have similar names, so you want to make sure the fund you look up is really the one you are interested in evaluating.

Step 2 **Check the fund's Weiss Investment Rating.** Turn to Section I, the Index of Closed-End Mutual Funds, and locate the fund you are evaluating. This section contains all closed-end mutual funds analyzed by Weiss including those that did not receive a Weiss Investment Rating. All funds are listed in alphabetical order by the name of the fund with the ticker symbol following the name for additional verification. Once you have located your specific fund, the first column after the ticker symbol shows its Weiss Investment Rating. Turn to *About the Weiss Investment Ratings* on page 7 for information about what this rating means.

Step 3 **Analyze the supporting data.** Following the Weiss Investment Rating are some of the various measures we have used in rating the fund. Refer to the Section I introduction (beginning on page 15) to see what each of these factors measures. In most cases, lower rated funds will have a low performance rating and/or a low risk rating (i.e., high volatility). Bear in mind, however, that the Weiss Investment Rating is the result of a complex computer-generated analysis which cannot be reproduced using only the data provided here.

When looking to identify a mutual fund that achieves your specific investing goals, we recommend the following:

Step 4 **Take our Investor Profile Quiz.** Turn to page 333 of the Appendix and take our Investor Profile Quiz to help determine your level of risk tolerance. After you have scored yourself, the last page of the quiz will refer you to the risk category in Section VII (Top-Rated Closed-End Mutual Funds by Risk Category) that is best for you. There you can choose a fund that has historically provided top-notch returns while keeping the risk at a level that is suited to your investment style.

Step 5 **View the 100 top-performing funds.** If your priority is to achieve the highest return, regardless of the amount of risk, turn to Section V which lists the top 100 closed-end mutual funds with the best financial performance. Keep in mind that past performance alone is not always a true indicator of the future since these funds have already experienced a run up in price and could be due for a correction.

Step 6 **View the 100 funds with the lowest risk.** On the other hand, if capital preservation is your top priority, turn to Section VI which lists the top 100 closed-end mutual funds with the lowest risk. These funds will have lower performance ratings than most other funds, but can provide a safe harbor for your savings.

Step 7 **View the top-rated funds by fund type.** If you are looking to invest in a particular type of mutual fund (e.g., corporate high-yield bond or emerging market), turn to Section VIII, Top-Rated Closed-End Mutual Funds by Fund Type. There you will find the top 100 closed-end mutual funds with the highest performance rating in each category. Please be careful to also consider the risk component when selecting a fund from one of these lists.

Step 8 **Refer back to Section I.** Once you have identified a particular fund that interests you, refer back to Section I, the Index of Closed-End Mutual Funds, for a more thorough analysis.

Always remember:

Step 9 **Read our warnings and cautions.** In order to use the Weiss Investment Ratings most effectively, we strongly recommend you consult the Important Warnings and Cautions listed on page 11. These are more than just "standard disclaimers." They are very important factors you should be aware of before using this Guide.

Step 10 **Stay up to date.** Periodically review the latest Weiss Investment Ratings for the funds that you own to make sure they are still in line with your investment goals and level of risk tolerance. For information on how to acquire follow-up reports on a particular mutual fund, call 1-800-289-9222 or visit www.WeissRatings.com.

About the Weiss Investment Ratings

The Weiss Investment Ratings represent a completely independent, unbiased opinion of a mutual fund's historical risk-adjusted performance. Each fund's rating is based on two primary components:

Primary Component #1

A fund's **Performance Rating** is based on its total return to shareholders over the last trailing three years, including share price appreciation and distributions to shareholders. This total return figure is stated net of the expenses and fees charged by the fund.

This adjusted return is then weighted to give more recent performance a slightly greater emphasis. Thus, two mutual funds may have provided identical returns to their shareholders over the last three years, but the one with the better performance in the last 12 months will receive a slightly higher performance rating.

Primary Component #2

The **Risk Rating** is based on the level of volatility in the fund's monthly returns, also over the last trailing three years. We use several statistical measures – standard deviation, semi-deviation and a drawdown factor – as our barometer of volatility. Funds with more volatility relative to other mutual funds are considered riskier, and thus receive a lower risk rating. By contrast, funds with very stable returns are considered less risky and receive a higher risk rating. In addition to considering the fund's volatility, the risk rating also considers the fund's discount/premium as compared to its historical average, as well as an assessment of the valuation and quality of the fund's holdings.

Note that none of the mutual funds listed in this publication have received a risk rating in the A (Excellent) range. This is because all closed-end mutual fund investments, by their very nature, involve at least some degree of risk.

Rarely will you ever find a mutual fund that has both a very high Performance Rating plus, at the same time, a very high Risk Rating. Therefore, the funds that receive the highest overall Weiss Investment Ratings are those that attain the ideal combination of both primary components. There is always a tradeoff between risk and reward. That is why we suggest you assess your own personal risk tolerance using the quiz on page 333 as a part of your decision-making process.

Keep in mind that while the Weiss Investment Ratings use the same rating scale as the Weiss Risk Ratings of financial institutions, the two ratings have totally independent meanings. The Weiss Risk Ratings assess the *future* financial stability of an insurer or bank as a way of helping investors place their money with a financially sound company and minimize the risk of loss. These ratings are derived without regard to the performance of the individual investments offered by the insurance companies, banks, or thrifts.

On the other hand, the Weiss Investment Ratings employ a ranking system to evaluate both safety and performance. Based on these measures, funds are divided into percentiles, and an individual performance rating and a risk rating are assigned to each fund. Then these measures are combined to derive a fund's composite percentile ranking. Finally, the Weiss Investment Ratings are assigned to their corresponding percentile rankings as shown on page 3.

How Our Ratings Differ From Those of Other Services

Balanced approach: The Weiss Investment Ratings are designed to meet the needs of aggressive *as well as* conservative investors. We realize that your investment goals can be different from those of other investors based upon your age, income, and tolerance for risk. Therefore, our ratings balance a fund's performance against the amount of risk it poses to identify those funds that have achieved the optimum mix of both factors. Some of these top funds have achieved excellent returns with only average risk. Others have achieved average returns with only moderate risk. Whatever your personal preferences, we can help you identify a top notch fund that meets your investing style.

Other investment rating firms give a far greater weight to performance and insufficient consideration to risk. In effect, they bet too heavily on a rising market and do not give enough consideration to the risk of a decline. While performance is obviously a very important factor to consider, we believe that the riskiness of a fund is also very important. Therefore, we weigh these two components more equally when assigning the Weiss Investment Ratings.

But we don't stop there. We also assign a separate performance rating and risk rating to each fund so you can focus on the component that is most important to you. In fact, Sections V, VI, and VII are designed specifically to help you select the best closed-end mutual funds based on these two factors. No other source gives you the cream of the crop in this manner.

Easy to use: Unlike those of other services, the Weiss Investment Ratings are extremely intuitive and easy to use. Our rating scale (A to E) is easily understood by members of the general public based on their familiarity with school grades. So, there are no stars to count and no numbering systems to interpret.

More funds: Weiss Ratings' *Guide to Closed-End Mutual Funds* tracks more closed-end mutual funds than any other publication – with updates that come out more frequently than those of other rating agencies. We've included more than 650 funds in this edition, all of which are updated every three months.

Recency: Recognizing that every fund's performance is going to have its peaks and valleys, superior long-term performance is a major consideration in the Weiss Investment Ratings. Even so, we do not give a fund a top rating solely because it did well 10 or 15 years ago. Times change and the top performing funds in the current economic environment are often very different from those of a decade ago. Thus, our ratings are designed to keep you abreast of the best funds available *today* and in the *near future,* not the distant past.

Thoroughness: One of the unique characteristics of closed-end funds is that they often trade either above (premium) or below (discount) their net asset value (NAV). Our ratings not only consider performance and risk factors of each fund, but we also evaluate the current premium or discount of each fund as compared to its historical average. This evaluation is factored into the overall rating and can help investors identify funds that may be overvalued or undervalued.

What Our Ratings Mean

A **Excellent.** The mutual fund has an excellent track record for maximizing performance while minimizing risk, thus delivering the best possible combination of total return on investment and reduced volatility. It has made the most of the recent economic environment to maximize risk-adjusted returns compared to other mutual funds. While past performance is just an indication – not a guarantee – we believe this fund is among the most likely to deliver superior performance relative to risk in the future.

B **Good.** The mutual fund has a good track record for balancing performance with risk. Compared to other mutual funds, it has achieved above-average returns given the level of risk in its underlying investments. While the risk-adjusted performance of any mutual fund is subject to change, we believe that this fund has proven to be a good investment in the recent past.

C **Fair.** In the trade-off between performance and risk, the mutual fund has a track record which is about average. It is neither significantly better nor significantly worse than most other mutual funds. With some funds in this category, the total return may be better than average, but this can be misleading since the higher return was achieved with higher than average risk. With other funds, the risk may be lower than average, but the returns are also lower. In short, based on recent history, there is no particular advantage to investing in this fund.

D **Weak.** The mutual fund has underperformed the universe of other funds given the level of risk in its underlying investments, resulting in a weak risk-adjusted performance. Thus, its investment strategy and/or management has not been attuned to capitalize on the recent economic environment. While the risk-adjusted performance of any mutual fund is subject to change, we believe that this fund has proven to be a bad investment over the recent past.

E **Very Weak.** The mutual fund has significantly underperformed most other funds given the level of risk in its underlying investments, resulting in a very weak risk-adjusted performance. Thus, its investment strategy and/or management has done just the opposite of what was needed to maximize returns in the recent economic environment. While the risk-adjusted performance of any mutual fund is subject to change, we believe this fund has proven to be a very bad investment in the recent past.

+ **The plus sign** is an indication that the fund is in the top third of its letter grade.

- **The minus sign** is an indication that the fund is in the bottom third of its letter grade.

U **Unrated.** The mutual fund is unrated because it is too new to make a reliable assessment of its risk-adjusted performance. Typically, a fund must be established for at least three years before it is eligible to receive a Weiss Investment Rating.

Important Warnings and Cautions

1. **A rating alone cannot tell the whole story.** Please read the explanatory information contained here, in the section introductions and in the appendix. It is provided in order to give you an understanding of our rating methodology as well as to paint a more complete picture of a mutual fund's strengths and weaknesses.

2. **Investment ratings shown in this Guide were current as of the publication date.** In the meantime, the rating may have been updated based on more recent data. Weiss offers a notification service for ratings changes on companies that you specify. For more information call 1-800-289-9222, visit www.WeissRatings.com or see the last section of this publication for details.

3. **When deciding to buy or sell shares in a specific mutual fund, your decision must be based on a wide variety of factors in addition to the Weiss Investment Rating**. These include any charges you may incur from switching funds, to what degree it meets your long-term planning needs, and what other choices are available to you.

4. **The Weiss Investment Ratings represent our opinion of a mutual fund's past risk-adjusted performance.** As such, a high rating means we feel that the mutual fund has performed very well for its shareholders compared to other closed-end mutual funds. A high rating is not a guarantee that a fund will continue to perform well, nor is a low rating a prediction of continued weak performance. The Weiss Investment Ratings are not deemed to be a recommendation concerning the purchase or sale of any mutual fund.

5. **A mutual fund's individual performance is not the only factor in determining its rating.** Since the Weiss Investment Ratings are based on performance relative to other funds, it is possible for a fund's rating to be upgraded or downgraded based strictly on the improved or deteriorated performance of other funds.

6. **All funds that have the same Weiss Investment Rating should be considered to be essentially equal from a risk/reward perspective.** This is true regardless of any differences in the underlying numbers which might appear to indicate greater strengths.

7. **Our rating standards are more consumer-oriented than those used by other rating agencies.** We make more conservative assumptions as we attempt to identify those funds that have historically provided superior returns with only little or moderate risk.

8. **We are an independent rating agency and do not depend on the cooperation of the managers operating the mutual funds we rate**. Our data are derived, for the most part, from price quotes obtained and documented on the open market. This is supplemented by information collected from the mutual fund prospectuses and regulatory filings. Although we seek to maintain an open line of communication with the mutual fund managers, we do not grant them the right to stop or influence publication of the ratings. This policy stems from the fact that this Guide is designed for the information of the consumer.

9. **The ratios and ratings contained in this edition of the *Guide to Closed-End Mutual Funds* reflect updates to previous editions**. Therefore, comparisons of ratios or ratings between this edition and previous editions may not be appropriate.

10. **This Guide does not cover open-end funds.** Because open-end funds represent a whole separate class of investments with unique risk profiles and performance expectations, they are available in separate publications. Please see our *Guide to Stock Mutual Funds* and our *Guide to Bond and Money Market Mutual Funds* for our analyses of open-end mutual funds.

Section I

Index of Closed-End Mutual Funds

An analysis of all rated and unrated

Closed-End Mutual Funds.

Funds are listed in alphabetical order.

Section I Contents

Left Pages

1. Fund Type The mutual fund's peer category based on an analysis of its investment portfolio.

COH	Corporate – High Yield	HL	Health
COI	Corporate – Inv. Grade	IN	Income
EM	Emerging Market	LP	Loan Participation
EN	Energy/Natural Resources	MTG	Mortgage
FS	Financial Services	MUH	Municipal – High Yield
FO	Foreign	MUN	Municipal – National
GEI	General – Inv. Grade	MUS	Municipal – Single State
GEN	General Bond	PM	Precious Metals
GL	Global	USA	U.S. Gov. – Agency
GR	Growth	UT	Utilities
GI	Growth and Income		

A blank fund type means that the mutual fund has not yet been categorized.

2. Fund Name The name of the mutual fund as stated in its prospectus, which can sometimes differ slightly from the name that the company uses for advertising. If you cannot find the particular mutual fund you are interested in, or if you have any doubts regarding the precise name, verify the information with your broker or on your account statement. Also, use the fund's ticker symbol for confirmation. (See column 3.)

3. Ticker Symbol The unique alphabetic symbol used for identifying and trading a specific mutual fund. No two funds can have the same ticker symbol.

A handful of funds currently show no associated ticker symbol. This means that the fund is either small or new since the NASD only assigns a ticker symbol to funds with at least $25 million in assets or 1,000 shareholders.

4. Overall Weiss Investment Rating Our overall rating is measured on a scale from A to E based on each fund's risk-adjusted performance. Please see page 10 for specific descriptions of each letter grade. Also, refer to page 7 for information on how our ratings are derived. Most important, when using this rating, please be sure to consider the warnings beginning on page 11 regarding the ratings' limitations and the underlying assumptions.

5. **Price** Closing price of the fund on the date shown.

6. **52-Week High** Highest price at which the fund has traded in the last 52 weeks.

7. **52-Week Low** Lowest price at which the fund has traded in the last 52 weeks.

8. **Performance Rating/Points** A letter grade rating based solely on the mutual fund's financial performance over the trailing three years, without any consideration for the amount of risk the fund poses. Like the overall Weiss Investment Rating, the Performance Rating is measured on a scale from A to E for ease of interpretation. The points score indicates where the Performance Rating falls on a scale of 0 to 10.

9. **3-Month Total Return** The total return the fund has provided to investors over the preceding 13 weeks. This total return figure is computed based on the fund's dividend distributions and share price appreciation/depreciation during the period, net of the expenses and fees it imposes on its shareholders. The 3-Month Total Return shown here is not annualized.

10. **6-Month Total Return** The total return the fund has provided investors over the preceding 26 weeks, not annualized.

11. **1-Year Total Return** The total return the fund has provided investors over the preceding 52 weeks.

12. **1-Year Total Return Percentile** The fund's percentile rank based on its one-year performance compared to that of all other closed-end funds in existence for at least one year. A score of 99 is the best possible, indicating that the fund outperformed 99% of the closed-end mutual funds. Zero is the worst possible percentile score.

13. **3-Year Total Return** The total annual return the fund has provided investors over the preceding 156 weeks.

14. **3-Year Total Return Percentile** The fund's percentile rank based on its three-year performance compared to that of all other closed-end funds in existence for at least three years. A score of 99 is the best possible, indicating that the fund outperformed 99% of the closed-end mutual funds. Zero is the worst possible percentile score.

15. **5-Year Total Return** The total annual return the fund has provided investors over the preceding 260 weeks.

16. **5-Year Total Return Percentile** The fund's percentile rank based on its five-year performance compared to that of all other closed-end funds in existence for at least five years. A score of 99 is the best possible, indicating that the fund outperformed 99% of the closed-end mutual funds. Zero is the worst possible percentile score.

Right Pages

1. Dividend Yield Most recent quarterly dividend to fund investors annualized, expressed as a percent of the fund's current share price. The dividend yield of a fund can have little correlation to the amount of dividends the fund has received from its underlying investments. Rather, dividend distributions are based on a fund's need to pass earnings from both dividends and gains on the sale of investments along to shareholders. Thus, these dividend distributions are included as a part of the fund's total return.

Keep in mind that dividend income may be taxed at a different rate than capital gains depending on your income tax bracket.

2. Expense Ratio The expense ratio is taken directly from each fund's annual report with no further calculation. It indicates the percentage of the fund's assets that are deducted each fiscal year to cover its expenses, although for practical purposes, it is actually accrued daily. Typical fund expenses include management fees and other costs incurred by the fund. Brokerage costs incurred by the fund to buy or sell shares of the underlying securities are not included in the expense ratio.

If a mutual fund's net assets are small, its expense ratio can be quite high because the fund must cover its expenses from a smaller asset base. Conversely, as the net assets of the fund grow, the expense percentage should ideally diminish since the expenses are being spread across a larger asset base.

Funds with higher expense ratios are generally less attractive since the expense ratio represents a hurdle that must be met before the investment becomes profitable to its shareholders. Since a fund's expenses affect its total return though, they are already factored into its Weiss Investment Rating.

3. Risk Rating/Points A letter grade rating based solely on the mutual fund's risk as determined by its monthly performance volatility over the trailing three years. The risk rating does not take into consideration the overall financial performance the fund has achieved or the total return it has provided to its shareholders. Like the overall Weiss Investment Rating, the Risk Rating is measured on a scale from A to E for ease of interpretation. The points score indicates where the Risk Rating falls on a scale of 0 to 10.

4. Standard Deviation

A statistical measure of the amount of volatility in a fund's monthly performance over the last trailing 36 months. In absolute terms, standard deviation provides a historical measure of a fund's deviation from its mean, or average, monthly total return over the period.

A high standard deviation indicates a high degree of volatility in the past, which usually means you should expect to see a high degree of volatility in the future as well. This translates into higher risk since a large negative swing could easily become a sizable loss in the event you need to liquidate your shares.

5. Beta

The level of correlation between the fund's monthly performance over the last trailing 36 months and the performance of its investment category as a whole.

A beta of 1.00 means that the fund's returns have matched those of the index one for one during the stock market's ups and downs. A beta of 1.10 means that on average the fund has outperformed the index by 10% during rising markets and underperformed it by 10% during falling markets. Conversely, a beta of 0.85 means that the fund has typically performed 15% worse than the overall market during up markets and 15% better during down markets.

6. Average Duration

Expressed in years, duration is a measure of a bond fund's sensitivity to interest rate fluctuations, or its level of interest rate risk.

The longer a fund's duration, the more sensitive the fund is to shifts in interest rates. For example, a fund with a duration of eight years is twice as sensitive to a change in rates as a fund with a four year duration.

7. NAV

The fund's net asset value (NAV) as of the date indicated. A fund's NAV is computed by dividing the value of the fund's asset holdings, less accrued fees and expenses, by the number of its shares outstanding.

Because a closed-end fund's shares trade on an exchange and the price is based on investor demand, the fund may trade at a price higher or lower than its NAV.

8. Net Assets

The total value (stated in millions of dollars) of all of the fund's asset holdings including stocks, bonds, cash, and other financial instruments, less accrued expenses and fees.

Larger funds have the advantage of being able to spread their expenses over a greater asset base so that the effect per share is lessened. On the other hand, if a fund becomes too large, it can be more difficult for the fund manager to buy and sell investments for the benefit of shareholders.

9. Premium/ Discount

A comparison of the fund's price to its NAV as of the date indicated. The premium (+) or discount (-) indicates the percentage the shares are trading above or below the fund's NAV per share.

If the price is above the fund's NAV, the fund is said to be trading at a premium. If the price is lower than the fund's NAV, the fund is trading at a discount.

10. 1-Year Average Premium/ Discount

The average of the fund's premium/discount over the preceding year.

It can be useful to compare the fund's current premium/discount to its one-year average. If the fund is currently trading at a premium/discount that is lower/higher than its one-year average, then there has been less demand for the fund in more recent times than over the past year. Conversely, if the fund is currently trading at a premium/discount that is higher/lower than its one-year average, this indicates that there has been greater demand for the fund in more recent times than over the past year.

11. Weighted Average Price-to-Earnings

The average of the price-to-earnings (P/E) ratios for the equity securities of the fund, where larger holdings are weighted more heavily than smaller holdings. A high P/E multiple indicates that investors have high expectations for future growth of the securities of that fund.

Compare this number to that of funds of the same type to get a feel for whether the equity securities of the fund might be overvalued or undervalued.

12. Cash %

The percentage of the fund's assets held in cash or money market funds as of the last reporting period. Investments in this area will tend to hamper the fund's returns while adding to its stability during market swings.

13. Stocks %

The percentage of the fund's assets held in common or preferred stocks as of the last reporting period. Since stocks are inherently riskier investments than the other categories, it is common for funds invested primarily or exclusively in stocks to receive a lower risk rating.

14. Bonds %

The percentage of the fund's assets held in bonds as of the last reporting period. This category includes corporate bonds, municipal bonds, and government bonds such as T-bills and T-bonds.

15. Other %

The percentage of the fund's assets invested as of the last reporting period in other types of financial instruments such as convertible securities, options, and warrants.

16. Portfolio Turnover Ratio

The average annual portion of the fund's holdings that have been moved from one specific investment to another over the past three years. This indicates the amount of buying and selling the fund manager engages in. A portfolio turnover ratio of 100% signifies that on average, the entire value of the fund's assets is turned over once during the course of a year.

A high portfolio turnover ratio has implications for shareholders since the fund is required to pass all realized earnings along to shareholders each year. Thus a high portfolio turnover ratio will result in higher annual distributions for shareholders, effectively increasing their annual taxable income. In contrast, a low turnover ratio means a higher level of unrealized gains that will not be taxable until you sell your shares in the fund.

17. Manager Quality Percentile

The manager quality percentile is based on a ranking of the fund's alpha, a statistical measure representing the difference between a fund's actual returns and its expected performance given its level of risk. Fund managers who have been able to exceed the fund's statistically expected performance receive a high percentile rank with 99 representing the highest possible score. At the other end of the spectrum, fund managers who have actually detracted from the fund's expected performance receive a low percentile rank with 0 representing the lowest possible score.

18. Manager Tenure

The number of years the current manager has been managing the fund. Since fund managers who deliver substandard returns are usually replaced, a long tenure is usually a good sign that shareholders are satisfied that the fund is achieving its stated objectives.

Fund Type	Fund Name (99 Pct = Best, 0 Pct = Worst)	Ticker Symbol	Overall Weiss Investment Rating	PRICE: Price As of 6/30/05	PRICE: 52 Week High	PRICE: 52 Week Low	PERFORMANCE: Performance Rating/Pts	% Total Return Through 6/30/05: 3 Mo	6 Mo	1Yr/Pct	Annualized: 3Yr/Pct	Annualized: 5Yr/Pct
COI	1838 Bond Debenture Fund	BDF	**D**	18.74	19.35	17.36	**D / 1.7**	3.45	3.28	14.36 / 35	5.88 / 12	8.95 / 34
COH	40/86 Strategic Income Fund	CFD	**B**	10.16	10.58	9.41	**B- / 7.5**	7.81	1.19	15.27 / 38	19.85 / 88	10.39 / 44
GL	Aberdeen Asia-Pacific Income Fund	FAX	**C**	6.35	8.00	5.65	**C+ / 6.9**	3.50	1.74	19.05 / 47	18.33 / 85	16.92 / 83
GL	Aberdeen Australia Equity Fund	IAF	**C+**	12.20	13.58	8.20	**A+ / 9.6**	0.81	10.55	51.75 / 99	31.89 / 97	20.13 / 93
GL	Aberdeen Global Income Fund	FCO	**C**	13.76	15.70	11.72	**C / 5.5**	1.32	-5.25	21.35 / 53	16.34 / 78	16.65 / 81
USA	ACM Government Opportunity Fund	AOF	**D-**	7.89	8.98	7.42	**E+ / 0.6**	6.23	4.07	4.51 / 11	3.98 / 5	11.13 / 47
USA	ACM Income Fund	ACG	**C-**	8.29	8.45	7.82	**C / 4.4**	4.87	6.01	15.12 / 38	12.16 / 58	15.30 / 72
GL	ACM Managed Dollar Income Fund	ADF	**C**	7.80	8.34	7.26	**C+ / 5.9**	7.90	4.20	6.13 / 13	16.77 / 79	10.55 / 45
GEN	ACM Managed Income Fund	AMF	**E+**	3.67	4.39	3.42	**E+ / 0.6**	7.81	-1.55	-4.63 / 3	5.77 / 12	0.45 / 13
MUN	ACM Municipal Securities Income Fd	AMU	**D**	10.73	12.47	9.95	**D- / 1.0**	6.95	7.24	3.13 / 11	2.83 / 6	5.95 / 36
IN	Adams Express Company	ADX	**D+**	12.91	13.99	12.07	**D / 1.8**	0.77	-0.77	8.64 / 20	8.51 / 26	-5.05 / 6
GI	Advent Claymore Convertible&Income	AVK	**U**	24.17	26.99	22.39	**U /**	5.09	-3.78	9.77 / 24	--	--
GL	Advent Claymore Enhanced Gr & Inc	LCM	**U**	17.51	N/A	N/A	**U /**	-1.55	--	--	--	--
GI	AEW Real Estate Income Fund	RIF	**U**	18.63	19.25	15.99	**U /**	7.34	3.53	25.14 / 62	--	--
GI	AIM Select Real Estate Income Fund	RRE	**C+**	16.84	17.78	14.80	**C+ / 6.1**	12.24	2.15	23.32 / 58	13.59 / 65	--
GR	Alliance All-Market Advantage Fd	AMO	**E+**	14.49	15.38	13.00	**E+ / 0.7**	4.04	0.70	5.74 / 13	4.49 / 7	-8.56 / 3
MUS	Alliance CA Municipal Income Fund	AKP	**A+**	14.87	15.15	12.82	**B / 8.1**	8.99	9.72	21.46 / 81	9.61 / 72	--
MUN	Alliance Nat Municipal Income Fund	AFB	**A+**	14.90	14.99	12.96	**B+ / 8.5**	7.87	11.84	22.30 / 84	10.26 / 76	--
MUS	Alliance NY Municipal Income Fund	AYN	**A-**	14.85	14.88	12.63	**B+ / 8.6**	11.36	12.61	24.47 / 90	9.44 / 71	--
GL	Alliance World Dollar Govt Fund	AWG	**C**	12.39	13.10	10.80	**C+ / 5.8**	9.70	2.20	21.56 / 53	13.61 / 66	13.98 / 65
GL	Alliance World Dollar Govt Fund II	AWF	**B-**	12.29	12.86	10.94	**B- / 7.5**	8.40	3.76	19.98 / 50	18.93 / 86	16.59 / 80
GEN	Allmerica Securities Trust	ALM	**C-**	9.42	9.74	8.70	**D- / 1.5**	5.50	3.74	13.07 / 31	4.99 / 8	6.29 / 26
MTG	American Income Fund	MRF	**C-**	8.28	8.60	7.78	**D / 1.7**	5.92	1.80	8.70 / 21	6.77 / 16	9.64 / 39
MUN	American Municipal Income Portfolio	XAA	**B-**	14.82	15.15	13.31	**C+ / 6.7**	6.03	7.48	16.50 / 63	8.60 / 64	11.29 / 85
MTG	American Select Portfolio	SLA	**D**	11.88	13.78	11.55	**E- / 0.2**	2.46	-3.09	2.99 / 9	2.81 / 4	9.58 / 39
MTG	American Strat Inc Portfolio	ASP	**D**	11.40	12.95	11.14	**E / 0.4**	1.72	-2.10	0.41 / 6	4.58 / 7	9.19 / 36
MTG	American Strat Inc Portfolio II	BSP	**D**	11.64	13.25	11.11	**E / 0.3**	3.32	-1.19	-0.84 / 5	3.61 / 5	10.21 / 43
MTG	American Strat Inc Portfolio III	CSP	**D+**	11.34	12.75	10.88	**E+ / 0.7**	1.83	-2.24	5.52 / 12	5.57 / 11	10.67 / 46
MUN	Apex Municipal Fund	APX	**A+**	9.36	9.44	8.20	**B+ / 8.6**	8.92	9.32	21.50 / 81	10.92 / 80	7.95 / 55
PM	ASA Limited	ASA	**E-**	38.59	45.81	33.15	**D / 1.8**	0.05	-4.83	8.40 / 20	8.77 / 28	22.47 / 97
FO	Asia Pacific Fund	APB	**C-**	15.21	16.22	11.58	**C+ / 6.2**	1.74	4.79	29.18 / 73	14.25 / 69	9.95 / 41
FO	Asia Tigers Fund	GRR	**C+**	12.19	12.79	9.00	**B / 7.6**	4.64	6.84	31.78 / 79	17.04 / 80	7.22 / 28
GI	Bancroft Convertible Fund	BCV	**D**	17.32	19.11	16.88	**E- / 0.0**	-1.21	-5.49	-2.20 / 5	0.65 / 1	2.79 / 16
MTG	BlackRock Advantage Term Trust	BAT	**D**	10.26	11.10	10.18	**E- / 0.2**	1.27	1.52	1.64 / 7	2.64 / 3	9.38 / 38
GEI	BlackRock Broad Inv Gr 2009 Tm Tr	BCT	**C-**	15.81	16.38	15.15	**D / 1.6**	2.72	2.72	9.13 / 22	7.10 / 18	13.19 / 60
MUS	BlackRock CA Insured Muni 2008 Term	BFC	**C**	16.06	16.72	15.64	**D+ / 2.5**	2.75	1.09	6.45 / 24	6.01 / 33	7.78 / 53
MUS	BlackRock CA Insured Muni Inc III	BCK	**U**	15.15	15.35	12.63	**U /**	10.82	15.32	25.56 / 92	--	--
MUS	BlackRock CA Inv Qual Muni Tr	RAA	**D**	14.26	14.95	12.70	**D+ / 2.8**	3.37	3.17	17.87 / 68	3.54 / 10	7.36 / 50
MUS	BlackRock CA Muni 2018 Income Trust	BJZ	**A-**	14.99	15.08	13.13	**B- / 7.4**	7.49	12.92	17.26 / 65	8.83 / 65	--
MUS	BlackRock CA Muni Bond Trust	BZA	**B+**	14.92	15.00	12.81	**B- / 7.4**	10.28	8.71	23.34 / 87	7.46 / 51	--
MUS	BlackRock CA Municipal Income Tr II	BCL	**U**	14.16	14.84	12.51	**U /**	5.26	4.70	20.14 / 77	--	--
MUS	BlackRock CA Municipal Income Trust	BFZ	**A**	14.55	14.68	12.50	**B+ / 8.4**	9.26	11.88	22.97 / 86	9.62 / 72	--
GEI	BlackRock Core Bond Trust	BHK	**C+**	14.32	14.37	12.92	**C+ / 5.6**	10.81	10.43	21.19 / 52	11.45 / 50	--
IN	BlackRock Dividend Achievers Trust	BDV	**U**	13.81	15.20	13.37	**U /**	-0.12	-3.69	4.58 / 11	--	--
MUS	BlackRock FL Insured Muni 2008 Term	BRF	**C-**	15.46	16.07	15.20	**D / 1.9**	0.96	1.33	6.05 / 23	5.33 / 23	6.22 / 39
MUS	BlackRock FL Insured Muni Inc III	BAF	**U**	14.99	15.40	12.42	**U /**	12.82	9.08	27.56 / 96	--	--
MUS	BlackRock FL Inv Qual Muni Tr	RFA	**B**	15.38	16.00	13.17	**B / 7.8**	9.20	13.18	24.21 / 89	7.54 / 52	10.15 / 75
MUS	BlackRock FL Muni 2020 Term Tr	BFO	**U**	14.37	16.25	13.83	**U /**	-2.88	-2.49	10.55 / 40	--	--
MUS	BlackRock FL Muni Bond Trust	BIE	**A-**	15.62	16.40	13.05	**B / 7.9**	8.60	9.03	25.96 / 93	8.10 / 59	--
MUS	BlackRock FL Municipal Income Trust	BBF	**B+**	15.29	15.30	12.76	**B / 7.8**	10.64	6.67	26.78 / 95	7.72 / 55	--
EN	Blackrock Global Energy&Resources	BGR	**U**	24.31	N/A	N/A	**U /**	5.26	--	--	--	--
LP	BlackRock Global Floating Rt Income	BGT	**U**	17.51	N/A	N/A	**U /**	-2.89	-2.12	--	--	--

N/A denotes number is not available

		RISK				NET ASSETS		VALUATION			ASSET					FUND MANAGER	
Incl. in Returns			3 Year					Premium / Discount									
Dividend Yield %	Expense Ratio	Risk Rating/ Pts	Standard Deviation	Beta	Avg Dura-tion	NAV as of 6/30/05	Total $(Mil)	As of 6/30/05	1 Year Average	Wtd Avg P/E	Cash %	Stocks %	Bonds %	Other %	Portfolio Turnover Ratio	Manager Quality Pct	Manager Tenure (Years)
6.05	0.89	C+ / 6.7	12.0	1.60	13.5	21.07	101	-11.06	-10.88	N/A	2	0	97	1	7	16	25
10.02	2.67	C+ / 6.0	18.3	2.27	5.5	11.25	80	-9.69	-10.31	N/A	0	0	100	0	92	4	7
6.67	1.19	C- / 4.2	19.0	1.42	N/A	6.66	1,775	-4.65	-3.03	N/A	0	0	100	0	5	75	19
8.55	1.47	D+ / 2.8	20.9	0.97	N/A	11.71	189	4.18	-2.98	N/A	1	98	0	1	12	97	20
5.37	1.70	C+ / 5.7	19.5	1.45	5.7	14.17	133	-2.89	-0.39	N/A	0	0	100	0	18	61	13
5.90	1.74	B- / 7.2	11.6	0.82	7.7	8.60	112	-8.26	-5.93	N/A	2	0	97	1	23	20	17
7.28	1.66	C+ / 5.8	13.8	0.86	N/A	8.35	1,888	-0.72	0.42	N/A	3	0	96	1	139	76	18
7.93	1.48	C+ / 5.7	19.3	0.70	7.0	8.15	179	-4.29	-1.26	N/A	0	0	99	1	33	88	12
5.83	1.98	C / 5.2	15.6	2.27	9.5	4.18	106	-12.20	-6.00	N/A	1	0	98	1	38	14	17
5.89	1.55	B- / 7.2	13.4	2.12	12.9	11.62	128	-7.66	-1.62	N/A	0	0	100	0	8	6	12
1.55	0.43	B- / 7.0	15.3	1.00	N/A	15.01	1,296	-13.99	-12.92	23.6	2	97	0	1	13	63	19
8.50	1.08	U /	N/A	N/A	4.2	25.63	577	-5.70	-4.15	11.0	3	0	30	67	29	N/A	2
5.49	1.26	U /	N/A	N/A	N/A	18.53	244	-5.50	N/A	N/A	4	39	28	29	53	N/A	0
7.34	1.23	U /	N/A	N/A	N/A	22.05	77	-15.51	-13.37	N/A	0	100	0	0	8	N/A	3
7.26	0.93	C+ / 5.8	17.6	0.42	N/A	19.90	799	-15.38	-13.62	57.2	0	74	0	26	19	90	3
8.94	1.78	C / 4.7	19.6	1.04	N/A	13.42	46	7.97	8.86	39.5	0	100	0	0	121	20	11
5.87	0.99	B- / 7.8	9.9	1.61	13.4	15.61	132	-4.74	-6.59	N/A	0	0	100	0	3	70	3
6.09	0.95	B- / 7.6	9.5	1.76	13.6	15.85	321	-5.99	-8.51	N/A	0	0	100	0	11	69	3
5.61	1.17	C+ / 6.4	12.0	2.02	N/A	15.52	74	-4.32	-7.89	N/A	0	0	100	0	6	57	3
6.08	1.59	C / 5.5	16.1	0.91	7.7	14.12	121	-12.25	-11.51	N/A	14	0	85	1	198	77	13
7.20	1.30	C+ / 5.8	15.7	0.88	8.9	14.09	917	-12.78	-11.59	N/A	7	0	92	1	147	89	12
5.79	0.76	B / 8.0	9.2	1.54	7.2	10.53	91	-10.54	-11.75	N/A	0	0	100	0	32	29	11
6.60	1.53	B / 8.4	7.9	1.95	N/A	8.99	84	-7.90	-7.96	N/A	1	0	99	0	92	48	5
6.10	1.23	B- / 7.8	11.9	1.83	11.8	15.88	91	-6.68	-7.07	N/A	0	0	100	0	36	52	12
7.02	1.87	B / 8.1	10.9	2.08	N/A	13.10	140	-9.31	-3.70	N/A	4	0	96	0	13	15	12
6.83	1.45	B- / 7.5	11.0	2.33	N/A	12.48	54	-8.65	-3.59	N/A	11	0	74	15	26	19	13
8.22	1.72	B- / 7.7	10.0	2.18	N/A	12.34	202	-5.67	-1.74	N/A	6	0	88	6	14	17	13
8.58	1.80	B / 8.2	9.7	2.01	N/A	12.04	260	-5.81	-1.38	N/A	1	0	93	6	22	33	12
6.08	0.80	B- / 7.6	8.3	1.35	12.4	9.80	187	-4.49	-6.68	N/A	2	0	97	1	14	78	7
1.55	1.03	E- / 0.0	33.3	1.47	N/A	43.43	480	-11.14	-12.48	N/A	1	0	0	99	2	14	17
0.98	2.01	C- / 4.2	25.5	1.05	N/A	17.01	172	-10.58	-10.74	N/A	0	100	0	0	73	69	1
0.00	2.04	C / 4.4	21.7	0.91	N/A	13.03	79	-6.45	-7.75	N/A	0	100	0	0	20	81	12
3.89	1.20	B / 8.3	14.0	0.49	7.5	20.40	111	-15.10	-11.94	N/A	12	0	0	88	38	25	19
5.85	1.29	B / 8.3	3.5	0.51	N/A	10.33	100	-0.68	-0.76	N/A	0	0	100	0	20	58	15
5.70	2.71	B / 8.1	6.3	1.11	N/A	15.20	45	4.01	1.56	N/A	0	0	100	0	168	66	12
4.78	1.05	B / 8.7	7.3	1.17	5.5	16.45	174	-2.37	-2.57	N/A	0	0	100	0	N/A	59	13
5.82	0.98	U /	N/A	N/A	N/A	15.14	78	0.07	-2.74	N/A	0	0	100	0	3	N/A	3
5.94	1.35	C+ / 5.7	12.8	1.95	N/A	14.53	15	-1.86	-3.03	N/A	0	0	100	0	3	9	12
4.92	1.01	B- / 7.6	10.3	1.55	N/A	15.32	98	-2.15	-5.03	N/A	0	0	100	0	9	64	4
6.38	1.03	B- / 7.3	11.2	1.90	N/A	15.97	53	-6.57	-6.56	N/A	0	0	100	0	6	42	3
6.90	1.02	U /	N/A	N/A	13.4	15.22	118	-6.96	-2.26	N/A	0	0	100	0	7	N/A	3
6.19	0.86	B- / 7.1	11.9	2.02	N/A	15.41	229	-5.58	-7.79	N/A	0	0	100	0	11	59	4
7.35	1.24	B- / 7.2	11.0	2.03	9.4	15.09	400	-5.10	-8.09	N/A	0	0	100	0	149	67	4
6.47	0.84	U /	N/A	N/A	N/A	14.58	798	-5.28	-1.00	19.7	0	99	0	1	24	N/A	2
4.85	1.07	B / 8.5	7.6	1.25	4.6	15.52	139	-0.39	-0.60	N/A	0	0	100	0	N/A	49	13
5.87	0.91	U /	N/A	N/A	N/A	15.16	130	-1.12	-2.38	N/A	0	0	100	0	N/A	N/A	3
5.59	1.28	C+ / 5.7	13.1	0.99	N/A	14.77	17	4.13	-3.36	N/A	0	0	100	0	3	72	12
5.67	1.21	U /	N/A	N/A	11.3	15.04	81	-4.45	2.42	N/A	0	0	100	0	9	N/A	2
5.88	1.01	B- / 7.1	11.5	1.80	13.9	16.23	53	-3.76	-6.55	N/A	0	0	100	0	N/A	57	3
5.95	0.91	B- / 7.0	12.2	2.05	13.9	15.73	104	-2.80	-6.57	N/A	0	0	100	0	N/A	33	4
6.12	1.29	U /	N/A	N/A	N/A	26.08	720	-6.79	N/A	N/A	43	56	0	1	13	N/A	N/A
5.69	1.26	U /	N/A	N/A	N/A	19.25	451	-9.04	N/A	N/A	0	0	100	0	11	N/A	1

N/A denotes number is not available

99 Pct = Best
0 Pct = Worst

Fund Type	Fund Name	Ticker Symbol	Overall Weiss Investment Rating	PRICE: Price As of 6/30/05	PRICE: 52 Week High	PRICE: 52 Week Low	PERFORMANCE: Performance Rating/Pts	% Total Return Through 6/30/05: 3 Mo	6 Mo	1Yr/Pct	Annualized: 3Yr/Pct	Annualized: 5Yr/Pct
HL	Blackrock Health Sciences Trust	BME	**U**	24.40	N/A	N/A	**U** /	--	--	--	--	--
COH	Blackrock High Income Shares	HIS	**C-**	2.84	3.24	2.47	**C+ / 6.3**	8.76	2.30	22.34 / 55	14.92 / 73	-1.37 / 10
COH	BlackRock High Yield Trust	BHY	**D-**	9.40	10.35	8.92	**D+ / 2.9**	4.32	3.54	10.97 / 26	10.13 / 38	6.60 / 27
GL	BlackRock Income Opportunity Trust	BNA	**C+**	11.25	11.42	10.42	**C / 4.6**	8.15	8.17	18.77 / 46	10.80 / 45	11.97 / 52
MTG	BlackRock Income Trust	BKT	**E+**	6.70	7.70	6.39	**E / 0.4**	-2.97	-1.67	6.60 / 15	4.95 / 8	10.70 / 46
MUN	BlackRock Insured Muni 2008 Tm Tr	BRM	**C**	16.10	16.61	15.73	**D+ / 2.3**	3.17	1.90	5.99 / 22	5.54 / 26	8.51 / 59
MUN	BlackRock Insured Muni Tm Tr	BMT	**C+**	11.17	11.80	10.60	**C / 4.3**	5.88	1.57	10.26 / 39	7.45 / 51	8.31 / 58
MUN	BlackRock Investment Qual Muni Tr	BKN	**A+**	16.61	16.61	13.64	**A+ / 9.6**	13.03	14.92	28.68 / 97	13.47 / 90	12.60 / 92
COH	BlackRock Limited Duration Income	BLW	**U**	18.22	20.42	17.50	**U** /	1.64	-4.94	7.13 / 16	--	--
MUS	BlackRock MD Muni Bond Trust	BZM	**B**	16.69	16.85	13.83	**B+ / 8.7**	10.72	10.04	26.28 / 94	9.81 / 73	--
MUN	BlackRock Muni 2020 Term Trust	BKK	**U**	14.70	15.83	13.75	**U** /	-0.41	0.34	11.86 / 45	--	--
MUN	BlackRock Muni Target Tm Tr	BMN	**C-**	10.18	10.87	10.13	**E / 0.5**	1.38	0.77	-1.13 / 5	3.38 / 9	5.70 / 34
MUN	BlackRock Municipal 2018 Income Tr	BPK	**A+**	15.70	15.84	13.99	**B / 8.0**	6.93	7.38	17.99 / 69	10.98 / 80	--
MUN	BlackRock Municipal Bond Trust	BBK	**A+**	16.09	16.37	13.30	**A / 9.5**	15.09	12.44	28.64 / 97	12.44 / 87	--
MUN	BlackRock Municipal Income Trust	BFK	**A**	15.15	15.24	12.55	**A- / 9.2**	10.80	10.60	28.30 / 96	11.60 / 84	--
MUN	BlackRock Municipal Income Trust II	BLE	**U**	15.15	15.25	12.80	**U** /	11.98	9.56	25.95 / 93	--	--
MUN	BlackRock Nat Insured Muni Inc III	BYM	**U**	15.19	15.28	12.85	**U** /	12.71	11.77	24.74 / 91	--	--
MUS	BlackRock NJ Inv Qual Muni Tr	RNJ	**B+**	15.56	15.70	13.15	**B+ / 8.6**	13.33	12.81	25.00 / 92	8.71 / 64	10.64 / 80
MUS	BlackRock NJ Muni Bond Trust	BLJ	**A**	15.55	16.14	12.82	**B+ / 8.7**	12.00	11.19	27.66 / 96	8.99 / 67	--
MUS	BlackRock NJ Municipal Income Trust	BNJ	**A**	15.39	15.44	13.22	**B / 8.1**	10.10	12.12	21.66 / 81	8.85 / 66	--
MUS	BlackRock NY Ins Muni Inc Trust III	BSE	**U**	15.10	15.40	12.77	**U** /	10.14	12.37	24.40 / 90	--	--
MUS	BlackRock NY Insured Muni 2008 Term	BLN	**C-**	15.83	16.37	15.30	**D / 2.0**	3.28	1.02	4.98 / 17	5.32 / 23	6.96 / 46
MUS	BlackRock NY Inv Qual Muni Tr	RNY	**B-**	14.79	14.90	13.02	**C+ / 6.2**	8.79	7.30	19.92 / 76	6.58 / 38	9.39 / 68
MUS	BlackRock NY Muni 2018 Income Trust	BLH	**B**	15.29	15.45	14.07	**C+ / 6.5**	4.93	4.44	13.88 / 53	9.75 / 73	--
MUS	BlackRock NY Muni Bond Trust	BQH	**A+**	15.21	15.27	12.94	**B+ / 8.9**	10.53	11.28	24.76 / 91	10.54 / 78	--
MUS	BlackRock NY Municipal Income Tr II	BFY	**U**	14.07	14.85	12.65	**U** /	6.52	2.32	17.58 / 67	--	--
MUS	BlackRock NY Municipal Income Trust	BNY	**A-**	15.13	15.15	13.02	**B+ / 8.4**	9.73	11.93	22.85 / 85	9.68 / 72	--
MUS	BlackRock PA Strategic Muni Tr	BPS	**C+**	15.36	15.92	13.89	**C+ / 6.8**	9.16	0.09	15.08 / 58	9.89 / 74	8.56 / 60
IN	BlackRock Preferred Opportunity Tr	BPP	**U**	24.70	25.99	22.00	**U** /	9.81	1.58	21.83 / 54	--	--
IN	BlackRock S&P Qual Rkg Glob Eq Mgd	BQY	**U**	13.87	15.01	13.25	**U** /	2.69	-0.26	-2.50 / 4	--	--
COH	BlackRock Strategic Bond Trust	BHD	**C-**	15.10	17.75	13.38	**C / 4.9**	12.87	-6.97	13.99 / 35	14.27 / 70	--
IN	BlackRock Strategic Div Achievers	BDT	**U**	13.93	15.00	12.67	**U** /	2.61	0.15	10.61 / 26	--	--
MUN	BlackRock Strategic Municipal Tr	BSD	**A**	16.40	16.60	13.15	**A+ / 9.6**	20.64	17.57	31.70 / 98	12.40 / 87	12.47 / 91
MUS	BlackRock VA Muni Bond Trust	BHV	**A**	17.27	17.40	14.40	**A- / 9.2**	12.00	13.31	25.93 / 93	11.16 / 81	--
FO	BLDRS Asia 50 ADR Index	ADRA	**U**	67.67	80.00	59.91	**U** /	-1.15	-0.44	4.56 / 11	--	--
FO	BLDRS Developed Mkts 100 ADR Index	ADRD	**U**	65.32	78.30	49.99	**U** /	-0.90	-0.63	11.89 / 28	--	--
EM	BLDRS Emerging Market 50 ADR Index	ADRE	**U**	90.10	95.99	55.00	**U** /	7.76	10.71	34.74 / 84	--	--
FO	BLDRS Europe 100 ADR Index	ADRU	**U**	66.70	71.95	56.35	**U** /	-0.22	0.70	14.81 / 37	--	--
GI	Blue Chip Value Fund	BLU	**D-**	6.24	6.94	5.86	**D+ / 2.5**	-2.44	-3.34	6.19 / 14	10.84 / 45	4.58 / 20
IN	Boulder Growth&Income Fund	BIF	**E+**	6.63	7.18	5.80	**E+ / 0.7**	0.61	-6.62	9.77 / 23	6.20 / 13	2.78 / 16
IN	Boulder Total Return Fund	BTF	**E+**	17.11	18.75	15.67	**E- / 0.1**	-1.89	-6.96	7.47 / 17	2.45 / 3	10.56 / 45
FO	Brazil Fund	BZF	**C-**	37.10	39.35	20.82	**A+ / 9.9**	9.47	11.70	80.66 / 99	46.52 / 99	21.10 / 96
GI	Calamos Convertible Opport&Income	CHI	**U**	19.41	21.93	17.30	**U** /	9.33	-0.78	16.10 / 40	--	--
GI	Calamos Convertible&High Income	CHY	**U**	16.34	17.27	14.52	**U** /	11.67	0.58	18.38 / 45	--	--
GI	Calamos Strategic Total Return Fund	CSQ	**U**	13.65	14.28	12.40	**U** /	7.06	4.45	10.02 / 24	--	--
FO	Canadian General Investments Ltd	T.CGI	**A+**	18.40	N/A	N/A	**A+ / 9.7**	9.89	21.95	47.72 / 98	29.43 / 97	18.56 / 90
GL	Canadian World Fund Limited	T.CWF	**E+**	4.10	N/A	N/A	**C- / 3.2**	-6.82	-1.91	19.88 / 50	12.24 / 58	-3.89 / 6
GI	Capital and Income Strategies Fund	CII	**U**	17.45	18.51	16.34	**U** /	2.85	1.21	6.21 / 14	--	--
GI	Castle Convertible Fund	CVF	**D**	22.15	24.69	21.41	**E- / 0.1**	-1.23	-3.61	2.58 / 8	1.97 / 2	5.72 / 24
FO	Central Europe & Russia Fund	CEE	**C+**	31.40	36.22	19.20	**A+ / 9.8**	6.40	19.89	46.25 / 98	34.81 / 98	18.50 / 90
PM	Central Fund of Canada	CEF	**D-**	5.40	6.14	5.10	**D- / 1.5**	0.93	-0.18	2.07 / 8	8.37 / 24	9.34 / 37
GR	Central Securities	CET	**D+**	23.78	24.25	20.90	**C- / 3.4**	3.46	4.50	10.58 / 25	11.08 / 47	-0.06 / 12

N/A denotes number is not available

		RISK				NET ASSETS		VALUATION			ASSET					FUND MANAGER	
Incl. in Returns			3 Year					Premium / Discount									
Dividend Yield %	Expense Ratio	Risk Rating/ Pts	Standard Deviation	Beta	Avg Dura- tion	NAV as of 6/30/05	Total $(Mil)	As of 6/30/05	1 Year Average	Wtd Avg P/E	Cash %	Stocks %	Bonds %	Other %	Portfolio Turnover Ratio	Manager Quality Pct	Manager Tenure (Years)
6.28	1.26	**U /**	N/A	N/A	N/A	25.08	184	-2.71	N/A	N/A	0	0	0	100	28	N/A	0
9.89	2.23	**C- / 3.4**	18.9	2.06	5.7	2.68	155	5.97	0.81	N/A	0	0	100	0	56	1	2
8.66	3.16	**C / 4.3**	19.6	0.95	5.4	7.65	48	22.88	20.89	N/A	0	0	100	0	57	37	7
7.41	1.43	**B- / 7.6**	10.0	0.62	8.8	12.10	408	-7.02	-7.95	N/A	0	0	100	0	216	78	14
9.04	2.05	**C+ / 5.8**	14.5	4.39	N/A	6.67	432	0.45	6.47	N/A	0	0	100	0	29	2	17
4.94	0.99	**B / 8.5**	7.3	1.39	4.3	16.34	456	-1.47	-2.56	N/A	0	0	100	0	4	44	13
5.14	1.02	**B / 8.1**	8.8	1.57	5.3	10.88	286	2.67	1.36	N/A	0	0	100	0	1	55	13
5.43	1.06	**C+ / 6.5**	13.5	2.05	13.4	15.96	265	4.07	-3.77	N/A	0	0	100	0	34	76	12
7.63	1.53	**U /**	N/A	N/A	N/A	19.48	709	-6.47	-2.79	N/A	0	0	100	0	36	N/A	2
5.26	1.14	**C / 5.1**	16.5	1.35	N/A	16.00	32	4.31	-2.24	N/A	0	0	100	0	1	71	3
6.31	1.09	**U /**	N/A	N/A	9.9	15.35	301	-4.23	1.58	N/A	0	0	100	0	51	N/A	2
4.72	0.96	**B+ / 9.0**	6.2	0.99	3.4	10.31	479	-1.26	-0.67	N/A	0	0	100	0	2	40	14
4.92	0.91	**B- / 7.9**	9.4	1.70	9.5	15.91	252	-1.32	-4.38	N/A	0	0	100	0	31	74	4
6.38	0.88	**C+ / 6.5**	12.6	2.12	N/A	16.11	160	-0.12	-3.63	N/A	0	0	100	0	40	72	3
6.32	0.82	**C+ / 6.4**	12.5	2.00	N/A	14.99	647	1.07	-1.81	N/A	0	0	100	0	22	72	4
6.62	0.94	**U /**	N/A	N/A	15.2	15.46	346	-2.01	-3.79	N/A	0	0	100	0	20	N/A	3
6.05	0.84	**U /**	N/A	N/A	N/A	15.45	399	-1.68	-4.64	N/A	0	0	100	0	25	N/A	3
5.18	1.33	**C+ / 5.7**	14.1	2.01	N/A	14.83	15	4.92	-1.54	N/A	0	0	100	0	10	40	12
5.98	1.10	**C+ / 6.5**	12.5	1.95	N/A	16.04	36	-3.05	-4.85	N/A	0	0	100	0	4	57	3
5.74	0.89	**B- / 7.1**	11.3	1.84	N/A	16.08	118	-4.29	-6.65	N/A	0	0	100	0	5	60	4
5.84	0.92	**U /**	N/A	N/A	N/A	15.25	96	-0.98	-2.84	N/A	0	0	100	0	9	N/A	3
4.73	1.03	**B / 8.5**	6.8	1.35	N/A	16.19	186	-2.22	-3.02	N/A	0	0	100	0	N/A	44	13
5.90	1.20	**B- / 7.1**	10.2	1.32	N/A	15.44	20	-4.21	-7.45	N/A	0	0	100	0	2	58	12
4.77	1.11	**B / 8.4**	9.5	1.51	N/A	16.25	57	-5.91	-5.29	N/A	0	0	100	0	N/A	72	4
6.04	1.09	**B- / 7.0**	11.4	1.86	N/A	16.02	43	-5.06	-8.31	N/A	0	0	100	0	N/A	67	3
6.43	1.06	**U /**	N/A	N/A	14.6	15.07	74	-6.64	-3.44	N/A	0	0	100	0	5	N/A	3
6.00	0.87	**C+ / 6.5**	11.8	2.06	N/A	15.68	194	-3.51	-7.26	N/A	0	0	100	0	8	53	4
5.82	1.03	**C+ / 6.7**	11.2	1.53	N/A	15.50	32	-0.90	-4.16	N/A	0	0	100	0	5	70	6
8.07	1.44	**U /**	N/A	N/A	11.0	25.12	474	-1.67	-5.02	N/A	0	0	0	100	88	N/A	2
5.33	1.14	**U /**	N/A	N/A	N/A	16.12	96	-13.96	-9.12	25.7	1	98	0	1	3	N/A	1
9.12	1.76	**C / 5.1**	17.2	1.87	5.4	14.30	99	5.59	7.77	N/A	0	0	100	0	21	3	3
6.45	0.97	**U /**	N/A	N/A	N/A	15.10	392	-7.75	-4.25	23.3	0	99	0	1	N/A	N/A	1
5.89	0.89	**C+ / 5.8**	14.2	2.32	N/A	15.87	114	3.34	-6.42	N/A	0	0	100	0	23	61	6
5.11	1.21	**C+ / 6.4**	12.0	1.13	13.7	16.21	25	6.54	1.21	N/A	0	0	100	0	N/A	79	3
3.13	0.30	**U /**	N/A	N/A	N/A	67.71	21	-0.06	0.08	N/A	0	100	0	0	N/A	N/A	3
4.30	0.30	**U /**	N/A	N/A	N/A	65.29	21	0.05	0.10	N/A	0	100	0	0	N/A	N/A	3
4.24	0.30	**U /**	N/A	N/A	N/A	90.06	50	0.04	0.01	N/A	0	100	0	0	N/A	N/A	3
4.69	0.30	**U /**	N/A	N/A	N/A	66.66	11	0.06	0.10	N/A	0	100	0	0	N/A	N/A	3
8.75	1.12	**C / 4.7**	21.0	1.21	N/A	5.65	157	10.44	16.76	21.1	0	100	0	0	115	73	3
0.00	2.38	**C / 4.3**	24.2	1.12	N/A	7.74	86	-14.34	-12.27	27.0	1	98	0	1	33	32	33
0.00	2.30	**C+ / 5.9**	16.8	0.75	N/A	20.49	246	-16.50	-13.34	23.8	17	82	0	1	25	22	6
2.06	1.51	**E+ / 0.6**	38.2	1.86	N/A	39.26	596	-5.50	-9.82	N/A	0	100	0	0	4	98	9
9.25	1.06	**U /**	13.8	0.47	6.0	16.66	741	16.51	14.49	15.4	0	0	61	39	22	N/A	3
8.93	1.23	**U /**	N/A	N/A	5.6	15.38	923	6.24	4.74	19.0	1	0	70	29	21	N/A	2
7.53	1.68	**U /**	N/A	N/A	5.2	14.80	2,227	-7.77	-6.83	18.0	0	47	51	2	43	N/A	1
1.30	N/A	**C+ / 6.7**	16.0	0.72	N/A	22.23	421	-17.23	-25.05	21.4	0	94	0	6	N/A	98	17
0.00	N/A	**D / 1.7**	23.3	0.32	N/A	5.53	19	-25.86	-24.04	46.4	4	95	0	1	N/A	87	11
6.83	2.19	**U /**	N/A	N/A	7.0	20.16	266	-13.44	-12.17	38.1	0	57	23	20	20	N/A	1
3.07	1.16	**B / 8.2**	12.8	0.39	7.0	26.22	57	-15.52	-12.55	24.5	3	15	0	82	23	46	4
0.55	1.27	**D+ / 2.4**	26.6	1.23	N/A	33.73	292	-6.91	-10.15	N/A	1	99	0	0	45	96	15
0.19	0.65	**C+ / 5.8**	19.9	0.85	N/A	5.40	418	0.00	6.46	N/A	2	0	0	98	N/A	46	6
0.25	0.55	**C+ / 5.6**	19.1	1.20	N/A	28.14	529	-15.49	-14.30	20.3	10	86	2	2	17	73	32

N/A denotes number is not available

99 Pct = Best
0 Pct = Worst

Fund Type	Fund Name	Ticker Symbol	Overall Weiss Investment Rating	PRICE: Price As of 6/30/05	PRICE: 52 Week High	PRICE: 52 Week Low	PERFORMANCE: Performance Rating/Pts	% Total Return Through 6/30/05: 3 Mo	6 Mo	1Yr/Pct	Annualized: 3Yr/Pct	Annualized: 5Yr/Pct
GI	Chartwell Dividend and Income Fund	CWF	**C**	10.59	10.75	8.91	**B- / 7.4**	12.62	9.59	31.72 / 78	13.99 / 68	11.15 / 48
FO	Chile Fund	CH	**B+**	15.03	15.66	11.96	**A+ / 9.7**	8.83	10.03	46.55 / 98	33.72 / 98	17.78 / 87
FO	China Fund	CHN	**C+**	28.73	35.25	25.43	**A+ / 9.6**	-4.84	-14.70	16.58 / 40	35.45 / 98	29.04 / 99
COH	CIM High Yield Securities	CIM	**D+**	4.00	4.79	3.82	**C- / 4.0**	2.85	-2.01	4.27 / 10	14.08 / 68	5.14 / 22
LP	Citigroup Investments Corp Loan	TLI	**D**	13.11	15.00	12.95	**E / 0.3**	-1.93	-3.99	-7.60 / 2	5.84 / 12	5.60 / 23
GI	Clough Global Allocation Fund	GLV	**U**	22.53	N/A	N/A	**U /**	3.64	4.54	--	--	--
GL	Clough Global Equity Fund	GLQ	**U**	20.05	N/A	N/A	**U /**	--	--	--	--	--
GI	Cohen&Steers Adv Inc Realty Fund	RLF	**B**	21.87	22.36	17.24	**A- / 9.0**	17.21	4.03	37.42 / 90	20.42 / 90	--
IN	Cohen&Steers Dividend Majors	DVM	**U**	17.84	N/A	N/A	**U /**	1.33	--	--	--	--
GI	Cohen&Steers Premium Income Realty	RPF	**U**	21.65	22.30	17.18	**U /**	14.53	4.86	37.88 / 91	--	--
GI	Cohen&Steers Quality Income Realty	RQI	**B-**	20.52	21.17	16.31	**A- / 9.1**	15.49	7.51	36.48 / 88	20.68 / 90	--
IN	Cohen&Steers REIT and Utility Inc	RTU	**U**	19.05	19.50	15.68	**U /**	14.18	6.85	23.30 / 58	--	--
IN	Cohen&Steers REIT& Preferred Income	RNP	**U**	26.65	27.39	22.89	**U /**	10.30	3.11	26.88 / 66	--	--
UT	Cohen&Steers Select Utility Fund	UTF	**U**	21.05	21.10	16.01	**U /**	12.27	12.21	36.07 / 87	--	--
GI	Cohen&Steers Total Return Realty	RFI	**B-**	19.80	20.24	16.51	**B / 7.7**	9.95	3.05	27.56 / 69	17.60 / 82	19.31 / 92
GL	Cohen&Steers Worldwide Realty Inc	RWF	**U**	20.50	N/A	N/A	**U /**	--	--	--	--	--
MUS	Colonial CA Insured Muni	CCA	**D**	14.53	14.60	13.16	**D / 2.1**	8.83	12.22	14.49 / 55	0.07 / 1	6.88 / 45
MUH	Colonial High Inc Muni Tr	CXE	**C-**	6.29	6.81	5.91	**D+ / 2.6**	2.41	1.95	12.16 / 46	4.91 / 21	7.88 / 53
MUN	Colonial Insured Muni	CFX	**D**	14.15	16.11	13.22	**E+ / 0.8**	6.98	5.80	6.02 / 22	2.08 / 4	8.24 / 58
COH	Colonial Interm High Inc	CIF	**C+**	3.44	3.75	3.20	**C / 5.5**	4.45	1.59	15.69 / 39	15.56 / 75	0.76 / 13
GL	Colonial InterMkt Inc Tr I	CMK	**C**	8.82	9.31	8.00	**C- / 3.9**	5.32	2.58	19.92 / 50	10.48 / 42	9.82 / 40
MUN	Colonial Invst Gr Muni Tr	CXH	**C+**	10.49	10.58	9.50	**C / 5.3**	5.83	8.51	17.63 / 67	6.19 / 35	9.96 / 73
MUH	Colonial Muni Inc Trust	CMU	**C-**	5.57	6.14	5.25	**D+ / 2.8**	2.79	1.80	12.20 / 47	5.47 / 25	6.42 / 40
IN	Cornerstone Strategic Value Fund	CLM	**D**	7.17	9.00	5.55	**C / 5.5**	8.25	-8.83	-3.77 / 3	18.63 / 85	-1.50 / 10
IN	Cornerstone Total Return Fund	CRF	**D**	15.48	19.00	11.10	**C+ / 6.5**	13.02	-6.95	5.10 / 12	18.82 / 86	13.29 / 61
COH	Corporate High Yield Fund	COY	**B-**	8.74	9.32	7.88	**B / 7.8**	10.86	4.54	18.39 / 46	19.44 / 88	9.52 / 38
COH	Corporate High Yield Fund III	CYE	**C+**	8.45	9.41	7.81	**B / 7.6**	8.51	2.25	18.67 / 46	19.40 / 88	8.00 / 32
COH	Corporate High Yield Fund V	HYV	**B-**	14.63	16.34	14.01	**B- / 7.2**	4.62	1.42	19.62 / 49	19.28 / 87	--
COH	Corporate High Yield VI	HYT	**U**	13.84	15.57	13.15	**U /**	6.13	-0.60	17.28 / 43	--	--
COH	Credit Suisse Asset Mgmt Income	CIK	**D+**	4.65	4.70	4.00	**C / 5.4**	11.33	10.11	24.21 / 60	10.32 / 41	5.52 / 23
COH	Credit Suisse High Yield Bond Fund	DHY	**C**	4.81	5.36	4.43	**C+ / 6.6**	10.27	-1.97	11.15 / 27	17.95 / 84	5.90 / 24
COH	Debt Strategies Fund I Inc	DSU	**C+**	6.52	7.09	5.88	**C+ / 6.7**	10.10	-2.64	13.26 / 32	18.03 / 84	10.59 / 46
IN	Defined Strategy Fund	DSF	**U**	16.92	N/A	N/A	**U /**	5.29	--	--	--	--
MUS	Delaware Inv AZ Muni Income	VAZ	**C**	15.57	16.68	13.85	**C / 4.6**	2.88	7.00	18.64 / 71	5.79 / 29	10.33 / 77
MUS	Delaware Inv CO Ins Muni Inc	VCF	**A-**	17.64	18.20	15.19	**B / 8.0**	5.28	1.44	23.63 / 87	11.27 / 81	13.19 / 94
GI	Delaware Inv Div & Inc	DDF	**D**	12.51	12.60	10.64	**C- / 3.7**	10.98	9.75	23.30 / 58	6.71 / 15	12.60 / 57
MUS	Delaware Inv FL Insured Muni Inc	VFL	**B+**	16.70	17.68	14.48	**B+ / 8.3**	13.26	2.96	21.90 / 82	10.32 / 76	13.81 / 96
GI	Delaware Inv Glob Div & Inc	DGF	**C+**	13.07	13.49	10.94	**C+ / 5.8**	8.58	10.80	27.51 / 68	11.10 / 48	12.97 / 59
MUS	Delaware Inv MN Muni Inc Fund II	VMM	**C+**	15.95	17.75	14.92	**C / 4.7**	-1.28	-0.21	13.57 / 51	9.33 / 70	11.29 / 85
MUS	Delaware Inv MN Muni Inc Fund III	VYM	**C**	14.94	16.95	13.66	**C / 4.3**	-4.66	1.30	14.10 / 53	9.00 / 67	11.02 / 83
MUS	Delaware Inv MN Muni Income	VMN	**C-**	14.93	17.25	14.14	**D+ / 2.3**	-0.40	-7.53	7.93 / 29	7.69 / 55	10.03 / 74
GR	Diamond Series Trust I	DIA	**D-**	102.86	109.83	97.27	**E / 0.5**	-1.02	-3.97	1.06 / 6	5.80 / 12	1.63 / 14
LP	Diversified Income Strat Port	DVF	**U**	16.78	N/A	N/A	**U /**	-6.16	--	--	--	--
GI	Dividend Capital Realty Income All	DCA	**U**	14.11	N/A	N/A	**U /**	-2.76	--	--	--	--
UT	DNP Select Income Fund Inc	DNP	**C+**	11.70	11.95	10.24	**C / 5.3**	12.08	3.31	18.21 / 45	12.65 / 61	11.71 / 51
IN	Dow 30 Premium & Dividend Income	DPD	**U**	19.84	N/A	N/A	**U /**	--	--	--	--	--
IN	Dreman/Claymore Dividend&Income	DCS	**U**	18.67	19.71	16.25	**U /**	4.67	5.61	18.90 / 47	--	--
COH	Dreyfus High Yield Strategies Fund	DHF	**D**	4.37	5.03	4.18	**C / 4.5**	1.88	-5.01	8.61 / 20	15.11 / 74	-1.31 / 10
MUN	Dreyfus Municipal Income	DMF	**C**	9.25	10.39	8.71	**C- / 3.6**	7.12	-4.78	8.28 / 30	7.54 / 52	11.41 / 86
MUN	Dreyfus Strategic Muni Bond Fund	DSM	**A-**	9.25	9.25	7.95	**B+ / 8.8**	13.53	14.47	24.27 / 90	9.07 / 67	10.01 / 73
MUN	Dreyfus Strategic Municipals	LEO	**C**	8.86	9.00	7.98	**C / 4.7**	12.13	9.39	17.91 / 68	3.60 / 11	9.42 / 68
MUN	DTF Tax Free Income	DTF	**C+**	15.90	16.59	14.26	**C+ / 5.9**	7.43	5.10	17.01 / 64	7.45 / 51	10.93 / 82

N/A denotes number is not available

		RISK				NET ASSETS		VALUATION			ASSET					FUND MANAGER	
Incl. in Returns			3 Year					Premium / Discount									
Dividend Yield %	Expense Ratio	Risk Rating/ Pts	Standard Deviation	Beta	Avg Dura- tion	NAV as of 6/30/05	Total $(Mil)	As of 6/30/05	1 Year Average	Wtd Avg P/E	Cash %	Stocks %	Bonds %	Other %	Portfolio Turnover Ratio	Manager Quality Pct	Manager Tenure (Years)
9.44	2.26	**C- / 3.9**	19.6	0.44	4.9	8.69	148	21.86	14.27	20.3	0	76	23	1	99	89	7
5.42	1.85	**C / 4.3**	29.2	1.28	N/A	17.00	159	-11.59	-10.68	3.5	2	97	0	1	36	95	1
0.69	1.40	**D+ / 2.3**	40.5	1.28	N/A	25.72	259	11.70	17.54	15.3	16	83	0	1	24	96	13
9.01	2.21	**C / 4.8**	16.9	1.87	5.2	4.35	28	-8.05	-5.27	N/A	0	0	100	0	55	3	7
5.53	2.31	**B / 8.2**	9.5	-48.34	N/A	14.32	143	-8.45	-2.02	N/A	0	0	100	0	53	96	7
4.73	N/A	**U /**	N/A	N/A	N/A	21.45	199	5.03	N/A	N/A	17	49	30	4	40	N/A	1
0.00	N/A	**U /**	N/A	N/A	N/A	19.58	N/A	2.40	N/A	N/A	0	0	0	100	N/A	N/A	0
8.11	0.91	**C / 4.7**	19.9	0.41	3.0	23.41	592	-6.58	-6.41	54.4	0	100	0	0	3	96	4
5.27	N/A	**U /**	N/A	N/A	N/A	20.08	N/A	-11.16	N/A	N/A	1	98	0	1	N/A	N/A	0
8.20	1.07	**U /**	N/A	N/A	N/A	24.22	754	-10.61	-9.11	55.2	0	100	0	0	5	N/A	3
7.93	1.04	**C / 4.3**	20.6	0.35	N/A	22.97	874	-10.67	-8.82	N/A	0	100	0	0	3	97	3
7.14	1.21	**U /**	N/A	N/A	16.1	22.32	1,266	-14.65	-11.99	35.9	0	100	0	0	36	N/A	1
8.65	1.29	**U /**	N/A	N/A	15.4	30.15	1,453	-11.61	-9.40	58.0	0	83	0	17	9	N/A	2
5.60	1.22	**U /**	N/A	N/A	18.3	24.25	969	-13.20	-11.81	21.3	0	100	0	0	28	N/A	1
6.56	0.92	**C+ / 5.7**	18.0	0.34	N/A	19.85	182	-0.25	0.51	52.4	2	77	0	21	3	94	12
4.73	N/A	**U /**	N/A	N/A	N/A	19.57	N/A	4.75	N/A	N/A	0	0	0	100	N/A	N/A	0
5.77	0.87	**C+ / 6.4**	13.4	1.73	12.1	15.31	42	-5.09	-7.86	N/A	0	0	100	0	16	5	N/A
6.53	1.58	**B / 8.0**	10.1	1.30	N/A	6.60	199	-4.70	-1.16	N/A	0	0	100	0	13	42	7
5.92	0.88	**B- / 7.4**	12.3	2.22	11.9	14.97	62	-5.48	-3.16	N/A	0	0	100	0	21	4	N/A
9.12	2.66	**B- / 7.0**	14.7	1.40	N/A	3.70	81	-7.03	-7.92	N/A	0	0	100	0	80	31	N/A
7.32	1.01	**B- / 7.8**	10.8	0.61	N/A	9.48	108	-6.96	-8.81	N/A	5	0	94	1	73	76	N/A
5.69	1.29	**B- / 7.3**	9.9	1.61	N/A	11.40	128	-7.98	-9.78	N/A	0	0	100	0	15	42	N/A
6.26	1.42	**B- / 7.6**	11.2	1.70	N/A	5.87	158	-5.11	-1.44	N/A	0	0	100	0	16	30	N/A
14.52	1.28	**C- / 3.0**	24.4	0.97	N/A	5.84	155	22.77	27.68	22.0	0	99	0	1	39	90	4
13.45	1.41	**D- / 1.3**	29.0	0.94	N/A	11.40	61	35.79	35.33	N/A	0	99	0	1	12	91	4
9.60	1.50	**C / 5.3**	17.7	2.05	N/A	8.64	313	1.16	-1.08	N/A	0	1	88	11	33	6	12
9.33	1.62	**C / 5.3**	16.0	1.92	4.8	8.56	336	-1.29	-2.13	12.5	0	1	88	11	31	12	7
9.80	1.85	**C+ / 6.1**	12.7	1.51	4.8	14.90	520	-1.81	-3.52	12.5	0	2	84	14	26	53	4
9.53	1.99	**U /**	N/A	N/A	4.9	14.81	553	-6.55	-7.53	12.5	0	1	88	11	26	N/A	2
9.91	0.78	**C- / 3.4**	17.6	1.31	5.3	4.31	227	7.89	0.80	7.6	0	0	100	0	58	8	16
10.37	3.00	**C- / 4.0**	17.4	1.78	4.9	4.26	230	12.91	12.69	N/A	0	0	100	0	6	18	7
9.61	1.83	**C+ / 6.0**	14.5	1.60	4.8	6.66	745	-2.10	-2.23	7.9	0	3	71	26	60	34	7
3.27	1.01	**U /**	N/A	N/A	N/A	18.34	137	-7.74	N/A	N/A	1	98	0	1	N/A	N/A	1
5.26	1.18	**C+ / 6.9**	13.9	1.83	13.7	15.50	45	0.45	1.00	N/A	0	0	100	0	8	35	12
5.42	1.03	**C+ / 6.9**	13.3	2.38	13.0	15.96	75	10.53	8.79	N/A	0	0	100	0	5	56	12
7.67	1.51	**C / 4.5**	19.9	0.37	5.6	12.98	167	-3.62	-7.59	26.7	2	59	27	12	89	75	5
5.73	1.24	**C+ / 6.1**	15.6	2.59	13.7	15.56	37	7.33	2.95	N/A	0	0	100	0	11	37	12
7.43	1.92	**C+ / 6.0**	15.3	0.30	6.0	13.46	81	-2.90	-7.40	25.9	1	64	34	1	78	86	6
5.45	1.00	**B- / 7.0**	14.3	2.14	13.4	15.40	108	3.57	7.93	N/A	0	0	100	0	15	48	12
5.25	1.33	**C+ / 6.8**	14.9	1.64	12.1	14.50	26	3.03	8.51	N/A	0	0	100	0	12	61	12
5.22	1.27	**B- / 7.3**	15.2	2.20	11.7	15.12	38	-1.26	5.38	N/A	0	0	100	0	12	27	13
1.33	0.18	**B- / 7.2**	14.6	1.01	N/A	102.91	6,680	-0.05	0.02	18.3	0	100	0	0	N/A	39	7
7.24	0.95	**U /**	N/A	N/A	N/A	17.93	227	-6.41	N/A	N/A	0	0	74	26	4	N/A	0
4.20	1.17	**U /**	N/A	N/A	N/A	14.59	169	-3.29	N/A	N/A	0	36	0	64	46	N/A	0
6.75	N/A	**B- / 7.3**	15.5	0.50	7.9	9.12	1,935	28.29	33.55	22.0	0	92	0	8	44	76	11
4.59	N/A	**U /**	N/A	N/A	N/A	19.13	N/A	3.71	N/A	N/A	0	99	0	1	N/A	N/A	0
6.86	1.48	**U /**	N/A	N/A	6.6	20.48	914	-8.84	-7.75	15.2	0	88	11	1	7	N/A	1
8.92	2.33	**C- / 3.7**	21.7	1.97	4.8	4.65	334	-6.02	-1.41	N/A	0	0	100	0	82	3	3
6.08	1.31	**B- / 7.1**	14.3	2.20	14.9	9.77	196	-5.32	0.79	N/A	0	0	100	0	9	27	17
6.52	1.25	**C+ / 6.1**	13.9	2.19	14.1	9.08	424	1.87	-3.64	N/A	0	0	100	0	40	47	9
6.24	1.26	**C+ / 6.8**	12.4	2.13	13.2	9.48	558	-6.54	-7.19	N/A	0	0	100	0	15	7	9
5.45	1.41	**C+ / 6.8**	13.8	2.15	13.1	16.98	143	-6.36	-7.71	N/A	0	0	100	0	12	33	14

N/A denotes number is not available

99 Pct = Best
0 Pct = Worst

Fund Type	Fund Name	Ticker Symbol	Overall Weiss Investment Rating	PRICE: Price As of 6/30/05	52 Week High	52 Week Low	PERFORMANCE: Performance Rating/Pts	% Total Return Through 6/30/05: 3 Mo	6 Mo	1Yr/Pct	Annualized: 3Yr/Pct	5Yr/Pct
GEI	Duff & Phelps Utilities & Crp Bd Tr	DUC	**C**	14.57	14.99	12.55	**C / 5.4**	14.66	1.14	24.22 / 60	11.26 / 49	13.48 / 62
MUS	Eaton Vance CA Muni Inc Tr	CEV	**B-**	14.99	15.85	13.90	**C+ / 6.0**	8.53	2.47	12.91 / 50	8.86 / 66	13.67 / 95
IN	Eaton Vance Enhanced Eqty Inc	EOI	**U**	19.94	N/A	N/A	**U /**	1.93	3.00	--	--	--
IN	Eaton Vance Enhanced Eqty Inc II	EOS	**U**	19.42	N/A	N/A	**U /**	2.16	--	--	--	--
MUS	Eaton Vance FL Muni Inc Tr	FEV	**B+**	15.55	16.20	13.85	**B / 7.9**	10.43	1.97	19.22 / 74	10.60 / 78	15.49 / 98
LP	Eaton Vance Floating Rate Income Tr	EFT	**U**	17.26	N/A	N/A	**U /**	-7.72	-4.44	--	--	--
MUS	Eaton Vance Insured CA Muni Bond	EVM	**U**	14.20	14.20	12.62	**U /**	8.66	8.92	18.68 / 72	--	--
MUS	Eaton Vance Insured CA Muni Bond II	EIA	**U**	15.60	15.95	13.16	**U /**	9.23	14.07	26.01 / 94	--	--
MUS	Eaton Vance Insured FL Muni Bond	EIF	**U**	15.70	16.01	12.91	**U /**	13.08	6.21	28.66 / 97	--	--
MUS	Eaton Vance Insured MA Muni Bond	MAB	**U**	16.80	19.25	14.43	**U /**	4.00	2.41	23.11 / 86	--	--
MUS	Eaton Vance Insured MI Muni Bond	MIW	**U**	15.91	17.25	14.08	**U /**	0.68	2.55	19.72 / 76	--	--
MUN	Eaton Vance Insured Muni Bond Fund	EIM	**U**	14.95	14.99	12.62	**U /**	12.12	12.73	24.41 / 90	--	--
MUN	Eaton Vance Insured Muni Bond II	EIV	**U**	16.09	16.29	13.38	**U /**	10.52	12.67	27.70 / 96	--	--
MUS	Eaton Vance Insured NJ Muni Bond	EMJ	**U**	16.49	17.96	14.02	**U /**	8.17	8.27	23.69 / 88	--	--
MUS	Eaton Vance Insured NY Muni Bond	ENX	**U**	14.38	14.50	12.35	**U /**	8.96	12.03	23.15 / 86	--	--
MUS	Eaton Vance Insured NY Muni Bond II	NYH	**U**	16.20	16.20	13.07	**U /**	12.41	15.43	31.29 / 98	--	--
MUS	Eaton Vance Insured OH Muni Bond	EIO	**U**	16.00	16.60	13.90	**U /**	5.76	1.75	19.36 / 74	--	--
MUS	Eaton Vance Insured PA Muni Bond	EIP	**U**	16.10	17.24	13.05	**U /**	7.99	0.40	27.44 / 96	--	--
GEI	Eaton Vance Limited Duration Income	EVV	**U**	17.93	19.48	17.25	**U /**	2.89	-1.15	7.02 / 16	--	--
MUS	Eaton Vance MA Muni Inc Tr	MMV	**C-**	15.78	18.85	14.80	**C- / 3.0**	-0.22	-7.68	11.29 / 43	8.45 / 63	13.36 / 95
MUS	Eaton Vance MI Muni Inc Tr	EMI	**C+**	15.46	17.20	15.28	**C / 4.5**	-5.07	-5.47	7.95 / 29	10.36 / 77	15.07 / 98
MUN	Eaton Vance Municipal Inc Tr	EVN	**A+**	16.67	16.93	14.66	**A / 9.3**	9.83	7.09	20.87 / 79	14.78 / 93	17.28 / 99
MUS	Eaton Vance NJ Muni Inc Tr	EVJ	**C+**	14.87	16.10	14.10	**C- / 4.2**	6.24	1.25	8.92 / 34	7.56 / 52	13.67 / 95
MUS	Eaton Vance NY Muni Inc Tr	EVY	**A**	16.70	16.70	13.85	**A- / 9.2**	14.27	11.67	27.07 / 95	11.14 / 81	16.66 / 99
MUS	Eaton Vance OH Muni Inc Tr	EVO	**C-**	15.69	17.50	14.20	**C- / 3.5**	-2.46	-1.95	16.61 / 64	7.34 / 49	13.54 / 95
MUS	Eaton Vance PA Muni Inc Tr	EVP	**B**	15.85	16.63	13.44	**B+ / 8.3**	2.25	2.82	25.40 / 92	12.24 / 86	15.20 / 98
LP	Eaton Vance Senior Floating Rate	EFR	**U**	17.47	20.49	17.46	**U /**	-10.41	-8.62	-6.09 / 2	--	--
LP	Eaton Vance Senior Income Trust	EVF	**D**	7.93	9.70	7.82	**E / 0.3**	-3.51	-6.99	-12.01 / 0	6.65 / 15	3.76 / 18
GL	Eaton Vance Sh Dur Diversified Inc	EVG	**U**	17.33	N/A	N/A	**U /**	-11.70	--	--	--	--
GL	Eaton Vance Tax Adv Glob Div Inc	ETG	**U**	19.29	20.30	16.10	**U /**	3.71	3.94	22.92 / 57	--	--
GL	Eaton Vance Tax Adv Global Div Opp	ETO	**U**	20.96	21.79	16.75	**U /**	6.43	9.30	28.18 / 71	--	--
IN	Eaton Vance Tax Advantage Div Inc	EVT	**U**	20.55	22.24	17.85	**U /**	4.17	1.10	18.81 / 47	--	--
IN	Eaton Vance Tax-Managed Buy-Write	ETB	**U**	19.95	N/A	N/A	**U /**	--	--	--	--	--
GI	Ellsworth Convertible Growth & Inc	ECF	**D**	7.49	8.25	7.15	**E- / 0.1**	0.41	-4.18	1.70 / 7	1.05 / 2	3.45 / 17
EM	Emerging Market Telecom Fund	ETF	**C**	10.10	10.60	7.20	**C+ / 6.3**	6.32	-0.49	30.32 / 76	14.26 / 69	-2.71 / 8
GR	Engex	EGX	**U**	9.40	14.15	7.50	**U /**	-10.48	-21.67	--	--	-22.44 / 1
IN	Enhanced Equity Yield Fund	EEF	**U**	20.03	N/A	N/A	**U /**	--	--	--	--	--
GR	Equus II	EQS	**C**	8.38	8.50	7.32	**C- / 3.8**	3.84	10.70	16.91 / 42	9.67 / 36	0.73 / 13
FO	Europe Fund	EF	**E+**	10.54	12.14	9.25	**D+ / 2.4**	-7.38	-1.86	8.79 / 21	10.62 / 43	-0.21 / 12
COH	Evergreen Income Advantage Fund	EAD	**U**	14.69	16.47	13.61	**U /**	7.28	-2.63	12.22 / 29	--	--
GL	Evergreen Managed Income Fund	ERC	**U**	17.35	19.00	16.60	**U /**	3.66	-1.13	8.94 / 21	--	--
UT	Evergreen Utilities&High Income	ERH	**U**	21.24	22.00	16.57	**U /**	8.92	8.22	29.07 / 73	--	--
IN	F&C/Claymore Preferred Sec Inc Fund	FFC	**U**	23.10	26.25	21.61	**U /**	4.64	-5.70	6.58 / 15	--	--
IN	F&C/Claymore Total Return Fund	FLC	**U**	21.95	24.95	21.07	**U /**	4.57	-6.05	5.95 / 13	--	--
MUN	Federated Prem Intermediate Muni	FPT	**U**	13.86	14.15	12.53	**U /**	9.60	12.72	15.77 / 60	--	--
MUN	Federated Premier Muni Income	FMN	**U**	15.45	15.85	12.95	**U /**	10.26	13.37	26.77 / 95	--	--
GR	Fidelity Nasdaq Comp Tracker Stock	ONEQ	**U**	80.93	86.67	69.73	**U /**	2.96	-5.13	1.21 / 6	--	--
IN	Fiduciary/Claymore Dynamic Eq Inc	HCE	**U**	19.43	N/A	N/A	**U /**	--	--	--	--	--
EN	Fiduciary/Claymore MLP Opp	FMO	**U**	19.92	N/A	N/A	**U /**	2.72	--	--	--	--
FS	First Financial Fund	FF	**B**	18.10	24.24	17.10	**A- / 9.1**	-0.66	-5.88	29.71 / 74	28.34 / 96	35.77 / 99
FO	First Israel Fund	ISL	**C**	14.38	17.40	11.49	**C+ / 6.3**	-11.78	-5.02	8.61 / 20	20.12 / 89	0.23 / 12
EN	First Trust Energy Income&Growth	FEN	**U**	23.08	N/A	N/A	**U /**	4.32	7.72	--	--	--

N/A denotes number is not available

		RISK				NET ASSETS		VALUATION			ASSET					FUND MANAGER	
Incl. in Returns			3 Year					Premium / Discount									
Dividend Yield %	Expense Ratio	Risk Rating/ Pts	Standard Deviation	Beta	Avg Dura-tion	NAV as of 6/30/05	Total $(Mil)	As of 6/30/05	1 Year Average	Wtd Avg P/E	Cash %	Stocks %	Bonds %	Other %	Portfolio Turnover Ratio	Manager Quality Pct	Manager Tenure (Years)
7.00	1.78	**C+ / 6.0**	14.3	2.12	10.2	13.21	363	10.30	5.81	N/A	0	0	100	0	17	64	9
5.90	1.77	**B- / 7.6**	13.9	2.43	11.6	15.80	108	-5.13	-2.72	N/A	0	0	100	0	17	35	6
6.12	N/A	**U /**	N/A	N/A	N/A	19.59	N/A	1.79	N/A	N/A	0	99	0	1	N/A	N/A	1
6.98	N/A	**U /**	N/A	N/A	N/A	18.86	N/A	2.97	N/A	N/A	0	100	0	0	N/A	N/A	0
5.72	N/A	**C+ / 6.6**	15.0	2.44	13.8	15.30	N/A	1.63	-0.20	N/A	0	0	100	0	N/A	50	6
6.37	0.93	**U /**	N/A	N/A	N/A	18.85	711	-8.44	N/A	N/A	0	0	100	0	83	N/A	1
5.96	0.83	**U /**	N/A	N/A	14.0	14.83	311	-4.25	-5.06	N/A	0	0	100	0	4	N/A	3
6.02	1.06	**U /**	N/A	N/A	13.8	15.05	56	3.65	-0.01	N/A	0	0	100	0	1	N/A	3
5.92	1.17	**U /**	N/A	N/A	12.3	15.12	38	3.84	1.28	N/A	0	0	100	0	11	N/A	3
5.57	1.25	**U /**	N/A	N/A	13.5	15.37	26	9.30	8.68	N/A	0	0	100	0	3	N/A	3
5.93	1.24	**U /**	N/A	N/A	12.1	15.32	22	3.85	4.69	N/A	0	0	100	0	4	N/A	3
6.26	0.77	**U /**	N/A	N/A	12.9	15.52	963	-3.67	-5.83	N/A	0	0	100	0	22	N/A	3
6.26	1.01	**U /**	N/A	N/A	14.2	15.65	150	2.81	-1.55	N/A	0	0	100	0	6	N/A	3
5.78	1.09	**U /**	N/A	N/A	12.1	15.57	39	5.91	2.45	N/A	0	0	100	0	4	N/A	3
5.78	0.86	**U /**	N/A	N/A	14.2	14.97	228	-3.94	-6.27	N/A	0	0	100	0	9	N/A	3
5.84	1.18	**U /**	N/A	N/A	14.3	15.49	38	4.58	-1.70	N/A	0	0	100	0	9	N/A	3
5.26	1.16	**U /**	N/A	N/A	13.4	14.98	37	6.81	3.98	N/A	0	0	100	0	4	N/A	3
5.84	1.12	**U /**	N/A	N/A	14.9	14.92	43	7.91	6.74	N/A	0	0	100	0	4	N/A	3
8.35	1.01	**U /**	N/A	N/A	N/A	18.46	2,060	-2.87	-0.76	N/A	2	0	97	1	60	N/A	2
5.66	1.86	**C+ / 7.0**	14.1	1.85	16.1	15.64	41	0.90	7.71	N/A	0	0	100	0	39	55	6
5.48	1.96	**B / 8.2**	10.7	1.64	12.6	15.26	31	1.31	7.75	N/A	0	0	100	0	5	65	6
6.77	1.78	**C+ / 6.9**	13.4	2.01	14.0	14.59	236	14.26	14.05	N/A	0	0	100	0	21	79	6
5.63	1.84	**B- / 7.7**	13.2	2.29	12.5	15.37	68	-3.25	0.56	N/A	0	0	100	0	52	26	6
5.91	1.78	**C+ / 6.2**	13.4	2.05	12.7	16.17	83	3.28	-2.01	N/A	0	0	100	0	31	70	6
5.56	1.90	**C+ / 6.3**	17.4	2.53	13.5	15.43	42	1.69	5.65	N/A	0	0	100	0	12	19	6
5.97	1.91	**C+ / 5.6**	16.4	2.30	12.8	15.09	40	5.04	2.76	N/A	0	0	100	0	8	63	6
7.00	1.14	**U /**	N/A	N/A	N/A	18.74	630	-6.78	3.80	N/A	0	0	100	0	37	N/A	2
6.12	3.08	**B- / 7.9**	11.7	-20.54	N/A	8.74	320	-9.27	0.99	N/A	5	0	94	1	38	91	7
5.60	0.95	**U /**	N/A	N/A	N/A	18.83	356	-7.97	N/A	N/A	6	0	93	1	70	N/A	0
6.86	1.08	**U /**	N/A	N/A	N/A	21.84	1,654	-11.68	-9.02	N/A	0	81	0	19	124	N/A	1
6.39	1.14	**U /**	N/A	N/A	N/A	24.14	341	-13.17	-10.80	21.2	0	81	0	19	110	N/A	1
6.41	1.38	**U /**	N/A	N/A	N/A	23.84	1,751	-13.80	-10.19	19.9	1	98	0	1	22	N/A	2
0.00	N/A	**U /**	N/A	N/A	N/A	19.52	N/A	2.20	N/A	N/A	0	0	0	100	N/A	N/A	0
3.62	1.20	**B- / 7.8**	12.7	0.49	7.3	8.73	108	-14.20	-11.70	15.7	0	4	6	90	32	38	19
0.00	1.99	**C / 4.6**	18.9	1.04	N/A	11.63	93	-13.16	-13.58	N/A	1	98	0	1	41	2	1
0.00	N/A	**U /**	64.9	1.18	N/A	9.91	9	-5.15	4.45	N/A	0	100	0	0	1	N/A	37
0.00	N/A	**U /**	N/A	N/A	N/A	19.20	N/A	4.32	N/A	N/A	9	90	0	1	N/A	N/A	0
6.91	3.55	**B- / 7.0**	14.0	0.57	N/A	11.61	69	-27.82	-26.32	N/A	0	30	57	13	N/A	78	13
7.34	1.22	**D+ / 2.7**	24.1	1.41	N/A	11.80	119	-10.68	-7.75	N/A	0	100	0	0	36	10	15
10.34	1.15	**U /**	N/A	N/A	N/A	14.65	967	0.27	-0.69	N/A	0	0	99	1	63	N/A	2
8.02	1.11	**U /**	N/A	N/A	N/A	19.54	824	-11.21	-10.46	N/A	1	0	98	1	44	N/A	2
5.55	1.56	**U /**	N/A	N/A	5.0	24.17	252	-12.12	-9.95	30.1	0	67	30	3	44	N/A	1
8.04	1.15	**U /**	N/A	N/A	N/A	23.92	1,022	-3.43	1.43	N/A	1	3	15	81	23	N/A	2
8.05	1.51	**U /**	N/A	N/A	14.1	23.81	230	-7.81	-2.22	17.1	2	0	25	73	79	N/A	2
5.70	0.89	**U /**	N/A	N/A	7.3	14.69	101	-5.65	-8.62	N/A	0	0	100	0	11	N/A	3
6.49	0.85	**U /**	N/A	N/A	12.3	15.35	90	0.65	-2.72	N/A	0	0	100	0	12	N/A	3
0.49	0.30	**U /**	N/A	N/A	N/A	80.97	134	-0.05	N/A	35.4	0	100	0	0	8	N/A	2
0.00	N/A	**U /**	N/A	N/A	N/A	19.62	N/A	-0.97	N/A	N/A	0	0	0	100	N/A	N/A	0
3.16	N/A	**U /**	N/A	N/A	N/A	20.28	N/A	-1.78	N/A	N/A	0	0	0	100	N/A	N/A	1
2.10	1.03	**C / 4.6**	22.3	0.98	N/A	17.71	399	2.20	2.97	20.6	6	93	0	1	79	97	19
0.00	2.28	**C / 4.8**	23.5	0.98	N/A	16.44	73	-12.53	-10.83	19.7	10	89	0	1	7	84	1
4.31	1.91	**U /**	N/A	N/A	N/A	23.22	137	-0.60	N/A	34.4	2	0	0	98	35	N/A	1

N/A denotes number is not available

Fund Type	Fund Name (99 Pct = Best, 0 Pct = Worst)	Ticker Symbol	Overall Weiss Investment Rating	PRICE: Price As of 6/30/05	PRICE: 52 Week High	PRICE: 52 Week Low	PERFORMANCE: Performance Rating/Pts	% Total Return Through 6/30/05: 3 Mo	6 Mo	1Yr/Pct	Annualized 3Yr/Pct	Annualized 5Yr/Pct
IN	First Trust Value Line 100 Fund	FVL	**U**	15.24	17.24	13.58	**U /**	--	-5.15	6.45 / 15	--	--
IN	First Trust Value Line Dividend	FVD	**U**	14.67	15.70	13.71	**U /**	3.87	0.85	14.70 / 37	--	--
GL	First Trust/Aberdeen Glob Opp Inc	FAM	**U**	17.85	N/A	N/A	**U /**	5.61	-4.85	--	--	--
IN	First Trust/Fid Asset Mgmt Cov Call	FFA	**U**	18.97	N/A	N/A	**U /**	-2.41	0.37	--	--	--
LP	First Trust/Four Corners Sr Fltg II	FCT	**U**	17.22	20.30	17.17	**U /**	-6.48	-2.12	-9.17 / 1	--	--
LP	First Trust/Four Corners Sr Fltg Rt	FCM	**U**	17.65	21.00	17.50	**U /**	-4.73	-3.71	-9.58 / 1	--	--
GI	First Trust/Ibbotson Eq Inc&Growth	FVI	**U**	20.11	21.66	16.00	**U /**	5.59	9.09	26.20 / 65	--	--
IN	Flaherty&Crumrine Preferred Inc Opp	PFO	**D+**	12.77	14.11	11.55	**D+ / 2.5**	8.67	-3.15	7.89 / 18	9.57 / 35	14.46 / 68
IN	Flaherty&Crumrine Preferred Income	PFD	**D**	16.75	19.00	15.25	**D+ / 2.6**	9.20	-4.29	2.53 / 8	10.76 / 45	14.73 / 69
LP	Floating Rate Income Strategies	FRA	**U**	17.45	19.75	17.44	**U /**	-8.61	-1.93	-4.93 / 2	--	--
LP	Floating Rate Income Strategies 2	FRB	**U**	17.66	N/A	N/A	**U /**	-5.25	-0.93	--	--	--
GEI	Fort Dearborn Inc. Secs.	FDI	**C-**	14.90	15.37	13.70	**D / 1.8**	6.56	2.83	15.35 / 39	5.46 / 10	9.13 / 36
GR	Foxby Corp	FXX	**E+**	2.18	2.28	2.01	**E- / 0.0**	-3.11	-2.68	1.40 / 7	-1.77 / 1	-23.58 / 1
GI	Franklin Multi-Income Trust	FMI	**B+**	9.35	9.36	6.91	**B+ / 8.3**	7.25	19.59	40.29 / 94	14.65 / 71	11.24 / 48
GEN	Franklin Templeton Ltd Duration Inc	FTF	**U**	13.67	15.01	13.20	**U /**	-1.73	-4.58	10.47 / 25	--	--
GI	Franklin Universal Trust	FT	**D-**	6.14	6.32	5.30	**C- / 3.0**	5.00	4.97	22.71 / 56	7.22 / 18	5.16 / 22
GI	Gabelli Convertible&Income Sec Fund	GCV	**E+**	9.50	10.77	8.84	**D- / 1.4**	4.79	6.71	4.22 / 10	6.82 / 16	9.99 / 42
IN	Gabelli Dividend & Income Trust	GDV	**U**	18.48	18.76	16.50	**U /**	5.23	8.04	13.05 / 31	--	--
GR	Gabelli Equity Trust	GAB	**E**	8.93	9.40	7.64	**D / 1.9**	0.76	3.56	17.44 / 43	6.27 / 14	6.72 / 27
PM	Gabelli Global Gold Nat Res&Income	GGN	**U**	19.65	N/A	N/A	**U /**	--	--	--	--	--
GL	Gabelli Global Multimedia Trust	GGT	**D+**	10.03	10.82	8.30	**C- / 4.2**	-0.09	-2.09	13.24 / 32	13.63 / 66	-2.94 / 7
UT	Gabelli Global Utility&Income Trust	GLU	**U**	19.25	20.13	17.90	**U /**	5.92	2.56	11.24 / 27	--	--
UT	Gabelli Utility Trust	GUT	**B**	10.00	10.24	8.57	**B / 8.2**	8.58	14.79	26.20 / 65	17.94 / 84	18.56 / 90
GR	General American Investors	GAM	**D+**	31.72	32.50	27.88	**D / 1.7**	3.73	2.38	8.89 / 21	7.17 / 18	2.89 / 17
FO	Germany Fund	GER	**E-**	7.77	8.48	6.29	**E+ / 0.6**	-2.87	-3.24	15.30 / 38	4.42 / 6	-6.71 / 5
EM	Global High Income Dollar Fund	GHI	**B-**	16.94	20.29	14.80	**B / 7.7**	3.50	-3.67	30.31 / 76	19.70 / 88	19.21 / 92
GL	Global Income Fund	GIF	**D-**	4.35	4.95	4.13	**E / 0.4**	2.55	-6.27	10.14 / 24	4.08 / 6	8.11 / 32
FO	Greater China Fund	GCH	**D+**	16.20	17.68	12.81	**B- / 7.5**	1.44	5.40	20.92 / 51	19.96 / 89	14.29 / 66
HL	H&Q Healthcare Investors	HQH	**D**	17.65	18.99	16.01	**C / 4.3**	10.70	1.69	12.32 / 30	12.46 / 59	2.83 / 16
HL	H&Q Life Sciences Investors	HQL	**C-**	15.89	17.00	13.77	**C / 5.3**	12.29	4.23	12.12 / 29	14.23 / 69	0.99 / 14
GL	Hartford Income Shares Fund Inc	HSF	**C**	7.75	7.95	7.06	**C / 4.7**	10.36	6.41	14.73 / 37	11.71 / 53	9.30 / 37
GL	Herzfeld Caribbean Basin Fund	CUBA	**B-**	6.30	6.66	4.00	**B+ / 8.9**	7.51	7.33	28.05 / 70	22.86 / 94	5.93 / 25
COH	High Income Opportunity Fund Inc.	HIO	**C-**	6.46	7.03	6.11	**C- / 3.2**	6.59	1.30	6.45 / 14	11.57 / 51	3.65 / 18
COH	High Yield Income Fund	HYI	**C+**	5.42	6.18	4.96	**C+ / 5.8**	10.88	-5.48	10.42 / 25	16.53 / 79	10.61 / 46
COH	High Yield Plus Fund	HYP	**C-**	4.00	4.75	3.80	**C+ / 5.7**	4.58	-8.42	9.03 / 22	17.45 / 82	2.54 / 16
GR	HOLDRS B2B Internet	BHH	**E-**	2.00	2.98	1.97	**E- / 0.0**	-18.06	-20.63	-9.46 / 1	-8.09 / 0	-43.03 / 0
HL	HOLDRS Biotech	BBH	**A+**	167.30	172.87	127.79	**A / 9.4**	15.70	10.68	16.87 / 41	27.32 / 96	-0.69 / 11
GR	HOLDRS Broadband	BDH	**D-**	15.33	17.30	13.16	**B- / 7.2**	8.81	-9.81	-4.47 / 3	22.85 / 94	-29.76 / 0
FO	HOLDRS Europe 2001	EKH	**D-**	63.10	66.20	52.85	**D / 2.1**	0.38	0.34	7.82 / 18	9.17 / 32	--
GR	HOLDRS Internet	HHH	**C**	55.94	72.48	49.15	**A- / 9.0**	5.75	-19.08	-10.32 / 0	32.31 / 97	-12.11 / 3
GR	HOLDRS Internet Architecture	IAH	**E**	34.23	38.36	29.70	**D / 1.6**	-1.82	-9.04	-1.73 / 5	10.35 / 41	-17.65 / 2
GR	HOLDRS Internet Infrastructure	IIH	**D-**	4.05	4.82	2.86	**B- / 7.4**	7.43	-10.99	10.36 / 25	21.65 / 92	-41.59 / 0
GR	HOLDRS Market 2000 +	MKH	**D-**	53.59	56.50	50.61	**E / 0.4**	0.34	-2.72	1.89 / 7	4.75 / 8	--
EN	HOLDRS Oil Services	OIH	**D+**	102.90	105.45	68.00	**A / 9.3**	10.26	20.08	44.01 / 97	19.31 / 87	--
HL	HOLDRS Pharmaceutical	PPH	**D-**	74.03	78.86	67.00	**E- / 0.1**	3.58	3.24	-3.62 / 3	0.37 / 1	-5.35 / 5
FS	HOLDRS Regional Bank	RKH	**D**	134.50	142.88	126.25	**D- / 1.2**	3.85	-4.03	5.62 / 12	7.19 / 18	10.29 / 44
GR	HOLDRS Retail	RTH	**E+**	94.62	102.15	83.80	**E / 0.5**	2.33	0.87	6.58 / 15	3.89 / 5	--
GR	HOLDRS Semiconductor	SMH	**E-**	34.10	38.05	27.78	**E / 0.3**	4.54	3.58	-8.22 / 1	4.07 / 6	-18.30 / 1
GR	HOLDRS Software	SWH	**E**	34.96	40.75	31.16	**D / 2.0**	1.14	-7.23	3.03 / 9	10.27 / 40	--
FO	HOLDRS TeleBras	TBH	**E+**	30.45	32.60	25.72	**C+ / 6.3**	14.03	2.92	16.96 / 42	14.75 / 72	-17.92 / 2
GR	HOLDRS Telecom	TTH	**E**	27.02	30.10	25.68	**E- / 0.1**	2.71	-6.90	7.27 / 16	2.01 / 2	-15.79 / 2
UT	HOLDRS Utilities	UTH	**C+**	109.69	111.12	80.08	**B / 8.0**	8.71	13.17	38.97 / 92	14.25 / 69	7.62 / 29

N/A denotes number is not available

		RISK				NET ASSETS		VALUATION			ASSET					FUND MANAGER	
Incl. in Returns			3 Year					Premium / Discount									
Dividend Yield %	Expense Ratio	Risk Rating/ Pts	Standard Deviation	Beta	Avg Dura- tion	NAV as of 6/30/05	Total $(Mil)	As of 6/30/05	1 Year Average	Wtd Avg P/E	Cash %	Stocks %	Bonds %	Other %	Portfolio Turnover Ratio	Manager Quality Pct	Manager Tenure (Years)
0.00	0.97	**U /**	N/A	N/A	N/A	17.52	316	-13.01	-9.48	25.8	0	99	0	1	220	N/A	2
2.72	0.93	**U /**	N/A	N/A	N/A	17.32	573	-15.30	-13.93	24.2	0	100	0	0	30	N/A	2
4.88	1.44	**U /**	N/A	N/A	N/A	19.22	333	-7.13	N/A	N/A	0	0	100	0	N/A	N/A	1
7.52	1.26	**U /**	N/A	N/A	N/A	18.74	395	1.23	N/A	36.5	0	100	0	0	73	N/A	1
5.90	1.54	**U /**	N/A	N/A	N/A	18.99	484	-9.32	-1.52	N/A	0	0	0	100	148	N/A	1
6.51	2.01	**U /**	N/A	N/A	N/A	19.11	95	-7.64	-0.17	N/A	0	0	0	100	141	N/A	2
0.20	1.09	**U /**	N/A	N/A	N/A	23.21	145	-13.36	-13.32	N/A	0	100	0	0	82	N/A	1
6.57	1.52	**C+ / 6.5**	16.7	-0.01	13.6	12.74	142	0.24	5.43	15.9	1	3	1	95	28	88	13
6.39	1.48	**C / 5.2**	21.5	0.17	13.7	16.02	159	4.56	11.08	17.8	1	4	0	95	27	89	14
6.56	1.97	**U /**	N/A	N/A	N/A	19.21	360	-9.16	-2.18	N/A	0	0	29	71	22	N/A	2
5.33	1.30	**U /**	N/A	N/A	N/A	19.38	207	-8.88	N/A	N/A	0	0	23	77	30	N/A	1
5.32	0.74	**B / 8.6**	9.4	1.68	9.5	16.69	142	-10.72	-10.57	N/A	0	0	99	1	44	34	4
0.00	5.27	**C / 5.5**	19.9	0.82	N/A	2.50	7	-12.80	-12.76	22.1	0	100	0	0	164	4	3
4.48	N/A	**C+ / 5.8**	18.9	0.55	5.2	9.53	53	-1.89	-9.77	20.8	1	42	52	5	27	90	16
8.02	1.21	**U /**	N/A	N/A	N/A	14.44	385	-5.33	-2.00	N/A	1	0	98	1	55	N/A	2
6.81	N/A	**C / 4.6**	18.7	0.38	5.1	6.98	196	-12.03	-12.55	20.9	1	24	70	5	19	77	17
8.06	1.61	**C / 4.9**	18.2	-0.01	6.7	8.00	97	18.75	17.05	18.3	0	28	29	43	57	86	16
5.38	1.12	**U /**	N/A	N/A	2.1	20.36	1,707	-9.23	-8.32	21.4	8	71	15	6	33	N/A	2
8.04	1.57	**D+ / 2.8**	22.2	1.25	4.1	8.33	1,219	7.20	6.22	27.4	0	92	0	8	29	28	19
2.84	N/A	**U /**	N/A	N/A	N/A	19.67	N/A	-0.10	N/A	N/A	0	0	0	100	N/A	N/A	0
2.38	1.87	**C / 5.0**	20.5	1.13	5.5	11.61	174	-13.61	-14.19	40.5	0	92	6	2	8	60	11
5.02	1.49	**U /**	N/A	N/A	6.8	21.37	64	-9.92	-5.74	18.2	0	88	10	2	17	N/A	1
7.29	2.04	**C / 5.5**	18.0	0.30	N/A	7.34	207	36.24	37.15	20.7	2	73	23	2	18	92	6
0.01	1.15	**B- / 7.6**	14.4	0.93	4.1	37.05	1,036	-14.39	-11.80	24.2	3	97	0	0	17	59	10
0.32	1.58	**D / 1.7**	29.8	1.69	N/A	8.86	140	-12.30	-12.99	N/A	0	99	0	1	205	N/A	1
8.30	1.43	**C / 5.3**	16.5	0.92	10.2	15.59	295	8.66	12.51	N/A	7	0	93	0	86	89	12
6.44	1.67	**C+ / 6.9**	13.6	1.05	4.3	4.59	37	-5.23	-6.13	N/A	0	0	100	0	97	7	5
1.28	2.28	**D- / 1.2**	34.0	1.17	N/A	18.46	216	-12.24	-9.26	N/A	4	95	0	1	66	82	13
7.95	1.60	**C- / 3.7**	21.4	0.96	N/A	18.01	361	-2.00	-2.06	151.0	8	76	0	16	37	80	1
7.81	1.78	**C- / 4.2**	21.4	0.98	N/A	16.19	190	-1.85	-1.84	167.5	15	66	0	19	27	83	1
7.14	0.77	**C+ / 6.9**	13.5	0.86	12.8	8.16	109	-5.02	-6.85	N/A	0	0	99	1	5	73	4
0.00	3.40	**C / 4.4**	20.7	0.50	N/A	7.24	12	-12.98	-13.44	23.3	0	100	0	0	14	95	11
8.36	1.25	**C+ / 6.1**	12.8	1.28	6.5	7.16	530	-9.78	-8.74	17.1	1	0	98	1	19	13	12
8.79	2.56	**C+ / 6.1**	19.5	1.98	N/A	5.59	67	-3.04	1.18	N/A	0	0	100	0	34	4	6
8.98	2.67	**C / 4.8**	17.5	2.18	5.3	3.87	62	3.36	9.08	N/A	0	0	100	0	56	2	3
14.73	N/A	**E- / 0.0**	49.3	2.54	N/A	2.00	32	0.00	N/A	N/A	0	100	0	0	N/A	N/A	5
0.00	N/A	**C+ / 6.6**	19.4	0.65	N/A	167.30	1,371	0.00	N/A	N/A	0	100	0	0	N/A	98	5
0.01	N/A	**E- / 0.0**	37.0	1.92	N/A	15.33	118	0.00	N/A	N/A	0	100	0	0	N/A	85	5
2.05	N/A	**C / 4.5**	20.8	1.23	N/A	63.10	19	0.00	N/A	N/A	0	100	0	0	N/A	11	4
0.00	N/A	**D+ / 2.7**	33.0	1.77	N/A	55.94	251	0.00	N/A	N/A	0	100	0	0	N/A	95	5
0.18	N/A	**D+ / 2.6**	27.6	1.68	N/A	34.23	83	0.00	N/A	N/A	0	100	0	0	N/A	33	5
0.00	N/A	**E- / 0.0**	52.0	2.91	N/A	4.05	37	0.00	N/A	N/A	0	100	0	0	N/A	46	5
1.38	N/A	**B- / 7.1**	15.1	1.03	N/A	53.59	54	0.00	N/A	N/A	0	100	0	0	N/A	27	5
0.88	N/A	**E- / 0.0**	24.3	1.09	N/A	102.90	933	0.00	N/A	N/A	0	100	0	0	N/A	33	4
2.23	N/A	**C+ / 6.5**	14.5	0.64	N/A	74.03	1,038	0.00	N/A	N/A	0	100	0	0	N/A	12	5
0.78	N/A	**C+ / 6.7**	14.1	0.87	N/A	134.50	200	0.00	N/A	N/A	0	100	0	0	N/A	49	5
0.09	N/A	**C / 4.7**	18.2	1.03	N/A	94.62	440	0.00	N/A	N/A	0	100	0	0	N/A	23	4
0.09	N/A	**E- / 0.0**	42.1	2.26	N/A	34.10	2,422	0.00	N/A	N/A	0	100	0	0	N/A	1	5
0.05	N/A	**D+ / 2.6**	29.4	1.81	N/A	34.96	202	0.00	N/A	N/A	0	100	0	0	N/A	30	4
0.87	N/A	**E- / 0.0**	45.6	1.92	N/A	30.45	763	0.00	N/A	N/A	0	100	0	0	N/A	6	7
0.21	N/A	**C- / 3.6**	24.4	1.39	N/A	27.02	202	0.00	N/A	N/A	0	100	0	0	N/A	5	5
2.39	N/A	**C- / 4.2**	17.3	0.96	N/A	109.69	405	0.00	N/A	N/A	0	100	0	0	N/A	52	5

N/A denotes number is not available

Fund Type	Fund Name (99 Pct = Best, 0 Pct = Worst)	Ticker Symbol	Overall Weiss Investment Rating	PRICE: Price As of 6/30/05	PRICE: 52 Week High	PRICE: 52 Week Low	PERFORMANCE: Performance Rating/Pts	% Total Return Through 6/30/05: 3 Mo	6 Mo	1Yr/Pct	Annualized: 3Yr/Pct	Annualized: 5Yr/Pct
GR	HOLDRS Wireless	WMH	**C+**	55.80	62.87	51.57	**B / 8.1**	4.84	-5.43	11.50 / 28	23.25 / 95	--
MTG	Hyperion 2005 Inv Gr Opp Tm Tr	HTO	**D+**	9.78	9.81	9.47	**E / 0.3**	1.27	0.97	3.95 / 10	2.65 / 3	8.55 / 33
MTG	Hyperion Strategic Mortgage Income	HSM	**U**	13.77	15.05	13.08	**U /**	4.33	-1.67	13.74 / 34	--	--
MTG	Hyperion Total Return Fund	HTR	**D+**	9.26	10.47	8.98	**D / 2.1**	-2.60	-1.03	13.50 / 33	9.20 / 33	14.28 / 66
FO	India Fund	IFN	**B-**	30.50	31.75	19.75	**A+ / 9.9**	17.53	7.61	50.84 / 99	50.94 / 99	18.32 / 89
FO	Indonesia Fund	IF	**C**	5.75	6.99	3.27	**A+ / 9.8**	0.88	10.58	56.91 / 99	40.95 / 99	11.75 / 52
GI	ING Clarion Glob Real Est Inc Fd	IGR	**U**	15.03	15.57	12.00	**U /**	8.75	5.81	33.37 / 82	--	--
GI	ING Clarion Real Estate Income	IIA	**U**	15.63	16.42	13.15	**U /**	9.63	2.87	25.04 / 62	--	--
GL	ING GLobal Equity Dividend Premium	IGD	**U**	19.99	N/A	N/A	**U /**	--	--	--	--	--
LP	ING Prime Rate Trust	PPR	**D+**	6.99	8.15	6.76	**D- / 1.3**	-1.64	-5.33	-7.80 / 2	10.17 / 39	2.53 / 15
MUN	Insured Municipal Income Fund	PIF	**C**	13.18	13.64	12.50	**D+ / 2.7**	5.68	4.13	11.64 / 44	4.04 / 14	8.41 / 59
MUN	Investment Grade Municipal Income	PPM	**C-**	13.67	14.60	13.01	**D+ / 2.3**	5.97	4.34	11.78 / 45	3.14 / 8	8.16 / 56
HL	iShares Biotechnology Index Fund	IBB	**E-**	67.57	76.19	61.22	**D- / 1.1**	2.85	-10.15	-8.95 / 1	9.83 / 37	--
GI	iShares Cohen&Steers Realty Major	ICF	**A-**	70.50	72.73	54.03	**A- / 9.0**	14.45	6.37	33.54 / 82	21.41 / 92	--
PM	iShares Comex Gold Trust	IAU	**U**	43.91	N/A	N/A	**U /**	3.39	--	--	--	--
IN	iShares DJ US Select Dividend Index	DVY	**U**	61.41	63.13	53.90	**U /**	4.43	1.56	15.23 / 38	--	--
IN	iShares Dow Jones Transportation	IYT	**U**	61.34	69.82	53.32	**U /**	-8.45	-9.80	8.36 / 20	--	--
GR	iShares Dow Jones US Basic Mtrls	IYM	**E**	46.50	54.50	42.04	**E / 0.3**	-8.96	-7.33	6.10 / 13	6.05 / 13	7.82 / 31
GR	iShares Dow Jones US Cns Gd Sct Idx	IYK	**D+**	52.30	54.75	46.70	**E+ / 0.9**	1.00	-0.82	2.41 / 8	6.42 / 14	6.51 / 27
GR	iShares Dow Jones US Cns Sv Sct Idx	IYC	**D-**	58.97	61.70	50.82	**E+ / 0.8**	0.83	-2.21	5.72 / 13	6.05 / 13	0.09 / 12
EN	iShares Dow Jones US Energy Sector	IYE	**B-**	77.92	80.22	54.70	**A / 9.3**	5.52	21.10	40.78 / 95	20.88 / 90	11.30 / 49
FS	iShares Dow Jones US Financial Sct	IYF	**D+**	94.37	98.20	85.85	**D / 2.1**	5.49	-2.24	7.17 / 16	8.92 / 29	7.75 / 30
FS	iShares Dow Jones US Financial Srv	IYG	**D+**	107.64	113.68	98.60	**D / 2.0**	4.26	-4.04	6.42 / 14	9.01 / 31	7.99 / 32
HL	iShares Dow Jones US Healthcare	IYH	**C-**	61.20	62.49	52.01	**D- / 1.5**	5.29	4.92	5.63 / 12	7.07 / 17	-0.49 / 12
GR	iShares Dow Jones US Industrial	IYJ	**D**	53.39	57.24	48.07	**D- / 1.2**	-3.72	-5.68	3.58 / 10	8.46 / 25	-1.07 / 11
GI	iShares Dow Jones US Real Estate	IYR	**B+**	62.82	65.07	49.34	**B+ / 8.5**	13.93	5.58	29.40 / 74	19.09 / 87	18.47 / 89
GR	iShares Dow Jones US Technology	IYW	**E-**	46.09	50.22	39.70	**D- / 1.4**	3.42	-4.71	-2.13 / 5	9.11 / 32	-18.16 / 1
GR	iShares Dow Jones US Telecom	IYZ	**E**	23.19	24.90	20.75	**D+ / 2.5**	2.97	-3.28	12.77 / 31	9.88 / 37	-15.69 / 3
GR	iShares Dow Jones US Total Mkt	IYY	**D+**	57.37	58.95	50.28	**D / 2.2**	2.42	-0.11	7.93 / 18	9.35 / 34	-1.84 / 9
UT	iShares Dow Jones US Utilities	IDU	**B**	76.12	77.21	57.74	**B- / 7.1**	8.83	12.06	33.36 / 82	12.74 / 62	6.38 / 26
FO	iShares FTSE/Xinhua China 25	FXI	**U**	56.46	N/A	N/A	**U /**	2.82	1.26	--	--	--
EN	iShares Goldman Sachs Nat Res Index	IGE	**C+**	76.30	78.49	55.56	**B+ / 8.7**	5.77	16.92	34.36 / 84	18.73 / 85	--
GR	iShares Goldman Sachs Ntwr Index Fd	IGN	**D**	27.70	31.85	23.26	**B- / 7.0**	9.53	-9.03	-10.27 / 0	22.96 / 94	--
GR	iShares Goldman Sachs Semicon Index	IGW	**E-**	53.60	59.60	43.70	**E- / 0.2**	4.91	0.71	-8.12 / 1	3.81 / 5	--
GR	iShares Goldman Sachs Software Indx	IGV	**E-**	38.38	43.45	31.08	**D+ / 2.6**	0.44	-9.13	3.02 / 9	12.04 / 56	--
GR	iShares Goldman Sachs Technology	IGM	**E-**	43.46	47.80	37.63	**D- / 1.2**	2.74	-6.46	-4.23 / 3	9.23 / 33	--
COI	iShares GS$ InvesTop Corp Bond	LQD	**U**	111.83	113.80	106.57	**U /**	3.91	2.02	9.01 / 21	--	--
GR	iShares KLD Select Social SM Index	KLD	**U**	50.97	N/A	N/A	**U /**	3.33	--	--	--	--
USA	iShares Lehman 1-3Yr Treasury Bond	SHY	**U**	81.23	82.28	80.62	**U /**	1.33	0.91	1.89 / 7	--	--
USA	iShares Lehman 20+Yr Treasury Bond	TLT	**U**	96.39	97.00	82.17	**U /**	10.40	11.17	21.38 / 53	--	--
USA	iShares Lehman 7-10Yr Treasury Bond	IEF	**U**	86.99	87.49	82.10	**U /**	5.78	3.83	9.11 / 22	--	--
GEI	iShares Lehman Aggregate Fund	AGG	**U**	103.32	103.50	99.41	**U /**	3.50	2.40	6.95 / 16	--	--
USA	iShares Lehman TIPS Bond Fund	TIP	**U**	107.00	107.90	100.52	**U /**	3.88	2.24	9.57 / 23	--	--
IN	iShares Morningstar Large Core	JKD	**U**	63.38	N/A	N/A	**U /**	0.25	-2.13	--	--	--
GR	iShares Morningstar Large Growth	JKE	**U**	58.04	N/A	N/A	**U /**	3.56	-1.80	--	--	--
IN	iShares Morningstar Large Value	JKF	**U**	66.58	N/A	N/A	**U /**	3.16	2.18	--	--	--
IN	iShares Morningstar Mid Core	JKG	**U**	67.03	N/A	N/A	**U /**	2.82	1.25	--	--	--
GR	iShares Morningstar Mid Growth	JKH	**U**	67.91	N/A	N/A	**U /**	3.92	2.46	--	--	--
IN	iShares Morningstar Mid Value	JKI	**U**	70.78	N/A	N/A	**U /**	5.05	5.98	--	--	--
IN	iShares Morningstar Small Core	JKJ	**U**	67.20	N/A	N/A	**U /**	1.32	-1.18	--	--	--
GR	iShares Morningstar Small Growth	JKK	**U**	61.51	N/A	N/A	**U /**	2.36	-3.41	--	--	--
IN	iShares Morningstar Small Value	JKL	**U**	67.46	N/A	N/A	**U /**	3.00	-0.95	--	--	--

N/A denotes number is not available

		RISK				NET ASSETS		VALUATION			ASSET					FUND MANAGER	
Incl. in Returns		Risk Rating/ Pts	3 Year		Avg Duration	NAV as of 6/30/05	Total $(Mil)	Premium / Discount		Wtd Avg P/E	Cash %	Stocks %	Bonds %	Other %	Portfolio Turnover Ratio	Manager Quality Pct	Manager Tenure (Years)
Dividend Yield %	Expense Ratio		Standard Deviation	Beta				As of 6/30/05	1 Year Average								
0.59	N/A	**C-** / **4.1**	25.6	1.54	N/A	55.80	74	0.00	N/A	N/A	0	100	0	0	N/A	90	5
0.12	1.30	**B** / **8.9**	3.6	0.88	N/A	9.89	167	-1.11	-1.39	N/A	18	0	40	42	299	48	8
9.21	1.83	**U** /	N/A	N/A	N/A	14.42	148	-4.51	-0.83	N/A	0	0	100	0	65	N/A	3
9.43	1.71	**C+** / **6.7**	13.1	3.21	N/A	9.10	282	1.76	9.12	N/A	0	0	100	0	80	41	7
5.09	1.64	**C-** / **3.5**	32.6	1.00	N/A	30.01	645	1.63	0.14	40.5	0	100	0	0	36	99	11
3.08	2.03	**D-** / **1.2**	41.8	1.22	N/A	6.06	42	-5.12	-1.13	N/A	2	97	0	1	44	99	2
8.15	0.82	**U** /	N/A	N/A	N/A	17.18	1,766	-12.51	-9.04	65.0	0	100	0	0	22	N/A	1
8.65	0.90	**U** /	N/A	N/A	12.3	18.05	263	-13.41	-9.20	69.7	0	100	0	0	22	N/A	2
3.12	N/A	**U** /	N/A	N/A	N/A	18.73	N/A	6.73	N/A	N/A	0	100	0	0	N/A	N/A	0
6.47	3.17	**B-** / **7.9**	11.1	-29.39	N/A	7.36	1,083	-5.03	2.56	N/A	0	0	0	100	93	96	6
5.00	1.51	**B** / **8.4**	9.0	1.52	9.5	15.33	308	-14.02	-13.36	N/A	13	0	86	1	50	23	9
5.45	1.61	**B-** / **7.8**	11.3	1.67	9.2	15.89	161	-13.97	-12.93	N/A	0	0	100	0	21	13	3
0.00	0.50	**D** / **1.6**	21.6	1.00	N/A	67.54	1,079	0.04	-0.02	83.7	0	100	0	0	14	72	4
5.10	0.35	**C+** / **5.9**	17.0	0.45	N/A	70.44	1,298	0.09	N/A	45.7	0	100	0	0	28	97	4
0.00	0.40	**U** /	N/A	N/A	N/A	43.98	174	-0.16	N/A	N/A	0	0	0	100	N/A	N/A	0
2.99	0.40	**U** /	N/A	N/A	N/A	61.35	6,371	0.10	0.09	16.7	0	100	0	0	20	N/A	2
0.85	0.60	**U** /	N/A	N/A	N/A	61.34	108	0.00	-0.01	21.0	0	100	0	0	5	N/A	2
1.75	0.60	**C-** / **3.0**	21.0	1.24	N/A	46.56	413	-0.13	0.02	23.0	0	100	0	0	6	24	5
1.61	0.60	**B-** / **7.8**	11.9	0.59	N/A	52.29	421	0.02	N/A	19.7	0	100	0	0	9	68	5
0.16	0.60	**C+** / **6.3**	16.9	1.08	N/A	59.03	251	-0.10	N/A	27.3	0	100	0	0	13	38	5
1.28	0.60	**C-** / **3.9**	19.4	0.99	N/A	77.81	639	0.14	0.05	18.3	0	100	0	0	3	60	5
1.77	0.60	**C+** / **6.9**	15.3	1.02	N/A	94.23	300	0.15	N/A	19.2	0	100	0	0	7	56	5
1.17	0.60	**C+** / **6.9**	15.6	1.03	N/A	107.69	142	-0.05	0.01	15.5	0	100	0	0	7	54	5
0.78	0.60	**B-** / **7.9**	10.7	0.55	N/A	61.22	1,169	-0.03	N/A	32.1	0	100	0	0	4	72	5
0.48	0.60	**C+** / **6.7**	15.8	1.03	N/A	53.43	237	-0.07	0.02	22.2	0	100	0	0	5	63	5
4.04	0.60	**C+** / **5.9**	16.8	0.49	N/A	63.13	737	-0.49	-0.11	49.4	0	100	0	0	16	95	5
0.23	0.60	**D-** / **1.4**	27.9	1.74	N/A	46.04	395	0.11	0.03	39.2	0	100	0	0	9	20	5
2.27	0.60	**D** / **1.8**	25.9	1.55	N/A	23.15	313	0.17	0.02	20.2	0	100	0	0	10	45	5
1.39	0.20	**B-** / **7.1**	14.3	1.01	N/A	57.39	415	-0.03	0.02	25.1	0	100	0	0	6	69	5
2.80	0.60	**C+** / **6.5**	16.6	0.88	N/A	76.16	646	-0.05	-0.02	19.8	0	100	0	0	7	50	5
0.00	0.74	**U** /	N/A	N/A	N/A	56.89	672	-0.76	N/A	N/A	0	100	0	0	9	N/A	1
1.15	0.50	**C-** / **3.8**	19.3	0.96	N/A	76.34	425	-0.05	0.04	22.7	0	100	0	0	3	53	4
0.00	0.50	**D-** / **1.4**	46.2	2.56	N/A	27.74	164	-0.14	-0.06	37.6	0	100	0	0	7	74	4
0.00	0.50	**D** / **1.6**	41.9	2.37	N/A	53.60	264	0.00	N/A	31.4	0	100	0	0	8	1	4
0.20	0.50	**E-** / **0.0**	28.0	1.70	N/A	38.35	137	0.08	-0.05	135.6	0	100	0	0	9	53	4
0.04	0.50	**D-** / **1.3**	28.6	1.81	N/A	43.41	183	0.12	0.04	42.3	0	100	0	0	4	18	4
4.61	0.15	**U** /	N/A	N/A	N/A	112.11	2,555	-0.25	0.23	N/A	0	0	100	0	32	N/A	3
1.30	0.50	**U** /	N/A	N/A	N/A	50.82	42	0.30	N/A	N/A	0	100	0	0	3	N/A	0
2.80	0.15	**U** /	N/A	N/A	N/A	81.17	2,729	0.07	0.05	N/A	0	0	100	0	106	N/A	3
4.33	0.15	**U** /	N/A	N/A	N/A	96.38	748	0.01	0.08	N/A	0	0	100	0	18	N/A	3
3.64	0.15	**U** /	N/A	N/A	N/A	86.98	767	0.01	0.06	N/A	0	0	100	0	121	N/A	3
4.04	0.20	**U** /	N/A	N/A	N/A	102.88	1,292	0.43	0.37	N/A	0	0	100	0	457	N/A	2
5.71	0.20	**U** /	N/A	N/A	N/A	106.89	2,006	0.10	0.18	N/A	0	0	100	0	32	N/A	2
1.24	0.20	**U** /	N/A	N/A	N/A	63.27	53	0.17	N/A	20.1	0	100	0	0	4	N/A	1
0.39	0.25	**U** /	N/A	N/A	N/A	57.81	49	0.40	N/A	37.5	0	100	0	0	19	N/A	1
2.86	0.25	**U** /	N/A	N/A	N/A	66.60	55	-0.03	N/A	15.2	0	100	0	0	2	N/A	1
0.97	0.25	**U** /	N/A	N/A	N/A	66.95	63	0.12	N/A	26.7	0	100	0	0	3	N/A	1
0.07	0.30	**U** /	N/A	N/A	N/A	67.80	31	0.16	N/A	35.3	0	100	0	0	11	N/A	1
2.54	0.30	**U** /	N/A	N/A	N/A	70.64	33	0.20	N/A	20.7	0	100	0	0	7	N/A	1
0.81	0.25	**U** /	N/A	N/A	N/A	67.33	37	-0.19	N/A	31.8	0	100	0	0	16	N/A	1
0.00	0.30	**U** /	N/A	N/A	N/A	61.61	25	-0.16	N/A	52.7	0	100	0	0	26	N/A	1
1.51	0.30	**U** /	N/A	N/A	N/A	67.63	34	-0.25	N/A	29.2	0	100	0	0	10	N/A	1

N/A denotes number is not available

Fund Type	Fund Name (99 Pct = Best, 0 Pct = Worst)	Ticker Symbol	Overall Weiss Investment Rating	PRICE: Price As of 6/30/05	52 Week High	52 Week Low	PERFORMANCE: Performance Rating/Pts	% Total Return Through 6/30/05: 3 Mo	6 Mo	1Yr/Pct	Annualized 3Yr/Pct	Annualized 5Yr/Pct
FO	iShares MSCI Australia Index	EWA	A	17.66	18.29	13.00	A / 9.3	4.31	8.21	36.87 / 89	24.75 / 95	13.56 / 63
FO	iShares MSCI Austria Index	EWO	C+	23.33	25.05	16.48	A+ / 9.7	3.23	3.05	39.40 / 92	37.92 / 99	25.33 / 98
FO	iShares MSCI Belgium Index	EWK	D-	17.81	19.59	13.78	C+ / 6.5	-5.06	-3.94	27.44 / 68	18.44 / 85	9.05 / 35
FO	iShares MSCI Brazil Index	EWZ	C-	23.94	25.99	14.11	A+ / 9.9	6.97	10.63	68.67 / 99	37.41 / 98	--
FO	iShares MSCI Canada Index	EWC	C+	18.29	18.81	13.72	B+ / 8.7	4.51	9.13	30.76 / 77	21.01 / 91	4.82 / 20
FO	iShares MSCI EAFE Index Fund	EFA	C-	52.50	55.36	44.47	D+ / 2.9	-1.13	-0.19	12.97 / 31	11.61 / 52	--
EM	iShares MSCI Emerging Markets Index	EEM	U	71.25	74.17	50.77	U /	6.87	7.56	35.63 / 87	--	--
FO	iShares MSCI EMU Index	EZU	E	70.36	75.59	57.45	C- / 3.0	-2.68	-2.26	16.78 / 41	11.67 / 52	--
FO	iShares MSCI France Index	EWQ	E	23.82	25.19	19.85	D+ / 2.8	-1.41	0.72	14.84 / 37	10.58 / 43	-2.06 / 9
FO	iShares MSCI Germany Index	EWG	E-	17.65	18.87	14.49	D- / 1.4	-1.84	-4.39	13.16 / 32	7.91 / 22	-3.03 / 7
FO	iShares MSCI Hong Kong Index	EWH	D+	12.32	12.50	9.81	C+ / 6.1	6.94	2.41	27.66 / 69	13.61 / 66	1.88 / 14
FO	iShares MSCI Italy Index	EWI	D-	24.22	26.99	19.62	C / 4.9	-4.27	-4.83	17.78 / 44	16.79 / 79	2.46 / 15
FO	iShares MSCI Japan Index	EWJ	E+	10.22	11.09	9.36	E+ / 0.6	-4.58	-3.22	-2.37 / 4	6.78 / 16	-6.95 / 4
FO	iShares MSCI Malaysia Index	EWM	E+	6.99	7.80	6.26	D / 2.0	2.04	-2.65	10.78 / 26	8.95 / 30	4.00 / 19
FO	iShares MSCI Mexico Index	EWW	C	26.57	28.09	18.28	A / 9.4	10.25	7.35	37.42 / 90	24.74 / 95	12.44 / 56
FO	iShares MSCI Netherlands Index	EWN	E-	18.40	20.25	15.11	E+ / 0.6	-2.02	0.27	13.65 / 34	3.75 / 5	-4.35 / 6
FO	iShares MSCI Pacific ex-Japan Idx	EPP	A+	94.11	96.49	72.00	B+ / 8.8	4.12	6.08	34.03 / 83	21.35 / 91	--
FO	iShares MSCI Singapore Index	EWS	B	7.61	7.67	6.05	B- / 7.1	3.68	6.88	29.85 / 75	15.90 / 77	3.08 / 17
FO	iShares MSCI South Africa	EZA	U	71.66	83.05	56.25	U /	-0.89	-9.06	27.65 / 69	--	--
FO	iShares MSCI South Korea Index	EWY	D-	32.68	34.80	21.59	B / 7.7	2.57	15.89	36.30 / 87	14.78 / 72	9.70 / 39
FO	iShares MSCI Spain Index	EWP	D+	33.76	36.50	26.72	B- / 7.2	-2.48	-3.79	21.92 / 54	21.56 / 92	7.09 / 28
FO	iShares MSCI Sweden Index	EWD	D-	20.25	21.78	15.84	B / 7.7	-1.51	-3.11	17.74 / 43	21.38 / 92	-3.70 / 7
FO	iShares MSCI Switzerland Index	EWL	D-	16.60	18.09	14.20	D- / 1.1	-1.31	-1.19	9.26 / 22	7.41 / 20	1.40 / 14
FO	iShares MSCI Taiwan Index	EWT	E-	12.34	13.00	9.51	D+ / 2.4	7.03	6.56	15.89 / 39	6.27 / 14	-6.91 / 5
FO	iShares MSCI UK Index	EWU	C-	18.07	18.92	15.40	C- / 3.3	0.06	0.72	13.69 / 34	11.80 / 54	2.08 / 15
IN	iShares NYSE 100 Index Fund	NY	U	63.25	65.60	58.06	U /	1.54	-0.71	5.40 / 12	--	--
IN	iShares NYSE Composite Index Fund	NYC	U	66.30	68.45	57.20	U /	2.16	1.94	12.58 / 30	--	--
GR	iShares Russell 1000	IWB	C-	64.40	66.32	56.79	D / 2.2	2.50	0.06	8.28 / 20	9.18 / 32	-1.97 / 9
GR	iShares Russell 1000 Growth	IWF	D	47.82	49.45	43.06	D- / 1.0	2.29	-1.75	1.51 / 7	6.98 / 17	-10.50 / 3
IN	iShares Russell 1000 Value	IWD	C-	66.58	68.81	57.34	C- / 3.2	2.46	1.48	14.46 / 36	10.90 / 47	6.00 / 25
GR	iShares Russell 2000	IWM	D-	62.21	65.33	51.34	C- / 3.4	2.14	-3.02	8.03 / 19	12.43 / 59	5.00 / 21
GR	iShares Russell 2000 Growth	IWO	E	63.50	67.99	52.02	D / 2.1	1.32	-4.89	2.99 / 9	10.47 / 42	--
GR	iShares Russell 2000 Value	IWN	D	63.10	65.41	52.19	C / 4.4	3.18	-0.91	13.25 / 32	13.52 / 65	--
GR	iShares Russell 3000	IWV	D+	68.35	70.34	59.84	D / 2.2	2.52	-0.13	8.03 / 19	9.33 / 34	-1.43 / 10
GR	iShares Russell 3000 Growth	IWZ	D	38.78	40.08	34.70	D- / 1.0	2.32	-1.96	1.32 / 7	6.96 / 17	--
GR	iShares Russell 3000 Value	IWW	C-	86.82	89.48	74.55	C- / 3.0	2.14	1.44	14.05 / 35	10.71 / 44	--
GR	iShares Russell Midcap Growth Index	IWP	C	84.87	86.98	68.08	C / 4.6	2.64	1.52	9.65 / 23	14.36 / 70	--
GR	iShares Russell Midcap Index	IWR	C+	81.12	83.06	64.79	C+ / 5.7	3.71	3.60	16.41 / 40	15.47 / 75	--
GR	iShares Russell Midcap Value Index	IWS	B-	116.86	119.56	93.03	C+ / 6.5	4.56	5.12	21.09 / 52	16.11 / 77	--
IN	iShares S&P 100 Index Fund	OEF	D+	55.77	N/A	N/A	E+ / 0.8	0.75	-1.93	2.86 / 9	6.35 / 14	--
IN	iShares S&P 1500 Index Fund	ISI	U	105.74	108.93	93.36	U /	2.41	-0.11	7.46 / 17	--	--
GR	iShares S&P 500	IVV	D+	119.00	123.36	106.64	D / 1.8	2.05	-0.71	6.72 / 15	8.23 / 23	-2.45 / 8
GR	iShares S&P 500/Barra Growth	IVW	D	50.50	58.99	51.98	E+ / 0.7	0.54	-1.98	1.99 / 8	5.94 / 13	-7.72 / 4
GR	iShares S&P 500/Barra Value	IVE	D+	62.17	63.97	54.17	D+ / 2.6	3.63	0.24	11.00 / 26	9.91 / 37	3.02 / 17
FO	iShares S&P Europe 350 Index Fund	IEV	E+	74.40	78.75	62.21	C- / 3.1	-0.89	-0.57	14.75 / 37	11.71 / 53	--
IN	iShares S&P Global 100	IOO	D	60.30	63.69	54.30	D- / 1.4	-0.26	-1.29	6.33 / 14	7.89 / 22	--
EN	iShares S&P Global Energy Sector	IXC	B-	86.99	88.84	62.75	B+ / 8.9	6.23	18.27	36.75 / 88	19.50 / 88	--
FS	iShares S&P Global Financials Sect	IXG	E+	65.00	67.60	56.45	D+ / 2.4	1.33	-2.06	11.20 / 27	10.18 / 39	--
HL	iShares S&P Global Healthcare Sect	IXJ	C-	50.15	51.38	44.01	E+ / 0.8	3.06	3.10	4.84 / 11	5.35 / 9	--
GL	iShares S&P Global Technology Sect	IXN	E-	48.77	52.93	42.50	D- / 1.1	2.24	-4.84	-2.82 / 4	8.50 / 25	--
GL	iShares S&P Global Telecomm Sect	IXP	D-	49.24	53.96	43.30	C- / 3.6	-1.22	-6.99	11.92 / 29	13.07 / 63	--
FO	iShares S&P Latin American 40 Idx	ILF	C-	90.69	93.94	57.00	A+ / 9.8	12.27	14.41	58.53 / 99	32.02 / 97	--

N/A denotes number is not available

		RISK				NET ASSETS		VALUATION			ASSET					FUND MANAGER	
Incl. in Returns			3 Year					Premium / Discount									
Dividend Yield %	Expense Ratio	Risk Rating/ Pts	Standard Deviation	Beta	Avg Dura-tion	NAV as of 6/30/05	Total $(Mil)	As of 6/30/05	1 Year Average	Wtd Avg P/E	Cash %	Stocks %	Bonds %	Other %	Portfolio Turnover Ratio	Manager Quality Pct	Manager Tenure (Years)
3.25	0.58	**C+ / 6.2**	15.8	0.85	N/A	17.70	345	-0.23	0.25	N/A	0	100	0	0	11	93	9
0.36	0.58	**D+ / 2.8**	18.8	0.87	N/A	23.41	189	-0.34	0.14	N/A	0	100	0	0	5	99	9
1.59	0.58	**E / 0.4**	23.6	1.30	N/A	18.02	56	-1.17	0.38	N/A	0	100	0	0	5	74	9
1.86	0.74	**E- / 0.0**	43.5	2.07	N/A	24.04	467	-0.42	N/A	N/A	0	100	0	0	13	91	5
1.09	0.58	**C- / 4.1**	18.7	0.97	N/A	18.24	314	0.27	0.22	19.6	0	100	0	0	2	87	9
1.53	0.35	**C+ / 6.8**	15.6	1.00	N/A	52.53	13,763	-0.06	0.31	18.2	0	100	0	0	3	54	4
1.12	0.76	**U /**	N/A	N/A	N/A	71.29	4,579	-0.06	0.08	N/A	0	100	0	0	8	N/A	2
1.83	0.58	**D- / 1.0**	22.2	1.36	N/A	70.79	507	-0.61	0.17	N/A	0	100	0	0	5	21	5
1.25	0.58	**D- / 1.3**	21.6	1.31	N/A	23.79	54	0.13	0.11	N/A	0	100	0	0	4	17	9
1.10	0.58	**E- / 0.0**	30.6	1.79	N/A	17.69	156	-0.23	-0.01	N/A	0	100	0	0	2	1	9
2.19	0.58	**D+ / 2.9**	18.6	0.78	N/A	12.42	643	-0.81	0.12	N/A	0	100	0	0	3	78	9
2.61	0.58	**D+ / 2.5**	19.3	1.05	N/A	24.34	39	-0.49	0.08	N/A	0	100	0	0	8	79	9
0.42	0.58	**C / 4.7**	17.2	0.67	N/A	10.29	6,914	-0.68	0.01	18.2	0	100	0	0	1	43	9
2.28	0.58	**C- / 3.0**	18.4	0.58	N/A	6.99	321	0.00	0.23	N/A	0	100	0	0	5	66	9
1.02	0.58	**D / 1.7**	20.9	1.11	N/A	26.65	281	-0.30	0.05	N/A	0	100	0	0	6	90	9
1.40	0.58	**E- / 0.0**	24.2	1.45	N/A	18.46	52	-0.33	0.16	N/A	0	100	0	0	1	1	9
3.20	0.50	**B- / 7.0**	13.3	0.72	N/A	94.24	1,179	-0.14	0.31	N/A	0	100	0	0	7	92	4
3.64	0.58	**C+ / 6.4**	15.2	0.75	N/A	7.59	236	0.26	0.27	N/A	0	100	0	0	6	83	9
1.67	0.74	**U /**	N/A	N/A	N/A	71.74	149	-0.11	0.33	N/A	0	100	0	0	3	N/A	2
0.31	0.74	**E- / 0.0**	29.2	1.45	N/A	32.60	641	0.25	0.18	N/A	0	100	0	0	4	29	5
1.79	0.58	**D / 1.8**	20.7	1.19	N/A	33.85	67	-0.27	0.09	N/A	0	100	0	0	5	85	9
0.73	0.58	**E- / 0.0**	28.7	1.62	N/A	20.62	63	-1.79	0.21	N/A	0	100	0	0	3	68	9
0.52	0.58	**C+ / 5.7**	16.9	0.99	N/A	16.63	63	-0.18	0.51	N/A	0	100	0	0	1	18	9
0.66	0.76	**E- / 0.0**	25.2	1.03	N/A	12.53	837	-1.52	-0.08	N/A	0	100	0	0	6	8	5
1.92	0.58	**C+ / 6.6**	14.6	0.88	N/A	18.16	569	-0.50	0.45	N/A	0	100	0	0	3	64	9
1.84	0.20	**U /**	N/A	N/A	N/A	63.10	28	0.24	-0.01	19.2	0	100	0	0	3	N/A	1
1.98	0.25	**U /**	N/A	N/A	N/A	65.79	6	0.78	0.16	23.4	0	100	0	0	3	N/A	1
1.10	0.15	**B- / 7.3**	13.5	0.95	N/A	64.41	1,985	-0.02	0.03	24.4	0	100	0	0	5	70	5
0.68	0.20	**B- / 7.1**	13.7	0.94	N/A	47.84	3,130	-0.04	0.04	29.2	0	100	0	0	14	57	5
1.69	0.20	**B- / 7.1**	14.6	1.01	N/A	66.68	4,791	-0.15	0.02	19.5	0	100	0	0	15	75	5
0.92	0.20	**C- / 3.4**	19.4	1.18	N/A	62.65	6,908	-0.70	-0.05	39.5	0	100	0	0	17	77	5
0.47	0.25	**D+ / 2.6**	21.2	1.26	N/A	63.92	2,106	-0.66	-0.06	45.4	0	100	0	0	22	68	5
1.33	0.25	**C- / 3.9**	18.5	1.10	N/A	63.35	2,711	-0.39	-0.04	33.9	0	100	0	0	23	82	5
1.19	0.20	**B- / 7.1**	14.3	1.01	N/A	68.35	1,957	0.00	0.03	25.5	0	100	0	0	5	68	5
0.43	0.25	**C+ / 6.8**	14.8	1.02	N/A	38.76	129	0.05	0.02	30.4	0	100	0	0	16	52	5
1.14	0.25	**B- / 7.1**	14.7	1.02	N/A	86.89	364	-0.08	0.03	20.6	0	100	0	0	16	74	5
0.27	0.25	**C+ / 6.4**	16.4	1.06	N/A	84.81	842	0.07	0.04	29.6	0	100	0	0	27	83	4
0.98	0.20	**C+ / 6.9**	14.8	0.97	N/A	81.15	1,202	-0.04	0.03	26.3	0	100	0	0	15	87	4
1.44	0.25	**B- / 7.0**	14.7	0.95	N/A	116.96	1,149	-0.09	0.03	23.1	0	100	0	0	20	88	4
1.65	0.20	**B- / 7.8**	14.5	1.01	N/A	55.84	795	-0.13	N/A	19.9	0	100	0	0	6	45	5
0.89	0.20	**U /**	N/A	N/A	N/A	105.47	73	0.26	N/A	24.1	0	100	0	0	5	N/A	1
1.30	0.09	**B- / 7.3**	13.7	0.97	N/A	119.08	12,514	-0.07	0.02	23.3	0	100	0	0	6	63	5
0.89	0.18	**B- / 7.3**	13.2	0.92	N/A	56.49	2,341	0.02	0.06	23.7	0	100	0	0	22	47	5
1.47	0.18	**C+ / 6.7**	15.9	1.09	N/A	62.21	2,704	-0.06	0.03	22.9	0	100	0	0	5	68	5
1.81	0.60	**C- / 3.4**	17.6	1.08	N/A	74.64	1,182	-0.32	0.35	N/A	0	100	0	0	5	49	5
1.70	0.40	**C+ / 6.8**	15.5	1.07	N/A	60.25	343	0.08	0.11	19.1	0	100	0	0	4	54	5
1.47	0.65	**C / 4.5**	17.9	0.90	N/A	86.94	323	0.06	0.22	16.0	0	100	0	0	5	66	4
1.37	0.65	**C- / 3.8**	19.5	1.25	N/A	64.79	71	0.32	0.23	15.9	0	100	0	0	5	47	4
0.73	0.65	**B / 8.9**	11.3	0.55	N/A	50.12	229	0.06	0.34	27.6	0	100	0	0	10	62	4
1.29	0.66	**D- / 1.4**	26.5	1.33	N/A	48.74	43	0.06	0.36	38.8	0	100	0	0	7	6	4
1.35	0.65	**C- / 3.3**	20.8	1.08	N/A	49.10	42	0.29	0.32	16.6	0	100	0	0	13	60	4
1.01	0.50	**E- / 0.0**	25.9	1.37	N/A	90.25	336	0.49	0.58	N/A	0	100	0	0	6	94	4

N/A denotes number is not available

Fund Type	Fund Name (99 Pct = Best; 0 Pct = Worst)	Ticker Symbol	Overall Weiss Investment Rating	PRICE: Price As of 6/30/05	PRICE: 52 Week High	PRICE: 52 Week Low	PERFORMANCE: Performance Rating/Pts	% Total Return Through 6/30/05: 3 Mo	6 Mo	1Yr/Pct	Annualized: 3Yr/Pct	Annualized: 5Yr/Pct
GR	iShares S&P MidCap 400	IJH	C	67.60	69.90	54.92	C- / 4.1	3.45	3.14	13.34 / 32	12.50 / 60	7.90 / 31
GR	iShares S&P MidCap 400/Barra Growth	IJK	C-	68.46	70.70	55.58	C- / 3.0	2.77	2.92	11.08 / 27	10.95 / 47	--
GR	iShares S&P MidCap 400/Barra Value	IJJ	C	65.64	67.91	53.34	C / 4.8	4.20	3.63	14.77 / 37	13.82 / 67	--
GR	iShares S&P SmallCap 600	IJR	D	53.70	56.09	43.47	C- / 4.0	1.48	-0.27	11.96 / 29	12.95 / 63	9.84 / 40
GR	iShares S&P SmallCap 600/Barra Gwth	IJT	C	106.60	111.65	84.73	C / 4.4	1.31	-0.20	11.07 / 27	14.19 / 68	--
GR	iShares S&P SmallCap 600/BarraValue	IJS	D-	60.43	63.10	49.53	C- / 3.2	2.24	-0.19	13.24 / 32	11.52 / 51	--
FO	iShares S&P/Topix 150 Index Fund	ITF	E	88.09	95.50	81.31	E+ / 0.6	-3.85	-3.34	-2.85 / 4	6.76 / 15	--
FS	J Hancock Bank & Thrift Oppty Fd	BTO	C+	9.77	10.90	9.15	C+ / 6.2	6.05	-2.34	18.38 / 45	16.97 / 80	20.51 / 94
FS	J Hancock Financial Trends Fund	JHFT	D	15.72	17.54	14.49	D+ / 2.9	2.28	-6.26	10.88 / 26	11.35 / 50	15.30 / 72
GEI	J Hancock Income Securities Tr	JHS	C-	14.98	16.17	14.32	D / 1.9	5.97	-2.22	11.02 / 26	7.76 / 21	9.97 / 41
GEI	J Hancock Investors Trust	JHI	D+	19.98	23.95	19.42	D / 2.1	0.73	-7.81	8.88 / 21	9.56 / 35	11.00 / 47
GL	J Hancock Patriot Global Div Fd	PGD	C	13.20	14.83	11.60	C- / 4.2	8.27	-3.35	19.71 / 49	11.83 / 55	12.59 / 56
IN	J Hancock Patriot Pref Div Fd	PPF	C	13.76	14.20	12.15	C / 5.5	12.68	2.02	18.84 / 47	12.91 / 62	14.05 / 65
IN	J Hancock Patriot Prem Div Fd I	PDF	C-	9.30	10.09	8.65	D / 1.9	5.35	-2.52	11.70 / 28	7.55 / 20	10.01 / 42
IN	J Hancock Patriot Prem Div Fd II	PDT	C+	12.07	12.30	10.05	C+ / 6.5	7.79	7.68	27.68 / 69	13.59 / 65	13.66 / 64
UT	J Hancock Patriot Select Div Tr	DIV	D+	13.65	15.45	12.25	D / 1.6	10.16	-6.82	5.68 / 12	7.95 / 22	10.17 / 43
IN	J Hancock Preferred Equity Inc	HPI	U	23.20	25.90	21.25	U /	9.49	-2.28	8.27 / 20	--	--
IN	J Hancock Preferred Income II	HPF	U	23.19	25.89	21.37	U /	8.53	-3.54	9.69 / 23	--	--
IN	J Hancock Preferred Income III	HPS	U	22.08	24.73	20.40	U /	7.60	2.68	11.35 / 27	--	--
IN	J Hancock Tax Advantage Div Income	HTD	U	17.89	18.50	15.78	U /	8.84	4.93	19.78 / 50	--	--
FO	Japan Equity Fund	JEQ	E	6.08	6.72	5.73	E- / 0.2	-3.80	-4.40	-6.17 / 2	4.68 / 8	-4.58 / 6
FO	Japan Smaller Cap Fund Inc.	JOF	E	10.78	13.44	9.85	E+ / 0.7	-6.91	-8.95	-18.40 / 0	10.50 / 42	5.36 / 22
FO	JF China Region Fund	JFC	C-	12.82	13.73	10.34	B / 8.2	1.02	-0.47	13.35 / 33	22.94 / 94	10.41 / 44
EN	Kayne Anderson MLP	KYN	U	0.00	N/A	N/A	U /	3.78	11.19	--	--	--
FO	Korea Equity Fund	KEF	C	6.99	8.05	3.85	A- / 9.0	3.56	19.28	46.54 / 98	18.70 / 85	13.26 / 61
FO	Korea Fund	KF	C	27.28	28.97	16.59	A / 9.5	3.57	18.22	49.47 / 98	22.48 / 93	20.11 / 93
FO	Latin America Equity Fund	LAQ	C+	23.00	24.74	14.20	A+ / 9.7	7.93	12.30	64.53 / 99	29.30 / 97	14.45 / 67
FO	Latin American Discovery Fund	LDF	C+	20.01	21.81	12.42	A+ / 9.8	8.69	10.07	63.53 / 99	34.65 / 98	16.12 / 79
GL	Lazard Global Total Return&Income	LGI	U	18.50	19.95	16.02	U /	-2.02	-0.27	14.99 / 38	--	--
COH	Lehman Brothers First Trust Inc Opp	LBC	U	15.17	16.49	14.16	U /	9.73	-1.70	14.38 / 36	--	--
IN	Liberty All-Star Equity Fund	USA	D-	8.92	9.65	8.05	C- / 3.3	3.09	-1.82	7.70 / 17	12.10 / 57	4.28 / 20
GR	Liberty All-Star Growth Fund	ASG	E+	5.89	6.80	5.51	E+ / 0.9	-0.84	-4.82	2.12 / 8	7.10 / 18	-2.46 / 8
COI	Lincoln National Income Fund	LND	D-	11.80	13.38	11.30	D- / 1.0	-0.35	-4.19	3.28 / 9	6.99 / 17	12.16 / 54
MUS	MA Health & Education Tax-Exempt Tr	MHE	C+	15.06	16.40	13.07	C+ / 6.6	11.45	-3.28	22.24 / 83	8.17 / 61	10.53 / 79
GL	Macquarie/First Trust Glob Util Div	MFD	U	20.94	22.65	16.90	U /	5.77	3.14	30.64 / 76	--	--
IN	Madison Strategic Sector Premium	MSP	U	19.85	N/A	N/A	U /	--	--	--	--	--
IN	Madison/Claymore Covered Call	MCN	U	15.15	N/A	N/A	U /	3.34	8.45	--	--	--
FO	Malaysia Fund	MF	E+	5.64	6.80	4.82	D+ / 2.6	-5.69	-11.60	8.35 / 20	11.95 / 56	5.02 / 21
COH	Managed High Income Portfolio	MHY	D+	6.35	6.99	5.96	C- / 3.6	6.63	2.57	9.34 / 23	11.80 / 54	4.07 / 19
GL	Managed High Yield Plus Fund	HYF	C	5.16	6.32	4.98	B- / 7.0	3.15	-7.01	14.44 / 36	19.64 / 88	0.77 / 13
MUN	Managed Municipals Portfolio	MMU	C	10.76	11.43	10.48	C- / 3.0	2.84	4.42	6.10 / 23	6.80 / 41	7.99 / 55
MUN	MBIA Cptl/Claymore Mgd Dur Inv Gr	MZF	U	12.86	13.74	11.80	U /	7.35	2.81	3.77 / 13	--	--
FO	Mexico Equity & Income Fund	MXF	C+	17.16	10.27	11.50	A / 9.4	5.60	2.20	42.76 / 96	26.45 / 96	11.88 / 52
FO	Mexico Fund	MXF	C+	23.65	24.32	18.35	A- / 9.0	8.59	9.65	30.29 / 75	22.24 / 93	18.97 / 91
GEN	MFS Charter Income Trust	MCR	C-	8.70	9.06	8.23	D / 2.0	4.83	0.66	11.97 / 29	7.28 / 19	7.33 / 29
GL	MFS Government Markets Income Trust	MGF	C-	6.62	6.77	6.37	E+ / 0.9	4.30	2.61	8.14 / 19	4.54 / 7	7.59 / 29
GL	MFS Intermediate Income Trust	MIN	D+	6.51	6.66	6.22	E / 0.5	4.44	4.24	7.31 / 16	2.48 / 3	7.04 / 28
GEN	MFS Multimarket Income Trust	MMT	C	6.29	6.50	5.82	D+ / 2.9	6.82	1.86	14.29 / 35	9.09 / 32	7.77 / 31
MUH	MFS Municipal Income Trust	MFM	A-	8.26	8.40	7.23	B+ / 8.4	14.32	10.63	21.69 / 82	9.08 / 67	9.35 / 67
GI	MFS Special Value Trust	MFV	C	10.77	12.25	10.16	C+ / 6.4	0.56	-4.67	10.42 / 25	18.96 / 86	5.18 / 22
MUS	Minnesota Municipal Inc Portfolio	MXA	B	16.07	16.42	13.88	B- / 7.0	9.70	6.83	21.20 / 80	7.54 / 52	11.58 / 88
MUS	Minnesota Municipal Income Fund II	MXN	U	14.69	15.00	12.63	U /	5.99	9.71	22.70 / 85	--	--

N/A denotes number is not available

Incl. in Returns: Dividend Yield %	Incl. in Returns: Expense Ratio	RISK: Risk Rating/ Pts	RISK: 3 Year Standard Deviation	RISK: 3 Year Beta	RISK: Avg Dura- tion	NET ASSETS: NAV as of 6/30/05	NET ASSETS: Total $(Mil)	VALUATION: Premium / Discount As of 6/30/05	VALUATION: Premium / Discount 1 Year Average	VALUATION: Wtd Avg P/E	ASSET: Cash %	ASSET: Stocks %	ASSET: Bonds %	ASSET: Other %	Portfolio Turnover Ratio	FUND MANAGER: Manager Quality Pct	FUND MANAGER: Manager Tenure (Years)
0.91	0.20	**C+ / 6.9**	14.7	0.95	N/A	67.68	2,416	-0.12	N/A	28.1	0	100	0	0	10	81	5
0.57	0.25	**B- / 7.2**	13.5	0.83	N/A	68.52	1,112	-0.09	-0.01	30.6	0	100	0	0	34	80	5
1.58	0.25	**C+ / 6.6**	15.8	1.01	N/A	65.71	1,853	-0.11	-0.01	25.6	0	100	0	0	10	83	5
0.76	0.20	**C / 4.4**	17.4	1.00	N/A	53.94	3,245	-0.44	-0.05	32.4	0	100	0	0	14	82	5
0.82	0.25	**C+ / 6.3**	16.5	0.96	N/A	106.81	991	-0.20	-0.01	32.5	0	100	0	0	45	85	5
0.70	0.25	**C- / 3.8**	18.9	1.10	N/A	60.56	1,572	-0.21	-0.05	32.4	0	100	0	0	13	76	5
0.39	0.50	**C- / 3.6**	17.1	0.54	N/A	88.28	95	-0.22	0.14	N/A	0	100	0	0	4	55	4
1.16	1.32	**C+ / 6.2**	16.1	0.90	N/A	10.49	876	-6.86	-7.88	15.6	1	98	0	1	3	87	11
1.25	1.22	**C / 5.4**	20.1	0.82	N/A	18.60	76	-15.48	-13.08	22.5	2	97	0	1	10	78	14
6.88	1.14	**B- / 7.6**	10.6	2.06	8.8	15.81	180	-5.25	-4.67	15.6	2	0	92	6	135	41	N/A
7.28	1.16	**B- / 7.1**	11.6	1.73	6.7	20.68	173	-3.38	1.51	15.6	2	0	96	2	128	65	N/A
6.25	1.78	**B- / 7.3**	15.7	0.25	N/A	14.35	118	-8.01	-2.60	18.7	0	33	0	67	3	87	13
6.28	1.83	**C+ / 6.1**	17.5	-0.05	N/A	14.37	102	-4.24	-5.09	19.6	0	13	0	87	3	92	12
5.94	1.69	**B- / 7.8**	15.7	0.24	N/A	9.91	147	-6.16	-0.61	19.2	0	36	0	64	5	80	17
6.46	1.71	**C+ / 6.7**	16.2	0.24	N/A	12.50	182	-3.44	-3.61	18.0	0	36	0	64	2	90	16
6.53	1.74	**B- / 7.1**	15.7	0.39	N/A	15.06	148	-9.36	-2.10	18.7	0	38	0	62	20	69	15
7.98	1.02	**U /**	N/A	N/A	N/A	25.48	665	-8.95	-4.60	N/A	2	3	9	86	8	N/A	3
7.93	1.08	**U /**	N/A	N/A	3.0	25.69	551	-9.73	-5.32	15.2	0	2	14	84	4	N/A	3
8.07	1.03	**U /**	N/A	N/A	2.6	24.14	754	-8.53	-3.88	16.5	0	0	15	85	5	N/A	2
6.38	0.95	**U /**	N/A	N/A	N/A	20.83	862	-14.11	-11.19	16.9	0	77	0	23	42	N/A	1
0.00	1.07	**C- / 4.0**	25.3	1.00	N/A	6.58	92	-7.60	-4.08	N/A	0	100	0	0	35	6	5
0.00	1.54	**D+ / 2.4**	34.5	1.33	N/A	11.71	184	-7.94	5.57	N/A	2	97	0	1	86	14	6
0.00	2.22	**D- / 1.3**	40.9	1.10	N/A	14.87	64	-13.79	-9.84	N/A	0	100	0	0	169	88	13
4.09	1.20	**U /**	N/A	N/A	N/A	0.00	793		N/A	N/A	0	100	0	0	12	N/A	1
0.00	2.27	**D / 2.1**	25.1	1.02	N/A	7.41	59	-5.67	-8.49	N/A	3	96	0	1	16	84	6
1.65	1.24	**D- / 1.1**	26.9	1.26	N/A	29.13	1,153	-6.35	-7.95	N/A	0	100	0	0	6	84	14
1.97	1.41	**D+ / 2.6**	25.4	1.30	N/A	26.63	154	-13.63	-13.99	N/A	1	98	0	1	70	93	1
0.22	1.45	**D+ / 2.6**	26.4	1.35	N/A	22.95	190	-12.81	-13.21	N/A	1	83	0	16	60	96	13
6.76	1.57	**U /**	N/A	N/A	N/A	20.51	209	-9.80	-8.14	18.7	2	97	0	1	7	N/A	1
10.22	1.48	**U /**	N/A	N/A	6.1	14.84	191	2.22	2.72	N/A	0	0	100	0	107	N/A	2
9.33	1.01	**C- / 3.9**	21.7	1.28	10.6	8.68	1,372	2.76	3.69	43.8	0	97	0	3	57	73	19
9.52	1.31	**C / 4.3**	22.6	1.20	N/A	5.75	165	2.43	5.53	33.7	0	100	0	0	28	37	10
5.28	1.76	**C+ / 6.6**	14.9	1.30	7.7	13.44	100	-12.20	-6.38	15.5	2	0	97	1	262	32	33
5.31	N/A	**C+ / 6.8**	13.9	1.75	15.1	14.10	N/A	6.81	7.66	N/A	0	0	100	0	N/A	45	9
7.79	2.51	**U /**	N/A	N/A	N/A	23.58	207	-11.20	-9.46	18.9	0	69	0	31	30	N/A	1
0.00	N/A	**U /**	N/A	N/A	N/A	19.83	N/A	0.10	N/A	N/A	0	0	0	100	N/A	N/A	0
6.95	1.24	**U /**	N/A	N/A	N/A	14.76	280	2.64	N/A	N/A	10	89	0	1	33	N/A	1
0.69	1.50	**D / 2.2**	27.8	0.91	N/A	5.77	59	-2.25	-1.64	N/A	3	96	0	1	24	64	18
8.16	1.26	**C+ / 5.7**	12.2	1.23	6.3	6.95	329	-8.63	-8.35	17.1	4	0	95	1	41	18	12
11.07	2.02	**C- / 4.2**	14.6	0.60	4.8	4.94	229	4.45	9.86	6.3	0	0	100	0	19	93	7
5.14	1.33	**B / 8.3**	9.2	1.20	12.5	11.69	492	-7.96	-7.43	N/A	0	0	100	0	1	61	13
5.17	1.48	**U /**	N/A	N/A	11.7	14.82	117	-13.23	-9.06	N/A	0	0	100	0	10	N/A	2
0.00	1.79	**C- / 3.2**	24.7	1.04	N/A	19.88	46	-13.68	-11.42	N/A	0	100	0	0	127	94	15
0.17	1.44	**D+ / 2.8**	20.0	1.00	N/A	27.09	431	-12.70	-12.52	N/A	2	97	0	1	14	89	24
5.71	0.80	**B / 8.5**	7.5	1.43	9.2	9.77	558	-10.95	-9.88	N/A	12	0	88	0	70	62	4
4.59	N/A	**B+ / 9.2**	6.9	0.45	N/A	7.49	399	-11.62	-11.36	N/A	9	0	95	N/A	71	56	3
5.51	0.87	**B / 8.3**	7.5	0.45	N/A	7.22	873	-9.83	-10.27	N/A	2	0	98	0	21	32	3
6.05	0.91	**B- / 7.8**	8.1	1.26	7.1	6.91	555	-8.97	-9.56	12.9	5	0	95	0	38	74	3
6.63	1.48	**C+ / 6.5**	13.0	2.01	11.8	8.01	318	3.12	-1.25	N/A	0	0	100	0	7	50	8
8.95	1.44	**C / 4.9**	18.0	0.79	5.3	10.00	66	7.70	12.72	54.0	1	30	69	0	28	93	4
5.57	1.17	**C+ / 6.6**	12.3	1.83	10.4	15.48	64	3.81	0.81	N/A	0	0	100	0	19	45	12
5.20	1.53	**U /**	N/A	N/A	12.8	15.32	22	-4.11	-5.20	N/A	0	0	100	0	13	N/A	3

N/A denotes number is not available

Fund Type	Fund Name (99 Pct = Best; 0 Pct = Worst)	Ticker Symbol	Overall Weiss Investment Rating	PRICE: Price As of 6/30/05	PRICE: 52 Week High	PRICE: 52 Week Low	PERFORMANCE: Performance Rating/Pts	% Total Return Through 6/30/05: 3 Mo	6 Mo	1Yr/Pct	Annualized: 3Yr/Pct	Annualized: 5Yr/Pct
GEI	Montgomery Street Inc. Sec.	MTS	**D+**	18.11	19.56	17.04	**D- / 1.2**	5.80	0.93	10.92 / 26	5.47 / 10	9.89 / 41
FO	Morgan Stanley Asia Pacific Fund	APF	**C-**	13.05	14.02	10.19	**C / 5.5**	0.69	1.48	19.66 / 49	15.59 / 76	5.90 / 24
MUS	Morgan Stanley CA Insured Muni Inc	IIC	**C+**	13.89	13.94	12.67	**C / 4.6**	7.21	10.84	13.74 / 52	5.15 / 22	7.55 / 51
MUS	Morgan Stanley CA Muni Sec	ICS	**C+**	14.09	14.80	13.04	**C- / 3.4**	2.42	4.17	14.23 / 54	5.45 / 25	7.02 / 47
MUS	Morgan Stanley CA Qual Muni Sec	IQC	**B+**	14.30	14.42	13.28	**C+ / 5.6**	2.93	4.46	13.78 / 52	8.77 / 65	8.39 / 58
FO	Morgan Stanley Eastern Europe	RNE	**C+**	29.85	32.85	24.18	**A+ / 9.8**	5.66	17.29	31.07 / 77	38.86 / 99	23.47 / 98
EM	Morgan Stanley Emerging Markets	MSF	**C+**	18.11	20.27	12.47	**A / 9.3**	4.08	5.11	39.60 / 93	24.43 / 95	8.67 / 34
EM	Morgan Stanley Emerging Mkts Debt	MSD	**B+**	9.97	10.51	8.23	**B+ / 8.6**	7.90	6.43	28.11 / 70	21.23 / 91	18.01 / 88
GL	Morgan Stanley Global Opp Bond Fund	MGB	**E+**	7.80	13.45	7.12	**C / 4.4**	-2.55	-17.27	13.93 / 35	15.54 / 75	7.85 / 31
USA	Morgan Stanley Govt Inc Tr	GVT	**C-**	8.92	9.11	8.60	**E+ / 0.9**	3.74	3.43	7.74 / 17	4.45 / 7	7.25 / 29
COH	Morgan Stanley High Yield Fund	MSY	**C-**	6.31	6.75	5.81	**C- / 4.1**	8.08	0.32	18.17 / 45	11.26 / 49	-1.24 / 11
COI	Morgan Stanley Income Sec	ICB	**C-**	15.88	16.70	14.90	**D / 1.9**	6.66	5.30	13.03 / 31	5.66 / 11	6.52 / 27
FO	Morgan Stanley India Inv Fund	IIF	**C+**	33.42	33.65	19.50	**A+ / 9.9**	16.73	11.40	65.14 / 99	54.11 / 99	29.60 / 99
MUN	Morgan Stanley Insured Muni Bond	IMB	**C**	13.98	14.27	13.18	**C- / 3.5**	5.97	4.27	11.69 / 44	5.27 / 23	7.41 / 50
MUN	Morgan Stanley Insured Muni Inc Tr	IIM	**B**	14.23	14.45	13.30	**C / 5.4**	7.51	7.01	12.77 / 49	7.30 / 48	8.24 / 57
MUN	Morgan Stanley Insured Muni Sec	IMS	**C+**	14.48	14.60	13.20	**C / 4.5**	6.87	7.30	14.43 / 55	5.70 / 28	8.24 / 57
MUN	Morgan Stanley Insured Muni Tr	IMT	**C+**	13.93	14.14	13.05	**C / 4.4**	6.28	6.66	13.18 / 51	5.89 / 31	7.31 / 49
MUN	Morgan Stanley Muni Inc Op	OIA	**B+**	8.10	8.17	6.81	**B / 7.8**	10.64	11.14	26.34 / 94	6.96 / 44	6.49 / 41
MUN	Morgan Stanley Muni Inc Op II	OIB	**B**	8.14	8.30	7.40	**C+ / 6.1**	8.85	9.64	15.00 / 57	7.08 / 46	9.22 / 65
MUN	Morgan Stanley Muni Inc Op III	OIC	**B-**	8.86	9.07	8.11	**C+ / 5.9**	8.85	10.89	15.95 / 62	6.35 / 36	8.56 / 60
MUN	Morgan Stanley Muni Inv Tr	IQT	**C+**	13.91	14.13	13.02	**C / 4.8**	7.68	6.45	13.86 / 52	6.24 / 36	7.50 / 51
MUN	Morgan Stanley Muni Prem Inc Tr	PIA	**C+**	9.12	9.49	8.49	**C / 4.8**	6.17	5.23	12.22 / 47	6.97 / 45	9.74 / 70
MUS	Morgan Stanley NY Qual Muni Sec	IQN	**C+**	13.77	13.91	12.70	**C / 4.9**	7.08	3.34	14.43 / 55	6.87 / 43	7.89 / 54
MUN	Morgan Stanley Qual Muni Inc Tr	IQI	**B**	13.93	14.16	13.07	**C / 5.2**	7.59	6.43	12.92 / 50	7.04 / 45	8.46 / 59
MUN	Morgan Stanley Qual Muni Sec	IQM	**B**	14.40	14.85	13.23	**C+ / 6.0**	7.54	6.70	14.65 / 56	7.81 / 56	9.93 / 72
MUN	Muni Intermediate Duration Fund	MUI	**U**	14.15	14.30	12.46	**U /**	7.65	11.10	21.12 / 80	--	--
MUS	Muni NY Intermediate Duration Fund	MNE	**U**	13.63	13.80	12.48	**U /**	8.01	8.90	13.70 / 52	--	--
MUN	MuniAssets Fund	MUA	**A+**	13.45	13.51	11.14	**A / 9.3**	12.91	11.90	28.55 / 97	11.50 / 83	10.73 / 80
MUN	Municipal Advantage Fund	MAF	**C**	12.95	13.44	12.23	**C- / 4.0**	3.64	5.10	12.57 / 48	6.30 / 36	10.05 / 74
MUN	Municipal High Income Fund	MHF	**C-**	7.21	7.48	6.97	**D- / 1.5**	3.13	6.48	8.67 / 32	2.59 / 6	5.85 / 35
MUN	MuniEnhanced Fund	MEN	**B+**	11.43	11.50	9.90	**B / 7.6**	8.78	9.39	22.35 / 84	8.36 / 62	10.40 / 78
MUS	MuniHoldings CA Insured Fund II	MUC	**B-**	14.77	15.00	13.20	**C+ / 6.6**	7.29	5.73	18.82 / 73	8.14 / 60	10.53 / 79
MUS	MuniHoldings FL Insured Fund	MFL	**A-**	15.57	15.84	13.51	**B+ / 8.5**	10.67	6.28	22.65 / 85	10.65 / 79	14.53 / 97
MUN	MuniHoldings Fund	MHD	**A+**	16.71	16.80	14.20	**A / 9.5**	10.36	9.32	25.09 / 92	14.87 / 94	12.17 / 90
MUN	MuniHoldings Fund II	MUH	**A+**	15.32	15.49	12.83	**A+ / 9.6**	10.67	10.64	27.08 / 95	14.47 / 93	13.96 / 96
MUN	MuniHoldings Insured Fund	MUS	**A-**	14.29	14.44	12.26	**B / 8.0**	8.17	4.52	22.46 / 84	10.10 / 75	11.14 / 84
MUN	MuniHoldings Insured Fund II	MUE	**B+**	13.70	13.70	12.09	**B- / 7.4**	9.83	7.75	20.27 / 78	8.60 / 64	12.63 / 92
MUS	MuniHoldings NJ Insured Fund	MUJ	**A**	15.59	15.69	13.52	**B+ / 8.6**	12.06	7.53	21.69 / 82	10.87 / 79	13.40 / 95
MUS	MuniHoldings NY Insured Fund	MHN	**A-**	14.96	15.24	13.21	**B / 8.0**	9.46	10.89	19.68 / 75	9.24 / 69	12.21 / 90
MUN	MuniVest Fund	MVF	**A+**	9.94	10.00	8.45	**A- / 9.1**	12.37	10.83	26.19 / 94	11.34 / 82	12.89 / 93
MUN	MuniVest Fund II	MVT	**A+**	16.20	16.44	13.75	**A / 9.5**	11.73	12.26	24.93 / 91	14.19 / 92	14.72 / 97
MUS	MuniYield AZ Fund	MZA	**A-**	15.76	16.10	13.40	**B+ / 8.5**	11.69	9.03	25.61 / 92	9.35 / 70	14.67 / 97
MUS	MuniYield CA Fund	MYC	**C-**	13.91	14.64	13.24	**D+ / 2.4**	3.10	2.54	11.36 / 43	4.40 / 16	7.95 / 55
MUS	MuniYield CA Insured Fund	MCA	**A-**	14.22	14.35	12.57	**B- / 7.3**	8.12	11.10	19.95 / 77	8.19 / 61	7.80 / 53
MUS	MuniYield FL Fund	MYF	**A**	15.06	15.07	12.64	**A- / 9.0**	12.83	10.20	26.38 / 94	10.66 / 79	13.21 / 94
MUS	MuniYield FL Insured Fund	MFT	**B+**	15.45	15.84	13.23	**B+ / 8.3**	10.06	10.51	24.04 / 89	9.32 / 70	11.93 / 89
MUN	MuniYield Fund	MYD	**A+**	14.99	15.10	12.44	**A- / 9.2**	12.10	11.47	29.19 / 97	11.30 / 81	11.40 / 86
MUN	MuniYield Insured Fund	MYI	**A**	15.14	15.17	13.18	**B / 7.9**	10.07	10.56	22.18 / 83	8.40 / 62	11.03 / 83
MUS	MuniYield MI Insured Fund	MIY	**B-**	15.49	15.60	13.87	**C+ / 6.9**	7.27	3.91	17.48 / 66	9.16 / 68	12.54 / 92
MUS	MuniYield MI Insured Fund II	MYM	**B+**	14.70	14.80	13.18	**B- / 7.3**	10.04	5.21	17.41 / 66	9.35 / 70	11:75 / 88
MUS	MuniYield NJ Fund	MYJ	**B+**	15.31	15.35	13.57	**B- / 7.2**	11.48	9.44	18.63 / 71	7.88 / 57	10.77 / 80
MUS	MuniYield NJ Insured Fund	MJI	**B**	15.65	15.80	13.50	**B- / 7.3**	11.14	8.27	21.68 / 81	7.65 / 54	10.09 / 74

N/A denotes number is not available

Incl. in Returns: Dividend Yield %	Incl. in Returns: Expense Ratio	RISK: Risk Rating/ Pts	RISK: 3 Year Standard Deviation	RISK: 3 Year Beta	RISK: Avg Duration	NET ASSETS: NAV as of 6/30/05	NET ASSETS: Total $(Mil)	VALUATION: Premium / Discount As of 6/30/05	VALUATION: Premium / Discount 1 Year Average	VALUATION: Wtd Avg P/E	ASSET: Cash %	ASSET: Stocks %	ASSET: Bonds %	ASSET: Other %	ASSET: Portfolio Turnover Ratio	FUND MANAGER: Manager Quality Pct	FUND MANAGER: Manager Tenure (Years)
6.38	N/A	B- / 7.4	9.9	1.45	7.1	19.83	204	-8.67	-6.70	N/A	0	0	97	3	149	43	32
0.05	1.18	C / 4.7	19.4	0.87	N/A	14.73	520	-11.41	-11.89	N/A	3	94	0	3	25	80	7
5.16	0.80	B- / 7.4	11.1	1.86	12.5	15.45	174	-10.10	-11.28	N/A	0	0	100	0	14	21	12
4.66	0.56	B+ / 9.1	6.5	1.08	12.0	15.47	56	-8.92	-9.56	N/A	0	0	100	0	18	58	11
5.87	0.80	B+ / 9.1	8.4	1.62	12.2	15.80	146	-9.49	-8.13	N/A	0	0	100	0	10	63	12
0.00	1.92	D+ / 2.3	28.9	1.33	N/A	31.66	107	-5.72	-8.93	N/A	5	92	1	2	128	98	9
0.37	1.53	D+ / 2.7	28.5	1.50	N/A	20.49	349	-11.62	-9.89	N/A	2	93	0	5	57	2	14
7.24	1.22	C / 5.4	15.6	0.94	7.1	10.80	229	-7.69	-8.26	N/A	0	0	100	0	118	91	12
7.10	1.91	D / 1.6	33.2	0.62	6.5	8.13	34	-4.06	8.79	N/A	0	0	100	0	91	87	11
4.67	0.72	B+ / 9.5	4.9	0.34	N/A	9.93	325	-10.17	-9.50	N/A	4	0	95	1	150	63	17
8.60	1.45	C+ / 5.6	14.9	1.55	5.0	6.83	83	-7.61	-9.53	N/A	0	0	100	0	55	5	3
6.12	0.67	B / 8.4	9.5	1.21	7.5	17.65	179	-10.03	-9.53	N/A	2	0	97	1	50	30	32
0.47	1.40	D+ / 2.3	33.4	1.17	N/A	31.31	465	6.74	2.57	N/A	3	96	0	1	52	99	11
5.45	1.01	B- / 7.7	11.6	2.16	11.1	15.81	68	-11.57	-11.02	N/A	0	0	100	0	10	17	14
5.66	0.83	B / 8.3	9.7	1.82	11.6	16.00	357	-11.06	-10.70	N/A	0	0	100	0	10	44	12
4.34	0.49	B- / 7.7	9.1	1.51	N/A	15.52	109	-6.70	-8.91	N/A	0	0	100	0	2	41	11
5.81	0.79	B / 8.4	9.0	1.64	11.0	15.67	293	-11.10	-11.00	N/A	0	0	100	0	14	36	13
6.26	0.91	C+ / 6.9	11.7	1.63	14.1	8.02	157	1.00	-4.20	N/A	0	0	100	0	14	50	17
5.84	0.89	B / 8.5	10.4	1.57	13.5	8.95	148	-9.05	-9.83	N/A	0	0	100	0	16	54	12
5.73	0.93	B- / 7.8	10.7	1.73	13.1	9.69	84	-8.57	-10.16	N/A	0	0	100	0	17	38	15
5.80	0.87	B- / 7.9	10.0	1.84	10.6	15.80	238	-11.96	-11.68	N/A	0	0	100	0	10	30	14
5.87	1.40	B / 8.2	10.0	1.88	11.9	10.50	187	-13.14	-11.76	N/A	0	0	100	0	26	39	12
5.42	0.89	B / 8.1	10.4	1.90	11.7	15.68	67	-12.18	-11.54	N/A	0	0	100	0	28	36	12
5.80	0.89	B / 8.4	10.0	1.95	11.4	15.81	401	-11.89	-11.31	N/A	0	0	100	0	4	34	13
5.85	0.81	B / 8.7	9.1	1.79	11.1	16.38	237	-12.09	-11.77	N/A	0	0	100	0	10	47	12
6.15	0.85	U /	N/A	N/A	11.0	15.57	578	-9.12	-10.49	N/A	0	0	99	1	32	N/A	2
5.23	1.15	U /	N/A	N/A	9.0	15.11	62	-9.79	-11.72	N/A	3	0	96	1	6	N/A	2
6.08	0.67	B- / 7.2	9.1	1.23	12.4	13.49	263	-0.30	-3.95	N/A	1	0	98	1	12	82	12
5.57	1.34	B- / 7.7	10.9	2.00	12.4	14.94	107	-13.32	-12.68	N/A	0	0	100	0	2	23	12
5.63	0.83	B / 8.4	8.9	1.11	12.9	7.90	167	-8.73	-7.64	N/A	0	0	100	0	27	27	17
6.34	1.01	B- / 7.1	11.1	2.04	12.7	11.86	348	-3.63	-6.84	N/A	0	0	99	1	40	46	16
6.33	1.09	B- / 7.3	11.0	1.89	12.7	15.40	624	-4.09	-5.50	N/A	2	0	97	1	22	52	7
6.34	1.17	C+ / 6.5	11.6	2.18	12.6	15.42	579	0.97	-2.25	N/A	4	0	95	1	7	59	8
6.87	1.13	B- / 7.2	11.1	1.94	12.4	16.51	225	1.21	-1.27	N/A	1	0	98	1	36	80	6
6.85	1.19	C+ / 6.9	11.7	1.98	12.1	15.13	166	1.26	-1.61	N/A	1	0	98	1	19	78	7
6.35	1.24	B- / 7.0	12.1	2.15	10.6	14.53	186	-1.65	-5.00	N/A	1	0	98	1	52	56	6
6.38	1.15	B- / 7.2	11.8	2.21	11.5	14.51	318	-5.58	-8.38	N/A	2	0	97	1	21	37	6
6.04	1.21	B- / 7.0	12.5	2.48	10.7	15.82	333	-1.45	-4.36	N/A	0	0	100	0	22	49	7
6.28	1.14	B- / 7.0	10.9	1.94	12.2	15.60	477	-4.10	-8.13	N/A	3	0	96	1	12	58	8
6.68	1.01	B- / 7.1	10.7	2.02	12.1	10.23	619	-2.83	-6.26	N/A	2	0	97	1	24	69	17
6.81	1.05	C+ / 6.8	11.3	2.15	14.0	15.60	307	3.85	0.13	N/A	2	0	97	1	39	75	6
5.85	1.18	C+ / 6.3	14.3	2.22	12.0	15.05	67	4.72	1.03	N/A	0	0	99	1	10	45	12
5.85	0.96	B / 8.1	10.3	1.98	12.0	15.22	321	-8.61	-6.89	N/A	1	0	98	1	22	12	13
6.14	0.94	B- / 7.6	9.9	1.79	12.6	15.38	523	-7.54	-9.95	N/A	3	0	96	1	20	53	13
6.13	1.03	C+ / 6.3	13.1	2.47	14.1	15.43	207	-2.40	-7.33	N/A	4	0	95	1	20	46	13
5.80	1.16	C+ / 6.4	12.1	2.09	12.9	15.28	128	1.11	-3.13	N/A	3	0	96	1	28	51	13
6.66	1.01	B- / 7.4	9.4	1.38	12.6	14.91	653	0.54	-3.62	N/A	1	0	98	1	16	77	14
6.30	1.00	B- / 7.7	10.6	1.92	12.9	15.94	1,058	-5.02	-7.28	N/A	1	0	98	1	63	51	13
6.18	1.08	B- / 7.5	10.4	2.04	12.3	16.01	287	-3.25	-3.95	N/A	1	0	98	1	19	55	13
6.03	1.07	B- / 7.0	11.9	2.23	11.2	15.17	181	-3.10	-5.16	N/A	1	0	98	1	10	49	13
6.07	1.02	B- / 7.3	11.1	2.00	12.6	15.92	217	-3.83	-5.91	N/A	0	0	100	0	15	42	13
5.92	1.15	C+ / 6.6	13.3	2.19	11.0	15.71	136	-0.38	-2.97	N/A	0	0	100	0	28	31	13

N/A denotes number is not available

Fund Type	Fund Name (99 Pct = Best, 0 Pct = Worst)	Ticker Symbol	Overall Weiss Investment Rating	PRICE: Price As of 6/30/05	52 Week High	52 Week Low	PERFORMANCE: Performance Rating/Pts	% Total Return Through 6/30/05: 3 Mo	6 Mo	1Yr/Pct	Annualized 3Yr/Pct	Annualized 5Yr/Pct
MUS	MuniYield NY Insured Fund	MYN	B-	13.57	13.65	12.25	C+ / 6.3	8.98	9.62	17.64 / 67	6.66 / 40	10.19 / 75
MUS	MuniYield PA Insured Fund	MPA	B	15.99	16.37	14.05	B- / 7.3	10.09	4.32	21.01 / 80	8.72 / 64	12.29 / 91
MUN	MuniYield Quality Fund	MQY	B+	15.27	15.40	13.09	B+ / 8.4	10.79	9.74	24.12 / 89	9.36 / 71	11.96 / 89
MUN	MuniYield Quality Fund II	MQT	A+	13.37	13.50	11.51	B+ / 8.9	11.71	11.88	24.18 / 89	11.04 / 80	10.17 / 75
GR	MVC Capital	MVC	C-	0.00	10.50	8.85	D- / 1.1	4.48	8.53	6.17 / 14	5.35 / 9	-7.09 / 4
GR	NAIC Growth Fund	GRF	E-	8.55	N/A	N/A	E- / 0.0	-3.43	-1.57	-3.56 / 4	-3.63 / 0	-1.25 / 10
GR	Nasdaq 100 Trust Series I	QQQQ	E+	36.97	40.68	32.00	D+ / 2.8	2.02	-6.93	0.07 / 6	12.71 / 61	-16.75 / 2
MUS	Neuberger Berman CA Inter Muni Fund	NBW	U	13.73	13.93	12.39	U /	8.59	8.78	16.30 / 62	--	--
IN	Neuberger Berman Dividend Advantage	NDD	U	20.15	20.48	16.35	U /	10.85	4.68	30.09 / 75	--	--
COH	Neuberger Berman Income Opportunity	NOX	U	14.75	15.25	13.31	U /	11.98	3.35	24.16 / 59	--	--
MUN	Neuberger Berman Intermediate Muni	NBH	U	14.03	14.08	12.43	U /	8.99	10.95	18.06 / 70	--	--
MUS	Neuberger Berman NY Int Muni	NBO	U	13.57	13.69	12.32	U /	7.15	8.75	14.98 / 57	--	--
GI	Neuberger Berman Real Est Secs Inc	NRO	U	14.64	15.09	12.50	U /	13.64	3.27	26.25 / 65	--	--
GI	Neuberger Berman Real Estate Income	NRL	U	21.55	21.97	17.26	U /	16.41	4.85	35.10 / 85	--	--
GI	Neuberger Berman Realty Income Fund	NRI	U	18.54	19.09	15.61	U /	15.70	3.68	26.97 / 66	--	--
COH	New America High Income Fund	HYB	D-	2.13	2.29	1.91	C / 4.7	8.13	1.77	22.92 / 57	11.22 / 48	3.86 / 18
FO	New Germany Fund	GF	C	9.18	9.79	6.90	B+ / 8.9	1.65	4.62	27.62 / 69	24.15 / 95	-6.33 / 5
IN	NFJ Dividend Interest & Premium Str	NFJ	U	23.25	N/A	N/A	U /	-4.92	--	--	--	--
GI	Nicholas-Applegate Conv&Income II	NCZ	U	14.63	15.94	13.40	U /	8.63	-1.52	16.91 / 42	--	--
GI	Nicholas-Applegate Convertible&Inc	NCV	U	15.24	17.40	14.27	U /	4.57	-2.36	16.76 / 41	--	--
FO	Nicholas-Applegate Intl & Prem Str	NAI	U	23.79	N/A	N/A	U /	--	--	--	--	--
MUS	Nuveen AZ Div Adv Muni	NFZ	C+	16.27	16.90	13.77	C+ / 6.4	3.54	7.71	23.87 / 88	6.99 / 45	--
MUS	Nuveen AZ Div Adv Muni Fund 2	NKR	C+	15.70	17.10	14.15	C / 5.1	9.43	3.58	18.68 / 72	5.85 / 30	--
MUS	Nuveen AZ Div Adv Muni Fund 3	NXE	U	14.63	15.25	12.80	U /	10.30	7.01	21.45 / 80	--	--
MUS	Nuveen AZ Prem Inc Muni	NAZ	D+	15.41	16.86	14.40	D- / 1.3	1.44	3.41	12.39 / 48	2.39 / 5	7.59 / 51
MUS	Nuveen CA Div Adv Muni	NAC	A	15.59	15.70	13.86	B / 8.0	10.02	8.61	20.04 / 77	9.58 / 72	10.24 / 76
MUS	Nuveen CA Div Adv Muni 2	NVX	B+	14.59	14.99	12.93	B- / 7.1	7.97	11.03	18.51 / 71	7.87 / 57	--
MUS	Nuveen CA Div Adv Muni 3	NZH	B-	13.96	14.13	12.28	C+ / 6.9	7.42	10.05	19.43 / 75	7.62 / 53	--
MUS	Nuveen CA Inv Quality Muni	NQC	B-	15.06	15.80	13.49	C+ / 6.0	7.69	9.11	19.04 / 74	6.43 / 37	7.27 / 48
MUS	Nuveen CA Muni Market Opportunity	NCO	B-	14.99	15.29	13.45	C+ / 6.0	6.90	8.76	18.54 / 71	6.70 / 40	6.56 / 43
MUS	Nuveen CA Muni Value	NCA	B-	9.90	9.94	8.73	C+ / 6.2	7.28	10.97	19.66 / 75	6.21 / 35	7.88 / 54
MUS	Nuveen CA Performance Plus Muni	NCP	C+	14.55	14.99	13.25	C / 5.5	5.42	7.50	18.17 / 70	6.59 / 39	6.50 / 42
MUS	Nuveen CA Prem Inc Muni	NCU	B+	14.16	14.84	12.50	B- / 7.1	10.05	9.70	20.44 / 78	7.41 / 50	8.60 / 61
MUS	Nuveen CA Quality Inc Muni	NUC	C+	15.23	15.85	14.04	C / 4.7	6.75	6.44	15.95 / 62	5.78 / 29	6.79 / 45
MUS	Nuveen CA Select Quality Muni	NVC	C+	15.04	15.48	13.68	C+ / 5.7	6.30	7.05	18.23 / 70	6.82 / 42	7.74 / 52
MUS	Nuveen CA Select Tax-Free Inc Port	NXC	C-	13.94	14.00	12.75	D+ / 2.6	5.69	9.44	15.49 / 59	2.05 / 4	5.14 / 31
MUS	Nuveen CT Div Adv Muni	NFC	C-	15.97	17.40	14.45	C- / 4.0	0.58	6.96	16.68 / 64	5.74 / 28	--
MUS	Nuveen CT Div Adv Muni Fund 2	NGK	C	16.00	16.79	14.66	C / 5.0	3.63	7.08	14.90 / 57	7.06 / 46	--
MUS	Nuveen CT Div Adv Muni Fund 3	NGO	U	14.40	15.10	13.20	U /	0.70	8.28	14.89 / 56	--	--
MUS	Nuveen CT Prem Inc Muni	NTC	C-	16.07	17.00	14.40	C- / 3.3	2.78	6.60	15.32 / 59	4.53 / 17	8.24 / 58
MUN	Nuveen Div Adv Muni	NAD	B-	15.20	15.45	13.75	C+ / 6.3	11.26	6.67	15.17 / 58	7.25 / 48	11.45 / 87
MUN	Nuveen Div Adv Muni 3	NZF	A+	14.92	14.95	13.14	B / 7.9	9.99	9.55	21.16 / 80	8.90 / 67	--
GI	Nuveen Diversified Dividend&Income	JDD	U	15.21	15.86	13.22	U /	10.09	3.54	23.75 / 59	--	--
MUN	Nuveen Dividend Advantage Muni 2	NXZ	A+	16.00	16.00	13.28	B+ / 8.8	10.73	7.00	23.48 / 87	11.25 / 81	--
IN	Nuveen Equity Premium Income Fund	JPZ	U	20.09	N/A	N/A	U /	3.48	3.68	--	--	--
IN	Nuveen Equity Premium Opportunity	JSN	U	19.60	N/A	N/A	U /	3.17	--	--	--	--
MUS	Nuveen FL Investment Quality Muni	NQF	C	15.54	16.40	13.95	C+ / 5.7	8.77	6.11	17.20 / 65	6.66 / 40	9.05 / 64
MUS	Nuveen FL Quality Inc Muni	NUF	C	15.35	16.24	13.60	C+ / 5.6	11.24	4.81	18.67 / 72	5.88 / 31	8.78 / 62
LP	Nuveen Floating Rate Income Fund	JFR	U	13.33	14.99	13.23	U /	-6.68	0.27	-3.48 / 4	--	--
LP	Nuveen Floating Rate Income Opp	JRO	U	13.16	N/A	N/A	U /	-4.19	-2.15	--	--	--
MUS	Nuveen GA Div Adv Muni	NZX	B+	16.00	17.05	13.49	B / 8.1	10.70	3.94	23.82 / 88	9.83 / 74	--
MUS	Nuveen GA Div Adv Muni Fund 2	NKG	U	13.99	14.97	12.70	U /	4.52	6.87	15.06 / 57	--	--

N/A denotes number is not available

Incl. in Returns: Dividend Yield %	Incl. in Returns: Expense Ratio	RISK: Risk Rating/ Pts	RISK: 3 Year Standard Deviation	RISK: 3 Year Beta	RISK: Avg Dura-tion	NET ASSETS: NAV as of 6/30/05	NET ASSETS: Total $(Mil)	VALUATION: Premium / Discount As of 6/30/05	VALUATION: Premium / Discount 1 Year Average	VALUATION: Wtd Avg P/E	ASSET: Cash %	ASSET: Stocks %	ASSET: Bonds %	ASSET: Other %	Portfolio Turnover Ratio	FUND MANAGER: Manager Quality Pct	FUND MANAGER: Manager Tenure (Years)
6.18	0.94	**B- / 7.7**	9.5	1.65	12.2	14.90	582	-8.93	-11.36	N/A	2	0	97	1	16	44	13
5.96	1.11	**C+ / 6.6**	14.6	2.45	12.2	16.29	185	-1.84	-3.71	N/A	2	0	97	1	24	29	13
6.31	0.94	**C+ / 6.3**	11.4	1.92	N/A	15.57	469	-1.93	-5.60	N/A	1	0	98	1	15	59	13
6.41	1.02	**B- / 7.2**	10.9	2.02	11.1	13.83	307	-3.33	-7.60	N/A	1	0	98	1	11	66	13
1.20	3.43	**B / 8.9**	12.0	0.12	N/A	0.00	116		-1.17	N/A	60	19	21	0	N/A	79	2
3.57	1.80	**D / 1.6**	27.1	0.73	N/A	9.57	27	-10.66	-14.29	27.3	0	96	2	2	7	2	15
0.19	0.20	**D / 2.1**	22.7	1.42	N/A	36.96	19,957	0.03	0.01	38.0	0	100	0	0	N/A	69	6
5.50	0.95	**U /**	N/A	N/A	8.5	15.21	102	-9.73	-11.65	N/A	1	0	98	1	N/A	N/A	3
5.97	1.24	**U /**	N/A	N/A	N/A	23.45	128	-14.07	-11.19	66.5	5	93	0	2	30	N/A	1
8.69	1.14	**U /**	N/A	N/A	5.6	16.60	279	-11.14	-10.63	93.5	3	38	45	14	27	N/A	2
5.69	0.81	**U /**	N/A	N/A	8.7	15.25	312	-8.00	-10.17	N/A	1	0	98	1	N/A	N/A	3
5.74	1.00	**U /**	N/A	N/A	8.8	15.04	83	-9.77	-11.38	N/A	1	0	98	1	N/A	N/A	3
8.11	1.09	**U /**	N/A	N/A	N/A	17.31	533	-15.42	-10.73	82.7	1	72	0	27	3	N/A	2
6.42	6.79	**U /**	N/A	N/A	N/A	24.62	94	-12.47	-11.97	79.6	2	80	0	18	2	N/A	3
7.18	1.05	**U /**	N/A	N/A	N/A	22.10	558	-16.11	-13.44	72.1	1	72	0	27	1	N/A	2
9.91	0.87	**C- / 3.0**	23.4	2.17	N/A	2.15	212	-0.93	-4.00	N/A	0	0	100	0	71	N/A	13
3.00	1.24	**D / 1.8**	28.5	1.59	N/A	10.72	266	-14.37	-15.27	N/A	4	96	0	0	58	80	15
6.70	N/A	**U /**	N/A	N/A	N/A	23.18	N/A	0.30	N/A	N/A	5	73	0	22	N/A	N/A	0
10.20	1.36	**U /**	N/A	N/A	5.5	14.49	897	0.97	-0.63	12.2	0	0	45	55	34	N/A	2
10.55	1.24	**U /**	N/A	N/A	N/A	14.92	1,086	2.14	1.25	N/A	4	0	44	52	70	N/A	2
0.00	N/A	**U /**	N/A	N/A	N/A	23.61	N/A	0.76	N/A	N/A	0	0	0	100	N/A	N/A	0
5.35	0.83	**C+ / 6.6**	15.4	1.99	11.0	15.62	24	4.16	2.85	N/A	0	0	100	0	N/A	50	4
5.42	0.79	**C+ / 6.9**	14.5	2.05	10.3	15.80	38	-0.63	-0.93	N/A	0	0	100	0	N/A	22	3
5.23	0.74	**U /**	N/A	N/A	10.8	14.76	45	-0.88	-3.20	N/A	0	0	100	0	N/A	N/A	3
5.00	1.19	**B- / 7.5**	14.0	1.89	11.2	14.72	66	4.69	8.71	N/A	0	0	100	0	N/A	7	13
6.35	0.74	**B- / 7.2**	11.7	2.14	12.5	15.98	374	-2.44	-4.95	N/A	0	0	100	0	N/A	47	6
6.20	0.70	**B- / 7.3**	11.7	2.10	11.1	15.57	230	-6.29	-8.09	N/A	0	0	100	0	N/A	36	3
6.16	0.70	**B- / 7.7**	10.8	1.98	11.5	15.31	369	-8.82	-9.70	N/A	0	0	100	0	N/A	40	3
5.75	1.20	**B- / 7.6**	11.1	1.73	11.8	15.89	216	-5.22	-6.20	N/A	0	0	100	0	N/A	39	3
6.06	1.25	**B- / 7.3**	13.0	2.25	12.4	16.14	131	-7.13	-7.76	N/A	0	0	100	0	N/A	19	3
4.69	0.63	**B- / 7.1**	11.1	1.91	12.5	10.32	260	-4.07	-8.09	N/A	0	0	100	0	N/A	25	3
5.82	1.22	**B- / 7.4**	13.2	2.39	11.2	15.78	204	-7.79	-7.77	N/A	0	0	100	0	N/A	13	3
5.94	1.19	**B- / 7.1**	13.1	2.04	11.5	15.07	87	-6.04	-7.07	N/A	0	0	100	0	N/A	31	3
5.98	1.19	**B- / 7.3**	12.7	2.29	12.3	16.01	352	-4.87	-3.82	N/A	0	0	100	0	N/A	12	3
6.09	1.18	**B- / 7.2**	13.6	2.48	12.3	15.97	369	-5.82	-5.83	N/A	0	0	100	0	N/A	16	3
4.72	0.38	**B- / 7.2**	10.6	1.38	10.2	14.89	93	-6.38	-8.39	N/A	0	0	100	0	N/A	14	13
5.31	0.82	**C+ / 6.5**	15.3	2.32	11.3	15.45	40	3.37	3.64	N/A	0	0	100	0	N/A	13	4
5.24	0.81	**C+ / 6.6**	13.9	1.80	10.5	15.70	36	1.91	1.66	N/A	0	0	100	0	N/A	43	3
5.02	0.75	**U /**	N/A	N/A	10.8	14.86	65	-3.10	-3.21	N/A	0	0	100	0	N/A	N/A	3
4.95	1.23	**C+ / 6.5**	14.6	1.62	11.5	15.31	82	4.96	4.54	N/A	0	0	99	1	N/A	26	6
6.42	0.77	**B- / 7.0**	13.5	2.43	12.1	15.72	618	-3.31	-4.47	N/A	0	0	100	0	N/A	20	3
6.44	0.67	**B- / 7.7**	9.9	1.68	13.1	15.76	636	-5.33	-6.75	N/A	0	0	99	1	N/A	62	3
8.08	1.00	**U /**	N/A	N/A	6.8	16.77	339	-9.30	-7.58	39.4	0	52	8	40	N/A	N/A	2
6.43	0.67	**B- / 7.3**	10.9	2.00	14.7	16.16	474	-0.99	-2.92	N/A	0	0	100	0	N/A	67	4
7.36	0.66	**U /**	N/A	N/A	N/A	18.90	720	6.30	N/A	N/A	0	100	0	0	N/A	N/A	1
7.20	N/A	**U /**	N/A	N/A	N/A	18.85	1,228	3.98	N/A	N/A	0	0	0	100	N/A	N/A	0
5.70	1.21	**C+ / 5.8**	18.4	3.18	12.1	15.64	259	-0.64	-0.10	N/A	0	0	100	0	N/A	4	0
5.66	1.22	**C+ / 5.8**	17.3	3.11	10.9	15.73	225	-2.42	-1.58	N/A	0	0	100	0	N/A	4	0
6.77	1.11	**U /**	N/A	N/A	N/A	14.02	664	-4.92	1.98	N/A	0	8	13	79	N/A	N/A	1
6.25	N/A	**U /**	N/A	N/A	N/A	13.96	397	-5.73	N/A	N/A	0	0	0	100	N/A	N/A	1
5.18	0.80	**C+ / 6.3**	14.1	2.10	11.0	15.36	30	4.17	0.74	N/A	0	0	100	0	N/A	67	4
5.03	0.74	**U /**	N/A	N/A	12.1	14.77	67	-5.28	-4.05	N/A	0	0	100	0	N/A	N/A	3

N/A denotes number is not available

99 Pct = Best
0 Pct = Worst

Fund Type	Fund Name	Ticker Symbol	Overall Weiss Investment Rating	PRICE: Price As of 6/30/05	PRICE: 52 Week High	PRICE: 52 Week Low	PERFORMANCE: Performance Rating/Pts	% Total Return Through 6/30/05: 3 Mo	6 Mo	1Yr/Pct	Annualized: 3Yr/Pct	Annualized: 5Yr/Pct
MUS	Nuveen GA Prem Inc Muni	NPG	B	16.95	17.85	14.41	B- / 7.2	12.67	7.31	23.09 / 86	6.95 / 44	11.08 / 84
MUS	Nuveen Insured CA Div Adv Muni Fund	NKL	C+	14.77	15.40	13.09	C / 5.2	3.76	6.71	18.99 / 73	6.44 / 38	--
MUS	Nuveen Insured CA Prem Inc Muni	NPC	C+	15.62	16.60	13.75	C / 5.4	4.03	4.10	20.46 / 78	6.86 / 43	7.98 / 55
MUS	Nuveen Insured CA Prem Inc Muni 2	NCL	C	14.77	15.67	13.18	C- / 3.8	2.97	0.74	18.70 / 72	5.83 / 30	8.56 / 60
MUS	Nuveen Insured CA T/F Adv Muni Fd	NKX	U	14.17	15.25	12.84	U /	2.96	1.73	16.35 / 63	--	--
MUN	Nuveen Insured Div Adv Muni Fund	NVG	B-	14.70	15.08	13.30	C+ / 6.0	9.73	8.45	17.38 / 66	6.50 / 38	--
MUS	Nuveen Insured FL Prem Inc Muni	NFL	B+	16.47	16.90	14.10	B / 8.2	13.09	9.66	24.22 / 90	8.28 / 61	11.40 / 86
MUS	Nuveen Insured FL T/F Adv Muni Fd	NWF	U	13.90	15.00	12.76	U /	6.78	5.75	12.44 / 48	--	--
MUS	Nuveen Insured MA T/F Adv Muni Fd	NGX	U	15.48	17.25	14.25	U /	0.47	-1.27	15.17 / 58	--	--
MUN	Nuveen Insured Muni Opportunity	NIO	B-	15.65	16.20	14.09	C+ / 5.9	10.47	4.72	16.42 / 63	7.08 / 46	10.67 / 80
MUS	Nuveen Insured NY Div Adv Muni Fund	NKO	A-	15.14	15.37	13.22	B / 7.7	11.36	12.54	22.46 / 84	7.32 / 49	--
MUS	Nuveen Insured NY Prem Inc Muni	NNF	B+	15.80	15.89	13.67	B / 7.6	11.53	10.65	23.43 / 87	7.28 / 48	10.34 / 77
MUS	Nuveen Insured NY T/F Adv Muni Fd	NRK	U	13.97	14.59	12.47	U /	3.98	9.33	18.13 / 70	--	--
MUN	Nuveen Insured Prem Inc Muni 2	NPX	C	13.56	14.25	12.51	C- / 4.2	6.73	5.83	14.84 / 56	5.44 / 24	10.41 / 78
MUN	Nuveen Insured Quality Muni	NQI	B+	16.22	16.48	14.21	B- / 7.5	11.59	7.44	21.36 / 80	8.10 / 59	11.34 / 86
MUN	Nuveen Insured T/F Adv Muni Fund	NEA	U	14.46	15.10	12.85	U /	9.12	10.93	16.50 / 63	--	--
MUN	Nuveen Investment Quality Muni	NQM	B-	15.15	15.45	13.55	C+ / 6.6	10.03	8.35	17.73 / 67	7.26 / 48	10.82 / 81
MUS	Nuveen MA Div Adv Muni	NMB	B-	16.80	19.00	14.54	C+ / 6.8	10.09	8.36	22.16 / 83	6.64 / 39	--
MUS	Nuveen MA Prem Inc Muni	NMT	C+	15.72	17.32	13.87	C / 5.0	9.41	3.76	18.66 / 72	5.60 / 27	8.19 / 57
MUS	Nuveen MD Div Adv Muni	NFM	C+	16.29	16.62	14.00	C+ / 6.7	5.97	8.64	20.18 / 77	7.67 / 54	--
MUS	Nuveen MD Div Adv Muni 2	NZR	C+	15.93	16.30	13.97	C+ / 6.8	7.31	7.15	19.80 / 76	7.84 / 56	--
MUS	Nuveen MD Div Adv Muni Fund 3	NWI	U	14.61	15.80	12.92	U /	6.25	9.72	18.55 / 71	--	--
MUS	Nuveen MD Prem Inc Muni	NMY	C-	15.72	16.73	14.36	D+ / 2.9	4.15	-1.32	14.69 / 56	5.37 / 24	8.81 / 63
MUS	Nuveen MI Div Adv Muni	NZW	B-	15.57	16.50	13.46	C+ / 6.1	4.26	4.75	22.12 / 83	7.40 / 50	--
MUS	Nuveen MI Prem Inc Muni	NMP	C+	15.44	16.25	13.72	C+ / 5.7	7.18	4.15	18.94 / 73	6.94 / 44	10.90 / 82
MUS	Nuveen MI Quality Inc Muni	NUM	C	15.86	17.27	14.59	C- / 3.7	4.31	0.76	15.80 / 60	5.98 / 33	9.50 / 69
MUS	Nuveen MO Prem Inc Muni	NOM	C+	17.38	19.05	15.17	C / 5.1	4.82	-3.51	20.85 / 79	7.67 / 54	11.51 / 87
MUN	Nuveen Muni Advantage	NMA	B+	15.59	15.86	13.97	B- / 7.0	8.90	6.69	18.96 / 73	8.25 / 61	11.81 / 88
MUH	Nuveen Muni High Income Opportunity	NMZ	U	15.67	15.78	13.40	U /	7.58	8.12	25.64 / 93	--	--
MUN	Nuveen Muni Income	NMI	C+	10.68	11.25	9.33	C+ / 6.7	10.35	11.34	17.81 / 67	6.81 / 42	4.50 / 28
MUN	Nuveen Muni Market Opportunity	NMO	B-	14.68	15.00	13.18	C+ / 6.4	10.82	8.69	16.47 / 63	6.94 / 44	9.48 / 68
MUN	Nuveen Muni Value	NUV	B	9.57	9.62	8.69	C / 5.0	6.83	7.82	15.95 / 61	6.06 / 33	8.68 / 62
MUS	Nuveen NC Div Adv Muni	NRB	A-	17.33	17.45	14.67	B / 8.2	5.23	6.38	24.75 / 91	10.47 / 78	--
MUS	Nuveen NC Div Adv Muni 2	NNO	B	16.60	16.74	14.75	B- / 7.0	6.53	7.36	11.25 / 43	10.12 / 75	--
MUS	Nuveen NC Div Adv Muni Fund 3	NII	U	14.96	15.65	13.54	U /	7.46	1.38	15.94 / 61	--	--
MUS	Nuveen NC Prem Inc Muni	NNC	C-	16.65	17.75	14.40	C- / 4.1	4.77	-1.73	20.65 / 79	5.68 / 27	10.01 / 73
MUS	Nuveen NJ Div Adv Muni	NXJ	B-	15.07	15.97	13.54	C+ / 6.8	7.72	4.26	18.49 / 71	8.73 / 64	--
MUS	Nuveen NJ Div Adv Muni Fund 2	NUJ	B	15.64	16.13	13.67	B- / 7.5	12.98	8.02	19.90 / 76	8.07 / 59	--
MUS	Nuveen NJ Investment Quality Muni	NQJ	C+	15.20	15.99	13.99	C / 5.0	5.03	4.12	16.02 / 62	7.19 / 47	8.51 / 60
MUS	Nuveen NJ Prem Inc Muni	NNJ	B-	15.62	16.25	14.00	C+ / 6.0	5.89	6.54	19.48 / 75	7.18 / 47	9.80 / 71
MUS	Nuveen NY Div Adv Muni	NAN	B+	15.93	16.09	14.14	B- / 7.3	8.36	6.48	19.11 / 74	9.16 / 68	11.15 / 84
MUS	Nuveen NY Div Adv Muni 2	NXK	A	15.54	15.54	13.47	B / 8.2	10.38	6.92	20.88 / 79	10.06 / 75	--
MUS	Nuveen NY Investment Quality Muni	NQN	B-	15.50	16.12	14.13	C+ / 6.1	6.67	5.32	18.01 / 70	7.69 / 55	9.84 / 71
MUS	Nuveen NY Muni Value	NNY	B-	9.68	9.78	8.54	C+ / 5.9	7.91	9.26	17.01 / 65	6.70 / 41	7.80 / 53
MUS	Nuveen NY Performance Plus Muni	NNP	B	16.02	16.42	14.26	B- / 7.1	10.53	7.45	19.22 / 74	7.85 / 56	10.84 / 81
MUS	Nuveen NY Quality Inc Muni	NUN	B-	15.00	15.25	13.52	C+ / 6.7	7.26	9.37	17.82 / 68	7.74 / 56	9.29 / 67
MUS	Nuveen NY Select Quality Muni	NVN	C+	15.48	15.64	14.03	C+ / 6.8	7.54	8.12	17.88 / 68	8.06 / 58	10.00 / 73
MUS	Nuveen NY Select Tax-Free Inc Port	NXN	C+	14.15	14.80	12.69	C / 5.0	5.98	7.31	16.48 / 63	6.15 / 34	7.32 / 49
MUS	Nuveen OH Div Adv Muni	NXI	C+	16.24	18.10	14.16	C+ / 6.6	9.31	-0.30	18.51 / 71	8.83 / 65	--
MUS	Nuveen OH Div Adv Muni 2	NBJ	B	16.06	17.16	13.75	B- / 7.3	5.42	1.41	23.90 / 89	9.69 / 73	--
MUS	Nuveen OH Div Adv Muni Fund 3	NVJ	C	15.71	17.40	13.40	C / 5.3	2.16	-2.11	24.13 / 89	7.60 / 53	--
MUS	Nuveen OH Quality Inc Muni	NUO	C-	17.14	18.99	15.60	D+ / 2.5	7.85	-3.13	15.84 / 61	3.70 / 12	7.91 / 54

N/A denotes number is not available

Incl. in Returns		RISK				NET ASSETS		VALUATION			ASSET					FUND MANAGER	
Dividend Yield %	Expense Ratio	Risk Rating/ Pts	3 Year Standard Deviation	3 Year Beta	Avg Duration	NAV as of 6/30/05	Total $(Mil)	Premium / Discount As of 6/30/05	Premium / Discount 1 Year Average	Wtd Avg P/E	Cash %	Stocks %	Bonds %	Other %	Portfolio Turnover Ratio	Manager Quality Pct	Manager Tenure (Years)
4.94	1.22	**C+ / 6.5**	15.1	1.43	12.0	15.25	58	11.15	7.63	N/A	0	0	100	0	N/A	52	12
5.81	0.71	**B- / 7.4**	12.7	2.01	12.1	15.80	241	-6.52	-6.09	N/A	0	0	100	0	N/A	26	3
5.66	1.14	**C+ / 6.4**	15.7	2.57	12.8	16.27	105	-4.00	-3.52	N/A	0	0	100	0	N/A	12	1
5.57	1.16	**C+ / 6.7**	16.4	2.46	11.7	15.40	196	-4.09	-1.56	N/A	0	0	100	0	N/A	9	1
5.55	0.72	**U /**	N/A	N/A	12.3	15.17	89	-6.59	-3.76	N/A	0	0	100	0	N/A	N/A	3
5.74	0.69	**B- / 7.5**	12.0	2.18	12.2	15.80	471	-6.96	-7.52	N/A	0	0	100	0	N/A	20	1
5.23	1.15	**C+ / 5.9**	16.8	2.90	11.4	16.26	234	1.29	-1.96	N/A	0	0	100	0	N/A	13	1
5.01	0.74	**U /**	N/A	N/A	11.3	14.77	57	-5.89	-3.71	N/A	0	0	100	0	N/A	N/A	1
4.95	0.79	**U /**	N/A	N/A	12.7	14.97	41	3.41	7.86	N/A	0	0	100	0	N/A	N/A	1
5.69	1.15	**B- / 7.0**	12.9	2.19	13.6	16.11	1,307	-2.86	-3.59	N/A	0	0	100	0	N/A	22	1
5.45	0.72	**B- / 7.2**	12.9	1.81	12.3	15.94	127	-5.02	-7.46	N/A	0	0	100	0	N/A	38	3
5.38	1.19	**C+ / 6.7**	12.7	2.10	11.9	16.12	134	-1.99	-6.13	N/A	0	0	100	0	N/A	24	6
5.19	0.75	**U /**	N/A	N/A	N/A	15.20	53	-8.09	-7.74	N/A	0	0	100	0	N/A	N/A	3
5.85	1.15	**B- / 7.1**	12.9	1.85	11.5	14.50	541	-6.48	-5.63	N/A	0	0	100	0	N/A	24	1
5.79	1.18	**C+ / 6.7**	13.6	2.18	13.9	15.88	607	2.14	-0.31	N/A	0	0	100	0	N/A	29	1
5.38	0.70	**U /**	N/A	N/A	13.0	15.08	279	-4.11	-3.99	N/A	0	0	99	1	N/A	N/A	1
6.07	1.19	**B- / 7.1**	12.3	2.33	12.3	16.05	574	-5.61	-6.39	N/A	0	0	100	0	N/A	21	3
5.20	0.85	**B- / 7.1**	10.7	1.09	12.1	15.67	31	7.21	5.48	N/A	0	0	100	0	N/A	70	3
5.27	1.22	**B- / 7.1**	14.0	2.17	11.8	15.16	72	3.69	4.79	N/A	0	0	100	0	N/A	18	3
5.34	0.79	**C+ / 6.0**	16.5	1.58	12.5	15.19	63	7.24	5.10	N/A	0	0	100	0	N/A	51	4
5.51	0.76	**C+ / 6.6**	13.7	1.71	11.6	15.51	65	2.71	-0.17	N/A	0	0	100	0	N/A	51	4
4.90	0.74	**U /**	N/A	N/A	11.7	14.91	80	-2.01	-3.71	N/A	0	0	100	0	N/A	N/A	3
5.18	1.22	**C+ / 6.8**	16.6	2.40	11.7	15.17	161	3.63	6.25	N/A	0	0	100	0	N/A	10	6
5.50	0.81	**B- / 7.7**	11.7	1.22	12.5	15.62	32	-0.32	0.10	N/A	0	0	100	0	N/A	73	0
5.45	1.17	**B- / 7.0**	12.6	2.07	12.2	15.78	122	-2.15	-1.91	N/A	0	0	100	0	N/A	25	0
5.37	1.20	**B- / 7.7**	13.0	1.97	11.9	16.14	189	-1.73	0.12	N/A	0	0	100	0	N/A	26	0
5.15	1.27	**C+ / 6.6**	14.9	1.66	11.4	15.15	34	14.72	14.78	N/A	0	0	100	0	N/A	48	12
6.36	1.17	**B- / 7.3**	12.1	2.11	13.3	16.15	695	-3.47	-4.09	N/A	0	0	100	0	N/A	40	3
6.82	0.72	**U /**	N/A	N/A	13.4	15.56	362	0.71	0.66	N/A	0	0	100	0	N/A	N/A	2
4.99	0.77	**C+ / 6.9**	12.1	1.71	11.8	11.04	90	-3.26	-6.62	N/A	0	0	100	0	N/A	39	4
6.11	1.17	**B- / 7.1**	12.5	2.06	12.2	15.63	712	-6.08	-7.81	N/A	0	0	100	0	N/A	32	3
4.87	0.60	**B / 8.8**	7.7	1.29	12.7	10.37	2,024	-7.71	-8.65	N/A	0	0	100	0	N/A	54	18
5.33	0.80	**C+ / 6.7**	12.4	1.81	11.1	15.51	35	11.73	7.96	N/A	0	0	100	0	N/A	65	4
5.32	0.77	**C+ / 6.7**	10.4	1.55	N/A	15.61	58	6.34	2.80	N/A	0	0	100	0	N/A	67	4
4.89	0.75	**U /**	N/A	N/A	11.1	14.85	58	0.74	1.74	N/A	0	0	100	0	N/A	N/A	3
4.90	1.22	**C+ / 6.4**	14.6	2.15	11.5	15.20	96	9.54	10.25	N/A	0	0	100	0	N/A	15	12
5.58	0.73	**B- / 7.2**	13.0	2.09	11.9	15.64	103	-3.64	-2.45	N/A	0	0	100	0	N/A	51	3
5.77	0.77	**C+ / 6.2**	12.6	1.78	N/A	15.80	71	-1.01	-2.92	N/A	0	0	100	0	N/A	57	3
5.74	1.19	**B- / 7.6**	11.9	1.96	11.8	15.61	319	-2.63	-0.53	N/A	0	0	99	1	N/A	35	3
5.41	1.17	**B- / 7.3**	12.3	2.07	10.8	16.05	193	-2.68	-2.83	N/A	0	0	99	1	N/A	31	3
6.13	0.78	**C+ / 6.7**	14.0	2.41	12.1	16.08	148	-0.93	-3.11	N/A	0	0	100	0	N/A	38	6
6.04	0.73	**C+ / 6.9**	12.8	2.04	12.7	15.86	102	-2.02	-4.71	N/A	0	0	100	0	N/A	61	4
5.76	1.17	**B- / 7.2**	12.0	2.02	11.6	16.21	287	-4.38	-5.37	N/A	0	0	100	0	N/A	36	6
4.40	0.67	**B- / 7.8**	8.4	1.39	12.9	10.16	154	-4.72	-7.98	N/A	0	0	100	0	N/A	55	6
6.06	1.19	**C+ / 6.7**	13.9	2.44	12.2	16.74	251	-4.30	-5.65	N/A	0	0	100	0	N/A	22	6
5.59	1.18	**B- / 7.2**	12.3	2.16	12.1	16.00	385	-6.25	-7.47	N/A	0	0	100	0	N/A	28	6
5.62	1.17	**C+ / 6.7**	14.2	2.50	12.6	16.24	380	-4.68	-6.34	N/A	0	0	100	0	N/A	19	6
4.28	0.40	**B- / 7.7**	11.4	1.58	11.3	14.60	57	-3.08	-5.55	N/A	0	0	100	0	N/A	44	3
5.78	0.74	**C+ / 6.2**	16.2	2.31	11.7	15.74	67	3.18	3.60	N/A	0	0	100	0	N/A	32	4
5.41	0.78	**C+ / 6.5**	15.3	2.72	10.5	15.60	49	2.95	2.01	N/A	0	0	100	0	N/A	16	4
5.27	0.78	**C+ / 6.1**	16.8	2.34	10.8	15.75	34	-0.25	0.42	N/A	0	0	100	0	N/A	22	3
5.34	1.17	**C+ / 6.9**	14.5	2.03	12.0	16.80	163	2.02	4.08	N/A	0	0	99	1	N/A	9	14

N/A denotes number is not available

Fund Type	Fund Name (99 Pct = Best, 0 Pct = Worst)	Ticker Symbol	Overall Weiss Investment Rating	PRICE: Price As of 6/30/05	PRICE: 52 Week High	PRICE: 52 Week Low	PERFORMANCE: Performance Rating/Pts	% Total Return Through 6/30/05: 3 Mo	6 Mo	1Yr/Pct	Annualized: 3Yr/Pct	Annualized: 5Yr/Pct
MUS	Nuveen PA Div Adv Muni	NXM	**A**	16.10	16.85	14.30	**B+** / **8.4**	9.72	5.87	22.85 / 85	10.62 / 78	--
MUS	Nuveen PA Div Adv Muni Fund 2	NVY	**C+**	14.98	16.33	13.35	**C+** / **6.4**	10.88	5.00	17.92 / 69	7.35 / 50	--
MUS	Nuveen PA Investment Quality Muni	NQP	**C**	14.84	15.95	13.45	**C-** / **3.9**	6.37	-0.15	16.63 / 64	5.78 / 29	7.18 / 47
MUS	Nuveen PA Prem Inc Muni 2	NPY	**C+**	15.21	16.20	13.70	**C** / **5.2**	0.87	1.50	19.14 / 74	8.13 / 60	11.25 / 85
MUN	Nuveen Performance Plus Muni	NPP	**B-**	14.79	15.25	13.35	**C+** / **6.1**	9.87	7.53	16.40 / 63	6.92 / 44	11.25 / 85
GI	Nuveen Preferred&Convertible Inc 2	JQC	**U**	13.10	14.49	12.25	**U** /	7.91	0.27	11.49 / 28	--	--
GI	Nuveen Preferred&Convertible Income	JPC	**U**	13.44	14.99	12.26	**U** /	9.75	1.67	13.36 / 33	--	--
MUN	Nuveen Prem Inc Muni	NPI	**C+**	14.33	14.56	13.02	**C** / **5.3**	5.03	8.52	17.27 / 65	6.47 / 38	10.61 / 79
MUN	Nuveen Prem Inc Muni 4	NPT	**C+**	12.54	12.88	11.48	**C-** / **4.1**	7.53	9.45	15.82 / 61	4.19 / 15	7.33 / 49
MUN	Nuveen Premier Insured Muni Inc	NIF	**C+**	15.69	16.20	14.15	**C+** / **6.4**	8.64	10.66	17.90 / 68	6.79 / 41	10.99 / 83
MUN	Nuveen Premier Muni Inc	NPF	**C+**	14.09	14.75	13.20	**C** / **4.4**	7.28	6.64	14.22 / 54	5.55 / 26	8.65 / 61
MUN	Nuveen Premium Income Muni 2	NPM	**B-**	14.66	14.68	13.15	**C+** / **6.7**	9.46	8.15	18.74 / 72	7.36 / 50	9.58 / 69
MUN	Nuveen Quality Inc Muni	NQU	**B-**	14.45	14.76	12.80	**C+** / **5.6**	7.96	6.64	16.54 / 64	6.70 / 40	8.84 / 63
IN	Nuveen Quality Preferred Income	JTP	**U**	14.04	15.09	12.50	**U** /	10.70	6.61	14.48 / 36	--	--
IN	Nuveen Quality Preferred Income 2	JPS	**U**	14.41	15.64	12.90	**U** /	10.52	4.94	14.98 / 38	--	--
IN	Nuveen Quality Preferred Income 3	JHP	**U**	14.55	15.50	13.16	**U** /	9.91	6.48	17.93 / 44	--	--
GI	Nuveen Real Estate Inc Fund	JRS	**B**	20.11	21.22	16.50	**B** / **8.1**	13.40	1.56	31.77 / 78	17.42 / 82	--
MUN	Nuveen Select Maturities Muni	NIM	**C**	9.72	10.20	9.10	**D+** / **2.7**	4.67	6.99	11.28 / 43	3.83 / 12	3.80 / 24
MUN	Nuveen Select Quality Muni	NQS	**B-**	15.12	15.29	13.45	**C+** / **6.9**	10.87	6.45	16.52 / 64	8.12 / 59	10.45 / 78
MUN	Nuveen Select T-F Inc Portf	NXP	**C+**	14.00	14.40	13.17	**C-** / **3.7**	5.36	6.83	11.70 / 44	5.44 / 24	5.80 / 34
MUN	Nuveen Select T-F Inc Portf 2	NXQ	**C**	13.51	13.61	12.66	**C-** / **3.1**	5.21	6.85	11.01 / 42	4.69 / 19	5.57 / 33
MUN	Nuveen Select Tax-Free Inc 3	NXR	**C+**	13.44	13.46	12.50	**C-** / **4.2**	6.38	7.72	11.63 / 44	5.82 / 30	5.95 / 36
LP	Nuveen Sr Inc	NSL	**C-**	8.57	10.05	8.54	**D** / **1.6**	-5.99	-4.14	-5.91 / 2	10.90 / 47	6.03 / 25
IN	Nuveen Tax-Advant Tot Ret Strat Fd	JTA	**U**	19.75	20.00	16.63	**U** /	5.43	6.73	22.89 / 56	--	--
LP	Nuveen Tax-Advantaged Floating Rate	JFP	**U**	13.25	N/A	N/A	**U** /	--	--	--	--	--
MUS	Nuveen TX Quality Inc Muni	NTX	**B+**	15.96	16.36	13.92	**B** / **7.6**	11.07	10.30	21.62 / 81	7.88 / 57	11.52 / 87
MUS	Nuveen VA Div Adv Muni 2	NNB	**A-**	17.00	17.50	14.75	**B+** / **8.4**	9.04	4.61	22.45 / 84	11.14 / 81	--
MUS	Nuveen VA Div Adv Muni Fund	NGB	**B+**	17.47	18.20	14.95	**B+** / **8.3**	1.82	4.51	23.72 / 88	12.22 / 86	--
MUS	Nuveen VA Premium Income Municipal	NPV	**C**	17.34	18.37	14.87	**C** / **5.1**	5.82	0.61	20.12 / 77	6.85 / 42	9.93 / 72
COH	Pacholder High Yield Fund	PHF	**C**	9.68	10.13	8.50	**B** / **8.1**	15.41	3.09	20.22 / 50	19.28 / 87	9.93 / 41
EN	Petroleum and Resources Corp.	PEO	**A**	30.01	30.52	23.58	**B** / **7.8**	5.12	16.28	30.76 / 77	15.59 / 76	10.32 / 44
MUS	PIMCO CA Municipal Income Fund	PCQ	**B-**	14.75	14.91	12.72	**C+** / **6.9**	6.90	12.41	22.28 / 83	6.62 / 39	--
MUS	PIMCO CA Municipal Income Fund II	PCK	**U**	14.87	15.00	12.85	**U** /	7.00	10.16	23.14 / 86	--	--
MUS	PIMCO CA Municipal Income Fund III	PZC	**U**	14.65	14.95	12.81	**U** /	5.46	10.13	22.17 / 83	--	--
MTG	PIMCO Commercial Mortgage Trust	PCM	**C-**	14.34	14.49	12.77	**C** / **4.3**	9.48	12.69	18.56 / 46	8.86 / 28	13.31 / 61
COI	PIMCO Corporate Income Fund	PCN	**C+**	15.40	16.03	13.52	**C+** / **6.4**	12.38	6.32	24.49 / 61	13.06 / 63	--
COH	PIMCO Corporate Opportunity Fund	PTY	**U**	17.07	18.09	15.09	**U** /	12.39	3.60	22.06 / 54	--	--
LP	PIMCO Floating Rate Income Fund	PFL	**U**	18.34	22.13	18.05	**U** /	-10.05	-8.11	-4.96 / 2	--	--
LP	PIMCO Floating Rate Strategy Fund	PFN	**U**	17.53	N/A	N/A	**U** /	-7.82	-7.22	--	--	--
COH	PIMCO High Income Fund	PHK	**U**	14.68	15.34	13.41	**U** /	9.13	4.48	22.70 / 50	--	--
MUN	PIMCO Municipal Income Fund	PMF	**A+**	15.54	15.67	13.02	**B+** / **8.6**	10.08	13.25	27.28 / 95	9.08 / 68	--
MUN	PIMCO Municipal Income Fund II	PML	**U**	15.33	15.37	13.10	**U** /	8.66	10.69	25.35 / 92	--	--
MUN	PIMCO National Muni Income Fund III	PMX	**U**	16.12	15.15	13.11	**U** /	8.53	10.63	23.11 / 86	--	--
MUS	PIMCO NY Muni Income Fund	PNF	**A**	14.89	14.99	12.50	**B+** / **8.8**	11.67	18.78	25.83 / 93	8.40 / 63	--
MUS	PIMCO NY Municipal Income Fund II	PNI	**U**	15.12	15.70	12.80	**U** /	9.65	12.40	26.00 / 93	--	--
MUS	PIMCO NY Municipal Income Fund III	PYN	**U**	15.39	15.50	12.79	**U** /	11.47	10.94	27.17 / 95	--	--
GL	PIMCO Strategic Glob Gov Fund	RCS	**C-**	12.67	13.29	10.17	**C+** / **6.6**	10.11	8.31	31.45 / 78	12.24 / 58	17.00 / 84
LP	Pioneer Floating Rate Trust	PHD	**U**	17.25	N/A	N/A	**U** /	-5.49	--	--	--	--
COH	Pioneer High Income Trust	PHT	**B-**	16.20	17.15	14.46	**B-** / **7.5**	12.91	2.50	19.09 / 48	18.29 / 84	--
GEI	Pioneer Interest Shares	MUO	**C-**	11.43	11.90	10.52	**D** / **1.7**	7.12	3.60	13.67 / 34	5.06 / 9	8.30 / 32
MUH	Pioneer Municipal High Income Adv	MAV	**U**	14.70	15.00	12.78	**U** /	5.17	8.82	23.89 / 88	--	--
MUH	Pioneer Municipal High Income Trust	MHI	**U**	14.80	15.19	13.15	**U** /	5.96	6.72	20.40 / 78	--	--

N/A denotes number is not available

		RISK				NET ASSETS		VALUATION			ASSET					FUND MANAGER	
Incl. in Returns			3 Year					Premium / Discount									
Dividend Yield %	Expense Ratio	Risk Rating/ Pts	Standard Deviation	Beta	Avg Dura- tion	NAV as of 6/30/05	Total $(Mil)	As of 6/30/05	1 Year Average	Wtd Avg P/E	Cash %	Stocks %	Bonds %	Other %	Portfolio Turnover Ratio	Manager Quality Pct	Manager Tenure (Years)
5.76	0.78	**C+ / 6.7**	14.0	2.54	11.4	15.95	53	0.94	-0.84	N/A	0	0	100	0	N/A	43	3
5.40	0.77	**C+ / 6.8**	14.7	2.55	10.7	15.90	59	-5.79	-5.32	N/A	0	0	100	0	N/A	13	3
5.30	1.21	**B- / 7.0**	14.3	2.49	11.8	15.74	256	-5.72	-4.04	N/A	0	0	100	0	N/A	11	3
5.62	1.19	**C+ / 6.7**	14.0	2.37	11.7	15.33	242	-0.78	-0.20	N/A	0	0	99	1	N/A	24	3
6.25	1.14	**B- / 7.4**	12.3	2.24	11.8	16.07	963	-7.97	-8.12	N/A	0	0	99	1	N/A	23	3
8.13	0.98	**U /**	N/A	N/A	7.2	14.46	2,044	-9.41	-7.51	14.8	0	2	10	88	N/A	N/A	2
8.09	1.01	**U /**	N/A	N/A	N/A	14.58	1,463	-7.82	-6.36	N/A	0	1	10	89	N/A	N/A	2
6.09	1.18	**B- / 7.5**	11.4	2.13	11.7	15.45	985	-7.25	-6.83	N/A	0	0	100	0	N/A	21	17
6.13	1.25	**B- / 7.6**	11.7	2.00	12.1	13.88	600	-9.65	-8.30	N/A	0	0	99	1	N/A	11	3
5.70	1.19	**C+ / 6.7**	13.4	2.32	11.8	15.96	310	-1.69	-3.44	N/A	0	0	100	0	N/A	17	1
5.91	1.25	**B- / 7.6**	12.0	2.12	10.2	15.58	313	-9.56	-8.02	N/A	0	0	100	0	N/A	17	14
6.05	1.19	**B- / 7.5**	11.1	2.06	10.5	15.68	644	-6.51	-7.46	N/A	0	0	100	0	N/A	34	3
6.10	1.18	**B- / 7.7**	11.2	1.93	12.4	15.73	853	-8.14	-7.85	N/A	0	0	99	1	N/A	30	3
8.01	1.02	**U /**	12.6	0.03	N/A	14.65	946	-4.16	-4.36	N/A	0	1	0	99	N/A	N/A	3
7.97	0.95	**U /**	N/A	N/A	N/A	15.41	1,844	-6.49	-6.10	N/A	0	1	0	99	N/A	N/A	3
7.97	1.07	**U /**	N/A	N/A	9.3	14.82	351	-1.82	-2.64	15.5	0	0	0	100	N/A	N/A	3
8.00	0.91	**C+ / 5.6**	17.8	0.24	N/A	22.41	634	-10.26	-7.44	50.7	0	71	0	29	N/A	95	4
4.82	0.60	**B / 8.4**	9.2	1.21	10.6	10.36	128	-6.18	-7.27	N/A	0	0	100	0	N/A	38	4
6.29	1.18	**B- / 7.5**	11.4	2.08	13.3	15.90	539	-4.91	-5.91	N/A	0	0	99	1	N/A	42	3
4.87	0.32	**B / 8.1**	8.7	1.35	11.4	14.95	245	-6.35	-6.80	N/A	0	0	99	1	N/A	46	6
4.87	0.36	**B / 8.2**	8.5	1.44	12.1	14.69	259	-8.03	-8.99	N/A	0	0	100	0	N/A	33	6
4.81	0.36	**B / 8.3**	8.7	1.51	11.4	14.56	189	-7.69	-9.01	N/A	0	0	100	0	N/A	39	6
7.03	2.38	**B- / 7.8**	12.9	-27.23	N/A	8.46	252	1.30	10.89	N/A	0	9	8	83	N/A	97	4
6.03	1.83	**U /**	N/A	N/A	3.8	21.27	295	-7.15	-9.13	20.6	0	73	3	24	N/A	N/A	1
3.91	N/A	**U /**	N/A	N/A	N/A	14.09	195	-5.96	N/A	N/A	0	0	0	100	N/A	N/A	0
5.43	1.14	**C+ / 6.4**	12.9	1.65	11.9	15.64	148	2.05	-1.26	N/A	0	0	100	0	N/A	58	14
4.93	0.74	**C+ / 6.5**	14.2	1.99	11.6	15.77	90	7.80	4.97	N/A	0	0	100	0	N/A	71	4
5.26	0.80	**C+ / 6.3**	15.1	2.11	11.8	15.55	49	12.35	12.71	N/A	0	0	100	0	N/A	65	4
4.73	1.18	**C+ / 6.5**	14.3	1.76	11.9	15.89	141	9.13	9.08	N/A	0	0	100	0	N/A	43	6
9.50	3.03	**C- / 3.3**	23.5	1.93	4.9	9.10	123	6.37	3.23	8.9	0	0	100	0	73	9	5
1.74	0.56	**B- / 7.3**	18.1	0.86	N/A	32.60	619	-7.94	-7.42	21.0	8	91	0	1	13	44	19
6.20	1.00	**B- / 7.2**	10.6	1.62	N/A	14.79	260	-0.27	-2.31	N/A	0	0	100	0	5	48	4
6.51	1.07	**U /**	9.7	1.56	N/A	14.77	425	0.68	-0.41	N/A	0	0	100	0	4	N/A	3
6.45	1.08	**U /**	N/A	N/A	N/A	14.86	311	-1.41	-1.75	N/A	0	0	100	0	6	N/A	3
8.04	1.75	**C / 5.3**	14.4	3.14	N/A	12.50	140	14.72	10.52	N/A	0	0	100	0	24	25	12
9.24	1.13	**C+ / 6.1**	15.1	1.81	N/A	15.20	530	1.32	-1.26	N/A	0	0	100	0	89	53	4
9.64	1.13	**U /**	N/A	N/A	N/A	16.29	1,093	4.79	1.78	N/A	13	0	86	1	64	N/A	3
7.92	1.51	**U /**	N/A	N/A	N/A	19.35	354	-5.22	5.09	N/A	10	0	30	60	39	N/A	2
6.42	1.16	**U /**	N/A	N/A	N/A	18.76	793	-6.56	N/A	N/A	18	0	81	1	11	N/A	1
10.75	1.26	**U /**	N/A	N/A	N/A	15.23	1,716	-3.61	-5.86	N/A	4	0	94	2	40	N/A	2
6.18	0.97	**B- / 7.6**	10.9	1.67	14.8	15.11	361	2.85	0.04	N/A	1	0	98	1	11	66	4
6.56	1.04	**U /**	10.1	1.64	13.1	14.94	838	2.61	0.14	N/A	1	0	98	1	6	N/A	3
6.53	1.05	**U /**	N/A	N/A	N/A	14.76	455	2.44	-0.76	N/A	3	0	96	1	1	N/A	3
6.00	1.12	**C+ / 6.3**	12.3	1.80	14.5	13.94	102	6.81	0.17	N/A	2	0	97	1	10	56	4
6.42	1.16	**U /**	10.6	1.53	15.2	14.76	145	2.44	0.33	N/A	1	0	98	1	10	N/A	3
6.19	1.25	**U /**	N/A	N/A	15.0	15.17	82	1.45	-2.16	N/A	3	0	96	1	3	N/A	3
7.28	1.06	**C- / 3.6**	17.3	0.65	N/A	10.88	399	16.45	7.98	N/A	0	0	100	0	224	76	11
4.37	N/A	**U /**	N/A	N/A	N/A	18.95	N/A	-8.97	N/A	N/A	0	0	0	100	N/A	N/A	N/A
10.02	1.00	**C / 5.5**	13.3	1.38	6.4	16.15	438	0.31	-0.81	N/A	0	0	98	2	54	61	N/A
5.59	0.77	**B / 8.3**	9.1	1.51	N/A	12.60	97	-9.29	-10.25	N/A	2	0	97	1	47	35	12
6.78	1.18	**U /**	N/A	N/A	15.0	15.28	332	-3.80	-0.59	N/A	0	0	100	0	39	N/A	2
6.45	1.04	**U /**	N/A	N/A	14.6	15.86	346	-6.68	-4.99	N/A	0	0	99	1	25	N/A	2

N/A denotes number is not available

				PRICE			PERFORMANCE					
	99 Pct = Best 0 Pct = Worst				52 Week			% Total Return Through 6/30/05				
											Annualized	
Fund Type	Fund Name	Ticker Symbol	Overall Weiss Investment Rating	Price As of 6/30/05	High	Low	Performance Rating/Pts	3 Mo	6 Mo	1Yr/Pct	3Yr/Pct	5Yr/Pct
GI	Pioneer Tax Advantage Balanced Tr	PBF	U	13.52	13.59	11.40	U /	8.91	9.08	24.34 / 60	--	--
IN	Power Shares Dynamic Market Portf	PWC	U	41.93	43.07	33.50	U /	4.57	5.04	14.66 / 37	--	--
GR	Power Shares Dynamic OTC Portfolio	PWO	U	45.88	47.40	34.29	U /	4.27	3.15	14.99 / 38	--	--
FO	Power Shares Gldn Drgn Hltr USX Chn	PGJ	U	13.64	N/A	N/A	U /	3.16	--	--	--	--
IN	Power Shares High Yld Eq Div Ach	PEY	U	14.88	N/A	N/A	U /	4.33	--	--	--	--
IN	Powershares Dynamic Large Cap Value	PWV	U	15.16	N/A	N/A	U /	--	--	--	--	--
GR	PowerShares Dynamic Lg Cap Growth	PWB	U	14.84	N/A	N/A	U /	--	--	--	--	--
GR	PowerShares Dynamic Mid Cap Growth	PWJ	U	15.10	N/A	N/A	U /	--	--	--	--	--
GR	PowerShares Dynamic Mid Cap Value	PWP	U	15.24	N/A	N/A	U /	--	--	--	--	--
GR	PowerShares Dynamic Sm Cap Growth	PWT	U	15.15	N/A	N/A	U /	--	--	--	--	--
GR	PowerShares Dynamic Small Cap Value	PWY	U	14.92	N/A	N/A	U /	--	--	--	--	--
EN	PowerShares Wilder Clean Energy	PBW	U	14.61	N/A	N/A	U /	--	--	--	--	--
IN	Preferred Income Strategies Fund	PSY	U	21.76	23.35	20.50	U /	6.36	4.20	12.25 / 29	--	--
IN	Preferred&Corporate Inc Strategy II	PSW	U	22.00	23.79	20.58	U /	8.32	4.47	12.31 / 30	--	--
COH	Prospect Street High Inc Portfolio	PHY	E-	3.40	4.00	3.00	D- / 1.5	5.45	1.12	23.31 / 58	3.40 / 4	2.95 / 17
GL	Prospect Street Income Shares	CNN	D-	5.99	7.00	5.52	D / 2.0	4.72	-1.72	13.61 / 33	7.49 / 20	3.71 / 18
MUS	Putnam CA Inv Grade Muni	PCA	C+	13.65	14.03	12.48	C- / 3.9	4.01	5.87	14.97 / 57	5.46 / 25	5.86 / 35
GI	Putnam High Income Bond Fund	PCF	C+	7.80	8.20	7.17	C+ / 5.8	8.22	1.10	16.90 / 41	15.29 / 74	9.53 / 38
MUH	Putnam High Yield Municipal Trust	PYM	C	7.17	7.19	6.31	C / 4.9	11.27	11.30	18.80 / 73	3.63 / 11	5.41 / 32
MUN	Putnam Investment Grade Muni Tr	PGM	D	9.67	10.09	9.13	D- / 1.3	6.76	6.81	9.86 / 38	1.12 / 2	6.05 / 37
COH	Putnam Managed High Yield Trust	PTM	D+	8.16	8.53	7.61	D+ / 2.7	7.93	2.31	12.56 / 30	8.62 / 27	4.28 / 19
MUN	Putnam Managed Muni Inc Tr	PMM	B+	7.88	7.99	6.85	B / 7.9	14.21	14.08	21.46 / 81	6.88 / 43	4.23 / 27
GEN	Putnam Master Intermediate Inc Tr	PIM	C-	6.50	6.85	6.21	D+ / 2.3	4.05	2.49	8.26 / 19	8.97 / 30	9.20 / 37
MUN	Putnam Muni Opp Tr	PMO	C-	12.03	13.26	11.40	D+ / 2.3	6.15	1.94	6.39 / 24	4.83 / 20	7.14 / 47
MUN	Putnam Municipal Bond Fund	PMG	B-	12.74	13.49	11.62	C+ / 5.8	10.04	3.33	15.85 / 61	7.35 / 49	10.20 / 76
MUS	Putnam NY Inv Gr Muni Tr	PMN	C+	12.17	12.17	11.30	C- / 3.6	6.53	6.03	13.45 / 51	4.75 / 19	5.53 / 33
GEN	Putnam Premier Income Trust	PPT	C	6.51	6.81	6.00	C- / 3.3	5.61	4.24	15.88 / 39	9.50 / 34	9.38 / 38
MUN	Putnam Tax-Free Health Care Fund	PMH	C+	12.25	12.32	11.63	C- / 3.3	4.73	4.88	9.36 / 36	5.71 / 28	6.34 / 40
UT	Reaves Utility Income Trust	UTG	U	20.92	21.29	15.80	U /	10.81	9.75	37.99 / 91	--	--
GI	Renaissance Cap Growth & Inc III	RENN	E+	11.25	14.25	13.00	C / 4.3	-0.45	-2.97	-2.37 / 4	16.31 / 78	4.82 / 20
COH	RMK Advantage Income Fund	RMA	U	16.03	N/A	N/A	U /	10.37	5.47	--	--	--
COH	RMK High Income Fund	RMH	U	17.50	18.66	15.50	U /	14.23	3.64	27.31 / 67	--	--
COH	RMK Strategic Income Fund	RSF	U	16.14	17.55	14.58	U /	10.91	0.15	24.20 / 60	--	--
FS	RMR F.I.R.E. Fund	RFR	U	20.78	N/A	N/A	U /	7.46	-11.24	--	--	--
IN	RMR Hospitality&Real Estate Fund	RHR	U	19.46	20.00	17.22	U /	10.82	3.30	21.38 / 53	--	--
GI	RMR Real Estate Fund	RMR	U	14.08	14.86	12.20	U /	9.57	1.43	22.31 / 55	--	--
GR	Royce Focus Trust	FUND	C-	8.47	11.79	8.36	C / 5.4	-14.11	-14.72	16.85 / 41	18.29 / 84	20.20 / 94
GR	Royce Micro-Cap Trust	RMT	D-	13.59	16.35	11.86	C / 5.3	-1.32	-4.24	14.30 / 35	16.09 / 77	20.17 / 93
GR	Royce Value Trust	RVT	D+	18.70	20.80	16.70	C / 4.9	1.00	-4.69	19.03 / 47	15.67 / 76	18.25 / 88
IN	Rydex S&P Equal Weight ETF	RSP	U	155.04	158.82	130.36	U /	2.82	0.33	10.17 / 24	--	--
IN	S&P 500 Covered Call Fund Inc	BEP	U	19.20	N/A	N/A	U /	--	--	--	--	--
GR	S&P 500 GEARED Fund	GRE	U	19.32	N/A	N/A	U /	5.57	-2.33	--	--	--
GL	Salomon Br 2008 Wldwide $ Gov Tm Tr	SBG	B	11.19	11.37	10.52	C- / 3.8	4.80	2.99	11.46 / 28	12.18 / 58	14.77 / 70
GI	Salomon Br Capital&Income	SCD	U	16.75	17.76	15.74	U /	5.48	1.00	6.20 / 14	--	--
EM	Salomon Br Emerging Market Debt	ESD	U	18.29	19.96	15.63	U /	5.42	1.61	23.81 / 59	--	--
EM	Salomon Br Emerging Markets Income	EMD	C-	16.38	20.52	15.30	C / 5.2	-2.59	-15.11	10.08 / 24	17.72 / 83	16.97 / 83
EM	Salomon Br Emerging Mkts Floating	EFL	C	12.54	14.48	11.90	C- / 4.1	1.01	-5.96	7.96 / 18	14.42 / 71	10.31 / 44
EM	Salomon Br Emerging Mkts Income II	EDF	D+	13.35	17.04	12.37	C- / 3.6	-11.28	-13.69	2.54 / 8	15.88 / 76	16.63 / 81
GR	Salomon Br Fund	SBF	D	12.88	13.15	11.36	D / 1.6	2.62	0.24	6.44 / 14	7.79 / 22	-2.76 / 8
GL	Salomon Br Global High Income	EHI	U	13.03	14.95	12.40	U /	1.53	-5.27	10.30 / 25	--	--
GL	Salomon Br Global Partners Income	GDF	C	12.87	14.84	12.33	C / 5.1	-2.03	-5.71	2.30 / 8	17.73 / 83	15.99 / 78
GL	Salomon Br High Inc Fd II	HIX	C-	10.81	12.54	10.21	C- / 3.9	2.33	-6.38	-0.39 / 6	15.17 / 74	11.24 / 49

N/A denotes number is not available

Incl. in Returns		RISK				NET ASSETS		VALUATION			ASSET					FUND MANAGER	
			3 Year					Premium / Discount									
Dividend Yield %	Expense Ratio	Risk Rating/ Pts	Standard Deviation	Beta	Avg Dura- tion	NAV as of 6/30/05	Total $(Mil)	As of 6/30/05	1 Year Average	Wtd Avg P/E	Cash %	Stocks %	Bonds %	Other %	Portfolio Turnover Ratio	Manager Quality Pct	Manager Tenure (Years)
6.12	1.04	**U /**	N/A	N/A	13.1	15.21	418	-11.11	-11.91	16.7	0	29	51	20	63	N/A	1
1.02	0.60	**U /**	N/A	N/A	N/A	41.90	284	0.07	0.14	18.3	0	99	0	1	94	N/A	2
0.00	0.60	**U /**	N/A	N/A	N/A	45.93	66	-0.11	0.10	23.4	0	99	0	1	112	N/A	2
0.72	0.70	**U /**	N/A	N/A	N/A	13.61	49	0.22	N/A	N/A	0	100	0	0	9	N/A	1
5.13	0.60	**U /**	N/A	N/A	N/A	14.86	314	0.13	N/A	N/A	0	99	0	1	21	N/A	1
1.65	0.63	**U /**	N/A	N/A	N/A	15.14	10	0.13	N/A	N/A	0	100	0	0	N/A	N/A	0
0.00	0.63	**U /**	N/A	N/A	N/A	14.83	8	0.07	N/A	N/A	0	100	0	0	2	N/A	0
0.00	0.63	**U /**	N/A	N/A	N/A	15.09	8	0.07	N/A	N/A	0	100	0	0	1	N/A	0
1.26	0.63	**U /**	N/A	N/A	N/A	15.23	10	0.07	N/A	N/A	0	100	0	0	1	N/A	0
0.00	0.63	**U /**	N/A	N/A	N/A	15.13	10	0.13	N/A	N/A	0	100	0	0	N/A	N/A	0
0.91	0.63	**U /**	N/A	N/A	N/A	14.90	10	0.13	N/A	N/A	0	100	0	0	N/A	N/A	0
0.00	0.70	**U /**	N/A	N/A	N/A	14.61	27	0.00	N/A	N/A	0	100	0	0	9	N/A	0
9.07	1.20	**U /**	N/A	N/A	15.3	23.02	945	-5.47	-5.72	20.3	0	0	17	83	13	N/A	2
9.06	1.25	**U /**	N/A	N/A	14.6	23.12	240	-4.84	-6.18	N/A	0	0	23	77	13	N/A	2
8.72	1.06	**D- / 1.2**	37.2	1.58	5.1	3.58	107	-5.03	0.64	77.1	0	0	100	0	28	N/A	17
7.85	1.36	**C / 4.8**	18.6	1.03	8.9	6.63	66	-9.65	-6.87	25.0	0	0	100	0	41	34	32
4.79	1.21	**B / 8.3**	8.7	1.50	13.0	15.47	70	-11.76	-11.13	N/A	0	0	100	0	50	41	9
7.18	1.06	**C+ / 6.9**	10.4	0.34	4.1	8.50	198	-8.24	-9.66	12.1	3	0	43	54	50	92	15
5.28	1.19	**C+ / 6.7**	10.4	1.80	12.0	7.86	172	-8.78	-13.05	3.8	0	0	100	0	25	11	9
5.06	1.39	**C+ / 6.8**	12.9	2.26	10.9	11.10	230	-12.88	-10.50	N/A	0	0	100	0	30	3	9
7.16	1.16	**C+ / 5.9**	14.1	1.42	5.4	9.10	70	-10.33	-10.42	22.7	3	2	91	4	62	3	12
5.24	1.28	**C+ / 6.9**	12.2	1.91	12.1	8.33	390	-5.40	-11.22	N/A	0	0	98	2	30	30	9
6.49	0.84	**B- / 7.2**	10.5	1.35	8.1	7.14	714	-8.96	-8.65	22.6	6	0	93	1	219	71	6
5.61	1.40	**B / 8.1**	11.2	1.90	12.3	13.34	213	-9.82	-5.74	N/A	0	0	100	0	30	16	9
6.13	1.35	**B- / 7.5**	12.4	2.13	11.5	14.03	239	-9.19	-8.55	N/A	0	0	100	0	31	27	9
4.32	1.39	**B / 8.3**	9.6	1.59	12.2	13.91	39	-12.51	-12.89	N/A	0	0	100	0	36	25	6
5.57	0.84	**B / 8.2**	10.4	1.57	N/A	7.17	1,030	-9.21	-9.96	N/A	5	0	93	2	244	67	9
4.49	0.84	**B+ / 9.2**	6.3	1.09	10.1	14.19	192	-13.67	-13.84	N/A	1	0	98	1	62	60	9
5.67	1.45	**U /**	N/A	N/A	3.2	22.55	490	-7.23	-6.86	20.6	0	100	0	0	33	N/A	1
3.46	3.08	**E+ / 0.8**	38.2	0.56	N/A	13.62	64	-17.40	-16.91	N/A	0	73	0	27	19	92	9
9.00	0.94	**U /**	N/A	N/A	N/A	14.18	404	13.05	N/A	N/A	2	7	87	4	57	N/A	1
10.29	2.12	**U /**	N/A	N/A	12.6	14.75	314	18.64	12.29	18.5	1	7	86	6	73	N/A	2
11.15	1.70	**U /**	N/A	N/A	12.7	14.03	360	15.04	12.97	18.4	1	10	86	3	69	N/A	1
5.92	1.69	**U /**	N/A	N/A	N/A	23.30	113	-10.82	N/A	N/A	2	64	0	34	36	N/A	N/A
7.61	1.69	**U /**	N/A	N/A	8.2	23.17	113	-16.01	-13.22	108.3	1	54	20	25	36	N/A	1
8.40	1.69	**U /**	N/A	N/A	N/A	16.54	113	-14.87	-9.43	118.3	1	76	0	23	36	N/A	2
2.81	1.53	**C / 4.8**	22.4	1.14	4.1	8.81	106	-3.86	1.19	25.5	8	67	21	4	52	89	3
8.93	1.62	**D / 2.2**	25.9	1.48	N/A	13.34	290	1.87	1.45	N/A	6	77	0	17	32	81	12
8.47	1.51	**C- / 3.7**	20.0	1.31	5.7	17.42	993	7.35	6.58	45.7	5	88	2	5	30	82	19
0.97	0.40	**U /**	N/A	N/A	N/A	155.12	708	-0.05	-0.01	27.5	0	100	0	0	25	N/A	2
21.02	N/A	**U /**	N/A	N/A	N/A	18.09	N/A	6.14	N/A	N/A	0	0	0	100	N/A	N/A	0
0.74	1.11	**U /**	N/A	N/A	N/A	19.73	138	-2.08	N/A	N/A	0	100	0	0	2	N/A	1
7.72	0.87	**B+ / 9.7**	7.1	0.51	N/A	11.53	393	-2.95	-0.42	N/A	0	0	100	0	45	84	12
7.08	2.27	**U /**	N/A	N/A	6.4	19.60	614	-14.54	-10.22	38.5	0	56	43	1	33	N/A	1
7.93	1.89	**U /**	N/A	N/A	8.9	20.15	540	-9.23	-3.36	N/A	3	0	96	1	19	N/A	2
7.63	2.52	**C / 5.1**	22.1	1.48	8.2	16.92	71	-3.19	9.10	N/A	1	0	98	1	51	73	13
5.74	2.40	**C+ / 6.7**	16.2	0.71	N/A	13.96	61	-10.17	-4.04	N/A	0	0	99	1	136	83	11
7.84	2.19	**C+ / 5.8**	16.5	1.20	8.4	14.64	350	-8.81	8.62	N/A	2	0	97	1	54	75	12
0.92	0.62	**C+ / 6.3**	16.0	1.11	N/A	14.85	1,505	-13.27	-14.33	26.6	1	98	0	1	44	55	-24
7.74	2.05	**U /**	N/A	N/A	N/A	14.82	460	-12.08	-6.36	N/A	0	0	99	1	31	N/A	2
8.04	2.55	**C+ / 5.8**	16.8	1.04	7.3	12.82	199	0.39	11.43	102.0	2	0	97	1	26	83	12
8.93	2.69	**C+ / 5.7**	15.8	0.64	6.4	11.54	862	-6.33	2.60	102.0	4	0	95	1	54	86	7

N/A denotes number is not available

99 Pct = Best
0 Pct = Worst

Fund Type	Fund Name	Ticker Symbol	Overall Weiss Investment Rating	PRICE: Price As of 6/30/05	PRICE: 52 Week High	PRICE: 52 Week Low	PERFORMANCE: Performance Rating/Pts	% Total Return Through 6/30/05: 3 Mo	6 Mo	1Yr/Pct	Annualized: 3Yr/Pct	Annualized: 5Yr/Pct
COH	Salomon Br High Income Fund	HIF	**D-**	9.43	12.00	8.91	**D- / 1.4**	5.19	-2.66	-8.33 / 1	9.45 / 34	4.60 / 20
GL	Salomon Br Inflation Mgmt	IMF	**U**	17.90	19.80	17.28	**U /**	4.62	1.55	-3.64 / 3	--	--
MUN	Salomon Br Municipal Partners	MNP	**B-**	13.88	14.20	12.11	**C+ / 6.9**	9.55	7.89	15.43 / 59	8.34 / 62	9.85 / 71
MUN	Salomon Br Municipal Partners II	MPT	**B-**	13.50	13.67	12.33	**C+ / 6.2**	9.18	6.65	14.56 / 55	7.69 / 55	9.65 / 70
GL	Salomon Br Var Rt Strat Fd	GFY	**U**	17.17	N/A	N/A	**U /**	-1.61	-8.92	--	--	--
GL	Salomon Br Worldwide Inc Fd	SBW	**C**	15.16	17.73	14.33	**C+ / 5.8**	-1.11	-7.39	13.82 / 34	17.43 / 82	17.57 / 86
GL	Scudder Global Commodities Fund	GCS	**U**	13.90	N/A	N/A	**U /**	-4.40	4.40	--	--	--
EM	Scudder Global High Income Fund	LBF	**B**	7.91	8.06	6.27	**B+ / 8.9**	14.36	3.25	34.74 / 85	20.30 / 89	21.16 / 96
COH	Scudder High Income Trust	KHI	**B-**	7.31	7.52	6.20	**B+ / 8.5**	17.34	7.09	26.71 / 66	18.53 / 85	9.20 / 37
GL	Scudder Multi-Market Income Trust	KMM	**B+**	10.21	10.60	7.66	**A- / 9.2**	2.31	15.02	42.62 / 96	21.05 / 91	14.63 / 69
MUN	Scudder Municipal Income Trust	KTF	**A**	12.74	12.74	11.10	**A- / 9.1**	13.02	13.06	22.60 / 85	11.54 / 83	9.64 / 70
FO	Scudder New Asia Fund	SAF	**B-**	15.82	16.38	11.61	**B+ / 8.3**	3.89	9.25	26.66 / 65	20.06 / 89	5.53 / 23
GI	Scudder Real Estate Fund	SRQ	**U**	21.61	22.94	18.07	**U /**	13.05	5.04	34.10 / 83	--	--
GI	Scudder Real Estate Fund II	SRO	**U**	16.54	16.99	13.40	**U /**	13.07	5.08	32.86 / 80	--	--
GL	Scudder Strategic Income Fund	KST	**B**	14.01	14.33	11.50	**B+ / 8.7**	7.38	6.79	32.08 / 79	20.89 / 91	8.78 / 34
MUN	Scudder Strategic Municipal Inc Tr	KSM	**A+**	13.66	13.90	11.54	**A+ / 9.6**	12.96	14.26	26.81 / 95	13.43 / 90	12.44 / 91
MUN	Seligman Quality Municipal Fund	SQF	**C**	12.27	12.60	11.50	**D+ / 2.7**	4.86	3.28	9.32 / 35	4.94 / 21	7.29 / 48
MUN	Seligman Select Municipal Fund	SEL	**C**	10.34	11.00	10.03	**D+ / 2.7**	2.19	4.30	8.84 / 33	5.45 / 24	8.67 / 62
COH	Senior High Income Portfolio	ARK	**B-**	5.93	6.38	5.40	**B- / 7.0**	9.24	2.59	16.61 / 41	17.79 / 83	9.09 / 35
FO	Singapore Fund	SGF	**B-**	8.91	9.60	7.36	**B / 7.8**	-0.89	3.36	24.29 / 60	20.77 / 90	6.10 / 25
MUN	Smith Barney Intermediate Muni	SBI	**C**	9.63	9.80	8.93	**C- / 3.8**	7.45	5.74	10.81 / 41	5.59 / 27	8.05 / 56
IN	Source Capital	SOR	**D**	69.45	72.75	62.75	**C- / 3.7**	0.61	4.26	16.17 / 40	11.71 / 53	16.12 / 78
FO	Spain Fund	SNF	**C**	12.45	16.30	9.90	**B+ / 8.7**	12.58	-4.52	27.50 / 68	22.65 / 93	9.16 / 36
GR	SPDR 500	SPY	**D**	118.98	170.76	106.59	**D / 1.8**	1.98	-0.69	6.62 / 15	8.20 / 23	-2.42 / 8
GR	SPDR Consumer Discretionary	XLY	**E**	32.84	35.55	28.90	**E+ / 0.9**	-0.10	-5.51	3.83 / 10	6.86 / 16	5.95 / 25
GR	SPDR Consumer Staples	XLP	**D**	22.74	23.80	21.18	**E- / 0.2**	-0.26	-0.41	0.90 / 6	2.56 / 3	-0.49 / 11
EN	SPDR Energy	XLE	**B-**	44.94	46.15	30.56	**A / 9.5**	7.25	23.91	44.57 / 97	21.81 / 92	10.07 / 42
FS	SPDR Financial	XLF	**D**	29.31	30.79	27.00	**D- / 1.3**	4.92	-3.06	4.88 / 11	7.50 / 20	6.20 / 26
GR	SPDR Health Care	XLV	**D+**	31.10	31.77	26.70	**E+ / 0.8**	4.68	4.46	3.46 / 10	5.24 / 9	1.86 / 14
GR	SPDR Industrial	XLI	**D**	29.29	31.50	26.55	**D- / 1.3**	-3.64	-5.70	4.40 / 11	8.67 / 27	2.04 / 15
GR	SPDR Materials	XLB	**E**	27.34	32.00	24.99	**D- / 1.0**	-9.18	-7.52	5.89 / 13	7.84 / 22	9.58 / 39
GR	SPDR Mid Cap 400	MDY	**C**	123.21	127.13	100.45	**C- / 3.8**	3.08	2.88	12.57 / 30	12.32 / 58	7.75 / 30
GR	SPDR Technology	XLK	**E-**	19.99	21.88	17.86	**D- / 1.5**	3.20	-5.53	-0.49 / 5	9.20 / 32	-17.59 / 2
UT	SPDR Utilities	XLU	**C**	31.12	31.92	23.31	**B- / 7.2**	9.23	12.83	35.48 / 86	12.77 / 62	6.35 / 26
GI	SSB Real Estate Income Fund Inc	RIT	**U**	18.11	18.55	15.77	**U /**	11.54	3.91	22.47 / 55	--	--
GL	Strategic Global Income Fund	SGL	**C-**	13.25	15.98	12.01	**C / 4.9**	0.87	-6.91	24.92 / 62	14.58 / 71	16.85 / 82
GL	streetTRACKS DJ Global Titan	DGT	**D**	63.21	66.30	58.36	**E+ / 0.9**	0.83	-0.73	4.68 / 11	6.18 / 13	--
GR	streetTRACKS DJ US Lg Cap Growth	ELG	**D-**	46.51	48.72	43.15	**E / 0.5**	1.82	-3.22	-0.47 / 6	5.47 / 11	--
GR	streetTRACKS DJ US Lg Cap Value	ELV	**C-**	136.14	140.36	121.04	**D+ / 2.3**	3.01	0.91	11.00 / 26	8.87 / 28	--
GR	streetTRACKS DJ US Small Cap Growth	DSG	**E+**	74.74	77.08	61.42	**C- / 3.2**	1.22	-0.39	8.80 / 21	11.91 / 55	--
GR	streetTRACKS DJ US Small Cap Value	DSV	**C-**	174.03	188.49	154.88	**C / 5.0**	2.62	-2.45	14.29 / 35	15.03 / 73	--
FO	streetTRACKS EURO STOXX 50	FEZ	**U**	38.20	42.00	31.71	**U /**	-2.83	-2.59	14.57 / 36	--	--
PM	streetTRACKS Gold Shares	GLD	**U**	43.90	N/A	N/A	**U /**	3.56	-0.84	--	--	--
GR	streetTRACKS MS Technology Index	MTK	**E**	47.33	50.80	39.31	**D+ / 2.8**	4.25	-5.49	-1.87 / 5	12.52 / 60	--
IN	streetTRACKS SPDR O-STRIP ETF	OOO	**U**	50.25	N/A	N/A	**U /**	2.74	-5.86	--	--	--
FO	streetTRACKS STOXX 50	FEU	**U**	36.86	39.29	31.30	**U /**	-0.04	-0.26	13.93 / 34	--	--
GR	streetTRACKS Total Market ETF	TMW	**D+**	85.14	87.63	75.87	**D / 1.6**	2.27	0.32	7.68 / 17	7.69 / 21	--
GI	streetTRACKS Wilshire REIT	RWR	**C+**	194.85	198.82	151.00	**B+ / 8.8**	14.30	6.82	31.89 / 79	19.98 / 89	--
FO	Swiss Helvetia Fund	SWZ	**D+**	13.69	15.22	12.15	**C- / 3.5**	-2.01	-3.02	13.56 / 33	13.40 / 64	5.05 / 22
FO	Taiwan Fund	TWN	**E+**	13.69	14.09	9.90	**C- / 3.5**	6.87	6.79	23.73 / 59	7.32 / 19	-6.06 / 5
FO	Taiwan Greater China Fund	TFC	**D-**	5.17	5.21	3.91	**D+ / 2.7**	5.08	11.18	19.42 / 49	6.02 / 13	-8.49 / 4
GI	TCW Convertible Securities Fund	CVT	**E**	5.09	5.48	4.50	**E- / 0.0**	-0.95	-0.80	9.29 / 22	-0.90 / 1	-3.58 / 7

N/A denotes number is not available

Incl. in Returns		RISK				NET ASSETS		VALUATION			ASSET					FUND MANAGER	
			3 Year					Premium / Discount									
Dividend Yield %	Expense Ratio	Risk Rating/ Pts	Standard Deviation	Beta	Avg Dura- tion	NAV as of 6/30/05	Total $(Mil)	As of 6/30/05	1 Year Average	Wtd Avg P/E	Cash %	Stocks %	Bonds %	Other %	Portfolio Turnover Ratio	Manager Quality Pct	Manager Tenure (Years)
7.56	1.41	**C+ / 5.7**	15.0	1.29	6.2	10.49	55	-10.10	-2.51	102.0	5	0	94	1	56	7	12
5.39	N/A	**U /**	N/A	N/A	N/A	19.74	189	-9.32	-5.52	N/A	13	0	86	1	N/A	N/A	1
6.03	1.32	**B- / 7.1**	10.7	1.77	12.7	15.32	88	-9.40	-11.98	N/A	0	0	100	0	38	56	11
6.00	1.33	**B- / 7.7**	10.3	1.77	11.3	14.95	90	-9.70	-12.28	N/A	0	0	100	0	31	50	11
5.36	N/A	**U /**	N/A	N/A	N/A	19.00	N/A	-9.63	N/A	N/A	10	0	89	1	N/A	N/A	1
7.66	2.31	**C+ / 5.9**	16.7	1.16	8.2	16.42	204	-7.67	3.53	N/A	3	0	96	1	28	81	12
0.19	1.20	**U /**	N/A	N/A	N/A	16.34	391	-14.93	N/A	20.0	17	83	0	0	71	N/A	1
7.22	2.70	**C / 4.9**	18.3	1.19	7.7	8.80	83	-10.11	-9.99	N/A	7	0	93	0	142	84	13
9.21	1.71	**C / 4.7**	19.1	1.64	5.6	5.95	195	22.86	17.41	N/A	1	1	98	0	135	28	17
7.72	1.05	**C / 4.9**	11.8	0.65	6.1	9.68	195	5.48	-1.71	N/A	3	0	95	2	187	93	16
6.28	1.06	**C+ / 6.5**	12.9	2.03	11.1	12.56	482	1.43	-3.63	N/A	0	0	100	0	25	70	7
0.44	1.81	**C / 5.1**	24.4	1.09	N/A	17.96	150	-11.92	-12.98	4.9	0	100	0	0	92	84	18
7.22	1.11	**U /**	N/A	N/A	N/A	25.64	404	-15.72	-12.70	47.6	0	82	0	18	29	N/A	3
7.50	1.16	**U /**	N/A	N/A	N/A	19.64	761	-15.78	-12.98	55.3	1	85	0	14	43	N/A	2
7.63	2.20	**C / 5.0**	15.5	0.61	6.5	13.90	48	0.79	-1.85	N/A	5	0	95	0	193	94	11
6.47	1.25	**B- / 7.1**	10.9	1.74	12.4	12.52	133	9.11	2.56	N/A	0	0	100	0	15	81	7
4.64	1.66	**B / 8.6**	9.1	1.70	12.4	14.38	67	-14.67	-13.78	N/A	0	0	100	0	8	24	14
5.52	1.91	**B / 8.5**	8.6	1.55	15.7	11.84	157	-12.67	-11.35	N/A	0	0	100	0	4	35	15
9.46	1.69	**C+ / 6.4**	15.0	1.69	N/A	5.99	350	-1.00	-3.11	N/A	0	0	64	36	54	20	12
2.48	1.76	**C / 5.5**	18.8	0.57	N/A	10.27	95	-13.24	-14.23	N/A	0	100	0	0	18	91	5
6.33	1.07	**B- / 7.1**	11.2	1.50	9.1	9.78	141	-1.53	-5.59	N/A	0	0	100	0	32	41	13
5.71	0.95	**C / 4.9**	19.1	0.97	4.8	62.34	528	11.41	12.27	22.4	2	89	4	5	23	79	9
8.24	1.95	**D / 2.0**	23.3	1.14	N/A	9.87	88	26.14	22.87	N/A	0	100	0	0	27	88	17
1.64	0.11	**C+ / 6.8**	13.9	0.98	N/A	119.09	45,716	-0.09	0.01	N/A	0	100	0	0	2	62	12
0.60	0.26	**C- / 3.3**	17.6	1.14	N/A	32.86	364	-0.06	0.02	N/A	0	100	0	0	10	41	7
1.97	0.25	**B / 8.2**	9.8	0.50	N/A	22.71	762	0.13	0.02	19.9	0	100	0	0	13	43	7
1.27	0.25	**C- / 3.8**	19.6	1.01	N/A	44.93	2,057	0.02	0.01	17.8	0	100	0	0	4	65	7
2.38	0.25	**C+ / 6.8**	15.8	1.04	N/A	29.29	1,483	0.07	N/A	16.0	0	100	0	0	5	40	7
1.24	0.25	**B- / 7.9**	10.9	0.54	N/A	31.09	1,279	0.03	0.02	28.1	0	100	0	0	3	62	7
1.02	0.26	**B- / 7.0**	14.9	0.96	N/A	29.28	771	0.03	-0.01	20.7	0	100	0	0	3	66	7
2.08	0.26	**C- / 3.2**	20.7	1.25	N/A	27.34	843	0.00	N/A	20.1	0	100	0	0	2	40	7
0.89	0.25	**C+ / 6.9**	14.9	0.96	N/A	123.57	6,536	-0.29	-0.02	28.3	0	100	0	0	16	81	10
0.56	0.26	**D- / 1.5**	25.8	1.65	N/A	19.96	1,040	0.15	-0.01	35.5	0	100	0	0	6	27	7
3.16	0.26	**C / 4.4**	17.8	0.98	N/A	31.09	1,830	0.10	N/A	19.8	0	100	0	0	3	36	7
7.11	1.02	**U /**	N/A	N/A	N/A	21.41	233	-15.41	-12.49	N/A	0	71	0	29	6	N/A	3
7.44	1.16	**C / 4.6**	18.1	1.43	N/A	11.89	240	11.44	11.43	N/A	6	0	93	1	189	49	13
2.14	0.51	**B- / 7.0**	14.7	0.86	N/A	63.27	93	-0.09	0.10	19.1	0	100	0	0	2	21	5
0.81	0.21	**C+ / 6.6**	15.6	1.05	N/A	46.30	82	0.45	0.03	26.5	0	100	0	0	13	31	5
2.18	0.22	**B- / 7.1**	14.4	0.99	N/A	135.91	123	0.17	N/A	20.8	0	100	0	0	11	64	5
0.42	0.26	**C- / 3.3**	20.1	1.26	N/A	74.79	57	-0.07	0.04	32.5	0	100	0	0	14	75	5
2.16	0.26	**C / 4.4**	17.0	0.99	N/A	174.93	99	-0.51	-0.09	36.1	0	100	0	0	15	86	5
6.97	0.33	**U /**	N/A	N/A	N/A	38.34	141	-0.37	0.05	N/A	0	100	0	0	3	N/A	1
0.00	N/A	**U /**	N/A	N/A	N/A	43.95	N/A	-0.11	N/A	N/A	0	0	0	100	N/A	N/A	1
0.05	0.51	**E+ / 0.7**	31.3	1.98	N/A	47.41	30	-0.17	-0.02	74.1	0	100	0	0	18	35	5
0.18	0.35	**U /**	N/A	N/A	N/A	50.06	56	0.38	N/A	N/A	0	100	0	0	7	N/A	1
4.93	0.33	**U /**	N/A	N/A	N/A	36.92	30	-0.16	0.28	N/A	0	100	0	0	1	N/A	1
1.70	0.21	**B- / 7.2**	14.0	0.99	N/A	85.04	120	0.12	0.01	20.0	0	100	0	0	3	60	5
4.19	0.26	**C- / 3.9**	17.2	0.41	N/A	194.89	535	-0.02	0.01	60.6	0	100	0	0	6	95	4
0.15	1.14	**C+ / 5.6**	17.5	1.05	N/A	16.05	402	-14.70	-14.86	N/A	3	96	0	1	41	64	9
0.22	1.97	**D+ / 2.6**	27.5	1.14	N/A	15.58	245	-12.13	-11.53	N/A	0	100	0	0	36	8	1
0.20	2.79	**C / 4.8**	20.0	0.76	N/A	5.57	116	-7.18	-8.91	N/A	0	100	0	0	137	24	16
8.06	0.90	**C- / 3.1**	26.2	1.12	7.0	5.51	281	-7.62	-9.26	N/A	2	0	0	98	91	3	8

N/A denotes number is not available

Fund Type	Fund Name (99 Pct = Best, 0 Pct = Worst)	Ticker Symbol	Overall Weiss Investment Rating	PRICE: Price As of 6/30/05	PRICE: 52 Week High	PRICE: 52 Week Low	PERFORMANCE: Performance Rating/Pts	% Total Return Through 6/30/05: 3 Mo	6 Mo	1Yr/Pct	Annualized: 3Yr/Pct	Annualized: 5Yr/Pct
FO	Templeton Dragon Fund	TDF	C+	17.99	18.36	13.50	A / 9.5	4.29	5.32	32.87 / 80	28.90 / 96	23.12 / 97
EM	Templeton Emerging Markets Fd	EMF	C	17.48	18.97	12.02	A / 9.4	4.36	9.06	45.84 / 98	24.37 / 95	14.27 / 66
EM	Templeton Emerging Markets Income	TEI	C+	13.93	14.67	11.48	B / 7.6	9.64	3.67	26.81 / 66	17.45 / 82	17.31 / 85
GL	Templeton Global Income Fd	GIM	D+	8.87	10.05	7.84	C- / 3.7	1.82	-5.61	20.04 / 50	12.51 / 60	15.69 / 76
FO	Templeton Russia&East European Fund	TRF	C+	40.02	45.80	31.85	A+ / 9.8	9.33	16.46	28.90 / 72	38.99 / 99	28.72 / 99
FO	Thai Capital Fund	TF	C-	9.52	11.74	6.35	A+ / 9.7	3.70	12.49	40.61 / 94	34.72 / 98	7.77 / 30
FO	Thai Fund	TTF	C-	9.69	11.60	7.05	A / 9.4	-0.31	4.64	22.58 / 56	28.98 / 96	14.23 / 66
FO	The New Ireland Fund	IRL	B+	21.20	22.80	15.10	A- / 9.2	-2.12	3.77	36.97 / 89	25.91 / 96	14.24 / 66
FO	Third Canadian General Invst Tr	T.THD	C-	28.95	N/A	N/A	A- / 9.1	-0.77	14.96	37.81 / 91	22.53 / 93	19.75 / 93
EN	Tortoise Energy Infrastr Corp	TYG	U	0.00	31.35	24.50	U /	5.76	15.15	--	--	--
GL	Transamerica Income Shares	TAI	D-	22.19	23.66	21.20	E / 0.4	5.27	2.62	9.64 / 23	1.44 / 2	7.71 / 30
IN	Tri-Continental Corporation	TY	D-	17.83	18.45	15.79	E+ / 0.7	1.41	-1.27	7.98 / 18	4.84 / 8	-2.11 / 9
GI	TS&W/Claymore Tax-Adv Balanced Fund	TYW	U	13.70	14.31	12.75	U /	4.31	5.31	11.86 / 28	--	--
FO	Turkish Investment Fund	TKF	C	15.89	21.39	8.95	A+ / 9.9	-3.99	-0.38	74.90 / 99	55.92 / 99	7.67 / 29
GR	Tuxis Corporation	TUX	E-	0.00	9.41	6.11	E- / 0.1	7.20	28.93	13.14 / 31	-3.52 / 0	2.02 / 15
MUN	Van Kampen Adv Muni Inc	VKA	C	14.85	15.39	14.03	C- / 3.6	5.99	5.48	12.44 / 48	5.03 / 21	10.25 / 76
MUN	Van Kampen Adv Muni Inc II	VKI	C	13.78	14.85	13.07	C- / 3.6	1.25	4.43	12.14 / 46	6.32 / 36	10.89 / 82
MUS	Van Kampen Adv PA Muni	VAP	D	14.70	16.20	14.03	D / 1.8	6.13	1.58	10.22 / 39	3.03 / 7	8.40 / 58
COI	Van Kampen Bond	VBF	C-	17.71	18.41	16.58	D / 1.7	6.90	3.29	12.46 / 30	5.47 / 10	8.38 / 33
MUS	Van Kampen CA Muni	VKC	C	9.53	11.00	8.61	C- / 3.5	4.62	1.63	16.62 / 64	5.05 / 21	9.51 / 69
MUS	Van Kampen CA Qual Muni	VQC	C+	16.40	17.25	14.92	C / 4.7	4.90	5.22	15.83 / 61	6.36 / 37	8.86 / 63
MUS	Van Kampen CA Val Muni Inc	VCV	C+	15.26	15.72	14.30	C / 4.5	4.92	7.50	13.47 / 51	6.19 / 35	8.91 / 64
MUS	Van Kampen FL Qual Muni	VFM	B-	14.99	15.55	13.59	C+ / 5.6	4.61	4.40	16.25 / 62	7.90 / 57	10.07 / 74
COH	Van Kampen High Income Trust	VIT	D-	3.68	4.60	3.40	D- / 1.2	8.11	-6.24	7.78 / 17	6.94 / 16	4.98 / 21
COH	Van Kampen High Income Trust II	VLT	D-	4.75	5.38	4.20	C- / 3.1	9.17	-2.83	20.65 / 51	8.74 / 27	3.95 / 19
GEN	Van Kampen Income Trust	VIN	C-	5.81	6.13	5.36	D- / 1.2	4.14	2.90	13.30 / 32	4.66 / 7	4.84 / 21
MUN	Van Kampen Invmt Grade Muni	VIG	C+	9.06	9.25	8.40	C / 4.6	7.67	4.04	13.66 / 51	6.44 / 38	6.54 / 42
MUS	Van Kampen MA Value Muni Inc	VMV	C	16.56	18.70	14.25	C / 5.1	4.93	-3.12	23.08 / 86	7.07 / 46	10.37 / 77
MUN	Van Kampen Muni Income	VMT	C+	9.09	9.56	8.59	C / 4.8	5.82	4.10	11.59 / 44	7.62 / 53	7.48 / 50
MUN	Van Kampen Muni Opp	VMO	C	14.96	15.54	14.10	C- / 4.1	5.91	5.14	12.55 / 48	6.02 / 33	10.22 / 76
MUN	Van Kampen Muni Opp II	VOT	C+	13.60	14.40	12.72	C- / 4.0	8.23	2.90	13.83 / 52	5.45 / 24	10.86 / 81
MUN	Van Kampen Muni Trust	VKQ	C+	14.41	15.35	13.52	C- / 3.8	7.32	2.60	12.54 / 48	5.85 / 30	8.17 / 56
MUS	Van Kampen NY Qual Muni	VNM	C+	14.86	15.50	13.91	C / 5.2	7.59	5.21	15.48 / 59	6.78 / 41	9.79 / 71
MUS	Van Kampen NY Val Muni Inc	VNV	C+	14.83	15.50	13.87	C- / 4.0	5.52	3.19	13.99 / 53	5.90 / 31	8.98 / 64
MUS	Van Kampen OH Qual Muni	VOQ	C+	16.62	17.44	14.39	C+ / 5.6	9.93	9.64	21.97 / 82	4.40 / 15	9.04 / 64
MUS	Van Kampen OH Val Muni Inc	VOV	C-	15.00	16.83	13.50	C- / 3.3	1.67	-0.56	17.78 / 67	5.54 / 26	9.84 / 71
MUS	Van Kampen PA Qual Muni	VPQ	D+	14.91	15.90	14.14	D- / 1.3	4.15	4.33	9.48 / 36	2.24 / 4	7.59 / 51
MUS	Van Kampen PA Val Muni Inc	VPV	C-	15.00	16.35	14.21	D / 2.2	3.42	-1.43	11.81 / 45	4.65 / 18	10.25 / 77
MUN	Van Kampen Sel Sector Muni	VKL	C	12.62	12.90	11.80	C- / 3.1	5.11	3.95	12.72 / 49	4.81 / 19	10.18 / 75
LP	Van Kampen Senior Inc Tr	VVR	C-	7.90	8.96	7.52	D- / 1.0	4.98	-3.82	-5.58 / 2	9.13 / 32	5.70 / 24
MUN	Van Kampen Strat Sect Muni	VKS	C-	12.84	13.30	12.15	D+ / 2.4	5.53	4.36	11.15 / 42	3.50 / 10	9.38 / 67
MUS	Van Kampen Tr for Inv Gr CA Muni	VIC	C	15.02	15.26	13.82	C / 4.8	6.98	8.31	14.41 / 54	5.78 / 29	6.68 / 43
MUN	Van Kampen Trust for Ins Muni	VIM	D+	14.80	16.05	13.95	D / 2.2	5.36	3.72	11.22 / 42	3.50 / 10	7.87 / 53
MUS	Van Kampen Trust for Inv FL Muni	VTF	C	15.14	15.86	14.29	C / 4.5	5.46	4.25	12.39 / 47	7.06 / 46	9.45 / 68
MUN	Van Kampen Trust for Inv Muni	VGM	C+	15.01	15.58	14.22	C- / 3.9	5.85	3.37	12.12 / 46	6.18 / 35	9.97 / 73
MUS	Van Kampen Trust for Inv NJ Muni	VTJ	C	16.53	17.50	15.45	C- / 3.4	6.71	2.87	10.76 / 40	5.57 / 26	8.81 / 63
MUS	Van Kampen Trust for Inv NY Muni	VTN	C	15.48	15.95	14.42	C / 4.6	7.74	7.64	12.81 / 49	5.86 / 31	7.93 / 54
MUS	Van Kampen Trust for Inv PA Muni	VTP	C-	15.09	15.99	14.09	C- / 3.4	6.32	5.54	14.38 / 54	4.28 / 15	9.19 / 65
MUN	Van Kampen Value Muni Inc Trust	VKV	C	13.73	14.82	12.90	C- / 3.1	6.86	5.13	10.51 / 40	4.70 / 19	10.15 / 75
IN	Vanguard Consumer Discret VIPERs	VCR	U	53.01	55.40	44.73	U /	1.73	-2.63	7.94 / 18	--	--
IN	Vanguard Consumer Staples VIPERs	VDC	U	55.24	56.82	49.90	U /	1.08	1.67	4.09 / 10	--	--
EM	Vanguard Emerging Markets VIPERs	VWO	U	49.00	N/A	N/A	U /	--	--	--	--	--

N/A denotes number is not available

Incl. in Returns		RISK				NET ASSETS		VALUATION			ASSET					FUND MANAGER	
Dividend Yield %	Expense Ratio	Risk Rating/ Pts	3 Year Standard Deviation	3 Year Beta	Avg Duration	NAV as of 6/30/05	Total $(Mil)	Premium / Discount As of 6/30/05	Premium / Discount 1 Year Average	Wtd Avg P/E	Cash %	Stocks %	Bonds %	Other %	Portfolio Turnover Ratio	Manager Quality Pct	Manager Tenure (Years)
0.78	1.52	**D+ / 2.5**	29.1	1.07	N/A	19.85	706	-9.37	-10.70	N/A	2	97	0	1	19	94	11
1.06	1.55	**D- / 1.3**	32.8	1.58	N/A	17.15	306	1.92	0.88	N/A	3	90	0	7	15	1	18
7.20	1.09	**C / 4.8**	16.6	0.99	7.6	14.00	675	-0.50	-2.58	N/A	0	0	100	0	15	85	9
5.41	0.75	**C / 5.3**	17.4	1.44	N/A	9.09	1,246	-2.42	-1.46	N/A	3	0	96	1	21	37	9
0.00	1.80	**D / 2.2**	32.6	1.29	N/A	38.16	219	4.87	2.42	N/A	7	92	0	1	8	98	10
0.45	2.26	**E / 0.3**	48.8	1.89	N/A	8.68	28	9.68	-1.69	N/A	0	100	0	0	11	85	4
1.31	1.73	**E+ / 0.7**	42.0	1.64	N/A	8.29	110	16.89	11.36	N/A	1	98	0	1	36	86	17
0.14	1.43	**C / 5.1**	20.5	1.08	N/A	24.64	111	-13.96	-13.38	N/A	0	97	0	3	4	93	15
1.03	N/A	**D- / 1.1**	22.2	0.76	N/A	36.96	130	-21.67	-15.44	N/A	0	90	0	10	N/A	92	17
5.65	N/A	**U /**	N/A	N/A	N/A	0.00	337		N/A	N/A	0	0	0	100	1	N/A	1
7.09	0.72	**B- / 7.2**	12.1	0.45	6.8	23.45	146	-5.37	-5.79	N/A	12	0	84	4	59	21	27
1.35	0.66	**C+ / 6.5**	15.6	1.05	N/A	21.43	2,471	-16.80	-16.42	36.2	1	98	0	1	47	26	1
6.82	1.36	**U /**	N/A	N/A	13.6	15.32	238	-10.57	-9.82	19.7	0	46	53	1	75	N/A	1
0.49	1.20	**E+ / 0.8**	56.4	1.86	N/A	14.63	68	8.61	11.87	N/A	0	100	0	0	28	99	16
0.00	5.09	**D- / 1.4**	21.5	0.31	N/A	0.00	9		-18.64	N/A	64	0	0	36	N/A	7	3
6.10	1.17	**B- / 7.0**	13.4	2.46	11.4	17.03	321	-12.80	-11.54	N/A	1	0	98	1	32	8	10
6.07	1.30	**B- / 7.3**	14.1	2.12	11.7	15.10	122	-8.74	-5.61	N/A	3	0	96	1	38	19	12
5.09	1.29	**C+ / 6.7**	14.5	2.34	11.0	17.15	74	-14.29	-11.21	N/A	1	0	98	1	20	5	13
5.61	0.62	**B- / 7.9**	9.8	1.34	7.5	19.66	224	-9.92	-10.28	N/A	3	0	97	0	34	23	35
5.32	1.63	**B- / 7.1**	13.6	2.27	10.2	10.72	34	-11.10	-9.75	N/A	5	0	94	1	14	10	13
5.91	1.09	**B- / 7.7**	11.3	1.77	10.5	17.29	165	-5.15	-4.95	N/A	1	0	98	1	28	36	13
5.79	1.26	**B- / 7.7**	11.8	1.90	9.6	17.10	102	-10.76	-9.62	N/A	1	0	98	1	20	28	9
5.27	1.13	**B- / 7.8**	10.3	1.75	11.8	16.89	109	-11.25	-10.86	N/A	1	0	98	1	18	52	14
9.47	1.99	**C / 5.4**	23.0	2.38	4.7	3.58	52	2.79	9.34	N/A	3	0	96	1	86	N/A	16
9.25	2.12	**C- / 4.1**	23.6	2.37	4.7	4.51	39	5.32	4.42	N/A	3	0	96	1	86	N/A	16
5.70	0.92	**B / 8.4**	8.6	1.12	7.0	6.50	101	-10.62	-11.68	N/A	4	0	94	2	225	47	17
5.44	1.39	**B / 8.1**	11.4	2.05	11.7	10.48	50	-13.55	-13.41	N/A	2	0	97	1	24	23	16
5.20	1.39	**C+ / 6.3**	15.4	2.28	11.8	16.50	44	0.36	2.68	N/A	3	0	96	1	12	29	9
5.74	1.21	**B- / 7.7**	11.6	2.22	8.4	10.55	300	-13.84	-12.55	N/A	1	0	98	1	22	26	17
5.92	1.16	**C+ / 6.9**	13.6	2.40	11.3	17.05	259	-12.26	-11.47	N/A	1	0	98	1	28	10	10
6.05	1.27	**B- / 7.7**	12.1	2.11	11.3	15.41	178	-11.75	-9.23	N/A	1	0	98	1	14	15	10
5.75	1.06	**B / 8.2**	11.1	2.10	10.4	16.71	600	-13.76	-12.06	N/A	1	0	98	1	32	18	14
5.38	1.16	**B- / 7.4**	12.6	2.04	11.3	17.07	95	-12.95	-11.54	N/A	9	0	90	1	64	28	10
5.34	1.31	**B- / 7.8**	10.7	1.76	10.9	16.90	72	-12.25	-11.03	N/A	1	0	98	1	34	32	12
5.06	1.21	**C+ / 6.2**	14.2	2.17	9.6	17.30	74	-3.93	-5.93	N/A	1	0	98	1	8	9	9
5.02	1.62	**C+ / 6.1**	15.9	2.38	10.8	15.85	26	-5.36	-3.15	N/A	2	0	97	1	8	10	12
5.43	1.13	**B- / 7.5**	12.1	1.66	11.3	17.03	139	-12.45	-9.57	N/A	0	0	99	1	22	10	9
5.32	1.36	**B- / 7.5**	13.6	1.93	11.2	16.50	73	-9.09	-5.19	N/A	2	0	97	1	24	16	12
5.81	1.25	**B / 8.0**	11.3	2.03	12.1	14.66	68	-13.92	-12.70	N/A	2	0	97	1	32	14	9
6.28	2.88	**B / 8.6**	9.4	-40.54	N/A	8.64	1,559	-8.56	-1.17	N/A	2	1	0	97	100	98	6
6.06	1.21	**B- / 7.1**	13.6	2.04	N/A	14.89	159	-13.77	-12.05	N/A	2	0	97	1	24	8	9
5.58	1.31	**C+ / 6.7**	14.5	2.63	11.0	16.74	77	-10.27	-10.00	N/A	2	0	97	1	32	7	13
5.46	1.18	**C+ / 6.6**	16.0	2.50	10.5	16.65	161	-11.11	-9.22	N/A	2	0	97	1	32	5	13
4.98	1.26	**B- / 7.1**	14.0	2.45	10.7	17.57	96	-13.83	-11.92	N/A	2	0	97	1	20	15	9
5.75	1.12	**B- / 7.8**	11.9	2.26	10.9	17.42	465	-13.83	-12.70	N/A	1	0	98	1	28	15	9
5.52	1.24	**B- / 7.5**	12.4	2.27	8.9	18.44	111	-10.36	-8.98	N/A	3	0	96	1	8	15	10
5.75	1.23	**C+ / 6.7**	14.2	2.36	11.1	17.40	106	-11.03	-10.17	N/A	1	0	98	1	48	12	13
5.49	1.21	**C+ / 6.7**	13.6	2.24	11.4	17.16	126	-12.06	-11.17	N/A	3	0	96	1	16	9	9
5.92	1.17	**B- / 7.6**	12.8	2.10	11.0	15.94	370	-13.86	-10.86	N/A	2	0	97	1	18	11	12
0.66	0.28	**U /**	N/A	N/A	N/A	52.85	16	0.30	0.05	27.1	0	100	0	0	17	N/A	1
1.55	0.27	**U /**	N/A	N/A	N/A	55.04	28	0.36	0.07	21.2	0	100	0	0	16	N/A	1
0.00	N/A	**U /**	N/A	N/A	N/A	49.02	N/A	-0.04	N/A	N/A	0	100	0	0	N/A	N/A	0

N/A denotes number is not available

				PRICE			PERFORMANCE					
99 Pct = Best *0 Pct = Worst*			Overall Weiss Investment Rating	Price As of 6/30/05	52 Week		Performance Rating/Pts	% Total Return Through 6/30/05			Annualized	
Fund Type	Fund Name	Ticker Symbol			High	Low		3 Mo	6 Mo	1Yr/Pct	3Yr/Pct	5Yr/Pct
EN	Vanguard Energy VIPERs	VDE	**U**	64.33	N/A	N/A	**U** /	6.19	21.61	--	--	--
IN	Vanguard Extended Market VIPERs	VXF	**C**	83.10	85.15	66.91	**C** / **5.2**	3.97	1.11	13.63 / 33	14.96 / 73	--
FS	Vanguard Financials VIPERs	VFH	**U**	52.40	54.55	47.75	**U** /	5.20	-2.34	8.00 / 19	--	--
GR	Vanguard Growth VIPERs	VUG	**U**	50.43	52.15	44.92	**U** /	2.25	-1.15	2.73 / 9	--	--
HL	Vanguard Health Care VIPERs	VHT	**U**	52.43	53.39	44.14	**U** /	5.22	5.30	5.61 / 12	--	--
IN	Vanguard Industrials VIPERs	VIS	**U**	52.36	N/A	N/A	**U** /	-3.39	-5.11	--	--	--
GR	Vanguard Information Tech VIPERs	VGT	**U**	44.50	48.42	38.80	**U** /	2.13	-5.32	-3.62 / 3	--	--
GR	Vanguard Large Cap VIPERs	VV	**U**	52.92	54.10	46.28	**U** /	2.86	0.36	8.17 / 19	--	--
IN	Vanguard Materials VIPERs	VAW	**U**	54.24	63.50	48.95	**U** /	-9.99	-8.13	6.63 / 15	--	--
GR	Vanguard Mid Cap VIPERs	VO	**U**	58.97	60.18	46.29	**U** /	3.86	3.60	17.85 / 44	--	--
FO	Vanguard Pacific VIPERs	VPL	**U**	48.84	N/A	N/A	**U** /	--	--	--	--	--
GI	Vanguard REIT VIPERs	VNQ	**U**	58.93	N/A	N/A	**U** /	14.43	5.88	--	--	--
GR	Vanguard Small Cap Growth VIPERs	VBK	**U**	52.93	54.73	42.00	**U** /	1.96	-1.56	7.41 / 17	--	--
GR	Vanguard Small Cap Value VIPERs	VBR	**U**	58.17	59.96	48.15	**U** /	3.10	0.17	15.90 / 39	--	--
GR	Vanguard Small Cap VIPERs	VB	**U**	55.54	57.31	45.25	**U** /	2.66	-0.51	11.31 / 27	--	--
GR	Vanguard Telecom Serv VIPERs	VOX	**U**	53.00	N/A	N/A	**U** /	4.06	-3.99	--	--	--
IN	Vanguard Total Stock Market VIPERs	VTI	**D+**	117.05	120.01	101.90	**D+** / **2.4**	2.45	-0.30	8.04 / 19	9.64 / 36	--
UT	Vanguard Utilities VIPERs	VPU	**U**	65.25	66.16	49.94	**U** /	8.97	11.97	33.04 / 81	--	--
IN	Vanguard Value VIPERs	VTV	**U**	55.28	56.54	47.81	**U** /	3.02	1.44	12.78 / 31	--	--
GEI	Western Asset Income Fund	PAI	**C-**	14.81	15.86	13.85	**D+** / **2.9**	8.01	1.28	17.08 / 42	8.48 / 25	11.36 / 50
GEI	Western Asset Premier Bond Fund	WEA	**C-**	14.85	16.50	13.60	**C-** / **3.2**	7.96	-3.64	16.72 / 41	10.15 / 39	--
USA	Western Asset/Claymore US Tr Inf	WIA	**U**	13.00	14.18	12.57	**U** /	0.20	1.12	7.10 / 16	--	--
USA	Western Asset/Claymore US Tr Inf 2	WIW	**U**	12.60	13.85	11.94	**U** /	-1.10	1.69	10.41 / 25	--	--
GL	Z-Seven Fund	ZSEV	**E**	4.35	N/A	N/A	**E-** / **0.0**	-4.40	-5.43	7.94 / 18	0.39 / 1	-10.13 / 3
COH	Zenix Income Fund	ZIF	**D+**	3.24	4.08	3.07	**C** / **4.3**	2.40	-5.47	-1.26 / 5	16.07 / 77	5.57 / 23
GR	Zweig Fund	ZF	**D-**	5.38	5.59	4.67	**D-** / **1.1**	1.12	1.87	21.65 / 53	3.20 / 4	-3.12 / 7
GI	Zweig Total Return Fund	ZTR	**E+**	5.12	5.36	4.99	**E** / **0.4**	1.86	1.26	11.70 / 28	2.21 / 2	4.00 / 19

N/A denotes number is not available

Incl. in Returns		RISK				NET ASSETS		VALUATION			ASSET					FUND MANAGER	
Dividend Yield %	Expense Ratio	Risk Rating/ Pts	3 Year Standard Deviation	3 Year Beta	Avg Dura- tion	NAV as of 6/30/05	Total $(Mil)	Premium / Discount As of 6/30/05	Premium / Discount 1 Year Average	Wtd Avg P/E	Cash %	Stocks %	Bonds %	Other %	Portfolio Turnover Ratio	Manager Quality Pct	Manager Tenure (Years)
0.45	0.28	**U** /	N/A	N/A	N/A	64.20	76	0.20	N/A	N/A	0	100	0	0	10	N/A	1
0.96	0.20	**C+** / **6.2**	15.7	0.99	N/A	83.40	231	-0.36	-0.02	N/A	0	100	0	0	17	86	4
1.46	0.27	**U** /	N/A	N/A	N/A	52.37	26	0.06	0.01	19.8	0	100	0	0	7	N/A	1
0.72	0.15	**U** /	N/A	N/A	N/A	50.41	104	0.04	0.03	N/A	0	100	0	0	24	N/A	1
0.25	0.27	**U** /	N/A	N/A	N/A	52.39	75	0.08	0.05	N/A	0	100	0	0	23	N/A	1
0.81	0.28	**U** /	N/A	N/A	N/A	52.47	11	-0.21	N/A	N/A	0	100	0	0	6	N/A	1
0.13	0.27	**U** /	N/A	N/A	N/A	44.47	22	0.07	0.02	38.7	0	100	0	0	6	N/A	1
1.44	0.12	**U** /	N/A	N/A	N/A	52.75	48	0.32	0.04	N/A	0	100	0	0	5	N/A	1
1.79	0.27	**U** /	N/A	N/A	N/A	54.41	31	-0.31	0.04	22.1	0	100	0	0	6	N/A	1
1.07	0.18	**U** /	N/A	N/A	N/A	59.02	58	-0.08	0.03	N/A	0	100	0	0	16	N/A	1
0.00	N/A	**U** /	N/A	N/A	N/A	48.29	N/A	1.14	N/A	N/A	0	100	0	0	N/A	N/A	0
4.39	0.18	**U** /	N/A	N/A	N/A	58.85	198	0.14	N/A	N/A	0	100	0	0	13	N/A	1
0.16	0.22	**U** /	N/A	N/A	N/A	53.15	92	-0.41	0.05	N/A	0	100	0	0	41	N/A	1
0.03	0.22	**U** /	N/A	N/A	N/A	58.42	47	-0.43	-0.03	N/A	0	100	0	0	30	N/A	1
0.02	0.18	**U** /	N/A	N/A	N/A	55.70	186	-0.29	0.01	N/A	0	100	0	0	19	N/A	1
1.02	0.28	**U** /	N/A	N/A	N/A	53.12	16	-0.23	N/A	N/A	0	100	0	0	41	N/A	1
1.38	0.13	**C+** / **6.8**	14.0	0.98	N/A	117.20	4,259	-0.13	0.01	N/A	0	100	0	0	4	71	4
2.41	0.27	**U** /	N/A	N/A	N/A	65.30	61	-0.08	0.01	N/A	0	100	0	0	10	N/A	1
2.33	0.15	**U** /	N/A	N/A	N/A	55.18	406	0.18	0.02	N/A	0	100	0	0	18	N/A	1
5.73	0.76	**B-** / **7.6**	11.3	1.37	8.4	16.11	153	-8.07	-8.51	N/A	2	0	97	1	81	71	32
7.32	1.17	**B-** / **7.2**	13.4	1.47	8.0	15.35	177	-3.26	-0.94	N/A	0	0	100	0	39	77	3
6.02	1.12	**U** /	N/A	N/A	N/A	14.26	421	-8.84	-6.15	N/A	0	0	98	2	88	N/A	2
6.52	1.25	**U** /	N/A	N/A	N/A	13.89	857	-9.29	-6.33	N/A	0	0	95	5	108	N/A	1
0.00	3.80	**C-** / **3.1**	25.0	0.58	N/A	5.52	10	-21.20	-17.66	25.3	22	77	0	1	N/A	16	21
9.97	2.14	**C** / **4.8**	19.9	1.86	6.5	3.03	57	6.93	15.41	17.5	3	0	96	1	29	6	17
11.14	1.38	**C** / **5.5**	14.9	0.74	12.0	5.77	441	-6.76	-8.42	18.2	9	74	17	0	89	29	19
10.53	1.28	**C+** / **5.8**	14.8	0.21	6.2	5.44	522	-5.88	-6.10	16.8	4	29	67	0	76	58	17

N/A denotes number is not available

Section II

Analysis of Closed-End Mutual Funds

A summary analysis of all

Closed-End Mutual Funds

receiving a Weiss Investment Rating.

Funds are listed in alphabetical order.

Section II Contents

1. Fund Name The name of the mutual fund as stated in its prospectus, which can sometimes differ slightly from the name that the company uses for advertising. If you cannot find the paritcular mutual fund you are interested in, or if you have any doubts regarding the precise name, verify the information with your broker or on your account statement. Also, use the fund's ticker symbol for confirmation.

2. Ticker Symbol The unique alphabetic symbol used for identifying and trading a specific mutual fund. No two funds can have the same ticker symbol.

A handful of funds currently show no associated ticker symbol. This means that the fund is either small or new since the NASD only assigns a ticker symbol to funds with at least $25 million in assets or 1,000 shareholders.

3. Weiss Investment Rating Our overall rating is measured on a scale from A to E based on each fund's risk-adjusted performance. Please see page 10 for specific descriptions of each letter grade. Also refer to page 7 for information on how our ratings are derived. Most important, when using this rating, please be sure to consider the warnings beginning on page 11 regarding the ratings' limitations and the underlying assumptions.

4. Fund Family The umbrella group of mutual funds to which the fund belongs.

5. Fund Type The mutual fund's peer category based on an analysis of its investment portfolio.

COH	Corporate – High Yield	HL	Health
COI	Corporate – Inv. Grade	IN	Income
EM	Emerging Market	LP	Loan Participation
EN	Energy/Natural Resources	MTG	Mortgage
FS	Financial Services	MUH	Municipal – High Yield
FO	Foreign	MUN	Municipal – National
GEI	General – Inv. Grade	MUS	Municipal – Single State
GEN	General Bond	PM	Precious Metals
GL	Global	USA	U.S. Gov. – Agency
GR	Growth	UT	Utilities
GI	Growth and Income		

A blank fund type means that the mutual fund has not yet been categorized.

6. Inception Date The date on which the fund began.

7. Major Rating Factors A synopsis of the key ratios and sub-factors that have most influenced the rating of a particular mutual fund, including an examination of the fund's performance, risk, and managerial performance. There may be additional factors which have influenced the rating but do not appear due to space limitations.

How to Read the Annualized Total Return Graph

The annualized total return graph provides a clearer picture of a fund's yearly financial performance. In addition to the solid line denoting the fund's calendar year returns for the last six years, the graph also shows the yearly return for a benchmark index for easy comparison using a dotted line. The S&P 500 Composite Index is used for closed-end mutual funds that are primarily invested in stocks. One of two indexes is shown for funds with the majority of their assets held in bonds. Municipal bond funds display the Lehman Brothers Municipals Index, and other bond funds will show the Lehman Brothers Aggregate Bond Index.

The top of the shaded area of the graph denotes the average returns for all funds within the same fund type. If the solid line falls into the shaded area, that means that the fund has performed below the average for its type.

How to Read the Historical Data Table

Data Date:
The quarter-end or year-end as of date used for evaluating the mutual fund.

Price:
The fund's share price as of the date indicated. A fund's price is determined by investor demand. The fund may trade at a price higher or lower than its net asset value (NAV).

Risk Rating/Pts:
A letter grade rating based on the mutual fund's risk as determined by its monthly performance volatility over the trailing three years. Pts is a points rank where 0=worst and 10=best.

Data Date	Weiss Investment Rating	Net Assets ($Mil)	Price	Performance Rating/Pts	Total Return Y-T-D	Risk Rating/Pts
6-05	B+	126.6	8.91	A- / 9.2	52.38%	C+ / 6.0
2004	B	87.35	14.30	C / 5.4	4.71%	B / 8.3
2003	D+	284.1	6.90	C- / 3.2	5.19%	C / 4.6

Weiss Investment Rating:
Our overall opinion of the fund's risk-adjusted performance at the specified time period.

Net Assets $(Mil):
The total value of all of the fund's asset holdings (in millions) including stocks, bonds, cash, and other financial instruments, less accrued expenses and fees.

Performance Rating/Pts:
A letter grade rating based solely on the mutual fund's return to shareholders over the trailing three years, without any consideration for the amount of risk the fund poses. Pts is a points rank where 0=worst and 10=best.

Total Return Y-T-D:
The fund's total return to shareholders from the first full week of the calendar year specified to the most recently completed full week.

1838 Bond Debenture Fund (BDF) D Weak

Fund Family: MBIA Capital Management
Fund Type: Corporate - Investment Grade
Inception Date: October 13, 1971

Major Rating Factors:
Disappointing performance is the major factor driving the D (Weak) Weiss Investment Rating for 1838 Bond Debenture Fund. The fund currently has a performance rating of D (Weak) based on an annualized return of 5.88% over the last three years and a total return of 2.89% year to date 2005. Factored into the performance evaluation is an expense ratio of 0.89% (low).

The fund's risk rating is currently C+ (Fair). It carries a beta of 1.60, meaning it is expected to move 16.0% for every 10% move in the market. Volatility, as measured by both the semi-deviation and a drawdown factor, is considered low. As of June 30, 2005, 1838 Bond Debenture Fund traded at a discount of 11.06% below its net asset value, which is better than its one-year historical average discount of 10.88%.

John H. Donaldson has been running the fund for 25 years and currently receives a manager quality ranking of 16 (0=worst, 99=best). This fund offers only a moderate level of risk but investors looking for strong performance are still waiting.

Data Date	Weiss Investment Rating	Net Assets ($Mil)	Price	Performance Rating/Pts	Total Return Y-T-D	Risk Rating/Pts
6-05	D	101.18	18.74	D / 1.7	2.89%	C+ / 6.7
2004	D+	101.35	18.50	D+ / 2.4	4.76%	B- / 7.4
2003	D+	79.56	19.05	D / 1.8	4.82%	B / 8.1

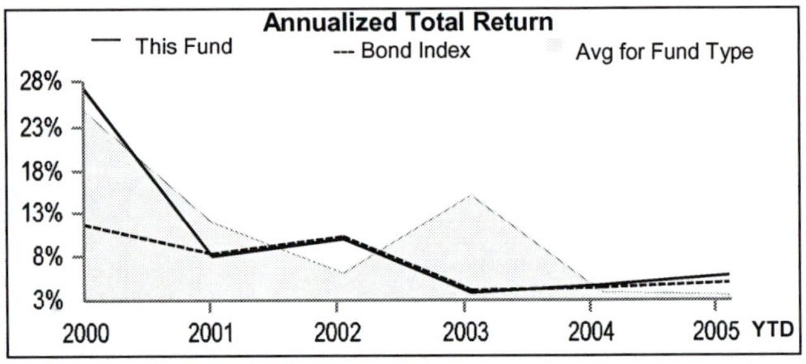

40/86 Strategic Income Fund (CFD) B Good

Fund Family: 40/86 Advisors, Inc
Fund Type: Corporate - High Yield
Inception Date: July 28, 1998

Major Rating Factors:
Strong performance is the major factor driving the B (Good) Weiss Investment Rating for 40/86 Strategic Income Fund. The fund currently has a performance rating of B- (Good) based on an annualized return of 19.85% over the last three years and a total return of 0.98% year to date 2005. Factored into the performance evaluation is an expense ratio of 2.67% (high).

The fund's risk rating is currently C+ (Fair). It carries a beta of 2.27, meaning it is expected to move 22.7% for every 10% move in the market. Volatility, as measured by both the semi-deviation and a drawdown factor, is considered low. As of June 30, 2005, 40/86 Strategic Income Fund traded at a discount of 9.69% below its net asset value, which is worse than its one-year historical average discount of 10.31%.

This fund has been team managed for 7 years and currently receives a manager quality ranking of 4 (0=worst, 99=best). If you desire only a moderate level of risk and strong performance, then this fund is an excellent option.

Data Date	Weiss Investment Rating	Net Assets ($Mil)	Price	Performance Rating/Pts	Total Return Y-T-D	Risk Rating/Pts
6-05	B	79.64	10.16	B- / 7.5	0.98%	C+ / 6.0
2004	C-	73.88	10.44	C+ / 5.9	2.75%	C / 4.5

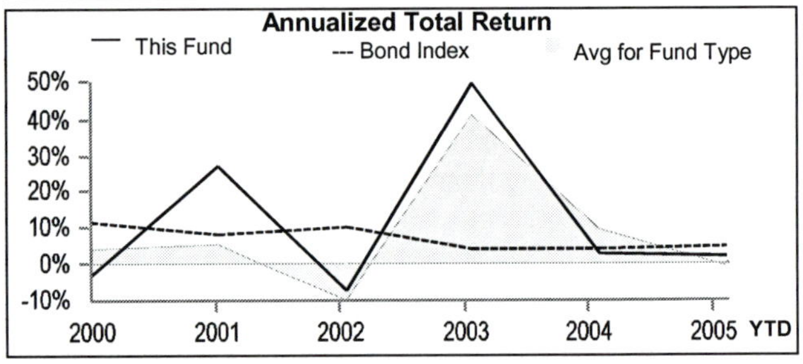

Aberdeen Asia-Pacific Income Fund (FAX) C Fair

Fund Family: Aberdeen Asset Management Limited
Fund Type: Global
Inception Date: April 16, 1986

Major Rating Factors:
Middle of the road best describes Aberdeen Asia-Pacific Income Fund whose Weiss Investment Rating is currently a C (Fair). The fund currently has a performance rating of C+ (Fair) based on an annualized return of 18.33% over the last three years and a total return of 0.72% year to date 2005. Factored into the performance evaluation is an expense ratio of 1.19% (average).

The fund's risk rating is currently C- (Fair). It carries a beta of 1.42, meaning it is expected to move 14.2% for every 10% move in the market. Volatility, as measured by both the semi-deviation and a drawdown factor, is considered average. As of June 30, 2005, Aberdeen Asia-Pacific Income Fund traded at a discount of 4.65% below its net asset value, which is better than its one-year historical average discount of 3.03%.

Aberdeen Asset Management has been running the fund for 19 years and currently receives a manager quality ranking of 75 (0=worst, 99=best). If you desire an average level of risk, then this fund may be an option.

Data Date	Weiss Investment Rating	Net Assets ($Mil)	Price	Performance Rating/Pts	Total Return Y-T-D	Risk Rating/Pts
6-05	C	1775.32	6.35	C+ / 6.9	0.72%	C- / 4.2
2004	B	1624.53	6.48	A- / 9.2	9.25%	C / 4.6
2003	B+	1613.98	6.38	A / 9.3	47.86%	C+ / 5.9

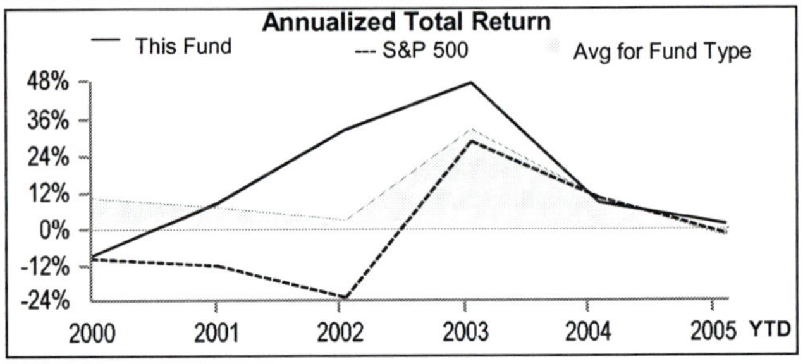

Aberdeen Australia Equity Fund (IAF) C+ Fair

Fund Family: Aberdeen Asset Management Limited
Fund Type: Global
Inception Date: December 19, 1985

Major Rating Factors:
Aberdeen Australia Equity Fund has adopted a risky asset allocation strategy and currently receives an overall Weiss Investment Rating of C+ (Fair). The fund has shown an above average level of volatility, as measured by both semi-deviation and drawdown factors. It carries a beta of 0.97, meaning that its performance tracks fairly well with that of the overall stock market. As of June 30, 2005, Aberdeen Australia Equity Fund traded at a premium of 4.18% above its net asset value, which is worse than its one-year historical average discount of 2.98%. The high level of risk (D+, Weak) did however, reward investors with excellent performance.
The fund's performance rating is currently A+ (Excellent). It has registered an annualized return of 31.89% over the last three years and is up 7.30% year to date 2005. Factored into the performance evaluation is an expense ratio of 1.47% (average).
Aberdeen Asset Management has been running the fund for 20 years and currently receives a manager quality ranking of 97 (0=worst, 99=best). If you are comfortable owning a high risk investment, this fund may be an option.

Data Date	Weiss Investment Rating	Net Assets ($Mil)	Price	Performance Rating/Pts	Total Return Y-T-D	Risk Rating/Pts
6-05	C+	188.72	12.20	A+ / 9.6	7.30%	D+ / 2.8
2004	B	164.48	11.65	A+ / 9.8	40.20%	C / 4.3
2003	B+	157.42	8.91	A- / 9.2	52.38%	C+ / 6.1

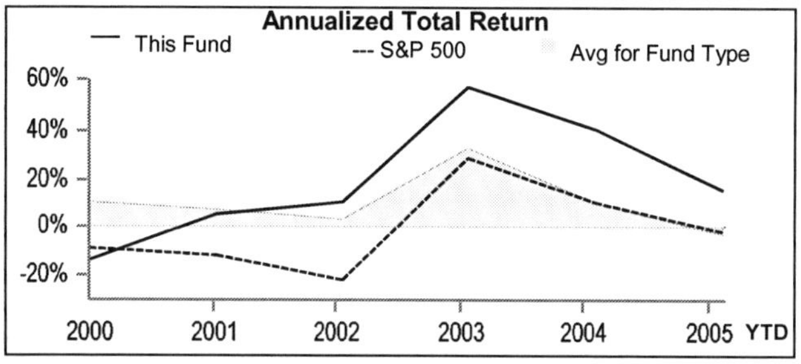

Aberdeen Global Income Fund (FCO) C Fair

Fund Family: Aberdeen Asset Management Limited
Fund Type: Global
Inception Date: February 28, 1992

Major Rating Factors:
Middle of the road best describes Aberdeen Global Income Fund whose Weiss Investment Rating is currently a C (Fair). The fund currently has a performance rating of C (Fair) based on an annualized return of 16.34% over the last three years and a total return of -5.14% year to date 2005. Factored into the performance evaluation is an expense ratio of 1.70% (above average).
The fund's risk rating is currently C+ (Fair). It carries a beta of 1.45, meaning it is expected to move 14.5% for every 10% move in the market. Volatility, as measured by both the semi-deviation and a drawdown factor, is considered low. As of June 30, 2005, Aberdeen Global Income Fund traded at a discount of 2.89% below its net asset value, which is better than its one-year historical average discount of .39%.
Aberdeen Asset Management has been running the fund for 13 years and currently receives a manager quality ranking of 61 (0=worst, 99=best). If you desire an average level of risk, then this fund may be an option.

Data Date	Weiss Investment Rating	Net Assets ($Mil)	Price	Performance Rating/Pts	Total Return Y-T-D	Risk Rating/Pts
6-05	C	133.03	13.76	C / 5.5	-5.14%	C+ / 5.7
2004	B	117.02	14.82	A- / 9.2	10.09%	C / 5.2
2003	A-	115.18	13.93	A- / 9.2	48.02%	C+ / 6.3

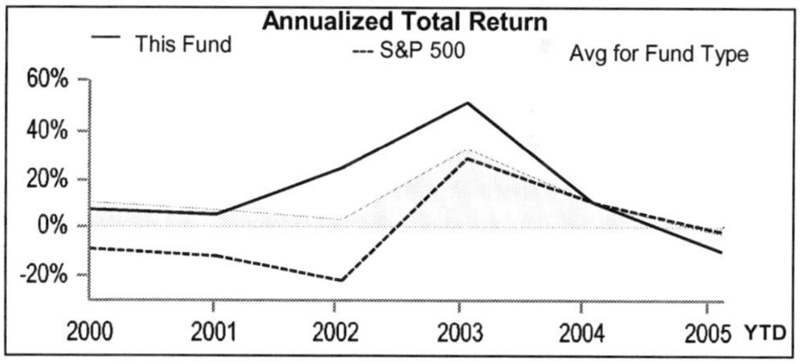

ACM Government Opportunity Fund (AOF) D- Weak

Fund Family: Alliance Capital Management L.P.
Fund Type: US Government/Agency
Inception Date: August 19, 1988

Major Rating Factors:
Very poor performance is the major factor driving the D- (Weak) Weiss Investment Rating for ACM Government Opportunity Fund. The fund currently has a performance rating of E+ (Very Weak) based on an annualized return of 3.98% over the last three years and a total return of 3.01% year to date 2005. Factored into the performance evaluation is an expense ratio of 1.74% (above average).
The fund's risk rating is currently B- (Good). It carries a beta of 0.82, meaning the fund's expected move will be 8.2% for every 10% move in the market. Volatility, as measured by both the semi-deviation and a drawdown factor, is considered low. As of June 30, 2005, ACM Government Opportunity Fund traded at a discount of 8.26% below its net asset value, which is better than its one-year historical average discount of 5.93%.
Doug Peebles has been running the fund for 17 years and currently receives a manager quality ranking of 20 (0=worst, 99=best). This fund offers only a moderate level of risk but investors looking for strong performance are still waiting.

Data Date	Weiss Investment Rating	Net Assets ($Mil)	Price	Performance Rating/Pts	Total Return Y-T-D	Risk Rating/Pts
6-05	D-	112.11	7.89	E+ / 0.6	3.01%	B- / 7.2
2004	D+	106.99	7.91	D- / 1.4	-5.49%	B- / 7.9
2003	B-	108.34	9.08	C+ / 5.7	12.33%	B- / 7.9

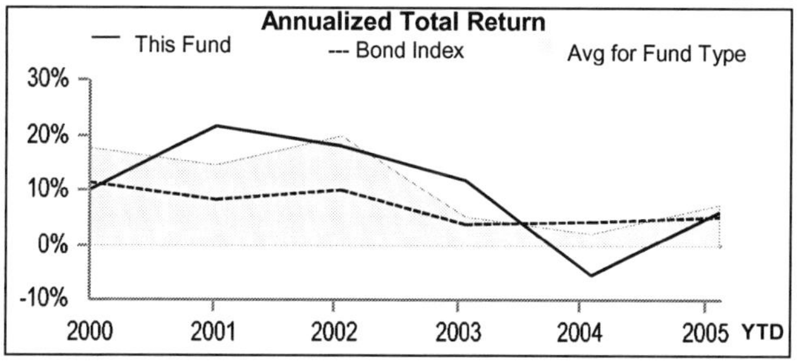

ACM Income Fund (ACG) C- Fair

Fund Family: Alliance Capital Management L.P.
Fund Type: US Government/Agency
Inception Date: August 28, 1987

Major Rating Factors:
Middle of the road best describes ACM Income Fund whose Weiss Investment Rating is currently a C- (Fair). The fund currently has a performance rating of C (Fair) based on an annualized return of 12.16% over the last three years and a total return of 6.01% year to date 2005. Factored into the performance evaluation is an expense ratio of 1.66% (above average).

The fund's risk rating is currently C+ (Fair). It carries a beta of 0.86, meaning the fund's expected move will be 8.6% for every 10% move in the market. Volatility, as measured by both the semi-deviation and a drawdown factor, is considered low. As of June 30, 2005, ACM Income Fund traded at a discount of .72% below its net asset value, which is better than its one-year historical average premium of .42%.

Andrew M. Aran has been running the fund for 18 years and currently receives a manager quality ranking of 76 (0=worst, 99=best). If you desire an average level of risk, then this fund may be an option.

Data Date	Weiss Investment Rating	Net Assets ($Mil)	Price	Performance Rating/Pts	Total Return Y-T-D	Risk Rating/Pts
6-05	C-	1888.27	8.29	C / 4.4	6.01%	C+ / 5.8
2004	C+	1780.44	8.16	C+ / 6.2	4.51%	C+ / 6.8
2003	C+	1958.50	8.51	C+ / 5.9	11.60%	B- / 7.4

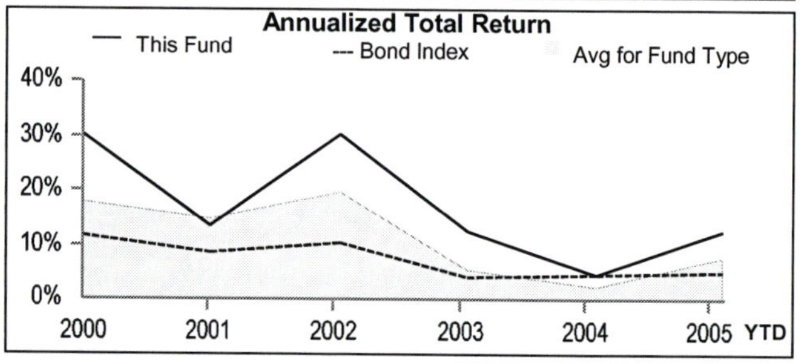

ACM Managed Dollar Income Fund (ADF) C Fair

Fund Family: Alliance Capital Management L.P.
Fund Type: Global
Inception Date: October 22, 1993

Major Rating Factors:
Middle of the road best describes ACM Managed Dollar Income Fund whose Weiss Investment Rating is currently a C (Fair). The fund currently has a performance rating of C+ (Fair) based on an annualized return of 16.77% over the last three years and a total return of 3.27% year to date 2005. Factored into the performance evaluation is an expense ratio of 1.48% (average).

The fund's risk rating is currently C+ (Fair). It carries a beta of 0.70, meaning the fund's expected move will be 7.0% for every 10% move in the market. Volatility, as measured by both the semi-deviation and a drawdown factor, is considered low. As of June 30, 2005, ACM Managed Dollar Income Fund traded at a discount of 4.29% below its net asset value, which is better than its one-year historical average discount of 1.26%.

Jim Kennedy has been running the fund for 12 years and currently receives a manager quality ranking of 88 (0=worst, 99=best). If you desire an average level of risk, then this fund may be an option.

Data Date	Weiss Investment Rating	Net Assets ($Mil)	Price	Performance Rating/Pts	Total Return Y-T-D	Risk Rating/Pts
6-05	C	179.31	7.80	C+ / 5.9	3.27%	C+ / 5.7
2004	D+	178.74	7.89	C / 5.1	4.18%	C / 4.6
2003	C+	173.18	8.40	B+ / 8.7	48.83%	C / 4.8

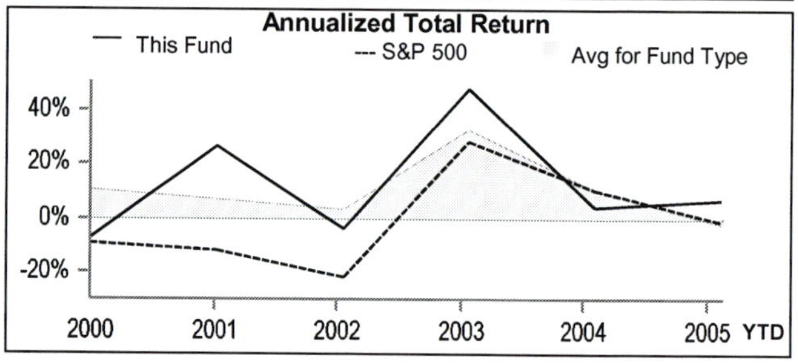

ACM Managed Income Fund (AMF) E+ Very Weak

Fund Family: Alliance Capital Management L.P.
Fund Type: General Bond
Inception Date: October 3, 1988

Major Rating Factors:
Very poor performance is the major factor driving the E+ (Very Weak) Weiss Investment Rating for ACM Managed Income Fund. The fund currently has a performance rating of E+ (Very Weak) based on an annualized return of 5.77% over the last three years and a total return of -3.06% year to date 2005. Factored into the performance evaluation is an expense ratio of 1.98% (high).

The fund's risk rating is currently C (Fair). It carries a beta of 2.27, meaning it is expected to move 22.7% for every 10% move in the market. Volatility, as measured by both the semi-deviation and a drawdown factor, is considered average. As of June 30, 2005, ACM Managed Income Fund traded at a discount of 12.20% below its net asset value, which is better than its one-year historical average discount of 6.00%.

Jim Kennedy has been running the fund for 17 years and currently receives a manager quality ranking of 14 (0=worst, 99=best). This fund offers an average level of risk but investors looking for strong performance will be frustrated.

Data Date	Weiss Investment Rating	Net Assets ($Mil)	Price	Performance Rating/Pts	Total Return Y-T-D	Risk Rating/Pts
6-05	E+	106.02	3.67	E+ / 0.6	-3.06%	C / 5.2
2004	D-	104.85	3.92	D- / 1.0	-11.60%	C+ / 5.9
2003	C	103.12	5.14	B- / 7.1	36.00%	C / 4.8

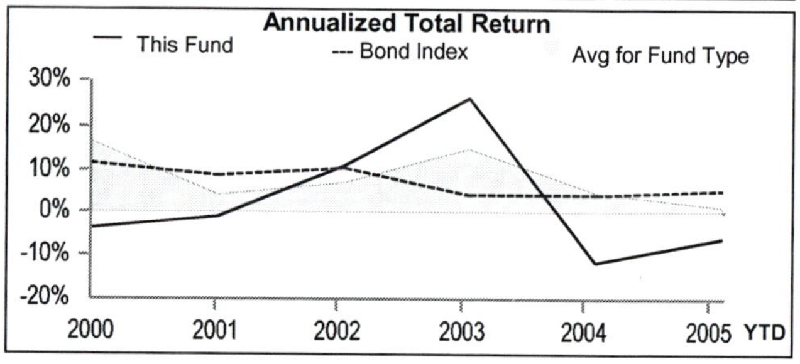

ACM Municipal Securities Income Fd (AMU) — D — Weak

Fund Family: Alliance Capital Management L.P.
Fund Type: Municipal - National
Inception Date: April 29, 1993

Data Date	Weiss Investment Rating	Net Assets ($Mil)	Price	Perfor-mance Rating/Pts	Total Return Y-T-D	Risk Rating/Pts
6-05	D	127.90	10.73	D- / 1.0	2.67%	B- / 7.2
2004	D	121.70	10.80	E+ / 0.7	-0.87%	B / 8.1
2003	C-	122.32	11.65	D / 2.1	8.27%	B / 8.5

Major Rating Factors:
Disappointing performance is the major factor driving the D (Weak) Weiss Investment Rating for ACM Municipal Securities Income Fd. The fund currently has a performance rating of D- (Weak) based on an annualized return of 2.83% over the last three years and a total return of 2.67% year to date 2005. Factored into the performance evaluation is an expense ratio of 1.55% (average).

The fund's risk rating is currently B- (Good). It carries a beta of 2.12, meaning it is expected to move 21.2% for every 10% move in the market. Volatility, as measured by both the semi-deviation and a drawdown factor, is considered low. As of June 30, 2005, ACM Municipal Securities Income Fd traded at a discount of 7.66% below its net asset value, which is better than its one-year historical average discount of 1.62%.

David Dowden has been running the fund for 12 years and currently receives a manager quality ranking of 6 (0=worst, 99=best). This fund offers only a moderate level of risk but investors looking for strong performance are still waiting.

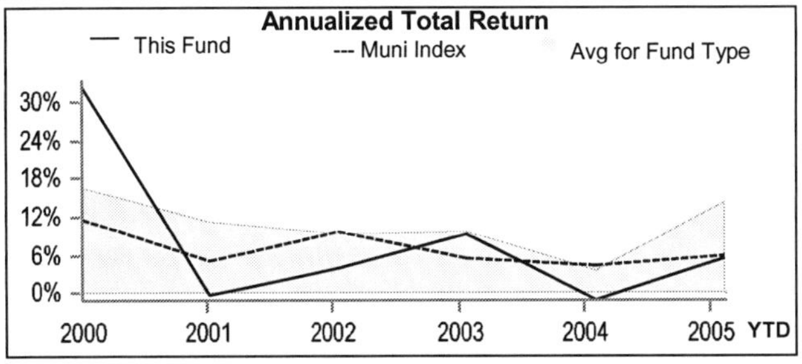

Adams Express Company (ADX) — D+ — Weak

Fund Family: Adams Express/Petroleum & Resources
Fund Type: Income
Inception Date: N/A

Data Date	Weiss Investment Rating	Net Assets ($Mil)	Price	Perfor-mance Rating/Pts	Total Return Y-T-D	Risk Rating/Pts
6-05	D+	1295.55	12.91	D / 1.8	-0.85%	B- / 7.0
2004	D	1248.43	13.12	D+ / 2.7	13.11%	C+ / 6.0
2003	D-	1082.41	12.35	E / 0.5	24.66%	C / 4.7

Major Rating Factors:
Disappointing performance is the major factor driving the D+ (Weak) Weiss Investment Rating for Adams Express Company. The fund currently has a performance rating of D (Weak) based on an annualized return of 8.51% over the last three years and a total return of -0.85% year to date 2005. Factored into the performance evaluation is an expense ratio of 0.43% (very low).

The fund's risk rating is currently B- (Good). It carries a beta of 1.00, meaning that its performance tracks fairly well with that of the overall stock market. Volatility, as measured by both the semi-deviation and a drawdown factor, is considered low. As of June 30, 2005, Adams Express Company traded at a discount of 13.99% below its net asset value, which is better than its one-year historical average discount of 12.92%.

Douglas G. Ober has been running the fund for 19 years and currently receives a manager quality ranking of 63 (0=worst, 99=best). This fund offers only a moderate level of risk but investors looking for strong performance are still waiting.

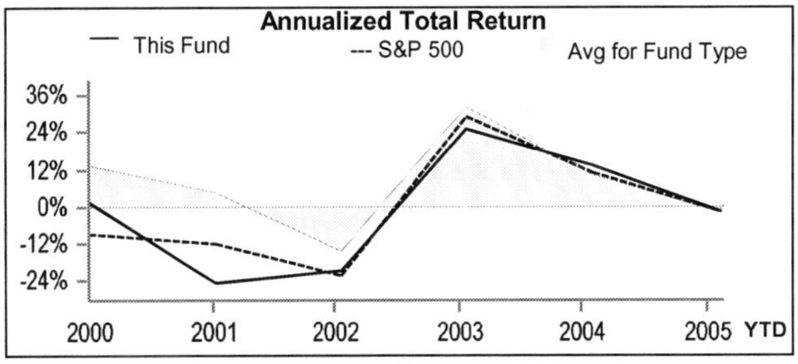

AIM Select Real Estate Income Fund (RRE) — C+ — Fair

Fund Family: AIM Advisors, Inc.
Fund Type: Growth and Income
Inception Date: May 31, 2002

Data Date	Weiss Investment Rating	Net Assets ($Mil)	Price	Perfor-mance Rating/Pts	Total Return Y-T-D	Risk Rating/Pts
6-05	C+	799.36	16.84	C+ / 6.1	-0.01%	C+ / 5.8

Major Rating Factors:
Middle of the road best describes AIM Select Real Estate Income Fund whose Weiss Investment Rating is currently a C+ (Fair). The fund currently has a performance rating of C+ (Fair) based on an annualized return of 13.59% over the last three years and a total return of -0.01% year to date 2005. Factored into the performance evaluation is an expense ratio of 0.93% (low).

The fund's risk rating is currently C+ (Fair). It carries a beta of 0.42, meaning the fund's expected move will be 4.2% for every 10% move in the market. Volatility, as measured by both the semi-deviation and a drawdown factor, is considered low. As of June 30, 2005, AIM Select Real Estate Income Fund traded at a discount of 15.38% below its net asset value, which is better than its one-year historical average discount of 13.62%.

James W. Trowbridge has been running the fund for 3 years and currently receives a manager quality ranking of 90 (0=worst, 99=best). If you desire an average level of risk, then this fund may be an option.

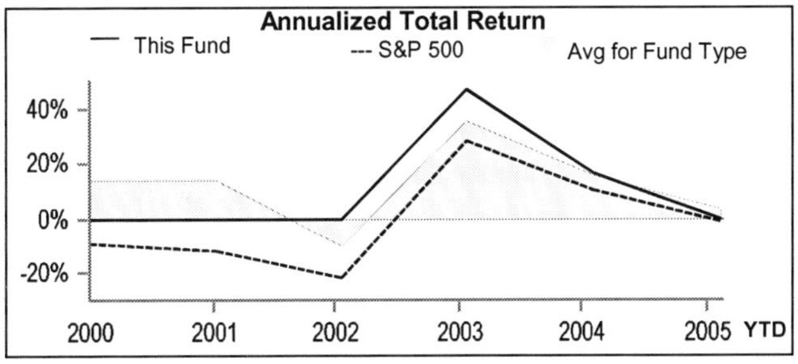

Alliance All-Market Advantage Fd (AMO) E+ Very Weak

Fund Family: Alliance Capital Management L.P.
Fund Type: Growth
Inception Date: November 4, 1994

Major Rating Factors:
Very poor performance is the major factor driving the E+ (Very Weak) Weiss Investment Rating for Alliance All-Market Advantage Fd. The fund currently has a performance rating of E+ (Very Weak) based on an annualized return of 4.49% over the last three years and a total return of 1.21% year to date 2005. Factored into the performance evaluation is an expense ratio of 1.78% (above average).

The fund's risk rating is currently C (Fair). It carries a beta of 1.04, meaning that its performance tracks fairly well with that of the overall stock market. Volatility, as measured by both the semi-deviation and a drawdown factor, is considered average. As of June 30, 2005, Alliance All-Market Advantage Fd traded at a premium of 7.97% above its net asset value, which is better than its one-year historical average premium of 8.86%.

Michael Reilly has been running the fund for 11 years and currently receives a manager quality ranking of 20 (0=worst, 99=best). This fund offers an average level of risk but investors looking for strong performance will be frustrated.

Data Date	Weiss Investment Rating	Net Assets ($Mil)	Price	Perfor-mance Rating/Pts	Total Return Y-T-D	Risk Rating/Pts
6-05	E+	45.88	14.49	E+ / 0.7	1.21%	C / 4.7
2004	E+	52.65	14.70	E / 0.4	12.47%	C- / 3.6
2003	E+	49.80	14.87	E- / 0.1	25.56%	C- / 3.3

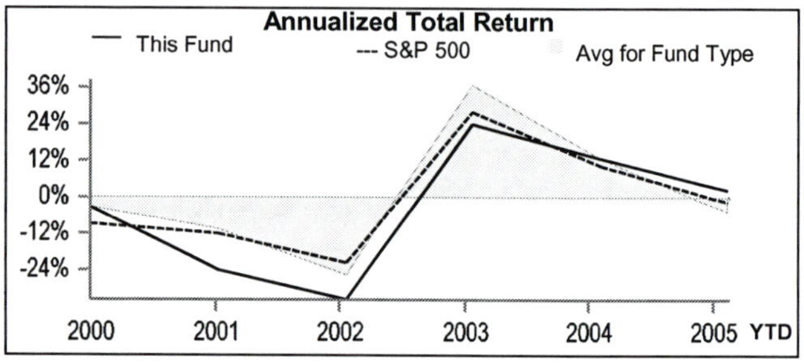

Alliance CA Municipal Income Fund (AKP) A+ Excellent

Fund Family: Alliance Capital Management L.P.
Fund Type: Municipal - Single State
Inception Date: January 29, 2002

Major Rating Factors:
Strong performance is the major factor driving the A+ (Excellent) Weiss Investment Rating for Alliance CA Municipal Income Fund. The fund currently has a performance rating of B (Good) based on an annualized return of 9.61% over the last three years and a total return of 8.56% year to date 2005. Factored into the performance evaluation is an expense ratio of 0.99% (low).

The fund's risk rating is currently B- (Good). It carries a beta of 1.61, meaning it is expected to move 16.1% for every 10% move in the market. Volatility, as measured by both the semi-deviation and a drawdown factor, is considered low. As of June 30, 2005, Alliance CA Municipal Income Fund traded at a discount of 4.74% below its net asset value, which is worse than its one-year historical average discount of 6.59%.

David Dowden has been running the fund for 3 years and currently receives a manager quality ranking of 70 (0=worst, 99=best). If you desire only a moderate level of risk and strong performance, then this fund is an excellent option.

Data Date	Weiss Investment Rating	Net Assets ($Mil)	Price	Perfor-mance Rating/Pts	Total Return Y-T-D	Risk Rating/Pts
6-05	A+	131.56	14.87	B / 8.1	8.56%	B- / 7.8

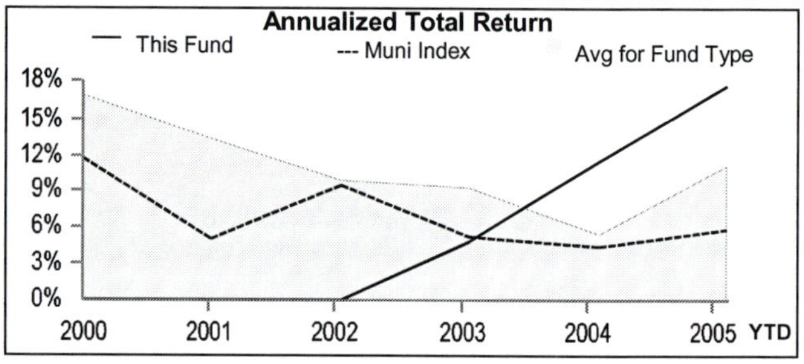

Alliance Nat Municipal Income Fund (AFB) A+ Excellent

Fund Family: Alliance Capital Management L.P.
Fund Type: Municipal - National
Inception Date: January 28, 2002

Major Rating Factors:
Strong performance is the major factor driving the A+ (Excellent) Weiss Investment Rating for Alliance Nat Municipal Income Fund. The fund currently has a performance rating of B+ (Good) based on an annualized return of 10.26% over the last three years and a total return of 10.56% year to date 2005. Factored into the performance evaluation is an expense ratio of 0.95% (low).

The fund's risk rating is currently B- (Good). It carries a beta of 1.76, meaning it is expected to move 17.6% for every 10% move in the market. Volatility, as measured by both the semi-deviation and a drawdown factor, is considered low. As of June 30, 2005, Alliance Nat Municipal Income Fund traded at a discount of 5.99% below its net asset value, which is worse than its one-year historical average discount of 8.51%.

David Dowden has been running the fund for 3 years and currently receives a manager quality ranking of 69 (0=worst, 99=best). If you desire only a moderate level of risk and strong performance, then this fund is an excellent option.

Data Date	Weiss Investment Rating	Net Assets ($Mil)	Price	Perfor-mance Rating/Pts	Total Return Y-T-D	Risk Rating/Pts
6-05	A+	320.94	14.90	B+ / 8.5	10.56%	B- / 7.8

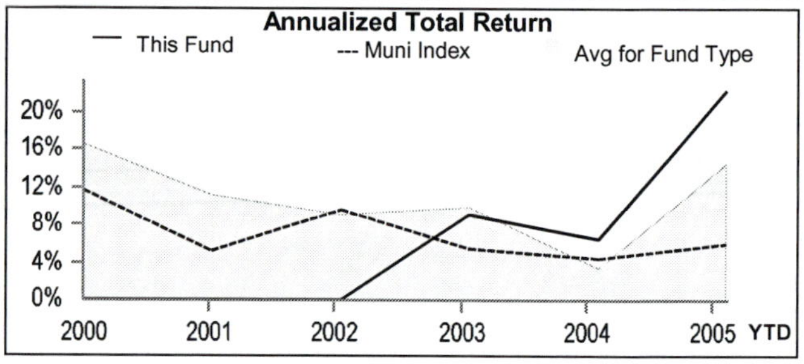

Alliance NY Municipal Income Fund (AYN) A- Excellent

Fund Family: Alliance Capital Management L.P.
Fund Type: Municipal - Single State
Inception Date: January 29, 2002

Data Date	Weiss Investment Rating	Net Assets ($Mil)	Price	Performance Rating/Pts	Total Return Y-T-D	Risk Rating/Pts
6-05	A-	74.09	14.85	B+ / 8.6	13.02%	C+ / 6.4

Major Rating Factors:
Strong performance is the major factor driving the A- (Excellent) Weiss Investment Rating for Alliance NY Municipal Income Fund. The fund currently has a performance rating of B+ (Good) based on an annualized return of 9.44% over the last three years and a total return of 13.02% year to date 2005. Factored into the performance evaluation is an expense ratio of 1.17% (low).

The fund's risk rating is currently C+ (Fair). It carries a beta of 2.02, meaning it is expected to move 20.2% for every 10% move in the market. Volatility, as measured by both the semi-deviation and a drawdown factor, is considered low. As of June 30, 2005, Alliance NY Municipal Income Fund traded at a discount of 4.32% below its net asset value, which is worse than its one-year historical average discount of 7.89%.

David Dowden has been running the fund for 3 years and currently receives a manager quality ranking of 57 (0=worst, 99=best). If you desire only a moderate level of risk and strong performance, then this fund is an excellent option.

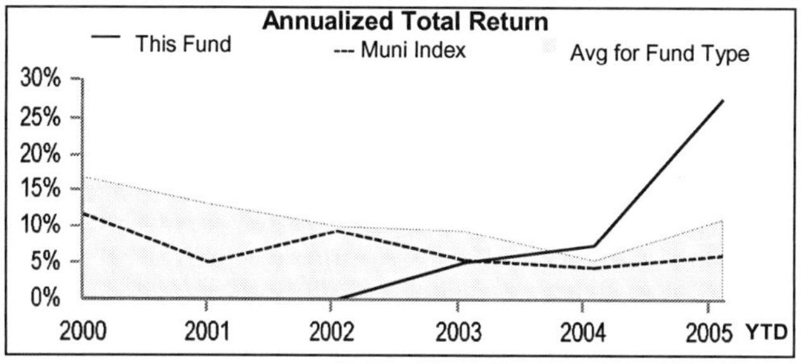

Alliance World Dollar Govt Fund (AWG) C Fair

Fund Family: Alliance Capital Management L.P.
Fund Type: Global
Inception Date: October 30, 1992

Data Date	Weiss Investment Rating	Net Assets ($Mil)	Price	Performance Rating/Pts	Total Return Y-T-D	Risk Rating/Pts
6-05	C	121.27	12.39	C+ / 5.8	0.99%	C / 5.5
2004	C+	113.88	12.69	C+ / 6.7	-0.08%	C+ / 6.0
2003	A-	115.99	13.45	B+ / 8.7	41.38%	C+ / 6.7

Major Rating Factors:
Middle of the road best describes Alliance World Dollar Govt Fund whose Weiss Investment Rating is currently a C (Fair). The fund currently has a performance rating of C+ (Fair) based on an annualized return of 13.61% over the last three years and a total return of 0.99% year to date 2005. Factored into the performance evaluation is an expense ratio of 1.59% (above average).

The fund's risk rating is currently C (Fair). It carries a beta of 0.91, meaning that its performance tracks fairly well with that of the overall stock market. Volatility, as measured by both the semi-deviation and a drawdown factor, is considered average. As of June 30, 2005, Alliance World Dollar Govt Fund traded at a discount of 12.25% below its net asset value, which is better than its one-year historical average discount of 11.51%.

Paul DeNoon has been running the fund for 13 years and currently receives a manager quality ranking of 77 (0=worst, 99=best). If you desire an average level of risk, then this fund may be an option.

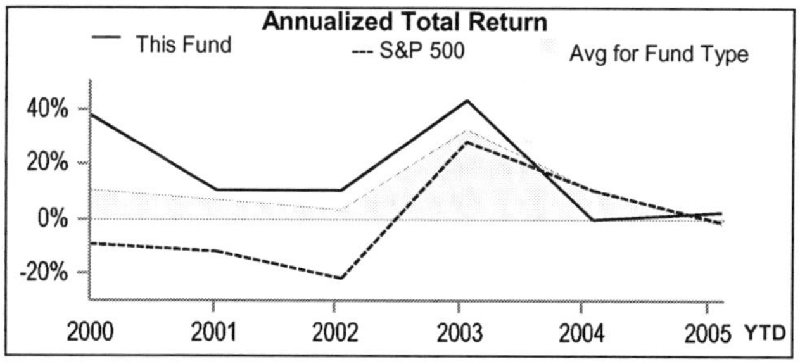

Alliance World Dollar Govt Fund II (AWF) B- Good

Fund Family: Alliance Capital Management L.P.
Fund Type: Global
Inception Date: July 27, 1993

Data Date	Weiss Investment Rating	Net Assets ($Mil)	Price	Performance Rating/Pts	Total Return Y-T-D	Risk Rating/Pts
6-05	B-	916.84	12.29	B- / 7.5	2.75%	C+ / 5.8
2004	B	908.88	12.38	B / 7.7	2.71%	C+ / 6.0
2003	B+	998.04	13.00	A / 9.3	45.90%	C+ / 6.0

Major Rating Factors:
Strong performance is the major factor driving the B- (Good) Weiss Investment Rating for Alliance World Dollar Govt Fund II. The fund currently has a performance rating of B- (Good) based on an annualized return of 18.93% over the last three years and a total return of 2.75% year to date 2005. Factored into the performance evaluation is an expense ratio of 1.30% (average).

The fund's risk rating is currently C+ (Fair). It carries a beta of 0.88, meaning the fund's expected move will be 8.8% for every 10% move in the market. Volatility, as measured by both the semi-deviation and a drawdown factor, is considered low. As of June 30, 2005, Alliance World Dollar Govt Fund II traded at a discount of 12.78% below its net asset value, which is better than its one-year historical average discount of 11.59%.

Paul DeNoon has been running the fund for 12 years and currently receives a manager quality ranking of 89 (0=worst, 99=best). If you desire only a moderate level of risk and strong performance, then this fund is an excellent option.

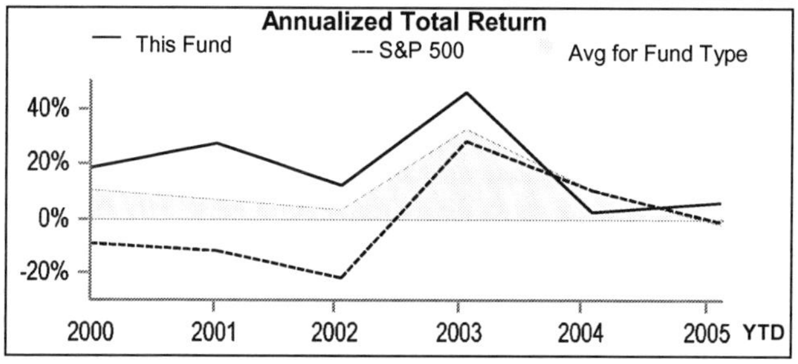

Allmerica Securities Trust (ALM) C- Fair

Fund Family: Allmerica Asset Management
Fund Type: General Bond
Inception Date: February 28, 1973

Major Rating Factors:
Disappointing performance is the major factor driving the C- (Fair) Weiss Investment Rating for Allmerica Securities Trust. The fund currently has a performance rating of D- (Weak) based on an annualized return of 4.99% over the last three years and a total return of -0.42% year to date 2005. Factored into the performance evaluation is an expense ratio of 0.76% (very low).

The fund's risk rating is currently B (Good). It carries a beta of 1.54, meaning it is expected to move 15.4% for every 10% move in the market. Volatility, as measured by both the semi-deviation and a drawdown factor, is considered low. As of June 30, 2005, Allmerica Securities Trust traded at a discount of 10.54% below its net asset value, which is worse than its one-year historical average discount of 11.75%.

Lisa Coleman has been running the fund for 11 years and currently receives a manager quality ranking of 29 (0=worst, 99=best). This fund offers only a moderate level of risk but investors looking for strong performance are still waiting.

Data Date	Weiss Investment Rating	Net Assets ($Mil)	Price	Performance Rating/Pts	Total Return Y-T-D	Risk Rating/Pts
6-05	C-	90.99	9.42	D- / 1.5	-0.42%	B / 8.0
2004	D+	88.89	9.74	D / 2.1	5.89%	B- / 7.8
2003	C-	94.05	9.71	D / 1.9	8.88%	B / 8.4

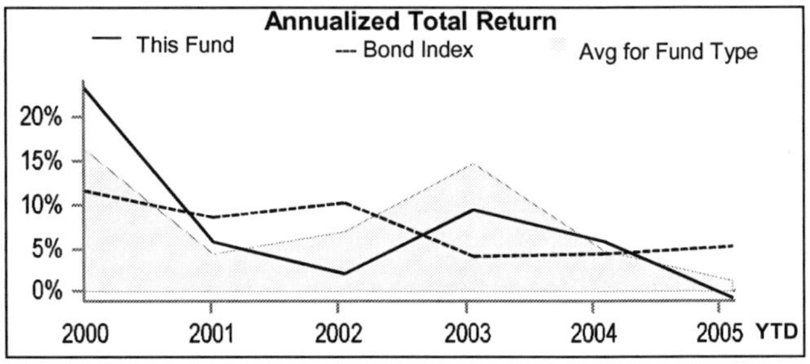

American Income Fund (MRF) C- Fair

Fund Family: US Bancorp Asset Management
Fund Type: Mortgage
Inception Date: December 27, 1988

Major Rating Factors:
Disappointing performance is the major factor driving the C- (Fair) Weiss Investment Rating for American Income Fund. The fund currently has a performance rating of D (Weak) based on an annualized return of 6.77% over the last three years and a total return of 2.41% year to date 2005. Factored into the performance evaluation is an expense ratio of 1.53% (average).

The fund's risk rating is currently B (Good). It carries a beta of 1.95, meaning it is expected to move 19.5% for every 10% move in the market. Volatility, as measured by both the semi-deviation and a drawdown factor, is considered low. As of June 30, 2005, American Income Fund traded at a discount of 7.90% below its net asset value, which is worse than its one-year historical average discount of 7.96%.

Chris Neuharth has been running the fund for 5 years and currently receives a manager quality ranking of 48 (0=worst, 99=best). This fund offers only a moderate level of risk but investors looking for strong performance are still waiting.

Data Date	Weiss Investment Rating	Net Assets ($Mil)	Price	Performance Rating/Pts	Total Return Y-T-D	Risk Rating/Pts
6-05	C-	83.85	8.28	D / 1.7	2.41%	B / 8.4
2004	C	84.99	8.32	D+ / 2.3	4.10%	B+ / 9.1
2003	C	85.67	8.70	D+ / 2.9	8.63%	B / 8.9

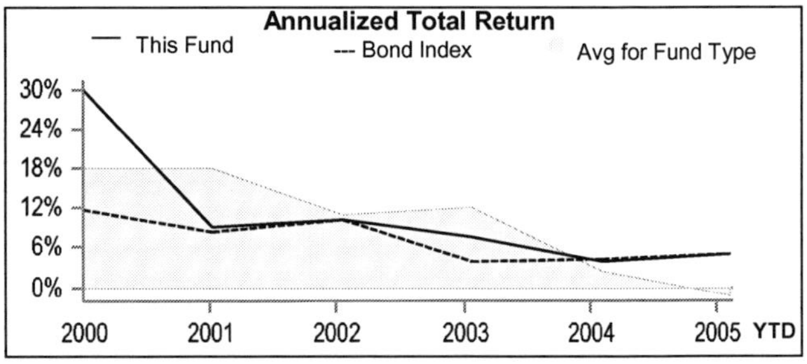

American Municipal Income Portfolio (XAA) B- Good

Fund Family: US Bancorp Asset Management
Fund Type: Municipal - National
Inception Date: June 18, 1993

Major Rating Factors:
American Municipal Income Portfolio receives a Weiss Investment Rating of B- (Good). The fund currently has a performance rating of C+ (Fair) based on an annualized return of 8.60% over the last three years and a total return of 6.43% year to date 2005. Factored into the performance evaluation is an expense ratio of 1.23% (average).

The fund's risk rating is currently B- (Good). It carries a beta of 1.83, meaning it is expected to move 18.3% for every 10% move in the market. Volatility, as measured by both the semi-deviation and a drawdown factor, is considered low. As of June 30, 2005, American Municipal Income Portfolio traded at a discount of 6.68% below its net asset value, which is worse than its one-year historical average discount of 7.07%.

Douglas J. White has been running the fund for 12 years and currently receives a manager quality ranking of 52 (0=worst, 99=best). If you desire an average level of risk, then this fund may be an option.

Data Date	Weiss Investment Rating	Net Assets ($Mil)	Price	Performance Rating/Pts	Total Return Y-T-D	Risk Rating/Pts
6-05	B-	90.64	14.82	C+ / 6.7	6.43%	B- / 7.8
2004	B	87.35	14.30	C / 5.4	4.71%	B / 8.3
2003	B	84.41	14.59	C+ / 6.6	5.85%	B / 8.8

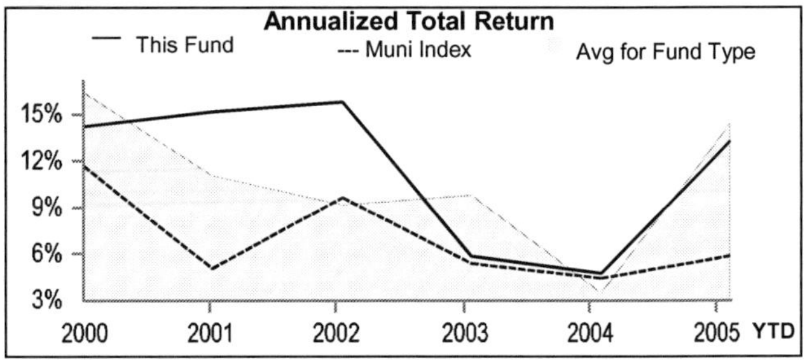

American Select Portfolio (SLA) D Weak

Fund Family: US Bancorp Asset Management
Fund Type: Mortgage
Inception Date: September 14, 1993

Major Rating Factors:
Very poor performance is the major factor driving the D (Weak) Weiss Investment Rating for American Select Portfolio. The fund currently has a performance rating of E - (Very Weak) based on an annualized return of 2.81% over the last three years and a total return of -4.53% year to date 2005. Factored into the performance evaluation is an expense ratio of 1.87% (above average).

The fund's risk rating is currently B (Good). It carries a beta of 2.08, meaning it is expected to move 20.8% for every 10% move in the market. Volatility, as measured by both the semi-deviation and a drawdown factor, is considered low. As of June 30, 2005, American Select Portfolio traded at a discount of 9.31% below its net asset value, which is better than its one-year historical average discount of 3.70%.

John Wenker has been running the fund for 12 years and currently receives a manager quality ranking of 15 (0=worst, 99=best). This fund offers only a moderate level of risk but investors looking for strong performance are still waiting.

Data Date	Weiss Investment Rating	Net Assets ($Mil)	Price	Performance Rating/Pts	Total Return Y-T-D	Risk Rating/Pts
6-05	D	140.06	11.88	E- / 0.2	-4.53%	B / 8.1
2004	D+	142.11	12.81	D / 1.9	-0.86%	B- / 7.7
2003	C+	144.62	13.63	C / 4.7	12.92%	B- / 7.7

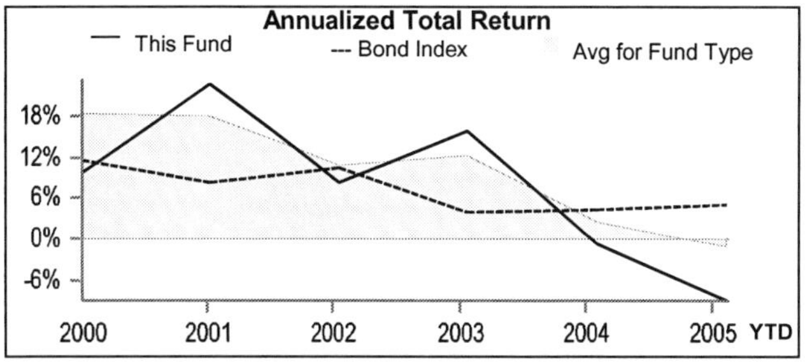

American Strat Inc Portfolio (ASP) D Weak

Fund Family: US Bancorp Asset Management
Fund Type: Mortgage
Inception Date: December 20, 1991

Major Rating Factors:
Very poor performance is the major factor driving the D (Weak) Weiss Investment Rating for American Strat Inc Portfolio. The fund currently has a performance rating of E (Very Weak) based on an annualized return of 4.58% over the last three years and a total return of -2.67% year to date 2005. Factored into the performance evaluation is an expense ratio of 1.45% (average).

The fund's risk rating is currently B- (Good). It carries a beta of 2.33, meaning it is expected to move 23.3% for every 10% move in the market. Volatility, as measured by both the semi-deviation and a drawdown factor, is considered low. As of June 30, 2005, American Strat Inc Portfolio traded at a discount of 8.65% below its net asset value, which is better than its one-year historical average discount of 3.59%.

John Wenker has been running the fund for 13 years and currently receives a manager quality ranking of 19 (0=worst, 99=best). This fund offers only a moderate level of risk but investors looking for strong performance are still waiting.

Data Date	Weiss Investment Rating	Net Assets ($Mil)	Price	Performance Rating/Pts	Total Return Y-T-D	Risk Rating/Pts
6-05	D	53.50	11.40	E / 0.4	-2.67%	B- / 7.5
2004	D	53.15	12.06	D- / 1.2	-1.50%	B- / 7.5
2003	C	53.41	12.65	C- / 3.7	13.92%	B / 8.0

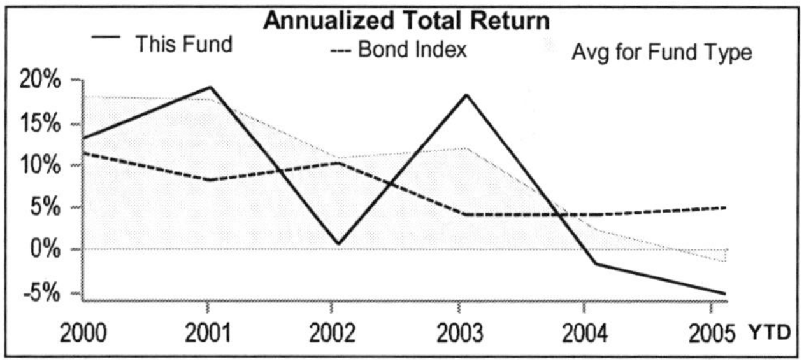

American Strat Inc Portfolio II (BSP) D Weak

Fund Family: US Bancorp Asset Management
Fund Type: Mortgage
Inception Date: July 23, 1992

Major Rating Factors:
Very poor performance is the major factor driving the D (Weak) Weiss Investment Rating for American Strat Inc Portfolio II. The fund currently has a performance rating of E (Very Weak) based on an annualized return of 3.61% over the last three years and a total return of -2.71% year to date 2005. Factored into the performance evaluation is an expense ratio of 1.72% (above average).

The fund's risk rating is currently B- (Good). It carries a beta of 2.18, meaning it is expected to move 21.8% for every 10% move in the market. Volatility, as measured by both the semi-deviation and a drawdown factor, is considered low. As of June 30, 2005, American Strat Inc Portfolio II traded at a discount of 5.67% below its net asset value, which is better than its one-year historical average discount of 1.74%.

John Wenker has been running the fund for 13 years and currently receives a manager quality ranking of 17 (0=worst, 99=best). This fund offers only a moderate level of risk but investors looking for strong performance are still waiting.

Data Date	Weiss Investment Rating	Net Assets ($Mil)	Price	Performance Rating/Pts	Total Return Y-T-D	Risk Rating/Pts
6-05	D	201.58	11.64	E / 0.3	-2.71%	B- / 7.7
2004	D+	207.42	12.38	D / 1.8	-3.37%	B / 8.0
2003	C+	209.39	13.80	C / 5.4	18.47%	B- / 7.5

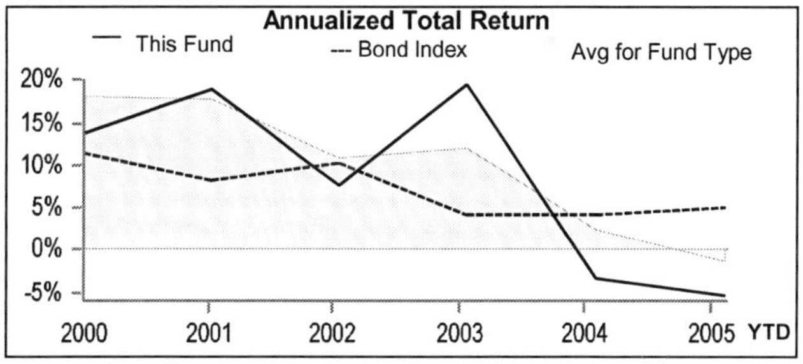

American Strat Inc Portfolio III (CSP) D+ Weak

Fund Family: US Bancorp Asset Management
Fund Type: Mortgage
Inception Date: March 18, 1993

Major Rating Factors:
Very poor performance is the major factor driving the D+ (Weak) Weiss Investment Rating for American Strat Inc Portfolio III. The fund currently has a performance rating of E+ (Very Weak) based on an annualized return of 5.57% over the last three years and a total return of -4.62% year to date 2005. Factored into the performance evaluation is an expense ratio of 1.80% (above average).

The fund's risk rating is currently B (Good). It carries a beta of 2.01, meaning it is expected to move 20.1% for every 10% move in the market. Volatility, as measured by both the semi-deviation and a drawdown factor, is considered low. As of June 30, 2005, American Strat Inc Portfolio III traded at a discount of 5.81% below its net asset value, which is better than its one-year historical average discount of 1.38%.

John Wenker has been running the fund for 12 years and currently receives a manager quality ranking of 33 (0=worst, 99=best). This fund offers only a moderate level of risk but investors looking for strong performance are still waiting.

Data Date	Weiss Investment Rating	Net Assets ($Mil)	Price	Performance Rating/Pts	Total Return Y-T-D	Risk Rating/Pts
6-05	D+	260.14	11.34	E+ / 0.7	-4.62%	B / 8.2
2004	C-	264.77	12.31	C- / 3.3	3.04%	B- / 7.4
2003	C+	267.23	13.15	C+ / 5.7	19.90%	B- / 7.6

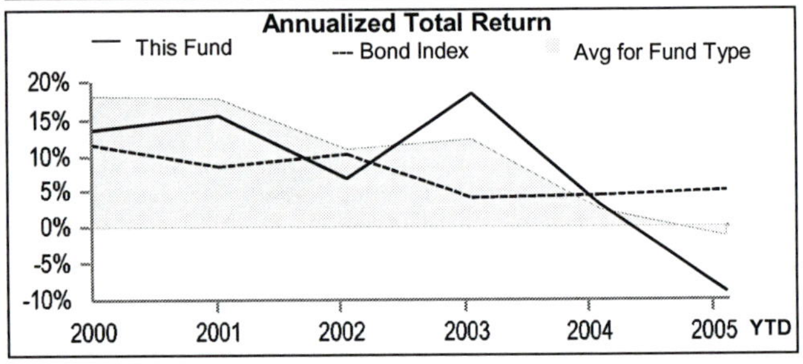

Apex Municipal Fund (APX) A+ Excellent

Fund Family: Merrill Lynch Investment Managers
Fund Type: Municipal - National
Inception Date: July 25, 1989

Major Rating Factors:
Strong performance is the major factor driving the A+ (Excellent) Weiss Investment Rating for Apex Municipal Fund. The fund currently has a performance rating of B+ (Good) based on an annualized return of 10.92% over the last three years and a total return of 9.32% year to date 2005. Factored into the performance evaluation is an expense ratio of 0.80% (very low).

The fund's risk rating is currently B- (Good). It carries a beta of 1.35, meaning it is expected to move 13.5% for every 10% move in the market. Volatility, as measured by both the semi-deviation and a drawdown factor, is considered low. As of June 30, 2005, Apex Municipal Fund traded at a discount of 4.49% below its net asset value, which is worse than its one-year historical average discount of 6.68%.

Theodore R. Jaeckel Jr. has been running the fund for 7 years and currently receives a manager quality ranking of 78 (0=worst, 99=best). If you desire only a moderate level of risk and strong performance, then this fund is an excellent option.

Data Date	Weiss Investment Rating	Net Assets ($Mil)	Price	Performance Rating/Pts	Total Return Y-T-D	Risk Rating/Pts
6-05	A+	186.76	9.36	B+ / 8.6	9.32%	B- / 7.6
2004	B	178.98	8.84	C+ / 6.8	12.20%	B / 8.1
2003	C+	176.12	8.38	C / 5.0	12.97%	B / 8.1

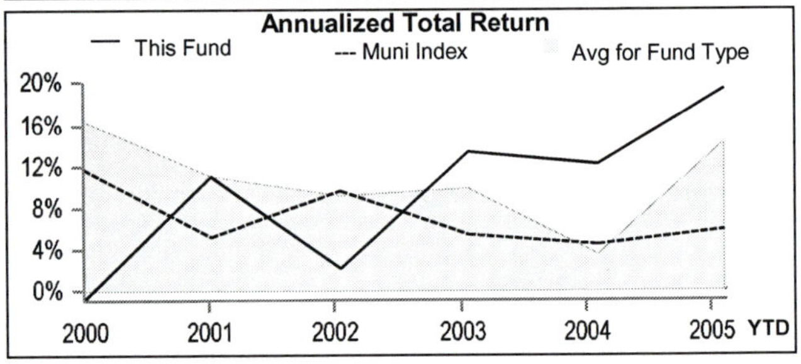

ASA Limited (ASA) E- Very Weak

Fund Family: ASA Limited
Fund Type: Precious Metals
Inception Date: September 1, 1958

Major Rating Factors:
ASA Limited has adopted a very risky asset allocation strategy and currently receives an overall Weiss Investment Rating of E- (Very Weak). The fund has a high level of volatility, with a standard deviation of 33.25. It carries a beta of 1.47, meaning it is expected to move 14.7% for every 10% move in the market. As of June 30, 2005, ASA Limited traded at a discount of 11.14% below its net asset value, which is worse than its one-year historical average discount of 12.48%. Unfortunately, the high level of risk (E-, Very Weak) failed to pay off as investors endured poor performance.

The fund's performance rating is currently D (Weak). It has registered an annualized return of 8.77% over the last three years but is down -4.06% year to date 2005. Factored into the performance evaluation is an expense ratio of 1.03% (low).

Ronald L. McCarthy has been running the fund for 17 years and currently receives a manager quality ranking of 14 (0=worst, 99=best). If you can tolerate very high levels of risk in the hope of improved future returns, holding this fund may be an option.

Data Date	Weiss Investment Rating	Net Assets ($Mil)	Price	Performance Rating/Pts	Total Return Y-T-D	Risk Rating/Pts
6-05	E-	479.53	38.59	D / 1.8	-4.06%	E- / 0.0
2004	D	412.38	40.35	B+ / 8.9	-10.11%	E- / 0.0
2003	D+	347.76	44.30	A+ / 9.6	11.84%	E- / 0.0

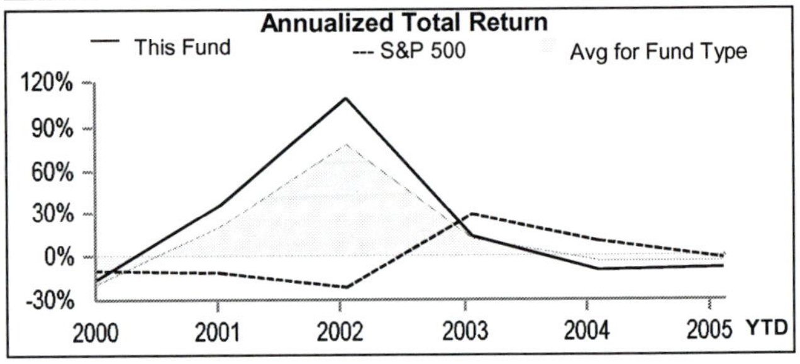

Asia Pacific Fund (APB) C- Fair

Fund Family: Altman Group
Fund Type: Foreign
Inception Date: April 30, 1987

Data Date	Weiss Investment Rating	Net Assets ($Mil)	Price	Performance Rating/Pts	Total Return Y-T-D	Risk Rating/Pts
6-05	C-	171.93	15.21	C+ / 6.2	3.89%	C- / 4.2
2004	C+	150.78	14.64	B / 8.0	4.15%	C / 5.0
2003	C+	128.94	13.76	A / 9.3	54.95%	C- / 3.7

Major Rating Factors:
Middle of the road best describes Asia Pacific Fund whose Weiss Investment Rating is currently a C- (Fair). The fund currently has a performance rating of C+ (Fair) based on an annualized return of 14.25% over the last three years and a total return of 3.89% year to date 2005. Factored into the performance evaluation is an expense ratio of 2.01% (high).

The fund's risk rating is currently C- (Fair). It carries a beta of 1.05, meaning that its performance tracks fairly well with that of the overall stock market. Volatility, as measured by both the semi-deviation and a drawdown factor, is considered average. As of June 30, 2005, Asia Pacific Fund traded at a discount of 10.58% below its net asset value, which is worse than its one-year historical average discount of 10.74%.

Khiem Do has been running the fund for 1 year and currently receives a manager quality ranking of 69 (0=worst, 99=best). If you desire an average level of risk, then this fund may be an option.

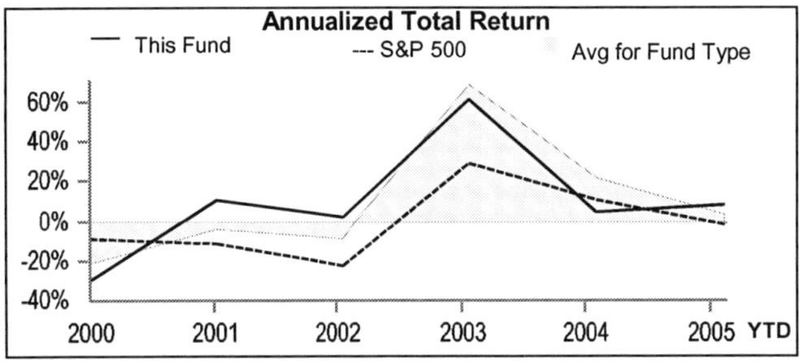

Asia Tigers Fund (GRR) C+ Fair

Fund Family: Advantage Advisers, Inc.
Fund Type: Foreign
Inception Date: November 19, 1993

Data Date	Weiss Investment Rating	Net Assets ($Mil)	Price	Performance Rating/Pts	Total Return Y-T-D	Risk Rating/Pts
6-05	C+	78.65	12.19	B / 7.6	5.09%	C / 4.4
2004	B	86.46	11.60	B / 7.9	10.48%	C+ / 5.9
2003	B-	91.48	10.07	B+ / 8.6	49.12%	C / 5.1

Major Rating Factors:
Strong performance is the major factor driving the C+ (Fair) Weiss Investment Rating for Asia Tigers Fund. The fund currently has a performance rating of B (Good) based on an annualized return of 17.04% over the last three years and a total return of 5.09% year to date 2005. Factored into the performance evaluation is an expense ratio of 2.04% (high).

The fund's risk rating is currently C (Fair). It carries a beta of 0.91, meaning that its performance tracks fairly well with that of the overall stock market. Volatility, as measured by both the semi-deviation and a drawdown factor, is considered average. As of June 30, 2005, Asia Tigers Fund traded at a discount of 6.45% below its net asset value, which is worse than its one-year historical average discount of 7.75%.

Punita Kumar-Sinha has been running the fund for 12 years and currently receives a manager quality ranking of 81 (0=worst, 99=best). If you desire an average level of risk and strong performance, then this fund is a good option.

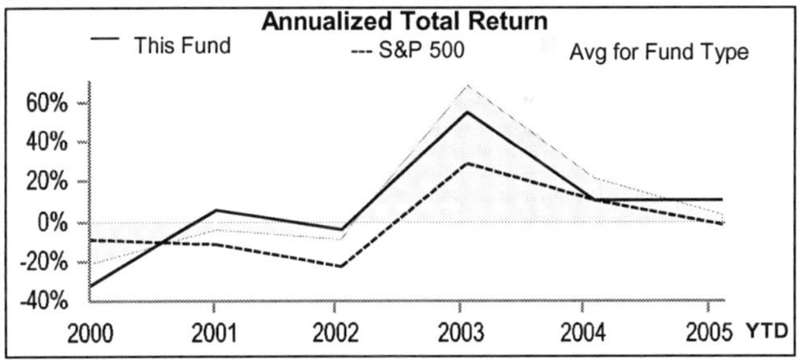

Bancroft Convertible Fund (BCV) D Weak

Fund Family: Davis/Dinsmore Management Co.
Fund Type: Growth and Income
Inception Date: October 4, 1971

Data Date	Weiss Investment Rating	Net Assets ($Mil)	Price	Performance Rating/Pts	Total Return Y-T-D	Risk Rating/Pts
6-05	D	111.32	17.32	E- / 0.0	-7.62%	B / 8.3
2004	D	115.55	19.11	E+ / 0.9	6.05%	B- / 7.0
2003	D	98.49	18.67	D- / 1.3	10.55%	C+ / 6.6

Major Rating Factors:
Very poor performance is the major factor driving the D (Weak) Weiss Investment Rating for Bancroft Convertible Fund. The fund currently has a performance rating of E- (Very Weak) based on an annualized return of 0.65% over the last three years and a total return of -7.62% year to date 2005. Factored into the performance evaluation is an expense ratio of 1.20% (average).

The fund's risk rating is currently B (Good). It carries a beta of 0.49, meaning the fund's expected move will be 4.9% for every 10% move in the market. Volatility, as measured by both the semi-deviation and a drawdown factor, is considered low. As of June 30, 2005, Bancroft Convertible Fund traded at a discount of 15.10% below its net asset value, which is better than its one-year historical average discount of 11.94%.

Thomas H. Dinsmore has been running the fund for 19 years and currently receives a manager quality ranking of 25 (0=worst, 99=best). This fund offers only a moderate level of risk but investors looking for strong performance are still waiting.

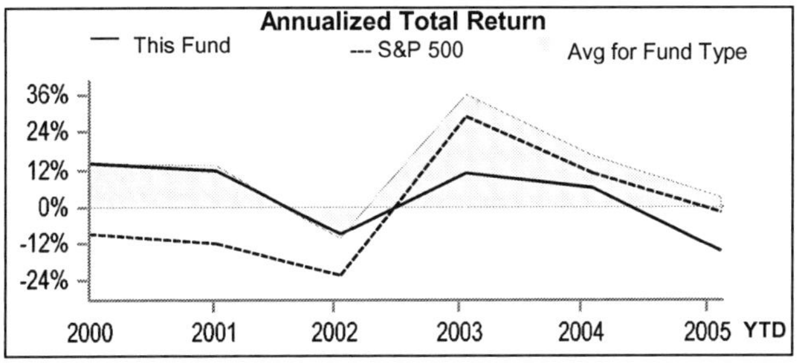

BlackRock Advantage Term Trust (BAT) D Weak

Fund Family: BlackRock Advisors, Inc.
Fund Type: Mortgage
Inception Date: April 20, 1990

Data Date	Weiss Investment Rating	Net Assets ($Mil)	Price	Perfor-mance Rating/Pts	Total Return Y-T-D	Risk Rating/Pts
6-05	D	99.73	10.26	E- / 0.2	0.48%	B / 8.3
2004	D+	105.71	10.47	D- / 1.4	1.54%	B / 8.4
2003	C	113.03	11.23	D+ / 2.7	0.65%	B / 8.8

Major Rating Factors:

Very poor performance is the major factor driving the D (Weak) Weiss Investment Rating for BlackRock Advantage Term Trust. The fund currently has a performance rating of E- (Very Weak) based on an annualized return of 2.64% over the last three years and a total return of 0.48% year to date 2005. Factored into the performance evaluation is an expense ratio of 1.29% (average).

The fund's risk rating is currently B (Good). It carries a beta of 0.51, meaning the fund's expected move will be 5.1% for every 10% move in the market. Volatility, as measured by both the semi-deviation and a drawdown factor, is considered low. As of June 30, 2005, BlackRock Advantage Term Trust traded at a discount of .68% below its net asset value, which is worse than its one-year historical average discount of .76%.

Robert S. Kapito has been running the fund for 15 years and currently receives a manager quality ranking of 58 (0=worst, 99=best). This fund offers only a moderate level of risk but investors looking for strong performance are still waiting.

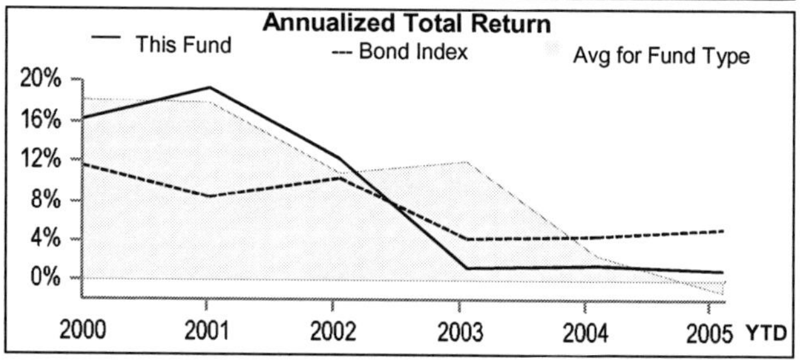

BlackRock Broad Inv Gr 2009 Tm Tr (BCT) C- Fair

Fund Family: BlackRock Advisors, Inc.
Fund Type: General - Investment Grade
Inception Date: June 18, 1993

Data Date	Weiss Investment Rating	Net Assets ($Mil)	Price	Perfor-mance Rating/Pts	Total Return Y-T-D	Risk Rating/Pts
6-05	C-	45.15	15.81	D / 1.6	2.55%	B / 8.1
2004	C	46.56	15.80	C- / 3.4	5.19%	B / 8.4
2003	C	47.38	15.90	C- / 3.6	6.94%	B / 8.3

Major Rating Factors:

Disappointing performance is the major factor driving the C- (Fair) Weiss Investment Rating for BlackRock Broad Inv Gr 2009 Tm Tr. The fund currently has a performance rating of D (Weak) based on an annualized return of 7.10% over the last three years and a total return of 2.55% year to date 2005. Factored into the performance evaluation is an expense ratio of 2.71% (high).

The fund's risk rating is currently B (Good). It carries a beta of 1.11, meaning it is expected to move 11.1% for every 10% move in the market. Volatility, as measured by both the semi-deviation and a drawdown factor, is considered low. As of June 30, 2005, BlackRock Broad Inv Gr 2009 Tm Tr traded at a premium of 4.01% above its net asset value, which is worse than its one-year historical average premium of 1.56%.

Robert S. Kapito has been running the fund for 12 years and currently receives a manager quality ranking of 66 (0=worst, 99=best). This fund offers only a moderate level of risk but investors looking for strong performance are still waiting.

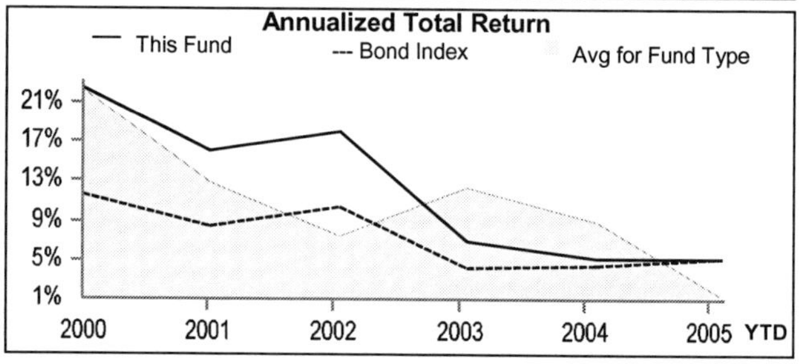

BlackRock CA Insured Muni 2008 Term (BFC) C Fair

Fund Family: BlackRock Advisors, Inc.
Fund Type: Municipal - Single State
Inception Date: September 28, 1992

Data Date	Weiss Investment Rating	Net Assets ($Mil)	Price	Perfor-mance Rating/Pts	Total Return Y-T-D	Risk Rating/Pts
6-05	C	174.41	16.06	D+ / 2.5	1.23%	B / 8.7
2004	C	171.37	16.25	C- / 3.1	-0.17%	B / 8.8
2003	C+	182.77	16.87	C / 4.6	9.54%	B / 8.3

Major Rating Factors:

Disappointing performance is the major factor driving the C (Fair) Weiss Investment Rating for BlackRock CA Insured Muni 2008 Term. The fund currently has a performance rating of D+ (Weak) based on an annualized return of 6.01% over the last three years and a total return of 1.23% year to date 2005. Factored into the performance evaluation is an expense ratio of 1.05% (low).

The fund's risk rating is currently B (Good). It carries a beta of 1.17, meaning it is expected to move 11.7% for every 10% move in the market. Volatility, as measured by both the semi-deviation and a drawdown factor, is considered low. As of June 30, 2005, BlackRock CA Insured Muni 2008 Term traded at a discount of 2.37% below its net asset value, which is worse than its one-year historical average discount of 2.57%.

Kevin M. Klingert has been running the fund for 13 years and currently receives a manager quality ranking of 59 (0=worst, 99=best). This fund offers only a moderate level of risk but investors looking for strong performance are still waiting.

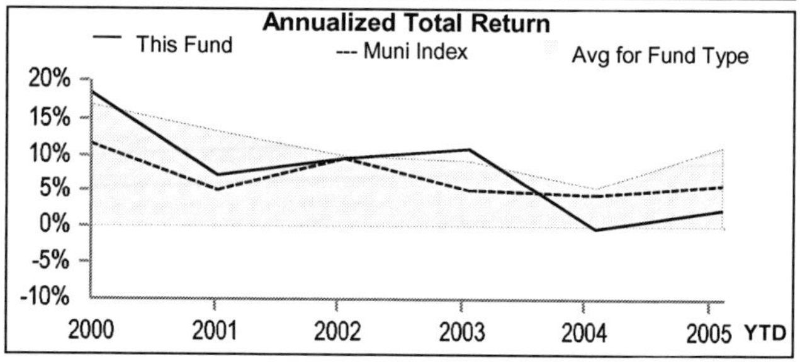

BlackRock CA Inv Qual Muni Tr (RAA) — D — Weak

Fund Family: BlackRock Advisors, Inc.
Fund Type: Municipal - Single State
Inception Date: May 28, 1993

Data Date	Weiss Investment Rating	Net Assets ($Mil)	Price	Performance Rating/Pts	Total Return Y-T-D	Risk Rating/Pts
6-05	D	14.63	14.26	D+ / 2.8	3.47%	C+ / 5.7
2004	C-	14.40	14.20	C- / 3.1	10.79%	B- / 7.0
2003	C-	14.67	13.69	D+ / 2.6	5.22%	B / 8.6

Major Rating Factors:

Disappointing performance is the major factor driving the D (Weak) Weiss Investment Rating for BlackRock CA Inv Qual Muni Tr. The fund currently has a performance rating of D+ (Weak) based on an annualized return of 3.54% over the last three years and a total return of 3.47% year to date 2005. Factored into the performance evaluation is an expense ratio of 1.35% (average).

The fund's risk rating is currently C+ (Fair). It carries a beta of 1.95, meaning it is expected to move 19.5% for every 10% move in the market. Volatility, as measured by both the semi-deviation and a drawdown factor, is considered low. As of June 30, 2005, BlackRock CA Inv Qual Muni Tr traded at a discount of 1.86% below its net asset value, which is worse than its one-year historical average discount of 3.03%.

Kevin Klingert has been running the fund for 12 years and currently receives a manager quality ranking of 9 (0=worst, 99=best). This fund offers only a moderate level of risk but investors looking for strong performance are still waiting.

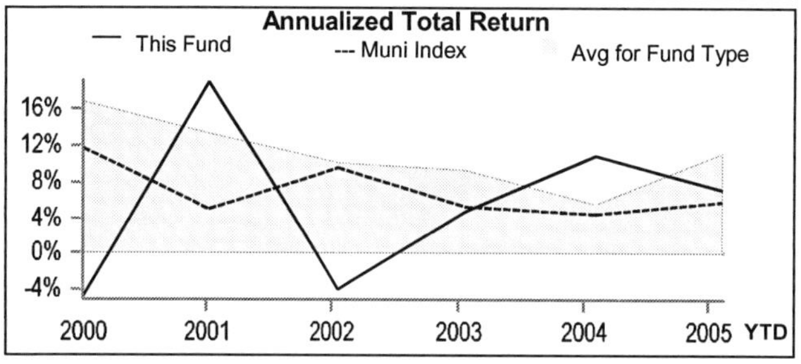

BlackRock CA Muni 2018 Income Trust (BJZ) — A- — Excellent

Fund Family: BlackRock Advisors, Inc.
Fund Type: Municipal - Single State
Inception Date: October 26, 2001

Data Date	Weiss Investment Rating	Net Assets ($Mil)	Price	Performance Rating/Pts	Total Return Y-T-D	Risk Rating/Pts
6-05	A-	97.59	14.99	B- / 7.4	10.65%	B- / 7.6
2004	B-	92.40	13.89	C / 4.3	9.07%	B / 8.9

Major Rating Factors:

Strong performance is the major factor driving the A- (Excellent) Weiss Investment Rating for BlackRock CA Muni 2018 Income Trust. The fund currently has a performance rating of B- (Good) based on an annualized return of 8.83% over the last three years and a total return of 10.65% year to date 2005. Factored into the performance evaluation is an expense ratio of 1.01% (low).

The fund's risk rating is currently B- (Good). It carries a beta of 1.55, meaning it is expected to move 15.5% for every 10% move in the market. Volatility, as measured by both the semi-deviation and a drawdown factor, is considered low. As of June 30, 2005, BlackRock CA Muni 2018 Income Trust traded at a discount of 2.15% below its net asset value, which is worse than its one-year historical average discount of 5.03%.

Kevin Klingert has been running the fund for 4 years and currently receives a manager quality ranking of 64 (0=worst, 99=best). If you desire only a moderate level of risk and strong performance, then this fund is an excellent option.

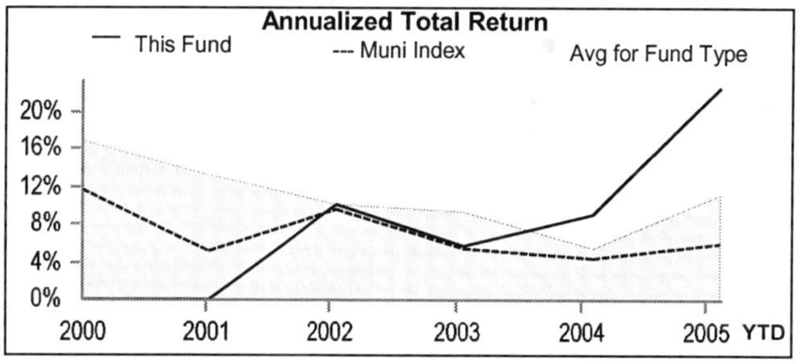

BlackRock CA Muni Bond Trust (BZA) — B+ — Good

Fund Family: BlackRock Advisors, Inc.
Fund Type: Municipal - Single State
Inception Date: April 25, 2002

Data Date	Weiss Investment Rating	Net Assets ($Mil)	Price	Performance Rating/Pts	Total Return Y-T-D	Risk Rating/Pts
6-05	B+	52.58	14.92	B- / 7.4	9.01%	B- / 7.3

Major Rating Factors:

Strong performance is the major factor driving the B+ (Good) Weiss Investment Rating for BlackRock CA Muni Bond Trust. The fund currently has a performance rating of B- (Good) based on an annualized return of 7.46% over the last three years and a total return of 9.01% year to date 2005. Factored into the performance evaluation is an expense ratio of 1.03% (low).

The fund's risk rating is currently B- (Good). It carries a beta of 1.90, meaning it is expected to move 19.0% for every 10% move in the market. Volatility, as measured by both the semi-deviation and a drawdown factor, is considered low. As of June 30, 2005, BlackRock CA Muni Bond Trust traded at a discount of 6.57% below its net asset value, which is better than its one-year historical average discount of 6.56%.

Kevin M. Klingert has been running the fund for 3 years and currently receives a manager quality ranking of 42 (0=worst, 99=best). If you desire only a moderate level of risk and strong performance, then this fund is an excellent option.

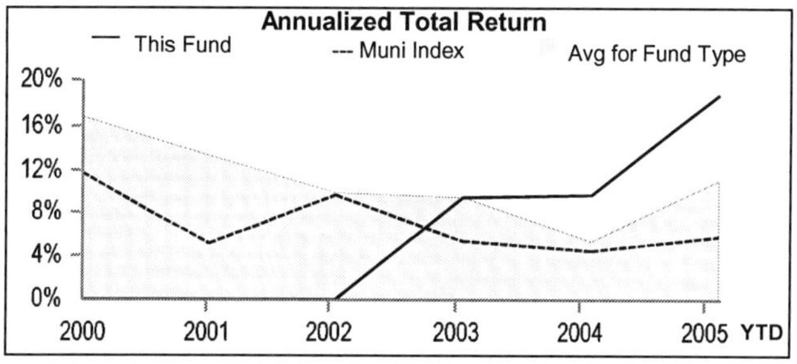

BlackRock CA Municipal Income Trust (BFZ) A Excellent

Fund Family: BlackRock Advisors, Inc.
Fund Type: Municipal - Single State
Inception Date: July 27, 2001

Major Rating Factors:
Strong performance is the major factor driving the A (Excellent) Weiss Investment Rating for BlackRock CA Municipal Income Trust. The fund currently has a performance rating of B+ (Good) based on an annualized return of 9.62% over the last three years and a total return of 11.30% year to date 2005. Factored into the performance evaluation is an expense ratio of 0.86% (very low).

The fund's risk rating is currently B- (Good). It carries a beta of 2.02, meaning it is expected to move 20.2% for every 10% move in the market. Volatility, as measured by both the semi-deviation and a drawdown factor, is considered low. As of June 30, 2005, BlackRock CA Municipal Income Trust traded at a discount of 5.58% below its net asset value, which is worse than its one-year historical average discount of 7.79%.

Kevin M. Klingert has been running the fund for 4 years and currently receives a manager quality ranking of 59 (0=worst, 99=best). If you desire only a moderate level of risk and strong performance, then this fund is an excellent option.

Data Date	Weiss Investment Rating	Net Assets ($Mil)	Price	Perfor-mance Rating/Pts	Total Return Y-T-D	Risk Rating/Pts
6-05	A	228.90	14.55	B+ / 8.4	11.30%	B- / 7.1
2004	C+	213.41	13.50	C / 4.5	7.61%	B- / 7.9

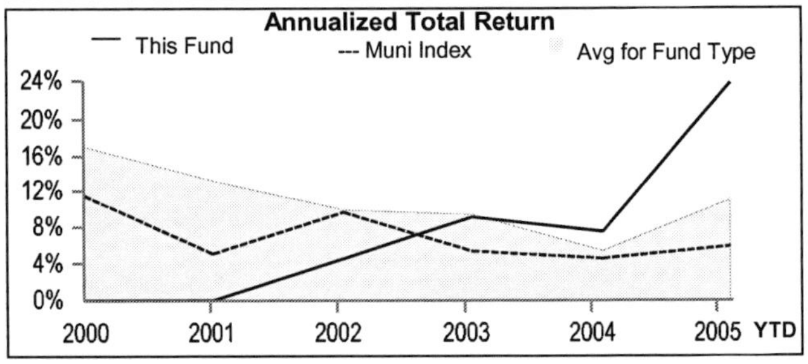

BlackRock Core Bond Trust (BHK) C+ Fair

Fund Family: BlackRock Advisors, Inc.
Fund Type: General - Investment Grade
Inception Date: November 29, 2001

Major Rating Factors:
Middle of the road best describes BlackRock Core Bond Trust whose Weiss Investment Rating is currently a C+ (Fair). The fund currently has a performance rating of C+ (Fair) based on an annualized return of 11.45% over the last three years and a total return of 9.08% year to date 2005. Factored into the performance evaluation is an expense ratio of 1.24% (average).

The fund's risk rating is currently B- (Good). It carries a beta of 2.03, meaning it is expected to move 20.3% for every 10% move in the market. Volatility, as measured by both the semi-deviation and a drawdown factor, is considered low. As of June 30, 2005, BlackRock Core Bond Trust traded at a discount of 5.10% below its net asset value, which is worse than its one-year historical average discount of 8.09%.

This fund has been team managed for 4 years and currently receives a manager quality ranking of 67 (0=worst, 99=best). If you desire an average level of risk, then this fund may be an option.

Data Date	Weiss Investment Rating	Net Assets ($Mil)	Price	Perfor-mance Rating/Pts	Total Return Y-T-D	Risk Rating/Pts
6-05	C+	400.48	14.32	C+ / 5.6	9.08%	B- / 7.2
2004	C-	395.10	13.55	D / 2.2	8.08%	B / 8.1

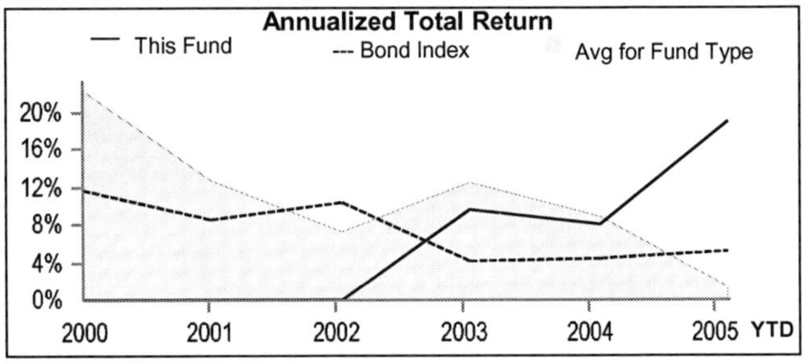

BlackRock FL Insured Muni 2008 Term (BRF) C- Fair

Fund Family: BlackRock Advisors, Inc.
Fund Type: Municipal - Single State
Inception Date: September 28, 1992

Major Rating Factors:
Disappointing performance is the major factor driving the C- (Fair) Weiss Investment Rating for BlackRock FL Insured Muni 2008 Term. The fund currently has a performance rating of D (Weak) based on an annualized return of 5.33% over the last three years and a total return of -0.08% year to date 2005. Factored into the performance evaluation is an expense ratio of 1.07% (low).

The fund's risk rating is currently B (Good). It carries a beta of 1.25, meaning it is expected to move 12.5% for every 10% move in the market. Volatility, as measured by both the semi-deviation and a drawdown factor, is considered low. As of June 30, 2005, BlackRock FL Insured Muni 2008 Term traded at a discount of .39% below its net asset value, which is worse than its one-year historical average discount of .60%.

Kevin M. Klingert has been running the fund for 13 years and currently receives a manager quality ranking of 49 (0=worst, 99=best). This fund offers only a moderate level of risk but investors looking for strong performance are still waiting.

Data Date	Weiss Investment Rating	Net Assets ($Mil)	Price	Perfor-mance Rating/Pts	Total Return Y-T-D	Risk Rating/Pts
6-05	C-	138.54	15.46	D / 1.9	-0.08%	B / 8.5
2004	C+	136.48	15.85	C- / 4.0	3.08%	B / 8.6
2003	B-	146.93	16.30	C+ / 5.7	8.37%	B / 8.2

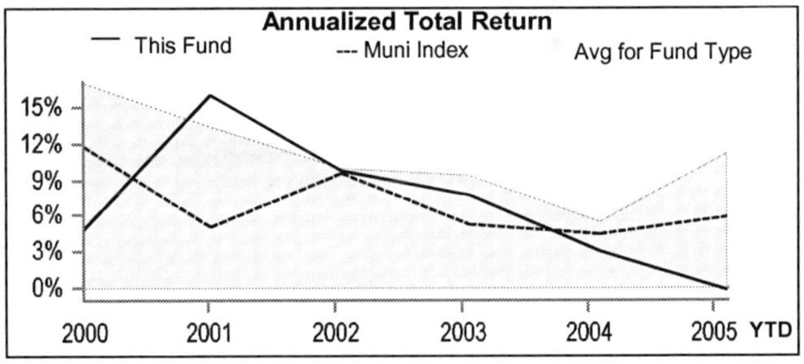

BlackRock FL Inv Qual Muni Tr (RFA) B Good

Fund Family: BlackRock Advisors, Inc.
Fund Type: Municipal - Single State
Inception Date: May 28, 1993

Data Date	Weiss Investment Rating	Net Assets ($Mil)	Price	Performance Rating/Pts	Total Return Y-T-D	Risk Rating/Pts
6-05	B	16.67	15.38	B / 7.8	11.88%	C+ / 5.7
2004	C-	16.87	14.15	D+ / 2.3	-0.78%	B- / 7.8
2003	B	17.35	15.54	C+ / 6.3	16.39%	B / 8.1

Major Rating Factors:
Strong performance is the major factor driving the B (Good) Weiss Investment Rating for BlackRock FL Inv Qual Muni Tr. The fund currently has a performance rating of B (Good) based on an annualized return of 7.54% over the last three years and a total return of 11.88% year to date 2005. Factored into the performance evaluation is an expense ratio of 1.28% (average).

The fund's risk rating is currently C+ (Fair). It carries a beta of 0.99, meaning that its performance tracks fairly well with that of the overall stock market. Volatility, as measured by both the semi-deviation and a drawdown factor, is considered low. As of June 30, 2005, BlackRock FL Inv Qual Muni Tr traded at a premium of 4.13% above its net asset value, which is worse than its one-year historical average discount of 3.36%.

Kevin Klingert has been running the fund for 12 years and currently receives a manager quality ranking of 72 (0=worst, 99=best). If you desire only a moderate level of risk and strong performance, then this fund is an excellent option.

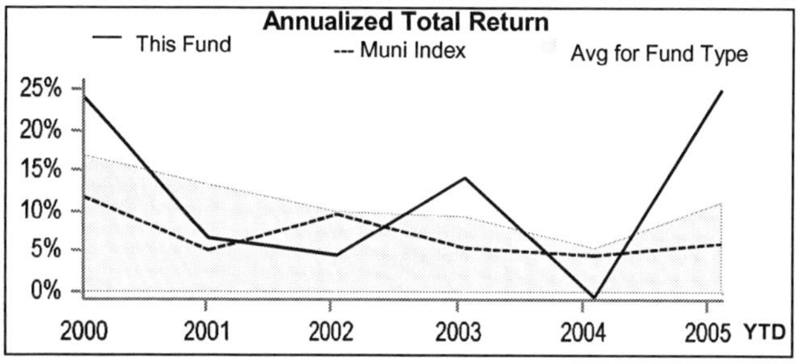

BlackRock FL Muni Bond Trust (BIE) A- Excellent

Fund Family: BlackRock Advisors, Inc.
Fund Type: Municipal - Single State
Inception Date: April 25, 2002

Data Date	Weiss Investment Rating	Net Assets ($Mil)	Price	Performance Rating/Pts	Total Return Y-T-D	Risk Rating/Pts
6-05	A-	53.16	15.62	B / 7.9	8.08%	B- / 7.1

Major Rating Factors:
Strong performance is the major factor driving the A- (Excellent) Weiss Investment Rating for BlackRock FL Muni Bond Trust. The fund currently has a performance rating of B (Good) based on an annualized return of 8.10% over the last three years and a total return of 8.08% year to date 2005. Factored into the performance evaluation is an expense ratio of 1.01% (low).

The fund's risk rating is currently B- (Good). It carries a beta of 1.80, meaning it is expected to move 18.0% for every 10% move in the market. Volatility, as measured by both the semi-deviation and a drawdown factor, is considered low. As of June 30, 2005, BlackRock FL Muni Bond Trust traded at a discount of 3.76% below its net asset value, which is worse than its one-year historical average discount of 6.55%.

Kevin M. Klingert has been running the fund for 3 years and currently receives a manager quality ranking of 57 (0=worst, 99=best). If you desire only a moderate level of risk and strong performance, then this fund is an excellent option.

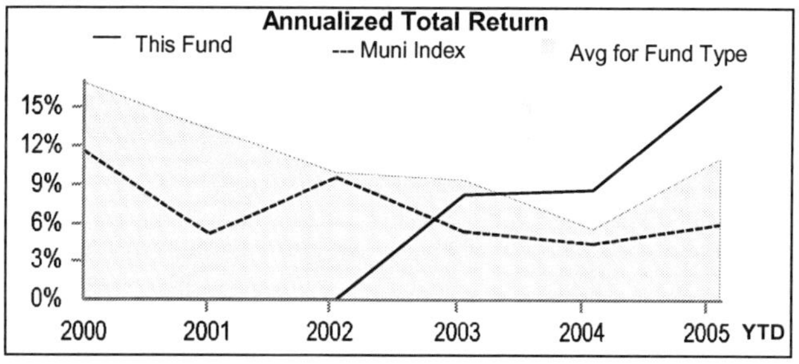

BlackRock FL Municipal Income Trust (BBF) B+ Good

Fund Family: BlackRock Advisors, Inc.
Fund Type: Municipal - Single State
Inception Date: July 27, 2001

Data Date	Weiss Investment Rating	Net Assets ($Mil)	Price	Performance Rating/Pts	Total Return Y-T-D	Risk Rating/Pts
6-05	B+	104.10	15.29	B / 7.8	5.81%	B- / 7.0
2004	A	99.05	14.90	B / 8.0	14.08%	B- / 7.4

Major Rating Factors:
Strong performance is the major factor driving the B+ (Good) Weiss Investment Rating for BlackRock FL Municipal Income Trust. The fund currently has a performance rating of B (Good) based on an annualized return of 7.72% over the last three years and a total return of 5.81% year to date 2005. Factored into the performance evaluation is an expense ratio of 0.91% (low).

The fund's risk rating is currently B- (Good). It carries a beta of 2.05, meaning it is expected to move 20.5% for every 10% move in the market. Volatility, as measured by both the semi-deviation and a drawdown factor, is considered low. As of June 30, 2005, BlackRock FL Municipal Income Trust traded at a discount of 2.80% below its net asset value, which is worse than its one-year historical average discount of 6.57%.

Kevin M. Klingert has been running the fund for 4 years and currently receives a manager quality ranking of 33 (0=worst, 99=best). If you desire only a moderate level of risk and strong performance, then this fund is an excellent option.

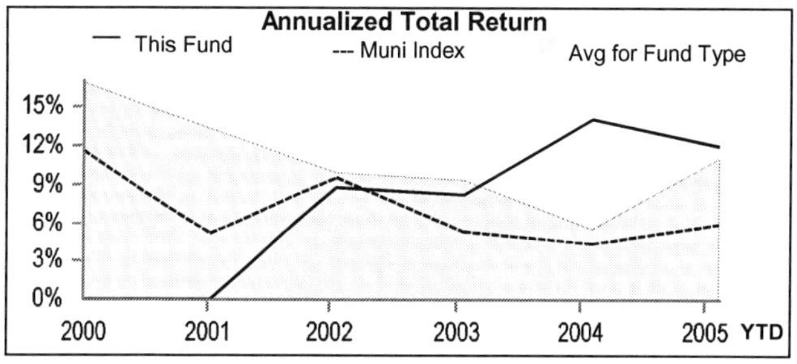

Blackrock High Income Shares (HIS) C- Fair

Fund Family: BlackRock Advisors, Inc.
Fund Type: Corporate - High Yield
Inception Date: August 10, 1988

Data Date	Weiss Investment Rating	Net Assets ($Mil)	Price	Performance Rating/Pts	Total Return Y-T-D	Risk Rating/Pts
6-05	C-	155.30	2.84	C+ / 6.3	3.01%	C- / 3.4
2004	E+	147.66	2.90	D / 2.2	12.37%	D / 1.7
2003	D-	146.68	2.91	C- / 3.1	39.32%	D+ / 2.6

Major Rating Factors:
Middle of the road best describes Blackrock High Income Shares whose Weiss Investment Rating is currently a C- (Fair). The fund currently has a performance rating of C+ (Fair) based on an annualized return of 14.92% over the last three years and a total return of 3.01% year to date 2005. Factored into the performance evaluation is an expense ratio of 2.23% (high).

The fund's risk rating is currently C- (Fair). It carries a beta of 2.06, meaning it is expected to move 20.6% for every 10% move in the market. Volatility, as measured by both the semi-deviation and a drawdown factor, is considered average. As of June 30, 2005, Blackrock High Income Shares traded at a premium of 5.97% above its net asset value, which is worse than its one-year historical average premium of .81%.

Frank Whitley has been running the fund for 2 years and currently receives a manager quality ranking of 1 (0=worst, 99=best). If you desire an average level of risk, then this fund may be an option.

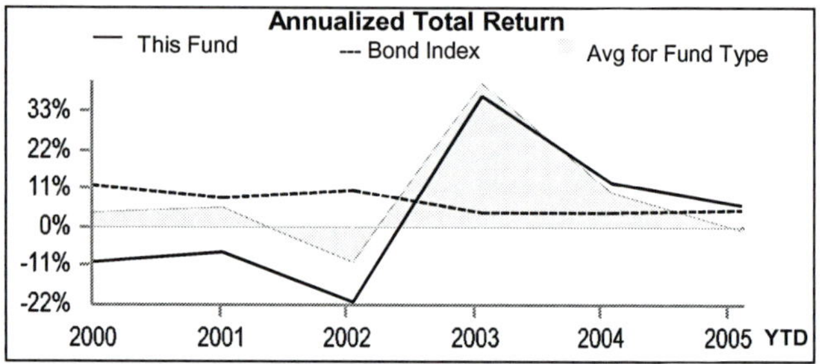

BlackRock High Yield Trust (BHY) D- Weak

Fund Family: BlackRock Advisors, Inc.
Fund Type: Corporate - High Yield
Inception Date: December 18, 1998

Data Date	Weiss Investment Rating	Net Assets ($Mil)	Price	Performance Rating/Pts	Total Return Y-T-D	Risk Rating/Pts
6-05	D-	48.12	9.40	D+ / 2.9	4.08%	C / 4.3
2004	D-	49.72	9.45	D+ / 2.9	-2.40%	C- / 4.1
2003	D	44.44	10.56	C- / 4.1	24.55%	C- / 3.6

Major Rating Factors:
Disappointing performance is the major factor driving the D- (Weak) Weiss Investment Rating for BlackRock High Yield Trust. The fund currently has a performance rating of D+ (Weak) based on an annualized return of 10.13% over the last three years and a total return of 4.08% year to date 2005. Factored into the performance evaluation is an expense ratio of 3.16% (high).

The fund's risk rating is currently C (Fair). It carries a beta of 0.95, meaning that its performance tracks fairly well with that of the overall stock market. Volatility, as measured by both the semi-deviation and a drawdown factor, is considered average. As of June 30, 2005, BlackRock High Yield Trust traded at a premium of 22.88% above its net asset value, which is worse than its one-year historical average premium of 20.89%.

Robert S. Kapito/Schaney has been running the fund for 7 years and currently receives a manager quality ranking of 37 (0=worst, 99=best). This fund offers an average level of risk but investors looking for strong performance will be frustrated.

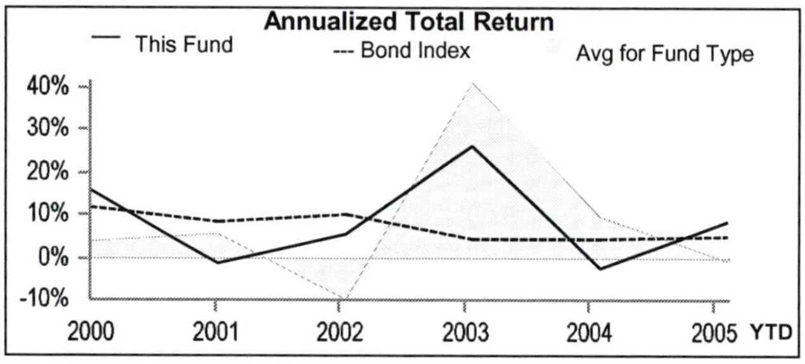

BlackRock Income Opportunity Trust (BNA) C+ Fair

Fund Family: BlackRock Advisors, Inc.
Fund Type: Global
Inception Date: December 20, 1991

Data Date	Weiss Investment Rating	Net Assets ($Mil)	Price	Performance Rating/Pts	Total Return Y-T-D	Risk Rating/Pts
6-05	C+	408.45	11.25	C / 4.6	7.01%	B- / 7.6
2004	B-	410.88	10.85	C+ / 5.7	8.44%	B- / 7.9
2003	C-	410.98	11.05	C- / 3.4	11.86%	B- / 7.8

Major Rating Factors:
Middle of the road best describes BlackRock Income Opportunity Trust whose Weiss Investment Rating is currently a C+ (Fair). The fund currently has a performance rating of C (Fair) based on an annualized return of 10.80% over the last three years and a total return of 7.01% year to date 2005. Factored into the performance evaluation is an expense ratio of 1.43% (average).

The fund's risk rating is currently B- (Good). It carries a beta of 0.62, meaning the fund's expected move will be 6.2% for every 10% move in the market. Volatility, as measured by both the semi-deviation and a drawdown factor, is considered low. As of June 30, 2005, BlackRock Income Opportunity Trust traded at a discount of 7.02% below its net asset value, which is worse than its one-year historical average discount of 7.95%.

This fund has been team managed for 14 years and currently receives a manager quality ranking of 78 (0=worst, 99=best). If you desire an average level of risk, then this fund may be an option.

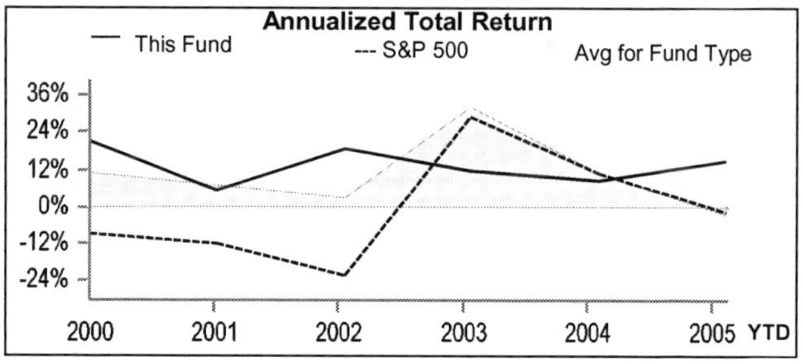

BlackRock Income Trust (BKT) E+ Very Weak

Fund Family: BlackRock Advisors, Inc.
Fund Type: Mortgage
Inception Date: July 22, 1988

Major Rating Factors:
Very poor performance is the major factor driving the E+ (Very Weak) Weiss Investment Rating for BlackRock Income Trust. The fund currently has a performance rating of E (Very Weak) based on an annualized return of 4.95% over the last three years and a total return of -3.32% year to date 2005. Factored into the performance evaluation is an expense ratio of 2.05% (high).

The fund's risk rating is currently C+ (Fair). It carries a beta of 4.39, meaning it is expected to move 43.9% for every 10% move in the market. Volatility, as measured by both the semi-deviation and a drawdown factor, is considered low. As of June 30, 2005, BlackRock Income Trust traded at a premium of .45% above its net asset value, which is better than its one-year historical average premium of 6.47%.

Keith T. Anderson has been running the fund for 17 years and currently receives a manager quality ranking of 2 (0=worst, 99=best). This fund offers only a moderate level of risk but investors looking for strong performance are still waiting.

Data Date	Weiss Investment Rating	Net Assets ($Mil)	Price	Performance Rating/Pts	Total Return Y-T-D	Risk Rating/Pts
6-05	E+	431.56	6.70	E / 0.4	-3.32%	C+ / 5.8
2004	D+	444.52	7.19	C- / 3.5	4.67%	C+ / 6.2
2003	C	457.31	7.55	C- / 4.0	4.36%	B- / 7.6

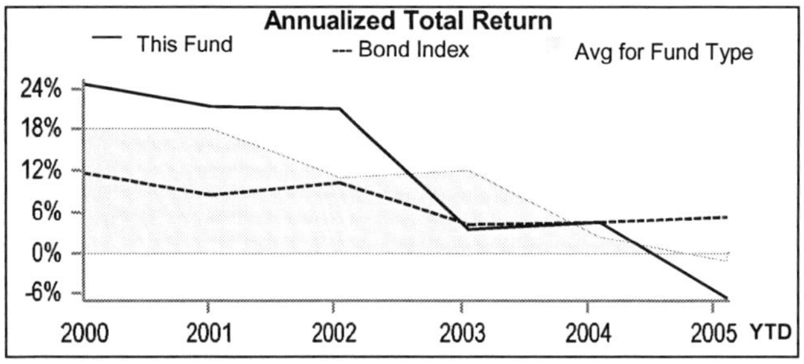

BlackRock Insured Muni 2008 Tm Tr (BRM) C Fair

Fund Family: BlackRock Advisors, Inc.
Fund Type: Municipal - National
Inception Date: September 18, 1992

Major Rating Factors:
Disappointing performance is the major factor driving the C (Fair) Weiss Investment Rating for BlackRock Insured Muni 2008 Tm Tr. The fund currently has a performance rating of D+ (Weak) based on an annualized return of 5.54% over the last three years and a total return of 1.18% year to date 2005. Factored into the performance evaluation is an expense ratio of 0.99% (low).

The fund's risk rating is currently B (Good). It carries a beta of 1.39, meaning it is expected to move 13.9% for every 10% move in the market. Volatility, as measured by both the semi-deviation and a drawdown factor, is considered low. As of June 30, 2005, BlackRock Insured Muni 2008 Tm Tr traded at a discount of 1.47% below its net asset value, which is worse than its one-year historical average discount of 2.56%.

Kevin Klingert has been running the fund for 13 years and currently receives a manager quality ranking of 44 (0=worst, 99=best). This fund offers only a moderate level of risk but investors looking for strong performance are still waiting.

Data Date	Weiss Investment Rating	Net Assets ($Mil)	Price	Performance Rating/Pts	Total Return Y-T-D	Risk Rating/Pts
6-05	C	455.66	16.10	D+ / 2.3	1.18%	B / 8.5
2004	C+	453.69	16.31	C- / 4.1	-0.07%	B / 8.8
2003	B-	488.88	17.15	C+ / 5.6	10.57%	B / 8.2

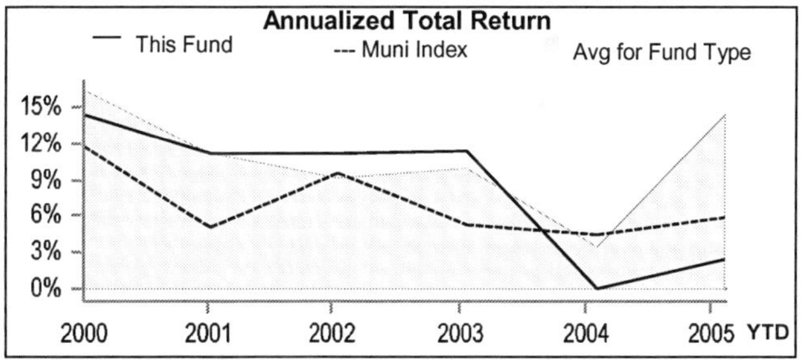

BlackRock Insured Muni Tm Tr (BMT) C+ Fair

Fund Family: BlackRock Advisors, Inc.
Fund Type: Municipal - National
Inception Date: February 28, 1992

Major Rating Factors:
Middle of the road best describes BlackRock Insured Muni Tm Tr whose Weiss Investment Rating is currently a C+ (Fair). The fund currently has a performance rating of C (Fair) based on an annualized return of 7.45% over the last three years and a total return of 1.49% year to date 2005. Factored into the performance evaluation is an expense ratio of 1.02% (low).

The fund's risk rating is currently B (Good). It carries a beta of 1.57, meaning it is expected to move 15.7% for every 10% move in the market. Volatility, as measured by both the semi-deviation and a drawdown factor, is considered low. As of June 30, 2005, BlackRock Insured Muni Tm Tr traded at a premium of 2.67% above its net asset value, which is worse than its one-year historical average premium of 1.36%.

Kevin Klingert has been running the fund for 13 years and currently receives a manager quality ranking of 55 (0=worst, 99=best). If you desire an average level of risk, then this fund may be an option.

Data Date	Weiss Investment Rating	Net Assets ($Mil)	Price	Performance Rating/Pts	Total Return Y-T-D	Risk Rating/Pts
6-05	C+	286.13	11.17	C / 4.3	1.49%	B / 8.1
2004	B	281.32	11.30	C+ / 6.1	7.96%	B / 8.1
2003	C	300.30	11.15	C- / 3.8	8.16%	B / 8.3

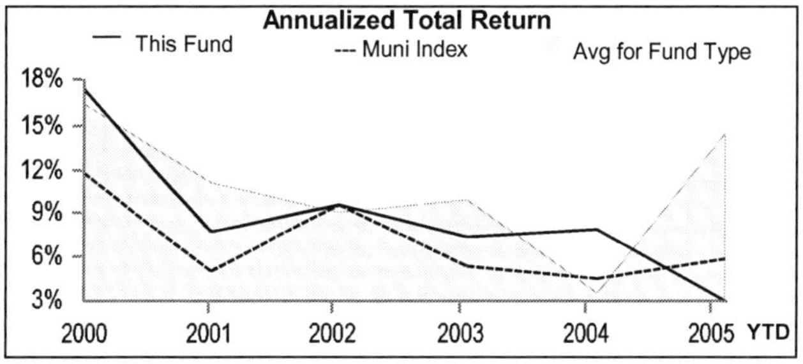

BlackRock Investment Qual Muni Tr (BKN) A+ Excellent

Fund Family: BlackRock Advisors, Inc.
Fund Type: Municipal - National
Inception Date: February 19, 1993

Data Date	Weiss Investment Rating	Net Assets ($Mil)	Price	Perfor-mance Rating/Pts	Total Return Y-T-D	Risk Rating/Pts
6-05	A+	264.82	16.61	A+ / 9.6	15.70%	C+ / 6.5
2004	A-	257.44	14.78	B- / 7.4	8.03%	B- / 7.7
2003	B	255.32	14.52	C+ / 6.0	12.02%	B / 8.4

Major Rating Factors:

Exceptional performance is the major factor driving the A+ (Excellent) Weiss Investment Rating for BlackRock Investment Qual Muni Tr. The fund currently has a performance rating of A+ (Excellent) based on an annualized return of 13.47% over the last three years and a total return of 15.70% year to date 2005. Factored into the performance evaluation is an expense ratio of 1.06% (low).

The fund's risk rating is currently C+ (Fair). It carries a beta of 2.05, meaning it is expected to move 20.5% for every 10% move in the market. Volatility, as measured by both the semi-deviation and a drawdown factor, is considered low. As of June 30, 2005, BlackRock Investment Qual Muni Tr traded at a premium of 4.07% above its net asset value, which is worse than its one-year historical average discount of 3.77%.

Kevin Klingert has been running the fund for 12 years and currently receives a manager quality ranking of 76 (0=worst, 99=best). If you desire only a moderate level of risk and strong performance, then this fund is an excellent option.

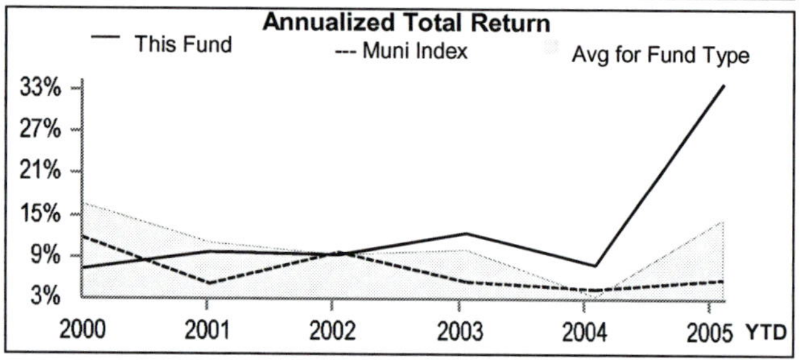

BlackRock MD Muni Bond Trust (BZM) B Good

Fund Family: BlackRock Advisors, Inc.
Fund Type: Municipal - Single State
Inception Date: April 25, 2002

Data Date	Weiss Investment Rating	Net Assets ($Mil)	Price	Perfor-mance Rating/Pts	Total Return Y-T-D	Risk Rating/Pts
6-05	B	31.94	16.69	B+ / 8.7	8.03%	C / 5.1

Major Rating Factors:

Strong performance is the major factor driving the B (Good) Weiss Investment Rating for BlackRock MD Muni Bond Trust. The fund currently has a performance rating of B+ (Good) based on an annualized return of 9.81% over the last three years and a total return of 8.03% year to date 2005. Factored into the performance evaluation is an expense ratio of 1.14% (low).

The fund's risk rating is currently C (Fair). It carries a beta of 1.35, meaning it is expected to move 13.5% for every 10% move in the market. Volatility, as measured by both the semi-deviation and a drawdown factor, is considered average. As of June 30, 2005, BlackRock MD Muni Bond Trust traded at a premium of 4.31% above its net asset value, which is worse than its one-year historical average discount of 2.24%.

Kevin M. Klingert has been running the fund for 3 years and currently receives a manager quality ranking of 71 (0=worst, 99=best). If you desire an average level of risk and strong performance, then this fund is a good option.

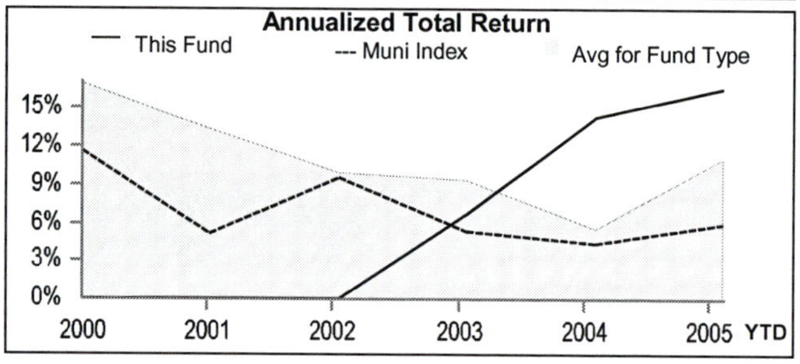

BlackRock Muni Target Tm Tr (BMN) C- Fair

Fund Family: BlackRock Advisors, Inc.
Fund Type: Municipal - National
Inception Date: September 20, 1991

Data Date	Weiss Investment Rating	Net Assets ($Mil)	Price	Perfor-mance Rating/Pts	Total Return Y-T-D	Risk Rating/Pts
6-05	C-	479.04	10.18	E / 0.5	-0.67%	B+ / 9.0
2004	C	481.56	10.49	D+ / 2.4	0.44%	B+ / 9.0
2003	C+	509.65	10.95	C- / 4.1	5.02%	B / 8.6

Major Rating Factors:

Very poor performance is the major factor driving the C- (Fair) Weiss Investment Rating for BlackRock Muni Target Tm Tr. The fund currently has a performance rating of E (Very Weak) based on an annualized return of 3.38% over the last three years and a total return of -0.67% year to date 2005. Factored into the performance evaluation is an expense ratio of 0.96% (low).

The fund's risk rating is currently B+ (Good). It carries a beta of 0.99, meaning that its performance tracks fairly well with that of the overall stock market. Volatility, as measured by both the semi-deviation and a drawdown factor, is considered very low. As of June 30, 2005, BlackRock Muni Target Tm Tr traded at a discount of 1.26% below its net asset value, which is better than its one-year historical average discount of .67%.

Kevin Klingert has been running the fund for 14 years and currently receives a manager quality ranking of 40 (0=worst, 99=best). This fund offers only a moderate level of risk but investors looking for strong performance are still waiting.

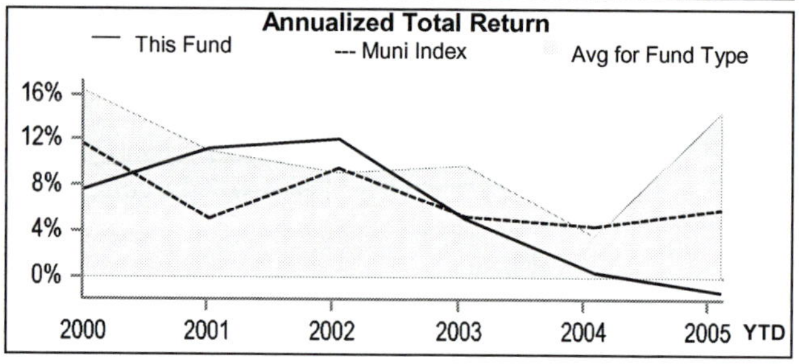

BlackRock Municipal 2018 Income Tr (BPK) A+ Excellent

Fund Family: BlackRock Advisors, Inc.
Fund Type: Municipal - National
Inception Date: October 26, 2001

Data Date	Weiss Investment Rating	Net Assets ($Mil)	Price	Perfor-mance Rating/Pts	Total Return Y-T-D	Risk Rating/Pts
6-05	A+	251.56	15.70	B / 8.0	6.24%	B- / 7.9
2004	A+	239.78	15.16	B- / 7.0	11.26%	B / 8.5

Major Rating Factors:
Strong performance is the major factor driving the A+ (Excellent) Weiss Investment Rating for BlackRock Municipal 2018 Income Tr. The fund currently has a performance rating of B (Good) based on an annualized return of 10.98% over the last three years and a total return of 6.24% year to date 2005. Factored into the performance evaluation is an expense ratio of 0.91% (low).

The fund's risk rating is currently B- (Good). It carries a beta of 1.70, meaning it is expected to move 17.0% for every 10% move in the market. Volatility, as measured by both the semi-deviation and a drawdown factor, is considered low. As of June 30, 2005, BlackRock Municipal 2018 Income Tr traded at a discount of 1.32% below its net asset value, which is worse than its one-year historical average discount of 4.38%.

Kevin Klingert has been running the fund for 4 years and currently receives a manager quality ranking of 74 (0=worst, 99=best). If you desire only a moderate level of risk and strong performance, then this fund is an excellent option.

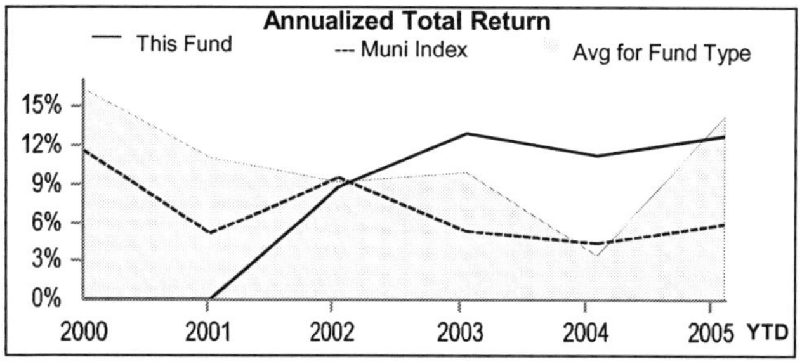

BlackRock Municipal Bond Trust (BBK) A+ Excellent

Fund Family: BlackRock Advisors, Inc.
Fund Type: Municipal - National
Inception Date: April 25, 2002

Data Date	Weiss Investment Rating	Net Assets ($Mil)	Price	Perfor-mance Rating/Pts	Total Return Y-T-D	Risk Rating/Pts
6-05	A+	160.20	16.09	A / 9.5	11.76%	C+ / 6.5

Major Rating Factors:
Exceptional performance is the major factor driving the A+ (Excellent) Weiss Investment Rating for BlackRock Municipal Bond Trust. The fund currently has a performance rating of A (Excellent) based on an annualized return of 12.44% over the last three years and a total return of 11.76% year to date 2005. Factored into the performance evaluation is an expense ratio of 0.88% (low).

The fund's risk rating is currently C+ (Fair). It carries a beta of 2.12, meaning it is expected to move 21.2% for every 10% move in the market. Volatility, as measured by both the semi-deviation and a drawdown factor, is considered low. As of June 30, 2005, BlackRock Municipal Bond Trust traded at a discount of .12% below its net asset value, which is worse than its one-year historical average discount of 3.63%.

Kevin M. Klingert has been running the fund for 3 years and currently receives a manager quality ranking of 72 (0=worst, 99=best). If you desire only a moderate level of risk and strong performance, then this fund is an excellent option.

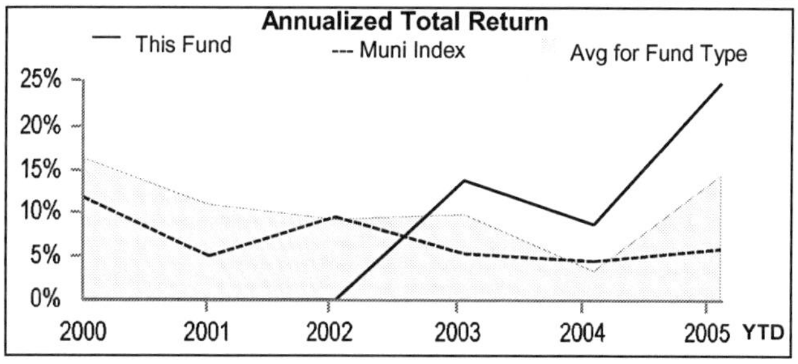

BlackRock Municipal Income Trust (BFK) A Excellent

Fund Family: BlackRock Advisors, Inc.
Fund Type: Municipal - National
Inception Date: July 27, 2001

Data Date	Weiss Investment Rating	Net Assets ($Mil)	Price	Perfor-mance Rating/Pts	Total Return Y-T-D	Risk Rating/Pts
6-05	A	647.35	15.15	A- / 9.2	9.59%	C+ / 6.4
2004	B-	614.32	14.29	C+ / 6.9	11.83%	B- / 7.3

Major Rating Factors:
Exceptional performance is the major factor driving the A (Excellent) Weiss Investment Rating for BlackRock Municipal Income Trust. The fund currently has a performance rating of A- (Excellent) based on an annualized return of 11.60% over the last three years and a total return of 9.59% year to date 2005. Factored into the performance evaluation is an expense ratio of 0.82% (very low).

The fund's risk rating is currently C+ (Fair). It carries a beta of 2.00, meaning it is expected to move 20.0% for every 10% move in the market. Volatility, as measured by both the semi-deviation and a drawdown factor, is considered low. As of June 30, 2005, BlackRock Municipal Income Trust traded at a premium of 1.07% above its net asset value, which is worse than its one-year historical average discount of 1.81%.

Kevin M. Klingert has been running the fund for 4 years and currently receives a manager quality ranking of 72 (0=worst, 99=best). If you desire only a moderate level of risk and strong performance, then this fund is an excellent option.

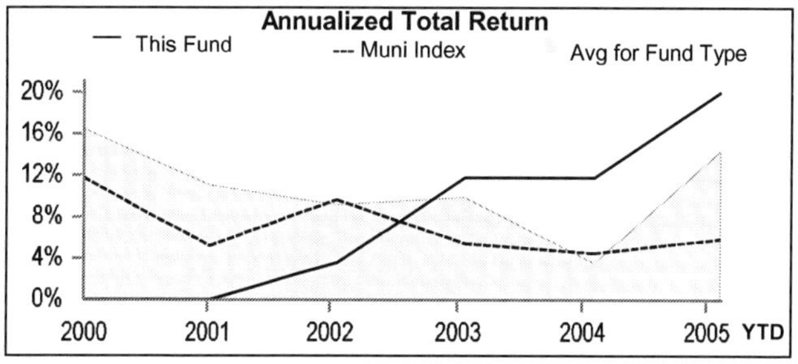

BlackRock NJ Inv Qual Muni Tr (RNJ) B+ Good

Fund Family: BlackRock Advisors, Inc.
Fund Type: Municipal - Single State
Inception Date: May 28, 1993

Major Rating Factors:

Strong performance is the major factor driving the B+ (Good) Weiss Investment Rating for BlackRock NJ Inv Qual Muni Tr. The fund currently has a performance rating of B+ (Good) based on an annualized return of 8.71% over the last three years and a total return of 9.19% year to date 2005. Factored into the performance evaluation is an expense ratio of 1.33% (average).

The fund's risk rating is currently C+ (Fair). It carries a beta of 2.01, meaning it is expected to move 20.1% for every 10% move in the market. Volatility, as measured by both the semi-deviation and a drawdown factor, is considered low. As of June 30, 2005, BlackRock NJ Inv Qual Muni Tr traded at a premium of 4.92% above its net asset value, which is worse than its one-year historical average discount of 1.54%.

Kevin Klingert has been running the fund for 12 years and currently receives a manager quality ranking of 40 (0=worst, 99=best). If you desire only a moderate level of risk and strong performance, then this fund is an excellent option.

Data Date	Weiss Investment Rating	Net Assets ($Mil)	Price	Performance Rating/Pts	Total Return Y-T-D	Risk Rating/Pts
6-05	B+	14.89	15.56	B+ / 8.6	9.19%	C+ / 5.7
2004	C+	14.91	14.65	C+ / 5.7	5.90%	B- / 7.0

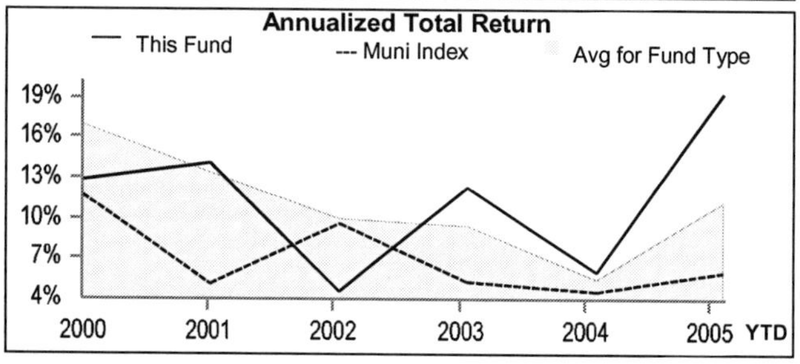

BlackRock NJ Muni Bond Trust (BLJ) A Excellent

Fund Family: BlackRock Advisors, Inc.
Fund Type: Municipal - Single State
Inception Date: April 25, 2002

Major Rating Factors:

Strong performance is the major factor driving the A (Excellent) Weiss Investment Rating for BlackRock NJ Muni Bond Trust. The fund currently has a performance rating of B+ (Good) based on an annualized return of 8.99% over the last three years and a total return of 7.10% year to date 2005. Factored into the performance evaluation is an expense ratio of 1.10% (low).

The fund's risk rating is currently C+ (Fair). It carries a beta of 1.95, meaning it is expected to move 19.5% for every 10% move in the market. Volatility, as measured by both the semi-deviation and a drawdown factor, is considered low. As of June 30, 2005, BlackRock NJ Muni Bond Trust traded at a discount of 3.05% below its net asset value, which is worse than its one-year historical average discount of 4.85%.

Kevin M. Klingert has been running the fund for 3 years and currently receives a manager quality ranking of 57 (0=worst, 99=best). If you desire only a moderate level of risk and strong performance, then this fund is an excellent option.

Data Date	Weiss Investment Rating	Net Assets ($Mil)	Price	Performance Rating/Pts	Total Return Y-T-D	Risk Rating/Pts
6-05	A	35.81	15.55	B+ / 8.7	7.10%	C+ / 6.5

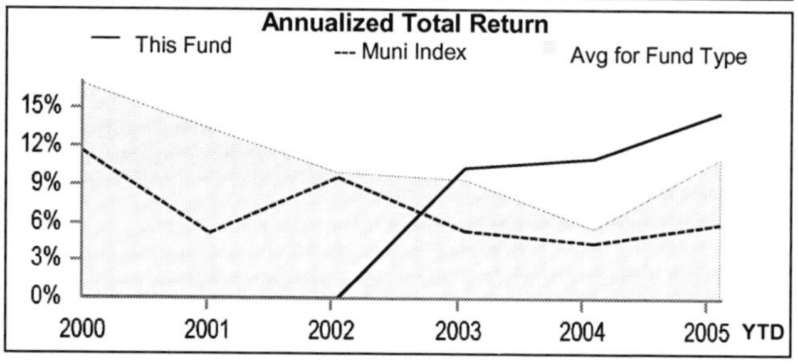

BlackRock NJ Municipal Income Trust (BNJ) A Excellent

Fund Family: BlackRock Advisors, Inc.
Fund Type: Municipal - Single State
Inception Date: July 27, 2001

Major Rating Factors:

Strong performance is the major factor driving the A (Excellent) Weiss Investment Rating for BlackRock NJ Municipal Income Trust. The fund currently has a performance rating of B (Good) based on an annualized return of 8.85% over the last three years and a total return of 10.32% year to date 2005. Factored into the performance evaluation is an expense ratio of 0.89% (low).

The fund's risk rating is currently B- (Good). It carries a beta of 1.84, meaning it is expected to move 18.4% for every 10% move in the market. Volatility, as measured by both the semi-deviation and a drawdown factor, is considered low. As of June 30, 2005, BlackRock NJ Municipal Income Trust traded at a discount of 4.29% below its net asset value, which is worse than its one-year historical average discount of 6.65%.

Kevin M. Klingert has been running the fund for 4 years and currently receives a manager quality ranking of 60 (0=worst, 99=best). If you desire only a moderate level of risk and strong performance, then this fund is an excellent option.

Data Date	Weiss Investment Rating	Net Assets ($Mil)	Price	Performance Rating/Pts	Total Return Y-T-D	Risk Rating/Pts
6-05	A	118.03	15.39	B / 8.1	10.32%	B- / 7.1
2004	B-	110.20	14.38	C+ / 5.6	8.00%	B- / 7.9

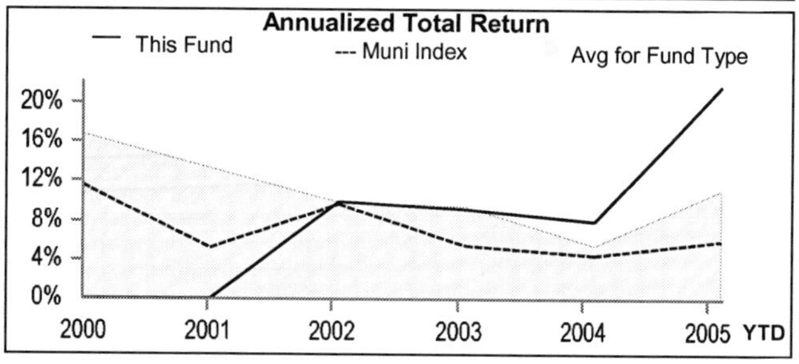

BlackRock NY Insured Muni 2008 Term (BLN) C- Fair

Fund Family: BlackRock Advisors, Inc.
Fund Type: Municipal - Single State
Inception Date: September 25, 1992

Data Date	Weiss Investment Rating	Net Assets ($Mil)	Price	Performance Rating/Pts	Total Return Y-T-D	Risk Rating/Pts
6-05	C-	186.42	15.83	D / 2.0	0.75%	B / 8.5
2004	C+	184.98	16.09	C- / 3.4	0.06%	B+ / 9.0
2003	C+	196.08	16.96	C / 5.0	9.71%	B / 8.1

Major Rating Factors:
Disappointing performance is the major factor driving the C- (Fair) Weiss Investment Rating for BlackRock NY Insured Muni 2008 Term. The fund currently has a performance rating of D (Weak) based on an annualized return of 5.32% over the last three years and a total return of 0.75% year to date 2005. Factored into the performance evaluation is an expense ratio of 1.03% (low).

The fund's risk rating is currently B (Good). It carries a beta of 1.35, meaning it is expected to move 13.5% for every 10% move in the market. Volatility, as measured by both the semi-deviation and a drawdown factor, is considered low. As of June 30, 2005, BlackRock NY Insured Muni 2008 Term traded at a discount of 2.22% below its net asset value, which is worse than its one-year historical average discount of 3.02%.

This fund has been team managed for 13 years and currently receives a manager quality ranking of 44 (0=worst, 99=best). This fund offers only a moderate level of risk but investors looking for strong performance are still waiting.

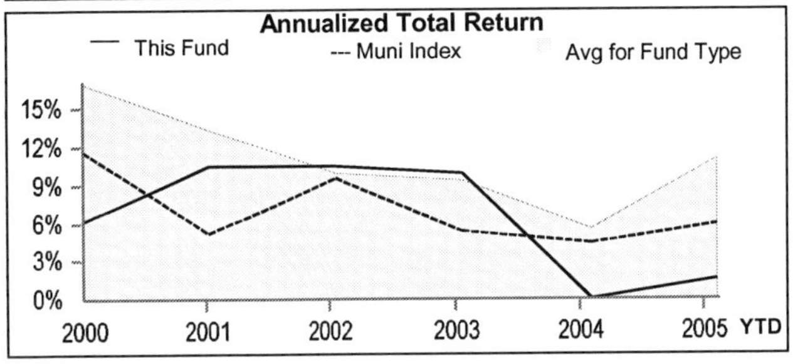

BlackRock NY Inv Qual Muni Tr (RNY) B- Good

Fund Family: BlackRock Advisors, Inc.
Fund Type: Municipal - Single State
Inception Date: May 28, 1993

Data Date	Weiss Investment Rating	Net Assets ($Mil)	Price	Performance Rating/Pts	Total Return Y-T-D	Risk Rating/Pts
6-05	B-	20.07	14.79	C+ / 6.2	8.52%	B- / 7.1
2004	C+	19.81	14.05	C- / 3.7	4.61%	B / 8.5
2003	C+	20.05	14.35	C- / 3.9	6.35%	B / 8.7

Major Rating Factors:
BlackRock NY Inv Qual Muni Tr receives a Weiss Investment Rating of B- (Good). The fund currently has a performance rating of C+ (Fair) based on an annualized return of 6.58% over the last three years and a total return of 8.52% year to date 2005. Factored into the performance evaluation is an expense ratio of 1.20% (average).

The fund's risk rating is currently B- (Good). It carries a beta of 1.32, meaning it is expected to move 13.2% for every 10% move in the market. Volatility, as measured by both the semi-deviation and a drawdown factor, is considered low. As of June 30, 2005, BlackRock NY Inv Qual Muni Tr traded at a discount of 4.21% below its net asset value, which is worse than its one-year historical average discount of 7.45%.

Kevin Klingert has been running the fund for 12 years and currently receives a manager quality ranking of 58 (0=worst, 99=best). If you desire an average level of risk, then this fund may be an option.

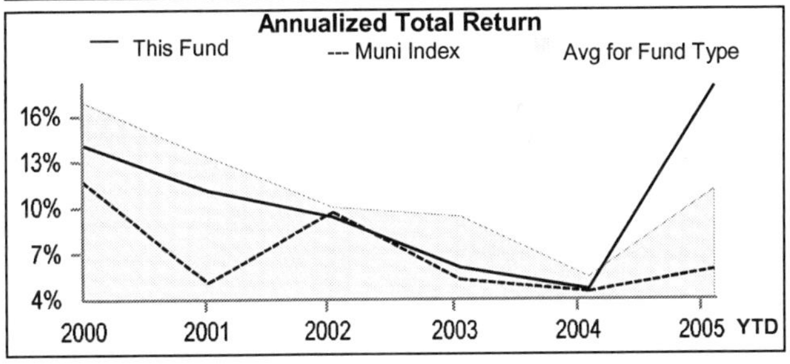

BlackRock NY Muni 2018 Income Trust (BLH) B Good

Fund Family: BlackRock Advisors, Inc.
Fund Type: Municipal - Single State
Inception Date: October 26, 2001

Data Date	Weiss Investment Rating	Net Assets ($Mil)	Price	Performance Rating/Pts	Total Return Y-T-D	Risk Rating/Pts
6-05	B	57.30	15.29	C+ / 6.5	5.71%	B / 8.4
2004	B+	54.39	14.82	C+ / 5.6	5.98%	B / 8.8

Major Rating Factors:
BlackRock NY Muni 2018 Income Trust receives a Weiss Investment Rating of B (Good). The fund currently has a performance rating of C+ (Fair) based on an annualized return of 9.75% over the last three years and a total return of 5.71% year to date 2005. Factored into the performance evaluation is an expense ratio of 1.11% (low).

The fund's risk rating is currently B (Good). It carries a beta of 1.51, meaning it is expected to move 15.1% for every 10% move in the market. Volatility, as measured by both the semi-deviation and a drawdown factor, is considered low. As of June 30, 2005, BlackRock NY Muni 2018 Income Trust traded at a discount of 5.91% below its net asset value, which is better than its one-year historical average discount of 5.29%.

Kevin Klingert has been running the fund for 4 years and currently receives a manager quality ranking of 72 (0=worst, 99=best). If you desire an average level of risk, then this fund may be an option.

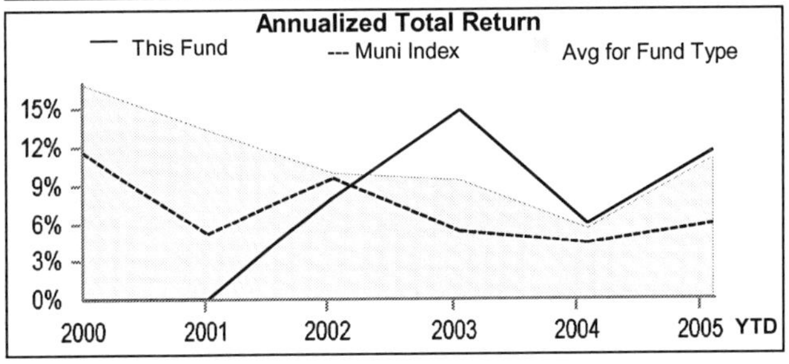

BlackRock NY Muni Bond Trust (BQH) A+ Excellent

Fund Family: BlackRock Advisors, Inc.
Fund Type: Municipal - Single State
Inception Date: April 25, 2002

Data Date	Weiss Investment Rating	Net Assets ($Mil)	Price	Perfor-mance Rating/Pts	Total Return Y-T-D	Risk Rating/Pts
6-05	A+	42.67	15.21	B+ / 8.9	11.04%	B- / 7.0

Major Rating Factors:
Strong performance is the major factor driving the A+ (Excellent) Weiss Investment Rating for BlackRock NY Muni Bond Trust. The fund currently has a performance rating of B+ (Good) based on an annualized return of 10.54% over the last three years and a total return of 11.04% year to date 2005. Factored into the performance evaluation is an expense ratio of 1.09% (low).

The fund's risk rating is currently B- (Good). It carries a beta of 1.86, meaning it is expected to move 18.6% for every 10% move in the market. Volatility, as measured by both the semi-deviation and a drawdown factor, is considered low. As of June 30, 2005, BlackRock NY Muni Bond Trust traded at a discount of 5.06% below its net asset value, which is worse than its one-year historical average discount of 8.31%.

Kevin M. Klingert has been running the fund for 3 years and currently receives a manager quality ranking of 67 (0=worst, 99=best). If you desire only a moderate level of risk and strong performance, then this fund is an excellent option.

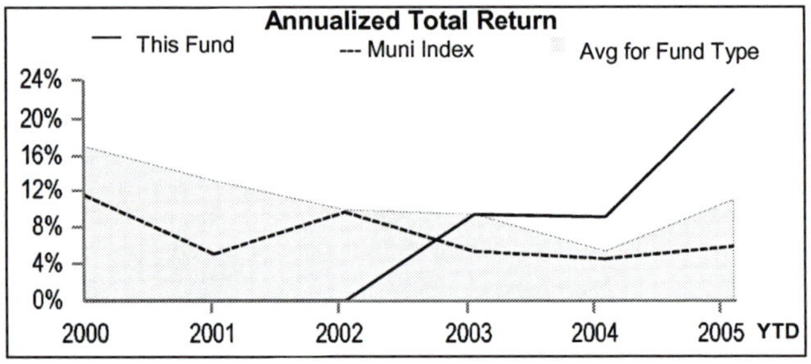

BlackRock NY Municipal Income Trust (BNY) A- Excellent

Fund Family: BlackRock Advisors, Inc.
Fund Type: Municipal - Single State
Inception Date: July 27, 2001

Data Date	Weiss Investment Rating	Net Assets ($Mil)	Price	Perfor-mance Rating/Pts	Total Return Y-T-D	Risk Rating/Pts
6-05	A-	194.29	15.13	B+ / 8.4	12.41%	C+ / 6.5
2004	C	185.86	13.88	C / 4.4	7.45%	B- / 7.5

Major Rating Factors:
Strong performance is the major factor driving the A- (Excellent) Weiss Investment Rating for BlackRock NY Municipal Income Trust. The fund currently has a performance rating of B+ (Good) based on an annualized return of 9.68% over the last three years and a total return of 12.41% year to date 2005. Factored into the performance evaluation is an expense ratio of 0.87% (low).

The fund's risk rating is currently C+ (Fair). It carries a beta of 2.06, meaning it is expected to move 20.6% for every 10% move in the market. Volatility, as measured by both the semi-deviation and a drawdown factor, is considered low. As of June 30, 2005, BlackRock NY Municipal Income Trust traded at a discount of 3.51% below its net asset value, which is worse than its one-year historical average discount of 7.26%.

Kevin M. Klingert has been running the fund for 4 years and currently receives a manager quality ranking of 53 (0=worst, 99=best). If you desire only a moderate level of risk and strong performance, then this fund is an excellent option.

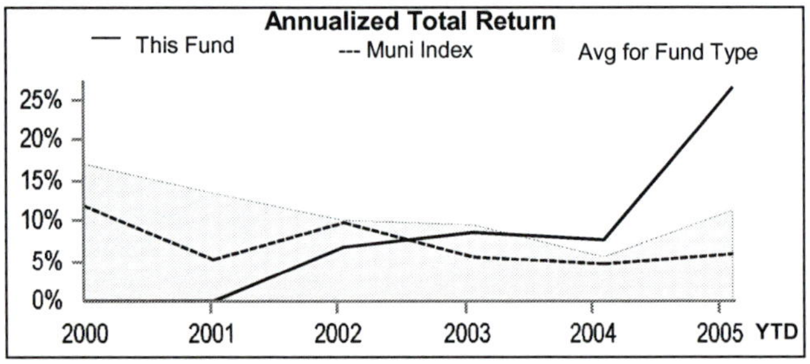

BlackRock PA Strategic Muni Tr (BPS) C+ Fair

Fund Family: BlackRock Advisors, Inc.
Fund Type: Municipal - Single State
Inception Date: August 27, 1999

Data Date	Weiss Investment Rating	Net Assets ($Mil)	Price	Perfor-mance Rating/Pts	Total Return Y-T-D	Risk Rating/Pts
6-05	C+	31.86	15.36	C+ / 6.8	0.73%	C+ / 6.7
2004	A-	31.31	15.70	B / 7.6	10.17%	B- / 7.5
2003	B	32.82	15.05	C+ / 6.0	11.45%	B / 8.4

Major Rating Factors:
Middle of the road best describes BlackRock PA Strategic Muni Tr whose Weiss Investment Rating is currently a C+ (Fair). The fund currently has a performance rating of C+ (Fair) based on an annualized return of 9.89% over the last three years and a total return of 0.73% year to date 2005. Factored into the performance evaluation is an expense ratio of 1.03% (low).

The fund's risk rating is currently C+ (Fair). It carries a beta of 1.53, meaning it is expected to move 15.3% for every 10% move in the market. Volatility, as measured by both the semi-deviation and a drawdown factor, is considered low. As of June 30, 2005, BlackRock PA Strategic Muni Tr traded at a discount of .90% below its net asset value, which is worse than its one-year historical average discount of 4.16%.

Kevin M. Klingert has been running the fund for 6 years and currently receives a manager quality ranking of 70 (0=worst, 99=best). If you desire an average level of risk, then this fund may be an option.

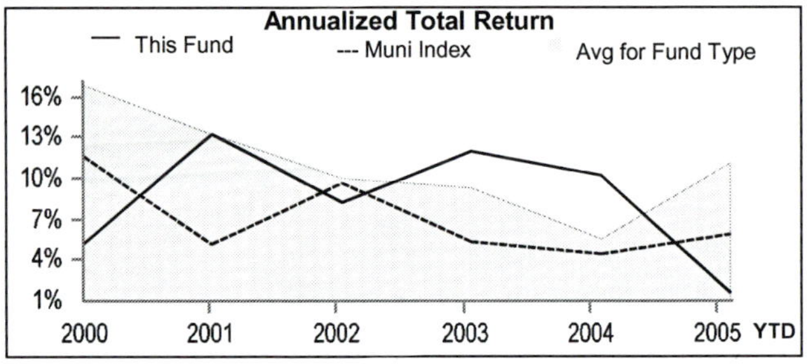

BlackRock Strategic Bond Trust (BHD) C- Fair

Fund Family: BlackRock Advisors, Inc.
Fund Type: Corporate - High Yield
Inception Date: February 27, 2002

Data Date	Weiss Investment Rating	Net Assets ($Mil)	Price	Perfor-mance Rating/Pts	Total Return Y-T-D	Risk Rating/Pts
6-05	C-	99.20	15.10	C / 4.9	-7.89%	C / 5.1

Major Rating Factors:
Middle of the road best describes BlackRock Strategic Bond Trust whose Weiss Investment Rating is currently a C- (Fair). The fund currently has a performance rating of C (Fair) based on an annualized return of 14.27% over the last three years and a total return of -7.89% year to date 2005. Factored into the performance evaluation is an expense ratio of 1.76% (above average).

The fund's risk rating is currently C (Fair). It carries a beta of 1.87, meaning it is expected to move 18.7% for every 10% move in the market. Volatility, as measured by both the semi-deviation and a drawdown factor, is considered average. As of June 30, 2005, BlackRock Strategic Bond Trust traded at a premium of 5.59% above its net asset value, which is better than its one-year historical average premium of 7.77%.

This fund has been team managed for 3 years and currently receives a manager quality ranking of 3 (0=worst, 99=best). If you desire an average level of risk, then this fund may be an option.

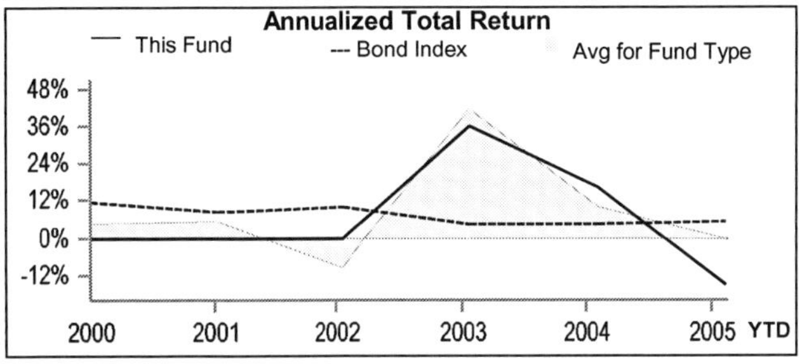

BlackRock Strategic Municipal Tr (BSD) A Excellent

Fund Family: BlackRock Advisors, Inc.
Fund Type: Municipal - National
Inception Date: August 27, 1999

Data Date	Weiss Investment Rating	Net Assets ($Mil)	Price	Perfor-mance Rating/Pts	Total Return Y-T-D	Risk Rating/Pts
6-05	A	113.69	16.40	A+ / 9.6	16.60%	C+ / 5.8
2004	B	107.93	14.52	C+ / 6.0	5.65%	B- / 7.7
2003	B-	114.40	14.62	C / 5.1	13.29%	B / 8.6

Major Rating Factors:
Exceptional performance is the major factor driving the A (Excellent) Weiss Investment Rating for BlackRock Strategic Municipal Tr. The fund currently has a performance rating of A+ (Excellent) based on an annualized return of 12.40% over the last three years and a total return of 16.60% year to date 2005. Factored into the performance evaluation is an expense ratio of 0.89% (low).

The fund's risk rating is currently C+ (Fair). It carries a beta of 2.32, meaning it is expected to move 23.2% for every 10% move in the market. Volatility, as measured by both the semi-deviation and a drawdown factor, is considered low. As of June 30, 2005, BlackRock Strategic Municipal Tr traded at a premium of 3.34% above its net asset value, which is worse than its one-year historical average discount of 6.42%.

Kevin M. Klingert has been running the fund for 6 years and currently receives a manager quality ranking of 61 (0=worst, 99=best). If you desire only a moderate level of risk and strong performance, then this fund is an excellent option.

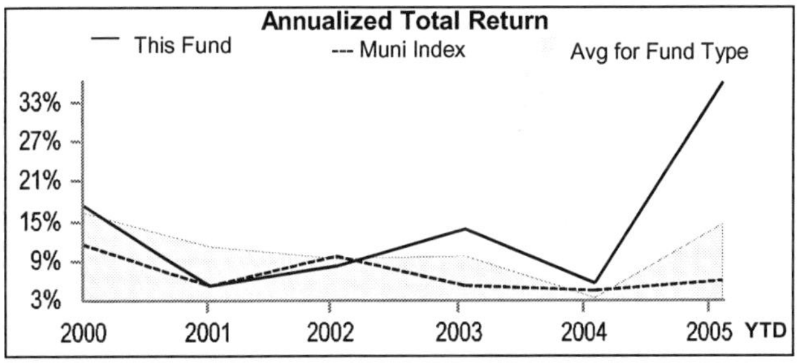

BlackRock VA Muni Bond Trust (BHV) A Excellent

Fund Family: BlackRock Advisors, Inc.
Fund Type: Municipal - Single State
Inception Date: April 25, 2002

Data Date	Weiss Investment Rating	Net Assets ($Mil)	Price	Perfor-mance Rating/Pts	Total Return Y-T-D	Risk Rating/Pts
6-05	A	24.52	17.27	A- / 9.2	12.30%	C+ / 6.4

Major Rating Factors:
Exceptional performance is the major factor driving the A (Excellent) Weiss Investment Rating for BlackRock VA Muni Bond Trust. The fund currently has a performance rating of A- (Excellent) based on an annualized return of 11.16% over the last three years and a total return of 12.30% year to date 2005. Factored into the performance evaluation is an expense ratio of 1.21% (average).

The fund's risk rating is currently C+ (Fair). It carries a beta of 1.13, meaning it is expected to move 11.3% for every 10% move in the market. Volatility, as measured by both the semi-deviation and a drawdown factor, is considered low. As of June 30, 2005, BlackRock VA Muni Bond Trust traded at a premium of 6.54% above its net asset value, which is worse than its one-year historical average premium of 1.21%.

Kevin M. Klingert has been running the fund for 3 years and currently receives a manager quality ranking of 79 (0=worst, 99=best). If you desire only a moderate level of risk and strong performance, then this fund is an excellent option.

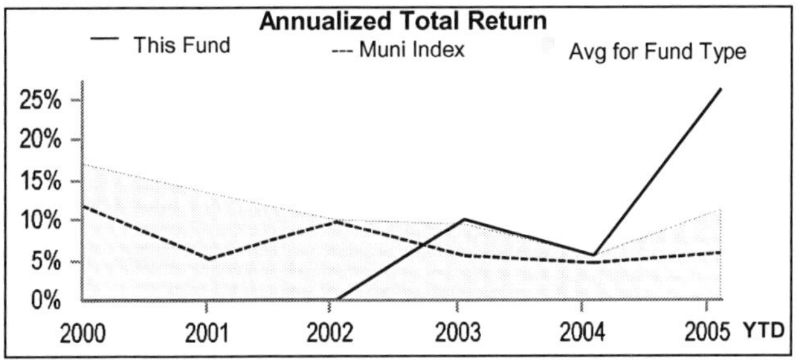

Blue Chip Value Fund (BLU) D- Weak

Fund Family: Denver Investment Advisors, LLC
Fund Type: Growth and Income
Inception Date: April 15, 1987

Major Rating Factors:
Disappointing performance is the major factor driving the D- (Weak) Weiss Investment Rating for Blue Chip Value Fund. The fund currently has a performance rating of D+ (Weak) based on an annualized return of 10.84% over the last three years and a total return of -4.34% year to date 2005. Factored into the performance evaluation is an expense ratio of 1.12% (low).

The fund's risk rating is currently C (Fair). It carries a beta of 1.21, meaning it is expected to move 12.1% for every 10% move in the market. Volatility, as measured by both the semi-deviation and a drawdown factor, is considered average. As of June 30, 2005, Blue Chip Value Fund traded at a premium of 10.44% above its net asset value, which is better than its one-year historical average premium of 16.76%.

Mark M. Adelmann has been running the fund for 3 years and currently receives a manager quality ranking of 73 (0=worst, 99=best). This fund offers an average level of risk but investors looking for strong performance will be frustrated.

Data Date	Weiss Investment Rating	Net Assets ($Mil)	Price	Performance Rating/Pts	Total Return Y-T-D	Risk Rating/Pts
6-05	D-	156.90	6.24	D+ / 2.5	-4.34%	C / 4.7
2004	D	151.64	6.68	C / 4.7	19.20%	C- / 3.5
2003	D+	136.66	6.19	C- / 3.8	44.58%	C / 4.3

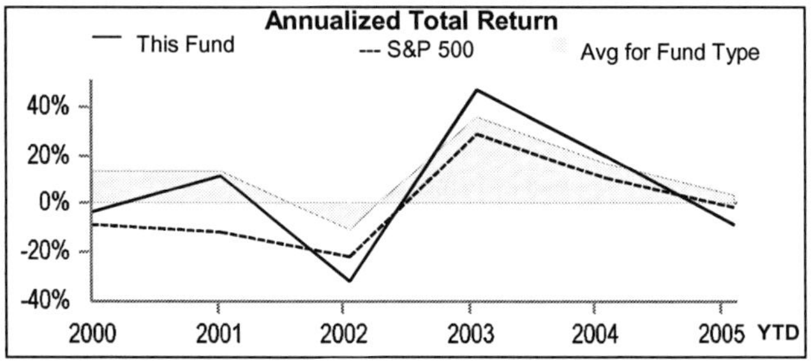

Boulder Growth&Income Fund (BIF) E+ Very Weak

Fund Family: Boulder Investment Advisers
Fund Type: Income
Inception Date: December 7, 1972

Major Rating Factors:
Very poor performance is the major factor driving the E+ (Very Weak) Weiss Investment Rating for Boulder Growth&Income Fund. The fund currently has a performance rating of E+ (Very Weak) based on an annualized return of 6.20% over the last three years and a total return of -6.88% year to date 2005. Factored into the performance evaluation is an expense ratio of 2.38% (high).

The fund's risk rating is currently C (Fair). It carries a beta of 1.12, meaning it is expected to move 11.2% for every 10% move in the market. Volatility, as measured by both the semi-deviation and a drawdown factor, is considered average. As of June 30, 2005, Boulder Growth&Income Fund traded at a discount of 14.34% below its net asset value, which is better than its one-year historical average discount of 12.27%.

Stewart Horejsi has been running the fund for 33 years and currently receives a manager quality ranking of 32 (0=worst, 99=best). This fund offers an average level of risk but investors looking for strong performance will be frustrated.

Data Date	Weiss Investment Rating	Net Assets ($Mil)	Price	Performance Rating/Pts	Total Return Y-T-D	Risk Rating/Pts
6-05	E+	85.90	6.63	E+ / 0.7	-6.88%	C / 4.3
2004	D-	80.81	7.12	C / 4.3	13.02%	D+ / 2.7
2003	D-	64.36	5.86	D- / 1.4	33.58%	C / 4.3

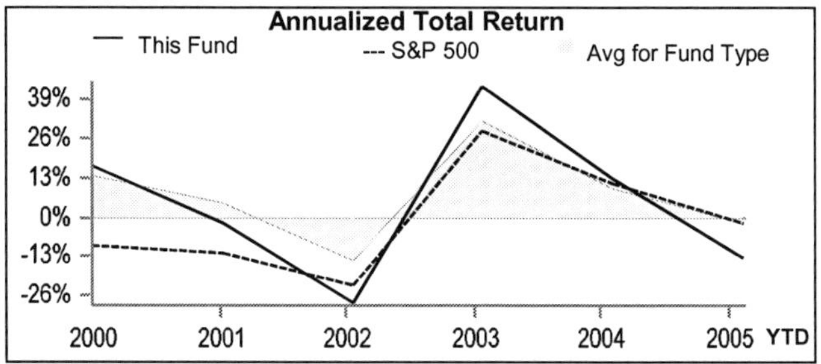

Boulder Total Return Fund (BTF) E+ Very Weak

Fund Family: Boulder Investment Advisers
Fund Type: Income
Inception Date: February 12, 1993

Major Rating Factors:
Very poor performance is the major factor driving the E+ (Very Weak) Weiss Investment Rating for Boulder Total Return Fund. The fund currently has a performance rating of E- (Very Weak) based on an annualized return of 2.45% over the last three years and a total return of -8.75% year to date 2005. Factored into the performance evaluation is an expense ratio of 2.30% (high).

The fund's risk rating is currently C+ (Fair). It carries a beta of 0.75, meaning the fund's expected move will be 7.5% for every 10% move in the market. Volatility, as measured by both the semi-deviation and a drawdown factor, is considered low. As of June 30, 2005, Boulder Total Return Fund traded at a discount of 16.50% below its net asset value, which is better than its one-year historical average discount of 13.34%.

Stewart Horejsi has been running the fund for 6 years and currently receives a manager quality ranking of 22 (0=worst, 99=best). This fund offers only a moderate level of risk but investors looking for strong performance are still waiting.

Data Date	Weiss Investment Rating	Net Assets ($Mil)	Price	Performance Rating/Pts	Total Return Y-T-D	Risk Rating/Pts
6-05	E+	245.63	17.11	E- / 0.1	-8.75%	C+ / 5.9
2004	C-	237.61	18.75	C / 5.4	23.11%	C / 4.8
2003	C-	148.93	14.96	C- / 3.8	23.85%	C+ / 6.2

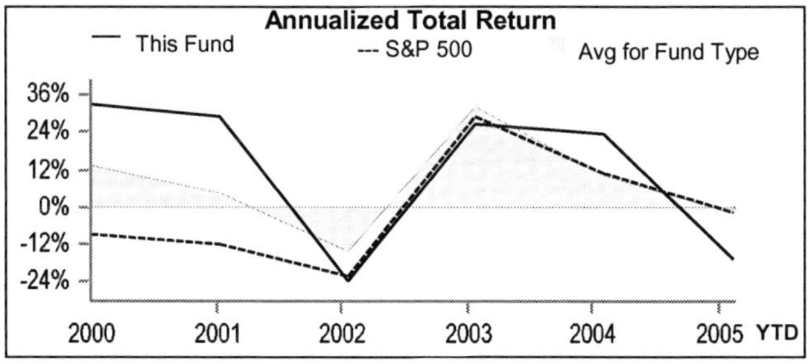

Brazil Fund (BZF) C- Fair

Fund Family: Deutsche Asset Management
Fund Type: Foreign
Inception Date: April 8, 1988

Major Rating Factors:
Brazil Fund has adopted a very risky asset allocation strategy and currently receives an overall Weiss Investment Rating of C- (Fair). The fund has shown a high level of volatility, as measured by both semi-deviation and drawdown factors. It carries a beta of 1.86, meaning it is expected to move 18.6% for every 10% move in the market. As of June 30, 2005, Brazil Fund traded at a discount of 5.50% below its net asset value, which is worse than its one-year historical average discount of 9.82%. The high level of risk (E+, Very Weak) did however, reward investors with excellent performance.

The fund's performance rating is currently A+ (Excellent). It has registered an annualized return of 46.52% over the last three years and is up 7.94% year to date 2005. Factored into the performance evaluation is an expense ratio of 1.51% (average).

Paul Rogers has been running the fund for 9 years and currently receives a manager quality ranking of 98 (0=worst, 99=best). If you are comfortable owning a very high risk investment, this fund may be an option.

Data Date	Weiss Investment Rating	Net Assets ($Mil)	Price	Performance Rating/Pts	Total Return Y-T-D	Risk Rating/Pts
6-05	C-	595.95	37.10	A+ / 9.9	7.94%	E+ / 0.6
2004	C-	415.44	34.37	A+ / 9.8	47.88%	E+ / 0.7
2003	C	292.55	23.85	A+ / 9.6	114.67%	D+ / 2.5

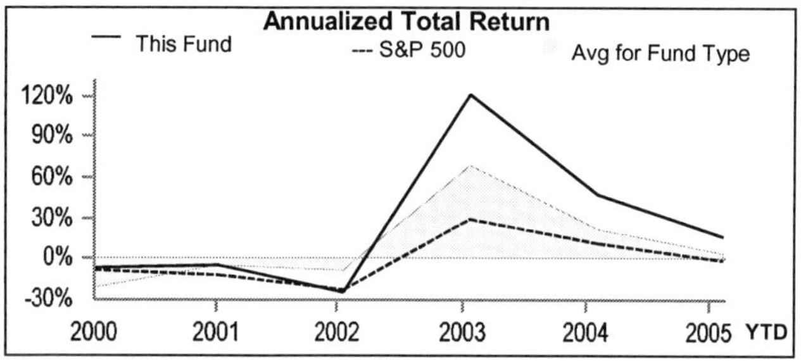

Canadian General Investments Ltd (T.CGI) A+ Excellent

Fund Family: Morgan Meighen & Associates Limited
Fund Type: Foreign
Inception Date: January 15, 1930

Major Rating Factors:
Exceptional performance is the major factor driving the A+ (Excellent) Weiss Investment Rating for Canadian General Investments Ltd. The fund currently has a performance rating of A+ (Excellent) based on an annualized return of 29.43% over the last three years and a total return of 19.98% year to date 2005.

The fund's risk rating is currently C+ (Fair). It carries a beta of 0.72, meaning the fund's expected move will be 7.2% for every 10% move in the market. Volatility, as measured by standard deviation, is considered low for equity funds at 16.01. As of June 30, 2005, Canadian General Investments Ltd traded at a discount of 17.23% below its net asset value, which is worse than its one-year historical average discount of 25.05%.

Michael A Smedley has been running the fund for 17 years and currently receives a manager quality ranking of 98 (0=worst, 99=best). If you desire only a moderate level of risk and strong performance, then this fund is an excellent option.

Data Date	Weiss Investment Rating	Net Assets ($Mil)	Price	Performance Rating/Pts	Total Return Y-T-D	Risk Rating/Pts
6-05	A+	420.87	18.40	A+ / 9.7	19.98%	C+ / 6.7
2004	A+	420.87	15.44	A / 9.3	28.54%	C+ / 6.9
2003	C+	302.22	12.73	B+ / 8.9	58.96%	C / 4.6

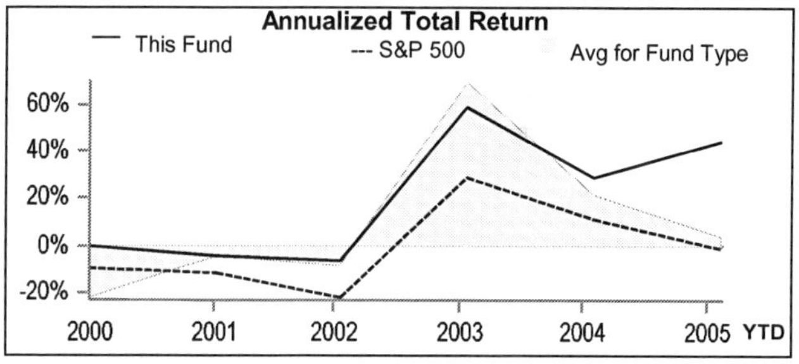

Canadian World Fund Limited (T.CWF) E+ Very Weak

Fund Family: Morgan Meighen & Associates Limited
Fund Type: Global
Inception Date: April 1, 1994

Major Rating Factors:
Canadian World Fund Limited has adopted a very risky asset allocation strategy and currently receives an overall Weiss Investment Rating of E+ (Very Weak). The fund has a high level of volatility, with a standard deviation of 23.31. It carries a beta of 0.32, meaning the fund's expected move will be 3.2% for every 10% move in the market. As of June 30, 2005, Canadian World Fund Limited traded at a discount of 25.86% below its net asset value, which is better than its one-year historical average discount of 24.04%. Unfortunately, the high level of risk (D, Weak) has only provided investors with average performance.

The fund's performance rating is currently C- (Fair). It has registered an annualized return of 12.24% over the last three years and is up 2.50% year to date 2005.

Michael A. Smedley has been running the fund for 11 years and currently receives a manager quality ranking of 87 (0=worst, 99=best). If you are comfortable owning a very high risk investment, then this fund may be an option.

Data Date	Weiss Investment Rating	Net Assets ($Mil)	Price	Performance Rating/Pts	Total Return Y-T-D	Risk Rating/Pts
6-05	E+	19.31	4.10	C- / 3.2	2.50%	D / 1.7
2004	E+	19.31	4.00	C / 4.3	11.11%	D / 1.6
2003	E	14.54	3.10	E+ / 0.6	17.87%	D- / 1.0

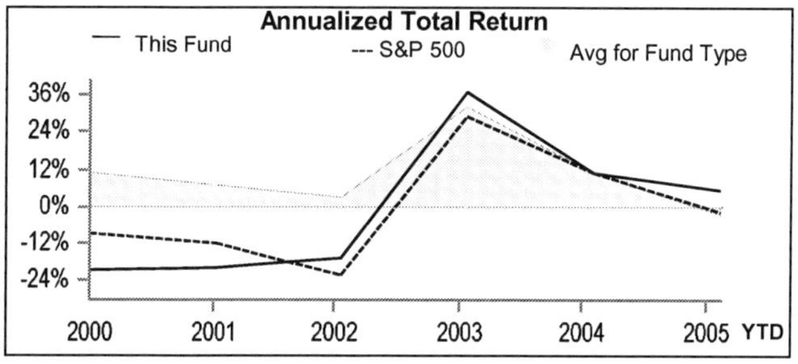

Castle Convertible Fund (CVF) D Weak

Fund Family: Fred Alger Management, Inc.
Fund Type: Growth and Income
Inception Date: November 1, 1971

Major Rating Factors:
Very poor performance is the major factor driving the D (Weak) Weiss Investment Rating for Castle Convertible Fund. The fund currently has a performance rating of E- (Very Weak) based on an annualized return of 1.97% over the last three years and a total return of -9.15% year to date 2005. Factored into the performance evaluation is an expense ratio of 1.16% (low).

The fund's risk rating is currently B (Good). It carries a beta of 0.39, meaning the fund's expected move will be 3.9% for every 10% move in the market. Volatility, as measured by both the semi-deviation and a drawdown factor, is considered low. As of June 30, 2005, Castle Convertible Fund traded at a discount of 15.52% below its net asset value, which is better than its one-year historical average discount of 12.55%.

Alison Barbi has been running the fund for 4 years and currently receives a manager quality ranking of 46 (0=worst, 99=best). This fund offers only a moderate level of risk but investors looking for strong performance are still waiting.

Data Date	Weiss Investment Rating	Net Assets ($Mil)	Price	Performance Rating/Pts	Total Return Y-T-D	Risk Rating/Pts
6-05	D	57.31	22.15	E- / 0.1	-9.15%	B / 8.2
2004	C-	57.05	24.57	C- / 3.3	12.21%	C+ / 6.7
2003	D+	55.05	22.53	D / 2.1	12.03%	C+ / 6.6

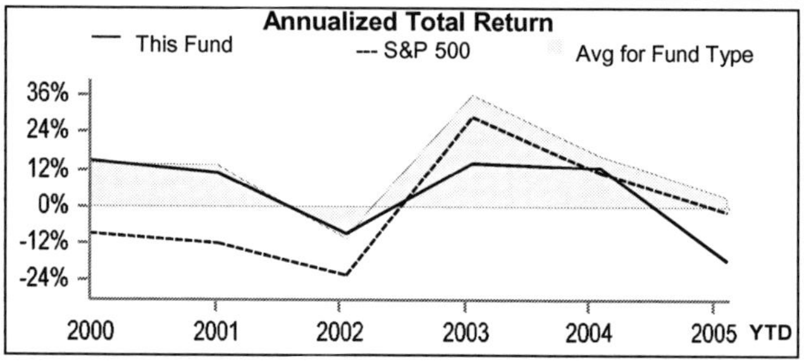

Central Europe & Russia Fund (CEE) C+ Fair

Fund Family: Deutsche Bank Group
Fund Type: Foreign
Inception Date: February 1, 1990

Major Rating Factors:
Central Europe & Russia Fund has adopted a risky asset allocation strategy and currently receives an overall Weiss Investment Rating of C+ (Fair). The fund has shown an above average level of volatility, as measured by both semi-deviation and drawdown factors. It carries a beta of 1.23, meaning it is expected to move 12.3% for every 10% move in the market. As of June 30, 2005, Central Europe & Russia Fund traded at a discount of 6.91% below its net asset value, which is worse than its one-year historical average discount of 10.15%. The high level of risk (D+, Weak) did however, reward investors with excellent performance.

The fund's performance rating is currently A+ (Excellent). It has registered an annualized return of 34.81% over the last three years and is up 12.14% year to date 2005. Factored into the performance evaluation is an expense ratio of 1.27% (average).

Sandra M. Schaufler has been running the fund for 15 years and currently receives a manager quality ranking of 96 (0=worst, 99=best). If you are comfortable owning a high risk investment, this fund may be an option.

Data Date	Weiss Investment Rating	Net Assets ($Mil)	Price	Performance Rating/Pts	Total Return Y-T-D	Risk Rating/Pts
6-05	C+	292.08	31.40	A+ / 9.8	12.14%	D+ / 2.4
2004	A-	252.15	28.00	A+ / 9.7	29.98%	C / 5.4
2003	B-	177.77	22.92	A / 9.5	59.63%	C / 4.6

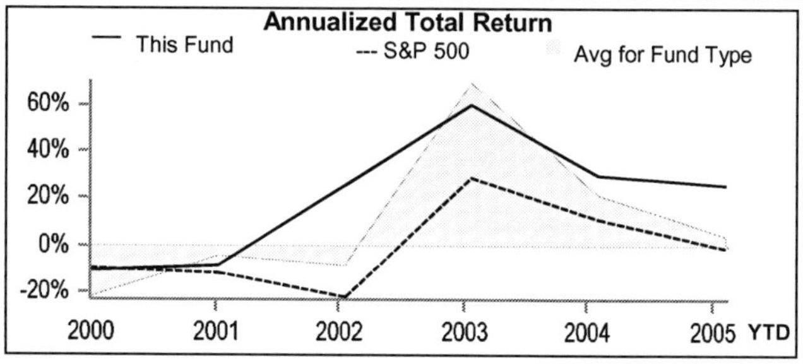

Central Fund of Canada (CEF) D- Weak

Fund Family: Central Group Alberta Ltd
Fund Type: Precious Metals
Inception Date: September 14, 1983

Major Rating Factors:
Disappointing performance is the major factor driving the D- (Weak) Weiss Investment Rating for Central Fund of Canada. The fund currently has a performance rating of D- (Weak) based on an annualized return of 8.37% over the last three years and a total return of -1.28% year to date 2005. Factored into the performance evaluation is an expense ratio of 0.65% (very low).

The fund's risk rating is currently C+ (Fair). It carries a beta of 0.85, meaning the fund's expected move will be 8.5% for every 10% move in the market. Volatility, as measured by both the semi-deviation and a drawdown factor, is considered low. As of June 30, 2005, Central Fund of Canada traded at a price exactly equal to its net asset value, which is better than its one-year historical average premium of 6.46%.

Stefan Spicer has been running the fund for 6 years and currently receives a manager quality ranking of 46 (0=worst, 99=best). This fund offers only a moderate level of risk but investors looking for strong performance are still waiting.

Data Date	Weiss Investment Rating	Net Assets ($Mil)	Price	Performance Rating/Pts	Total Return Y-T-D	Risk Rating/Pts
6-05	D-	418.35	5.40	D- / 1.5	-1.28%	C+ / 5.8
2004	C+	382.29	5.47	C+ / 6.8	4.38%	C+ / 6.3
2003	C+	173.22	5.15	C+ / 6.5	8.20%	C+ / 6.8

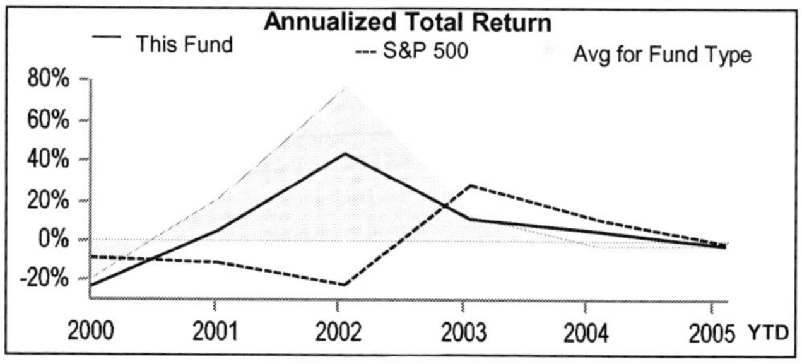

Central Securities (CET) D+ Weak

Fund Family: Central Securities Corporation
Fund Type: Growth
Inception Date: N/A

Major Rating Factors:
Central Securities receives a Weiss Investment Rating of D+ (Weak). The fund currently has a performance rating of C- (Fair) based on an annualized return of 11.08% over the last three years and a total return of 4.95% year to date 2005. Factored into the performance evaluation is an expense ratio of 0.55% (very low).

The fund's risk rating is currently C+ (Fair). It carries a beta of 1.20, meaning it is expected to move 12.0% for every 10% move in the market. Volatility, as measured by both the semi-deviation and a drawdown factor, is considered low. As of June 30, 2005, Central Securities traded at a discount of 15.49% below its net asset value, which is better than its one-year historical average discount of 14.30%.

Wilmot H. Kidd has been running the fund for 32 years and currently receives a manager quality ranking of 73 (0=worst, 99=best). If you desire an average level of risk, then this fund may be an option.

Data Date	Weiss Investment Rating	Net Assets ($Mil)	Price	Performance Rating/Pts	Total Return Y-T-D	Risk Rating/Pts
6-05	D+	529.47	23.78	C- / 3.4	4.95%	C+ / 5.6
2004	D-	526.78	22.85	D / 2.0	15.75%	C- / 4.2
2003	D-	421.97	20.65	D- / 1.2	35.68%	C / 4.5

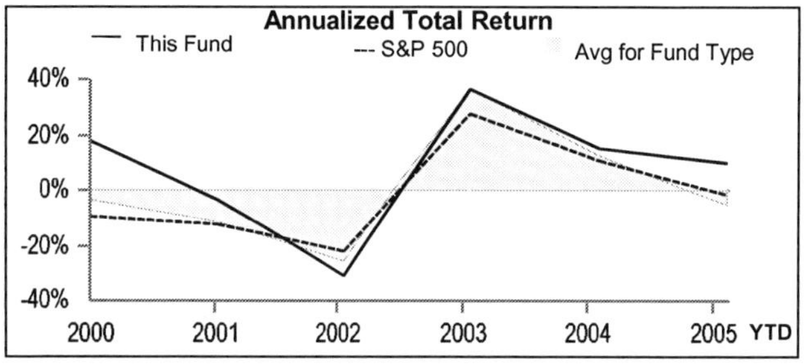

Chartwell Dividend and Income Fund (CWF) C Fair

Fund Family: Chartwell Investment Partners, L.P.
Fund Type: Growth and Income
Inception Date: June 24, 1998

Major Rating Factors:
Strong performance is the major factor driving the C (Fair) Weiss Investment Rating for Chartwell Dividend and Income Fund. The fund currently has a performance rating of B- (Good) based on an annualized return of 13.99% over the last three years and a total return of 10.24% year to date 2005. Factored into the performance evaluation is an expense ratio of 2.26% (high).

The fund's risk rating is currently C- (Fair). It carries a beta of 0.44, meaning the fund's expected move will be 4.4% for every 10% move in the market. Volatility, as measured by both the semi-deviation and a drawdown factor, is considered average. As of June 30, 2005, Chartwell Dividend and Income Fund traded at a premium of 21.86% above its net asset value, which is worse than its one-year historical average premium of 14.27%.

Bernard P. Schaffer has been running the fund for 7 years and currently receives a manager quality ranking of 89 (0=worst, 99=best). If you desire an average level of risk and strong performance, then this fund is a good option.

Data Date	Weiss Investment Rating	Net Assets ($Mil)	Price	Performance Rating/Pts	Total Return Y-T-D	Risk Rating/Pts
6-05	C	148.14	10.59	B- / 7.4	10.24%	C- / 3.9
2004	D	138.65	10.12	C / 4.8	16.18%	C- / 3.0
2003	C	130.73	9.71	B- / 7.2	48.31%	C- / 4.2

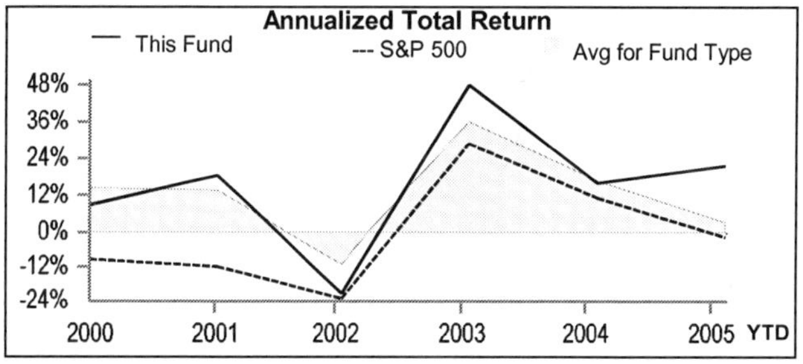

Chile Fund (CH) B+ Good

Fund Family: Credit Suisse Asset Management,LLC
Fund Type: Foreign
Inception Date: September 27, 1989

Major Rating Factors:
Exceptional performance is the major factor driving the B+ (Good) Weiss Investment Rating for Chile Fund. The fund currently has a performance rating of A+ (Excellent) based on an annualized return of 33.72% over the last three years and a total return of 7.43% year to date 2005. Factored into the performance evaluation is an expense ratio of 1.85% (above average).

The fund's risk rating is currently C (Fair). It carries a beta of 1.28, meaning it is expected to move 12.8% for every 10% move in the market. Volatility, as measured by both the semi-deviation and a drawdown factor, is considered average. As of June 30, 2005, Chile Fund traded at a discount of 11.59% below its net asset value, which is better than its one-year historical average discount of 10.68%.

Mathew J.K. Hickman has been running the fund for 1 year and currently receives a manager quality ranking of 95 (0=worst, 99=best). If you desire an average level of risk and strong performance, then this fund is a good option.

Data Date	Weiss Investment Rating	Net Assets ($Mil)	Price	Performance Rating/Pts	Total Return Y-T-D	Risk Rating/Pts
6-05	B+	158.98	15.03	A+ / 9.7	7.43%	C / 4.3
2004	B-	140.34	13.99	A- / 9.2	16.26%	C- / 4.2
2003	C+	107.63	13.74	A+ / 9.7	96.16%	C- / 3.0

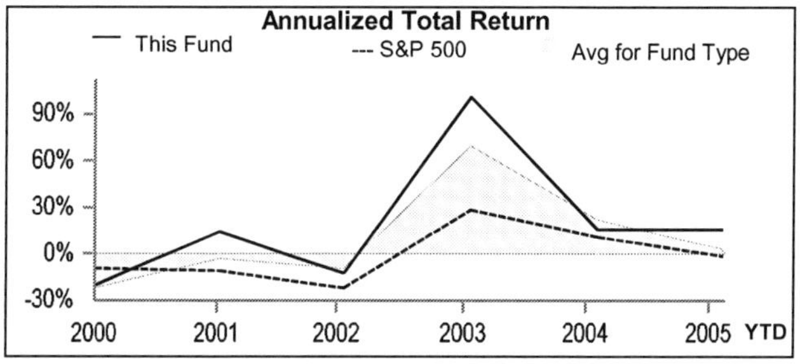

China Fund (CHN) — C+ — Fair

Fund Family: Asia Direct Capital Mgmt&Martin Cur
Fund Type: Foreign
Inception Date: July 10, 1992

Major Rating Factors:
China Fund has adopted a risky asset allocation strategy and currently receives an overall Weiss Investment Rating of C+ (Fair). The fund has shown an above average level of volatility, as measured by both semi-deviation and drawdown factors. It carries a beta of 1.28, meaning it is expected to move 12.8% for every 10% move in the market. As of June 30, 2005, China Fund traded at a premium of 11.70% above its net asset value, which is better than its one-year historical average premium of 17.54%. The high level of risk (D+, Weak) did however, reward investors with excellent performance.

The fund's performance rating is currently A+ (Excellent). It has registered an annualized return of 35.45% over the last three years but is down -12.19% year to date 2005. Factored into the performance evaluation is an expense ratio of 1.40% (average).

Chris Ruffle has been running the fund for 13 years and currently receives a manager quality ranking of 96 (0=worst, 99=best). If you are comfortable owning a high risk investment, this fund may be an option.

Data Date	Weiss Investment Rating	Net Assets ($Mil)	Price	Performance Rating/Pts	Total Return Y-T-D	Risk Rating/Pts
6-05	C+	258.79	28.73	A+ / 9.6	-12.19%	D+ / 2.3
2004	C+	256.64	32.72	A+ / 9.8	-10.29%	D+ / 2.7
2003	C	271.30	40.30	A+ / 9.9	193.09%	D+ / 2.5

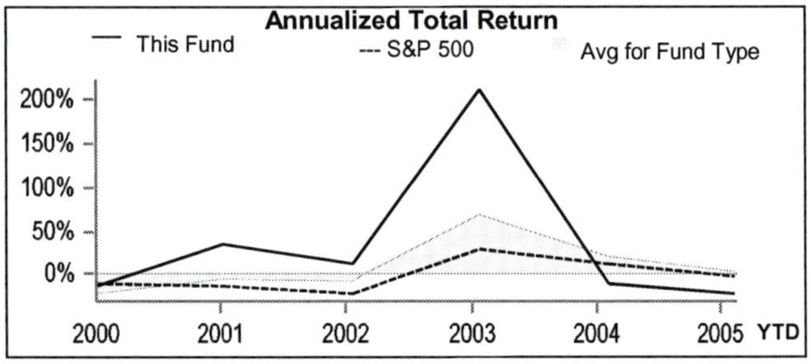

CIM High Yield Securities (CIM) — D+ — Weak

Fund Family: INVESCO (NY) Inc.
Fund Type: Corporate - High Yield
Inception Date: November 12, 1987

Major Rating Factors:
CIM High Yield Securities receives a Weiss Investment Rating of D+ (Weak). The fund currently has a performance rating of C- (Fair) based on an annualized return of 14.08% over the last three years and a total return of -2.24% year to date 2005. Factored into the performance evaluation is an expense ratio of 2.21% (high).

The fund's risk rating is currently C (Fair). It carries a beta of 1.87, meaning it is expected to move 18.7% for every 10% move in the market. Volatility, as measured by both the semi-deviation and a drawdown factor, is considered average. As of June 30, 2005, CIM High Yield Securities traded at a discount of 8.05% below its net asset value, which is better than its one-year historical average discount of 5.27%.

Chang-Hock Lau has been running the fund for 7 years and currently receives a manager quality ranking of 3 (0=worst, 99=best). If you desire an average level of risk, then this fund may be an option.

Data Date	Weiss Investment Rating	Net Assets ($Mil)	Price	Performance Rating/Pts	Total Return Y-T-D	Risk Rating/Pts
6-05	D+	28.41	4.00	C- / 4.0	-2.24%	C / 4.8
2004	D-	26.60	4.28	C- / 3.1	-1.36%	C / 4.4
2003	C	26.10	4.84	B / 7.6	48.84%	C- / 3.8

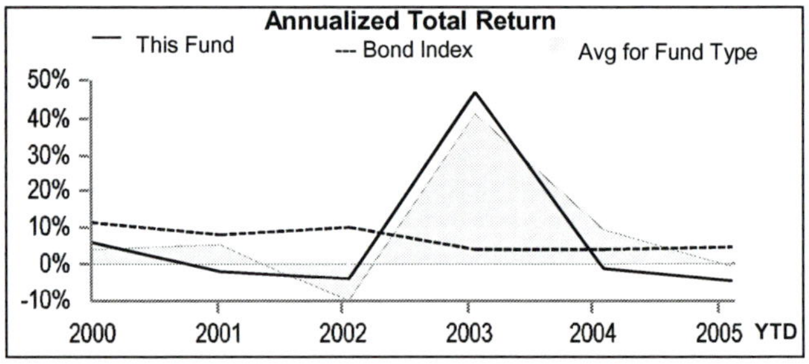

Citigroup Investments Corp Loan (TLI) — D — Weak

Fund Family: SSBC Fund Management Inc.
Fund Type: Loan Participation
Inception Date: November 24, 1998

Major Rating Factors:
Very poor performance is the major factor driving the D (Weak) Weiss Investment Rating for Citigroup Investments Corp Loan. The fund currently has a performance rating of E (Very Weak) based on an annualized return of 5.84% over the last three years and a total return of -4.05% year to date 2005. Factored into the performance evaluation is an expense ratio of 2.31% (high).

The fund's risk rating is currently B (Good). It carries a beta of -48.34, meaning the fund's expected move will be -483.4% for every 10% move in the market. Volatility, as measured by both the semi-deviation and a drawdown factor, is considered low. As of June 30, 2005, Citigroup Investments Corp Loan traded at a discount of 8.45% below its net asset value, which is better than its one-year historical average discount of 2.02%.

Glenn Marchak has been running the fund for 7 years and currently receives a manager quality ranking of 96 (0=worst, 99=best). This fund offers only a moderate level of risk but investors looking for strong performance are still waiting.

Data Date	Weiss Investment Rating	Net Assets ($Mil)	Price	Performance Rating/Pts	Total Return Y-T-D	Risk Rating/Pts
6-05	D	142.99	13.11	E / 0.3	-4.05%	B / 8.2
2004	C-	141.22	14.02	D / 2.0	-2.57%	B / 8.2
2003	C+	136.48	15.20	C+ / 6.2	38.17%	C+ / 6.4

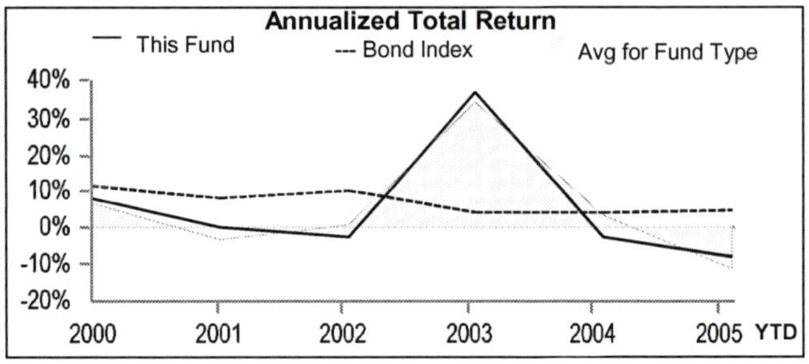

Cohen&Steers Adv Inc Realty Fund (RLF) B Good

Fund Family: Cohen & Steers Cap
Fund Type: Growth and Income
Inception Date: May 25, 2001

Data Date	Weiss Investment Rating	Net Assets ($Mil)	Price	Performance Rating/Pts	Total Return Y-T-D	Risk Rating/Pts
6-05	B	592.14	21.87	A- / 9.0	2.68%	C / 4.7
2004	A	489.38	22.25	A / 9.5	31.95%	C+ / 6.0

Major Rating Factors:
Exceptional performance is the major factor driving the B (Good) Weiss Investment Rating for Cohen&Steers Adv Inc Realty Fund. The fund currently has a performance rating of A- (Excellent) based on an annualized return of 20.42% over the last three years and a total return of 2.68% year to date 2005. Factored into the performance evaluation is an expense ratio of 0.91% (low).

The fund's risk rating is currently C (Fair). It carries a beta of 0.41, meaning the fund's expected move will be 4.1% for every 10% move in the market. Volatility, as measured by both the semi-deviation and a drawdown factor, is considered average. As of June 30, 2005, Cohen&Steers Adv Inc Realty Fund traded at a discount of 6.58% below its net asset value, which is better than its one-year historical average discount of 6.41%.

Joseph M. Harvey has been running the fund for 4 years and currently receives a manager quality ranking of 96 (0=worst, 99=best). If you desire an average level of risk and strong performance, then this fund is a good option.

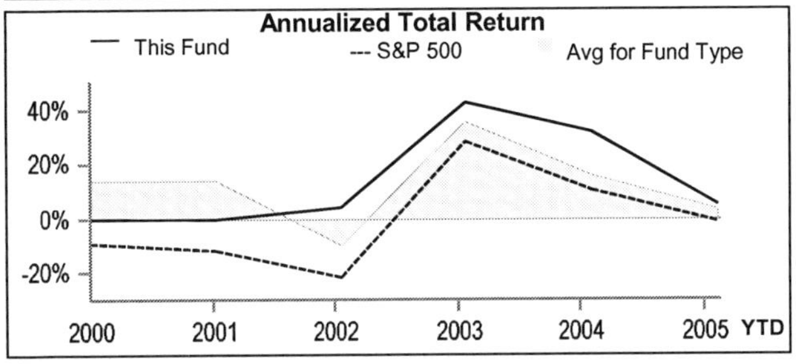

Cohen&Steers Quality Income Realty (RQI) B- Good

Fund Family: Cohen & Steers Cap
Fund Type: Growth and Income
Inception Date: February 26, 2002

Data Date	Weiss Investment Rating	Net Assets ($Mil)	Price	Performance Rating/Pts	Total Return Y-T-D	Risk Rating/Pts
6-05	B-	874.24	20.52	A- / 9.1	3.86%	C / 4.3

Major Rating Factors:
Exceptional performance is the major factor driving the B- (Good) Weiss Investment Rating for Cohen&Steers Quality Income Realty. The fund currently has a performance rating of A- (Excellent) based on an annualized return of 20.68% over the last three years and a total return of 3.86% year to date 2005. Factored into the performance evaluation is an expense ratio of 1.04% (low).

The fund's risk rating is currently C (Fair). It carries a beta of 0.35, meaning the fund's expected move will be 3.5% for every 10% move in the market. Volatility, as measured by both the semi-deviation and a drawdown factor, is considered average. As of June 30, 2005, Cohen&Steers Quality Income Realty traded at a discount of 10.67% below its net asset value, which is better than its one-year historical average discount of 8.82%.

Joseph M. Harvey has been running the fund for 3 years and currently receives a manager quality ranking of 97 (0=worst, 99=best). If you desire an average level of risk and strong performance, then this fund is a good option.

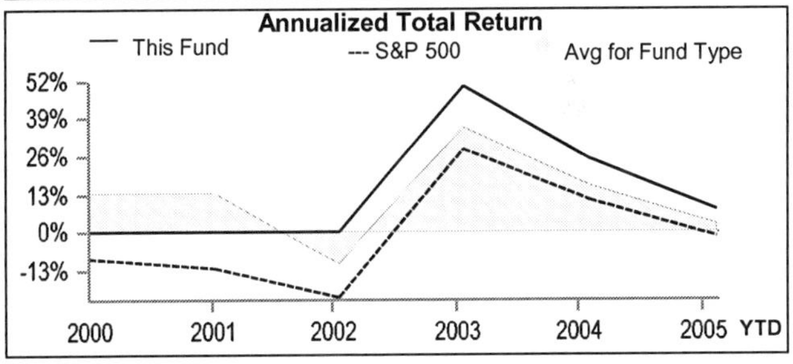

Cohen&Steers Total Return Realty (RFI) B- Good

Fund Family: Cohen & Steers Cap
Fund Type: Growth and Income
Inception Date: September 17, 1993

Data Date	Weiss Investment Rating	Net Assets ($Mil)	Price	Performance Rating/Pts	Total Return Y-T-D	Risk Rating/Pts
6-05	B-	182.36	19.80	B / 7.7	1.93%	C+ / 5.7
2004	A-	158.65	20.12	B+ / 8.6	20.92%	C+ / 6.5
2003	A+	137.99	17.30	B+ / 8.5	30.49%	B- / 7.6

Major Rating Factors:
Strong performance is the major factor driving the B- (Good) Weiss Investment Rating for Cohen&Steers Total Return Realty. The fund currently has a performance rating of B (Good) based on an annualized return of 17.60% over the last three years and a total return of 1.93% year to date 2005. Factored into the performance evaluation is an expense ratio of 0.92% (low).

The fund's risk rating is currently C+ (Fair). It carries a beta of 0.34, meaning the fund's expected move will be 3.4% for every 10% move in the market. Volatility, as measured by both the semi-deviation and a drawdown factor, is considered low. As of June 30, 2005, Cohen&Steers Total Return Realty traded at a discount of .25% below its net asset value, which is better than its one-year historical average premium of .51%.

Joseph M. Harvey has been running the fund for 12 years and currently receives a manager quality ranking of 94 (0=worst, 99=best). If you desire only a moderate level of risk and strong performance, then this fund is an excellent option.

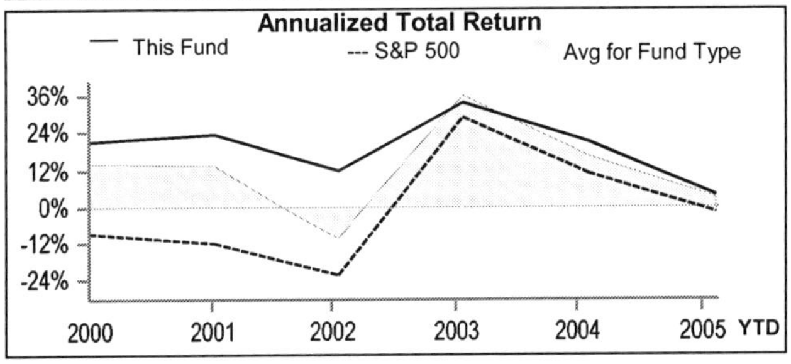

Colonial CA Insured Muni (CCA) — D — Weak

Fund Family: Colonial Management Associates Inc
Fund Type: Municipal - Single State
Inception Date: October 28, 1999

Major Rating Factors:
Disappointing performance is the major factor driving the D (Weak) Weiss Investment Rating for Colonial CA Insured Muni. The fund currently has a performance rating of D (Weak) based on an annualized return of 0.07% over the last three years and a total return of 10.40% year to date 2005. Factored into the performance evaluation is an expense ratio of 0.87% (low).

The fund's risk rating is currently C+ (Fair). It carries a beta of 1.73, meaning it is expected to move 17.3% for every 10% move in the market. Volatility, as measured by both the semi-deviation and a drawdown factor, is considered low. As of June 30, 2005, Colonial CA Insured Muni traded at a discount of 5.09% below its net asset value, which is worse than its one-year historical average discount of 7.86%.

Kimberly Campbell currently receives a manager quality ranking of 5 (0=worst, 99=best). This fund offers only a moderate level of risk but investors looking for strong performance are still waiting.

Data Date	Weiss Investment Rating	Net Assets ($Mil)	Price	Performance Rating/Pts	Total Return Y-T-D	Risk Rating/Pts
6-05	D	41.63	14.53	D / 2.1	10.40%	C+ / 6.4
2004	D-	40.16	13.56	E / 0.3	-6.00%	B- / 7.1
2003	C+	45.08	15.46	C / 5.1	2.30%	B- / 7.9

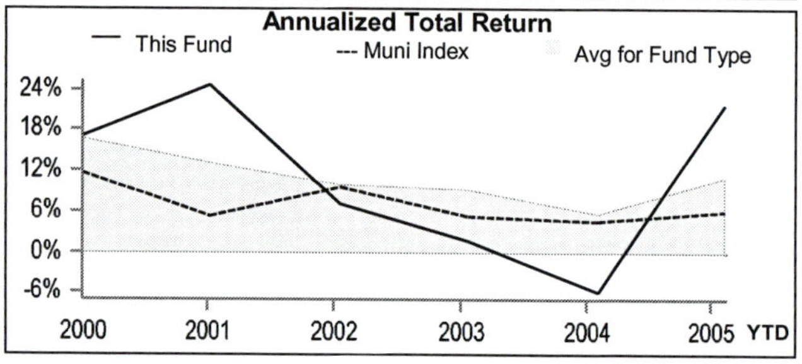

Colonial High Inc Muni Tr (CXE) — C- — Fair

Fund Family: Colonial Management Associates Inc
Fund Type: Municipal - High Yield
Inception Date: February 16, 1989

Major Rating Factors:
Disappointing performance is the major factor driving the C- (Fair) Weiss Investment Rating for Colonial High Inc Muni Tr. The fund currently has a performance rating of D+ (Weak) based on an annualized return of 4.91% over the last three years and a total return of 3.02% year to date 2005. Factored into the performance evaluation is an expense ratio of 1.58% (above average).

The fund's risk rating is currently B (Good). It carries a beta of 1.30, meaning it is expected to move 13.0% for every 10% move in the market. Volatility, as measured by both the semi-deviation and a drawdown factor, is considered low. As of June 30, 2005, Colonial High Inc Muni Tr traded at a discount of 4.70% below its net asset value, which is better than its one-year historical average discount of 1.16%.

Maureen Newman has been running the fund for 7 years and currently receives a manager quality ranking of 42 (0=worst, 99=best). This fund offers only a moderate level of risk but investors looking for strong performance are still waiting.

Data Date	Weiss Investment Rating	Net Assets ($Mil)	Price	Performance Rating/Pts	Total Return Y-T-D	Risk Rating/Pts
6-05	C-	199.10	6.29	D+ / 2.6	3.02%	B / 8.0
2004	B-	195.05	6.29	C / 5.3	5.76%	B / 8.0
2003	C+	198.97	6.48	C / 4.5	10.14%	B / 8.3

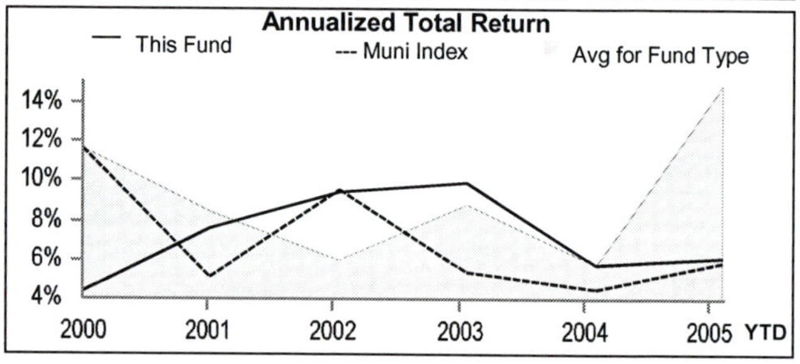

Colonial Insured Muni (CFX) — D — Weak

Fund Family: Colonial Management Associates Inc
Fund Type: Municipal - National
Inception Date: October 28, 1999

Major Rating Factors:
Very poor performance is the major factor driving the D (Weak) Weiss Investment Rating for Colonial Insured Muni. The fund currently has a performance rating of E+ (Very Weak) based on an annualized return of 2.08% over the last three years and a total return of 5.34% year to date 2005. Factored into the performance evaluation is an expense ratio of 0.88% (low).

The fund's risk rating is currently B- (Good). It carries a beta of 2.22, meaning it is expected to move 22.2% for every 10% move in the market. Volatility, as measured by both the semi-deviation and a drawdown factor, is considered low. As of June 30, 2005, Colonial Insured Muni traded at a discount of 5.48% below its net asset value, which is better than its one-year historical average discount of 3.16%.

Kimberly Campbell currently receives a manager quality ranking of 4 (0=worst, 99=best). This fund offers only a moderate level of risk but investors looking for strong performance are still waiting.

Data Date	Weiss Investment Rating	Net Assets ($Mil)	Price	Performance Rating/Pts	Total Return Y-T-D	Risk Rating/Pts
6-05	D	61.86	14.15	E+ / 0.8	5.34%	B- / 7.4
2004	D	60.52	13.86	E+ / 0.6	-3.57%	B / 8.1
2003	B	66.29	15.35	C+ / 6.8	7.98%	B / 8.4

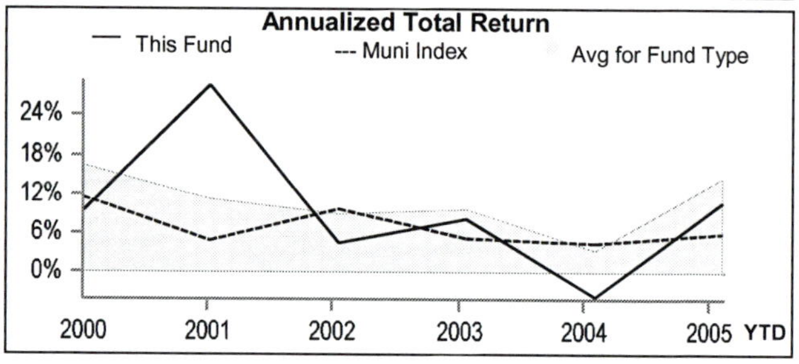

Colonial Interm High Inc (CIF) C+ Fair

Fund Family: Colonial Management Associates Inc
Fund Type: Corporate - High Yield
Inception Date: July 21, 1988

Major Rating Factors:
Middle of the road best describes Colonial Interm High Inc whose Weiss Investment Rating is currently a C+ (Fair). The fund currently has a performance rating of C (Fair) based on an annualized return of 15.56% over the last three years and a total return of -1.36% year to date 2005. Factored into the performance evaluation is an expense ratio of 2.66% (high).

The fund's risk rating is currently B- (Good). It carries a beta of 1.40, meaning it is expected to move 14.0% for every 10% move in the market. Volatility, as measured by both the semi-deviation and a drawdown factor, is considered low. As of June 30, 2005, Colonial Interm High Inc traded at a discount of 7.03% below its net asset value, which is worse than its one-year historical average discount of 7.92%.

Kevin Cronk currently receives a manager quality ranking of 31 (0=worst, 99=best). If you desire an average level of risk, then this fund may be an option.

Data Date	Weiss Investment Rating	Net Assets ($Mil)	Price	Performance Rating/Pts	Total Return Y-T-D	Risk Rating/Pts
6-05	C+	81.23	3.44	C / 5.5	-1.36%	B- / 7.0
2004	D	74.42	3.62	C- / 4.1	9.09%	C- / 3.7
2003	D	74.95	3.68	C- / 3.5	37.89%	C- / 3.2

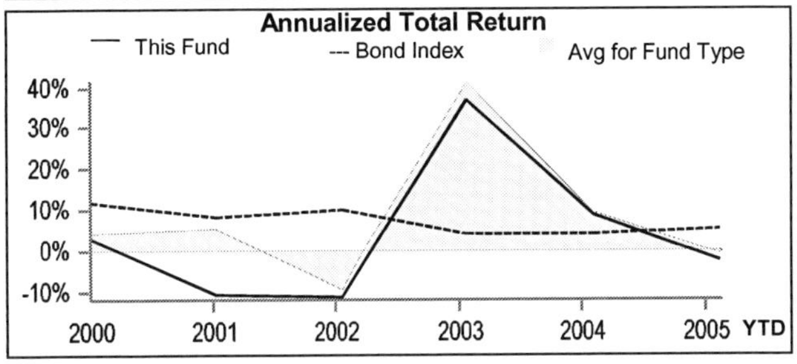

Colonial InterMkt Inc Tr I (CMK) C Fair

Fund Family: Colonial Management Associates Inc
Fund Type: Global
Inception Date: September 22, 1989

Major Rating Factors:
Middle of the road best describes Colonial InterMkt Inc Tr I whose Weiss Investment Rating is currently a C (Fair). The fund currently has a performance rating of C- (Fair) based on an annualized return of 10.48% over the last three years and a total return of -0.43% year to date 2005. Factored into the performance evaluation is an expense ratio of 1.01% (low).

The fund's risk rating is currently B- (Good). It carries a beta of 0.61, meaning the fund's expected move will be 6.1% for every 10% move in the market. Volatility, as measured by both the semi-deviation and a drawdown factor, is considered low. As of June 30, 2005, Colonial InterMkt Inc Tr I traded at a discount of 6.96% below its net asset value, which is worse than its one-year historical average discount of 8.81%.

Laura Ostrander currently receives a manager quality ranking of 76 (0=worst, 99=best). If you desire an average level of risk, then this fund may be an option.

Data Date	Weiss Investment Rating	Net Assets ($Mil)	Price	Performance Rating/Pts	Total Return Y-T-D	Risk Rating/Pts
6-05	C	107.80	8.82	C- / 3.9	-0.43%	B- / 7.8
2004	B-	101.95	9.19	C+ / 6.6	12.61%	B- / 7.9
2003	C	103.73	8.89	C- / 4.1	16.05%	B- / 7.3

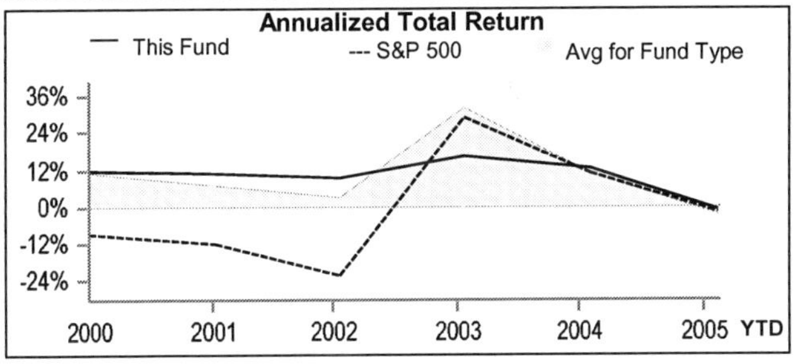

Colonial Invst Gr Muni Tr (CXH) C+ Fair

Fund Family: Colonial Management Associates Inc
Fund Type: Municipal - National
Inception Date: May 26, 1989

Major Rating Factors:
Middle of the road best describes Colonial Invst Gr Muni Tr whose Weiss Investment Rating is currently a C+ (Fair). The fund currently has a performance rating of C (Fair) based on an annualized return of 6.19% over the last three years and a total return of 6.17% year to date 2005. Factored into the performance evaluation is an expense ratio of 1.29% (average).

The fund's risk rating is currently B- (Good). It carries a beta of 1.61, meaning it is expected to move 16.1% for every 10% move in the market. Volatility, as measured by both the semi-deviation and a drawdown factor, is considered low. As of June 30, 2005, Colonial Invst Gr Muni Tr traded at a discount of 7.98% below its net asset value, which is worse than its one-year historical average discount of 9.78%.

Maureen Newman currently receives a manager quality ranking of 42 (0=worst, 99=best). If you desire an average level of risk, then this fund may be an option.

Data Date	Weiss Investment Rating	Net Assets ($Mil)	Price	Performance Rating/Pts	Total Return Y-T-D	Risk Rating/Pts
6-05	C+	128.16	10.49	C / 5.3	6.17%	B- / 7.3
2004	C	125.57	10.19	C- / 3.6	3.97%	B / 8.1
2003	B-	131.97	10.43	C / 4.9	9.20%	B / 8.7

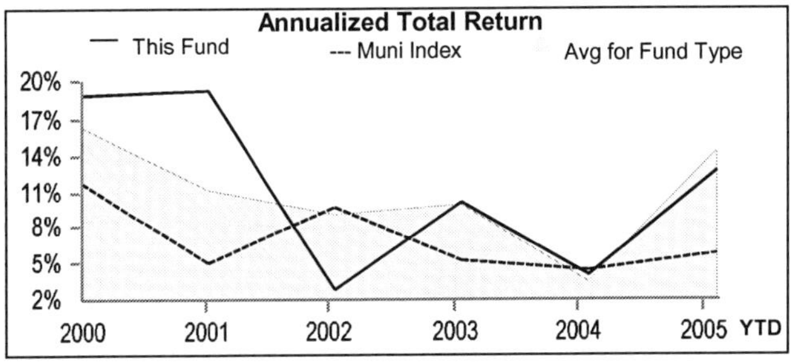

Colonial Muni Inc Trust (CMU) — C- Fair

Fund Family: Colonial Management Associates Inc
Fund Type: Municipal - High Yield
Inception Date: March 19, 1987

Major Rating Factors:
Disappointing performance is the major factor driving the C- (Fair) Weiss Investment Rating for Colonial Muni Inc Trust. The fund currently has a performance rating of D+ (Weak) based on an annualized return of 5.47% over the last three years and a total return of 0.75% year to date 2005. Factored into the performance evaluation is an expense ratio of 1.42% (average).

The fund's risk rating is currently B- (Good). It carries a beta of 1.70, meaning it is expected to move 17.0% for every 10% move in the market. Volatility, as measured by both the semi-deviation and a drawdown factor, is considered low. As of June 30, 2005, Colonial Muni Inc Trust traded at a discount of 5.11% below its net asset value, which is better than its one-year historical average discount of 1.44%.

Maureen Newman currently receives a manager quality ranking of 30 (0=worst, 99=best). This fund offers only a moderate level of risk but investors looking for strong performance are still waiting.

Data Date	Weiss Investment Rating	Net Assets ($Mil)	Price	Performance Rating/Pts	Total Return Y-T-D	Risk Rating/Pts
6-05	C-	157.76	5.57	D+ / 2.8	0.75%	B- / 7.6
2004	B-	153.43	5.69	C+ / 6.6	8.05%	B- / 7.8
2003	C+	161.99	5.70	C / 4.3	8.43%	B / 8.3

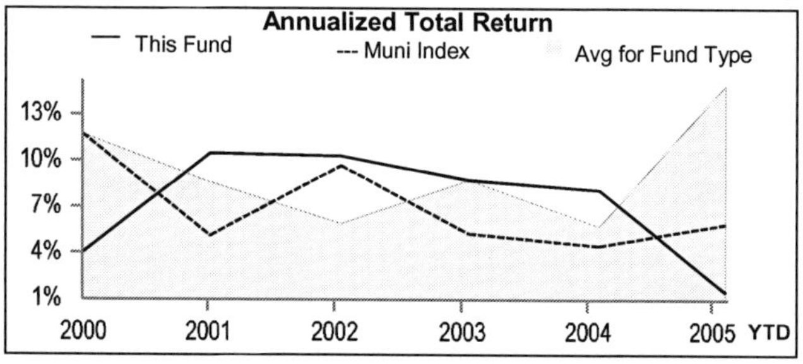

Cornerstone Strategic Value Fund (CLM) — D Weak

Fund Family: Cornerstone Advisors Inc.
Fund Type: Income
Inception Date: July 1, 1987

Major Rating Factors:
Cornerstone Strategic Value Fund receives a Weiss Investment Rating of D (Weak). The fund currently has a performance rating of C (Fair) based on an annualized return of 18.63% over the last three years and a total return of -9.05% year to date 2005. Factored into the performance evaluation is an expense ratio of 1.28% (average).

The fund's risk rating is currently C- (Fair). It carries a beta of 0.97, meaning that its performance tracks fairly well with that of the overall stock market. Volatility, as measured by both the semi-deviation and a drawdown factor, is considered average. As of June 30, 2005, Cornerstone Strategic Value Fund traded at a premium of 22.77% above its net asset value, which is better than its one-year historical average premium of 27.68%.

Ralph W Bradshaw has been running the fund for 4 years and currently receives a manager quality ranking of 90 (0=worst, 99=best). If you desire an average level of risk, then this fund may be an option.

Data Date	Weiss Investment Rating	Net Assets ($Mil)	Price	Performance Rating/Pts	Total Return Y-T-D	Risk Rating/Pts
6-05	D	154.69	7.17	C / 5.5	-9.05%	C- / 3.0
2004	C	154.34	8.51	C+ / 6.9	7.48%	C / 4.9
2003	C-	25.01	8.67	C+ / 6.7	71.61%	C- / 3.5

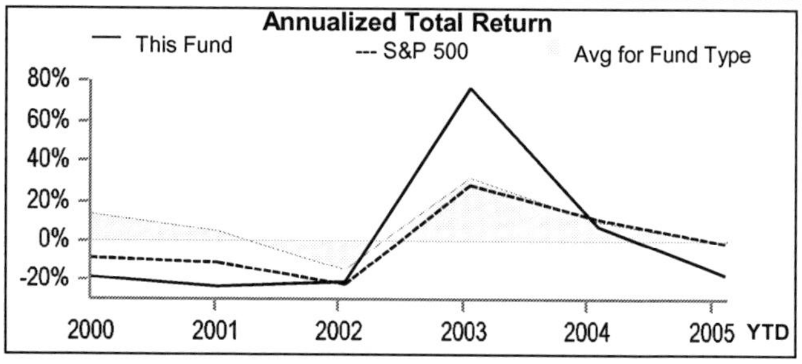

Cornerstone Total Return Fund (CRF) — D Weak

Fund Family: Cornerstone Advisors Inc.
Fund Type: Income
Inception Date: May 30, 1973

Major Rating Factors:
Cornerstone Total Return Fund has adopted a very risky asset allocation strategy and currently receives an overall Weiss Investment Rating of D (Weak). The fund has a high level of volatility, as measured by both semi-deviation and drawdown factors. It carries a beta of 0.94, meaning that its performance tracks fairly well with that of the overall stock market. As of June 30, 2005, Cornerstone Total Return Fund traded at a premium of 35.79% above its net asset value, which is worse than its one-year historical average premium of 35.33%. Unfortunately, the high level of risk (D-, Weak) has only provided investors with average performance.

The fund's performance rating is currently C+ (Fair). It has registered an annualized return of 18.82% over the last three years but is down -7.10% year to date 2005. Factored into the performance evaluation is an expense ratio of 1.41% (average).

Ralph W. Bradshaw has been running the fund for 4 years and currently receives a manager quality ranking of 91 (0=worst, 99=best). If you are comfortable owning a very high risk investment, then this fund may be an option.

Data Date	Weiss Investment Rating	Net Assets ($Mil)	Price	Performance Rating/Pts	Total Return Y-T-D	Risk Rating/Pts
6-05	D	61.37	15.48	C+ / 6.5	-7.10%	D- / 1.3
2004	C+	62.45	17.95	B / 8.2	13.79%	C- / 4.1
2003	B-	61.85	17.75	A / 9.4	81.40%	C / 4.3

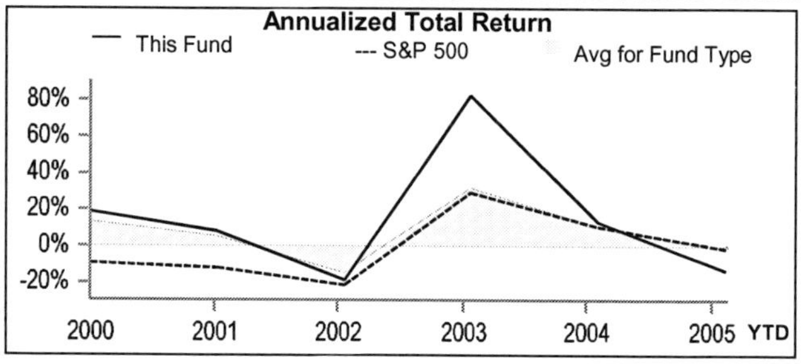

Corporate High Yield Fund (COY) B- Good

Fund Family: Merrill Lynch Investment Managers
Fund Type: Corporate - High Yield
Inception Date: June 30, 1993

Data Date	Weiss Investment Rating	Net Assets ($Mil)	Price	Performance Rating/Pts	Total Return Y-T-D	Risk Rating/Pts
6-05	B-	312.67	8.74	B / 7.8	4.03%	C / 5.3
2004	D+	291.65	8.77	C / 4.6	1.48%	C / 4.8
2003	C+	293.88	9.75	B+ / 8.6	56.70%	C- / 4.2

Major Rating Factors:
Strong performance is the major factor driving the B- (Good) Weiss Investment Rating for Corporate High Yield Fund. The fund currently has a performance rating of B (Good) based on an annualized return of 19.44% over the last three years and a total return of 4.03% year to date 2005. Factored into the performance evaluation is an expense ratio of 1.50% (average).

The fund's risk rating is currently C (Fair). It carries a beta of 2.05, meaning it is expected to move 20.5% for every 10% move in the market. Volatility, as measured by both the semi-deviation and a drawdown factor, is considered average. As of June 30, 2005, Corporate High Yield Fund traded at a premium of 1.16% above its net asset value, which is worse than its one-year historical average discount of 1.08%.

Dan Evans has been running the fund for 12 years and currently receives a manager quality ranking of 6 (0=worst, 99=best). If you desire an average level of risk and strong performance, then this fund is a good option.

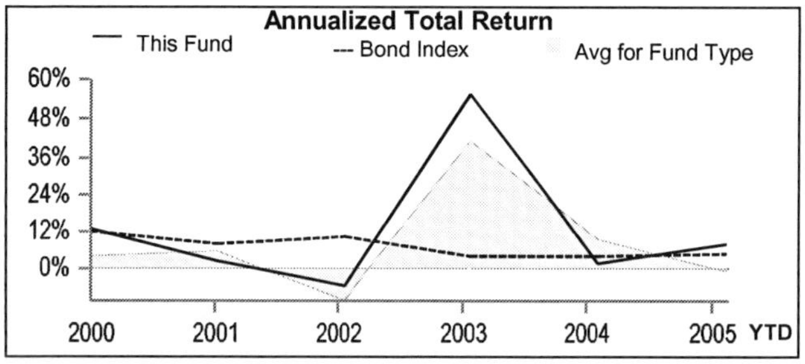

Corporate High Yield Fund III (CYE) C+ Fair

Fund Family: Merrill Lynch Investment Managers
Fund Type: Corporate - High Yield
Inception Date: February 2, 1998

Data Date	Weiss Investment Rating	Net Assets ($Mil)	Price	Performance Rating/Pts	Total Return Y-T-D	Risk Rating/Pts
6-05	C+	336.08	8.45	B / 7.6	0.24%	C / 5.3
2004	C	313.58	8.80	C+ / 6.6	11.35%	C / 4.9
2003	C-	312.92	8.79	C+ / 6.9	42.47%	C- / 4.1

Major Rating Factors:
Strong performance is the major factor driving the C+ (Fair) Weiss Investment Rating for Corporate High Yield Fund III. The fund currently has a performance rating of B (Good) based on an annualized return of 19.40% over the last three years and a total return of 0.24% year to date 2005. Factored into the performance evaluation is an expense ratio of 1.62% (above average).

The fund's risk rating is currently C (Fair). It carries a beta of 1.92, meaning it is expected to move 19.2% for every 10% move in the market. Volatility, as measured by both the semi-deviation and a drawdown factor, is considered average. As of June 30, 2005, Corporate High Yield Fund III traded at a discount of 1.29% below its net asset value, which is worse than its one-year historical average discount of 2.13%.

Dan Evans has been running the fund for 7 years and currently receives a manager quality ranking of 12 (0=worst, 99=best). If you desire an average level of risk and strong performance, then this fund is a good option.

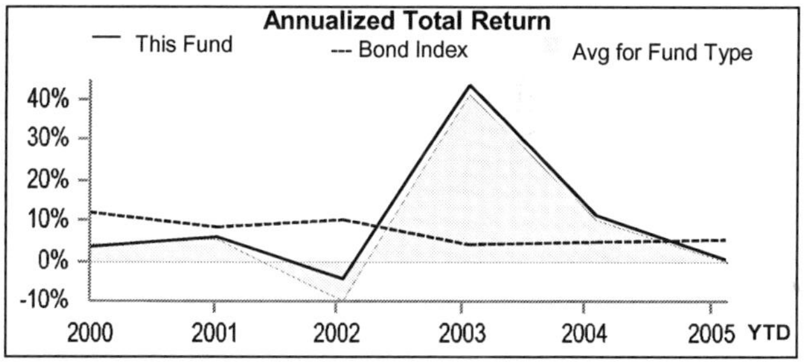

Corporate High Yield Fund V (HYV) B- Good

Fund Family: Merrill Lynch Investment Managers
Fund Type: Corporate - High Yield
Inception Date: December 3, 2001

Data Date	Weiss Investment Rating	Net Assets ($Mil)	Price	Performance Rating/Pts	Total Return Y-T-D	Risk Rating/Pts
6-05	B-	520.42	14.63	B- / 7.2	-2.28%	C+ / 6.1

Major Rating Factors:
Strong performance is the major factor driving the B- (Good) Weiss Investment Rating for Corporate High Yield Fund V. The fund currently has a performance rating of B- (Good) based on an annualized return of 19.28% over the last three years and a total return of -2.28% year to date 2005. Factored into the performance evaluation is an expense ratio of 1.85% (above average).

The fund's risk rating is currently C+ (Fair). It carries a beta of 1.51, meaning it is expected to move 15.1% for every 10% move in the market. Volatility, as measured by both the semi-deviation and a drawdown factor, is considered low. As of June 30, 2005, Corporate High Yield Fund V traded at a discount of 1.81% below its net asset value, which is worse than its one-year historical average discount of 3.52%.

Dan Evans has been running the fund for 4 years and currently receives a manager quality ranking of 53 (0=worst, 99=best). If you desire only a moderate level of risk and strong performance, then this fund is an excellent option.

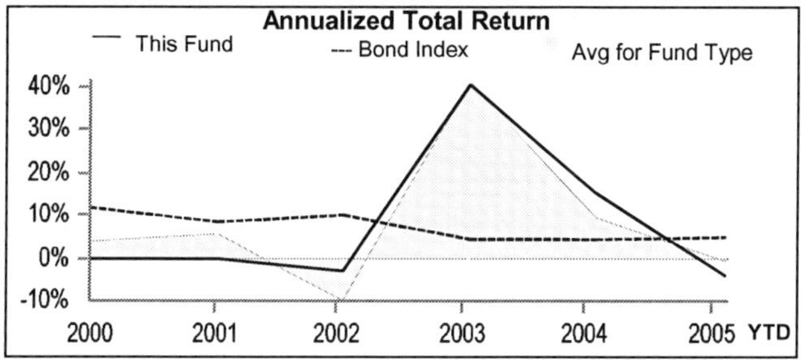

Credit Suisse Asset Mgmt Income (CIK) D+ Weak

Fund Family: Credit Suisse Asset Management
Fund Type: Corporate - High Yield
Inception Date: April 8, 1987

Data Date	Weiss Investment Rating	Net Assets ($Mil)	Price	Performance Rating/Pts	Total Return Y-T-D	Risk Rating/Pts
6-05	D+	227.37	4.65	C / 5.4	9.62%	C- / 3.4
2004	E+	215.76	4.45	D / 1.7	8.97%	C- / 3.3
2003	D	212.90	4.49	C- / 3.2	28.70%	C- / 3.8

Major Rating Factors:

Credit Suisse Asset Mgmt Income receives a Weiss Investment Rating of D+ (Weak). The fund currently has a performance rating of C (Fair) based on an annualized return of 10.32% over the last three years and a total return of 9.62% year to date 2005. Factored into the performance evaluation is an expense ratio of 0.78% (very low).

The fund's risk rating is currently C- (Fair). It carries a beta of 1.31, meaning it is expected to move 13.1% for every 10% move in the market. Volatility, as measured by both the semi-deviation and a drawdown factor, is considered average. As of June 30, 2005, Credit Suisse Asset Mgmt Income traded at a premium of 7.89% above its net asset value, which is worse than its one-year historical average premium of .80%.

Richard J. Lindquist has been running the fund for 16 years and currently receives a manager quality ranking of 8 (0=worst, 99=best). If you desire an average level of risk, then this fund may be an option.

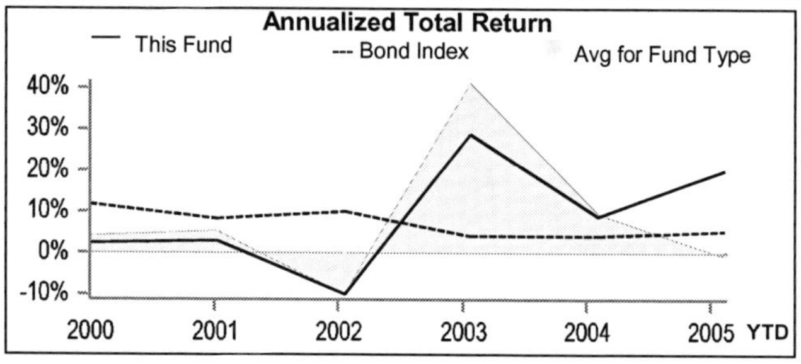

Credit Suisse High Yield Bond Fund (DHY) C Fair

Fund Family: Credit Suisse Asset Management, LLC
Fund Type: Corporate - High Yield
Inception Date: July 29, 1998

Data Date	Weiss Investment Rating	Net Assets ($Mil)	Price	Performance Rating/Pts	Total Return Y-T-D	Risk Rating/Pts
6-05	C	230.45	4.81	C+ / 6.6	-0.62%	C- / 4.0
2004	D	236.83	5.12	C / 5.5	8.27%	D+ / 2.5
2003	C-	229.26	5.28	B+ / 8.4	44.95%	D+ / 2.6

Major Rating Factors:

Middle of the road best describes Credit Suisse High Yield Bond Fund whose Weiss Investment Rating is currently a C (Fair). The fund currently has a performance rating of C+ (Fair) based on an annualized return of 17.95% over the last three years and a total return of -0.62% year to date 2005. Factored into the performance evaluation is an expense ratio of 3.00% (high).

The fund's risk rating is currently C- (Fair). It carries a beta of 1.78, meaning it is expected to move 17.8% for every 10% move in the market. Volatility, as measured by both the semi-deviation and a drawdown factor, is considered average. As of June 30, 2005, Credit Suisse High Yield Bond Fund traded at a premium of 12.91% above its net asset value, which is worse than its one-year historical average premium of 12.69%.

Richard Lindquist has been running the fund for 7 years and currently receives a manager quality ranking of 18 (0=worst, 99=best). If you desire an average level of risk, then this fund may be an option.

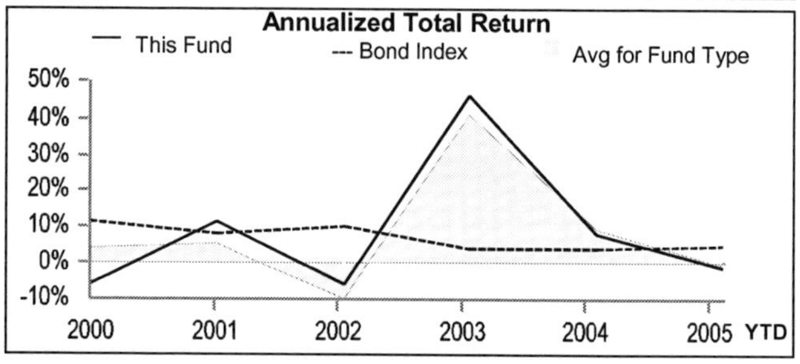

Debt Strategies Fund I Inc (DSU) C+ Fair

Fund Family: Merrill Lynch Investment Managers
Fund Type: Corporate - High Yield
Inception Date: March 24, 1998

Data Date	Weiss Investment Rating	Net Assets ($Mil)	Price	Performance Rating/Pts	Total Return Y-T-D	Risk Rating/Pts
6-05	C+	745.26	6.52	C+ / 6.7	-2.96%	C+ / 6.0
2004	C	710.24	7.00	C+ / 6.7	10.36%	C / 4.8
2003	C	635.96	7.03	B / 7.8	40.81%	C- / 4.1

Major Rating Factors:

Middle of the road best describes Debt Strategies Fund I Inc whose Weiss Investment Rating is currently a C+ (Fair). The fund currently has a performance rating of C+ (Fair) based on an annualized return of 18.03% over the last three years and a total return of -2.96% year to date 2005. Factored into the performance evaluation is an expense ratio of 1.83% (above average).

The fund's risk rating is currently C+ (Fair). It carries a beta of 1.60, meaning it is expected to move 16.0% for every 10% move in the market. Volatility, as measured by both the semi-deviation and a drawdown factor, is considered low. As of June 30, 2005, Debt Strategies Fund I Inc traded at a discount of 2.10% below its net asset value, which is worse than its one-year historical average discount of 2.23%.

Joe Matteo has been running the fund for 7 years and currently receives a manager quality ranking of 34 (0=worst, 99=best). If you desire an average level of risk, then this fund may be an option.

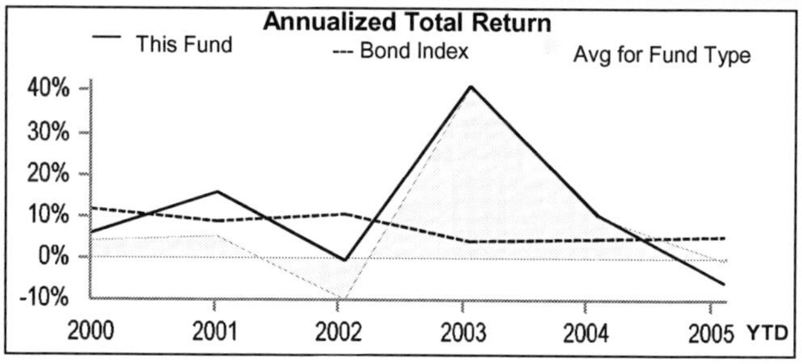

Delaware Inv AZ Muni Income (VAZ) C Fair

Fund Family: Delaware Investments
Fund Type: Municipal - Single State
Inception Date: February 26, 1993

Major Rating Factors:
Middle of the road best describes Delaware Inv AZ Muni Income whose Weiss Investment Rating is currently a C (Fair). The fund currently has a performance rating of C (Fair) based on an annualized return of 5.79% over the last three years and a total return of 3.81% year to date 2005. Factored into the performance evaluation is an expense ratio of 1.18% (low).

The fund's risk rating is currently C+ (Fair). It carries a beta of 1.83, meaning it is expected to move 18.3% for every 10% move in the market. Volatility, as measured by both the semi-deviation and a drawdown factor, is considered low. As of June 30, 2005, Delaware Inv AZ Muni Income traded at a premium of .45% above its net asset value, which is better than its one-year historical average premium of 1.00%.

Andrew M. McCullagh, Jr. has been running the fund for 12 years and currently receives a manager quality ranking of 35 (0=worst, 99=best). If you desire an average level of risk, then this fund may be an option.

Data Date	Weiss Investment Rating	Net Assets ($Mil)	Price	Performance Rating/Pts	Total Return Y-T-D	Risk Rating/Pts
6-05	C	44.94	15.57	C / 4.6	3.81%	C+ / 6.9
2004	C+	45.40	15.46	C / 4.8	3.58%	B- / 7.6
2003	B-	45.50	15.90	C+ / 6.3	11.56%	B- / 7.7

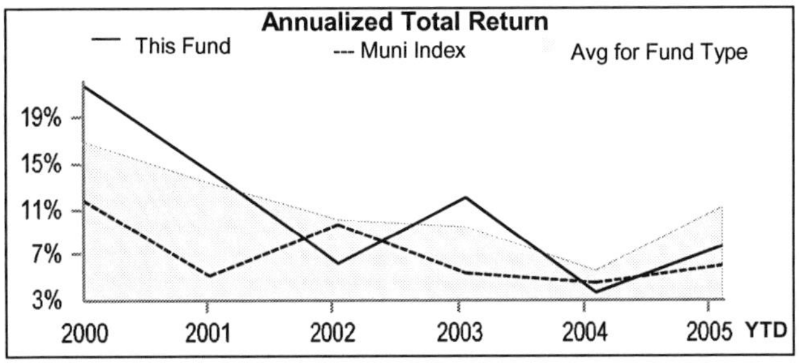

Delaware Inv CO Ins Muni Inc (VCF) A- Excellent

Fund Family: Delaware Investments
Fund Type: Municipal - Single State
Inception Date: July 29, 1993

Major Rating Factors:
Strong performance is the major factor driving the A- (Excellent) Weiss Investment Rating for Delaware Inv CO Ins Muni Inc. The fund currently has a performance rating of B (Good) based on an annualized return of 11.27% over the last three years and a total return of 1.95% year to date 2005. Factored into the performance evaluation is an expense ratio of 1.03% (low).

The fund's risk rating is currently C+ (Fair). It carries a beta of 2.38, meaning it is expected to move 23.8% for every 10% move in the market. Volatility, as measured by both the semi-deviation and a drawdown factor, is considered low. As of June 30, 2005, Delaware Inv CO Ins Muni Inc traded at a premium of 10.53% above its net asset value, which is worse than its one-year historical average premium of 8.79%.

Andrew M. McCullagh, Jr. has been running the fund for 12 years and currently receives a manager quality ranking of 56 (0=worst, 99=best). If you desire only a moderate level of risk and strong performance, then this fund is an excellent option.

Data Date	Weiss Investment Rating	Net Assets ($Mil)	Price	Performance Rating/Pts	Total Return Y-T-D	Risk Rating/Pts
6-05	A-	75.36	17.64	B / 8.0	1.95%	C+ / 6.9
2004	A+	76.65	17.81	B+ / 8.8	16.20%	C+ / 6.9
2003	B+	76.70	16.42	B- / 7.1	3.41%	B- / 7.9

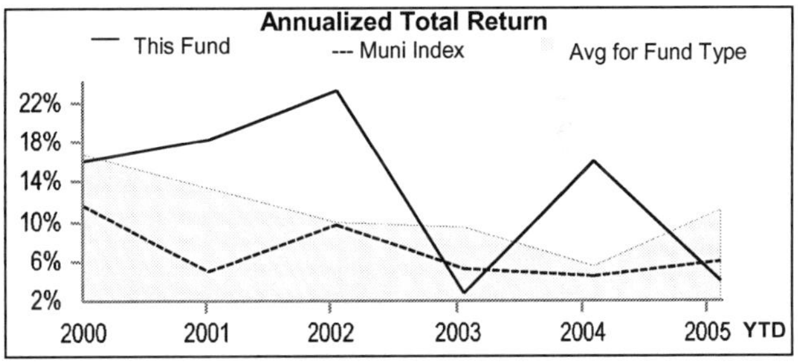

Delaware Inv Div & Inc (DDF) D Weak

Fund Family: Delaware Investments
Fund Type: Growth and Income
Inception Date: March 19, 1993

Major Rating Factors:
Delaware Inv Div & Inc receives a Weiss Investment Rating of D (Weak). The fund currently has a performance rating of C- (Fair) based on an annualized return of 6.71% over the last three years and a total return of 7.30% year to date 2005. Factored into the performance evaluation is an expense ratio of 1.51% (average).

The fund's risk rating is currently C (Fair). It carries a beta of 0.37, meaning the fund's expected move will be 3.7% for every 10% move in the market. Volatility, as measured by both the semi-deviation and a drawdown factor, is considered average. As of June 30, 2005, Delaware Inv Div & Inc traded at a discount of 3.62% below its net asset value, which is worse than its one-year historical average discount of 7.59%.

Peter Andersen has been running the fund for 5 years and currently receives a manager quality ranking of 75 (0=worst, 99=best). If you desire an average level of risk, then this fund may be an option.

Data Date	Weiss Investment Rating	Net Assets ($Mil)	Price	Performance Rating/Pts	Total Return Y-T-D	Risk Rating/Pts
6-05	D	166.93	12.51	C- / 3.7	7.30%	C / 4.5
2004	D	153.92	12.13	D+ / 2.8	8.86%	C / 5.0
2003	C-	150.60	11.96	C / 4.6	26.42%	C+ / 5.8

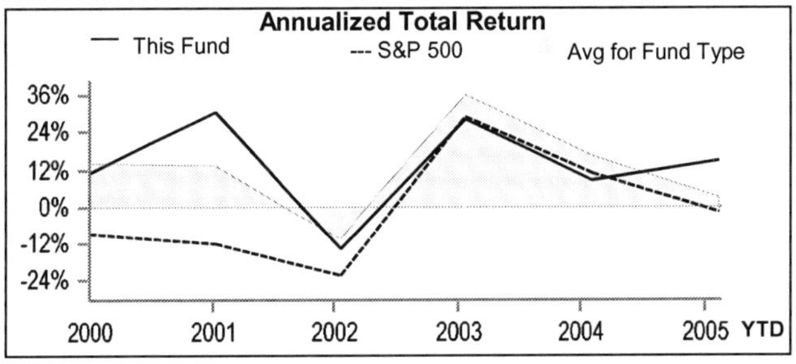

Delaware Inv FL Insured Muni Inc (VFL) B+ Good

Fund Family: Delaware Investments
Fund Type: Municipal - Single State
Inception Date: February 26, 1993

Data Date	Weiss Investment Rating	Net Assets ($Mil)	Price	Perfor-mance Rating/Pts	Total Return Y-T-D	Risk Rating/Pts
6-05	B+	37.17	16.70	B+ / 8.3	-0.03%	C+ / 6.1
2004	A	38.29	17.25	B+ / 8.9	14.69%	C+ / 6.6
2003	B	39.26	16.06	B- / 7.3	12.13%	B- / 7.4

Major Rating Factors:
Strong performance is the major factor driving the B+ (Good) Weiss Investment Rating for Delaware Inv FL Insured Muni Inc. The fund currently has a performance rating of B+ (Good) based on an annualized return of 10.32% over the last three years and a total return of -0.03% year to date 2005. Factored into the performance evaluation is an expense ratio of 1.24% (average).

The fund's risk rating is currently C+ (Fair). It carries a beta of 2.59, meaning it is expected to move 25.9% for every 10% move in the market. Volatility, as measured by both the semi-deviation and a drawdown factor, is considered low. As of June 30, 2005, Delaware Inv FL Insured Muni Inc traded at a premium of 7.33% above its net asset value, which is worse than its one-year historical average premium of 2.95%.

Denise Franchetti has been running the fund for 12 years and currently receives a manager quality ranking of 37 (0=worst, 99=best). If you desire only a moderate level of risk and strong performance, then this fund is an excellent option.

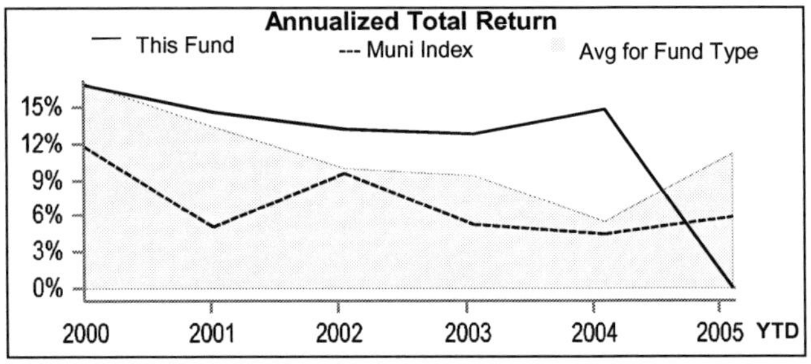

Delaware Inv Glob Div & Inc (DGF) C+ Fair

Fund Family: Delaware Investments
Fund Type: Growth and Income
Inception Date: February 28, 1994

Data Date	Weiss Investment Rating	Net Assets ($Mil)	Price	Perfor-mance Rating/Pts	Total Return Y-T-D	Risk Rating/Pts
6-05	C+	81.32	13.07	C+ / 5.8	7.97%	C+ / 6.0
2004	C+	73.27	12.57	C+ / 5.9	10.08%	C+ / 6.3
2003	C	71.69	12.04	C+ / 5.8	27.84%	C+ / 6.5

Major Rating Factors:
Middle of the road best describes Delaware Inv Glob Div & Inc whose Weiss Investment Rating is currently a C+ (Fair). The fund currently has a performance rating of C+ (Fair) based on an annualized return of 11.10% over the last three years and a total return of 7.97% year to date 2005. Factored into the performance evaluation is an expense ratio of 1.92% (above average).

The fund's risk rating is currently C+ (Fair). It carries a beta of 0.30, meaning the fund's expected move will be 3.0% for every 10% move in the market. Volatility, as measured by both the semi-deviation and a drawdown factor, is considered low. As of June 30, 2005, Delaware Inv Glob Div & Inc traded at a discount of 2.90% below its net asset value, which is worse than its one-year historical average discount of 7.40%.

This fund has been team managed for 6 years and currently receives a manager quality ranking of 86 (0=worst, 99=best). If you desire an average level of risk, then this fund may be an option.

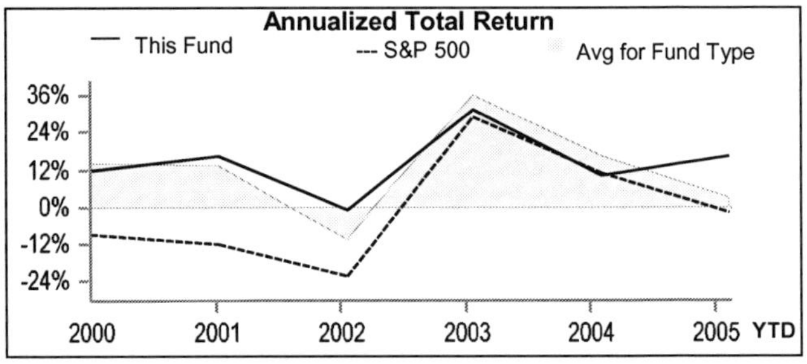

Delaware Inv MN Muni Inc Fund II (VMM) C+ Fair

Fund Family: Delaware Investments
Fund Type: Municipal - Single State
Inception Date: February 26, 1993

Data Date	Weiss Investment Rating	Net Assets ($Mil)	Price	Perfor-mance Rating/Pts	Total Return Y-T-D	Risk Rating/Pts
6-05	C+	107.96	15.95	C / 4.7	-3.14%	B- / 7.0
2004	A	109.51	17.00	B+ / 8.6	12.36%	C+ / 6.9
2003	A-	109.10	16.37	B / 8.2	13.73%	B- / 7.4

Major Rating Factors:
Middle of the road best describes Delaware Inv MN Muni Inc Fund II whose Weiss Investment Rating is currently a C+ (Fair). The fund currently has a performance rating of C (Fair) based on an annualized return of 0.33% over the last three years and a total return of -3.14% year to date 2005. Factored into the performance evaluation is an expense ratio of 1.00% (low).

The fund's risk rating is currently B- (Good). It carries a beta of 2.14, meaning it is expected to move 21.4% for every 10% move in the market. Volatility, as measured by both the semi-deviation and a drawdown factor, is considered low. As of June 30, 2005, Delaware Inv MN Muni Inc Fund II traded at a premium of 3.57% above its net asset value, which is better than its one-year historical average premium of 7.93%.

Denise Franchetti has been running the fund for 12 years and currently receives a manager quality ranking of 48 (0=worst, 99=best). If you desire an average level of risk, then this fund may be an option.

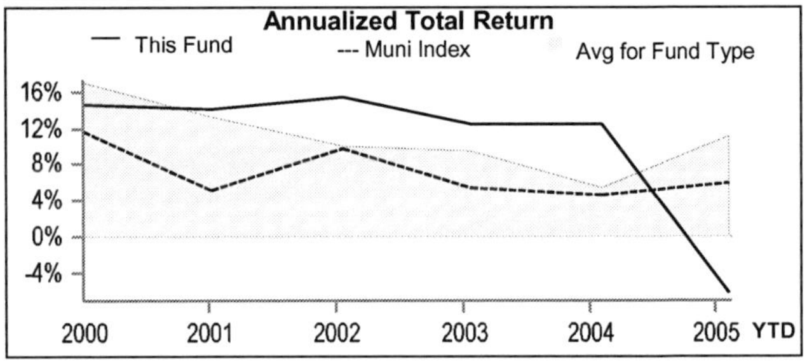

Delaware Inv MN Muni Inc Fund III (VYM) — C — Fair

Fund Family: Delaware Investments
Fund Type: Municipal - Single State
Inception Date: October 29, 1993

Major Rating Factors:
Middle of the road best describes Delaware Inv MN Muni Inc Fund III whose Weiss Investment Rating is currently a C (Fair). The fund currently has a performance rating of C (Fair) based on an annualized return of 9.00% over the last three years and a total return of -0.02% year to date 2005. Factored into the performance evaluation is an expense ratio of 1.33% (average).

The fund's risk rating is currently C+ (Fair). It carries a beta of 1.64, meaning it is expected to move 16.4% for every 10% move in the market. Volatility, as measured by both the semi-deviation and a drawdown factor, is considered low. As of June 30, 2005, Delaware Inv MN Muni Inc Fund III traded at a premium of 3.03% above its net asset value, which is better than its one-year historical average premium of 8.51%.

Denise Franchetti has been running the fund for 12 years and currently receives a manager quality ranking of 61 (0=worst, 99=best). If you desire an average level of risk, then this fund may be an option.

Data Date	Weiss Investment Rating	Net Assets ($Mil)	Price	Performance Rating/Pts	Total Return Y-T-D	Risk Rating/Pts
6-05	C	25.72	14.94	C / 4.3	-0.02%	C+ / 6.8
2004	B+	26.15	15.40	B+ / 8.3	5.14%	C+ / 6.6
2003	A-	26.29	15.55	B+ / 8.5	17.08%	B- / 7.1

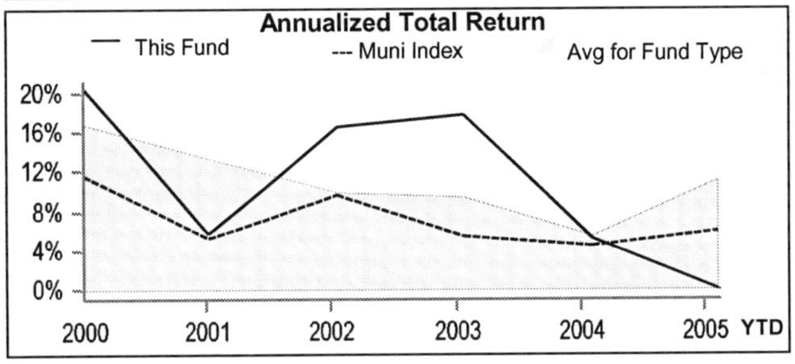

Delaware Inv MN Muni Income (VMN) — C- — Fair

Fund Family: Delaware Investments
Fund Type: Municipal - Single State
Inception Date: May 1, 1992

Major Rating Factors:
Disappointing performance is the major factor driving the C- (Fair) Weiss Investment Rating for Delaware Inv MN Muni Income. The fund currently has a performance rating of D+ (Weak) based on an annualized return of 7.69% over the last three years and a total return of -8.36% year to date 2005. Factored into the performance evaluation is an expense ratio of 1.27% (average).

The fund's risk rating is currently B- (Good). It carries a beta of 2.20, meaning it is expected to move 22.0% for every 10% move in the market. Volatility, as measured by both the semi-deviation and a drawdown factor, is considered low. As of June 30, 2005, Delaware Inv MN Muni Income traded at a discount of 1.26% below its net asset value, which is better than its one-year historical average premium of 5.38%.

Denise Franchetti has been running the fund for 13 years and currently receives a manager quality ranking of 27 (0=worst, 99=best). This fund offers only a moderate level of risk but investors looking for strong performance are still waiting.

Data Date	Weiss Investment Rating	Net Assets ($Mil)	Price	Performance Rating/Pts	Total Return Y-T-D	Risk Rating/Pts
6-05	C-	37.74	14.93	D+ / 2.3	-8.36%	B- / 7.3
2004	A+	38.43	16.75	B+ / 8.8	14.30%	B- / 7.0
2003	B	39.38	15.65	B- / 7.4	10.39%	B- / 7.3

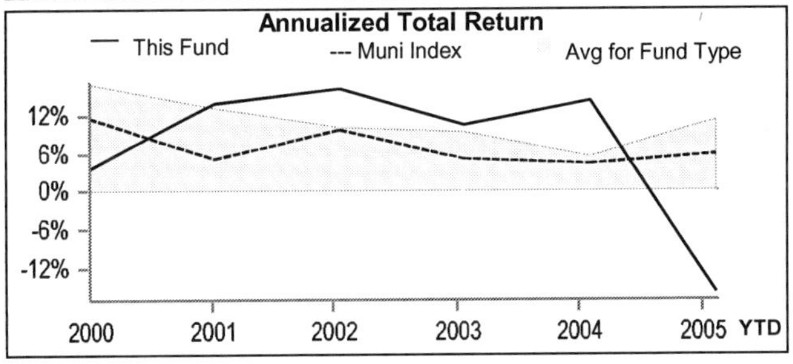

Diamond Series Trust I (DIA) — D- — Weak

Fund Family: State Street Bank & Trust Co.
Fund Type: Growth
Inception Date: January 27, 1998

Major Rating Factors:
Very poor performance is the major factor driving the D- (Weak) Weiss Investment Rating for Diamond Series Trust I. The fund currently has a performance rating of E (Very Weak) based on an annualized return of 5.80% over the last three years and a total return of -3.39% year to date 2005. Factored into the performance evaluation is an expense ratio of 0.18% (very low).

The fund's risk rating is currently B- (Good). It carries a beta of 1.01, meaning that its performance tracks fairly well with that of the overall stock market. Volatility, as measured by both the semi-deviation and a drawdown factor, is considered low. As of June 30, 2005, Diamond Series Trust I traded at a discount of .05% below its net asset value, which is better than its one-year historical average premium of .02%.

State Street Bank has been running the fund for 7 years and currently receives a manager quality ranking of 39 (0=worst, 99=best). This fund offers only a moderate level of risk but investors looking for strong performance are still waiting.

Data Date	Weiss Investment Rating	Net Assets ($Mil)	Price	Performance Rating/Pts	Total Return Y-T-D	Risk Rating/Pts
6-05	D-	6680.16	102.86	E / 0.5	-3.39%	B- / 7.2
2004	D	7546.89	107.51	D- / 1.2	5.01%	C+ / 6.5
2003	D+	6030.40	103.27	D+ / 2.8	26.29%	C+ / 5.8

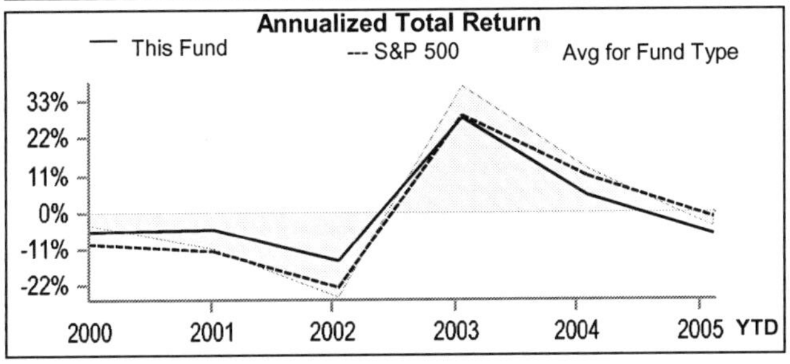

DNP Select Income Fund Inc (DNP) C+ Fair

Fund Family: Duff & Phelps Investment Mgmt Co.
Fund Type: Utilities
Inception Date: January 28, 1987

Major Rating Factors:
Middle of the road best describes DNP Select Income Fund Inc whose Weiss Investment Rating is currently a C+ (Fair). The fund currently has a performance rating of C (Fair) based on an annualized return of 12.65% over the last three years and a total return of 1.11% year to date 2005.

The fund's risk rating is currently B- (Good). It carries a beta of 0.50, meaning the fund's expected move will be 5.0% for every 10% move in the market. Volatility, as measured by both the semi-deviation and a drawdown factor, is considered low. As of June 30, 2005, DNP Select Income Fund Inc traded at a premium of 28.29% above its net asset value, which is better than its one-year historical average premium of 33.55%.

T. Brooks Beittel has been running the fund for 11 years and currently receives a manager quality ranking of 76 (0=worst, 99=best). If you desire an average level of risk, then this fund may be an option.

Data Date	Weiss Investment Rating	Net Assets ($Mil)	Price	Performance Rating/Pts	Total Return Y-T-D	Risk Rating/Pts
6-05	C+	1935.44	11.70	C / 5.3	1.11%	B- / 7.3
2004	C	1703.96	0.00	C+ / 6.4	17.22%	C / 5.3
2003	C-	1688.55	11.00	C- / 3.3	19.29%	C+ / 6.7

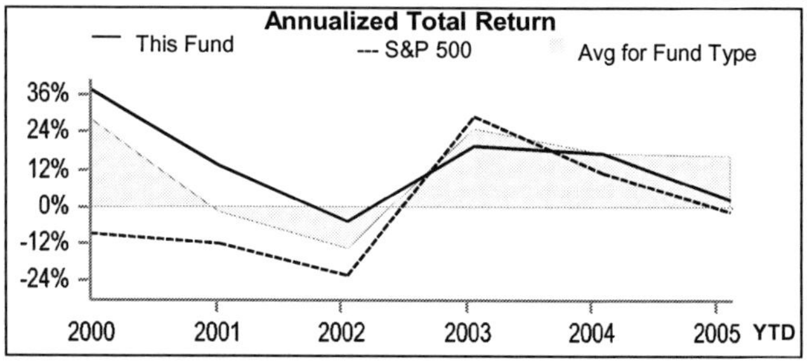

Dreyfus High Yield Strategies Fund (DHF) D Weak

Fund Family: Dreyfus Corporation
Fund Type: Corporate - High Yield
Inception Date: April 29, 1998

Major Rating Factors:
Dreyfus High Yield Strategies Fund receives a Weiss Investment Rating of D (Weak). The fund currently has a performance rating of C (Fair) based on an annualized return of 15.11% over the last three years and a total return of -4.41% year to date 2005. Factored into the performance evaluation is an expense ratio of 2.33% (high).

The fund's risk rating is currently C- (Fair). It carries a beta of 1.97, meaning it is expected to move 19.7% for every 10% move in the market. Volatility, as measured by both the semi-deviation and a drawdown factor, is considered average. As of June 30, 2005, Dreyfus High Yield Strategies Fund traded at a discount of 6.02% below its net asset value, which is better than its one-year historical average discount of 1.41%.

Gerald E. Thunelius has been running the fund for 3 years and currently receives a manager quality ranking of 3 (0=worst, 99=best). If you desire an average level of risk, then this fund may be an option.

Data Date	Weiss Investment Rating	Net Assets ($Mil)	Price	Performance Rating/Pts	Total Return Y-T-D	Risk Rating/Pts
6-05	D	333.87	4.37	C / 4.5	-4.41%	C- / 3.7
2004	E+	340.04	4.77	D+ / 2.9	-2.11%	D+ / 2.5
2003	C-	325.03	5.45	B / 8.1	63.77%	D / 2.0

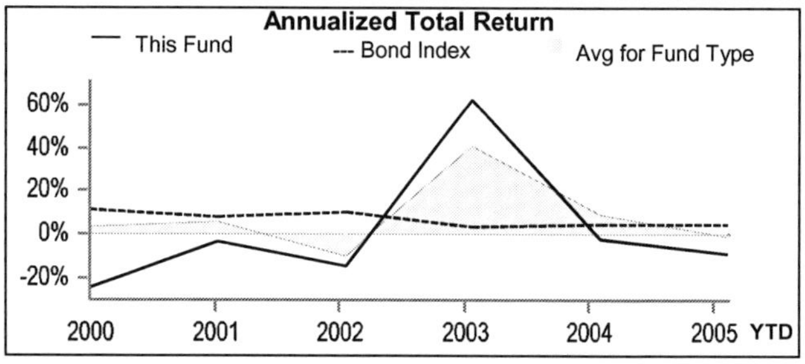

Dreyfus Municipal Income (DMF) C Fair

Fund Family: Dreyfus Corporation
Fund Type: Municipal - National
Inception Date: October 24, 1988

Major Rating Factors:
Middle of the road best describes Dreyfus Municipal Income whose Weiss Investment Rating is currently a C (Fair). The fund currently has a performance rating of C- (Fair) based on an annualized return of 7.54% over the last three years and a total return of -4.49% year to date 2005. Factored into the performance evaluation is an expense ratio of 1.31% (average).

The fund's risk rating is currently B- (Good). It carries a beta of 2.20, meaning it is expected to move 22.0% for every 10% move in the market. Volatility, as measured by both the semi-deviation and a drawdown factor, is considered low. As of June 30, 2005, Dreyfus Municipal Income traded at a discount of 5.32% below its net asset value, which is better than its one-year historical average premium of .79%.

A. Paul Disdier has been running the fund for 17 years and currently receives a manager quality ranking of 27 (0=worst, 99=best). If you desire an average level of risk, then this fund may be an option.

Data Date	Weiss Investment Rating	Net Assets ($Mil)	Price	Performance Rating/Pts	Total Return Y-T-D	Risk Rating/Pts
6-05	C	196.03	9.25	C- / 3.5	-4.49%	B- / 7.1
2004	A	195.40	10.00	B+ / 8.4	9.00%	B- / 7.0
2003	A	194.39	9.78	B / 8.2	18.53%	B- / 7.8

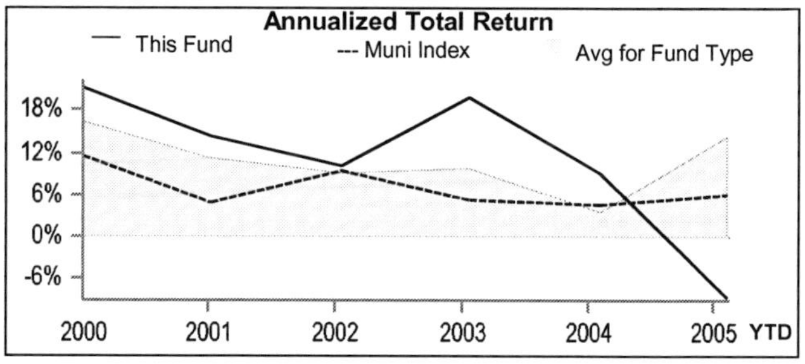

Dreyfus Strategic Muni Bond Fund (DSM) | A- | Excellent

Fund Family: Dreyfus Corporation
Fund Type: Municipal - National
Inception Date: November 22, 1989

Data Date	Weiss Investment Rating	Net Assets ($Mil)	Price	Performance Rating/Pts	Total Return Y-T-D	Risk Rating/Pts
6-05	A-	423.56	9.25	B+ / 8.8	12.59%	C+ / 6.1
2004	C+	412.83	8.51	C / 4.7	3.74%	B- / 7.4
2003	C+	428.30	8.84	C / 5.2	17.51%	B- / 7.5

Major Rating Factors:
Strong performance is the major factor driving the A- (Excellent) Weiss Investment Rating for Dreyfus Strategic Muni Bond Fund. The fund currently has a performance rating of B+ (Good) based on an annualized return of 9.07% over the last three years and a total return of 12.59% year to date 2005. Factored into the performance evaluation is an expense ratio of 1.25% (average).

The fund's risk rating is currently C+ (Fair). It carries a beta of 2.19, meaning it is expected to move 21.9% for every 10% move in the market. Volatility, as measured by both the semi-deviation and a drawdown factor, is considered low. As of June 30, 2005, Dreyfus Strategic Muni Bond Fund traded at a premium of 1.87% above its net asset value, which is worse than its one-year historical average discount of 3.64%.

Paul Disdier has been running the fund for 9 years and currently receives a manager quality ranking of 47 (0=worst, 99=best). If you desire only a moderate level of risk and strong performance, then this fund is an excellent option.

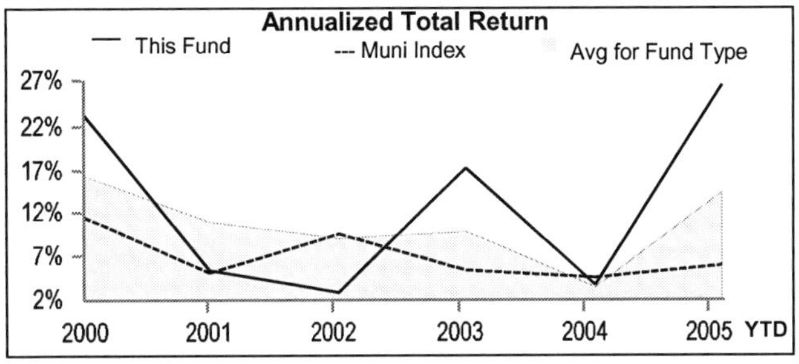

Dreyfus Strategic Municipals (LEO) | C | Fair

Fund Family: Dreyfus Corporation
Fund Type: Municipal - National
Inception Date: September 28, 1987

Data Date	Weiss Investment Rating	Net Assets ($Mil)	Price	Performance Rating/Pts	Total Return Y-T-D	Risk Rating/Pts
6-05	C	558.37	8.86	C / 4.7	8.74%	C+ / 6.8
2004	D	556.24	8.42	E+ / 0.9	-8.09%	B- / 7.5
2003	B	549.68	9.80	C+ / 6.6	9.26%	B / 8.2

Major Rating Factors:
Middle of the road best describes Dreyfus Strategic Municipals whose Weiss Investment Rating is currently a C (Fair). The fund currently has a performance rating of C (Fair) based on an annualized return of 3.60% over the last three years and a total return of 8.74% year to date 2005. Factored into the performance evaluation is an expense ratio of 1.26% (average).

The fund's risk rating is currently C+ (Fair). It carries a beta of 2.13, meaning it is expected to move 21.3% for every 10% move in the market. Volatility, as measured by both the semi-deviation and a drawdown factor, is considered low. As of June 30, 2005, Dreyfus Strategic Municipals traded at a discount of 6.54% below its net asset value, which is worse than its one-year historical average discount of 7.19%.

Paul Disdier has been running the fund for 9 years and currently receives a manager quality ranking of 7 (0=worst, 99=best). If you desire an average level of risk, then this fund may be an option.

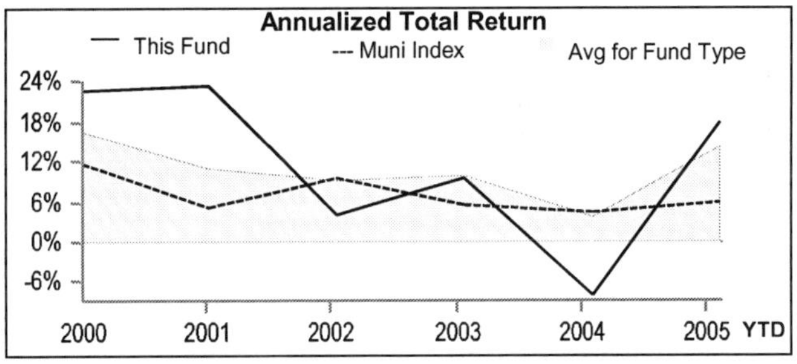

DTF Tax Free Income (DTF) | C+ | Fair

Fund Family: Duff & Phelps Investment Mgmt Co.
Fund Type: Municipal - National
Inception Date: November 22, 1991

Data Date	Weiss Investment Rating	Net Assets ($Mil)	Price	Performance Rating/Pts	Total Return Y-T-D	Risk Rating/Pts
6-05	C+	143.29	15.90	C+ / 5.9	5.03%	C+ / 6.8
2004	B-	141.11	15.61	C+ / 6.6	4.53%	B- / 7.6
2003	B+	144.82	15.89	C+ / 6.5	8.91%	B / 8.4

Major Rating Factors:
Middle of the road best describes DTF Tax Free Income whose Weiss Investment Rating is currently a C+ (Fair). The fund currently has a performance rating of C+ (Fair) based on an annualized return of 7.45% over the last three years and a total return of 5.03% year to date 2005. Factored into the performance evaluation is an expense ratio of 1.41% (average).

The fund's risk rating is currently C+ (Fair). It carries a beta of 2.15, meaning it is expected to move 21.5% for every 10% move in the market. Volatility, as measured by both the semi-deviation and a drawdown factor, is considered low. As of June 30, 2005, DTF Tax Free Income traded at a discount of 6.36% below its net asset value, which is worse than its one-year historical average discount of 7.71%.

James D. Wehr has been running the fund for 14 years and currently receives a manager quality ranking of 33 (0=worst, 99=best). If you desire an average level of risk, then this fund may be an option.

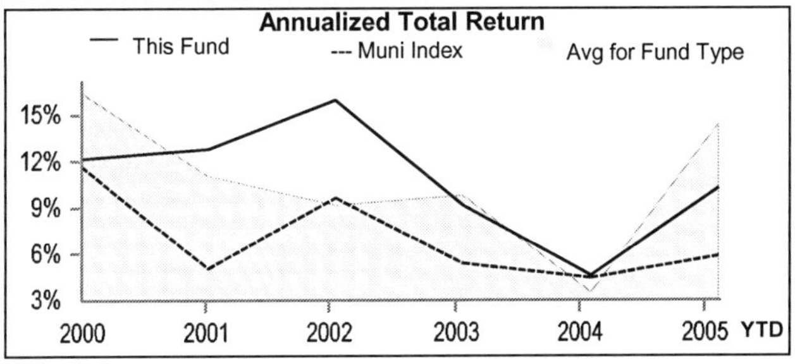

Duff & Phelps Utilities & Crp Bd Tr (DUC) C Fair

Fund Family: Duff & Phelps Investment Mgmt Co.
Fund Type: General - Investment Grade
Inception Date: January 22, 1993

Major Rating Factors:
Middle of the road best describes Duff & Phelps Utilities & Crp Bd Tr whose Weiss Investment Rating is currently a C (Fair). The fund currently has a performance rating of C (Fair) based on an annualized return of 11.26% over the last three years and a total return of 2.93% year to date 2005. Factored into the performance evaluation is an expense ratio of 1.78% (above average).

The fund's risk rating is currently C+ (Fair). It carries a beta of 2.12, meaning it is expected to move 21.2% for every 10% move in the market. Volatility, as measured by both the semi-deviation and a drawdown factor, is considered low. As of June 30, 2005, Duff & Phelps Utilities & Crp Bd Tr traded at a premium of 10.30% above its net asset value, which is worse than its one-year historical average premium of 5.81%.

Daniel J. Petrisko has been running the fund for 9 years and currently receives a manager quality ranking of 64 (0=worst, 99=best). If you desire an average level of risk, then this fund may be an option.

Data Date	Weiss Investment Rating	Net Assets ($Mil)	Price	Performance Rating/Pts	Total Return Y-T-D	Risk Rating/Pts
6-05	C	362.60	14.57	C / 5.4	2.93%	C+ / 6.0
2004	C+	353.06	14.70	C / 5.1	5.66%	B- / 7.0
2003	C	377.37	14.72	C / 4.5	20.45%	B- / 7.9

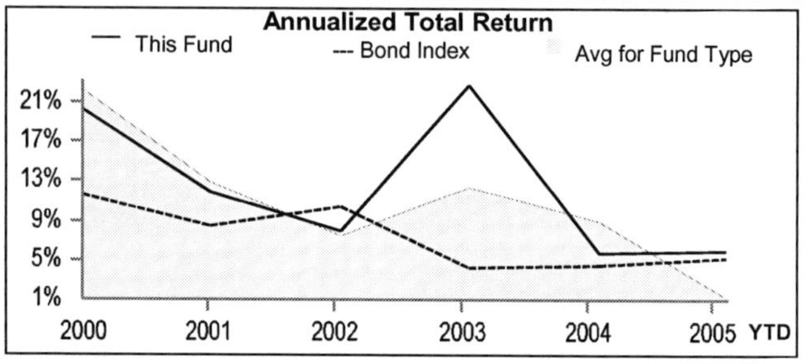

Eaton Vance CA Muni Inc Tr (CEV) B- Good

Fund Family: Eaton Vance Mgmt.
Fund Type: Municipal - Single State
Inception Date: January 29, 1999

Major Rating Factors:
Eaton Vance CA Muni Inc Tr receives a Weiss Investment Rating of B- (Good). The fund currently has a performance rating of C+ (Fair) based on an annualized return of 8.86% over the last three years and a total return of 3.02% year to date 2005. Factored into the performance evaluation is an expense ratio of 1.77% (above average).

The fund's risk rating is currently B- (Good). It carries a beta of 2.43, meaning it is expected to move 24.3% for every 10% move in the market. Volatility, as measured by both the semi-deviation and a drawdown factor, is considered low. As of June 30, 2005, Eaton Vance CA Muni Inc Tr traded at a discount of 5.13% below its net asset value, which is better than its one-year historical average discount of 2.72%.

Cynthia J. Clemson has been running the fund for 6 years and currently receives a manager quality ranking of 35 (0=worst, 99=best). If you desire an average level of risk, then this fund may be an option.

Data Date	Weiss Investment Rating	Net Assets ($Mil)	Price	Performance Rating/Pts	Total Return Y-T-D	Risk Rating/Pts
6-05	B-	108.19	14.99	C+ / 6.0	3.02%	B- / 7.6
2004	B-	105.34	15.02	C+ / 6.3	5.25%	B- / 7.8
2003	A+	109.99	15.20	B+ / 8.6	16.18%	B / 8.0

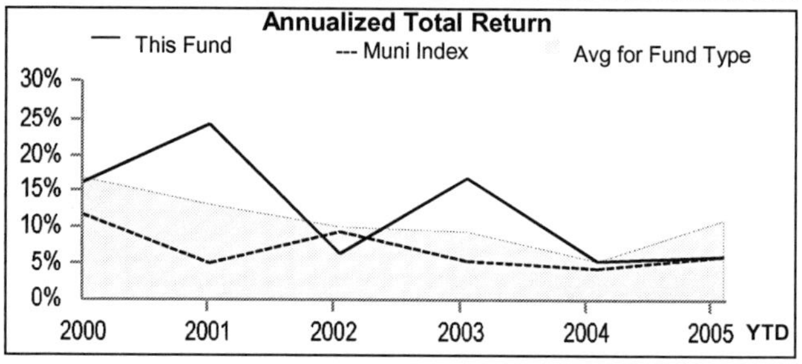

Eaton Vance FL Muni Inc Tr (FEV) B+ Good

Fund Family: Eaton Vance Mgmt.
Fund Type: Municipal - Single State
Inception Date: January 29, 1999

Major Rating Factors:
Strong performance is the major factor driving the B+ (Good) Weiss Investment Rating for Eaton Vance FL Muni Inc Tr. The fund currently has a performance rating of B (Good) based on an annualized return of 10.60% over the last three years and a total return of 1.84% year to date 2005.

The fund's risk rating is currently C+ (Fair). It carries a beta of 2.44, meaning it is expected to move 24.4% for every 10% move in the market. Volatility, as measured by both the semi-deviation and a drawdown factor, is considered low. As of June 30, 2005, Eaton Vance FL Muni Inc Tr traded at a premium of 1.63% above its net asset value, which is worse than its one-year historical average discount of .20%.

Cynthia J. Clemson has been running the fund for 6 years and currently receives a manager quality ranking of 50 (0=worst, 99=best). If you desire only a moderate level of risk and strong performance, then this fund is an excellent option.

Data Date	Weiss Investment Rating	Net Assets ($Mil)	Price	Performance Rating/Pts	Total Return Y-T-D	Risk Rating/Pts
6-05	B+	0.00	15.55	B / 7.9	1.84%	C+ / 6.6
2004	A+	62.95	15.76	B+ / 8.7	9.16%	B- / 7.0
2003	A+	65.90	15.50	B+ / 8.7	10.76%	B / 8.1

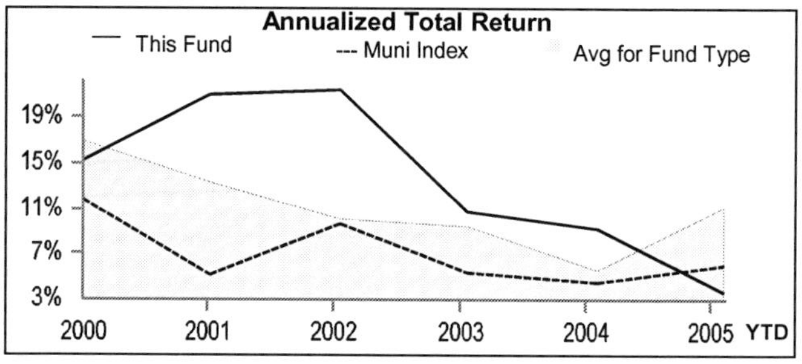

Eaton Vance MA Muni Inc Tr (MMV) C- Fair

Fund Family: Eaton Vance Mgmt.
Fund Type: Municipal - Single State
Inception Date: January 29, 1999

Major Rating Factors:
Middle of the road best describes Eaton Vance MA Muni Inc Tr whose Weiss Investment Rating is currently a C- (Fair). The fund currently has a performance rating of C- (Fair) based on an annualized return of 8.45% over the last three years and a total return of -6.45% year to date 2005. Factored into the performance evaluation is an expense ratio of 1.86% (above average).

The fund's risk rating is currently C+ (Fair). It carries a beta of 1.85, meaning it is expected to move 18.5% for every 10% move in the market. Volatility, as measured by both the semi-deviation and a drawdown factor, is considered low. As of June 30, 2005, Eaton Vance MA Muni Inc Tr traded at a premium of .90% above its net asset value, which is better than its one-year historical average premium of 7.71%.

Robert B. MacIntosh has been running the fund for 6 years and currently receives a manager quality ranking of 55 (0=worst, 99=best). If you desire an average level of risk, then this fund may be an option.

Data Date	Weiss Investment Rating	Net Assets ($Mil)	Price	Performance Rating/Pts	Total Return Y-T-D	Risk Rating/Pts
6-05	C-	40.66	15.78	C- / 3.0	-6.45%	C+ / 7.0
2004	A+	39.23	17.37	A- / 9.0	20.27%	C+ / 6.8
2003	A+	41.04	15.49	B+ / 8.5	7.03%	B / 8.5

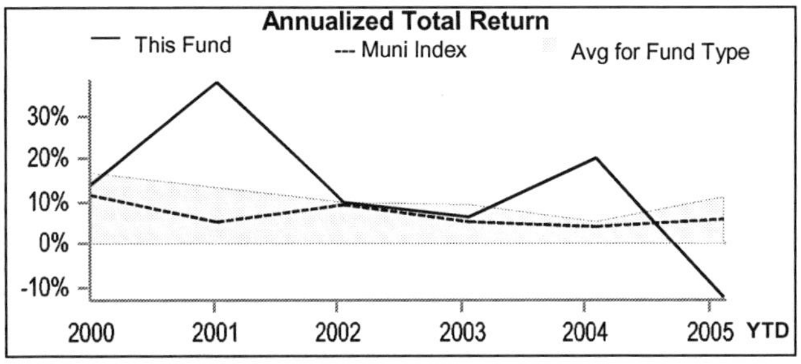

Eaton Vance MI Muni Inc Tr (EMI) C+ Fair

Fund Family: Eaton Vance Mgmt.
Fund Type: Municipal - Single State
Inception Date: January 29, 1999

Major Rating Factors:
Middle of the road best describes Eaton Vance MI Muni Inc Tr whose Weiss Investment Rating is currently a C+ (Fair). The fund currently has a performance rating of C (Fair) based on an annualized return of 10.36% over the last three years and a total return of -4.11% year to date 2005. Factored into the performance evaluation is an expense ratio of 1.96% (above average).

The fund's risk rating is currently B (Good). It carries a beta of 1.64, meaning it is expected to move 16.4% for every 10% move in the market. Volatility, as measured by both the semi-deviation and a drawdown factor, is considered low. As of June 30, 2005, Eaton Vance MI Muni Inc Tr traded at a premium of 1.31% above its net asset value, which is better than its one-year historical average premium of 7.75%.

William H. Ahern Jr. has been running the fund for 6 years and currently receives a manager quality ranking of 65 (0=worst, 99=best). If you desire an average level of risk, then this fund may be an option.

Data Date	Weiss Investment Rating	Net Assets ($Mil)	Price	Performance Rating/Pts	Total Return Y-T-D	Risk Rating/Pts
6-05	C+	31.36	15.46	C / 4.5	-4.11%	B / 8.2
2004	A+	30.56	16.60	B+ / 8.8	9.31%	B- / 7.7
2003	A+	31.96	16.00	A- / 9.0	18.28%	B- / 7.8

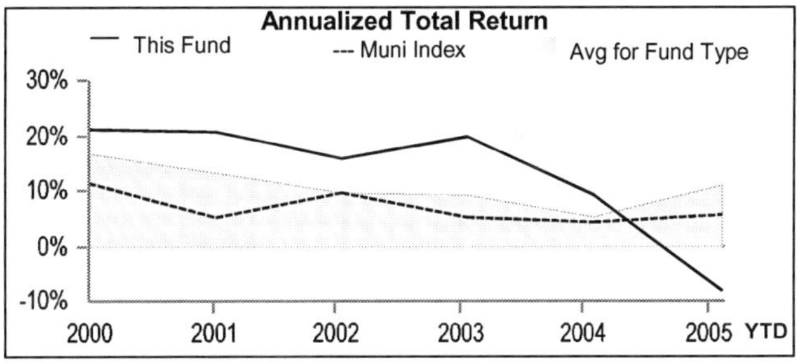

Eaton Vance Municipal Inc Tr (EVN) A+ Excellent

Fund Family: Eaton Vance Mgmt.
Fund Type: Municipal - National
Inception Date: January 29, 1999

Major Rating Factors:
Exceptional performance is the major factor driving the A+ (Excellent) Weiss Investment Rating for Eaton Vance Municipal Inc Tr. The fund currently has a performance rating of A (Excellent) based on an annualized return of 14.78% over the last three years and a total return of 5.59% year to date 2005. Factored into the performance evaluation is an expense ratio of 1.78% (above average).

The fund's risk rating is currently C+ (Fair). It carries a beta of 2.01, meaning it is expected to move 20.1% for every 10% move in the market. Volatility, as measured by both the semi-deviation and a drawdown factor, is considered low. As of June 30, 2005, Eaton Vance Municipal Inc Tr traded at a premium of 14.26% above its net asset value, which is worse than its one-year historical average premium of 14.05%.

Tom Metzold has been running the fund for 6 years and currently receives a manager quality ranking of 79 (0=worst, 99=best). If you desire only a moderate level of risk and strong performance, then this fund is an excellent option.

Data Date	Weiss Investment Rating	Net Assets ($Mil)	Price	Performance Rating/Pts	Total Return Y-T-D	Risk Rating/Pts
6-05	A+	236.30	16.67	A / 9.3	5.59%	C+ / 6.9
2004	A+	226.08	16.40	B+ / 8.7	12.44%	B- / 7.1
2003	A+	236.56	15.74	A- / 9.0	19.76%	B- / 7.8

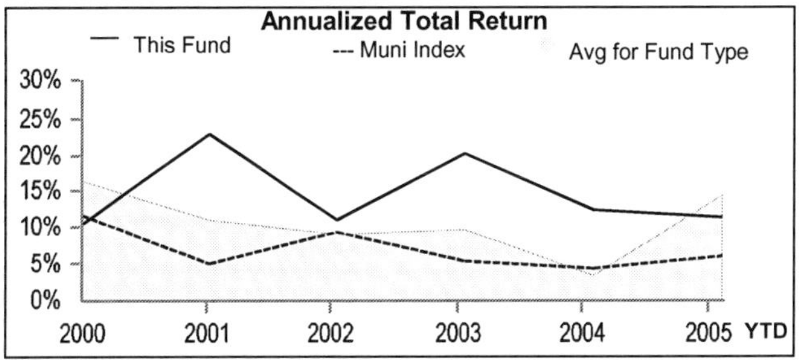

Eaton Vance NJ Muni Inc Tr (EVJ) C+ Fair

Fund Family: Eaton Vance Mgmt.
Fund Type: Municipal - Single State
Inception Date: January 29, 1999

Major Rating Factors:
Middle of the road best describes Eaton Vance NJ Muni Inc Tr whose Weiss Investment Rating is currently a C+ (Fair). The fund currently has a performance rating of C- (Fair) based on an annualized return of 7.56% over the last three years and a total return of -1.04% year to date 2005. Factored into the performance evaluation is an expense ratio of 1.84% (above average).

The fund's risk rating is currently B- (Good). It carries a beta of 2.29, meaning it is expected to move 22.9% for every 10% move in the market. Volatility, as measured by both the semi-deviation and a drawdown factor, is considered low. As of June 30, 2005, Eaton Vance NJ Muni Inc Tr traded at a discount of 3.25% below its net asset value, which is better than its one-year historical average premium of .56%.

Robert B. Macintosh has been running the fund for 6 years and currently receives a manager quality ranking of 26 (0=worst, 99=best). If you desire an average level of risk, then this fund may be an option.

Data Date	Weiss Investment Rating	Net Assets ($Mil)	Price	Performance Rating/Pts	Total Return Y-T-D	Risk Rating/Pts
6-05	C+	68.30	14.87	C- / 4.2	-1.04%	B- / 7.7
2004	A+	65.42	15.50	B / 8.2	4.83%	B- / 7.4
2003	A+	69.50	16.10	A- / 9.2	15.69%	B- / 7.3

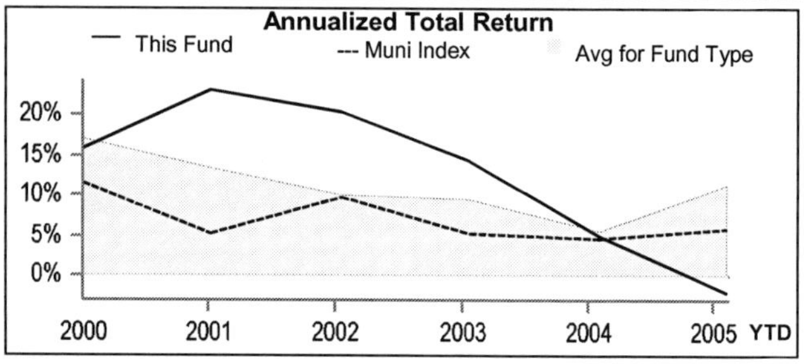

Eaton Vance NY Muni Inc Tr (EVY) A Excellent

Fund Family: Eaton Vance Mgmt.
Fund Type: Municipal - Single State
Inception Date: January 29, 1999

Major Rating Factors:
Exceptional performance is the major factor driving the A (Excellent) Weiss Investment Rating for Eaton Vance NY Muni Inc Tr. The fund currently has a performance rating of A- (Excellent) based on an annualized return of 11.14% over the last three years and a total return of 12.40% year to date 2005. Factored into the performance evaluation is an expense ratio of 1.78% (above average).

The fund's risk rating is currently C+ (Fair). It carries a beta of 2.05, meaning it is expected to move 20.5% for every 10% move in the market. Volatility, as measured by both the semi-deviation and a drawdown factor, is considered low. As of June 30, 2005, Eaton Vance NY Muni Inc Tr traded at a premium of 3.28% above its net asset value, which is worse than its one-year historical average discount of 2.01%.

Thomas J. Fetter has been running the fund for 6 years and currently receives a manager quality ranking of 70 (0=worst, 99=best). If you desire only a moderate level of risk and strong performance, then this fund is an excellent option.

Data Date	Weiss Investment Rating	Net Assets ($Mil)	Price	Performance Rating/Pts	Total Return Y-T-D	Risk Rating/Pts
6-05	A	83.04	16.70	A- / 9.2	12.40%	C+ / 6.2
2004	B+	80.00	15.35	B- / 7.1	5.83%	B- / 7.4
2003	A+	84.74	15.40	B+ / 8.7	12.44%	B / 8.0

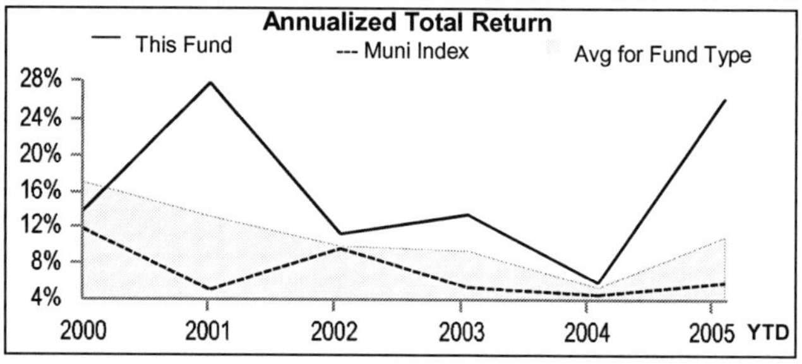

Eaton Vance OH Muni Inc Tr (EVO) C- Fair

Fund Family: Eaton Vance Mgmt.
Fund Type: Municipal - Single State
Inception Date: January 29, 1999

Major Rating Factors:
Middle of the road best describes Eaton Vance OH Muni Inc Tr whose Weiss Investment Rating is currently a C- (Fair). The fund currently has a performance rating of C- (Fair) based on an annualized return of 7.34% over the last three years and a total return of -1.71% year to date 2005. Factored into the performance evaluation is an expense ratio of 1.90% (above average).

The fund's risk rating is currently C+ (Fair). It carries a beta of 2.53, meaning it is expected to move 25.3% for every 10% move in the market. Volatility, as measured by both the semi-deviation and a drawdown factor, is considered low. As of June 30, 2005, Eaton Vance OH Muni Inc Tr traded at a premium of 1.69% above its net asset value, which is better than its one-year historical average premium of 5.65%.

Thomas J. Fetter has been running the fund for 6 years and currently receives a manager quality ranking of 19 (0=worst, 99=best). If you desire an average level of risk, then this fund may be an option.

Data Date	Weiss Investment Rating	Net Assets ($Mil)	Price	Performance Rating/Pts	Total Return Y-T-D	Risk Rating/Pts
6-05	C-	42.44	15.69	C- / 3.5	-1.71%	C+ / 6.3
2004	A	40.47	16.46	B+ / 8.9	10.46%	C+ / 6.6
2003	A+	42.30	15.73	B+ / 8.6	8.52%	B- / 7.9

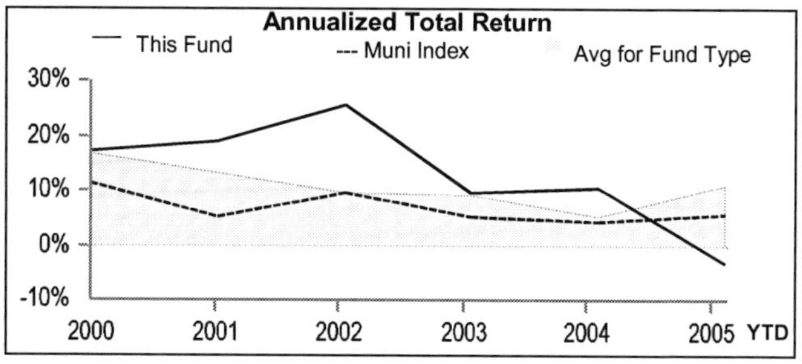

Eaton Vance PA Muni Inc Tr (EVP) B Good

Fund Family: Eaton Vance Mgmt.
Fund Type: Municipal - Single State
Inception Date: January 29, 1999

Major Rating Factors:
Strong performance is the major factor driving the B (Good) Weiss Investment Rating for Eaton Vance PA Muni Inc Tr. The fund currently has a performance rating of B+ (Good) based on an annualized return of 12.24% over the last three years and a total return of 3.73% year to date 2005. Factored into the performance evaluation is an expense ratio of 1.91% (above average).

The fund's risk rating is currently C+ (Fair). It carries a beta of 2.30, meaning it is expected to move 23.0% for every 10% move in the market. Volatility, as measured by both the semi-deviation and a drawdown factor, is considered low. As of June 30, 2005, Eaton Vance PA Muni Inc Tr traded at a premium of 5.04% above its net asset value, which is worse than its one-year historical average premium of 2.76%.

Thomas M. Metzold has been running the fund for 6 years and currently receives a manager quality ranking of 63 (0=worst, 99=best). If you desire only a moderate level of risk and strong performance, then this fund is an excellent option.

Data Date	Weiss Investment Rating	Net Assets ($Mil)	Price	Performance Rating/Pts	Total Return Y-T-D	Risk Rating/Pts
6-05	B	40.02	15.85	B+ / 8.3	3.73%	C+ / 5.6
2004	B+	38.96	15.78	B+ / 8.3	0.38%	C+ / 6.3
2003	A+	40.67	16.83	A+ / 9.6	27.25%	B- / 7.0

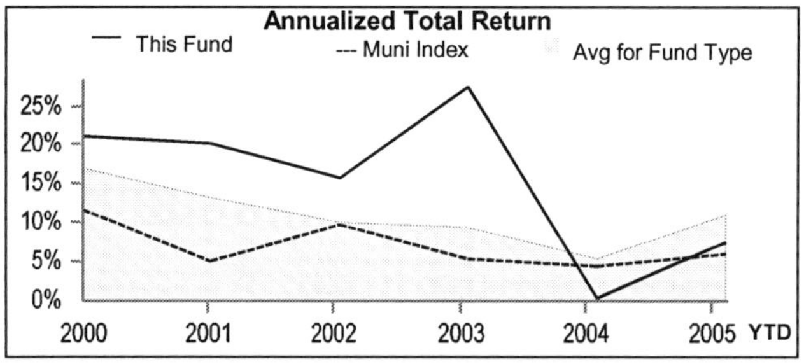

Eaton Vance Senior Income Trust (EVF) D Weak

Fund Family: Eaton Vance Mgmt.
Fund Type: Loan Participation
Inception Date: October 30, 1998

Major Rating Factors:
Very poor performance is the major factor driving the D (Weak) Weiss Investment Rating for Eaton Vance Senior Income Trust. The fund currently has a performance rating of E (Very Weak) based on an annualized return of 6.65% over the last three years and a total return of -6.99% year to date 2005. Factored into the performance evaluation is an expense ratio of 3.08% (high).

The fund's risk rating is currently B- (Good). It carries a beta of -20.54, meaning the fund's expected move will be -205.4% for every 10% move in the market. Volatility, as measured by both the semi-deviation and a drawdown factor, is considered low. As of June 30, 2005, Eaton Vance Senior Income Trust traded at a discount of 9.27% below its net asset value, which is better than its one-year historical average premium of .99%.

Payson F. Swaffield has been running the fund for 7 years and currently receives a manager quality ranking of 91 (0=worst, 99=best). This fund offers only a moderate level of risk but investors looking for strong performance are still waiting.

Data Date	Weiss Investment Rating	Net Assets ($Mil)	Price	Performance Rating/Pts	Total Return Y-T-D	Risk Rating/Pts
6-05	D	320.39	7.93	E / 0.3	-6.99%	B- / 7.9
2004	D+	318.79	8.73	D+ / 2.4	-0.62%	C+ / 6.9
2003	C-	306.44	9.36	C / 5.3	27.81%	C / 5.4

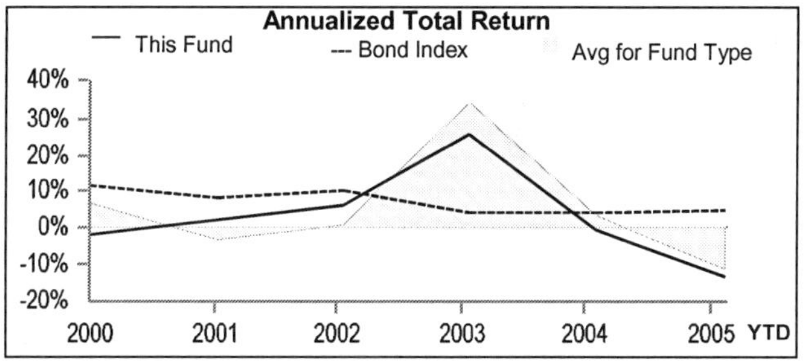

Ellsworth Convertible Growth & Inc (ECF) D Weak

Fund Family: Davis/Dinsmore Management Co.
Fund Type: Growth and Income
Inception Date: June 30, 1986

Major Rating Factors:
Very poor performance is the major factor driving the D (Weak) Weiss Investment Rating for Ellsworth Convertible Growth & Inc. The fund currently has a performance rating of E- (Very Weak) based on an annualized return of 1.05% over the last three years and a total return of -5.60% year to date 2005. Factored into the performance evaluation is an expense ratio of 1.20% (average).

The fund's risk rating is currently B- (Good). It carries a beta of 0.49, meaning the fund's expected move will be 4.9% for every 10% move in the market. Volatility, as measured by both the semi-deviation and a drawdown factor, is considered low. As of June 30, 2005, Ellsworth Convertible Growth & Inc traded at a discount of 14.20% below its net asset value, which is better than its one-year historical average discount of 11.70%.

Thomas H. Dinsmore has been running the fund for 19 years and currently receives a manager quality ranking of 38 (0=worst, 99=best). This fund offers only a moderate level of risk but investors looking for strong performance are still waiting.

Data Date	Weiss Investment Rating	Net Assets ($Mil)	Price	Performance Rating/Pts	Total Return Y-T-D	Risk Rating/Pts
6-05	D	108.48	7.49	E- / 0.1	-5.60%	B- / 7.8
2004	D-	107.11	8.08	E+ / 0.8	4.81%	C+ / 6.7
2003	D+	89.80	7.95	D- / 1.5	12.35%	C+ / 6.9

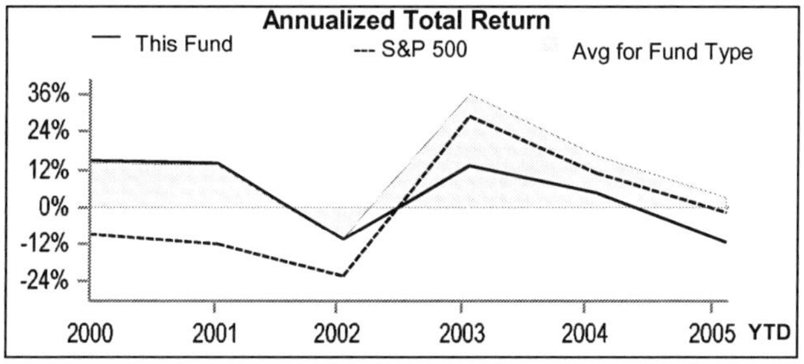

Emerging Market Telecom Fund (ETF) C Fair

Fund Family: Credit Suisse Asset Management
Fund Type: Emerging Market
Inception Date: June 25, 1992

Data Date	Weiss Investment Rating	Net Assets ($Mil)	Price	Perfor-mance Rating/Pts	Total Return Y-T-D	Risk Rating/Pts
6-05	C	93.24	10.10	C+ / 6.3	1.61%	C / 4.6
2004	B-	80.31	9.94	B+ / 8.5	33.24%	C / 4.9
2003	D-	74.90	7.11	E+ / 0.8	23.44%	C / 4.4

Major Rating Factors:
Middle of the road best describes Emerging Market Telecom Fund whose Weiss Investment Rating is currently a C (Fair). The fund currently has a performance rating of C+ (Fair) based on an annualized return of 14.26% over the last three years and a total return of 1.61% year to date 2005. Factored into the performance evaluation is an expense ratio of 1.99% (high).

The fund's risk rating is currently C (Fair). It carries a beta of 1.04, meaning that its performance tracks fairly well with that of the overall stock market. Volatility, as measured by both the semi-deviation and a drawdown factor, is considered average. As of June 30, 2005, Emerging Market Telecom Fund traded at a discount of 13.16% below its net asset value, which is worse than its one-year historical average discount of 13.58%.

Emily Alejos (CIO) has been running the fund for 1 year and currently receives a manager quality ranking of 2 (0=worst, 99=best). If you desire an average level of risk, then this fund may be an option.

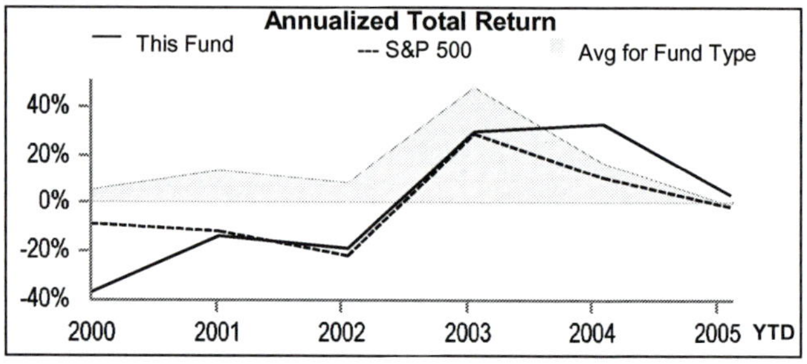

Equus II (EQS) C Fair

Fund Family: Equus Capital Mgmt Corporation
Fund Type: Growth
Inception Date: September 11, 1992

Data Date	Weiss Investment Rating	Net Assets ($Mil)	Price	Perfor-mance Rating/Pts	Total Return Y-T-D	Risk Rating/Pts
6-05	C	68.60	8.38	C- / 3.8	8.69%	B- / 7.0
2004	D	70.53	7.71	D- / 1.4	2.75%	C+ / 6.6
2003	D	76.95	7.89	D- / 1.3	29.36%	C+ / 6.4

Major Rating Factors:
Middle of the road best describes Equus II whose Weiss Investment Rating is currently a C (Fair). The fund currently has a performance rating of C- (Fair) based on an annualized return of 9.67% over the last three years and a total return of 8.69% year to date 2005. Factored into the performance evaluation is an expense ratio of 3.55% (high).

The fund's risk rating is currently B- (Good). It carries a beta of 0.57, meaning the fund's expected move will be 5.7% for every 10% move in the market. Volatility, as measured by both the semi-deviation and a drawdown factor, is considered low. As of June 30, 2005, Equus II traded at a discount of 27.82% below its net asset value, which is better than its one-year historical average discount of 26.32%.

Gary L. Forbes has been running the fund for 13 years and currently receives a manager quality ranking of 78 (0=worst, 99=best). If you desire an average level of risk, then this fund may be an option.

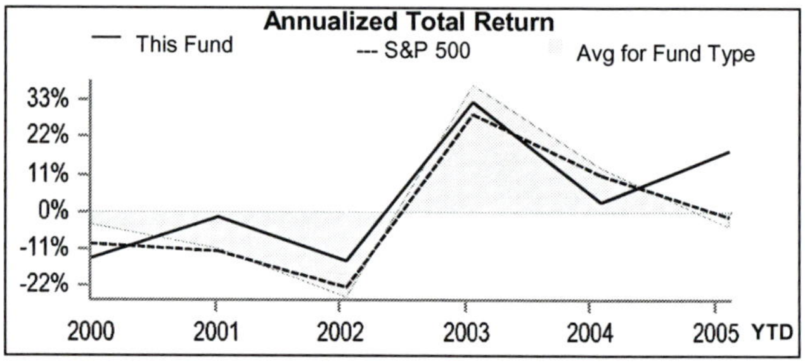

Europe Fund (EF) E+ Very Weak

Fund Family: Merrill Lynch Investment Managers
Fund Type: Foreign
Inception Date: May 3, 1990

Data Date	Weiss Investment Rating	Net Assets ($Mil)	Price	Perfor-mance Rating/Pts	Total Return Y-T-D	Risk Rating/Pts
6-05	E+	119.29	10.54	D+ / 2.4	-7.05%	D+ / 2.7
2004	C-	112.61	11.34	C+ / 6.2	22.50%	C- / 4.0
2003	D-	92.41	9.88	D / 1.8	47.48%	C- / 3.9

Major Rating Factors:
Europe Fund has adopted a risky asset allocation strategy and currently receives an overall Weiss Investment Rating of E+ (Very Weak). The fund has an above average level of volatility, as measured by both semi-deviation and drawdown factors. It carries a beta of 1.41, meaning it is expected to move 14.1% for every 10% move in the market. As of June 30, 2005, Europe Fund traded at a discount of 10.68% below its net asset value, which is better than its one-year historical average discount of 7.75%. Unfortunately, the high level of risk (D+, Weak) failed to pay off as investors endured poor performance.

The fund's performance rating is currently D+ (Weak). It has registered an annualized return of 10.62% over the last three years but is down -7.05% year to date 2005. Factored into the performance evaluation is an expense ratio of 1.22% (average).

Michel Legros has been running the fund for 15 years and currently receives a manager quality ranking of 10 (0=worst, 99=best). If you can tolerate high levels of risk in the hope of improved future returns, holding this fund may be an option.

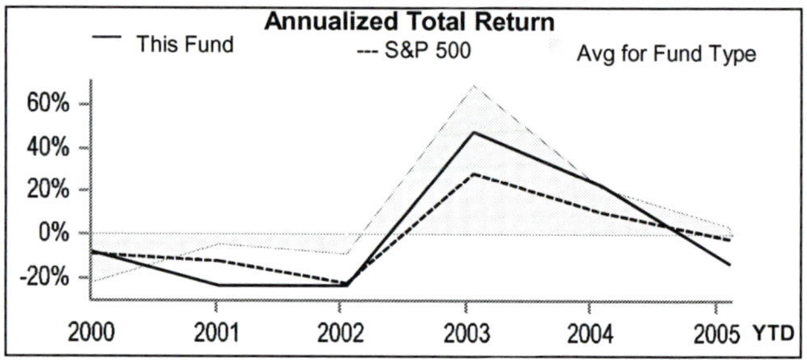

First Financial Fund (FF) B Good

Fund Family: Wellington Mang. Co
Fund Type: Financial Services
Inception Date: May 1, 1986

Data Date	Weiss Investment Rating	Net Assets ($Mil)	Price	Perfor-mance Rating/Pts	Total Return Y-T-D	Risk Rating/Pts
6-05	B	398.63	18.10	A- / 9.1	-15.74%	C / 4.6
2004	B+	467.67	21.48	A+ / 9.9	53.50%	C / 4.6
2003	A-	414.70	17.42	A+ / 9.7	52.29%	C+ / 5.9

Major Rating Factors:
Exceptional performance is the major factor driving the B (Good) Weiss Investment Rating for First Financial Fund. The fund currently has a performance rating of A- (Excellent) based on an annualized return of 28.34% over the last three years and a total return of -15.74% year to date 2005. Factored into the performance evaluation is an expense ratio of 1.03% (low).

The fund's risk rating is currently C (Fair). It carries a beta of 0.98, meaning that its performance tracks fairly well with that of the overall stock market. Volatility, as measured by both the semi-deviation and a drawdown factor, is considered average. As of June 30, 2005, First Financial Fund traded at a premium of 2.20% above its net asset value, which is better than its one-year historical average premium of 2.97%.

Nicholas C. Adams has been running the fund for 19 years and currently receives a manager quality ranking of 97 (0=worst, 99=best). If you desire an average level of risk and strong performance, then this fund is a good option.

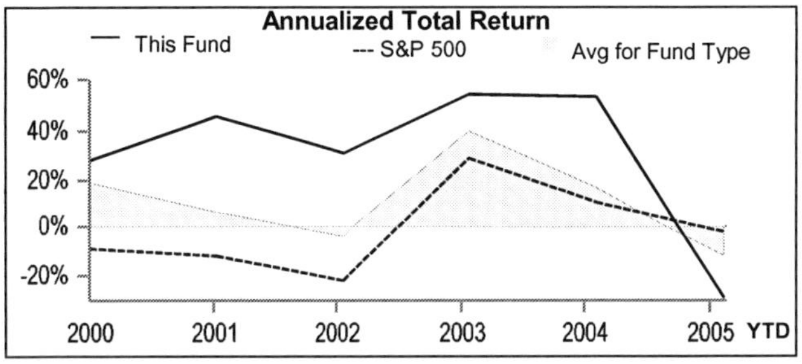

First Israel Fund (ISL) C Fair

Fund Family: Credit Suisse Asset Management
Fund Type: Foreign
Inception Date: October 29, 1992

Data Date	Weiss Investment Rating	Net Assets ($Mil)	Price	Perfor-mance Rating/Pts	Total Return Y-T-D	Risk Rating/Pts
6-05	C	73.00	14.38	C+ / 6.3	-6.14%	C / 4.8
2004	C+	60.77	15.32	B / 7.6	24.35%	C / 4.8
2003	D	52.60	11.93	D+ / 2.3	60.90%	C / 4.6

Major Rating Factors:
Middle of the road best describes First Israel Fund whose Weiss Investment Rating is currently a C (Fair). The fund currently has a performance rating of C+ (Fair) based on an annualized return of 20.12% over the last three years and a total return of -6.14% year to date 2005. Factored into the performance evaluation is an expense ratio of 2.28% (high).

The fund's risk rating is currently C (Fair). It carries a beta of 0.98, meaning that its performance tracks fairly well with that of the overall stock market. Volatility, as measured by both the semi-deviation and a drawdown factor, is considered average. As of June 30, 2005, First Israel Fund traded at a discount of 12.53% below its net asset value, which is better than its one-year historical average discount of 10.83%.

Neil Gregson has been running the fund for 1 year and currently receives a manager quality ranking of 84 (0=worst, 99=best). If you desire an average level of risk, then this fund may be an option.

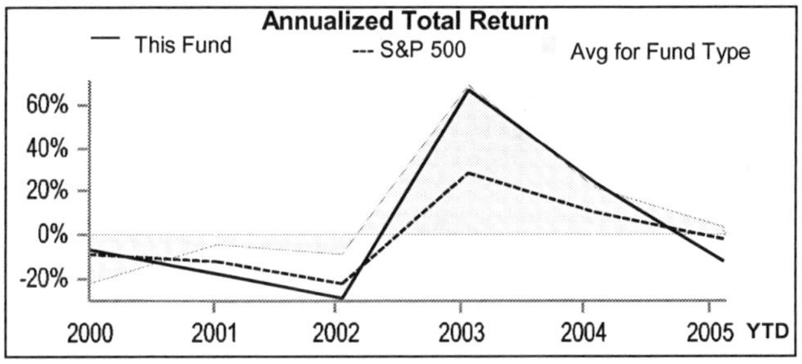

Flaherty&Crumrine Preferred Inc Opp (PFO) D+ Weak

Fund Family: Flaherty & Crumrine
Fund Type: Income
Inception Date: February 13, 1992

Data Date	Weiss Investment Rating	Net Assets ($Mil)	Price	Perfor-mance Rating/Pts	Total Return Y-T-D	Risk Rating/Pts
6-05	D+	142.15	12.77	D+ / 2.5	-2.07%	C+ / 6.5
2004	C+	141.26	13.50	C / 5.2	1.15%	B- / 7.1
2003	A+	144.30	14.11	B+ / 8.3	24.30%	B / 8.0

Major Rating Factors:
Disappointing performance is the major factor driving the D+ (Weak) Weiss Investment Rating for Flaherty&Crumrine Preferred Inc Opp. The fund currently has a performance rating of D+ (Weak) based on an annualized return of 9.57% over the last three years and a total return of -2.07% year to date 2005. Factored into the performance evaluation is an expense ratio of 1.52% (average).

The fund's risk rating is currently C+ (Fair). It carries a beta of -0.01, meaning the fund's expected move will be -0.1% for every 10% move in the market. Volatility, as measured by both the semi-deviation and a drawdown factor, is considered low. As of June 30, 2005, Flaherty&Crumrine Preferred Inc Opp traded at a premium of .24% above its net asset value, which is better than its one-year historical average premium of 5.43%.

Donald F. Crumrine has been running the fund for 13 years and currently receives a manager quality ranking of 88 (0=worst, 99=best). This fund offers only a moderate level of risk but investors looking for strong performance are still waiting.

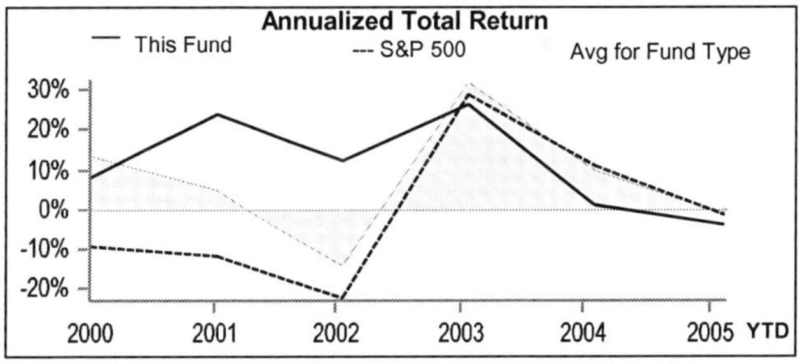

Flaherty&Crumrine Preferred Income (PFD) D Weak

Fund Family: Flaherty & Crumrine
Fund Type: Income
Inception Date: January 31, 1991

Major Rating Factors:

Disappointing performance is the major factor driving the D (Weak) Weiss Investment Rating for Flaherty&Crumrine Preferred Income. The fund currently has a performance rating of D+ (Weak) based on an annualized return of 10.76% over the last three years and a total return of -5.08% year to date 2005. Factored into the performance evaluation is an expense ratio of 1.48% (average).

The fund's risk rating is currently C (Fair). It carries a beta of 0.17, meaning the fund's expected move will be 1.7% for every 10% move in the market. Volatility, as measured by both the semi-deviation and a drawdown factor, is considered average. As of June 30, 2005, Flaherty&Crumrine Preferred Income traded at a premium of 4.56% above its net asset value, which is better than its one-year historical average premium of 11.08%.

Donald F. Crumrine has been running the fund for 14 years and currently receives a manager quality ranking of 89 (0=worst, 99=best). This fund offers an average level of risk but investors looking for strong performance will be frustrated.

Data Date	Weiss Investment Rating	Net Assets ($Mil)	Price	Perfor-mance Rating/Pts	Total Return Y-T-D	Risk Rating/Pts
6-05	D	159.10	16.75	D+ / 2.6	-5.08%	C / 5.2
2004	C+	157.77	18.25	C+ / 6.5	6.49%	C+ / 5.8
2003	A+	160.92	18.40	B+ / 8.9	30.90%	B- / 7.7

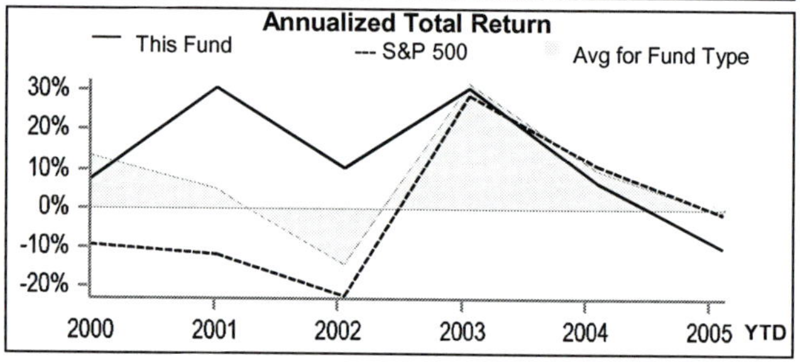

Fort Dearborn Inc. Secs. (FDI) C- Fair

Fund Family: UBS Global Asset Management
Fund Type: General - Investment Grade
Inception Date: December 31, 1972

Major Rating Factors:

Disappointing performance is the major factor driving the C- (Fair) Weiss Investment Rating for Fort Dearborn Inc. Secs.. The fund currently has a performance rating of D (Weak) based on an annualized return of 5.46% over the last three years and a total return of 2.14% year to date 2005. Factored into the performance evaluation is an expense ratio of 0.74% (very low).

The fund's risk rating is currently B (Good). It carries a beta of 1.68, meaning it is expected to move 16.8% for every 10% move in the market. Volatility, as measured by both the semi-deviation and a drawdown factor, is considered low. As of June 30, 2005, Fort Dearborn Inc. Secs. traded at a discount of 10.72% below its net asset value, which is better than its one-year historical average discount of 10.57%.

Craig G. Ellinger has been running the fund for 4 years and currently receives a manager quality ranking of 34 (0=worst, 99=best). This fund offers only a moderate level of risk but investors looking for strong performance are still waiting.

Data Date	Weiss Investment Rating	Net Assets ($Mil)	Price	Perfor-mance Rating/Pts	Total Return Y-T-D	Risk Rating/Pts
6-05	C-	141.94	14.90	D / 1.8	2.14%	B / 8.6
2004	C	144.59	14.99	D+ / 2.8	7.04%	B / 8.5
2003	C	144.47	14.84	D+ / 2.7	5.87%	B+ / 9.1

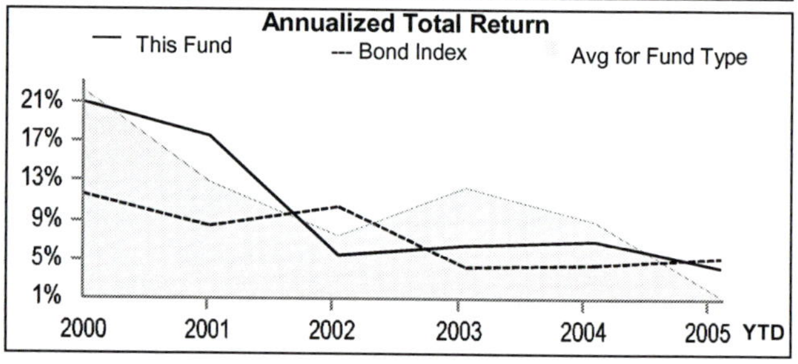

Foxby Corp (FXX) E+ Very Weak

Fund Family: CEF Advisers, Inc
Fund Type: Growth
Inception Date: October 29, 1999

Major Rating Factors:

Very poor performance is the major factor driving the E+ (Very Weak) Weiss Investment Rating for Foxby Corp. The fund currently has a performance rating of E- (Very Weak) based on an annualized return of -1.77% over the last three years and a total return of -1.80% year to date 2005. Factored into the performance evaluation is an expense ratio of 5.27% (high).

The fund's risk rating is currently C (Fair). It carries a beta of 0.82, meaning the fund's expected move will be 8.2% for every 10% move in the market. Volatility, as measured by both the semi-deviation and a drawdown factor, is considered average. As of June 30, 2005, Foxby Corp traded at a discount of 12.80% below its net asset value, which is better than its one-year historical average discount of 12.76%.

Investment Policy Committee has been running the fund for 3 years and currently receives a manager quality ranking of 4 (0=worst, 99=best). This fund offers an average level of risk but investors looking for strong performance will be frustrated.

Data Date	Weiss Investment Rating	Net Assets ($Mil)	Price	Perfor-mance Rating/Pts	Total Return Y-T-D	Risk Rating/Pts
6-05	E+	6.70	2.18	E- / 0.0	-1.80%	C / 5.5
2004	E	6.42	2.22	E- / 0.0	-7.50%	D+ / 2.4
2003	E-	6.73	2.38	E- / 0.1	14.98%	D- / 1.1

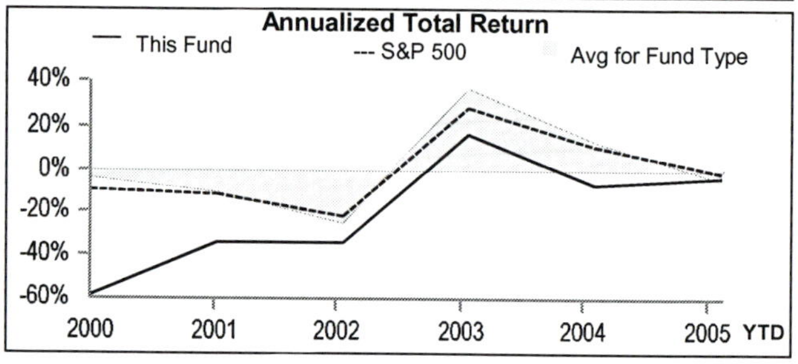

Franklin Multi-Income Trust (FMI) B+ Good

Fund Family: Templeton Investment Management
Fund Type: Growth and Income
Inception Date: October 24, 1989

Data Date	Weiss Investment Rating	Net Assets ($Mil)	Price	Performance Rating/Pts	Total Return Y-T-D	Risk Rating/Pts
6-05	B+	53.45	9.35	B+ / 8.3	18.47%	C+ / 5.8
2004	D	50.29	8.05	C- / 3.7	13.99%	C / 4.5
2003	D+	44.60	7.44	D+ / 2.9	28.02%	C / 5.4

Major Rating Factors:
Strong performance is the major factor driving the B+ (Good) Weiss Investment Rating for Franklin Multi-Income Trust. The fund currently has a performance rating of B+ (Good) based on an annualized return of 14.65% over the last three years and a total return of 18.47% year to date 2005.

The fund's risk rating is currently C+ (Fair). It carries a beta of 0.55, meaning the fund's expected move will be 5.5% for every 10% move in the market. Volatility, as measured by both the semi-deviation and a drawdown factor, is considered low. As of June 30, 2005, Franklin Multi-Income Trust traded at a discount of 1.89% below its net asset value, which is worse than its one-year historical average discount of 9.77%.

Chris Molumphy has been running the fund for 16 years and currently receives a manager quality ranking of 90 (0=worst, 99=best). If you desire only a moderate level of risk and strong performance, then this fund is an excellent option.

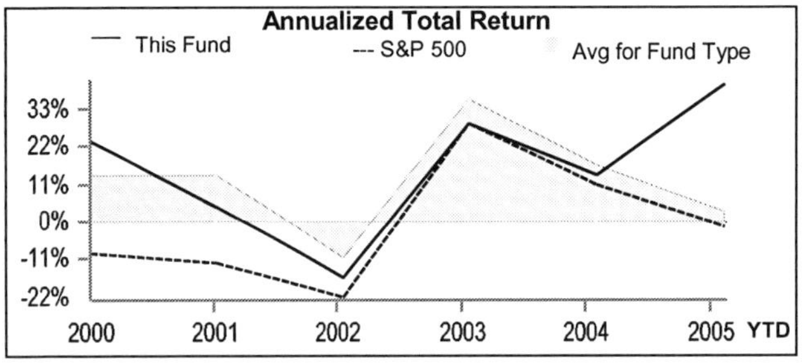

Franklin Universal Trust (FT) D- Weak

Fund Family: Templeton Investment Management
Fund Type: Growth and Income
Inception Date: September 23, 1988

Data Date	Weiss Investment Rating	Net Assets ($Mil)	Price	Performance Rating/Pts	Total Return Y-T-D	Risk Rating/Pts
6-05	D-	195.64	6.14	C- / 3.0	4.62%	C / 4.6
2004	E	180.85	6.04	E+ / 0.6	10.37%	D / 2.2
2003	D	158.36	5.76	D+ / 2.3	21.10%	C / 4.4

Major Rating Factors:
Franklin Universal Trust receives a Weiss Investment Rating of D- (Weak). The fund currently has a performance rating of C- (Fair) based on an annualized return of 7.22% over the last three years and a total return of 4.62% year to date 2005.

The fund's risk rating is currently C (Fair). It carries a beta of 0.38, meaning the fund's expected move will be 3.8% for every 10% move in the market. Volatility, as measured by both the semi-deviation and a drawdown factor, is considered average. As of June 30, 2005, Franklin Universal Trust traded at a discount of 12.03% below its net asset value, which is worse than its one-year historical average discount of 12.55%.

Chris Molumphy has been running the fund for 17 years and currently receives a manager quality ranking of 77 (0=worst, 99=best). If you desire an average level of risk, then this fund may be an option.

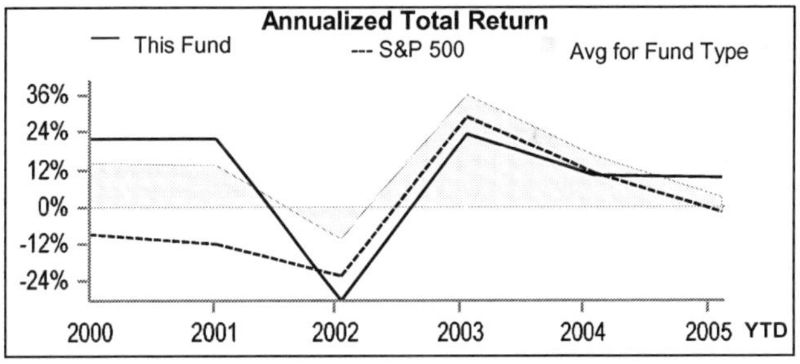

Gabelli Convertible&Income Sec Fund (GCV) E+ Very Weak

Fund Family: Gabelli Funds, LLC
Fund Type: Growth and Income
Inception Date: July 3, 1989

Data Date	Weiss Investment Rating	Net Assets ($Mil)	Price	Performance Rating/Pts	Total Return Y-T-D	Risk Rating/Pts
6-05	E+	97.43	9.50	D- / 1.4	7.52%	C / 4.9
2004	E+	98.40	9.24	E / 0.5	-4.77%	C / 5.1
2003	C	100.00	10.32	C+ / 5.9	31.66%	C+ / 6.3

Major Rating Factors:
Disappointing performance is the major factor driving the E+ (Very Weak) Weiss Investment Rating for Gabelli Convertible&Income Sec Fund. The fund currently has a performance rating of D- (Weak) based on an annualized return of 6.82% over the last three years and a total return of 7.52% year to date 2005. Factored into the performance evaluation is an expense ratio of 1.61% (above average).

The fund's risk rating is currently C (Fair). It carries a beta of -0.01, meaning the fund's expected move will be -0.1% for every 10% move in the market. Volatility, as measured by both the semi-deviation and a drawdown factor, is considered average. As of June 30, 2005, Gabelli Convertible&Income Sec Fund traded at a premium of 18.75% above its net asset value, which is worse than its one-year historical average premium of 17.05%.

Mario J. Gabelli has been running the fund for 16 years and currently receives a manager quality ranking of 86 (0=worst, 99=best). This fund offers an average level of risk but investors looking for strong performance will be frustrated.

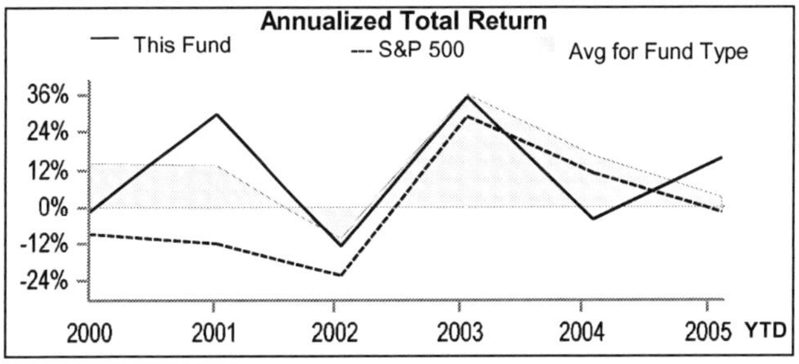

Gabelli Equity Trust (GAB) E Very Weak

Fund Family: Gabelli Funds, LLC
Fund Type: Growth
Inception Date: August 14, 1986

Data Date	Weiss Investment Rating	Net Assets ($Mil)	Price	Performance Rating/Pts	Total Return Y-T-D	Risk Rating/Pts
6-05	E	1219.48	8.93	D / 1.9	3.21%	D+ / 2.8
2004	D	1117.27	9.02	C / 4.7	24.04%	C- / 3.0
2003	D	921.58	7.93	D+ / 2.7	27.59%	C- / 3.2

Major Rating Factors:
Gabelli Equity Trust has adopted a risky asset allocation strategy and currently receives an overall Weiss Investment Rating of E (Very Weak). The fund has an above average level of volatility, as measured by both semi-deviation and drawdown factors. It carries a beta of 1.25, meaning it is expected to move 12.5% for every 10% move in the market. As of June 30, 2005, Gabelli Equity Trust traded at a premium of 7.20% above its net asset value, which is worse than its one-year historical average premium of 6.22%. Unfortunately, the high level of risk (D+, Weak) failed to pay off as investors endured poor performance.

The fund's performance rating is currently D (Weak). It has registered an annualized return of 6.27% over the last three years and is up 3.21% year to date 2005. Factored into the performance evaluation is an expense ratio of 1.57% (above average).

Mario J. Gabelli has been running the fund for 19 years and currently receives a manager quality ranking of 28 (0=worst, 99=best). If you can tolerate high levels of risk in the hope of improved future returns, holding this fund may be an option.

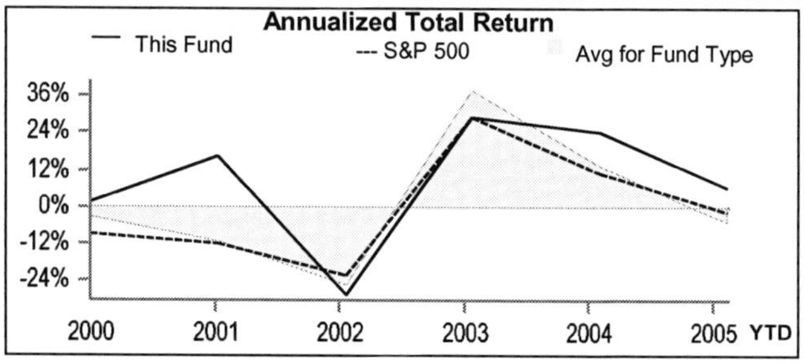

Gabelli Global Multimedia Trust (GGT) D+ Weak

Fund Family: Gabelli Funds, LLC
Fund Type: Global
Inception Date: November 15, 1994

Data Date	Weiss Investment Rating	Net Assets ($Mil)	Price	Performance Rating/Pts	Total Return Y-T-D	Risk Rating/Pts
6-05	D+	173.91	10.03	C- / 4.2	-3.83%	C / 5.0
2004	D-	153.76	10.68	C- / 3.1	17.75%	C- / 3.2
2003	E+	128.18	8.92	D- / 1.1	39.37%	D+ / 2.8

Major Rating Factors:
Gabelli Global Multimedia Trust receives a Weiss Investment Rating of D+ (Weak). The fund currently has a performance rating of C- (Fair) based on an annualized return of 13.63% over the last three years and a total return of -3.83% year to date 2005. Factored into the performance evaluation is an expense ratio of 1.87% (above average).

The fund's risk rating is currently C (Fair). It carries a beta of 1.13, meaning it is expected to move 11.3% for every 10% move in the market. Volatility, as measured by both the semi-deviation and a drawdown factor, is considered average. As of June 30, 2005, Gabelli Global Multimedia Trust traded at a discount of 13.61% below its net asset value, which is worse than its one-year historical average discount of 14.19%.

Mario J. Gabelli has been running the fund for 11 years and currently receives a manager quality ranking of 60 (0=worst, 99=best). If you desire an average level of risk, then this fund may be an option.

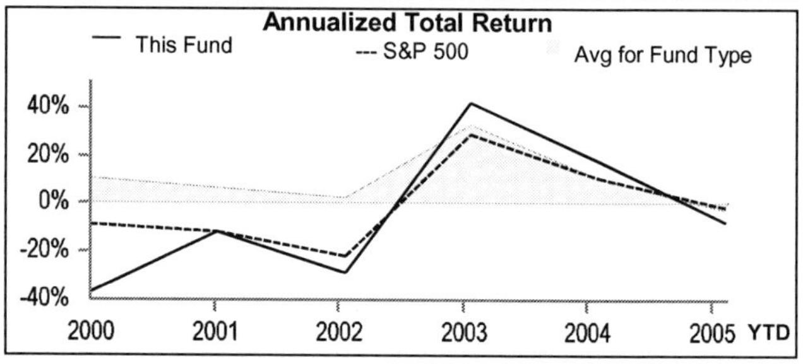

Gabelli Utility Trust (GUT) B Good

Fund Family: Gabelli Funds, LLC
Fund Type: Utilities
Inception Date: July 7, 1999

Data Date	Weiss Investment Rating	Net Assets ($Mil)	Price	Performance Rating/Pts	Total Return Y-T-D	Risk Rating/Pts
6-05	B	206.96	10.00	B / 8.2	11.83%	C / 5.5
2004	C	154.03	9.30	C+ / 6.5	11.30%	C / 5.2
2003	C	101.26	9.35	C+ / 6.3	23.37%	C+ / 5.9

Major Rating Factors:
Strong performance is the major factor driving the B (Good) Weiss Investment Rating for Gabelli Utility Trust. The fund currently has a performance rating of B (Good) based on an annualized return of 17.04% over the last three years and a total return of 11.83% year to date 2005. Factored into the performance evaluation is an expense ratio of 2.04% (high).

The fund's risk rating is currently C (Fair). It carries a beta of 0.30, meaning the fund's expected move will be 3.0% for every 10% move in the market. Volatility, as measured by both the semi-deviation and a drawdown factor, is considered average. As of June 30, 2005, Gabelli Utility Trust traded at a premium of 36.24% above its net asset value, which is better than its one-year historical average premium of 37.15%.

Mario J. Gabelli has been running the fund for 6 years and currently receives a manager quality ranking of 92 (0=worst, 99=best). If you desire an average level of risk and strong performance, then this fund is a good option.

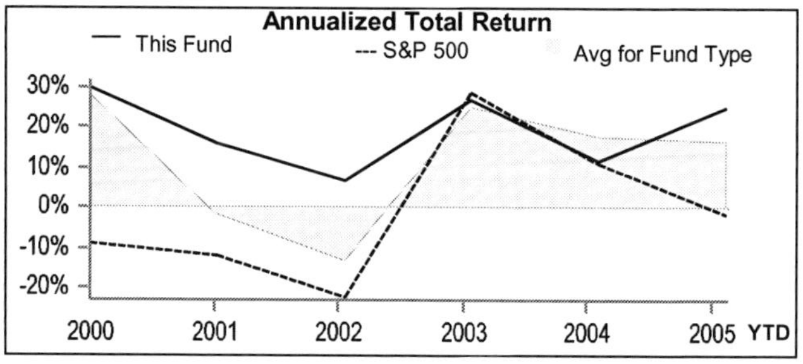

General American Investors (GAM) D+ Weak

Fund Family: General American Investors Company
Fund Type: Growth
Inception Date: N/A

Major Rating Factors:
Disappointing performance is the major factor driving the D+ (Weak) Weiss Investment Rating for General American Investors. The fund currently has a performance rating of D (Weak) based on an annualized return of 7.17% over the last three years and a total return of 2.16% year to date 2005. Factored into the performance evaluation is an expense ratio of 1.15% (low).

The fund's risk rating is currently B- (Good). It carries a beta of 0.93, meaning that its performance tracks fairly well with that of the overall stock market. Volatility, as measured by both the semi-deviation and a drawdown factor, is considered low. As of June 30, 2005, General American Investors traded at a discount of 14.39% below its net asset value, which is better than its one-year historical average discount of 11.80%.

Spencer Davidson has been running the fund for 10 years and currently receives a manager quality ranking of 59 (0=worst, 99=best). This fund offers only a moderate level of risk but investors looking for strong performance are still waiting.

Data Date	Weiss Investment Rating	Net Assets ($Mil)	Price	Perfor-mance Rating/Pts	Total Return Y-T-D	Risk Rating/Pts
6-05	D+	1036.39	31.72	D / 1.7	2.16%	B- / 7.6
2004	D-	982.93	31.32	E+ / 0.6	8.77%	C+ / 6.0
2003	D	901.00	29.26	D- / 1.0	24.98%	C+ / 6.0

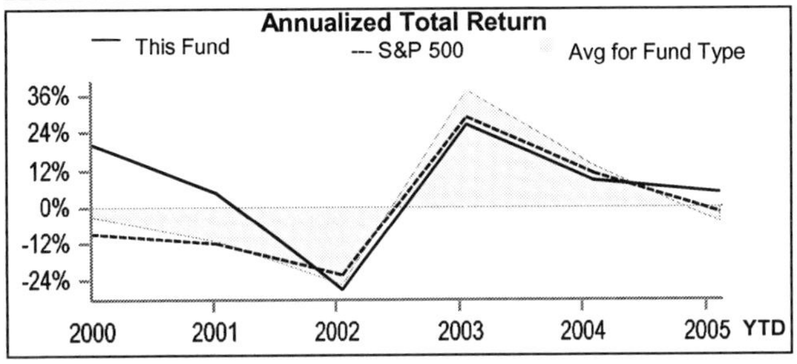

Germany Fund (GER) E- Very Weak

Fund Family: Deutsche Bank Group
Fund Type: Foreign
Inception Date: July 23, 1986

Major Rating Factors:
Germany Fund has adopted a very risky asset allocation strategy and currently receives an overall Weiss Investment Rating of E- (Very Weak). The fund has a high level of volatility, as measured by both semi-deviation and drawdown factors. It carries a beta of 1.69, meaning it is expected to move 16.9% for every 10% move in the market. As of June 30, 2005, Germany Fund traded at a discount of 12.30% below its net asset value, which is worse than its one-year historical average discount of 12.99%. Unfortunately, the high level of risk (D, Weak) failed to pay off as investors endured very poor performance.

The fund's performance rating is currently E+ (Very Weak). It has registered an annualized return of 4.42% over the last three years but is down -4.19% year to date 2005. Factored into the performance evaluation is an expense ratio of 1.58% (above average).

Sandra M. Schaufler has been running the fund for 1 year and currently receives a manager quality ranking of 0 (0=worst, 99=best). If you can tolerate very high levels of risk in the hope of improved future returns, holding this fund may be an option.

Data Date	Weiss Investment Rating	Net Assets ($Mil)	Price	Perfor-mance Rating/Pts	Total Return Y-T-D	Risk Rating/Pts
6-05	E-	140.04	7.77	E+ / 0.6	-4.19%	D / 1.7
2004	E	120.87	8.11	D / 1.8	7.26%	D / 1.9
2003	D-	99.87	7.39	D / 2.0	63.50%	D+ / 2.3

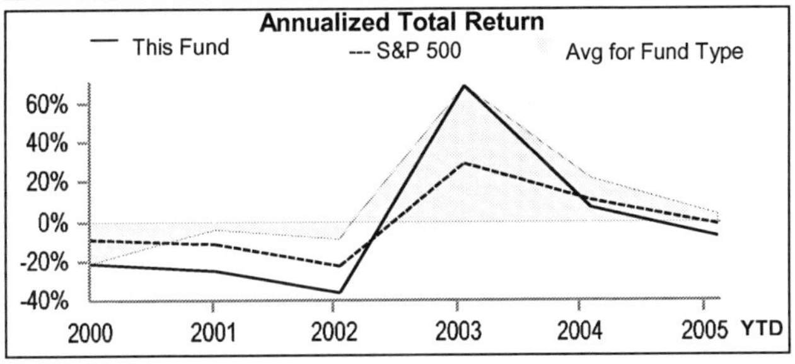

Global High Income Dollar Fund (GHI) B- Good

Fund Family: UBS Global Asset Management
Fund Type: Emerging Market
Inception Date: September 30, 1993

Major Rating Factors:
Strong performance is the major factor driving the B- (Good) Weiss Investment Rating for Global High Income Dollar Fund. The fund currently has a performance rating of B (Good) based on an annualized return of 19.70% over the last three years and a total return of -9.22% year to date 2005. Factored into the performance evaluation is an expense ratio of 1.43% (average).

The fund's risk rating is currently C (Fair). It carries a beta of 0.92, meaning that its performance tracks fairly well with that of the overall stock market. Volatility, as measured by both the semi-deviation and a drawdown factor, is considered average. As of June 30, 2005, Global High Income Dollar Fund traded at a premium of 8.66% above its net asset value, which is better than its one-year historical average premium of 12.51%.

Maria-Mednikov Loucks/Uwe Schi has been running the fund for 12 years and currently receives a manager quality ranking of 89 (0=worst, 99=best). If you desire an average level of risk and strong performance, then this fund is a good option.

Data Date	Weiss Investment Rating	Net Assets ($Mil)	Price	Perfor-mance Rating/Pts	Total Return Y-T-D	Risk Rating/Pts
6-05	B-	294.53	16.94	B / 7.7	-9.22%	C / 5.3
2004	B+	298.18	19.60	A+ / 9.6	27.79%	C / 5.0
2003	B+	309.52	18.16	A- / 9.0	39.25%	C+ / 6.1

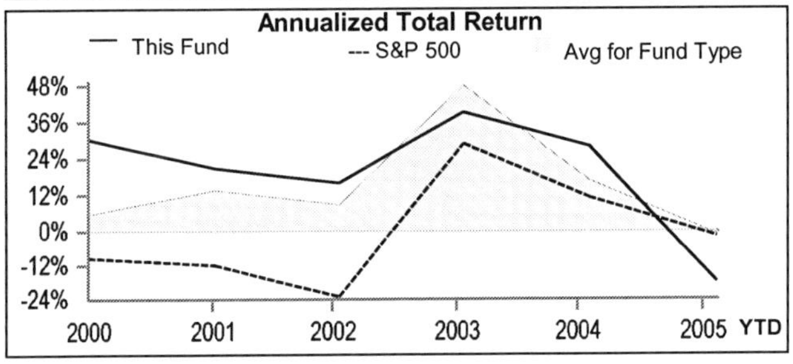

Global Income Fund (GIF) | D- | Weak

Fund Family: CEF Advisers, Inc
Fund Type: Global
Inception Date: February 7, 1997

Major Rating Factors:

Very poor performance is the major factor driving the D- (Weak) Weiss Investment Rating for Global Income Fund. The fund currently has a performance rating of E (Very Weak) based on an annualized return of 4.08% over the last three years and a total return of -6.85% year to date 2005. Factored into the performance evaluation is an expense ratio of 1.67% (above average).

The fund's risk rating is currently C+ (Fair). It carries a beta of 1.05, meaning that its performance tracks fairly well with that of the overall stock market. Volatility, as measured by both the semi-deviation and a drawdown factor, is considered low. As of June 30, 2005, Global Income Fund traded at a discount of 5.23% below its net asset value, which is worse than its one-year historical average discount of 6.13%.

Marion E. Morris has been running the fund for 5 years and currently receives a manager quality ranking of 7 (0=worst, 99=best). This fund offers only a moderate level of risk but investors looking for strong performance are still waiting.

Data Date	Weiss Investment Rating	Net Assets ($Mil)	Price	Perfor-mance Rating/Pts	Total Return Y-T-D	Risk Rating/Pts
6-05	D-	36.67	4.35	E / 0.4	-6.85%	C+ / 6.9
2004	C-	34.15	4.82	C- / 4.2	4.85%	C+ / 6.7
2003	C-	28.27	4.90	C- / 3.5	14.65%	B- / 7.0

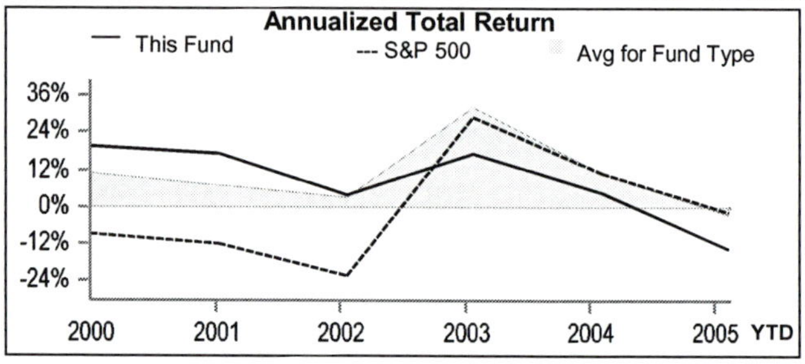

Greater China Fund (GCH) | D+ | Weak

Fund Family: Baring International Investment Mgm
Fund Type: Foreign
Inception Date: July 15, 1992

Major Rating Factors:

Greater China Fund has adopted a very risky asset allocation strategy and currently receives an overall Weiss Investment Rating of D+ (Weak). The fund has shown a high level of volatility, as measured by both semi-deviation and drawdown factors. It carries a beta of 1.17, meaning it is expected to move 11.7% for every 10% move in the market. As of June 30, 2005, Greater China Fund traded at a discount of 12.24% below its net asset value, which is better than its one-year historical average discount of 9.26%. The high level of risk (D-, Weak) did however, reward investors with excellent performance.

The fund's performance rating is currently B- (Good). It has registered an annualized return of 19.96% over the last three years and is up 2.86% year to date 2005. Factored into the performance evaluation is an expense ratio of 2.28% (high).

Wilfred Sit has been running the fund for 13 years and currently receives a manager quality ranking of 82 (0=worst, 99=best). If you are comfortable owning a very high risk investment, this fund may be an option.

Data Date	Weiss Investment Rating	Net Assets ($Mil)	Price	Perfor-mance Rating/Pts	Total Return Y-T-D	Risk Rating/Pts
6-05	D+	216.43	16.20	B- / 7.5	2.86%	D- / 1.2
2004	C-	197.88	15.75	B / 7.8	-14.72%	D+ / 2.6
2003	C	146.53	18.26	A+ / 9.8	109.19%	D+ / 2.7

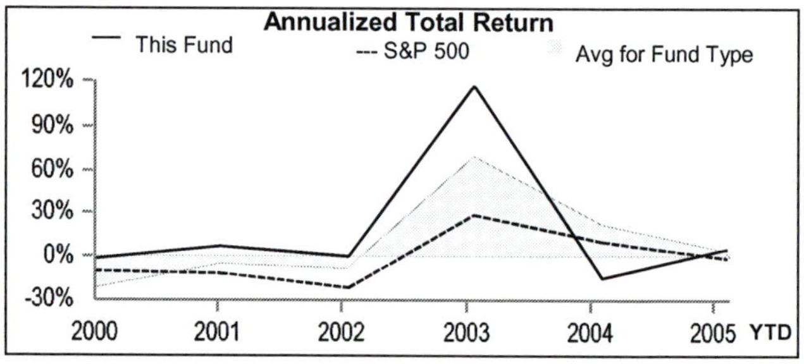

H&Q Healthcare Investors (HQH) | D | Weak

Fund Family: Hambrecht & Quist Capital Mgmt, LLC
Fund Type: Health
Inception Date: April 23, 1987

Major Rating Factors:

H&Q Healthcare Investors receives a Weiss Investment Rating of D (Weak). The fund currently has a performance rating of C (Fair) based on an annualized return of 12.46% over the last three years and a total return of 0.69% year to date 2005. Factored into the performance evaluation is an expense ratio of 1.60% (above average).

The fund's risk rating is currently C- (Fair). It carries a beta of 0.96, meaning that its performance tracks fairly well with that of the overall stock market. Volatility, as measured by both the semi-deviation and a drawdown factor, is considered average. As of June 30, 2005, H&Q Healthcare Investors traded at a discount of 2.00% below its net asset value, which is worse than its one-year historical average discount of 2.06%.

Daniel R. Omstead has been running the fund for 1 year and currently receives a manager quality ranking of 80 (0=worst, 99=best). If you desire an average level of risk, then this fund may be an option.

Data Date	Weiss Investment Rating	Net Assets ($Mil)	Price	Perfor-mance Rating/Pts	Total Return Y-T-D	Risk Rating/Pts
6-05	D	361.39	17.65	C / 4.3	0.69%	C- / 3.7
2004	E	369.30	18.28	E+ / 0.8	9.66%	D+ / 2.7
2003	D	286.76	18.08	C- / 3.4	44.50%	D+ / 2.9

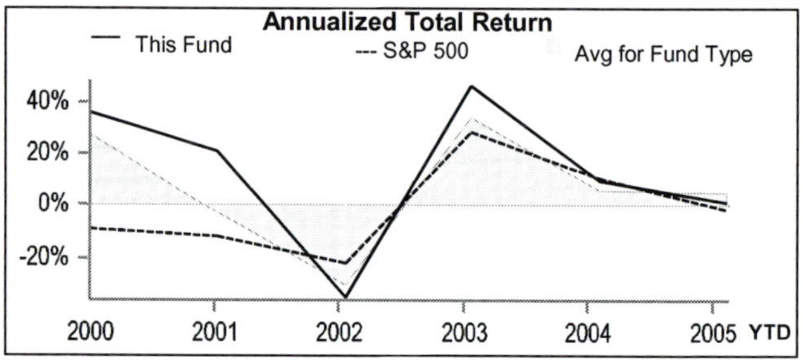

H&Q Life Sciences Investors (HQL) C- Fair

Fund Family: Hambrecht & Quist Capital Mgmt, LLC
Fund Type: Health
Inception Date: May 1, 1992

Major Rating Factors:
Middle of the road best describes H&Q Life Sciences Investors whose Weiss Investment Rating is currently a C- (Fair). The fund currently has a performance rating of C (Fair) based on an annualized return of 14.23% over the last three years and a total return of 4.56% year to date 2005. Factored into the performance evaluation is an expense ratio of 1.78% (above average).

The fund's risk rating is currently C- (Fair). It carries a beta of 0.98, meaning that its performance tracks fairly well with that of the overall stock market. Volatility, as measured by both the semi-deviation and a drawdown factor, is considered average. As of June 30, 2005, H&Q Life Sciences Investors traded at a discount of 1.85% below its net asset value, which is better than its one-year historical average discount of 1.84%.

Daniel R. Omstead has been running the fund for 1 year and currently receives a manager quality ranking of 83 (0=worst, 99=best). If you desire an average level of risk, then this fund may be an option.

Data Date	Weiss Investment Rating	Net Assets ($Mil)	Price	Perfor-mance Rating/Pts	Total Return Y-T-D	Risk Rating/Pts
6-05	C-	190.19	15.89	C / 5.3	4.56%	C- / 4.2
2004	E	191.84	15.85	D- / 1.0	11.15%	D+ / 2.8
2003	D	190.35	15.60	C- / 3.1	42.62%	D+ / 2.8

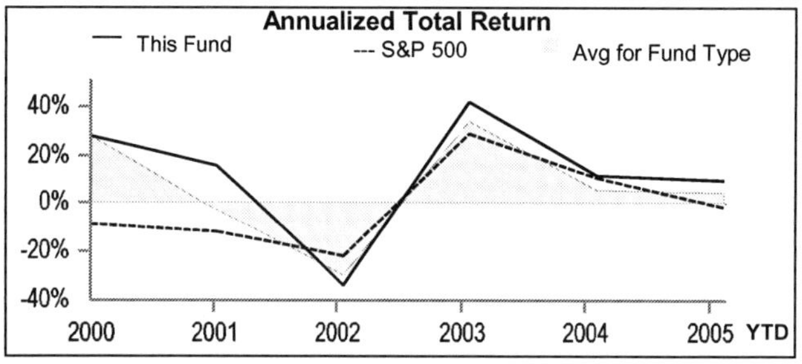

Hartford Income Shares Fund Inc (HSF) C Fair

Fund Family: Hartford Investment Financial Serv.
Fund Type: Global
Inception Date: October 1, 1972

Major Rating Factors:
Middle of the road best describes Hartford Income Shares Fund Inc whose Weiss Investment Rating is currently a C (Fair). The fund currently has a performance rating of C (Fair) based on an annualized return of 11.71% over the last three years and a total return of 4.34% year to date 2005. Factored into the performance evaluation is an expense ratio of 0.77% (very low).

The fund's risk rating is currently C+ (Fair). It carries a beta of 0.86, meaning the fund's expected move will be 8.6% for every 10% move in the market. Volatility, as measured by both the semi-deviation and a drawdown factor, is considered low. As of June 30, 2005, Hartford Income Shares Fund Inc traded at a discount of 5.02% below its net asset value, which is worse than its one-year historical average discount of 6.85%.

Mark Niland has been running the fund for 4 years and currently receives a manager quality ranking of 73 (0=worst, 99=best). If you desire an average level of risk, then this fund may be an option.

Data Date	Weiss Investment Rating	Net Assets ($Mil)	Price	Perfor-mance Rating/Pts	Total Return Y-T-D	Risk Rating/Pts
6-05	C	108.73	7.75	C / 4.7	4.34%	C+ / 6.9
2004	C-	102.99	7.70	C- / 3.2	8.41%	B- / 7.1
2003	C-	99.05	7.62	C- / 3.7	20.24%	B- / 7.6

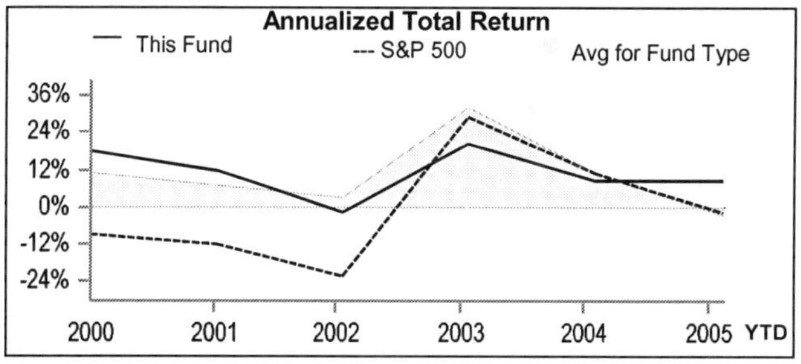

Herzfeld Caribbean Basin Fund (CUBA) B- Good

Fund Family: Herzfeld/Cuba
Fund Type: Global
Inception Date: April 22, 1994

Major Rating Factors:
Strong performance is the major factor driving the B- (Good) Weiss Investment Rating for Herzfeld Caribbean Basin Fund. The fund currently has a performance rating of B+ (Good) based on an annualized return of 22.86% over the last three years and a total return of 5.00% year to date 2005. Factored into the performance evaluation is an expense ratio of 3.40% (high).

The fund's risk rating is currently C (Fair). It carries a beta of 0.50, meaning the fund's expected move will be 5.0% for every 10% move in the market. Volatility, as measured by both the semi-deviation and a drawdown factor, is considered average. As of June 30, 2005, Herzfeld Caribbean Basin Fund traded at a discount of 12.98% below its net asset value, which is worse than its one-year historical average discount of 13.44%.

Thomas J. Herzfeld has been running the fund for 11 years and currently receives a manager quality ranking of 95 (0=worst, 99=best). If you desire an average level of risk and strong performance, then this fund is a good option.

Data Date	Weiss Investment Rating	Net Assets ($Mil)	Price	Perfor-mance Rating/Pts	Total Return Y-T-D	Risk Rating/Pts
6-05	B-	11.72	6.30	B+ / 8.9	5.00%	C / 4.4
2004	B	9.11	6.00	A- / 9.0	26.32%	C / 4.7
2003	C	6.63	4.75	B / 8.0	43.12%	C- / 3.9

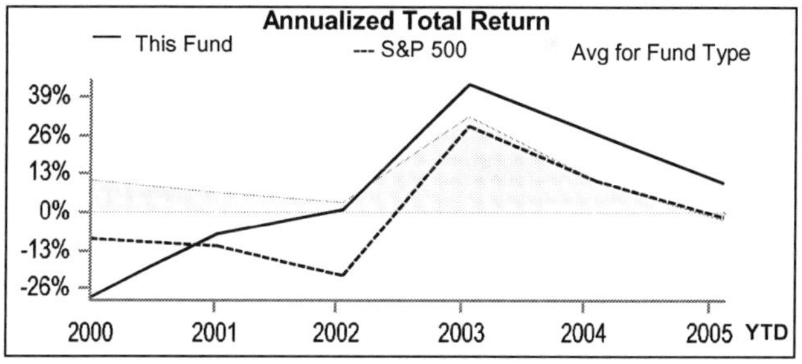

High Income Opportunity Fund Inc. (HIO) C- Fair

Fund Family: SSBC Fund Management Inc.
Fund Type: Corporate - High Yield
Inception Date: November 16, 1993

Data Date	Weiss Investment Rating	Net Assets ($Mil)	Price	Perfor-mance Rating/Pts	Total Return Y-T-D	Risk Rating/Pts
6-05	C-	529.90	6.46	C- / 3.2	0.24%	C+ / 6.1
2004	D-	538.16	6.72	D- / 1.3	2.23%	C / 5.3
2003	D	522.72	7.14	D+ / 2.4	25.32%	C / 4.9

Major Rating Factors:
Middle of the road best describes High Income Opportunity Fund Inc. whose Weiss Investment Rating is currently a C- (Fair). The fund currently has a performance rating of C- (Fair) based on an annualized return of 11.57% over the last three years and a total return of 0.24% year to date 2005. Factored into the performance evaluation is an expense ratio of 1.25% (average).

The fund's risk rating is currently C+ (Fair). It carries a beta of 1.28, meaning it is expected to move 12.8% for every 10% move in the market. Volatility, as measured by both the semi-deviation and a drawdown factor, is considered low. As of June 30, 2005, High Income Opportunity Fund Inc. traded at a discount of 9.78% below its net asset value, which is better than its one-year historical average discount of 8.74%.

Beth Semmel has been running the fund for 12 years and currently receives a manager quality ranking of 13 (0=worst, 99=best). If you desire an average level of risk, then this fund may be an option.

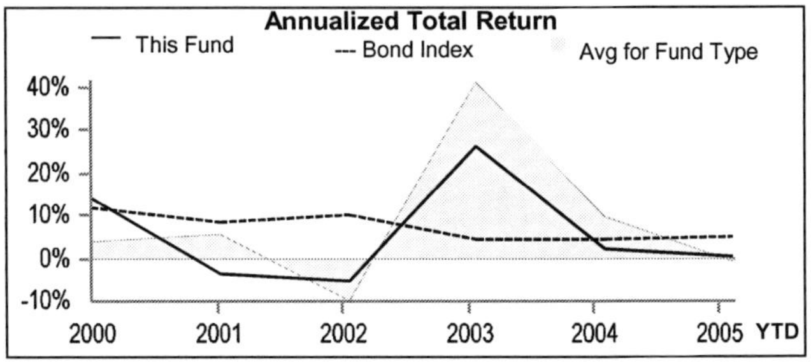

High Yield Income Fund (HYI) C+ Fair

Fund Family: Prudential Investments Fund Mgt, LL
Fund Type: Corporate - High Yield
Inception Date: October 30, 1987

Data Date	Weiss Investment Rating	Net Assets ($Mil)	Price	Perfor-mance Rating/Pts	Total Return Y-T-D	Risk Rating/Pts
6-05	C+	67.06	5.42	C+ / 5.8	-6.11%	C+ / 6.1
2004	D+	64.47	6.04	C / 5.1	7.83%	C / 4.4
2003	C	60.45	5.99	B- / 7.4	29.25%	C / 4.5

Major Rating Factors:
Middle of the road best describes High Yield Income Fund whose Weiss Investment Rating is currently a C+ (Fair). The fund currently has a performance rating of C+ (Fair) based on an annualized return of 16.53% over the last three years and a total return of -6.11% year to date 2005. Factored into the performance evaluation is an expense ratio of 2.56% (high).

The fund's risk rating is currently C+ (Fair). It carries a beta of 1.98, meaning it is expected to move 19.8% for every 10% move in the market. Volatility, as measured by both the semi-deviation and a drawdown factor, is considered low. As of June 30, 2005, High Yield Income Fund traded at a discount of 3.04% below its net asset value, which is better than its one-year historical average premium of 1.18%.

George Edwards has been running the fund for 6 years and currently receives a manager quality ranking of 4 (0=worst, 99=best). If you desire an average level of risk, then this fund may be an option.

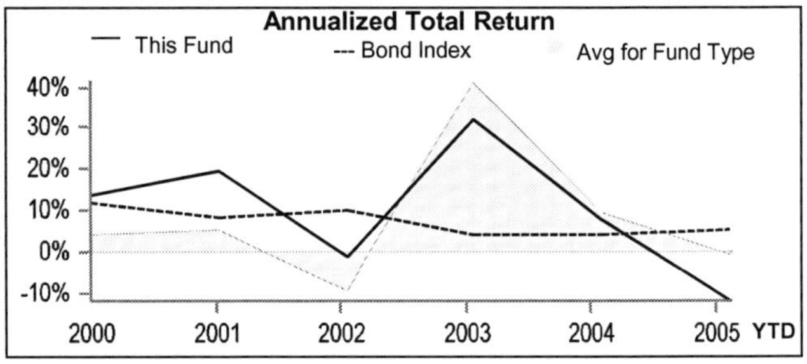

High Yield Plus Fund (HYP) C- Fair

Fund Family: Wellington Mang. Co
Fund Type: Corporate - High Yield
Inception Date: April 22, 1988

Data Date	Weiss Investment Rating	Net Assets ($Mil)	Price	Perfor-mance Rating/Pts	Total Return Y-T-D	Risk Rating/Pts
6-05	C-	61.74	4.00	C+ / 5.7	-7.76%	C / 4.8
2004	D-	63.45	4.53	C- / 4.1	7.79%	D / 2.2
2003	C-	60.39	4.72	B- / 7.2	59.80%	D+ / 2.7

Major Rating Factors:
Middle of the road best describes High Yield Plus Fund whose Weiss Investment Rating is currently a C- (Fair). The fund currently has a performance rating of C+ (Fair) based on an annualized return of 17.45% over the last three years and a total return of -7.76% year to date 2005. Factored into the performance evaluation is an expense ratio of 2.67% (high).

The fund's risk rating is currently C (Fair). It carries a beta of 2.18, meaning it is expected to move 21.8% for every 10% move in the market. Volatility, as measured by both the semi-deviation and a drawdown factor, is considered average. As of June 30, 2005, High Yield Plus Fund traded at a premium of 3.36% above its net asset value, which is better than its one-year historical average premium of 9.08%.

Earl A. McEvoy has been running the fund for 3 years and currently receives a manager quality ranking of 2 (0=worst, 99=best). If you desire an average level of risk, then this fund may be an option.

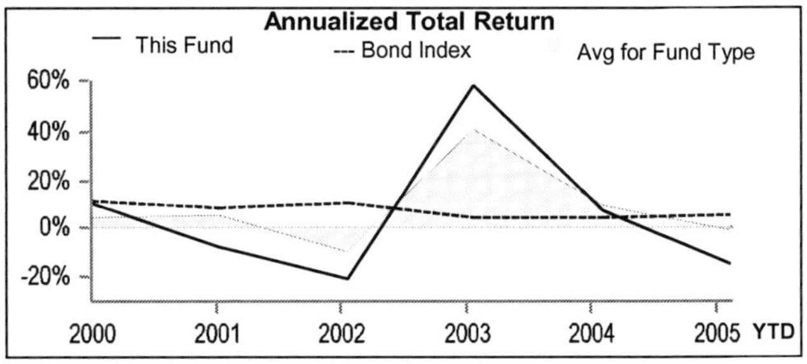

HOLDRS B2B Internet (BHH) E- Very Weak

Fund Family: Merril Lynch
Fund Type: Growth
Inception Date: February 24, 2000

Data Date	Weiss Investment Rating	Net Assets ($Mil)	Price	Performance Rating/Pts	Total Return Y-T-D	Risk Rating/Pts
6-05	E-	32.29	2.00	E- / 0.0	-20.07%	E- / 0.0
2004	E-	32.29	2.85	E- / 0.0	5.91%	E- / 0.0
2003	E-	35.31	2.73	E- / 0.0	37.88%	E- / 0.0

Major Rating Factors:
HOLDRS B2B Internet has adopted a very risky asset allocation strategy and currently receives an overall Weiss Investment Rating of E- (Very Weak). The fund has a high level of volatility, as measured by both semi-deviation and drawdown factors. It carries a beta of 2.54, meaning it is expected to move 25.4% for every 10% move in the market. As of June 30, 2005, HOLDRS B2B Internet traded at a price exactly equal to its net asset value. Unfortunately, the high level of risk (E-, Very Weak) failed to pay off as investors endured very poor performance.

The fund's performance rating is currently E- (Very Weak). It has registered an annualized return of -8.09% over the last three years and is down -20.07% year to date 2005.

Merrill Lynch, Pierce, Fenner has been running the fund for 5 years and currently receives a manager quality ranking of 0 (0=worst, 99=best). If you can tolerate very high levels of risk in the hope of improved future returns, holding this fund may be an option.

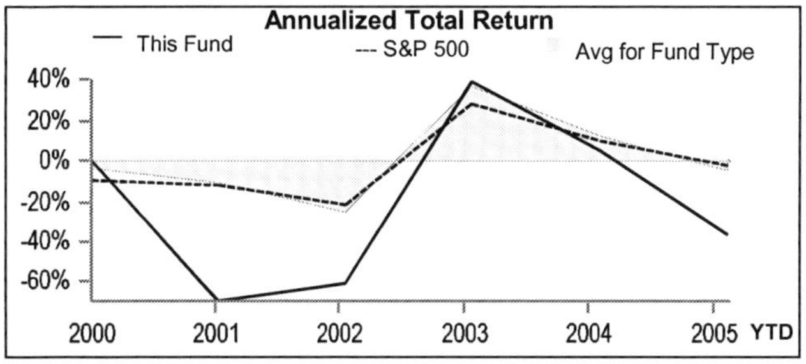

HOLDRS Biotech (BBH) A+ Excellent

Fund Family: Merril Lynch
Fund Type: Health
Inception Date: November 23, 1999

Data Date	Weiss Investment Rating	Net Assets ($Mil)	Price	Performance Rating/Pts	Total Return Y-T-D	Risk Rating/Pts
6-05	A+	1370.78	167.30	A / 9.4	9.40%	C+ / 6.6
2004	E+	1370.78	152.92	C- / 3.0	13.01%	D+ / 2.4
2003	E+	1500.93	135.49	D- / 1.0	60.23%	D / 1.7

Major Rating Factors:
Exceptional performance is the major factor driving the A+ (Excellent) Weiss Investment Rating for HOLDRS Biotech. The fund currently has a performance rating of A (Excellent) based on an annualized return of 27.32% over the last three years and a total return of 9.40% year to date 2005.

The fund's risk rating is currently C+ (Fair). It carries a beta of 0.65, meaning the fund's expected move will be 6.5% for every 10% move in the market. Volatility, as measured by both the semi-deviation and a drawdown factor, is considered low. As of June 30, 2005, HOLDRS Biotech traded at a price exactly equal to its net asset value.

Merrill Lynch, Pierce, Fenner has been running the fund for 5 years and currently receives a manager quality ranking of 98 (0=worst, 99=best). If you desire only a moderate level of risk and strong performance, then this fund is an excellent option.

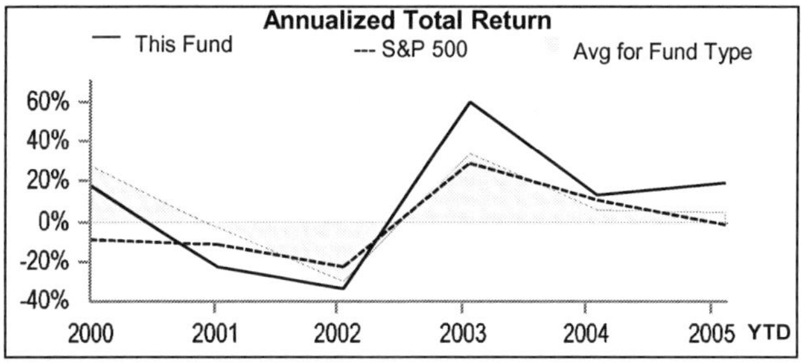

HOLDRS Broadband (BDH) D- Weak

Fund Family: Merril Lynch
Fund Type: Growth
Inception Date: April 6, 2000

Data Date	Weiss Investment Rating	Net Assets ($Mil)	Price	Performance Rating/Pts	Total Return Y-T-D	Risk Rating/Pts
6-05	D-	117.59	15.33	B- / 7.2	-8.19%	E- / 0.0
2004	E-	117.59	16.70	E / 0.5	24.16%	E- / 0.0
2003	E-	70.02	13.20	E- / 0.0	74.83%	E- / 0.0

Major Rating Factors:
HOLDRS Broadband has adopted a very risky asset allocation strategy and currently receives an overall Weiss Investment Rating of D- (Weak). The fund has shown a high level of volatility, as measured by both semi-deviation and drawdown factors. It carries a beta of 1.92, meaning it is expected to move 19.2% for every 10% move in the market. As of June 30, 2005, HOLDRS Broadband traded at a price exactly equal to its net asset value. The high level of risk (E-, Very Weak) did however, reward investors with excellent performance.

The fund's performance rating is currently B- (Good). It has registered an annualized return of 22.85% over the last three years but is down -8.19% year to date 2005.

Merrill Lynch, Pierce, Fenner has been running the fund for 5 years and currently receives a manager quality ranking of 85 (0=worst, 99=best). If you are comfortable owning a very high risk investment, this fund may be an option.

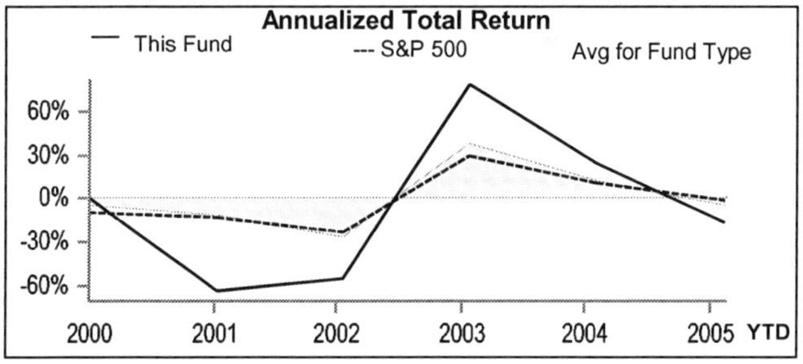

HOLDRS Europe 2001 (EKH) D- Weak

Fund Family: Merril Lynch
Fund Type: Foreign
Inception Date: January 18, 2001

Major Rating Factors:
Disappointing performance is the major factor driving the D- (Weak) Weiss Investment Rating for HOLDRS Europe 2001. The fund currently has a performance rating of D (Weak) based on an annualized return of 9.17% over the last three years and a total return of 0.09% year to date 2005.

The fund's risk rating is currently C (Fair). It carries a beta of 1.23, meaning it is expected to move 12.3% for every 10% move in the market. Volatility, as measured by both the semi-deviation and a drawdown factor, is considered average. As of June 30, 2005, HOLDRS Europe 2001 traded at a price exactly equal to its net asset value.

Merrill Lynch, Pierce, Fenner has been running the fund for 4 years and currently receives a manager quality ranking of 11 (0=worst, 99=best). This fund offers an average level of risk but investors looking for strong performance will be frustrated.

Data Date	Weiss Investment Rating	Net Assets ($Mil)	Price	Perfor-mance Rating/Pts	Total Return Y-T-D	Risk Rating/Pts
6-05	D-	18.80	63.10	D / 2.1	0.09%	C / 4.5
2004	E	18.80	63.65	E+ / 0.7	6.49%	D+ / 2.6

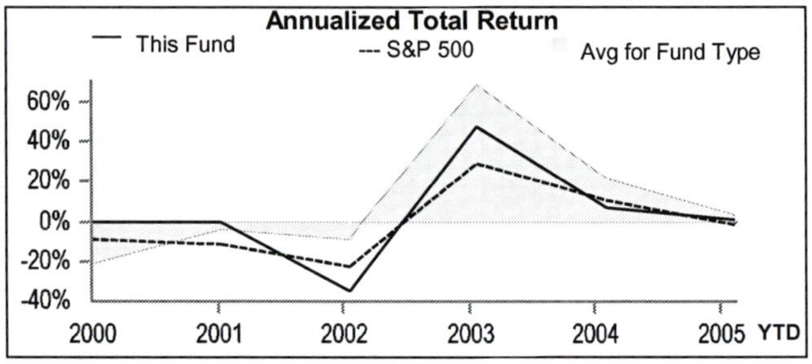

HOLDRS Internet (HHH) C Fair

Fund Family: Merril Lynch
Fund Type: Growth
Inception Date: September 24, 1999

Major Rating Factors:
HOLDRS Internet has adopted a risky asset allocation strategy and currently receives an overall Weiss Investment Rating of C (Fair). The fund has shown an above average level of volatility, as measured by both semi-deviation and drawdown factors. It carries a beta of 1.77, meaning it is expected to move 17.7% for every 10% move in the market. As of June 30, 2005, HOLDRS Internet traded at a price exactly equal to its net asset value. The high level of risk (D+, Weak) did however, reward investors with excellent performance.

The fund's performance rating is currently A- (Excellent). It has registered an annualized return of 32.31% over the last three years but is down -21.55% year to date 2005.

Merrill Lynch, Pierce, Fenner has been running the fund for 5 years and currently receives a manager quality ranking of 95 (0=worst, 99=best). If you are comfortable owning a high risk investment, this fund may be an option.

Data Date	Weiss Investment Rating	Net Assets ($Mil)	Price	Perfor-mance Rating/Pts	Total Return Y-T-D	Risk Rating/Pts
6-05	C	250.76	55.94	A- / 9.0	-21.55%	D+ / 2.7
2004	C-	250.76	71.31	A / 9.5	42.08%	D- / 1.0
2003	D+	203.21	49.72	A- / 9.2	101.03%	E / 0.4

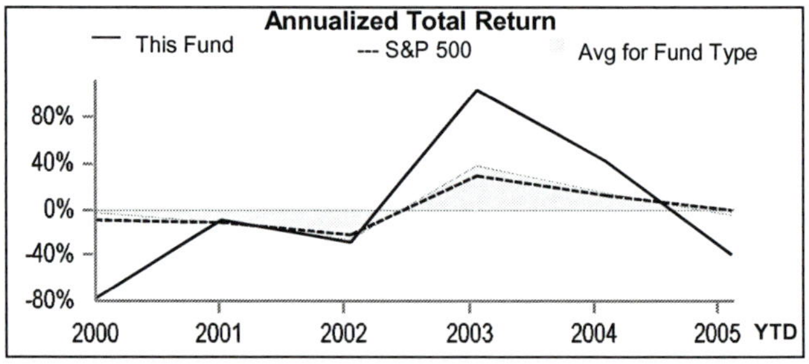

HOLDRS Internet Architecture (IAH) E Very Weak

Fund Family: Merril Lynch
Fund Type: Growth
Inception Date: February 25, 2000

Major Rating Factors:
HOLDRS Internet Architecture has adopted a risky asset allocation strategy and currently receives an overall Weiss Investment Rating of E (Very Weak). The fund has an above average level of volatility, as measured by both semi-deviation and drawdown factors. It carries a beta of 1.68, meaning it is expected to move 16.8% for every 10% move in the market. As of June 30, 2005, HOLDRS Internet Architecture traded at a price exactly equal to its net asset value. Unfortunately, the high level of risk (D+, Weak) failed to pay off as investors endured poor performance.

The fund's performance rating is currently D (Weak). It has registered an annualized return of 10.35% over the last three years but is down -9.57% year to date 2005.

Merrill Lynch, Pierce, Fenner has been running the fund for 5 years and currently receives a manager quality ranking of 33 (0=worst, 99=best). If you can tolerate high levels of risk in the hope of improved future returns, holding this fund may be an option.

Data Date	Weiss Investment Rating	Net Assets ($Mil)	Price	Perfor-mance Rating/Pts	Total Return Y-T-D	Risk Rating/Pts
6-05	E	83.04	34.23	D / 1.6	-9.57%	D+ / 2.6
2004	E-	83.04	37.90	E / 0.4	5.50%	E+ / 0.6
2003	E-	54.64	35.80	E / 0.3	39.19%	E- / 0.0

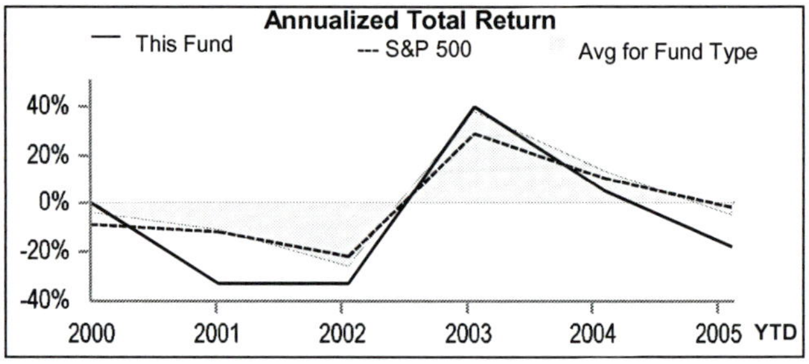

HOLDRS Internet Infrastructure (IIH) D- Weak

Fund Family: Merril Lynch
Fund Type: Growth
Inception Date: February 25, 2000

Major Rating Factors:

HOLDRS Internet Infrastructure has adopted a very risky asset allocation strategy and currently receives an overall Weiss Investment Rating of D- (Weak). The fund has shown a high level of volatility, as measured by both semi-deviation and drawdown factors. It carries a beta of 2.91, meaning it is expected to move 29.1% for every 10% move in the market. As of June 30, 2005, HOLDRS Internet Infrastructure traded at a price exactly equal to its net asset value. The high level of risk (E-, Very Weak) did however, reward investors with excellent performance.

The fund's performance rating is currently B- (Good). It has registered an annualized return of 21.65% over the last three years but is down -11.96% year to date 2005.

Merrill Lynch, Pierce, Fenner has been running the fund for 5 years and currently receives a manager quality ranking of 46 (0=worst, 99=best). If you are comfortable owning a very high risk investment, this fund may be an option.

Data Date	Weiss Investment Rating	Net Assets ($Mil)	Price	Performance Rating/Pts	Total Return Y-T-D	Risk Rating/Pts
6-05	D-	37.14	4.05	B- / 7.4	-11.96%	E- / 0.0
2004	E-	37.14	4.60	E- / 0.2	21.94%	E- / 0.0
2003	E-	29.02	3.76	E- / 0.0	58.52%	E- / 0.0

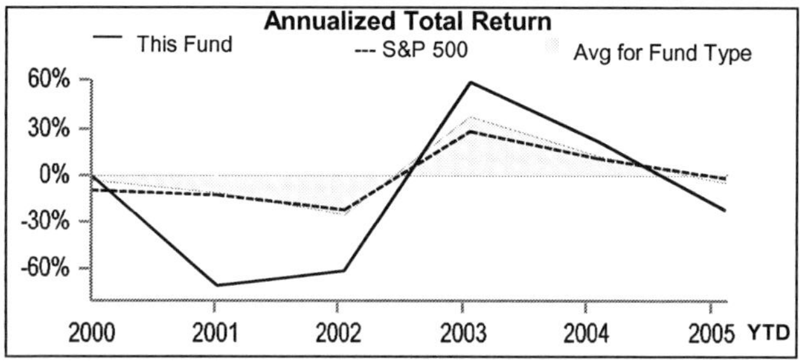

HOLDRS Market 2000 + (MKH) D- Weak

Fund Family: Merril Lynch
Fund Type: Growth
Inception Date: August 30, 2000

Major Rating Factors:

Very poor performance is the major factor driving the D- (Weak) Weiss Investment Rating for HOLDRS Market 2000 +. The fund currently has a performance rating of E (Very Weak) based on an annualized return of 4.75% over the last three years and a total return of -3.33% year to date 2005.

The fund's risk rating is currently B- (Good). It carries a beta of 1.03, meaning that its performance tracks fairly well with that of the overall stock market. Volatility, as measured by both the semi-deviation and a drawdown factor, is considered low. As of June 30, 2005, HOLDRS Market 2000 + traded at a price exactly equal to its net asset value.

Merrill Lynch, Pierce, Fenner has been running the fund for 5 years and currently receives a manager quality ranking of 27 (0=worst, 99=best). This fund offers only a moderate level of risk but investors looking for strong performance are still waiting.

Data Date	Weiss Investment Rating	Net Assets ($Mil)	Price	Performance Rating/Pts	Total Return Y-T-D	Risk Rating/Pts
6-05	D-	54.48	53.59	E / 0.4	-3.33%	B- / 7.1
2004	E+	54.48	55.88	E / 0.4	5.45%	C / 4.5
2003	D-	69.94	53.24	E / 0.4	20.17%	C- / 3.8

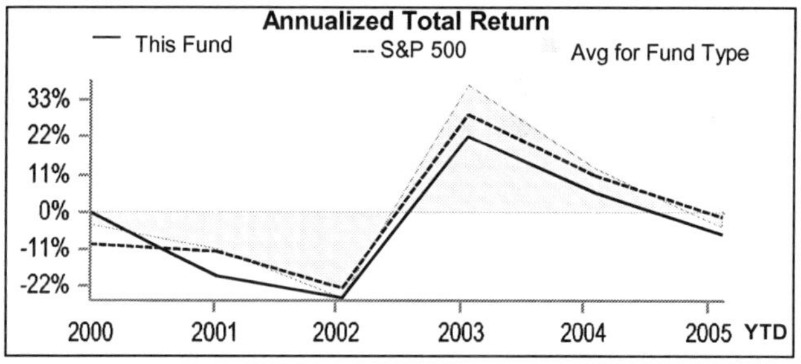

HOLDRS Oil Services (OIH) D+ Weak

Fund Family: Merril Lynch
Fund Type: Energy/Natural Resources
Inception Date: February 6, 2001

Major Rating Factors:

HOLDRS Oil Services has adopted a very risky asset allocation strategy and currently receives an overall Weiss Investment Rating of D+ (Weak). The fund has shown a high level of volatility, with a standard deviation of 24.34. It carries a beta of 1.09, meaning that its performance tracks fairly well with that of the overall stock market. As of June 30, 2005, HOLDRS Oil Services traded at a price exactly equal to its net asset value. The high level of risk (E-, Very Weak) did however, reward investors with excellent performance.

The fund's performance rating is currently A (Excellent). It has registered an annualized return of 19.31% over the last three years and is up 21.19% year to date 2005.

Merrill Lynch, Pierce, Fenner & has been running the fund for 4 years and currently receives a manager quality ranking of 33 (0=worst, 99=best). If you are comfortable owning a very high risk investment, this fund may be an option.

Data Date	Weiss Investment Rating	Net Assets ($Mil)	Price	Performance Rating/Pts	Total Return Y-T-D	Risk Rating/Pts
6-05	D+	932.99	102.90	A / 9.3	21.19%	E- / 0.0
2004	D	932.99	85.07	B+ / 8.3	37.84%	E- / 0.0

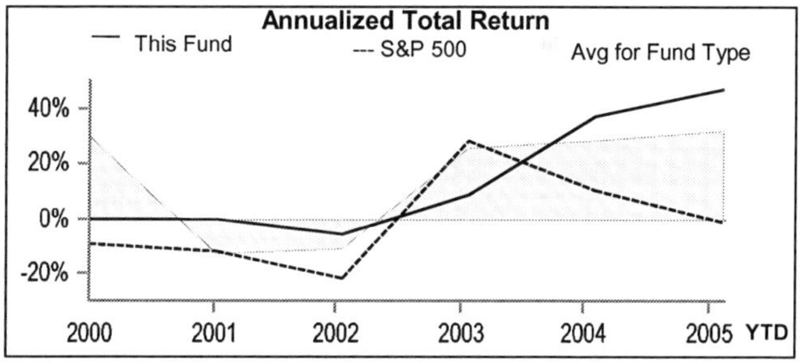

HOLDRS Pharmaceutical (PPH) D- Weak

Fund Family: Merril Lynch
Fund Type: Health
Inception Date: February 1, 2000

Major Rating Factors:
Very poor performance is the major factor driving the D- (Weak) Weiss Investment Rating for HOLDRS Pharmaceutical. The fund currently has a performance rating of E- (Very Weak) based on an annualized return of 0.37% over the last three years and a total return of 2.73% year to date 2005.

The fund's risk rating is currently C+ (Fair). It carries a beta of 0.64, meaning the fund's expected move will be 6.4% for every 10% move in the market. Volatility, as measured by both the semi-deviation and a drawdown factor, is considered low. As of June 30, 2005, HOLDRS Pharmaceutical traded at a price exactly equal to its net asset value.

Merrill Lynch, Pierce, Fenner has been running the fund for 5 years and currently receives a manager quality ranking of 12 (0=worst, 99=best). This fund offers only a moderate level of risk but investors looking for strong performance are still waiting.

Data Date	Weiss Investment Rating	Net Assets ($Mil)	Price	Performance Rating/Pts	Total Return Y-T-D	Risk Rating/Pts
6-05	D-	1037.69	74.03	E- / 0.1	2.73%	C+ / 6.5
2004	E+	1037.69	72.69	E- / 0.0	-6.92%	C- / 4.1
2003	D-	519.32	78.30	E- / 0.2	7.60%	C / 4.7

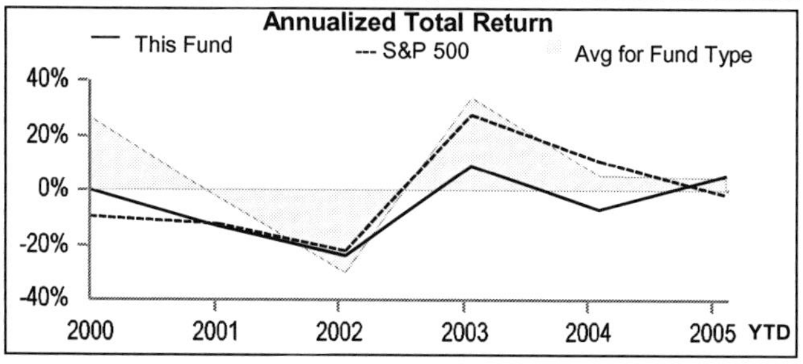

HOLDRS Regional Bank (RKH) D Weak

Fund Family: Merril Lynch
Fund Type: Financial Services
Inception Date: June 26, 2000

Major Rating Factors:
Disappointing performance is the major factor driving the D (Weak) Weiss Investment Rating for HOLDRS Regional Bank. The fund currently has a performance rating of D- (Weak) based on an annualized return of 7.19% over the last three years and a total return of -4.12% year to date 2005.

The fund's risk rating is currently C+ (Fair). It carries a beta of 0.87, meaning the fund's expected move will be 8.7% for every 10% move in the market. Volatility, as measured by both the semi-deviation and a drawdown factor, is considered low. As of June 30, 2005, HOLDRS Regional Bank traded at a price exactly equal to its net asset value.

Merrill Lynch, Pierce, Fenner has been running the fund for 5 years and currently receives a manager quality ranking of 49 (0=worst, 99=best). This fund offers only a moderate level of risk but investors looking for strong performance are still waiting.

Data Date	Weiss Investment Rating	Net Assets ($Mil)	Price	Performance Rating/Pts	Total Return Y-T-D	Risk Rating/Pts
6-05	D	200.11	134.50	D- / 1.2	-4.12%	C+ / 6.7
2004	C	200.11	141.95	C / 5.0	9.52%	C+ / 6.6
2003	C-	225.31	130.72	C- / 4.2	29.77%	C+ / 6.6

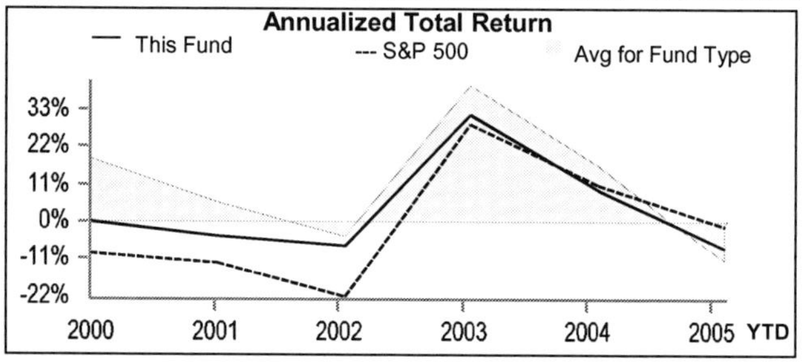

HOLDRS Retail (RTH) E+ Very Weak

Fund Family: Merril Lynch
Fund Type: Growth
Inception Date: May 2, 2001

Major Rating Factors:
Very poor performance is the major factor driving the E+ (Very Weak) Weiss Investment Rating for HOLDRS Retail. The fund currently has a performance rating of E (Very Weak) based on an annualized return of 3.89% over the last three years and a total return of -0.56% year to date 2005.

The fund's risk rating is currently C (Fair). It carries a beta of 1.03, meaning that its performance tracks fairly well with that of the overall stock market. Volatility, as measured by both the semi-deviation and a drawdown factor, is considered average. As of June 30, 2005, HOLDRS Retail traded at a price exactly equal to its net asset value.

Merrill Lynch, Pierce, Fenner has been running the fund for 4 years and currently receives a manager quality ranking of 23 (0=worst, 99=best). This fund offers an average level of risk but investors looking for strong performance will be frustrated.

Data Date	Weiss Investment Rating	Net Assets ($Mil)	Price	Performance Rating/Pts	Total Return Y-T-D	Risk Rating/Pts
6-05	E+	439.61	94.62	E / 0.5	-0.56%	C / 4.7
2004	D-	439.61	98.61	D / 1.6	9.95%	C / 4.4

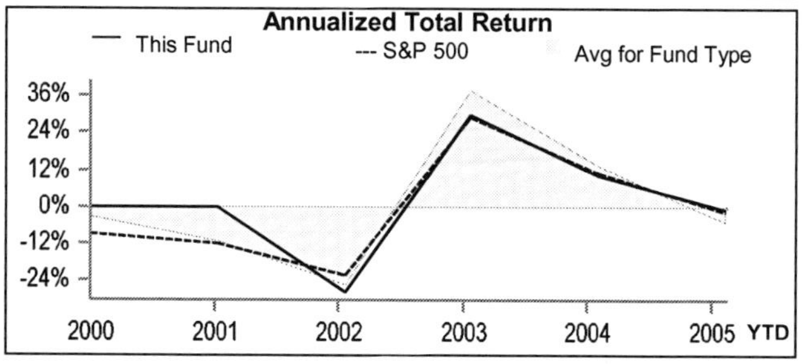

HOLDRS Semiconductor (SMH) E- Very Weak

Fund Family: Merril Lynch
Fund Type: Growth
Inception Date: May 26, 2000

Data Date	Weiss Investment Rating	Net Assets ($Mil)	Price	Performance Rating/Pts	Total Return Y-T-D	Risk Rating/Pts
6-05	E-	2422.17	34.10	E / 0.3	2.37%	E- / 0.0
2004	E-	2422.17	33.37	E- / 0.0	-19.46%	E- / 0.0
2003	E+	872.13	40.92	D+ / 2.9	84.74%	E- / 0.0

Major Rating Factors:
HOLDRS Semiconductor has adopted a very risky asset allocation strategy and currently receives an overall Weiss Investment Rating of E- (Very Weak). The fund has a high level of volatility, as measured by both semi-deviation and drawdown factors. It carries a beta of 2.26, meaning it is expected to move 22.6% for every 10% move in the market. As of June 30, 2005, HOLDRS Semiconductor traded at a price exactly equal to its net asset value. Unfortunately, the high level of risk (E-, Very Weak) failed to pay off as investors endured very poor performance.

The fund's performance rating is currently E (Very Weak). It has registered an annualized return of 4.07% over the last three years and is up 2.37% year to date 2005.

Merrill Lynch, Pierce, Fenner has been running the fund for 5 years and currently receives a manager quality ranking of 1 (0=worst, 99=best). If you can tolerate very high levels of risk in the hope of improved future returns, holding this fund may be an option.

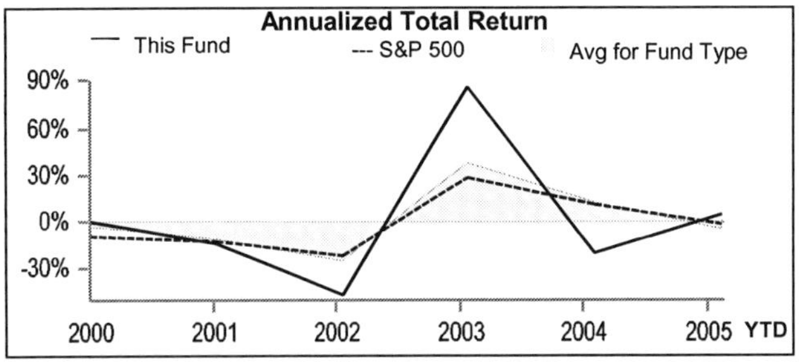

HOLDRS Software (SWH) E Very Weak

Fund Family: Merril Lynch
Fund Type: Growth
Inception Date: September 27, 2000

Data Date	Weiss Investment Rating	Net Assets ($Mil)	Price	Performance Rating/Pts	Total Return Y-T-D	Risk Rating/Pts
6-05	E	201.68	34.96	D / 2.0	-7.71%	D+ / 2.6
2004	E-	201.68	40.24	E / 0.3	8.21%	E- / 0.0
2003	E-	326.87	37.64	E / 0.3	42.88%	E- / 0.0

Major Rating Factors:
HOLDRS Software has adopted a risky asset allocation strategy and currently receives an overall Weiss Investment Rating of E (Very Weak). The fund has an above average level of volatility, as measured by both semi-deviation and drawdown factors. It carries a beta of 1.81, meaning it is expected to move 18.1% for every 10% move in the market. As of June 30, 2005, HOLDRS Software traded at a price exactly equal to its net asset value. Unfortunately, the high level of risk (D+, Weak) failed to pay off as investors endured poor performance.

The fund's performance rating is currently D (Weak). It has registered an annualized return of 10.27% over the last three years but is down -7.71% year to date 2005.

Merrill Lynch, Pierce, Fenner has been running the fund for 4 years and currently receives a manager quality ranking of 30 (0=worst, 99=best). If you can tolerate high levels of risk in the hope of improved future returns, holding this fund may be an option.

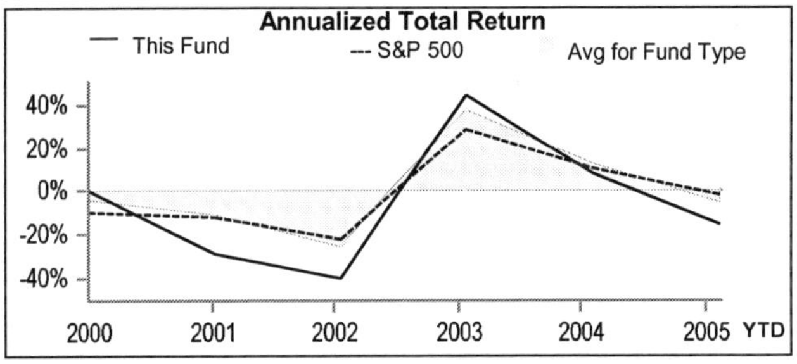

HOLDRS TeleBras (TBH) E+ Very Weak

Fund Family: Merril Lynch
Fund Type: Foreign
Inception Date: July 28, 1998

Data Date	Weiss Investment Rating	Net Assets ($Mil)	Price	Performance Rating/Pts	Total Return Y-T-D	Risk Rating/Pts
6-05	E+	763.15	30.45	C+ / 6.3	0.28%	E- / 0.0
2004	E-	763.15	32.18	E- / 0.1	-3.36%	E- / 0.0
2003	E-	770.02	33.29	E / 0.3	79.90%	E- / 0.0

Major Rating Factors:
HOLDRS TeleBras has adopted a very risky asset allocation strategy and currently receives an overall Weiss Investment Rating of E+ (Very Weak). The fund has a high level of volatility, with a standard deviation of 45.61. It carries a beta of 1.92, meaning it is expected to move 19.2% for every 10% move in the market. As of June 30, 2005, HOLDRS TeleBras traded at a price exactly equal to its net asset value. Unfortunately, the high level of risk (E-, Very Weak) has only provided investors with average performance.

The fund's performance rating is currently C+ (Fair). It has registered an annualized return of 14.75% over the last three years and is up 0.28% year to date 2005.

Merrill Lynch, Pierce, Fenner has been running the fund for 7 years and currently receives a manager quality ranking of 6 (0=worst, 99=best). If you are comfortable owning a very high risk investment, then this fund may be an option.

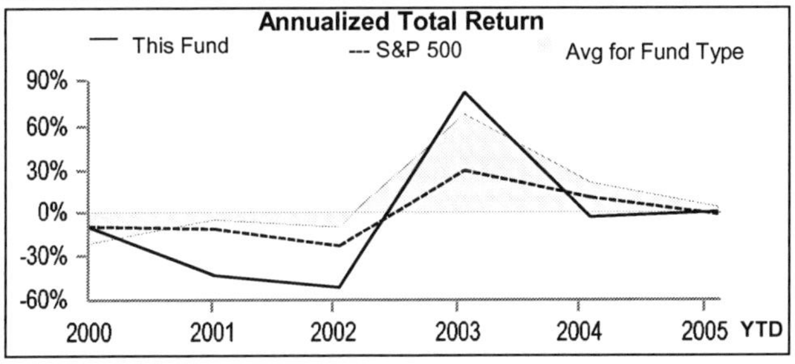

HOLDRS Telecom (TTH) E Very Weak

Fund Family: Merril Lynch
Fund Type: Growth
Inception Date: February 2, 2000

Major Rating Factors:
Very poor performance is the major factor driving the E (Very Weak) Weiss Investment Rating for HOLDRS Telecom. The fund currently has a performance rating of E- (Very Weak) based on an annualized return of 2.01% over the last three years and a total return of -6.37% year to date 2005.

The fund's risk rating is currently C- (Fair). It carries a beta of 1.39, meaning it is expected to move 13.9% for every 10% move in the market. Volatility, as measured by both the semi-deviation and a drawdown factor, is considered average. As of June 30, 2005, HOLDRS Telecom traded at a price exactly equal to its net asset value.

Merrill Lynch, Pierce, Fenner has been running the fund for 5 years and currently receives a manager quality ranking of 5 (0=worst, 99=best). This fund offers an average level of risk but investors looking for strong performance will be frustrated.

Data Date	Weiss Investment Rating	Net Assets ($Mil)	Price	Perfor-mance Rating/Pts	Total Return Y-T-D	Risk Rating/Pts
6-05	E	202.45	27.02	E- / 0.1	-6.37%	C- / 3.6
2004	E-	202.45	29.18	E- / 0.0	12.91%	E+ / 0.9
2003	E-	162.48	26.42	E- / 0.0	2.37%	D- / 1.4

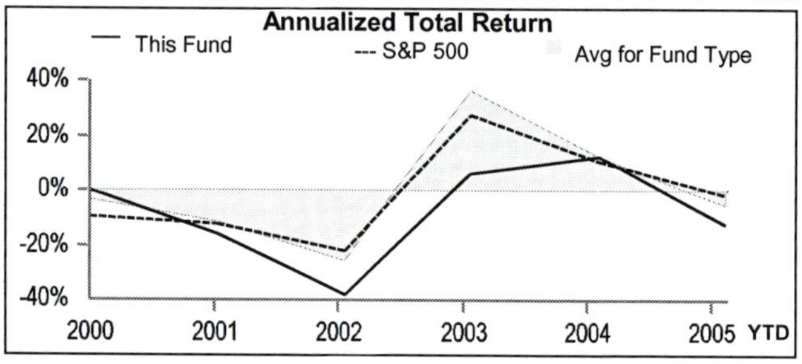

HOLDRS Utilities (UTH) C+ Fair

Fund Family: Merril Lynch
Fund Type: Utilities
Inception Date: June 26, 2000

Major Rating Factors:
Strong performance is the major factor driving the C+ (Fair) Weiss Investment Rating for HOLDRS Utilities. The fund currently has a performance rating of B (Good) based on an annualized return of 14.25% over the last three years and a total return of 13.79% year to date 2005.

The fund's risk rating is currently C- (Fair). It carries a beta of 0.96, meaning that its performance tracks fairly well with that of the overall stock market. Volatility, as measured by both the semi-deviation and a drawdown factor, is considered average. As of June 30, 2005, HOLDRS Utilities traded at a price exactly equal to its net asset value.

Merrill Lynch, Pierce, Fenner has been running the fund for 5 years and currently receives a manager quality ranking of 52 (0=worst, 99=best). If you desire an average level of risk and strong performance, then this fund is a good option.

Data Date	Weiss Investment Rating	Net Assets ($Mil)	Price	Perfor-mance Rating/Pts	Total Return Y-T-D	Risk Rating/Pts
6-05	C+	405.22	109.69	B / 8.0	13.79%	C- / 4.2
2004	D+	405.22	97.68	C+ / 6.5	27.90%	D+ / 2.7
2003	E+	273.37	77.71	E / 0.3	25.07%	C- / 3.3

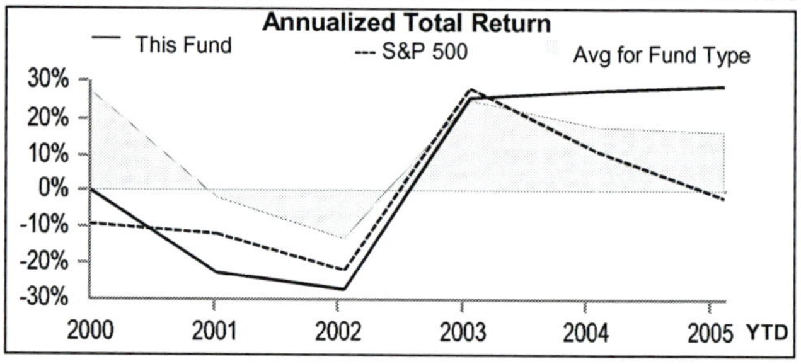

HOLDRS Wireless (WMH) C+ Fair

Fund Family: Merril Lynch
Fund Type: Growth
Inception Date: November 1, 2000

Major Rating Factors:
Strong performance is the major factor driving the C+ (Fair) Weiss Investment Rating for HOLDRS Wireless. The fund currently has a performance rating of B (Good) based on an annualized return of 23.25% over the last three years and a total return of -4.82% year to date 2005.

The fund's risk rating is currently C- (Fair). It carries a beta of 1.54, meaning it is expected to move 15.4% for every 10% move in the market. Volatility, as measured by both the semi-deviation and a drawdown factor, is considered average. As of June 30, 2005, HOLDRS Wireless traded at a price exactly equal to its net asset value.

Merrill Lynch, Pierce, Fenner has been running the fund for 5 years and currently receives a manager quality ranking of 90 (0=worst, 99=best). If you desire an average level of risk and strong performance, then this fund is a good option.

Data Date	Weiss Investment Rating	Net Assets ($Mil)	Price	Perfor-mance Rating/Pts	Total Return Y-T-D	Risk Rating/Pts
6-05	C+	73.76	55.80	B / 8.1	-4.82%	C- / 4.1
2004	D-	73.76	59.15	C / 5.3	37.07%	D- / 1.1
2003	E-	55.71	47.24	E- / 0.2	36.23%	E+ / 0.7

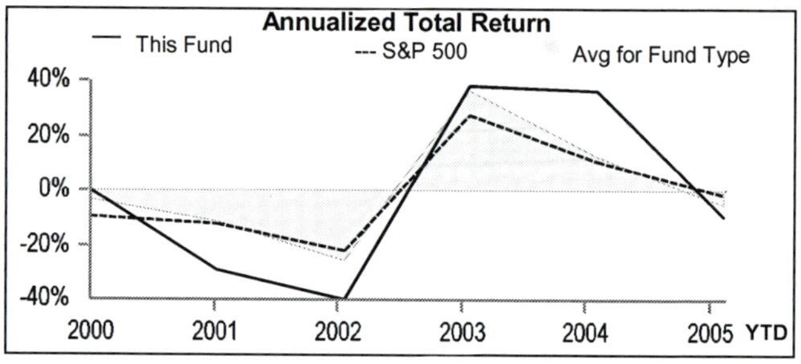

Hyperion 2005 Inv Gr Opp Tm Tr (HTO) D+ Weak

Fund Family: Hyperion Capital Management
Fund Type: Mortgage
Inception Date: February 19, 1993

Major Rating Factors:
Very poor performance is the major factor driving the D+ (Weak) Weiss Investment Rating for Hyperion 2005 Inv Gr Opp Tm Tr. The fund currently has a performance rating of E (Very Weak) based on an annualized return of 2.65% over the last three years and a total return of 0.76% year to date 2005. Factored into the performance evaluation is an expense ratio of 1.30% (average).

The fund's risk rating is currently B (Good). It carries a beta of 0.88, meaning the fund's expected move will be 8.8% for every 10% move in the market. Volatility, as measured by both the semi-deviation and a drawdown factor, is considered low. As of June 30, 2005, Hyperion 2005 Inv Gr Opp Tm Tr traded at a discount of 1.11% below its net asset value, which is worse than its one-year historical average discount of 1.39%.

Clifford E. Lai has been running the fund for 8 years and currently receives a manager quality ranking of 48 (0=worst, 99=best). This fund offers only a moderate level of risk but investors looking for strong performance are still waiting.

Data Date	Weiss Investment Rating	Net Assets ($Mil)	Price	Performance Rating/Pts	Total Return Y-T-D	Risk Rating/Pts
6-05	D+	166.86	9.78	E / 0.3	0.76%	B / 8.9
2004	C-	166.15	9.73	D- / 1.0	3.10%	B / 8.9
2003	C-	165.49	9.61	D+ / 2.3	0.67%	B / 8.8

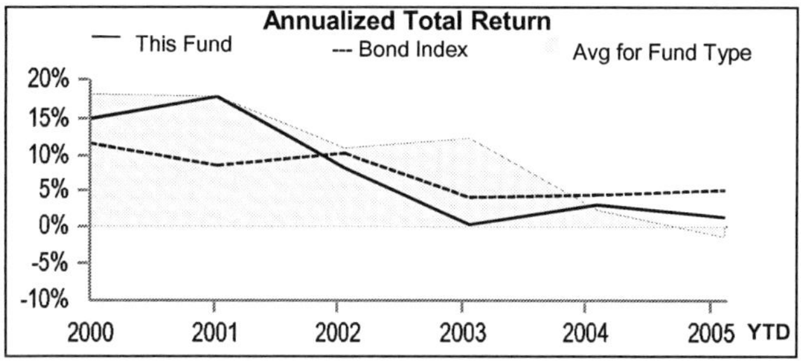

Hyperion Total Return Fund (HTR) D+ Weak

Fund Family: Hyperion Capital Management
Fund Type: Mortgage
Inception Date: August 4, 1989

Major Rating Factors:
Disappointing performance is the major factor driving the D+ (Weak) Weiss Investment Rating for Hyperion Total Return Fund. The fund currently has a performance rating of D (Weak) based on an annualized return of 9.20% over the last three years and a total return of -3.75% year to date 2005. Factored into the performance evaluation is an expense ratio of 1.71% (above average).

The fund's risk rating is currently C+ (Fair). It carries a beta of 3.21, meaning it is expected to move 32.1% for every 10% move in the market. Volatility, as measured by both the semi-deviation and a drawdown factor, is considered low. As of June 30, 2005, Hyperion Total Return Fund traded at a premium of 1.76% above its net asset value, which is better than its one-year historical average premium of 9.12%.

John H. Dolan has been running the fund for 7 years and currently receives a manager quality ranking of 41 (0=worst, 99=best). This fund offers only a moderate level of risk but investors looking for strong performance are still waiting.

Data Date	Weiss Investment Rating	Net Assets ($Mil)	Price	Performance Rating/Pts	Total Return Y-T-D	Risk Rating/Pts
6-05	D+	281.54	9.26	D / 2.1	-3.75%	C+ / 6.7
2004	C+	279.92	9.88	C+ / 6.5	5.42%	C+ / 6.8
2003	B-	285.15	10.35	B- / 7.0	20.63%	B- / 7.3

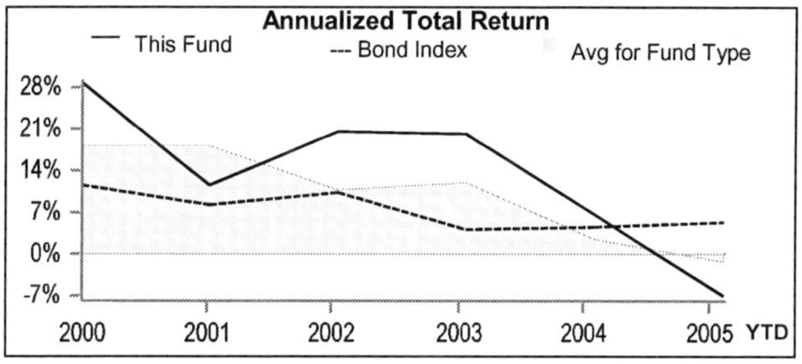

India Fund (IFN) B- Good

Fund Family: Advantage Advisers, Inc.
Fund Type: Foreign
Inception Date: February 15, 1994

Major Rating Factors:
Exceptional performance is the major factor driving the B- (Good) Weiss Investment Rating for India Fund. The fund currently has a performance rating of A+ (Excellent) based on an annualized return of 50.94% over the last three years and a total return of 2.94% year to date 2005. Factored into the performance evaluation is an expense ratio of 1.64% (above average).

The fund's risk rating is currently C- (Fair). It carries a beta of 1.00, meaning that its performance tracks fairly well with that of the overall stock market. Volatility, as measured by both the semi-deviation and a drawdown factor, is considered average. As of June 30, 2005, India Fund traded at a premium of 1.63% above its net asset value, which is worse than its one-year historical average premium of .14%.

Punita Kumar-Sinha has been running the fund for 11 years and currently receives a manager quality ranking of 99 (0=worst, 99=best). If you desire an average level of risk and strong performance, then this fund is a good option.

Data Date	Weiss Investment Rating	Net Assets ($Mil)	Price	Performance Rating/Pts	Total Return Y-T-D	Risk Rating/Pts
6-05	B-	644.67	30.50	A+ / 9.9	2.94%	C- / 3.5
2004	B+	461.82	29.63	A+ / 9.8	23.75%	C / 4.9
2003	C+	391.71	23.99	A+ / 9.8	127.81%	C- / 3.6

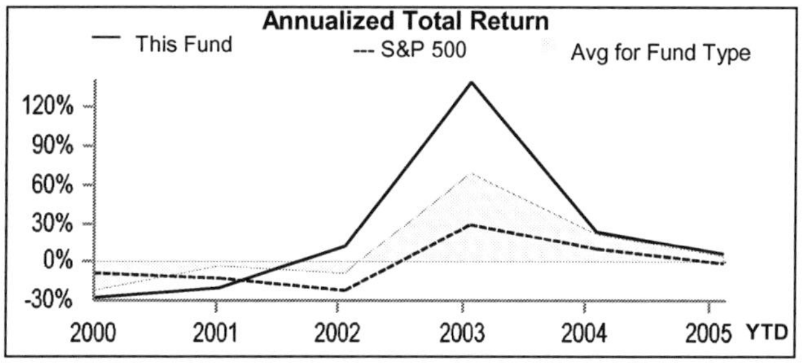

Indonesia Fund (IF) C Fair

Fund Family: Credit Suisse Asset Management
Fund Type: Foreign
Inception Date: March 9, 1990

Major Rating Factors:
Indonesia Fund has adopted a very risky asset allocation strategy and currently receives an overall Weiss Investment Rating of C (Fair). The fund has shown a high level of volatility, as measured by both semi-deviation and drawdown factors. It carries a beta of 1.22, meaning it is expected to move 12.2% for every 10% move in the market. As of June 30, 2005, Indonesia Fund traded at a discount of 5.12% below its net asset value, which is better than its one-year historical average discount of 1.13%. The high level of risk (D-, Weak) did however, reward investors with excellent performance.

The fund's performance rating is currently A+ (Excellent). It has registered an annualized return of 40.95% over the last three years and is up 12.09% year to date 2005. Factored into the performance evaluation is an expense ratio of 2.03% (high).

Boon-Hong Yeo (CIO) has been running the fund for 2 years and currently receives a manager quality ranking of 99 (0=worst, 99=best). If you are comfortable owning a very high risk investment, this fund may be an option.

Data Date	Weiss Investment Rating	Net Assets ($Mil)	Price	Perfor-mance Rating/Pts	Total Return Y-T-D	Risk Rating/Pts
6-05	C	42.02	5.75	A+ / 9.8	12.09%	D- / 1.2
2004	C-	30.65	5.13	A+ / 9.9	8.95%	D- / 1.1
2003	C-	23.84	5.90	A+ / 9.9	259.47%	E / 0.3

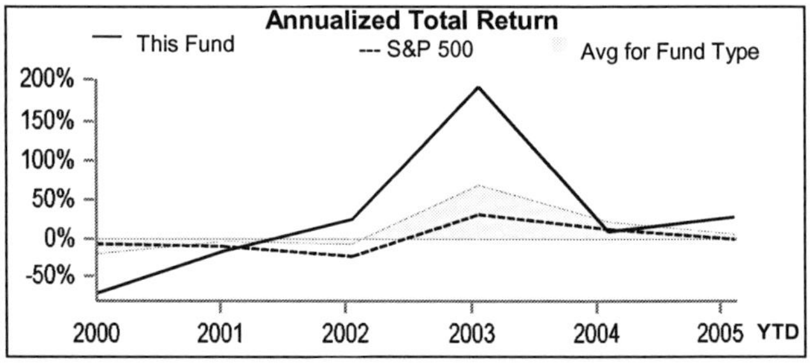

ING Prime Rate Trust (PPR) D+ Weak

Fund Family: ING Clarion Real Estate Securities
Fund Type: Loan Participation
Inception Date: May 12, 1988

Major Rating Factors:
Disappointing performance is the major factor driving the D+ (Weak) Weiss Investment Rating for ING Prime Rate Trust. The fund currently has a performance rating of D- (Weak) based on an annualized return of 10.17% over the last three years and a total return of -4.15% year to date 2005. Factored into the performance evaluation is an expense ratio of 3.17% (high).

The fund's risk rating is currently B- (Good). It carries a beta of -29.39, meaning the fund's expected move will be -293.9% for every 10% move in the market. Volatility, as measured by both the semi-deviation and a drawdown factor, is considered low. As of June 30, 2005, ING Prime Rate Trust traded at a discount of 5.03% below its net asset value, which is better than its one-year historical average premium of 2.56%.

Dan Norman has been running the fund for 6 years and currently receives a manager quality ranking of 96 (0=worst, 99=best). This fund offers only a moderate level of risk but investors looking for strong performance are still waiting.

Data Date	Weiss Investment Rating	Net Assets ($Mil)	Price	Perfor-mance Rating/Pts	Total Return Y-T-D	Risk Rating/Pts
6-05	D+	1082.75	6.99	D- / 1.3	-4.15%	B- / 7.9
2004	D+	1037.83	7.48	D+ / 2.5	-0.18%	C+ / 6.8
2003	C	963.75	7.98	C+ / 6.5	38.25%	C / 5.2

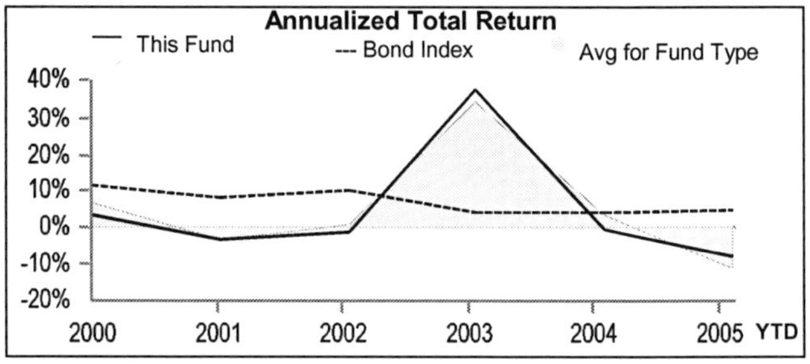

Insured Municipal Income Fund (PIF) C Fair

Fund Family: UBS Global Asset Management
Fund Type: Municipal - National
Inception Date: June 8, 1993

Major Rating Factors:
Disappointing performance is the major factor driving the C (Fair) Weiss Investment Rating for Insured Municipal Income Fund. The fund currently has a performance rating of D+ (Weak) based on an annualized return of 4.04% over the last three years and a total return of 1.70% year to date 2005. Factored into the performance evaluation is an expense ratio of 1.51% (average).

The fund's risk rating is currently B (Good). It carries a beta of 1.52, meaning it is expected to move 15.2% for every 10% move in the market. Volatility, as measured by both the semi-deviation and a drawdown factor, is considered low. As of June 30, 2005, Insured Municipal Income Fund traded at a discount of 14.02% below its net asset value, which is better than its one-year historical average discount of 13.36%.

ELBRIDGE T. GERRY III has been running the fund for 9 years and currently receives a manager quality ranking of 23 (0=worst, 99=best). This fund offers only a moderate level of risk but investors looking for strong performance are still waiting.

Data Date	Weiss Investment Rating	Net Assets ($Mil)	Price	Perfor-mance Rating/Pts	Total Return Y-T-D	Risk Rating/Pts
6-05	C	308.03	13.18	D+ / 2.7	1.70%	B / 8.4
2004	C	314.74	13.30	C- / 3.5	-0.08%	B / 8.4
2003	C+	323.08	13.96	C / 4.5	7.68%	B+ / 9.0

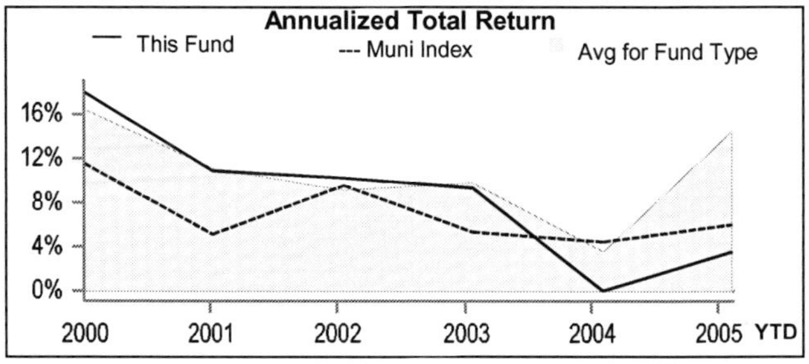

Investment Grade Municipal Income (PPM) C- Fair

Fund Family: UBS Global Asset Management
Fund Type: Municipal - National
Inception Date: November 6, 1992

Data Date	Weiss Investment Rating	Net Assets ($Mil)	Price	Performance Rating/Pts	Total Return Y-T-D	Risk Rating/Pts
6-05	C-	160.52	13.67	D+ / 2.3	3.49%	B- / 7.8
2004	C-	163.74	13.58	D- / 1.5	-4.32%	B / 8.4
2003	B	168.89	14.80	C / 4.8	7.27%	B+ / 9.8

Major Rating Factors:
Disappointing performance is the major factor driving the C- (Fair) Weiss Investment Rating for Investment Grade Municipal Income. The fund currently has a performance rating of D+ (Weak) based on an annualized return of 3.14% over the last three years and a total return of 3.49% year to date 2005. Factored into the performance evaluation is an expense ratio of 1.61% (above average).

The fund's risk rating is currently B- (Good). It carries a beta of 1.67, meaning it is expected to move 16.7% for every 10% move in the market. Volatility, as measured by both the semi-deviation and a drawdown factor, is considered low. As of June 30, 2005, Investment Grade Municipal Income traded at a discount of 13.97% below its net asset value, which is better than its one-year historical average discount of 12.93%.

William Veronda has been running the fund for 3 years and currently receives a manager quality ranking of 13 (0=worst, 99=best). This fund offers only a moderate level of risk but investors looking for strong performance are still waiting.

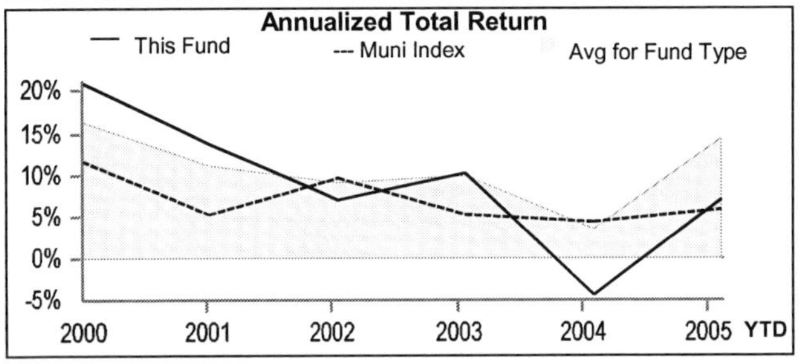

iShares Biotechnology Index Fund (IBB) E- Very Weak

Fund Family: Barclays Global Fund Advisors
Fund Type: Health
Inception Date: February 5, 2001

Data Date	Weiss Investment Rating	Net Assets ($Mil)	Price	Performance Rating/Pts	Total Return Y-T-D	Risk Rating/Pts
6-05	E-	1079.20	67.57	D- / 1.1	-10.38%	D / 1.6
2004	E	1204.10	75.40	E- / 0.1	4.79%	D / 1.6

Major Rating Factors:
iShares Biotechnology Index Fund has adopted a very risky asset allocation strategy and currently receives an overall Weiss Investment Rating of E- (Very Weak). The fund has a high level of volatility, with a standard deviation of 21.58. It carries a beta of 1.00, meaning that its performance tracks fairly well with that of the overall stock market. As of June 30, 2005, iShares Biotechnology Index Fund traded at a premium of .04% above its net asset value, which is worse than its one-year historical average discount of .02%. Unfortunately, the high level of risk (D, Weak) failed to pay off as investors endured poor performance.

The fund's performance rating is currently D- (Weak). It has registered an annualized return of 9.83% over the last three years but is down -10.38% year to date 2005. Factored into the performance evaluation is an expense ratio of 0.50% (very low).

Index Strategies Group has been running the fund for 4 years and currently receives a manager quality ranking of 72 (0=worst, 99=best). If you can tolerate very high levels of risk in the hope of improved future returns, holding this fund may be an option.

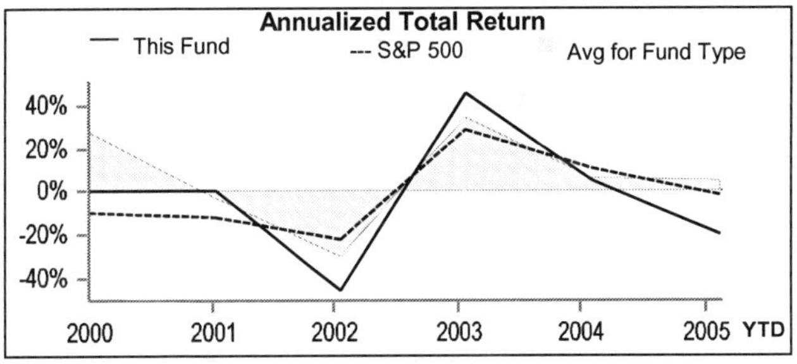

iShares Cohen&Steers Realty Major (ICF) A- Excellent

Fund Family: Barclays Global Fund Advisors
Fund Type: Growth and Income
Inception Date: January 29, 2001

Data Date	Weiss Investment Rating	Net Assets ($Mil)	Price	Performance Rating/Pts	Total Return Y-T-D	Risk Rating/Pts
6-05	A-	1298.08	70.50	A- / 9.0	5.71%	C+ / 5.9
2004	A+	724.45	136.31	A / 9.4	34.58%	C+ / 6.7

Major Rating Factors:
Exceptional performance is the major factor driving the A- (Excellent) Weiss Investment Rating for iShares Cohen&Steers Realty Major. The fund currently has a performance rating of A- (Excellent) based on an annualized return of 21.41% over the last three years and a total return of 5.71% year to date 2005. Factored into the performance evaluation is an expense ratio of 0.35% (very low).

The fund's risk rating is currently C+ (Fair). It carries a beta of 0.45, meaning the fund's expected move will be 4.5% for every 10% move in the market. Volatility, as measured by standard deviation, is considered low for equity funds at 16.96. As of June 30, 2005, iShares Cohen&Steers Realty Major traded at a premium of .09% above its net asset value.

Index Strategies Group has been running the fund for 4 years and currently receives a manager quality ranking of 97 (0=worst, 99=best). If you desire only a moderate level of risk and strong performance, then this fund is an excellent option.

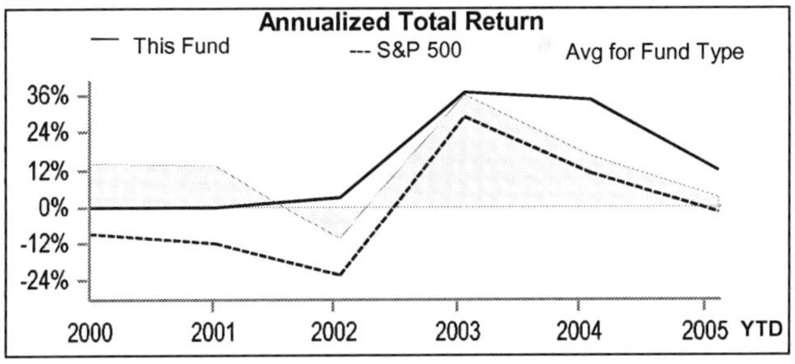

iShares Dow Jones US Basic Mtrls (IYM) — E — Very Weak

Fund Family: Barclays Global Fund Advisors
Fund Type: Growth
Inception Date: June 12, 2000

Major Rating Factors:
Very poor performance is the major factor driving the E (Very Weak) Weiss Investment Rating for iShares Dow Jones US Basic Mtrls. The fund currently has a performance rating of E (Very Weak) based on an annualized return of 6.05% over the last three years and a total return of -7.06% year to date 2005. Factored into the performance evaluation is an expense ratio of 0.60% (very low).

The fund's risk rating is currently C- (Fair). It carries a beta of 1.24, meaning it is expected to move 12.4% for every 10% move in the market. Volatility, as measured by standard deviation, is considered average for equity funds at 20.96. As of June 30, 2005, iShares Dow Jones US Basic Mtrls traded at a discount of .13% below its net asset value, which is better than its one-year historical average premium of .02%.

Index Strategies Group has been running the fund for 5 years and currently receives a manager quality ranking of 24 (0=worst, 99=best). This fund offers an average level of risk but investors looking for strong performance will be frustrated.

Data Date	Weiss Investment Rating	Net Assets ($Mil)	Price	Performance Rating/Pts	Total Return Y-T-D	Risk Rating/Pts
6-05	E	412.85	46.50	E / 0.3	-7.06%	C- / 3.0
2004	D	316.84	50.36	C / 5.0	12.23%	C- / 3.4
2003	D+	234.18	45.10	C+ / 6.4	33.19%	D / 1.7

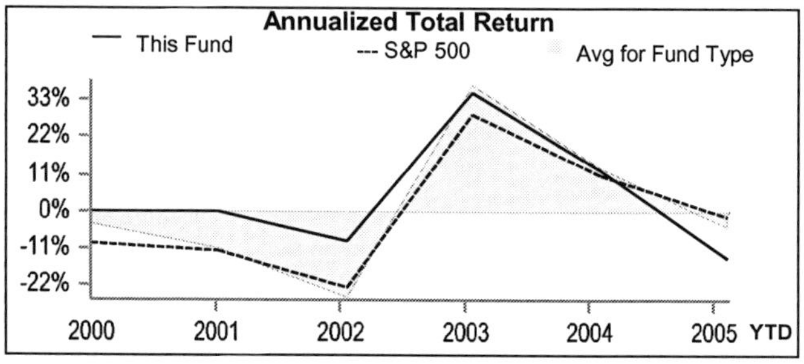

iShares Dow Jones US Cns Gd Sct Idx (IYK) — D+ — Weak

Fund Family: Barclays Global Fund Advisors
Fund Type: Growth
Inception Date: June 12, 2000

Major Rating Factors:
Very poor performance is the major factor driving the D+ (Weak) Weiss Investment Rating for iShares Dow Jones US Cns Gd Sct Idx. The fund currently has a performance rating of E+ (Very Weak) based on an annualized return of 6.42% over the last three years and a total return of -1.15% year to date 2005. Factored into the performance evaluation is an expense ratio of 0.60% (very low).

The fund's risk rating is currently B- (Good). It carries a beta of 0.59, meaning the fund's expected move will be 5.9% for every 10% move in the market. Volatility, as measured by standard deviation, is considered low for equity funds at 11.91. As of June 30, 2005, iShares Dow Jones US Cns Gd Sct Idx traded at a premium of .02% above its net asset value.

Index Strategies Group has been running the fund for 5 years and currently receives a manager quality ranking of 68 (0=worst, 99=best). This fund offers only a moderate level of risk but investors looking for strong performance are still waiting.

Data Date	Weiss Investment Rating	Net Assets ($Mil)	Price	Performance Rating/Pts	Total Return Y-T-D	Risk Rating/Pts
6-05	D+	421.10	52.30	E+ / 0.9	-1.15%	B- / 7.8
2004	C+	289.57	53.32	C / 4.3	11.97%	B- / 7.8
2003	C-	135.11	47.99	C- / 3.0	19.84%	B- / 7.2

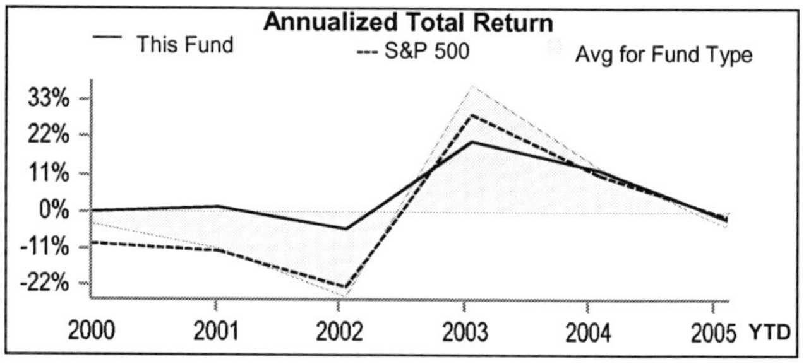

iShares Dow Jones US Cns Sv Sct Idx (IYC) — D- — Weak

Fund Family: Barclays Global Fund Advisors
Fund Type: Growth
Inception Date: June 12, 2000

Major Rating Factors:
Very poor performance is the major factor driving the D- (Weak) Weiss Investment Rating for iShares Dow Jones US Cns Sv Sct Idx. The fund currently has a performance rating of E+ (Very Weak) based on an annualized return of 6.05% over the last three years and a total return of -3.54% year to date 2005. Factored into the performance evaluation is an expense ratio of 0.60% (very low).

The fund's risk rating is currently C+ (Fair). It carries a beta of 1.08, meaning that its performance tracks fairly well with that of the overall stock market. Volatility, as measured by standard deviation, is considered low for equity funds at 16.89. As of June 30, 2005, iShares Dow Jones US Cns Sv Sct Idx traded at a discount of .10% below its net asset value.

Index Strategies Group has been running the fund for 5 years and currently receives a manager quality ranking of 38 (0=worst, 99=best). This fund offers only a moderate level of risk but investors looking for strong performance are still waiting.

Data Date	Weiss Investment Rating	Net Assets ($Mil)	Price	Performance Rating/Pts	Total Return Y-T-D	Risk Rating/Pts
6-05	D-	251.21	58.97	E+ / 0.8	-3.54%	C+ / 6.3
2004	D-	219.39	61.19	D / 1.7	10.72%	C / 4.7
2003	E+	149.22	54.81	D / 1.6	31.18%	D- / 1.4

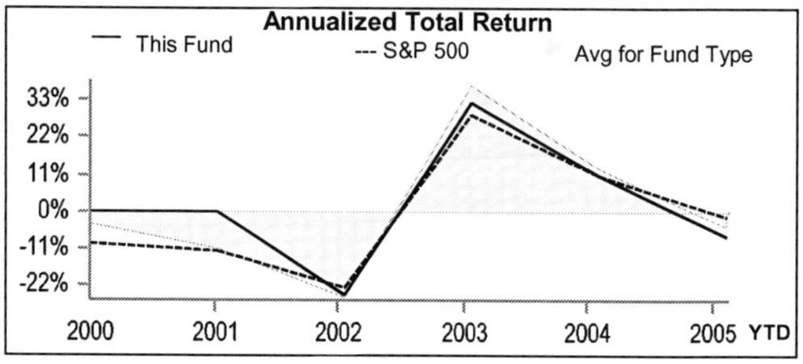

iShares Dow Jones US Energy Sector (IYE) B- Good

Fund Family: Barclays Global Fund Advisors
Fund Type: Energy/Natural Resources
Inception Date: June 12, 2000

Data Date	Weiss Investment Rating	Net Assets ($Mil)	Price	Performance Rating/Pts	Total Return Y-T-D	Risk Rating/Pts
6-05	B-	638.77	77.92	A / 9.3	21.85%	C- / 3.9
2004	C	348.52	64.30	B / 7.6	31.73%	C / 4.4
2003	D-	156.19	48.98	D- / 1.2	26.41%	C- / 3.2

Major Rating Factors:
Exceptional performance is the major factor driving the B- (Good) Weiss Investment Rating for iShares Dow Jones US Energy Sector. The fund currently has a performance rating of A (Excellent) based on an annualized return of 20.88% over the last three years and a total return of 21.85% year to date 2005. Factored into the performance evaluation is an expense ratio of 0.60% (very low).

The fund's risk rating is currently C- (Fair). It carries a beta of 0.99, meaning that its performance tracks fairly well with that of the overall stock market. Volatility, as measured by standard deviation, is considered average for equity funds at 19.37. As of June 30, 2005, iShares Dow Jones US Energy Sector traded at a premium of .14% above its net asset value, which is worse than its one-year historical average premium of .05%.

Index Strategies Group has been running the fund for 5 years and currently receives a manager quality ranking of 60 (0=worst, 99=best). If you desire an average level of risk and strong performance, then this fund is a good option.

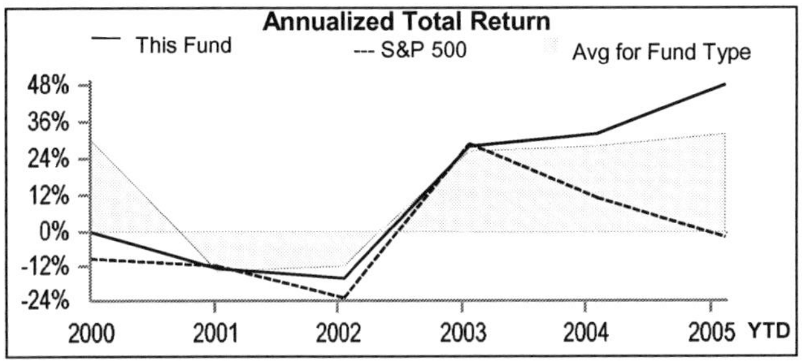

iShares Dow Jones US Financial Sct (IYF) D+ Weak

Fund Family: Barclays Global Fund Advisors
Fund Type: Financial Services
Inception Date: May 22, 2000

Data Date	Weiss Investment Rating	Net Assets ($Mil)	Price	Performance Rating/Pts	Total Return Y-T-D	Risk Rating/Pts
6-05	D+	299.91	94.37	D / 2.1	-2.51%	C+ / 6.9
2004	C	258.08	97.68	C / 4.5	13.01%	C+ / 6.9
2003	D	203.31	86.90	D+ / 2.9	29.79%	C / 4.7

Major Rating Factors:
Disappointing performance is the major factor driving the D+ (Weak) Weiss Investment Rating for iShares Dow Jones US Financial Sct. The fund currently has a performance rating of D (Weak) based on an annualized return of 8.92% over the last three years and a total return of -2.51% year to date 2005. Factored into the performance evaluation is an expense ratio of 0.60% (very low).

The fund's risk rating is currently C+ (Fair). It carries a beta of 1.02, meaning that its performance tracks fairly well with that of the overall stock market. Volatility, as measured by standard deviation, is considered low for equity funds at 15.31. As of June 30, 2005, iShares Dow Jones US Financial Sct traded at a premium of .15% above its net asset value.

Index Strategies Group has been running the fund for 5 years and currently receives a manager quality ranking of 56 (0=worst, 99=best). This fund offers only a moderate level of risk but investors looking for strong performance are still waiting.

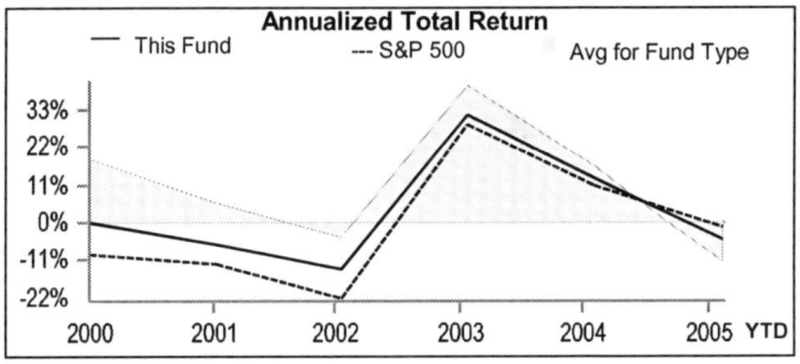

iShares Dow Jones US Financial Srv (IYG) D+ Weak

Fund Family: Barclays Global Fund Advisors
Fund Type: Financial Services
Inception Date: June 12, 2000

Data Date	Weiss Investment Rating	Net Assets ($Mil)	Price	Performance Rating/Pts	Total Return Y-T-D	Risk Rating/Pts
6-05	D+	141.65	107.64	D / 2.0	-4.15%	C+ / 6.9
2004	C	110.67	113.15	C / 4.8	11.87%	C+ / 6.7
2003	D	89.79	101.44	C- / 3.2	31.93%	C- / 4.2

Major Rating Factors:
Disappointing performance is the major factor driving the D+ (Weak) Weiss Investment Rating for iShares Dow Jones US Financial Srv. The fund currently has a performance rating of D (Weak) based on an annualized return of 9.01% over the last three years and a total return of -4.15% year to date 2005. Factored into the performance evaluation is an expense ratio of 0.60% (very low).

The fund's risk rating is currently C+ (Fair). It carries a beta of 1.03, meaning that its performance tracks fairly well with that of the overall stock market. Volatility, as measured by standard deviation, is considered low for equity funds at 15.64. As of June 30, 2005, iShares Dow Jones US Financial Srv traded at a discount of .05% below its net asset value, which is better than its one-year historical average premium of .01%.

Index Strategies Group has been running the fund for 5 years and currently receives a manager quality ranking of 54 (0=worst, 99=best). This fund offers only a moderate level of risk but investors looking for strong performance are still waiting.

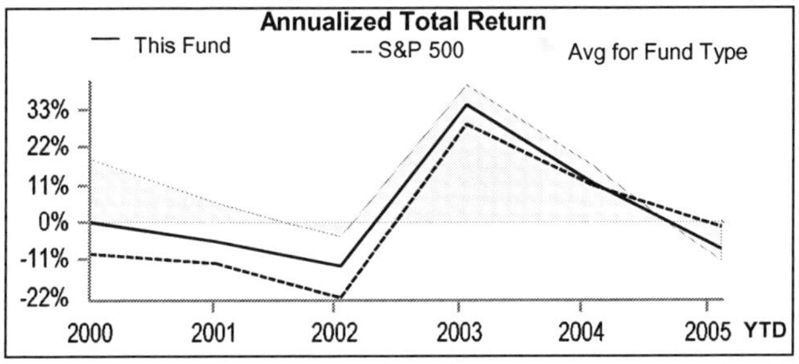

iShares Dow Jones US Healthcare (IYH) C- Fair

Fund Family: Barclays Global Fund Advisors
Fund Type: Health
Inception Date: June 12, 2000

Major Rating Factors:
Disappointing performance is the major factor driving the C- (Fair) Weiss Investment Rating for iShares Dow Jones US Healthcare. The fund currently has a performance rating of D- (Weak) based on an annualized return of 7.07% over the last three years and a total return of 4.15% year to date 2005. Factored into the performance evaluation is an expense ratio of 0.60% (very low).

The fund's risk rating is currently B- (Good). It carries a beta of 0.55, meaning the fund's expected move will be 5.5% for every 10% move in the market. Volatility, as measured by standard deviation, is considered low for equity funds at 10.74. As of June 30, 2005, iShares Dow Jones US Healthcare traded at a discount of .03% below its net asset value.

Index Strategies Group has been running the fund for 5 years and currently receives a manager quality ranking of 72 (0=worst, 99=best). This fund offers only a moderate level of risk but investors looking for strong performance are still waiting.

Data Date	Weiss Investment Rating	Net Assets ($Mil)	Price	Perfor-mance Rating/Pts	Total Return Y-T-D	Risk Rating/Pts
6-05	C-	1169.28	61.20	D- / 1.5	4.15%	B- / 7.9
2004	D	651.80	58.99	E / 0.4	4.21%	B- / 7.5
2003	D	420.67	56.34	E / 0.5	17.01%	C+ / 6.7

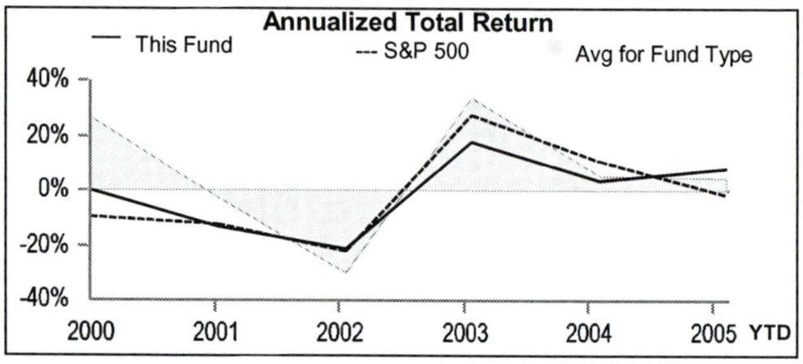

iShares Dow Jones US Industrial (IYJ) D Weak

Fund Family: Barclays Global Fund Advisors
Fund Type: Growth
Inception Date: June 12, 2000

Major Rating Factors:
Disappointing performance is the major factor driving the D (Weak) Weiss Investment Rating for iShares Dow Jones US Industrial. The fund currently has a performance rating of D- (Weak) based on an annualized return of 8.46% over the last three years and a total return of -5.31% year to date 2005. Factored into the performance evaluation is an expense ratio of 0.60% (very low).

The fund's risk rating is currently C+ (Fair). It carries a beta of 1.03, meaning that its performance tracks fairly well with that of the overall stock market. Volatility, as measured by standard deviation, is considered low for equity funds at 15.78. As of June 30, 2005, iShares Dow Jones US Industrial traded at a discount of .07% below its net asset value, which is better than its one-year historical average premium of .02%.

Index Strategies Group has been running the fund for 5 years and currently receives a manager quality ranking of 63 (0=worst, 99=best). This fund offers only a moderate level of risk but investors looking for strong performance are still waiting.

Data Date	Weiss Investment Rating	Net Assets ($Mil)	Price	Perfor-mance Rating/Pts	Total Return Y-T-D	Risk Rating/Pts
6-05	D	236.84	53.39	D- / 1.2	-5.31%	C+ / 6.7
2004	D	157.38	56.60	C- / 3.5	16.34%	C / 4.7
2003	E+	146.20	48.58	D- / 1.1	30.96%	D / 2.1

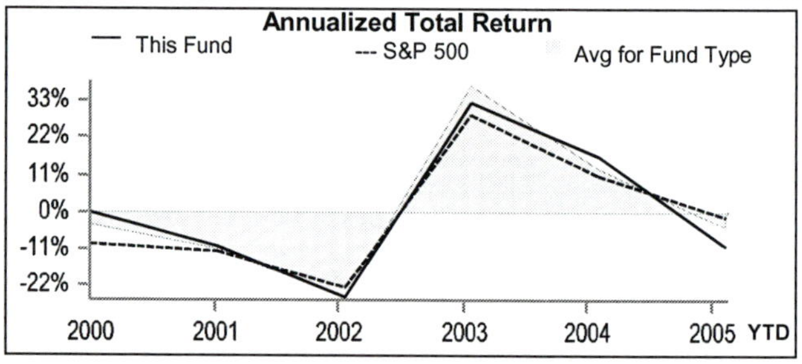

iShares Dow Jones US Real Estate (IYR) B+ Good

Fund Family: Barclays Global Fund Advisors
Fund Type: Growth and Income
Inception Date: June 12, 2000

Major Rating Factors:
Strong performance is the major factor driving the B+ (Good) Weiss Investment Rating for iShares Dow Jones US Real Estate. The fund currently has a performance rating of B+ (Good) based on an annualized return of 19.09% over the last three years and a total return of 4.21% year to date 2005. Factored into the performance evaluation is an expense ratio of 0.60% (very low).

The fund's risk rating is currently C+ (Fair). It carries a beta of 0.49, meaning the fund's expected move will be 4.9% for every 10% move in the market. Volatility, as measured by standard deviation, is considered low for equity funds at 16.79. As of June 30, 2005, iShares Dow Jones US Real Estate traded at a discount of .49% below its net asset value, which is better than its one-year historical average discount of .11%.

Index Strategies Group has been running the fund for 5 years and currently receives a manager quality ranking of 95 (0=worst, 99=best). If you desire only a moderate level of risk and strong performance, then this fund is an excellent option.

Data Date	Weiss Investment Rating	Net Assets ($Mil)	Price	Perfor-mance Rating/Pts	Total Return Y-T-D	Risk Rating/Pts
6-05	B+	736.78	62.82	B+ / 8.5	4.21%	C+ / 5.9
2004	A+	419.09	123.20	A- / 9.1	30.09%	C+ / 6.7
2003	A	331.04	99.07	B / 7.9	35.09%	B- / 7.7

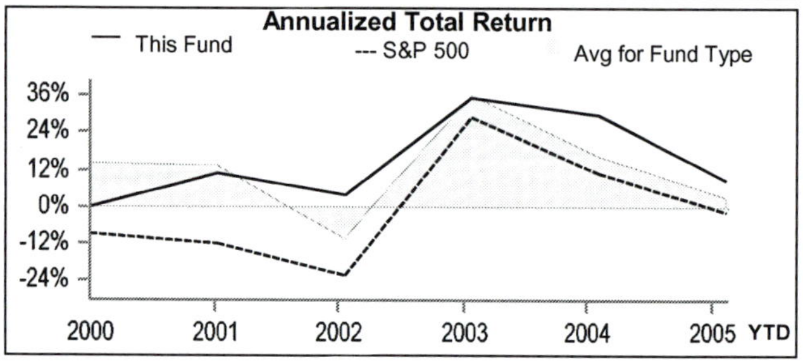

iShares Dow Jones US Technology (IYW) E- Very Weak

Fund Family: Barclays Global Fund Advisors
Fund Type: Growth
Inception Date: May 15, 2000

Data Date	Weiss Investment Rating	Net Assets ($Mil)	Price	Performance Rating/Pts	Total Return Y-T-D	Risk Rating/Pts
6-05	E-	395.01	46.09	D- / 1.4	-4.73%	D- / 1.4
2004	E-	322.54	48.46	E- / 0.1	1.34%	D- / 1.4
2003	E	330.22	48.04	E / 0.5	47.82%	D- / 1.1

Major Rating Factors:
iShares Dow Jones US Technology has adopted a very risky asset allocation strategy and currently receives an overall Weiss Investment Rating of E- (Very Weak). The fund has a high level of volatility, with a standard deviation of 27.85. It carries a beta of 1.74, meaning it is expected to move 17.4% for every 10% move in the market. As of June 30, 2005, iShares Dow Jones US Technology traded at a premium of .11% above its net asset value, which is worse than its one-year historical average premium of .03%. Unfortunately, the high level of risk (D-, Weak) failed to pay off as investors endured poor performance.

The fund's performance rating is currently D- (Weak). It has registered an annualized return of 9.11% over the last three years but is down -4.73% year to date 2005. Factored into the performance evaluation is an expense ratio of 0.60% (very low).

Index Strategies Group has been running the fund for 5 years and currently receives a manager quality ranking of 20 (0=worst, 99=best). If you can tolerate very high levels of risk in the hope of improved future returns, holding this fund may be an option.

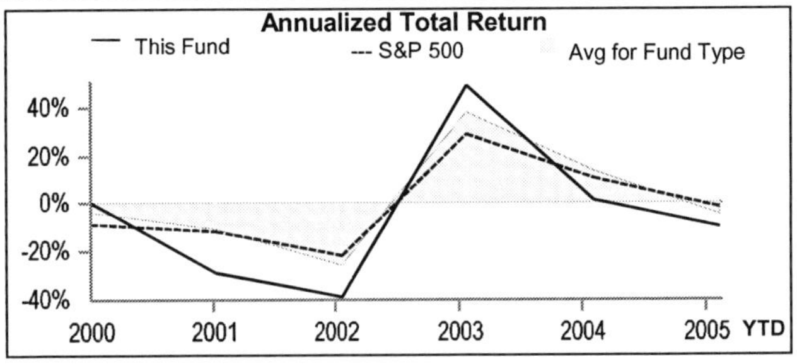

iShares Dow Jones US Telecom (IYZ) E Very Weak

Fund Family: Barclays Global Fund Advisors
Fund Type: Growth
Inception Date: May 22, 2000

Data Date	Weiss Investment Rating	Net Assets ($Mil)	Price	Performance Rating/Pts	Total Return Y-T-D	Risk Rating/Pts
6-05	E	313.38	23.19	D+ / 2.5	-3.48%	D / 1.8
2004	E-	215.76	24.30	E- / 0.2	18.28%	E+ / 0.6
2003	E	110.36	20.50	E- / 0.1	10.03%	D- / 1.5

Major Rating Factors:
iShares Dow Jones US Telecom has adopted a very risky asset allocation strategy and currently receives an overall Weiss Investment Rating of E (Very Weak). The fund has a high level of volatility, with a standard deviation of 25.91. It carries a beta of 1.55, meaning it is expected to move 15.5% for every 10% move in the market. As of June 30, 2005, iShares Dow Jones US Telecom traded at a premium of .17% above its net asset value, which is worse than its one-year historical average premium of .02%. Unfortunately, the high level of risk (D, Weak) failed to pay off as investors endured poor performance.

The fund's performance rating is currently D+ (Weak). It has registered an annualized return of 9.88% over the last three years but is down -3.48% year to date 2005. Factored into the performance evaluation is an expense ratio of 0.60% (very low).

Index Strategies Group has been running the fund for 5 years and currently receives a manager quality ranking of 45 (0=worst, 99=best). If you can tolerate very high levels of risk in the hope of improved future returns, holding this fund may be an option.

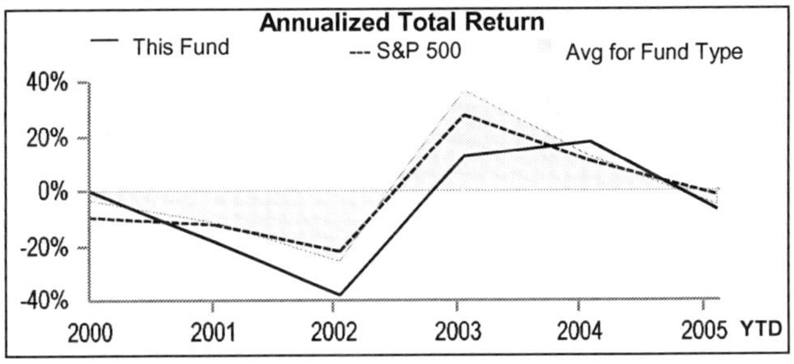

iShares Dow Jones US Total Mkt (IYY) D+ Weak

Fund Family: Barclays Global Fund Advisors
Fund Type: Growth
Inception Date: June 12, 2000

Data Date	Weiss Investment Rating	Net Assets ($Mil)	Price	Performance Rating/Pts	Total Return Y-T-D	Risk Rating/Pts
6-05	D+	414.90	57.37	D / 2.2	-0.39%	B- / 7.1
2004	D+	381.16	58.00	D+ / 2.6	11.89%	C+ / 6.7
2003	D-	279.38	52.03	E+ / 0.9	28.65%	C- / 3.2

Major Rating Factors:
Disappointing performance is the major factor driving the D+ (Weak) Weiss Investment Rating for iShares Dow Jones US Total Mkt. The fund currently has a performance rating of D (Weak) based on an annualized return of 9.35% over the last three years and a total return of -0.39% year to date 2005. Factored into the performance evaluation is an expense ratio of 0.20% (very low).

The fund's risk rating is currently B- (Good). It carries a beta of 1.01, meaning that its performance tracks fairly well with that of the overall stock market. Volatility, as measured by standard deviation, is considered low for equity funds at 14.33. As of June 30, 2005, iShares Dow Jones US Total Mkt traded at a discount of .03% below its net asset value, which is better than its one-year historical average premium of .02%.

Index Strategies Group has been running the fund for 5 years and currently receives a manager quality ranking of 69 (0=worst, 99=best). This fund offers only a moderate level of risk but investors looking for strong performance are still waiting.

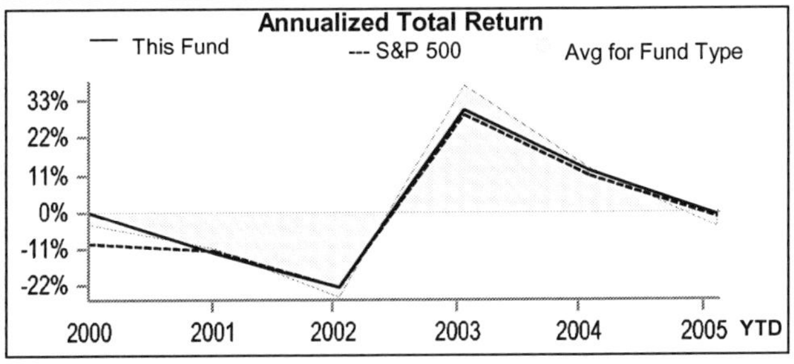

iShares Dow Jones US Utilities (IDU) B Good

Fund Family: Barclays Global Fund Advisors
Fund Type: Utilities
Inception Date: June 12, 2000

Data Date	Weiss Investment Rating	Net Assets ($Mil)	Price	Performance Rating/Pts	Total Return Y-T-D	Risk Rating/Pts
6-05	B	645.87	76.12	B- / 7.1	12.42%	C+ / 6.5
2004	C-	440.49	68.70	C+ / 5.8	23.07%	C / 4.4
2003	E+	439.18	57.21	E / 0.4	23.68%	C- / 3.3

Major Rating Factors:

Strong performance is the major factor driving the B (Good) Weiss Investment Rating for iShares Dow Jones US Utilities. The fund currently has a performance rating of B- (Good) based on an annualized return of 12.74% over the last three years and a total return of 12.42% year to date 2005. Factored into the performance evaluation is an expense ratio of 0.60% (very low).

The fund's risk rating is currently C+ (Fair). It carries a beta of 0.88, meaning the fund's expected move will be 8.8% for every 10% move in the market. Volatility, as measured by standard deviation, is considered low for equity funds at 16.55. As of June 30, 2005, iShares Dow Jones US Utilities traded at a discount of .05% below its net asset value, which is better than its one-year historical average discount of .02%.

Index Strategies Group has been running the fund for 5 years and currently receives a manager quality ranking of 50 (0=worst, 99=best). If you desire only a moderate level of risk and strong performance, then this fund is an excellent option.

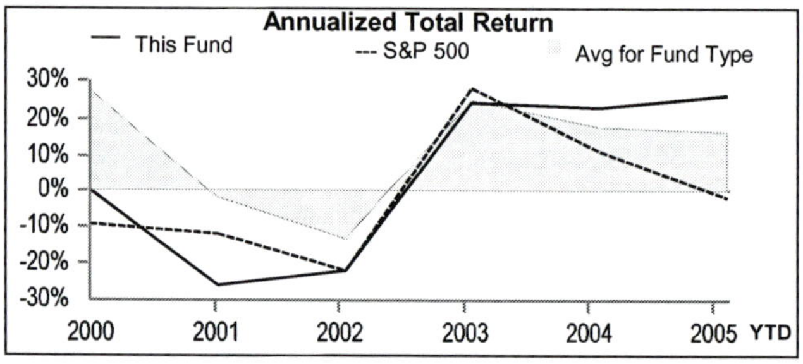

iShares Goldman Sachs Nat Res Index (IGE) C+ Fair

Fund Family: Barclays Global Fund Advisors
Fund Type: Energy/Natural Resources
Inception Date: October 22, 2001

Data Date	Weiss Investment Rating	Net Assets ($Mil)	Price	Performance Rating/Pts	Total Return Y-T-D	Risk Rating/Pts
6-05	C+	424.73	76.30	B+ / 8.7	16.90%	C- / 3.8
2004	C	263.27	131.29	B- / 7.4	24.38%	C / 4.4

Major Rating Factors:

Strong performance is the major factor driving the C+ (Fair) Weiss Investment Rating for iShares Goldman Sachs Nat Res Index. The fund currently has a performance rating of B+ (Good) based on an annualized return of 18.73% over the last three years and a total return of 16.90% year to date 2005. Factored into the performance evaluation is an expense ratio of 0.50% (very low).

The fund's risk rating is currently C- (Fair). It carries a beta of 0.96, meaning that its performance tracks fairly well with that of the overall stock market. Volatility, as measured by standard deviation, is considered average for equity funds at 19.27. As of June 30, 2005, iShares Goldman Sachs Nat Res Index traded at a discount of .05% below its net asset value, which is better than its one-year historical average premium of .04%.

Index Strategies Group has been running the fund for 4 years and currently receives a manager quality ranking of 53 (0=worst, 99=best). If you desire an average level of risk and strong performance, then this fund is a good option.

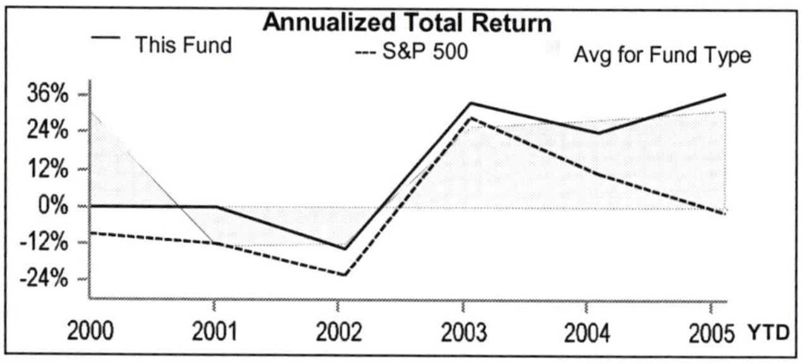

iShares Goldman Sachs Ntwr Index Fd (IGN) D Weak

Fund Family: Barclays Global Fund Advisors
Fund Type: Growth
Inception Date: July 10, 2001

Data Date	Weiss Investment Rating	Net Assets ($Mil)	Price	Performance Rating/Pts	Total Return Y-T-D	Risk Rating/Pts
6-05	D	163.70	27.70	B- / 7.0	-8.55%	D- / 1.4
2004	E-	146.99	30.29	E- / 0.2	9.71%	D- / 1.4

Major Rating Factors:

iShares Goldman Sachs Ntwr Index Fd has adopted a very risky asset allocation strategy and currently receives an overall Weiss Investment Rating of D (Weak). The fund has shown a high level of volatility, with a standard deviation of 46.17. It carries a beta of 2.56, meaning it is expected to move 25.6% for every 10% move in the market. As of June 30, 2005, iShares Goldman Sachs Ntwr Index Fd traded at a discount of .14% below its net asset value, which is better than its one-year historical average discount of .06%. The high level of risk (D-, Weak) did however, reward investors with excellent performance.

The fund's performance rating is currently B- (Good). It has registered an annualized return of 22.96% over the last three years but is down -8.55% year to date 2005. Factored into the performance evaluation is an expense ratio of 0.50% (very low).

Index Strategies Group has been running the fund for 4 years and currently receives a manager quality ranking of 74 (0=worst, 99=best). If you are comfortable owning a very high risk investment, this fund may be an option.

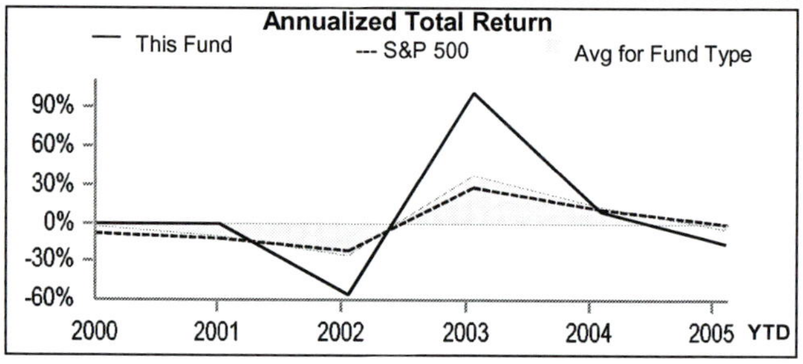

iShares Goldman Sachs Semicon Index (IGW) E- Very Weak

Fund Family: Barclays Global Fund Advisors
Fund Type: Growth
Inception Date: July 10, 2001

Data Date	Weiss Investment Rating	Net Assets ($Mil)	Price	Performance Rating/Pts	Total Return Y-T-D	Risk Rating/Pts
6-05	E-	264.31	53.60	E- / 0.2	-0.37%	D / 1.6
2004	E	124.07	53.80	E- / 0.0	-14.26%	D / 1.7

Major Rating Factors:
iShares Goldman Sachs Semicon Index has adopted a very risky asset allocation strategy and currently receives an overall Weiss Investment Rating of E- (Very Weak). The fund has a high level of volatility, with a standard deviation of 41.91. It carries a beta of 2.37, meaning it is expected to move 23.7% for every 10% move in the market. As of June 30, 2005, iShares Goldman Sachs Semicon Index traded at a price exactly equal to its net asset value. Unfortunately, the high level of risk (D, Weak) failed to pay off as investors endured very poor performance.

The fund's performance rating is currently E- (Very Weak). It has registered an annualized return of 3.81% over the last three years but is down -0.37% year to date 2005. Factored into the performance evaluation is an expense ratio of 0.50% (very low).

Index Strategies Group has been running the fund for 4 years and currently receives a manager quality ranking of 1 (0=worst, 99=best). If you can tolerate very high levels of risk in the hope of improved future returns, holding this fund may be an option.

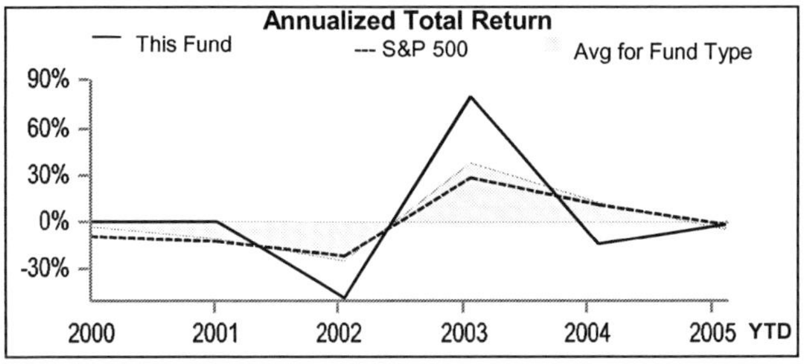

iShares Goldman Sachs Software Indx (IGV) E- Very Weak

Fund Family: Barclays Global Fund Advisors
Fund Type: Growth
Inception Date: July 10, 2001

Data Date	Weiss Investment Rating	Net Assets ($Mil)	Price	Performance Rating/Pts	Total Return Y-T-D	Risk Rating/Pts
6-05	E-	137.07	38.38	D+ / 2.6	-9.92%	E- / 0.0
2004	E-	115.08	42.65	E / 0.5	13.49%	E- / 0.0

Major Rating Factors:
iShares Goldman Sachs Software Indx has adopted a very risky asset allocation strategy and currently receives an overall Weiss Investment Rating of E- (Very Weak). The fund has a high level of volatility, with a standard deviation of 27.96. It carries a beta of 1.70, meaning it is expected to move 17.0% for every 10% move in the market. As of June 30, 2005, iShares Goldman Sachs Software Indx traded at a premium of .08% above its net asset value, which is worse than its one-year historical average discount of .05%. Unfortunately, the high level of risk (E-, Very Weak) failed to pay off as investors endured poor performance.

The fund's performance rating is currently D+ (Weak). It has registered an annualized return of 12.04% over the last three years but is down -9.92% year to date 2005. Factored into the performance evaluation is an expense ratio of 0.50% (very low).

Index Strategies Group has been running the fund for 4 years and currently receives a manager quality ranking of 53 (0=worst, 99=best). If you can tolerate very high levels of risk in the hope of improved future returns, holding this fund may be an option.

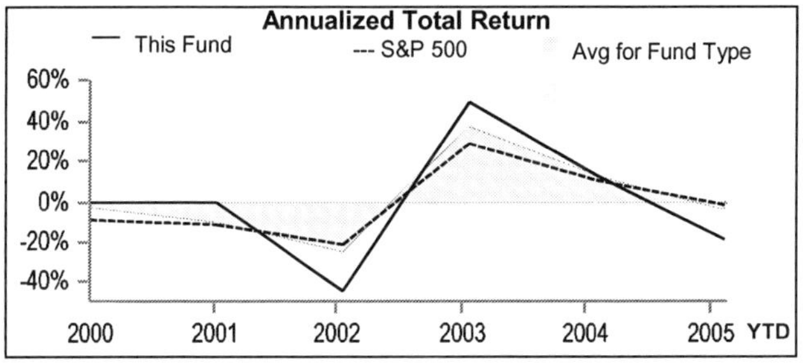

iShares Goldman Sachs Technology (IGM) E- Very Weak

Fund Family: Barclays Global Fund Advisors
Fund Type: Growth
Inception Date: March 13, 2001

Data Date	Weiss Investment Rating	Net Assets ($Mil)	Price	Performance Rating/Pts	Total Return Y-T-D	Risk Rating/Pts
6-05	E-	183.24	43.46	D- / 1.2	-6.85%	D- / 1.3
2004	E-	185.97	46.71	E- / 0.2	2.59%	D- / 1.3

Major Rating Factors:
iShares Goldman Sachs Technology has adopted a very risky asset allocation strategy and currently receives an overall Weiss Investment Rating of E- (Very Weak). The fund has a high level of volatility, with a standard deviation of 28.55. It carries a beta of 1.81, meaning it is expected to move 18.1% for every 10% move in the market. As of June 30, 2005, iShares Goldman Sachs Technology traded at a premium of .12% above its net asset value, which is worse than its one-year historical average premium of .04%. Unfortunately, the high level of risk (D-, Weak) failed to pay off as investors endured poor performance.

The fund's performance rating is currently D- (Weak). It has registered an annualized return of 9.23% over the last three years but is down -6.85% year to date 2005. Factored into the performance evaluation is an expense ratio of 0.50% (very low).

Index Strategies Group has been running the fund for 4 years and currently receives a manager quality ranking of 18 (0=worst, 99=best). If you can tolerate very high levels of risk in the hope of improved future returns, holding this fund may be an option.

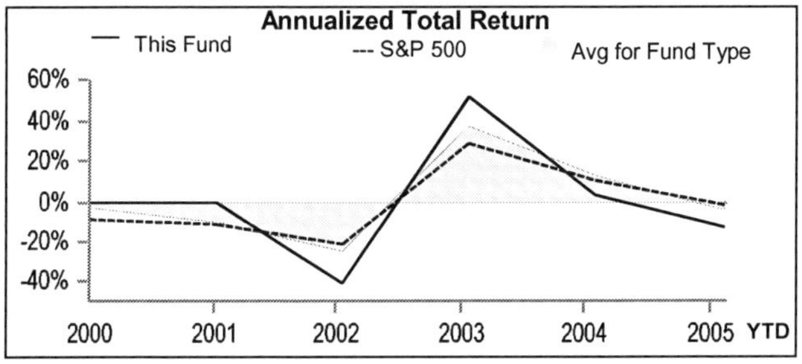

iShares MSCI Australia Index (EWA) A Excellent

Fund Family: Barclays Global Fund Advisors
Fund Type: Foreign
Inception Date: March 12, 1996

Major Rating Factors:
Exceptional performance is the major factor driving the A (Excellent) Weiss Investment Rating for iShares MSCI Australia Index. The fund currently has a performance rating of A (Excellent) based on an annualized return of 24.75% over the last three years and a total return of 5.75% year to date 2005. Factored into the performance evaluation is an expense ratio of 0.58% (very low).

The fund's risk rating is currently C+ (Fair). It carries a beta of 0.85, meaning the fund's expected move will be 8.5% for every 10% move in the market. Volatility, as measured by standard deviation, is considered low for equity funds at 15.79. As of June 30, 2005, iShares MSCI Australia Index traded at a discount of .23% below its net asset value, which is better than its one-year historical average premium of .25%.

Index Strategies Group has been running the fund for 9 years and currently receives a manager quality ranking of 93 (0=worst, 99=best). If you desire only a moderate level of risk and strong performance, then this fund is an excellent option.

Data Date	Weiss Investment Rating	Net Assets ($Mil)	Price	Performance Rating/Pts	Total Return Y-T-D	Risk Rating/Pts
6-05	A	344.70	17.66	A / 9.3	5.75%	C+ / 6.2
2004	A	179.00	16.70	A / 9.3	29.33%	C+ / 6.2
2003	D+	87.54	13.05	B+ / 8.4	48.59%	E+ / 0.6

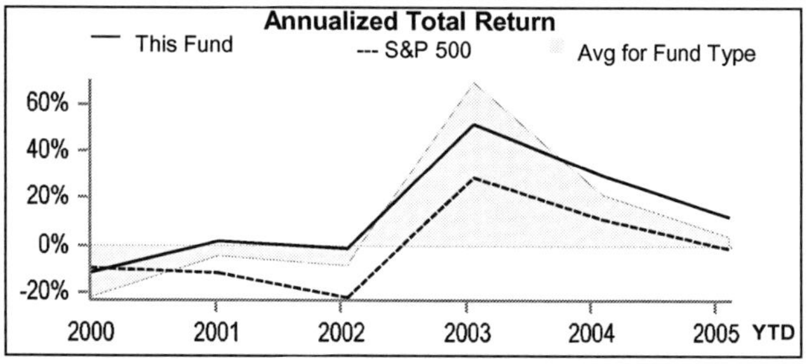

iShares MSCI Austria Index (EWO) C+ Fair

Fund Family: Barclays Global Fund Advisors
Fund Type: Foreign
Inception Date: March 12, 1996

Major Rating Factors:
iShares MSCI Austria Index has adopted a risky asset allocation strategy and currently receives an overall Weiss Investment Rating of C+ (Fair). The fund has shown an above average level of volatility, with a standard deviation of 18.75. It carries a beta of 0.87, meaning the fund's expected move will be 8.7% for every 10% move in the market. As of June 30, 2005, iShares MSCI Austria Index traded at a discount of .34% below its net asset value, which is better than its one-year historical average premium of .14%. The high level of risk (D+, Weak) did however, reward investors with excellent performance.

The fund's performance rating is currently A+ (Excellent). It has registered an annualized return of 37.92% over the last three years and is up 1.35% year to date 2005. Factored into the performance evaluation is an expense ratio of 0.58% (very low).

Index Strategies Group has been running the fund for 9 years and currently receives a manager quality ranking of 99 (0=worst, 99=best). If you are comfortable owning a high risk investment, this fund may be an option.

Data Date	Weiss Investment Rating	Net Assets ($Mil)	Price	Performance Rating/Pts	Total Return Y-T-D	Risk Rating/Pts
6-05	C+	188.72	23.33	A+ / 9.7	1.35%	D+ / 2.8
2004	B-	57.92	23.02	A+ / 9.9	73.09%	C- / 3.6
2003	C	22.29	13.34	A / 9.4	56.95%	D / 2.0

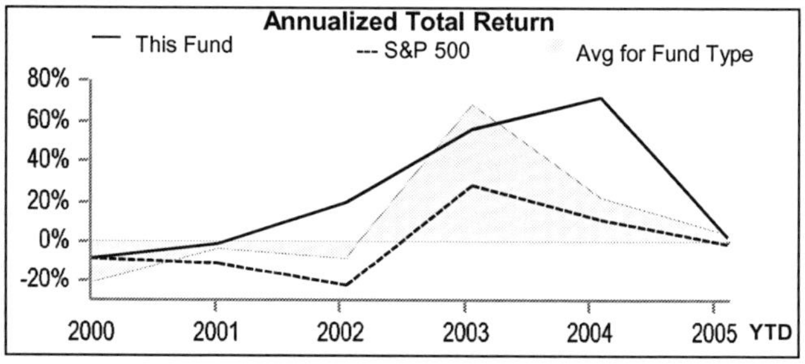

iShares MSCI Belgium Index (EWK) D- Weak

Fund Family: Barclays Global Fund Advisors
Fund Type: Foreign
Inception Date: March 12, 1996

Major Rating Factors:
iShares MSCI Belgium Index has adopted a very risky asset allocation strategy and currently receives an overall Weiss Investment Rating of D- (Weak). The fund has a high level of volatility, with a standard deviation of 23.55. It carries a beta of 1.30, meaning it is expected to move 13.0% for every 10% move in the market. As of June 30, 2005, iShares MSCI Belgium Index traded at a discount of 1.17% below its net asset value, which is better than its one-year historical average premium of .38%. Unfortunately, the high level of risk (E, Very Weak) has only provided investors with average performance.

The fund's performance rating is currently C+ (Fair). It has registered an annualized return of 18.44% over the last three years but is down -4.04% year to date 2005. Factored into the performance evaluation is an expense ratio of 0.58% (very low).

Index Strategies Group has been running the fund for 9 years and currently receives a manager quality ranking of 74 (0=worst, 99=best). If you are comfortable owning a very high risk investment, then this fund may be an option.

Data Date	Weiss Investment Rating	Net Assets ($Mil)	Price	Performance Rating/Pts	Total Return Y-T-D	Risk Rating/Pts
6-05	D-	56.49	17.81	C+ / 6.5	-4.04%	E / 0.4
2004	C-	24.81	18.56	A+ / 9.6	45.53%	E / 0.4
2003	D-	21.87	12.73	C / 5.4	39.24%	E- / 0.0

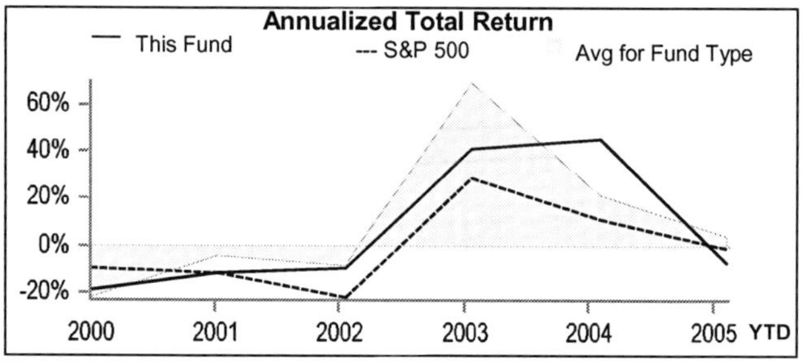

iShares MSCI Brazil Index (EWZ) C- Fair

Fund Family: Barclays Global Fund Advisors
Fund Type: Foreign
Inception Date: July 10, 2000

Major Rating Factors:
iShares MSCI Brazil Index has adopted a very risky asset allocation strategy and currently receives an overall Weiss Investment Rating of C- (Fair). The fund has shown a high level of volatility, with a standard deviation of 43.49. It carries a beta of 2.07, meaning it is expected to move 20.7% for every 10% move in the market. As of June 30, 2005, iShares MSCI Brazil Index traded at a discount of .42% below its net asset value. The high level of risk (E-, Very Weak) did however, reward investors with excellent performance.

The fund's performance rating is currently A+ (Excellent). It has registered an annualized return of 37.41% over the last three years and is up 7.64% year to date 2005. Factored into the performance evaluation is an expense ratio of 0.74% (very low).

Index Strategies Group has been running the fund for 5 years and currently receives a manager quality ranking of 91 (0=worst, 99=best). If you are comfortable owning a very high risk investment, this fund may be an option.

Data Date	Weiss Investment Rating	Net Assets ($Mil)	Price	Performance Rating/Pts	Total Return Y-T-D	Risk Rating/Pts
6-05	C-	467.49	23.94	A+ / 9.9	7.64%	E- / 0.0
2004	C	209.50	22.24	A- / 9.1	33.55%	D / 2.0
2003	D+	103.04	16.63	A / 9.4	111.65%	E- / 0.0

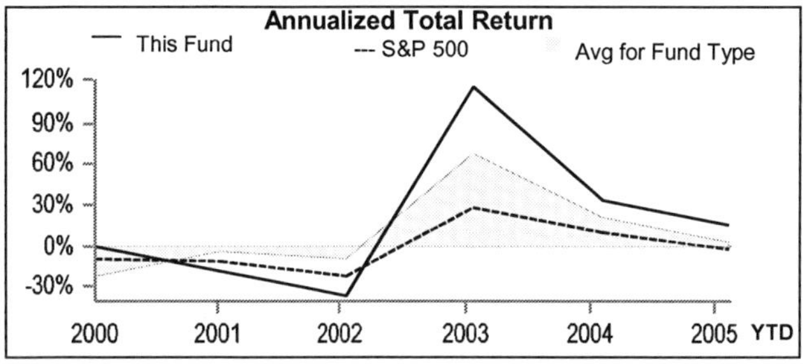

iShares MSCI Canada Index (EWC) C+ Fair

Fund Family: Barclays Global Fund Advisors
Fund Type: Foreign
Inception Date: March 12, 1996

Major Rating Factors:
Strong performance is the major factor driving the C+ (Fair) Weiss Investment Rating for iShares MSCI Canada Index. The fund currently has a performance rating of B+ (Good) based on an annualized return of 21.01% over the last three years and a total return of 5.78% year to date 2005. Factored into the performance evaluation is an expense ratio of 0.58% (very low).

The fund's risk rating is currently C- (Fair). It carries a beta of 0.97, meaning that its performance tracks fairly well with that of the overall stock market. Volatility, as measured by standard deviation, is considered average for equity funds at 18.74. As of June 30, 2005, iShares MSCI Canada Index traded at a premium of .27% above its net asset value, which is worse than its one-year historical average premium of .22%.

Index Strategies Group has been running the fund for 9 years and currently receives a manager quality ranking of 87 (0=worst, 99=best). If you desire an average level of risk and strong performance, then this fund is a good option.

Data Date	Weiss Investment Rating	Net Assets ($Mil)	Price	Performance Rating/Pts	Total Return Y-T-D	Risk Rating/Pts
6-05	C+	314.00	18.29	B+ / 8.7	5.78%	C- / 4.1
2004	C+	325.30	17.29	B / 8.1	22.74%	C / 4.4
2003	D	503.41	14.00	C / 5.2	50.49%	D / 2.0

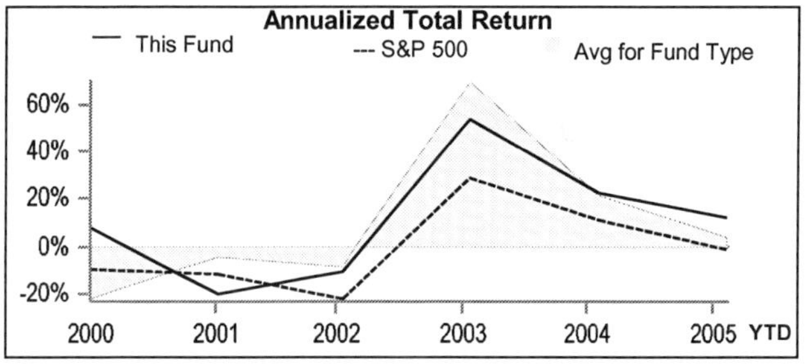

iShares MSCI EAFE Index Fund (EFA) C- Fair

Fund Family: Barclays Global Fund Advisors
Fund Type: Foreign
Inception Date: August 14, 2001

Major Rating Factors:
Disappointing performance is the major factor driving the C- (Fair) Weiss Investment Rating for iShares MSCI EAFE Index Fund. The fund currently has a performance rating of D+ (Weak) based on an annualized return of 11.61% over the last three years and a total return of -1.71% year to date 2005. Factored into the performance evaluation is an expense ratio of 0.35% (very low).

The fund's risk rating is currently C+ (Fair). It carries a beta of 1.00, meaning that its performance tracks fairly well with that of the overall stock market. Volatility, as measured by standard deviation, is considered low for equity funds at 15.59. As of June 30, 2005, iShares MSCI EAFE Index Fund traded at a discount of .06% below its net asset value, which is better than its one-year historical average premium of .31%.

Index Strategies Group has been running the fund for 4 years and currently receives a manager quality ranking of 54 (0=worst, 99=best). This fund offers only a moderate level of risk but investors looking for strong performance are still waiting.

Data Date	Weiss Investment Rating	Net Assets ($Mil)	Price	Performance Rating/Pts	Total Return Y-T-D	Risk Rating/Pts
6-05	C-	13763.27	52.50	D+ / 2.9	-1.71%	C+ / 6.8
2004	C+	8733.74	160.25	B- / 7.2	18.93%	C / 5.0

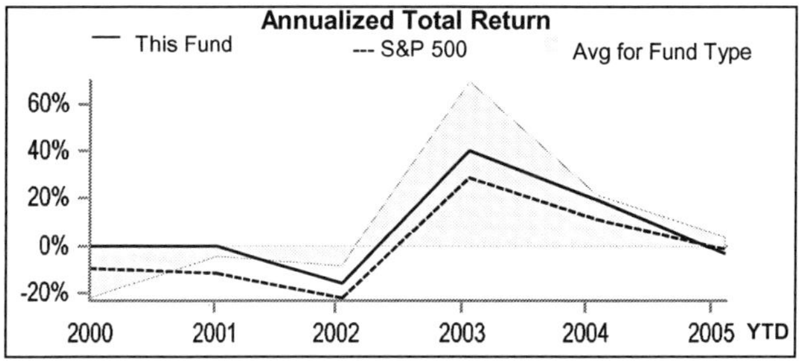

iShares MSCI EMU Index (EZU) E Very Weak

Fund Family: Barclays Global Fund Advisors
Fund Type: Foreign
Inception Date: July 25, 2000

Major Rating Factors:
iShares MSCI EMU Index has adopted a very risky asset allocation strategy and currently receives an overall Weiss Investment Rating of E (Very Weak). The fund has a high level of volatility, with a standard deviation of 22.17. It carries a beta of 1.36, meaning it is expected to move 13.6% for every 10% move in the market. As of June 30, 2005, iShares MSCI EMU Index traded at a discount of .61% below its net asset value, which is better than its one-year historical average premium of .17%. Unfortunately, the high level of risk (D-, Weak) has only provided investors with average performance.

The fund's performance rating is currently C- (Fair). It has registered an annualized return of 11.67% over the last three years but is down -3.09% year to date 2005. Factored into the performance evaluation is an expense ratio of 0.58% (very low).

Index Strategies Group has been running the fund for 5 years and currently receives a manager quality ranking of 21 (0=worst, 99=best). If you are comfortable owning a very high risk investment, then this fund may be an option.

Data Date	Weiss Investment Rating	Net Assets ($Mil)	Price	Performance Rating/Pts	Total Return Y-T-D	Risk Rating/Pts
6-05	E	506.97	70.36	C- / 3.0	-3.09%	D- / 1.0
2004	D	326.61	72.60	B- / 7.2	20.66%	E+ / 0.6
2003	E-	165.39	59.74	D- / 1.3	39.18%	E- / 0.2

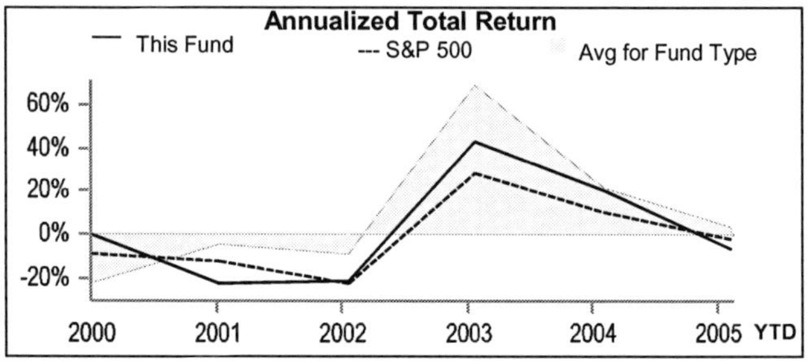

iShares MSCI France Index (EWQ) E Very Weak

Fund Family: Barclays Global Fund Advisors
Fund Type: Foreign
Inception Date: March 12, 1996

Major Rating Factors:
iShares MSCI France Index has adopted a very risky asset allocation strategy and currently receives an overall Weiss Investment Rating of E (Very Weak). The fund has a high level of volatility, with a standard deviation of 21.58. It carries a beta of 1.31, meaning it is expected to move 13.1% for every 10% move in the market. As of June 30, 2005, iShares MSCI France Index traded at a premium of .13% above its net asset value, which is worse than its one-year historical average premium of .11%. Unfortunately, the high level of risk (D-, Weak) failed to pay off as investors endured poor performance.

The fund's performance rating is currently D+ (Weak). It has registered an annualized return of 10.58% over the last three years but is down -0.25% year to date 2005. Factored into the performance evaluation is an expense ratio of 0.58% (very low).

Index Strategies Group has been running the fund for 9 years and currently receives a manager quality ranking of 17 (0=worst, 99=best). If you can tolerate very high levels of risk in the hope of improved future returns, holding this fund may be an option.

Data Date	Weiss Investment Rating	Net Assets ($Mil)	Price	Performance Rating/Pts	Total Return Y-T-D	Risk Rating/Pts
6-05	E	54.22	23.82	D+ / 2.8	-0.25%	D- / 1.3
2004	D-	61.20	23.88	C+ / 6.2	18.58%	D- / 1.2
2003	E	54.08	20.00	D- / 1.2	37.07%	D- / 1.5

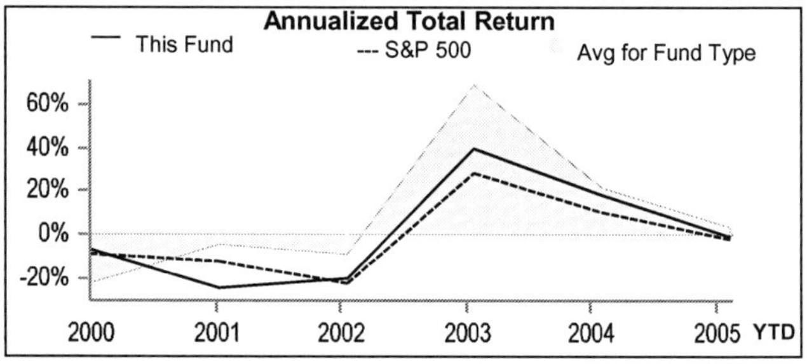

iShares MSCI Germany Index (EWG) E- Very Weak

Fund Family: Barclays Global Fund Advisors
Fund Type: Foreign
Inception Date: March 12, 1996

Major Rating Factors:
iShares MSCI Germany Index has adopted a very risky asset allocation strategy and currently receives an overall Weiss Investment Rating of E- (Very Weak). The fund has a high level of volatility, with a standard deviation of 30.56. It carries a beta of 1.79, meaning it is expected to move 17.9% for every 10% move in the market. As of June 30, 2005, iShares MSCI Germany Index traded at a discount of .23% below its net asset value, which is better than its one-year historical average discount of .01%. Unfortunately, the high level of risk (E-, Very Weak) failed to pay off as investors endured poor performance.

The fund's performance rating is currently D- (Weak). It has registered an annualized return of 7.91% over the last three years but is down -5.26% year to date 2005. Factored into the performance evaluation is an expense ratio of 0.58% (very low).

Index Strategies Group has been running the fund for 9 years and currently receives a manager quality ranking of 1 (0=worst, 99=best). If you can tolerate very high levels of risk in the hope of improved future returns, holding this fund may be an option.

Data Date	Weiss Investment Rating	Net Assets ($Mil)	Price	Performance Rating/Pts	Total Return Y-T-D	Risk Rating/Pts
6-05	E-	155.71	17.65	D- / 1.4	-5.26%	E- / 0.0
2004	E+	98.76	18.63	C / 4.7	16.28%	E- / 0.0
2003	E	101.80	15.85	D+ / 2.5	63.15%	E- / 0.0

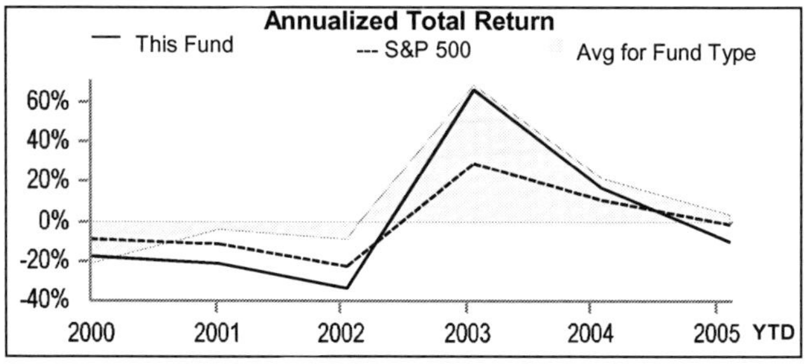

iShares MSCI Hong Kong Index (EWH) D+ Weak

Fund Family: Barclays Global Fund Advisors
Fund Type: Foreign
Inception Date: March 12, 1996

Major Rating Factors:
iShares MSCI Hong Kong Index has adopted a risky asset allocation strategy and currently receives an overall Weiss Investment Rating of D+ (Weak). The fund has an above average level of volatility, with a standard deviation of 18.59. It carries a beta of 0.78, meaning the fund's expected move will be 7.8% for every 10% move in the market. As of June 30, 2005, iShares MSCI Hong Kong Index traded at a discount of .81% below its net asset value, which is better than its one-year historical average premium of .12%. Unfortunately, the high level of risk (D+, Weak) has only provided investors with average performance.

The fund's performance rating is currently C+ (Fair). It has registered an annualized return of 13.61% over the last three years and is up 1.90% year to date 2005. Factored into the performance evaluation is an expense ratio of 0.58% (very low).

Index Strategies Group has been running the fund for 9 years and currently receives a manager quality ranking of 78 (0=worst, 99=best). If you are comfortable owning a high risk investment, then this fund may be an option.

Data Date	Weiss Investment Rating	Net Assets ($Mil)	Price	Perfor-mance Rating/Pts	Total Return Y-T-D	Risk Rating/Pts
6-05	D+	643.14	12.32	C+ / 6.1	1.90%	D+ / 2.9
2004	D	449.92	12.09	C+ / 6.2	23.65%	D+ / 2.4
2003	E+	250.63	9.90	D- / 1.4	35.30%	D- / 1.4

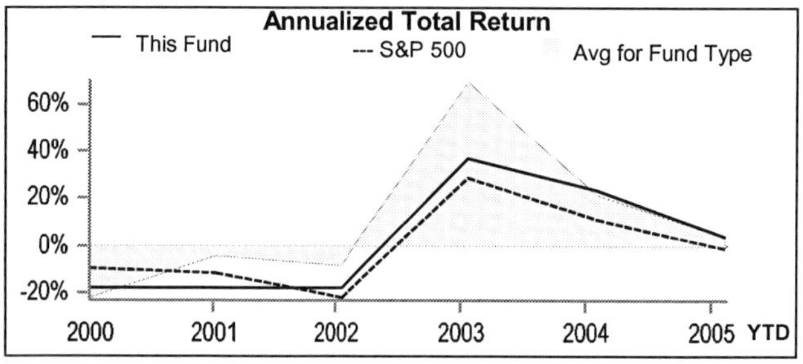

iShares MSCI Italy Index (EWI) D- Weak

Fund Family: Barclays Global Fund Advisors
Fund Type: Foreign
Inception Date: March 12, 1996

Major Rating Factors:
iShares MSCI Italy Index has adopted a risky asset allocation strategy and currently receives an overall Weiss Investment Rating of D- (Weak). The fund has an above average level of volatility, with a standard deviation of 19.31. It carries a beta of 1.05, meaning that its performance tracks fairly well with that of the overall stock market. As of June 30, 2005, iShares MSCI Italy Index traded at a discount of .49% below its net asset value, which is better than its one-year historical average premium of .08%. Unfortunately, the high level of risk (D+, Weak) has only provided investors with average performance.

The fund's performance rating is currently C (Fair). It has registered an annualized return of 16.79% over the last three years but is down -5.39% year to date 2005. Factored into the performance evaluation is an expense ratio of 0.58% (very low).

Index Strategies Group has been running the fund for 9 years and currently receives a manager quality ranking of 79 (0=worst, 99=best). If you are comfortable owning a high risk investment, then this fund may be an option.

Data Date	Weiss Investment Rating	Net Assets ($Mil)	Price	Perfor-mance Rating/Pts	Total Return Y-T-D	Risk Rating/Pts
6-05	D-	38.72	24.22	C / 4.9	-5.39%	D+ / 2.5
2004	C	27.28	25.60	A- / 9.1	33.08%	D+ / 2.7
2003	E	30.00	19.67	D / 1.6	38.94%	E+ / 0.9

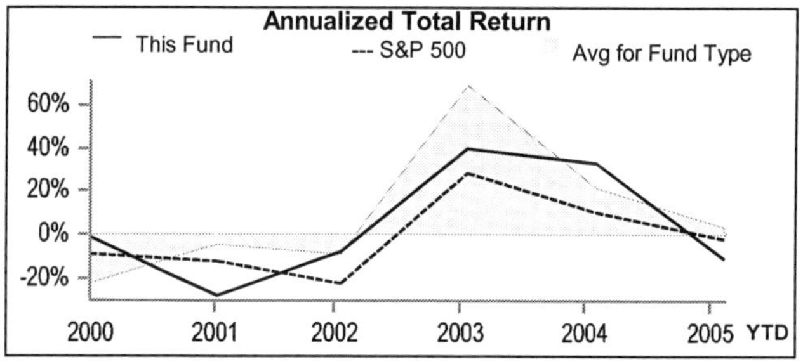

iShares MSCI Japan Index (EWJ) E+ Very Weak

Fund Family: Barclays Global Fund Advisors
Fund Type: Foreign
Inception Date: March 12, 1996

Major Rating Factors:
Very poor performance is the major factor driving the E+ (Very Weak) Weiss Investment Rating for iShares MSCI Japan Index. The fund currently has a performance rating of E+ (Very Weak) based on an annualized return of 6.78% over the last three years and a total return of -6.41% year to date 2005. Factored into the performance evaluation is an expense ratio of 0.58% (very low).

The fund's risk rating is currently C (Fair). It carries a beta of 0.67, meaning the fund's expected move will be 6.7% for every 10% move in the market. Volatility, as measured by standard deviation, is considered average for equity funds at 17.21. As of June 30, 2005, iShares MSCI Japan Index traded at a discount of .68% below its net asset value, which is better than its one-year historical average premium of .01%.

Index Strategies Group has been running the fund for 9 years and currently receives a manager quality ranking of 43 (0=worst, 99=best). This fund offers an average level of risk but investors looking for strong performance will be frustrated.

Data Date	Weiss Investment Rating	Net Assets ($Mil)	Price	Perfor-mance Rating/Pts	Total Return Y-T-D	Risk Rating/Pts
6-05	E+	6914.20	10.22	E+ / 0.6	-6.41%	C / 4.7
2004	D	5863.33	10.92	C+ / 5.6	13.73%	D+ / 2.4
2003	E+	1726.86	9.41	D- / 1.1	35.42%	D / 2.2

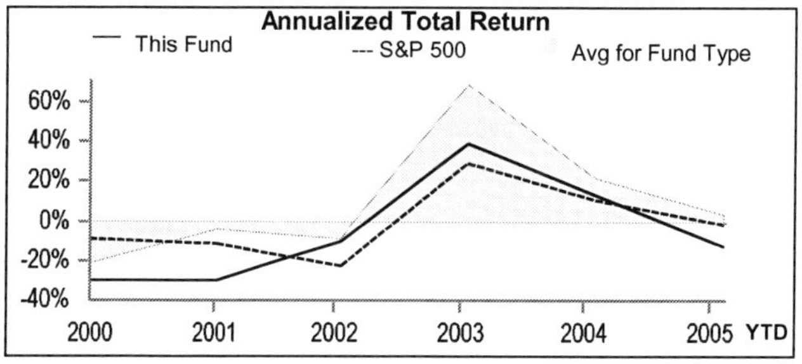

iShares MSCI Malaysia Index (EWM) E+ Very Weak

Fund Family: Barclays Global Fund Advisors
Fund Type: Foreign
Inception Date: March 12, 1996

Data Date	Weiss Investment Rating	Net Assets ($Mil)	Price	Performance Rating/Pts	Total Return Y-T-D	Risk Rating/Pts
6-05	E+	320.92	6.99	D / 2.0	-2.24%	C- / 3.0
2004	D+	224.22	7.15	B- / 7.0	13.32%	D / 2.1
2003	D-	99.73	6.23	C- / 4.1	26.18%	E- / 0.0

Major Rating Factors:
Disappointing performance is the major factor driving the E+ (Very Weak) Weiss Investment Rating for iShares MSCI Malaysia Index. The fund currently has a performance rating of D (Weak) based on an annualized return of 8.95% over the last three years and a total return of -2.24% year to date 2005. Factored into the performance evaluation is an expense ratio of 0.58% (very low).

The fund's risk rating is currently C- (Fair). It carries a beta of 0.58, meaning the fund's expected move will be 5.8% for every 10% move in the market. Volatility, as measured by standard deviation, is considered average for equity funds at 18.42. As of June 30, 2005, iShares MSCI Malaysia Index traded at a price exactly equal to its net asset value, which is better than its one-year historical average premium of .23%.

Index Strategies Group has been running the fund for 9 years and currently receives a manager quality ranking of 66 (0=worst, 99=best). This fund offers an average level of risk but investors looking for strong performance will be frustrated.

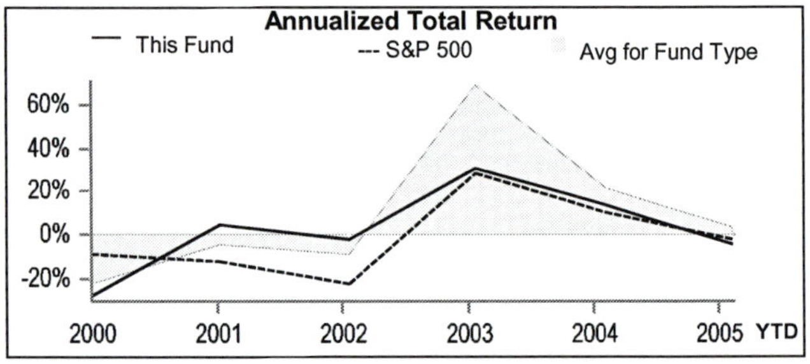

iShares MSCI Mexico Index (EWW) C Fair

Fund Family: Barclays Global Fund Advisors
Fund Type: Foreign
Inception Date: March 12, 1996

Data Date	Weiss Investment Rating	Net Assets ($Mil)	Price	Performance Rating/Pts	Total Return Y-T-D	Risk Rating/Pts
6-05	C	280.77	26.57	A / 9.4	5.60%	D / 1.7
2004	C-	129.62	25.16	A / 9.4	48.95%	E+ / 0.8
2003	D-	60.16	16.55	C / 5.5	34.61%	E- / 0.0

Major Rating Factors:
iShares MSCI Mexico Index has adopted a very risky asset allocation strategy and currently receives an overall Weiss Investment Rating of C (Fair). The fund has shown a high level of volatility, with a standard deviation of 20.92. It carries a beta of 1.11, meaning it is expected to move 11.1% for every 10% move in the market. As of June 30, 2005, iShares MSCI Mexico Index traded at a discount of .30% below its net asset value, which is better than its one-year historical average premium of .05%. The high level of risk (D, Weak) did however, reward investors with excellent performance.

The fund's performance rating is currently A (Excellent). It has registered an annualized return of 24.74% over the last three years and is up 5.60% year to date 2005. Factored into the performance evaluation is an expense ratio of 0.58% (very low).

Index Strategies Group has been running the fund for 9 years and currently receives a manager quality ranking of 90 (0=worst, 99=best). If you are comfortable owning a very high risk investment, this fund may be an option.

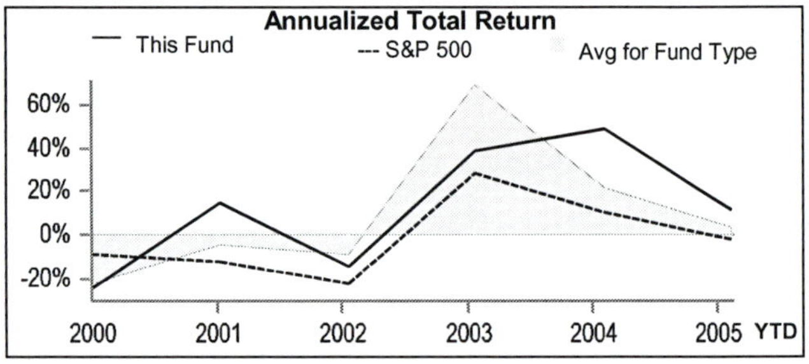

iShares MSCI Netherlands Index (EWN) E- Very Weak

Fund Family: Barclays Global Fund Advisors
Fund Type: Foreign
Inception Date: March 12, 1996

Data Date	Weiss Investment Rating	Net Assets ($Mil)	Price	Performance Rating/Pts	Total Return Y-T-D	Risk Rating/Pts
6-05	E-	51.66	18.40	E+ / 0.6	-0.05%	E- / 0.0
2004	E	28.27	18.41	D+ / 2.8	14.13%	E- / 0.0
2003	E-	18.60	16.00	E+ / 0.6	23.96%	E- / 0.0

Major Rating Factors:
iShares MSCI Netherlands Index has adopted a very risky asset allocation strategy and currently receives an overall Weiss Investment Rating of E- (Very Weak). The fund has a high level of volatility, with a standard deviation of 24.22. It carries a beta of 1.45, meaning it is expected to move 14.5% for every 10% move in the market. As of June 30, 2005, iShares MSCI Netherlands Index traded at a discount of .33% below its net asset value, which is better than its one-year historical average premium of .16%. Unfortunately, the high level of risk (E-, Very Weak) failed to pay off as investors endured very poor performance.

The fund's performance rating is currently E+ (Very Weak). It has registered an annualized return of 3.75% over the last three years but is down -0.05% year to date 2005. Factored into the performance evaluation is an expense ratio of 0.58% (very low).

Index Strategies Group has been running the fund for 9 years and currently receives a manager quality ranking of 1 (0=worst, 99=best). If you can tolerate very high levels of risk in the hope of improved future returns, holding this fund may be an option.

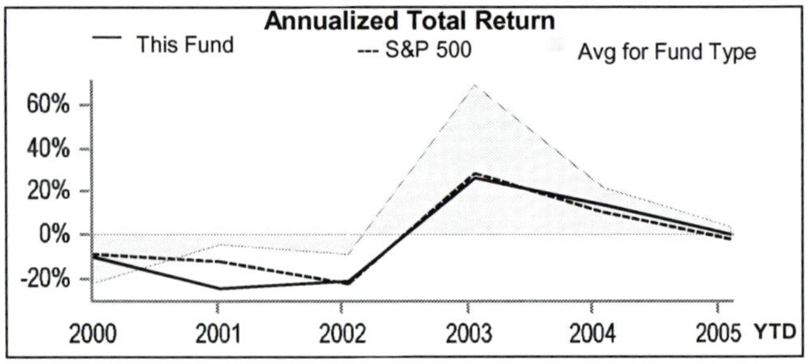

iShares MSCI Pacific ex-Japan Idx (EPP) A+ Excellent

Fund Family: Barclays Global Fund Advisors
Fund Type: Foreign
Inception Date: October 25, 2001

Major Rating Factors:
Strong performance is the major factor driving the A+ (Excellent) Weiss Investment Rating for iShares MSCI Pacific ex-Japan Idx. The fund currently has a performance rating of B+ (Good) based on an annualized return of 21.35% over the last three years and a total return of 4.37% year to date 2005. Factored into the performance evaluation is an expense ratio of 0.50% (very low).

The fund's risk rating is currently B- (Good). It carries a beta of 0.72, meaning the fund's expected move will be 7.2% for every 10% move in the market. Volatility, as measured by standard deviation, is considered low for equity funds at 13.31. As of June 30, 2005, iShares MSCI Pacific ex-Japan Idx traded at a discount of .14% below its net asset value, which is better than its one-year historical average premium of .31%.

Index Strategies Group has been running the fund for 4 years and currently receives a manager quality ranking of 92 (0=worst, 99=best). If you desire only a moderate level of risk and strong performance, then this fund is an excellent option.

Data Date	Weiss Investment Rating	Net Assets ($Mil)	Price	Performance Rating/Pts	Total Return Y-T-D	Risk Rating/Pts
6-05	A+	1178.98	94.11	B+ / 8.8	4.37%	B- / 7.0
2004	A+	651.25	90.17	B+ / 8.9	28.61%	C+ / 6.9

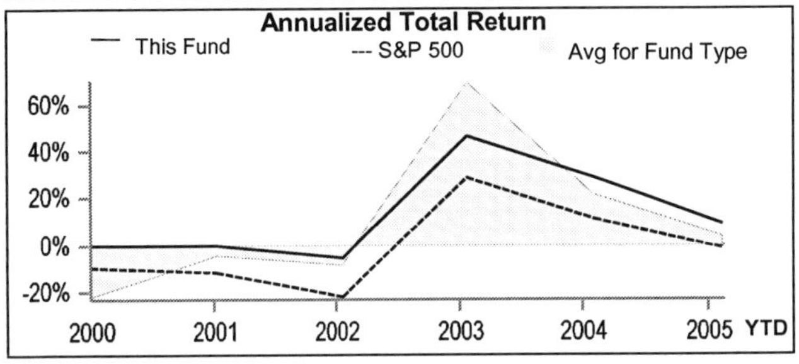

iShares MSCI Singapore Index (EWS) B Good

Fund Family: Barclays Global Fund Advisors
Fund Type: Foreign
Inception Date: March 12, 1996

Major Rating Factors:
Strong performance is the major factor driving the B (Good) Weiss Investment Rating for iShares MSCI Singapore Index. The fund currently has a performance rating of B- (Good) based on an annualized return of 15.90% over the last three years and a total return of 6.14% year to date 2005. Factored into the performance evaluation is an expense ratio of 0.58% (very low).

The fund's risk rating is currently C+ (Fair). It carries a beta of 0.75, meaning the fund's expected move will be 7.5% for every 10% move in the market. Volatility, as measured by standard deviation, is considered low for equity funds at 15.24. As of June 30, 2005, iShares MSCI Singapore Index traded at a premium of .26% above its net asset value, which is better than its one-year historical average premium of .27%.

Index Strategies Group has been running the fund for 9 years and currently receives a manager quality ranking of 83 (0=worst, 99=best). If you desire only a moderate level of risk and strong performance, then this fund is an excellent option.

Data Date	Weiss Investment Rating	Net Assets ($Mil)	Price	Performance Rating/Pts	Total Return Y-T-D	Risk Rating/Pts
6-05	B	235.86	7.61	B- / 7.1	6.14%	C+ / 6.4
2004	C-	170.05	7.17	B- / 7.5	24.17%	C- / 3.0
2003	E-	108.20	5.88	D / 1.6	40.52%	E- / 0.0

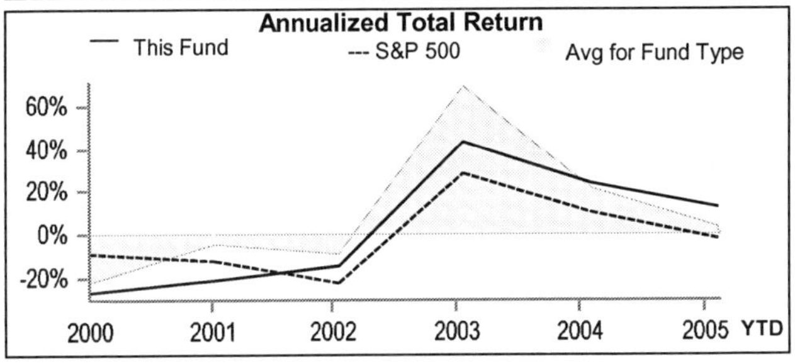

iShares MSCI South Korea Index (EWY) D- Weak

Fund Family: Barclays Global Fund Advisors
Fund Type: Foreign
Inception Date: May 9, 2000

Major Rating Factors:
iShares MSCI South Korea Index has adopted a very risky asset allocation strategy and currently receives an overall Weiss Investment Rating of D- (Weak). The fund has shown a high level of volatility, with a standard deviation of 29.21. It carries a beta of 1.45, meaning it is expected to move 14.5% for every 10% move in the market. As of June 30, 2005, iShares MSCI South Korea Index traded at a premium of .25% above its net asset value, which is worse than its one-year historical average premium of .18%. The high level of risk (E-, Very Weak) did however, reward investors with excellent performance.

The fund's performance rating is currently B (Good). It has registered an annualized return of 14.78% over the last three years and is up 11.73% year to date 2005. Factored into the performance evaluation is an expense ratio of 0.74% (very low).

Index Strategies Group has been running the fund for 5 years and currently receives a manager quality ranking of 29 (0=worst, 99=best). If you are comfortable owning a very high risk investment, this fund may be an option.

Data Date	Weiss Investment Rating	Net Assets ($Mil)	Price	Performance Rating/Pts	Total Return Y-T-D	Risk Rating/Pts
6-05	D-	640.83	32.68	B / 7.7	11.73%	E- / 0.0
2004	D+	315.46	29.25	B / 7.7	17.22%	D / 1.8
2003	D+	154.49	24.17	A- / 9.1	32.55%	E- / 0.0

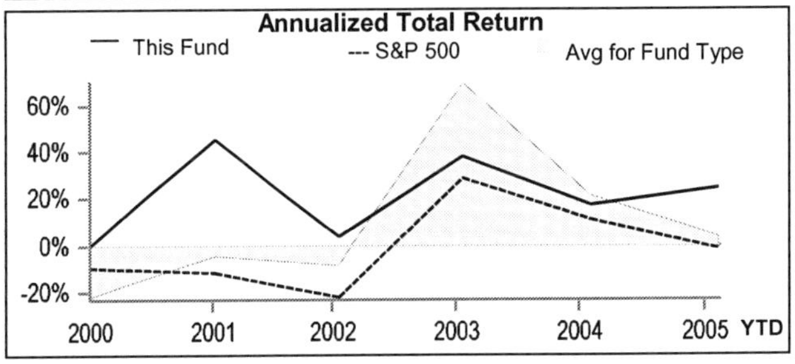

iShares MSCI Spain Index (EWP) D+ Weak

Fund Family: Barclays Global Fund Advisors
Fund Type: Foreign
Inception Date: March 12, 1996

Data Date	Weiss Investment Rating	Net Assets ($Mil)	Price	Performance Rating/Pts	Total Return Y-T-D	Risk Rating/Pts
6-05	D+	67.06	33.76	B- / 7.2	-4.36%	D / 1.8
2004	C-	45.46	35.30	A- / 9.2	30.11%	D / 1.6
2003	D	50.37	27.39	B / 7.7	56.21%	E- / 0.1

Major Rating Factors:
iShares MSCI Spain Index has adopted a very risky asset allocation strategy and currently receives an overall Weiss Investment Rating of D+ (Weak). The fund has shown a high level of volatility, with a standard deviation of 20.70. It carries a beta of 1.19, meaning it is expected to move 11.9% for every 10% move in the market. As of June 30, 2005, iShares MSCI Spain Index traded at a discount of .27% below its net asset value, which is better than its one-year historical average premium of .09%. The high level of risk (D, Weak) did however, reward investors with excellent performance.

The fund's performance rating is currently B- (Good). It has registered an annualized return of 21.56% over the last three years but is down -4.36% year to date 2005. Factored into the performance evaluation is an expense ratio of 0.58% (very low).

Index Strategies Group has been running the fund for 9 years and currently receives a manager quality ranking of 85 (0=worst, 99=best). If you are comfortable owning a very high risk investment, this fund may be an option.

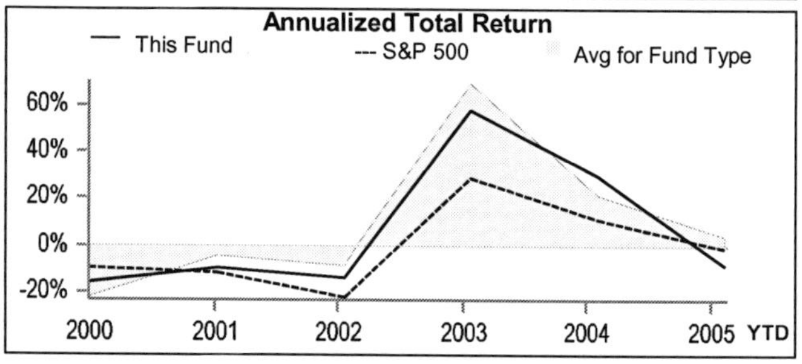

iShares MSCI Sweden Index (EWD) D- Weak

Fund Family: Barclays Global Fund Advisors
Fund Type: Foreign
Inception Date: March 12, 1996

Data Date	Weiss Investment Rating	Net Assets ($Mil)	Price	Performance Rating/Pts	Total Return Y-T-D	Risk Rating/Pts
6-05	D-	63.46	20.25	B / 7.7	-3.39%	E- / 0.0
2004	D	27.76	20.96	B+ / 8.6	35.30%	E- / 0.0
2003	E	16.99	15.14	D / 2.2	61.16%	E- / 0.0

Major Rating Factors:
iShares MSCI Sweden Index has adopted a very risky asset allocation strategy and currently receives an overall Weiss Investment Rating of D- (Weak). The fund has shown a high level of volatility, with a standard deviation of 28.69. It carries a beta of 1.62, meaning it is expected to move 16.2% for every 10% move in the market. As of June 30, 2005, iShares MSCI Sweden Index traded at a discount of 1.79% below its net asset value, which is better than its one-year historical average premium of .21%. The high level of risk (E-, Very Weak) did however, reward investors with excellent performance.

The fund's performance rating is currently B (Good). It has registered an annualized return of 21.38% over the last three years but is down -3.39% year to date 2005. Factored into the performance evaluation is an expense ratio of 0.58% (very low).

Index Strategies Group has been running the fund for 9 years and currently receives a manager quality ranking of 68 (0=worst, 99=best). If you are comfortable owning a very high risk investment, this fund may be an option.

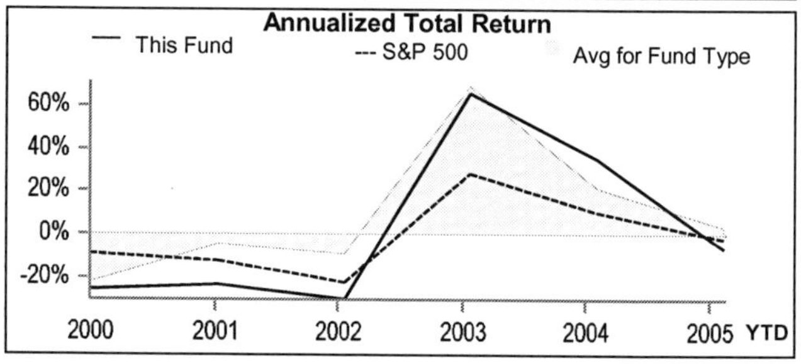

iShares MSCI Switzerland Index (EWL) D- Weak

Fund Family: Barclays Global Fund Advisors
Fund Type: Foreign
Inception Date: March 12, 1996

Data Date	Weiss Investment Rating	Net Assets ($Mil)	Price	Performance Rating/Pts	Total Return Y-T-D	Risk Rating/Pts
6-05	D-	63.25	16.60	D- / 1.1	-3.49%	C+ / 5.7
2004	C-	41.92	17.20	C+ / 6.8	17.28%	C- / 3.6
2003	D-	33.64	14.51	D- / 1.3	31.09%	C- / 3.9

Major Rating Factors:
Disappointing performance is the major factor driving the D- (Weak) Weiss Investment Rating for iShares MSCI Switzerland Index. The fund currently has a performance rating of D- (Weak) based on an annualized return of 7.41% over the last three years and a total return of -3.49% year to date 2005. Factored into the performance evaluation is an expense ratio of 0.58% (very low).

The fund's risk rating is currently C+ (Fair). It carries a beta of 0.99, meaning that its performance tracks fairly well with that of the overall stock market. Volatility, as measured by standard deviation, is considered low for equity funds at 16.87. As of June 30, 2005, iShares MSCI Switzerland Index traded at a discount of .18% below its net asset value, which is better than its one-year historical average premium of .51%.

Index Strategies Group has been running the fund for 9 years and currently receives a manager quality ranking of 18 (0=worst, 99=best). This fund offers only a moderate level of risk but investors looking for strong performance are still waiting.

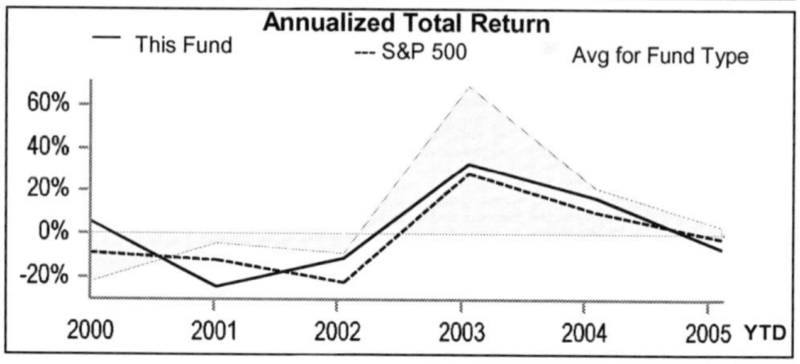

iShares MSCI Taiwan Index (EWT) E- Very Weak

Fund Family: Barclays Global Fund Advisors
Fund Type: Foreign
Inception Date: June 20, 2000

Data Date	Weiss Investment Rating	Net Assets ($Mil)	Price	Performance Rating/Pts	Total Return Y-T-D	Risk Rating/Pts
6-05	E-	837.32	12.34	D+ / 2.4	2.32%	E- / 0.0
2004	E-	390.23	12.06	D- / 1.3	8.02%	E- / 0.0
2003	E+	234.73	11.19	C- / 3.8	37.57%	E- / 0.0

Major Rating Factors:
iShares MSCI Taiwan Index has adopted a very risky asset allocation strategy and currently receives an overall Weiss Investment Rating of E- (Very Weak). The fund has a high level of volatility, with a standard deviation of 25.23. It carries a beta of 1.03, meaning that its performance tracks fairly well with that of the overall stock market. As of June 30, 2005, iShares MSCI Taiwan Index traded at a discount of 1.52% below its net asset value, which is better than its one-year historical average discount of .08%. Unfortunately, the high level of risk (E-, Very Weak) failed to pay off as investors endured poor performance.

The fund's performance rating is currently D+ (Weak). It has registered an annualized return of 6.27% over the last three years and is up 2.32% year to date 2005. Factored into the performance evaluation is an expense ratio of 0.76% (very low).

Index Strategy Team has been running the fund for 5 years and currently receives a manager quality ranking of 8 (0=worst, 99=best). If you can tolerate very high levels of risk in the hope of improved future returns, holding this fund may be an option.

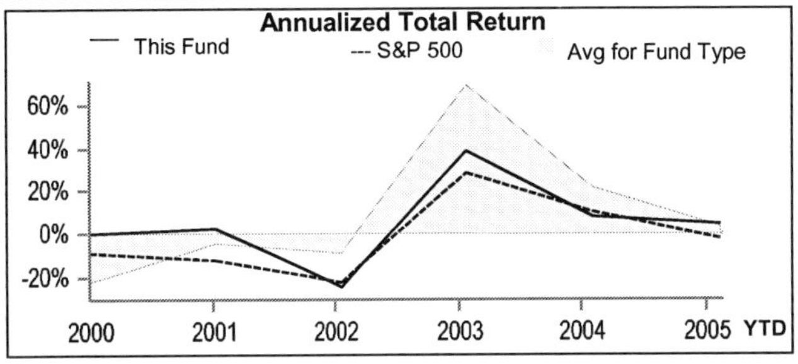

iShares MSCI UK Index (EWU) C- Fair

Fund Family: Barclays Global Fund Advisors
Fund Type: Foreign
Inception Date: March 12, 1996

Data Date	Weiss Investment Rating	Net Assets ($Mil)	Price	Performance Rating/Pts	Total Return Y-T-D	Risk Rating/Pts
6-05	C-	569.03	18.07	C- / 3.3	-0.11%	C+ / 6.6
2004	C+	452.87	18.09	C+ / 6.6	18.35%	C+ / 6.5
2003	D	150.81	15.28	D / 1.6	29.76%	C+ / 5.9

Major Rating Factors:
Middle of the road best describes iShares MSCI UK Index whose Weiss Investment Rating is currently a C- (Fair). The fund currently has a performance rating of C- (Fair) based on an annualized return of 11.80% over the last three years and a total return of -0.11% year to date 2005. Factored into the performance evaluation is an expense ratio of 0.58% (very low).

The fund's risk rating is currently C+ (Fair). It carries a beta of 0.88, meaning the fund's expected move will be 8.8% for every 10% move in the market. Volatility, as measured by standard deviation, is considered low for equity funds at 14.59. As of June 30, 2005, iShares MSCI UK Index traded at a discount of .50% below its net asset value, which is better than its one-year historical average premium of .45%.

Index Strategies Group has been running the fund for 9 years and currently receives a manager quality ranking of 64 (0=worst, 99=best). If you desire an average level of risk, then this fund may be an option.

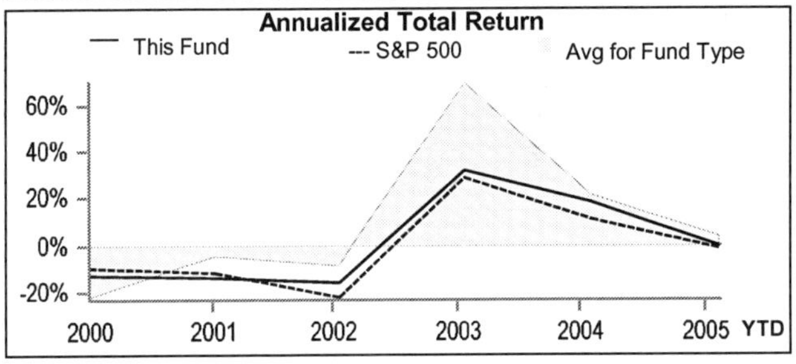

iShares Russell 1000 (IWB) C- Fair

Fund Family: Barclays Global Fund Advisors
Fund Type: Growth
Inception Date: May 15, 2000

Data Date	Weiss Investment Rating	Net Assets ($Mil)	Price	Performance Rating/Pts	Total Return Y-T-D	Risk Rating/Pts
6-05	C-	1984.79	64.40	D / 2.2	0.17%	B- / 7.3
2004	D+	1525.56	64.94	D / 2.2	10.97%	C+ / 6.9
2003	D-	1660.62	58.82	E+ / 0.9	27.90%	C- / 3.8

Major Rating Factors:
Disappointing performance is the major factor driving the C- (Fair) Weiss Investment Rating for iShares Russell 1000. The fund currently has a performance rating of D (Weak) based on an annualized return of 9.18% over the last three years and a total return of 0.17% year to date 2005. Factored into the performance evaluation is an expense ratio of 0.15% (very low).

The fund's risk rating is currently B- (Good). It carries a beta of 0.95, meaning that its performance tracks fairly well with that of the overall stock market. Volatility, as measured by standard deviation, is considered low for equity funds at 13.50. As of June 30, 2005, iShares Russell 1000 traded at a discount of .02% below its net asset value, which is better than its one-year historical average premium of .03%.

Index Strategies Group has been running the fund for 5 years and currently receives a manager quality ranking of 70 (0=worst, 99=best). This fund offers only a moderate level of risk but investors looking for strong performance are still waiting.

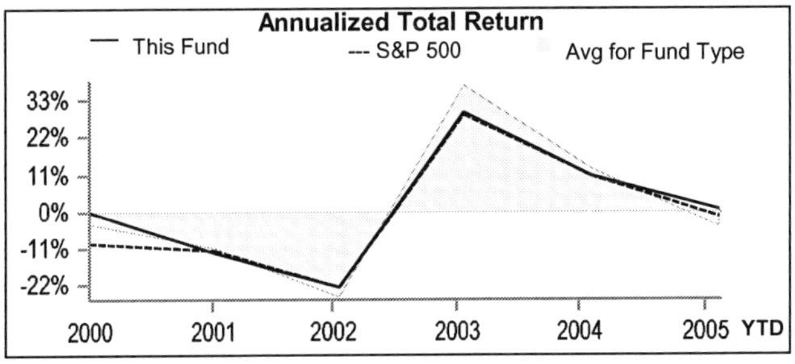

iShares Russell 1000 Growth (IWF) — D — Weak

Fund Family: Barclays Global Fund Advisors
Fund Type: Growth
Inception Date: May 22, 2000

Data Date	Weiss Investment Rating	Net Assets ($Mil)	Price	Performance Rating/Pts	Total Return Y-T-D	Risk Rating/Pts
6-05	D	3129.99	47.82	D- / 1.0	-2.25%	B- / 7.1
2004	D-	2263.77	49.15	E / 0.5	6.15%	C+ / 6.5
2003	E	1166.97	46.06	E / 0.4	27.79%	D- / 1.3

Major Rating Factors:
Disappointing performance is the major factor driving the D (Weak) Weiss Investment Rating for iShares Russell 1000 Growth. The fund currently has a performance rating of D- (Weak) based on an annualized return of 6.98% over the last three years and a total return of -2.25% year to date 2005. Factored into the performance evaluation is an expense ratio of 0.20% (very low).

The fund's risk rating is currently B- (Good). It carries a beta of 0.94, meaning that its performance tracks fairly well with that of the overall stock market. Volatility, as measured by standard deviation, is considered low for equity funds at 13.70. As of June 30, 2005, iShares Russell 1000 Growth traded at a discount of .04% below its net asset value, which is better than its one-year historical average premium of .04%.

Index Strategies Group has been running the fund for 5 years and currently receives a manager quality ranking of 57 (0=worst, 99=best). This fund offers only a moderate level of risk but investors looking for strong performance are still waiting.

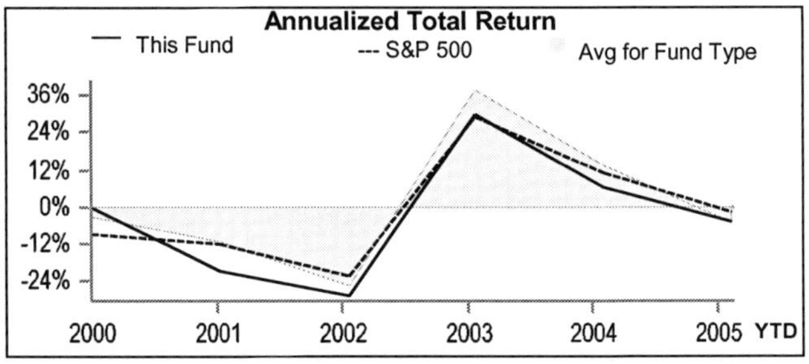

iShares Russell 1000 Value (IWD) — C- — Fair

Fund Family: Barclays Global Fund Advisors
Fund Type: Income
Inception Date: May 22, 2000

Data Date	Weiss Investment Rating	Net Assets ($Mil)	Price	Performance Rating/Pts	Total Return Y-T-D	Risk Rating/Pts
6-05	C-	4791.38	66.58	C- / 3.2	1.54%	B- / 7.1
2004	C	3466.95	66.37	C / 5.0	16.11%	C+ / 6.9
2003	D+	1673.74	57.58	D+ / 2.8	28.29%	C+ / 6.4

Major Rating Factors:
Middle of the road best describes iShares Russell 1000 Value whose Weiss Investment Rating is currently a C- (Fair). The fund currently has a performance rating of C- (Fair) based on an annualized return of 10.90% over the last three years and a total return of 1.54% year to date 2005. Factored into the performance evaluation is an expense ratio of 0.20% (very low).

The fund's risk rating is currently B- (Good). It carries a beta of 1.01, meaning that its performance tracks fairly well with that of the overall stock market. Volatility, as measured by standard deviation, is considered low for equity funds at 14.55. As of June 30, 2005, iShares Russell 1000 Value traded at a discount of .15% below its net asset value, which is better than its one-year historical average premium of .02%.

Index Strategies Group has been running the fund for 5 years and currently receives a manager quality ranking of 75 (0=worst, 99=best). If you desire an average level of risk, then this fund may be an option.

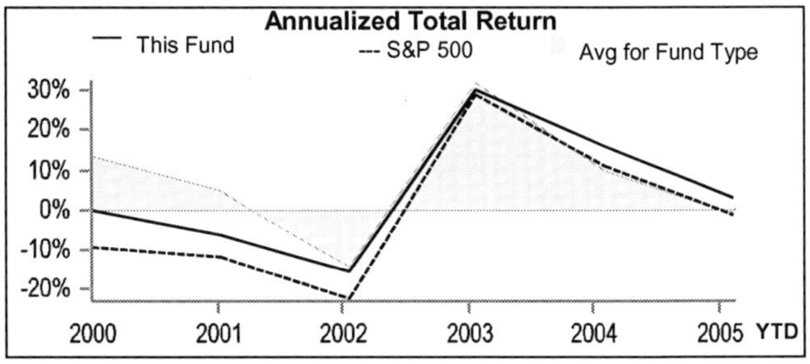

iShares Russell 2000 (IWM) — D- — Weak

Fund Family: Barclays Global Fund Advisors
Fund Type: Growth
Inception Date: May 22, 2000

Data Date	Weiss Investment Rating	Net Assets ($Mil)	Price	Performance Rating/Pts	Total Return Y-T-D	Risk Rating/Pts
6-05	D-	6908.11	62.21	C- / 3.4	-3.26%	C- / 3.4
2004	C-	6085.76	129.50	C+ / 6.4	18.04%	C- / 3.6
2003	D+	3539.77	110.47	C+ / 6.4	47.13%	D / 1.7

Major Rating Factors:
iShares Russell 2000 receives a Weiss Investment Rating of D- (Weak). The fund currently has a performance rating of C- (Fair) based on an annualized return of 12.43% over the last three years and a total return of -3.26% year to date 2005. Factored into the performance evaluation is an expense ratio of 0.20% (very low).

The fund's risk rating is currently C- (Fair). It carries a beta of 1.18, meaning it is expected to move 11.8% for every 10% move in the market. Volatility, as measured by standard deviation, is considered average for equity funds at 19.38. As of June 30, 2005, iShares Russell 2000 traded at a discount of .70% below its net asset value, which is better than its one-year historical average discount of .05%.

Index Strategies Group has been running the fund for 5 years and currently receives a manager quality ranking of 77 (0=worst, 99=best). If you desire an average level of risk, then this fund may be an option.

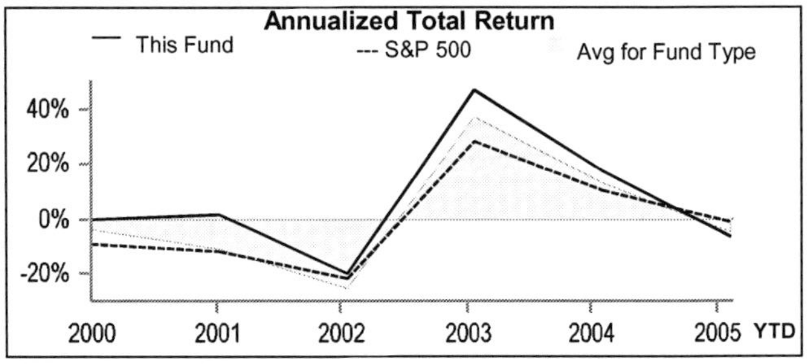

iShares Russell 2000 Growth (IWO) E Very Weak

Fund Family: Barclays Global Fund Advisors
Fund Type: Growth
Inception Date: July 24, 2000

Major Rating Factors:
iShares Russell 2000 Growth has adopted a risky asset allocation strategy and currently receives an overall Weiss Investment Rating of E (Very Weak). The fund has an above average level of volatility, with a standard deviation of 21.17. It carries a beta of 1.26, meaning it is expected to move 12.6% for every 10% move in the market. As of June 30, 2005, iShares Russell 2000 Growth traded at a discount of .66% below its net asset value, which is better than its one-year historical average discount of .06%. Unfortunately, the high level of risk (D+, Weak) failed to pay off as investors endured poor performance.

The fund's performance rating is currently D (Weak). It has registered an annualized return of 10.47% over the last three years but is down -5.39% year to date 2005. Factored into the performance evaluation is an expense ratio of 0.25% (very low).

Index Strategies Group has been running the fund for 5 years and currently receives a manager quality ranking of 68 (0=worst, 99=best). If you can tolerate high levels of risk in the hope of improved future returns, holding this fund may be an option.

Data Date	Weiss Investment Rating	Net Assets ($Mil)	Price	Performance Rating/Pts	Total Return Y-T-D	Risk Rating/Pts
6-05	E	2105.73	63.50	D / 2.1	-5.39%	D+ / 2.6
2004	E+	1755.83	67.30	C- / 3.4	13.86%	D+ / 2.5
2003	E+	1341.50	58.90	D / 1.9	48.38%	E+ / 0.9

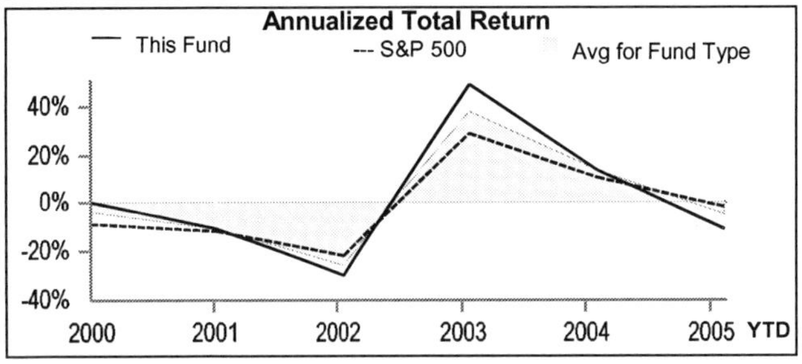

iShares Russell 2000 Value (IWN) D Weak

Fund Family: Barclays Global Fund Advisors
Fund Type: Growth
Inception Date: July 24, 2000

Major Rating Factors:
iShares Russell 2000 Value receives a Weiss Investment Rating of D (Weak). The fund currently has a performance rating of C (Fair) based on an annualized return of 13.52% over the last three years and a total return of -1.04% year to date 2005. Factored into the performance evaluation is an expense ratio of 0.25% (very low).

The fund's risk rating is currently C- (Fair). It carries a beta of 1.10, meaning it is expected to move 11.0% for every 10% move in the market. Volatility, as measured by standard deviation, is considered average for equity funds at 18.45. As of June 30, 2005, iShares Russell 2000 Value traded at a discount of .39% below its net asset value, which is better than its one-year historical average discount of .04%.

Index Strategies Group has been running the fund for 5 years and currently receives a manager quality ranking of 82 (0=worst, 99=best). If you desire an average level of risk, then this fund may be an option.

Data Date	Weiss Investment Rating	Net Assets ($Mil)	Price	Performance Rating/Pts	Total Return Y-T-D	Risk Rating/Pts
6-05	D	2711.33	63.10	C / 4.4	-1.04%	C- / 3.9
2004	C+	2180.34	192.96	B / 8.1	22.10%	C- / 4.2
2003	C	1125.33	160.78	B+ / 8.4	46.29%	C- / 3.3

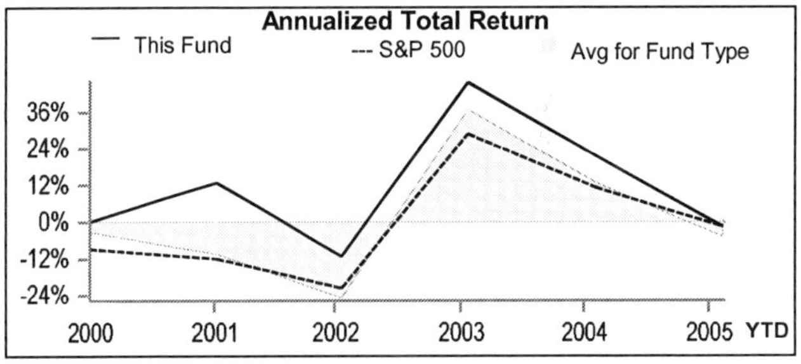

iShares Russell 3000 (IWV) D+ Weak

Fund Family: Barclays Global Fund Advisors
Fund Type: Growth
Inception Date: May 22, 2000

Major Rating Factors:
Disappointing performance is the major factor driving the D+ (Weak) Weiss Investment Rating for iShares Russell 3000. The fund currently has a performance rating of D (Weak) based on an annualized return of 9.33% over the last three years and a total return of -0.26% year to date 2005. Factored into the performance evaluation is an expense ratio of 0.20% (very low).

The fund's risk rating is currently B- (Good). It carries a beta of 1.01, meaning that its performance tracks fairly well with that of the overall stock market. Volatility, as measured by standard deviation, is considered low for equity funds at 14.26. As of June 30, 2005, iShares Russell 3000 traded at a price exactly equal to its net asset value, which is better than its one-year historical average premium of .03%.

Index Strategies Group has been running the fund for 5 years and currently receives a manager quality ranking of 68 (0=worst, 99=best). This fund offers only a moderate level of risk but investors looking for strong performance are still waiting.

Data Date	Weiss Investment Rating	Net Assets ($Mil)	Price	Performance Rating/Pts	Total Return Y-T-D	Risk Rating/Pts
6-05	D+	1957.32	68.35	D / 2.2	-0.26%	B- / 7.1
2004	D+	1543.87	69.15	D+ / 2.7	11.69%	C+ / 6.8
2003	D-	1095.17	62.10	D- / 1.0	28.84%	C- / 3.5

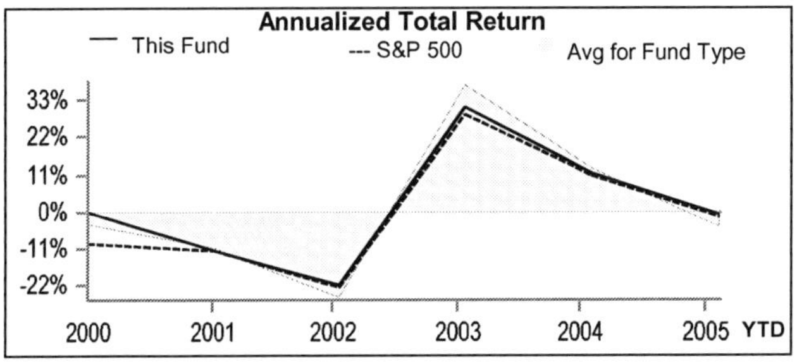

iShares Russell 3000 Growth (IWZ) — D Weak

Fund Family: Barclays Global Fund Advisors
Fund Type: Growth
Inception Date: July 24, 2000

Data Date	Weiss Investment Rating	Net Assets ($Mil)	Price	Performance Rating/Pts	Total Return Y-T-D	Risk Rating/Pts
6-05	D	129.22	38.78	D- / 1.0	-2.13%	C+ / 6.8
2004	D-	109.74	39.80	E+ / 0.6	6.40%	C+ / 6.3
2003	E	68.55	37.37	E / 0.5	28.84%	D- / 1.2

Major Rating Factors:
Disappointing performance is the major factor driving the D (Weak) Weiss Investment Rating for iShares Russell 3000 Growth. The fund currently has a performance rating of D- (Weak) based on an annualized return of 6.96% over the last three years and a total return of -2.13% year to date 2005. Factored into the performance evaluation is an expense ratio of 0.25% (very low).

The fund's risk rating is currently C+ (Fair). It carries a beta of 1.02, meaning that its performance tracks fairly well with that of the overall stock market. Volatility, as measured by standard deviation, is considered low for equity funds at 14.76. As of June 30, 2005, iShares Russell 3000 Growth traded at a premium of .05% above its net asset value, which is worse than its one-year historical average premium of .02%.

Index Strategies Group has been running the fund for 5 years and currently receives a manager quality ranking of 52 (0=worst, 99=best). This fund offers only a moderate level of risk but investors looking for strong performance are still waiting.

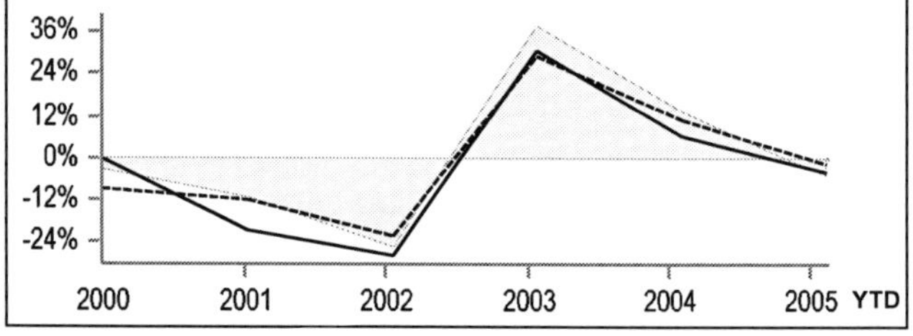

iShares Russell 3000 Value (IWW) — C- Fair

Fund Family: Barclays Global Fund Advisors
Fund Type: Growth
Inception Date: July 24, 2000

Data Date	Weiss Investment Rating	Net Assets ($Mil)	Price	Performance Rating/Pts	Total Return Y-T-D	Risk Rating/Pts
6-05	C-	364.05	86.82	C- / 3.0	1.21%	B- / 7.1
2004	C+	244.36	86.66	C / 5.4	16.70%	C+ / 6.9
2003	D+	130.08	74.61	D+ / 2.8	29.05%	C+ / 6.3

Major Rating Factors:
Middle of the road best describes iShares Russell 3000 Value whose Weiss Investment Rating is currently a C- (Fair). The fund currently has a performance rating of C- (Fair) based on an annualized return of 10.71% over the last three years and a total return of 1.21% year to date 2005. Factored into the performance evaluation is an expense ratio of 0.25% (very low).

The fund's risk rating is currently B- (Good). It carries a beta of 1.02, meaning that its performance tracks fairly well with that of the overall stock market. Volatility, as measured by standard deviation, is considered low for equity funds at 14.74. As of June 30, 2005, iShares Russell 3000 Value traded at a discount of .08% below its net asset value, which is better than its one-year historical average premium of .03%.

Index Strategies Group has been running the fund for 5 years and currently receives a manager quality ranking of 74 (0=worst, 99=best). If you desire an average level of risk, then this fund may be an option.

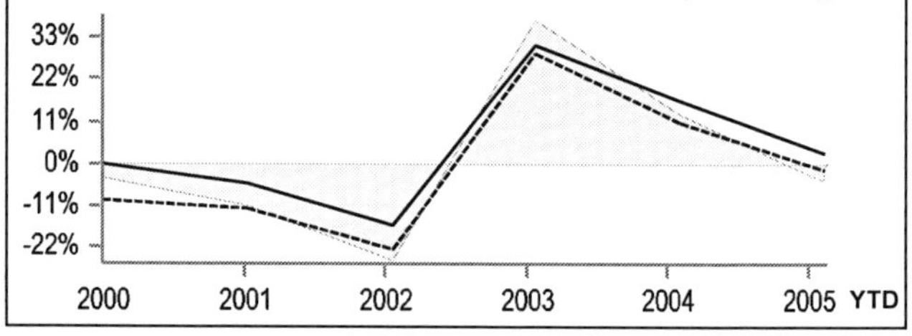

iShares Russell Midcap Growth Index (IWP) — C Fair

Fund Family: Barclays Global Fund Advisors
Fund Type: Growth
Inception Date: July 17, 2001

Data Date	Weiss Investment Rating	Net Assets ($Mil)	Price	Performance Rating/Pts	Total Return Y-T-D	Risk Rating/Pts
6-05	C	842.05	84.87	C / 4.6	0.63%	C+ / 6.4
2004	D	590.82	84.50	C- / 3.7	15.00%	C- / 4.0

Major Rating Factors:
Middle of the road best describes iShares Russell Midcap Growth Index whose Weiss Investment Rating is currently a C (Fair). The fund currently has a performance rating of C (Fair) based on an annualized return of 14.36% over the last three years and a total return of 0.63% year to date 2005. Factored into the performance evaluation is an expense ratio of 0.25% (very low).

The fund's risk rating is currently C+ (Fair). It carries a beta of 1.06, meaning that its performance tracks fairly well with that of the overall stock market. Volatility, as measured by standard deviation, is considered low for equity funds at 16.39. As of June 30, 2005, iShares Russell Midcap Growth Index traded at a premium of .07% above its net asset value, which is worse than its one-year historical average premium of .04%.

Index Strategies Group has been running the fund for 4 years and currently receives a manager quality ranking of 83 (0=worst, 99=best). If you desire an average level of risk, then this fund may be an option.

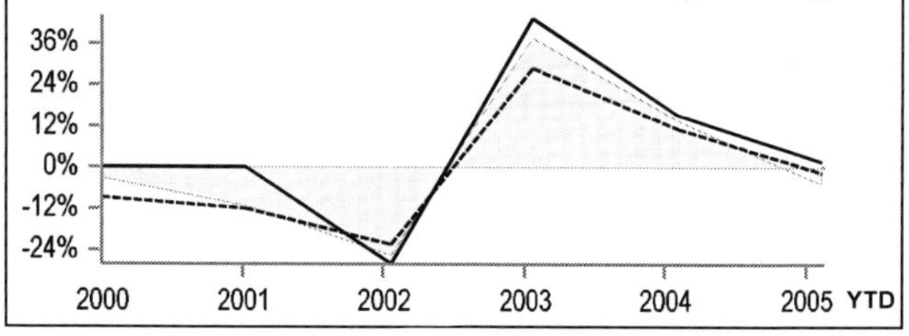

iShares Russell Midcap Index (IWR) C+ Fair

Fund Family: Barclays Global Fund Advisors
Fund Type: Growth
Inception Date: July 17, 2001

Data Date	Weiss Investment Rating	Net Assets ($Mil)	Price	Performance Rating/Pts	Total Return Y-T-D	Risk Rating/Pts
6-05	C+	1202.45	81.12	C+ / 5.7	2.96%	C+ / 6.9
2004	B	831.13	79.33	B- / 7.1	19.63%	C+ / 6.8

Major Rating Factors:
Middle of the road best describes iShares Russell Midcap Index whose Weiss Investment Rating is currently a C+ (Fair). The fund currently has a performance rating of C+ (Fair) based on an annualized return of 15.47% over the last three years and a total return of 2.96% year to date 2005. Factored into the performance evaluation is an expense ratio of 0.20% (very low).

The fund's risk rating is currently C+ (Fair). It carries a beta of 0.97, meaning that its performance tracks fairly well with that of the overall stock market. Volatility, as measured by standard deviation, is considered low for equity funds at 14.78. As of June 30, 2005, iShares Russell Midcap Index traded at a discount of .04% below its net asset value, which is better than its one-year historical average premium of .03%.

Index Strategies Group has been running the fund for 4 years and currently receives a manager quality ranking of 87 (0=worst, 99=best). If you desire an average level of risk, then this fund may be an option.

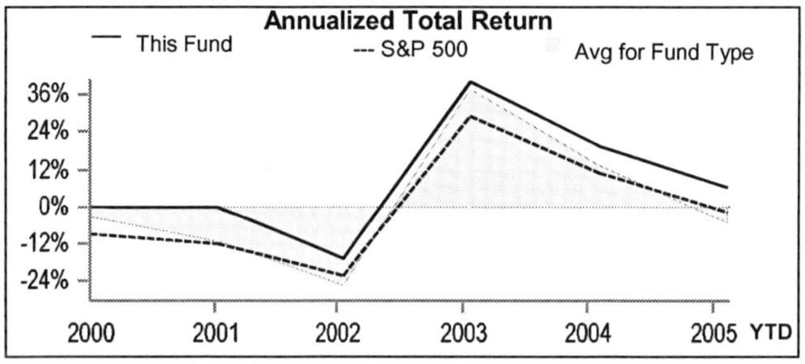

iShares Russell Midcap Value Index (IWS) B- Good

Fund Family: Barclays Global Fund Advisors
Fund Type: Growth
Inception Date: July 17, 2001

Data Date	Weiss Investment Rating	Net Assets ($Mil)	Price	Performance Rating/Pts	Total Return Y-T-D	Risk Rating/Pts
6-05	B-	1148.61	116.86	C+ / 6.5	4.52%	B- / 7.0
2004	A-	670.24	112.81	B / 8.2	22.97%	B- / 7.0

Major Rating Factors:
iShares Russell Midcap Value Index receives a Weiss Investment Rating of B- (Good). The fund currently has a performance rating of C+ (Fair) based on an annualized return of 16.11% over the last three years and a total return of 4.52% year to date 2005. Factored into the performance evaluation is an expense ratio of 0.25% (very low).

The fund's risk rating is currently B- (Good). It carries a beta of 0.95, meaning that its performance tracks fairly well with that of the overall stock market. Volatility, as measured by standard deviation, is considered low for equity funds at 14.72. As of June 30, 2005, iShares Russell Midcap Value Index traded at a discount of .09% below its net asset value, which is better than its one-year historical average premium of .03%.

Index Strategies Group has been running the fund for 4 years and currently receives a manager quality ranking of 88 (0=worst, 99=best). If you desire an average level of risk, then this fund may be an option.

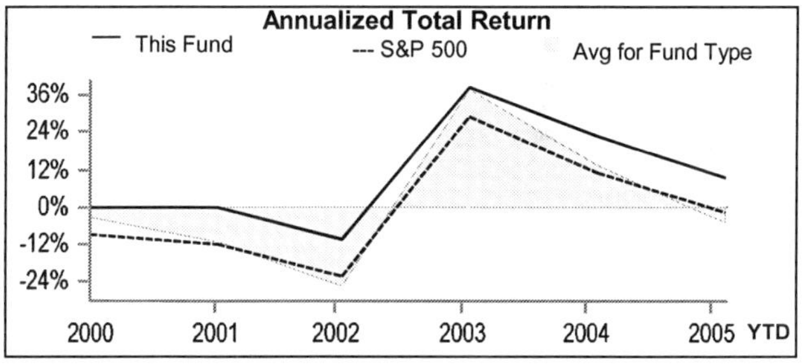

iShares S&P 100 Index Fund (OEF) D+ Weak

Fund Family: Barclays Global Fund Advisors
Fund Type: Income
Inception Date: October 23, 2000

Data Date	Weiss Investment Rating	Net Assets ($Mil)	Price	Performance Rating/Pts	Total Return Y-T-D	Risk Rating/Pts
6-05	D+	795.42	55.77	E+ / 0.8	-1.92%	B- / 7.8
2004	D-	689.53	57.38	E+ / 0.9	6.41%	C+ / 5.9
2003	E+	382.62	54.33	E+ / 0.7	24.23%	C- / 3.3

Major Rating Factors:
Very poor performance is the major factor driving the D+ (Weak) Weiss Investment Rating for iShares S&P 100 Index Fund. The fund currently has a performance rating of E+ (Very Weak) based on an annualized return of 6.35% over the last three years and a total return of -1.92% year to date 2005. Factored into the performance evaluation is an expense ratio of 0.20% (very low).

The fund's risk rating is currently B- (Good). It carries a beta of 1.01, meaning that its performance tracks fairly well with that of the overall stock market. Volatility, as measured by both the semi-deviation and a drawdown factor, is considered low. As of June 30, 2005, iShares S&P 100 Index Fund traded at a discount of .13% below its net asset value.

Index Strategies Group has been running the fund for 5 years and currently receives a manager quality ranking of 45 (0=worst, 99=best). This fund offers only a moderate level of risk but investors looking for strong performance are still waiting.

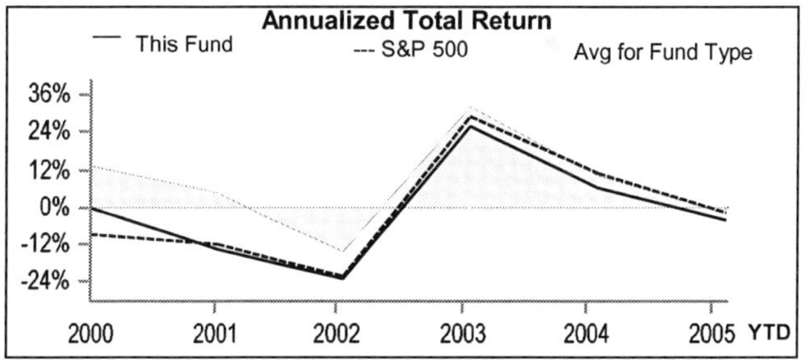

iShares S&P 500 (IVV) D+ Weak

Fund Family: Barclays Global Fund Advisors
Fund Type: Growth
Inception Date: May 15, 2000

Data Date	Weiss Investment Rating	Net Assets ($Mil)	Price	Performance Rating/Pts	Total Return Y-T-D	Risk Rating/Pts
6-05	D+	12513.83	119.00	D / 1.8	-0.71%	B- / 7.3
2004	D	9804.88	121.00	D / 1.8	10.77%	C+ / 6.9
2003	D-	6356.92	109.79	E+ / 0.9	26.33%	C- / 4.0

Major Rating Factors:
Disappointing performance is the major factor driving the D+ (Weak) Weiss Investment Rating for iShares S&P 500. The fund currently has a performance rating of D (Weak) based on an annualized return of 8.23% over the last three years and a total return of -0.71% year to date 2005. Factored into the performance evaluation is an expense ratio of 0.09% (very low).

The fund's risk rating is currently B- (Good). It carries a beta of 0.97, meaning that its performance tracks fairly well with that of the overall stock market. Volatility, as measured by standard deviation, is considered low for equity funds at 13.67. As of June 30, 2005, iShares S&P 500 traded at a discount of .07% below its net asset value, which is better than its one-year historical average premium of .02%.

Index Strategies Group has been running the fund for 5 years and currently receives a manager quality ranking of 63 (0=worst, 99=best). This fund offers only a moderate level of risk but investors looking for strong performance are still waiting.

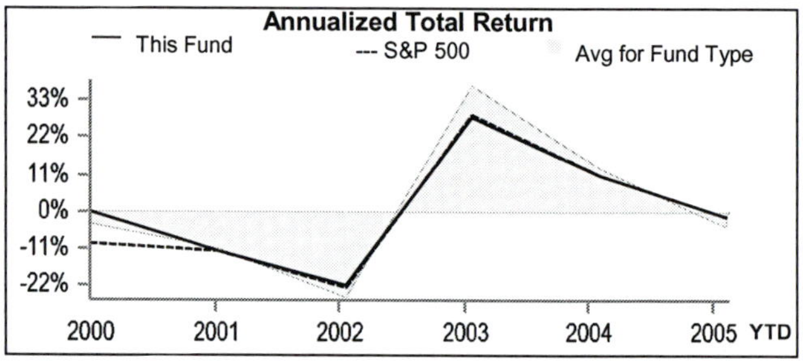

iShares S&P 500/Barra Growth (IVW) D Weak

Fund Family: Barclays Global Fund Advisors
Fund Type: Growth
Inception Date: May 22, 2000

Data Date	Weiss Investment Rating	Net Assets ($Mil)	Price	Performance Rating/Pts	Total Return Y-T-D	Risk Rating/Pts
6-05	D	2341.10	56.50	E+ / 0.7	-1.51%	B- / 7.3
2004	D-	1802.20	57.75	E+ / 0.6	5.66%	B- / 7.0
2003	D-	998.49	54.84	E+ / 0.7	23.58%	C- / 3.5

Major Rating Factors:
Very poor performance is the major factor driving the D (Weak) Weiss Investment Rating for iShares S&P 500/Barra Growth. The fund currently has a performance rating of E+ (Very Weak) based on an annualized return of 5.94% over the last three years and a total return of -1.51% year to date 2005. Factored into the performance evaluation is an expense ratio of 0.18% (very low).

The fund's risk rating is currently B- (Good). It carries a beta of 0.92, meaning that its performance tracks fairly well with that of the overall stock market. Volatility, as measured by standard deviation, is considered low for equity funds at 13.22. As of June 30, 2005, iShares S&P 500/Barra Growth traded at a premium of .02% above its net asset value, which is better than its one-year historical average premium of .06%.

Index Strategies Group has been running the fund for 5 years and currently receives a manager quality ranking of 47 (0=worst, 99=best). This fund offers only a moderate level of risk but investors looking for strong performance are still waiting.

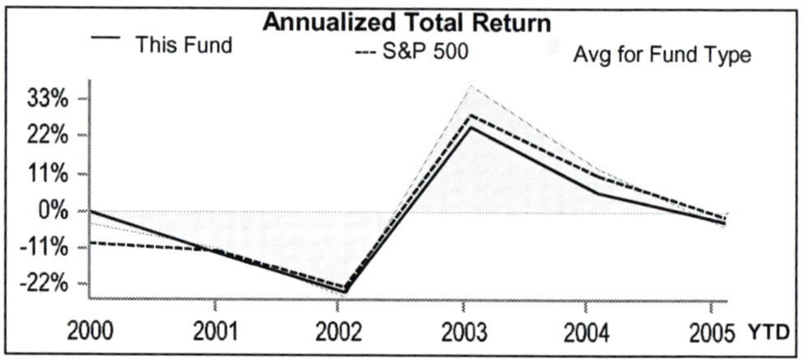

iShares S&P 500/Barra Value (IVE) D+ Weak

Fund Family: Barclays Global Fund Advisors
Fund Type: Growth
Inception Date: May 22, 2000

Data Date	Weiss Investment Rating	Net Assets ($Mil)	Price	Performance Rating/Pts	Total Return Y-T-D	Risk Rating/Pts
6-05	D+	2704.49	62.17	D+ / 2.6	-0.01%	C+ / 6.7
2004	C-	2494.31	62.88	C- / 3.6	15.62%	C+ / 6.3
2003	D-	1159.07	54.65	D- / 1.2	29.35%	C- / 3.7

Major Rating Factors:
Disappointing performance is the major factor driving the D+ (Weak) Weiss Investment Rating for iShares S&P 500/Barra Value. The fund currently has a performance rating of D+ (Weak) based on an annualized return of 9.91% over the last three years and a total return of -0.01% year to date 2005. Factored into the performance evaluation is an expense ratio of 0.18% (very low).

The fund's risk rating is currently C+ (Fair). It carries a beta of 1.09, meaning that its performance tracks fairly well with that of the overall stock market. Volatility, as measured by standard deviation, is considered low for equity funds at 15.85. As of June 30, 2005, iShares S&P 500/Barra Value traded at a discount of .06% below its net asset value, which is better than its one-year historical average premium of .03%.

Index Strategies Group has been running the fund for 5 years and currently receives a manager quality ranking of 68 (0=worst, 99=best). This fund offers only a moderate level of risk but investors looking for strong performance are still waiting.

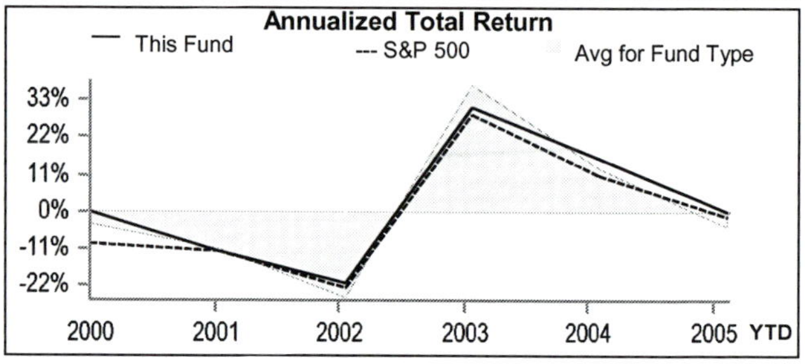

iShares S&P Europe 350 Index Fund (IEV) E+ Very Weak

Fund Family: Barclays Global Fund Advisors
Fund Type: Foreign
Inception Date: July 25, 2000

Data Date	Weiss Investment Rating	Net Assets ($Mil)	Price	Performance Rating/Pts	Total Return Y-T-D	Risk Rating/Pts
6-05	E+	1182.05	74.40	C- / 3.1	-1.13%	C- / 3.4
2004	C-	851.92	75.25	C+ / 6.7	19.40%	C- / 3.9
2003	D-	512.12	63.30	D- / 1.4	35.70%	D+ / 2.9

Major Rating Factors:
iShares S&P Europe 350 Index Fund receives a Weiss Investment Rating of E+ (Very Weak). The fund currently has a performance rating of C- (Fair) based on an annualized return of 11.71% over the last three years and a total return of -1.13% year to date 2005. Factored into the performance evaluation is an expense ratio of 0.60% (very low).

The fund's risk rating is currently C- (Fair). It carries a beta of 1.08, meaning that its performance tracks fairly well with that of the overall stock market. Volatility, as measured by standard deviation, is considered average for equity funds at 17.55. As of June 30, 2005, iShares S&P Europe 350 Index Fund traded at a discount of .32% below its net asset value, which is better than its one-year historical average premium of .35%.

Index Strategies Group has been running the fund for 5 years and currently receives a manager quality ranking of 49 (0=worst, 99=best). If you desire an average level of risk, then this fund may be an option.

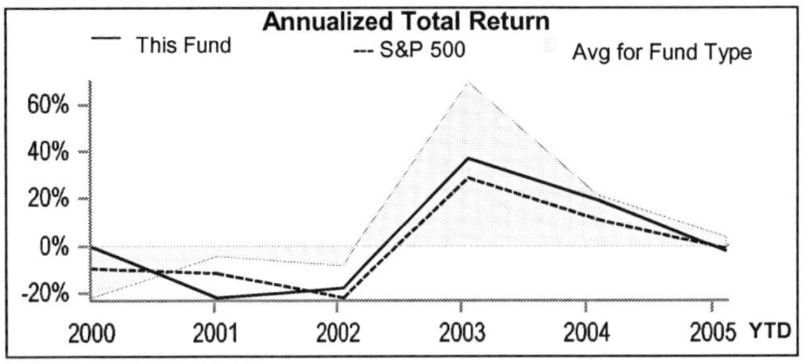

iShares S&P Global 100 (IOO) D Weak

Fund Family: Barclays Global Fund Advisors
Fund Type: Income
Inception Date: December 5, 2000

Data Date	Weiss Investment Rating	Net Assets ($Mil)	Price	Performance Rating/Pts	Total Return Y-T-D	Risk Rating/Pts
6-05	D	342.78	60.30	D- / 1.4	-1.95%	C+ / 6.8
2004	D-	189.31	61.50	D- / 1.1	8.93%	C+ / 6.5

Major Rating Factors:
Disappointing performance is the major factor driving the D (Weak) Weiss Investment Rating for iShares S&P Global 100. The fund currently has a performance rating of D- (Weak) based on an annualized return of 7.89% over the last three years and a total return of -1.95% year to date 2005. Factored into the performance evaluation is an expense ratio of 0.40% (very low).

The fund's risk rating is currently C+ (Fair). It carries a beta of 1.07, meaning that its performance tracks fairly well with that of the overall stock market. Volatility, as measured by standard deviation, is considered low for equity funds at 15.52. As of June 30, 2005, iShares S&P Global 100 traded at a premium of .08% above its net asset value, which is better than its one-year historical average premium of .11%.

Index Strategies Group has been running the fund for 5 years and currently receives a manager quality ranking of 54 (0=worst, 99=best). This fund offers only a moderate level of risk but investors looking for strong performance are still waiting.

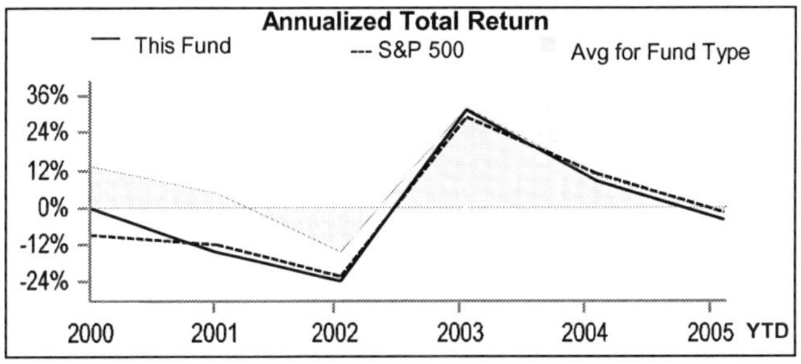

iShares S&P Global Energy Sector (IXC) B- Good

Fund Family: Barclays Global Fund Advisors
Fund Type: Energy/Natural Resources
Inception Date: November 12, 2001

Data Date	Weiss Investment Rating	Net Assets ($Mil)	Price	Performance Rating/Pts	Total Return Y-T-D	Risk Rating/Pts
6-05	B-	323.30	86.99	B+ / 8.9	18.92%	C / 4.5
2004	B+	223.31	73.15	B / 8.2	26.48%	C+ / 6.6

Major Rating Factors:
Strong performance is the major factor driving the B- (Good) Weiss Investment Rating for iShares S&P Global Energy Sector. The fund currently has a performance rating of B+ (Good) based on an annualized return of 19.50% over the last three years and a total return of 18.92% year to date 2005. Factored into the performance evaluation is an expense ratio of 0.65% (very low).

The fund's risk rating is currently C (Fair). It carries a beta of 0.90, meaning that its performance tracks fairly well with that of the overall stock market. Volatility, as measured by standard deviation, is considered average for equity funds at 17.89. As of June 30, 2005, iShares S&P Global Energy Sector traded at a premium of .06% above its net asset value, which is better than its one-year historical average premium of .22%.

Index Strategies Group has been running the fund for 4 years and currently receives a manager quality ranking of 66 (0=worst, 99=best). If you desire an average level of risk and strong performance, then this fund is a good option.

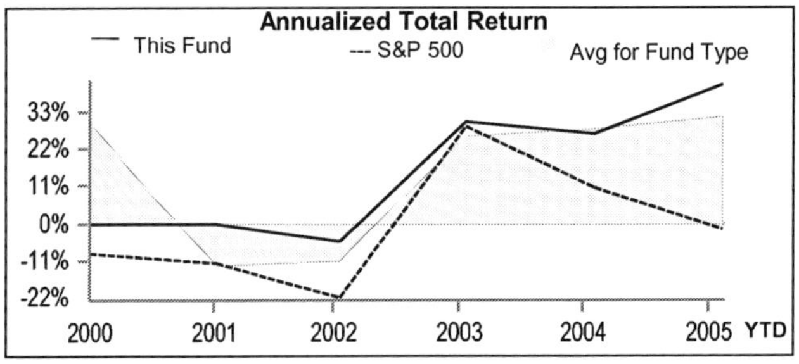

iShares S&P Global Financials Sect (IXG) E+ Very Weak

Fund Family: Barclays Global Fund Advisors
Fund Type: Financial Services
Inception Date: November 12, 2001

Major Rating Factors:
Disappointing performance is the major factor driving the E+ (Very Weak) Weiss Investment Rating for iShares S&P Global Financials Sect. The fund currently has a performance rating of D+ (Weak) based on an annualized return of 10.18% over the last three years and a total return of -2.91% year to date 2005. Factored into the performance evaluation is an expense ratio of 0.65% (very low).

The fund's risk rating is currently C- (Fair). It carries a beta of 1.25, meaning it is expected to move 12.5% for every 10% move in the market. Volatility, as measured by standard deviation, is considered average for equity funds at 19.48. As of June 30, 2005, iShares S&P Global Financials Sect traded at a premium of .32% above its net asset value, which is worse than its one-year historical average premium of .23%.

Index Strategies Group has been running the fund for 4 years and currently receives a manager quality ranking of 47 (0=worst, 99=best). This fund offers an average level of risk but investors looking for strong performance will be frustrated.

Data Date	Weiss Investment Rating	Net Assets ($Mil)	Price	Performance Rating/Pts	Total Return Y-T-D	Risk Rating/Pts
6-05	E+	70.64	65.00	D+ / 2.4	-2.91%	C- / 3.8
2004	C-	32.78	66.95	C+ / 6.4	16.30%	C- / 3.6

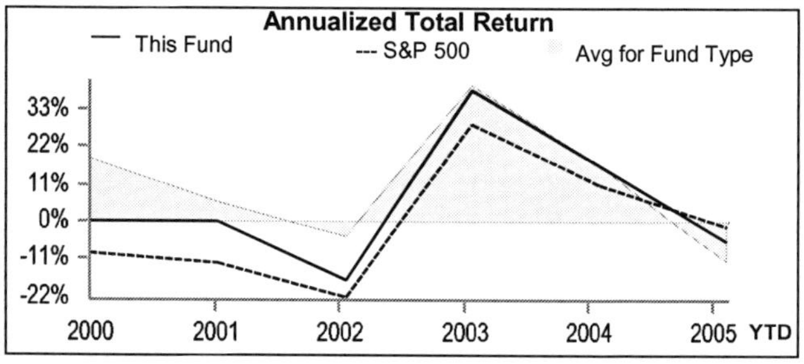

iShares S&P Global Healthcare Sect (IXJ) C- Fair

Fund Family: Barclays Global Fund Advisors
Fund Type: Health
Inception Date: November 13, 2001

Major Rating Factors:
Very poor performance is the major factor driving the C- (Fair) Weiss Investment Rating for iShares S&P Global Healthcare Sect. The fund currently has a performance rating of E+ (Very Weak) based on an annualized return of 5.35% over the last three years and a total return of 1.91% year to date 2005. Factored into the performance evaluation is an expense ratio of 0.65% (very low).

The fund's risk rating is currently B (Good). It carries a beta of 0.55, meaning the fund's expected move will be 5.5% for every 10% move in the market. Volatility, as measured by both the semi-deviation and a drawdown factor, is considered low. As of June 30, 2005, iShares S&P Global Healthcare Sect traded at a premium of .06% above its net asset value, which is better than its one-year historical average premium of .34%.

Index Strategies Group has been running the fund for 4 years and currently receives a manager quality ranking of 62 (0=worst, 99=best). This fund offers only a moderate level of risk but investors looking for strong performance are still waiting.

Data Date	Weiss Investment Rating	Net Assets ($Mil)	Price	Performance Rating/Pts	Total Return Y-T-D	Risk Rating/Pts
6-05	C-	228.61	50.15	E+ / 0.8	1.91%	B / 8.9
2004	D	141.61	49.21	E+ / 0.7	3.98%	B- / 7.0

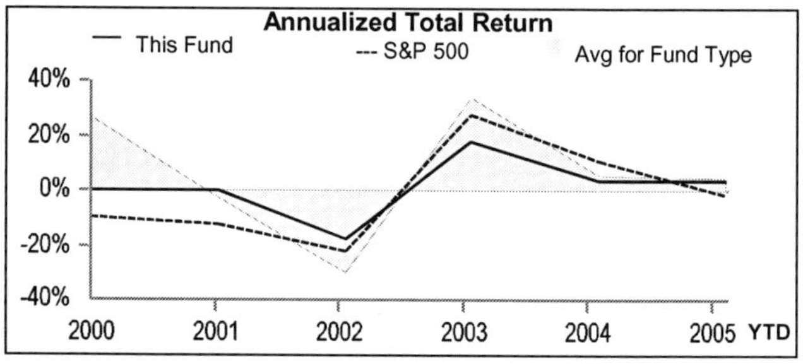

iShares S&P Global Technology Sect (IXN) E- Very Weak

Fund Family: Barclays Global Fund Advisors
Fund Type: Global
Inception Date: November 12, 2001

Major Rating Factors:
iShares S&P Global Technology Sect has adopted a very risky asset allocation strategy and currently receives an overall Weiss Investment Rating of E- (Very Weak). The fund has a high level of volatility, with a standard deviation of 26.50. It carries a beta of 1.33, meaning it is expected to move 13.3% for every 10% move in the market. As of June 30, 2005, iShares S&P Global Technology Sect traded at a premium of .06% above its net asset value, which is better than its one-year historical average premium of .36%. Unfortunately, the high level of risk (D-, Weak) failed to pay off as investors endured poor performance.

The fund's performance rating is currently D- (Weak). It has registered an annualized return of 8.50% over the last three years but is down -5.28% year to date 2005. Factored into the performance evaluation is an expense ratio of 0.66% (very low).

Index Strategies Group has been running the fund for 4 years and currently receives a manager quality ranking of 6 (0=worst, 99=best). If you can tolerate very high levels of risk in the hope of improved future returns, holding this fund may be an option.

Data Date	Weiss Investment Rating	Net Assets ($Mil)	Price	Performance Rating/Pts	Total Return Y-T-D	Risk Rating/Pts
6-05	E-	42.89	48.77	D- / 1.1	-5.28%	D- / 1.4
2004	E-	25.17	51.49	E- / 0.2	2.82%	D- / 1.4

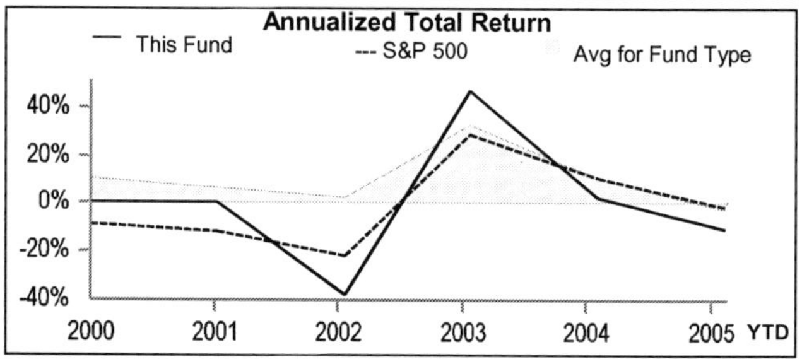

iShares S&P Global Telecomm Sect (IXP) D- Weak

Fund Family: Barclays Global Fund Advisors
Fund Type: Global
Inception Date: November 12, 2001

Data Date	Weiss Investment Rating	Net Assets ($Mil)	Price	Performance Rating/Pts	Total Return Y-T-D	Risk Rating/Pts
6-05	D-	42.50	49.24	C- / 3.6	-7.95%	C- / 3.3
2004	E	20.73	53.49	D / 2.0	18.96%	E- / 0.0

Major Rating Factors:
iShares S&P Global Telecomm Sect receives a Weiss Investment Rating of D- (Weak). The fund currently has a performance rating of C- (Fair) based on an annualized return of 13.07% over the last three years and a total return of -7.95% year to date 2005. Factored into the performance evaluation is an expense ratio of 0.65% (very low).

The fund's risk rating is currently C- (Fair). It carries a beta of 1.08, meaning that its performance tracks fairly well with that of the overall stock market. Volatility, as measured by standard deviation, is considered average for equity funds at 20.83. As of June 30, 2005, iShares S&P Global Telecomm Sect traded at a premium of .29% above its net asset value, which is better than its one-year historical average premium of .32%.

Index Strategies Group has been running the fund for 4 years and currently receives a manager quality ranking of 60 (0=worst, 99=best). If you desire an average level of risk, then this fund may be an option.

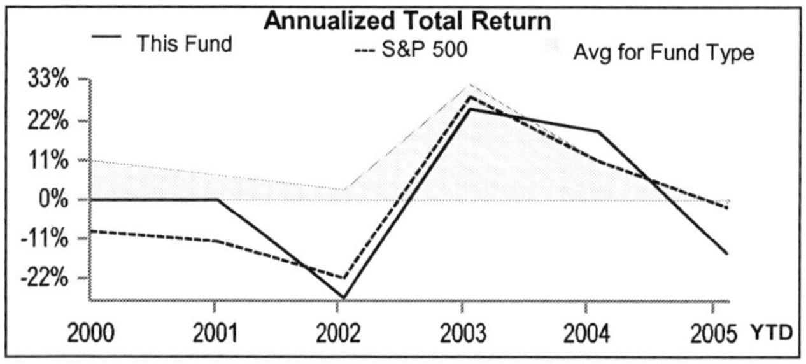

iShares S&P Latin American 40 Idx (ILF) C- Fair

Fund Family: Barclays Global Fund Advisors
Fund Type: Foreign
Inception Date: October 25, 2001

Data Date	Weiss Investment Rating	Net Assets ($Mil)	Price	Performance Rating/Pts	Total Return Y-T-D	Risk Rating/Pts
6-05	C-	335.56	90.69	A+ / 9.8	12.59%	E- / 0.0
2004	C-	106.00	80.55	A- / 9.0	38.51%	D- / 1.0

Major Rating Factors:
iShares S&P Latin American 40 Idx has adopted a very risky asset allocation strategy and currently receives an overall Weiss Investment Rating of C- (Fair). The fund has shown a high level of volatility, with a standard deviation of 25.91. It carries a beta of 1.37, meaning it is expected to move 13.7% for every 10% move in the market. As of June 30, 2005, iShares S&P Latin American 40 Idx traded at a premium of .49% above its net asset value, which is better than its one-year historical average premium of .58%. The high level of risk (E-, Very Weak) did however, reward investors with excellent performance.

The fund's performance rating is currently A+ (Excellent). It has registered an annualized return of 32.02% over the last three years and is up 12.59% year to date 2005. Factored into the performance evaluation is an expense ratio of 0.50% (very low).

Index Strategies Group has been running the fund for 4 years and currently receives a manager quality ranking of 94 (0=worst, 99=best). If you are comfortable owning a very high risk investment, this fund may be an option.

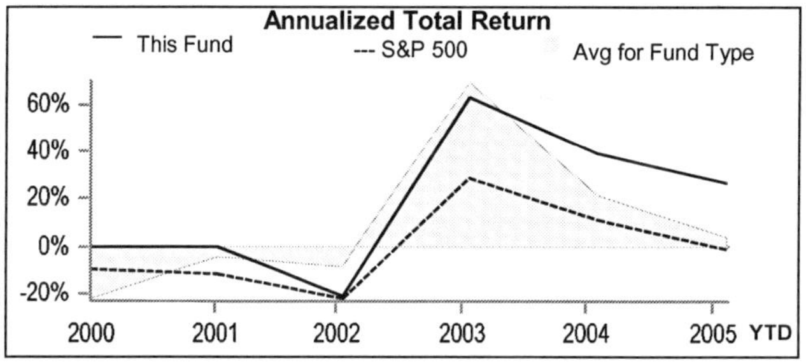

iShares S&P MidCap 400 (IJH) C Fair

Fund Family: Barclays Global Fund Advisors
Fund Type: Growth
Inception Date: May 22, 2000

Data Date	Weiss Investment Rating	Net Assets ($Mil)	Price	Performance Rating/Pts	Total Return Y-T-D	Risk Rating/Pts
6-05	C	2416.34	67.60	C- / 4.1	2.76%	C+ / 6.9
2004	C+	1916.96	132.32	C+ / 5.8	16.07%	C+ / 6.9
2003	D	1077.58	114.79	C / 4.3	34.57%	C- / 3.4

Major Rating Factors:
Middle of the road best describes iShares S&P MidCap 400 whose Weiss Investment Rating is currently a C (Fair). The fund currently has a performance rating of C- (Fair) based on an annualized return of 12.50% over the last three years and a total return of 2.76% year to date 2005. Factored into the performance evaluation is an expense ratio of 0.20% (very low).

The fund's risk rating is currently C+ (Fair). It carries a beta of 0.95, meaning that its performance tracks fairly well with that of the overall stock market. Volatility, as measured by standard deviation, is considered low for equity funds at 14.71. As of June 30, 2005, iShares S&P MidCap 400 traded at a discount of .12% below its net asset value.

Index Strategies Group has been running the fund for 5 years and currently receives a manager quality ranking of 81 (0=worst, 99=best). If you desire an average level of risk, then this fund may be an option.

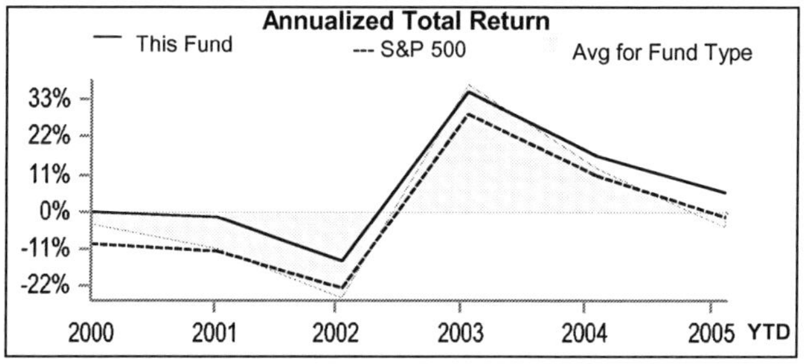

iShares S&P MidCap 400/Barra Growth (IJK) C- Fair

Fund Family: Barclays Global Fund Advisors
Fund Type: Growth
Inception Date: July 24, 2000

Major Rating Factors:
Middle of the road best describes iShares S&P MidCap 400/Barra Growth whose Weiss Investment Rating is currently a C- (Fair). The fund currently has a performance rating of C- (Fair) based on an annualized return of 10.95% over the last three years and a total return of 2.26% year to date 2005. Factored into the performance evaluation is an expense ratio of 0.25% (very low).

The fund's risk rating is currently B- (Good). It carries a beta of 0.83, meaning the fund's expected move will be 8.3% for every 10% move in the market. Volatility, as measured by standard deviation, is considered low for equity funds at 13.49. As of June 30, 2005, iShares S&P MidCap 400/Barra Growth traded at a discount of .09% below its net asset value, which is better than its one-year historical average discount of .01%.

Index Strategies Group has been running the fund for 5 years and currently receives a manager quality ranking of 80 (0=worst, 99=best). If you desire an average level of risk, then this fund may be an option.

Data Date	Weiss Investment Rating	Net Assets ($Mil)	Price	Performance Rating/Pts	Total Return Y-T-D	Risk Rating/Pts
6-05	C-	1112.26	68.46	C- / 3.0	2.26%	B- / 7.2
2004	C-	914.39	134.40	C- / 3.6	13.75%	B- / 7.0
2003	E+	476.92	118.19	D- / 1.4	29.75%	D+ / 2.6

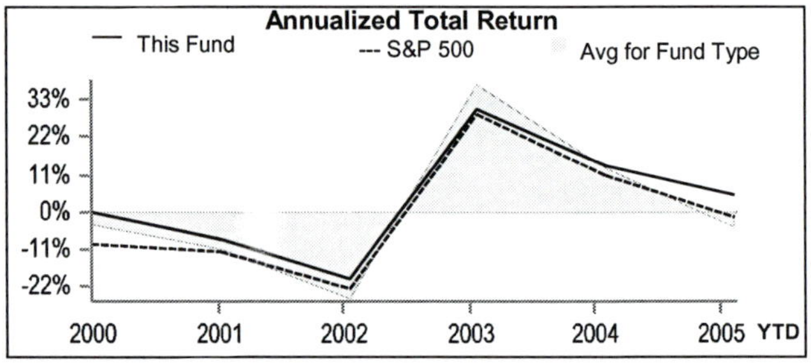

iShares S&P MidCap 400/Barra Value (IJJ) C Fair

Fund Family: Barclays Global Fund Advisors
Fund Type: Growth
Inception Date: July 24, 2000

Major Rating Factors:
Middle of the road best describes iShares S&P MidCap 400/Barra Value whose Weiss Investment Rating is currently a C (Fair). The fund currently has a performance rating of C (Fair) based on an annualized return of 13.82% over the last three years and a total return of 2.98% year to date 2005. Factored into the performance evaluation is an expense ratio of 0.25% (very low).

The fund's risk rating is currently C+ (Fair). It carries a beta of 1.01, meaning that its performance tracks fairly well with that of the overall stock market. Volatility, as measured by standard deviation, is considered low for equity funds at 15.84. As of June 30, 2005, iShares S&P MidCap 400/Barra Value traded at a discount of .11% below its net asset value, which is better than its one-year historical average discount of .01%.

Index Strategies Group has been running the fund for 5 years and currently receives a manager quality ranking of 83 (0=worst, 99=best). If you desire an average level of risk, then this fund may be an option.

Data Date	Weiss Investment Rating	Net Assets ($Mil)	Price	Performance Rating/Pts	Total Return Y-T-D	Risk Rating/Pts
6-05	C	1852.99	65.64	C / 4.8	2.98%	C+ / 6.6
2004	B	1429.54	128.50	B- / 7.3	17.92%	C+ / 6.6
2003	C-	740.41	109.30	B- / 7.1	38.53%	C- / 3.7

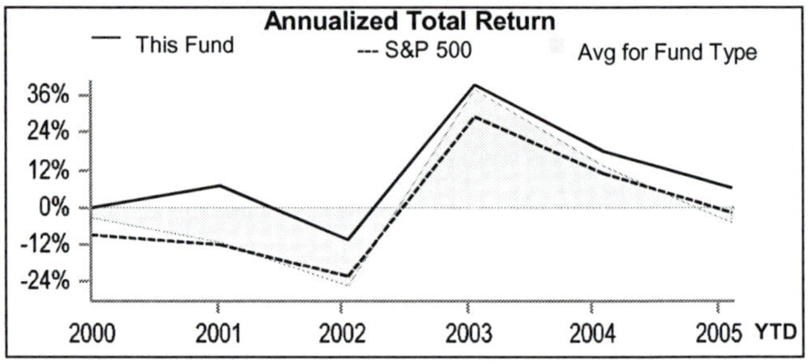

iShares S&P SmallCap 600 (IJR) D Weak

Fund Family: Barclays Global Fund Advisors
Fund Type: Growth
Inception Date: May 22, 2000

Major Rating Factors:
iShares S&P SmallCap 600 receives a Weiss Investment Rating of D (Weak). The fund currently has a performance rating of C- (Fair) based on an annualized return of 12.95% over the last three years and a total return of -0.49% year to date 2005. Factored into the performance evaluation is an expense ratio of 0.20% (very low).

The fund's risk rating is currently C (Fair). It carries a beta of 1.00, meaning that its performance tracks fairly well with that of the overall stock market. Volatility, as measured by standard deviation, is considered average for equity funds at 17.36. As of June 30, 2005, iShares S&P SmallCap 600 traded at a discount of .44% below its net asset value, which is better than its one-year historical average discount of .05%.

Index Strategies Group has been running the fund for 5 years and currently receives a manager quality ranking of 82 (0=worst, 99=best). If you desire an average level of risk, then this fund may be an option.

Data Date	Weiss Investment Rating	Net Assets ($Mil)	Price	Performance Rating/Pts	Total Return Y-T-D	Risk Rating/Pts
6-05	D	3245.47	53.70	C- / 4.0	-0.49%	C / 4.4
2004	C	2437.65	162.71	B- / 7.3	22.39%	C / 4.4
2003	D+	1646.16	133.98	C+ / 6.5	38.47%	D+ / 2.9

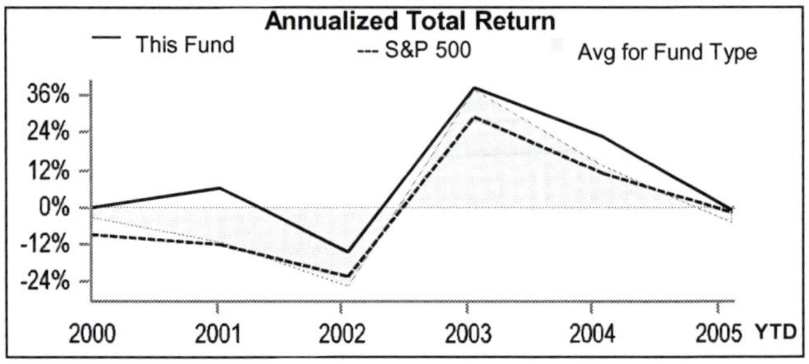

iShares S&P SmallCap 600/Barra Gwth (IJT) C Fair

Fund Family: Barclays Global Fund Advisors
Fund Type: Growth
Inception Date: July 24, 2000

Data Date	Weiss Investment Rating	Net Assets ($Mil)	Price	Performance Rating/Pts	Total Return Y-T-D	Risk Rating/Pts
6-05	C	990.54	106.60	C / 4.4	-0.13%	C+ / 6.3
2004	C	755.92	107.10	B- / 7.0	21.16%	C / 4.7
2003	D	499.23	88.32	C / 4.4	36.27%	D+ / 2.9

Major Rating Factors:
Middle of the road best describes iShares S&P SmallCap 600/Barra Gwth whose Weiss Investment Rating is currently a C (Fair). The fund currently has a performance rating of C (Fair) based on an annualized return of 14.19% over the last three years and a total return of -0.13% year to date 2005. Factored into the performance evaluation is an expense ratio of 0.25% (very low).

The fund's risk rating is currently C+ (Fair). It carries a beta of 0.96, meaning that its performance tracks fairly well with that of the overall stock market. Volatility, as measured by standard deviation, is considered low for equity funds at 16.53. As of June 30, 2005, iShares S&P SmallCap 600/Barra Gwth traded at a discount of .20% below its net asset value, which is better than its one-year historical average discount of .01%.

Index Strategies Group has been running the fund for 5 years and currently receives a manager quality ranking of 85 (0=worst, 99=best). If you desire an average level of risk, then this fund may be an option.

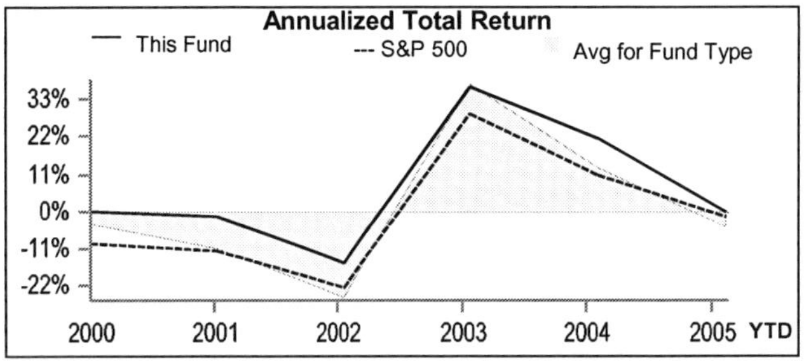

iShares S&P SmallCap 600/BarraValue (IJS) D- Weak

Fund Family: Barclays Global Fund Advisors
Fund Type: Growth
Inception Date: July 24, 2000

Data Date	Weiss Investment Rating	Net Assets ($Mil)	Price	Performance Rating/Pts	Total Return Y-T-D	Risk Rating/Pts
6-05	D-	1572.41	60.43	C- / 3.2	-0.24%	C- / 3.8
2004	C	1281.61	121.80	B- / 7.4	22.57%	C- / 3.8
2003	D+	687.10	100.39	B- / 7.2	39.25%	D+ / 2.4

Major Rating Factors:
iShares S&P SmallCap 600/BarraValue receives a Weiss Investment Rating of D - (Weak). The fund currently has a performance rating of C- (Fair) based on an annualized return of 11.52% over the last three years and a total return of -0.24% year to date 2005. Factored into the performance evaluation is an expense ratio of 0.25% (very low).

The fund's risk rating is currently C- (Fair). It carries a beta of 1.10, meaning it is expected to move 11.0% for every 10% move in the market. Volatility, as measured by standard deviation, is considered average for equity funds at 18.86. As of June 30, 2005, iShares S&P SmallCap 600/BarraValue traded at a discount of .21% below its net asset value, which is better than its one-year historical average discount of .05%.

Index Strategies Group has been running the fund for 5 years and currently receives a manager quality ranking of 76 (0=worst, 99=best). If you desire an average level of risk, then this fund may be an option.

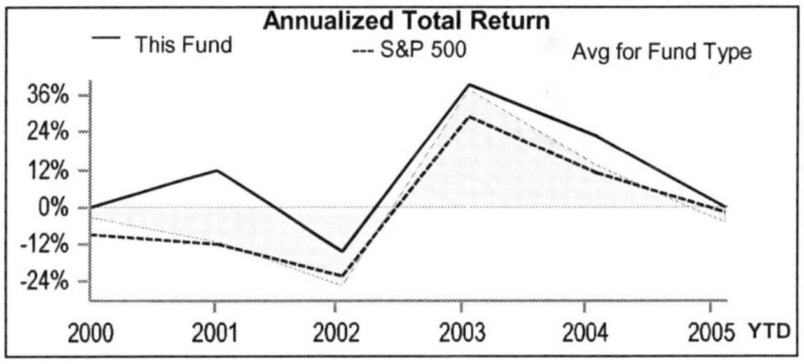

iShares S&P/Topix 150 Index Fund (ITF) E Very Weak

Fund Family: Barclays Global Fund Advisors
Fund Type: Foreign
Inception Date: October 23, 2001

Data Date	Weiss Investment Rating	Net Assets ($Mil)	Price	Performance Rating/Pts	Total Return Y-T-D	Risk Rating/Pts
6-05	E	95.25	88.09	E+ / 0.6	-6.18%	C- / 3.6
2004	D-	87.64	93.89	C / 4.8	12.68%	D / 2.1

Major Rating Factors:
Very poor performance is the major factor driving the E (Very Weak) Weiss Investment Rating for iShares S&P/Topix 150 Index Fund. The fund currently has a performance rating of E+ (Very Weak) based on an annualized return of 6.76% over the last three years and a total return of -6.18% year to date 2005. Factored into the performance evaluation is an expense ratio of 0.50% (very low).

The fund's risk rating is currently C- (Fair). It carries a beta of 0.54, meaning the fund's expected move will be 5.4% for every 10% move in the market. Volatility, as measured by standard deviation, is considered average for equity funds at 17.06. As of June 30, 2005, iShares S&P/Topix 150 Index Fund traded at a discount of .22% below its net asset value, which is better than its one-year historical average premium of .14%.

Index Strategies Group has been running the fund for 4 years and currently receives a manager quality ranking of 55 (0=worst, 99=best). This fund offers an average level of risk but investors looking for strong performance will be frustrated.

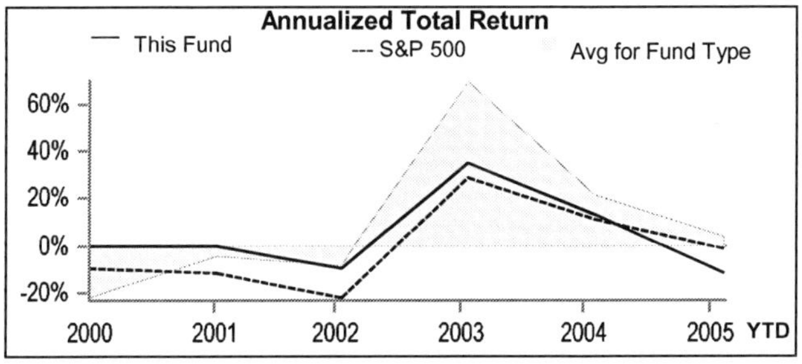

J Hancock Bank & Thrift Oppty Fd (BTO) C+ Fair

Fund Family: John Hancock Advisors,LLC
Fund Type: Financial Services
Inception Date: August 16, 1994

Major Rating Factors:
Middle of the road best describes J Hancock Bank & Thrift Oppty Fd whose Weiss Investment Rating is currently a C+ (Fair). The fund currently has a performance rating of C+ (Fair) based on an annualized return of 16.97% over the last three years and a total return of -4.06% year to date 2005. Factored into the performance evaluation is an expense ratio of 1.32% (average).

The fund's risk rating is currently C+ (Fair). It carries a beta of 0.90, meaning that its performance tracks fairly well with that of the overall stock market. Volatility, as measured by both the semi-deviation and a drawdown factor, is considered low. As of June 30, 2005, J Hancock Bank & Thrift Oppty Fd traded at a discount of 6.86% below its net asset value, which is worse than its one-year historical average discount of 7.88%.

James K. Schmidt, CFA has been running the fund for 11 years and currently receives a manager quality ranking of 87 (0=worst, 99=best). If you desire an average level of risk, then this fund may be an option.

Data Date	Weiss Investment Rating	Net Assets ($Mil)	Price	Performance Rating/Pts	Total Return Y-T-D	Risk Rating/Pts
6-05	C+	875.99	9.77	C+ / 6.2	-4.06%	C+ / 6.2
2004	A-	865.14	10.79	B+ / 8.7	16.25%	C+ / 6.5
2003	B	923.43	10.25	B+ / 8.8	44.78%	C+ / 5.9

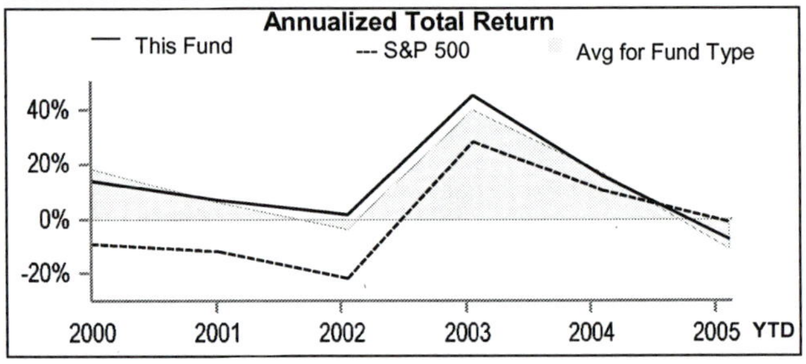

J Hancock Financial Trends Fund (JHFT) D Weak

Fund Family: John Hancock Advisors,LLC
Fund Type: Financial Services
Inception Date: August 23, 1989

Major Rating Factors:
Disappointing performance is the major factor driving the D (Weak) Weiss Investment Rating for J Hancock Financial Trends Fund. The fund currently has a performance rating of D+ (Weak) based on an annualized return of 11.35% over the last three years and a total return of -10.12% year to date 2005. Factored into the performance evaluation is an expense ratio of 1.22% (average).

The fund's risk rating is currently C (Fair). It carries a beta of 0.82, meaning the fund's expected move will be 8.2% for every 10% move in the market. Volatility, as measured by both the semi-deviation and a drawdown factor, is considered average. As of June 30, 2005, J Hancock Financial Trends Fund traded at a discount of 15.48% below its net asset value, which is better than its one-year historical average discount of 13.08%.

James K. Schmidt,CFA has been running the fund for 14 years and currently receives a manager quality ranking of 78 (0=worst, 99=best). This fund offers an average level of risk but investors looking for strong performance will be frustrated.

Data Date	Weiss Investment Rating	Net Assets ($Mil)	Price	Performance Rating/Pts	Total Return Y-T-D	Risk Rating/Pts
6-05	D	76.23	15.72	D+ / 2.9	-10.12%	C / 5.4
2004	B-	72.89	17.49	B- / 7.5	1.51%	C+ / 5.7
2003	B-	63.87	16.07	B / 8.0	36.04%	C+ / 5.6

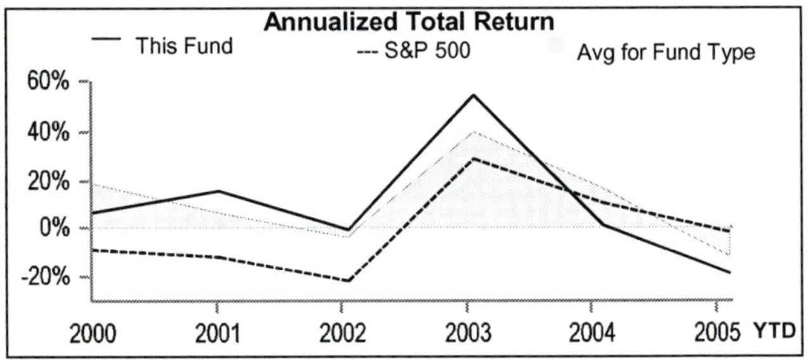

J Hancock Income Securities Tr (JHS) C- Fair

Fund Family: John Hancock Advisors,LLC
Fund Type: General - Investment Grade
Inception Date: February 14, 1973

Major Rating Factors:
Disappointing performance is the major factor driving the C- (Fair) Weiss Investment Rating for J Hancock Income Securities Tr. The fund currently has a performance rating of D (Weak) based on an annualized return of 7.76% over the last three years and a total return of -0.98% year to date 2005. Factored into the performance evaluation is an expense ratio of 1.14% (low).

The fund's risk rating is currently B- (Good). It carries a beta of 2.06, meaning it is expected to move 20.6% for every 10% move in the market. Volatility, as measured by both the semi-deviation and a drawdown factor, is considered low. As of June 30, 2005, J Hancock Income Securities Tr traded at a discount of 5.25% below its net asset value, which is better than its one-year historical average discount of 4.67%.

Barry H. Evans, CFA currently receives a manager quality ranking of 41 (0=worst, 99=best). This fund offers only a moderate level of risk but investors looking for strong performance are still waiting.

Data Date	Weiss Investment Rating	Net Assets ($Mil)	Price	Performance Rating/Pts	Total Return Y-T-D	Risk Rating/Pts
6-05	C-	180.39	14.98	D / 1.9	-0.98%	B- / 7.6
2004	C+	174.60	15.68	C / 4.9	9.96%	B- / 7.5
2003	C	187.56	15.42	C- / 3.2	13.65%	B / 8.3

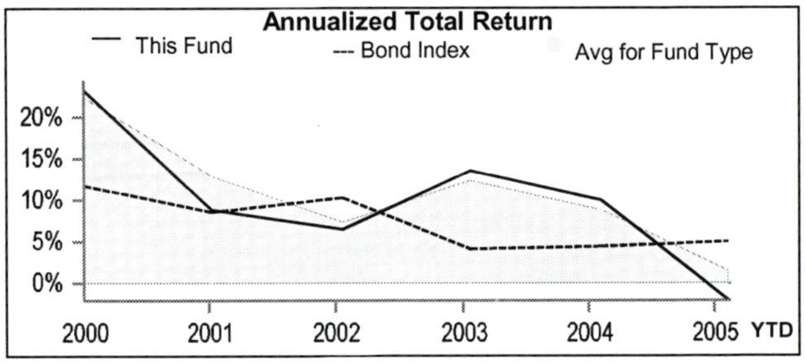

J Hancock Investors Trust (JHI) — D+ — Weak

Fund Family: John Hancock Advisors,LLC
Fund Type: General - Investment Grade
Inception Date: January 21, 1971

Major Rating Factors:
Disappointing performance is the major factor driving the D+ (Weak) Weiss Investment Rating for J Hancock Investors Trust. The fund currently has a performance rating of D (Weak) based on an annualized return of 9.56% over the last three years and a total return of -7.69% year to date 2005. Factored into the performance evaluation is an expense ratio of 1.16% (low).

The fund's risk rating is currently B- (Good). It carries a beta of 1.73, meaning it is expected to move 17.3% for every 10% move in the market. Volatility, as measured by both the semi-deviation and a drawdown factor, is considered low. As of June 30, 2005, J Hancock Investors Trust traded at a discount of 3.38% below its net asset value, which is better than its one-year historical average premium of 1.51%.

Barry H. Evans, CFA currently receives a manager quality ranking of 65 (0=worst, 99=best). This fund offers only a moderate level of risk but investors looking for strong performance are still waiting.

Data Date	Weiss Investment Rating	Net Assets ($Mil)	Price	Perfor-mance Rating/Pts	Total Return Y-T-D	Risk Rating/Pts
6-05	D+	173.16	19.98	D / 2.1	-7.69%	B- / 7.1
2004	B+	167.14	22.46	B / 7.8	21.63%	C+ / 6.9
2003	C-	179.89	20.14	C- / 3.3	16.03%	B- / 7.8

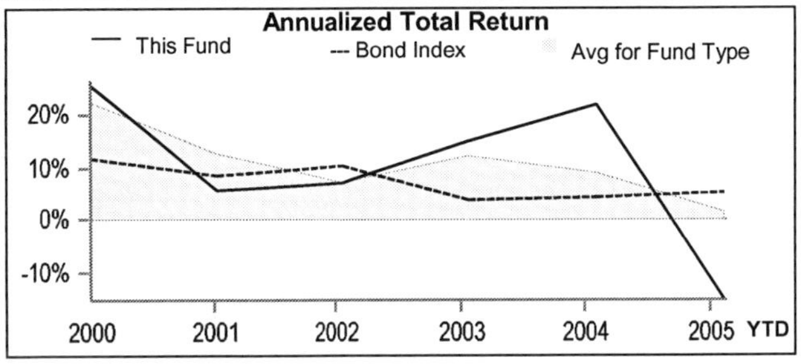

J Hancock Patriot Global Div Fd (PGD) — C — Fair

Fund Family: John Hancock Advisors,LLC
Fund Type: Global
Inception Date: August 3, 1992

Major Rating Factors:
Middle of the road best describes J Hancock Patriot Global Div Fd whose Weiss Investment Rating is currently a C (Fair). The fund currently has a performance rating of C- (Fair) based on an annualized return of 11.83% over the last three years and a total return of -2.94% year to date 2005. Factored into the performance evaluation is an expense ratio of 1.78% (above average).

The fund's risk rating is currently B- (Good). It carries a beta of 0.25, meaning the fund's expected move will be 2.5% for every 10% move in the market. Volatility, as measured by both the semi-deviation and a drawdown factor, is considered low. As of June 30, 2005, J Hancock Patriot Global Div Fd traded at a discount of 8.01% below its net asset value, which is better than its one-year historical average discount of 2.60%.

Mark T. Maloney has been running the fund for 13 years and currently receives a manager quality ranking of 87 (0=worst, 99=best). If you desire an average level of risk, then this fund may be an option.

Data Date	Weiss Investment Rating	Net Assets ($Mil)	Price	Perfor-mance Rating/Pts	Total Return Y-T-D	Risk Rating/Pts
6-05	C	118.14	13.20	C- / 4.2	-2.94%	B- / 7.3
2004	B-	106.51	14.07	C+ / 6.4	14.75%	B- / 7.2
2003	C	103.15	13.09	C / 4.6	23.24%	B- / 7.8

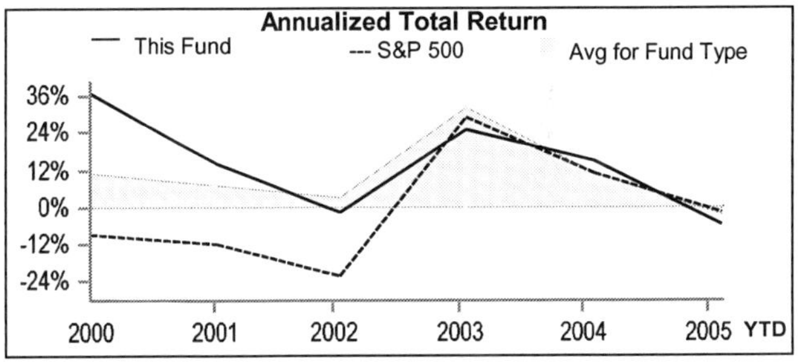

J Hancock Patriot Pref Div Fd (PPF) — C — Fair

Fund Family: John Hancock Advisors,LLC
Fund Type: Income
Inception Date: June 1, 1993

Major Rating Factors:
Middle of the road best describes J Hancock Patriot Pref Div Fd whose Weiss Investment Rating is currently a C (Fair). The fund currently has a performance rating of C (Fair) based on an annualized return of 12.91% over the last three years and a total return of 1.51% year to date 2005. Factored into the performance evaluation is an expense ratio of 1.83% (above average).

The fund's risk rating is currently C+ (Fair). It carries a beta of -0.05, meaning the fund's expected move will be -0.5% for every 10% move in the market. Volatility, as measured by both the semi-deviation and a drawdown factor, is considered low. As of June 30, 2005, J Hancock Patriot Pref Div Fd traded at a discount of 4.24% below its net asset value, which is worse than its one-year historical average discount of 5.09%.

Mark T. Maloney has been running the fund for 12 years and currently receives a manager quality ranking of 92 (0=worst, 99=best). If you desire an average level of risk, then this fund may be an option.

Data Date	Weiss Investment Rating	Net Assets ($Mil)	Price	Perfor-mance Rating/Pts	Total Return Y-T-D	Risk Rating/Pts
6-05	C	101.53	13.76	C / 5.5	1.51%	C+ / 6.1
2004	C+	94.15	14.00	C / 5.5	8.28%	C+ / 6.8
2003	B-	97.87	13.41	C+ / 6.2	22.41%	B- / 7.7

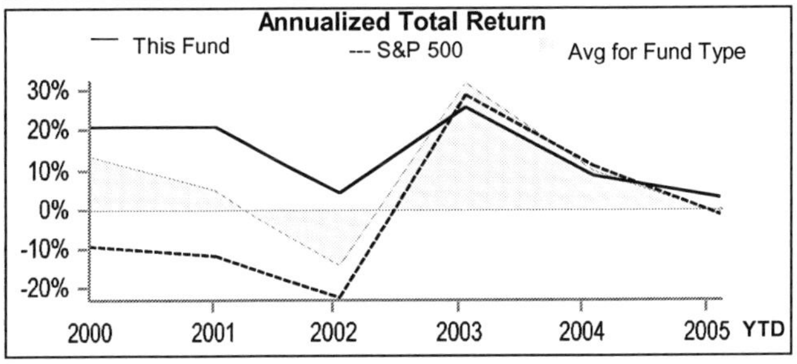

J Hancock Patriot Prem Div Fd I (PDF) C- Fair

Fund Family: John Hancock Advisors,LLC
Fund Type: Income
Inception Date: October 28, 1988

Data Date	Weiss Investment Rating	Net Assets ($Mil)	Price	Performance Rating/Pts	Total Return Y-T-D	Risk Rating/Pts
6-05	C-	146.70	9.30	D / 1.9	-3.98%	B- / 7.8
2004	C	141.07	10.00	C / 4.5	10.47%	B- / 7.0
2003	C	133.63	9.85	C+ / 5.7	27.61%	C+ / 6.7

Major Rating Factors:
Disappointing performance is the major factor driving the C- (Fair) Weiss Investment Rating for J Hancock Patriot Prem Div Fd I. The fund currently has a performance rating of D (Weak) based on an annualized return of 7.55% over the last three years and a total return of -3.98% year to date 2005. Factored into the performance evaluation is an expense ratio of 1.69% (above average).

The fund's risk rating is currently B- (Good). It carries a beta of 0.24, meaning the fund's expected move will be 2.4% for every 10% move in the market. Volatility, as measured by both the semi-deviation and a drawdown factor, is considered low. As of June 30, 2005, J Hancock Patriot Prem Div Fd I traded at a discount of 6.16% below its net asset value, which is better than its one-year historical average discount of .61%.

Mark T. Maloney has been running the fund for 17 years and currently receives a manager quality ranking of 80 (0=worst, 99=best). This fund offers only a moderate level of risk but investors looking for strong performance are still waiting.

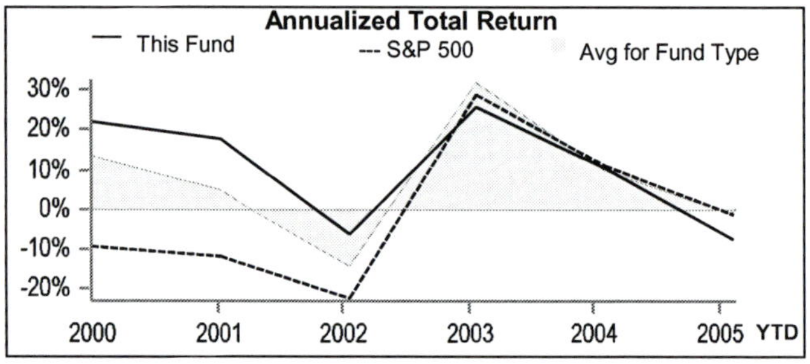

J Hancock Patriot Prem Div Fd II (PDT) C+ Fair

Fund Family: John Hancock Advisors,LLC
Fund Type: Income
Inception Date: December 14, 1989

Data Date	Weiss Investment Rating	Net Assets ($Mil)	Price	Performance Rating/Pts	Total Return Y-T-D	Risk Rating/Pts
6-05	C+	182.01	12.07	C+ / 6.5	8.34%	C+ / 6.7
2004	C	169.69	11.51	C / 4.6	9.15%	B- / 7.3
2003	C+	165.34	11.46	C / 5.3	27.50%	B- / 7.4

Major Rating Factors:
Middle of the road best describes J Hancock Patriot Prem Div Fd II whose Weiss Investment Rating is currently a C+ (Fair). The fund currently has a performance rating of C+ (Fair) based on an annualized return of 13.59% over the last three years and a total return of 8.34% year to date 2005. Factored into the performance evaluation is an expense ratio of 1.71% (above average).

The fund's risk rating is currently C+ (Fair). It carries a beta of 0.24, meaning the fund's expected move will be 2.4% for every 10% move in the market. Volatility, as measured by both the semi-deviation and a drawdown factor, is considered low. As of June 30, 2005, J Hancock Patriot Prem Div Fd II traded at a discount of 3.44% below its net asset value, which is worse than its one-year historical average discount of 3.61%.

Mark T. Maloney has been running the fund for 16 years and currently receives a manager quality ranking of 90 (0=worst, 99=best). If you desire an average level of risk, then this fund may be an option.

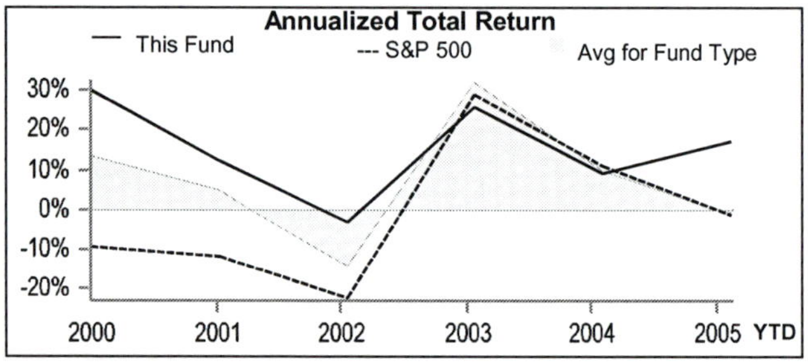

J Hancock Patriot Select Div Tr (DIV) D+ Weak

Fund Family: John Hancock Advisors,LLC
Fund Type: Utilities
Inception Date: July 25, 1990

Data Date	Weiss Investment Rating	Net Assets ($Mil)	Price	Performance Rating/Pts	Total Return Y-T-D	Risk Rating/Pts
6-05	D+	147.71	13.65	D / 1.6	-3.03%	B- / 7.1
2004	C-	133.43	14.55	D+ / 2.7	2.01%	B- / 7.7
2003	B+	136.58	15.75	B / 7.8	30.71%	B- / 7.4

Major Rating Factors:
Disappointing performance is the major factor driving the D+ (Weak) Weiss Investment Rating for J Hancock Patriot Select Div Tr. The fund currently has a performance rating of D (Weak) based on an annualized return of 7.95% over the last three years and a total return of -3.03% year to date 2005. Factored into the performance evaluation is an expense ratio of 1.74% (above average).

The fund's risk rating is currently B- (Good). It carries a beta of 0.39, meaning the fund's expected move will be 3.9% for every 10% move in the market. Volatility, as measured by both the semi-deviation and a drawdown factor, is considered low. As of June 30, 2005, J Hancock Patriot Select Div Tr traded at a discount of 9.36% below its net asset value, which is better than its one-year historical average discount of 2.10%.

Mark T. Maloney has been running the fund for 15 years and currently receives a manager quality ranking of 69 (0=worst, 99=best). This fund offers only a moderate level of risk but investors looking for strong performance are still waiting.

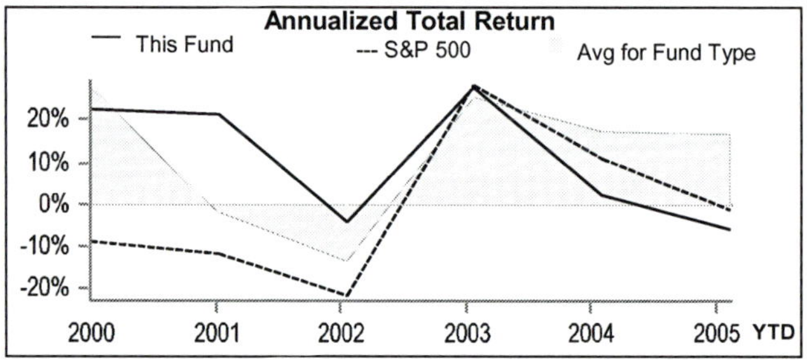

Japan Equity Fund (JEQ) — E — Very Weak

Fund Family: Daiwa SB Investments
Fund Type: Foreign
Inception Date: July 24, 1992

Major Rating Factors:
Very poor performance is the major factor driving the E (Very Weak) Weiss Investment Rating for Japan Equity Fund. The fund currently has a performance rating of E- (Very Weak) based on an annualized return of 4.68% over the last three years and a total return of -8.16% year to date 2005. Factored into the performance evaluation is an expense ratio of 1.07% (low).

The fund's risk rating is currently C- (Fair). It carries a beta of 1.00, meaning that its performance tracks fairly well with that of the overall stock market. Volatility, as measured by both the semi-deviation and a drawdown factor, is considered average. As of June 30, 2005, Japan Equity Fund traded at a discount of 7.60% below its net asset value, which is better than its one-year historical average discount of 4.08%.

Mr. Hosaka has been running the fund for 5 years and currently receives a manager quality ranking of 6 (0=worst, 99=best). This fund offers an average level of risk but investors looking for strong performance will be frustrated.

Data Date	Weiss Investment Rating	Net Assets ($Mil)	Price	Performance Rating/Pts	Total Return Y-T-D	Risk Rating/Pts
6-05	E	92.49	6.08	E- / 0.2	-8.16%	C- / 4.0
2004	D-	95.27	6.53	C- / 3.3	-2.39%	C- / 3.0
2003	D	64.92	6.40	C- / 3.6	46.12%	C / 4.4

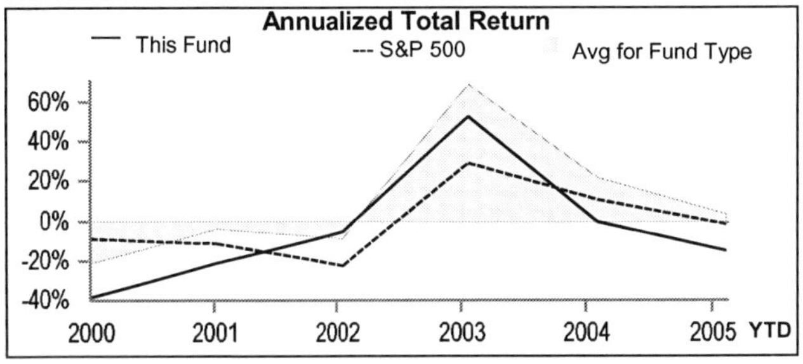

Japan Smaller Cap Fund Inc. (JOF) — E — Very Weak

Fund Family: Nomura Asset Management Co Ltd
Fund Type: Foreign
Inception Date: March 15, 1990

Major Rating Factors:
Japan Smaller Cap Fund Inc. has adopted a risky asset allocation strategy and currently receives an overall Weiss Investment Rating of E (Very Weak). The fund has an above average level of volatility, as measured by both semi-deviation and drawdown factors. It carries a beta of 1.33, meaning it is expected to move 13.3% for every 10% move in the market. As of June 30, 2005, Japan Smaller Cap Fund Inc. traded at a discount of 7.94% below its net asset value, which is better than its one-year historical average premium of 5.57%. Unfortunately, the high level of risk (D+, Weak) failed to pay off as investors endured very poor performance.

The fund's performance rating is currently E+ (Very Weak). It has registered an annualized return of 10.50% over the last three years but is down -10.91% year to date 2005. Factored into the performance evaluation is an expense ratio of 1.54% (average).

Nobuo Katayama has been running the fund for 6 years and currently receives a manager quality ranking of 14 (0=worst, 99=best). If you can tolerate high levels of risk in the hope of improved future returns, holding this fund may be an option.

Data Date	Weiss Investment Rating	Net Assets ($Mil)	Price	Performance Rating/Pts	Total Return Y-T-D	Risk Rating/Pts
6-05	E	183.72	10.78	E+ / 0.7	-10.91%	D+ / 2.4
2004	C-	168.08	12.10	B+ / 8.9	11.01%	D / 1.9
2003	C	121.72	10.04	A- / 9.2	64.59%	C- / 3.1

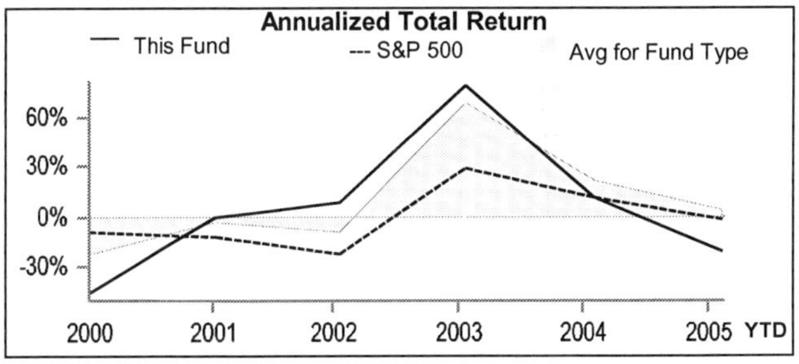

JF China Region Fund (JFC) — C- — Fair

Fund Family: Jardine Fleming Int'l Mgmt Inc.
Fund Type: Foreign
Inception Date: July 16, 1992

Major Rating Factors:
JF China Region Fund has adopted a very risky asset allocation strategy and currently receives an overall Weiss Investment Rating of C- (Fair). The fund has shown a high level of volatility, as measured by both semi-deviation and drawdown factors. It carries a beta of 1.10, meaning it is expected to move 11.0% for every 10% move in the market. As of June 30, 2005, JF China Region Fund traded at a discount of 13.79% below its net asset value, which is better than its one-year historical average discount of 9.84%. The high level of risk (D-, Weak) did however, reward investors with excellent performance.

The fund's performance rating is currently B (Good). It has registered an annualized return of 22.94% over the last three years and is up 0.16% year to date 2005. Factored into the performance evaluation is an expense ratio of 2.22% (high).

Douglas Eu has been running the fund for 13 years and currently receives a manager quality ranking of 88 (0=worst, 99=best). If you are comfortable owning a very high risk investment, this fund may be an option.

Data Date	Weiss Investment Rating	Net Assets ($Mil)	Price	Performance Rating/Pts	Total Return Y-T-D	Risk Rating/Pts
6-05	C-	64.49	12.82	B / 8.2	0.16%	D- / 1.3
2004	D+	56.73	12.80	B / 7.6	-29.20%	D- / 1.3
2003	C+	42.62	16.42	A+ / 9.9	152.62%	D+ / 2.9

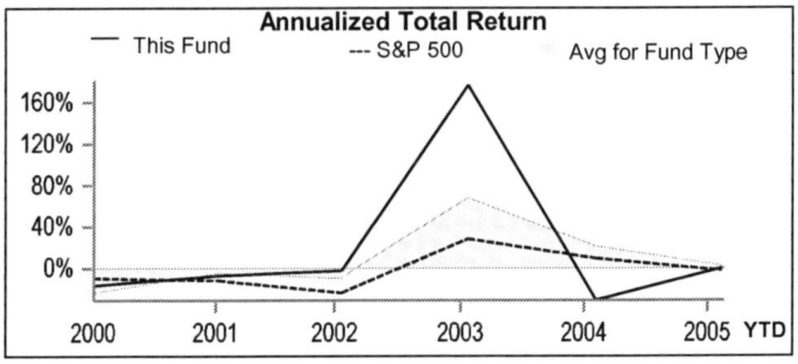

Korea Equity Fund (KEF) C Fair

Fund Family: Nomura Asset Management Co Ltd
Fund Type: Foreign
Inception Date: November 24, 1993

Data Date	Weiss Investment Rating	Net Assets ($Mil)	Price	Performance Rating/Pts	Total Return Y-T-D	Risk Rating/Pts
6-05	C	59.01	6.99	A- / 9.0	13.66%	D / 2.1
2004	C+	49.34	6.15	B+ / 8.5	23.49%	C- / 4.1
2003	B-	45.20	4.77	A- / 9.1	31.77%	C / 4.7

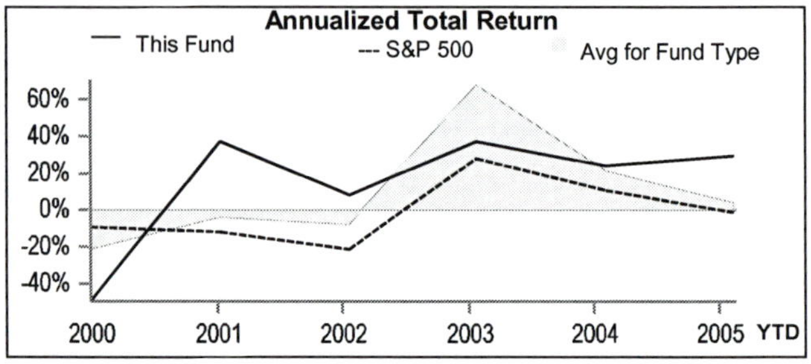

Major Rating Factors:

Korea Equity Fund has adopted a very risky asset allocation strategy and currently receives an overall Weiss Investment Rating of C (Fair). The fund has shown a high level of volatility, as measured by both semi-deviation and drawdown factors. It carries a beta of 1.02, meaning that its performance tracks fairly well with that of the overall stock market. As of June 30, 2005, Korea Equity Fund traded at a discount of 5.67% below its net asset value, which is worse than its one-year historical average discount of 8.49%. The high level of risk (D, Weak) did however, reward investors with excellent performance.

The fund's performance rating is currently A- (Excellent). It has registered an annualized return of 18.70% over the last three years and is up 13.66% year to date 2005. Factored into the performance evaluation is an expense ratio of 2.27% (high).

Nobuo Katayama has been running the fund for 6 years and currently receives a manager quality ranking of 84 (0=worst, 99=best). If you are comfortable owning a very high risk investment, this fund may be an option.

Korea Fund (KF) C Fair

Fund Family: Deutsche Asset Management
Fund Type: Foreign
Inception Date: August 29, 1984

Data Date	Weiss Investment Rating	Net Assets ($Mil)	Price	Performance Rating/Pts	Total Return Y-T-D	Risk Rating/Pts
6-05	C	1153.42	27.28	A / 9.5	13.38%	D- / 1.1
2004	B-	963.13	24.06	A / 9.3	34.75%	C- / 4.2
2003	C+	878.64	17.51	B+ / 8.9	26.43%	C- / 4.1

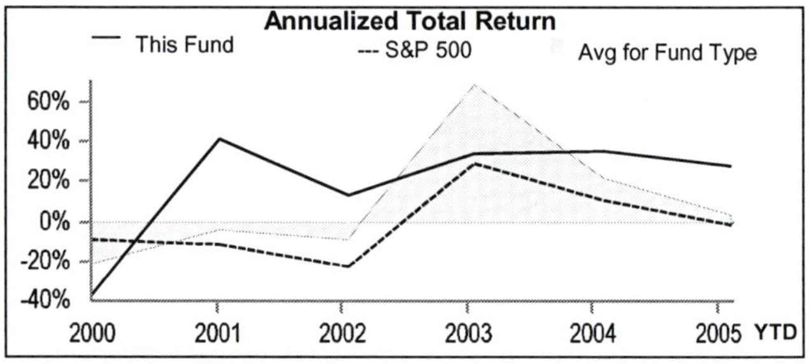

Major Rating Factors:

Korea Fund has adopted a very risky asset allocation strategy and currently receives an overall Weiss Investment Rating of C (Fair). The fund has shown a high level of volatility, as measured by both semi-deviation and drawdown factors. It carries a beta of 1.26, meaning it is expected to move 12.6% for every 10% move in the market. As of June 30, 2005, Korea Fund traded at a discount of 6.35% below its net asset value, which is worse than its one-year historical average discount of 7.95%. The high level of risk (D-, Weak) did however, reward investors with excellent performance.

The fund's performance rating is currently A (Excellent). It has registered an annualized return of 22.48% over the last three years and is up 13.38% year to date 2005. Factored into the performance evaluation is an expense ratio of 1.24% (average).

Terrence S. Gray has been running the fund for 14 years and currently receives a manager quality ranking of 84 (0=worst, 99=best). If you are comfortable owning a very high risk investment, this fund may be an option.

Latin America Equity Fund (LAQ) C+ Fair

Fund Family: Credit Suisse Asset Management
Fund Type: Foreign
Inception Date: October 30, 1991

Data Date	Weiss Investment Rating	Net Assets ($Mil)	Price	Performance Rating/Pts	Total Return Y-T-D	Risk Rating/Pts
6-05	C+	154.21	23.00	A+ / 9.7	6.24%	D+ / 2.6
2004	C+	111.09	21.65	A / 9.4	45.19%	C- / 3.5
2003	C	86.29	14.75	B- / 7.3	54.01%	C / 4.3

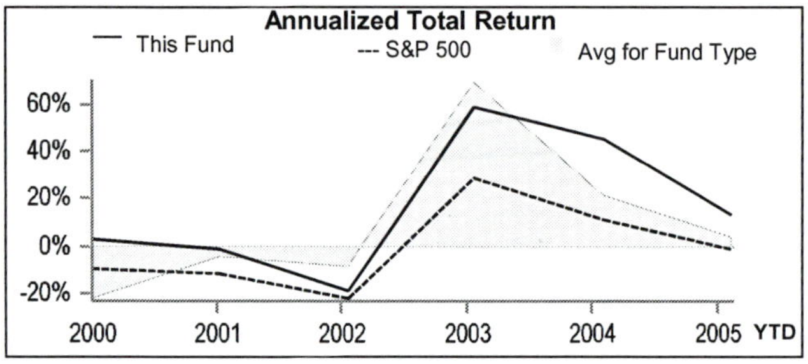

Major Rating Factors:

Latin America Equity Fund has adopted a risky asset allocation strategy and currently receives an overall Weiss Investment Rating of C+ (Fair). The fund has shown an above average level of volatility, as measured by both semi-deviation and drawdown factors. It carries a beta of 1.30, meaning it is expected to move 13.0% for every 10% move in the market. As of June 30, 2005, Latin America Equity Fund traded at a discount of 13.63% below its net asset value, which is worse than its one-year historical average discount of 13.99%. The high level of risk (D+, Weak) did however, reward investors with excellent performance.

The fund's performance rating is currently A+ (Excellent). It has registered an annualized return of 29.30% over the last three years and is up 6.24% year to date 2005. Factored into the performance evaluation is an expense ratio of 1.41% (average).

Emily Alejos has been running the fund for 1 year and currently receives a manager quality ranking of 93 (0=worst, 99=best). If you are comfortable owning a high risk investment, this fund may be an option.

Latin American Discovery Fund (LDF) C+ Fair

Fund Family: Morgan Stanley Invesment Advisors,I
Fund Type: Foreign
Inception Date: June 23, 1992

Data Date	Weiss Investment Rating	Net Assets ($Mil)	Price	Performance Rating/Pts	Total Return Y-T-D	Risk Rating/Pts
6-05	C+	190.49	20.01	A+ / 9.8	9.52%	D+ / 2.6
2004	B	137.06	18.27	A / 9.5	45.08%	C- / 4.1
2003	B-	119.61	12.49	B+ / 8.8	68.41%	C / 4.9

Major Rating Factors:
Latin American Discovery Fund has adopted a risky asset allocation strategy and currently receives an overall Weiss Investment Rating of C+ (Fair). The fund has shown an above average level of volatility, as measured by both semi-deviation and drawdown factors. It carries a beta of 1.35, meaning it is expected to move 13.5% for every 10% move in the market. As of June 30, 2005, Latin American Discovery Fund traded at a discount of 12.81% below its net asset value, which is worse than its one-year historical average discount of 13.21%. The high level of risk (D+, Weak) did however, reward investors with excellent performance.

The fund's performance rating is currently A+ (Excellent). It has registered an annualized return of 34.65% over the last three years and is up 9.52% year to date 2005. Factored into the performance evaluation is an expense ratio of 1.45% (average).

Ana Piedrahita has been running the fund for 13 years and currently receives a manager quality ranking of 96 (0=worst, 99=best). If you are comfortable owning a high risk investment, this fund may be an option.

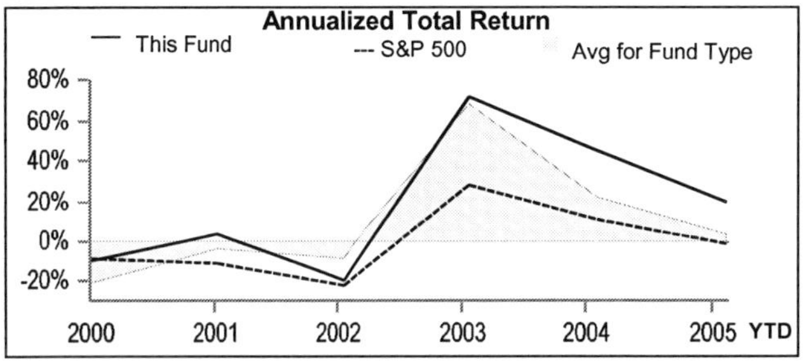

Liberty All-Star Equity Fund (USA) D- Weak

Fund Family: Banc of America Investment Advisors
Fund Type: Income
Inception Date: November 3, 1986

Data Date	Weiss Investment Rating	Net Assets ($Mil)	Price	Performance Rating/Pts	Total Return Y-T-D	Risk Rating/Pts
6-05	D-	1372.19	8.92	C- / 3.3	-1.93%	C- / 3.9
2004	E+	1176.16	9.56	D / 2.2	12.39%	D+ / 2.9
2003	D+	975.50	9.40	C / 4.8	55.68%	C- / 3.8

Major Rating Factors:
Liberty All-Star Equity Fund receives a Weiss Investment Rating of D- (Weak). The fund currently has a performance rating of C- (Fair) based on an annualized return of 12.10% over the last three years and a total return of -1.93% year to date 2005. Factored into the performance evaluation is an expense ratio of 1.01% (low).

The fund's risk rating is currently C- (Fair). It carries a beta of 1.28, meaning it is expected to move 12.8% for every 10% move in the market. Volatility, as measured by both the semi-deviation and a drawdown factor, is considered average. As of June 30, 2005, Liberty All-Star Equity Fund traded at a premium of 2.76% above its net asset value, which is better than its one-year historical average premium of 3.69%.

This fund has been team managed for 19 years and currently receives a manager quality ranking of 73 (0=worst, 99=best). If you desire an average level of risk, then this fund may be an option.

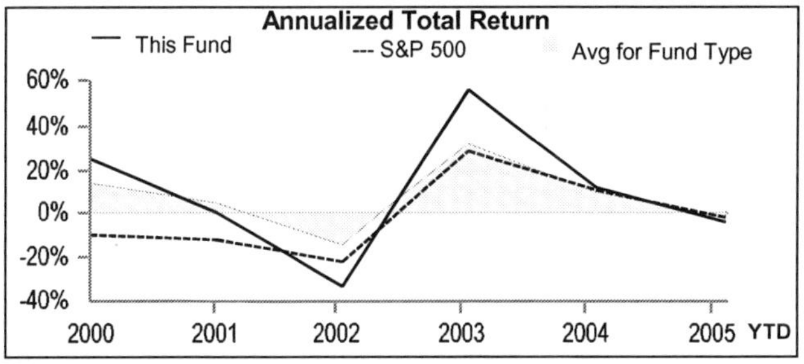

Liberty All-Star Growth Fund (ASG) E+ Very Weak

Fund Family: Banc of America Investment Advisors
Fund Type: Growth
Inception Date: March 14, 1986

Data Date	Weiss Investment Rating	Net Assets ($Mil)	Price	Performance Rating/Pts	Total Return Y-T-D	Risk Rating/Pts
6-05	E+	164.65	5.89	E+ / 0.9	-6.26%	C / 4.3
2004	E+	161.47	6.61	D- / 1.2	6.90%	D+ / 2.9
2003	E+	127.25	6.55	D / 1.8	43.74%	D / 2.0

Major Rating Factors:
Very poor performance is the major factor driving the E+ (Very Weak) Weiss Investment Rating for Liberty All-Star Growth Fund. The fund currently has a performance rating of E+ (Very Weak) based on an annualized return of 7.10% over the last three years and a total return of -6.26% year to date 2005. Factored into the performance evaluation is an expense ratio of 1.31% (average).

The fund's risk rating is currently C (Fair). It carries a beta of 1.20, meaning it is expected to move 12.0% for every 10% move in the market. Volatility, as measured by both the semi-deviation and a drawdown factor, is considered average. As of June 30, 2005, Liberty All-Star Growth Fund traded at a premium of 2.43% above its net asset value, which is better than its one-year historical average premium of 5.53%.

This fund has been team managed for 10 years and currently receives a manager quality ranking of 37 (0=worst, 99=best). This fund offers an average level of risk but investors looking for strong performance will be frustrated.

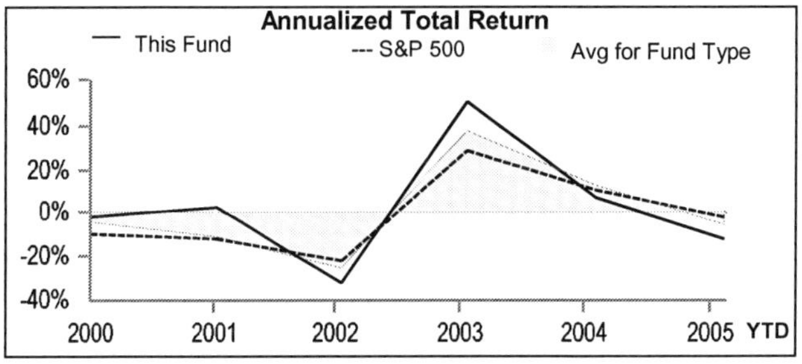

Lincoln National Income Fund (LND) D- Weak

Fund Family: Lincoln Investment Mgmt Co
Fund Type: Corporate - Investment Grade
Inception Date: November 10, 1972

Data Date	Weiss Investment Rating	Net Assets ($Mil)	Price	Performance Rating/Pts	Total Return Y-T-D	Risk Rating/Pts
6-05	D-	99.93	11.80	D- / 1.0	-5.47%	C+ / 6.6
2004	C	96.85	12.50	C- / 4.1	-7.95%	B- / 7.5
2003	A-	105.20	15.10	B / 8.2	26.43%	B- / 7.3

Major Rating Factors:
Disappointing performance is the major factor driving the D- (Weak) Weiss Investment Rating for Lincoln National Income Fund. The fund currently has a performance rating of D- (Weak) based on an annualized return of 6.99% over the last three years and a total return of -5.47% year to date 2005. Factored into the performance evaluation is an expense ratio of 1.76% (above average).

The fund's risk rating is currently C+ (Fair). It carries a beta of 1.30, meaning it is expected to move 13.0% for every 10% move in the market. Volatility, as measured by both the semi-deviation and a drawdown factor, is considered low. As of June 30, 2005, Lincoln National Income Fund traded at a discount of 12.20% below its net asset value, which is better than its one-year historical average discount of 6.38%.

Ryan Brist has been running the fund for 33 years and currently receives a manager quality ranking of 32 (0=worst, 99=best). This fund offers only a moderate level of risk but investors looking for strong performance are still waiting.

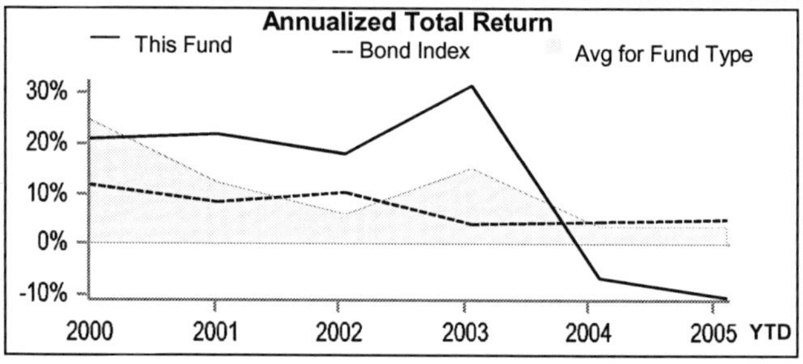

MA Health & Education Tax-Exempt Tr (MHE) C+ Fair

Fund Family: Merrill Lynch Investment Managers
Fund Type: Municipal - Single State
Inception Date: July 23, 1993

Data Date	Weiss Investment Rating	Net Assets ($Mil)	Price	Performance Rating/Pts	Total Return Y-T-D	Risk Rating/Pts
6-05	C+	0.00	15.06	C+ / 6.6	-4.71%	C+ / 6.8
2003	B+	32.75	15.08	B / 7.8	18.75%	B- / 7.5

Major Rating Factors:
Middle of the road best describes MA Health & Education Tax-Exempt Tr whose Weiss Investment Rating is currently a C+ (Fair). The fund currently has a performance rating of C+ (Fair) based on an annualized return of 8.17% over the last three years and a total return of -4.71% year to date 2005.

The fund's risk rating is currently C+ (Fair). It carries a beta of 1.75, meaning it is expected to move 17.5% for every 10% move in the market. Volatility, as measured by both the semi-deviation and a drawdown factor, is considered low. As of June 30, 2005, MA Health & Education Tax-Exempt Tr traded at a premium of 6.81% above its net asset value, which is better than its one-year historical average premium of 7.66%.

Robert MacIntosh has been running the fund for 9 years and currently receives a manager quality ranking of 45 (0=worst, 99=best). If you desire an average level of risk, then this fund may be an option.

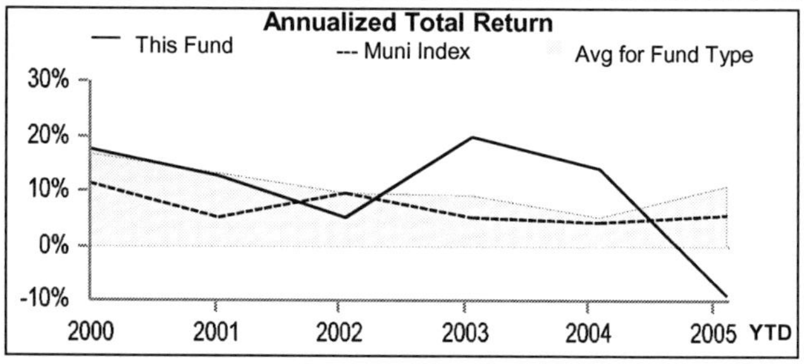

Malaysia Fund (MF) E+ Very Weak

Fund Family: Morgan Stanley Investment Mgmt., In
Fund Type: Foreign
Inception Date: May 4, 1987

Data Date	Weiss Investment Rating	Net Assets ($Mil)	Price	Performance Rating/Pts	Total Return Y-T-D	Risk Rating/Pts
6-05	E+	59.02	5.64	D+ / 2.6	-9.18%	D / 2.2
2004	C	55.91	6.21	B / 7.8	4.41%	C- / 3.3
2003	C+	49.16	5.81	A / 9.4	55.34%	C- / 3.4

Major Rating Factors:
Malaysia Fund has adopted a very risky asset allocation strategy and currently receives an overall Weiss Investment Rating of E+ (Very Weak). The fund has a high level of volatility, as measured by both semi-deviation and drawdown factors. It carries a beta of 0.91, meaning that its performance tracks fairly well with that of the overall stock market. As of June 30, 2005, Malaysia Fund traded at a discount of 2.25% below its net asset value, which is better than its one-year historical average discount of 1.64%. Unfortunately, the high level of risk (D, Weak) failed to pay off as investors endured poor performance.

The fund's performance rating is currently D+ (Weak). It has registered an annualized return of 11.95% over the last three years but is down -9.18% year to date 2005. Factored into the performance evaluation is an expense ratio of 1.50% (average).

Ashutosh Sinha has been running the fund for 18 years and currently receives a manager quality ranking of 64 (0=worst, 99=best). If you can tolerate very high levels of risk in the hope of improved future returns, holding this fund may be an option.

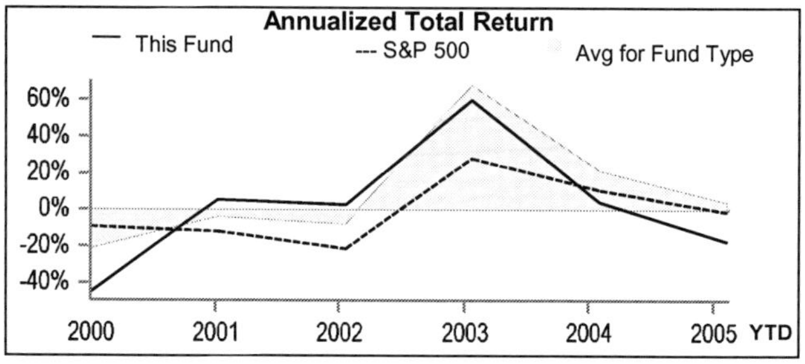

Managed High Income Portfolio (MHY) D+ Weak

Fund Family: Smith Barney Advisers, Inc.
Fund Type: Corporate - High Yield
Inception Date: March 26, 1993

Data Date	Weiss Investment Rating	Net Assets ($Mil)	Price	Perfor-mance Rating/Pts	Total Return Y-T-D	Risk Rating/Pts
6-05	D+	328.60	6.35	C- / 3.6	0.70%	C+ / 5.7
2004	D-	321.14	6.57	D / 1.8	3.27%	C / 5.5
2003	D	308.78	6.96	D+ / 2.4	23.87%	C / 5.0

Major Rating Factors:
Managed High Income Portfolio receives a Weiss Investment Rating of D+ (Weak). The fund currently has a performance rating of C- (Fair) based on an annualized return of 11.80% over the last three years and a total return of 0.70% year to date 2005. Factored into the performance evaluation is an expense ratio of 1.26% (average).

The fund's risk rating is currently C+ (Fair). It carries a beta of 1.23, meaning it is expected to move 12.3% for every 10% move in the market. Volatility, as measured by both the semi-deviation and a drawdown factor, is considered low. As of June 30, 2005, Managed High Income Portfolio traded at a discount of 8.63% below its net asset value, which is better than its one-year historical average discount of 8.35%.

Beth Semmel has been running the fund for 12 years and currently receives a manager quality ranking of 18 (0=worst, 99=best). If you desire an average level of risk, then this fund may be an option.

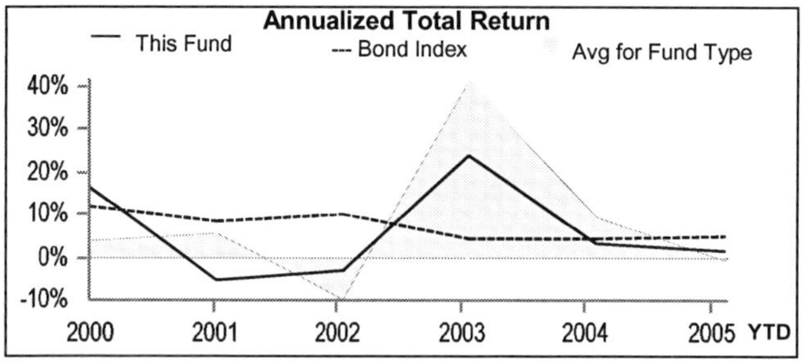

Managed High Yield Plus Fund (HYF) C Fair

Fund Family: UBS Global Asset Management
Fund Type: Global
Inception Date: June 26, 1998

Data Date	Weiss Investment Rating	Net Assets ($Mil)	Price	Perfor-mance Rating/Pts	Total Return Y-T-D	Risk Rating/Pts
6-05	C	228.78	5.16	B- / 7.0	-6.70%	C- / 4.2
2004	D+	214.43	6.11	B- / 7.5	19.69%	D / 2.1
2003	C-	212.23	5.74	B- / 7.4	49.82%	C- / 3.1

Major Rating Factors:
Strong performance is the major factor driving the C (Fair) Weiss Investment Rating for Managed High Yield Plus Fund. The fund currently has a performance rating of B- (Good) based on an annualized return of 19.64% over the last three years and a total return of -6.70% year to date 2005. Factored into the performance evaluation is an expense ratio of 2.02% (high).

The fund's risk rating is currently C- (Fair). It carries a beta of 0.60, meaning the fund's expected move will be 6.0% for every 10% move in the market. Volatility, as measured by both the semi-deviation and a drawdown factor, is considered average. As of June 30, 2005, Managed High Yield Plus Fund traded at a premium of 4.45% above its net asset value, which is better than its one-year historical average premium of 9.86%.

Marianne Rossi has been running the fund for 7 years and currently receives a manager quality ranking of 93 (0=worst, 99=best). If you desire an average level of risk and strong performance, then this fund is a good option.

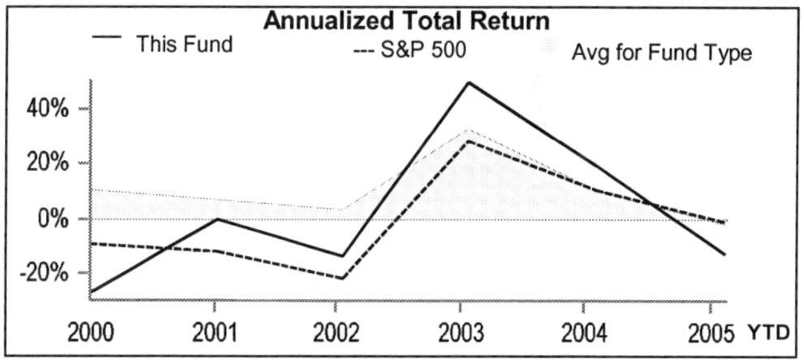

Managed Municipals Portfolio (MMU) C Fair

Fund Family: Smith Barney Advisers, Inc.
Fund Type: Municipal - National
Inception Date: June 25, 1992

Data Date	Weiss Investment Rating	Net Assets ($Mil)	Price	Perfor-mance Rating/Pts	Total Return Y-T-D	Risk Rating/Pts
6-05	C	492.07	10.76	C- / 3.0	3.25%	B / 8.3
2004	C+	491.76	10.72	C- / 3.9	0.38%	B / 8.5
2003	B+	507.10	11.37	B- / 7.1	13.70%	B / 8.2

Major Rating Factors:
Middle of the road best describes Managed Municipals Portfolio whose Weiss Investment Rating is currently a C (Fair). The fund currently has a performance rating of C- (Fair) based on an annualized return of 6.80% over the last three years and a total return of 3.25% year to date 2005. Factored into the performance evaluation is an expense ratio of 1.33% (average).

The fund's risk rating is currently B (Good). It carries a beta of 1.20, meaning it is expected to move 12.0% for every 10% move in the market. Volatility, as measured by both the semi-deviation and a drawdown factor, is considered low. As of June 30, 2005, Managed Municipals Portfolio traded at a discount of 7.96% below its net asset value, which is better than its one-year historical average discount of 7.43%.

Joseph P. Deane/David Fare has been running the fund for 13 years and currently receives a manager quality ranking of 61 (0=worst, 99=best). If you desire an average level of risk, then this fund may be an option.

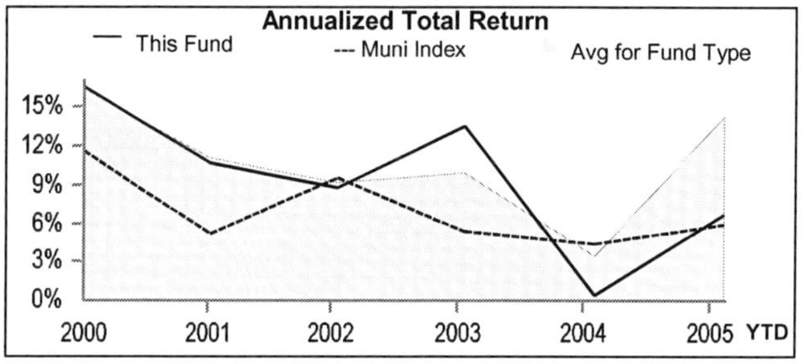

Mexico Equity & Income Fund (MXE) C+ Fair

Fund Family: Phicardo Asset Management
Fund Type: Foreign
Inception Date: August 21, 1990

Major Rating Factors:
Exceptional performance is the major factor driving the C+ (Fair) Weiss Investment Rating for Mexico Equity & Income Fund. The fund currently has a performance rating of A (Excellent) based on an annualized return of 26.45% over the last three years and a total return of -0.46% year to date 2005. Factored into the performance evaluation is an expense ratio of 1.79% (above average).

The fund's risk rating is currently C- (Fair). It carries a beta of 1.04, meaning that its performance tracks fairly well with that of the overall stock market. Volatility, as measured by both the semi-deviation and a drawdown factor, is considered average. As of June 30, 2005, Mexico Equity & Income Fund traded at a discount of 13.68% below its net asset value, which is better than its one-year historical average discount of 11.42%.

Eugenia Pichardo has been running the fund for 15 years and currently receives a manager quality ranking of 94 (0=worst, 99=best). If you desire an average level of risk and strong performance, then this fund is a good option.

Data Date	Weiss Investment Rating	Net Assets ($Mil)	Price	Performance Rating/Pts	Total Return Y-T-D	Risk Rating/Pts
6-05	C+	45.63	17.16	A / 9.4	-0.46%	C- / 3.2
2004	B+	33.78	17.24	A+ / 9.7	66.57%	C / 5.0
2003	C-	25.10	10.12	C / 4.9	33.01%	C+ / 5.7

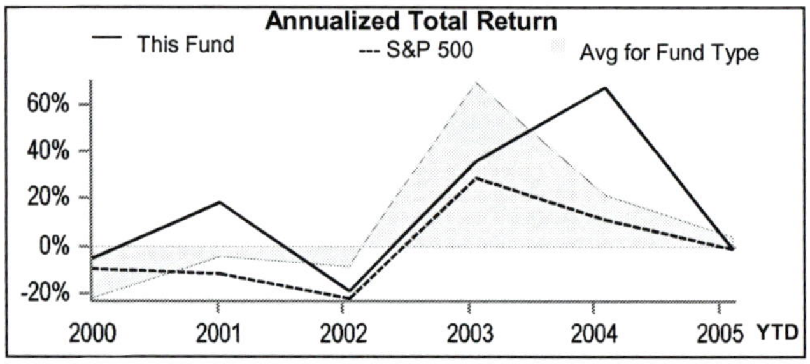

Mexico Fund (MXF) C+ Fair

Fund Family: Impulsora del Fondo Mexico, S.A. de
Fund Type: Foreign
Inception Date: June 11, 1981

Major Rating Factors:
Mexico Fund has adopted a risky asset allocation strategy and currently receives an overall Weiss Investment Rating of C+ (Fair). The fund has shown an above average level of volatility, as measured by both semi-deviation and drawdown factors. It carries a beta of 1.00, meaning that its performance tracks fairly well with that of the overall stock market. As of June 30, 2005, Mexico Fund traded at a discount of 12.70% below its net asset value, which is better than its one-year historical average discount of 12.52%. The high level of risk (D+, Weak) did however, reward investors with excellent performance.

The fund's performance rating is currently A- (Excellent). It has registered an annualized return of 22.24% over the last three years and is up 9.29% year to date 2005. Factored into the performance evaluation is an expense ratio of 1.44% (average).

Carlos H. Woodworth has been running the fund for 24 years and currently receives a manager quality ranking of 89 (0=worst, 99=best). If you are comfortable owning a high risk investment, this fund may be an option.

Data Date	Weiss Investment Rating	Net Assets ($Mil)	Price	Performance Rating/Pts	Total Return Y-T-D	Risk Rating/Pts
6-05	C+	431.10	23.65	A- / 9.0	9.29%	D+ / 2.8
2004	C	301.75	21.64	A- / 9.0	40.40%	C- / 3.0
2003	C	269.76	16.00	B- / 7.5	38.00%	C- / 3.8

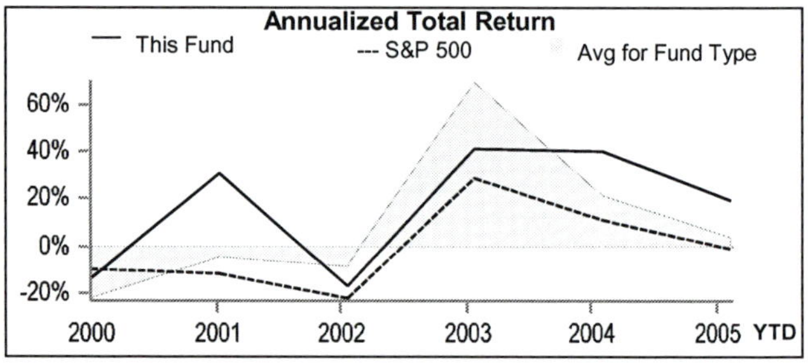

MFS Charter Income Trust (MCR) C- Fair

Fund Family: MFS Investment Management
Fund Type: General Bond
Inception Date: July 21, 1989

Major Rating Factors:
Disappointing performance is the major factor driving the C- (Fair) Weiss Investment Rating for MFS Charter Income Trust. The fund currently has a performance rating of D (Weak) based on an annualized return of 7.28% over the last three years and a total return of 1.57% year to date 2005. Factored into the performance evaluation is an expense ratio of 0.80% (very low).

The fund's risk rating is currently B (Good). It carries a beta of 1.43, meaning it is expected to move 14.3% for every 10% move in the market. Volatility, as measured by both the semi-deviation and a drawdown factor, is considered low. As of June 30, 2005, MFS Charter Income Trust traded at a discount of 10.95% below its net asset value, which is better than its one-year historical average discount of 9.88%.

S. Bryant has been running the fund for 4 years and currently receives a manager quality ranking of 62 (0=worst, 99=best). This fund offers only a moderate level of risk but investors looking for strong performance are still waiting.

Data Date	Weiss Investment Rating	Net Assets ($Mil)	Price	Performance Rating/Pts	Total Return Y-T-D	Risk Rating/Pts
6-05	C-	558.44	8.70	D / 2.0	1.57%	B / 8.5
2004	C+	548.21	8.82	C- / 3.2	6.41%	B / 8.8
2003	C-	561.90	8.80	D+ / 2.7	12.38%	B / 8.2

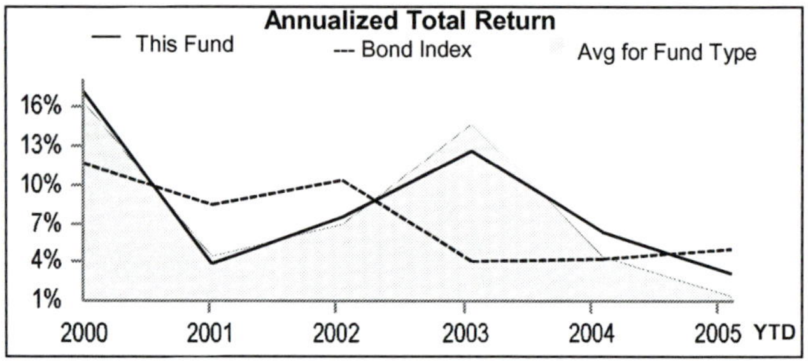

MFS Government Markets Income Trust (MGF) C- Fair

Fund Family: MFS Investment Management
Fund Type: Global
Inception Date: May 28, 1987

Major Rating Factors:
Very poor performance is the major factor driving the C- (Fair) Weiss Investment Rating for MFS Government Markets Income Trust. The fund currently has a performance rating of E+ (Very Weak) based on an annualized return of 4.54% over the last three years and a total return of 1.99% year to date 2005.

The fund's risk rating is currently B+ (Good). It carries a beta of 0.45, meaning the fund's expected move will be 4.5% for every 10% move in the market. Volatility, as measured by both the semi-deviation and a drawdown factor, is considered very low. As of June 30, 2005, MFS Government Markets Income Trust traded at a discount of 11.62% below its net asset value, which is better than its one-year historical average discount of 11.36%.

James J. Calmes has been running the fund for 3 years and currently receives a manager quality ranking of 56 (0=worst, 99=best). This fund offers only a moderate level of risk but investors looking for strong performance are still waiting.

Data Date	Weiss Investment Rating	Net Assets ($Mil)	Price	Performance Rating/Pts	Total Return Y-T-D	Risk Rating/Pts
6-05	C-	399.06	6.62	E+ / 0.9	1.99%	B+ / 9.2
2004	C	398.72	6.64	D / 2.0	2.80%	B+ / 9.3
2003	C	414.10	6.74	D / 1.9	1.85%	B+ / 9.5

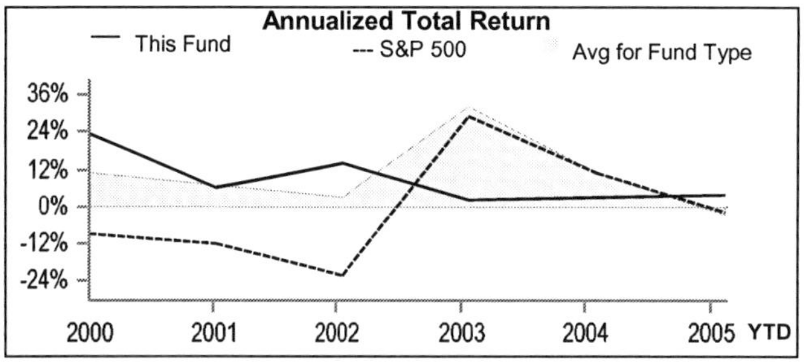

MFS Intermediate Income Trust (MIN) D+ Weak

Fund Family: MFS Investment Management
Fund Type: Global
Inception Date: March 18, 1988

Major Rating Factors:
Very poor performance is the major factor driving the D+ (Weak) Weiss Investment Rating for MFS Intermediate Income Trust. The fund currently has a performance rating of E (Very Weak) based on an annualized return of 2.48% over the last three years and a total return of 3.27% year to date 2005. Factored into the performance evaluation is an expense ratio of 0.87% (low).

The fund's risk rating is currently B (Good). It carries a beta of 0.45, meaning the fund's expected move will be 4.5% for every 10% move in the market. Volatility, as measured by both the semi-deviation and a drawdown factor, is considered low. As of June 30, 2005, MFS Intermediate Income Trust traded at a discount of 9.83% below its net asset value, which is worse than its one-year historical average discount of 10.27%.

James J. Calmas has been running the fund for 3 years and currently receives a manager quality ranking of 32 (0=worst, 99=best). This fund offers only a moderate level of risk but investors looking for strong performance are still waiting.

Data Date	Weiss Investment Rating	Net Assets ($Mil)	Price	Performance Rating/Pts	Total Return Y-T-D	Risk Rating/Pts
6-05	D+	873.01	6.51	E / 0.5	3.27%	B / 8.3
2004	D+	918.54	6.48	D- / 1.1	0.40%	B / 8.7
2003	C-	936.65	6.80	D / 1.8	1.45%	B+ / 9.2

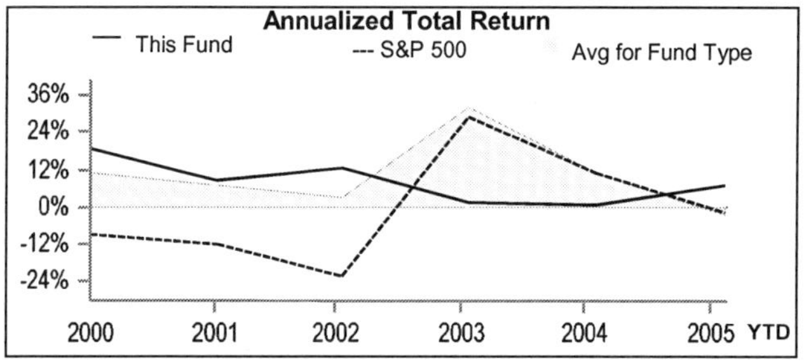

MFS Multimarket Income Trust (MMT) C Fair

Fund Family: MFS Investment Management
Fund Type: General Bond
Inception Date: March 12, 1987

Major Rating Factors:
Disappointing performance is the major factor driving the C (Fair) Weiss Investment Rating for MFS Multimarket Income Trust. The fund currently has a performance rating of D+ (Weak) based on an annualized return of 9.09% over the last three years and a total return of 2.51% year to date 2005. Factored into the performance evaluation is an expense ratio of 0.91% (low).

The fund's risk rating is currently B- (Good). It carries a beta of 1.26, meaning it is expected to move 12.6% for every 10% move in the market. Volatility, as measured by both the semi-deviation and a drawdown factor, is considered low. As of June 30, 2005, MFS Multimarket Income Trust traded at a discount of 8.97% below its net asset value, which is worse than its one-year historical average discount of 9.56%.

Peter C. Vaream has been running the fund for 3 years and currently receives a manager quality ranking of 74 (0=worst, 99=best). This fund offers only a moderate level of risk but investors looking for strong performance are still waiting.

Data Date	Weiss Investment Rating	Net Assets ($Mil)	Price	Performance Rating/Pts	Total Return Y-T-D	Risk Rating/Pts
6-05	C	554.72	6.29	D+ / 2.9	2.51%	B- / 7.8
2004	C	563.59	6.33	C- / 3.3	6.52%	B- / 7.8
2003	D+	563.76	6.36	C- / 3.0	14.58%	C+ / 6.2

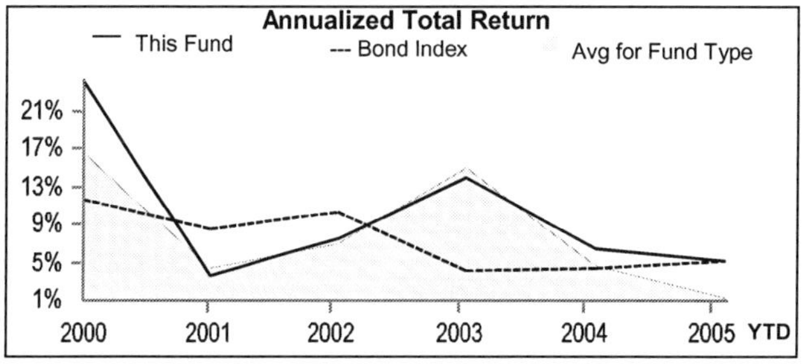

MFS Municipal Income Trust (MFM) A- Excellent

Fund Family: MFS Investment Management
Fund Type: Municipal - High Yield
Inception Date: November 25, 1986

Major Rating Factors:
Strong performance is the major factor driving the A- (Excellent) Weiss Investment Rating for MFS Municipal Income Trust. The fund currently has a performance rating of B+ (Good) based on an annualized return of 9.08% over the last three years and a total return of 11.20% year to date 2005. Factored into the performance evaluation is an expense ratio of 1.48% (average).

The fund's risk rating is currently C+ (Fair). It carries a beta of 2.01, meaning it is expected to move 20.1% for every 10% move in the market. Volatility, as measured by both the semi-deviation and a drawdown factor, is considered low. As of June 30, 2005, MFS Municipal Income Trust traded at a premium of 3.12% above its net asset value, which is worse than its one-year historical average discount of 1.25%.

Michael W. Roberge has been running the fund for 8 years and currently receives a manager quality ranking of 50 (0=worst, 99=best). If you desire only a moderate level of risk and strong performance, then this fund is an excellent option.

Data Date	Weiss Investment Rating	Net Assets ($Mil)	Price	Performance Rating/Pts	Total Return Y-T-D	Risk Rating/Pts
6-05	A-	318.23	8.26	B+ / 8.4	11.20%	C+ / 6.5
2004	C+	306.46	7.69	C / 5.1	8.27%	B- / 7.7
2003	C	300.44	7.51	C- / 4.2	12.87%	B / 8.1

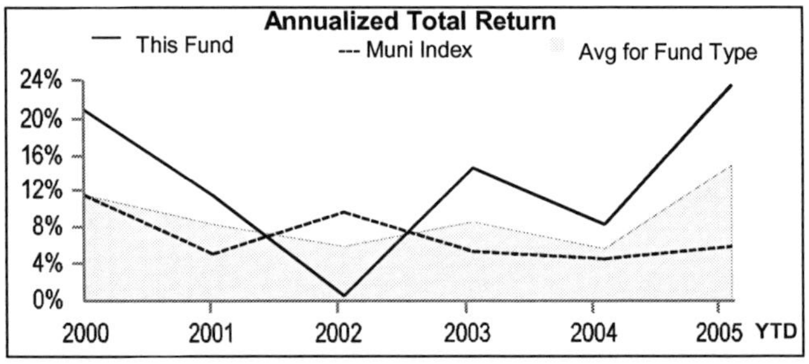

MFS Special Value Trust (MFV) C Fair

Fund Family: MFS Investment Management
Fund Type: Growth and Income
Inception Date: November 30, 1989

Major Rating Factors:
Middle of the road best describes MFS Special Value Trust whose Weiss Investment Rating is currently a C (Fair). The fund currently has a performance rating of C+ (Fair) based on an annualized return of 18.96% over the last three years and a total return of -5.15% year to date 2005. Factored into the performance evaluation is an expense ratio of 1.44% (average).

The fund's risk rating is currently C (Fair). It carries a beta of 0.79, meaning the fund's expected move will be 7.9% for every 10% move in the market. Volatility, as measured by both the semi-deviation and a drawdown factor, is considered average. As of June 30, 2005, MFS Special Value Trust traded at a premium of 7.70% above its net asset value, which is better than its one-year historical average premium of 12.72%.

John F. Addeo has been running the fund for 4 years and currently receives a manager quality ranking of 93 (0=worst, 99=best). If you desire an average level of risk, then this fund may be an option.

Data Date	Weiss Investment Rating	Net Assets ($Mil)	Price	Performance Rating/Pts	Total Return Y-T-D	Risk Rating/Pts
6-05	C	65.85	10.77	C+ / 6.4	-5.15%	C / 4.9
2004	C	67.89	11.91	B / 8.0	21.63%	C- / 3.8
2003	D	57.47	10.74	C / 5.3	55.13%	D+ / 2.4

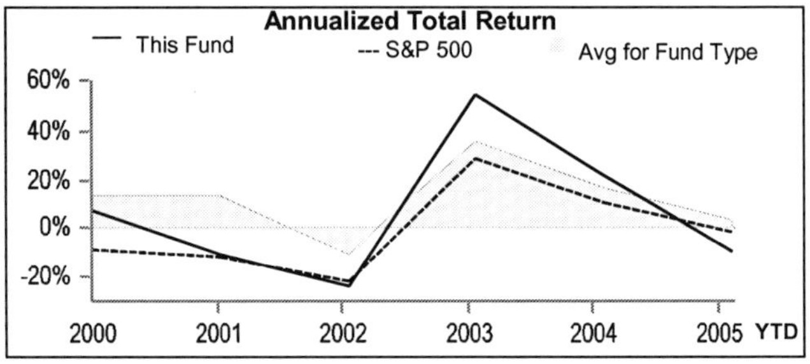

Minnesota Municipal Inc Portfolio (MXA) B Good

Fund Family: US Bancorp Asset Management
Fund Type: Municipal - Single State
Inception Date: June 25, 1993

Major Rating Factors:
Strong performance is the major factor driving the B (Good) Weiss Investment Rating for Minnesota Municipal Inc Portfolio. The fund currently has a performance rating of B- (Good) based on an annualized return of 7.54% over the last three years and a total return of 6.69% year to date 2005. Factored into the performance evaluation is an expense ratio of 1.17% (low).

The fund's risk rating is currently C+ (Fair). It carries a beta of 1.83, meaning it is expected to move 18.3% for every 10% move in the market. Volatility, as measured by both the semi-deviation and a drawdown factor, is considered low. As of June 30, 2005, Minnesota Municipal Inc Portfolio traded at a premium of 3.81% above its net asset value, which is worse than its one-year historical average premium of .81%.

Douglas J. White has been running the fund for 12 years and currently receives a manager quality ranking of 45 (0=worst, 99=best). If you desire only a moderate level of risk and strong performance, then this fund is an excellent option.

Data Date	Weiss Investment Rating	Net Assets ($Mil)	Price	Performance Rating/Pts	Total Return Y-T-D	Risk Rating/Pts
6-05	B	64.37	16.07	B- / 7.0	6.69%	C+ / 6.6
2004	B+	62.32	15.45	B- / 7.0	4.77%	B- / 7.5
2003	A	61.21	15.75	B- / 7.3	8.04%	B / 8.7

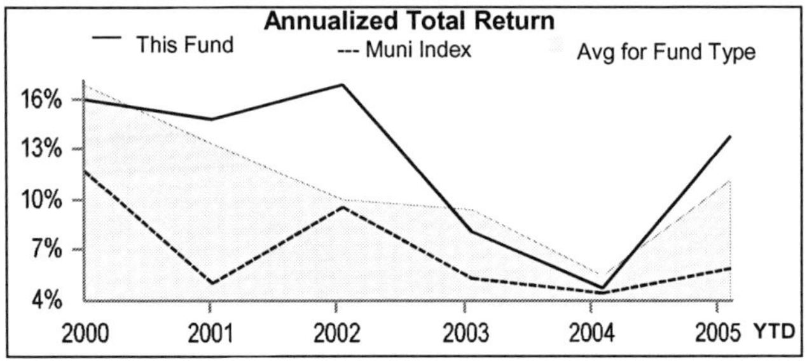

Montgomery Street Inc. Sec. (MTS) D+ Weak

Fund Family: Deutsche Asset Management
Fund Type: General - Investment Grade
Inception Date: February 14, 1973

Data Date	Weiss Investment Rating	Net Assets ($Mil)	Price	Performance Rating/Pts	Total Return Y-T-D	Risk Rating/Pts
6-05	D+	203.81	18.11	D- / 1.2	0.27%	B- / 7.4
2004	D+	201.55	18.36	D / 2.1	5.81%	B- / 7.7
2003	C-	211.49	18.42	D+ / 2.6	3.78%	B / 8.4

Major Rating Factors:
Disappointing performance is the major factor driving the D+ (Weak) Weiss Investment Rating for Montgomery Street Inc. Sec.. The fund currently has a performance rating of D- (Weak) based on an annualized return of 5.47% over the last three years and a total return of 0.27% year to date 2005.

The fund's risk rating is currently B- (Good). It carries a beta of 1.45, meaning it is expected to move 14.5% for every 10% move in the market. Volatility, as measured by both the semi-deviation and a drawdown factor, is considered low. As of June 30, 2005, Montgomery Street Inc. Sec. traded at a discount of 8.67% below its net asset value, which is better than its one-year historical average discount of 6.70%.

Gary Bartlett has been running the fund for 32 years and currently receives a manager quality ranking of 43 (0=worst, 99=best). This fund offers only a moderate level of risk but investors looking for strong performance are still waiting.

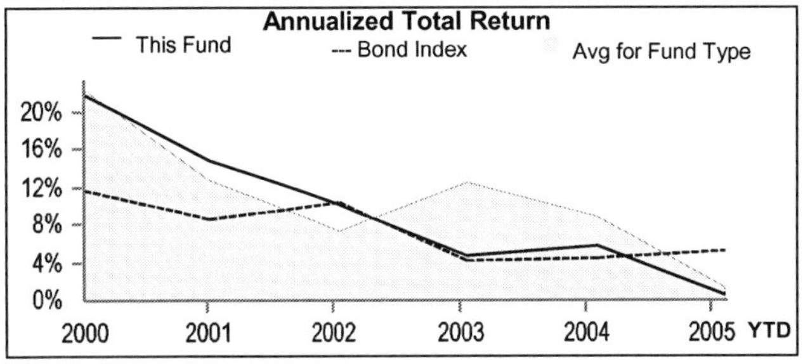

Morgan Stanley Asia Pacific Fund (APF) C- Fair

Fund Family: Morgan Stanley Invesment Advisors,I
Fund Type: Foreign
Inception Date: July 26, 1994

Data Date	Weiss Investment Rating	Net Assets ($Mil)	Price	Performance Rating/Pts	Total Return Y-T-D	Risk Rating/Pts
6-05	C-	520.13	13.05	C / 5.5	1.87%	C / 4.7
2004	B+	462.72	12.81	B+ / 8.5	19.06%	C+ / 6.2
2003	C	338.66	10.55	C+ / 6.9	47.77%	C / 4.9

Major Rating Factors:
Middle of the road best describes Morgan Stanley Asia Pacific Fund whose Weiss Investment Rating is currently a C- (Fair). The fund currently has a performance rating of C (Fair) based on an annualized return of 15.59% over the last three years and a total return of 1.87% year to date 2005. Factored into the performance evaluation is an expense ratio of 1.18% (low).

The fund's risk rating is currently C (Fair). It carries a beta of 0.87, meaning the fund's expected move will be 8.7% for every 10% move in the market. Volatility, as measured by both the semi-deviation and a drawdown factor, is considered average. As of June 30, 2005, Morgan Stanley Asia Pacific Fund traded at a discount of 11.41% below its net asset value, which is worse than its one-year historical average discount of 11.89%.

Ashutosh Sinha has been running the fund for 7 years and currently receives a manager quality ranking of 80 (0=worst, 99=best). If you desire an average level of risk, then this fund may be an option.

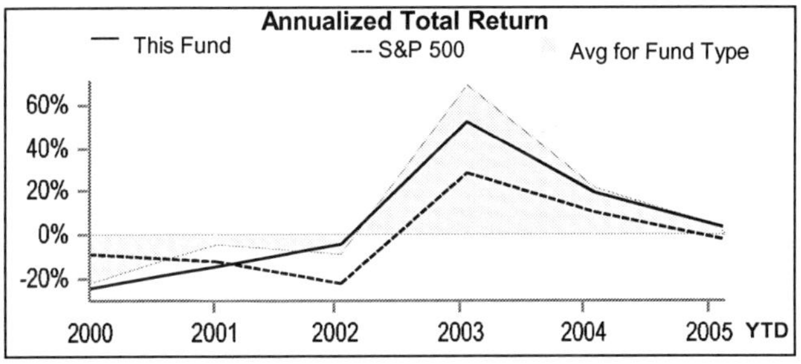

Morgan Stanley CA Insured Muni Inc (IIC) C+ Fair

Fund Family: Morgan Stanley Invesment Advisors,I
Fund Type: Municipal - Single State
Inception Date: February 26, 1993

Data Date	Weiss Investment Rating	Net Assets ($Mil)	Price	Performance Rating/Pts	Total Return Y-T-D	Risk Rating/Pts
6-05	C+	173.82	13.89	C / 4.6	8.40%	B- / 7.4
2004	D+	172.78	13.16	D- / 1.3	1.38%	B / 8.1
2003	C-	178.54	13.75	D / 2.2	1.75%	B+ / 9.1

Major Rating Factors:
Middle of the road best describes Morgan Stanley CA Insured Muni Inc whose Weiss Investment Rating is currently a C+ (Fair). The fund currently has a performance rating of C (Fair) based on an annualized return of 5.15% over the last three years and a total return of 8.40% year to date 2005. Factored into the performance evaluation is an expense ratio of 0.80% (very low).

The fund's risk rating is currently B- (Good). It carries a beta of 1.86, meaning it is expected to move 18.6% for every 10% move in the market. Volatility, as measured by both the semi-deviation and a drawdown factor, is considered low. As of June 30, 2005, Morgan Stanley CA Insured Muni Inc traded at a discount of 10.10% below its net asset value, which is worse than its one-year historical average discount of 11.28%.

James Willison has been running the fund for 12 years and currently receives a manager quality ranking of 21 (0=worst, 99=best). If you desire an average level of risk, then this fund may be an option.

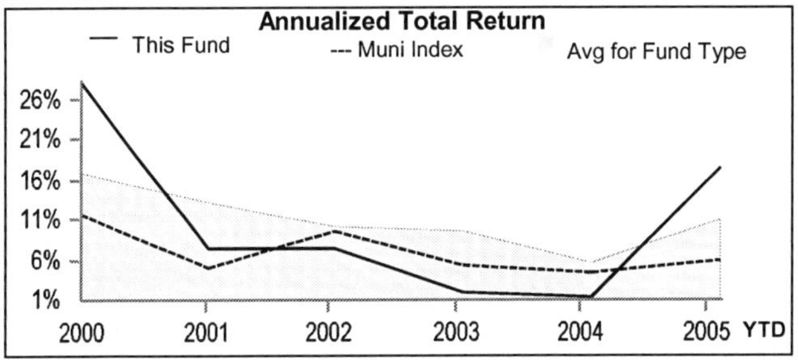

Morgan Stanley CA Muni Sec (ICS) C+ Fair

Fund Family: Morgan Stanley Invesment Advisors,I
Fund Type: Municipal - Single State
Inception Date: February 28, 1994

Major Rating Factors:
Middle of the road best describes Morgan Stanley CA Muni Sec whose Weiss Investment Rating is currently a C+ (Fair). The fund currently has a performance rating of C- (Fair) based on an annualized return of 5.45% over the last three years and a total return of 5.39% year to date 2005. Factored into the performance evaluation is an expense ratio of 0.56% (very low).

The fund's risk rating is currently B+ (Good). It carries a beta of 1.08, meaning that its performance tracks fairly well with that of the overall stock market. Volatility, as measured by both the semi-deviation and a drawdown factor, is considered very low. As of June 30, 2005, Morgan Stanley CA Muni Sec traded at a discount of 8.92% below its net asset value, which is worse than its one-year historical average discount of 9.56%.

James Willison has been running the fund for 11 years and currently receives a manager quality ranking of 58 (0=worst, 99=best). If you desire an average level of risk, then this fund may be an option.

Data Date	Weiss Investment Rating	Net Assets ($Mil)	Price	Performance Rating/Pts	Total Return Y-T-D	Risk Rating/Pts
6-05	C+	56.24	14.09	C- / 3.4	5.39%	B+ / 9.1
2004	C	55.98	13.69	D+ / 2.6	4.13%	B+ / 9.0
2003	C	57.92	13.83	D+ / 2.8	3.56%	B+ / 9.1

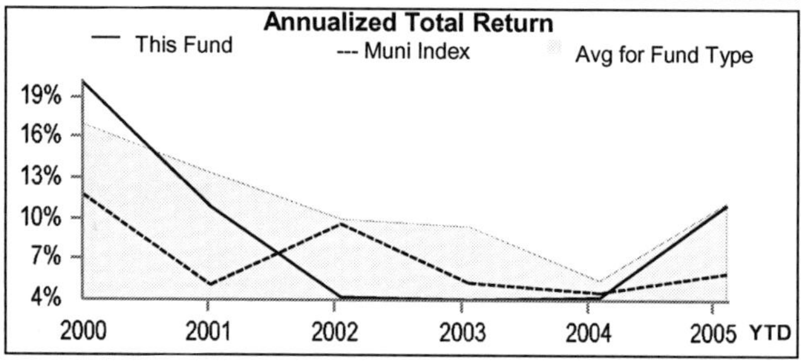

Morgan Stanley CA Qual Muni Sec (IQC) B+ Good

Fund Family: Morgan Stanley Invesment Advisors,I
Fund Type: Municipal - Single State
Inception Date: September 29, 1993

Major Rating Factors:
Morgan Stanley CA Qual Muni Sec receives a Weiss Investment Rating of B+ (Good). The fund currently has a performance rating of C+ (Fair) based on an annualized return of 8.77% over the last three years and a total return of 5.29% year to date 2005. Factored into the performance evaluation is an expense ratio of 0.80% (very low).

The fund's risk rating is currently B+ (Good). It carries a beta of 1.62, meaning it is expected to move 16.2% for every 10% move in the market. Volatility, as measured by both the semi-deviation and a drawdown factor, is considered very low. As of June 30, 2005, Morgan Stanley CA Qual Muni Sec traded at a discount of 9.49% below its net asset value, which is better than its one-year historical average discount of 8.13%.

James Willison has been running the fund for 12 years and currently receives a manager quality ranking of 63 (0=worst, 99=best). If you desire an average level of risk, then this fund may be an option.

Data Date	Weiss Investment Rating	Net Assets ($Mil)	Price	Performance Rating/Pts	Total Return Y-T-D	Risk Rating/Pts
6-05	B+	145.66	14.30	C+ / 5.6	5.29%	B+ / 9.1
2004	B	142.45	13.99	C / 5.0	6.24%	B+ / 9.0
2003	C+	146.01	13.94	C / 4.6	6.62%	B / 8.7

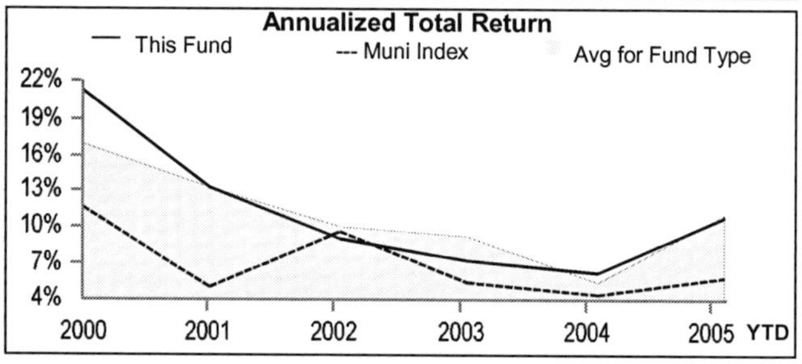

Morgan Stanley Eastern Europe (RNE) C+ Fair

Fund Family: Morgan Stanley Invesment Advisors,I
Fund Type: Foreign
Inception Date: September 30, 1996

Major Rating Factors:
Morgan Stanley Eastern Europe has adopted a risky asset allocation strategy and currently receives an overall Weiss Investment Rating of C+ (Fair). The fund has shown an above average level of volatility, as measured by both semi-deviation and drawdown factors. It carries a beta of 1.33, meaning it is expected to move 13.3% for every 10% move in the market. As of June 30, 2005, Morgan Stanley Eastern Europe traded at a discount of 5.72% below its net asset value, which is worse than its one-year historical average discount of 8.93%. The high level of risk (D+, Weak) did however, reward investors with excellent performance.

The fund's performance rating is currently A+ (Excellent). It has registered an annualized return of 38.86% over the last three years and is up 8.03% year to date 2005. Factored into the performance evaluation is an expense ratio of 1.92% (above average).

Eric Carlson has been running the fund for 9 years and currently receives a manager quality ranking of 98 (0=worst, 99=best). If you are comfortable owning a high risk investment, this fund may be an option.

Data Date	Weiss Investment Rating	Net Assets ($Mil)	Price	Performance Rating/Pts	Total Return Y-T-D	Risk Rating/Pts
6-05	C+	107.27	29.85	A+ / 9.8	8.03%	D+ / 2.3
2004	B	108.89	27.63	A+ / 9.8	44.47%	C / 4.4
2003	B	93.56	24.99	A+ / 9.7	76.00%	C / 4.8

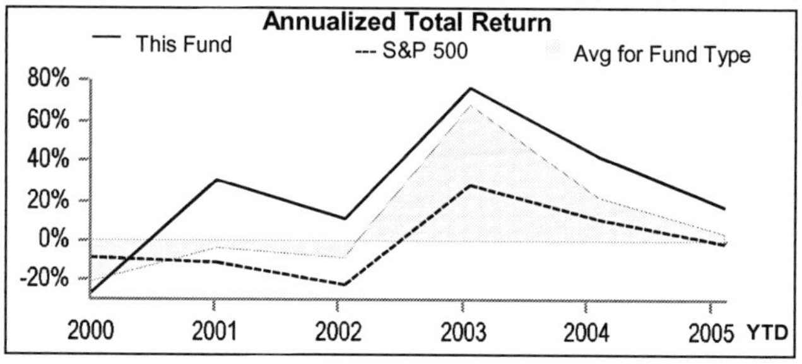

Morgan Stanley Emerging Markets (MSF) C+ Fair

Fund Family: Morgan Stanley Invesment Advisors,I
Fund Type: Emerging Market
Inception Date: November 1, 1991

Major Rating Factors:
Morgan Stanley Emerging Markets has adopted a risky asset allocation strategy and currently receives an overall Weiss Investment Rating of C+ (Fair). The fund has shown an above average level of volatility, as measured by both semi-deviation and drawdown factors. It carries a beta of 1.50, meaning it is expected to move 15.0% for every 10% move in the market. As of June 30, 2005, Morgan Stanley Emerging Markets traded at a discount of 11.62% below its net asset value, which is better than its one-year historical average discount of 9.89%. The high level of risk (D+, Weak) did however, reward investors with excellent performance.

The fund's performance rating is currently A (Excellent). It has registered an annualized return of 24.43% over the last three years and is up 3.07% year to date 2005. Factored into the performance evaluation is an expense ratio of 1.53% (average).

Ashutosh Sinha has been running the fund for 14 years and currently receives a manager quality ranking of 2 (0=worst, 99=best). If you are comfortable owning a high risk investment, this fund may be an option.

Data Date	Weiss Investment Rating	Net Assets ($Mil)	Price	Performance Rating/Pts	Total Return Y-T-D	Risk Rating/Pts
6-05	C+	348.93	18.11	A / 9.3	3.07%	D+ / 2.7
2004	B	275.48	17.57	A- / 9.2	20.11%	C / 5.1
2003	C+	209.86	14.35	A / 9.5	74.13%	C- / 3.6

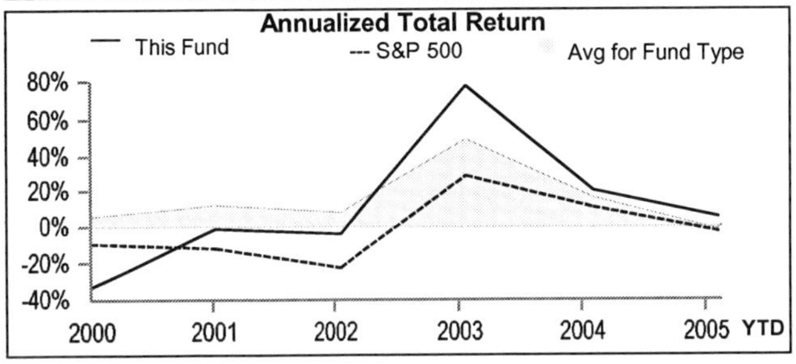

Morgan Stanley Emerging Mkts Debt (MSD) B+ Good

Fund Family: Morgan Stanley Invesment Advisors,I
Fund Type: Emerging Market
Inception Date: July 23, 1993

Major Rating Factors:
Strong performance is the major factor driving the B+ (Good) Weiss Investment Rating for Morgan Stanley Emerging Mkts Debt. The fund currently has a performance rating of B+ (Good) based on an annualized return of 21.23% over the last three years and a total return of 5.77% year to date 2005. Factored into the performance evaluation is an expense ratio of 1.22% (average).

The fund's risk rating is currently C (Fair). It carries a beta of 0.94, meaning that its performance tracks fairly well with that of the overall stock market. Volatility, as measured by both the semi-deviation and a drawdown factor, is considered average. As of June 30, 2005, Morgan Stanley Emerging Mkts Debt traded at a discount of 7.69% below its net asset value, which is worse than its one-year historical average discount of 8.26%.

Eric J. Baurmeister has been running the fund for 12 years and currently receives a manager quality ranking of 91 (0=worst, 99=best). If you desire an average level of risk and strong performance, then this fund is a good option.

Data Date	Weiss Investment Rating	Net Assets ($Mil)	Price	Performance Rating/Pts	Total Return Y-T-D	Risk Rating/Pts
6-05	B+	229.04	9.97	B+ / 8.6	5.77%	C / 5.4
2004	B	210.42	9.61	B / 8.0	8.14%	C+ / 5.7
2003	B	216.27	9.61	B+ / 8.9	38.31%	C+ / 5.8

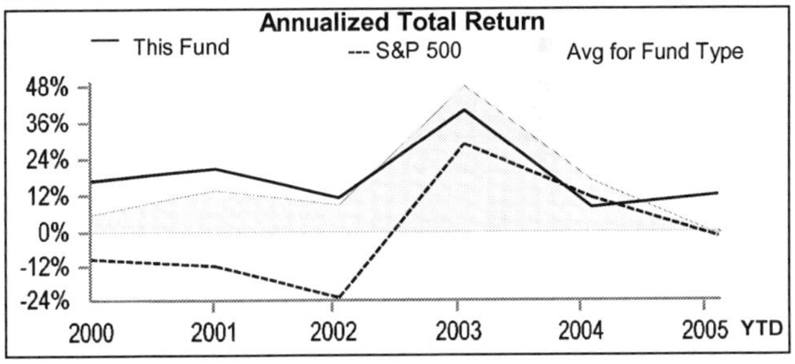

Morgan Stanley Global Opp Bond Fund (MGB) E+ Very Weak

Fund Family: Morgan Stanley Invesment Advisors,I
Fund Type: Global
Inception Date: May 27, 1994

Major Rating Factors:
Morgan Stanley Global Opp Bond Fund has adopted a very risky asset allocation strategy and currently receives an overall Weiss Investment Rating of E+ (Very Weak). The fund has a high level of volatility, as measured by both semi-deviation and drawdown factors. It carries a beta of 0.62, meaning the fund's expected move will be 6.2% for every 10% move in the market. As of June 30, 2005, Morgan Stanley Global Opp Bond Fund traded at a discount of 4.06% below its net asset value, which is better than its one-year historical average premium of 8.79%. Unfortunately, the high level of risk (D, Weak) has only provided investors with average performance.

The fund's performance rating is currently C (Fair). It has registered an annualized return of 15.54% over the last three years but is down -22.52% year to date 2005. Factored into the performance evaluation is an expense ratio of 1.91% (above average).

Thomas Bennett has been running the fund for 11 years and currently receives a manager quality ranking of 87 (0=worst, 99=best). If you are comfortable owning a very high risk investment, then this fund may be an option.

Data Date	Weiss Investment Rating	Net Assets ($Mil)	Price	Performance Rating/Pts	Total Return Y-T-D	Risk Rating/Pts
6-05	E+	33.86	7.80	C / 4.4	-22.52%	D / 1.6
2004	C+	31.50	10.25	A / 9.4	42.83%	C- / 3.4
2003	C-	30.98	7.74	C+ / 6.1	41.54%	C / 4.3

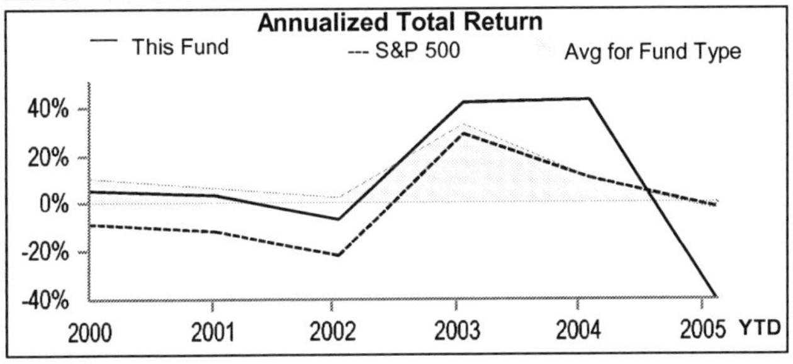

Morgan Stanley Govt Inc Tr (GVT) C- Fair

Fund Family: Morgan Stanley Invesment Advisors,I
Fund Type: US Government/Agency
Inception Date: February 2, 1988

Major Rating Factors:
Very poor performance is the major factor driving the C- (Fair) Weiss Investment Rating for Morgan Stanley Govt Inc Tr. The fund currently has a performance rating of E+ (Very Weak) based on an annualized return of 4.45% over the last three years and a total return of 3.49% year to date 2005. Factored into the performance evaluation is an expense ratio of 0.72% (very low).

The fund's risk rating is currently B+ (Good). It carries a beta of 0.34, meaning the fund's expected move will be 3.4% for every 10% move in the market. Volatility, as measured by both the semi-deviation and a drawdown factor, is considered very low. As of June 30, 2005, Morgan Stanley Govt Inc Tr traded at a discount of 10.17% below its net asset value, which is better than its one-year historical average discount of 9.50%.

Jaidip Singh has been running the fund for 17 years and currently receives a manager quality ranking of 63 (0=worst, 99=best). This fund offers only a moderate level of risk but investors looking for strong performance are still waiting.

Data Date	Weiss Investment Rating	Net Assets ($Mil)	Price	Performance Rating/Pts	Total Return Y-T-D	Risk Rating/Pts
6-05	C-	324.61	8.92	E+ / 0.9	3.49%	B+ / 9.5
2004	C-	334.71	8.79	D- / 1.5	2.32%	B+ / 9.6
2003	C-	350.47	9.01	D / 2.1	2.56%	B / 8.4

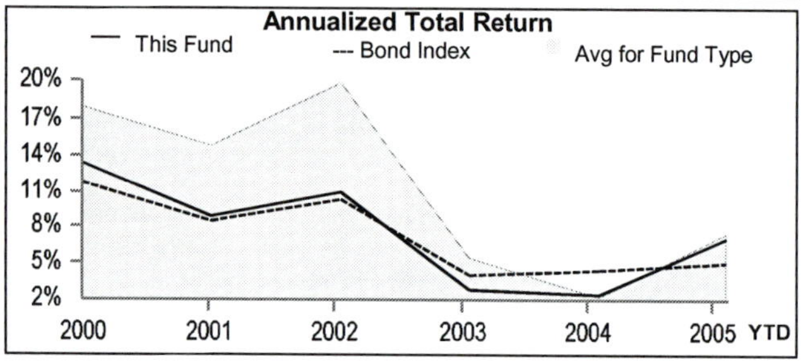

Morgan Stanley High Yield Fund (MSY) C- Fair

Fund Family: Morgan Stanley Invesment Advisors,I
Fund Type: Corporate - High Yield
Inception Date: November 30, 1993

Major Rating Factors:
Middle of the road best describes Morgan Stanley High Yield Fund whose Weiss Investment Rating is currently a C- (Fair). The fund currently has a performance rating of C- (Fair) based on an annualized return of 11.26% over the last three years and a total return of 0.47% year to date 2005. Factored into the performance evaluation is an expense ratio of 1.45% (average).

The fund's risk rating is currently C+ (Fair). It carries a beta of 1.55, meaning it is expected to move 15.5% for every 10% move in the market. Volatility, as measured by both the semi-deviation and a drawdown factor, is considered low. As of June 30, 2005, Morgan Stanley High Yield Fund traded at a discount of 7.61% below its net asset value, which is worse than its one-year historical average discount of 9.53%.

Deanna Loughnane has been running the fund for 3 years and currently receives a manager quality ranking of 5 (0=worst, 99=best). If you desire an average level of risk, then this fund may be an option.

Data Date	Weiss Investment Rating	Net Assets ($Mil)	Price	Performance Rating/Pts	Total Return Y-T-D	Risk Rating/Pts
6-05	C-	83.49	6.31	C- / 4.1	0.47%	C+ / 5.6
2004	E+	79.83	6.51	D- / 1.4	10.30%	C- / 3.3
2003	D-	76.44	6.54	D- / 1.4	33.07%	C- / 3.7

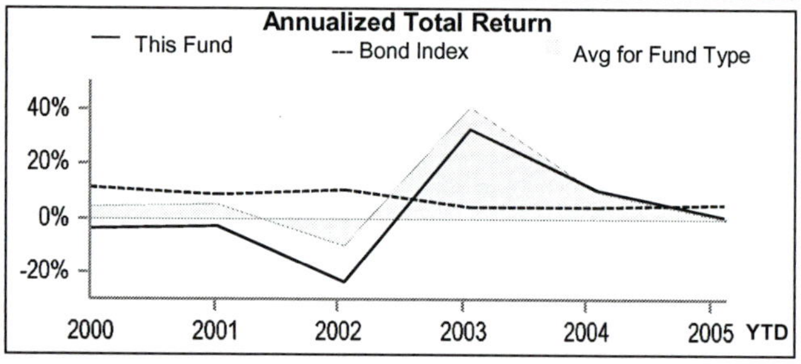

Morgan Stanley Income Sec (ICB) C- Fair

Fund Family: Morgan Stanley Invesment Advisors,I
Fund Type: Corporate - Investment Grade
Inception Date: April 6, 1973

Major Rating Factors:
Disappointing performance is the major factor driving the C- (Fair) Weiss Investment Rating for Morgan Stanley Income Sec. The fund currently has a performance rating of D (Weak) based on an annualized return of 5.66% over the last three years and a total return of 3.04% year to date 2005. Factored into the performance evaluation is an expense ratio of 0.67% (very low).

The fund's risk rating is currently B (Good). It carries a beta of 1.21, meaning it is expected to move 12.1% for every 10% move in the market. Volatility, as measured by both the semi-deviation and a drawdown factor, is considered low. As of June 30, 2005, Morgan Stanley Income Sec traded at a discount of 10.03% below its net asset value, which is better than its one-year historical average discount of 9.53%.

Stephen Esser has been running the fund for 32 years and currently receives a manager quality ranking of 30 (0=worst, 99=best). This fund offers only a moderate level of risk but investors looking for strong performance are still waiting.

Data Date	Weiss Investment Rating	Net Assets ($Mil)	Price	Performance Rating/Pts	Total Return Y-T-D	Risk Rating/Pts
6-05	C-	179.01	15.88	D / 1.9	3.04%	B / 8.4
2004	C-	185.95	15.81	D / 1.8	4.61%	B / 8.1
2003	D+	190.30	16.17	D / 2.1	15.35%	B- / 7.8

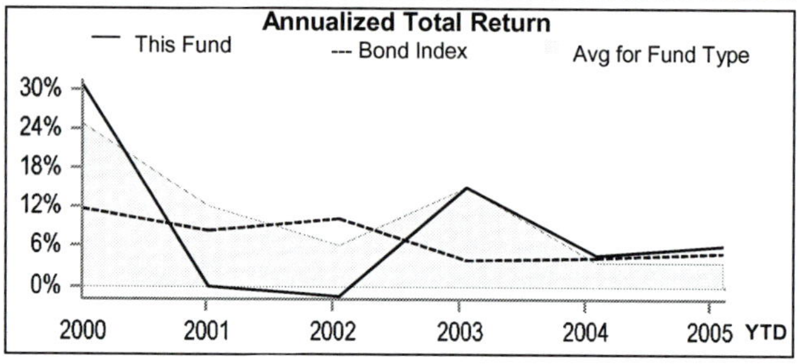

Morgan Stanley India Inv Fund (IIF) C+ Fair

Fund Family: Morgan Stanley Invesment Advisors,I
Fund Type: Foreign
Inception Date: February 25, 1994

Major Rating Factors:
Morgan Stanley India Inv Fund has adopted a risky asset allocation strategy and currently receives an overall Weiss Investment Rating of C+ (Fair). The fund has shown an above average level of volatility, as measured by both semi-deviation and drawdown factors. It carries a beta of 1.17, meaning it is expected to move 11.7% for every 10% move in the market. As of June 30, 2005, Morgan Stanley India Inv Fund traded at a premium of 6.74% above its net asset value, which is worse than its one-year historical average premium of 2.57%. The high level of risk (D+, Weak) did however, reward investors with excellent performance.

The fund's performance rating is currently A+ (Excellent). It has registered an annualized return of 54.11% over the last three years and is up 7.95% year to date 2005. Factored into the performance evaluation is an expense ratio of 1.40% (average).

Amay Hattangadi has been running the fund for 11 years and currently receives a manager quality ranking of 99 (0=worst, 99=best). If you are comfortable owning a high risk investment, this fund may be an option.

Data Date	Weiss Investment Rating	Net Assets ($Mil)	Price	Performance Rating/Pts	Total Return Y-T-D	Risk Rating/Pts
6-05	C+	465.45	33.42	A+ / 9.9	7.95%	D+ / 2.3
2004	B	309.09	30.96	A+ / 9.9	17.03%	C- / 4.0
2003	C	220.47	26.23	A+ / 9.9	166.42%	D+ / 2.4

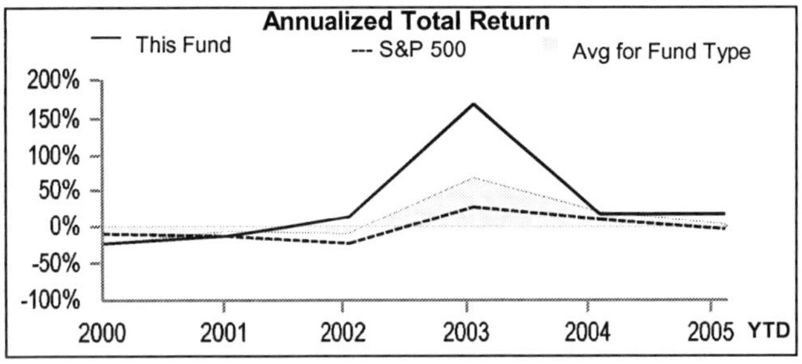

Morgan Stanley Insured Muni Bond (IMB) C Fair

Fund Family: Morgan Stanley Invesment Advisors,I
Fund Type: Municipal - National
Inception Date: February 28, 1991

Major Rating Factors:
Middle of the road best describes Morgan Stanley Insured Muni Bond whose Weiss Investment Rating is currently a C (Fair). The fund currently has a performance rating of C- (Fair) based on an annualized return of 5.27% over the last three years and a total return of 4.12% year to date 2005. Factored into the performance evaluation is an expense ratio of 1.01% (low).

The fund's risk rating is currently B- (Good). It carries a beta of 2.16, meaning it is expected to move 21.6% for every 10% move in the market. Volatility, as measured by both the semi-deviation and a drawdown factor, is considered low. As of June 30, 2005, Morgan Stanley Insured Muni Bond traded at a discount of 11.57% below its net asset value, which is better than its one-year historical average discount of 11.02%.

James Willison has been running the fund for 14 years and currently receives a manager quality ranking of 17 (0=worst, 99=best). If you desire an average level of risk, then this fund may be an option.

Data Date	Weiss Investment Rating	Net Assets ($Mil)	Price	Performance Rating/Pts	Total Return Y-T-D	Risk Rating/Pts
6-05	C	67.78	13.98	C- / 3.5	4.12%	B- / 7.7
2004	C	69.12	13.81	C- / 3.6	-1.32%	B / 8.1
2003	C+	71.94	14.80	C / 4.7	4.72%	B / 8.6

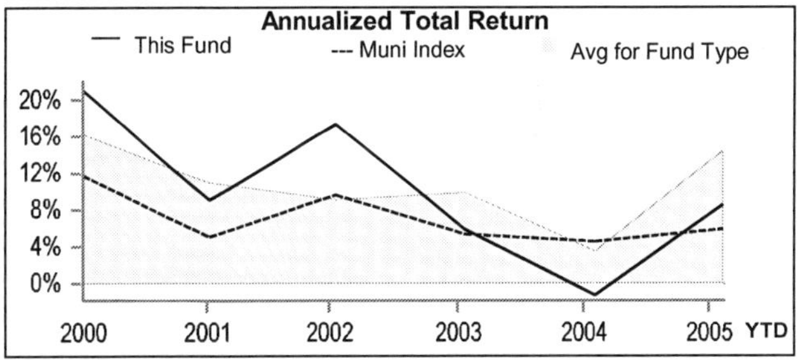

Morgan Stanley Insured Muni Inc Tr (IIM) B Good

Fund Family: Morgan Stanley Invesment Advisors,I
Fund Type: Municipal - National
Inception Date: February 26, 1993

Major Rating Factors:
Morgan Stanley Insured Muni Inc Tr receives a Weiss Investment Rating of B (Good). The fund currently has a performance rating of C (Fair) based on an annualized return of 7.30% over the last three years and a total return of 5.39% year to date 2005. Factored into the performance evaluation is an expense ratio of 0.83% (very low).

The fund's risk rating is currently B (Good). It carries a beta of 1.82, meaning it is expected to move 18.2% for every 10% move in the market. Volatility, as measured by both the semi-deviation and a drawdown factor, is considered low. As of June 30, 2005, Morgan Stanley Insured Muni Inc Tr traded at a discount of 11.06% below its net asset value, which is better than its one-year historical average discount of 10.70%.

James Willison has been running the fund for 12 years and currently receives a manager quality ranking of 44 (0=worst, 99=best). If you desire an average level of risk, then this fund may be an option.

Data Date	Weiss Investment Rating	Net Assets ($Mil)	Price	Performance Rating/Pts	Total Return Y-T-D	Risk Rating/Pts
6-05	B	357.16	14.23	C / 5.4	5.39%	B / 8.3
2004	C+	362.95	13.90	C / 4.3	-0.46%	B / 8.6
2003	B	382.15	14.82	C+ / 6.2	12.30%	B / 8.4

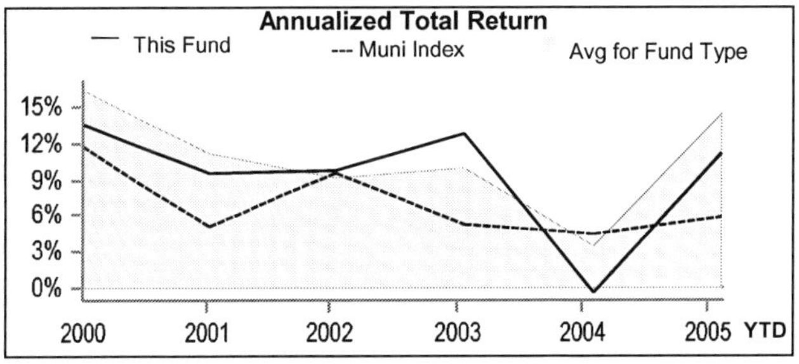

Morgan Stanley Insured Muni Sec (IMS) C+ Fair

Fund Family: Morgan Stanley Invesment Advisors,I
Fund Type: Municipal - National
Inception Date: February 28, 1994

Major Rating Factors:
Middle of the road best describes Morgan Stanley Insured Muni Sec whose Weiss Investment Rating is currently a C+ (Fair). The fund currently has a performance rating of C (Fair) based on an annualized return of 5.70% over the last three years and a total return of 7.23% year to date 2005. Factored into the performance evaluation is an expense ratio of 0.49% (very low).

The fund's risk rating is currently B- (Good). It carries a beta of 1.51, meaning it is expected to move 15.1% for every 10% move in the market. Volatility, as measured by both the semi-deviation and a drawdown factor, is considered low. As of June 30, 2005, Morgan Stanley Insured Muni Sec traded at a discount of 6.70% below its net asset value, which is worse than its one-year historical average discount of 8.91%.

James Willison has been running the fund for 11 years and currently receives a manager quality ranking of 41 (0=worst, 99=best). If you desire an average level of risk, then this fund may be an option.

Data Date	Weiss Investment Rating	Net Assets ($Mil)	Price	Performance Rating/Pts	Total Return Y-T-D	Risk Rating/Pts
6-05	C+	109.44	14.48	C / 4.5	7.23%	B- / 7.7
2004	C	111.64	13.81	D+ / 2.6	-1.00%	B / 8.8
2003	C+	116.77	14.60	C / 4.7	8.93%	B / 8.6

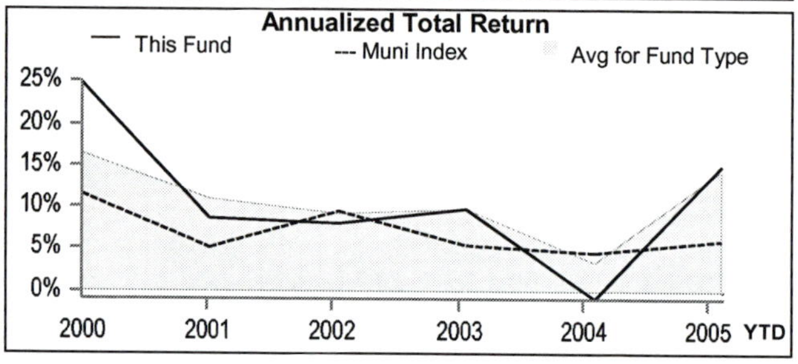

Morgan Stanley Insured Muni Tr (IMT) C+ Fair

Fund Family: Morgan Stanley Invesment Advisors,I
Fund Type: Municipal - National
Inception Date: February 28, 1992

Major Rating Factors:
Middle of the road best describes Morgan Stanley Insured Muni Tr whose Weiss Investment Rating is currently a C+ (Fair). The fund currently has a performance rating of C (Fair) based on an annualized return of 5.89% over the last three years and a total return of 5.02% year to date 2005. Factored into the performance evaluation is an expense ratio of 0.79% (very low).

The fund's risk rating is currently B (Good). It carries a beta of 1.64, meaning it is expected to move 16.4% for every 10% move in the market. Volatility, as measured by both the semi-deviation and a drawdown factor, is considered low. As of June 30, 2005, Morgan Stanley Insured Muni Tr traded at a discount of 11.10% below its net asset value, which is better than its one-year historical average discount of 11.00%.

James Willison has been running the fund for 13 years and currently receives a manager quality ranking of 36 (0=worst, 99=best). If you desire an average level of risk, then this fund may be an option.

Data Date	Weiss Investment Rating	Net Assets ($Mil)	Price	Performance Rating/Pts	Total Return Y-T-D	Risk Rating/Pts
6-05	C+	293.25	13.93	C / 4.4	5.02%	B / 8.4
2004	C	298.36	13.66	D+ / 2.9	-0.22%	B / 8.8
2003	C	309.30	14.54	C- / 3.2	7.89%	B+ / 9.0

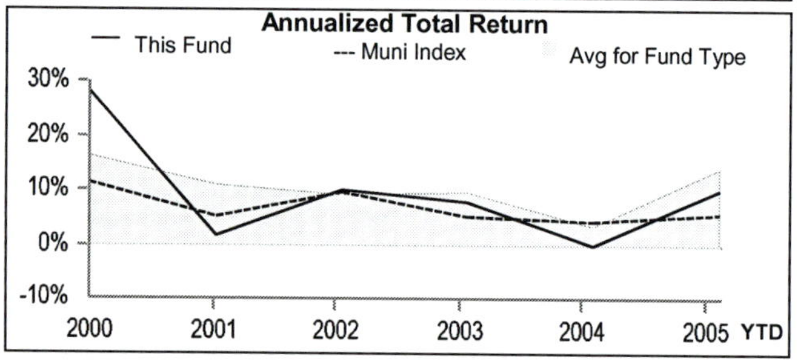

Morgan Stanley Muni Inc Op (OIA) B+ Good

Fund Family: Morgan Stanley Invesment Advisors,I
Fund Type: Municipal - National
Inception Date: September 19, 1988

Major Rating Factors:
Strong performance is the major factor driving the B+ (Good) Weiss Investment Rating for Morgan Stanley Muni Inc Op. The fund currently has a performance rating of B (Good) based on an annualized return of 6.96% over the last three years and a total return of 10.40% year to date 2005. Factored into the performance evaluation is an expense ratio of 0.91% (low).

The fund's risk rating is currently C+ (Fair). It carries a beta of 1.63, meaning it is expected to move 16.3% for every 10% move in the market. Volatility, as measured by both the semi-deviation and a drawdown factor, is considered low. As of June 30, 2005, Morgan Stanley Muni Inc Op traded at a premium of 1.00% above its net asset value, which is worse than its one-year historical average discount of 4.20%.

Gerard Lian has been running the fund for 17 years and currently receives a manager quality ranking of 50 (0=worst, 99=best). If you desire only a moderate level of risk and strong performance, then this fund is an excellent option.

Data Date	Weiss Investment Rating	Net Assets ($Mil)	Price	Performance Rating/Pts	Total Return Y-T-D	Risk Rating/Pts
6-05	B+	157.09	8.10	B / 7.8	10.40%	C+ / 6.9
2004	C+	156.27	7.58	C / 4.9	12.84%	B- / 7.7
2003	D+	159.70	7.20	D- / 1.0	2.97%	B / 8.4

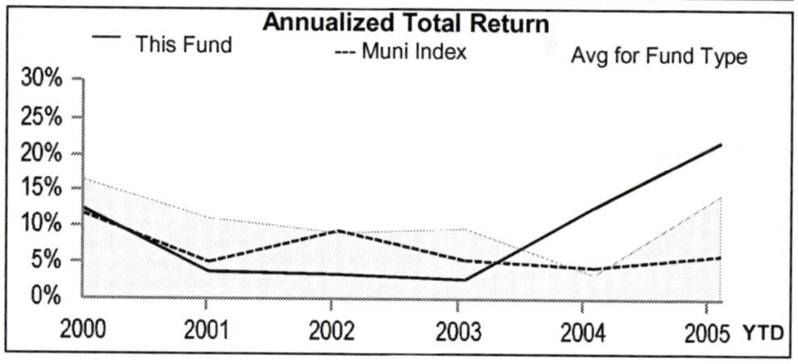

Morgan Stanley Muni Inc Op II (OIB) B Good

Fund Family: Morgan Stanley Invesment Advisors,I
Fund Type: Municipal - National
Inception Date: June 30, 1989

Major Rating Factors:
Morgan Stanley Muni Inc Op II receives a Weiss Investment Rating of B (Good). The fund currently has a performance rating of C+ (Fair) based on an annualized return of 7.08% over the last three years and a total return of 7.67% year to date 2005. Factored into the performance evaluation is an expense ratio of 0.89% (low).

The fund's risk rating is currently B (Good). It carries a beta of 1.57, meaning it is expected to move 15.7% for every 10% move in the market. Volatility, as measured by both the semi-deviation and a drawdown factor, is considered low. As of June 30, 2005, Morgan Stanley Muni Inc Op II traded at a discount of 9.05% below its net asset value, which is worse than its one-year historical average discount of 9.83%.

James F. Willison has been running the fund for 12 years and currently receives a manager quality ranking of 54 (0=worst, 99=best). If you desire an average level of risk, then this fund may be an option.

Data Date	Weiss Investment Rating	Net Assets ($Mil)	Price	Perfor-mance Rating/Pts	Total Return Y-T-D	Risk Rating/Pts
6-05	B	148.17	8.14	C+ / 6.1	7.67%	B / 8.5
2004	C+	147.28	7.79	C- / 4.2	7.63%	B / 8.9
2003	C	146.55	7.64	C- / 3.1	6.11%	B+ / 9.2

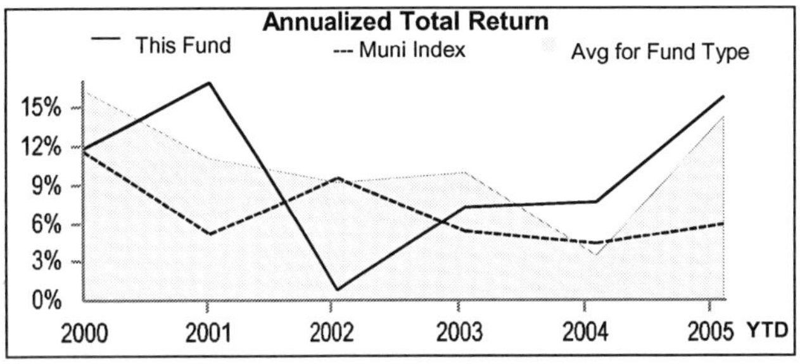

Morgan Stanley Muni Inc Op III (OIC) B- Good

Fund Family: Morgan Stanley Invesment Advisors,I
Fund Type: Municipal - National
Inception Date: April 30, 1990

Major Rating Factors:
Morgan Stanley Muni Inc Op III receives a Weiss Investment Rating of B- (Good). The fund currently has a performance rating of C+ (Fair) based on an annualized return of 6.35% over the last three years and a total return of 9.43% year to date 2005. Factored into the performance evaluation is an expense ratio of 0.93% (low).

The fund's risk rating is currently B- (Good). It carries a beta of 1.73, meaning it is expected to move 17.3% for every 10% move in the market. Volatility, as measured by both the semi-deviation and a drawdown factor, is considered low. As of June 30, 2005, Morgan Stanley Muni Inc Op III traded at a discount of 8.57% below its net asset value, which is worse than its one-year historical average discount of 10.16%.

Gerard Lian has been running the fund for 15 years and currently receives a manager quality ranking of 38 (0=worst, 99=best). If you desire an average level of risk, then this fund may be an option.

Data Date	Weiss Investment Rating	Net Assets ($Mil)	Price	Perfor-mance Rating/Pts	Total Return Y-T-D	Risk Rating/Pts
6-05	B-	84.38	8.86	C+ / 5.9	9.43%	B- / 7.8
2004	C-	84.70	8.34	D / 2.0	3.71%	B / 8.5
2003	C	85.25	8.60	C- / 3.0	6.88%	B / 8.9

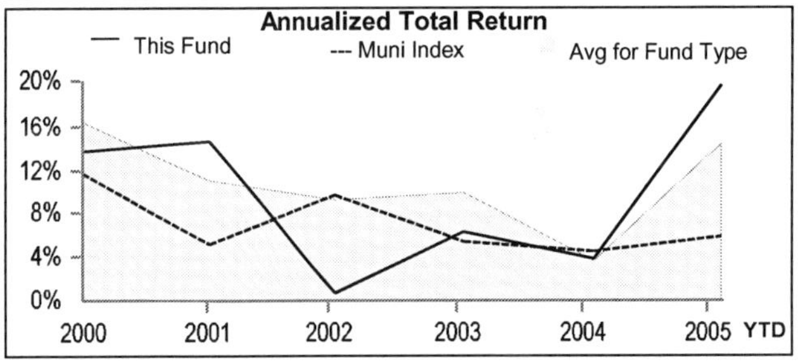

Morgan Stanley Muni Inv Tr (IQT) C+ Fair

Fund Family: Morgan Stanley Invesment Advisors,I
Fund Type: Municipal - National
Inception Date: September 27, 1991

Major Rating Factors:
Middle of the road best describes Morgan Stanley Muni Inv Tr whose Weiss Investment Rating is currently a C+ (Fair). The fund currently has a performance rating of C (Fair) based on an annualized return of 6.24% over the last three years and a total return of 6.29% year to date 2005. Factored into the performance evaluation is an expense ratio of 0.87% (low).

The fund's risk rating is currently B- (Good). It carries a beta of 1.84, meaning it is expected to move 18.4% for every 10% move in the market. Volatility, as measured by both the semi-deviation and a drawdown factor, is considered low. As of June 30, 2005, Morgan Stanley Muni Inv Tr traded at a discount of 11.96% below its net asset value, which is better than its one-year historical average discount of 11.68%.

James Willison has been running the fund for 14 years and currently receives a manager quality ranking of 30 (0=worst, 99=best). If you desire an average level of risk, then this fund may be an option.

Data Date	Weiss Investment Rating	Net Assets ($Mil)	Price	Perfor-mance Rating/Pts	Total Return Y-T-D	Risk Rating/Pts
6-05	C+	237.84	13.91	C / 4.8	6.29%	B- / 7.9
2004	C-	240.19	13.48	D / 1.9	1.08%	B / 8.3
2003	C+	249.85	14.25	C- / 3.3	7.18%	B+ / 9.2

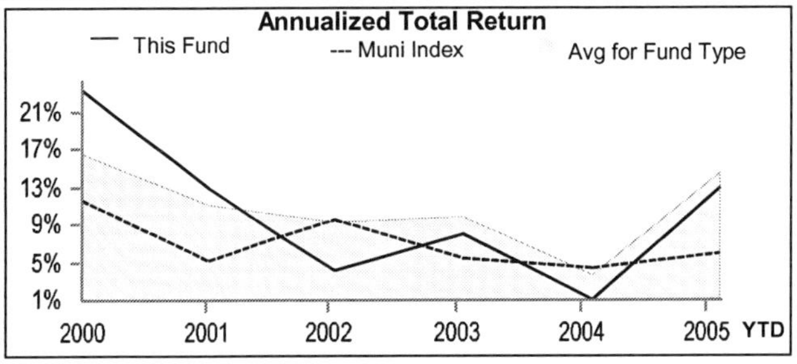

Morgan Stanley Muni Prem Inc Tr (PIA) C+ Fair

Fund Family: Morgan Stanley Invesment Advisors,I
Fund Type: Municipal - National
Inception Date: February 1, 1989

Major Rating Factors:
Middle of the road best describes Morgan Stanley Muni Prem Inc Tr whose Weiss Investment Rating is currently a C+ (Fair). The fund currently has a performance rating of C (Fair) based on an annualized return of 6.97% over the last three years and a total return of 3.83% year to date 2005. Factored into the performance evaluation is an expense ratio of 1.40% (average).

The fund's risk rating is currently B (Good). It carries a beta of 1.88, meaning it is expected to move 18.8% for every 10% move in the market. Volatility, as measured by both the semi-deviation and a drawdown factor, is considered low. As of June 30, 2005, Morgan Stanley Muni Prem Inc Tr traded at a discount of 13.14% below its net asset value, which is better than its one-year historical average discount of 11.76%.

James Willison has been running the fund for 12 years and currently receives a manager quality ranking of 39 (0=worst, 99=best). If you desire an average level of risk, then this fund may be an option.

Data Date	Weiss Investment Rating	Net Assets ($Mil)	Price	Perfor-mance Rating/Pts	Total Return Y-T-D	Risk Rating/Pts
6-05	C+	187.28	9.12	C / 4.8	3.83%	B / 8.2
2004	C+	186.76	9.05	C / 4.4	1.06%	B / 8.3
2003	B+	200.92	9.47	C+ / 6.2	14.37%	B / 8.6

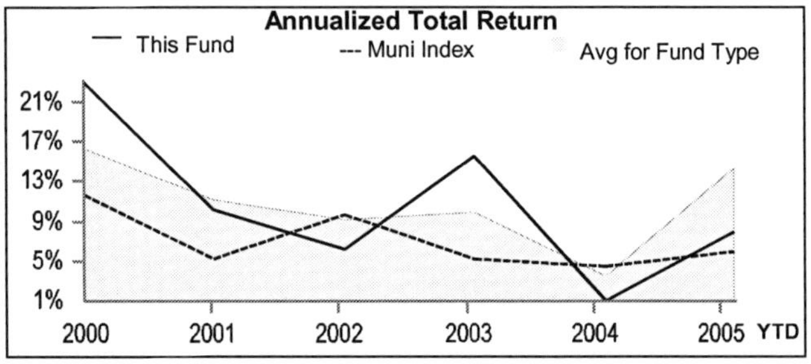

Morgan Stanley NY Qual Muni Sec (IQN) C+ Fair

Fund Family: Morgan Stanley Invesment Advisors,I
Fund Type: Municipal - Single State
Inception Date: September 29, 1993

Major Rating Factors:
Middle of the road best describes Morgan Stanley NY Qual Muni Sec whose Weiss Investment Rating is currently a C+ (Fair). The fund currently has a performance rating of C (Fair) based on an annualized return of 6.87% over the last three years and a total return of 3.34% year to date 2005. Factored into the performance evaluation is an expense ratio of 0.89% (low).

The fund's risk rating is currently B (Good). It carries a beta of 1.90, meaning it is expected to move 19.0% for every 10% move in the market. Volatility, as measured by both the semi-deviation and a drawdown factor, is considered low. As of June 30, 2005, Morgan Stanley NY Qual Muni Sec traded at a discount of 12.18% below its net asset value, which is better than its one-year historical average discount of 11.54%.

James Willison has been running the fund for 12 years and currently receives a manager quality ranking of 36 (0=worst, 99=best). If you desire an average level of risk, then this fund may be an option.

Data Date	Weiss Investment Rating	Net Assets ($Mil)	Price	Perfor-mance Rating/Pts	Total Return Y-T-D	Risk Rating/Pts
6-05	C+	67.36	13.77	C / 4.9	3.34%	B / 8.1
2004	B-	65.80	13.70	C / 5.5	6.14%	B- / 7.9
2003	C+	67.51	13.64	C- / 3.9	6.35%	B+ / 9.1

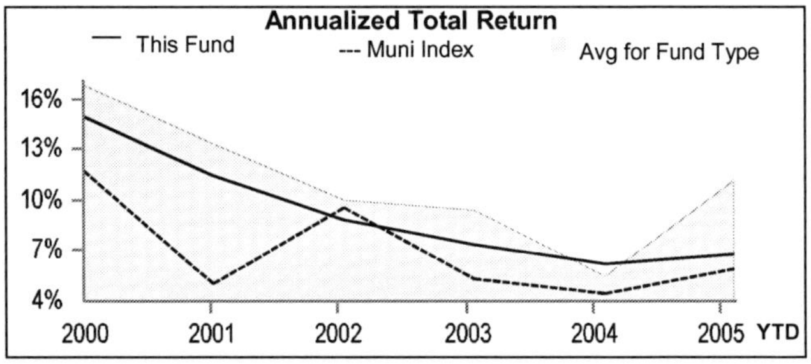

Morgan Stanley Qual Muni Inc Tr (IQI) B Good

Fund Family: Morgan Stanley Invesment Advisors,I
Fund Type: Municipal - National
Inception Date: September 29, 1992

Major Rating Factors:
Morgan Stanley Qual Muni Inc Tr receives a Weiss Investment Rating of B (Good). The fund currently has a performance rating of C (Fair) based on an annualized return of 7.01% over the last three years and a total return of 6.20% year to date 2005. Factored into the performance evaluation is an expense ratio of 0.89% (low).

The fund's risk rating is currently B (Good). It carries a beta of 1.95, meaning it is expected to move 19.5% for every 10% move in the market. Volatility, as measured by both the semi-deviation and a drawdown factor, is considered low. As of June 30, 2005, Morgan Stanley Qual Muni Inc Tr traded at a discount of 11.89% below its net asset value, which is better than its one-year historical average discount of 11.31%.

James Willison has been running the fund for 13 years and currently receives a manager quality ranking of 34 (0=worst, 99=best). If you desire an average level of risk, then this fund may be an option.

Data Date	Weiss Investment Rating	Net Assets ($Mil)	Price	Perfor-mance Rating/Pts	Total Return Y-T-D	Risk Rating/Pts
6-05	B	401.22	13.93	C / 5.2	6.20%	B / 8.4
2004	C	405.19	13.51	C- / 3.0	0.94%	B / 8.7
2003	D-	430.35	14.28	C / 5.0	11.10%	B / 8.7

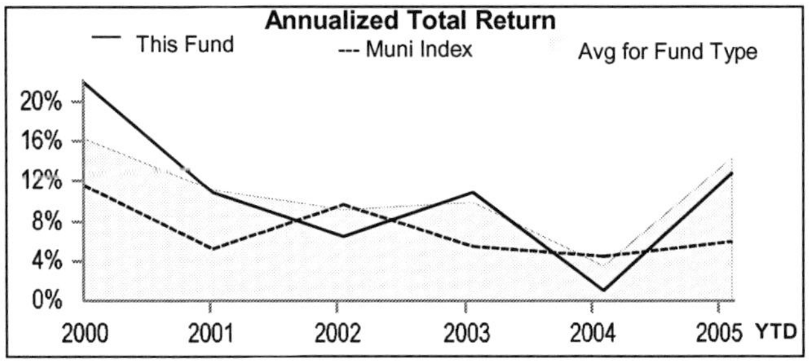

Morgan Stanley Qual Muni Sec (IQM) B Good

Fund Family: Morgan Stanley Invesment Advisors,I
Fund Type: Municipal - National
Inception Date: September 29, 1993

Data Date	Weiss Investment Rating	Net Assets ($Mil)	Price	Performance Rating/Pts	Total Return Y-T-D	Risk Rating/Pts
6-05	B	236.56	14.40	C+ / 6.0	5.71%	B / 8.7
2004	B	233.81	14.03	C / 5.3	4.73%	B / 8.9
2003	B-	240.57	14.22	C / 4.8	8.47%	B+ / 9.3

Major Rating Factors:
Morgan Stanley Qual Muni Sec receives a Weiss Investment Rating of B (Good). The fund currently has a performance rating of C+ (Fair) based on an annualized return of 7.81% over the last three years and a total return of 5.71% year to date 2005. Factored into the performance evaluation is an expense ratio of 0.81% (very low).

The fund's risk rating is currently B (Good). It carries a beta of 1.79, meaning it is expected to move 17.9% for every 10% move in the market. Volatility, as measured by both the semi-deviation and a drawdown factor, is considered low. As of June 30, 2005, Morgan Stanley Qual Muni Sec traded at a discount of 12.09% below its net asset value, which is better than its one-year historical average discount of 11.77%.

James Willison has been running the fund for 12 years and currently receives a manager quality ranking of 47 (0=worst, 99=best). If you desire an average level of risk, then this fund may be an option.

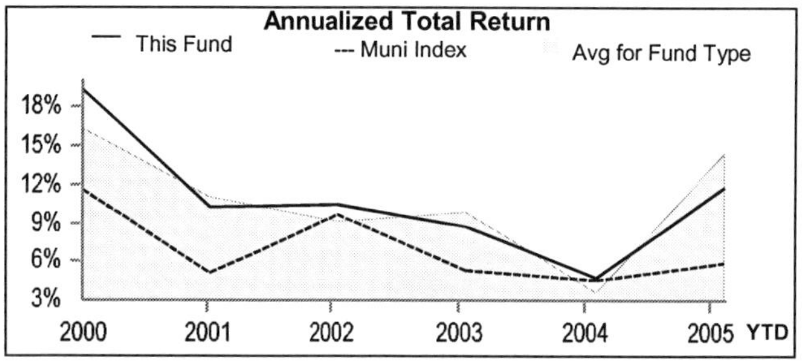

MuniAssets Fund (MUA) A+ Excellent

Fund Family: Merrill Lynch Investment Managers
Fund Type: Municipal - National
Inception Date: June 25, 1993

Data Date	Weiss Investment Rating	Net Assets ($Mil)	Price	Performance Rating/Pts	Total Return Y-T-D	Risk Rating/Pts
6-05	A+	263.06	13.45	A / 9.3	11.19%	B- / 7.2
2004	A+	252.20	12.49	B+ / 8.4	16.06%	B / 8.0
2003	C-	252.49	11.49	D / 2.1	5.52%	B / 8.2

Major Rating Factors:
Exceptional performance is the major factor driving the A+ (Excellent) Weiss Investment Rating for MuniAssets Fund. The fund currently has a performance rating of A (Excellent) based on an annualized return of 11.50% over the last three years and a total return of 11.19% year to date 2005. Factored into the performance evaluation is an expense ratio of 0.67% (very low).

The fund's risk rating is currently B- (Good). It carries a beta of 1.23, meaning it is expected to move 12.3% for every 10% move in the market. Volatility, as measured by both the semi-deviation and a drawdown factor, is considered low. As of June 30, 2005, MuniAssets Fund traded at a discount of .30% below its net asset value, which is worse than its one-year historical average discount of 3.95%.

Ted Jaeckel has been running the fund for 12 years and currently receives a manager quality ranking of 82 (0=worst, 99=best). If you desire only a moderate level of risk and strong performance, then this fund is an excellent option.

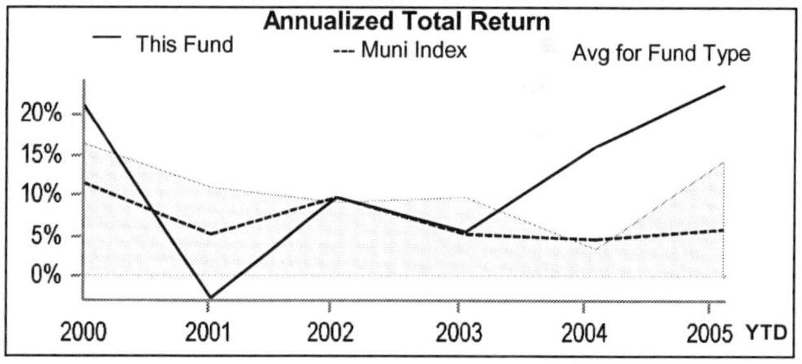

Municipal Advantage Fund (MAF) C Fair

Fund Family: PIMCO Advisors L.P.
Fund Type: Municipal - National
Inception Date: April 30, 1993

Data Date	Weiss Investment Rating	Net Assets ($Mil)	Price	Performance Rating/Pts	Total Return Y-T-D	Risk Rating/Pts
6-05	C	107.13	12.95	C- / 4.0	2.42%	B- / 7.7
2004	C+	105.18	13.00	C / 4.3	-0.36%	B- / 7.9
2003	B+	108.32	13.88	C+ / 6.3	11.86%	B / 8.6

Major Rating Factors:
Middle of the road best describes Municipal Advantage Fund whose Weiss Investment Rating is currently a C (Fair). The fund currently has a performance rating of C- (Fair) based on an annualized return of 6.30% over the last three years and a total return of 2.42% year to date 2005. Factored into the performance evaluation is an expense ratio of 1.34% (average).

The fund's risk rating is currently B- (Good). It carries a beta of 2.00, meaning it is expected to move 20.0% for every 10% move in the market. Volatility, as measured by both the semi-deviation and a drawdown factor, is considered low. As of June 30, 2005, Municipal Advantage Fund traded at a discount of 13.32% below its net asset value, which is better than its one-year historical average discount of 12.68%.

Matthew Greenwald has been running the fund for 12 years and currently receives a manager quality ranking of 23 (0=worst, 99=best). If you desire an average level of risk, then this fund may be an option.

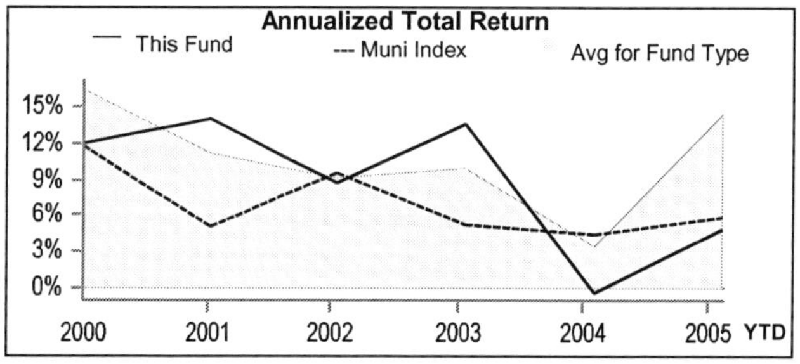

Municipal High Income Fund (MHF) C- Fair

Fund Family: Smith Barney Mutual Funds Mgmt. Inc
Fund Type: Municipal - National
Inception Date: November 25, 1988

Major Rating Factors:
Disappointing performance is the major factor driving the C- (Fair) Weiss Investment Rating for Municipal High Income Fund. The fund currently has a performance rating of D- (Weak) based on an annualized return of 2.59% over the last three years and a total return of 4.10% year to date 2005. Factored into the performance evaluation is an expense ratio of 0.83% (very low).

The fund's risk rating is currently B (Good). It carries a beta of 1.11, meaning it is expected to move 11.1% for every 10% move in the market. Volatility, as measured by both the semi-deviation and a drawdown factor, is considered low. As of June 30, 2005, Municipal High Income Fund traded at a discount of 8.73% below its net asset value, which is better than its one-year historical average discount of 7.64%.

Lawrence T. McDermott has been running the fund for 17 years and currently receives a manager quality ranking of 27 (0=worst, 99=best). This fund offers only a moderate level of risk but investors looking for strong performance are still waiting.

Data Date	Weiss Investment Rating	Net Assets ($Mil)	Price	Performance Rating/Pts	Total Return Y-T-D	Risk Rating/Pts
6-05	C-	166.96	7.21	D- / 1.5	4.10%	B / 8.4
2004	D+	164.38	7.15	E+ / 0.7	-0.73%	B / 8.7
2003	C-	165.81	7.70	D+ / 2.4	8.51%	B / 8.0

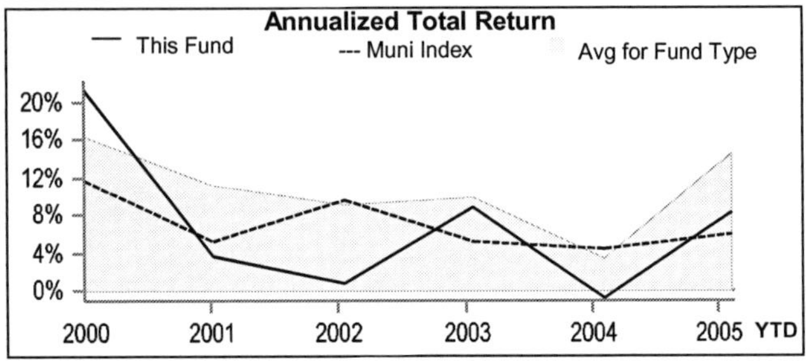

MuniEnhanced Fund (MEN) B+ Good

Fund Family: Merrill Lynch Investment Managers
Fund Type: Municipal - National
Inception Date: March 2, 1989

Major Rating Factors:
Strong performance is the major factor driving the B+ (Good) Weiss Investment Rating for MuniEnhanced Fund. The fund currently has a performance rating of B (Good) based on an annualized return of 8.36% over the last three years and a total return of 8.89% year to date 2005. Factored into the performance evaluation is an expense ratio of 1.01% (low).

The fund's risk rating is currently B- (Good). It carries a beta of 2.04, meaning it is expected to move 20.4% for every 10% move in the market. Volatility, as measured by both the semi-deviation and a drawdown factor, is considered low. As of June 30, 2005, MuniEnhanced Fund traded at a discount of 3.63% below its net asset value, which is worse than its one-year historical average discount of 6.84%.

Mike Kalinoski has been running the fund for 16 years and currently receives a manager quality ranking of 46 (0=worst, 99=best). If you desire only a moderate level of risk and strong performance, then this fund is an excellent option.

Data Date	Weiss Investment Rating	Net Assets ($Mil)	Price	Performance Rating/Pts	Total Return Y-T-D	Risk Rating/Pts
6-05	B+	348.03	11.43	B / 7.6	8.89%	B- / 7.1
2004	B	333.84	10.85	C+ / 5.9	7.45%	B / 8.0
2003	C+	328.14	10.80	C- / 3.6	8.17%	B / 8.8

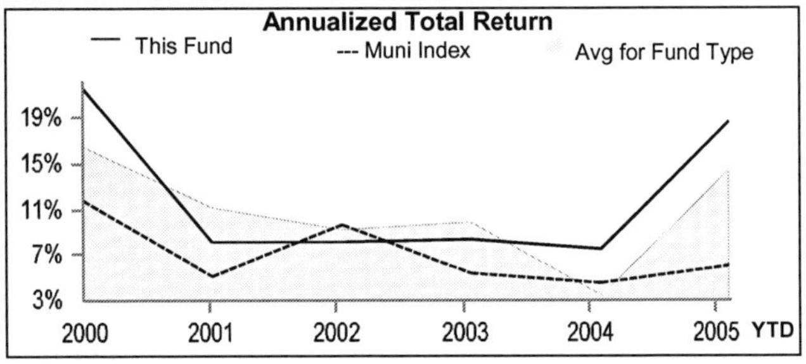

MuniHoldings CA Insured Fund II (MUC) B- Good

Fund Family: Merrill Lynch Investment Managers
Fund Type: Municipal - Single State
Inception Date: March 6, 1998

Major Rating Factors:
MuniHoldings CA Insured Fund II receives a Weiss Investment Rating of B- (Good). The fund currently has a performance rating of C+ (Fair) based on an annualized return of 8.14% over the last three years and a total return of 7.52% year to date 2005. Factored into the performance evaluation is an expense ratio of 1.09% (low).

The fund's risk rating is currently B- (Good). It carries a beta of 1.89, meaning it is expected to move 18.9% for every 10% move in the market. Volatility, as measured by both the semi-deviation and a drawdown factor, is considered low. As of June 30, 2005, MuniHoldings CA Insured Fund II traded at a discount of 4.09% below its net asset value, which is worse than its one-year historical average discount of 5.50%.

Walter O'Connor has been running the fund for 7 years and currently receives a manager quality ranking of 52 (0=worst, 99=best). If you desire an average level of risk, then this fund may be an option.

Data Date	Weiss Investment Rating	Net Assets ($Mil)	Price	Performance Rating/Pts	Total Return Y-T-D	Risk Rating/Pts
6-05	B-	624.14	14.77	C+ / 6.6	7.52%	B- / 7.3
2004	C	598.91	14.19	C- / 3.5	4.09%	B- / 7.8
2003	B-	631.57	14.33	C / 5.2	9.09%	B / 8.5

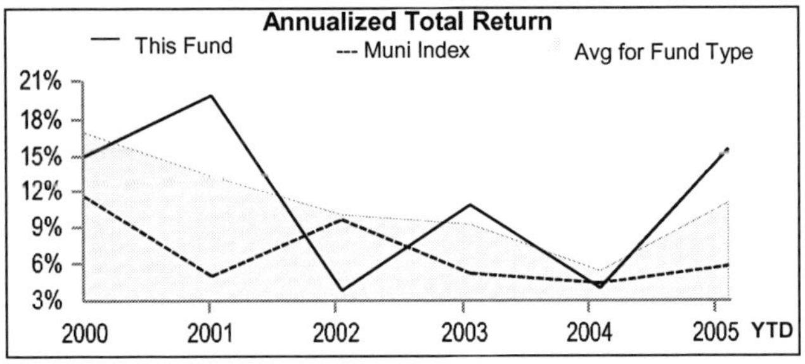

MuniHoldings FL Insured Fund (MFL) A- Excellent

Fund Family: Merrill Lynch Investment Managers
Fund Type: Municipal - Single State
Inception Date: September 29, 1997

Major Rating Factors:
Strong performance is the major factor driving the A- (Excellent) Weiss Investment Rating for MuniHoldings FL Insured Fund. The fund currently has a performance rating of B+ (Good) based on an annualized return of 10.65% over the last three years and a total return of 5.86% year to date 2005. Factored into the performance evaluation is an expense ratio of 1.17% (low).

The fund's risk rating is currently C+ (Fair). It carries a beta of 2.18, meaning it is expected to move 21.8% for every 10% move in the market. Volatility, as measured by both the semi-deviation and a drawdown factor, is considered low. As of June 30, 2005, MuniHoldings FL Insured Fund traded at a premium of .97% above its net asset value, which is worse than its one-year historical average discount of 2.25%.

Bob Sneeden has been running the fund for 8 years and currently receives a manager quality ranking of 59 (0=worst, 99=best). If you desire only a moderate level of risk and strong performance, then this fund is an excellent option.

Data Date	Weiss Investment Rating	Net Assets ($Mil)	Price	Performance Rating/Pts	Total Return Y-T-D	Risk Rating/Pts
6-05	A-	578.99	15.57	B+ / 8.5	5.86%	C+ / 6.5
2004	B+	578.51	15.20	B- / 7.4	10.48%	B- / 7.0
2003	B+	565.99	14.73	B- / 7.2	9.43%	B / 8.1

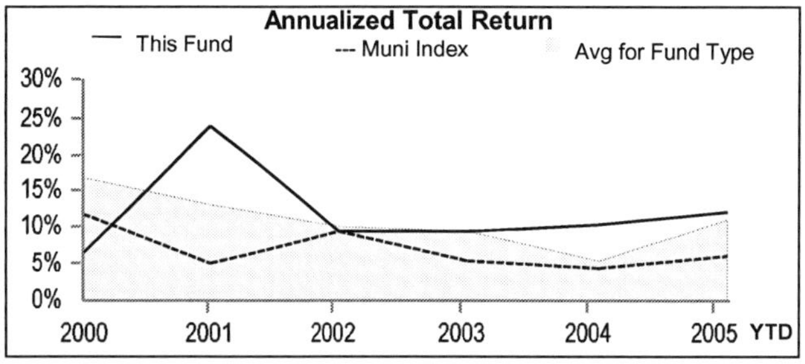

MuniHoldings Fund (MHD) A+ Excellent

Fund Family: Merrill Lynch Investment Managers
Fund Type: Municipal - National
Inception Date: May 2, 1997

Major Rating Factors:
Exceptional performance is the major factor driving the A+ (Excellent) Weiss Investment Rating for MuniHoldings Fund. The fund currently has a performance rating of A (Excellent) based on an annualized return of 14.87% over the last three years and a total return of 8.84% year to date 2005. Factored into the performance evaluation is an expense ratio of 1.13% (low).

The fund's risk rating is currently B- (Good). It carries a beta of 1.94, meaning it is expected to move 19.4% for every 10% move in the market. Volatility, as measured by both the semi-deviation and a drawdown factor, is considered low. As of June 30, 2005, MuniHoldings Fund traded at a premium of 1.21% above its net asset value, which is worse than its one-year historical average discount of 1.27%.

Robert A. DiMella has been running the fund for 6 years and currently receives a manager quality ranking of 80 (0=worst, 99=best). If you desire only a moderate level of risk and strong performance, then this fund is an excellent option.

Data Date	Weiss Investment Rating	Net Assets ($Mil)	Price	Performance Rating/Pts	Total Return Y-T-D	Risk Rating/Pts
6-05	A+	225.22	16.71	A / 9.5	8.84%	B- / 7.2
2004	A+	214.47	15.91	B+ / 8.4	11.29%	B- / 7.6
2003	A+	213.87	15.30	B+ / 8.8	19.72%	B- / 7.9

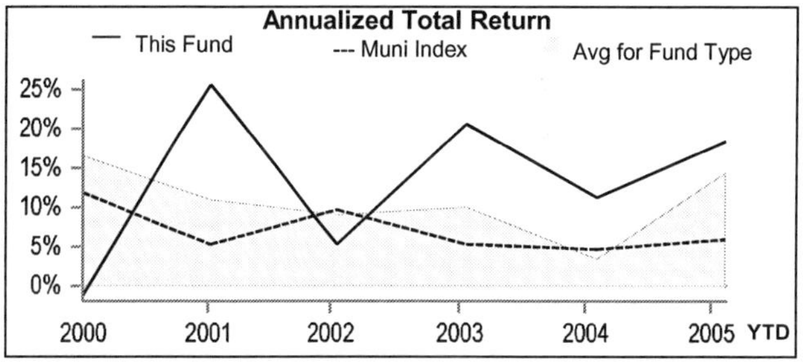

MuniHoldings Fund II (MUH) A+ Excellent

Fund Family: Merrill Lynch Investment Managers
Fund Type: Municipal - National
Inception Date: February 27, 1998

Major Rating Factors:
Exceptional performance is the major factor driving the A+ (Excellent) Weiss Investment Rating for MuniHoldings Fund II. The fund currently has a performance rating of A+ (Excellent) based on an annualized return of 14.47% over the last three years and a total return of 10.41% year to date 2005. Factored into the performance evaluation is an expense ratio of 1.19% (average).

The fund's risk rating is currently C+ (Fair). It carries a beta of 1.98, meaning it is expected to move 19.8% for every 10% move in the market. Volatility, as measured by both the semi-deviation and a drawdown factor, is considered low. As of June 30, 2005, MuniHoldings Fund II traded at a premium of 1.26% above its net asset value, which is worse than its one-year historical average discount of 1.61%.

Robert DiMella has been running the fund for 7 years and currently receives a manager quality ranking of 78 (0=worst, 99=best). If you desire only a moderate level of risk and strong performance, then this fund is an excellent option.

Data Date	Weiss Investment Rating	Net Assets ($Mil)	Price	Performance Rating/Pts	Total Return Y-T-D	Risk Rating/Pts
6-05	A+	165.61	15.32	A+ / 9.6	10.41%	C+ / 6.9
2004	A+	155.58	14.38	B+ / 8.3	8.33%	B- / 7.7
2003	A+	149.26	14.15	B+ / 8.5	22.38%	B- / 7.7

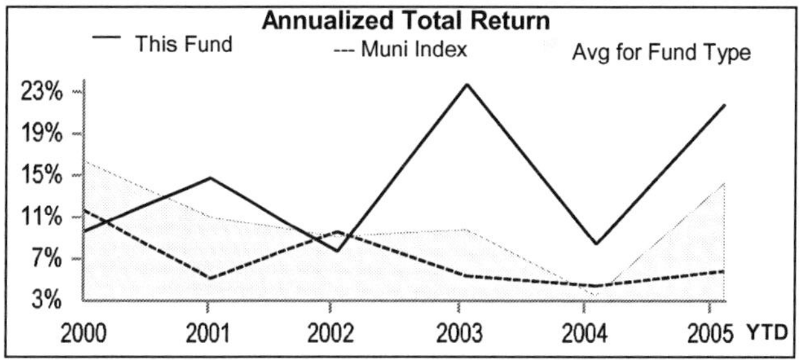

MuniHoldings Insured Fund (MUS) A- Excellent

Fund Family: Merrill Lynch Investment Managers
Fund Type: Municipal - National
Inception Date: May 15, 1998

Major Rating Factors:
Strong performance is the major factor driving the A- (Excellent) Weiss Investment Rating for MuniHoldings Insured Fund. The fund currently has a performance rating of B (Good) based on an annualized return of 10.10% over the last three years and a total return of 3.64% year to date 2005. Factored into the performance evaluation is an expense ratio of 1.24% (average).

The fund's risk rating is currently B- (Good). It carries a beta of 2.15, meaning it is expected to move 21.5% for every 10% move in the market. Volatility, as measured by both the semi-deviation and a drawdown factor, is considered low. As of June 30, 2005, MuniHoldings Insured Fund traded at a discount of 1.65% below its net asset value, which is worse than its one-year historical average discount of 5.00%.

Robert A. DiMella has been running the fund for 6 years and currently receives a manager quality ranking of 56 (0=worst, 99=best). If you desire only a moderate level of risk and strong performance, then this fund is an excellent option.

Data Date	Weiss Investment Rating	Net Assets ($Mil)	Price	Performance Rating/Pts	Total Return Y-T-D	Risk Rating/Pts
6-05	A-	185.82	14.29	B / 8.0	3.64%	B- / 7.0
2004	B+	181.73	14.25	B / 7.6	11.53%	B- / 7.3
2003	A	184.23	13.73	B- / 7.4	14.01%	B / 8.4

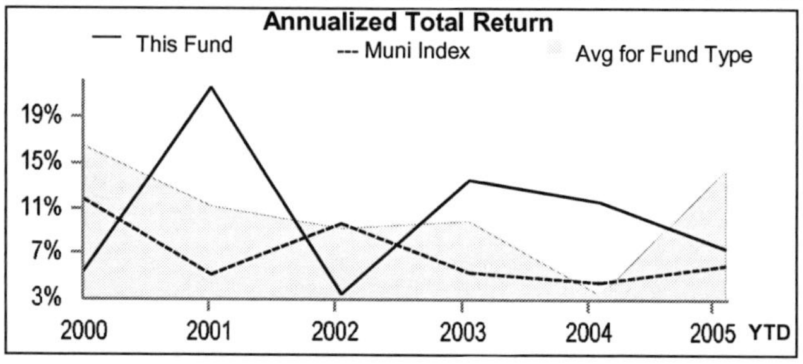

MuniHoldings Insured Fund II (MUE) B+ Good

Fund Family: Merrill Lynch Investment Managers
Fund Type: Municipal - National
Inception Date: March 9, 1999

Major Rating Factors:
Strong performance is the major factor driving the B+ (Good) Weiss Investment Rating for MuniHoldings Insured Fund II. The fund currently has a performance rating of B- (Good) based on an annualized return of 8.60% over the last three years and a total return of 7.02% year to date 2005. Factored into the performance evaluation is an expense ratio of 1.15% (low).

The fund's risk rating is currently B- (Good). It carries a beta of 2.21, meaning it is expected to move 22.1% for every 10% move in the market. Volatility, as measured by both the semi-deviation and a drawdown factor, is considered low. As of June 30, 2005, MuniHoldings Insured Fund II traded at a discount of 5.58% below its net asset value, which is worse than its one-year historical average discount of 8.38%.

Robert A. DiMella has been running the fund for 6 years and currently receives a manager quality ranking of 37 (0=worst, 99=best). If you desire only a moderate level of risk and strong performance, then this fund is an excellent option.

Data Date	Weiss Investment Rating	Net Assets ($Mil)	Price	Performance Rating/Pts	Total Return Y-T-D	Risk Rating/Pts
6-05	B+	317.62	13.70	B- / 7.4	7.02%	B- / 7.2
2004	B	322.07	13.23	C+ / 5.7	5.71%	B / 8.0
2003	B	321.27	13.32	C+ / 6.6	10.64%	B / 8.6

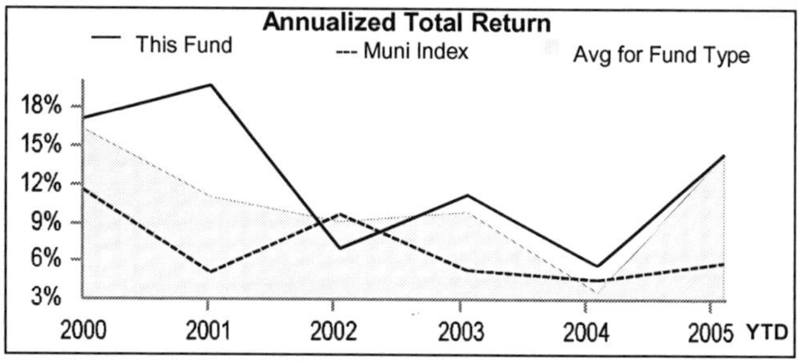

MuniHoldings NJ Insured Fund (MUJ) A Excellent

Fund Family: Merrill Lynch Investment Managers
Fund Type: Municipal - Single State
Inception Date: March 6, 1998

Major Rating Factors:
Strong performance is the major factor driving the A (Excellent) Weiss Investment Rating for MuniHoldings NJ Insured Fund. The fund currently has a performance rating of B+ (Good) based on an annualized return of 10.87% over the last three years and a total return of 6.67% year to date 2005. Factored into the performance evaluation is an expense ratio of 1.21% (average).

The fund's risk rating is currently B- (Good). It carries a beta of 2.48, meaning it is expected to move 24.8% for every 10% move in the market. Volatility, as measured by both the semi-deviation and a drawdown factor, is considered low. As of June 30, 2005, MuniHoldings NJ Insured Fund traded at a discount of 1.45% below its net asset value, which is worse than its one-year historical average discount of 4.36%.

Ted R. Jaeckel has been running the fund for 7 years and currently receives a manager quality ranking of 49 (0=worst, 99=best). If you desire only a moderate level of risk and strong performance, then this fund is an excellent option.

Data Date	Weiss Investment Rating	Net Assets ($Mil)	Price	Performance Rating/Pts	Total Return Y-T-D	Risk Rating/Pts
6-05	A	332.97	15.59	B+ / 8.6	6.67%	B- / 7.0
2004	A	316.17	15.08	B / 7.7	10.69%	B- / 7.6
2003	B	304.13	14.39	C+ / 6.8	10.09%	B / 8.2

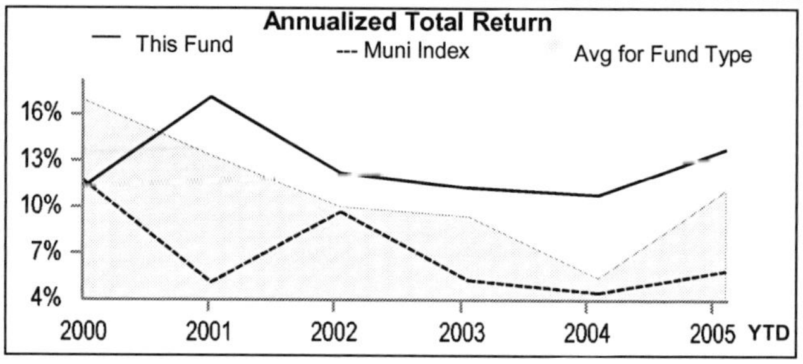

MuniHoldings NY Insured Fund (MHN) A- Excellent

Fund Family: Merrill Lynch Investment Managers
Fund Type: Municipal - Single State
Inception Date: September 26, 1997

Major Rating Factors:
Strong performance is the major factor driving the A- (Excellent) Weiss Investment Rating for MuniHoldings NY Insured Fund. The fund currently has a performance rating of B (Good) based on an annualized return of 9.24% over the last three years and a total return of 9.95% year to date 2005. Factored into the performance evaluation is an expense ratio of 1.14% (low).

The fund's risk rating is currently B- (Good). It carries a beta of 1.94, meaning it is expected to move 19.4% for every 10% move in the market. Volatility, as measured by both the semi-deviation and a drawdown factor, is considered low. As of June 30, 2005, MuniHoldings NY Insured Fund traded at a discount of 4.10% below its net asset value, which is worse than its one-year historical average discount of 8.13%.

Roberto Roffo has been running the fund for 8 years and currently receives a manager quality ranking of 58 (0=worst, 99=best). If you desire only a moderate level of risk and strong performance, then this fund is an excellent option.

Data Date	Weiss Investment Rating	Net Assets ($Mil)	Price	Performance Rating/Pts	Total Return Y-T-D	Risk Rating/Pts
6-05	A-	477.50	14.96	B / 8.0	9.95%	B- / 7.0
2004	B-	474.36	14.06	C / 5.4	5.90%	B / 8.0
2003	C+	467.51	14.18	C / 4.5	8.70%	B / 8.7

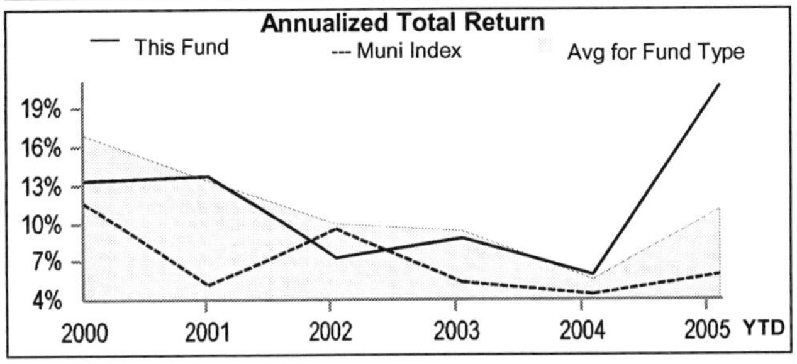

MuniVest Fund (MVF) A+ Excellent

Fund Family: Merrill Lynch Investment Managers
Fund Type: Municipal - National
Inception Date: September 23, 1988

Major Rating Factors:
Exceptional performance is the major factor driving the A+ (Excellent) Weiss Investment Rating for MuniVest Fund. The fund currently has a performance rating of A- (Excellent) based on an annualized return of 11.34% over the last three years and a total return of 8.83% year to date 2005. Factored into the performance evaluation is an expense ratio of 1.01% (low).

The fund's risk rating is currently B- (Good). It carries a beta of 2.02, meaning it is expected to move 20.2% for every 10% move in the market. Volatility, as measured by both the semi-deviation and a drawdown factor, is considered low. As of June 30, 2005, MuniVest Fund traded at a discount of 2.83% below its net asset value, which is worse than its one-year historical average discount of 6.26%.

Fred Stuebe has been running the fund for 17 years and currently receives a manager quality ranking of 69 (0=worst, 99=best). If you desire only a moderate level of risk and strong performance, then this fund is an excellent option.

Data Date	Weiss Investment Rating	Net Assets ($Mil)	Price	Performance Rating/Pts	Total Return Y-T-D	Risk Rating/Pts
6-05	A+	619.10	9.94	A- / 9.1	8.83%	B- / 7.1
2004	A	607.84	9.46	B- / 7.5	10.98%	B- / 7.7
2003	B-	585.02	9.10	C / 4.7	9.70%	B / 8.9

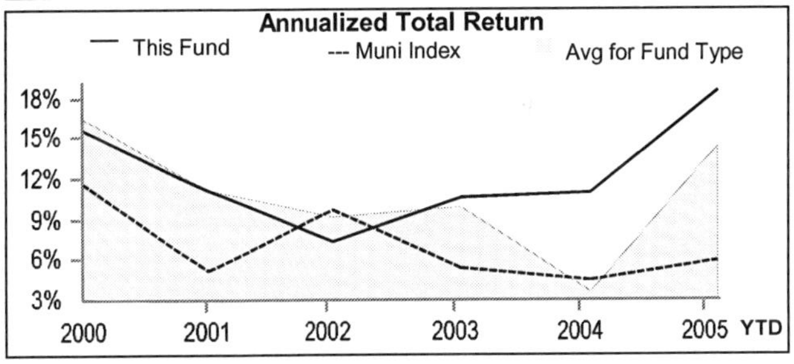

MuniVest Fund II (MVT) A+ Excellent

Fund Family: Merrill Lynch Investment Managers
Fund Type: Municipal - National
Inception Date: March 26, 1993

Major Rating Factors:
Exceptional performance is the major factor driving the A+ (Excellent) Weiss Investment Rating for MuniVest Fund II. The fund currently has a performance rating of A (Excellent) based on an annualized return of 14.19% over the last three years and a total return of 10.20% year to date 2005. Factored into the performance evaluation is an expense ratio of 1.05% (low).

The fund's risk rating is currently C+ (Fair). It carries a beta of 2.15, meaning it is expected to move 21.5% for every 10% move in the market. Volatility, as measured by both the semi-deviation and a drawdown factor, is considered low. As of June 30, 2005, MuniVest Fund II traded at a premium of 3.85% above its net asset value, which is worse than its one-year historical average premium of .13%.

Fred K. Stuebe has been running the fund for 6 years and currently receives a manager quality ranking of 75 (0=worst, 99=best). If you desire only a moderate level of risk and strong performance, then this fund is an excellent option.

Data Date	Weiss Investment Rating	Net Assets ($Mil)	Price	Performance Rating/Pts	Total Return Y-T-D	Risk Rating/Pts
6-05	A+	306.81	16.20	A / 9.5	10.20%	C+ / 6.8
2004	A+	293.94	15.24	B+ / 8.6	11.70%	B- / 7.5
2003	A	293.75	14.58	B / 7.6	15.38%	B / 8.2

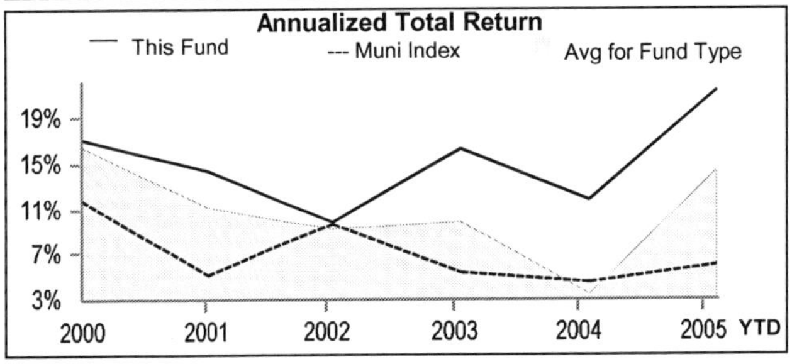

MuniYield AZ Fund (MZA) A- Excellent

Fund Family: Merrill Lynch Investment Managers
Fund Type: Municipal - Single State
Inception Date: October 29, 1993

Major Rating Factors:
Strong performance is the major factor driving the A- (Excellent) Weiss Investment Rating for MuniYield AZ Fund. The fund currently has a performance rating of B+ (Good) based on an annualized return of 9.35% over the last three years and a total return of 7.80% year to date 2005. Factored into the performance evaluation is an expense ratio of 1.18% (low).

The fund's risk rating is currently C+ (Fair). It carries a beta of 2.22, meaning it is expected to move 22.2% for every 10% move in the market. Volatility, as measured by both the semi-deviation and a drawdown factor, is considered low. As of June 30, 2005, MuniYield AZ Fund traded at a premium of 4.72% above its net asset value, which is worse than its one-year historical average premium of 1.03%.

Mike Kalinoski has been running the fund for 12 years and currently receives a manager quality ranking of 45 (0=worst, 99=best). If you desire only a moderate level of risk and strong performance, then this fund is an excellent option.

Data Date	Weiss Investment Rating	Net Assets ($Mil)	Price	Performance Rating/Pts	Total Return Y-T-D	Risk Rating/Pts
6-05	A-	66.74	15.76	B+ / 8.5	7.80%	C+ / 6.3
2004	A	64.51	15.08	B / 8.1	8.04%	B- / 7.2
2003	A+	65.23	14.94	B+ / 8.3	14.88%	B- / 7.8

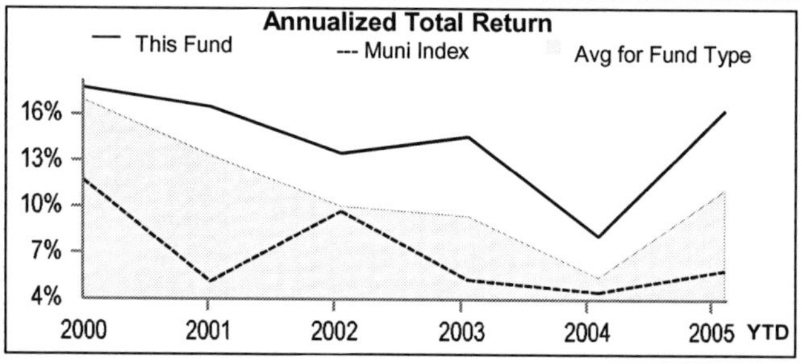

MuniYield CA Fund (MYC) C- Fair

Fund Family: Merrill Lynch Investment Managers
Fund Type: Municipal - Single State
Inception Date: February 28, 1992

Major Rating Factors:
Disappointing performance is the major factor driving the C- (Fair) Weiss Investment Rating for MuniYield CA Fund. The fund currently has a performance rating of D+ (Weak) based on an annualized return of 4.40% over the last three years and a total return of 1.09% year to date 2005. Factored into the performance evaluation is an expense ratio of 0.96% (low).

The fund's risk rating is currently B (Good). It carries a beta of 1.98, meaning it is expected to move 19.8% for every 10% move in the market. Volatility, as measured by both the semi-deviation and a drawdown factor, is considered low. As of June 30, 2005, MuniYield CA Fund traded at a discount of 8.61% below its net asset value, which is better than its one-year historical average discount of 6.89%.

Walter O'Connor has been running the fund for 13 years and currently receives a manager quality ranking of 12 (0=worst, 99=best). This fund offers only a moderate level of risk but investors looking for strong performance are still waiting.

Data Date	Weiss Investment Rating	Net Assets ($Mil)	Price	Performance Rating/Pts	Total Return Y-T-D	Risk Rating/Pts
6-05	C-	320.72	13.91	D+ / 2.4	1.09%	B / 8.1
2004	C	316.27	14.20	C- / 3.3	5.68%	B / 8.0
2003	C	323.16	14.38	C- / 3.3	5.89%	B / 8.9

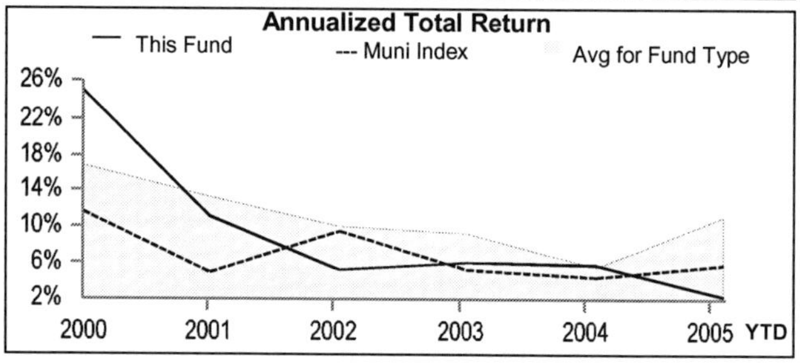

MuniYield CA Insured Fund (MCA) A- Excellent

Fund Family: Merrill Lynch Investment Managers
Fund Type: Municipal - Single State
Inception Date: October 6, 1992

Major Rating Factors:
Strong performance is the major factor driving the A- (Excellent) Weiss Investment Rating for MuniYield CA Insured Fund. The fund currently has a performance rating of B- (Good) based on an annualized return of 8.19% over the last three years and a total return of 10.10% year to date 2005. Factored into the performance evaluation is an expense ratio of 0.94% (low).

The fund's risk rating is currently B- (Good). It carries a beta of 1.79, meaning it is expected to move 17.9% for every 10% move in the market. Volatility, as measured by both the semi-deviation and a drawdown factor, is considered low. As of June 30, 2005, MuniYield CA Insured Fund traded at a discount of 7.54% below its net asset value, which is worse than its one-year historical average discount of 9.95%.

Walter O'Connor has been running the fund for 13 years and currently receives a manager quality ranking of 53 (0=worst, 99=best). If you desire only a moderate level of risk and strong performance, then this fund is an excellent option.

Data Date	Weiss Investment Rating	Net Assets ($Mil)	Price	Performance Rating/Pts	Total Return Y-T-D	Risk Rating/Pts
6-05	A-	523.39	14.22	B- / 7.3	10.10%	B- / 7.6
2004	C-	505.31	13.33	D / 2.1	1.83%	B / 8.2
2003	C-	518.79	13.92	D+ / 2.5	8.43%	B / 8.5

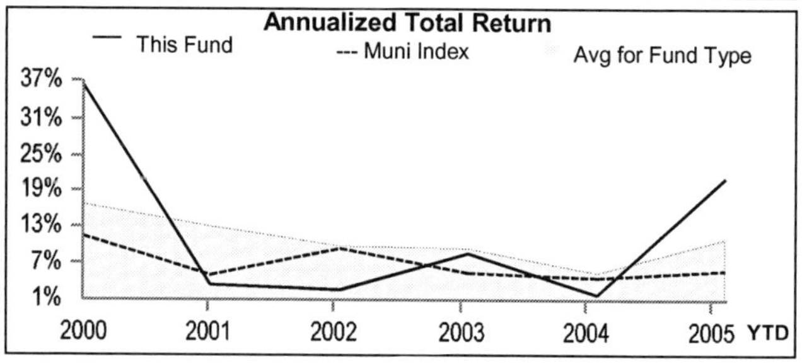

MuniYield FL Fund (MYF) A Excellent

Fund Family: Merrill Lynch Investment Managers
Fund Type: Municipal - Single State
Inception Date: February 28, 1992

Data Date	Weiss Investment Rating	Net Assets ($Mil)	Price	Performance Rating/Pts	Total Return Y-T-D	Risk Rating/Pts
6-05	A	207.39	15.06	A- / 9.0	9.58%	C+ / 6.3
2004	B-	199.57	14.19	C+ / 6.8	6.53%	B- / 7.3
2003	B-	202.89	14.28	C+ / 6.8	9.24%	B- / 7.7

Major Rating Factors:
Exceptional performance is the major factor driving the A (Excellent) Weiss Investment Rating for MuniYield FL Fund. The fund currently has a performance rating of A- (Excellent) based on an annualized return of 10.66% over the last three years and a total return of 9.58% year to date 2005. Factored into the performance evaluation is an expense ratio of 1.03% (low).

The fund's risk rating is currently C+ (Fair). It carries a beta of 2.47, meaning it is expected to move 24.7% for every 10% move in the market. Volatility, as measured by both the semi-deviation and a drawdown factor, is considered low. As of June 30, 2005, MuniYield FL Fund traded at a discount of 2.40% below its net asset value, which is worse than its one-year historical average discount of 7.33%.

Bob Sneeden has been running the fund for 13 years and currently receives a manager quality ranking of 46 (0=worst, 99=best). If you desire only a moderate level of risk and strong performance, then this fund is an excellent option.

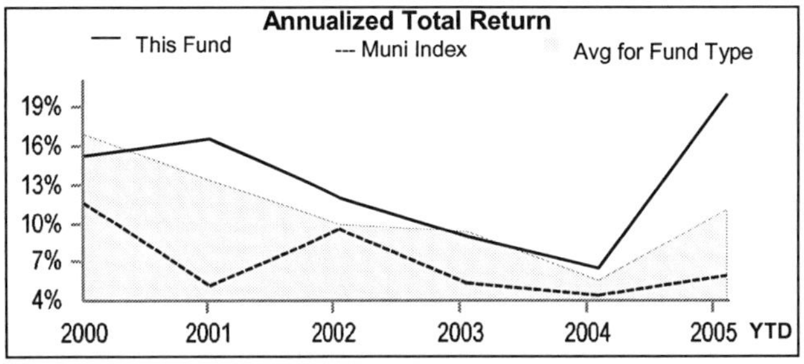

MuniYield FL Insured Fund (MFT) B+ Good

Fund Family: Merrill Lynch Investment Managers
Fund Type: Municipal - Single State
Inception Date: December 2, 1992

Data Date	Weiss Investment Rating	Net Assets ($Mil)	Price	Performance Rating/Pts	Total Return Y-T-D	Risk Rating/Pts
6-05	B+	128.04	15.45	B+ / 8.3	9.75%	C+ / 6.4
2004	C+	124.28	14.51	C / 5.5	6.16%	B- / 7.2
2003	C	126.92	14.44	C- / 3.6	2.67%	B / 8.4

Major Rating Factors:
Strong performance is the major factor driving the B+ (Good) Weiss Investment Rating for MuniYield FL Insured Fund. The fund currently has a performance rating of B+ (Good) based on an annualized return of 9.32% over the last three years and a total return of 9.75% year to date 2005. Factored into the performance evaluation is an expense ratio of 1.16% (low).

The fund's risk rating is currently C+ (Fair). It carries a beta of 2.09, meaning it is expected to move 20.9% for every 10% move in the market. Volatility, as measured by both the semi-deviation and a drawdown factor, is considered low. As of June 30, 2005, MuniYield FL Insured Fund traded at a premium of 1.11% above its net asset value, which is worse than its one-year historical average discount of 3.13%.

Robert Sneeden has been running the fund for 13 years and currently receives a manager quality ranking of 51 (0=worst, 99=best). If you desire only a moderate level of risk and strong performance, then this fund is an excellent option.

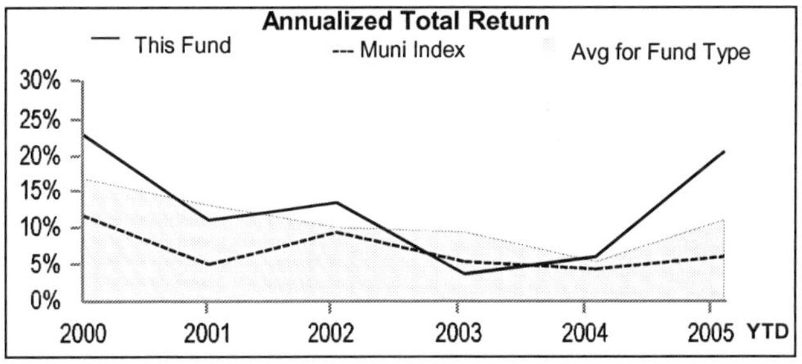

MuniYield Fund (MYD) A+ Excellent

Fund Family: Merrill Lynch Investment Managers
Fund Type: Municipal - National
Inception Date: December 20, 1991

Data Date	Weiss Investment Rating	Net Assets ($Mil)	Price	Performance Rating/Pts	Total Return Y-T-D	Risk Rating/Pts
6-05	A+	653.34	14.99	A- / 9.2	11.63%	B- / 7.4
2004	A+	609.84	13.90	B / 7.9	13.66%	B / 8.4
2003	C+	615.17	13.14	C- / 3.5	9.49%	B+ / 9.1

Major Rating Factors:
Exceptional performance is the major factor driving the A+ (Excellent) Weiss Investment Rating for MuniYield Fund. The fund currently has a performance rating of A- (Excellent) based on an annualized return of 11.30% over the last three years and a total return of 11.63% year to date 2005. Factored into the performance evaluation is an expense ratio of 1.01% (low).

The fund's risk rating is currently B- (Good). It carries a beta of 1.38, meaning it is expected to move 13.8% for every 10% move in the market. Volatility, as measured by both the semi-deviation and a drawdown factor, is considered low. As of June 30, 2005, MuniYield Fund traded at a premium of .54% above its net asset value, which is worse than its one-year historical average discount of 3.62%.

Roberto Roffo has been running the fund for 14 years and currently receives a manager quality ranking of 77 (0=worst, 99=best). If you desire only a moderate level of risk and strong performance, then this fund is an excellent option.

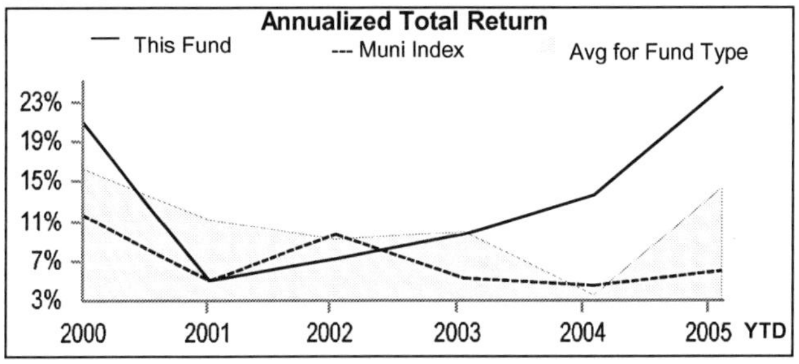

MuniYield Insured Fund (MYI) A Excellent

Fund Family: Merrill Lynch Investment Managers
Fund Type: Municipal - National
Inception Date: March 27, 1992

Major Rating Factors:
Strong performance is the major factor driving the A (Excellent) Weiss Investment Rating for MuniYield Insured Fund. The fund currently has a performance rating of B (Good) based on an annualized return of 8.40% over the last three years and a total return of 10.25% year to date 2005. Factored into the performance evaluation is an expense ratio of 1.00% (low).

The fund's risk rating is currently B- (Good). It carries a beta of 1.92, meaning it is expected to move 19.2% for every 10% move in the market. Volatility, as measured by both the semi-deviation and a drawdown factor, is considered low. As of June 30, 2005, MuniYield Insured Fund traded at a discount of 5.02% below its net asset value, which is worse than its one-year historical average discount of 7.28%.

William Bock has been running the fund for 13 years and currently receives a manager quality ranking of 51 (0=worst, 99=best). If you desire only a moderate level of risk and strong performance, then this fund is an excellent option.

Data Date	Weiss Investment Rating	Net Assets ($Mil)	Price	Performance Rating/Pts	Total Return Y-T-D	Risk Rating/Pts
6-05	A	1057.69	15.14	B / 7.9	10.25%	B- / 7.7
2004	C	935.64	14.19	C- / 3.2	3.43%	B / 8.2
2003	C+	953.66	14.66	C / 4.3	7.68%	B / 8.7

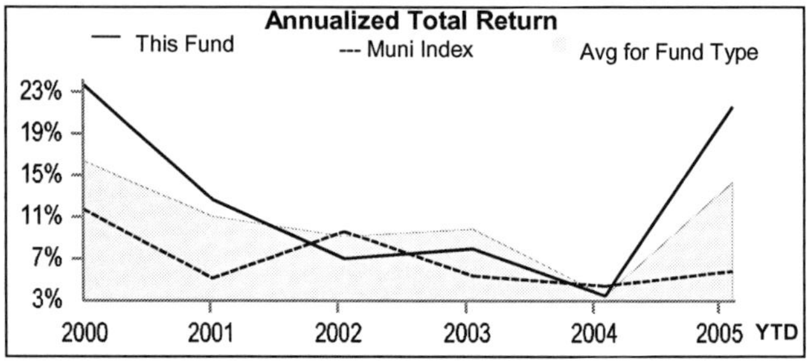

MuniYield MI Insured Fund (MIY) B- Good

Fund Family: Merrill Lynch Investment Managers
Fund Type: Municipal - Single State
Inception Date: October 30, 1992

Major Rating Factors:
MuniYield MI Insured Fund receives a Weiss Investment Rating of B- (Good). The fund currently has a performance rating of C+ (Fair) based on an annualized return of 9.16% over the last three years and a total return of 2.90% year to date 2005. Factored into the performance evaluation is an expense ratio of 1.08% (low).

The fund's risk rating is currently B- (Good). It carries a beta of 2.04, meaning it is expected to move 20.4% for every 10% move in the market. Volatility, as measured by both the semi-deviation and a drawdown factor, is considered low. As of June 30, 2005, MuniYield MI Insured Fund traded at a discount of 3.25% below its net asset value, which is worse than its one-year historical average discount of 3.95%.

Fred Stuebe has been running the fund for 13 years and currently receives a manager quality ranking of 55 (0=worst, 99=best). If you desire an average level of risk, then this fund may be an option.

Data Date	Weiss Investment Rating	Net Assets ($Mil)	Price	Performance Rating/Pts	Total Return Y-T-D	Risk Rating/Pts
6-05	B-	287.49	15.49	C+ / 6.9	2.90%	B- / 7.5
2004	A+	281.98	15.54	B / 8.2	10.72%	B- / 7.4
2003	B	289.36	14.98	C+ / 6.8	11.84%	B / 8.2

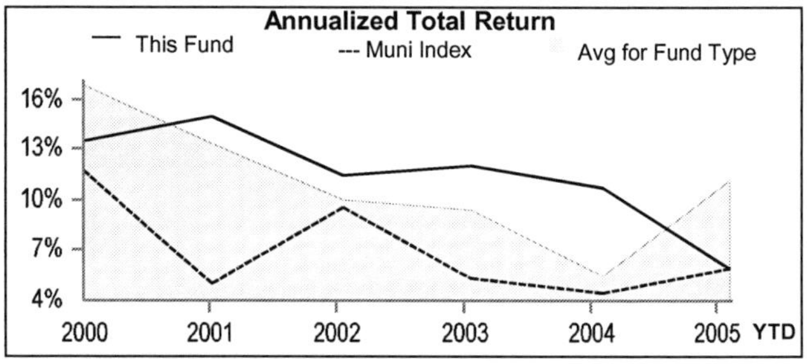

MuniYield MI Insured Fund II (MYM) B+ Good

Fund Family: Merrill Lynch Investment Managers
Fund Type: Municipal - Single State
Inception Date: February 28, 1992

Major Rating Factors:
Strong performance is the major factor driving the B+ (Good) Weiss Investment Rating for MuniYield MI Insured Fund II. The fund currently has a performance rating of B- (Good) based on an annualized return of 9.35% over the last three years and a total return of 4.92% year to date 2005. Factored into the performance evaluation is an expense ratio of 1.07% (low).

The fund's risk rating is currently B- (Good). It carries a beta of 2.23, meaning it is expected to move 22.3% for every 10% move in the market. Volatility, as measured by both the semi-deviation and a drawdown factor, is considered low. As of June 30, 2005, MuniYield MI Insured Fund II traded at a discount of 3.10% below its net asset value, which is worse than its one-year historical average discount of 5.16%.

Fred Stuebe has been running the fund for 13 years and currently receives a manager quality ranking of 49 (0=worst, 99=best). If you desire only a moderate level of risk and strong performance, then this fund is an excellent option.

Data Date	Weiss Investment Rating	Net Assets ($Mil)	Price	Performance Rating/Pts	Total Return Y-T-D	Risk Rating/Pts
6-05	B+	181.15	14.70	B- / 7.3	4.92%	B- / 7.0
2004	A-	178.38	14.46	B / 7.6	10.42%	B- / 7.5
2003	B-	183.24	13.90	C+ / 5.0	8.24%	B / 8.4

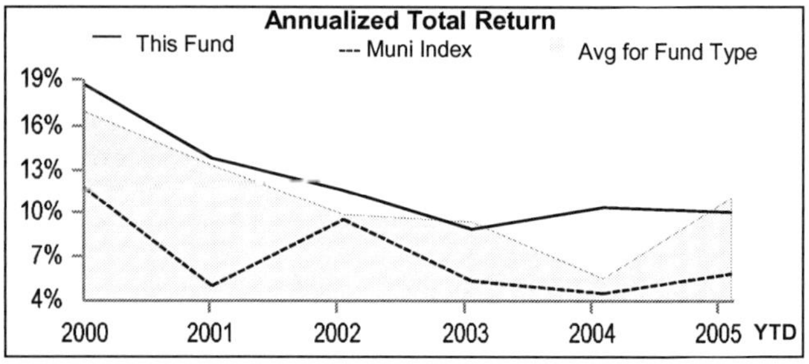

MuniYield NJ Fund (MYJ) B+ Good

Fund Family: Merrill Lynch Investment Managers
Fund Type: Municipal - Single State
Inception Date: May 18, 1992

Major Rating Factors:
Strong performance is the major factor driving the B+ (Good) Weiss Investment Rating for MuniYield NJ Fund. The fund currently has a performance rating of B- (Good) based on an annualized return of 7.88% over the last three years and a total return of 7.58% year to date 2005. Factored into the performance evaluation is an expense ratio of 1.02% (low).

The fund's risk rating is currently B- (Good). It carries a beta of 2.00, meaning it is expected to move 20.0% for every 10% move in the market. Volatility, as measured by both the semi-deviation and a drawdown factor, is considered low. As of June 30, 2005, MuniYield NJ Fund traded at a discount of 3.83% below its net asset value, which is worse than its one-year historical average discount of 5.91%.

Ted Jaeckel has been running the fund for 13 years and currently receives a manager quality ranking of 42 (0=worst, 99=best). If you desire only a moderate level of risk and strong performance, then this fund is an excellent option.

Data Date	Weiss Investment Rating	Net Assets ($Mil)	Price	Performance Rating/Pts	Total Return Y-T-D	Risk Rating/Pts
6-05	B+	216.62	15.31	B- / 7.2	7.58%	B- / 7.3
2004	B-	208.52	14.69	C+ / 5.6	8.28%	B / 8.0
2003	B-	218.64	14.35	C / 4.6	5.78%	B+ / 9.0

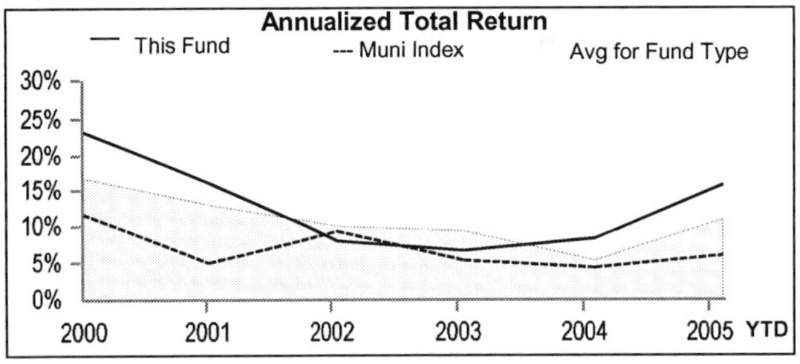

MuniYield NJ Insured Fund (MJI) B Good

Fund Family: Merrill Lynch Investment Managers
Fund Type: Municipal - Single State
Inception Date: November 2, 1992

Major Rating Factors:
Strong performance is the major factor driving the B (Good) Weiss Investment Rating for MuniYield NJ Insured Fund. The fund currently has a performance rating of B- (Good) based on an annualized return of 7.65% over the last three years and a total return of 6.06% year to date 2005. Factored into the performance evaluation is an expense ratio of 1.15% (low).

The fund's risk rating is currently C+ (Fair). It carries a beta of 2.19, meaning it is expected to move 21.9% for every 10% move in the market. Volatility, as measured by both the semi-deviation and a drawdown factor, is considered low. As of June 30, 2005, MuniYield NJ Insured Fund traded at a discount of .38% below its net asset value, which is worse than its one-year historical average discount of 2.97%.

Ted Jaeckel has been running the fund for 13 years and currently receives a manager quality ranking of 31 (0=worst, 99=best). If you desire only a moderate level of risk and strong performance, then this fund is an excellent option.

Data Date	Weiss Investment Rating	Net Assets ($Mil)	Price	Performance Rating/Pts	Total Return Y-T-D	Risk Rating/Pts
6-05	B	136.41	15.65	B- / 7.3	6.06%	C+ / 6.6
2004	C+	130.17	15.22	C / 5.3	7.70%	B- / 7.2
2003	C+	133.24	15.03	C / 4.7	8.52%	B / 8.6

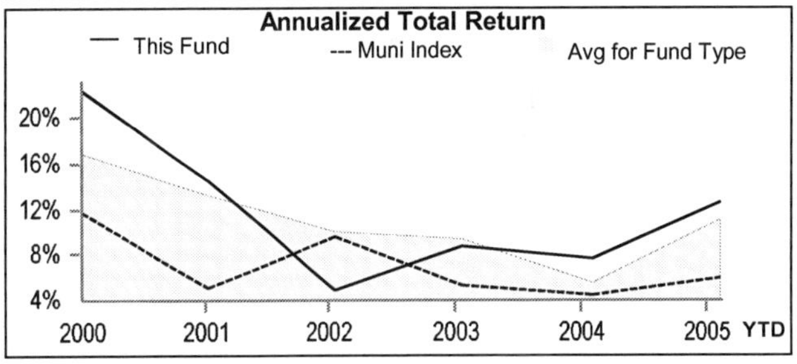

MuniYield NY Insured Fund (MYN) B- Good

Fund Family: Merrill Lynch Investment Managers
Fund Type: Municipal - Single State
Inception Date: February 20, 1992

Major Rating Factors:
MuniYield NY Insured Fund receives a Weiss Investment Rating of B- (Good). The fund currently has a performance rating of C+ (Fair) based on an annualized return of 6.66% over the last three years and a total return of 9.19% year to date 2005. Factored into the performance evaluation is an expense ratio of 0.94% (low).

The fund's risk rating is currently B- (Good). It carries a beta of 1.65, meaning it is expected to move 16.5% for every 10% move in the market. Volatility, as measured by both the semi-deviation and a drawdown factor, is considered low. As of June 30, 2005, MuniYield NY Insured Fund traded at a discount of 8.93% below its net asset value, which is worse than its one-year historical average discount of 11.36%.

Roberto Roffo has been running the fund for 13 years and currently receives a manager quality ranking of 44 (0=worst, 99=best). If you desire an average level of risk, then this fund may be an option.

Data Date	Weiss Investment Rating	Net Assets ($Mil)	Price	Performance Rating/Pts	Total Return Y-T-D	Risk Rating/Pts
6-05	B-	582.12	13.57	C+ / 6.3	9.19%	B- / 7.7
2004	C-	565.86	12.83	D+ / 2.3	1.73%	B / 8.6
2003	C	584.03	13.31	C- / 3.1	6.46%	B+ / 9.1

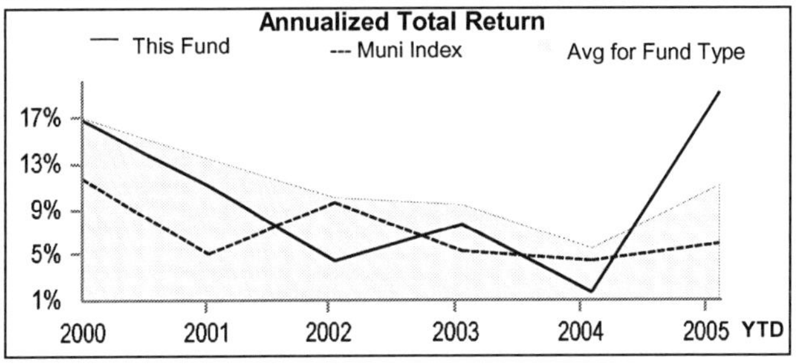

MuniYield PA Insured Fund (MPA) B Good

Fund Family: Merrill Lynch Investment Managers
Fund Type: Municipal - Single State
Inception Date: November 4, 1992

Major Rating Factors:
Strong performance is the major factor driving the B (Good) Weiss Investment Rating for MuniYield PA Insured Fund. The fund currently has a performance rating of B- (Good) based on an annualized return of 8.72% over the last three years and a total return of 3.09% year to date 2005. Factored into the performance evaluation is an expense ratio of 1.11% (low).

The fund's risk rating is currently C+ (Fair). It carries a beta of 2.45, meaning it is expected to move 24.5% for every 10% move in the market. Volatility, as measured by both the semi-deviation and a drawdown factor, is considered low. As of June 30, 2005, MuniYield PA Insured Fund traded at a discount of 1.84% below its net asset value, which is worse than its one-year historical average discount of 3.71%.

Bill Bock has been running the fund for 13 years and currently receives a manager quality ranking of 29 (0=worst, 99=best). If you desire only a moderate level of risk and strong performance, then this fund is an excellent option.

Data Date	Weiss Investment Rating	Net Assets ($Mil)	Price	Performance Rating/Pts	Total Return Y-T-D	Risk Rating/Pts
6-05	B	184.61	15.99	B- / 7.3	3.09%	C+ / 6.6
2004	B+	175.88	16.00	B / 7.9	9.64%	C+ / 6.9
2003	A+	178.34	15.50	B / 8.0	11.15%	B / 8.1

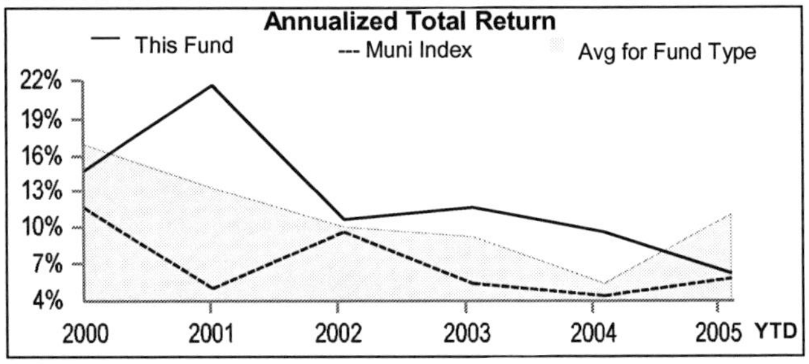

MuniYield Quality Fund (MQY) B+ Good

Fund Family: Merrill Lynch Investment Managers
Fund Type: Municipal - National
Inception Date: June 26, 1992

Major Rating Factors:
Strong performance is the major factor driving the B+ (Good) Weiss Investment Rating for MuniYield Quality Fund. The fund currently has a performance rating of B+ (Good) based on an annualized return of 9.36% over the last three years and a total return of 9.66% year to date 2005. Factored into the performance evaluation is an expense ratio of 0.94% (low).

The fund's risk rating is currently C+ (Fair). It carries a beta of 1.92, meaning it is expected to move 19.2% for every 10% move in the market. Volatility, as measured by both the semi-deviation and a drawdown factor, is considered low. As of June 30, 2005, MuniYield Quality Fund traded at a discount of 1.93% below its net asset value, which is worse than its one-year historical average discount of 5.60%.

Mike Kalinoski has been running the fund for 13 years and currently receives a manager quality ranking of 59 (0=worst, 99=best). If you desire only a moderate level of risk and strong performance, then this fund is an excellent option.

Data Date	Weiss Investment Rating	Net Assets ($Mil)	Price	Performance Rating/Pts	Total Return Y-T-D	Risk Rating/Pts
6-05	B+	468.97	15.27	B+ / 8.4	9.66%	C+ / 6.3
2004	B-	458.91	14.39	C+ / 6.3	5.59%	B- / 7.9
2003	B	467.37	14.51	C+ / 5.8	10.72%	B / 8.5

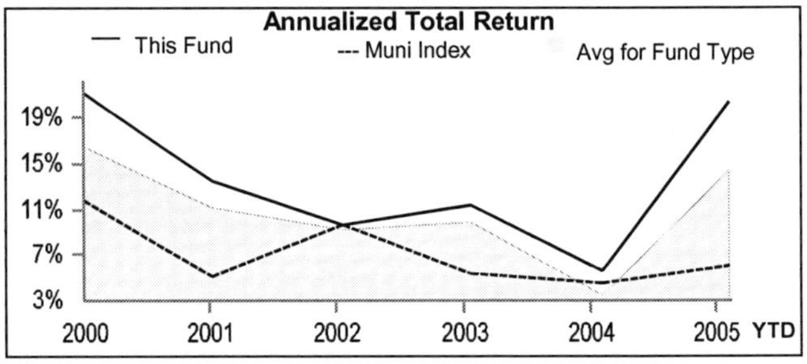

MuniYield Quality Fund II (MQT) A+ Excellent

Fund Family: Merrill Lynch Investment Managers
Fund Type: Municipal - National
Inception Date: August 28, 1992

Major Rating Factors:
Strong performance is the major factor driving the A+ (Excellent) Weiss Investment Rating for MuniYield Quality Fund II. The fund currently has a performance rating of B+ (Good) based on an annualized return of 11.04% over the last three years and a total return of 12.15% year to date 2005. Factored into the performance evaluation is an expense ratio of 1.02% (low).

The fund's risk rating is currently B- (Good). It carries a beta of 2.02, meaning it is expected to move 20.2% for every 10% move in the market. Volatility, as measured by both the semi-deviation and a drawdown factor, is considered low. As of June 30, 2005, MuniYield Quality Fund II traded at a discount of 3.33% below its net asset value, which is worse than its one-year historical average discount of 7.60%.

Mike Kalinoski has been running the fund for 13 years and currently receives a manager quality ranking of 66 (0=worst, 99=best). If you desire only a moderate level of risk and strong performance, then this fund is an excellent option.

Data Date	Weiss Investment Rating	Net Assets ($Mil)	Price	Performance Rating/Pts	Total Return Y-T-D	Risk Rating/Pts
6-05	A+	306.58	13.37	B+ / 8.9	12.15%	B- / 7.2
2004	B	296.06	12.33	C+ / 6.1	4.66%	B / 8.4
2003	C+	300.50	12.47	C / 5.1	9.86%	B / 8.4

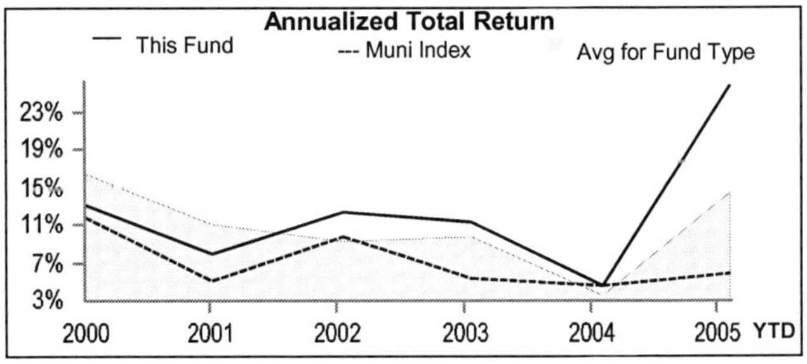

MVC Capital (MVC) C- Fair

Fund Family: MVC Capital, Inc
Fund Type: Growth
Inception Date: March 31, 2000

Major Rating Factors:
Disappointing performance is the major factor driving the C- (Fair) Weiss Investment Rating for MVC Capital. The fund currently has a performance rating of D- (Weak) based on an annualized return of 5.35% over the last three years and a total return of 7.93% year to date 2005. Factored into the performance evaluation is an expense ratio of 3.43% (high).

The fund's risk rating is currently B (Good). It carries a beta of 0.12, meaning the fund's expected move will be 1.2% for every 10% move in the market. Volatility, as measured by both the semi-deviation and a drawdown factor, is considered low. As of June 30, 2005, MVC Capital traded at a price exactly equal to its net asset value, which is worse than its one-year historical average discount of 1.17%.

Michael Tokarz has been running the fund for 2 years and currently receives a manager quality ranking of 79 (0=worst, 99=best). This fund offers only a moderate level of risk but investors looking for strong performance are still waiting.

Data Date	Weiss Investment Rating	Net Assets ($Mil)	Price	Performance Rating/Pts	Total Return Y-T-D	Risk Rating/Pts
6-05	C-	115.57	0.00	D- / 1.1	7.93%	B / 8.9
2004	E+	108.85	9.08	E / 0.3	15.12%	C+ / 5.6
2003	E+	141.67	7.90	E- / 0.1	-4.24%	C- / 3.9

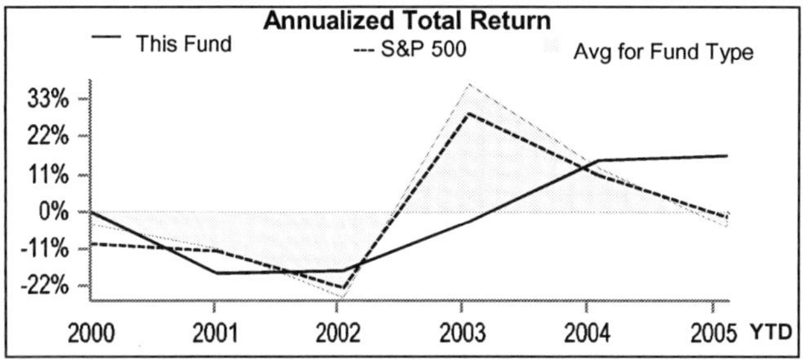

NAIC Growth Fund (GRF) E- Very Weak

Fund Family: Growth Fund Advisors
Fund Type: Growth
Inception Date: July 2, 1990

Major Rating Factors:
NAIC Growth Fund has adopted a very risky asset allocation strategy and currently receives an overall Weiss Investment Rating of E- (Very Weak). The fund has a high level of volatility, with a standard deviation of 27.12. It carries a beta of 0.73, meaning the fund's expected move will be 7.3% for every 10% move in the market. As of June 30, 2005, NAIC Growth Fund traded at a discount of 10.66% below its net asset value, which is worse than its one-year historical average discount of 14.29%. Unfortunately, the high level of risk (D, Weak) failed to pay off as investors endured very poor performance.

The fund's performance rating is currently E- (Very Weak). It has registered an annualized return of -3.63% over the last three years and is down -7.53% year to date 2005. Factored into the performance evaluation is an expense ratio of 1.80% (above average).

Kenneth S. Janke has been running the fund for 15 years and currently receives a manager quality ranking of 2 (0=worst, 99=best). If you can tolerate very high levels of risk in the hope of improved future returns, holding this fund may be an option.

Data Date	Weiss Investment Rating	Net Assets ($Mil)	Price	Performance Rating/Pts	Total Return Y-T-D	Risk Rating/Pts
6-05	E-	26.87	8.55	E- / 0.0	-7.53%	D / 1.6
2004	E	26.31	9.50	E+ / 0.8	2.22%	D- / 1.5
2003	E	22.60	9.30	E+ / 0.6	-7.78%	D / 1.7

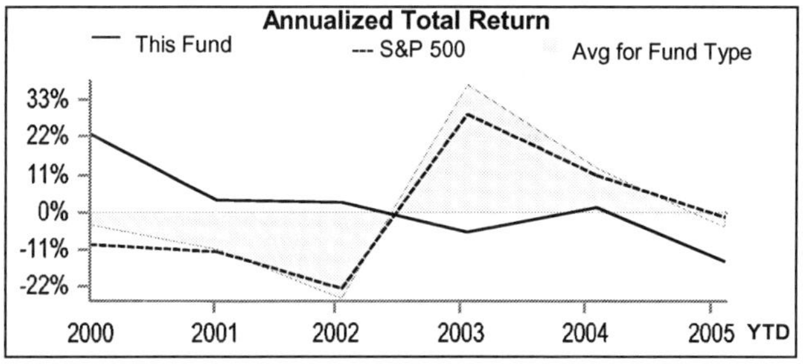

Nasdaq 100 Trust Series I (QQQQ) E+ Very Weak

Fund Family: Bank of New York
Fund Type: Growth
Inception Date: March 9, 1999

Major Rating Factors:
Nasdaq 100 Trust Series I has adopted a very risky asset allocation strategy and currently receives an overall Weiss Investment Rating of E+ (Very Weak). The fund has a high level of volatility, with a standard deviation of 22.73. It carries a beta of 1.42, meaning it is expected to move 14.2% for every 10% move in the market. As of June 30, 2005, Nasdaq 100 Trust Series I traded at a premium of .03% above its net asset value, which is worse than its one-year historical average premium of .01%. Unfortunately, the high level of risk (D, Weak) failed to pay off as investors endured poor performance.

The fund's performance rating is currently D+ (Weak). It has registered an annualized return of 12.71% over the last three years but is down -7.29% year to date 2005. Factored into the performance evaluation is an expense ratio of 0.20% (very low).

This fund has been team managed for 6 years and currently receives a manager quality ranking of 69 (0=worst, 99=best). If you can tolerate very high levels of risk in the hope of improved future returns, holding this fund may be an option.

Data Date	Weiss Investment Rating	Net Assets ($Mil)	Price	Performance Rating/Pts	Total Return Y-T-D	Risk Rating/Pts
6-05	E+	19957.13	36.97	D+ / 2.8	-7.29%	D / 2.1
2004	E	23030.12	39.92	E+ / 0.7	10.51%	D / 1.6
2003	E-	22081.40	35.85	E / 0.4	47.16%	E- / 0.1

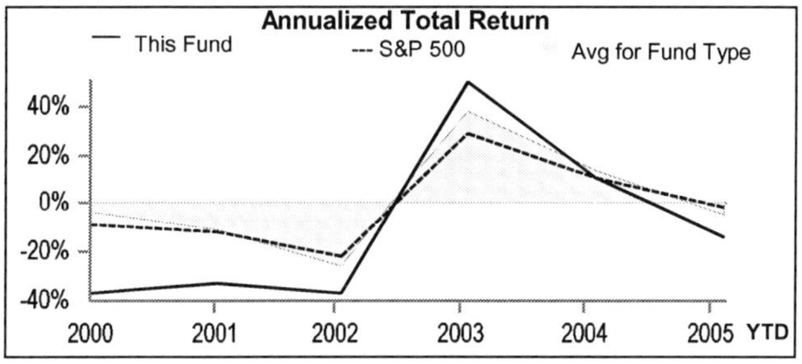

New America High Income Fund (HYB) D- Weak

Fund Family: T. Rowe Price, Inc.
Fund Type: Corporate - High Yield
Inception Date: February 26, 1988

Data Date	Weiss Investment Rating	Net Assets ($Mil)	Price	Performance Rating/Pts	Total Return Y-T-D	Risk Rating/Pts
6-05	D-	212.17	2.13	C / 4.7	1.37%	C- / 3.0
2004	D-	200.59	2.19	C- / 3.3	13.11%	C- / 3.0
2003	D	153.23	2.17	C- / 3.9	26.18%	C- / 3.4

Major Rating Factors:

New America High Income Fund receives a Weiss Investment Rating of D- (Weak). The fund currently has a performance rating of C (Fair) based on an annualized return of 11.22% over the last three years and a total return of 1.37% year to date 2005. Factored into the performance evaluation is an expense ratio of 0.87% (low).

The fund's risk rating is currently C- (Fair). It carries a beta of 2.17, meaning it is expected to move 21.7% for every 10% move in the market. Volatility, as measured by both the semi-deviation and a drawdown factor, is considered average. As of June 30, 2005, New America High Income Fund traded at a discount of .93% below its net asset value, which is worse than its one-year historical average discount of 4.00%.

Catherine A. Smith has been running the fund for 13 years and currently receives a manager quality ranking of 0 (0=worst, 99=best). If you desire an average level of risk, then this fund may be an option.

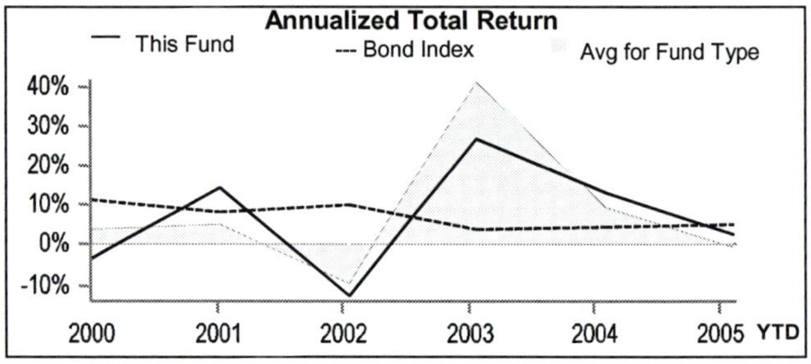

New Germany Fund (GF) C Fair

Fund Family: Deutsche Bank Group
Fund Type: Foreign
Inception Date: January 30, 1990

Data Date	Weiss Investment Rating	Net Assets ($Mil)	Price	Performance Rating/Pts	Total Return Y-T-D	Risk Rating/Pts
6-05	C	265.81	9.18	B+ / 8.9	3.00%	D / 1.8
2004	C-	240.93	9.05	B+ / 8.6	30.56%	D / 1.8
2003	D	168.74	7.10	C- / 3.7	100.73%	D / 2.1

Major Rating Factors:

New Germany Fund has adopted a very risky asset allocation strategy and currently receives an overall Weiss Investment Rating of C (Fair). The fund has shown a high level of volatility, as measured by both semi-deviation and drawdown factors. It carries a beta of 1.59, meaning it is expected to move 15.9% for every 10% move in the market. As of June 30, 2005, New Germany Fund traded at a discount of 14.37% below its net asset value, which is worse than its one-year historical average discount of 15.27%. The high level of risk (D, Weak) did however, reward investors with excellent performance.

The fund's performance rating is currently B+ (Good). It has registered an annualized return of 24.15% over the last three years and is up 3.00% year to date 2005. Factored into the performance evaluation is an expense ratio of 1.24% (average).

Sandra M. Schaufler has been running the fund for 15 years and currently receives a manager quality ranking of 80 (0=worst, 99=best). If you are comfortable owning a very high risk investment, this fund may be an option.

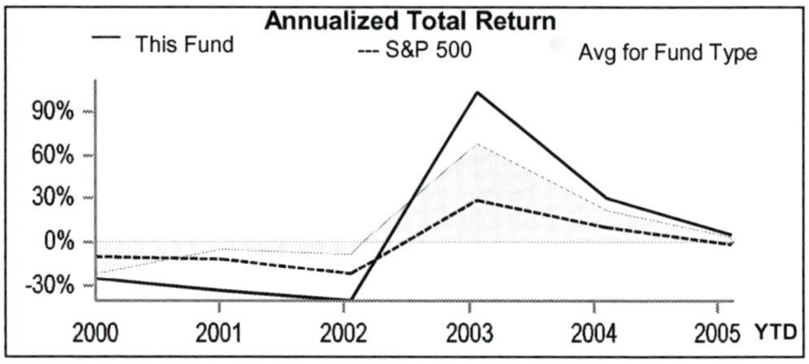

Nuveen AZ Div Adv Muni (NFZ) C+ Fair

Fund Family: Nuveen Advisory Corp.
Fund Type: Municipal - Single State
Inception Date: January 26, 2001

Data Date	Weiss Investment Rating	Net Assets ($Mil)	Price	Performance Rating/Pts	Total Return Y-T-D	Risk Rating/Pts
6-05	C+	24.12	16.27	C+ / 6.4	7.09%	C+ / 6.6
2004	C+	23.57	15.65	C / 4.7	-0.47%	B- / 7.5

Major Rating Factors:

Middle of the road best describes Nuveen AZ Div Adv Muni whose Weiss Investment Rating is currently a C+ (Fair). The fund currently has a performance rating of C+ (Fair) based on an annualized return of 6.99% over the last three years and a total return of 7.09% year to date 2005. Factored into the performance evaluation is an expense ratio of 0.83% (very low).

The fund's risk rating is currently C+ (Fair). It carries a beta of 1.99, meaning it is expected to move 19.9% for every 10% move in the market. Volatility, as measured by both the semi-deviation and a drawdown factor, is considered low. As of June 30, 2005, Nuveen AZ Div Adv Muni traded at a premium of 4.16% above its net asset value, which is worse than its one-year historical average premium of 2.85%.

Scott R. Romans, Ph.D has been running the fund for 4 years and currently receives a manager quality ranking of 50 (0=worst, 99=best). If you desire an average level of risk, then this fund may be an option.

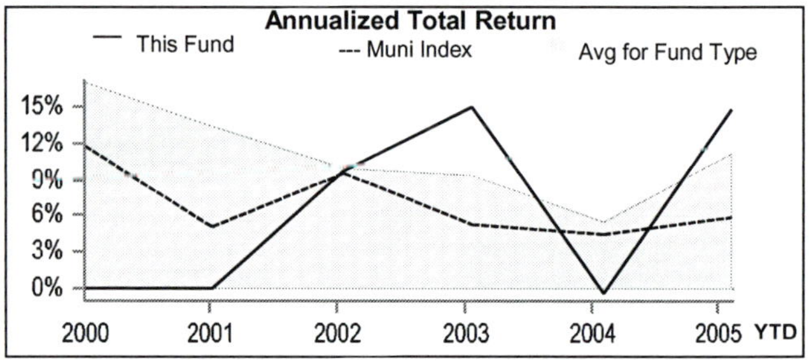

Nuveen AZ Div Adv Muni Fund 2 (NKR) C+ Fair

Fund Family: Nuveen Advisory Corp.
Fund Type: Municipal - Single State
Inception Date: March 25, 2002

Major Rating Factors:
Middle of the road best describes Nuveen AZ Div Adv Muni Fund 2 whose Weiss Investment Rating is currently a C+ (Fair). The fund currently has a performance rating of C (Fair) based on an annualized return of 5.85% over the last three years and a total return of 2.46% year to date 2005. Factored into the performance evaluation is an expense ratio of 0.79% (very low).

The fund's risk rating is currently C+ (Fair). It carries a beta of 2.05, meaning it is expected to move 20.5% for every 10% move in the market. Volatility, as measured by both the semi-deviation and a drawdown factor, is considered low. As of June 30, 2005, Nuveen AZ Div Adv Muni Fund 2 traded at a discount of .63% below its net asset value, which is worse than its one-year historical average discount of .93%.

Scott R. Romans, Ph.D has been running the fund for 3 years and currently receives a manager quality ranking of 22 (0=worst, 99=best). If you desire an average level of risk, then this fund may be an option.

Data Date	Weiss Investment Rating	Net Assets ($Mil)	Price	Performance Rating/Pts	Total Return Y-T-D	Risk Rating/Pts
6-05	C+	38.28	15.70	C / 5.1	2.46%	C+ / 6.9

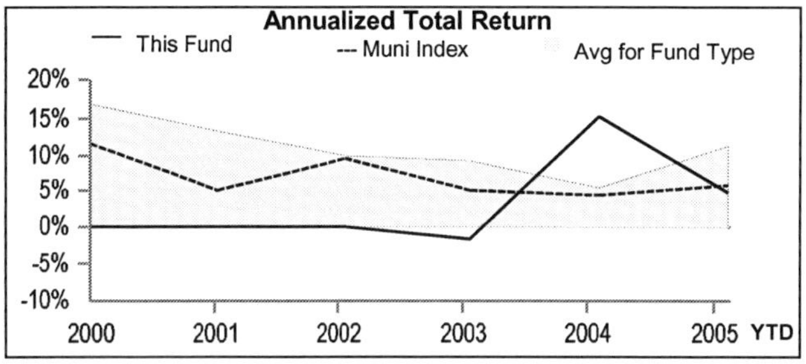

Nuveen AZ Prem Inc Muni (NAZ) D+ Weak

Fund Family: Nuveen Advisory Corp.
Fund Type: Municipal - Single State
Inception Date: November 19, 1992

Major Rating Factors:
Disappointing performance is the major factor driving the D+ (Weak) Weiss Investment Rating for Nuveen AZ Prem Inc Muni. The fund currently has a performance rating of D- (Weak) based on an annualized return of 2.39% over the last three years and a total return of 4.16% year to date 2005. Factored into the performance evaluation is an expense ratio of 1.19% (average).

The fund's risk rating is currently B- (Good). It carries a beta of 1.89, meaning it is expected to move 18.9% for every 10% move in the market. Volatility, as measured by both the semi-deviation and a drawdown factor, is considered low. As of June 30, 2005, Nuveen AZ Prem Inc Muni traded at a premium of 4.69% above its net asset value, which is better than its one-year historical average premium of 8.71%.

Scott R. Romans, Ph.D has been running the fund for 13 years and currently receives a manager quality ranking of 7 (0=worst, 99=best). This fund offers only a moderate level of risk but investors looking for strong performance are still waiting.

Data Date	Weiss Investment Rating	Net Assets ($Mil)	Price	Performance Rating/Pts	Total Return Y-T-D	Risk Rating/Pts
6-05	D+	65.59	15.41	D- / 1.3	4.16%	B- / 7.5
2004	D+	63.52	15.21	D- / 1.3	-0.06%	B / 8.1
2003	C	63.72	15.80	C- / 3.4	10.23%	B / 8.4

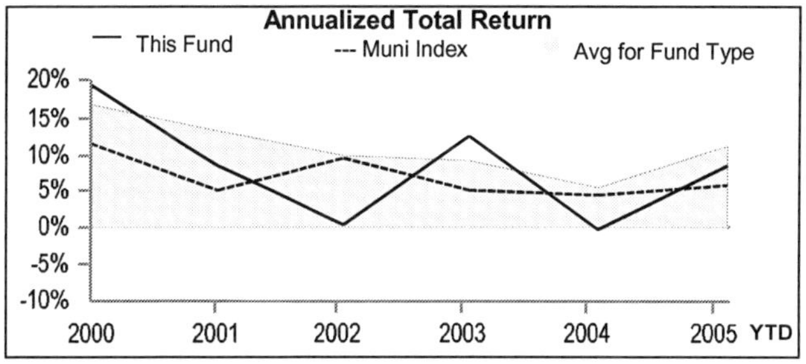

Nuveen CA Div Adv Muni (NAC) A Excellent

Fund Family: Nuveen Advisory Corp.
Fund Type: Municipal - Single State
Inception Date: May 26, 1999

Major Rating Factors:
Strong performance is the major factor driving the A (Excellent) Weiss Investment Rating for Nuveen CA Div Adv Muni. The fund currently has a performance rating of B (Good) based on an annualized return of 9.58% over the last three years and a total return of 8.10% year to date 2005. Factored into the performance evaluation is an expense ratio of 0.74% (very low).

The fund's risk rating is currently B- (Good). It carries a beta of 2.14, meaning it is expected to move 21.4% for every 10% move in the market. Volatility, as measured by both the semi-deviation and a drawdown factor, is considered low. As of June 30, 2005, Nuveen CA Div Adv Muni traded at a discount of 2.44% below its net asset value, which is worse than its one-year historical average discount of 4.95%.

Bill Fitzgerald has been running the fund for 6 years and currently receives a manager quality ranking of 47 (0=worst, 99=best). If you desire only a moderate level of risk and strong performance, then this fund is an excellent option.

Data Date	Weiss Investment Rating	Net Assets ($Mil)	Price	Performance Rating/Pts	Total Return Y-T-D	Risk Rating/Pts
6-05	A	373.98	15.59	B / 8.0	8.10%	B- / 7.2
2004	B	362.61	14.90	C+ / 5.8	4.25%	B / 8.0
2003	B-	365.50	15.21	C / 5.4	10.21%	B / 8.3

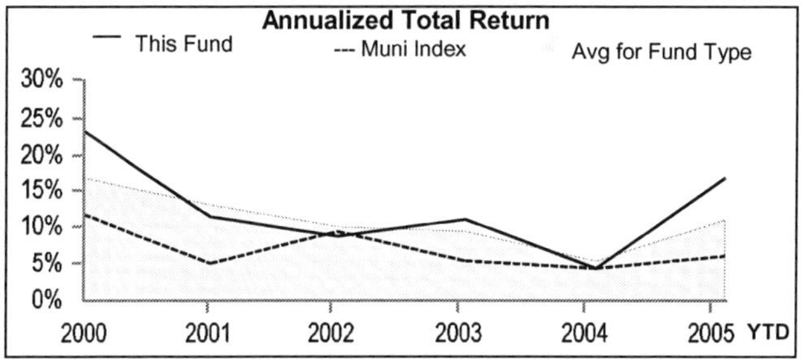

Nuveen CA Div Adv Muni 2 (NVX) B+ Good

Fund Family: Nuveen Advisory Corp.
Fund Type: Municipal - Single State
Inception Date: March 27, 2001

Major Rating Factors:
Strong performance is the major factor driving the B+ (Good) Weiss Investment Rating for Nuveen CA Div Adv Muni 2. The fund currently has a performance rating of B- (Good) based on an annualized return of 7.87% over the last three years and a total return of 12.02% year to date 2005. Factored into the performance evaluation is an expense ratio of 0.70% (very low).

The fund's risk rating is currently B- (Good). It carries a beta of 2.10, meaning it is expected to move 21.0% for every 10% move in the market. Volatility, as measured by both the semi-deviation and a drawdown factor, is considered low. As of June 30, 2005, Nuveen CA Div Adv Muni 2 traded at a discount of 6.29% below its net asset value, which is worse than its one-year historical average discount of 8.09%.

Scott Romans has been running the fund for 3 years and currently receives a manager quality ranking of 36 (0=worst, 99=best). If you desire only a moderate level of risk and strong performance, then this fund is an excellent option.

Data Date	Weiss Investment Rating	Net Assets ($Mil)	Price	Performance Rating/Pts	Total Return Y-T-D	Risk Rating/Pts
6-05	B+	230.17	14.59	B- / 7.1	12.02%	B- / 7.3
2004	C-	221.13	13.45	D+ / 2.6	2.52%	B / 8.4

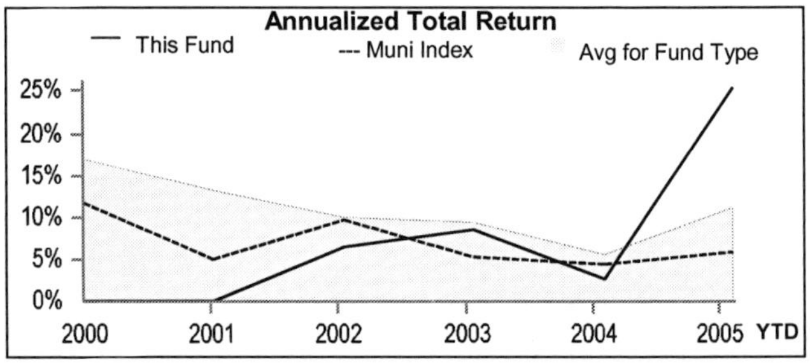

Nuveen CA Div Adv Muni 3 (NZH) B- Good

Fund Family: Nuveen Advisory Corp.
Fund Type: Municipal - Single State
Inception Date: September 25, 2001

Major Rating Factors:
Nuveen CA Div Adv Muni 3 receives a Weiss Investment Rating of B- (Good). The fund currently has a performance rating of C+ (Fair) based on an annualized return of 7.62% over the last three years and a total return of 9.63% year to date 2005. Factored into the performance evaluation is an expense ratio of 0.70% (very low).

The fund's risk rating is currently B- (Good). It carries a beta of 1.98, meaning it is expected to move 19.8% for every 10% move in the market. Volatility, as measured by both the semi-deviation and a drawdown factor, is considered low. As of June 30, 2005, Nuveen CA Div Adv Muni 3 traded at a discount of 8.82% below its net asset value, which is worse than its one-year historical average discount of 9.70%.

Scott Romans has been running the fund for 3 years and currently receives a manager quality ranking of 40 (0=worst, 99=best). If you desire an average level of risk, then this fund may be an option.

Data Date	Weiss Investment Rating	Net Assets ($Mil)	Price	Performance Rating/Pts	Total Return Y-T-D	Risk Rating/Pts
6-05	B-	369.30	13.96	C+ / 6.9	9.63%	B- / 7.7
2004	C	352.42	13.14	D+ / 2.9	4.77%	B / 8.3

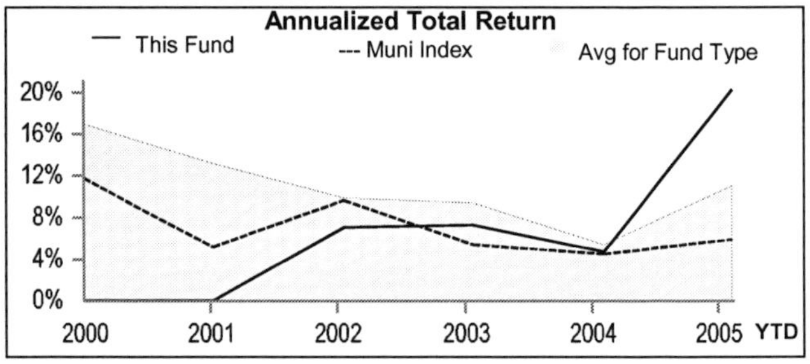

Nuveen CA Inv Quality Muni (NQC) B- Good

Fund Family: Nuveen Advisory Corp.
Fund Type: Municipal - Single State
Inception Date: November 20, 1990

Major Rating Factors:
Nuveen CA Inv Quality Muni receives a Weiss Investment Rating of B- (Good). The fund currently has a performance rating of C+ (Fair) based on an annualized return of 6.43% over the last three years and a total return of 9.57% year to date 2005. Factored into the performance evaluation is an expense ratio of 1.20% (average).

The fund's risk rating is currently B- (Good). It carries a beta of 1.73, meaning it is expected to move 17.3% for every 10% move in the market. Volatility, as measured by both the semi-deviation and a drawdown factor, is considered low. As of June 30, 2005, Nuveen CA Inv Quality Muni traded at a discount of 5.22% below its net asset value, which is worse than its one-year historical average discount of 6.20%.

Scott Romans has been running the fund for 3 years and currently receives a manager quality ranking of 39 (0=worst, 99=best). If you desire an average level of risk, then this fund may be an option.

Data Date	Weiss Investment Rating	Net Assets ($Mil)	Price	Performance Rating/Pts	Total Return Y-T-D	Risk Rating/Pts
6-05	B-	215.69	15.06	C+ / 6.0	9.57%	B- / 7.6
2004	C-	210.58	14.18	D+ / 2.3	2.88%	B / 8.4
2003	C-	212.51	14.83	D+ / 2.5	6.31%	B / 8.7

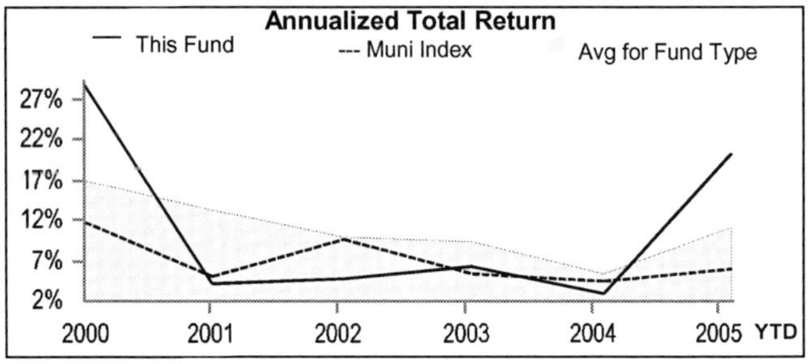

Nuveen CA Muni Market Opportunity (NCO) B- Good

Fund Family: Nuveen Advisory Corp.
Fund Type: Municipal - Single State
Inception Date: May 18, 1990

Major Rating Factors:
Nuveen CA Muni Market Opportunity receives a Weiss Investment Rating of B- (Good). The fund currently has a performance rating of C+ (Fair) based on an annualized return of 6.70% over the last three years and a total return of 9.53% year to date 2005. Factored into the performance evaluation is an expense ratio of 1.25% (average).

The fund's risk rating is currently B- (Good). It carries a beta of 2.25, meaning it is expected to move 22.5% for every 10% move in the market. Volatility, as measured by both the semi-deviation and a drawdown factor, is considered low. As of June 30, 2005, Nuveen CA Muni Market Opportunity traded at a discount of 7.13% below its net asset value, which is worse than its one-year historical average discount of 7.76%.

Scott Romans has been running the fund for 3 years and currently receives a manager quality ranking of 19 (0=worst, 99=best). If you desire an average level of risk, then this fund may be an option.

Data Date	Weiss Investment Rating	Net Assets ($Mil)	Price	Performance Rating/Pts	Total Return Y-T-D	Risk Rating/Pts
6-05	B-	131.50	14.99	C+ / 6.0	9.53%	B- / 7.3
2004	C-	126.65	14.12	D+ / 2.3	2.36%	B / 8.0
2003	C-	127.25	14.64	D / 2.2	7.43%	B / 8.4

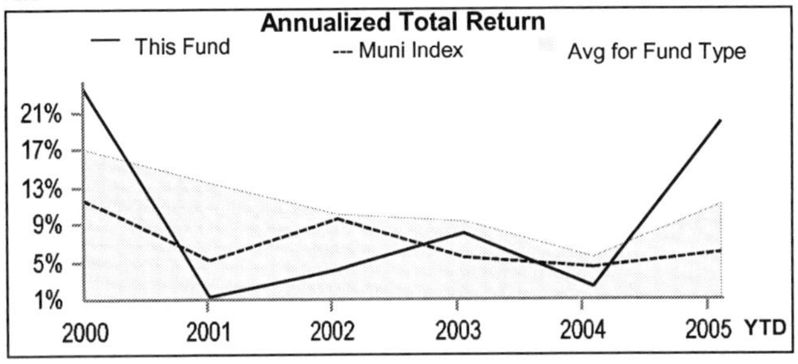

Nuveen CA Muni Value (NCA) B- Good

Fund Family: Nuveen Advisory Corp.
Fund Type: Municipal - Single State
Inception Date: October 7, 1987

Major Rating Factors:
Nuveen CA Muni Value receives a Weiss Investment Rating of B- (Good). The fund currently has a performance rating of C+ (Fair) based on an annualized return of 6.21% over the last three years and a total return of 9.77% year to date 2005. Factored into the performance evaluation is an expense ratio of 0.63% (very low).

The fund's risk rating is currently B- (Good). It carries a beta of 1.91, meaning it is expected to move 19.1% for every 10% move in the market. Volatility, as measured by both the semi-deviation and a drawdown factor, is considered low. As of June 30, 2005, Nuveen CA Muni Value traded at a discount of 4.07% below its net asset value, which is worse than its one-year historical average discount of 8.09%.

Scott Romans has been running the fund for 3 years and currently receives a manager quality ranking of 25 (0=worst, 99=best). If you desire an average level of risk, then this fund may be an option.

Data Date	Weiss Investment Rating	Net Assets ($Mil)	Price	Performance Rating/Pts	Total Return Y-T-D	Risk Rating/Pts
6-05	B-	260.40	9.90	C+ / 6.2	9.77%	B- / 7.1
2004	C-	256.90	9.24	D / 1.7	5.45%	B / 8.2
2003	C-	257.42	9.28	D+ / 2.3	2.40%	B / 8.8

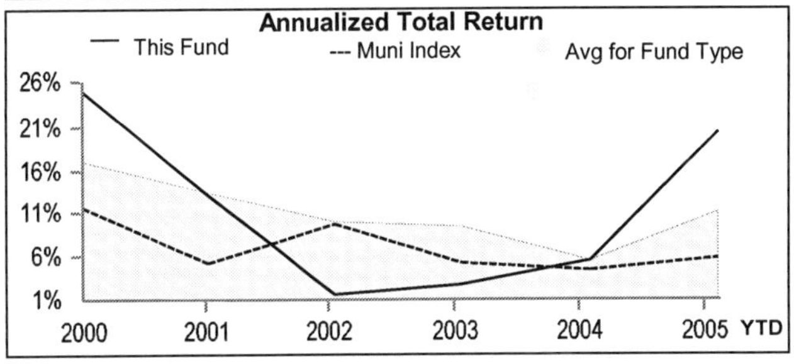

Nuveen CA Performance Plus Muni (NCP) C+ Fair

Fund Family: Nuveen Advisory Corp.
Fund Type: Municipal - Single State
Inception Date: November 17, 1989

Major Rating Factors:
Middle of the road best describes Nuveen CA Performance Plus Muni whose Weiss Investment Rating is currently a C+ (Fair). The fund currently has a performance rating of C (Fair) based on an annualized return of 6.59% over the last three years and a total return of 7.27% year to date 2005. Factored into the performance evaluation is an expense ratio of 1.22% (average).

The fund's risk rating is currently B- (Good). It carries a beta of 2.39, meaning it is expected to move 23.9% for every 10% move in the market. Volatility, as measured by both the semi-deviation and a drawdown factor, is considered low. As of June 30, 2005, Nuveen CA Performance Plus Muni traded at a discount of 7.79% below its net asset value, which is better than its one-year historical average discount of 7.77%.

Scott Romans has been running the fund for 3 years and currently receives a manager quality ranking of 13 (0=worst, 99=best). If you desire an average level of risk, then this fund may be an option.

Data Date	Weiss Investment Rating	Net Assets ($Mil)	Price	Performance Rating/Pts	Total Return Y-T-D	Risk Rating/Pts
6-05	C+	204.36	14.55	C / 5.5	7.27%	B- / 7.4
2004	C-	199.79	13.99	D+ / 2.8	3.82%	B / 8.1
2003	C	201.49	14.72	C- / 3.0	9.64%	B / 8.6

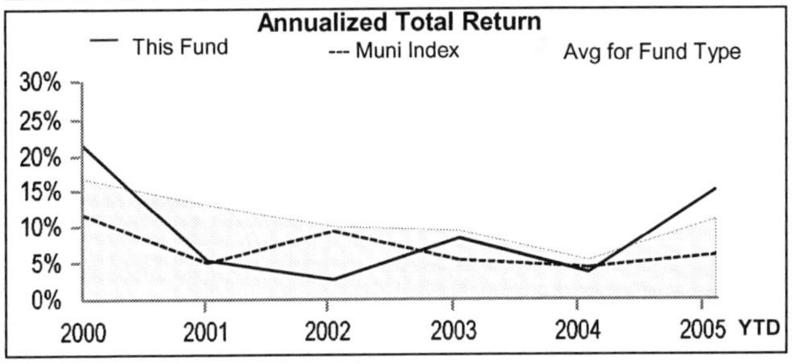

Nuveen CA Prem Inc Muni (NCU) B+ Good

Fund Family: Nuveen Advisory Corp.
Fund Type: Municipal - Single State
Inception Date: June 18, 1993

Major Rating Factors:
Strong performance is the major factor driving the B+ (Good) Weiss Investment Rating for Nuveen CA Prem Inc Muni. The fund currently has a performance rating of B- (Good) based on an annualized return of 7.41% over the last three years and a total return of 10.78% year to date 2005. Factored into the performance evaluation is an expense ratio of 1.19% (average).

The fund's risk rating is currently B- (Good). It carries a beta of 2.04, meaning it is expected to move 20.4% for every 10% move in the market. Volatility, as measured by both the semi-deviation and a drawdown factor, is considered low. As of June 30, 2005, Nuveen CA Prem Inc Muni traded at a discount of 6.04% below its net asset value, which is worse than its one-year historical average discount of 7.07%.

Scott Romans has been running the fund for 3 years and currently receives a manager quality ranking of 31 (0=worst, 99=best). If you desire only a moderate level of risk and strong performance, then this fund is an excellent option.

Data Date	Weiss Investment Rating	Net Assets ($Mil)	Price	Perfor-mance Rating/Pts	Total Return Y-T-D	Risk Rating/Pts
6-05	B+	86.96	14.16	B- / 7.1	10.78%	B- / 7.1
2004	C	83.68	13.18	C- / 3.0	2.97%	B / 8.2
2003	C	83.39	13.61	C- / 3.1	4.79%	B / 8.7

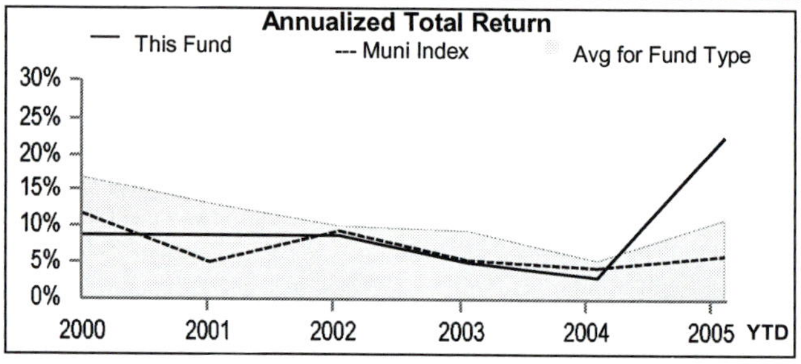

Nuveen CA Quality Inc Muni (NUC) C+ Fair

Fund Family: Nuveen Advisory Corp.
Fund Type: Municipal - Single State
Inception Date: November 20, 1991

Major Rating Factors:
Middle of the road best describes Nuveen CA Quality Inc Muni whose Weiss Investment Rating is currently a C+ (Fair). The fund currently has a performance rating of C (Fair) based on an annualized return of 5.78% over the last three years and a total return of 6.87% year to date 2005. Factored into the performance evaluation is an expense ratio of 1.19% (average).

The fund's risk rating is currently B- (Good). It carries a beta of 2.29, meaning it is expected to move 22.9% for every 10% move in the market. Volatility, as measured by both the semi-deviation and a drawdown factor, is considered low. As of June 30, 2005, Nuveen CA Quality Inc Muni traded at a discount of 4.87% below its net asset value, which is better than its one-year historical average discount of 3.82%.

Scott Romans has been running the fund for 3 years and currently receives a manager quality ranking of 12 (0=worst, 99=best). If you desire an average level of risk, then this fund may be an option.

Data Date	Weiss Investment Rating	Net Assets ($Mil)	Price	Perfor-mance Rating/Pts	Total Return Y-T-D	Risk Rating/Pts
6-05	C+	351.98	15.23	C / 4.7	6.87%	B- / 7.3
2004	C-	340.03	14.71	D / 2.1	1.76%	B / 8.0
2003	C-	341.90	15.31	D+ / 2.6	3.46%	B / 8.7

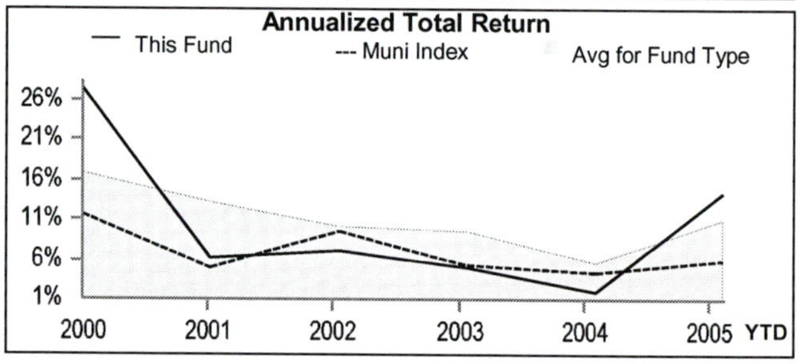

Nuveen CA Select Quality Muni (NVC) C+ Fair

Fund Family: Nuveen Advisory Corp.
Fund Type: Municipal - Single State
Inception Date: May 22, 1991

Major Rating Factors:
Middle of the road best describes Nuveen CA Select Quality Muni whose Weiss Investment Rating is currently a C+ (Fair). The fund currently has a performance rating of C+ (Fair) based on an annualized return of 6.82% over the last three years and a total return of 8.02% year to date 2005. Factored into the performance evaluation is an expense ratio of 1.18% (low).

The fund's risk rating is currently B- (Good). It carries a beta of 2.48, meaning it is expected to move 24.8% for every 10% move in the market. Volatility, as measured by both the semi-deviation and a drawdown factor, is considered low. As of June 30, 2005, Nuveen CA Select Quality Muni traded at a discount of 5.82% below its net asset value, which is worse than its one-year historical average discount of 5.83%.

Scott Romans has been running the fund for 3 years and currently receives a manager quality ranking of 16 (0=worst, 99=best). If you desire an average level of risk, then this fund may be an option.

Data Date	Weiss Investment Rating	Net Assets ($Mil)	Price	Perfor-mance Rating/Pts	Total Return Y-T-D	Risk Rating/Pts
6-05	C+	368.72	15.04	C+ / 5.7	8.02%	B- / 7.2
2004	C-	359.17	14.37	D+ / 2.4	2.02%	B- / 7.9
2003	C-	361.26	15.02	C- / 3.0	8.56%	B / 8.3

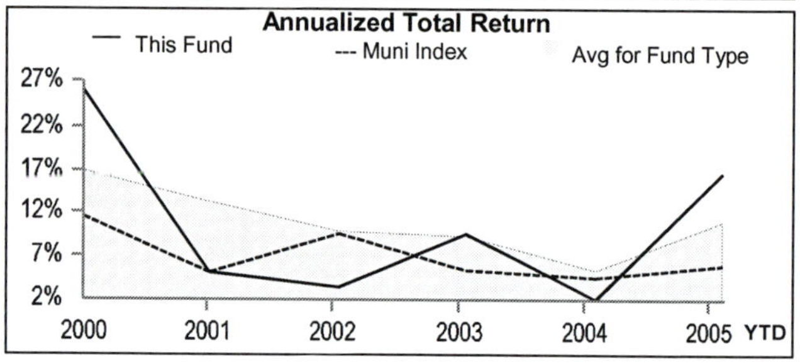

Nuveen CA Select Tax-Free Inc Port (NXC) — C- Fair

Fund Family: Nuveen Advisory Corp.
Fund Type: Municipal - Single State
Inception Date: June 19, 1992

Major Rating Factors:
Disappointing performance is the major factor driving the C- (Fair) Weiss Investment Rating for Nuveen CA Select Tax-Free Inc Port. The fund currently has a performance rating of D+ (Weak) based on an annualized return of 2.05% over the last three years and a total return of 9.10% year to date 2005. Factored into the performance evaluation is an expense ratio of 0.38% (very low).

The fund's risk rating is currently B- (Good). It carries a beta of 1.38, meaning it is expected to move 13.8% for every 10% move in the market. Volatility, as measured by both the semi-deviation and a drawdown factor, is considered low. As of June 30, 2005, Nuveen CA Select Tax-Free Inc Port traded at a discount of 6.38% below its net asset value, which is worse than its one-year historical average discount of 8.39%.

Scott Romans has been running the fund for 13 years and currently receives a manager quality ranking of 14 (0=worst, 99=best). This fund offers only a moderate level of risk but investors looking for strong performance are still waiting.

Data Date	Weiss Investment Rating	Net Assets ($Mil)	Price	Performance Rating/Pts	Total Return Y-T-D	Risk Rating/Pts
6-05	C-	93.16	13.94	D+ / 2.6	9.10%	B- / 7.2
2004	D	91.08	13.09	E+ / 0.9	3.79%	B / 8.0
2003	C-	91.14	13.40	D / 1.9	2.72%	B / 8.6

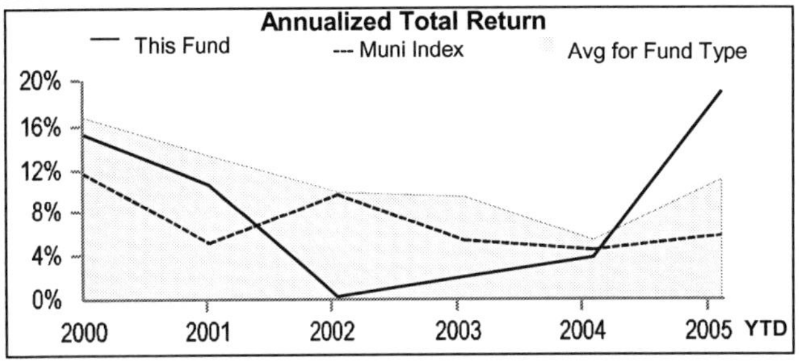

Nuveen CT Div Adv Muni (NFC) — C- Fair

Fund Family: Nuveen Advisory Corp.
Fund Type: Municipal - Single State
Inception Date: January 26, 2001

Major Rating Factors:
Middle of the road best describes Nuveen CT Div Adv Muni whose Weiss Investment Rating is currently a C- (Fair). The fund currently has a performance rating of C- (Fair) based on an annualized return of 5.74% over the last three years and a total return of 3.78% year to date 2005. Factored into the performance evaluation is an expense ratio of 0.82% (very low).

The fund's risk rating is currently C+ (Fair). It carries a beta of 2.32, meaning it is expected to move 23.2% for every 10% move in the market. Volatility, as measured by both the semi-deviation and a drawdown factor, is considered low. As of June 30, 2005, Nuveen CT Div Adv Muni traded at a premium of 3.37% above its net asset value, which is better than its one-year historical average premium of 3.64%.

Paul Brennan has been running the fund for 4 years and currently receives a manager quality ranking of 13 (0=worst, 99=best). If you desire an average level of risk, then this fund may be an option.

Data Date	Weiss Investment Rating	Net Assets ($Mil)	Price	Performance Rating/Pts	Total Return Y-T-D	Risk Rating/Pts
6-05	C-	39.63	15.97	C- / 4.0	3.78%	C+ / 6.5
2004	C-	38.50	15.83	C- / 3.8	3.90%	B- / 7.1

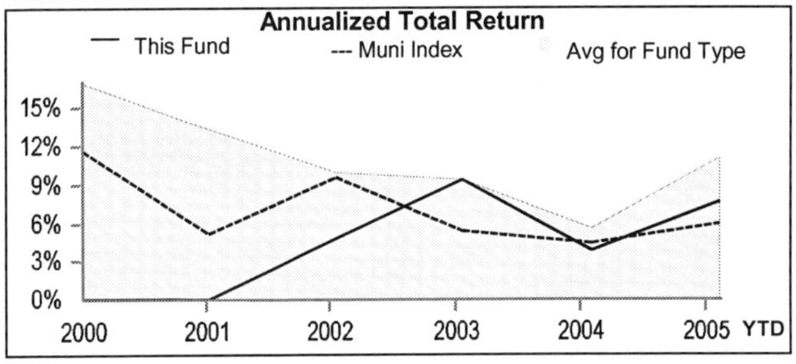

Nuveen CT Div Adv Muni Fund 2 (NGK) — C Fair

Fund Family: Nuveen Advisory Corp.
Fund Type: Municipal - Single State
Inception Date: March 25, 2002

Major Rating Factors:
Middle of the road best describes Nuveen CT Div Adv Muni Fund 2 whose Weiss Investment Rating is currently a C (Fair). The fund currently has a performance rating of C (Fair) based on an annualized return of 7.06% over the last three years and a total return of 4.76% year to date 2005. Factored into the performance evaluation is an expense ratio of 0.81% (very low).

The fund's risk rating is currently C+ (Fair). It carries a beta of 1.80, meaning it is expected to move 18.0% for every 10% move in the market. Volatility, as measured by both the semi-deviation and a drawdown factor, is considered low. As of June 30, 2005, Nuveen CT Div Adv Muni Fund 2 traded at a premium of 1.91% above its net asset value, which is worse than its one-year historical average premium of 1.66%.

Paul Brennan has been running the fund for 3 years and currently receives a manager quality ranking of 43 (0=worst, 99=best). If you desire an average level of risk, then this fund may be an option.

Data Date	Weiss Investment Rating	Net Assets ($Mil)	Price	Performance Rating/Pts	Total Return Y-T-D	Risk Rating/Pts
6-05	C	36.26	16.00	C / 5.0	4.76%	C+ / 6.6

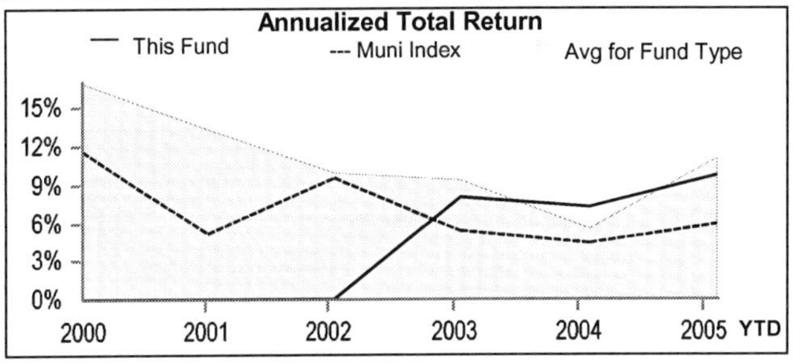

Nuveen CT Prem Inc Muni (NTC) C- Fair

Fund Family: Nuveen Advisory Corp.
Fund Type: Municipal - Single State
Inception Date: May 20, 1993

Major Rating Factors:
Middle of the road best describes Nuveen CT Prem Inc Muni whose Weiss Investment Rating is currently a C- (Fair). The fund currently has a performance rating of C- (Fair) based on an annualized return of 4.53% over the last three years and a total return of 8.63% year to date 2005. Factored into the performance evaluation is an expense ratio of 1.23% (average).

The fund's risk rating is currently C+ (Fair). It carries a beta of 1.62, meaning it is expected to move 16.2% for every 10% move in the market. Volatility, as measured by both the semi-deviation and a drawdown factor, is considered low. As of June 30, 2005, Nuveen CT Prem Inc Muni traded at a premium of 4.96% above its net asset value, which is worse than its one-year historical average premium of 4.54%.

Paul Brennan has been running the fund for 6 years and currently receives a manager quality ranking of 26 (0=worst, 99=best). If you desire an average level of risk, then this fund may be an option.

Data Date	Weiss Investment Rating	Net Assets ($Mil)	Price	Performance Rating/Pts	Total Return Y-T-D	Risk Rating/Pts
6-05	C-	81.85	16.07	C- / 3.3	8.63%	C+ / 6.5
2004	D+	79.98	15.21	D- / 1.5	-1.07%	B- / 7.6
2003	C+	81.08	16.38	C- / 4.0	4.68%	B+ / 9.1

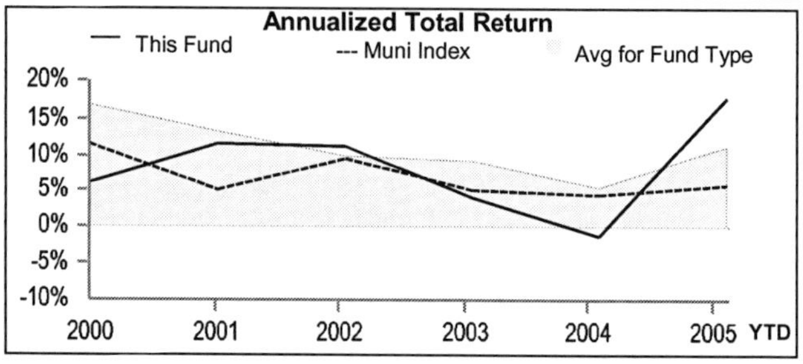

Nuveen Div Adv Muni (NAD) B- Good

Fund Family: Nuveen Advisory Corp.
Fund Type: Municipal - National
Inception Date: May 26, 1999

Major Rating Factors:
Nuveen Div Adv Muni receives a Weiss Investment Rating of B- (Good). The fund currently has a performance rating of C+ (Fair) based on an annualized return of 7.25% over the last three years and a total return of 5.74% year to date 2005. Factored into the performance evaluation is an expense ratio of 0.77% (very low).

The fund's risk rating is currently B- (Good). It carries a beta of 2.43, meaning it is expected to move 24.3% for every 10% move in the market. Volatility, as measured by both the semi-deviation and a drawdown factor, is considered low. As of June 30, 2005, Nuveen Div Adv Muni traded at a discount of 3.31% below its net asset value, which is worse than its one-year historical average discount of 4.47%.

Tom Spalding has been running the fund for 3 years and currently receives a manager quality ranking of 20 (0=worst, 99=best). If you desire an average level of risk, then this fund may be an option.

Data Date	Weiss Investment Rating	Net Assets ($Mil)	Price	Performance Rating/Pts	Total Return Y-T-D	Risk Rating/Pts
6-05	B-	618.40	15.20	C+ / 6.3	5.74%	B- / 7.0
2004	C	603.67	14.87	C- / 3.9	2.89%	B- / 7.7
2003	B	608.88	15.44	C+ / 5.6	10.44%	B / 8.7

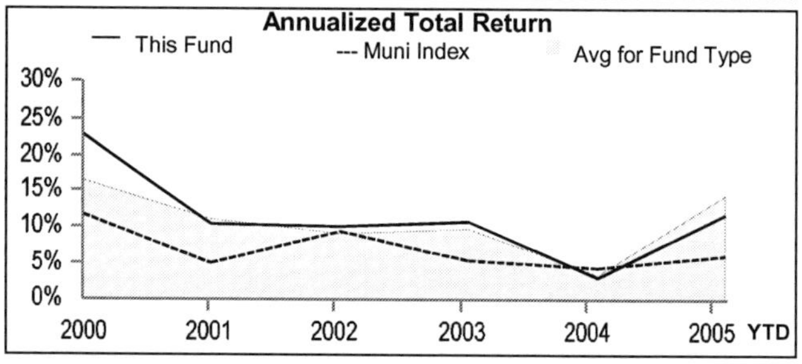

Nuveen Div Adv Muni 3 (NZF) A+ Excellent

Fund Family: Nuveen Advisory Corp.
Fund Type: Municipal - National
Inception Date: September 25, 2001

Major Rating Factors:
Strong performance is the major factor driving the A+ (Excellent) Weiss Investment Rating for Nuveen Div Adv Muni 3. The fund currently has a performance rating of B (Good) based on an annualized return of 8.90% over the last three years and a total return of 8.78% year to date 2005. Factored into the performance evaluation is an expense ratio of 0.67% (very low).

The fund's risk rating is currently B- (Good). It carries a beta of 1.68, meaning it is expected to move 16.8% for every 10% move in the market. Volatility, as measured by both the semi-deviation and a drawdown factor, is considered low. As of June 30, 2005, Nuveen Div Adv Muni 3 traded at a discount of 5.33% below its net asset value, which is worse than its one-year historical average discount of 6.75%.

Tom Spalding has been running the fund for 3 years and currently receives a manager quality ranking of 62 (0=worst, 99=best). If you desire only a moderate level of risk and strong performance, then this fund is an excellent option.

Data Date	Weiss Investment Rating	Net Assets ($Mil)	Price	Performance Rating/Pts	Total Return Y-T-D	Risk Rating/Pts
6-05	A+	635.62	14.92	B / 7.9	8.78%	B- / 7.7
2004	C+	609.65	14.18	C / 4.7	6.30%	B / 8.3

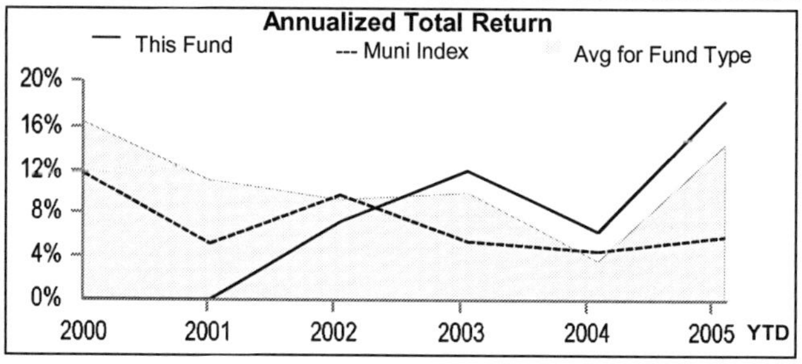

Nuveen Dividend Advantage Muni 2 (NXZ) A+ Excellent

Fund Family: Nuveen Advisory Corp.
Fund Type: Municipal - National
Inception Date: March 27, 2001

Data Date	Weiss Investment Rating	Net Assets ($Mil)	Price	Perfor-mance Rating/Pts	Total Return Y-T-D	Risk Rating/Pts
6-05	A+	473.95	16.00	B+ / 8.8	5.57%	B- / 7.3
2004	A	452.90	15.67	B / 8.0	10.14%	B- / 7.6

Major Rating Factors:
Strong performance is the major factor driving the A+ (Excellent) Weiss Investment Rating for Nuveen Dividend Advantage Muni 2. The fund currently has a performance rating of B+ (Good) based on an annualized return of 11.25% over the last three years and a total return of 5.57% year to date 2005. Factored into the performance evaluation is an expense ratio of 0.67% (very low).

The fund's risk rating is currently B- (Good). It carries a beta of 2.00, meaning it is expected to move 20.0% for every 10% move in the market. Volatility, as measured by both the semi-deviation and a drawdown factor, is considered low. As of June 30, 2005, Nuveen Dividend Advantage Muni 2 traded at a discount of .99% below its net asset value, which is worse than its one-year historical average discount of 2.92%.

Tom Spalding has been running the fund for 4 years and currently receives a manager quality ranking of 67 (0=worst, 99=best). If you desire only a moderate level of risk and strong performance, then this fund is an excellent option.

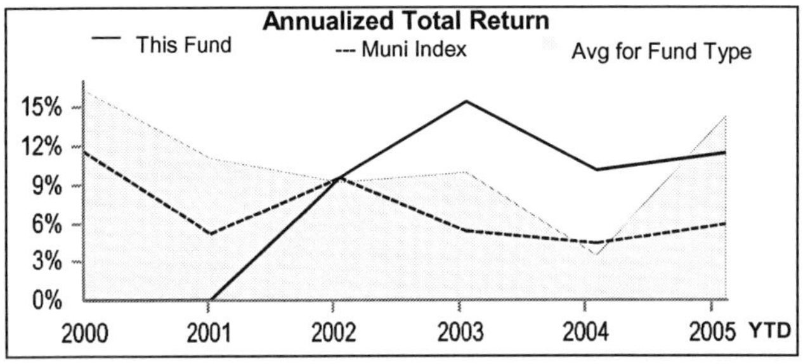

Nuveen FL Investment Quality Muni (NQF) C Fair

Fund Family: Nuveen Advisory Corp.
Fund Type: Municipal - Single State
Inception Date: February 21, 1991

Data Date	Weiss Investment Rating	Net Assets ($Mil)	Price	Perfor-mance Rating/Pts	Total Return Y-T-D	Risk Rating/Pts
6-05	C	259.07	15.54	C+ / 5.7	5.34%	C+ / 5.8
2004	C-	251.80	15.21	C- / 4.0	-2.08%	C+ / 6.2
2003	A-	256.04	16.78	B+ / 8.3	13.57%	B- / 7.2

Major Rating Factors:
Middle of the road best describes Nuveen FL Investment Quality Muni whose Weiss Investment Rating is currently a C (Fair). The fund currently has a performance rating of C+ (Fair) based on an annualized return of 6.66% over the last three years and a total return of 5.34% year to date 2005. Factored into the performance evaluation is an expense ratio of 1.21% (average).

The fund's risk rating is currently C+ (Fair). It carries a beta of 3.18, meaning it is expected to move 31.8% for every 10% move in the market. Volatility, as measured by both the semi-deviation and a drawdown factor, is considered low. As of June 30, 2005, Nuveen FL Investment Quality Muni traded at a discount of .64% below its net asset value, which is better than its one-year historical average discount of .10%.

Cathryn Steeves currently receives a manager quality ranking of 4 (0=worst, 99=best). If you desire an average level of risk, then this fund may be an option.

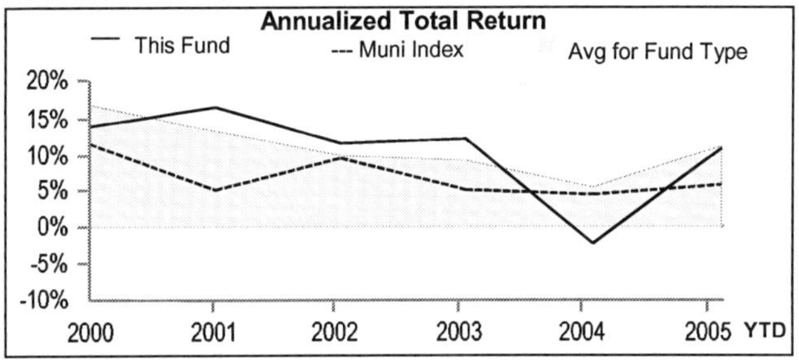

Nuveen FL Quality Inc Muni (NUF) C Fair

Fund Family: Nuveen Advisory Corp.
Fund Type: Municipal - Single State
Inception Date: October 17, 1991

Data Date	Weiss Investment Rating	Net Assets ($Mil)	Price	Perfor-mance Rating/Pts	Total Return Y-T-D	Risk Rating/Pts
6-05	C	224.79	15.35	C+ / 5.6	1.71%	C+ / 5.8
2004	C	218.13	15.55	C+ / 5.8	2.52%	C+ / 6.0
2003	C+	221.05	16.30	C+ / 5.8	6.97%	B- / 7.5

Major Rating Factors:
Middle of the road best describes Nuveen FL Quality Inc Muni whose Weiss Investment Rating is currently a C (Fair). The fund currently has a performance rating of C+ (Fair) based on an annualized return of 5.88% over the last three years and a total return of 1.71% year to date 2005. Factored into the performance evaluation is an expense ratio of 1.22% (average).

The fund's risk rating is currently C+ (Fair). It carries a beta of 3.11, meaning it is expected to move 31.1% for every 10% move in the market. Volatility, as measured by both the semi-deviation and a drawdown factor, is considered low. As of June 30, 2005, Nuveen FL Quality Inc Muni traded at a discount of 2.42% below its net asset value, which is better than its one-year historical average discount of 1.58%.

Cathryn Steeves currently receives a manager quality ranking of 4 (0=worst, 99=best). If you desire an average level of risk, then this fund may be an option.

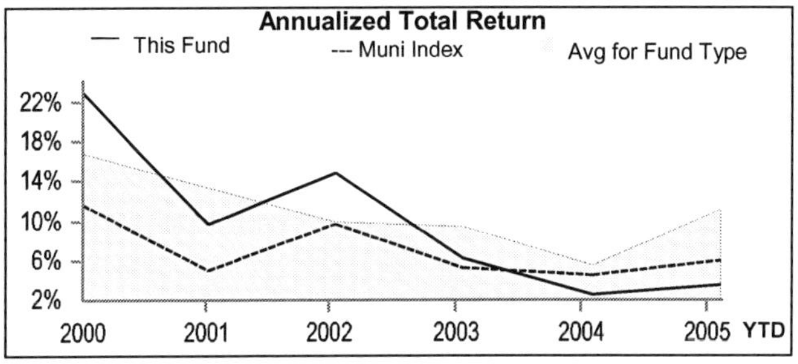

Nuveen GA Div Adv Muni (NZX) B+ Good

Fund Family: Nuveen Advisory Corp.
Fund Type: Municipal - Single State
Inception Date: September 25, 2001

Major Rating Factors:
Strong performance is the major factor driving the B+ (Good) Weiss Investment Rating for Nuveen GA Div Adv Muni. The fund currently has a performance rating of B (Good) based on an annualized return of 9.83% over the last three years and a total return of 6.43% year to date 2005. Factored into the performance evaluation is an expense ratio of 0.80% (very low).

The fund's risk rating is currently C+ (Fair). It carries a beta of 2.10, meaning it is expected to move 21.0% for every 10% move in the market. Volatility, as measured by both the semi-deviation and a drawdown factor, is considered low. As of June 30, 2005, Nuveen GA Div Adv Muni traded at a premium of 4.17% above its net asset value, which is worse than its one-year historical average premium of .74%.

Cathryn Steeves has been running the fund for 4 years and currently receives a manager quality ranking of 67 (0=worst, 99=best). If you desire only a moderate level of risk and strong performance, then this fund is an excellent option.

Data Date	Weiss Investment Rating	Net Assets ($Mil)	Price	Perfor-mance Rating/Pts	Total Return Y-T-D	Risk Rating/Pts
6-05	B+	30.13	16.00	B / 8.1	6.43%	C+ / 6.3
2004	B-	29.34	15.47	C+ / 6.5	6.68%	B- / 7.3

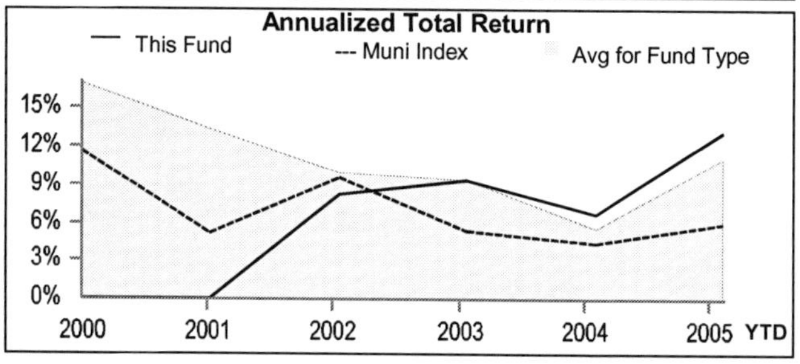

Nuveen GA Prem Inc Muni (NPG) B Good

Fund Family: Nuveen Advisory Corp.
Fund Type: Municipal - Single State
Inception Date: May 20, 1993

Major Rating Factors:
Strong performance is the major factor driving the B (Good) Weiss Investment Rating for Nuveen GA Prem Inc Muni. The fund currently has a performance rating of B- (Good) based on an annualized return of 6.95% over the last three years and a total return of 6.40% year to date 2005. Factored into the performance evaluation is an expense ratio of 1.22% (average).

The fund's risk rating is currently C+ (Fair). It carries a beta of 1.43, meaning it is expected to move 14.3% for every 10% move in the market. Volatility, as measured by both the semi-deviation and a drawdown factor, is considered low. As of June 30, 2005, Nuveen GA Prem Inc Muni traded at a premium of 11.15% above its net asset value, which is worse than its one-year historical average premium of 7.63%.

Cathryn Steeves has been running the fund for 12 years and currently receives a manager quality ranking of 52 (0=worst, 99=best). If you desire only a moderate level of risk and strong performance, then this fund is an excellent option.

Data Date	Weiss Investment Rating	Net Assets ($Mil)	Price	Perfor-mance Rating/Pts	Total Return Y-T-D	Risk Rating/Pts
6-05	B	57.89	16.95	B- / 7.2	6.40%	C+ / 6.5
2004	B-	56.22	16.38	C / 5.5	-0.12%	B- / 7.8
2003	A+	56.93	17.08	B / 8.2	13.82%	B / 8.1

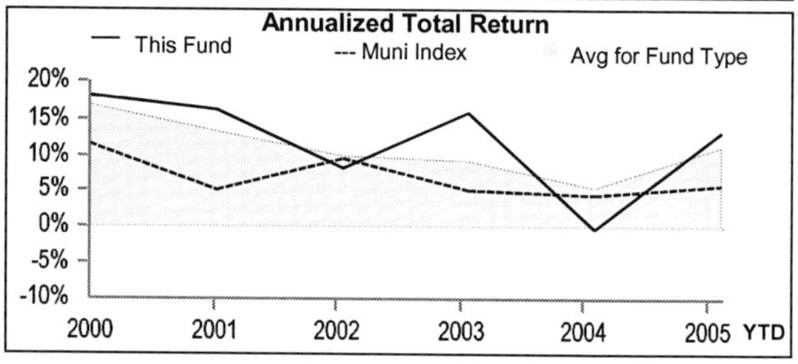

Nuveen Insured CA Div Adv Muni Fund (NKL) C+ Fair

Fund Family: Nuveen Advisory Corp.
Fund Type: Municipal - Single State
Inception Date: March 25, 2002

Major Rating Factors:
Middle of the road best describes Nuveen Insured CA Div Adv Muni Fund whose Weiss Investment Rating is currently a C+ (Fair). The fund currently has a performance rating of C (Fair) based on an annualized return of 6.44% over the last three years and a total return of 6.33% year to date 2005. Factored into the performance evaluation is an expense ratio of 0.71% (very low).

The fund's risk rating is currently B- (Good). It carries a beta of 2.01, meaning it is expected to move 20.1% for every 10% move in the market. Volatility, as measured by both the semi-deviation and a drawdown factor, is considered low. As of June 30, 2005, Nuveen Insured CA Div Adv Muni Fund traded at a discount of 6.52% below its net asset value, which is better than its one-year historical average discount of 6.09%.

Scott Romans has been running the fund for 3 years and currently receives a manager quality ranking of 26 (0=worst, 99=best). If you desire an average level of risk, then this fund may be an option.

Data Date	Weiss Investment Rating	Net Assets ($Mil)	Price	Perfor-mance Rating/Pts	Total Return Y-T-D	Risk Rating/Pts
6-05	C+	241.10	14.77	C / 5.2	6.33%	B- / 7.4

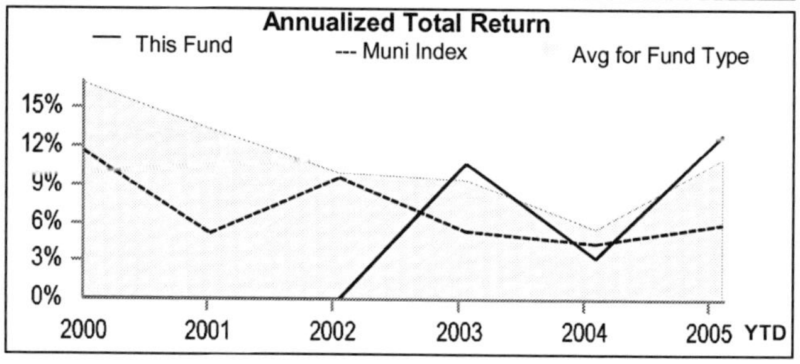

Nuveen Insured CA Prem Inc Muni (NPC) C+ Fair

Fund Family: Nuveen Advisory Corp.
Fund Type: Municipal - Single State
Inception Date: November 19, 1992

Data Date	Weiss Investment Rating	Net Assets ($Mil)	Price	Performance Rating/Pts	Total Return Y-T-D	Risk Rating/Pts
6-05	C+	105.13	15.62	C / 5.4	0.08%	C+ / 6.4
2004	C+	103.61	16.06	C+ / 6.6	6.84%	C+ / 6.8
2003	C+	104.85	16.07	C / 4.9	8.40%	B / 8.2

Major Rating Factors:
Middle of the road best describes Nuveen Insured CA Prem Inc Muni whose Weiss Investment Rating is currently a C+ (Fair). The fund currently has a performance rating of C (Fair) based on an annualized return of 6.86% over the last three years and a total return of 0.08% year to date 2005. Factored into the performance evaluation is an expense ratio of 1.14% (low).

The fund's risk rating is currently C+ (Fair). It carries a beta of 2.57, meaning it is expected to move 25.7% for every 10% move in the market. Volatility, as measured by both the semi-deviation and a drawdown factor, is considered low. As of June 30, 2005, Nuveen Insured CA Prem Inc Muni traded at a discount of 4.00% below its net asset value, which is better than its one-year historical average discount of 3.52%.

Daniel S. Solender,CFA has been running the fund for 1 year and currently receives a manager quality ranking of 12 (0=worst, 99=best). If you desire an average level of risk, then this fund may be an option.

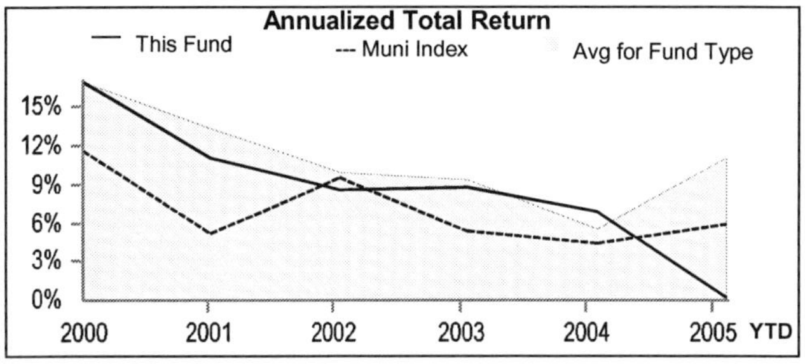

Nuveen Insured CA Prem Inc Muni 2 (NCL) C Fair

Fund Family: Nuveen Advisory Corp.
Fund Type: Municipal - Single State
Inception Date: March 18, 1993

Data Date	Weiss Investment Rating	Net Assets ($Mil)	Price	Performance Rating/Pts	Total Return Y-T-D	Risk Rating/Pts
6-05	C	195.81	14.77	C- / 3.8	-0.25%	C+ / 6.7
2004	C+	190.69	15.25	C+ / 6.0	3.33%	C+ / 6.9
2003	C+	193.78	15.43	C / 5.2	7.83%	B / 8.2

Major Rating Factors:
Middle of the road best describes Nuveen Insured CA Prem Inc Muni 2 whose Weiss Investment Rating is currently a C (Fair). The fund currently has a performance rating of C- (Fair) based on an annualized return of 5.83% over the last three years and a total return of -0.25% year to date 2005. Factored into the performance evaluation is an expense ratio of 1.16% (low).

The fund's risk rating is currently C+ (Fair). It carries a beta of 2.46, meaning it is expected to move 24.6% for every 10% move in the market. Volatility, as measured by both the semi-deviation and a drawdown factor, is considered low. As of June 30, 2005, Nuveen Insured CA Prem Inc Muni 2 traded at a discount of 4.09% below its net asset value, which is better than its one-year historical average discount of 1.56%.

Daniel S. Solender,CFA has been running the fund for 1 year and currently receives a manager quality ranking of 9 (0=worst, 99=best). If you desire an average level of risk, then this fund may be an option.

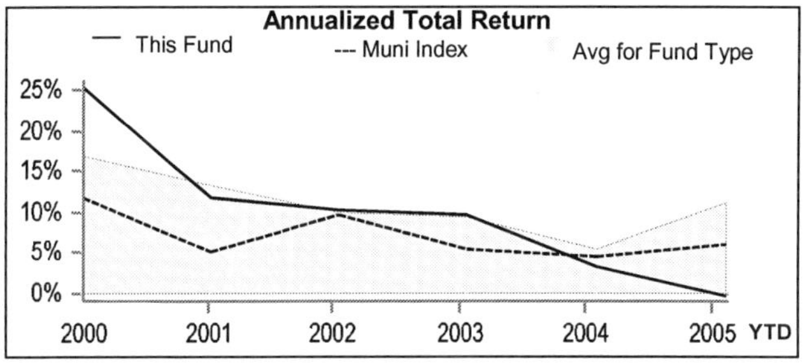

Nuveen Insured Div Adv Muni Fund (NVG) B- Good

Fund Family: Nuveen Advisory Corp.
Fund Type: Municipal - National
Inception Date: March 25, 2002

Data Date	Weiss Investment Rating	Net Assets ($Mil)	Price	Performance Rating/Pts	Total Return Y-T-D	Risk Rating/Pts
6-05	B-	470.77	14.70	C+ / 6.0	7.53%	B- / 7.5

Major Rating Factors:
Nuveen Insured Div Adv Muni Fund receives a Weiss Investment Rating of B- (Good). The fund currently has a performance rating of C+ (Fair) based on an annualized return of 6.50% over the last three years and a total return of 7.53% year to date 2005. Factored into the performance evaluation is an expense ratio of 0.69% (very low).

The fund's risk rating is currently B- (Good). It carries a beta of 2.18, meaning it is expected to move 21.8% for every 10% move in the market. Volatility, as measured by both the semi-deviation and a drawdown factor, is considered low. As of June 30, 2005, Nuveen Insured Div Adv Muni Fund traded at a discount of 6.96% below its net asset value, which is worse than its one-year historical average discount of 7.52%.

Daniel S. Solender,CFA has been running the fund for 1 year and currently receives a manager quality ranking of 20 (0=worst, 99=best). If you desire an average level of risk, then this fund may be an option.

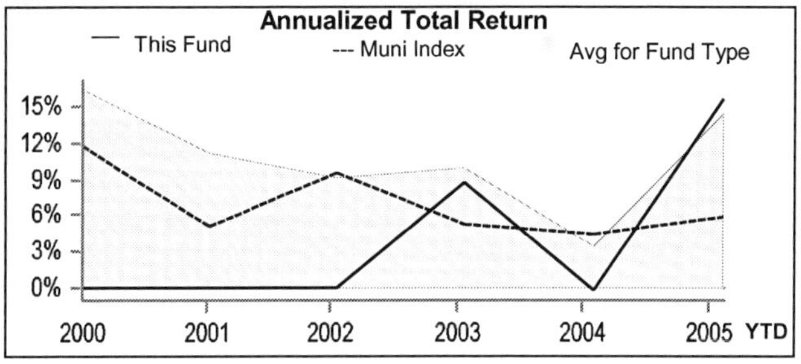

Nuveen Insured FL Prem Inc Muni (NFL) B+ Good

Fund Family: Nuveen Advisory Corp.
Fund Type: Municipal - Single State
Inception Date: December 18, 1992

Data Date	Weiss Investment Rating	Net Assets ($Mil)	Price	Performance Rating/Pts	Total Return Y-T-D	Risk Rating/Pts
6-05	B+	233.78	16.47	B / 8.2	5.50%	C+ / 5.9
2004	C+	230.25	16.07	C+ / 6.4	0.38%	C+ / 6.8
2003	B+	235.06	17.19	B / 7.9	12.74%	B- / 7.5

Major Rating Factors:
Strong performance is the major factor driving the B+ (Good) Weiss Investment Rating for Nuveen Insured FL Prem Inc Muni. The fund currently has a performance rating of B (Good) based on an annualized return of 8.28% over the last three years and a total return of 5.50% year to date 2005. Factored into the performance evaluation is an expense ratio of 1.15% (low).

The fund's risk rating is currently C+ (Fair). It carries a beta of 2.90, meaning it is expected to move 29.0% for every 10% move in the market. Volatility, as measured by both the semi-deviation and a drawdown factor, is considered low. As of June 30, 2005, Nuveen Insured FL Prem Inc Muni traded at a premium of 1.29% above its net asset value, which is worse than its one-year historical average discount of 1.96%.

Daniel S. Solender,CFA has been running the fund for 1 year and currently receives a manager quality ranking of 13 (0=worst, 99=best). If you desire only a moderate level of risk and strong performance, then this fund is an excellent option.

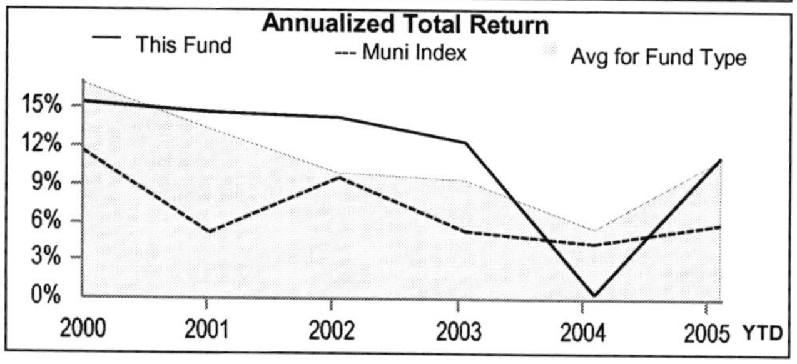

Nuveen Insured Muni Opportunity (NIO) B- Good

Fund Family: Nuveen Advisory Corp.
Fund Type: Municipal - National
Inception Date: September 19, 1991

Data Date	Weiss Investment Rating	Net Assets ($Mil)	Price	Performance Rating/Pts	Total Return Y-T-D	Risk Rating/Pts
6-05	B-	1307.19	15.65	C+ / 5.9	2.39%	B- / 7.0
2004	B+	1275.74	15.76	B- / 7.2	4.04%	B- / 7.5
2003	B	1307.82	15.96	C+ / 6.6	7.86%	B / 8.8

Major Rating Factors:
Nuveen Insured Muni Opportunity receives a Weiss Investment Rating of B- (Good). The fund currently has a performance rating of C+ (Fair) based on an annualized return of 7.08% over the last three years and a total return of 2.39% year to date 2005. Factored into the performance evaluation is an expense ratio of 1.15% (low).

The fund's risk rating is currently B- (Good). It carries a beta of 2.19, meaning it is expected to move 21.9% for every 10% move in the market. Volatility, as measured by both the semi-deviation and a drawdown factor, is considered low. As of June 30, 2005, Nuveen Insured Muni Opportunity traded at a discount of 2.86% below its net asset value, which is worse than its one-year historical average discount of 3.59%.

Daniel S. Solender,CFA has been running the fund for 1 year and currently receives a manager quality ranking of 22 (0=worst, 99=best). If you desire an average level of risk, then this fund may be an option.

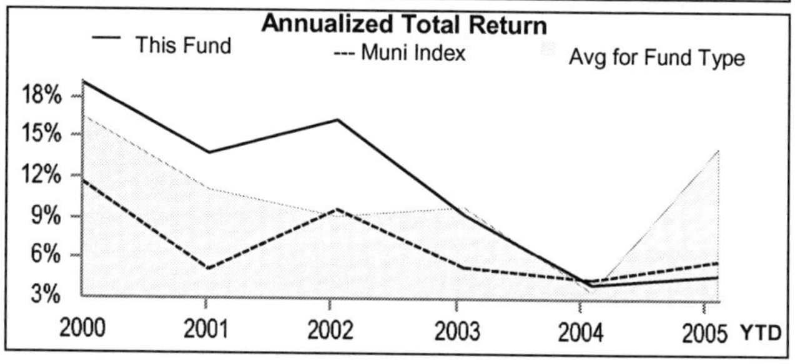

Nuveen Insured NY Div Adv Muni Fund (NKO) A- Excellent

Fund Family: Nuveen Advisory Corp.
Fund Type: Municipal - Single State
Inception Date: March 25, 2002

Data Date	Weiss Investment Rating	Net Assets ($Mil)	Price	Performance Rating/Pts	Total Return Y-T-D	Risk Rating/Pts
6-05	A-	126.81	15.14	B / 7.7	12.54%	B- / 7.2

Major Rating Factors:
Strong performance is the major factor driving the A- (Excellent) Weiss Investment Rating for Nuveen Insured NY Div Adv Muni Fund. The fund currently has a performance rating of B (Good) based on an annualized return of 7.32% over the last three years and a total return of 12.54% year to date 2005. Factored into the performance evaluation is an expense ratio of 0.72% (very low).

The fund's risk rating is currently B- (Good). It carries a beta of 1.81, meaning it is expected to move 18.1% for every 10% move in the market. Volatility, as measured by both the semi-deviation and a drawdown factor, is considered low. As of June 30, 2005, Nuveen Insured NY Div Adv Muni Fund traded at a discount of 5.02% below its net asset value, which is worse than its one-year historical average discount of 7.46%.

Paul Brennan has been running the fund for 3 years and currently receives a manager quality ranking of 30 (0=worst, 99=best). If you desire only a moderate level of risk and strong performance, then this fund is an excellent option.

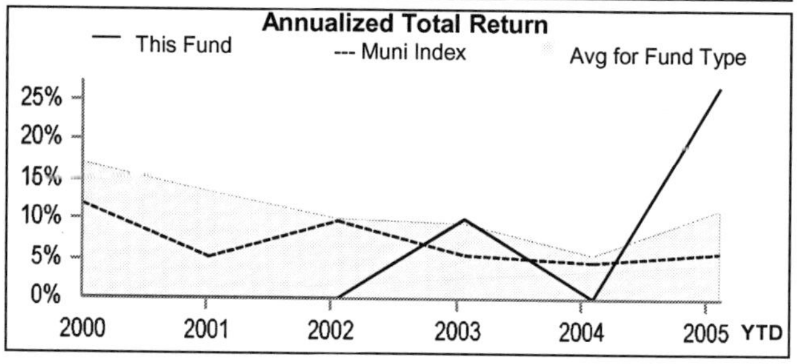

Nuveen Insured NY Prem Inc Muni (NNF) B+ Good

Fund Family: Nuveen Advisory Corp.
Fund Type: Municipal - Single State
Inception Date: December 18, 1992

Major Rating Factors:
Strong performance is the major factor driving the B+ (Good) Weiss Investment Rating for Nuveen Insured NY Prem Inc Muni. The fund currently has a performance rating of B (Good) based on an annualized return of 7.28% over the last three years and a total return of 7.43% year to date 2005. Factored into the performance evaluation is an expense ratio of 1.19% (average).

The fund's risk rating is currently C+ (Fair). It carries a beta of 2.10, meaning it is expected to move 21.0% for every 10% move in the market. Volatility, as measured by both the semi-deviation and a drawdown factor, is considered low. As of June 30, 2005, Nuveen Insured NY Prem Inc Muni traded at a discount of 1.99% below its net asset value, which is worse than its one-year historical average discount of 6.13%.

Paul Brennan has been running the fund for 6 years and currently receives a manager quality ranking of 24 (0=worst, 99=best). If you desire only a moderate level of risk and strong performance, then this fund is an excellent option.

Data Date	Weiss Investment Rating	Net Assets ($Mil)	Price	Performance Rating/Pts	Total Return Y-T-D	Risk Rating/Pts
6-05	B+	134.18	15.80	B / 7.6	7.43%	C+ / 6.7
2004	C+	132.35	15.15	C / 4.9	1.24%	B- / 7.7
2003	B+	135.18	15.91	C+ / 6.4	10.37%	B / 8.5

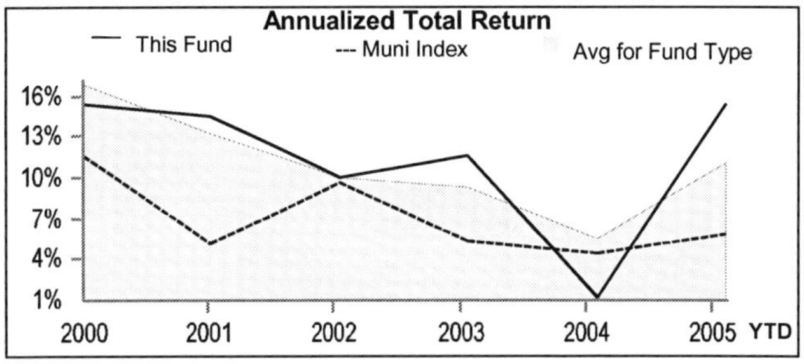

Nuveen Insured Prem Inc Muni 2 (NPX) C Fair

Fund Family: Nuveen Advisory Corp.
Fund Type: Municipal - National
Inception Date: July 22, 1993

Major Rating Factors:
Middle of the road best describes Nuveen Insured Prem Inc Muni 2 whose Weiss Investment Rating is currently a C (Fair). The fund currently has a performance rating of C- (Fair) based on an annualized return of 5.44% over the last three years and a total return of 5.99% year to date 2005. Factored into the performance evaluation is an expense ratio of 1.15% (low).

The fund's risk rating is currently B- (Good). It carries a beta of 1.85, meaning it is expected to move 18.5% for every 10% move in the market. Volatility, as measured by both the semi-deviation and a drawdown factor, is considered low. As of June 30, 2005, Nuveen Insured Prem Inc Muni 2 traded at a discount of 6.48% below its net asset value, which is better than its one-year historical average discount of 5.63%.

Daniel S. Solender,CFA has been running the fund for 1 year and currently receives a manager quality ranking of 24 (0=worst, 99=best). If you desire an average level of risk, then this fund may be an option.

Data Date	Weiss Investment Rating	Net Assets ($Mil)	Price	Performance Rating/Pts	Total Return Y-T-D	Risk Rating/Pts
6-05	C	541.33	13.56	C- / 4.2	5.99%	B- / 7.1
2004	C-	528.19	13.20	D+ / 2.5	-3.79%	B- / 7.9
2003	A	540.87	14.72	B- / 7.5	11.78%	B / 8.3

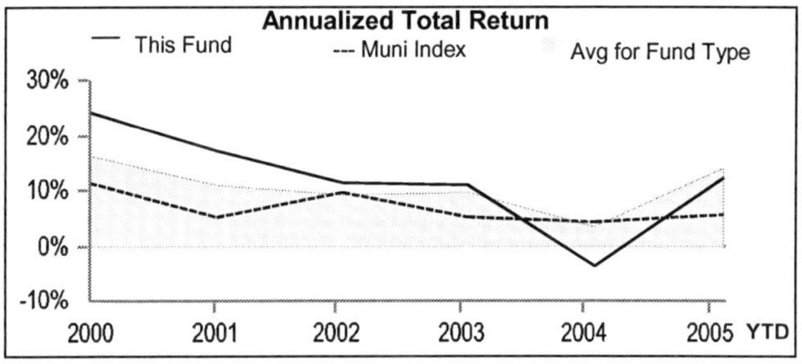

Nuveen Insured Quality Muni (NQI) B+ Good

Fund Family: Nuveen Advisory Corp.
Fund Type: Municipal - National
Inception Date: December 19, 1990

Major Rating Factors:
Strong performance is the major factor driving the B+ (Good) Weiss Investment Rating for Nuveen Insured Quality Muni. The fund currently has a performance rating of B- (Good) based on an annualized return of 8.10% over the last three years and a total return of 7.50% year to date 2005. Factored into the performance evaluation is an expense ratio of 1.18% (low).

The fund's risk rating is currently C+ (Fair). It carries a beta of 2.18, meaning it is expected to move 21.8% for every 10% move in the market. Volatility, as measured by both the semi-deviation and a drawdown factor, is considered low. As of June 30, 2005, Nuveen Insured Quality Muni traded at a premium of 2.14% above its net asset value, which is worse than its one-year historical average discount of .31%.

Daniel S. Solender,CFA has been running the fund for 1 year and currently receives a manager quality ranking of 29 (0=worst, 99=best). If you desire only a moderate level of risk and strong performance, then this fund is an excellent option.

Data Date	Weiss Investment Rating	Net Assets ($Mil)	Price	Performance Rating/Pts	Total Return Y-T-D	Risk Rating/Pts
6-05	B+	607.36	16.22	B- / 7.5	7.50%	C+ / 6.7
2004	B-	591.76	15.57	C+ / 5.8	0.03%	B- / 7.7
2003	A	607.83	16.76	B / 7.8	12.68%	B / 8.2

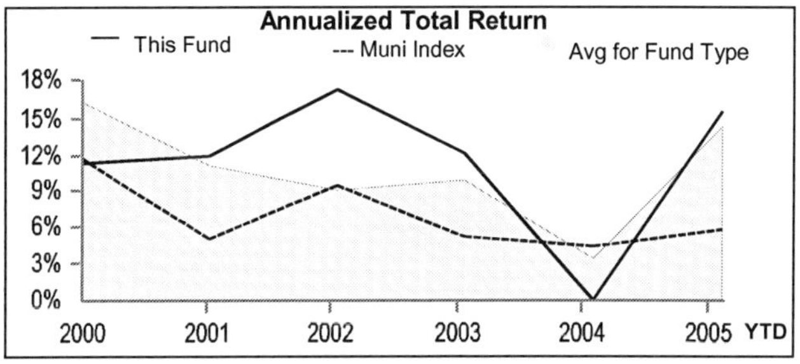

Nuveen Investment Quality Muni (NQM) B- Good

Fund Family: Nuveen Advisory Corp.
Fund Type: Municipal - National
Inception Date: June 21, 1990

Data Date	Weiss Investment Rating	Net Assets ($Mil)	Price	Performance Rating/Pts	Total Return Y-T-D	Risk Rating/Pts
6-05	B-	573.54	15.15	C+ / 6.6	5.86%	B- / 7.1
2004	B-	562.29	14.79	C+ / 5.6	3.72%	B- / 7.8
2003	B-	573.71	15.27	C / 5.5	8.71%	B / 8.7

Major Rating Factors:
Nuveen Investment Quality Muni receives a Weiss Investment Rating of B- (Good). The fund currently has a performance rating of C+ (Fair) based on an annualized return of 7.26% over the last three years and a total return of 5.86% year to date 2005. Factored into the performance evaluation is an expense ratio of 1.19% (average).

The fund's risk rating is currently B- (Good). It carries a beta of 2.33, meaning it is expected to move 23.3% for every 10% move in the market. Volatility, as measured by both the semi-deviation and a drawdown factor, is considered low. As of June 30, 2005, Nuveen Investment Quality Muni traded at a discount of 5.61% below its net asset value, which is worse than its one-year historical average discount of 6.39%.

Tom Spalding has been running the fund for 3 years and currently receives a manager quality ranking of 21 (0=worst, 99=best). If you desire an average level of risk, then this fund may be an option.

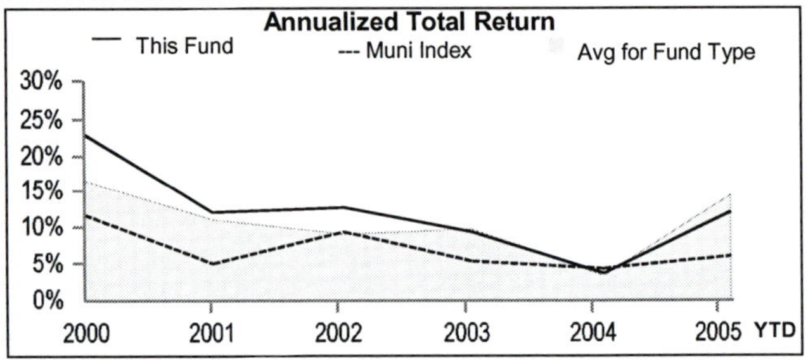

Nuveen MA Div Adv Muni (NMB) B- Good

Fund Family: Nuveen Advisory Corp.
Fund Type: Municipal - Single State
Inception Date: January 26, 2001

Data Date	Weiss Investment Rating	Net Assets ($Mil)	Price	Performance Rating/Pts	Total Return Y-T-D	Risk Rating/Pts
6-05	B-	30.70	16.80	C+ / 6.8	7.02%	B- / 7.1
2004	B+	30.05	16.14	C+ / 5.9	4.55%	B / 8.8

Major Rating Factors:
Nuveen MA Div Adv Muni receives a Weiss Investment Rating of B- (Good). The fund currently has a performance rating of C+ (Fair) based on an annualized return of 6.64% over the last three years and a total return of 7.02% year to date 2005. Factored into the performance evaluation is an expense ratio of 0.85% (very low).

The fund's risk rating is currently B- (Good). It carries a beta of 1.09, meaning that its performance tracks fairly well with that of the overall stock market. Volatility, as measured by both the semi-deviation and a drawdown factor, is considered low. As of June 30, 2005, Nuveen MA Div Adv Muni traded at a premium of 7.21% above its net asset value, which is worse than its one-year historical average premium of 5.48%.

Paul Brennan has been running the fund for 3 years and currently receives a manager quality ranking of 70 (0=worst, 99=best). If you desire an average level of risk, then this fund may be an option.

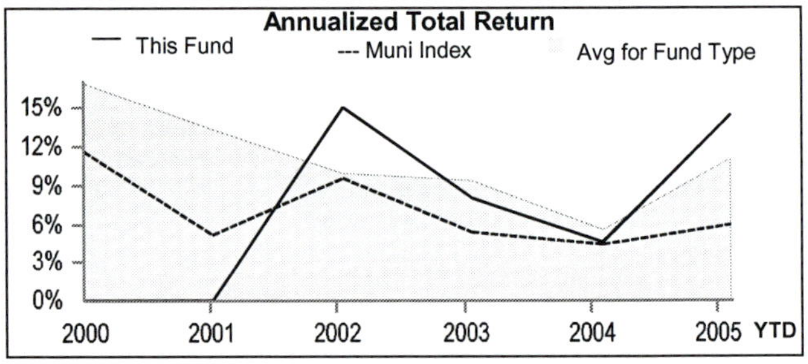

Nuveen MA Prem Inc Muni (NMT) C+ Fair

Fund Family: Nuveen Advisory Corp.
Fund Type: Municipal - Single State
Inception Date: March 18, 1993

Data Date	Weiss Investment Rating	Net Assets ($Mil)	Price	Performance Rating/Pts	Total Return Y-T-D	Risk Rating/Pts
6-05	C+	71.98	15.72	C / 5.0	2.18%	B- / 7.1
2004	B-	69.86	15.82	C+ / 5.7	8.02%	B- / 7.6
2003	C	70.67	15.36	C- / 3.2	2.89%	B / 8.8

Major Rating Factors:
Middle of the road best describes Nuveen MA Prem Inc Muni whose Weiss Investment Rating is currently a C+ (Fair). The fund currently has a performance rating of C (Fair) based on an annualized return of 5.60% over the last three years and a total return of 2.18% year to date 2005. Factored into the performance evaluation is an expense ratio of 1.22% (average).

The fund's risk rating is currently B- (Good). It carries a beta of 2.17, meaning it is expected to move 21.7% for every 10% move in the market. Volatility, as measured by both the semi-deviation and a drawdown factor, is considered low. As of June 30, 2005, Nuveen MA Prem Inc Muni traded at a premium of 3.69% above its net asset value, which is better than its one-year historical average premium of 4.79%.

Paul Brennan has been running the fund for 3 years and currently receives a manager quality ranking of 18 (0=worst, 99=best). If you desire an average level of risk, then this fund may be an option.

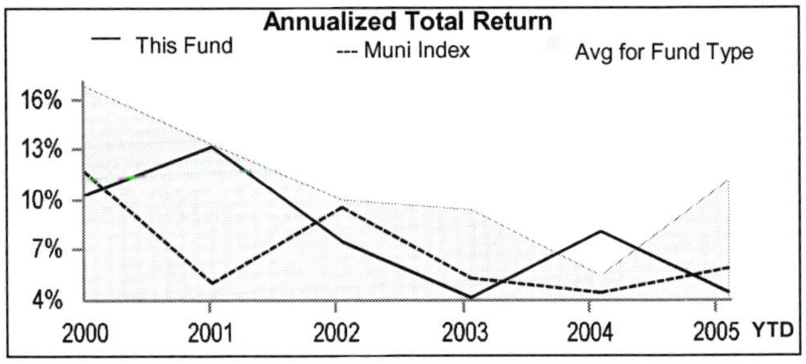

Nuveen MD Div Adv Muni (NFM) C+ Fair

Fund Family: Nuveen Advisory Corp.
Fund Type: Municipal - Single State
Inception Date: January 26, 2001

Major Rating Factors:
Middle of the road best describes Nuveen MD Div Adv Muni whose Weiss Investment Rating is currently a C+ (Fair). The fund currently has a performance rating of C+ (Fair) based on an annualized return of 7.67% over the last three years and a total return of 7.25% year to date 2005. Factored into the performance evaluation is an expense ratio of 0.79% (very low).

The fund's risk rating is currently C+ (Fair). It carries a beta of 1.58, meaning it is expected to move 15.8% for every 10% move in the market. Volatility, as measured by both the semi-deviation and a drawdown factor, is considered low. As of June 30, 2005, Nuveen MD Div Adv Muni traded at a premium of 7.24% above its net asset value, which is worse than its one-year historical average premium of 5.10%.

Paul Brennan has been running the fund for 4 years and currently receives a manager quality ranking of 51 (0=worst, 99=best). If you desire an average level of risk, then this fund may be an option.

Data Date	Weiss Investment Rating	Net Assets ($Mil)	Price	Performance Rating/Pts	Total Return Y-T-D	Risk Rating/Pts
6-05	C+	63.23	16.29	C+ / 6.7	7.25%	C+ / 6.0
2004	C-	61.71	15.65	C- / 3.8	-0.71%	B- / 7.0

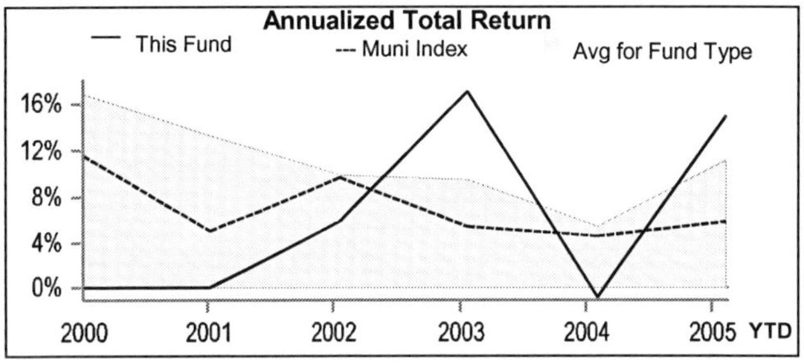

Nuveen MD Div Adv Muni 2 (NZR) C+ Fair

Fund Family: Nuveen Advisory Corp.
Fund Type: Municipal - Single State
Inception Date: September 25, 2001

Major Rating Factors:
Middle of the road best describes Nuveen MD Div Adv Muni 2 whose Weiss Investment Rating is currently a C+ (Fair). The fund currently has a performance rating of C+ (Fair) based on an annualized return of 7.84% over the last three years and a total return of 1.89% year to date 2005. Factored into the performance evaluation is an expense ratio of 0.76% (very low).

The fund's risk rating is currently C+ (Fair). It carries a beta of 1.71, meaning it is expected to move 17.1% for every 10% move in the market. Volatility, as measured by both the semi-deviation and a drawdown factor, is considered low. As of June 30, 2005, Nuveen MD Div Adv Muni 2 traded at a premium of 2.71% above its net asset value, which is worse than its one-year historical average discount of .17%.

Paul Brennan has been running the fund for 4 years and currently receives a manager quality ranking of 51 (0=worst, 99=best). If you desire an average level of risk, then this fund may be an option.

Data Date	Weiss Investment Rating	Net Assets ($Mil)	Price	Performance Rating/Pts	Total Return Y-T-D	Risk Rating/Pts
6-05	C+	64.65	15.93	C+ / 6.8	1.89%	C+ / 6.6
2004	A	63.19	16.09	B+ / 8.4	8.04%	B- / 7.1

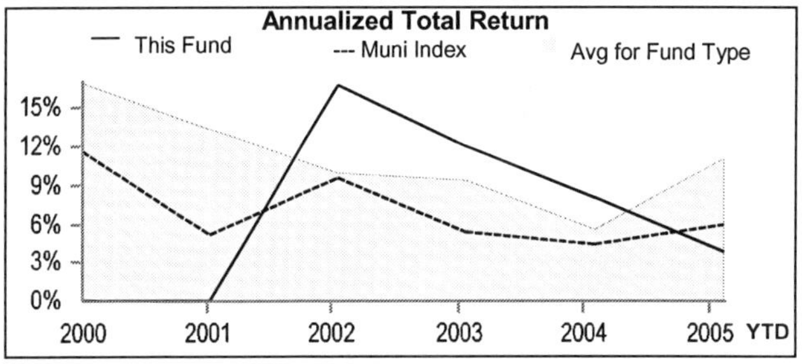

Nuveen MD Prem Inc Muni (NMY) C- Fair

Fund Family: Nuveen Advisory Corp.
Fund Type: Municipal - Single State
Inception Date: March 18, 1993

Major Rating Factors:
Disappointing performance is the major factor driving the C- (Fair) Weiss Investment Rating for Nuveen MD Prem Inc Muni. The fund currently has a performance rating of D+ (Weak) based on an annualized return of 5.37% over the last three years and a total return of -1.80% year to date 2005. Factored into the performance evaluation is an expense ratio of 1.22% (average).

The fund's risk rating is currently C+ (Fair). It carries a beta of 2.40, meaning it is expected to move 24.0% for every 10% move in the market. Volatility, as measured by both the semi-deviation and a drawdown factor, is considered low. As of June 30, 2005, Nuveen MD Prem Inc Muni traded at a premium of 3.63% above its net asset value, which is better than its one-year historical average premium of 6.25%.

Paul Brennan has been running the fund for 6 years and currently receives a manager quality ranking of 10 (0=worst, 99=best). This fund offers only a moderate level of risk but investors looking for strong performance are still waiting.

Data Date	Weiss Investment Rating	Net Assets ($Mil)	Price	Performance Rating/Pts	Total Return Y-T-D	Risk Rating/Pts
6-05	C-	160.73	15.72	D+ / 2.9	-1.80%	C+ / 6.8
2004	B-	156.02	16.48	C+ / 6.2	7.67%	B- / 7.0
2003	C	156.42	16.05	C- / 3.7	5.52%	B / 8.4

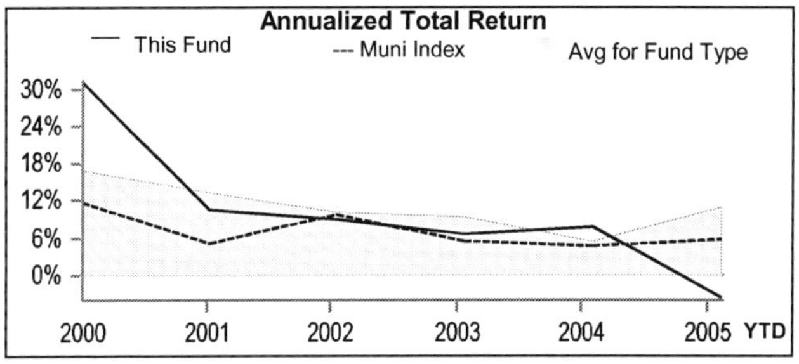

Nuveen MI Div Adv Muni (NZW) — B- Good

Fund Family: Nuveen Advisory Corp.
Fund Type: Municipal - Single State
Inception Date: September 25, 2001

Major Rating Factors:
Nuveen MI Div Adv Muni receives a Weiss Investment Rating of B- (Good). The fund currently has a performance rating of C+ (Fair) based on an annualized return of 7.40% over the last three years and a total return of 2.02% year to date 2005. Factored into the performance evaluation is an expense ratio of 0.81% (very low).

The fund's risk rating is currently B- (Good). It carries a beta of 1.22, meaning it is expected to move 12.2% for every 10% move in the market. Volatility, as measured by both the semi-deviation and a drawdown factor, is considered low. As of June 30, 2005, Nuveen MI Div Adv Muni traded at a discount of .32% below its net asset value, which is better than its one-year historical average premium of .10%.

Cathryn Steeves currently receives a manager quality ranking of 73 (0=worst, 99=best). If you desire an average level of risk, then this fund may be an option.

Data Date	Weiss Investment Rating	Net Assets ($Mil)	Price	Perfor-mance Rating/Pts	Total Return Y-T-D	Risk Rating/Pts
6-05	B-	32.11	15.57	C+ / 6.1	2.02%	B- / 7.7
2004	A+	31.07	15.71	B / 7.8	7.97%	B / 8.1

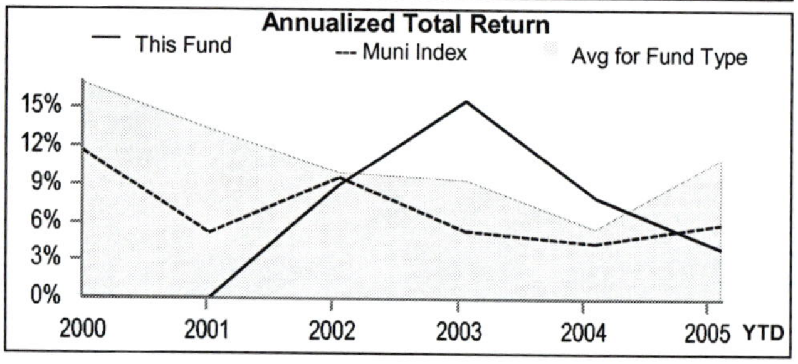

Nuveen MI Prem Inc Muni (NMP) — C+ Fair

Fund Family: Nuveen Advisory Corp.
Fund Type: Municipal - Single State
Inception Date: December 18, 1992

Major Rating Factors:
Middle of the road best describes Nuveen MI Prem Inc Muni whose Weiss Investment Rating is currently a C+ (Fair). The fund currently has a performance rating of C+ (Fair) based on an annualized return of 6.94% over the last three years and a total return of 5.04% year to date 2005. Factored into the performance evaluation is an expense ratio of 1.17% (low).

The fund's risk rating is currently B- (Good). It carries a beta of 2.07, meaning it is expected to move 20.7% for every 10% move in the market. Volatility, as measured by both the semi-deviation and a drawdown factor, is considered low. As of June 30, 2005, Nuveen MI Prem Inc Muni traded at a discount of 2.15% below its net asset value, which is better than its one-year historical average discount of 1.91%.

Cathryn Steeves currently receives a manager quality ranking of 25 (0=worst, 99=best). If you desire an average level of risk, then this fund may be an option.

Data Date	Weiss Investment Rating	Net Assets ($Mil)	Price	Perfor-mance Rating/Pts	Total Return Y-T-D	Risk Rating/Pts
6-05	C+	122.24	15.44	C+ / 5.7	5.04%	B- / 7.0
2004	B	119.05	15.13	C+ / 6.0	1.17%	B- / 7.7
2003	A	120.13	15.73	B / 8.1	14.12%	B- / 7.8

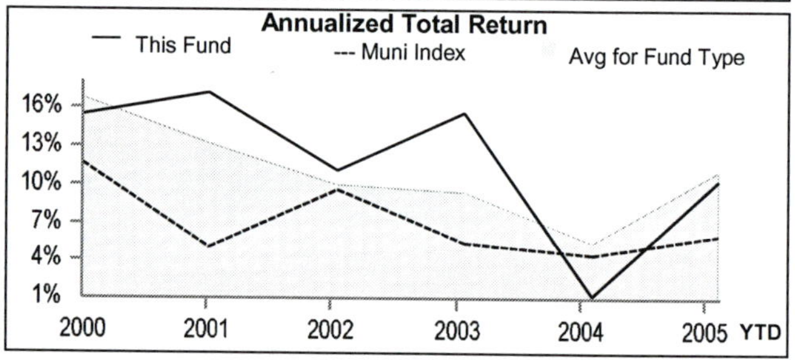

Nuveen MI Quality Inc Muni (NUM) — C Fair

Fund Family: Nuveen Advisory Corp.
Fund Type: Municipal - Single State
Inception Date: October 17, 1991

Major Rating Factors:
Middle of the road best describes Nuveen MI Quality Inc Muni whose Weiss Investment Rating is currently a C (Fair). The fund currently has a performance rating of C- (Fair) based on an annualized return of 5.98% over the last three years and a total return of -0.23% year to date 2005. Factored into the performance evaluation is an expense ratio of 1.20% (average).

The fund's risk rating is currently B- (Good). It carries a beta of 1.97, meaning it is expected to move 19.7% for every 10% move in the market. Volatility, as measured by both the semi-deviation and a drawdown factor, is considered low. As of June 30, 2005, Nuveen MI Quality Inc Muni traded at a discount of 1.73% below its net asset value, which is better than its one-year historical average premium of .12%.

Cathryn Steeves currently receives a manager quality ranking of 26 (0=worst, 99=best). If you desire an average level of risk, then this fund may be an option.

Data Date	Weiss Investment Rating	Net Assets ($Mil)	Price	Perfor-mance Rating/Pts	Total Return Y-T-D	Risk Rating/Pts
6-05	C	188.86	15.86	C- / 3.7	-0.23%	B- / 7.7
2004	A-	184.10	16.36	B- / 7.1	5.77%	B- / 7.8
2003	A	186.22	16.35	B- / 7.3	12.98%	B / 8.4

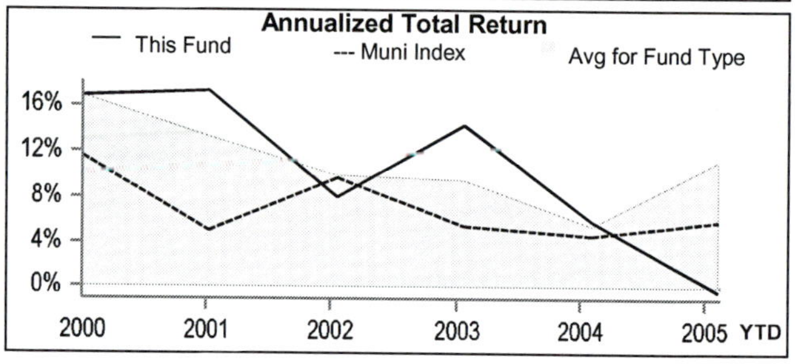

Nuveen MO Prem Inc Muni (NOM) — C+ Fair

Fund Family: Nuveen Advisory Corp.
Fund Type: Municipal - Single State
Inception Date: May 20, 1993

Major Rating Factors:
Middle of the road best describes Nuveen MO Prem Inc Muni whose Weiss Investment Rating is currently a C+ (Fair). The fund currently has a performance rating of C (Fair) based on an annualized return of 7.67% over the last three years and a total return of -6.05% year to date 2005. Factored into the performance evaluation is an expense ratio of 1.27% (average).

The fund's risk rating is currently C+ (Fair). It carries a beta of 1.66, meaning it is expected to move 16.6% for every 10% move in the market. Volatility, as measured by both the semi-deviation and a drawdown factor, is considered low. As of June 30, 2005, Nuveen MO Prem Inc Muni traded at a premium of 14.72% above its net asset value, which is better than its one-year historical average premium of 14.78%.

Scott R. Romans, Ph.D has been running the fund for 12 years and currently receives a manager quality ranking of 48 (0=worst, 99=best). If you desire an average level of risk, then this fund may be an option.

Data Date	Weiss Investment Rating	Net Assets ($Mil)	Price	Performance Rating/Pts	Total Return Y-T-D	Risk Rating/Pts
6-05	C+	34.31	17.38	C / 5.1	-6.05%	C+ / 6.6
2004	A+	33.46	19.00	A- / 9.1	17.16%	C+ / 6.7
2003	A+	33.55	17.15	B / 7.9	10.13%	B / 8.4

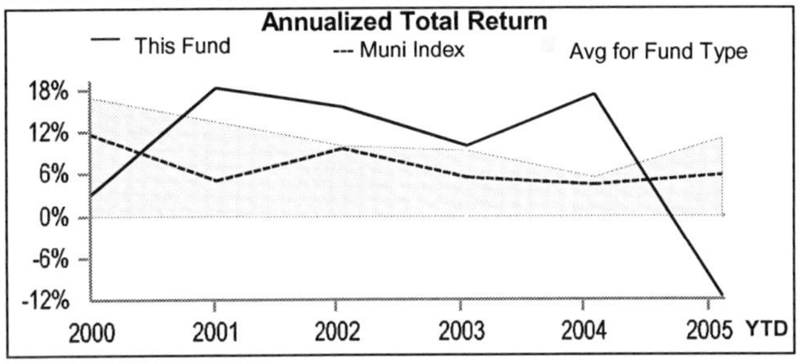

Nuveen Muni Advantage (NMA) — B+ Good

Fund Family: Nuveen Advisory Corp.
Fund Type: Municipal - National
Inception Date: December 20, 1989

Major Rating Factors:
Strong performance is the major factor driving the B+ (Good) Weiss Investment Rating for Nuveen Muni Advantage. The fund currently has a performance rating of B - (Good) based on an annualized return of 8.25% over the last three years and a total return of 5.37% year to date 2005. Factored into the performance evaluation is an expense ratio of 1.17% (low).

The fund's risk rating is currently B- (Good). It carries a beta of 2.11, meaning it is expected to move 21.1% for every 10% move in the market. Volatility, as measured by both the semi-deviation and a drawdown factor, is considered low. As of June 30, 2005, Nuveen Muni Advantage traded at a discount of 3.47% below its net asset value, which is worse than its one-year historical average discount of 4.09%.

Tom Spalding has been running the fund for 3 years and currently receives a manager quality ranking of 40 (0=worst, 99=best). If you desire only a moderate level of risk and strong performance, then this fund is an excellent option.

Data Date	Weiss Investment Rating	Net Assets ($Mil)	Price	Performance Rating/Pts	Total Return Y-T-D	Risk Rating/Pts
6-05	B+	695.37	15.59	B- / 7.0	5.37%	B- / 7.3
2004	B-	679.96	15.29	C+ / 6.7	4.63%	B- / 7.9
2003	B	685.38	15.52	C+ / 6.7	12.43%	B / 8.5

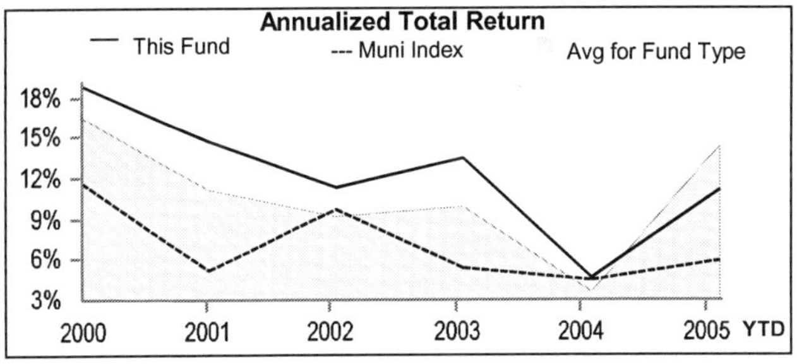

Nuveen Muni Income (NMI) — C+ Fair

Fund Family: Nuveen Advisory Corp.
Fund Type: Municipal - National
Inception Date: April 20, 1988

Major Rating Factors:
Middle of the road best describes Nuveen Muni Income whose Weiss Investment Rating is currently a C+ (Fair). The fund currently has a performance rating of C+ (Fair) based on an annualized return of 6.81% over the last three years and a total return of 11.22% year to date 2005. Factored into the performance evaluation is an expense ratio of 0.77% (very low).

The fund's risk rating is currently C+ (Fair). It carries a beta of 1.71, meaning it is expected to move 17.1% for every 10% move in the market. Volatility, as measured by both the semi-deviation and a drawdown factor, is considered low. As of June 30, 2005, Nuveen Muni Income traded at a discount of 3.26% below its net asset value, which is worse than its one-year historical average discount of 6.62%.

John Miller has been running the fund for 4 years and currently receives a manager quality ranking of 39 (0=worst, 99=best). If you desire an average level of risk, then this fund may be an option.

Data Date	Weiss Investment Rating	Net Assets ($Mil)	Price	Performance Rating/Pts	Total Return Y-T-D	Risk Rating/Pts
6-05	C+	89.60	10.68	C+ / 6.7	11.22%	C+ / 6.9
2004	D+	86.81	9.85	D / 1.7	7.79%	B- / 7.7
2003	D+	85.63	9.84	E+ / 0.8	4.08%	B- / 7.9

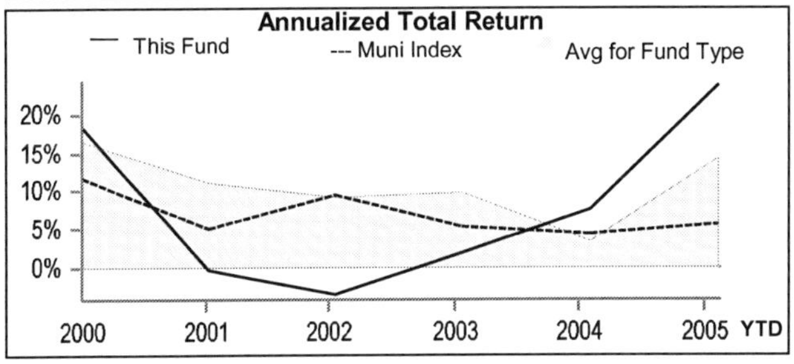

Nuveen Muni Market Opportunity (NMO) B- Good

Fund Family: Nuveen Advisory Corp.
Fund Type: Municipal - National
Inception Date: March 22, 1990

Major Rating Factors:
Nuveen Muni Market Opportunity receives a Weiss Investment Rating of B- (Good). The fund currently has a performance rating of C+ (Fair) based on an annualized return of 6.94% over the last three years and a total return of 7.69% year to date 2005. Factored into the performance evaluation is an expense ratio of 1.17% (low).

The fund's risk rating is currently B- (Good). It carries a beta of 2.06, meaning it is expected to move 20.6% for every 10% move in the market. Volatility, as measured by both the semi-deviation and a drawdown factor, is considered low. As of June 30, 2005, Nuveen Muni Market Opportunity traded at a discount of 6.08% below its net asset value, which is worse than its one-year historical average discount of 7.81%.

Tom Spalding has been running the fund for 3 years and currently receives a manager quality ranking of 32 (0=worst, 99=best). If you desire an average level of risk, then this fund may be an option.

Data Date	Weiss Investment Rating	Net Assets ($Mil)	Price	Performance Rating/Pts	Total Return Y-T-D	Risk Rating/Pts
6-05	B-	712.24	14.68	C+ / 6.4	7.69%	B- / 7.1
2004	C+	692.89	14.08	C- / 4.2	3.94%	B / 8.0
2003	C+	704.37	14.48	C / 4.4	11.34%	B / 8.9

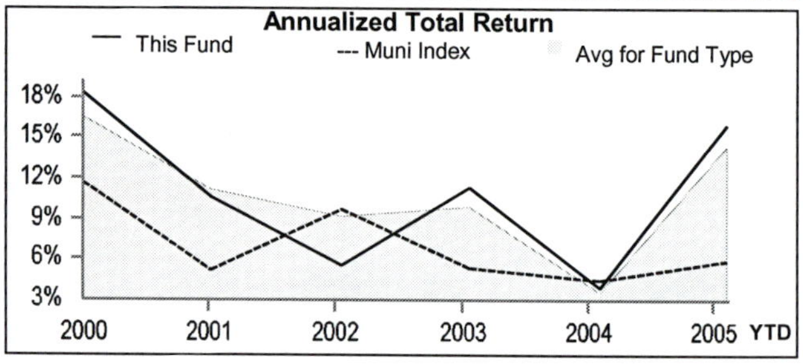

Nuveen Muni Value (NUV) B Good

Fund Family: Nuveen Advisory Corp.
Fund Type: Municipal - National
Inception Date: June 17, 1987

Major Rating Factors:
Nuveen Muni Value receives a Weiss Investment Rating of B (Good). The fund currently has a performance rating of C (Fair) based on an annualized return of 6.06% over the last three years and a total return of 6.77% year to date 2005. Factored into the performance evaluation is an expense ratio of 0.60% (very low).

The fund's risk rating is currently B (Good). It carries a beta of 1.29, meaning it is expected to move 12.9% for every 10% move in the market. Volatility, as measured by both the semi-deviation and a drawdown factor, is considered low. As of June 30, 2005, Nuveen Muni Value traded at a discount of 7.71% below its net asset value, which is worse than its one-year historical average discount of 8.65%.

Tom Spalding has been running the fund for 18 years and currently receives a manager quality ranking of 54 (0=worst, 99=best). If you desire an average level of risk, then this fund may be an option.

Data Date	Weiss Investment Rating	Net Assets ($Mil)	Price	Performance Rating/Pts	Total Return Y-T-D	Risk Rating/Pts
6-05	B	2024.31	9.57	C / 5.0	6.77%	B / 8.8
2004	C+	1958.65	9.19	C- / 3.8	4.51%	B+ / 9.1
2003	C+	1948.02	9.25	C- / 3.5	5.48%	B+ / 9.1

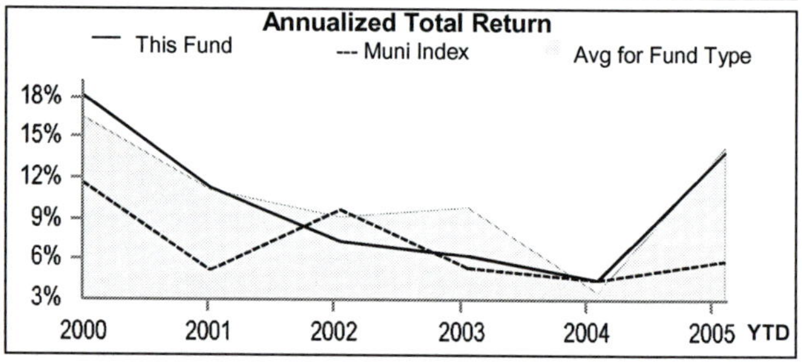

Nuveen NC Div Adv Muni (NRB) A- Excellent

Fund Family: Nuveen Advisory Corp.
Fund Type: Municipal - Single State
Inception Date: January 26, 2001

Major Rating Factors:
Strong performance is the major factor driving the A- (Excellent) Weiss Investment Rating for Nuveen NC Div Adv Muni. The fund currently has a performance rating of B (Good) based on an annualized return of 10.47% over the last three years and a total return of 7.08% year to date 2005. Factored into the performance evaluation is an expense ratio of 0.80% (very low).

The fund's risk rating is currently C+ (Fair). It carries a beta of 1.81, meaning it is expected to move 18.1% for every 10% move in the market. Volatility, as measured by both the semi-deviation and a drawdown factor, is considered low. As of June 30, 2005, Nuveen NC Div Adv Muni traded at a premium of 11.73% above its net asset value, which is worse than its one-year historical average premium of 7.96%.

Cathryn Steeves has been running the fund for 4 years and currently receives a manager quality ranking of 65 (0=worst, 99=best). If you desire only a moderate level of risk and strong performance, then this fund is an excellent option.

Data Date	Weiss Investment Rating	Net Assets ($Mil)	Price	Performance Rating/Pts	Total Return Y-T-D	Risk Rating/Pts
6-05	A-	34.93	17.33	B / 8.2	7.08%	C+ / 6.7
2004	B+	34.09	16.65	B- / 7.4	6.10%	B- / 7.3

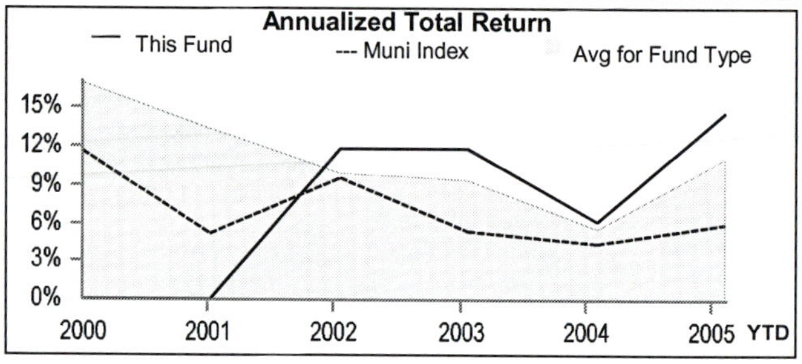

Nuveen NC Div Adv Muni 2 (NNO) B Good

Fund Family: Nuveen Advisory Corp.
Fund Type: Municipal - Single State
Inception Date: November 15, 2001

Major Rating Factors:
Strong performance is the major factor driving the B (Good) Weiss Investment Rating for Nuveen NC Div Adv Muni 2. The fund currently has a performance rating of B- (Good) based on an annualized return of 10.12% over the last three years and a total return of 8.17% year to date 2005. Factored into the performance evaluation is an expense ratio of 0.77% (very low).

The fund's risk rating is currently C+ (Fair). It carries a beta of 1.55, meaning it is expected to move 15.5% for every 10% move in the market. Volatility, as measured by both the semi-deviation and a drawdown factor, is considered low. As of June 30, 2005, Nuveen NC Div Adv Muni 2 traded at a premium of 6.34% above its net asset value, which is worse than its one-year historical average premium of 2.80%.

Cathryn Steeves has been running the fund for 4 years and currently receives a manager quality ranking of 67 (0=worst, 99=best). If you desire only a moderate level of risk and strong performance, then this fund is an excellent option.

Data Date	Weiss Investment Rating	Net Assets ($Mil)	Price	Performance Rating/Pts	Total Return Y-T-D	Risk Rating/Pts
6-05	B	58.31	16.60	B- / 7.0	8.17%	C+ / 6.7
2004	B	57.13	15.78	C+ / 6.7	6.12%	B / 8.2

Annualized Total Return

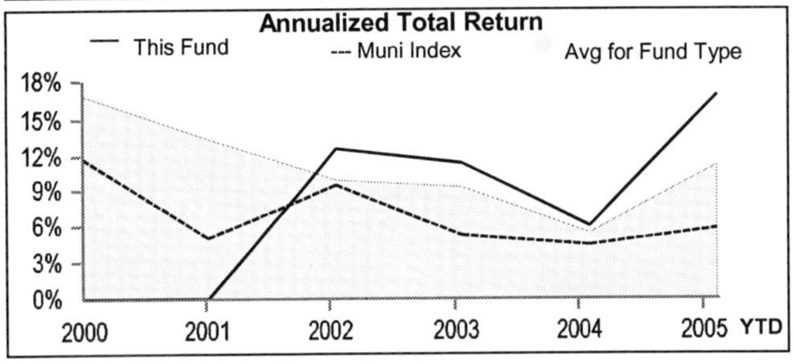

Nuveen NC Prem Inc Muni (NNC) C- Fair

Fund Family: Nuveen Advisory Corp.
Fund Type: Municipal - Single State
Inception Date: May 20, 1993

Major Rating Factors:
Middle of the road best describes Nuveen NC Prem Inc Muni whose Weiss Investment Rating is currently a C- (Fair). The fund currently has a performance rating of C- (Fair) based on an annualized return of 5.68% over the last three years and a total return of -2.01% year to date 2005. Factored into the performance evaluation is an expense ratio of 1.22% (average).

The fund's risk rating is currently C+ (Fair). It carries a beta of 2.15, meaning it is expected to move 21.5% for every 10% move in the market. Volatility, as measured by both the semi-deviation and a drawdown factor, is considered low. As of June 30, 2005, Nuveen NC Prem Inc Muni traded at a premium of 9.54% above its net asset value, which is better than its one-year historical average premium of 10.25%.

Cathryn Steeves has been running the fund for 12 years and currently receives a manager quality ranking of 15 (0=worst, 99=best). If you desire an average level of risk, then this fund may be an option.

Data Date	Weiss Investment Rating	Net Assets ($Mil)	Price	Performance Rating/Pts	Total Return Y-T-D	Risk Rating/Pts
6-05	C-	96.26	16.65	C- / 4.1	-2.01%	C+ / 6.4
2004	A-	94.20	17.45	B+ / 8.4	8.38%	C+ / 6.6
2003	A-	95.77	17.08	B / 7.7	14.48%	B- / 7.7

Annualized Total Return

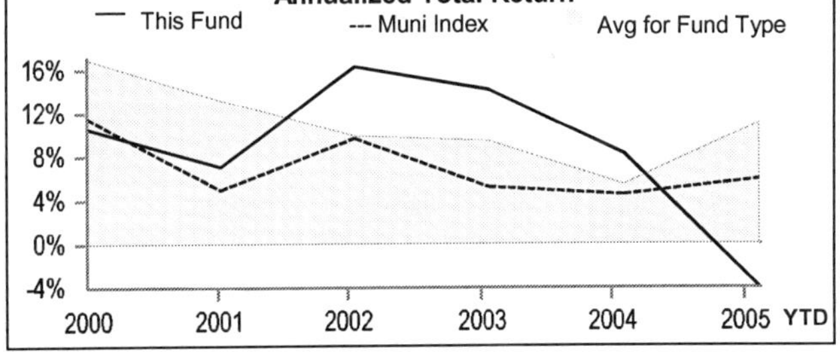

Nuveen NJ Div Adv Muni (NXJ) B- Good

Fund Family: Nuveen Advisory Corp.
Fund Type: Municipal - Single State
Inception Date: March 27, 2001

Major Rating Factors:
Nuveen NJ Div Adv Muni receives a Weiss Investment Rating of B- (Good). The fund currently has a performance rating of C+ (Fair) based on an annualized return of 8.73% over the last three years and a total return of 2.47% year to date 2005. Factored into the performance evaluation is an expense ratio of 0.73% (very low).

The fund's risk rating is currently B- (Good). It carries a beta of 2.09, meaning it is expected to move 20.9% for every 10% move in the market. Volatility, as measured by both the semi-deviation and a drawdown factor, is considered low. As of June 30, 2005, Nuveen NJ Div Adv Muni traded at a discount of 3.64% below its net asset value, which is better than its one-year historical average discount of 2.45%.

Paul Brennan has been running the fund for 3 years and currently receives a manager quality ranking of 51 (0=worst, 99=best). If you desire an average level of risk, then this fund may be an option.

Data Date	Weiss Investment Rating	Net Assets ($Mil)	Price	Performance Rating/Pts	Total Return Y-T-D	Risk Rating/Pts
6-05	B-	102.50	15.07	C+ / 6.8	2.47%	B- / 7.2
2004	B-	98.72	15.16	C+ / 6.0	6.19%	B- / 7.4

Annualized Total Return

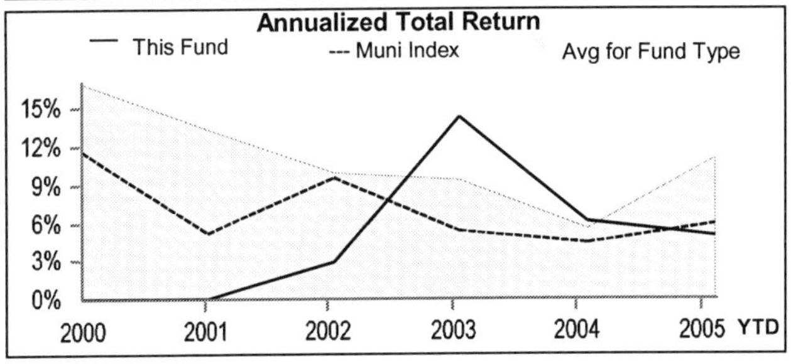

Nuveen NJ Div Adv Muni Fund 2 (NUJ) B Good

Fund Family: Nuveen Advisory Corp.
Fund Type: Municipal - Single State
Inception Date: March 25, 2002

Data Date	Weiss Investment Rating	Net Assets ($Mil)	Price	Performance Rating/Pts	Total Return Y-T-D	Risk Rating/Pts
6-05	B	71.23	15.64	B- / 7.5	7.59%	C+ / 6.2

Major Rating Factors:
Strong performance is the major factor driving the B (Good) Weiss Investment Rating for Nuveen NJ Div Adv Muni Fund 2. The fund currently has a performance rating of B- (Good) based on an annualized return of 8.07% over the last three years and a total return of 7.59% year to date 2005. Factored into the performance evaluation is an expense ratio of 0.77% (very low).

The fund's risk rating is currently C+ (Fair). It carries a beta of 1.78, meaning it is expected to move 17.8% for every 10% move in the market. Volatility, as measured by both the semi-deviation and a drawdown factor, is considered low. As of June 30, 2005, Nuveen NJ Div Adv Muni Fund 2 traded at a discount of 1.01% below its net asset value, which is worse than its one-year historical average discount of 2.92%.

Paul Brennan has been running the fund for 3 years and currently receives a manager quality ranking of 57 (0=worst, 99=best). If you desire only a moderate level of risk and strong performance, then this fund is an excellent option.

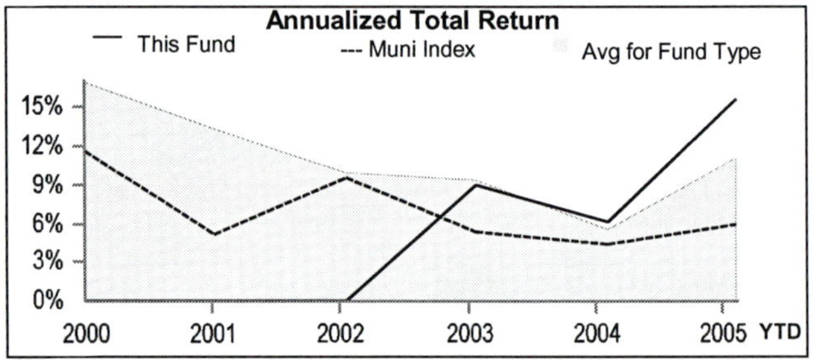

Nuveen NJ Investment Quality Muni (NQJ) C+ Fair

Fund Family: Nuveen Advisory Corp.
Fund Type: Municipal - Single State
Inception Date: February 21, 1991

Data Date	Weiss Investment Rating	Net Assets ($Mil)	Price	Performance Rating/Pts	Total Return Y-T-D	Risk Rating/Pts
6-05	C+	319.08	15.20	C / 5.0	2.69%	B- / 7.6
2004	C	310.45	15.26	C / 4.4	2.73%	B- / 7.6
2003	C+	313.79	15.75	C- / 4.1	12.81%	B / 8.5

Major Rating Factors:
Middle of the road best describes Nuveen NJ Investment Quality Muni whose Weiss Investment Rating is currently a C+ (Fair). The fund currently has a performance rating of C (Fair) based on an annualized return of 7.19% over the last three years and a total return of 2.69% year to date 2005. Factored into the performance evaluation is an expense ratio of 1.19% (average).

The fund's risk rating is currently B- (Good). It carries a beta of 1.96, meaning it is expected to move 19.6% for every 10% move in the market. Volatility, as measured by both the semi-deviation and a drawdown factor, is considered low. As of June 30, 2005, Nuveen NJ Investment Quality Muni traded at a discount of 2.63% below its net asset value, which is better than its one-year historical average discount of .53%.

Paul Brennan has been running the fund for 3 years and currently receives a manager quality ranking of 35 (0=worst, 99=best). If you desire an average level of risk, then this fund may be an option.

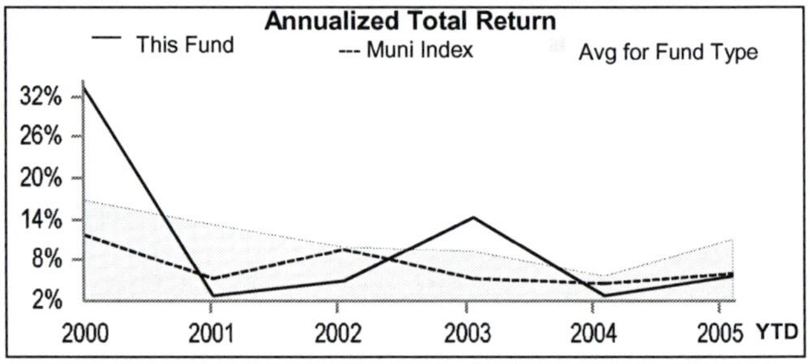

Nuveen NJ Prem Inc Muni (NNJ) B- Good

Fund Family: Nuveen Advisory Corp.
Fund Type: Municipal - Single State
Inception Date: December 18, 1992

Data Date	Weiss Investment Rating	Net Assets ($Mil)	Price	Performance Rating/Pts	Total Return Y-T-D	Risk Rating/Pts
6-05	B-	193.18	15.62	C+ / 6.0	1.63%	B- / 7.3
2004	B-	190.30	15.82	C+ / 6.8	4.74%	B- / 7.3
2003	B-	194.18	16.05	C+ / 5.6	12.21%	B / 8.5

Major Rating Factors:
Nuveen NJ Prem Inc Muni receives a Weiss Investment Rating of B- (Good). The fund currently has a performance rating of C+ (Fair) based on an annualized return of 7.18% over the last three years and a total return of 1.63% year to date 2005. Factored into the performance evaluation is an expense ratio of 1.17% (low).

The fund's risk rating is currently B- (Good). It carries a beta of 2.07, meaning it is expected to move 20.7% for every 10% move in the market. Volatility, as measured by both the semi-deviation and a drawdown factor, is considered low. As of June 30, 2005, Nuveen NJ Prem Inc Muni traded at a discount of 2.68% below its net asset value, which is worse than its one-year historical average discount of 2.83%.

Paul Brennan has been running the fund for 3 years and currently receives a manager quality ranking of 31 (0=worst, 99=best). If you desire an average level of risk, then this fund may be an option.

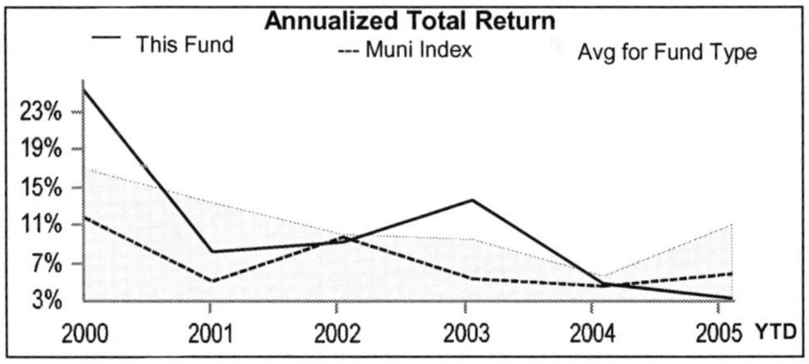

Nuveen NY Div Adv Muni (NAN) B+ Good

Fund Family: Nuveen Advisory Corp.
Fund Type: Municipal - Single State
Inception Date: May 26, 1999

Major Rating Factors:
Strong performance is the major factor driving the B+ (Good) Weiss Investment Rating for Nuveen NY Div Adv Muni. The fund currently has a performance rating of B- (Good) based on an annualized return of 9.16% over the last three years and a total return of 5.72% year to date 2005. Factored into the performance evaluation is an expense ratio of 0.78% (very low).

The fund's risk rating is currently C+ (Fair). It carries a beta of 2.41, meaning it is expected to move 24.1% for every 10% move in the market. Volatility, as measured by both the semi-deviation and a drawdown factor, is considered low. As of June 30, 2005, Nuveen NY Div Adv Muni traded at a discount of .93% below its net asset value, which is worse than its one-year historical average discount of 3.11%.

Paul Brennan has been running the fund for 6 years and currently receives a manager quality ranking of 38 (0=worst, 99=best). If you desire only a moderate level of risk and strong performance, then this fund is an excellent option.

Data Date	Weiss Investment Rating	Net Assets ($Mil)	Price	Performance Rating/Pts	Total Return Y-T-D	Risk Rating/Pts
6-05	B+	147.88	15.93	B- / 7.3	5.72%	C+ / 6.7
2004	B-	143.83	15.55	C+ / 6.9	3.89%	B- / 7.3
2003	B	145.84	15.88	C+ / 6.9	13.42%	B / 8.2

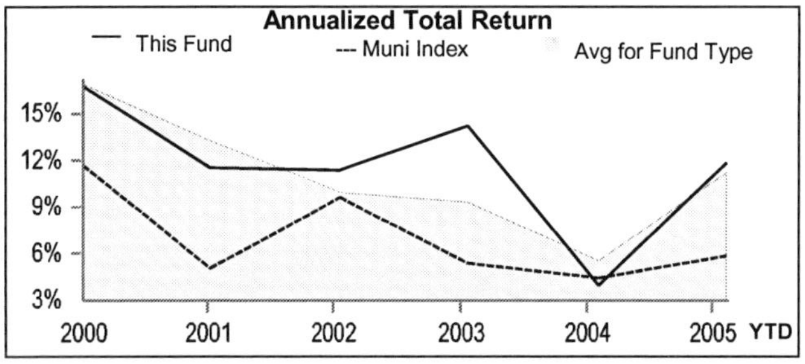

Nuveen NY Div Adv Muni 2 (NXK) A Excellent

Fund Family: Nuveen Advisory Corp.
Fund Type: Municipal - Single State
Inception Date: March 27, 2001

Major Rating Factors:
Strong performance is the major factor driving the A (Excellent) Weiss Investment Rating for Nuveen NY Div Adv Muni 2. The fund currently has a performance rating of B (Good) based on an annualized return of 10.06% over the last three years and a total return of 8.36% year to date 2005. Factored into the performance evaluation is an expense ratio of 0.73% (very low).

The fund's risk rating is currently C+ (Fair). It carries a beta of 2.04, meaning it is expected to move 20.4% for every 10% move in the market. Volatility, as measured by both the semi-deviation and a drawdown factor, is considered low. As of June 30, 2005, Nuveen NY Div Adv Muni 2 traded at a discount of 2.02% below its net asset value, which is worse than its one-year historical average discount of 4.71%.

Paul Brennan has been running the fund for 4 years and currently receives a manager quality ranking of 61 (0=worst, 99=best). If you desire only a moderate level of risk and strong performance, then this fund is an excellent option.

Data Date	Weiss Investment Rating	Net Assets ($Mil)	Price	Performance Rating/Pts	Total Return Y-T-D	Risk Rating/Pts
6-05	A	102.44	15.54	B / 8.2	8.36%	C+ / 6.9
2004	B-	99.49	14.80	C+ / 6.4	4.67%	B- / 7.7

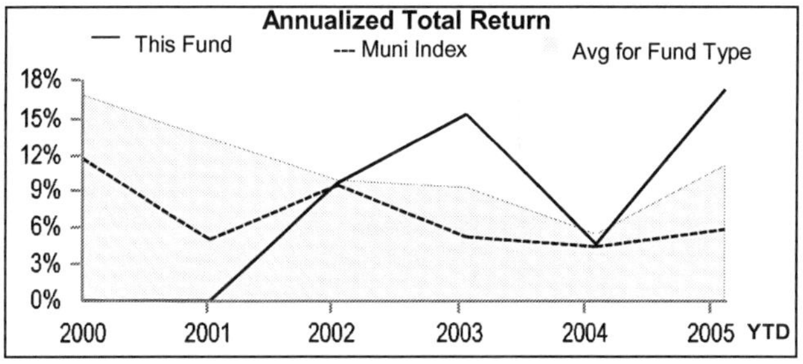

Nuveen NY Investment Quality Muni (NQN) B- Good

Fund Family: Nuveen Advisory Corp.
Fund Type: Municipal - Single State
Inception Date: November 20, 1990

Major Rating Factors:
Nuveen NY Investment Quality Muni receives a Weiss Investment Rating of B- (Good). The fund currently has a performance rating of C+ (Fair) based on an annualized return of 7.69% over the last three years and a total return of 3.21% year to date 2005. Factored into the performance evaluation is an expense ratio of 1.17% (low).

The fund's risk rating is currently B- (Good). It carries a beta of 2.02, meaning it is expected to move 20.2% for every 10% move in the market. Volatility, as measured by both the semi-deviation and a drawdown factor, is considered low. As of June 30, 2005, Nuveen NY Investment Quality Muni traded at a discount of 4.38% below its net asset value, which is worse than its one-year historical average discount of 5.37%.

Paul Brennan has been running the fund for 6 years and currently receives a manager quality ranking of 36 (0=worst, 99=best). If you desire an average level of risk, then this fund may be an option.

Data Date	Weiss Investment Rating	Net Assets ($Mil)	Price	Performance Rating/Pts	Total Return Y-T-D	Risk Rating/Pts
6-05	B-	286.97	15.50	C+ / 6.1	3.21%	B- / 7.2
2004	B+	286.52	15.49	B- / 7.0	5.55%	B- / 7.6
2003	A-	292.87	15.77	B- / 7.0	10.67%	B / 8.6

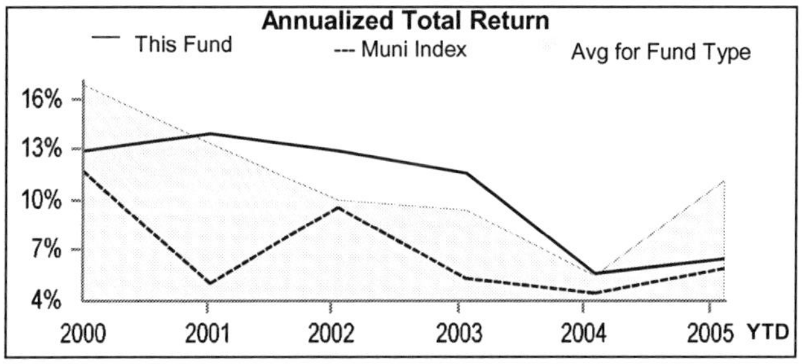

Nuveen NY Muni Value (NNY) B- Good

Fund Family: Nuveen Advisory Corp.
Fund Type: Municipal - Single State
Inception Date: October 7, 1987

Major Rating Factors:
Nuveen NY Muni Value receives a Weiss Investment Rating of B- (Good). The fund currently has a performance rating of C+ (Fair) based on an annualized return of 6.70% over the last three years and a total return of 10.35% year to date 2005. Factored into the performance evaluation is an expense ratio of 0.67% (very low).

The fund's risk rating is currently B- (Good). It carries a beta of 1.39, meaning it is expected to move 13.9% for every 10% move in the market. Volatility, as measured by both the semi-deviation and a drawdown factor, is considered low. As of June 30, 2005, Nuveen NY Muni Value traded at a discount of 4.72% below its net asset value, which is worse than its one-year historical average discount of 7.98%.

Paul Brennan has been running the fund for 6 years and currently receives a manager quality ranking of 55 (0=worst, 99=best). If you desire an average level of risk, then this fund may be an option.

Data Date	Weiss Investment Rating	Net Assets ($Mil)	Price	Perfor-mance Rating/Pts	Total Return Y-T-D	Risk Rating/Pts
6-05	B-	153.69	9.68	C+ / 5.9	10.35%	B- / 7.8
2004	C-	150.27	8.97	D / 1.6	1.64%	B / 8.9
2003	C+	151.75	9.25	C- / 3.4	6.64%	B+ / 9.0

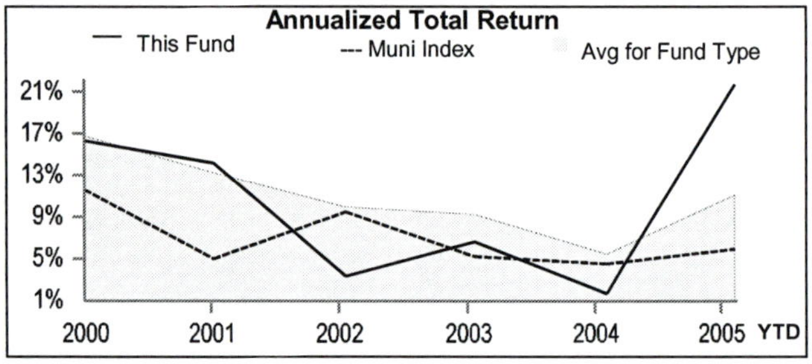

Nuveen NY Performance Plus Muni (NNP) B Good

Fund Family: Nuveen Advisory Corp.
Fund Type: Municipal - Single State
Inception Date: November 16, 1989

Major Rating Factors:
Strong performance is the major factor driving the B (Good) Weiss Investment Rating for Nuveen NY Performance Plus Muni. The fund currently has a performance rating of B- (Good) based on an annualized return of 7.85% over the last three years and a total return of 5.94% year to date 2005. Factored into the performance evaluation is an expense ratio of 1.19% (average).

The fund's risk rating is currently C+ (Fair). It carries a beta of 2.44, meaning it is expected to move 24.4% for every 10% move in the market. Volatility, as measured by both the semi-deviation and a drawdown factor, is considered low. As of June 30, 2005, Nuveen NY Performance Plus Muni traded at a discount of 4.30% below its net asset value, which is worse than its one-year historical average discount of 5.65%.

Paul Brennan has been running the fund for 6 years and currently receives a manager quality ranking of 22 (0=worst, 99=best). If you desire only a moderate level of risk and strong performance, then this fund is an excellent option.

Data Date	Weiss Investment Rating	Net Assets ($Mil)	Price	Perfor-mance Rating/Pts	Total Return Y-T-D	Risk Rating/Pts
6-05	B	250.62	16.02	B- / 7.1	5.94%	C+ / 6.7
2004	B-	244.31	15.61	C+ / 6.0	-0.35%	B- / 7.5
2003	A	247.93	16.54	B / 7.7	13.37%	B / 8.0

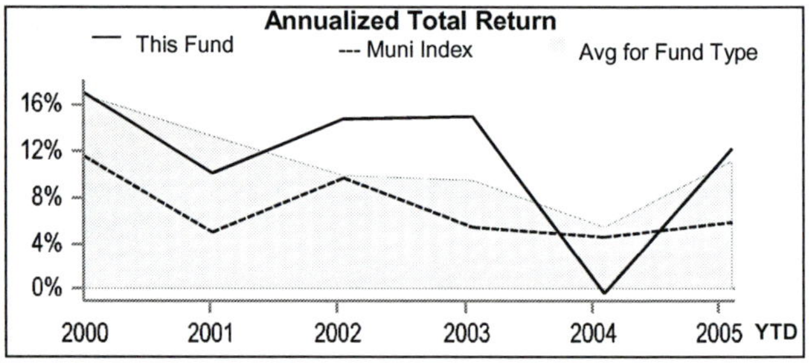

Nuveen NY Quality Inc Muni (NUN) B- Good

Fund Family: Nuveen Advisory Corp.
Fund Type: Municipal - Single State
Inception Date: November 25, 1991

Major Rating Factors:
Nuveen NY Quality Inc Muni receives a Weiss Investment Rating of B- (Good). The fund currently has a performance rating of C+ (Fair) based on an annualized return of 7.74% over the last three years and a total return of 7.02% year to date 2005. Factored into the performance evaluation is an expense ratio of 1.18% (low).

The fund's risk rating is currently B- (Good). It carries a beta of 2.16, meaning it is expected to move 21.6% for every 10% move in the market. Volatility, as measured by both the semi-deviation and a drawdown factor, is considered low. As of June 30, 2005, Nuveen NY Quality Inc Muni traded at a discount of 6.25% below its net asset value, which is worse than its one-year historical average discount of 7.47%.

Paul Brennan has been running the fund for 6 years and currently receives a manager quality ranking of 28 (0=worst, 99=best). If you desire an average level of risk, then this fund may be an option.

Data Date	Weiss Investment Rating	Net Assets ($Mil)	Price	Perfor-mance Rating/Pts	Total Return Y-T-D	Risk Rating/Pts
6-05	B-	385.13	15.00	C+ / 6.7	7.02%	B- / 7.2
2004	C+	376.78	14.44	C / 4.8	0.12%	B / 8.1
2003	B	385.55	15.14	C+ / 5.6	8.36%	B / 8.9

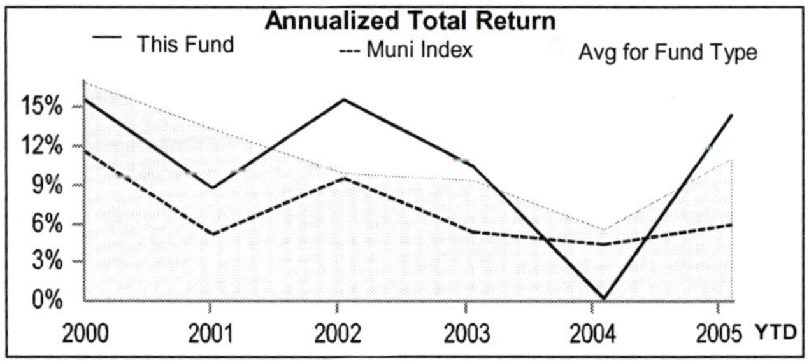

Nuveen NY Select Quality Muni (NVN) C+ Fair

Fund Family: Nuveen Advisory Corp.
Fund Type: Municipal - Single State
Inception Date: May 22, 1991

Data Date	Weiss Investment Rating	Net Assets ($Mil)	Price	Performance Rating/Pts	Total Return Y-T-D	Risk Rating/Pts
6-05	C+	380.23	15.48	C+ / 6.8	3.49%	C+ / 6.7
2004	B	372.69	15.42	B- / 7.0	3.77%	B- / 7.2
2003	B	379.36	15.68	C+ / 6.6	11.11%	B / 8.4

Major Rating Factors:
Middle of the road best describes Nuveen NY Select Quality Muni whose Weiss Investment Rating is currently a C+ (Fair). The fund currently has a performance rating of C+ (Fair) based on an annualized return of 8.06% over the last three years and a total return of 3.49% year to date 2005. Factored into the performance evaluation is an expense ratio of 1.17% (low).

The fund's risk rating is currently C+ (Fair). It carries a beta of 2.50, meaning it is expected to move 25.0% for every 10% move in the market. Volatility, as measured by both the semi-deviation and a drawdown factor, is considered low. As of June 30, 2005, Nuveen NY Select Quality Muni traded at a discount of 4.68% below its net asset value, which is worse than its one-year historical average discount of 6.34%.

Paul Brennan has been running the fund for 6 years and currently receives a manager quality ranking of 19 (0=worst, 99=best). If you desire an average level of risk, then this fund may be an option.

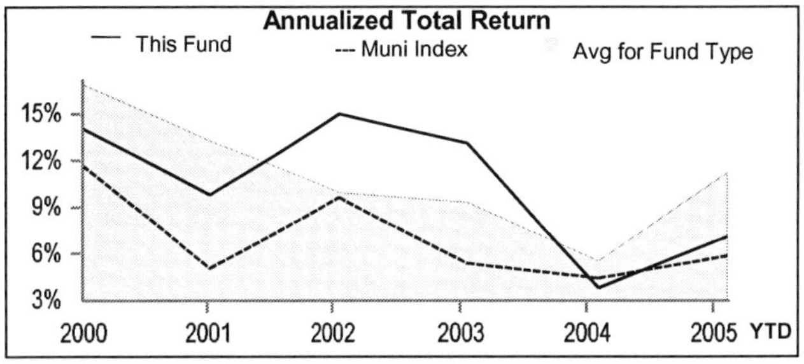

Nuveen NY Select Tax-Free Inc Port (NXN) C+ Fair

Fund Family: Nuveen Advisory Corp.
Fund Type: Municipal - Single State
Inception Date: June 19, 1992

Data Date	Weiss Investment Rating	Net Assets ($Mil)	Price	Performance Rating/Pts	Total Return Y-T-D	Risk Rating/Pts
6-05	C+	57.04	14.15	C / 5.0	9.76%	B- / 7.7
2004	D+	55.96	13.19	D- / 1.1	-3.58%	B / 8.7
2003	C+	56.73	14.20	C / 5.0	7.43%	B / 8.4

Major Rating Factors:
Middle of the road best describes Nuveen NY Select Tax-Free Inc Port whose Weiss Investment Rating is currently a C+ (Fair). The fund currently has a performance rating of C (Fair) based on an annualized return of 6.15% over the last three years and a total return of 9.76% year to date 2005. Factored into the performance evaluation is an expense ratio of 0.40% (very low).

The fund's risk rating is currently B- (Good). It carries a beta of 1.58, meaning it is expected to move 15.8% for every 10% move in the market. Volatility, as measured by both the semi-deviation and a drawdown factor, is considered low. As of June 30, 2005, Nuveen NY Select Tax-Free Inc Port traded at a discount of 3.08% below its net asset value, which is worse than its one-year historical average discount of 5.55%.

Paul Brennan has been running the fund for 3 years and currently receives a manager quality ranking of 44 (0=worst, 99=best). If you desire an average level of risk, then this fund may be an option.

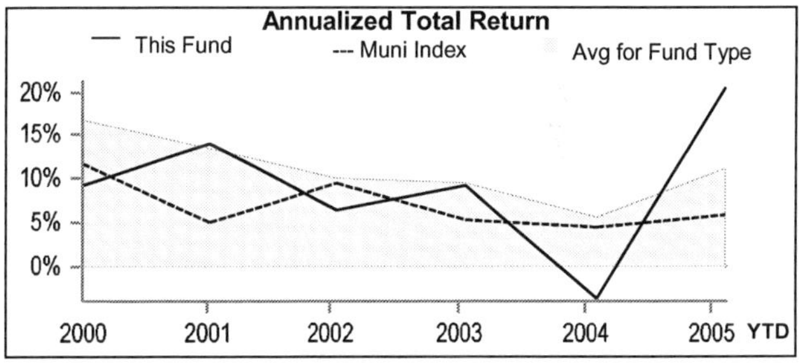

Nuveen OH Div Adv Muni (NXI) C+ Fair

Fund Family: Nuveen Advisory Corp.
Fund Type: Municipal - Single State
Inception Date: March 27, 2001

Data Date	Weiss Investment Rating	Net Assets ($Mil)	Price	Performance Rating/Pts	Total Return Y-T-D	Risk Rating/Pts
6-05	C+	66.69	16.24	C+ / 6.6	-5.69%	C+ / 6.2
2004	A-	64.81	17.75	B+ / 8.7	16.99%	C+ / 6.5

Major Rating Factors:
Middle of the road best describes Nuveen OH Div Adv Muni whose Weiss Investment Rating is currently a C+ (Fair). The fund currently has a performance rating of C+ (Fair) based on an annualized return of 8.83% over the last three years and a total return of -5.69% year to date 2005. Factored into the performance evaluation is an expense ratio of 0.74% (very low).

The fund's risk rating is currently C+ (Fair). It carries a beta of 2.31, meaning it is expected to move 23.1% for every 10% move in the market. Volatility, as measured by both the semi-deviation and a drawdown factor, is considered low. As of June 30, 2005, Nuveen OH Div Adv Muni traded at a premium of 3.18% above its net asset value, which is better than its one-year historical average premium of 3.60%.

Cathryn Steeves has been running the fund for 4 years and currently receives a manager quality ranking of 32 (0=worst, 99=best). If you desire an average level of risk, then this fund may be an option.

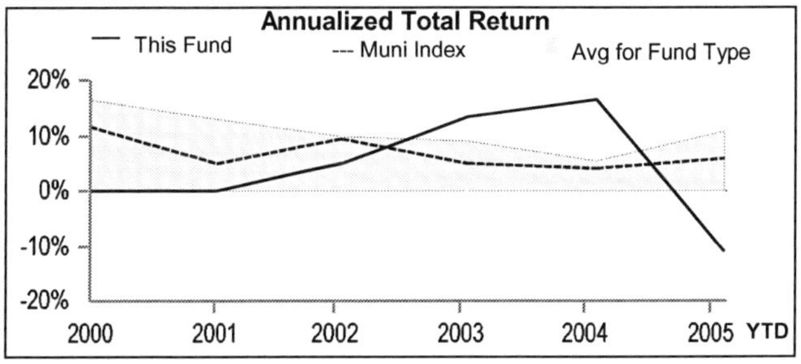

Nuveen OH Div Adv Muni 2 (NBJ) B Good

Fund Family: Nuveen Advisory Corp.
Fund Type: Municipal - Single State
Inception Date: September 25, 2001

Major Rating Factors:
Strong performance is the major factor driving the B (Good) Weiss Investment Rating for Nuveen OH Div Adv Muni 2. The fund currently has a performance rating of B- (Good) based on an annualized return of 9.69% over the last three years and a total return of -0.72% year to date 2005. Factored into the performance evaluation is an expense ratio of 0.78% (very low).

The fund's risk rating is currently C+ (Fair). It carries a beta of 2.72, meaning it is expected to move 27.2% for every 10% move in the market. Volatility, as measured by both the semi-deviation and a drawdown factor, is considered low. As of June 30, 2005, Nuveen OH Div Adv Muni 2 traded at a premium of 2.95% above its net asset value, which is worse than its one-year historical average premium of 2.01%.

Cathryn Steeves has been running the fund for 4 years and currently receives a manager quality ranking of 16 (0=worst, 99=best). If you desire only a moderate level of risk and strong performance, then this fund is an excellent option.

Data Date	Weiss Investment Rating	Net Assets ($Mil)	Price	Performance Rating/Pts	Total Return Y-T-D	Risk Rating/Pts
6-05	B	48.63	16.06	B- / 7.3	-0.72%	C+ / 6.5
2004	A-	47.12	16.65	B+ / 8.5	14.01%	C+ / 6.6

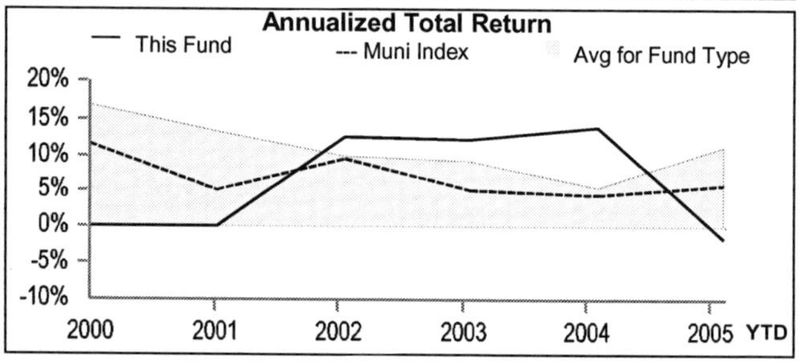

Nuveen OH Div Adv Muni Fund 3 (NVJ) C Fair

Fund Family: Nuveen Advisory Corp.
Fund Type: Municipal - Single State
Inception Date: March 25, 2002

Major Rating Factors:
Middle of the road best describes Nuveen OH Div Adv Muni Fund 3 whose Weiss Investment Rating is currently a C (Fair). The fund currently has a performance rating of C (Fair) based on an annualized return of 7.60% over the last three years and a total return of -4.26% year to date 2005. Factored into the performance evaluation is an expense ratio of 0.78% (very low).

The fund's risk rating is currently C+ (Fair). It carries a beta of 2.34, meaning it is expected to move 23.4% for every 10% move in the market. Volatility, as measured by both the semi-deviation and a drawdown factor, is considered low. As of June 30, 2005, Nuveen OH Div Adv Muni Fund 3 traded at a discount of .25% below its net asset value, which is better than its one-year historical average premium of .42%.

Cathryn Steeves has been running the fund for 3 years and currently receives a manager quality ranking of 22 (0=worst, 99=best). If you desire an average level of risk, then this fund may be an option.

Data Date	Weiss Investment Rating	Net Assets ($Mil)	Price	Performance Rating/Pts	Total Return Y-T-D	Risk Rating/Pts
6-05	C	34.07	15.71	C / 5.3	-4.26%	C+ / 6.1

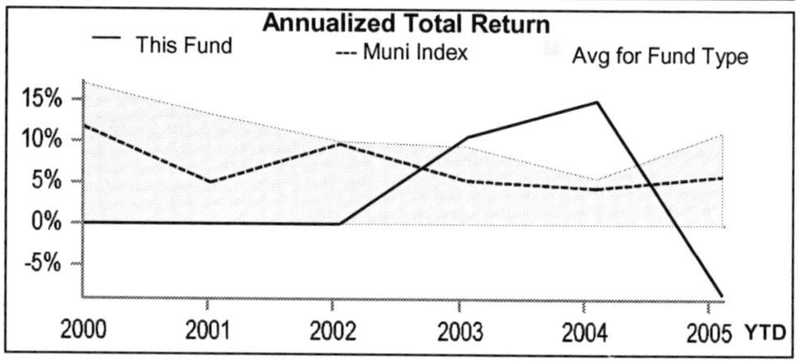

Nuveen OH Quality Inc Muni (NUO) C- Fair

Fund Family: Nuveen Advisory Corp.
Fund Type: Municipal - Single State
Inception Date: October 17, 1991

Major Rating Factors:
Disappointing performance is the major factor driving the C- (Fair) Weiss Investment Rating for Nuveen OH Quality Inc Muni. The fund currently has a performance rating of D+ (Weak) based on an annualized return of 3.70% over the last three years and a total return of -5.52% year to date 2005. Factored into the performance evaluation is an expense ratio of 1.17% (low).

The fund's risk rating is currently C+ (Fair). It carries a beta of 2.03, meaning it is expected to move 20.3% for every 10% move in the market. Volatility, as measured by both the semi-deviation and a drawdown factor, is considered low. As of June 30, 2005, Nuveen OH Quality Inc Muni traded at a premium of 2.02% above its net asset value, which is better than its one-year historical average premium of 4.08%.

Cathryn Steeves has been running the fund for 14 years and currently receives a manager quality ranking of 9 (0=worst, 99=best). This fund offers only a moderate level of risk but investors looking for strong performance are still waiting.

Data Date	Weiss Investment Rating	Net Assets ($Mil)	Price	Performance Rating/Pts	Total Return Y-T-D	Risk Rating/Pts
6-05	C-	163.03	17.14	D+ / 2.5	-5.52%	C+ / 6.9
2004	B+	158.93	18.67	B / 7.8	8.23%	C+ / 6.8
2003	B+	160.89	18.10	B / 7.6	15.85%	B- / 7.6

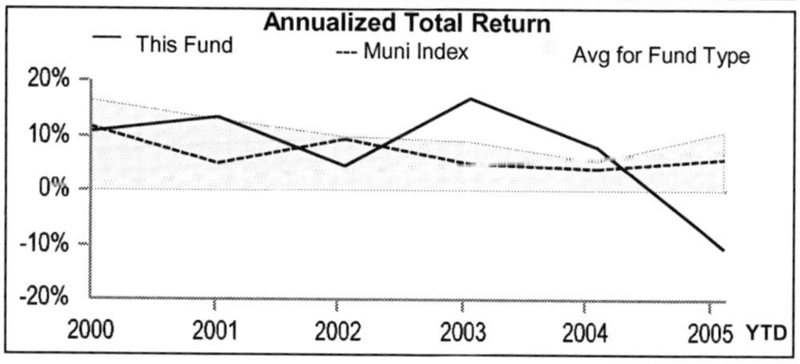

Nuveen PA Div Adv Muni (NXM) A Excellent

Fund Family: Nuveen Advisory Corp.
Fund Type: Municipal - Single State
Inception Date: March 27, 2001

Data Date	Weiss Investment Rating	Net Assets ($Mil)	Price	Perfor-mance Rating/Pts	Total Return Y-T-D	Risk Rating/Pts
6-05	A	52.71	16.10	B+ / 8.4	2.79%	C+ / 6.7
2004	A-	52.29	16.14	B / 7.9	8.10%	B- / 7.1

Major Rating Factors:
Strong performance is the major factor driving the A (Excellent) Weiss Investment Rating for Nuveen PA Div Adv Muni. The fund currently has a performance rating of B+ (Good) based on an annualized return of 10.62% over the last three years and a total return of 2.79% year to date 2005. Factored into the performance evaluation is an expense ratio of 0.78% (very low).

The fund's risk rating is currently C+ (Fair). It carries a beta of 2.54, meaning it is expected to move 25.4% for every 10% move in the market. Volatility, as measured by both the semi-deviation and a drawdown factor, is considered low. As of June 30, 2005, Nuveen PA Div Adv Muni traded at a premium of .94% above its net asset value, which is worse than its one-year historical average discount of .84%.

Paul Brennan has been running the fund for 3 years and currently receives a manager quality ranking of 43 (0=worst, 99=best). If you desire only a moderate level of risk and strong performance, then this fund is an excellent option.

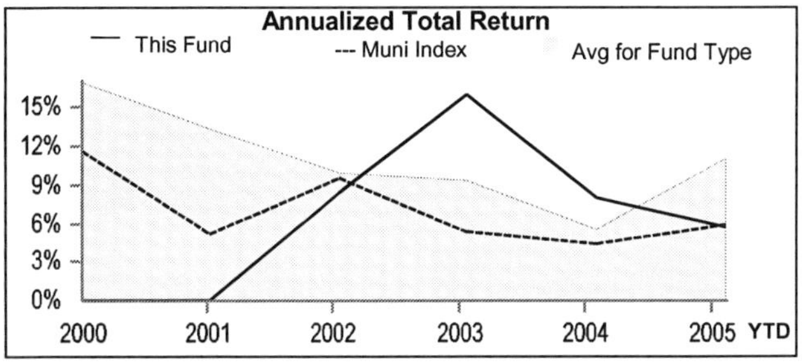

Nuveen PA Div Adv Muni Fund 2 (NVY) C+ Fair

Fund Family: Nuveen Advisory Corp.
Fund Type: Municipal - Single State
Inception Date: March 25, 2002

Data Date	Weiss Investment Rating	Net Assets ($Mil)	Price	Perfor-mance Rating/Pts	Total Return Y-T-D	Risk Rating/Pts
6-05	C+	59.17	14.98	C+ / 6.4	4.36%	C+ / 6.8

Major Rating Factors:
Middle of the road best describes Nuveen PA Div Adv Muni Fund 2 whose Weiss Investment Rating is currently a C+ (Fair). The fund currently has a performance rating of C+ (Fair) based on an annualized return of 7.35% over the last three years and a total return of 4.36% year to date 2005. Factored into the performance evaluation is an expense ratio of 0.77% (very low).

The fund's risk rating is currently C+ (Fair). It carries a beta of 2.55, meaning it is expected to move 25.5% for every 10% move in the market. Volatility, as measured by both the semi-deviation and a drawdown factor, is considered low. As of June 30, 2005, Nuveen PA Div Adv Muni Fund 2 traded at a discount of 5.79% below its net asset value, which is better than its one-year historical average discount of 5.32%.

Paul Brennan has been running the fund for 3 years and currently receives a manager quality ranking of 13 (0=worst, 99=best). If you desire an average level of risk, then this fund may be an option.

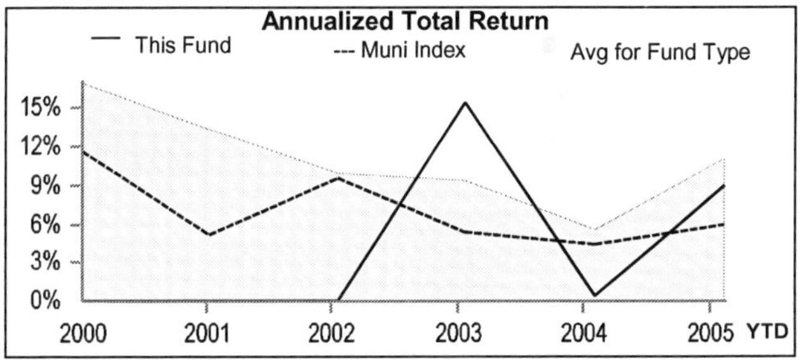

Nuveen PA Investment Quality Muni (NQP) C Fair

Fund Family: Nuveen Advisory Corp.
Fund Type: Municipal - Single State
Inception Date: February 21, 1991

Data Date	Weiss Investment Rating	Net Assets ($Mil)	Price	Perfor-mance Rating/Pts	Total Return Y-T-D	Risk Rating/Pts
6-05	C	256.37	14.84	C- / 3.9	-0.35%	B- / 7.0
2004	B-	250.62	15.33	C+ / 6.2	4.94%	B- / 7.1
2003	B	255.22	15.46	C+ / 6.0	11.40%	B / 8.4

Major Rating Factors:
Middle of the road best describes Nuveen PA Investment Quality Muni whose Weiss Investment Rating is currently a C (Fair). The fund currently has a performance rating of C- (Fair) based on an annualized return of 5.78% over the last three years and a total return of -0.35% year to date 2005. Factored into the performance evaluation is an expense ratio of 1.21% (average).

The fund's risk rating is currently B- (Good). It carries a beta of 2.49, meaning it is expected to move 24.9% for every 10% move in the market. Volatility, as measured by both the semi-deviation and a drawdown factor, is considered low. As of June 30, 2005, Nuveen PA Investment Quality Muni traded at a discount of 5.72% below its net asset value, which is better than its one-year historical average discount of 4.04%.

Paul Brennan has been running the fund for 3 years and currently receives a manager quality ranking of 11 (0=worst, 99=best). If you desire an average level of risk, then this fund may be an option.

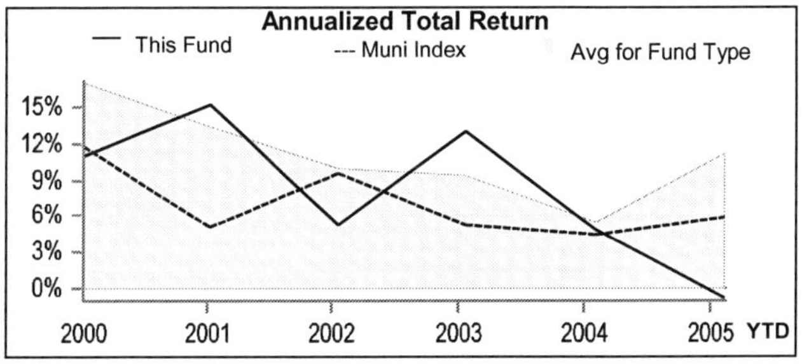

Nuveen PA Prem Inc Muni 2 (NPY) C+ Fair

Fund Family: Nuveen Advisory Corp.
Fund Type: Municipal - Single State
Inception Date: March 18, 1993

Major Rating Factors:
Middle of the road best describes Nuveen PA Prem Inc Muni 2 whose Weiss Investment Rating is currently a C+ (Fair). The fund currently has a performance rating of C (Fair) based on an annualized return of 8.13% over the last three years and a total return of 0.71% year to date 2005. Factored into the performance evaluation is an expense ratio of 1.19% (average).

The fund's risk rating is currently C+ (Fair). It carries a beta of 2.37, meaning it is expected to move 23.7% for every 10% move in the market. Volatility, as measured by both the semi-deviation and a drawdown factor, is considered low. As of June 30, 2005, Nuveen PA Prem Inc Muni 2 traded at a discount of .78% below its net asset value, which is better than its one-year historical average discount of .20%.

Paul Brennan has been running the fund for 3 years and currently receives a manager quality ranking of 24 (0=worst, 99=best). If you desire an average level of risk, then this fund may be an option.

Data Date	Weiss Investment Rating	Net Assets ($Mil)	Price	Performance Rating/Pts	Total Return Y-T-D	Risk Rating/Pts
6-05	C+	242.37	15.21	C / 5.2	0.71%	C+ / 6.7
2004	B+	239.10	15.56	B / 7.7	5.89%	C+ / 6.9
2003	A-	244.66	15.42	B- / 7.2	14.56%	B / 8.3

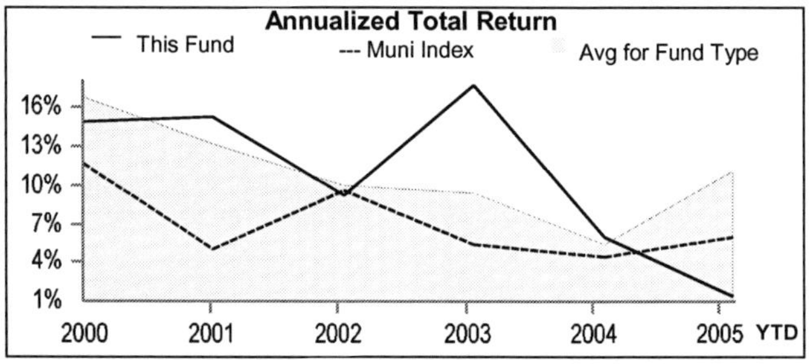

Nuveen Performance Plus Muni (NPP) B- Good

Fund Family: Nuveen Advisory Corp.
Fund Type: Municipal - National
Inception Date: June 22, 1989

Major Rating Factors:
Nuveen Performance Plus Muni receives a Weiss Investment Rating of B- (Good). The fund currently has a performance rating of C+ (Fair) based on an annualized return of 6.92% over the last three years and a total return of 5.45% year to date 2005. Factored into the performance evaluation is an expense ratio of 1.14% (low).

The fund's risk rating is currently B- (Good). It carries a beta of 2.24, meaning it is expected to move 22.4% for every 10% move in the market. Volatility, as measured by both the semi-deviation and a drawdown factor, is considered low. As of June 30, 2005, Nuveen Performance Plus Muni traded at a discount of 7.97% below its net asset value, which is worse than its one-year historical average discount of 8.12%.

Tom Spalding has been running the fund for 3 years and currently receives a manager quality ranking of 23 (0=worst, 99=best). If you desire an average level of risk, then this fund may be an option.

Data Date	Weiss Investment Rating	Net Assets ($Mil)	Price	Performance Rating/Pts	Total Return Y-T-D	Risk Rating/Pts
6-05	B-	962.99	14.79	C+ / 6.1	5.45%	B- / 7.4
2004	B-	934.06	14.49	C / 5.3	3.41%	B- / 7.9
2003	B	948.16	14.92	C+ / 5.9	11.65%	B / 8.5

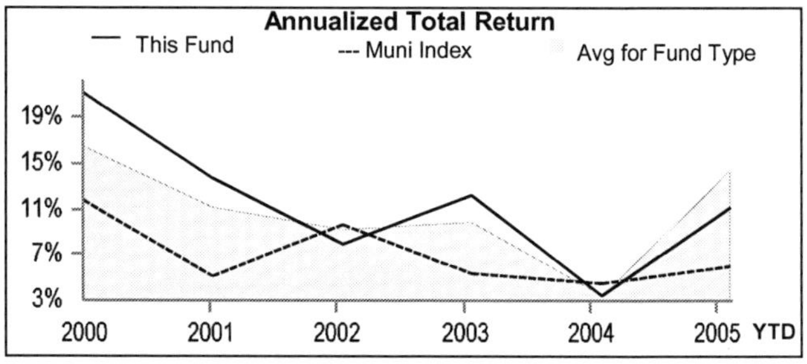

Nuveen Prem Inc Muni (NPI) C+ Fair

Fund Family: Nuveen Advisory Corp.
Fund Type: Municipal - National
Inception Date: July 21, 1988

Major Rating Factors:
Middle of the road best describes Nuveen Prem Inc Muni whose Weiss Investment Rating is currently a C+ (Fair). The fund currently has a performance rating of C (Fair) based on an annualized return of 6.47% over the last three years and a total return of 6.57% year to date 2005. Factored into the performance evaluation is an expense ratio of 1.18% (low).

The fund's risk rating is currently B- (Good). It carries a beta of 2.13, meaning it is expected to move 21.3% for every 10% move in the market. Volatility, as measured by both the semi-deviation and a drawdown factor, is considered low. As of June 30, 2005, Nuveen Prem Inc Muni traded at a discount of 7.25% below its net asset value, which is better than its one-year historical average discount of 6.83%.

Daniel Solender has been running the fund for 17 years and currently receives a manager quality ranking of 21 (0=worst, 99=best). If you desire an average level of risk, then this fund may be an option.

Data Date	Weiss Investment Rating	Net Assets ($Mil)	Price	Performance Rating/Pts	Total Return Y-T-D	Risk Rating/Pts
6-05	C+	985.40	14.33	C / 5.3	6.57%	B- / 7.5
2004	C	953.08	13.89	C- / 3.9	2.33%	B / 8.0
2003	C+	968.67	14.39	C / 4.9	9.73%	B / 8.6

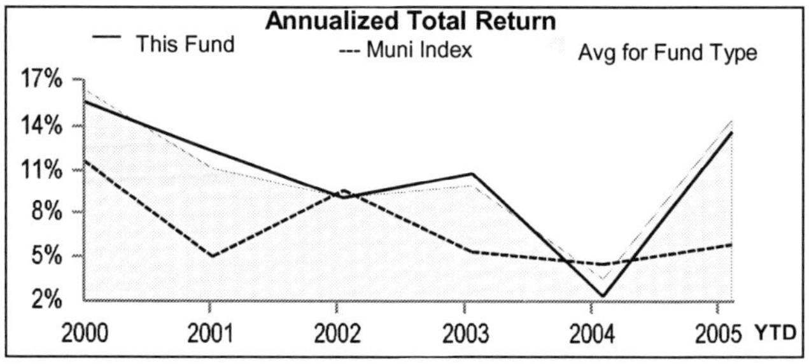

Nuveen Prem Inc Muni 4 (NPT) C+ Fair

Fund Family: Nuveen Advisory Corp.
Fund Type: Municipal - National
Inception Date: February 19, 1993

Major Rating Factors:
Middle of the road best describes Nuveen Prem Inc Muni 4 whose Weiss Investment Rating is currently a C+ (Fair). The fund currently has a performance rating of C- (Fair) based on an annualized return of 4.19% over the last three years and a total return of 6.22% year to date 2005. Factored into the performance evaluation is an expense ratio of 1.25% (average).

The fund's risk rating is currently B- (Good). It carries a beta of 2.00, meaning it is expected to move 20.0% for every 10% move in the market. Volatility, as measured by both the semi-deviation and a drawdown factor, is considered low. As of June 30, 2005, Nuveen Prem Inc Muni 4 traded at a discount of 9.65% below its net asset value, which is better than its one-year historical average discount of 8.30%.

Tom Spalding has been running the fund for 3 years and currently receives a manager quality ranking of 11 (0=worst, 99=best). If you desire an average level of risk, then this fund may be an option.

Data Date	Weiss Investment Rating	Net Assets ($Mil)	Price	Performance Rating/Pts	Total Return Y-T-D	Risk Rating/Pts
6-05	C+	600.24	12.54	C- / 4.1	6.22%	B- / 7.6
2004	D+	575.17	12.20	D / 1.6	2.68%	B / 8.1
2003	C	581.07	12.69	D+ / 2.5	4.01%	B+ / 9.0

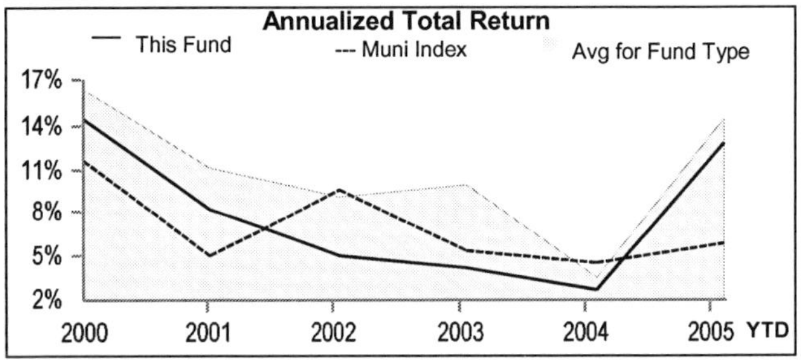

Nuveen Premier Insured Muni Inc (NIF) C+ Fair

Fund Family: Nuveen Advisory Corp.
Fund Type: Municipal - National
Inception Date: December 19, 1991

Major Rating Factors:
Middle of the road best describes Nuveen Premier Insured Muni Inc whose Weiss Investment Rating is currently a C+ (Fair). The fund currently has a performance rating of C+ (Fair) based on an annualized return of 6.79% over the last three years and a total return of 8.29% year to date 2005. Factored into the performance evaluation is an expense ratio of 1.19% (average).

The fund's risk rating is currently C+ (Fair). It carries a beta of 2.32, meaning it is expected to move 23.2% for every 10% move in the market. Volatility, as measured by both the semi-deviation and a drawdown factor, is considered low. As of June 30, 2005, Nuveen Premier Insured Muni Inc traded at a discount of 1.69% below its net asset value, which is worse than its one-year historical average discount of 3.44%.

Daniel S. Solender,CFA has been running the fund for 1 year and currently receives a manager quality ranking of 17 (0=worst, 99=best). If you desire an average level of risk, then this fund may be an option.

Data Date	Weiss Investment Rating	Net Assets ($Mil)	Price	Performance Rating/Pts	Total Return Y-T-D	Risk Rating/Pts
6-05	C+	309.80	15.69	C+ / 6.4	8.29%	C+ / 6.7
2004	C	303.47	14.94	C- / 3.7	-1.17%	B- / 7.9
2003	B	310.38	16.10	C+ / 5.9	7.98%	B / 8.4

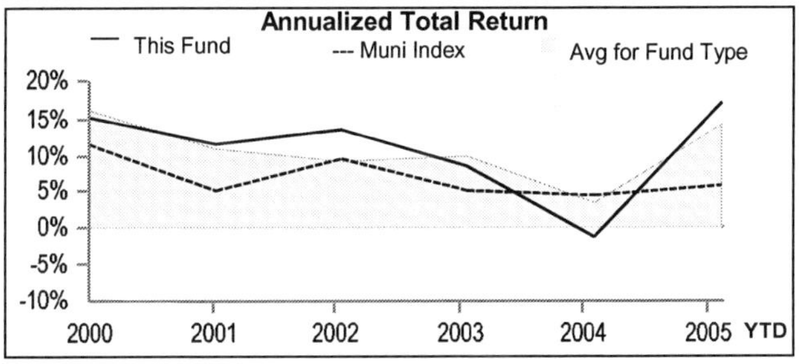

Nuveen Premier Muni Inc (NPF) C+ Fair

Fund Family: Nuveen Advisory Corp.
Fund Type: Municipal - National
Inception Date: December 19, 1991

Major Rating Factors:
Middle of the road best describes Nuveen Premier Muni Inc whose Weiss Investment Rating is currently a C+ (Fair). The fund currently has a performance rating of C (Fair) based on an annualized return of 5.55% over the last three years and a total return of 4.65% year to date 2005. Factored into the performance evaluation is an expense ratio of 1.25% (average).

The fund's risk rating is currently B- (Good). It carries a beta of 2.12, meaning it is expected to move 21.2% for every 10% move in the market. Volatility, as measured by both the semi-deviation and a drawdown factor, is considered low. As of June 30, 2005, Nuveen Premier Muni Inc traded at a discount of 9.56% below its net asset value, which is better than its one-year historical average discount of 8.02%.

Daniel Solender has been running the fund for 14 years and currently receives a manager quality ranking of 17 (0=worst, 99=best). If you desire an average level of risk, then this fund may be an option.

Data Date	Weiss Investment Rating	Net Assets ($Mil)	Price	Performance Rating/Pts	Total Return Y-T-D	Risk Rating/Pts
6-05	C+	312.90	14.09	C / 4.4	4.65%	B- / 7.6
2004	C	304.85	13.90	C- / 3.4	1.98%	B / 8.1
2003	C	311.79	14.58	C- / 3.3	6.97%	B+ / 9.1

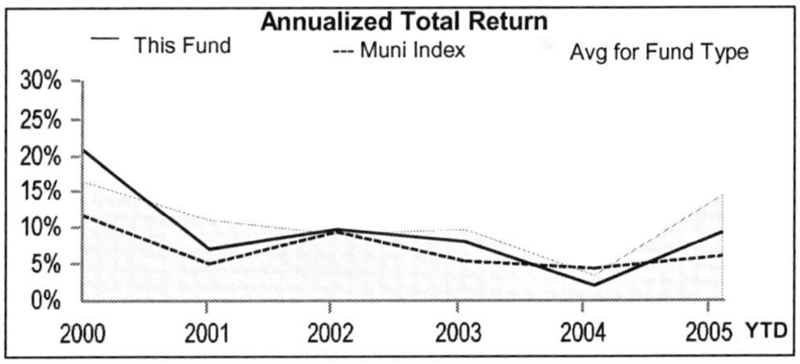

Nuveen Premium Income Muni 2 (NPM) B- Good

Fund Family: Nuveen Advisory Corp.
Fund Type: Municipal - National
Inception Date: July 24, 1992

Major Rating Factors:
Nuveen Premium Income Muni 2 receives a Weiss Investment Rating of B- (Good). The fund currently has a performance rating of C+ (Fair) based on an annualized return of 7.36% over the last three years and a total return of 7.62% year to date 2005. Factored into the performance evaluation is an expense ratio of 1.19% (average).

The fund's risk rating is currently B- (Good). It carries a beta of 2.06, meaning it is expected to move 20.6% for every 10% move in the market. Volatility, as measured by both the semi-deviation and a drawdown factor, is considered low. As of June 30, 2005, Nuveen Premium Income Muni 2 traded at a discount of 6.51% below its net asset value, which is worse than its one-year historical average discount of 7.46%.

Tom Spalding has been running the fund for 3 years and currently receives a manager quality ranking of 34 (0=worst, 99=best). If you desire an average level of risk, then this fund may be an option.

Data Date	Weiss Investment Rating	Net Assets ($Mil)	Price	Performance Rating/Pts	Total Return Y-T-D	Risk Rating/Pts
6-05	B-	644.02	14.66	C+ / 6.7	7.62%	B- / 7.5
2004	C+	624.56	14.08	C / 4.9	4.43%	B / 8.3
2003	C+	634.20	14.39	C- / 3.9	5.89%	B+ / 9.1

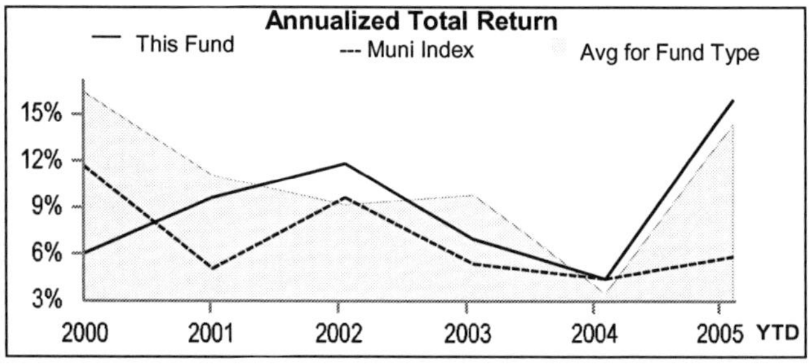

Nuveen Quality Inc Muni (NQU) B- Good

Fund Family: Nuveen Advisory Corp.
Fund Type: Municipal - National
Inception Date: June 20, 1991

Major Rating Factors:
Nuveen Quality Inc Muni receives a Weiss Investment Rating of B- (Good). The fund currently has a performance rating of C+ (Fair) based on an annualized return of 6.70% over the last three years and a total return of 5.66% year to date 2005. Factored into the performance evaluation is an expense ratio of 1.18% (low).

The fund's risk rating is currently B- (Good). It carries a beta of 1.93, meaning it is expected to move 19.3% for every 10% move in the market. Volatility, as measured by both the semi-deviation and a drawdown factor, is considered low. As of June 30, 2005, Nuveen Quality Inc Muni traded at a discount of 8.14% below its net asset value, which is better than its one-year historical average discount of 7.85%.

Tom Spalding has been running the fund for 3 years and currently receives a manager quality ranking of 30 (0=worst, 99=best). If you desire an average level of risk, then this fund may be an option.

Data Date	Weiss Investment Rating	Net Assets ($Mil)	Price	Performance Rating/Pts	Total Return Y-T-D	Risk Rating/Pts
6-05	B-	853.10	14.45	C+ / 5.6	5.66%	B- / 7.7
2004	C+	826.61	14.13	C- / 4.1	3.38%	B / 8.2
2003	C+	833.89	14.54	C- / 4.2	10.69%	B / 8.6

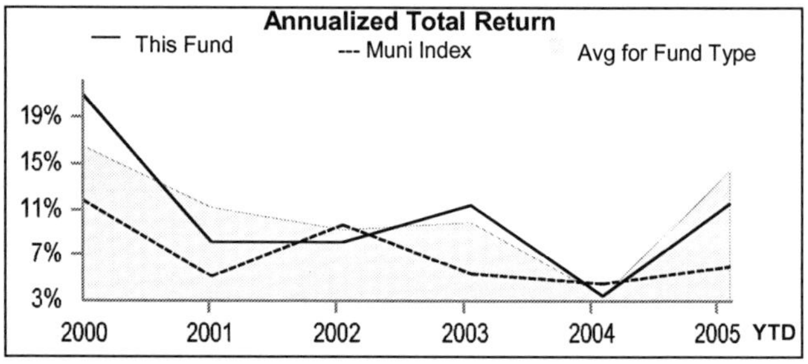

Nuveen Real Estate Inc Fund (JRS) B Good

Fund Family: Nuveen Advisory Corp.
Fund Type: Growth and Income
Inception Date: November 15, 2001

Major Rating Factors:
Strong performance is the major factor driving the B (Good) Weiss Investment Rating for Nuveen Real Estate Inc Fund. The fund currently has a performance rating of B (Good) based on an annualized return of 17.42% over the last three years and a total return of 1.02% year to date 2005. Factored into the performance evaluation is an expense ratio of 0.91% (low).

The fund's risk rating is currently C+ (Fair). It carries a beta of 0.24, meaning the fund's expected move will be 2.4% for every 10% move in the market. Volatility, as measured by both the semi-deviation and a drawdown factor, is considered low. As of June 30, 2005, Nuveen Real Estate Inc Fund traded at a discount of 10.26% below its net asset value, which is better than its one-year historical average discount of 7.44%.

Security Capital Research&Mgmt has been running the fund for 4 years and currently receives a manager quality ranking of 95 (0=worst, 99=best). If you desire only a moderate level of risk and strong performance, then this fund is an excellent option.

Data Date	Weiss Investment Rating	Net Assets ($Mil)	Price	Performance Rating/Pts	Total Return Y-T-D	Risk Rating/Pts
6-05	B	633.76	20.11	B / 8.1	1.02%	C+ / 5.6
2004	A	562.85	20.75	B+ / 8.8	19.84%	C+ / 6.4

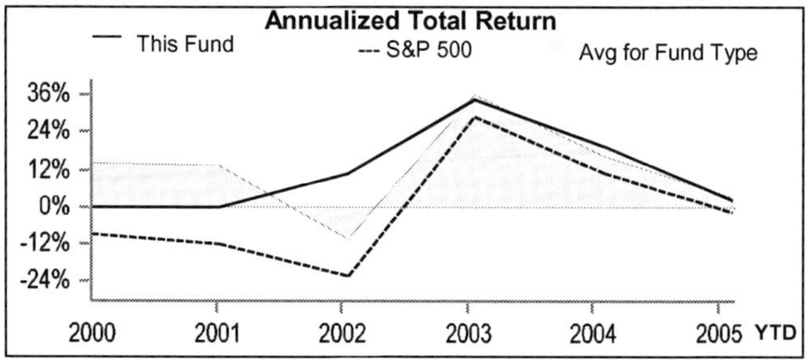

Nuveen Select Maturities Muni (NIM) C Fair

Fund Family: Nuveen Advisory Corp.
Fund Type: Municipal - National
Inception Date: September 18, 1992

Data Date	Weiss Investment Rating	Net Assets ($Mil)	Price	Perfor-mance Rating/Pts	Total Return Y-T-D	Risk Rating/Pts
6-05	C	128.43	9.72	D+ / 2.7	6.64%	B / 8.4
2004	D	127.13	9.34	E+ / 0.7	2.82%	B / 8.2
2003	D+	128.15	9.60	D- / 1.1	2.64%	B / 8.7

Major Rating Factors:
Disappointing performance is the major factor driving the C (Fair) Weiss Investment Rating for Nuveen Select Maturities Muni. The fund currently has a performance rating of D+ (Weak) based on an annualized return of 3.83% over the last three years and a total return of 6.64% year to date 2005. Factored into the performance evaluation is an expense ratio of 0.60% (very low).

The fund's risk rating is currently B (Good). It carries a beta of 1.21, meaning it is expected to move 12.1% for every 10% move in the market. Volatility, as measured by both the semi-deviation and a drawdown factor, is considered low. As of June 30, 2005, Nuveen Select Maturities Muni traded at a discount of 6.18% below its net asset value, which is worse than its one-year historical average discount of 7.27%.

John Miller has been running the fund for 4 years and currently receives a manager quality ranking of 38 (0=worst, 99=best). This fund offers only a moderate level of risk but investors looking for strong performance are still waiting.

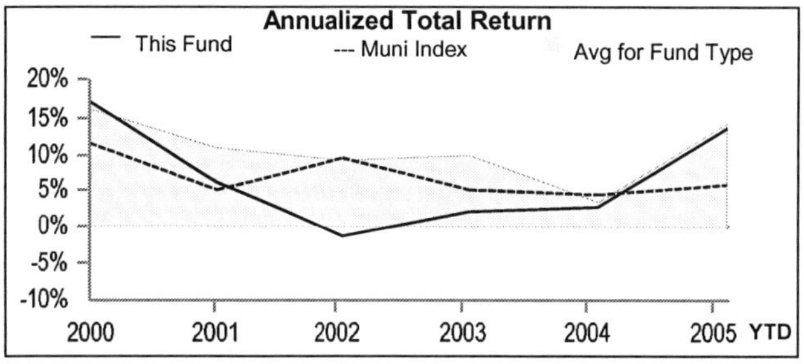

Nuveen Select Quality Muni (NQS) B- Good

Fund Family: Nuveen Advisory Corp.
Fund Type: Municipal - National
Inception Date: March 21, 1991

Data Date	Weiss Investment Rating	Net Assets ($Mil)	Price	Perfor-mance Rating/Pts	Total Return Y-T-D	Risk Rating/Pts
6-05	B-	539.04	15.12	C+ / 6.9	3.83%	B- / 7.5
2004	B-	524.06	15.05	C+ / 6.9	6.27%	B- / 7.8
2003	B	529.54	15.00	C+ / 5.8	10.41%	B / 8.8

Major Rating Factors:
Nuveen Select Quality Muni receives a Weiss Investment Rating of B- (Good). The fund currently has a performance rating of C+ (Fair) based on an annualized return of 8.12% over the last three years and a total return of 3.83% year to date 2005. Factored into the performance evaluation is an expense ratio of 1.18% (low).

The fund's risk rating is currently B- (Good). It carries a beta of 2.08, meaning it is expected to move 20.8% for every 10% move in the market. Volatility, as measured by both the semi-deviation and a drawdown factor, is considered low. As of June 30, 2005, Nuveen Select Quality Muni traded at a discount of 4.91% below its net asset value, which is worse than its one-year historical average discount of 5.91%.

Tom Spalding has been running the fund for 3 years and currently receives a manager quality ranking of 42 (0=worst, 99=best). If you desire an average level of risk, then this fund may be an option.

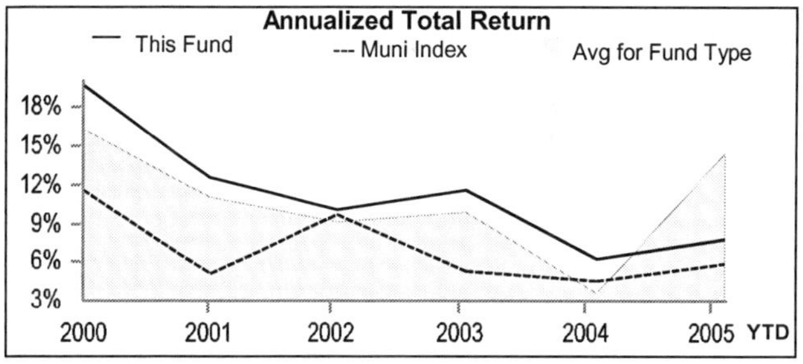

Nuveen Select T-F Inc Portf (NXP) C+ Fair

Fund Family: Nuveen Advisory Corp.
Fund Type: Municipal - National
Inception Date: March 19, 1992

Data Date	Weiss Investment Rating	Net Assets ($Mil)	Price	Perfor-mance Rating/Pts	Total Return Y-T-D	Risk Rating/Pts
6-05	C+	244.79	14.00	C- / 3.7	7.55%	B / 8.1
2004	C	240.74	13.34	D+ / 2.5	3.77%	B / 8.9
2003	C-	242.19	13.70	D / 1.7	4.98%	B / 8.9

Major Rating Factors:
Middle of the road best describes Nuveen Select T-F Inc Portf whose Weiss Investment Rating is currently a C+ (Fair). The fund currently has a performance rating of C- (Fair) based on an annualized return of 5.44% over the last three years and a total return of 7.55% year to date 2005. Factored into the performance evaluation is an expense ratio of 0.32% (very low).

The fund's risk rating is currently B (Good). It carries a beta of 1.35, meaning it is expected to move 13.5% for every 10% move in the market. Volatility, as measured by both the semi-deviation and a drawdown factor, is considered low. As of June 30, 2005, Nuveen Select T-F Inc Portf traded at a discount of 6.35% below its net asset value, which is worse than its one-year historical average discount of 6.80%.

Tom Spalding has been running the fund for 6 years and currently receives a manager quality ranking of 46 (0=worst, 99=best). If you desire an average level of risk, then this fund may be an option.

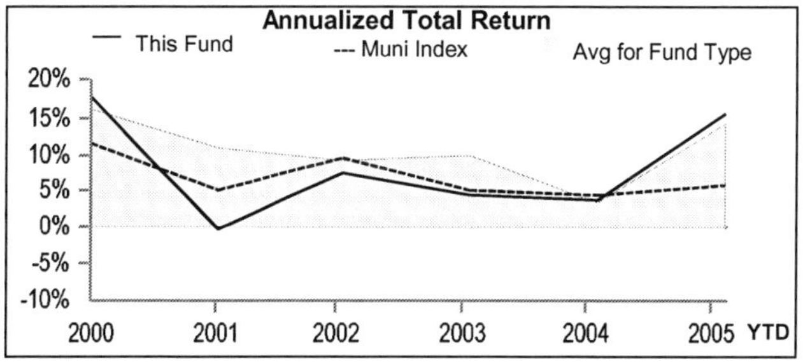

Nuveen Select T-F Inc Portf 2 (NXQ) C Fair

Fund Family: Nuveen Advisory Corp.
Fund Type: Municipal - National
Inception Date: May 21, 1992

Major Rating Factors:
Middle of the road best describes Nuveen Select T-F Inc Portf 2 whose Weiss Investment Rating is currently a C (Fair). The fund currently has a performance rating of C- (Fair) based on an annualized return of 4.69% over the last three years and a total return of 6.44% year to date 2005. Factored into the performance evaluation is an expense ratio of 0.36% (very low).

The fund's risk rating is currently B (Good). It carries a beta of 1.44, meaning it is expected to move 14.4% for every 10% move in the market. Volatility, as measured by both the semi-deviation and a drawdown factor, is considered low. As of June 30, 2005, Nuveen Select T-F Inc Portf 2 traded at a discount of 8.03% below its net asset value, which is worse than its one-year historical average discount of 8.99%.

Tom Spalding has been running the fund for 6 years and currently receives a manager quality ranking of 33 (0=worst, 99=best). If you desire an average level of risk, then this fund may be an option.

Data Date	Weiss Investment Rating	Net Assets ($Mil)	Price	Performance Rating/Pts	Total Return Y-T-D	Risk Rating/Pts
6-05	C	258.72	13.51	C- / 3.1	6.44%	B / 8.2
2004	C	252.94	13.01	D+ / 2.5	3.61%	B / 8.8
2003	C-	255.05	13.19	D / 1.8	4.01%	B+ / 9.1

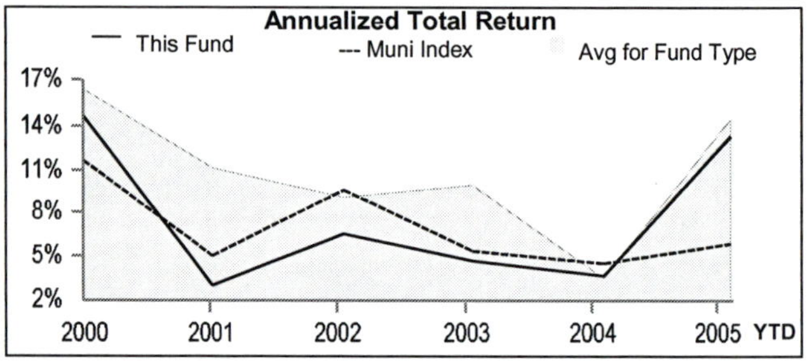

Nuveen Select Tax-Free Inc 3 (NXR) C+ Fair

Fund Family: Nuveen Advisory Corp.
Fund Type: Municipal - National
Inception Date: July 24, 1992

Major Rating Factors:
Middle of the road best describes Nuveen Select Tax-Free Inc 3 whose Weiss Investment Rating is currently a C+ (Fair). The fund currently has a performance rating of C- (Fair) based on an annualized return of 5.82% over the last three years and a total return of 6.63% year to date 2005. Factored into the performance evaluation is an expense ratio of 0.36% (very low).

The fund's risk rating is currently B (Good). It carries a beta of 1.51, meaning it is expected to move 15.1% for every 10% move in the market. Volatility, as measured by both the semi-deviation and a drawdown factor, is considered low. As of June 30, 2005, Nuveen Select Tax-Free Inc 3 traded at a discount of 7.69% below its net asset value, which is worse than its one-year historical average discount of 9.01%.

Tom Spalding has been running the fund for 6 years and currently receives a manager quality ranking of 39 (0=worst, 99=best). If you desire an average level of risk, then this fund may be an option.

Data Date	Weiss Investment Rating	Net Assets ($Mil)	Price	Performance Rating/Pts	Total Return Y-T-D	Risk Rating/Pts
6-05	C+	188.74	13.44	C- / 4.2	6.63%	B / 8.3
2004	C	184.30	12.92	D+ / 2.5	3.71%	B+ / 9.1
2003	C	185.53	13.09	D+ / 2.4	4.43%	B+ / 9.0

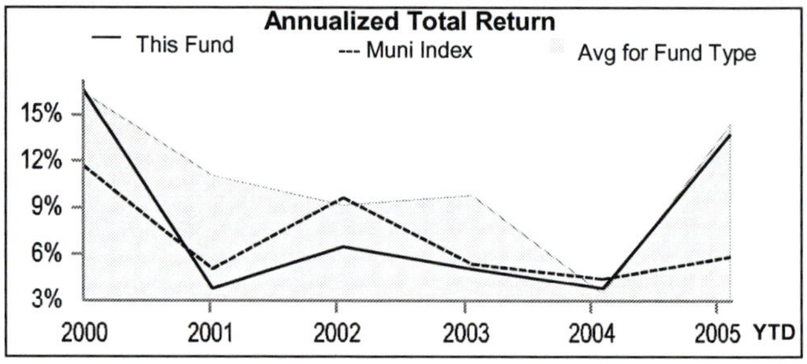

Nuveen Sr Inc (NSL) C- Fair

Fund Family: Nuveen Advisory Corp.
Fund Type: Loan Participation
Inception Date: October 27, 1999

Major Rating Factors:
Disappointing performance is the major factor driving the C- (Fair) Weiss Investment Rating for Nuveen Sr Inc. The fund currently has a performance rating of D (Weak) based on an annualized return of 10.90% over the last three years and a total return of -5.97% year to date 2005. Factored into the performance evaluation is an expense ratio of 2.38% (high).

The fund's risk rating is currently B- (Good). It carries a beta of -27.23, meaning the fund's expected move will be -272.3% for every 10% move in the market. Volatility, as measured by both the semi-deviation and a drawdown factor, is considered low. As of June 30, 2005, Nuveen Sr Inc traded at a premium of 1.30% above its net asset value, which is better than its one-year historical average premium of 10.89%.

Symphony Asset Management has been running the fund for 4 years and currently receives a manager quality ranking of 97 (0=worst, 99=best). This fund offers only a moderate level of risk but investors looking for strong performance are still waiting.

Data Date	Weiss Investment Rating	Net Assets ($Mil)	Price	Performance Rating/Pts	Total Return Y-T-D	Risk Rating/Pts
6-05	C-	252.44	8.57	D / 1.6	-5.97%	B- / 7.8
2004	C+	253.10	9.43	C / 5.4	6.98%	C+ / 6.7
2003	D+	242.39	9.23	C- / 3.8	36.14%	C / 5.3

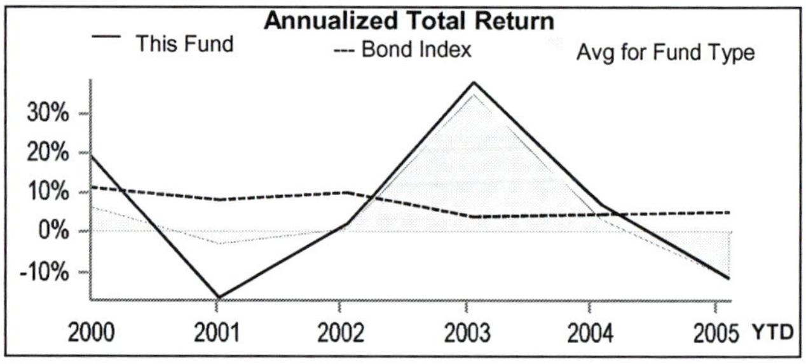

Nuveen TX Quality Inc Muni (NTX) B+ Good

Fund Family: Nuveen Advisory Corp.
Fund Type: Municipal - Single State
Inception Date: October 17, 1991

Major Rating Factors:
Strong performance is the major factor driving the B+ (Good) Weiss Investment Rating for Nuveen TX Quality Inc Muni. The fund currently has a performance rating of B (Good) based on an annualized return of 7.88% over the last three years and a total return of 9.56% year to date 2005. Factored into the performance evaluation is an expense ratio of 1.14% (low).

The fund's risk rating is currently C+ (Fair). It carries a beta of 1.65, meaning it is expected to move 16.5% for every 10% move in the market. Volatility, as measured by both the semi-deviation and a drawdown factor, is considered low. As of June 30, 2005, Nuveen TX Quality Inc Muni traded at a premium of 2.05% above its net asset value, which is worse than its one-year historical average discount of 1.26%.

Cathryn Steeves has been running the fund for 14 years and currently receives a manager quality ranking of 58 (0=worst, 99=best). If you desire only a moderate level of risk and strong performance, then this fund is an excellent option.

Data Date	Weiss Investment Rating	Net Assets ($Mil)	Price	Perfor-mance Rating/Pts	Total Return Y-T-D	Risk Rating/Pts
6-05	B+	148.39	15.96	B / 7.6	9.56%	C+ / 6.4
2004	C+	145.31	15.01	C / 5.2	1.66%	B- / 7.6
2003	B	146.74	15.25	C+ / 6.9	11.45%	B / 8.7

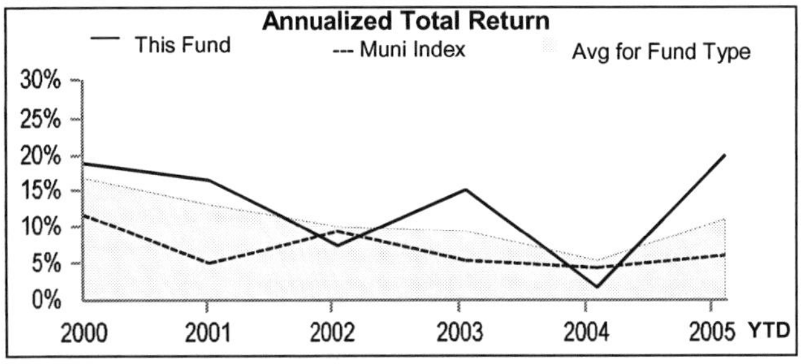

Nuveen VA Div Adv Muni 2 (NNB) A- Excellent

Fund Family: Nuveen Advisory Corp.
Fund Type: Municipal - Single State
Inception Date: November 15, 2001

Major Rating Factors:
Strong performance is the major factor driving the A- (Excellent) Weiss Investment Rating for Nuveen VA Div Adv Muni 2. The fund currently has a performance rating of B+ (Good) based on an annualized return of 11.14% over the last three years and a total return of 1.92% year to date 2005. Factored into the performance evaluation is an expense ratio of 0.74% (very low).

The fund's risk rating is currently C+ (Fair). It carries a beta of 1.99, meaning it is expected to move 19.9% for every 10% move in the market. Volatility, as measured by both the semi-deviation and a drawdown factor, is considered low. As of June 30, 2005, Nuveen VA Div Adv Muni 2 traded at a premium of 7.80% above its net asset value, which is worse than its one-year historical average premium of 4.97%.

Paul Brennan has been running the fund for 4 years and currently receives a manager quality ranking of 71 (0=worst, 99=best). If you desire only a moderate level of risk and strong performance, then this fund is an excellent option.

Data Date	Weiss Investment Rating	Net Assets ($Mil)	Price	Perfor-mance Rating/Pts	Total Return Y-T-D	Risk Rating/Pts
6-05	A-	90.08	17.00	B+ / 8.4	1.92%	C+ / 6.5
2004	A-	88.02	17.14	B+ / 8.3	6.77%	C+ / 6.7

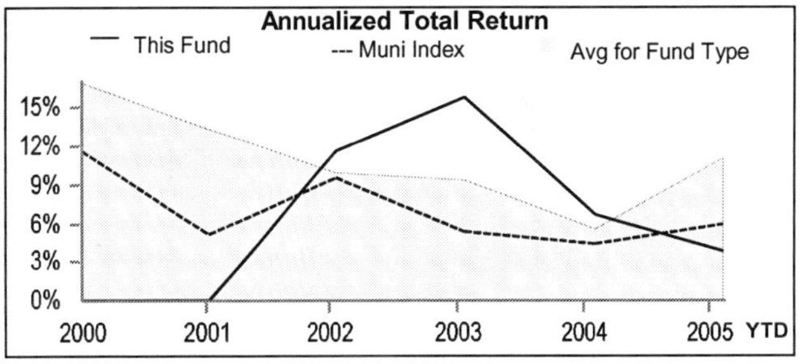

Nuveen VA Div Adv Muni Fund (NGB) B+ Good

Fund Family: Nuveen Advisory Corp.
Fund Type: Municipal - Single State
Inception Date: January 26, 2001

Major Rating Factors:
Strong performance is the major factor driving the B+ (Good) Weiss Investment Rating for Nuveen VA Div Adv Muni Fund. The fund currently has a performance rating of B+ (Good) based on an annualized return of 12.22% over the last three years and a total return of 0.76% year to date 2005. Factored into the performance evaluation is an expense ratio of 0.80% (very low).

The fund's risk rating is currently C+ (Fair). It carries a beta of 2.11, meaning it is expected to move 21.1% for every 10% move in the market. Volatility, as measured by both the semi-deviation and a drawdown factor, is considered low. As of June 30, 2005, Nuveen VA Div Adv Muni Fund traded at a premium of 12.35% above its net asset value, which is better than its one-year historical average premium of 12.71%.

Paul Brennan has been running the fund for 4 years and currently receives a manager quality ranking of 65 (0=worst, 99=best). If you desire only a moderate level of risk and strong performance, then this fund is an excellent option.

Data Date	Weiss Investment Rating	Net Assets ($Mil)	Price	Perfor-mance Rating/Pts	Total Return Y-T-D	Risk Rating/Pts
6-05	B+	48.78	17.47	B+ / 8.3	0.76%	C+ / 6.3
2004	A-	46.91	17.83	B+ / 8.5	11.29%	C+ / 6.5

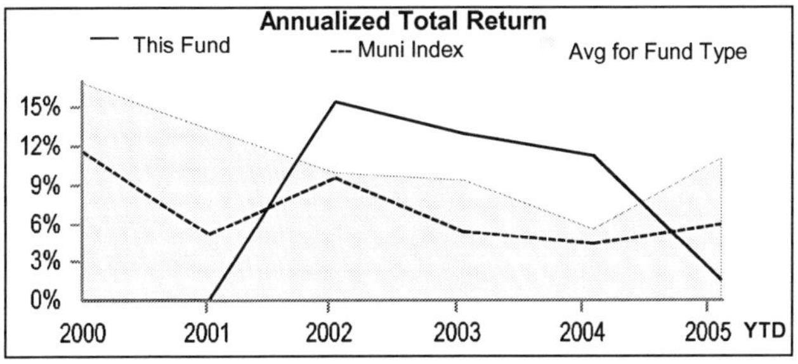

Nuveen VA Premium Income Municipal (NPV) C Fair

Fund Family: Nuveen Advisory Corp.
Fund Type: Municipal - Single State
Inception Date: March 18, 1993

Major Rating Factors:
Middle of the road best describes Nuveen VA Premium Income Municipal whose Weiss Investment Rating is currently a C (Fair). The fund currently has a performance rating of C (Fair) based on an annualized return of 6.85% over the last three years and a total return of 1.36% year to date 2005. Factored into the performance evaluation is an expense ratio of 1.18% (low).

The fund's risk rating is currently C+ (Fair). It carries a beta of 1.76, meaning it is expected to move 17.6% for every 10% move in the market. Volatility, as measured by both the semi-deviation and a drawdown factor, is considered low. As of June 30, 2005, Nuveen VA Premium Income Municipal traded at a premium of 9.13% above its net asset value, which is worse than its one-year historical average premium of 9.08%.

Paul Brennan has been running the fund for 6 years and currently receives a manager quality ranking of 43 (0=worst, 99=best). If you desire an average level of risk, then this fund may be an option.

Data Date	Weiss Investment Rating	Net Assets ($Mil)	Price	Performance Rating/Pts	Total Return Y-T-D	Risk Rating/Pts
6-05	C	141.02	17.34	C / 5.1	1.36%	C+ / 6.5
2004	B+	136.88	17.57	B- / 7.5	8.17%	C+ / 6.9
2003	C+	137.49	17.01	C / 4.4	3.24%	B / 8.7

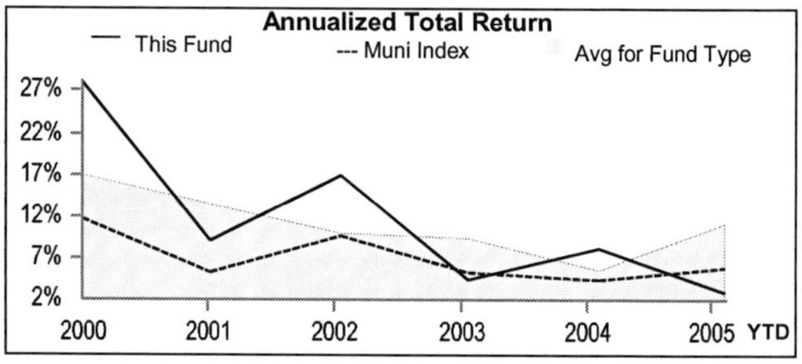

Pacholder High Yield Fund (PHF) C Fair

Fund Family: Pacholder Company, LLC
Fund Type: Corporate - High Yield
Inception Date: November 23, 1988

Major Rating Factors:
Strong performance is the major factor driving the C (Fair) Weiss Investment Rating for Pacholder High Yield Fund. The fund currently has a performance rating of B (Good) based on an annualized return of 19.28% over the last three years and a total return of 2.67% year to date 2005. Factored into the performance evaluation is an expense ratio of 3.03% (high).

The fund's risk rating is currently C- (Fair). It carries a beta of 1.93, meaning it is expected to move 19.3% for every 10% move in the market. Volatility, as measured by both the semi-deviation and a drawdown factor, is considered average. As of June 30, 2005, Pacholder High Yield Fund traded at a premium of 6.37% above its net asset value, which is worse than its one-year historical average premium of 3.23%.

William J. Morgan has been running the fund for 5 years and currently receives a manager quality ranking of 9 (0=worst, 99=best). If you desire an average level of risk and strong performance, then this fund is a good option.

Data Date	Weiss Investment Rating	Net Assets ($Mil)	Price	Performance Rating/Pts	Total Return Y-T-D	Risk Rating/Pts
6-05	C	123.18	9.68	B / 8.1	2.67%	C- / 3.3
2004	C-	112.38	9.69	B / 7.7	17.14%	D+ / 2.7
2003	C	96.59	9.16	B+ / 8.4	67.56%	C- / 3.1

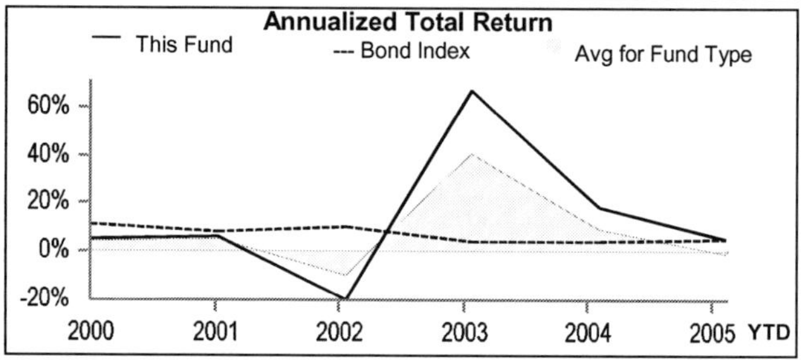

Petroleum and Resources Corp. (PEO) A Excellent

Fund Family: Adams Express/Petroleum & Resources
Fund Type: Energy/Natural Resources
Inception Date: N/A

Major Rating Factors:
Strong performance is the major factor driving the A (Excellent) Weiss Investment Rating for Petroleum and Resources Corp.. The fund currently has a performance rating of B (Good) based on an annualized return of 15.59% over the last three years and a total return of 17.45% year to date 2005. Factored into the performance evaluation is an expense ratio of 0.56% (very low).

The fund's risk rating is currently B (Good). It carries a beta of 0.86, meaning the fund's expected move will be 8.6% for every 10% move in the market. Volatility, as measured by both the semi-deviation and a drawdown factor, is considered low. As of June 30, 2005, Petroleum and Resources Corp. traded at a discount of 7.94% below its net asset value, which is better than its one-year historical average discount of 7.42%.

Douglas G. Ober has been running the fund for 19 years and currently receives a manager quality ranking of 44 (0=worst, 99=best). If you desire only a moderate level of risk and strong performance, then this fund is an excellent option.

Data Date	Weiss Investment Rating	Net Assets ($Mil)	Price	Performance Rating/Pts	Total Return Y-T-D	Risk Rating/Pts
6-05	A	618.89	30.01	B / 7.8	17.45%	B- / 7.3
2004	C	568.51	25.78	C / 4.6	14.33%	C+ / 6.6
2003	D	476.55	23.10	D+ / 2.7	27.55%	C / 5.2

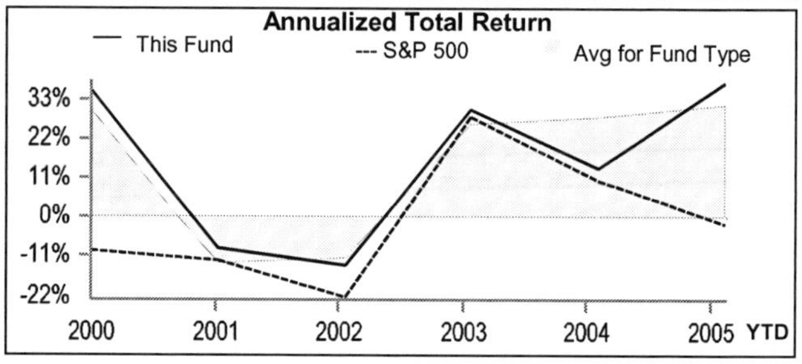

PIMCO CA Municipal Income Fund (PCQ) B- Good

Fund Family: PIMCO Advisors L.P.
Fund Type: Municipal - Single State
Inception Date: June 25, 2001

Major Rating Factors:
PIMCO CA Municipal Income Fund receives a Weiss Investment Rating of B- (Good). The fund currently has a performance rating of C+ (Fair) based on an annualized return of 6.62% over the last three years and a total return of 12.58% year to date 2005. Factored into the performance evaluation is an expense ratio of 1.00% (low).

The fund's risk rating is currently B- (Good). It carries a beta of 1.62, meaning it is expected to move 16.2% for every 10% move in the market. Volatility, as measured by both the semi-deviation and a drawdown factor, is considered low. As of June 30, 2005, PIMCO CA Municipal Income Fund traded at a discount of .27% below its net asset value, which is worse than its one-year historical average discount of 2.31%.

Mark V. McCray has been running the fund for 4 years and currently receives a manager quality ranking of 48 (0=worst, 99=best). If you desire an average level of risk, then this fund may be an option.

Data Date	Weiss Investment Rating	Net Assets ($Mil)	Price	Performance Rating/Pts	Total Return Y-T-D	Risk Rating/Pts
6-05	B-	259.98	14.75	C+ / 6.9	12.58%	B- / 7.2
2004	C-	247.86	13.53	D+ / 2.7	8.10%	B / 8.2

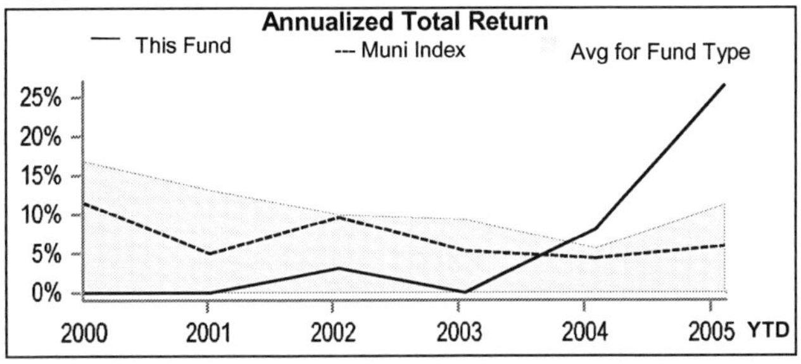

PIMCO Commercial Mortgage Trust (PCM) C- Fair

Fund Family: PIMCO Advisors L.P.
Fund Type: Mortgage
Inception Date: September 2, 1993

Major Rating Factors:
Middle of the road best describes PIMCO Commercial Mortgage Trust whose Weiss Investment Rating is currently a C- (Fair). The fund currently has a performance rating of C (Fair) based on an annualized return of 8.86% over the last three years and a total return of 12.79% year to date 2005. Factored into the performance evaluation is an expense ratio of 1.75% (above average).

The fund's risk rating is currently C (Fair). It carries a beta of 3.14, meaning it is expected to move 31.4% for every 10% move in the market. Volatility, as measured by both the semi-deviation and a drawdown factor, is considered average. As of June 30, 2005, PIMCO Commercial Mortgage Trust traded at a premium of 14.72% above its net asset value, which is worse than its one-year historical average premium of 10.52%.

Bill Powers has been running the fund for 12 years and currently receives a manager quality ranking of 25 (0=worst, 99=best). If you desire an average level of risk, then this fund may be an option.

Data Date	Weiss Investment Rating	Net Assets ($Mil)	Price	Performance Rating/Pts	Total Return Y-T-D	Risk Rating/Pts
6-05	C-	140.27	14.34	C / 4.3	12.79%	C / 5.3
2004	D	136.35	13.17	D / 1.7	-1.20%	B- / 7.0
2003	C	141.95	14.55	C / 4.8	9.60%	B- / 7.5

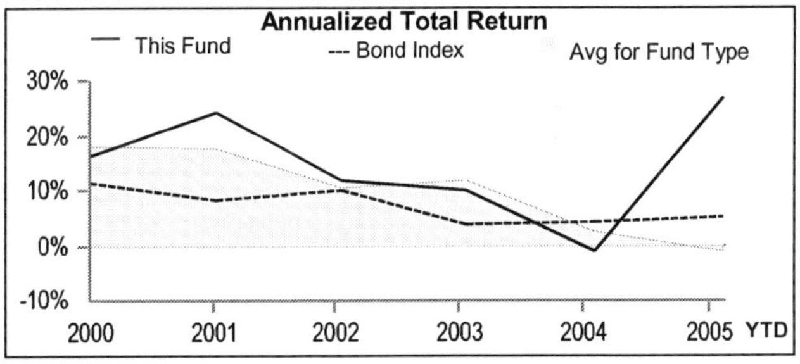

PIMCO Corporate Income Fund (PCN) C+ Fair

Fund Family: PIMCO Advisors L.P.
Fund Type: Corporate - Investment Grade
Inception Date: December 21, 2001

Major Rating Factors:
Middle of the road best describes PIMCO Corporate Income Fund whose Weiss Investment Rating is currently a C+ (Fair). The fund currently has a performance rating of C+ (Fair) based on an annualized return of 13.06% over the last three years and a total return of 5.05% year to date 2005. Factored into the performance evaluation is an expense ratio of 1.13% (low).

The fund's risk rating is currently C+ (Fair). It carries a beta of 1.81, meaning it is expected to move 18.1% for every 10% move in the market. Volatility, as measured by both the semi-deviation and a drawdown factor, is considered low. As of June 30, 2005, PIMCO Corporate Income Fund traded at a premium of 1.32% above its net asset value, which is worse than its one-year historical average discount of 1.26%.

David C. Hinman, CFA has been running the fund for 4 years and currently receives a manager quality ranking of 53 (0=worst, 99=best). If you desire an average level of risk, then this fund may be an option.

Data Date	Weiss Investment Rating	Net Assets ($Mil)	Price	Performance Rating/Pts	Total Return Y-T-D	Risk Rating/Pts
6-05	C+	529.87	15.40	C+ / 6.4	5.05%	C+ / 6.1

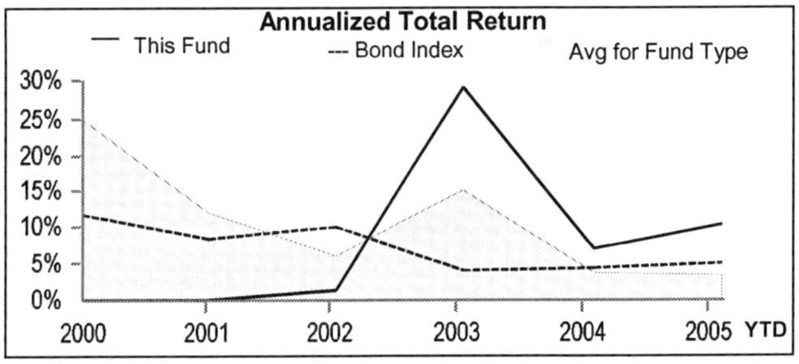

PIMCO Municipal Income Fund (PMF) A+ Excellent

Fund Family: PIMCO Advisors L.P.
Fund Type: Municipal - National
Inception Date: June 25, 2001

Data Date	Weiss Investment Rating	Net Assets ($Mil)	Price	Performance Rating/Pts	Total Return Y-T-D	Risk Rating/Pts
6-05	A+	360.70	15.54	B+ / 8.6	14.14%	B- / 7.6
2004	C+	341.78	14.07	C- / 4.0	8.97%	B / 8.6

Major Rating Factors:
Strong performance is the major factor driving the A+ (Excellent) Weiss Investment Rating for PIMCO Municipal Income Fund. The fund currently has a performance rating of B+ (Good) based on an annualized return of 9.08% over the last three years and a total return of 14.14% year to date 2005. Factored into the performance evaluation is an expense ratio of 0.97% (low).

The fund's risk rating is currently B- (Good). It carries a beta of 1.67, meaning it is expected to move 16.7% for every 10% move in the market. Volatility, as measured by both the semi-deviation and a drawdown factor, is considered low. As of June 30, 2005, PIMCO Municipal Income Fund traded at a premium of 2.85% above its net asset value, which is worse than its one-year historical average premium of .04%.

Mark V. McCray has been running the fund for 4 years and currently receives a manager quality ranking of 66 (0=worst, 99=best). If you desire only a moderate level of risk and strong performance, then this fund is an excellent option.

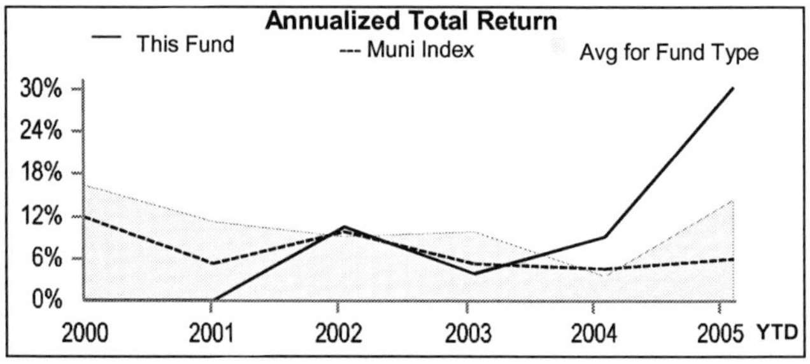

PIMCO NY Muni Income Fund (PNF) A Excellent

Fund Family: PIMCO Advisors L.P.
Fund Type: Municipal - Single State
Inception Date: June 25, 2001

Data Date	Weiss Investment Rating	Net Assets ($Mil)	Price	Performance Rating/Pts	Total Return Y-T-D	Risk Rating/Pts
6-05	A	102.11	14.89	B+ / 8.8	19.24%	C+ / 6.3
2004	C-	98.92	12.90	D / 1.9	3.46%	B / 8.1

Major Rating Factors:
Strong performance is the major factor driving the A (Excellent) Weiss Investment Rating for PIMCO NY Muni Income Fund. The fund currently has a performance rating of B+ (Good) based on an annualized return of 8.40% over the last three years and a total return of 19.24% year to date 2005. Factored into the performance evaluation is an expense ratio of 1.12% (low).

The fund's risk rating is currently C+ (Fair). It carries a beta of 1.80, meaning it is expected to move 18.0% for every 10% move in the market. Volatility, as measured by both the semi-deviation and a drawdown factor, is considered low. As of June 30, 2005, PIMCO NY Muni Income Fund traded at a premium of 6.81% above its net asset value, which is worse than its one-year historical average premium of .17%.

Mark V. McCray has been running the fund for 4 years and currently receives a manager quality ranking of 56 (0=worst, 99=best). If you desire only a moderate level of risk and strong performance, then this fund is an excellent option.

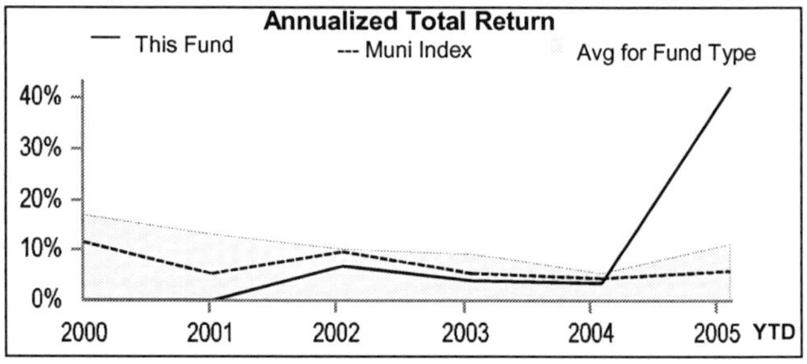

PIMCO Strategic Glob Gov Fund (RCS) C- Fair

Fund Family: PIMCO Advisors L.P.
Fund Type: Global
Inception Date: February 24, 1994

Data Date	Weiss Investment Rating	Net Assets ($Mil)	Price	Performance Rating/Pts	Total Return Y-T-D	Risk Rating/Pts
6-05	C-	399.27	12.67	C+ / 6.6	8.35%	C- / 3.6
2004	C	394.45	12.07	C+ / 6.1	6.11%	C / 5.3
2003	C+	386.44	12.28	C / 5.3	10.70%	B- / 7.4

Major Rating Factors:
Middle of the road best describes PIMCO Strategic Glob Gov Fund whose Weiss Investment Rating is currently a C- (Fair). The fund currently has a performance rating of C+ (Fair) based on an annualized return of 12.24% over the last three years and a total return of 8.35% year to date 2005. Factored into the performance evaluation is an expense ratio of 1.06% (low).

The fund's risk rating is currently C- (Fair). It carries a beta of 0.65, meaning the fund's expected move will be 6.5% for every 10% move in the market. Volatility, as measured by both the semi-deviation and a drawdown factor, is considered average. As of June 30, 2005, PIMCO Strategic Glob Gov Fund traded at a premium of 16.45% above its net asset value, which is worse than its one-year historical average premium of 7.98%.

Daniel J. Ivascyn has been running the fund for 11 years and currently receives a manager quality ranking of 76 (0=worst, 99=best). If you desire an average level of risk, then this fund may be an option.

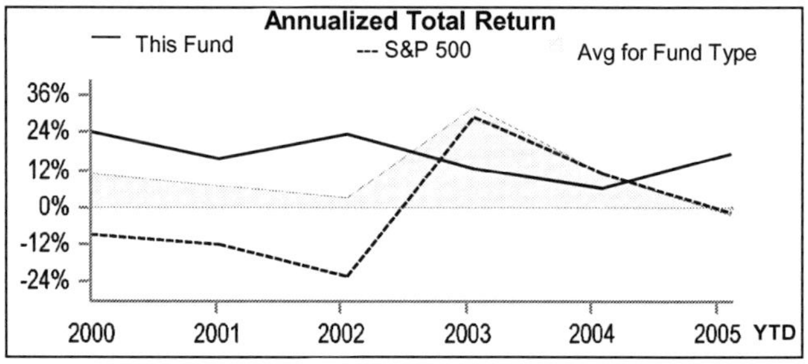

Pioneer High Income Trust (PHT) B- Good

Fund Family: Pioneer Management Corp.
Fund Type: Corporate - High Yield
Inception Date: April 25, 2002

Data Date	Weiss Investment Rating	Net Assets ($Mil)	Price	Perfor-mance Rating/Pts	Total Return Y-T-D	Risk Rating/Pts
6-05	B-	438.30	16.20	B- / 7.5	-0.08%	C / 5.5

Major Rating Factors:
Strong performance is the major factor driving the B- (Good) Weiss Investment Rating for Pioneer High Income Trust. The fund currently has a performance rating of B- (Good) based on an annualized return of 18.29% over the last three years and a total return of -0.08% year to date 2005. Factored into the performance evaluation is an expense ratio of 1.00% (low).

The fund's risk rating is currently C (Fair). It carries a beta of 1.38, meaning it is expected to move 13.8% for every 10% move in the market. Volatility, as measured by both the semi-deviation and a drawdown factor, is considered average. As of June 30, 2005, Pioneer High Income Trust traded at a premium of .31% above its net asset value, which is worse than its one-year historical average discount of .81%.

Ken Taubes currently receives a manager quality ranking of 61 (0=worst, 99=best). If you desire an average level of risk and strong performance, then this fund is a good option.

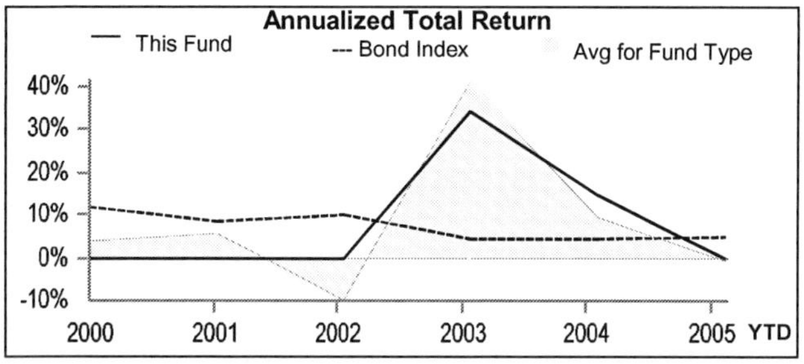

Pioneer Interest Shares (MUO) C- Fair

Fund Family: Pioneer Management Corp.
Fund Type: General - Investment Grade
Inception Date: November 3, 1971

Data Date	Weiss Investment Rating	Net Assets ($Mil)	Price	Perfor-mance Rating/Pts	Total Return Y-T-D	Risk Rating/Pts
6-05	C-	96.53	11.43	D / 1.7	2.78%	B / 8.3
2004	C-	91.20	11.45	D+ / 2.3	5.76%	B / 8.6
2003	C-	93.82	11.48	D+ / 2.6	8.42%	B / 8.3

Major Rating Factors:
Disappointing performance is the major factor driving the C- (Fair) Weiss Investment Rating for Pioneer Interest Shares. The fund currently has a performance rating of D (Weak) based on an annualized return of 5.06% over the last three years and a total return of 2.78% year to date 2005. Factored into the performance evaluation is an expense ratio of 0.77% (very low).

The fund's risk rating is currently B (Good). It carries a beta of 1.51, meaning it is expected to move 15.1% for every 10% move in the market. Volatility, as measured by both the semi-deviation and a drawdown factor, is considered low. As of June 30, 2005, Pioneer Interest Shares traded at a discount of 9.29% below its net asset value, which is worse than its one-year historical average discount of 10.25%.

Sherman B.Russ has been running the fund for 12 years and currently receives a manager quality ranking of 35 (0=worst, 99=best). This fund offers only a moderate level of risk but investors looking for strong performance are still waiting.

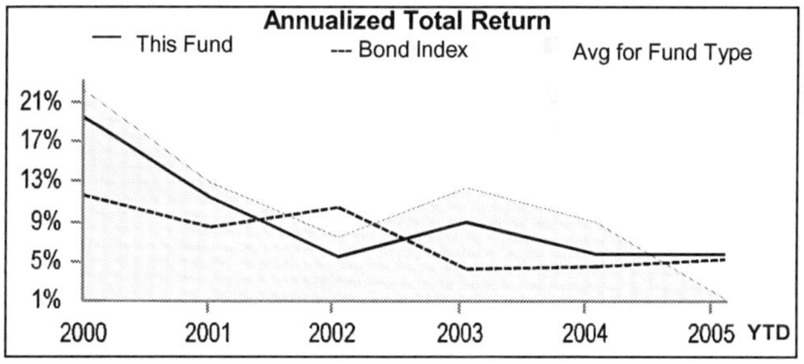

Prospect Street High Inc Portfolio (PHY) E- Very Weak

Fund Family: Highland Capital Management Corp
Fund Type: Corporate - High Yield
Inception Date: December 5, 1988

Data Date	Weiss Investment Rating	Net Assets ($Mil)	Price	Perfor-mance Rating/Pts	Total Return Y-T-D	Risk Rating/Pts
6-05	E-	106.77	3.40	D- / 1.5	0.26%	D- / 1.2
2004	E+	84.76	3.55	C / 4.5	23.44%	D- / 1.2
2003	D+	74.11	3.22	B / 8.1	66.36%	D- / 1.5

Major Rating Factors:
Prospect Street High Inc Portfolio has adopted a very risky asset allocation strategy and currently receives an overall Weiss Investment Rating of E- (Very Weak). The fund has a high level of volatility, as measured by both semi-deviation and drawdown factors. It carries a beta of 1.58, meaning it is expected to move 15.8% for every 10% move in the market. As of June 30, 2005, Prospect Street High Inc Portfolio traded at a discount of 5.03% below its net asset value, which is better than its one-year historical average premium of .64%. Unfortunately, the high level of risk (D-, Weak) failed to pay off as investors endured poor performance.

The fund's performance rating is currently D- (Weak). It has registered an annualized return of 3.40% over the last three years and is up 0.26% year to date 2005. Factored into the performance evaluation is an expense ratio of 1.06% (low).

Highland Capital Mgmt has been running the fund for 17 years and currently receives a manager quality ranking of 0 (0=worst, 99=best). If you can tolerate very high levels of risk in the hope of improved future returns, holding this fund may be an option.

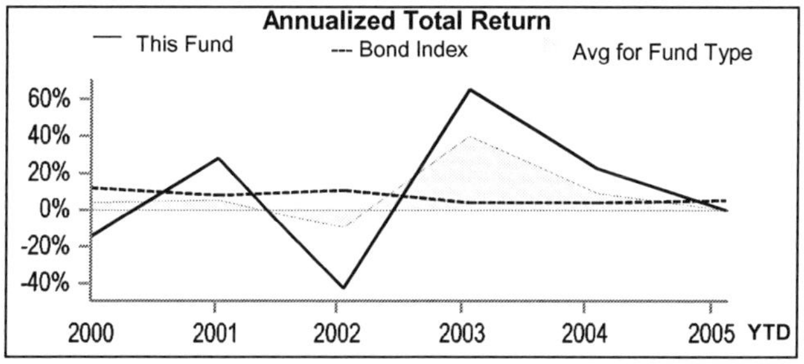

Prospect Street Income Shares (CNN) D- Weak

Fund Family: Highland Capital Management Corp
Fund Type: Global
Inception Date: May 15, 1973

Data Date	Weiss Investment Rating	Net Assets ($Mil)	Price	Performance Rating/Pts	Total Return Y-T-D	Risk Rating/Pts
6-05	D-	66.18	5.99	D / 2.0	-1.68%	C / 4.8
2004	C-	62.04	6.21	C / 4.6	7.77%	C+ / 5.9
2003	D+	62.29	6.43	C- / 3.4	27.03%	C+ / 5.6

Major Rating Factors:
Disappointing performance is the major factor driving the D- (Weak) Weiss Investment Rating for Prospect Street Income Shares. The fund currently has a performance rating of D (Weak) based on an annualized return of 7.49% over the last three years and a total return of -1.68% year to date 2005. Factored into the performance evaluation is an expense ratio of 1.36% (average).

The fund's risk rating is currently C (Fair). It carries a beta of 1.03, meaning that its performance tracks fairly well with that of the overall stock market. Volatility, as measured by both the semi-deviation and a drawdown factor, is considered average. As of June 30, 2005, Prospect Street Income Shares traded at a discount of 9.65% below its net asset value, which is better than its one-year historical average discount of 6.87%.

Highland Capital Mgmt has been running the fund for 32 years and currently receives a manager quality ranking of 34 (0=worst, 99=best). This fund offers an average level of risk but investors looking for strong performance will be frustrated.

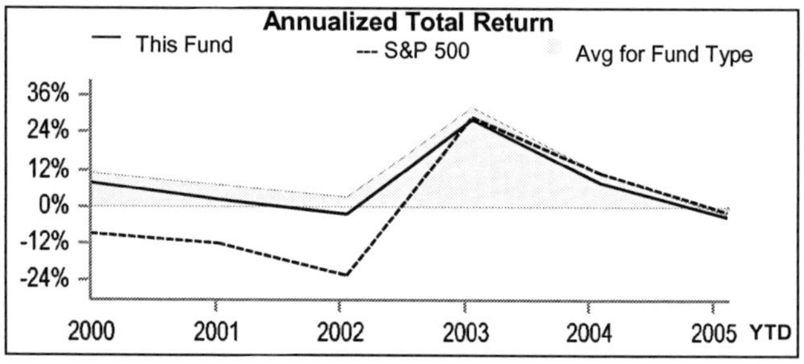

Putnam CA Inv Grade Muni (PCA) C+ Fair

Fund Family: Putnam Management Co.
Fund Type: Municipal - Single State
Inception Date: November 27, 1992

Data Date	Weiss Investment Rating	Net Assets ($Mil)	Price	Performance Rating/Pts	Total Return Y-T-D	Risk Rating/Pts
6-05	C+	70.29	13.65	C- / 3.9	4.52%	B / 8.3
2004	C	66.71	13.40	D+ / 2.7	5.30%	B / 8.4
2003	C-	67.67	13.46	D- / 1.5	4.32%	B / 8.5

Major Rating Factors:
Middle of the road best describes Putnam CA Inv Grade Muni whose Weiss Investment Rating is currently a C+ (Fair). The fund currently has a performance rating of C- (Fair) based on an annualized return of 5.46% over the last three years and a total return of 4.52% year to date 2005. Factored into the performance evaluation is an expense ratio of 1.21% (average).

The fund's risk rating is currently B (Good). It carries a beta of 1.50, meaning it is expected to move 15.0% for every 10% move in the market. Volatility, as measured by both the semi-deviation and a drawdown factor, is considered low. As of June 30, 2005, Putnam CA Inv Grade Muni traded at a discount of 11.76% below its net asset value, which is better than its one-year historical average discount of 11.13%.

Richard P. Wyke has been running the fund for 9 years and currently receives a manager quality ranking of 41 (0=worst, 99=best). If you desire an average level of risk, then this fund may be an option.

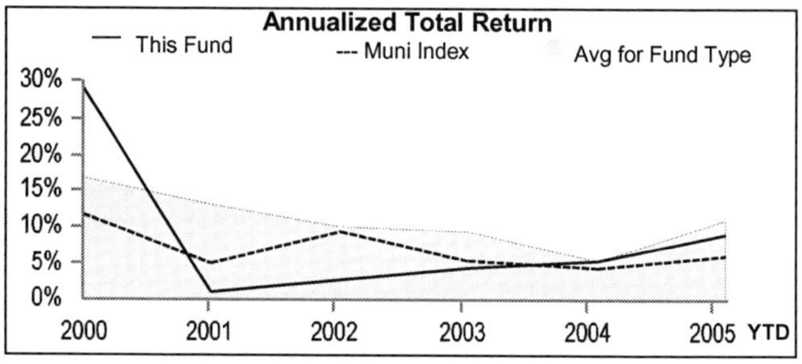

Putnam High Income Bond Fund (PCF) C+ Fair

Fund Family: Putnam Management Co.
Fund Type: Growth and Income
Inception Date: July 9, 1987

Data Date	Weiss Investment Rating	Net Assets ($Mil)	Price	Performance Rating/Pts	Total Return Y-T-D	Risk Rating/Pts
6-05	C+	198.22	7.80	C+ / 5.8	0.60%	C+ / 6.9
2004	C	115.78	8.04	C+ / 6.0	9.39%	C+ / 5.9
2003	C+	106.93	7.88	C+ / 6.0	31.85%	C+ / 6.5

Major Rating Factors:
Middle of the road best describes Putnam High Income Bond Fund whose Weiss Investment Rating is currently a C+ (Fair). The fund currently has a performance rating of C+ (Fair) based on an annualized return of 15.29% over the last three years and a total return of 0.60% year to date 2005. Factored into the performance evaluation is an expense ratio of 1.06% (low).

The fund's risk rating is currently C+ (Fair). It carries a beta of 0.34, meaning the fund's expected move will be 3.4% for every 10% move in the market. Volatility, as measured by both the semi-deviation and a drawdown factor, is considered low. As of June 30, 2005, Putnam High Income Bond Fund traded at a discount of 8.24% below its net asset value, which is worse than its one-year historical average discount of 9.66%.

Charles G. Pohl has been running the fund for 15 years and currently receives a manager quality ranking of 92 (0=worst, 99=best). If you desire an average level of risk, then this fund may be an option.

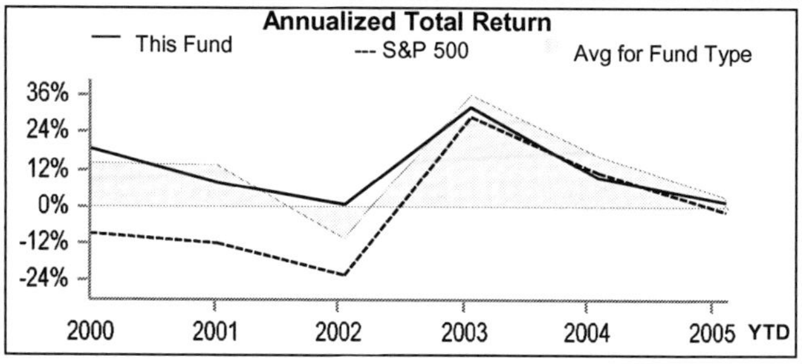

Putnam High Yield Municipal Trust (PYM) C Fair

Fund Family: Putnam Management Co.
Fund Type: Municipal - High Yield
Inception Date: May 25, 1989

Data Date	Weiss Investment Rating	Net Assets ($Mil)	Price	Performance Rating/Pts	Total Return Y-T-D	Risk Rating/Pts
6-05	C	171.80	7.17	C / 4.9	10.80%	C+ / 6.7
2004	D	170.72	6.65	D- / 1.0	2.31%	B- / 7.7
2003	D+	170.23	6.83	D- / 1.3	0.70%	B / 8.1

Major Rating Factors:
Middle of the road best describes Putnam High Yield Municipal Trust whose Weiss Investment Rating is currently a C (Fair). The fund currently has a performance rating of C (Fair) based on an annualized return of 3.63% over the last three years and a total return of 10.80% year to date 2005. Factored into the performance evaluation is an expense ratio of 1.19% (average).

The fund's risk rating is currently C+ (Fair). It carries a beta of 1.80, meaning it is expected to move 18.0% for every 10% move in the market. Volatility, as measured by both the semi-deviation and a drawdown factor, is considered low. As of June 30, 2005, Putnam High Yield Municipal Trust traded at a discount of 8.78% below its net asset value, which is worse than its one-year historical average discount of 13.05%.

Blake E. Anderson has been running the fund for 9 years and currently receives a manager quality ranking of 11 (0=worst, 99=best). If you desire an average level of risk, then this fund may be an option.

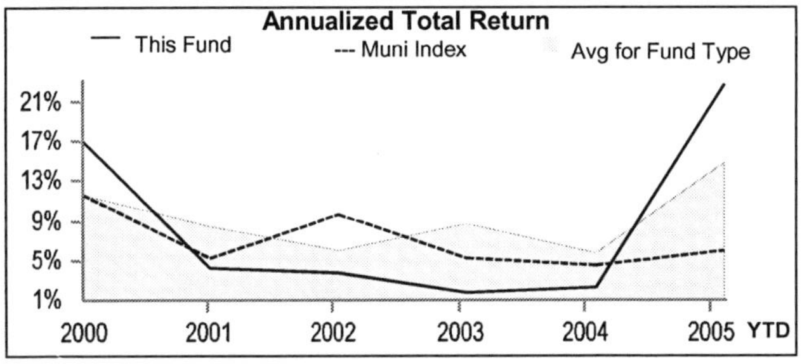

Putnam Investment Grade Muni Tr (PGM) D Weak

Fund Family: Putnam Management Co.
Fund Type: Municipal - National
Inception Date: October 26, 1989

Data Date	Weiss Investment Rating	Net Assets ($Mil)	Price	Performance Rating/Pts	Total Return Y-T-D	Risk Rating/Pts
6-05	D	229.94	9.67	D- / 1.3	4.46%	C+ / 6.8
2004	D	222.45	9.54	D- / 1.1	-5.15%	B- / 7.6
2003	C	229.14	10.81	C- / 4.0	7.97%	B / 8.2

Major Rating Factors:
Disappointing performance is the major factor driving the D (Weak) Weiss Investment Rating for Putnam Investment Grade Muni Tr. The fund currently has a performance rating of D- (Weak) based on an annualized return of 1.12% over the last three years and a total return of 4.46% year to date 2005. Factored into the performance evaluation is an expense ratio of 1.39% (average).

The fund's risk rating is currently C+ (Fair). It carries a beta of 2.26, meaning it is expected to move 22.6% for every 10% move in the market. Volatility, as measured by both the semi-deviation and a drawdown factor, is considered low. As of June 30, 2005, Putnam Investment Grade Muni Tr traded at a discount of 12.88% below its net asset value, which is better than its one-year historical average discount of 10.50%.

Richard P. Wyke has been running the fund for 9 years and currently receives a manager quality ranking of 3 (0=worst, 99=best). This fund offers only a moderate level of risk but investors looking for strong performance are still waiting.

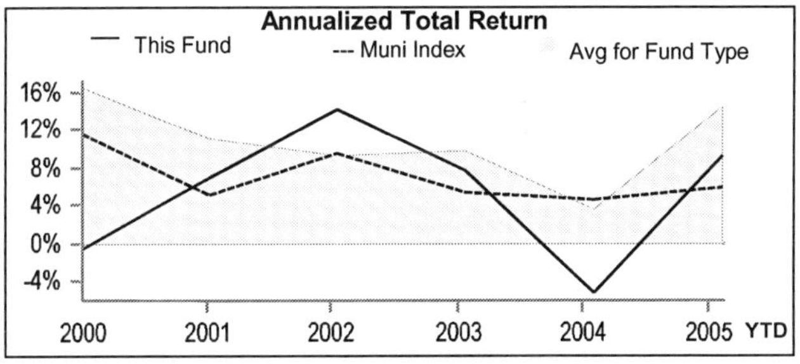

Putnam Managed High Yield Trust (PTM) D+ Weak

Fund Family: Putnam Management Co.
Fund Type: Corporate - High Yield
Inception Date: June 25, 1993

Data Date	Weiss Investment Rating	Net Assets ($Mil)	Price	Performance Rating/Pts	Total Return Y-T-D	Risk Rating/Pts
6-05	D+	69.62	8.16	D+ / 2.7	1.21%	C+ / 5.9
2004	D-	66.18	8.36	D- / 1.5	4.04%	C / 5.0
2003	D	66.69	8.65	D / 2.0	13.46%	C / 4.9

Major Rating Factors:
Disappointing performance is the major factor driving the D+ (Weak) Weiss Investment Rating for Putnam Managed High Yield Trust. The fund currently has a performance rating of D+ (Weak) based on an annualized return of 8.62% over the last three years and a total return of 1.21% year to date 2005. Factored into the performance evaluation is an expense ratio of 1.16% (low).

The fund's risk rating is currently C+ (Fair). It carries a beta of 1.42, meaning it is expected to move 14.2% for every 10% move in the market. Volatility, as measured by both the semi-deviation and a drawdown factor, is considered low. As of June 30, 2005, Putnam Managed High Yield Trust traded at a discount of 10.33% below its net asset value, which is worse than its one-year historical average discount of 10.42%.

Jennifer Leichter has been running the fund for 12 years and currently receives a manager quality ranking of 3 (0=worst, 99=best). This fund offers only a moderate level of risk but investors looking for strong performance are still waiting.

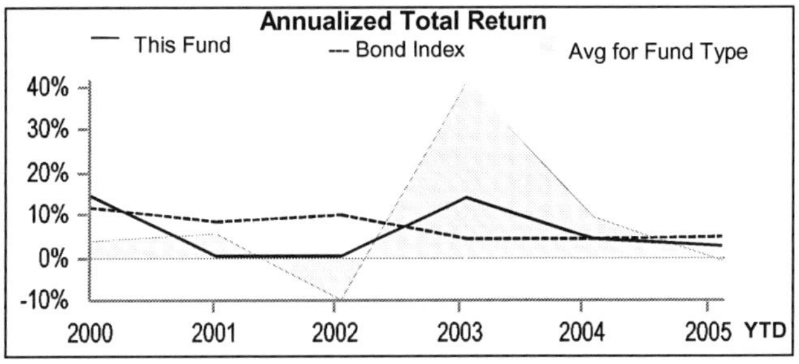

Putnam Managed Muni Inc Tr (PMM) B+ Good

Fund Family: Putnam Management Co.
Fund Type: Municipal - National
Inception Date: February 24, 1989

Data Date	Weiss Investment Rating	Net Assets ($Mil)	Price	Performance Rating/Pts	Total Return Y-T-D	Risk Rating/Pts
6-05	B+	390.03	7.88	B / 7.9	13.28%	C+ / 6.9
2004	D+	378.15	7.17	D- / 1.2	4.47%	B- / 7.8
2003	C-	376.87	7.43	D / 2.0	8.27%	B / 8.3

Major Rating Factors:
Strong performance is the major factor driving the B+ (Good) Weiss Investment Rating for Putnam Managed Muni Inc Tr. The fund currently has a performance rating of B (Good) based on an annualized return of 6.88% over the last three years and a total return of 13.28% year to date 2005. Factored into the performance evaluation is an expense ratio of 1.28% (average).

The fund's risk rating is currently C+ (Fair). It carries a beta of 1.91, meaning it is expected to move 19.1% for every 10% move in the market. Volatility, as measured by both the semi-deviation and a drawdown factor, is considered low. As of June 30, 2005, Putnam Managed Muni Inc Tr traded at a discount of 5.40% below its net asset value, which is worse than its one-year historical average discount of 11.22%.

Richard P. Wyke has been running the fund for 9 years and currently receives a manager quality ranking of 30 (0=worst, 99=best). If you desire only a moderate level of risk and strong performance, then this fund is an excellent option.

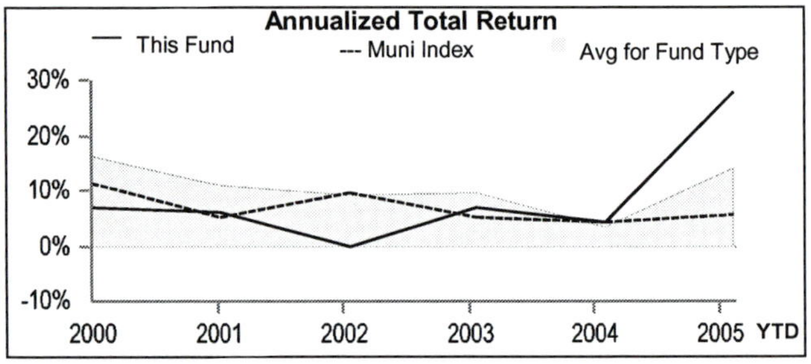

Putnam Master Intermediate Inc Tr (PIM) C- Fair

Fund Family: Putnam Management Co.
Fund Type: General Bond
Inception Date: April 29, 1988

Data Date	Weiss Investment Rating	Net Assets ($Mil)	Price	Performance Rating/Pts	Total Return Y-T-D	Risk Rating/Pts
6-05	C-	714.24	6.50	D+ / 2.3	2.34%	B- / 7.2
2004	C	715.60	6.56	C- / 3.7	6.34%	B- / 7.4
2003	C	700.69	6.58	C- / 3.6	15.70%	B / 8.6

Major Rating Factors:
Disappointing performance is the major factor driving the C- (Fair) Weiss Investment Rating for Putnam Master Intermediate Inc Tr. The fund currently has a performance rating of D+ (Weak) based on an annualized return of 8.97% over the last three years and a total return of 2.34% year to date 2005. Factored into the performance evaluation is an expense ratio of 0.84% (very low).

The fund's risk rating is currently B- (Good). It carries a beta of 1.35, meaning it is expected to move 13.5% for every 10% move in the market. Volatility, as measured by both the semi-deviation and a drawdown factor, is considered low. As of June 30, 2005, Putnam Master Intermediate Inc Tr traded at a discount of 8.96% below its net asset value, which is better than its one-year historical average discount of 8.65%.

David L. Waldman has been running the fund for 6 years and currently receives a manager quality ranking of 71 (0=worst, 99=best). This fund offers only a moderate level of risk but investors looking for strong performance are still waiting.

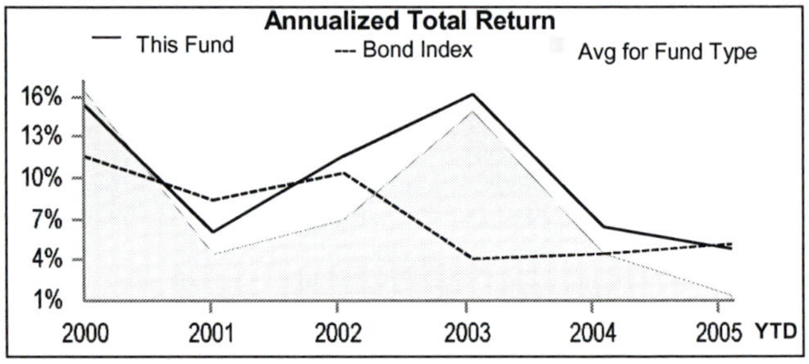

Putnam Muni Opp Tr (PMO) C- Fair

Fund Family: Putnam Management Co.
Fund Type: Municipal - National
Inception Date: May 28, 1993

Data Date	Weiss Investment Rating	Net Assets ($Mil)	Price	Performance Rating/Pts	Total Return Y-T-D	Risk Rating/Pts
6-05	C-	212.51	12.03	D+ / 2.3	1.19%	B / 8.1
2004	C	205.57	12.27	D+ / 2.9	1.27%	B / 8.4
2003	C	209.22	13.04	C- / 4.2	15.76%	B- / 7.9

Major Rating Factors:
Disappointing performance is the major factor driving the C- (Fair) Weiss Investment Rating for Putnam Muni Opp Tr. The fund currently has a performance rating of D+ (Weak) based on an annualized return of 4.83% over the last three years and a total return of 1.19% year to date 2005. Factored into the performance evaluation is an expense ratio of 1.40% (average).

The fund's risk rating is currently B (Good). It carries a beta of 1.90, meaning it is expected to move 19.0% for every 10% move in the market. Volatility, as measured by both the semi-deviation and a drawdown factor, is considered low. As of June 30, 2005, Putnam Muni Opp Tr traded at a discount of 9.82% below its net asset value, which is better than its one-year historical average discount of 5.74%.

Blake E. Anderson has been running the fund for 9 years and currently receives a manager quality ranking of 16 (0=worst, 99=best). This fund offers only a moderate level of risk but investors looking for strong performance are still waiting.

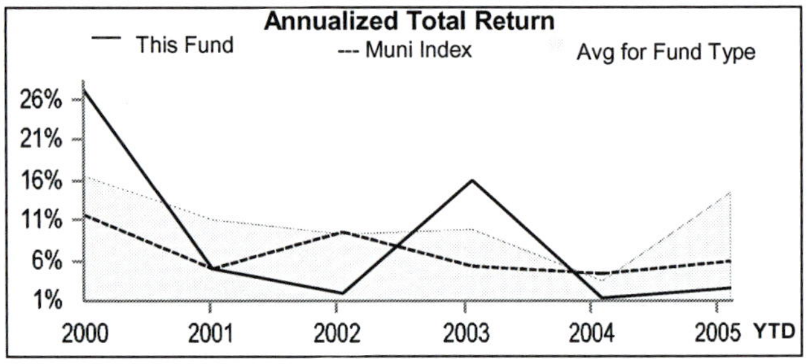

Putnam Municipal Bond Fund (PMG) B- Good

Fund Family: Putnam Management Co.
Fund Type: Municipal - National
Inception Date: November 27, 1992

Major Rating Factors:
Putnam Municipal Bond Fund receives a Weiss Investment Rating of B- (Good). The fund currently has a performance rating of C+ (Fair) based on an annualized return of 7.35% over the last three years and a total return of 3.01% year to date 2005. Factored into the performance evaluation is an expense ratio of 1.35% (average).

The fund's risk rating is currently B- (Good). It carries a beta of 2.13, meaning it is expected to move 21.3% for every 10% move in the market. Volatility, as measured by both the semi-deviation and a drawdown factor, is considered low. As of June 30, 2005, Putnam Municipal Bond Fund traded at a discount of 9.19% below its net asset value, which is better than its one-year historical average discount of 8.55%.

Richard P. Wyke has been running the fund for 9 years and currently receives a manager quality ranking of 27 (0=worst, 99=best). If you desire an average level of risk, then this fund may be an option.

Data Date	Weiss Investment Rating	Net Assets ($Mil)	Price	Performance Rating/Pts	Total Return Y-T-D	Risk Rating/Pts
6-05	B-	239.36	12.74	C+ / 5.8	3.01%	B- / 7.5
2004	A-	230.09	12.77	B- / 7.2	6.47%	B / 8.0
2003	B	230.95	12.74	C+ / 6.2	12.63%	B / 8.6

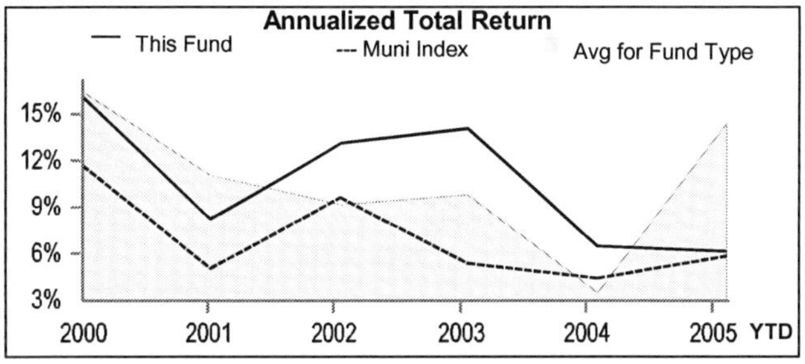

Putnam NY Inv Gr Muni Tr (PMN) C+ Fair

Fund Family: Putnam Management Co.
Fund Type: Municipal - Single State
Inception Date: November 27, 1992

Major Rating Factors:
Middle of the road best describes Putnam NY Inv Gr Muni Tr whose Weiss Investment Rating is currently a C+ (Fair). The fund currently has a performance rating of C- (Fair) based on an annualized return of 4.75% over the last three years and a total return of 5.22% year to date 2005. Factored into the performance evaluation is an expense ratio of 1.39% (average).

The fund's risk rating is currently B (Good). It carries a beta of 1.59, meaning it is expected to move 15.9% for every 10% move in the market. Volatility, as measured by both the semi-deviation and a drawdown factor, is considered low. As of June 30, 2005, Putnam NY Inv Gr Muni Tr traded at a discount of 12.51% below its net asset value, which is worse than its one-year historical average discount of 12.89%.

Richard P. Wyke has been running the fund for 6 years and currently receives a manager quality ranking of 25 (0=worst, 99=best). If you desire an average level of risk, then this fund may be an option.

Data Date	Weiss Investment Rating	Net Assets ($Mil)	Price	Performance Rating/Pts	Total Return Y-T-D	Risk Rating/Pts
6-05	C+	39.14	12.17	C- / 3.6	5.22%	B / 8.3
2004	C	37.53	11.85	D+ / 2.7	1.16%	B / 8.6
2003	C-	37.96	12.35	D+ / 2.8	9.56%	B / 8.4

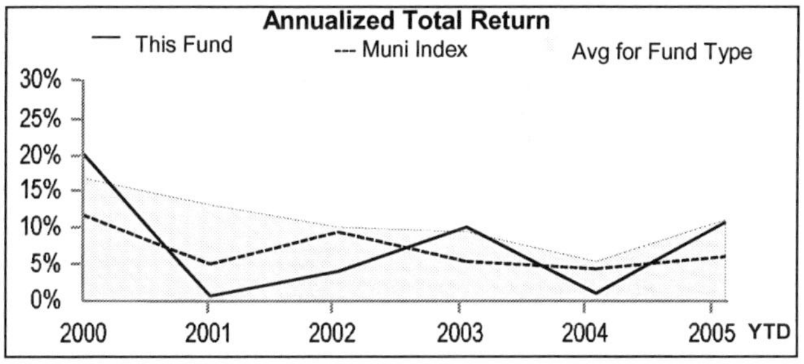

Putnam Premier Income Trust (PPT) C Fair

Fund Family: Putnam Management Co.
Fund Type: General Bond
Inception Date: February 26, 1988

Major Rating Factors:
Middle of the road best describes Putnam Premier Income Trust whose Weiss Investment Rating is currently a C (Fair). The fund currently has a performance rating of C- (Fair) based on an annualized return of 9.50% over the last three years and a total return of 3.29% year to date 2005. Factored into the performance evaluation is an expense ratio of 0.84% (very low).

The fund's risk rating is currently B (Good). It carries a beta of 1.57, meaning it is expected to move 15.7% for every 10% move in the market. Volatility, as measured by both the semi-deviation and a drawdown factor, is considered low. As of June 30, 2005, Putnam Premier Income Trust traded at a discount of 9.21% below its net asset value, which is worse than its one-year historical average discount of 9.96%.

Jin W. Ho has been running the fund for 9 years and currently receives a manager quality ranking of 67 (0=worst, 99=best). If you desire an average level of risk, then this fund may be an option.

Data Date	Weiss Investment Rating	Net Assets ($Mil)	Price	Performance Rating/Pts	Total Return Y-T-D	Risk Rating/Pts
6-05	C	1030.01	6.51	C- / 3.3	3.29%	B / 8.2
2004	C	992.68	6.58	C / 4.5	7.33%	B- / 7.4
2003	C-	952.73	6.58	C- / 3.7	15.96%	B- / 7.1

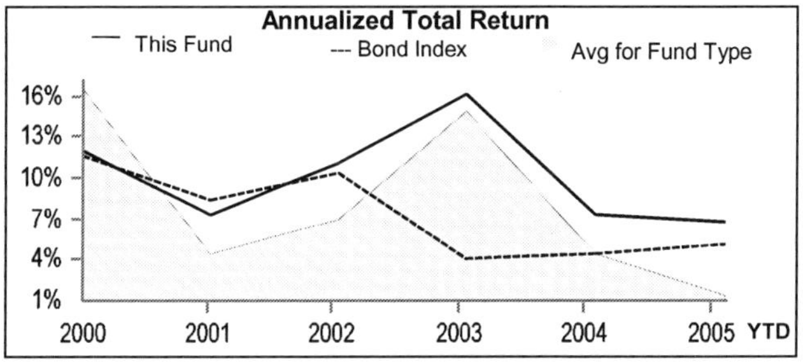

Putnam Tax-Free Health Care Fund (PMH) C+ Fair

Fund Family: Putnam Management Co.
Fund Type: Municipal - National
Inception Date: June 29, 1992

Major Rating Factors:
Middle of the road best describes Putnam Tax-Free Health Care Fund whose Weiss Investment Rating is currently a C+ (Fair). The fund currently has a performance rating of C- (Fair) based on an annualized return of 5.71% over the last three years and a total return of 4.71% year to date 2005. Factored into the performance evaluation is an expense ratio of 0.84% (very low).

The fund's risk rating is currently B+ (Good). It carries a beta of 1.09, meaning that its performance tracks fairly well with that of the overall stock market. Volatility, as measured by both the semi-deviation and a drawdown factor, is considered very low. As of June 30, 2005, Putnam Tax-Free Health Care Fund traded at a discount of 13.67% below its net asset value, which is worse than its one-year historical average discount of 13.84%.

Triet M. Nguyen has been running the fund for 9 years and currently receives a manager quality ranking of 60 (0=worst, 99=best). If you desire an average level of risk, then this fund may be an option.

Data Date	Weiss Investment Rating	Net Assets ($Mil)	Price	Perfor-mance Rating/Pts	Total Return Y-T-D	Risk Rating/Pts
6-05	C+	192.04	12.25	C- / 3.3	4.71%	B+ / 9.2
2004	C	189.31	11.97	D+ / 2.4	3.01%	B+ / 9.5
2003	C-	192.09	12.24	D+ / 2.6	8.85%	B / 8.7

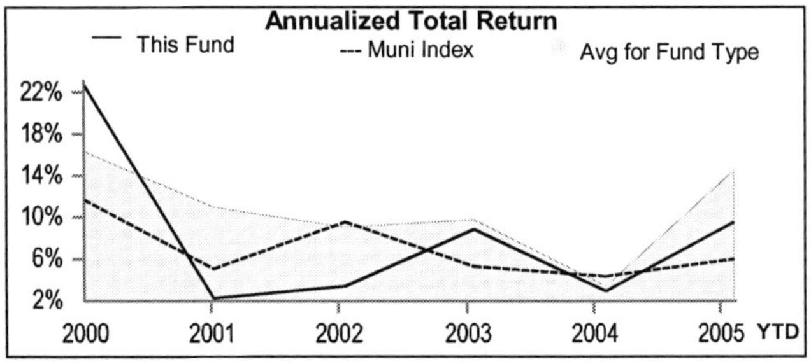

Renaissance Cap Growth & Inc III (RENN) E+ Very Weak

Fund Family: Renaissance Capital Group, Inc.
Fund Type: Growth and Income
Inception Date: September 30, 1996

Major Rating Factors:
Renaissance Cap Growth & Inc III has adopted a very risky asset allocation strategy and currently receives an overall Weiss Investment Rating of E+ (Very Weak). The fund has a high level of volatility, as measured by both semi-deviation and drawdown factors. It carries a beta of 0.56, meaning the fund's expected move will be 5.6% for every 10% move in the market. As of June 30, 2005, Renaissance Cap Growth & Inc III traded at a discount of 17.40% below its net asset value, which is better than its one-year historical average discount of 16.91%. Unfortunately, the high level of risk (E+, Very Weak) has only provided investors with average performance.

The fund's performance rating is currently C (Fair). It has registered an annualized return of 16.31% over the last three years but is down -11.70% year to date 2005. Factored into the performance evaluation is an expense ratio of 3.08% (high).

Russel Cleveland has been running the fund for 9 years and currently receives a manager quality ranking of 92 (0=worst, 99=best). If you are comfortable owning a very high risk investment, then this fund may be an option.

Data Date	Weiss Investment Rating	Net Assets ($Mil)	Price	Perfor-mance Rating/Pts	Total Return Y-T-D	Risk Rating/Pts
6-05	E+	64.36	11.25	C / 4.3	-11.70%	E+ / 0.8
2004	C	64.36	12.95	A+ / 9.6	38.70%	D / 1.6
2003	C+	50.49	13.70	A / 9.5	81.71%	C- / 3.4

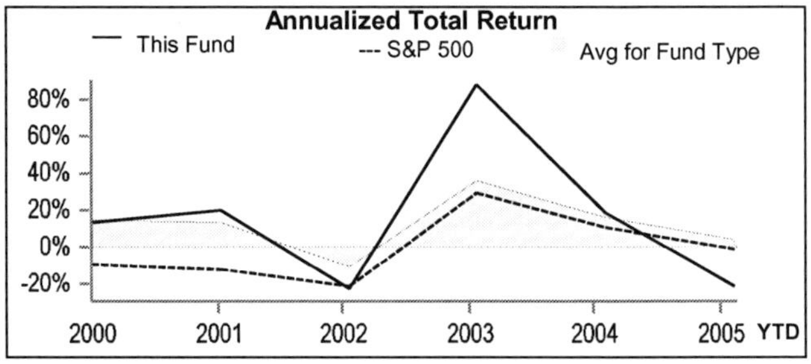

Royce Focus Trust (FUND) C- Fair

Fund Family: Royce & Associates, LLC
Fund Type: Growth
Inception Date: March 10, 1988

Major Rating Factors:
Middle of the road best describes Royce Focus Trust whose Weiss Investment Rating is currently a C- (Fair). The fund currently has a performance rating of C (Fair) based on an annualized return of 18.29% over the last three years and a total return of -16.95% year to date 2005. Factored into the performance evaluation is an expense ratio of 1.53% (average).

The fund's risk rating is currently C (Fair). It carries a beta of 1.14, meaning it is expected to move 11.4% for every 10% move in the market. Volatility, as measured by both the semi-deviation and a drawdown factor, is considered average. As of June 30, 2005, Royce Focus Trust traded at a discount of 3.86% below its net asset value, which is better than its one-year historical average premium of 1.19%.

Whitney George has been running the fund for 3 years and currently receives a manager quality ranking of 89 (0=worst, 99=best). If you desire an average level of risk, then this fund may be an option.

Data Date	Weiss Investment Rating	Net Assets ($Mil)	Price	Perfor-mance Rating/Pts	Total Return Y-T-D	Risk Rating/Pts
6-05	C-	105.85	8.47	C / 5.4	-16.95%	C / 4.8
2004	B+	95.54	10.47	A+ / 9.7	47.31%	C / 4.8
2003	B-	68.73	8.15	A- / 9.0	57.73%	C / 4.8

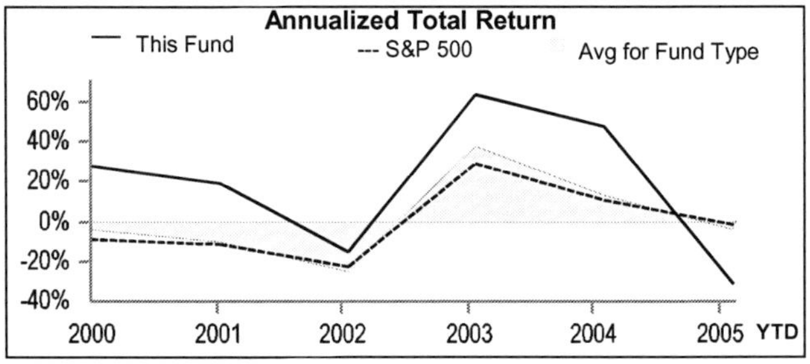

Royce Micro-Cap Trust (RMT) D- Weak

Fund Family: Royce & Associates, LLC
Fund Type: Growth
Inception Date: December 15, 1993

Major Rating Factors:

Royce Micro-Cap Trust has adopted a very risky asset allocation strategy and currently receives an overall Weiss Investment Rating of D- (Weak). The fund has a high level of volatility, as measured by both semi-deviation and drawdown factors. It carries a beta of 1.48, meaning it is expected to move 14.8% for every 10% move in the market. As of June 30, 2005, Royce Micro-Cap Trust traded at a premium of 1.87% above its net asset value, which is worse than its one-year historical average premium of 1.45%. Unfortunately, the high level of risk (D, Weak) has only provided investors with average performance.

The fund's performance rating is currently C (Fair). It has registered an annualized return of 16.09% over the last three years but is down -6.69% year to date 2005. Factored into the performance evaluation is an expense ratio of 1.62% (above average).

Charles M. Royce has been running the fund for 12 years and currently receives a manager quality ranking of 81 (0=worst, 99=best). If you are comfortable owning a very high risk investment, then this fund may be an option.

Data Date	Weiss Investment Rating	Net Assets ($Mil)	Price	Perfor-mance Rating/Pts	Total Return Y-T-D	Risk Rating/Pts
6-05	D-	290.36	13.59	C / 5.3	-6.69%	D / 2.2
2004	C+	270.91	15.24	A / 9.3	33.44%	C- / 3.2
2003	C+	196.72	12.44	A / 9.5	61.49%	C- / 3.8

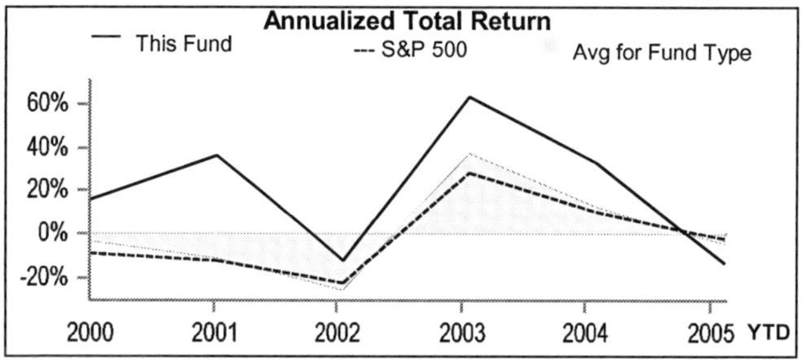

Royce Value Trust (RVT) D+ Weak

Fund Family: Royce & Associates, LLC
Fund Type: Growth
Inception Date: November 26, 1986

Major Rating Factors:

Royce Value Trust receives a Weiss Investment Rating of D+ (Weak). The fund currently has a performance rating of C (Fair) based on an annualized return of 15.67% over the last three years and a total return of -4.36% year to date 2005. Factored into the performance evaluation is an expense ratio of 1.51% (average).

The fund's risk rating is currently C- (Fair). It carries a beta of 1.31, meaning it is expected to move 13.1% for every 10% move in the market. Volatility, as measured by both the semi-deviation and a drawdown factor, is considered average. As of June 30, 2005, Royce Value Trust traded at a premium of 7.35% above its net asset value, which is worse than its one-year historical average premium of 6.58%.

Charles M. Royce has been running the fund for 19 years and currently receives a manager quality ranking of 82 (0=worst, 99=best). If you desire an average level of risk, then this fund may be an option.

Data Date	Weiss Investment Rating	Net Assets ($Mil)	Price	Perfor-mance Rating/Pts	Total Return Y-T-D	Risk Rating/Pts
6-05	D+	993.30	18.70	C / 4.9	-4.36%	C- / 3.7
2004	B-	916.41	20.44	A- / 9.0	29.00%	C / 4.3
2003	C+	699.22	16.74	B / 7.9	40.36%	C / 4.7

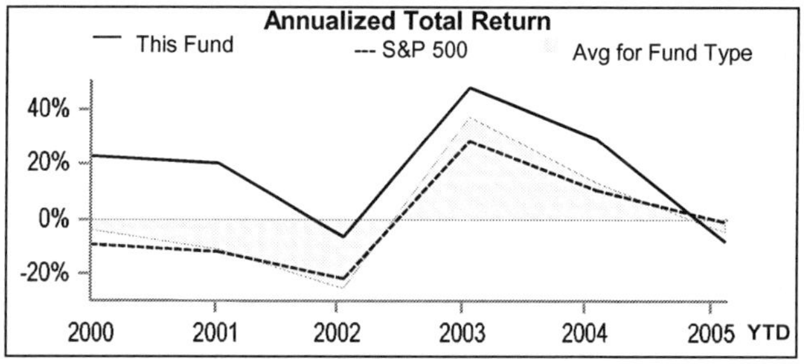

Salomon Br 2008 Wldwide $ Gov Tm Tr (SBG) B Good

Fund Family: Salomon Brothers Asset Management,
Fund Type: Global
Inception Date: August 20, 1993

Major Rating Factors:

Salomon Br 2008 Wldwide $ Gov Tm Tr receives a Weiss Investment Rating of B (Good). The fund currently has a performance rating of C- (Fair) based on an annualized return of 12.18% over the last three years and a total return of 3.17% year to date 2005. Factored into the performance evaluation is an expense ratio of 0.87% (low).

The fund's risk rating is currently B+ (Good). It carries a beta of 0.51, meaning the fund's expected move will be 5.1% for every 10% move in the market. Volatility, as measured by both the semi-deviation and a drawdown factor, is considered very low. As of June 30, 2005, Salomon Br 2008 Wldwide $ Gov Tm Tr traded at a discount of 2.95% below its net asset value, which is better than its one-year historical average discount of .42%.

Steven Guterman has been running the fund for 12 years and currently receives a manager quality ranking of 84 (0=worst, 99=best). If you desire an average level of risk, then this fund may be an option.

Data Date	Weiss Investment Rating	Net Assets ($Mil)	Price	Perfor-mance Rating/Pts	Total Return Y-T-D	Risk Rating/Pts
6-05	B	392.93	11.19	C- / 3.8	3.17%	B+ / 9.7
2004	B+	364.96	11.28	C+ / 6.1	10.52%	B+ / 9.5
2003	B	351.75	11.11	C / 5.2	16.08%	B+ / 9.1

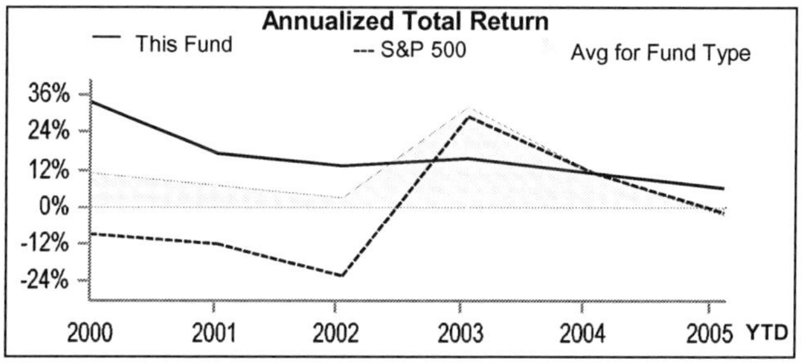

Salomon Br Emerging Markets Income (EMD) C- Fair

Fund Family: Salomon Brothers Asset Management,
Fund Type: Emerging Market
Inception Date: October 23, 1992

Major Rating Factors:
Middle of the road best describes Salomon Br Emerging Markets Income whose Weiss Investment Rating is currently a C- (Fair). The fund currently has a performance rating of C (Fair) based on an annualized return of 17.72% over the last three years and a total return of -15.82% year to date 2005. Factored into the performance evaluation is an expense ratio of 2.52% (high).

The fund's risk rating is currently C (Fair). It carries a beta of 1.48, meaning it is expected to move 14.8% for every 10% move in the market. Volatility, as measured by both the semi-deviation and a drawdown factor, is considered average. As of June 30, 2005, Salomon Br Emerging Markets Income traded at a discount of 3.19% below its net asset value, which is better than its one-year historical average premium of 9.10%.

Peter Wilby has been running the fund for 13 years and currently receives a manager quality ranking of 73 (0=worst, 99=best). If you desire an average level of risk, then this fund may be an option.

Data Date	Weiss Investment Rating	Net Assets ($Mil)	Price	Performance Rating/Pts	Total Return Y-T-D	Risk Rating/Pts
6-05	C-	70.63	16.38	C / 5.2	-15.82%	C / 5.1
2004	B	66.82	20.32	A+ / 9.6	23.04%	C / 4.4
2003	B+	63.82	18.32	A / 9.4	51.46%	C / 5.5

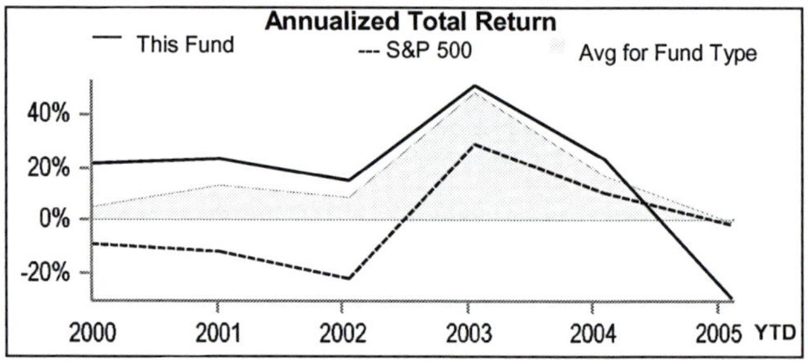

Salomon Br Emerging Mkts Floating (EFL) C Fair

Fund Family: Salomon Brothers Asset Management,
Fund Type: Emerging Market
Inception Date: March 18, 1994

Major Rating Factors:
Middle of the road best describes Salomon Br Emerging Mkts Floating whose Weiss Investment Rating is currently a C (Fair). The fund currently has a performance rating of C- (Fair) based on an annualized return of 14.42% over the last three years and a total return of -6.91% year to date 2005. Factored into the performance evaluation is an expense ratio of 2.40% (high).

The fund's risk rating is currently C+ (Fair). It carries a beta of 0.71, meaning the fund's expected move will be 7.1% for every 10% move in the market. Volatility, as measured by both the semi-deviation and a drawdown factor, is considered low. As of June 30, 2005, Salomon Br Emerging Mkts Floating traded at a discount of 10.17% below its net asset value, which is better than its one-year historical average discount of 4.04%.

Peter J. Wilby has been running the fund for 11 years and currently receives a manager quality ranking of 83 (0=worst, 99=best). If you desire an average level of risk, then this fund may be an option.

Data Date	Weiss Investment Rating	Net Assets ($Mil)	Price	Performance Rating/Pts	Total Return Y-T-D	Risk Rating/Pts
6-05	C	61.03	12.54	C- / 4.1	-6.91%	C+ / 6.7
2004	C+	57.35	13.91	B- / 7.3	13.15%	C / 5.2
2003	C+	55.15	13.20	B- / 7.5	42.28%	C / 5.4

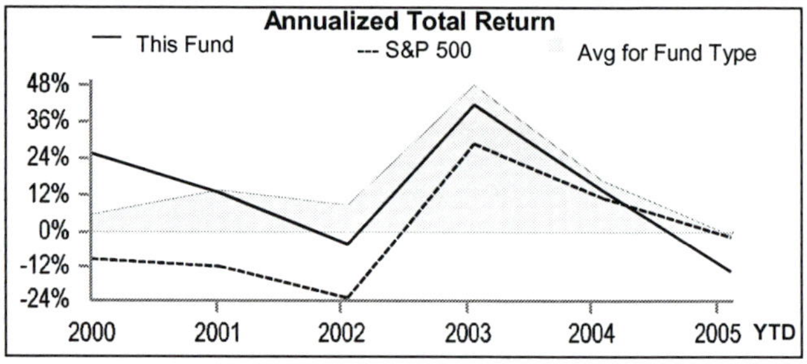

Salomon Br Emerging Mkts Income II (EDF) D+ Weak

Fund Family: Salomon Brothers Asset Management,
Fund Type: Emerging Market
Inception Date: June 25, 1993

Major Rating Factors:
Salomon Br Emerging Mkts Income II receives a Weiss Investment Rating of D+ (Weak). The fund currently has a performance rating of C- (Fair) based on an annualized return of 15.88% over the last three years and a total return of -15.11% year to date 2005. Factored into the performance evaluation is an expense ratio of 2.19% (high).

The fund's risk rating is currently C+ (Fair). It carries a beta of 1.20, meaning it is expected to move 12.0% for every 10% move in the market. Volatility, as measured by both the semi-deviation and a drawdown factor, is considered low. As of June 30, 2005, Salomon Br Emerging Mkts Income II traded at a discount of 8.81% below its net asset value, which is better than its one-year historical average premium of 8.62%.

Peter Wilby has been running the fund for 12 years and currently receives a manager quality ranking of 75 (0=worst, 99=best). If you desire an average level of risk, then this fund may be an option.

Data Date	Weiss Investment Rating	Net Assets ($Mil)	Price	Performance Rating/Pts	Total Return Y-T-D	Risk Rating/Pts
6-05	D+	349.93	13.35	C- / 3.6	-15.11%	C+ / 5.8
2004	B+	311.71	16.46	A- / 9.1	11.50%	C / 5.4
2003	B	339.11	16.47	A / 9.3	49.03%	C / 5.5

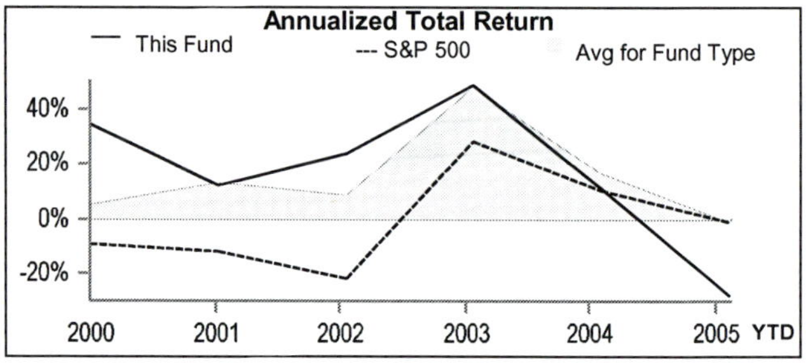

Salomon Br Fund (SBF) D Weak

Fund Family: Salomon Brothers Asset Management,
Fund Type: Growth
Inception Date: N/A

Data Date	Weiss Investment Rating	Net Assets ($Mil)	Price	Perfor-mance Rating/Pts	Total Return Y-T-D	Risk Rating/Pts
6-05	D	1504.80	12.88	D / 1.6	-0.46%	C+ / 6.3
2004	D-	1432.20	13.00	D / 1.6	9.25%	C / 5.3
2003	D-	1227.14	11.88	E+ / 0.6	31.85%	C / 5.2

Major Rating Factors:
Disappointing performance is the major factor driving the D (Weak) Weiss Investment Rating for Salomon Br Fund. The fund currently has a performance rating of D (Weak) based on an annualized return of 7.79% over the last three years and a total return of -0.46% year to date 2005. Factored into the performance evaluation is an expense ratio of 0.62% (very low).

The fund's risk rating is currently C+ (Fair). It carries a beta of 1.11, meaning it is expected to move 11.1% for every 10% move in the market. Volatility, as measured by both the semi-deviation and a drawdown factor, is considered low. As of June 30, 2005, Salomon Br Fund traded at a discount of 13.27% below its net asset value, which is worse than its one-year historical average discount of 14.33%.

Kevin Caliendo currently receives a manager quality ranking of 55 (0=worst, 99=best). This fund offers only a moderate level of risk but investors looking for strong performance are still waiting.

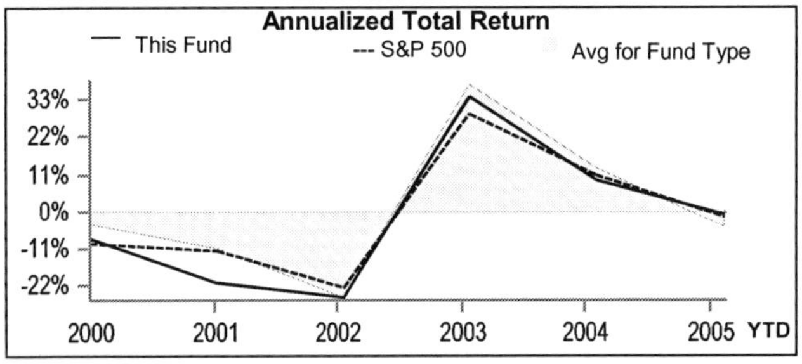

Salomon Br Global Partners Income (GDF) C Fair

Fund Family: Salomon Brothers Asset Management,
Fund Type: Global
Inception Date: October 22, 1993

Data Date	Weiss Investment Rating	Net Assets ($Mil)	Price	Perfor-mance Rating/Pts	Total Return Y-T-D	Risk Rating/Pts
6-05	C	198.57	12.87	C / 5.1	-5.94%	C+ / 5.8
2004	C+	184.94	14.32	B / 8.0	3.56%	C / 4.8
2003	B	174.35	15.20	A / 9.5	53.88%	C / 4.8

Major Rating Factors:
Middle of the road best describes Salomon Br Global Partners Income whose Weiss Investment Rating is currently a C (Fair). The fund currently has a performance rating of C (Fair) based on an annualized return of 17.73% over the last three years and a total return of -5.94% year to date 2005. Factored into the performance evaluation is an expense ratio of 2.55% (high).

The fund's risk rating is currently C+ (Fair). It carries a beta of 1.04, meaning that its performance tracks fairly well with that of the overall stock market. Volatility, as measured by both the semi-deviation and a drawdown factor, is considered low. As of June 30, 2005, Salomon Br Global Partners Income traded at a premium of .39% above its net asset value, which is better than its one-year historical average premium of 11.43%.

Peter Wilby has been running the fund for 12 years and currently receives a manager quality ranking of 83 (0=worst, 99=best). If you desire an average level of risk, then this fund may be an option.

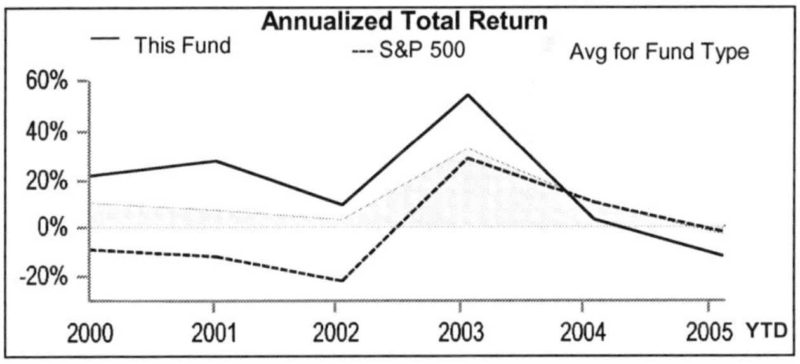

Salomon Br High Inc Fd II (HIX) C- Fair

Fund Family: Salomon Brothers Asset Management,
Fund Type: Global
Inception Date: May 22, 1998

Data Date	Weiss Investment Rating	Net Assets ($Mil)	Price	Perfor-mance Rating/Pts	Total Return Y-T-D	Risk Rating/Pts
6-05	C-	861.64	10.81	C- / 3.9	-6.69%	C+ / 5.7
2004	C+	839.02	12.17	C+ / 6.9	3.45%	C / 5.3
2003	C+	825.61	12.98	B+ / 8.8	46.97%	C / 4.5

Major Rating Factors:
Middle of the road best describes Salomon Br High Inc Fd II whose Weiss Investment Rating is currently a C- (Fair). The fund currently has a performance rating of C- (Fair) based on an annualized return of 15.17% over the last three years and a total return of -6.69% year to date 2005. Factored into the performance evaluation is an expense ratio of 2.69% (high).

The fund's risk rating is currently C+ (Fair). It carries a beta of 0.64, meaning the fund's expected move will be 6.4% for every 10% move in the market. Volatility, as measured by both the semi-deviation and a drawdown factor, is considered low. As of June 30, 2005, Salomon Br High Inc Fd II traded at a discount of 6.33% below its net asset value, which is better than its one-year historical average premium of 2.60%.

Peter J. Wilby has been running the fund for 7 years and currently receives a manager quality ranking of 86 (0=worst, 99=best). If you desire an average level of risk, then this fund may be an option.

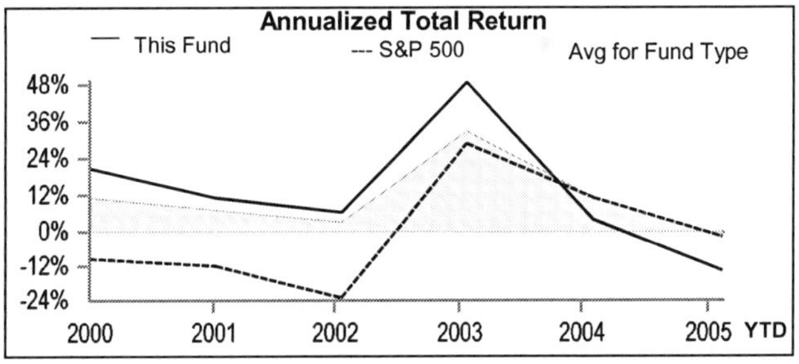

Salomon Br High Income Fund (HIF) D- Weak

Fund Family: Salomon Brothers Asset Management,
Fund Type: Corporate - High Yield
Inception Date: January 22, 1993

Data Date	Weiss Investment Rating	Net Assets ($Mil)	Price	Performance Rating/Pts	Total Return Y-T-D	Risk Rating/Pts
6-05	D-	55.11	9.43	D- / 1.4	-4.28%	C+ / 5.7
2004	D-	51.50	10.23	D- / 1.1	-2.70%	C / 5.0
2003	D+	51.01	11.47	C / 4.9	33.89%	C / 4.8

Major Rating Factors:
Disappointing performance is the major factor driving the D- (Weak) Weiss Investment Rating for Salomon Br High Income Fund. The fund currently has a performance rating of D- (Weak) based on an annualized return of 9.45% over the last three years and a total return of -4.28% year to date 2005. Factored into the performance evaluation is an expense ratio of 1.41% (average).

The fund's risk rating is currently C+ (Fair). It carries a beta of 1.29, meaning it is expected to move 12.9% for every 10% move in the market. Volatility, as measured by both the semi-deviation and a drawdown factor, is considered low. As of June 30, 2005, Salomon Br High Income Fund traded at a discount of 10.10% below its net asset value, which is better than its one-year historical average discount of 2.51%.

Peter Wilby has been running the fund for 12 years and currently receives a manager quality ranking of 7 (0=worst, 99=best). This fund offers only a moderate level of risk but investors looking for strong performance are still waiting.

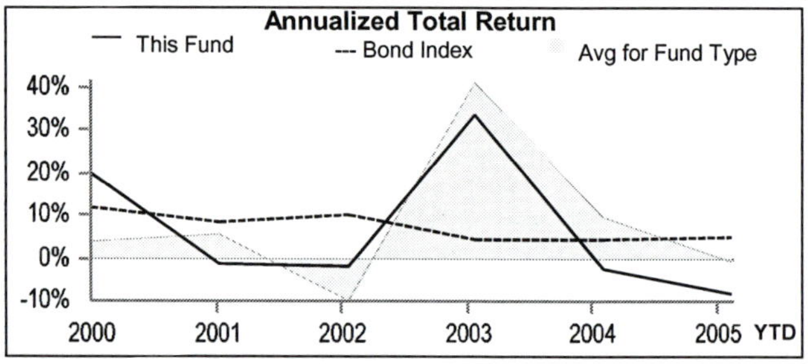

Salomon Br Municipal Partners (MNP) B- Good

Fund Family: Salomon Brothers Asset Management,
Fund Type: Municipal - National
Inception Date: January 29, 1993

Data Date	Weiss Investment Rating	Net Assets ($Mil)	Price	Performance Rating/Pts	Total Return Y-T-D	Risk Rating/Pts
6-05	B-	88.26	13.88	C+ / 6.9	6.45%	B- / 7.1
2004	B	85.73	13.45	C+ / 5.8	2.73%	B / 8.1
2003	B	90.18	13.89	C+ / 6.1	10.25%	B / 8.7

Major Rating Factors:
Salomon Br Municipal Partners receives a Weiss Investment Rating of B- (Good). The fund currently has a performance rating of C+ (Fair) based on an annualized return of 8.34% over the last three years and a total return of 6.45% year to date 2005. Factored into the performance evaluation is an expense ratio of 1.32% (average).

The fund's risk rating is currently B- (Good). It carries a beta of 1.77, meaning it is expected to move 17.7% for every 10% move in the market. Volatility, as measured by both the semi-deviation and a drawdown factor, is considered low. As of June 30, 2005, Salomon Br Municipal Partners traded at a discount of 9.40% below its net asset value, which is worse than its one-year historical average discount of 11.98%.

MaryBeth Whyte has been running the fund for 11 years and currently receives a manager quality ranking of 56 (0=worst, 99=best). If you desire an average level of risk, then this fund may be an option.

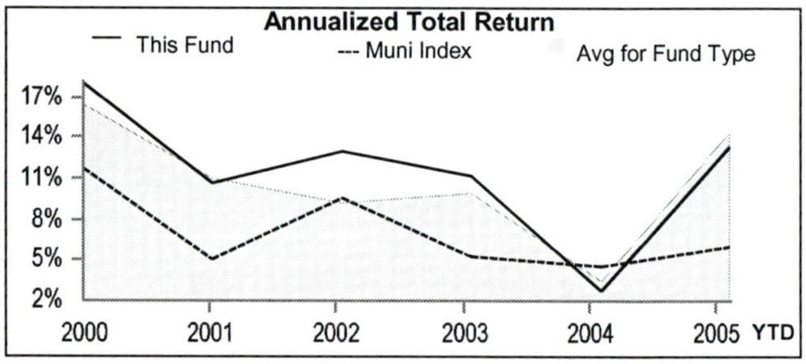

Salomon Br Municipal Partners II (MPT) B- Good

Fund Family: Salomon Brothers Asset Management,
Fund Type: Municipal - National
Inception Date: July 30, 1993

Data Date	Weiss Investment Rating	Net Assets ($Mil)	Price	Performance Rating/Pts	Total Return Y-T-D	Risk Rating/Pts
6-05	B-	89.81	13.50	C+ / 6.2	7.06%	B- / 7.7
2004	B-	87.04	13.01	C / 4.6	1.88%	B / 8.6
2003	B	92.09	13.58	C / 5.4	8.56%	B / 8.9

Major Rating Factors:
Salomon Br Municipal Partners II receives a Weiss Investment Rating of B- (Good). The fund currently has a performance rating of C+ (Fair) based on an annualized return of 7.69% over the last three years and a total return of 7.06% year to date 2005. Factored into the performance evaluation is an expense ratio of 1.33% (average).

The fund's risk rating is currently B- (Good). It carries a beta of 1.77, meaning it is expected to move 17.7% for every 10% move in the market. Volatility, as measured by both the semi-deviation and a drawdown factor, is considered low. As of June 30, 2005, Salomon Br Municipal Partners II traded at a discount of 9.70% below its net asset value, which is worse than its one-year historical average discount of 12.28%.

MaryBeth Whyte has been running the fund for 11 years and currently receives a manager quality ranking of 50 (0=worst, 99=best). If you desire an average level of risk, then this fund may be an option.

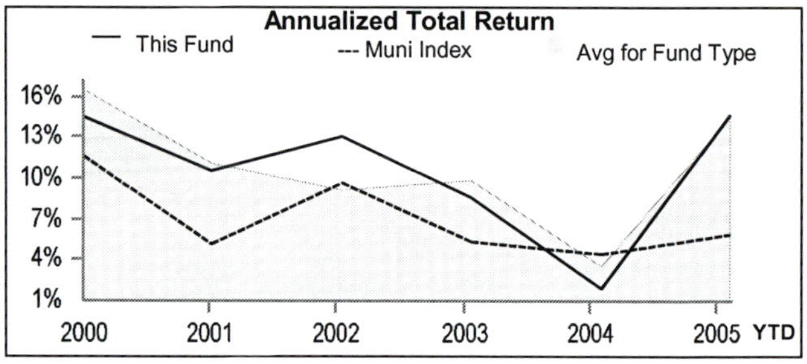

Salomon Br Worldwide Inc Fd (SBW) C Fair

Fund Family: Salomon Brothers Asset Management,
Fund Type: Global
Inception Date: December 23, 1993

Major Rating Factors:
Middle of the road best describes Salomon Br Worldwide Inc Fd whose Weiss Investment Rating is currently a C (Fair). The fund currently has a performance rating of C+ (Fair) based on an annualized return of 17.43% over the last three years and a total return of -8.83% year to date 2005. Factored into the performance evaluation is an expense ratio of 2.31% (high).

The fund's risk rating is currently C+ (Fair). It carries a beta of 1.16, meaning it is expected to move 11.6% for every 10% move in the market. Volatility, as measured by both the semi-deviation and a drawdown factor, is considered low. As of June 30, 2005, Salomon Br Worldwide Inc Fd traded at a discount of 7.67% below its net asset value, which is better than its one-year historical average premium of 3.53%.

Peter J. Wilby has been running the fund for 12 years and currently receives a manager quality ranking of 81 (0=worst, 99=best). If you desire an average level of risk, then this fund may be an option.

Data Date	Weiss Investment Rating	Net Assets ($Mil)	Price	Performance Rating/Pts	Total Return Y-T-D	Risk Rating/Pts
6-05	C	204.36	15.16	C+ / 5.8	-8.83%	C+ / 5.9
2004	B	188.46	17.37	B+ / 8.6	14.79%	C / 5.4
2003	B+	194.34	16.60	B+ / 8.9	39.25%	C+ / 6.3

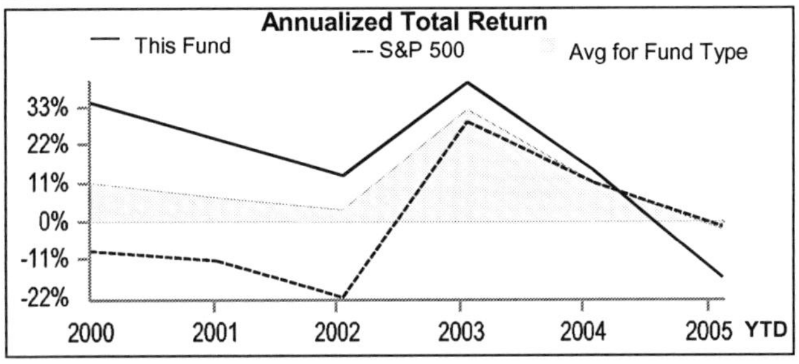

Scudder Global High Income Fund (LBF) B Good

Fund Family: Deutsche Asset Management
Fund Type: Emerging Market
Inception Date: July 31, 1992

Major Rating Factors:
Strong performance is the major factor driving the B (Good) Weiss Investment Rating for Scudder Global High Income Fund. The fund currently has a performance rating of B+ (Good) based on an annualized return of 20.30% over the last three years and a total return of 4.17% year to date 2005. Factored into the performance evaluation is an expense ratio of 2.70% (high).

The fund's risk rating is currently C (Fair). It carries a beta of 1.19, meaning it is expected to move 11.9% for every 10% move in the market. Volatility, as measured by both the semi-deviation and a drawdown factor, is considered average. As of June 30, 2005, Scudder Global High Income Fund traded at a discount of 10.11% below its net asset value, which is better than its one-year historical average discount of 9.99%.

Brett Diment has been running the fund for 13 years and currently receives a manager quality ranking of 84 (0=worst, 99=best). If you desire an average level of risk and strong performance, then this fund is a good option.

Data Date	Weiss Investment Rating	Net Assets ($Mil)	Price	Performance Rating/Pts	Total Return Y-T-D	Risk Rating/Pts
6-05	B	83.12	7.91	B+ / 8.9	4.17%	C / 4.9
2004	B	72.87	7.74	B+ / 8.8	10.83%	C / 5.1
2003	B	71.57	7.70	A- / 9.1	34.68%	C / 5.5

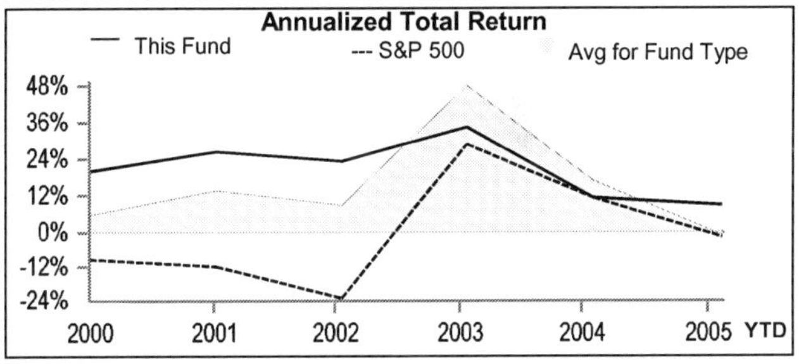

Scudder High Income Trust (KHI) B- Good

Fund Family: Deutsche Asset Management
Fund Type: Corporate - High Yield
Inception Date: April 21, 1988

Major Rating Factors:
Strong performance is the major factor driving the B- (Good) Weiss Investment Rating for Scudder High Income Trust. The fund currently has a performance rating of B+ (Good) based on an annualized return of 18.53% over the last three years and a total return of 8.06% year to date 2005. Factored into the performance evaluation is an expense ratio of 1.71% (above average).

The fund's risk rating is currently C (Fair). It carries a beta of 1.64, meaning it is expected to move 16.4% for every 10% move in the market. Volatility, as measured by both the semi-deviation and a drawdown factor, is considered average. As of June 30, 2005, Scudder High Income Trust traded at a premium of 22.86% above its net asset value, which is worse than its one-year historical average premium of 17.41%.

Andrew Cestone has been running the fund for 17 years and currently receives a manager quality ranking of 28 (0=worst, 99=best). If you desire an average level of risk and strong performance, then this fund is a good option.

Data Date	Weiss Investment Rating	Net Assets ($Mil)	Price	Performance Rating/Pts	Total Return Y-T-D	Risk Rating/Pts
6-05	B-	194.58	7.31	B+ / 8.5	8.06%	C / 4.7
2004	D-	180.36	7.04	C- / 3.9	3.81%	C- / 3.4
2003	C+	182.51	7.47	B / 8.2	54.21%	C / 4.7

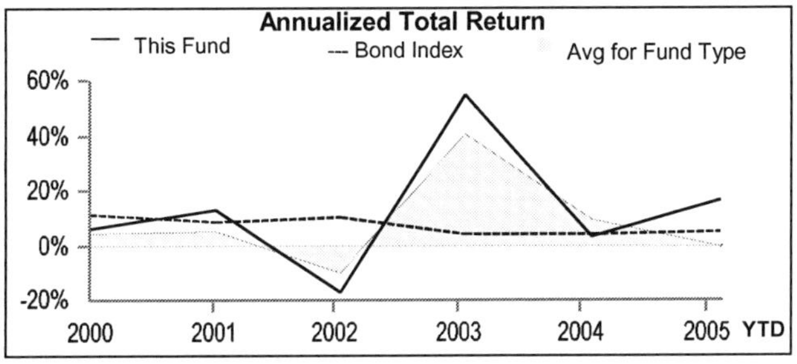

Scudder Multi-Market Income Trust (KMM) B+ Good

Fund Family: Deutsche Asset Management
Fund Type: Global
Inception Date: January 23, 1989

Data Date	Weiss Investment Rating	Net Assets ($Mil)	Price	Performance Rating/Pts	Total Return Y-T-D	Risk Rating/Pts
6-05	B+	194.66	10.21	A- / 9.2	12.82%	C / 4.9
2004	C+	174.61	9.42	B- / 7.1	17.26%	C+ / 5.8
2003	C-	179.19	8.75	C / 4.3	29.63%	C+ / 6.1

Major Rating Factors:
Exceptional performance is the major factor driving the B+ (Good) Weiss Investment Rating for Scudder Multi-Market Income Trust. The fund currently has a performance rating of A- (Excellent) based on an annualized return of 21.05% over the last three years and a total return of 12.82% year to date 2005. Factored into the performance evaluation is an expense ratio of 1.05% (low).

The fund's risk rating is currently C (Fair). It carries a beta of 0.65, meaning the fund's expected move will be 6.5% for every 10% move in the market. Volatility, as measured by both the semi-deviation and a drawdown factor, is considered average. As of June 30, 2005, Scudder Multi-Market Income Trust traded at a premium of 5.48% above its net asset value, which is worse than its one-year historical average discount of 1.71%.

Jan Faller has been running the fund for 16 years and currently receives a manager quality ranking of 93 (0=worst, 99=best). If you desire an average level of risk and strong performance, then this fund is a good option.

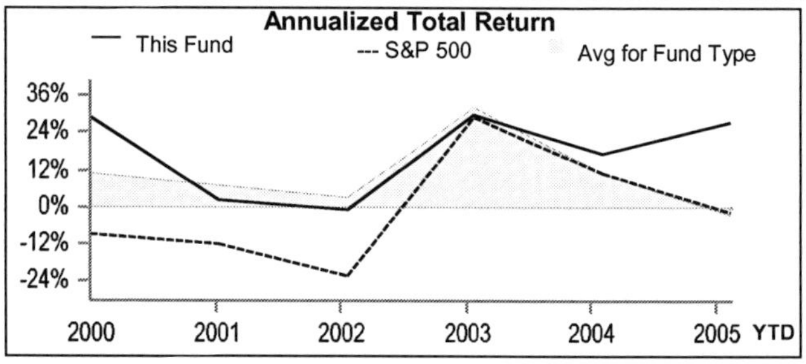

Scudder Municipal Income Trust (KTF) A Excellent

Fund Family: Deutsche Asset Management
Fund Type: Municipal - National
Inception Date: October 20, 1988

Data Date	Weiss Investment Rating	Net Assets ($Mil)	Price	Performance Rating/Pts	Total Return Y-T-D	Risk Rating/Pts
6-05	A	482.17	12.74	A- / 9.1	13.94%	C+ / 6.5
2004	C	471.33	11.56	C- / 4.1	-0.31%	B- / 7.9
2003	B+	488.93	12.25	B- / 7.4	15.86%	B- / 7.9

Major Rating Factors:
Exceptional performance is the major factor driving the A (Excellent) Weiss Investment Rating for Scudder Municipal Income Trust. The fund currently has a performance rating of A- (Excellent) based on an annualized return of 11.54% over the last three years and a total return of 13.94% year to date 2005. Factored into the performance evaluation is an expense ratio of 1.06% (low).

The fund's risk rating is currently C+ (Fair). It carries a beta of 2.03, meaning it is expected to move 20.3% for every 10% move in the market. Volatility, as measured by both the semi-deviation and a drawdown factor, is considered low. As of June 30, 2005, Scudder Municipal Income Trust traded at a premium of 1.43% above its net asset value, which is worse than its one-year historical average discount of 3.63%.

Philip G. Condon has been running the fund for 7 years and currently receives a manager quality ranking of 70 (0=worst, 99=best). If you desire only a moderate level of risk and strong performance, then this fund is an excellent option.

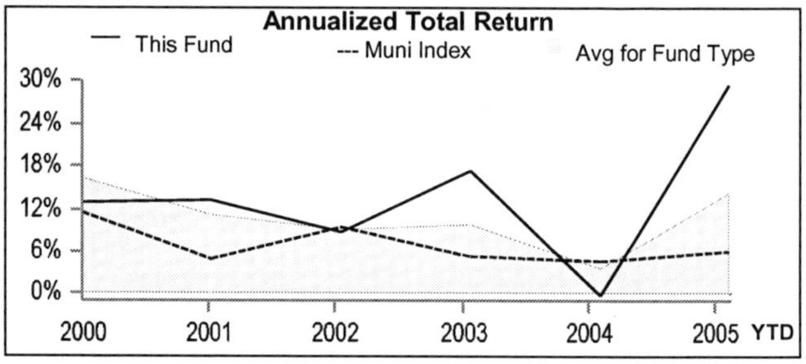

Scudder New Asia Fund (SAF) B- Good

Fund Family: Deutsche Asset Management
Fund Type: Foreign
Inception Date: June 18, 1987

Data Date	Weiss Investment Rating	Net Assets ($Mil)	Price	Performance Rating/Pts	Total Return Y-T-D	Risk Rating/Pts
6-05	B-	149.62	15.82	B+ / 8.3	7.18%	C / 5.1
2004	C+	129.29	14.83	B / 7.9	3.66%	C / 6.0
2003	C+	94.90	13.61	A / 9.3	76.52%	C- / 3.6

Major Rating Factors:
Strong performance is the major factor driving the B- (Good) Weiss Investment Rating for Scudder New Asia Fund. The fund currently has a performance rating of B+ (Good) based on an annualized return of 20.06% over the last three years and a total return of 7.18% year to date 2005. Factored into the performance evaluation is an expense ratio of 1.81% (above average).

The fund's risk rating is currently C (Fair). It carries a beta of 1.09, meaning that its performance tracks fairly well with that of the overall stock market. Volatility, as measured by both the semi-deviation and a drawdown factor, is considered average. As of June 30, 2005, Scudder New Asia Fund traded at a discount of 11.92% below its net asset value, which is worse than its one-year historical average discount of 12.98%.

Terrence Gray has been running the fund for 18 years and currently receives a manager quality ranking of 84 (0=worst, 99=best). If you desire an average level of risk and strong performance, then this fund is a good option.

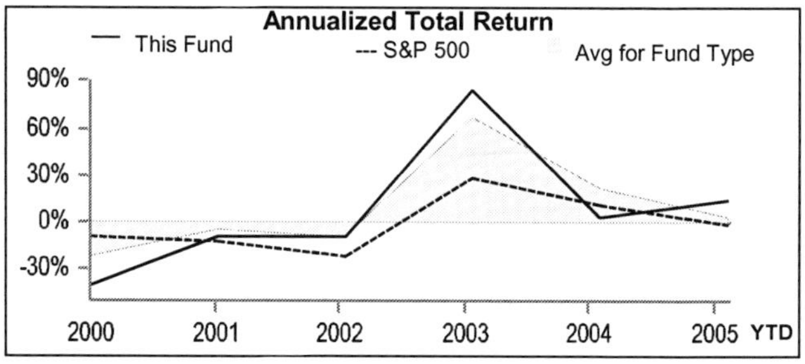

Scudder Strategic Income Fund (KST) B Good

Fund Family: Deutsche Asset Management
Fund Type: Global
Inception Date: April 25, 1994

Major Rating Factors:
Strong performance is the major factor driving the B (Good) Weiss Investment Rating for Scudder Strategic Income Fund. The fund currently has a performance rating of B+ (Good) based on an annualized return of 20.89% over the last three years and a total return of 5.63% year to date 2005. Factored into the performance evaluation is an expense ratio of 2.20% (high).

The fund's risk rating is currently C (Fair). It carries a beta of 0.61, meaning the fund's expected move will be 6.1% for every 10% move in the market. Volatility, as measured by both the semi-deviation and a drawdown factor, is considered average. As of June 30, 2005, Scudder Strategic Income Fund traded at a premium of .79% above its net asset value, which is worse than its one-year historical average discount of 1.85%.

Jan Faller has been running the fund for 11 years and currently receives a manager quality ranking of 94 (0=worst, 99=best). If you desire an average level of risk and strong performance, then this fund is a good option.

Data Date	Weiss Investment Rating	Net Assets ($Mil)	Price	Performance Rating/Pts	Total Return Y-T-D	Risk Rating/Pts
6-05	B	47.75	14.01	B+ / 8.7	5.63%	C / 5.0
2004	C+	42.82	13.80	B- / 7.3	10.97%	C / 5.4
2003	C+	44.34	13.52	B- / 7.5	37.73%	C / 5.2

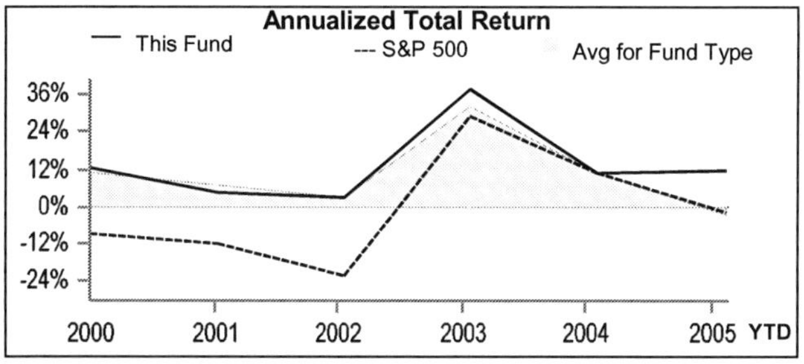

Scudder Strategic Municipal Inc Tr (KSM) A+ Excellent

Fund Family: Deutsche Asset Management
Fund Type: Municipal - National
Inception Date: March 22, 1989

Major Rating Factors:
Exceptional performance is the major factor driving the A+ (Excellent) Weiss Investment Rating for Scudder Strategic Municipal Inc Tr. The fund currently has a performance rating of A+ (Excellent) based on an annualized return of 13.43% over the last three years and a total return of 14.08% year to date 2005. Factored into the performance evaluation is an expense ratio of 1.25% (average).

The fund's risk rating is currently B- (Good). It carries a beta of 1.74, meaning it is expected to move 17.4% for every 10% move in the market. Volatility, as measured by both the semi-deviation and a drawdown factor, is considered low. As of June 30, 2005, Scudder Strategic Municipal Inc Tr traded at a premium of 9.11% above its net asset value, which is worse than its one-year historical average premium of 2.56%.

Philip G. Condon has been running the fund for 7 years and currently receives a manager quality ranking of 81 (0=worst, 99=best). If you desire only a moderate level of risk and strong performance, then this fund is an excellent option.

Data Date	Weiss Investment Rating	Net Assets ($Mil)	Price	Performance Rating/Pts	Total Return Y-T-D	Risk Rating/Pts
6-05	A+	133.03	13.66	A+ / 9.6	14.08%	B- / 7.1
2004	B	128.80	12.41	C+ / 6.3	2.51%	B / 8.4
2003	B+	132.10	12.94	B / 7.8	16.62%	B- / 7.6

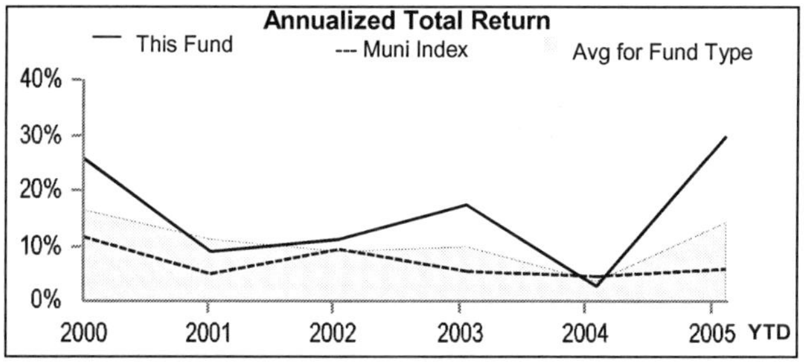

Seligman Quality Municipal Fund (SQF) C Fair

Fund Family: Seligman, J.W. & Co., Inc.
Fund Type: Municipal - National
Inception Date: November 25, 1991

Major Rating Factors:
Disappointing performance is the major factor driving the C (Fair) Weiss Investment Rating for Seligman Quality Municipal Fund. The fund currently has a performance rating of D+ (Weak) based on an annualized return of 4.94% over the last three years and a total return of 2.35% year to date 2005. Factored into the performance evaluation is an expense ratio of 1.66% (above average).

The fund's risk rating is currently B (Good). It carries a beta of 1.70, meaning it is expected to move 17.0% for every 10% move in the market. Volatility, as measured by both the semi-deviation and a drawdown factor, is considered low. As of June 30, 2005, Seligman Quality Municipal Fund traded at a discount of 14.67% below its net asset value, which is better than its one-year historical average discount of 13.78%.

Thomas G. Moles has been running the fund for 14 years and currently receives a manager quality ranking of 24 (0=worst, 99=best). This fund offers only a moderate level of risk but investors looking for strong performance are still waiting.

Data Date	Weiss Investment Rating	Net Assets ($Mil)	Price	Performance Rating/Pts	Total Return Y-T-D	Risk Rating/Pts
6-05	C	67.14	12.27	D+ / 2.7	2.35%	B / 8.6
2004	C	65.90	12.28	D+ / 2.6	-0.03%	B / 8.7
2003	C+	67.47	12.95	C / 4.4	8.42%	B / 8.9

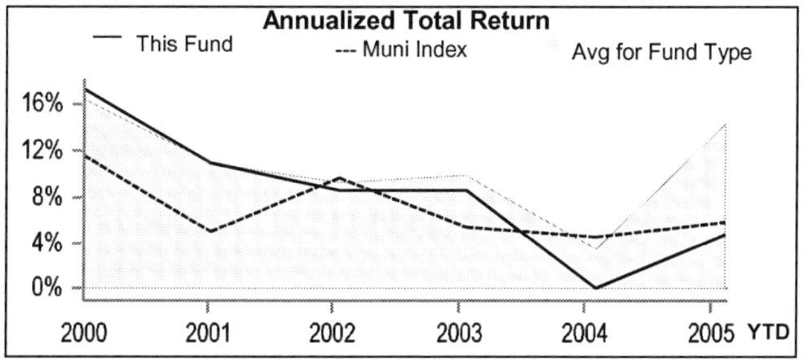

Seligman Select Municipal Fund (SEL) C Fair

Fund Family: Seligman, J.W. & Co., Inc.
Fund Type: Municipal - National
Inception Date: February 15, 1990

Major Rating Factors:
Disappointing performance is the major factor driving the C (Fair) Weiss Investment Rating for Seligman Select Municipal Fund. The fund currently has a performance rating of D+ (Weak) based on an annualized return of 5.45% over the last three years and a total return of 3.09% year to date 2005. Factored into the performance evaluation is an expense ratio of 1.91% (above average).

The fund's risk rating is currently B (Good). It carries a beta of 1.55, meaning it is expected to move 15.5% for every 10% move in the market. Volatility, as measured by both the semi-deviation and a drawdown factor, is considered low. As of June 30, 2005, Seligman Select Municipal Fund traded at a discount of 12.67% below its net asset value, which is better than its one-year historical average discount of 11.35%.

Thomas G. Moles has been running the fund for 15 years and currently receives a manager quality ranking of 35 (0=worst, 99=best). This fund offers only a moderate level of risk but investors looking for strong performance are still waiting.

Data Date	Weiss Investment Rating	Net Assets ($Mil)	Price	Performance Rating/Pts	Total Return Y-T-D	Risk Rating/Pts
6-05	C	156.66	10.34	D+ / 2.7	3.09%	B / 8.5
2004	C	154.61	10.35	C- / 3.1	-0.24%	B / 8.7
2003	C+	163.16	10.99	C / 5.1	8.82%	B / 8.3

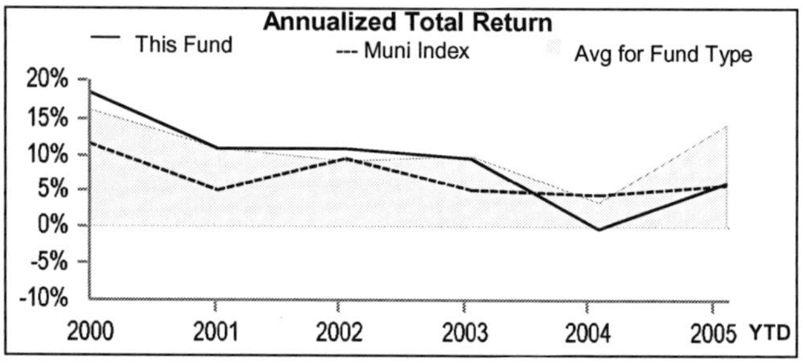

Senior High Income Portfolio (ARK) B- Good

Fund Family: Merrill Lynch Investment Managers
Fund Type: Corporate - High Yield
Inception Date: April 30, 1993

Major Rating Factors:
Strong performance is the major factor driving the B- (Good) Weiss Investment Rating for Senior High Income Portfolio. The fund currently has a performance rating of B- (Good) based on an annualized return of 17.79% over the last three years and a total return of 2.14% year to date 2005. Factored into the performance evaluation is an expense ratio of 1.69% (above average).

The fund's risk rating is currently C+ (Fair). It carries a beta of 1.69, meaning it is expected to move 16.9% for every 10% move in the market. Volatility, as measured by both the semi-deviation and a drawdown factor, is considered low. As of June 30, 2005, Senior High Income Portfolio traded at a discount of 1.00% below its net asset value, which is worse than its one-year historical average discount of 3.11%.

Joe Matteo has been running the fund for 12 years and currently receives a manager quality ranking of 20 (0=worst, 99=best). If you desire only a moderate level of risk and strong performance, then this fund is an excellent option.

Data Date	Weiss Investment Rating	Net Assets ($Mil)	Price	Performance Rating/Pts	Total Return Y-T-D	Risk Rating/Pts
6-05	B-	349.79	5.93	B- / 7.0	2.14%	C+ / 6.4
2004	C-	340.07	6.04	C+ / 6.1	5.79%	C / 5.0
2003	C	303.51	6.33	B / 8.0	46.09%	C- / 3.7

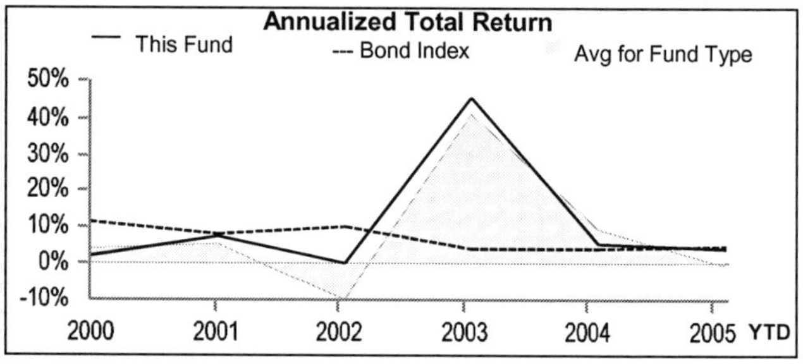

Singapore Fund (SGF) B- Good

Fund Family: DBS Asset Management(US) Pte. Ltd
Fund Type: Foreign
Inception Date: July 31, 1990

Major Rating Factors:
Strong performance is the major factor driving the B- (Good) Weiss Investment Rating for Singapore Fund. The fund currently has a performance rating of B (Good) based on an annualized return of 20.77% over the last three years and a total return of 1.83% year to date 2005. Factored into the performance evaluation is an expense ratio of 1.76% (above average).

The fund's risk rating is currently C (Fair). It carries a beta of 0.57, meaning the fund's expected move will be 5.7% for every 10% move in the market. Volatility, as measured by both the semi-deviation and a drawdown factor, is considered average. As of June 30, 2005, Singapore Fund traded at a discount of 13.24% below its net asset value, which is worse than its one-year historical average discount of 14.23%.

Roy Phua has been running the fund for 5 years and currently receives a manager quality ranking of 91 (0=worst, 99=best). If you desire an average level of risk and strong performance, then this fund is a good option.

Data Date	Weiss Investment Rating	Net Assets ($Mil)	Price	Performance Rating/Pts	Total Return Y-T-D	Risk Rating/Pts
6-05	B-	94.76	8.91	B / 7.8	1.83%	C / 5.5
2004	B	84.84	8.69	B+ / 8.4	18.01%	C / 5.5
2003	C-	54.05	7.38	B- / 7.0	59.04%	C- / 4.2

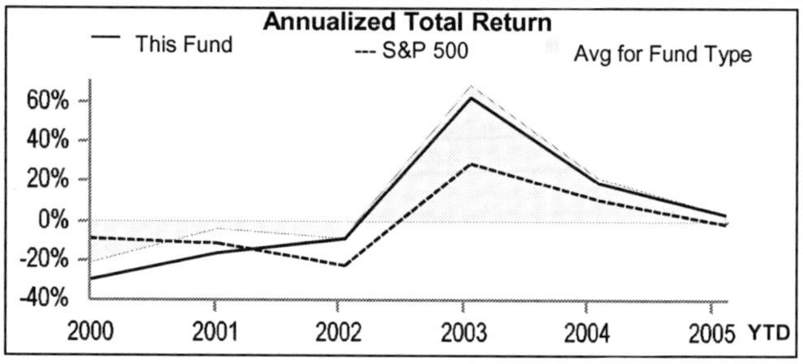

Smith Barney Intermediate Muni (SBI) C Fair

Fund Family: Smith Barney Mutual Funds Mgmt. Inc
Fund Type: Municipal - National
Inception Date: March 2, 1992

Data Date	Weiss Investment Rating	Net Assets ($Mil)	Price	Performance Rating/Pts	Total Return Y-T-D	Risk Rating/Pts
6-05	C	140.54	9.63	C- / 3.8	6.30%	B- / 7.1
2004	C-	140.21	9.36	D+ / 2.8	-2.16%	B / 8.1
2003	B	144.43	10.25	C+ / 6.7	14.02%	B / 8.1

Major Rating Factors:
Middle of the road best describes Smith Barney Intermediate Muni whose Weiss Investment Rating is currently a C (Fair). The fund currently has a performance rating of C- (Fair) based on an annualized return of 5.59% over the last three years and a total return of 6.30% year to date 2005. Factored into the performance evaluation is an expense ratio of 1.07% (low).

The fund's risk rating is currently B- (Good). It carries a beta of 1.50, meaning it is expected to move 15.0% for every 10% move in the market. Volatility, as measured by both the semi-deviation and a drawdown factor, is considered low. As of June 30, 2005, Smith Barney Intermediate Muni traded at a discount of 1.53% below its net asset value, which is worse than its one-year historical average discount of 5.59%.

Peter M. Coffey has been running the fund for 13 years and currently receives a manager quality ranking of 41 (0=worst, 99=best). If you desire an average level of risk, then this fund may be an option.

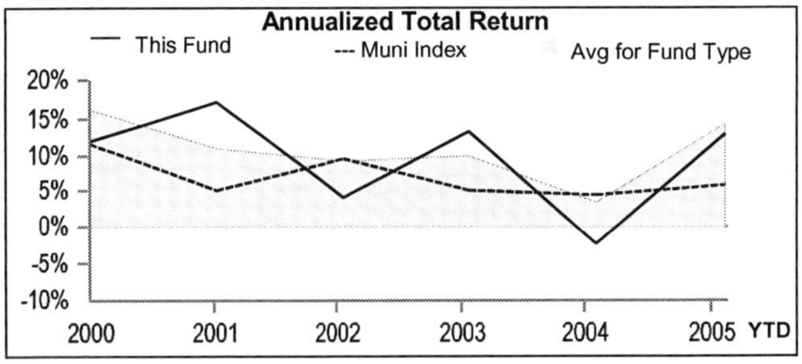

Source Capital (SOR) D Weak

Fund Family: First Pacific Advisors, Inc.
Fund Type: Income
Inception Date: October 24, 1968

Data Date	Weiss Investment Rating	Net Assets ($Mil)	Price	Performance Rating/Pts	Total Return Y-T-D	Risk Rating/Pts
6-05	D	527.58	69.45	C- / 3.7	-0.03%	C / 4.9
2004	C	498.02	71.54	B- / 7.4	28.36%	C / 4.6
2003	C-	387.43	58.96	C / 5.3	19.75%	C+ / 5.9

Major Rating Factors:
Source Capital receives a Weiss Investment Rating of D (Weak). The fund currently has a performance rating of C- (Fair) based on an annualized return of 11.71% over the last three years and a total return of -0.03% year to date 2005. Factored into the performance evaluation is an expense ratio of 0.95% (low).

The fund's risk rating is currently C (Fair). It carries a beta of 0.97, meaning that its performance tracks fairly well with that of the overall stock market. Volatility, as measured by both the semi-deviation and a drawdown factor, is considered average. As of June 30, 2005, Source Capital traded at a premium of 11.41% above its net asset value, which is better than its one-year historical average premium of 12.27%.

Eric Ende has been running the fund for 9 years and currently receives a manager quality ranking of 79 (0=worst, 99=best). If you desire an average level of risk, then this fund may be an option.

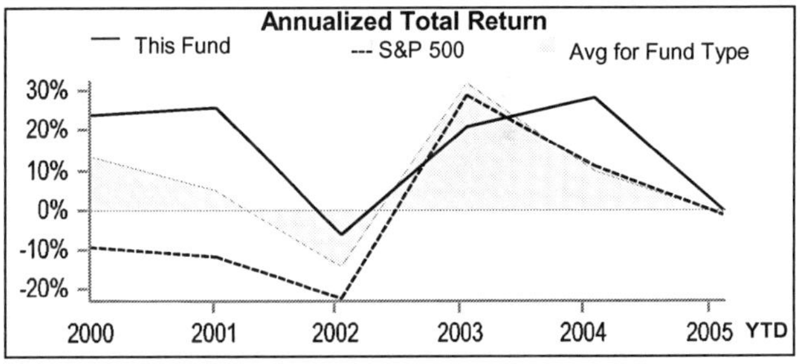

Spain Fund (SNF) C Fair

Fund Family: Alliance Capital Management L.P.
Fund Type: Foreign
Inception Date: June 28, 1988

Data Date	Weiss Investment Rating	Net Assets ($Mil)	Price	Performance Rating/Pts	Total Return Y-T-D	Risk Rating/Pts
6-05	C	87.80	12.45	B+ / 8.7	-4.75%	D / 2.0
2004	C+	77.89	13.38	A+ / 9.7	42.41%	C- / 3.2
2003	C	72.82	10.10	B+ / 8.7	65.02%	C- / 3.8

Major Rating Factors:
Spain Fund has adopted a very risky asset allocation strategy and currently receives an overall Weiss Investment Rating of C (Fair). The fund has shown a high level of volatility, as measured by both semi-deviation and drawdown factors. It carries a beta of 1.14, meaning it is expected to move 11.4% for every 10% move in the market. As of June 30, 2005, Spain Fund traded at a premium of 26.14% above its net asset value, which is worse than its one-year historical average premium of 22.87%. The high level of risk (D, Weak) did however, reward investors with excellent performance.

The fund's performance rating is currently B+ (Good). It has registered an annualized return of 22.65% over the last three years but is down -4.75% year to date 2005. Factored into the performance evaluation is an expense ratio of 1.95% (above average).

Christina Fernandez-Alepuz has been running the fund for 17 years and currently receives a manager quality ranking of 88 (0=worst, 99=best). If you are comfortable owning a very high risk investment, this fund may be an option.

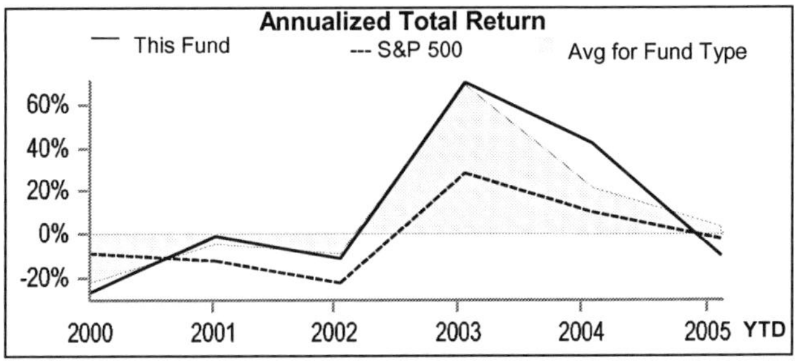

SPDR 500 (SPY) — D — Weak

Fund Family: State Street Bank & Trust Co.
Fund Type: Growth
Inception Date: January 29, 1993

Data Date	Weiss Investment Rating	Net Assets ($Mil)	Price	Performance Rating/Pts	Total Return Y-T-D	Risk Rating/Pts
6-05	D	45715.93	118.98	D / 1.8	-0.77%	C+ / 6.8
2004	D	46191.79	120.87	D / 1.9	10.71%	C+ / 6.4
2003	E+	38165.09	109.70	E+ / 0.9	26.34%	C- / 3.0

Major Rating Factors:

Disappointing performance is the major factor driving the D (Weak) Weiss Investment Rating for SPDR 500. The fund currently has a performance rating of D (Weak) based on an annualized return of 8.20% over the last three years and a total return of -0.77% year to date 2005. Factored into the performance evaluation is an expense ratio of 0.11% (very low).

The fund's risk rating is currently C+ (Fair). It carries a beta of 0.98, meaning that its performance tracks fairly well with that of the overall stock market. Volatility, as measured by standard deviation, is considered low for equity funds at 13.90. As of June 30, 2005, SPDR 500 traded at a discount of .09% below its net asset value, which is better than its one-year historical average premium of .01%.

State Street Bank has been running the fund for 12 years and currently receives a manager quality ranking of 62 (0=worst, 99=best). This fund offers only a moderate level of risk but investors looking for strong performance are still waiting.

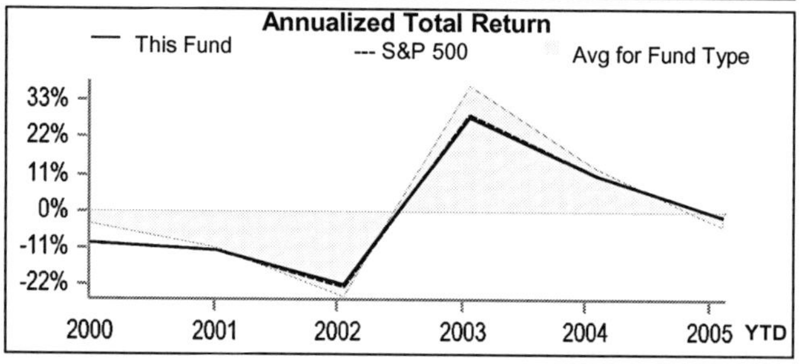

SPDR Consumer Discretionary (XLY) — E — Very Weak

Fund Family: State Street Bank & Trust Co.
Fund Type: Growth
Inception Date: December 14, 1998

Data Date	Weiss Investment Rating	Net Assets ($Mil)	Price	Performance Rating/Pts	Total Return Y-T-D	Risk Rating/Pts
6-05	E	363.76	32.84	E+ / 0.9	-6.66%	C- / 3.3
2004	D+	245.33	35.29	C / 5.1	12.88%	C / 4.7
2003	D	267.63	31.08	C / 5.4	35.39%	D+ / 2.3

Major Rating Factors:

Very poor performance is the major factor driving the E (Very Weak) Weiss Investment Rating for SPDR Consumer Discretionary. The fund currently has a performance rating of E+ (Very Weak) based on an annualized return of 6.86% over the last three years and a total return of -6.66% year to date 2005. Factored into the performance evaluation is an expense ratio of 0.26% (very low).

The fund's risk rating is currently C- (Fair). It carries a beta of 1.14, meaning it is expected to move 11.4% for every 10% move in the market. Volatility, as measured by standard deviation, is considered average for equity funds at 17.61. As of June 30, 2005, SPDR Consumer Discretionary traded at a discount of .06% below its net asset value, which is better than its one-year historical average premium of .02%.

State Street Bank has been running the fund for 7 years and currently receives a manager quality ranking of 41 (0=worst, 99=best). This fund offers an average level of risk but investors looking for strong performance will be frustrated.

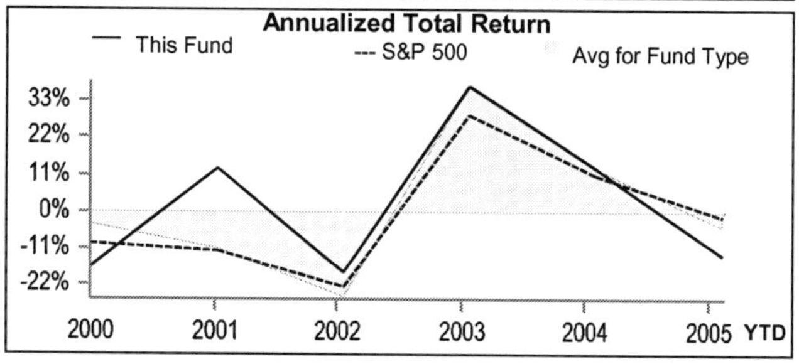

SPDR Consumer Staples (XLP) — D — Weak

Fund Family: State Street Bank & Trust Co.
Fund Type: Growth
Inception Date: December 14, 1998

Data Date	Weiss Investment Rating	Net Assets ($Mil)	Price	Performance Rating/Pts	Total Return Y-T-D	Risk Rating/Pts
6-05	D	761.53	22.74	E- / 0.2	-0.58%	B / 8.2
2004	D	600.72	23.08	E / 0.5	7.66%	B- / 7.7
2003	D	284.06	21.48	E / 0.4	9.64%	B- / 7.2

Major Rating Factors:

Very poor performance is the major factor driving the D (Weak) Weiss Investment Rating for SPDR Consumer Staples. The fund currently has a performance rating of E- (Very Weak) based on an annualized return of 2.56% over the last three years and a total return of -0.58% year to date 2005. Factored into the performance evaluation is an expense ratio of 0.25% (very low).

The fund's risk rating is currently B (Good). It carries a beta of 0.50, meaning the fund's expected move will be 5.0% for every 10% move in the market. Volatility, as measured by standard deviation, is considered low for equity funds at 9.78. As of June 30, 2005, SPDR Consumer Staples traded at a premium of .13% above its net asset value, which is worse than its one-year historical average premium of .02%.

State Street Bank has been running the fund for 7 years and currently receives a manager quality ranking of 43 (0=worst, 99=best). This fund offers only a moderate level of risk but investors looking for strong performance are still waiting.

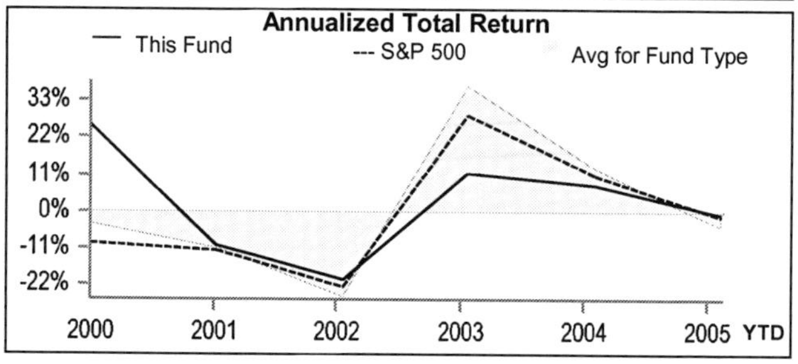

SPDR Energy (XLE) B- Good

Fund Family: State Street Bank & Trust Co.
Fund Type: Energy/Natural Resources
Inception Date: December 14, 1998

Data Date	Weiss Investment Rating	Net Assets ($Mil)	Price	Perfor-mance Rating/Pts	Total Return Y-T-D	Risk Rating/Pts
6-05	B-	2057.19	44.94	A / 9.5	24.56%	C- / 3.8
2004	C-	1302.53	36.32	B / 7.8	33.89%	C- / 3.1
2003	E+	392.15	27.36	E+ / 0.9	25.00%	D / 2.1

Major Rating Factors:
Exceptional performance is the major factor driving the B- (Good) Weiss Investment Rating for SPDR Energy. The fund currently has a performance rating of A (Excellent) based on an annualized return of 21.81% over the last three years and a total return of 24.56% year to date 2005. Factored into the performance evaluation is an expense ratio of 0.25% (very low).

The fund's risk rating is currently C- (Fair). It carries a beta of 1.01, meaning that its performance tracks fairly well with that of the overall stock market. Volatility, as measured by standard deviation, is considered average for equity funds at 19.61. As of June 30, 2005, SPDR Energy traded at a premium of .02% above its net asset value, which is worse than its one-year historical average premium of .01%.

State Street Bank has been running the fund for 7 years and currently receives a manager quality ranking of 65 (0=worst, 99=best). If you desire an average level of risk and strong performance, then this fund is a good option.

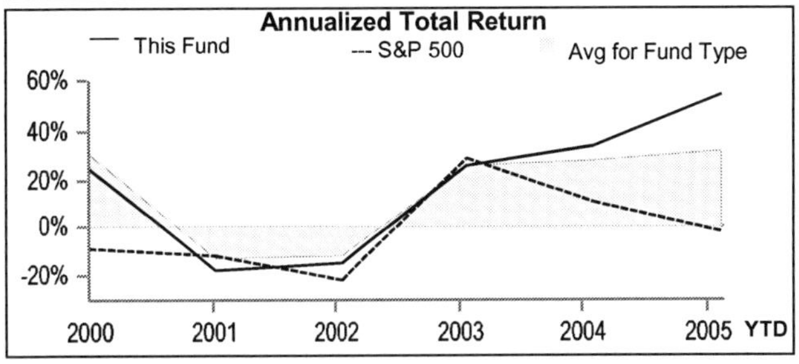

SPDR Financial (XLF) D Weak

Fund Family: State Street Bank & Trust Co.
Fund Type: Financial Services
Inception Date: December 14, 1998

Data Date	Weiss Investment Rating	Net Assets ($Mil)	Price	Perfor-mance Rating/Pts	Total Return Y-T-D	Risk Rating/Pts
6-05	D	1483.18	29.31	D- / 1.3	-2.90%	C+ / 6.8
2004	C-	841.79	30.53	C- / 3.2	10.91%	C+ / 6.8
2003	D	672.05	27.76	D- / 1.5	28.69%	C / 4.4

Major Rating Factors:
Disappointing performance is the major factor driving the D (Weak) Weiss Investment Rating for SPDR Financial. The fund currently has a performance rating of D- (Weak) based on an annualized return of 7.50% over the last three years and a total return of -2.90% year to date 2005. Factored into the performance evaluation is an expense ratio of 0.25% (very low).

The fund's risk rating is currently C+ (Fair). It carries a beta of 1.04, meaning that its performance tracks fairly well with that of the overall stock market. Volatility, as measured by standard deviation, is considered low for equity funds at 15.76. As of June 30, 2005, SPDR Financial traded at a premium of .07% above its net asset value.

State Street Bank has been running the fund for 7 years and currently receives a manager quality ranking of 40 (0=worst, 99=best). This fund offers only a moderate level of risk but investors looking for strong performance are still waiting.

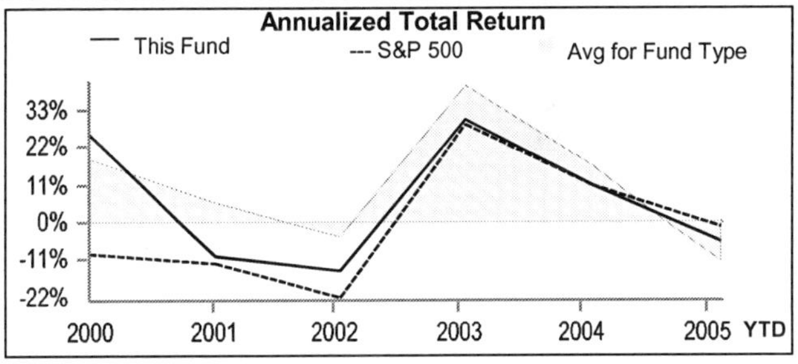

SPDR Health Care (XLV) D+ Weak

Fund Family: State Street Bank & Trust Co.
Fund Type: Growth
Inception Date: December 14, 1998

Data Date	Weiss Investment Rating	Net Assets ($Mil)	Price	Perfor-mance Rating/Pts	Total Return Y-T-D	Risk Rating/Pts
6-05	D+	1278.69	31.10	E+ / 0.8	3.66%	B- / 7.9
2004	D	748.85	30.19	D- / 1.0	1.31%	B- / 7.8
2003	D	331.11	29.70	D / 1.9	13.23%	C / 4.3

Major Rating Factors:
Very poor performance is the major factor driving the D+ (Weak) Weiss Investment Rating for SPDR Health Care. The fund currently has a performance rating of E+ (Very Weak) based on an annualized return of 5.24% over the last three years and a total return of 3.66% year to date 2005. Factored into the performance evaluation is an expense ratio of 0.25% (very low).

The fund's risk rating is currently B- (Good). It carries a beta of 0.54, meaning the fund's expected move will be 5.4% for every 10% move in the market. Volatility, as measured by standard deviation, is considered low for equity funds at 10.92. As of June 30, 2005, SPDR Health Care traded at a premium of .03% above its net asset value, which is worse than its one-year historical average premium of .02%.

State Street Bank has been running the fund for 7 years and currently receives a manager quality ranking of 62 (0=worst, 99=best). This fund offers only a moderate level of risk but investors looking for strong performance are still waiting.

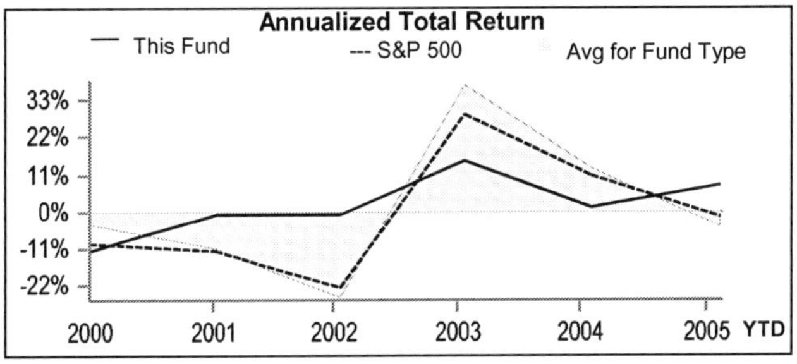

SPDR Industrial (XLI) D Weak

Fund Family: State Street Bank & Trust Co.
Fund Type: Growth
Inception Date: December 14, 1998

Major Rating Factors:
Disappointing performance is the major factor driving the D (Weak) Weiss Investment Rating for SPDR Industrial. The fund currently has a performance rating of D- (Weak) based on an annualized return of 8.67% over the last three years and a total return of -5.15% year to date 2005. Factored into the performance evaluation is an expense ratio of 0.26% (very low).

The fund's risk rating is currently B- (Good). It carries a beta of 0.96, meaning that its performance tracks fairly well with that of the overall stock market. Volatility, as measured by standard deviation, is considered low for equity funds at 14.92. As of June 30, 2005, SPDR Industrial traded at a premium of .03% above its net asset value, which is worse than its one-year historical average discount of .01%.

State Street Bank has been running the fund for 7 years and currently receives a manager quality ranking of 66 (0=worst, 99=best). This fund offers only a moderate level of risk but investors looking for strong performance are still waiting.

Data Date	Weiss Investment Rating	Net Assets ($Mil)	Price	Performance Rating/Pts	Total Return Y-T-D	Risk Rating/Pts
6-05	D	770.94	29.29	D- / 1.3	-5.15%	B- / 7.0
2004	C-	676.01	31.07	C- / 3.8	17.74%	C+ / 6.6
2003	E	548.63	26.55	D- / 1.2	30.79%	D- / 1.2

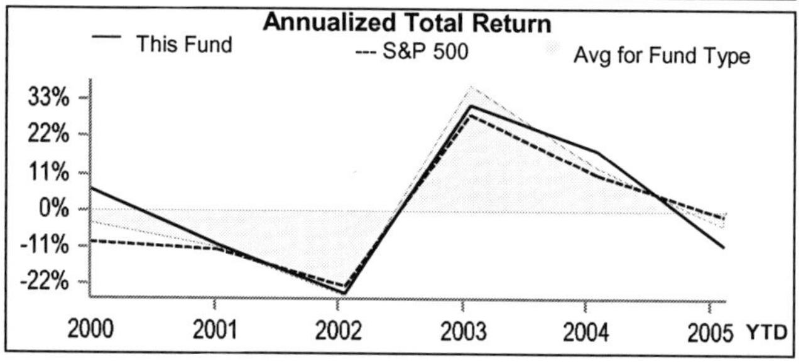

SPDR Materials (XLB) E Very Weak

Fund Family: State Street Bank & Trust Co.
Fund Type: Growth
Inception Date: December 14, 1998

Major Rating Factors:
Disappointing performance is the major factor driving the E (Very Weak) Weiss Investment Rating for SPDR Materials. The fund currently has a performance rating of D- (Weak) based on an annualized return of 7.84% over the last three years and a total return of -7.24% year to date 2005. Factored into the performance evaluation is an expense ratio of 0.26% (very low).

The fund's risk rating is currently C- (Fair). It carries a beta of 1.25, meaning it is expected to move 12.5% for every 10% move in the market. Volatility, as measured by standard deviation, is considered average for equity funds at 20.71. As of June 30, 2005, SPDR Materials traded at a price exactly equal to its net asset value.

State Street Bank has been running the fund for 7 years and currently receives a manager quality ranking of 40 (0=worst, 99=best). This fund offers an average level of risk but investors looking for strong performance will be frustrated.

Data Date	Weiss Investment Rating	Net Assets ($Mil)	Price	Performance Rating/Pts	Total Return Y-T-D	Risk Rating/Pts
6-05	E	842.98	27.34	D- / 1.0	-7.24%	C- / 3.2
2004	D+	674.70	29.73	C+ / 6.3	13.48%	C- / 3.5
2003	D+	557.09	26.48	B- / 7.5	36.23%	D- / 1.1

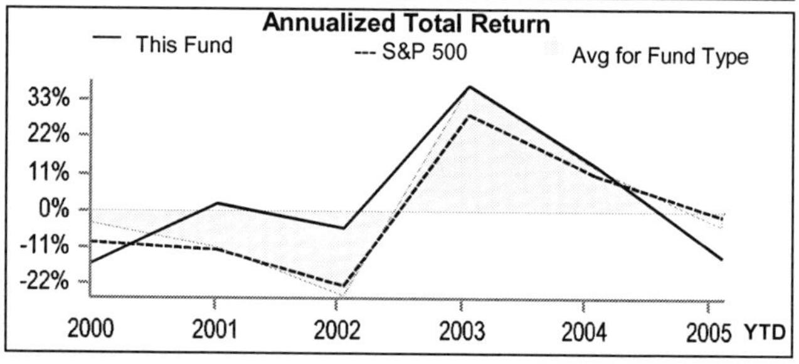

SPDR Mid Cap 400 (MDY) C Fair

Fund Family: Bank of New York
Fund Type: Growth
Inception Date: May 4, 1995

Major Rating Factors:
Middle of the road best describes SPDR Mid Cap 400 whose Weiss Investment Rating is currently a C (Fair). The fund currently has a performance rating of C- (Fair) based on an annualized return of 12.32% over the last three years and a total return of 2.42% year to date 2005. Factored into the performance evaluation is an expense ratio of 0.25% (very low).

The fund's risk rating is currently C+ (Fair). It carries a beta of 0.96, meaning that its performance tracks fairly well with that of the overall stock market. Volatility, as measured by standard deviation, is considered low for equity funds at 14.88. As of June 30, 2005, SPDR Mid Cap 400 traded at a discount of .29% below its net asset value, which is better than its one-year historical average discount of .02%.

This fund has been team managed for 10 years and currently receives a manager quality ranking of 81 (0=worst, 99=best). If you desire an average level of risk, then this fund may be an option.

Data Date	Weiss Investment Rating	Net Assets ($Mil)	Price	Performance Rating/Pts	Total Return Y-T-D	Risk Rating/Pts
6-05	C	6536.03	123.21	C- / 3.8	2.42%	C+ / 6.9
2004	C+	6884.67	121.00	C+ / 5.7	15.90%	C+ / 6.9
2003	D	5127.79	104.75	C / 4.3	34.42%	D+ / 2.7

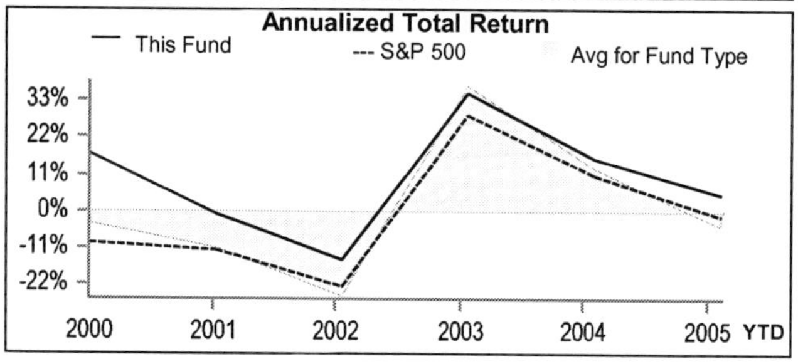

SPDR Technology (XLK) E- Very Weak

Fund Family: State Street Bank & Trust Co.
Fund Type: Growth
Inception Date: December 14, 1998

Major Rating Factors:
SPDR Technology has adopted a very risky asset allocation strategy and currently receives an overall Weiss Investment Rating of E- (Very Weak). The fund has a high level of volatility, with a standard deviation of 25.76. It carries a beta of 1.65, meaning it is expected to move 16.5% for every 10% move in the market. As of June 30, 2005, SPDR Technology traded at a premium of .15% above its net asset value, which is worse than its one-year historical average discount of .01%. Unfortunately, the high level of risk (D-, Weak) failed to pay off as investors endured poor performance.

The fund's performance rating is currently D- (Weak). It has registered an annualized return of 9.20% over the last three years but is down -5.31% year to date 2005. Factored into the performance evaluation is an expense ratio of 0.26% (very low).

State Street Bank has been running the fund for 7 years and currently receives a manager quality ranking of 27 (0=worst, 99=best). If you can tolerate very high levels of risk in the hope of improved future returns, holding this fund may be an option.

Data Date	Weiss Investment Rating	Net Assets ($Mil)	Price	Performance Rating/Pts	Total Return Y-T-D	Risk Rating/Pts
6-05	E-	1040.14	19.99	D- / 1.5	-5.31%	D- / 1.5
2004	E-	1049.90	21.11	E- / 0.1	5.66%	D- / 1.0
2003	E	1085.16	20.08	E / 0.3	36.64%	D- / 1.3

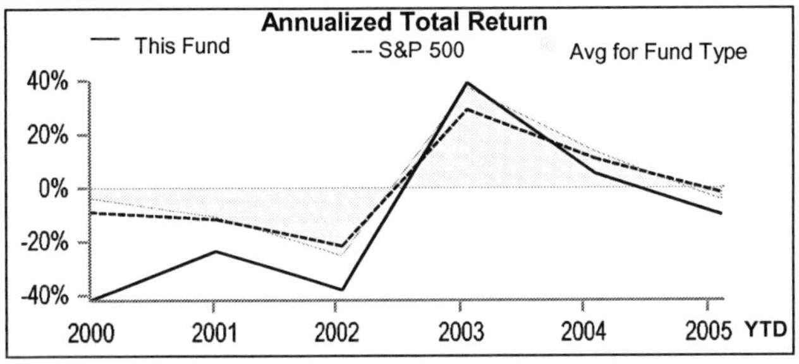

SPDR Utilities (XLU) C Fair

Fund Family: State Street Bank & Trust Co.
Fund Type: Utilities
Inception Date: December 14, 1998

Major Rating Factors:
Strong performance is the major factor driving the C (Fair) Weiss Investment Rating for SPDR Utilities. The fund currently has a performance rating of B- (Good) based on an annualized return of 12.77% over the last three years and a total return of 13.48% year to date 2005. Factored into the performance evaluation is an expense ratio of 0.26% (very low).

The fund's risk rating is currently C (Fair). It carries a beta of 0.98, meaning that its performance tracks fairly well with that of the overall stock market. Volatility, as measured by standard deviation, is considered average for equity funds at 17.84. As of June 30, 2005, SPDR Utilities traded at a premium of .10% above its net asset value.

State Street Bank has been running the fund for 7 years and currently receives a manager quality ranking of 36 (0=worst, 99=best). If you desire an average level of risk and strong performance, then this fund is a good option.

Data Date	Weiss Investment Rating	Net Assets ($Mil)	Price	Performance Rating/Pts	Total Return Y-T-D	Risk Rating/Pts
6-05	C	1830.04	31.12	B- / 7.2	13.48%	C / 4.4
2004	D	1123.76	27.85	C / 4.4	23.55%	C- / 4.0
2003	D-	1222.89	23.14	E / 0.5	25.42%	C- / 3.7

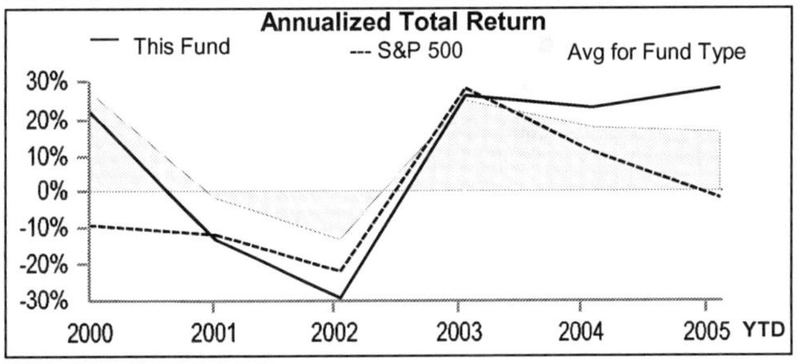

Strategic Global Income Fund (SGL) C- Fair

Fund Family: UBS Global Asset Management
Fund Type: Global
Inception Date: January 31, 1992

Major Rating Factors:
Middle of the road best describes Strategic Global Income Fund whose Weiss Investment Rating is currently a C- (Fair). The fund currently has a performance rating of C (Fair) based on an annualized return of 14.58% over the last three years and a total return of -11.71% year to date 2005. Factored into the performance evaluation is an expense ratio of 1.16% (low).

The fund's risk rating is currently C (Fair). It carries a beta of 1.43, meaning it is expected to move 14.3% for every 10% move in the market. Volatility, as measured by both the semi-deviation and a drawdown factor, is considered average. As of June 30, 2005, Strategic Global Income Fund traded at a premium of 11.44% above its net asset value, which is worse than its one-year historical average premium of 11.43%.

This fund has been team managed for 13 years and currently receives a manager quality ranking of 49 (0=worst, 99=best). If you desire an average level of risk, then this fund may be an option.

Data Date	Weiss Investment Rating	Net Assets ($Mil)	Price	Performance Rating/Pts	Total Return Y-T-D	Risk Rating/Pts
6-05	C-	239.54	13.25	C / 4.9	-11.71%	C / 4.6
2004	B+	228.06	15.70	A / 9.4	20.62%	C / 5.3
2003	A-	236.10	14.74	B / 8.1	21.69%	B- / 7.5

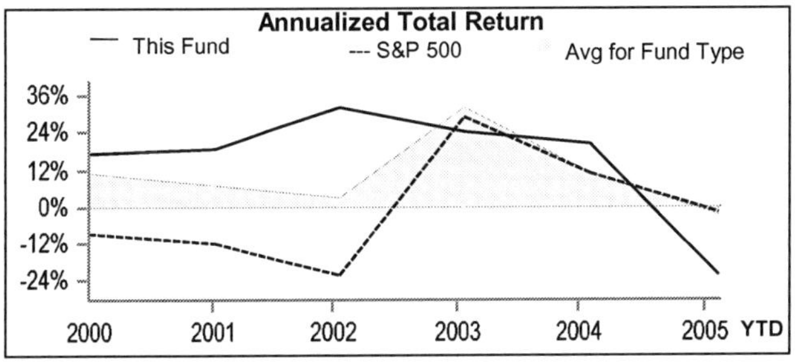

streetTRACKS DJ Global Titan (DGT) D Weak

Fund Family: State Street Bank Global Advisors
Fund Type: Global
Inception Date: September 29, 2000

Data Date	Weiss Investment Rating	Net Assets ($Mil)	Price	Performance Rating/Pts	Total Return Y-T-D	Risk Rating/Pts
6-05	D	93.38	63.21	E+ / 0.9	-0.81%	B- / 7.0
2004	D-	67.58	64.43	E+ / 0.9	7.38%	C+ / 6.5
2003	D-	19.87	60.40	E+ / 0.7	23.37%	C- / 3.6

Major Rating Factors:
Very poor performance is the major factor driving the D (Weak) Weiss Investment Rating for streetTRACKS DJ Global Titan. The fund currently has a performance rating of E+ (Very Weak) based on an annualized return of 6.18% over the last three years and a total return of -0.81% year to date 2005. Factored into the performance evaluation is an expense ratio of 0.51% (very low).

The fund's risk rating is currently B- (Good). It carries a beta of 0.86, meaning the fund's expected move will be 8.6% for every 10% move in the market. Volatility, as measured by standard deviation, is considered low for equity funds at 14.67. As of June 30, 2005, streetTRACKS DJ Global Titan traded at a discount of .09% below its net asset value, which is better than its one-year historical average premium of .10%.

AGUSTIN J. FLEITES has been running the fund for 5 years and currently receives a manager quality ranking of 21 (0=worst, 99=best). This fund offers only a moderate level of risk but investors looking for strong performance are still waiting.

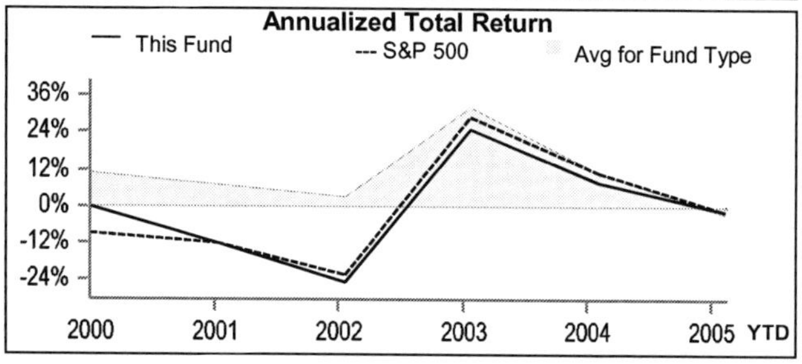

streetTRACKS DJ US Lg Cap Growth (ELG) D- Weak

Fund Family: State Street Bank Global Advisors
Fund Type: Growth
Inception Date: September 25, 2000

Data Date	Weiss Investment Rating	Net Assets ($Mil)	Price	Performance Rating/Pts	Total Return Y-T-D	Risk Rating/Pts
6-05	D-	82.15	46.51	E / 0.5	-3.62%	C+ / 6.6
2004	E+	68.97	48.45	E / 0.3	5.26%	C- / 4.2
2003	E	31.37	46.13	E- / 0.2	26.92%	D- / 1.3

Major Rating Factors:
Very poor performance is the major factor driving the D- (Weak) Weiss Investment Rating for streetTRACKS DJ US Lg Cap Growth. The fund currently has a performance rating of E (Very Weak) based on an annualized return of 5.47% over the last three years and a total return of -3.62% year to date 2005. Factored into the performance evaluation is an expense ratio of 0.21% (very low).

The fund's risk rating is currently C+ (Fair). It carries a beta of 1.05, meaning that its performance tracks fairly well with that of the overall stock market. Volatility, as measured by standard deviation, is considered low for equity funds at 15.58. As of June 30, 2005, streetTRACKS DJ US Lg Cap Growth traded at a premium of .45% above its net asset value, which is worse than its one-year historical average premium of .03%.

AGUSTIN J. FLEITES has been running the fund for 5 years and currently receives a manager quality ranking of 31 (0=worst, 99=best). This fund offers only a moderate level of risk but investors looking for strong performance are still waiting.

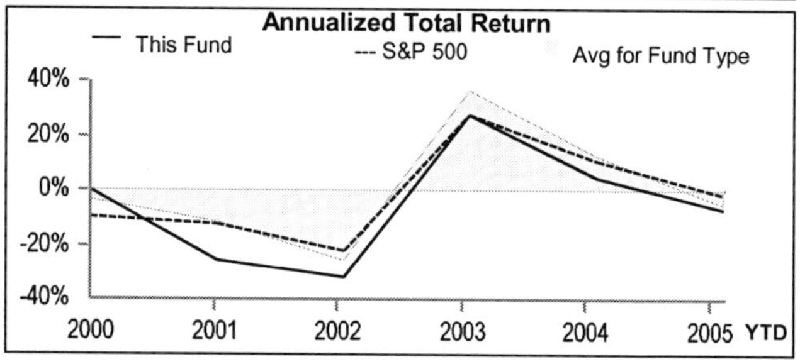

streetTRACKS DJ US Lg Cap Value (ELV) C- Fair

Fund Family: State Street Bank Global Advisors
Fund Type: Growth
Inception Date: September 25, 2000

Data Date	Weiss Investment Rating	Net Assets ($Mil)	Price	Performance Rating/Pts	Total Return Y-T-D	Risk Rating/Pts
6-05	C-	122.88	136.14	D+ / 2.3	0.82%	B- / 7.1
2004	D+	94.37	136.66	C- / 3.0	13.20%	C+ / 6.7
2003	D	80.93	121.61	D- / 1.0	23.17%	C+ / 6.5

Major Rating Factors:
Disappointing performance is the major factor driving the C- (Fair) Weiss Investment Rating for streetTRACKS DJ US Lg Cap Value. The fund currently has a performance rating of D+ (Weak) based on an annualized return of 8.87% over the last three years and a total return of 0.82% year to date 2005. Factored into the performance evaluation is an expense ratio of 0.22% (very low).

The fund's risk rating is currently B- (Good). It carries a beta of 0.99, meaning that its performance tracks fairly well with that of the overall stock market. Volatility, as measured by standard deviation, is considered low for equity funds at 14.42. As of June 30, 2005, streetTRACKS DJ US Lg Cap Value traded at a premium of .17% above its net asset value.

AGUSTIN J. FLEITES has been running the fund for 5 years and currently receives a manager quality ranking of 64 (0=worst, 99=best). This fund offers only a moderate level of risk but investors looking for strong performance are still waiting.

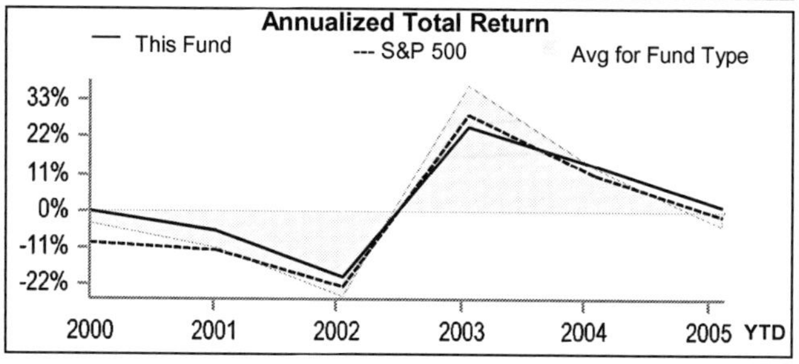

streetTRACKS DJ US Small Cap Growth (DSG) E+ Very Weak

Fund Family: State Street Bank Global Advisors
Fund Type: Growth
Inception Date: September 25, 2000

Data Date	Weiss Investment Rating	Net Assets ($Mil)	Price	Perfor-mance Rating/Pts	Total Return Y-T-D	Risk Rating/Pts
6-05	E+	56.80	74.74	C- / 3.2	-1.15%	C- / 3.3
2004	E+	55.94	75.75	D / 1.7	14.83%	D+ / 2.3
2003	E	41.66	65.67	D- / 1.1	46.37%	D- / 1.3

Major Rating Factors:
streetTRACKS DJ US Small Cap Growth receives a Weiss Investment Rating of E+ (Very Weak). The fund currently has a performance rating of C- (Fair) based on an annualized return of 11.91% over the last three years and a total return of -1.15% year to date 2005. Factored into the performance evaluation is an expense ratio of 0.26% (very low).

The fund's risk rating is currently C- (Fair). It carries a beta of 1.26, meaning it is expected to move 12.6% for every 10% move in the market. Volatility, as measured by standard deviation, is considered average for equity funds at 20.14. As of June 30, 2005, streetTRACKS DJ US Small Cap Growth traded at a discount of .07% below its net asset value, which is better than its one-year historical average premium of .04%.

AGUSTIN J. FLEITES has been running the fund for 5 years and currently receives a manager quality ranking of 75 (0=worst, 99=best). If you desire an average level of risk, then this fund may be an option.

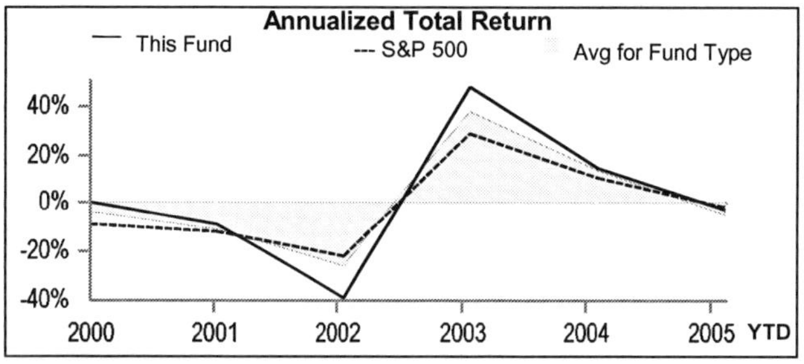

streetTRACKS DJ US Small Cap Value (DSV) C- Fair

Fund Family: State Street Bank Global Advisors
Fund Type: Growth
Inception Date: September 25, 2000

Data Date	Weiss Investment Rating	Net Assets ($Mil)	Price	Perfor-mance Rating/Pts	Total Return Y-T-D	Risk Rating/Pts
6-05	C-	99.48	174.03	C / 5.0	-3.07%	C / 4.4
2004	B+	76.93	181.21	B / 8.2	18.12%	C+ / 6.6
2003	B	45.79	161.25	B+ / 8.5	41.80%	C+ / 6.1

Major Rating Factors:
Middle of the road best describes streetTRACKS DJ US Small Cap Value whose Weiss Investment Rating is currently a C- (Fair). The fund currently has a performance rating of C (Fair) based on an annualized return of 15.03% over the last three years and a total return of -3.07% year to date 2005. Factored into the performance evaluation is an expense ratio of 0.26% (very low).

The fund's risk rating is currently C (Fair). It carries a beta of 0.99, meaning that its performance tracks fairly well with that of the overall stock market. Volatility, as measured by standard deviation, is considered average for equity funds at 17.02. As of June 30, 2005, streetTRACKS DJ US Small Cap Value traded at a discount of .51% below its net asset value, which is better than its one-year historical average discount of .09%.

AGUSTIN J. FLEITES has been running the fund for 5 years and currently receives a manager quality ranking of 86 (0=worst, 99=best). If you desire an average level of risk, then this fund may be an option.

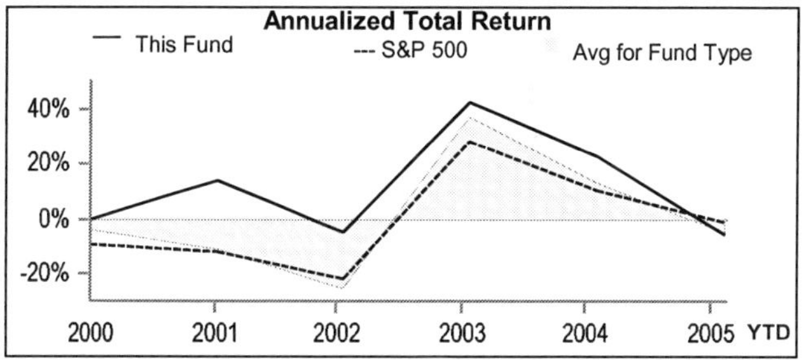

streetTRACKS MS Technology Index (MTK) E Very Weak

Fund Family: State Street Bank Global Advisors
Fund Type: Growth
Inception Date: September 25, 2000

Data Date	Weiss Investment Rating	Net Assets ($Mil)	Price	Perfor-mance Rating/Pts	Total Return Y-T-D	Risk Rating/Pts
6-05	E	30.32	47.33	D+ / 2.8	-6.29%	E+ / 0.7
2004	E-	24.60	50.52	E / 0.3	6.59%	E / 0.3
2003	E-	24.92	46.87	E+ / 0.8	63.60%	E / 0.4

Major Rating Factors:
streetTRACKS MS Technology Index has adopted a very risky asset allocation strategy and currently receives an overall Weiss Investment Rating of E (Very Weak). The fund has a high level of volatility, with a standard deviation of 31.31. It carries a beta of 1.98, meaning it is expected to move 19.8% for every 10% move in the market. As of June 30, 2005, streetTRACKS MS Technology Index traded at a discount of .17% below its net asset value, which is better than its one-year historical average discount of .02%. Unfortunately, the high level of risk (E+, Very Weak) failed to pay off as investors endured poor performance.

The fund's performance rating is currently D+ (Weak). It has registered an annualized return of 12.52% over the last three years but is down -6.29% year to date 2005. Factored into the performance evaluation is an expense ratio of 0.51% (very low).

AGUSTIN J. FLEITES has been running the fund for 5 years and currently receives a manager quality ranking of 35 (0=worst, 99=best). If you can tolerate very high levels of risk in the hope of improved future returns, holding this fund may be an option.

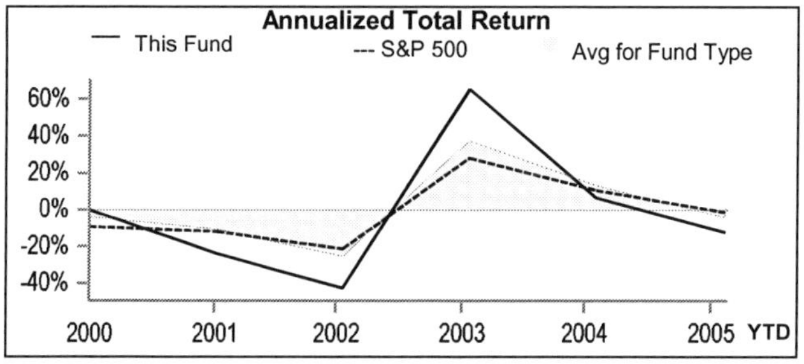

streetTRACKS Total Market ETF (TMW) D+ Weak

Fund Family: State Street Bank Global Advisors
Fund Type: Growth
Inception Date: October 4, 2000

Data Date	Weiss Investment Rating	Net Assets ($Mil)	Price	Perfor-mance Rating/Pts	Total Return Y-T-D	Risk Rating/Pts
6-05	D+	119.88	85.14	D / 1.6	-0.13%	B- / 7.2
2004	D+	113.23	85.94	D / 1.9	10.56%	B- / 7.0
2003	D-	94.07	78.09	E+ / 0.8	25.22%	C- / 4.1

Major Rating Factors:

Disappointing performance is the major factor driving the D+ (Weak) Weiss Investment Rating for streetTRACKS Total Market ETF. The fund currently has a performance rating of D (Weak) based on an annualized return of 7.69% over the last three years and a total return of -0.13% year to date 2005. Factored into the performance evaluation is an expense ratio of 0.21% (very low).

The fund's risk rating is currently B- (Good). It carries a beta of 0.99, meaning that its performance tracks fairly well with that of the overall stock market. Volatility, as measured by standard deviation, is considered low for equity funds at 14.04. As of June 30, 2005, streetTRACKS Total Market ETF traded at a premium of .12% above its net asset value, which is worse than its one-year historical average premium of .01%.

AGUSTIN J. FLEITES has been running the fund for 5 years and currently receives a manager quality ranking of 60 (0=worst, 99=best). This fund offers only a moderate level of risk but investors looking for strong performance are still waiting.

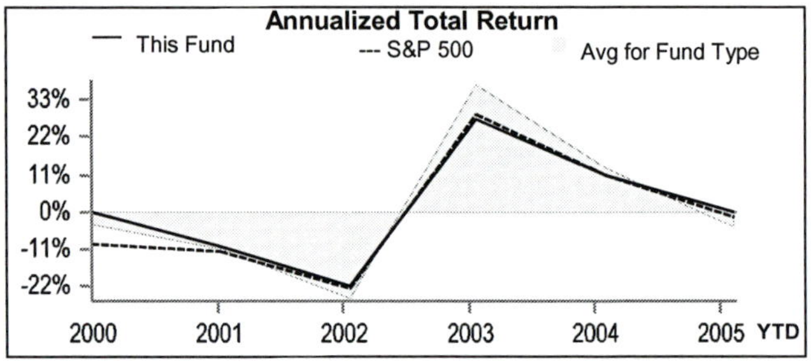

streetTRACKS Wilshire REIT (RWR) C+ Fair

Fund Family: State Street Bank Global Advisors
Fund Type: Growth and Income
Inception Date: April 23, 2001

Data Date	Weiss Investment Rating	Net Assets ($Mil)	Price	Perfor-mance Rating/Pts	Total Return Y-T-D	Risk Rating/Pts
6-05	C+	535.09	194.85	B+ / 8.8	5.70%	C- / 3.9
2004	A+	462.47	187.58	A- / 9.2	32.43%	C+ / 6.5

Major Rating Factors:

Strong performance is the major factor driving the C+ (Fair) Weiss Investment Rating for streetTRACKS Wilshire REIT. The fund currently has a performance rating of B+ (Good) based on an annualized return of 19.98% over the last three years and a total return of 5.70% year to date 2005. Factored into the performance evaluation is an expense ratio of 0.26% (very low).

The fund's risk rating is currently C- (Fair). It carries a beta of 0.41, meaning the fund's expected move will be 4.1% for every 10% move in the market. Volatility, as measured by standard deviation, is considered average for equity funds at 17.20. As of June 30, 2005, streetTRACKS Wilshire REIT traded at a discount of .02% below its net asset value, which is better than its one-year historical average premium of .01%.

Patrick Donnelly has been running the fund for 4 years and currently receives a manager quality ranking of 95 (0=worst, 99=best). If you desire an average level of risk and strong performance, then this fund is a good option.

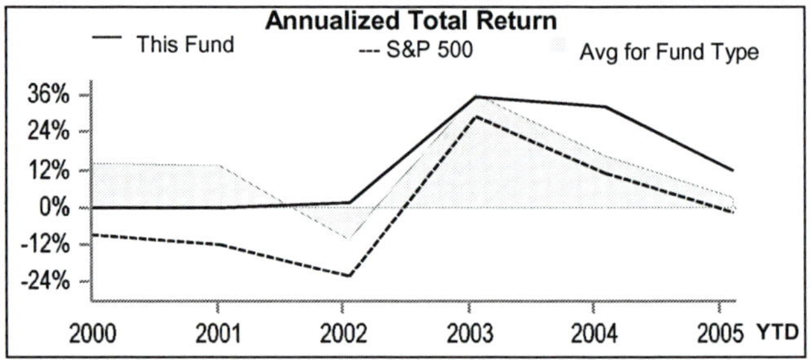

Swiss Helvetia Fund (SWZ) D+ Weak

Fund Family: Hottinger Capital Corp.
Fund Type: Foreign
Inception Date: August 27, 1987

Data Date	Weiss Investment Rating	Net Assets ($Mil)	Price	Perfor-mance Rating/Pts	Total Return Y-T-D	Risk Rating/Pts
6-05	D+	401.51	13.69	C- / 3.5	-6.27%	C+ / 5.6
2004	B	375.31	14.95	B+ / 8.8	23.50%	C / 5.1
2003	D+	299.53	12.55	C- / 4.0	38.08%	C+ / 5.6

Major Rating Factors:

Swiss Helvetia Fund receives a Weiss Investment Rating of D+ (Weak). The fund currently has a performance rating of C- (Fair) based on an annualized return of 13.40% over the last three years and a total return of -6.27% year to date 2005. Factored into the performance evaluation is an expense ratio of 1.14% (low).

The fund's risk rating is currently C+ (Fair). It carries a beta of 1.05, meaning that its performance tracks fairly well with that of the overall stock market. Volatility, as measured by both the semi-deviation and a drawdown factor, is considered low. As of June 30, 2005, Swiss Helvetia Fund traded at a discount of 14.70% below its net asset value, which is worse than its one-year historical average discount of 14.86%.

Philippe Comby has been running the fund for 9 years and currently receives a manager quality ranking of 64 (0=worst, 99=best). If you desire an average level of risk, then this fund may be an option.

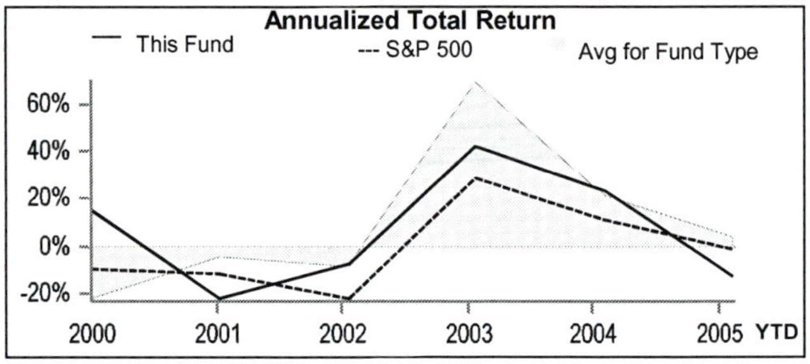

Taiwan Fund (TWN) E+ Very Weak

Fund Family: HSBC Asset Management
Fund Type: Foreign
Inception Date: December 5, 1986

Data Date	Weiss Investment Rating	Net Assets ($Mil)	Price	Performance Rating/Pts	Total Return Y-T-D	Risk Rating/Pts
6-05	E+	245.21	13.69	C- / 3.5	3.32%	D+ / 2.6
2004	E	209.17	13.25	D- / 1.5	11.61%	D+ / 2.3
2003	D+	209.85	11.90	C / 5.1	35.23%	C- / 3.0

Major Rating Factors:
Taiwan Fund has adopted a risky asset allocation strategy and currently receives an overall Weiss Investment Rating of E+ (Very Weak). The fund has an above average level of volatility, as measured by both semi-deviation and drawdown factors. It carries a beta of 1.14, meaning it is expected to move 11.4% for every 10% move in the market. As of June 30, 2005, Taiwan Fund traded at a discount of 12.13% below its net asset value, which is better than its one-year historical average discount of 11.53%. Unfortunately, the high level of risk (D+, Weak) has only provided investors with average performance.

The fund's performance rating is currently C- (Fair). It has registered an annualized return of 7.32% over the last three years and is up 3.32% year to date 2005. Factored into the performance evaluation is an expense ratio of 1.97% (above average).

Victor Shih has been running the fund for 1 year and currently receives a manager quality ranking of 8 (0=worst, 99=best). If you are comfortable owning a high risk investment, then this fund may be an option.

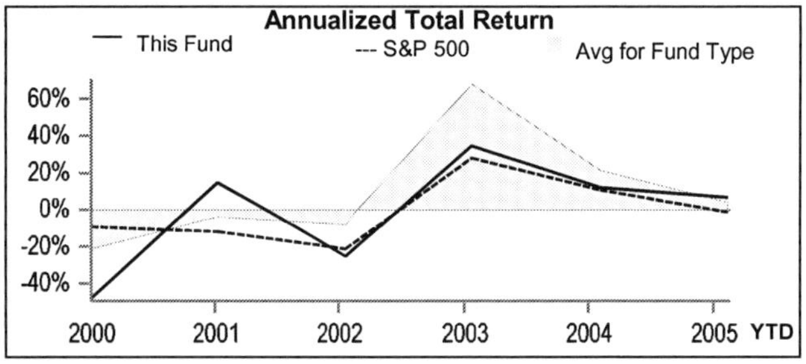

Taiwan Greater China Fund (TFC) D- Weak

Fund Family: Altman Group
Fund Type: Foreign
Inception Date: May 18, 1989

Data Date	Weiss Investment Rating	Net Assets ($Mil)	Price	Performance Rating/Pts	Total Return Y-T-D	Risk Rating/Pts
6-05	D-	116.47	5.17	D+ / 2.7	5.51%	C / 4.8
2004	E+	154.15	4.90	E+ / 0.8	3.42%	C- / 4.1
2003	D-	143.37	4.64	D / 2.0	16.08%	C- / 3.5

Major Rating Factors:
Disappointing performance is the major factor driving the D- (Weak) Weiss Investment Rating for Taiwan Greater China Fund. The fund currently has a performance rating of D+ (Weak) based on an annualized return of 6.02% over the last three years and a total return of 5.51% year to date 2005. Factored into the performance evaluation is an expense ratio of 2.79% (high).

The fund's risk rating is currently C (Fair). It carries a beta of 0.76, meaning the fund's expected move will be 7.6% for every 10% move in the market. Volatility, as measured by both the semi-deviation and a drawdown factor, is considered average. As of June 30, 2005, Taiwan Greater China Fund traded at a discount of 7.18% below its net asset value, which is worse than its one-year historical average discount of 8.91%.

Steven R. Champion has been running the fund for 16 years and currently receives a manager quality ranking of 24 (0=worst, 99=best). This fund offers an average level of risk but investors looking for strong performance will be frustrated.

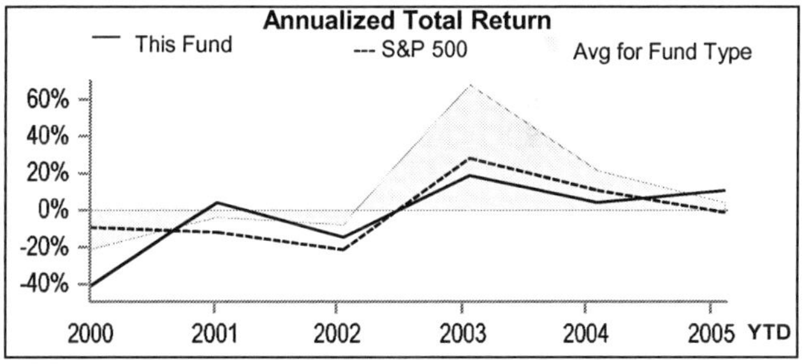

TCW Convertible Securities Fund (CVT) E Very Weak

Fund Family: TCW Funds Management, Inc.
Fund Type: Growth and Income
Inception Date: February 26, 1987

Data Date	Weiss Investment Rating	Net Assets ($Mil)	Price	Performance Rating/Pts	Total Return Y-T-D	Risk Rating/Pts
6-05	E	280.87	5.09	E- / 0.0	-3.17%	C- / 3.1
2004	E	278.54	5.36	E- / 0.1	12.78%	D / 1.9
2003	E	259.28	5.00	E- / 0.2	25.86%	D / 2.1

Major Rating Factors:
Very poor performance is the major factor driving the E (Very Weak) Weiss Investment Rating for TCW Convertible Securities Fund. The fund currently has a performance rating of E- (Very Weak) based on an annualized return of -0.90% over the last three years and a total return of -3.17% year to date 2005. Factored into the performance evaluation is an expense ratio of 0.90% (low).

The fund's risk rating is currently C- (Fair). It carries a beta of 1.12, meaning it is expected to move 11.2% for every 10% move in the market. Volatility, as measured by both the semi-deviation and a drawdown factor, is considered average. As of June 30, 2005, TCW Convertible Securities Fund traded at a discount of 7.62% below its net asset value, which is worse than its one-year historical average discount of 9.26%.

Thomas D. Lyon, CFA has been running the fund for 8 years and currently receives a manager quality ranking of 3 (0=worst, 99=best). This fund offers an average level of risk but investors looking for strong performance will be frustrated.

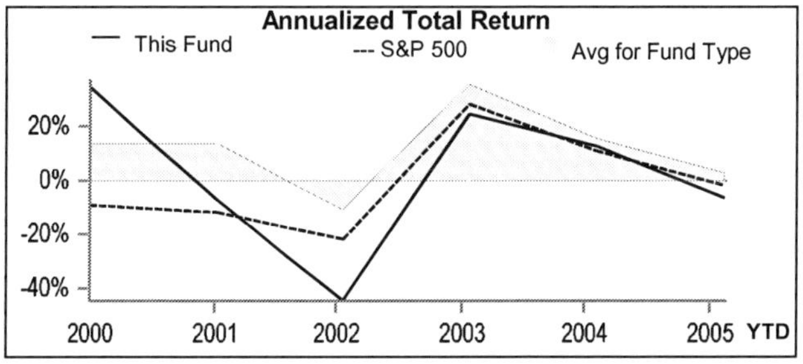

Templeton Dragon Fund (TDF) C+ Fair

Fund Family: Templeton Investment Management
Fund Type: Foreign
Inception Date: September 21, 1994

Major Rating Factors:
Templeton Dragon Fund has adopted a risky asset allocation strategy and currently receives an overall Weiss Investment Rating of C+ (Fair). The fund has shown an above average level of volatility, as measured by both semi-deviation and drawdown factors. It carries a beta of 1.07, meaning that its performance tracks fairly well with that of the overall stock market. As of June 30, 2005, Templeton Dragon Fund traded at a discount of 9.37% below its net asset value, which is worse than its one-year historical average discount of 10.70%. The high level of risk (D+, Weak) did however, reward investors with excellent performance.

The fund's performance rating is currently A (Excellent). It has registered an annualized return of 28.90% over the last three years and is up 3.88% year to date 2005. Factored into the performance evaluation is an expense ratio of 1.52% (average).

J. Mark Mobius has been running the fund for 11 years and currently receives a manager quality ranking of 94 (0=worst, 99=best). If you are comfortable owning a high risk investment, this fund may be an option.

Data Date	Weiss Investment Rating	Net Assets ($Mil)	Price	Performance Rating/Pts	Total Return Y-T-D	Risk Rating/Pts
6-05	C+	706.14	17.99	A / 9.5	3.88%	D+ / 2.5
2004	C+	626.29	17.47	A / 9.5	0.28%	C- / 3.6
2003	C+	439.21	17.40	A+ / 9.7	95.39%	C- / 3.7

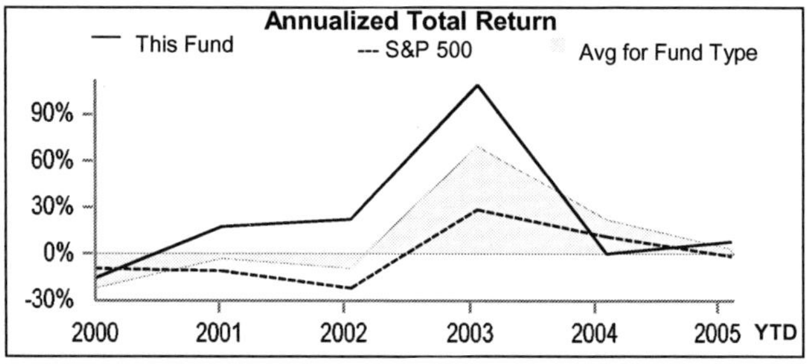

Templeton Emerging Markets Fd (EMF) C Fair

Fund Family: Templeton Investment Management
Fund Type: Emerging Market
Inception Date: February 26, 1987

Major Rating Factors:
Templeton Emerging Markets Fd has adopted a very risky asset allocation strategy and currently receives an overall Weiss Investment Rating of C (Fair). The fund has shown a high level of volatility, as measured by both semi-deviation and drawdown factors. It carries a beta of 1.58, meaning it is expected to move 15.8% for every 10% move in the market. As of June 30, 2005, Templeton Emerging Markets Fd traded at a premium of 1.92% above its net asset value, which is worse than its one-year historical average premium of .88%. The high level of risk (D-, Weak) did however, reward investors with excellent performance.

The fund's performance rating is currently A (Excellent). It has registered an annualized return of 24.37% over the last three years and is up 5.94% year to date 2005. Factored into the performance evaluation is an expense ratio of 1.55% (average).

J. Mark Mobius has been running the fund for 18 years and currently receives a manager quality ranking of 1 (0=worst, 99=best). If you are comfortable owning a very high risk investment, this fund may be an option.

Data Date	Weiss Investment Rating	Net Assets ($Mil)	Price	Performance Rating/Pts	Total Return Y-T-D	Risk Rating/Pts
6-05	C	306.19	17.48	A / 9.4	5.94%	D- / 1.3
2004	C+	236.85	16.50	A / 9.4	16.27%	C- / 3.6
2003	B-	191.08	14.00	A+ / 9.6	83.91%	C / 4.6

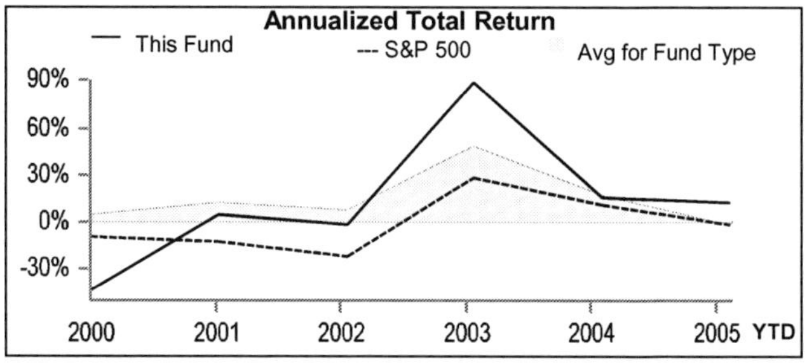

Templeton Emerging Markets Income (TEI) C+ Fair

Fund Family: Templeton Investment Management
Fund Type: Emerging Market
Inception Date: September 23, 1993

Major Rating Factors:
Strong performance is the major factor driving the C+ (Fair) Weiss Investment Rating for Templeton Emerging Markets Income. The fund currently has a performance rating of B (Good) based on an annualized return of 17.45% over the last three years and a total return of 3.19% year to date 2005. Factored into the performance evaluation is an expense ratio of 1.09% (low).

The fund's risk rating is currently C (Fair). It carries a beta of 0.99, meaning that its performance tracks fairly well with that of the overall stock market. Volatility, as measured by both the semi-deviation and a drawdown factor, is considered average. As of June 30, 2005, Templeton Emerging Markets Income traded at a discount of .50% below its net asset value, which is worse than its one-year historical average discount of 2.58%.

Umran Demirors has been running the fund for 9 years and currently receives a manager quality ranking of 85 (0=worst, 99=best). If you desire an average level of risk and strong performance, then this fund is a good option.

Data Date	Weiss Investment Rating	Net Assets ($Mil)	Price	Performance Rating/Pts	Total Return Y-T-D	Risk Rating/Pts
6-05	C+	674.60	13.93	B / 7.6	3.19%	C / 4.8
2004	B-	624.11	13.76	B / 8.1	10.62%	C / 5.5
2003	B+	591.03	13.49	B+ / 8.3	24.02%	C+ / 6.7

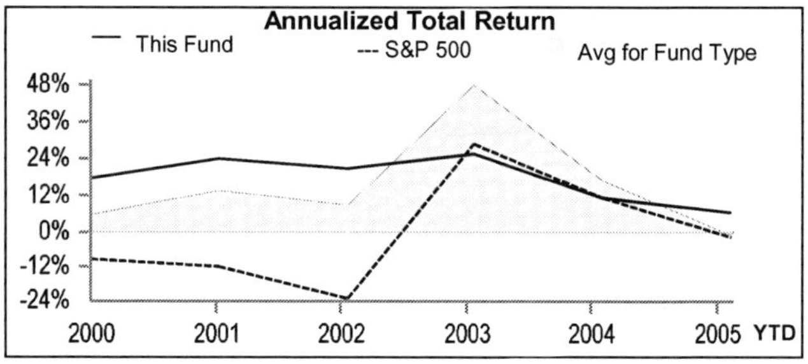

Templeton Global Income Fd (GIM) D+ Weak

Fund Family: Templeton Investment Management
Fund Type: Global
Inception Date: March 24, 1988

Data Date	Weiss Investment Rating	Net Assets ($Mil)	Price	Performance Rating/Pts	Total Return Y-T-D	Risk Rating/Pts
6-05	D+	1245.83	8.87	C- / 3.7	-8.27%	C / 5.3
2004	A	1136.98	9.93	A- / 9.0	11.86%	C+ / 6.4
2003	A	1058.79	9.48	A- / 9.0	31.51%	C+ / 6.7

Major Rating Factors:
Templeton Global Income Fd receives a Weiss Investment Rating of D+ (Weak). The fund currently has a performance rating of C- (Fair) based on an annualized return of 12.51% over the last three years and a total return of -8.27% year to date 2005. Factored into the performance evaluation is an expense ratio of 0.75% (very low).

The fund's risk rating is currently C (Fair). It carries a beta of 1.44, meaning it is expected to move 14.4% for every 10% move in the market. Volatility, as measured by both the semi-deviation and a drawdown factor, is considered average. As of June 30, 2005, Templeton Global Income Fd traded at a discount of 2.42% below its net asset value, which is better than its one-year historical average discount of 1.46%.

Tom Dickson has been running the fund for 9 years and currently receives a manager quality ranking of 37 (0=worst, 99=best). If you desire an average level of risk, then this fund may be an option.

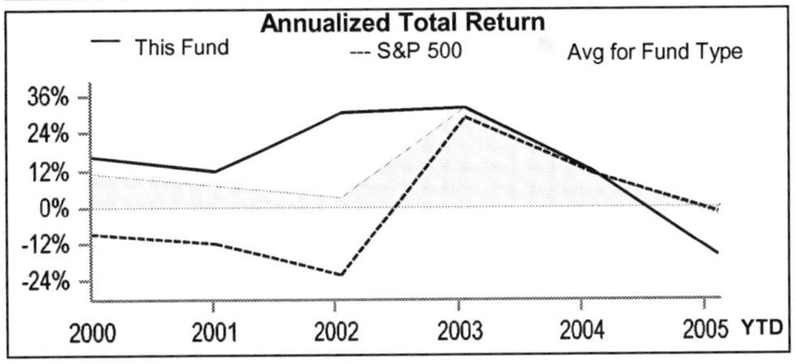

Templeton Russia&East European Fund (TRF) C+ Fair

Fund Family: Templeton Investment Management
Fund Type: Foreign
Inception Date: June 15, 1995

Data Date	Weiss Investment Rating	Net Assets ($Mil)	Price	Performance Rating/Pts	Total Return Y-T-D	Risk Rating/Pts
6-05	C+	218.58	40.02	A+ / 9.8	6.78%	D / 2.2
2004	C+	203.82	39.60	A+ / 9.8	41.64%	D+ / 2.7
2003	B	171.62	32.37	A+ / 9.7	70.43%	C / 4.8

Major Rating Factors:
Templeton Russia&East European Fund has adopted a very risky asset allocation strategy and currently receives an overall Weiss Investment Rating of C+ (Fair). The fund has shown a high level of volatility, as measured by both semi-deviation and drawdown factors. It carries a beta of 1.29, meaning it is expected to move 12.9% for every 10% move in the market. As of June 30, 2005, Templeton Russia&East European Fund traded at a premium of 4.87% above its net asset value, which is worse than its one-year historical average premium of 2.42%. The high level of risk (D, Weak) did however, reward investors with excellent performance.

The fund's performance rating is currently A+ (Excellent). It has registered an annualized return of 38.99% over the last three years and is up 6.78% year to date 2005. Factored into the performance evaluation is an expense ratio of 1.80% (above average).

J. Mark Mobius has been running the fund for 10 years and currently receives a manager quality ranking of 98 (0=worst, 99=best). If you are comfortable owning a very high risk investment, this fund may be an option.

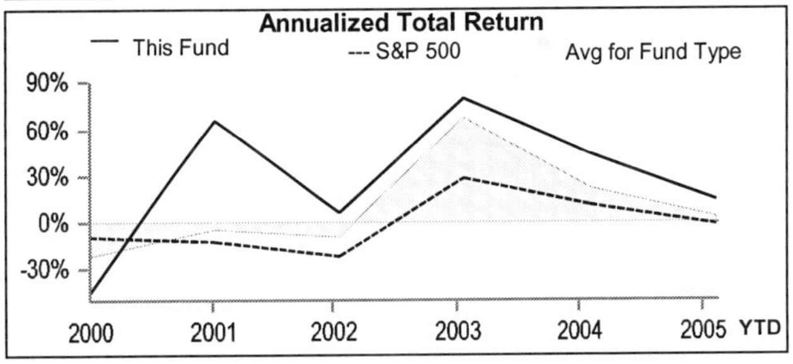

Thai Capital Fund (TF) C- Fair

Fund Family: SCB Asset Management Co, Ltd
Fund Type: Foreign
Inception Date: May 30, 1990

Data Date	Weiss Investment Rating	Net Assets ($Mil)	Price	Performance Rating/Pts	Total Return Y-T-D	Risk Rating/Pts
6-05	C-	27.89	9.52	A+ / 9.7	12.13%	E / 0.3
2004	C+	25.33	8.36	A+ / 9.7	-9.19%	D+ / 2.9
2003	C-	17.86	8.26	A+ / 9.8	108.06%	E / 0.4

Major Rating Factors:
Thai Capital Fund has adopted a very risky asset allocation strategy and currently receives an overall Weiss Investment Rating of C- (Fair). The fund has shown a high level of volatility, as measured by both semi-deviation and drawdown factors. It carries a beta of 1.89, meaning it is expected to move 18.9% for every 10% move in the market. As of June 30, 2005, Thai Capital Fund traded at a premium of 9.68% above its net asset value, which is worse than its one-year historical average discount of 1.69%. The high level of risk (E, Very Weak) did however, reward investors with excellent performance.

The fund's performance rating is currently A+ (Excellent). It has registered an annualized return of 34.72% over the last three years and is up 12.13% year to date 2005. Factored into the performance evaluation is an expense ratio of 2.26% (high).

Cholathee Pornrojnangkool has been running the fund for 4 years and currently receives a manager quality ranking of 85 (0=worst, 99=best). If you are comfortable owning a very high risk investment, this fund may be an option.

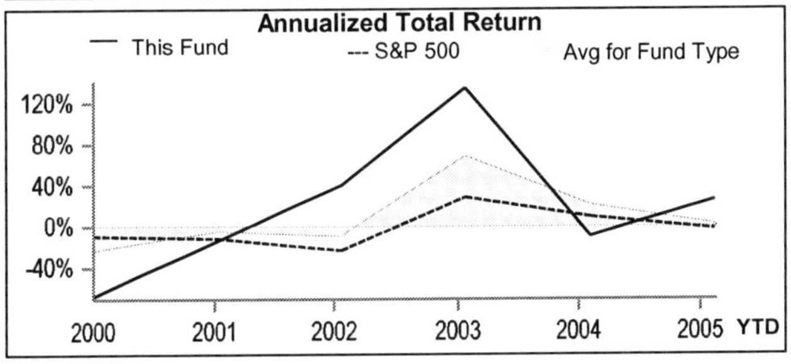

Thai Fund (TTF) C- Fair

Fund Family: Morgan Stanley Invesment Advisors,I
Fund Type: Foreign
Inception Date: February 17, 1988

Data Date	Weiss Investment Rating	Net Assets ($Mil)	Price	Perfor-mance Rating/Pts	Total Return Y-T-D	Risk Rating/Pts
6-05	C-	110.40	9.69	A / 9.4	8.27%	E+ / 0.7
2004	C-	101.55	8.95	A / 9.5	-12.72%	D- / 1.3
2003	C-	68.71	9.93	A+ / 9.9	188.22%	D- / 1.2

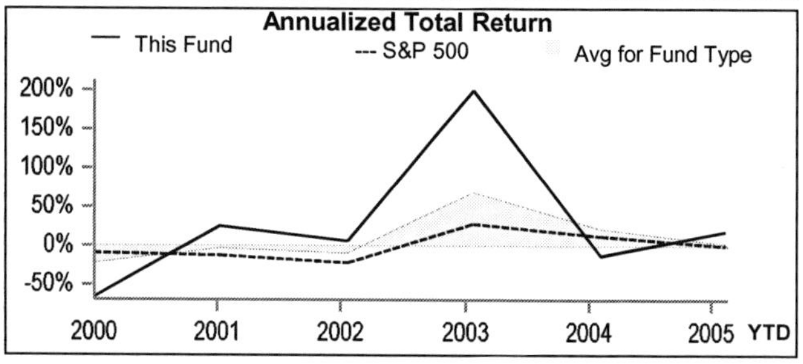

Major Rating Factors:
Thai Fund has adopted a very risky asset allocation strategy and currently receives an overall Weiss Investment Rating of C- (Fair). The fund has shown a high level of volatility, as measured by both semi-deviation and drawdown factors. It carries a beta of 1.64, meaning it is expected to move 16.4% for every 10% move in the market. As of June 30, 2005, Thai Fund traded at a premium of 16.89% above its net asset value, which is worse than its one-year historical average premium of 11.36%. The high level of risk (E+, Very Weak) did however, reward investors with excellent performance.

The fund's performance rating is currently A (Excellent). It has registered an annualized return of 28.98% over the last three years and is up 8.27% year to date 2005. Factored into the performance evaluation is an expense ratio of 1.73% (above average).

Ashutosh Sinha has been running the fund for 17 years and currently receives a manager quality ranking of 86 (0=worst, 99=best). If you are comfortable owning a very high risk investment, this fund may be an option.

The New Ireland Fund (IRL) B+ Good

Fund Family: Bank of Ireland Asset Management Lt
Fund Type: Foreign
Inception Date: March 29, 1990

Data Date	Weiss Investment Rating	Net Assets ($Mil)	Price	Perfor-mance Rating/Pts	Total Return Y-T-D	Risk Rating/Pts
6-05	B+	110.86	21.20	A- / 9.2	0.43%	C / 5.1
2004	A	83.70	21.11	A+ / 9.6	41.97%	C+ / 5.9
2003	C	77.79	14.59	B- / 7.3	60.27%	C / 4.6

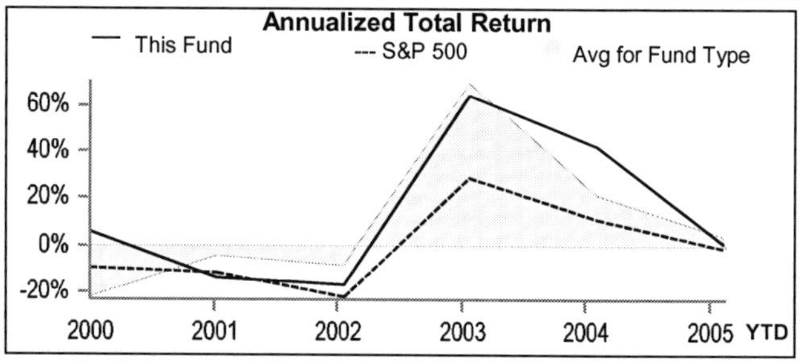

Major Rating Factors:
Exceptional performance is the major factor driving the B+ (Good) Weiss Investment Rating for The New Ireland Fund. The fund currently has a performance rating of A- (Excellent) based on an annualized return of 25.91% over the last three years and a total return of 0.43% year to date 2005. Factored into the performance evaluation is an expense ratio of 1.43% (average).

The fund's risk rating is currently C (Fair). It carries a beta of 1.08, meaning that its performance tracks fairly well with that of the overall stock market. Volatility, as measured by both the semi-deviation and a drawdown factor, is considered average. As of June 30, 2005, The New Ireland Fund traded at a discount of 13.96% below its net asset value, which is better than its one-year historical average discount of 13.38%.

Bank of Ireland Asset Mgmt has been running the fund for 15 years and currently receives a manager quality ranking of 93 (0=worst, 99=best). If you desire an average level of risk and strong performance, then this fund is a good option.

Third Canadian General Invst Tr (T.THD) C- Fair

Fund Family: Morgan Meighen & Associates Limited
Fund Type: Foreign
Inception Date: N/A

Data Date	Weiss Investment Rating	Net Assets ($Mil)	Price	Perfor-mance Rating/Pts	Total Return Y-T-D	Risk Rating/Pts
6-05	C-	130.38	28.95	A- / 9.1	12.56%	D- / 1.1
2004	C	130.38	25.85	A / 9.3	32.45%	D / 2.2
2003	C	93.35	19.60	B+ / 8.6	36.73%	C- / 3.2

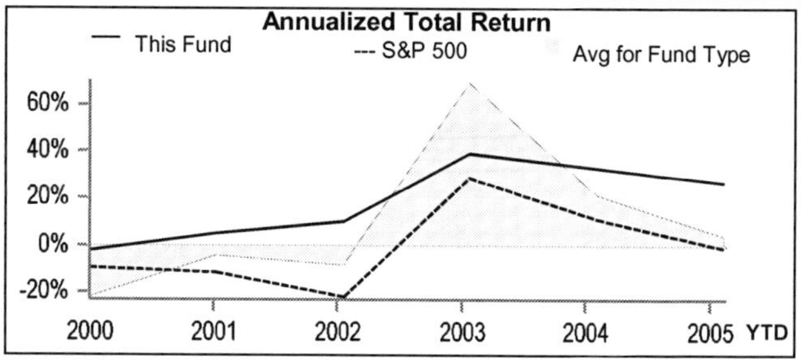

Major Rating Factors:
Third Canadian General Invst Tr has adopted a very risky asset allocation strategy and currently receives an overall Weiss Investment Rating of C- (Fair). The fund has shown a high level of volatility, with a standard deviation of 22.17. It carries a beta of 0.76, meaning the fund's expected move will be 7.6% for every 10% move in the market. As of June 30, 2005, Third Canadian General Invst Tr traded at a discount of 21.67% below its net asset value, which is better than its one-year historical average discount of 15.44%. The high level of risk (D-, Weak) did however, reward investors with excellent performance.

The fund's performance rating is currently A- (Excellent). It has registered an annualized return of 22.53% over the last three years and is up 12.56% year to date 2005.

Michael A. Smedley has been running the fund for 17 years and currently receives a manager quality ranking of 92 (0=worst, 99=best). If you are comfortable owning a very high risk investment, this fund may be an option.

Transamerica Income Shares (TAI) D- Weak

Fund Family: Transamerica Investment Management,
Fund Type: Global
Inception Date: February 28, 1978

Major Rating Factors:
Very poor performance is the major factor driving the D- (Weak) Weiss Investment Rating for Transamerica Income Shares. The fund currently has a performance rating of E (Very Weak) based on an annualized return of 1.44% over the last three years and a total return of 2.38% year to date 2005. Factored into the performance evaluation is an expense ratio of 0.72% (very low).

The fund's risk rating is currently B- (Good). It carries a beta of 0.45, meaning the fund's expected move will be 4.5% for every 10% move in the market. Volatility, as measured by both the semi-deviation and a drawdown factor, is considered low. As of June 30, 2005, Transamerica Income Shares traded at a discount of 5.37% below its net asset value, which is worse than its one-year historical average discount of 5.79%.

Peter Lopez has been running the fund for 27 years and currently receives a manager quality ranking of 21 (0=worst, 99=best). This fund offers only a moderate level of risk but investors looking for strong performance are still waiting.

Data Date	Weiss Investment Rating	Net Assets ($Mil)	Price	Performance Rating/Pts	Total Return Y-T-D	Risk Rating/Pts
6-05	D-	146.38	22.19	E / 0.4	2.38%	B- / 7.2
2004	D	150.34	22.32	E+ / 0.9	1.06%	B- / 7.6
2003	D+	150.73	23.70	D- / 1.5	0.01%	B / 8.1

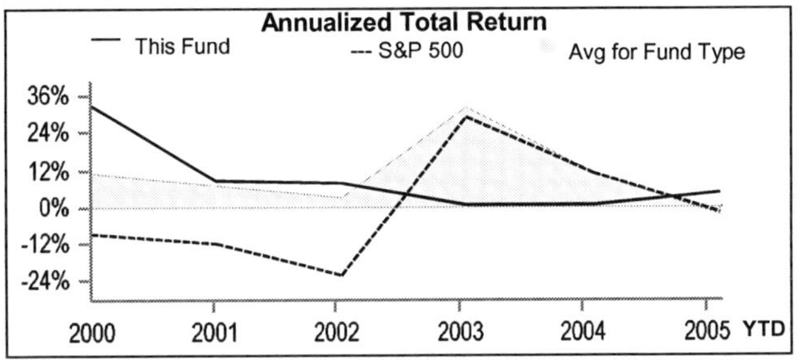

Tri-Continental Corporation (TY) D- Weak

Fund Family: Seligman, J.W. & Co., Inc.
Fund Type: Income
Inception Date: N/A

Major Rating Factors:
Very poor performance is the major factor driving the D- (Weak) Weiss Investment Rating for Tri-Continental Corporation. The fund currently has a performance rating of E+ (Very Weak) based on an annualized return of 4.84% over the last three years and a total return of -1.86% year to date 2005. Factored into the performance evaluation is an expense ratio of 0.66% (very low).

The fund's risk rating is currently C+ (Fair). It carries a beta of 1.05, meaning that its performance tracks fairly well with that of the overall stock market. Volatility, as measured by both the semi-deviation and a drawdown factor, is considered low. As of June 30, 2005, Tri-Continental Corporation traded at a discount of 16.80% below its net asset value, which is better than its one-year historical average discount of 16.42%.

John B. Cunningham, CFA has been running the fund for 1 year and currently receives a manager quality ranking of 26 (0=worst, 99=best). This fund offers only a moderate level of risk but investors looking for strong performance are still waiting.

Data Date	Weiss Investment Rating	Net Assets ($Mil)	Price	Performance Rating/Pts	Total Return Y-T-D	Risk Rating/Pts
6-05	D-	2470.78	17.83	E+ / 0.7	-1.86%	C+ / 6.5
2004	E+	2353.19	18.28	E+ / 0.8	12.95%	C / 5.0
2003	D	2062.87	16.15	E+ / 0.7	23.31%	C / 5.4

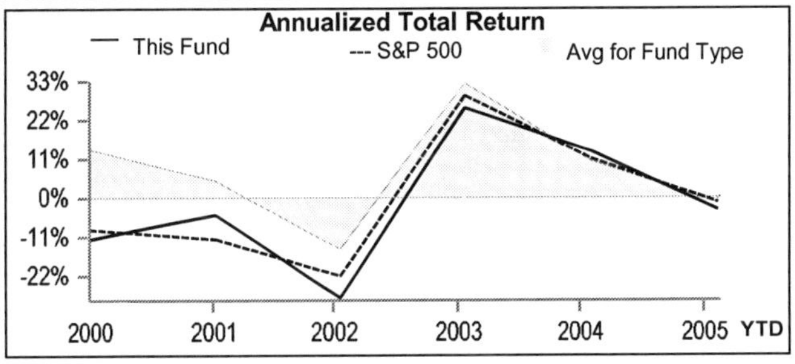

Turkish Investment Fund (TKF) C Fair

Fund Family: Morgan Stanley Invesment Advisors,I
Fund Type: Foreign
Inception Date: December 5, 1989

Major Rating Factors:
Turkish Investment Fund has adopted a very risky asset allocation strategy and currently receives an overall Weiss Investment Rating of C (Fair). The fund has shown a high level of volatility, as measured by both semi-deviation and drawdown factors. It carries a beta of 1.86, meaning it is expected to move 18.6% for every 10% move in the market. As of June 30, 2005, Turkish Investment Fund traded at a premium of 8.61% above its net asset value, which is better than its one-year historical average premium of 11.87%. The high level of risk (E+, Very Weak) did however, reward investors with excellent performance.

The fund's performance rating is currently A+ (Excellent). It has registered an annualized return of 55.92% over the last three years but is down -8.94% year to date 2005. Factored into the performance evaluation is an expense ratio of 1.20% (average).

Eric Carlson has been running the fund for 16 years and currently receives a manager quality ranking of 99 (0=worst, 99=best). If you are comfortable owning a very high risk investment, this fund may be an option.

Data Date	Weiss Investment Rating	Net Assets ($Mil)	Price	Performance Rating/Pts	Total Return Y-T-D	Risk Rating/Pts
6-05	C	68.40	15.89	A+ / 9.9	-8.94%	E+ / 0.8
2004	C-	50.81	17.45	A+ / 9.9	63.83%	E+ / 0.6
2003	C-	40.17	10.78	A+ / 9.8	168.64%	E+ / 0.6

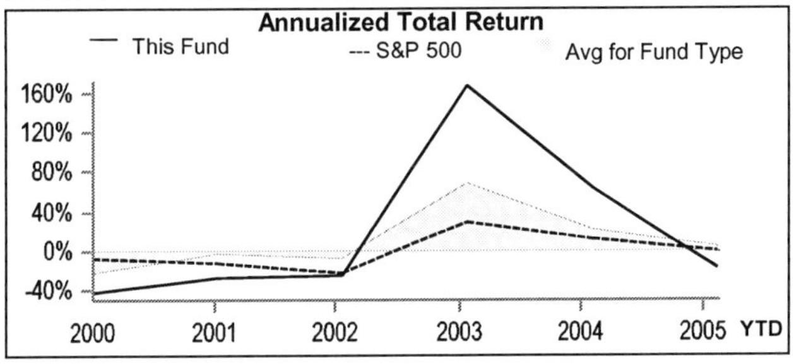

Tuxis Corporation (TUX) — E- Very Weak

Fund Family: Tuxis
Fund Type: Growth
Inception Date: November 8, 1996

Data Date	Weiss Investment Rating	Net Assets ($Mil)	Price	Perfor-mance Rating/Pts	Total Return Y-T-D	Risk Rating/Pts
6-05	E-	9.11	0.00	E- / 0.1	19.46%	D- / 1.4
2004	E	9.32	0.00	E- / 0.1	-3.91%	D / 2.1
2003	D-	9.34	7.88	E- / 0.2	-14.61%	C / 5.3

Major Rating Factors:
Tuxis Corporation has adopted a very risky asset allocation strategy and currently receives an overall Weiss Investment Rating of E- (Very Weak). The fund has a high level of volatility, as measured by both semi-deviation and drawdown factors. It carries a beta of 0.31, meaning the fund's expected move will be 3.1% for every 10% move in the market. As of June 30, 2005, Tuxis Corporation traded at a price exactly equal to its net asset value, which is worse than its one-year historical average discount of 18.64%. Unfortunately, the high level of risk (D-, Weak) failed to pay off as investors endured very poor performance.

The fund's performance rating is currently E- (Very Weak). It has registered an annualized return of -3.52% over the last three years and is up 19.46% year to date 2005. Factored into the performance evaluation is an expense ratio of 5.09% (high).

Mark C. Winmill has been running the fund for 3 years and currently receives a manager quality ranking of 7 (0=worst, 99=best). If you can tolerate very high levels of risk in the hope of improved future returns, holding this fund may be an option.

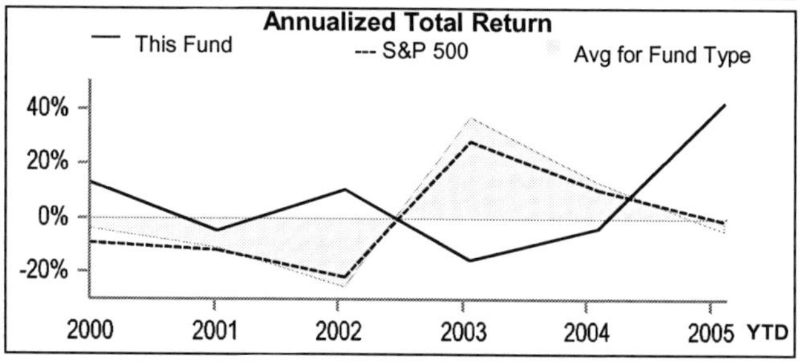

Van Kampen Adv Muni Inc (VKA) — C Fair

Fund Family: Van Kampen Asset Management
Fund Type: Municipal - National
Inception Date: September 25, 1992

Data Date	Weiss Investment Rating	Net Assets ($Mil)	Price	Perfor-mance Rating/Pts	Total Return Y-T-D	Risk Rating/Pts
6-05	C	321.41	14.85	C- / 3.6	5.63%	B- / 7.0
2004	C-	310.84	14.53	C- / 3.2	-5.18%	B- / 7.8
2003	A-	319.55	16.29	B / 7.6	10.70%	B- / 7.9

Major Rating Factors:
Middle of the road best describes Van Kampen Adv Muni Inc whose Weiss Investment Rating is currently a C (Fair). The fund currently has a performance rating of C- (Fair) based on an annualized return of 5.03% over the last three years and a total return of 5.63% year to date 2005. Factored into the performance evaluation is an expense ratio of 1.17% (low).

The fund's risk rating is currently B- (Good). It carries a beta of 2.46, meaning it is expected to move 24.6% for every 10% move in the market. Volatility, as measured by both the semi-deviation and a drawdown factor, is considered low. As of June 30, 2005, Van Kampen Adv Muni Inc traded at a discount of 12.80% below its net asset value, which is better than its one-year historical average discount of 11.54%.

Brian Neely has been running the fund for 10 years and currently receives a manager quality ranking of 8 (0=worst, 99=best). If you desire an average level of risk, then this fund may be an option.

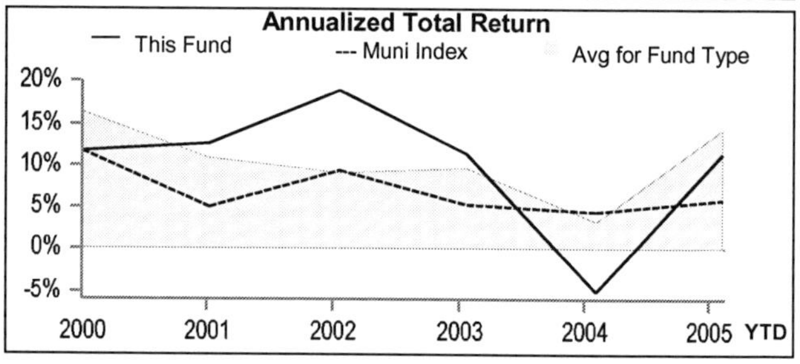

Van Kampen Adv Muni Inc II (VKI) — C Fair

Fund Family: Van Kampen Asset Management
Fund Type: Municipal - National
Inception Date: August 27, 1993

Data Date	Weiss Investment Rating	Net Assets ($Mil)	Price	Perfor-mance Rating/Pts	Total Return Y-T-D	Risk Rating/Pts
6-05	C	121.86	13.78	C- / 3.6	5.75%	B- / 7.3
2004	C	117.92	13.47	C- / 3.4	-4.23%	B- / 7.8
2003	A+	119.99	15.38	B+ / 8.8	13.58%	B- / 7.5

Major Rating Factors:
Middle of the road best describes Van Kampen Adv Muni Inc II whose Weiss Investment Rating is currently a C (Fair). The fund currently has a performance rating of C- (Fair) based on an annualized return of 6.32% over the last three years and a total return of 5.75% year to date 2005. Factored into the performance evaluation is an expense ratio of 1.30% (average).

The fund's risk rating is currently B- (Good). It carries a beta of 2.12, meaning it is expected to move 21.2% for every 10% move in the market. Volatility, as measured by both the semi-deviation and a drawdown factor, is considered low. As of June 30, 2005, Van Kampen Adv Muni Inc II traded at a discount of 8.74% below its net asset value, which is better than its one-year historical average discount of 5.61%.

Brian Neely has been running the fund for 12 years and currently receives a manager quality ranking of 19 (0=worst, 99=best). If you desire an average level of risk, then this fund may be an option.

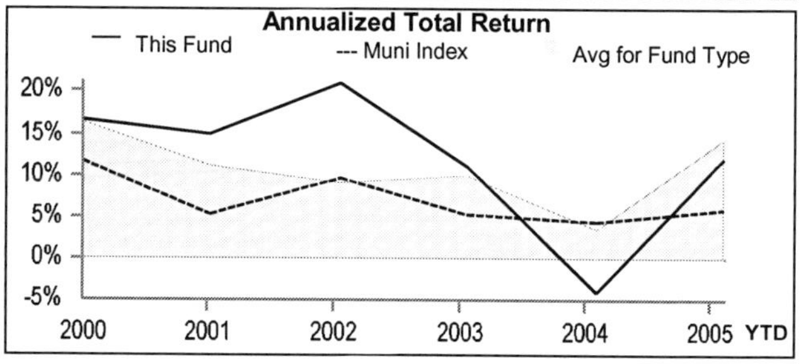

Van Kampen Adv PA Muni (VAP) D Weak

Fund Family: Van Kampen Asset Management
Fund Type: Municipal - Single State
Inception Date: September 25, 1992

Major Rating Factors:
Disappointing performance is the major factor driving the D (Weak) Weiss Investment Rating for Van Kampen Adv PA Muni. The fund currently has a performance rating of D (Weak) based on an annualized return of 3.03% over the last three years and a total return of 1.31% year to date 2005. Factored into the performance evaluation is an expense ratio of 1.29% (average).

The fund's risk rating is currently C+ (Fair). It carries a beta of 2.34, meaning it is expected to move 23.4% for every 10% move in the market. Volatility, as measured by both the semi-deviation and a drawdown factor, is considered low. As of June 30, 2005, Van Kampen Adv PA Muni traded at a discount of 14.29% below its net asset value, which is better than its one-year historical average discount of 11.21%.

Dennis Pietrzak has been running the fund for 13 years and currently receives a manager quality ranking of 5 (0=worst, 99=best). This fund offers only a moderate level of risk but investors looking for strong performance are still waiting.

Data Date	Weiss Investment Rating	Net Assets ($Mil)	Price	Performance Rating/Pts	Total Return Y-T-D	Risk Rating/Pts
6-05	D	73.89	14.70	D / 1.8	1.31%	C+ / 6.7
2004	C-	71.77	14.92	C- / 3.1	-0.56%	B- / 7.5
2003	C+	74.93	16.20	C / 5.0	6.68%	B / 8.2

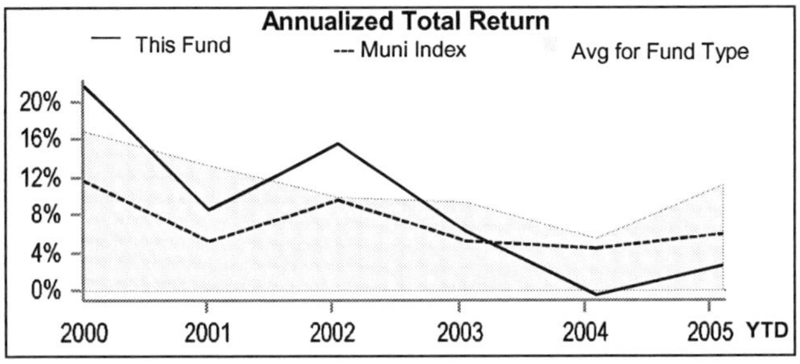

Van Kampen Bond (VBF) C- Fair

Fund Family: Van Kampen Asset Management
Fund Type: Corporate - Investment Grade
Inception Date: July 9, 1970

Major Rating Factors:
Disappointing performance is the major factor driving the C- (Fair) Weiss Investment Rating for Van Kampen Bond. The fund currently has a performance rating of D (Weak) based on an annualized return of 5.47% over the last three years and a total return of 2.37% year to date 2005. Factored into the performance evaluation is an expense ratio of 0.62% (very low).

The fund's risk rating is currently B- (Good). It carries a beta of 1.34, meaning it is expected to move 13.4% for every 10% move in the market. Volatility, as measured by both the semi-deviation and a drawdown factor, is considered low. As of June 30, 2005, Van Kampen Bond traded at a discount of 9.92% below its net asset value, which is worse than its one-year historical average discount of 10.28%.

This fund has been team managed for 35 years and currently receives a manager quality ranking of 23 (0=worst, 99=best). This fund offers only a moderate level of risk but investors looking for strong performance are still waiting.

Data Date	Weiss Investment Rating	Net Assets ($Mil)	Price	Performance Rating/Pts	Total Return Y-T-D	Risk Rating/Pts
6-05	C-	223.68	17.71	D / 1.7	2.37%	B- / 7.9
2004	D+	217.55	17.80	D- / 1.5	7.01%	B / 8.1
2003	C-	224.70	17.98	D / 2.2	3.79%	B / 8.6

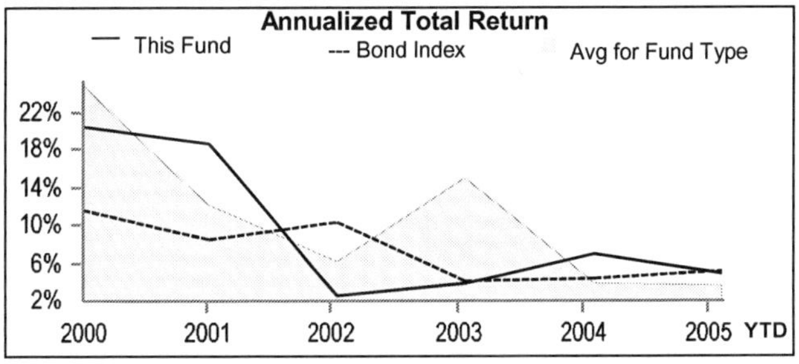

Van Kampen CA Muni (VKC) C Fair

Fund Family: Van Kampen Asset Management
Fund Type: Municipal - Single State
Inception Date: November 1, 1988

Major Rating Factors:
Middle of the road best describes Van Kampen CA Muni whose Weiss Investment Rating is currently a C (Fair). The fund currently has a performance rating of C- (Fair) based on an annualized return of 5.05% over the last three years and a total return of -0.23% year to date 2005. Factored into the performance evaluation is an expense ratio of 1.63% (above average).

The fund's risk rating is currently B- (Good). It carries a beta of 2.27, meaning it is expected to move 22.7% for every 10% move in the market. Volatility, as measured by both the semi-deviation and a drawdown factor, is considered low. As of June 30, 2005, Van Kampen CA Muni traded at a discount of 11.10% below its net asset value, which is better than its one-year historical average discount of 9.75%.

Joseph Piraro has been running the fund for 13 years and currently receives a manager quality ranking of 10 (0=worst, 99=best). If you desire an average level of risk, then this fund may be an option.

Data Date	Weiss Investment Rating	Net Assets ($Mil)	Price	Performance Rating/Pts	Total Return Y-T-D	Risk Rating/Pts
6-05	C	34.20	9.53	C- / 3.5	-0.23%	B- / 7.1
2004	B+	32.50	9.83	B- / 7.3	4.95%	B- / 7.3
2003	B	35.01	9.80	C+ / 6.3	7.24%	B / 8.3

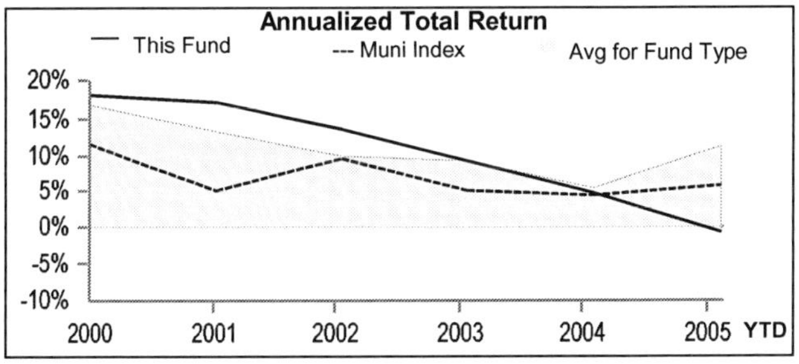

Van Kampen CA Qual Muni (VQC) C+ Fair

Fund Family: Van Kampen Asset Management
Fund Type: Municipal - Single State
Inception Date: September 27, 1991

Major Rating Factors:
Middle of the road best describes Van Kampen CA Qual Muni whose Weiss Investment Rating is currently a C+ (Fair). The fund currently has a performance rating of C (Fair) based on an annualized return of 6.36% over the last three years and a total return of 5.74% year to date 2005. Factored into the performance evaluation is an expense ratio of 1.09% (low).

The fund's risk rating is currently B- (Good). It carries a beta of 1.77, meaning it is expected to move 17.7% for every 10% move in the market. Volatility, as measured by both the semi-deviation and a drawdown factor, is considered low. As of June 30, 2005, Van Kampen CA Qual Muni traded at a discount of 5.15% below its net asset value, which is better than its one-year historical average discount of 4.95%.

Joseph A. Piraro has been running the fund for 13 years and currently receives a manager quality ranking of 36 (0=worst, 99=best). If you desire an average level of risk, then this fund may be an option.

Data Date	Weiss Investment Rating	Net Assets ($Mil)	Price	Performance Rating/Pts	Total Return Y-T-D	Risk Rating/Pts
6-05	C+	165.42	16.40	C / 4.7	5.74%	B- / 7.7
2004	C+	160.32	16.01	C / 4.4	-1.67%	B / 8.0
2003	B-	164.33	16.60	C / 5.5	5.47%	B / 8.3

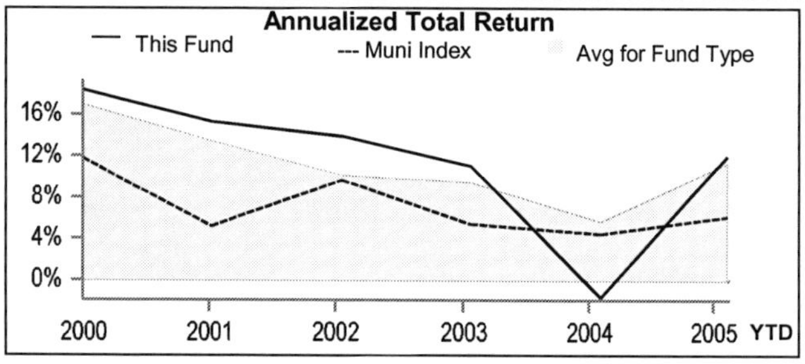

Van Kampen CA Val Muni Inc (VCV) C+ Fair

Fund Family: Van Kampen Asset Management
Fund Type: Municipal - Single State
Inception Date: April 30, 1993

Major Rating Factors:
Middle of the road best describes Van Kampen CA Val Muni Inc whose Weiss Investment Rating is currently a C+ (Fair). The fund currently has a performance rating of C (Fair) based on an annualized return of 6.19% over the last three years and a total return of 6.69% year to date 2005. Factored into the performance evaluation is an expense ratio of 1.26% (average).

The fund's risk rating is currently B- (Good). It carries a beta of 1.90, meaning it is expected to move 19.0% for every 10% move in the market. Volatility, as measured by both the semi-deviation and a drawdown factor, is considered low. As of June 30, 2005, Van Kampen CA Val Muni Inc traded at a discount of 10.76% below its net asset value, which is better than its one-year historical average discount of 9.62%.

Joseph A. Piraro has been running the fund for 9 years and currently receives a manager quality ranking of 28 (0=worst, 99=best). If you desire an average level of risk, then this fund may be an option.

Data Date	Weiss Investment Rating	Net Assets ($Mil)	Price	Performance Rating/Pts	Total Return Y-T-D	Risk Rating/Pts
6-05	C+	101.85	15.26	C / 4.5	6.69%	B- / 7.7
2004	C-	97.51	14.76	D / 2.2	-6.32%	B / 8.3
2003	B+	101.57	16.90	B- / 7.1	14.65%	B- / 7.8

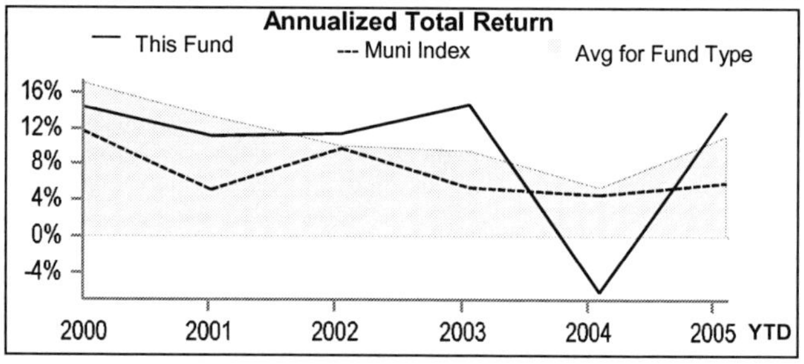

Van Kampen FL Qual Muni (VFM) B- Good

Fund Family: Van Kampen Asset Management
Fund Type: Municipal - Single State
Inception Date: September 27, 1991

Major Rating Factors:
Van Kampen FL Qual Muni receives a Weiss Investment Rating of B- (Good). The fund currently has a performance rating of C+ (Fair) based on an annualized return of 7.90% over the last three years and a total return of 5.12% year to date 2005. Factored into the performance evaluation is an expense ratio of 1.13% (low).

The fund's risk rating is currently B- (Good). It carries a beta of 1.75, meaning it is expected to move 17.5% for every 10% move in the market. Volatility, as measured by both the semi-deviation and a drawdown factor, is considered low. As of June 30, 2005, Van Kampen FL Qual Muni traded at a discount of 11.25% below its net asset value, which is better than its one-year historical average discount of 10.86%.

Brian Neely has been running the fund for 14 years and currently receives a manager quality ranking of 52 (0=worst, 99=best). If you desire an average level of risk, then this fund may be an option.

Data Date	Weiss Investment Rating	Net Assets ($Mil)	Price	Performance Rating/Pts	Total Return Y-T-D	Risk Rating/Pts
6-05	B-	108.77	14.99	C+ / 5.6	5.12%	B- / 7.8
2004	C+	105.51	14.68	C- / 4.2	2.80%	B / 8.1
2003	B-	108.47	15.29	C+ / 6.1	10.19%	B / 8.1

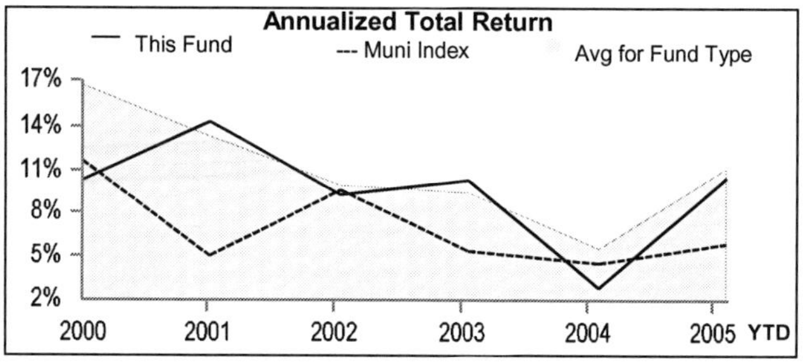

Van Kampen High Income Trust (VIT) D- Weak

Fund Family: Van Kampen Asset Management
Fund Type: Corporate - High Yield
Inception Date: January 26, 1989

Data Date	Weiss Investment Rating	Net Assets ($Mil)	Price	Performance Rating/Pts	Total Return Y-T-D	Risk Rating/Pts
6-05	D-	51.99	3.68	D- / 1.2	-5.56%	C / 5.4
2004	E+	48.27	4.09	D / 2.1	7.73%	C- / 3.2
2003	C	47.54	4.28	B+ / 8.4	52.89%	C- / 4.0

Major Rating Factors:
Disappointing performance is the major factor driving the D- (Weak) Weiss Investment Rating for Van Kampen High Income Trust. The fund currently has a performance rating of D- (Weak) based on an annualized return of 6.94% over the last three years and a total return of -5.56% year to date 2005. Factored into the performance evaluation is an expense ratio of 1.99% (high).

The fund's risk rating is currently C (Fair). It carries a beta of 2.38, meaning it is expected to move 23.8% for every 10% move in the market. Volatility, as measured by both the semi-deviation and a drawdown factor, is considered average. As of June 30, 2005, Van Kampen High Income Trust traded at a premium of 2.79% above its net asset value, which is better than its one-year historical average premium of 9.34%.

This fund has been team managed for 16 years and currently receives a manager quality ranking of 0 (0=worst, 99=best). This fund offers an average level of risk but investors looking for strong performance will be frustrated.

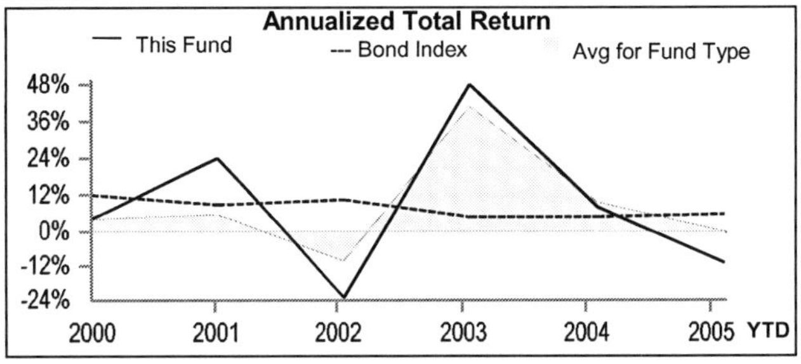

Van Kampen High Income Trust II (VLT) D- Weak

Fund Family: Van Kampen Asset Management
Fund Type: Corporate - High Yield
Inception Date: April 28, 1989

Data Date	Weiss Investment Rating	Net Assets ($Mil)	Price	Performance Rating/Pts	Total Return Y-T-D	Risk Rating/Pts
6-05	D-	38.60	4.75	C- / 3.1	-3.01%	C- / 4.1
2004	D-	35.83	5.14	C- / 3.5	11.29%	C- / 3.0
2003	C-	35.23	5.19	C+ / 6.9	40.87%	C- / 3.9

Major Rating Factors:
Van Kampen High Income Trust II receives a Weiss Investment Rating of D- (Weak). The fund currently has a performance rating of C- (Fair) based on an annualized return of 8.74% over the last three years and a total return of -3.01% year to date 2005. Factored into the performance evaluation is an expense ratio of 2.12% (high).

The fund's risk rating is currently C- (Fair). It carries a beta of 2.37, meaning it is expected to move 23.7% for every 10% move in the market. Volatility, as measured by both the semi-deviation and a drawdown factor, is considered average. As of June 30, 2005, Van Kampen High Income Trust II traded at a premium of 5.32% above its net asset value, which is worse than its one-year historical average premium of 4.42%.

This fund has been team managed for 16 years and currently receives a manager quality ranking of 0 (0=worst, 99=best). If you desire an average level of risk, then this fund may be an option.

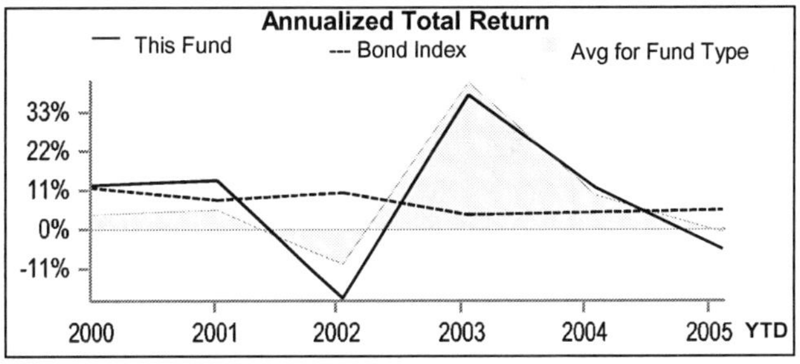

Van Kampen Income Trust (VIN) C- Fair

Fund Family: Van Kampen Asset Management
Fund Type: General Bond
Inception Date: April 22, 1988

Data Date	Weiss Investment Rating	Net Assets ($Mil)	Price	Performance Rating/Pts	Total Return Y-T-D	Risk Rating/Pts
6-05	C-	101.15	5.81	D- / 1.2	2.19%	B / 8.4
2004	D+	97.71	5.85	D- / 1.3	6.30%	B / 8.0
2003	D+	98.36	5.85	D / 1.7	9.24%	C+ / 6.9

Major Rating Factors:
Disappointing performance is the major factor driving the C- (Fair) Weiss Investment Rating for Van Kampen Income Trust. The fund currently has a performance rating of D- (Weak) based on an annualized return of 4.66% over the last three years and a total return of 2.19% year to date 2005. Factored into the performance evaluation is an expense ratio of 0.92% (low).

The fund's risk rating is currently B (Good). It carries a beta of 1.12, meaning it is expected to move 11.2% for every 10% move in the market. Volatility, as measured by both the semi-deviation and a drawdown factor, is considered low. As of June 30, 2005, Van Kampen Income Trust traded at a discount of 10.62% below its net asset value, which is worse than its one-year historical average discount of 11.68%.

Bob Hickey has been running the fund for 17 years and currently receives a manager quality ranking of 47 (0=worst, 99=best). This fund offers only a moderate level of risk but investors looking for strong performance are still waiting.

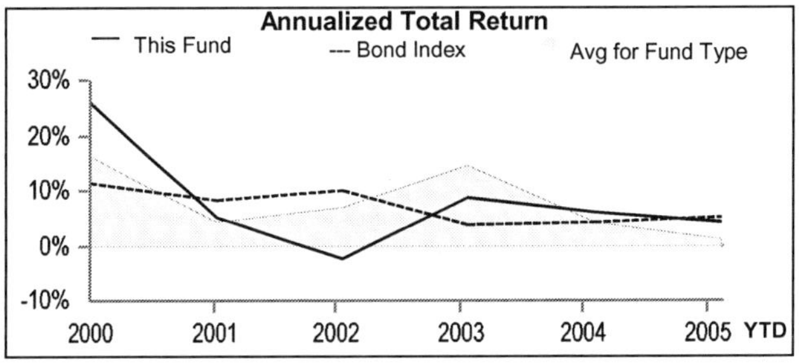

Van Kampen Invmt Grade Muni (VIG) C+ Fair

Fund Family: Van Kampen Asset Management
Fund Type: Municipal - National
Inception Date: November 30, 1989

Data Date	Weiss Investment Rating	Net Assets ($Mil)	Price	Performance Rating/Pts	Total Return Y-T-D	Risk Rating/Pts
6-05	C+	49.95	9.06	C / 4.6	3.69%	B / 8.1
2004	B-	48.43	8.98	C / 5.0	3.42%	B / 8.4
2003	C+	49.12	9.10	C / 4.5	8.58%	B / 8.6

Major Rating Factors:
Middle of the road best describes Van Kampen Invmt Grade Muni whose Weiss Investment Rating is currently a C+ (Fair). The fund currently has a performance rating of C (Fair) based on an annualized return of 6.44% over the last three years and a total return of 3.69% year to date 2005. Factored into the performance evaluation is an expense ratio of 1.39% (average).

The fund's risk rating is currently B (Good). It carries a beta of 2.05, meaning it is expected to move 20.5% for every 10% move in the market. Volatility, as measured by both the semi-deviation and a drawdown factor, is considered low. As of June 30, 2005, Van Kampen Invmt Grade Muni traded at a discount of 13.55% below its net asset value, which is better than its one-year historical average discount of 13.41%.

Tom Byron has been running the fund for 16 years and currently receives a manager quality ranking of 23 (0=worst, 99=best). If you desire an average level of risk, then this fund may be an option.

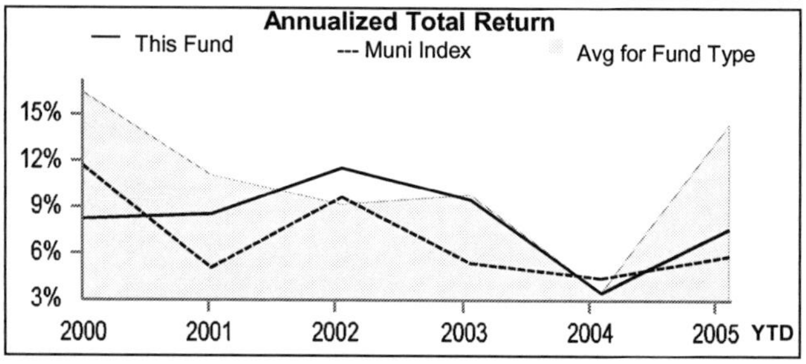

Van Kampen MA Value Muni Inc (VMV) C Fair

Fund Family: Van Kampen Asset Management
Fund Type: Municipal - Single State
Inception Date: April 30, 1993

Data Date	Weiss Investment Rating	Net Assets ($Mil)	Price	Performance Rating/Pts	Total Return Y-T-D	Risk Rating/Pts
6-05	C	43.81	16.56	C / 5.1	-4.69%	C+ / 6.3
2004	A	42.27	17.89	B+ / 8.7	13.54%	C+ / 6.6
2003	B	43.12	16.70	C+ / 6.1	6.78%	B / 8.2

Major Rating Factors:
Middle of the road best describes Van Kampen MA Value Muni Inc whose Weiss Investment Rating is currently a C (Fair). The fund currently has a performance rating of C (Fair) based on an annualized return of 7.07% over the last three years and a total return of -4.69% year to date 2005. Factored into the performance evaluation is an expense ratio of 1.39% (average).

The fund's risk rating is currently C+ (Fair). It carries a beta of 2.28, meaning it is expected to move 22.8% for every 10% move in the market. Volatility, as measured by both the semi-deviation and a drawdown factor, is considered low. As of June 30, 2005, Van Kampen MA Value Muni Inc traded at a premium of .36% above its net asset value, which is better than its one-year historical average premium of 2.68%.

Timothy D. Haney has been running the fund for 9 years and currently receives a manager quality ranking of 29 (0=worst, 99=best). If you desire an average level of risk, then this fund may be an option.

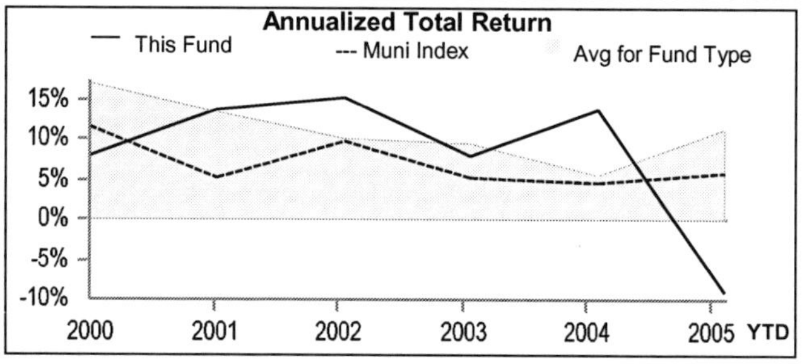

Van Kampen Muni Income (VMT) C+ Fair

Fund Family: Van Kampen Asset Management
Fund Type: Municipal - National
Inception Date: August 19, 1988

Data Date	Weiss Investment Rating	Net Assets ($Mil)	Price	Performance Rating/Pts	Total Return Y-T-D	Risk Rating/Pts
6-05	C+	300.48	9.09	C / 4.8	3.76%	B- / 7.7
2004	B-	288.18	9.04	C / 5.2	1.82%	B / 8.1
2003	B	307.89	9.47	C+ / 6.1	11.94%	B / 8.5

Major Rating Factors:
Middle of the road best describes Van Kampen Muni Income whose Weiss Investment Rating is currently a C+ (Fair). The fund currently has a performance rating of C (Fair) based on an annualized return of 7.62% over the last three years and a total return of 3.76% year to date 2005. Factored into the performance evaluation is an expense ratio of 1.21% (average).

The fund's risk rating is currently B- (Good). It carries a beta of 2.22, meaning it is expected to move 22.2% for every 10% move in the market. Volatility, as measured by both the semi-deviation and a drawdown factor, is considered low. As of June 30, 2005, Van Kampen Muni Income traded at a discount of 13.84% below its net asset value, which is better than its one-year historical average discount of 12.55%.

Tom Byron has been running the fund for 17 years and currently receives a manager quality ranking of 26 (0=worst, 99=best). If you desire an average level of risk, then this fund may be an option.

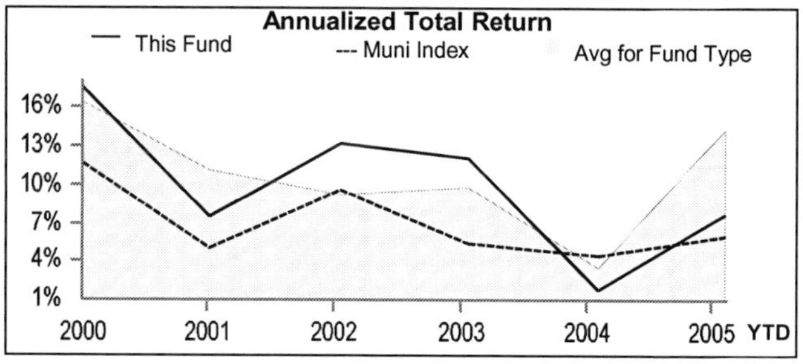

Van Kampen Muni Opp (VMO) C Fair

Fund Family: Van Kampen Asset Management
Fund Type: Municipal - National
Inception Date: April 24, 1992

Major Rating Factors:
Middle of the road best describes Van Kampen Muni Opp whose Weiss Investment Rating is currently a C (Fair). The fund currently has a performance rating of C- (Fair) based on an annualized return of 6.02% over the last three years and a total return of 5.43% year to date 2005. Factored into the performance evaluation is an expense ratio of 1.16% (low).

The fund's risk rating is currently C+ (Fair). It carries a beta of 2.40, meaning it is expected to move 24.0% for every 10% move in the market. Volatility, as measured by both the semi-deviation and a drawdown factor, is considered low. As of June 30, 2005, Van Kampen Muni Opp traded at a discount of 12.26% below its net asset value, which is better than its one-year historical average discount of 11.47%.

Dennis Pietrzak has been running the fund for 10 years and currently receives a manager quality ranking of 10 (0=worst, 99=best). If you desire an average level of risk, then this fund may be an option.

Data Date	Weiss Investment Rating	Net Assets ($Mil)	Price	Performance Rating/Pts	Total Return Y-T-D	Risk Rating/Pts
6-05	C	258.74	14.96	C- / 4.1	5.43%	C+ / 6.9
2004	C-	250.33	14.66	C- / 3.0	-5.74%	B- / 7.6
2003	A-	261.31	16.70	B / 7.7	13.60%	B- / 7.7

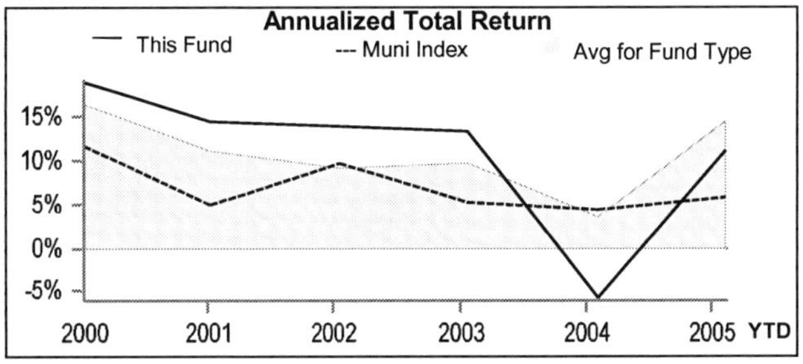

Van Kampen Muni Opp II (VOT) C+ Fair

Fund Family: Van Kampen Asset Management
Fund Type: Municipal - National
Inception Date: June 25, 1993

Major Rating Factors:
Middle of the road best describes Van Kampen Muni Opp II whose Weiss Investment Rating is currently a C+ (Fair). The fund currently has a performance rating of C- (Fair) based on an annualized return of 5.45% over the last three years and a total return of 2.23% year to date 2005. Factored into the performance evaluation is an expense ratio of 1.27% (average).

The fund's risk rating is currently B- (Good). It carries a beta of 2.11, meaning it is expected to move 21.1% for every 10% move in the market. Volatility, as measured by both the semi-deviation and a drawdown factor, is considered low. As of June 30, 2005, Van Kampen Muni Opp II traded at a discount of 11.75% below its net asset value, which is better than its one-year historical average discount of 9.23%.

Tim Haney has been running the fund for 10 years and currently receives a manager quality ranking of 15 (0=worst, 99=best). If you desire an average level of risk, then this fund may be an option.

Data Date	Weiss Investment Rating	Net Assets ($Mil)	Price	Performance Rating/Pts	Total Return Y-T-D	Risk Rating/Pts
6-05	C+	177.65	13.60	C- / 4.0	2.23%	B- / 7.7
2004	B-	171.56	13.75	C+ / 5.6	1.78%	B / 8.0
2003	B+	175.40	14.59	B- / 7.0	11.16%	B- / 7.8

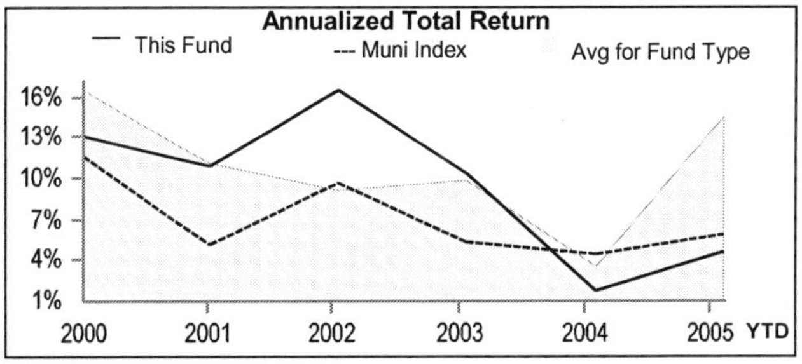

Van Kampen Muni Trust (VKQ) C+ Fair

Fund Family: Van Kampen Asset Management
Fund Type: Municipal - National
Inception Date: September 27, 1991

Major Rating Factors:
Middle of the road best describes Van Kampen Muni Trust whose Weiss Investment Rating is currently a C+ (Fair). The fund currently has a performance rating of C- (Fair) based on an annualized return of 5.85% over the last three years and a total return of 1.27% year to date 2005. Factored into the performance evaluation is an expense ratio of 1.06% (low).

The fund's risk rating is currently B (Good). It carries a beta of 2.10, meaning it is expected to move 21.0% for every 10% move in the market. Volatility, as measured by both the semi-deviation and a drawdown factor, is considered low. As of June 30, 2005, Van Kampen Muni Trust traded at a discount of 13.76% below its net asset value, which is better than its one-year historical average discount of 12.06%.

David C. Johnson has been running the fund for 14 years and currently receives a manager quality ranking of 18 (0=worst, 99=best). If you desire an average level of risk, then this fund may be an option.

Data Date	Weiss Investment Rating	Net Assets ($Mil)	Price	Performance Rating/Pts	Total Return Y-T-D	Risk Rating/Pts
6-05	C+	599.71	14.41	C- / 3.8	1.27%	B / 8.2
2004	B	578.64	14.68	C+ / 6.8	5.83%	B / 8.2
2003	B-	590.88	14.77	C+ / 5.6	9.13%	B / 8.4

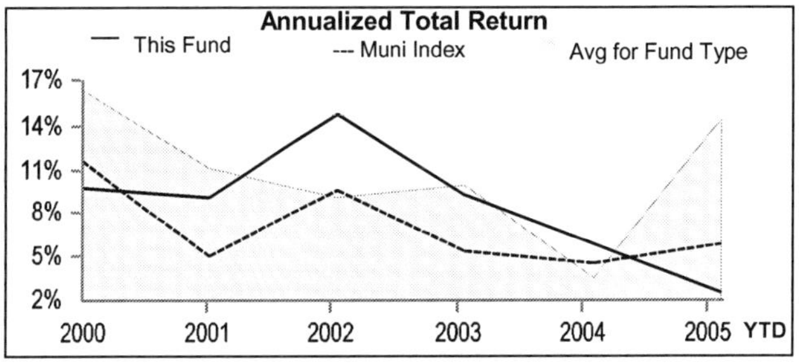

Van Kampen NY Qual Muni (VNM) C+ Fair

Fund Family: Van Kampen Asset Management
Fund Type: Municipal - Single State
Inception Date: September 27, 1991

Major Rating Factors:
Middle of the road best describes Van Kampen NY Qual Muni whose Weiss Investment Rating is currently a C+ (Fair). The fund currently has a performance rating of C (Fair) based on an annualized return of 6.78% over the last three years and a total return of 3.72% year to date 2005. Factored into the performance evaluation is an expense ratio of 1.16% (low).

The fund's risk rating is currently B- (Good). It carries a beta of 2.04, meaning it is expected to move 20.4% for every 10% move in the market. Volatility, as measured by both the semi-deviation and a drawdown factor, is considered low. As of June 30, 2005, Van Kampen NY Qual Muni traded at a discount of 12.95% below its net asset value, which is better than its one-year historical average discount of 11.54%.

Dennis Pietrzak has been running the fund for 10 years and currently receives a manager quality ranking of 28 (0=worst, 99=best). If you desire an average level of risk, then this fund may be an option.

Data Date	Weiss Investment Rating	Net Assets ($Mil)	Price	Performance Rating/Pts	Total Return Y-T-D	Risk Rating/Pts
6-05	C+	95.02	14.86	C / 5.2	3.72%	B- / 7.4
2004	B	92.83	14.75	C+ / 5.9	5.14%	B- / 7.9
2003	C+	95.95	15.17	C / 4.8	6.10%	B / 8.4

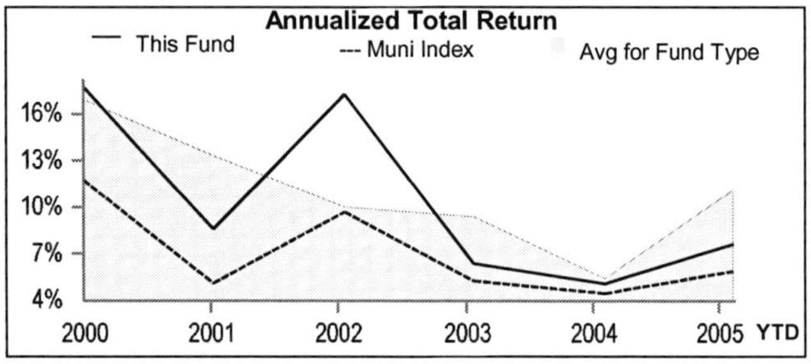

Van Kampen NY Val Muni Inc (VNV) C+ Fair

Fund Family: Van Kampen Asset Management
Fund Type: Municipal - Single State
Inception Date: April 30, 1993

Major Rating Factors:
Middle of the road best describes Van Kampen NY Val Muni Inc whose Weiss Investment Rating is currently a C+ (Fair). The fund currently has a performance rating of C- (Fair) based on an annualized return of 5.90% over the last three years and a total return of 3.89% year to date 2005. Factored into the performance evaluation is an expense ratio of 1.31% (average).

The fund's risk rating is currently B- (Good). It carries a beta of 1.76, meaning it is expected to move 17.6% for every 10% move in the market. Volatility, as measured by both the semi-deviation and a drawdown factor, is considered low. As of June 30, 2005, Van Kampen NY Val Muni Inc traded at a discount of 12.25% below its net asset value, which is better than its one-year historical average discount of 11.03%.

David C. Johnson has been running the fund for 12 years and currently receives a manager quality ranking of 32 (0=worst, 99=best). If you desire an average level of risk, then this fund may be an option.

Data Date	Weiss Investment Rating	Net Assets ($Mil)	Price	Performance Rating/Pts	Total Return Y-T-D	Risk Rating/Pts
6-05	C+	71.52	14.83	C- / 4.0	3.89%	B- / 7.8
2004	C+	69.50	14.71	C- / 4.0	1.18%	B / 8.1
2003	C+	70.82	15.49	C- / 3.9	10.24%	B / 8.6

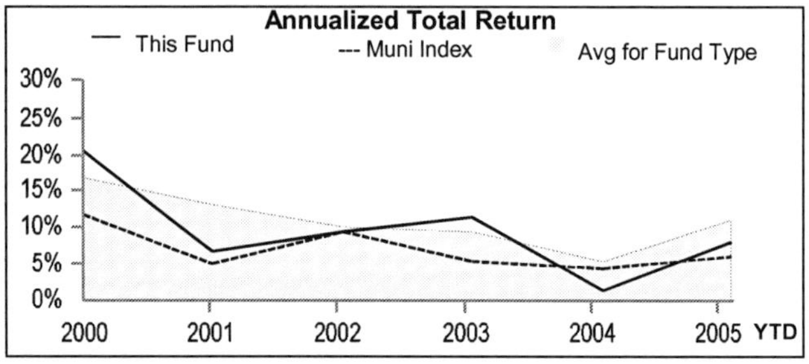

Van Kampen OH Qual Muni (VOQ) C+ Fair

Fund Family: Van Kampen Asset Management
Fund Type: Municipal - Single State
Inception Date: September 27, 1991

Major Rating Factors:
Middle of the road best describes Van Kampen OH Qual Muni whose Weiss Investment Rating is currently a C+ (Fair). The fund currently has a performance rating of C+ (Fair) based on an annualized return of 4.40% over the last three years and a total return of 5.44% year to date 2005. Factored into the performance evaluation is an expense ratio of 1.21% (average).

The fund's risk rating is currently C+ (Fair). It carries a beta of 2.17, meaning it is expected to move 21.7% for every 10% move in the market. Volatility, as measured by both the semi-deviation and a drawdown factor, is considered low. As of June 30, 2005, Van Kampen OH Qual Muni traded at a discount of 3.93% below its net asset value, which is worse than its one-year historical average discount of 5.93%.

Timothy D. Haney has been running the fund for 9 years and currently receives a manager quality ranking of 9 (0=worst, 99=best). If you desire an average level of risk, then this fund may be an option.

Data Date	Weiss Investment Rating	Net Assets ($Mil)	Price	Performance Rating/Pts	Total Return Y-T-D	Risk Rating/Pts
6-05	C+	74.00	16.62	C+ / 5.6	5.44%	C+ / 6.2
2004	C+	70.62	16.20	C / 5.4	5.78%	B- / 7.3
2003	C+	72.98	16.26	C- / 4.2	1.09%	B / 8.4

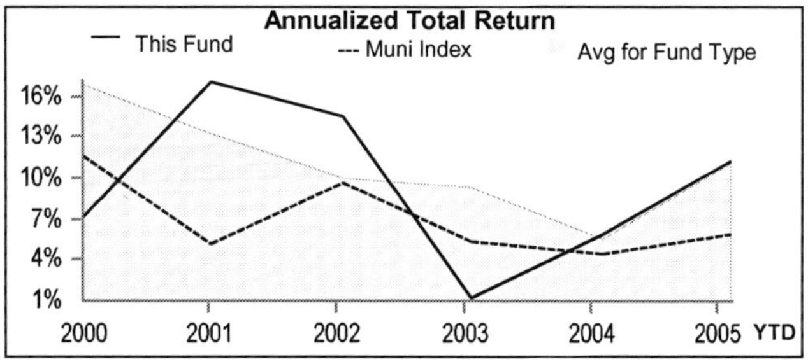

Van Kampen OH Val Muni Inc (VOV) C- Fair

Fund Family: Van Kampen Asset Management
Fund Type: Municipal - Single State
Inception Date: April 30, 1993

Major Rating Factors:
Middle of the road best describes Van Kampen OH Val Muni Inc whose Weiss Investment Rating is currently a C- (Fair). The fund currently has a performance rating of C- (Fair) based on an annualized return of 5.54% over the last three years and a total return of -2.14% year to date 2005. Factored into the performance evaluation is an expense ratio of 1.62% (above average).

The fund's risk rating is currently C+ (Fair). It carries a beta of 2.38, meaning it is expected to move 23.8% for every 10% move in the market. Volatility, as measured by both the semi-deviation and a drawdown factor, is considered low. As of June 30, 2005, Van Kampen OH Val Muni Inc traded at a discount of 5.36% below its net asset value, which is better than its one-year historical average discount of 3.15%.

Tim Haney has been running the fund for 12 years and currently receives a manager quality ranking of 10 (0=worst, 99=best). If you desire an average level of risk, then this fund may be an option.

Data Date	Weiss Investment Rating	Net Assets ($Mil)	Price	Performance Rating/Pts	Total Return Y-T-D	Risk Rating/Pts
6-05	C-	26.44	15.00	C- / 3.3	-2.14%	C+ / 6.1
2004	B+	25.24	15.75	B / 8.1	5.51%	C+ / 6.7
2003	B+	25.74	16.02	B / 7.7	11.46%	B- / 7.6

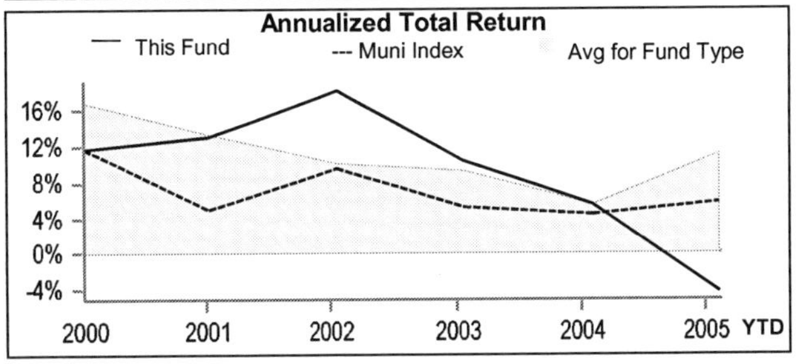

Van Kampen PA Qual Muni (VPQ) D+ Weak

Fund Family: Van Kampen Asset Management
Fund Type: Municipal - Single State
Inception Date: September 27, 1991

Major Rating Factors:
Disappointing performance is the major factor driving the D+ (Weak) Weiss Investment Rating for Van Kampen PA Qual Muni. The fund currently has a performance rating of D- (Weak) based on an annualized return of 2.24% over the last three years and a total return of 2.59% year to date 2005. Factored into the performance evaluation is an expense ratio of 1.13% (low).

The fund's risk rating is currently B- (Good). It carries a beta of 1.66, meaning it is expected to move 16.6% for every 10% move in the market. Volatility, as measured by both the semi-deviation and a drawdown factor, is considered low. As of June 30, 2005, Van Kampen PA Qual Muni traded at a discount of 12.45% below its net asset value, which is better than its one-year historical average discount of 9.57%.

Dennis S. Pietrzak has been running the fund for 9 years and currently receives a manager quality ranking of 10 (0=worst, 99=best). This fund offers only a moderate level of risk but investors looking for strong performance are still waiting.

Data Date	Weiss Investment Rating	Net Assets ($Mil)	Price	Performance Rating/Pts	Total Return Y-T-D	Risk Rating/Pts
6-05	D+	138.98	14.91	D- / 1.3	2.59%	B- / 7.5
2004	C-	133.89	14.96	D+ / 2.5	-4.05%	B / 8.1
2003	A	138.41	16.86	B / 8.0	12.42%	B- / 7.7

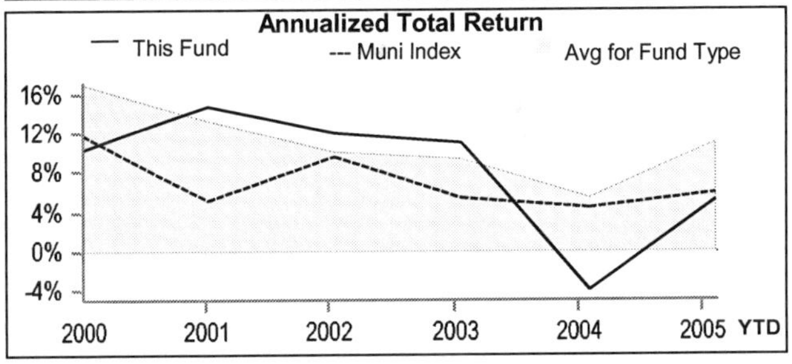

Van Kampen PA Val Muni Inc (VPV) C- Fair

Fund Family: Van Kampen Asset Management
Fund Type: Municipal - Single State
Inception Date: April 30, 1993

Major Rating Factors:
Disappointing performance is the major factor driving the C- (Fair) Weiss Investment Rating for Van Kampen PA Val Muni Inc. The fund currently has a performance rating of D (Weak) based on an annualized return of 4.65% over the last three years and a total return of -3.82% year to date 2005. Factored into the performance evaluation is an expense ratio of 1.36% (average).

The fund's risk rating is currently B- (Good). It carries a beta of 1.93, meaning it is expected to move 19.3% for every 10% move in the market. Volatility, as measured by both the semi-deviation and a drawdown factor, is considered low. As of June 30, 2005, Van Kampen PA Val Muni Inc traded at a discount of 9.09% below its net asset value, which is better than its one-year historical average discount of 5.19%.

Dennis Pietrzak has been running the fund for 12 years and currently receives a manager quality ranking of 16 (0=worst, 99=best). This fund offers only a moderate level of risk but investors looking for strong performance are still waiting.

Data Date	Weiss Investment Rating	Net Assets ($Mil)	Price	Performance Rating/Pts	Total Return Y-T-D	Risk Rating/Pts
6-05	C-	72.93	15.00	D / 2.2	-3.82%	B- / 7.5
2004	B+	70.67	16.06	B- / 7.2	6.41%	B- / 7.4
2003	A+	72.46	16.15	B / 7.9	10.87%	B / 8.1

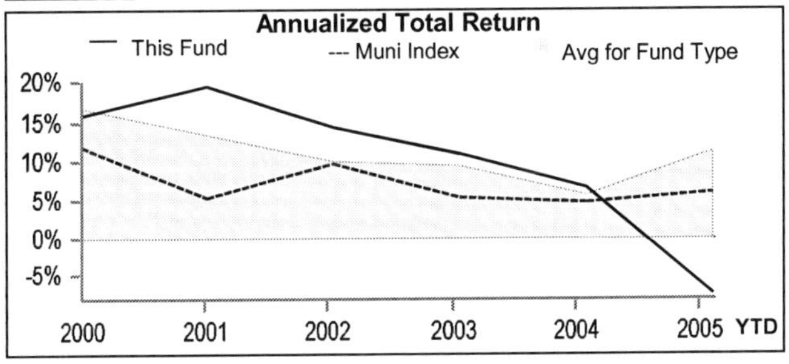

Van Kampen Sel Sector Muni (VKL) C Fair

Fund Family: Van Kampen Asset Management
Fund Type: Municipal - National
Inception Date: November 26, 1993

Major Rating Factors:
Middle of the road best describes Van Kampen Sel Sector Muni whose Weiss Investment Rating is currently a C (Fair). The fund currently has a performance rating of C- (Fair) based on an annualized return of 4.81% over the last three years and a total return of 4.03% year to date 2005. Factored into the performance evaluation is an expense ratio of 1.25% (average).

The fund's risk rating is currently B (Good). It carries a beta of 2.03, meaning it is expected to move 20.3% for every 10% move in the market. Volatility, as measured by both the semi-deviation and a drawdown factor, is considered low. As of June 30, 2005, Van Kampen Sel Sector Muni traded at a discount of 13.92% below its net asset value, which is better than its one-year historical average discount of 12.70%.

Dennis S. Pietrzak has been running the fund for 9 years and currently receives a manager quality ranking of 14 (0=worst, 99=best). If you desire an average level of risk, then this fund may be an option.

Data Date	Weiss Investment Rating	Net Assets ($Mil)	Price	Performance Rating/Pts	Total Return Y-T-D	Risk Rating/Pts
6-05	C	67.70	12.62	C- / 3.1	4.03%	B / 8.0
2004	C+	65.01	12.51	C / 4.5	2.81%	B / 8.4
2003	B	66.00	12.89	C+ / 5.7	5.51%	B / 8.9

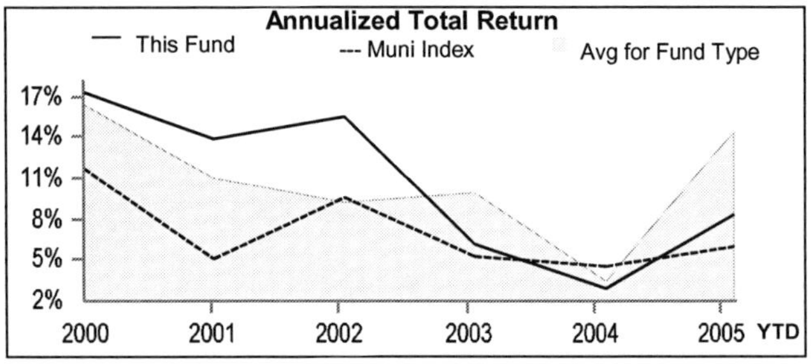

Van Kampen Senior Inc Tr (VVR) C- Fair

Fund Family: Van Kampen Asset Management
Fund Type: Loan Participation
Inception Date: June 23, 1998

Major Rating Factors:
Disappointing performance is the major factor driving the C- (Fair) Weiss Investment Rating for Van Kampen Senior Inc Tr. The fund currently has a performance rating of D- (Weak) based on an annualized return of 9.13% over the last three years and a total return of -3.46% year to date 2005. Factored into the performance evaluation is an expense ratio of 2.88% (high).

The fund's risk rating is currently B (Good). It carries a beta of -40.54, meaning the fund's expected move will be -405.4% for every 10% move in the market. Volatility, as measured by both the semi-deviation and a drawdown factor, is considered low. As of June 30, 2005, Van Kampen Senior Inc Tr traded at a discount of 8.56% below its net asset value, which is better than its one-year historical average discount of 1.17%.

Howard Tiffen has been running the fund for 6 years and currently receives a manager quality ranking of 98 (0=worst, 99=best). This fund offers only a moderate level of risk but investors looking for strong performance are still waiting.

Data Date	Weiss Investment Rating	Net Assets ($Mil)	Price	Performance Rating/Pts	Total Return Y-T-D	Risk Rating/Pts
6-05	C-	1559.41	7.90	D- / 1.0	-3.46%	B / 8.6
2004	C	1554.11	8.42	C- / 3.6	2.55%	B / 8.1
2003	C+	1458.59	8.62	C+ / 6.4	35.11%	C+ / 6.3

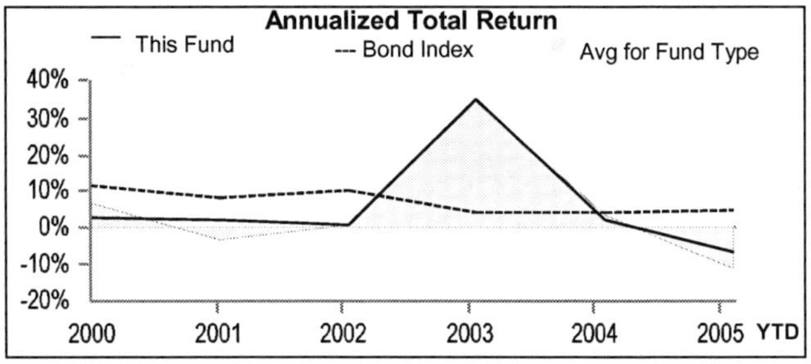

Van Kampen Strat Sect Muni (VKS) C- Fair

Fund Family: Van Kampen Asset Management
Fund Type: Municipal - National
Inception Date: January 22, 1993

Major Rating Factors:
Disappointing performance is the major factor driving the C- (Fair) Weiss Investment Rating for Van Kampen Strat Sect Muni. The fund currently has a performance rating of D+ (Weak) based on an annualized return of 3.50% over the last three years and a total return of 4.94% year to date 2005. Factored into the performance evaluation is an expense ratio of 1.21% (average).

The fund's risk rating is currently B- (Good). It carries a beta of 2.04, meaning it is expected to move 20.4% for every 10% move in the market. Volatility, as measured by both the semi-deviation and a drawdown factor, is considered low. As of June 30, 2005, Van Kampen Strat Sect Muni traded at a discount of 13.77% below its net asset value, which is better than its one-year historical average discount of 12.05%.

Timothy D. Haney has been running the fund for 9 years and currently receives a manager quality ranking of 8 (0=worst, 99=best). This fund offers only a moderate level of risk but investors looking for strong performance are still waiting.

Data Date	Weiss Investment Rating	Net Assets ($Mil)	Price	Performance Rating/Pts	Total Return Y-T-D	Risk Rating/Pts
6-05	C-	159.04	12.84	D+ / 2.4	4.94%	B- / 7.1
2004	C-	153.31	12.63	D / 2.1	-3.54%	B- / 7.9
2003	B	156.56	14.03	C+ / 6.8	7.95%	B / 8.4

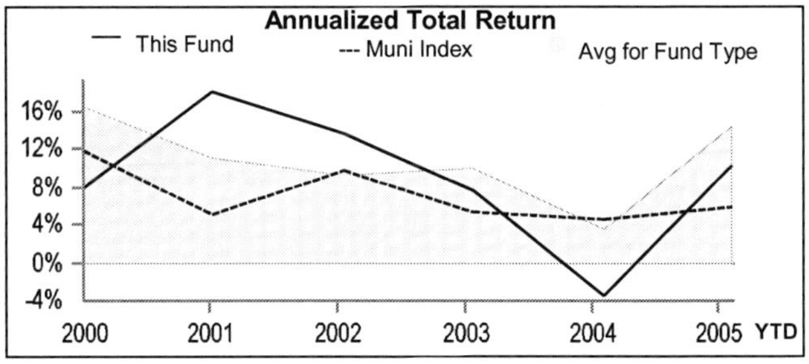

Van Kampen Tr for Inv Gr CA Muni (VIC) C Fair

Fund Family: Van Kampen Asset Management
Fund Type: Municipal - Single State
Inception Date: March 27, 1992

Data Date	Weiss Investment Rating	Net Assets ($Mil)	Price	Performance Rating/Pts	Total Return Y-T-D	Risk Rating/Pts
6-05	C	77.17	15.02	C / 4.8	8.01%	C+ / 6.7
2004	D+	73.54	14.34	D- / 1.2	-6.57%	B- / 7.7
2003	C	75.55	16.35	C / 4.4	11.55%	B- / 7.8

Major Rating Factors:
Middle of the road best describes Van Kampen Tr for Inv Gr CA Muni whose Weiss Investment Rating is currently a C (Fair). The fund currently has a performance rating of C (Fair) based on an annualized return of 5.78% over the last three years and a total return of 8.01% year to date 2005. Factored into the performance evaluation is an expense ratio of 1.31% (average).

The fund's risk rating is currently C+ (Fair). It carries a beta of 2.63, meaning it is expected to move 26.3% for every 10% move in the market. Volatility, as measured by both the semi-deviation and a drawdown factor, is considered low. As of June 30, 2005, Van Kampen Tr for Inv Gr CA Muni traded at a discount of 10.27% below its net asset value, which is better than its one-year historical average discount of 10.00%.

Joseph A. Piraro has been running the fund for 13 years and currently receives a manager quality ranking of 7 (0=worst, 99=best). If you desire an average level of risk, then this fund may be an option.

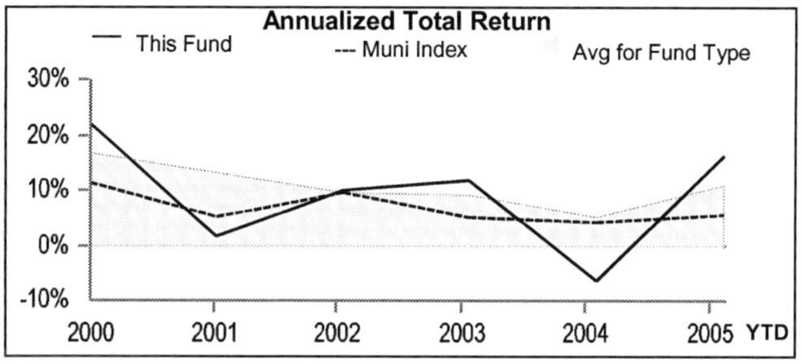

Van Kampen Trust for Ins Muni (VIM) D+ Weak

Fund Family: Van Kampen Asset Management
Fund Type: Municipal - National
Inception Date: January 24, 1992

Data Date	Weiss Investment Rating	Net Assets ($Mil)	Price	Performance Rating/Pts	Total Return Y-T-D	Risk Rating/Pts
6-05	D+	161.44	14.80	D / 2.2	4.57%	C+ / 6.6
2004	D	156.49	14.58	D- / 1.4	-10.64%	B- / 7.4
2003	A	160.35	17.30	B / 8.1	7.11%	B- / 7.7

Major Rating Factors:
Disappointing performance is the major factor driving the D+ (Weak) Weiss Investment Rating for Van Kampen Trust for Ins Muni. The fund currently has a performance rating of D (Weak) based on an annualized return of 3.50% over the last three years and a total return of 4.57% year to date 2005. Factored into the performance evaluation is an expense ratio of 1.18% (low).

The fund's risk rating is currently C+ (Fair). It carries a beta of 2.50, meaning it is expected to move 25.0% for every 10% move in the market. Volatility, as measured by both the semi-deviation and a drawdown factor, is considered low. As of June 30, 2005, Van Kampen Trust for Ins Muni traded at a discount of 11.11% below its net asset value, which is better than its one-year historical average discount of 9.22%.

Joseph A. Piraro has been running the fund for 13 years and currently receives a manager quality ranking of 5 (0=worst, 99=best). This fund offers only a moderate level of risk but investors looking for strong performance are still waiting.

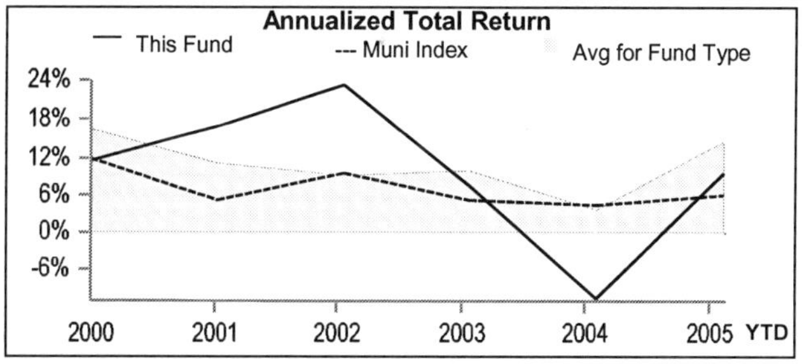

Van Kampen Trust for Inv FL Muni (VTF) C Fair

Fund Family: Van Kampen Asset Management
Fund Type: Municipal - Single State
Inception Date: March 27, 1992

Data Date	Weiss Investment Rating	Net Assets ($Mil)	Price	Performance Rating/Pts	Total Return Y-T-D	Risk Rating/Pts
6-05	C	96.42	15.14	C / 4.5	3.08%	B- / 7.1
2004	C	91.91	15.10	C- / 4.0	-4.67%	B- / 7.5
2003	A	95.43	16.89	B+ / 8.3	15.00%	B- / 7.4

Major Rating Factors:
Middle of the road best describes Van Kampen Trust for Inv FL Muni whose Weiss Investment Rating is currently a C (Fair). The fund currently has a performance rating of C (Fair) based on an annualized return of 7.06% over the last three years and a total return of 3.08% year to date 2005. Factored into the performance evaluation is an expense ratio of 1.26% (average).

The fund's risk rating is currently B- (Good). It carries a beta of 2.45, meaning it is expected to move 24.5% for every 10% move in the market. Volatility, as measured by both the semi-deviation and a drawdown factor, is considered low. As of June 30, 2005, Van Kampen Trust for Inv FL Muni traded at a discount of 13.83% below its net asset value, which is better than its one-year historical average discount of 11.92%.

Thomas M. Byron has been running the fund for 9 years and currently receives a manager quality ranking of 15 (0=worst, 99=best). If you desire an average level of risk, then this fund may be an option.

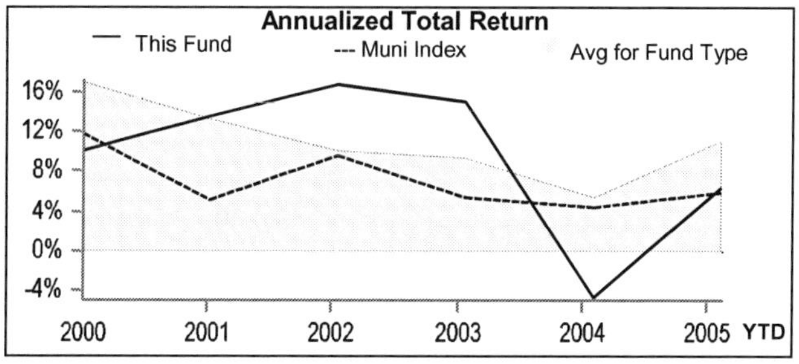

Van Kampen Trust for Inv Muni (VGM) C+ Fair

Fund Family: Van Kampen Asset Management
Fund Type: Municipal - National
Inception Date: January 24, 1992

Major Rating Factors:
Middle of the road best describes Van Kampen Trust for Inv Muni whose Weiss Investment Rating is currently a C+ (Fair). The fund currently has a performance rating of C- (Fair) based on an annualized return of 6.18% over the last three years and a total return of 3.65% year to date 2005. Factored into the performance evaluation is an expense ratio of 1.12% (low).

The fund's risk rating is currently B- (Good). It carries a beta of 2.26, meaning it is expected to move 22.6% for every 10% move in the market. Volatility, as measured by both the semi-deviation and a drawdown factor, is considered low. As of June 30, 2005, Van Kampen Trust for Inv Muni traded at a discount of 13.83% below its net asset value, which is better than its one-year historical average discount of 12.70%.

Thomas M. Byron has been running the fund for 9 years and currently receives a manager quality ranking of 15 (0=worst, 99=best). If you desire an average level of risk, then this fund may be an option.

Data Date	Weiss Investment Rating	Net Assets ($Mil)	Price	Performance Rating/Pts	Total Return Y-T-D	Risk Rating/Pts
6-05	C+	464.71	15.01	C- / 3.9	3.65%	B- / 7.8
2004	B-	450.23	14.95	C / 4.9	1.35%	B / 8.2
2003	B	463.33	15.60	C+ / 5.9	6.07%	B / 8.4

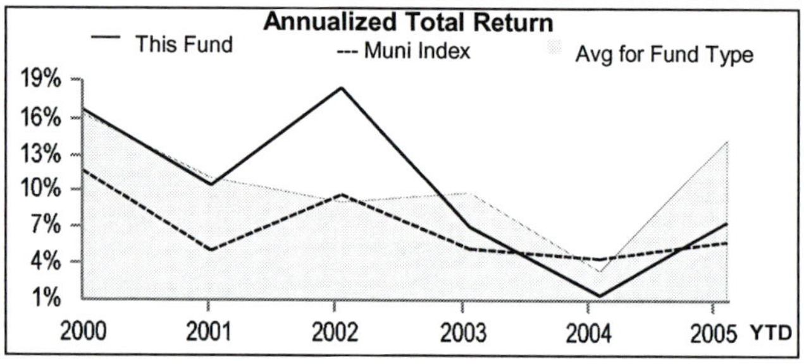

Van Kampen Trust for Inv NJ Muni (VTJ) C Fair

Fund Family: Van Kampen Asset Management
Fund Type: Municipal - Single State
Inception Date: March 27, 1992

Major Rating Factors:
Middle of the road best describes Van Kampen Trust for Inv NJ Muni whose Weiss Investment Rating is currently a C (Fair). The fund currently has a performance rating of C- (Fair) based on an annualized return of 5.57% over the last three years and a total return of 2.13% year to date 2005. Factored into the performance evaluation is an expense ratio of 1.24% (average).

The fund's risk rating is currently B- (Good). It carries a beta of 2.27, meaning it is expected to move 22.7% for every 10% move in the market. Volatility, as measured by both the semi-deviation and a drawdown factor, is considered low. As of June 30, 2005, Van Kampen Trust for Inv NJ Muni traded at a discount of 10.36% below its net asset value, which is better than its one-year historical average discount of 8.98%.

Tim Haney has been running the fund for 10 years and currently receives a manager quality ranking of 15 (0=worst, 99=best). If you desire an average level of risk, then this fund may be an option.

Data Date	Weiss Investment Rating	Net Assets ($Mil)	Price	Performance Rating/Pts	Total Return Y-T-D	Risk Rating/Pts
6-05	C	111.08	16.53	C- / 3.4	2.13%	B- / 7.5
2004	C+	107.15	16.68	C / 5.2	3.97%	B- / 7.9
2003	B+	109.56	17.11	C+ / 6.4	5.35%	B / 8.4

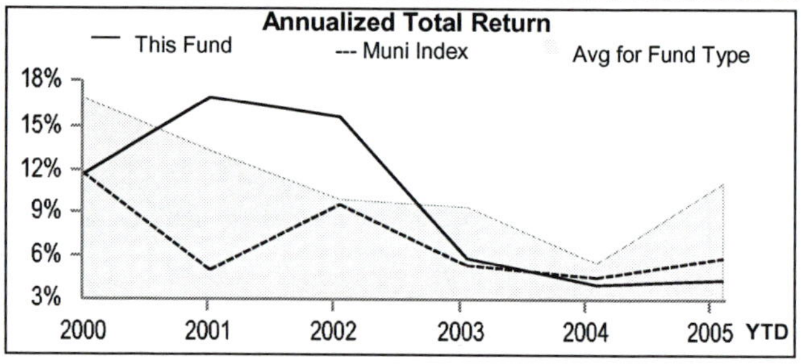

Van Kampen Trust for Inv NY Muni (VTN) C Fair

Fund Family: Van Kampen Asset Management
Fund Type: Municipal - Single State
Inception Date: March 27, 1992

Major Rating Factors:
Middle of the road best describes Van Kampen Trust for Inv NY Muni whose Weiss Investment Rating is currently a C (Fair). The fund currently has a performance rating of C (Fair) based on an annualized return of 5.86% over the last three years and a total return of 6.78% year to date 2005. Factored into the performance evaluation is an expense ratio of 1.23% (average).

The fund's risk rating is currently C+ (Fair). It carries a beta of 2.36, meaning it is expected to move 23.6% for every 10% move in the market. Volatility, as measured by both the semi-deviation and a drawdown factor, is considered low. As of June 30, 2005, Van Kampen Trust for Inv NY Muni traded at a discount of 11.03% below its net asset value, which is better than its one-year historical average discount of 10.17%.

Dennis S. Pietrzak has been running the fund for 13 years and currently receives a manager quality ranking of 12 (0=worst, 99=best). If you desire an average level of risk, then this fund may be an option.

Data Date	Weiss Investment Rating	Net Assets ($Mil)	Price	Performance Rating/Pts	Total Return Y-T-D	Risk Rating/Pts
6-05	C	106.36	15.48	C / 4.6	6.78%	C+ / 6.7
2004	D+	102.83	14.96	D / 1.9	-7.16%	B- / 7.5
2003	B+	107.77	17.35	B / 7.6	14.09%	B- / 7.5

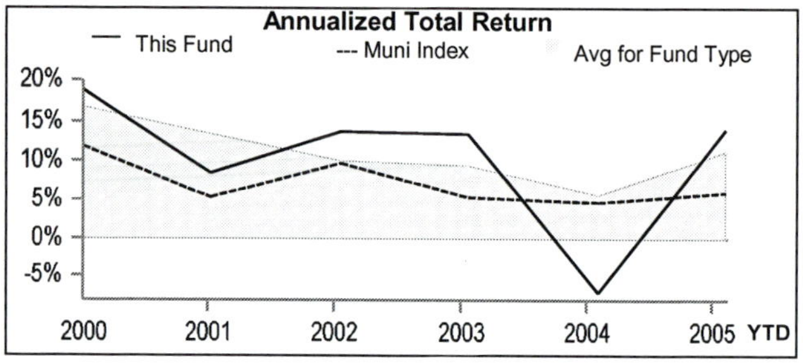

Van Kampen Trust for Inv PA Muni (VTP) — C- Fair

Fund Family: Van Kampen Asset Management
Fund Type: Municipal - Single State
Inception Date: March 27, 1992

Major Rating Factors:
Middle of the road best describes Van Kampen Trust for Inv PA Muni whose Weiss Investment Rating is currently a C- (Fair). The fund currently has a performance rating of C- (Fair) based on an annualized return of 4.28% over the last three years and a total return of 3.22% year to date 2005. Factored into the performance evaluation is an expense ratio of 1.21% (average).

The fund's risk rating is currently C+ (Fair). It carries a beta of 2.24, meaning it is expected to move 22.4% for every 10% move in the market. Volatility, as measured by both the semi-deviation and a drawdown factor, is considered low. As of June 30, 2005, Van Kampen Trust for Inv PA Muni traded at a discount of 12.06% below its net asset value, which is better than its one-year historical average discount of 11.17%.

Dennis S. Pietrzak has been running the fund for 9 years and currently receives a manager quality ranking of 9 (0=worst, 99=best). If you desire an average level of risk, then this fund may be an option.

Data Date	Weiss Investment Rating	Net Assets ($Mil)	Price	Performance Rating/Pts	Total Return Y-T-D	Risk Rating/Pts
6-05	C-	125.70	15.09	C- / 3.4	3.22%	C+ / 6.7
2004	C	123.49	15.06	C- / 3.9	2.00%	B- / 7.4
2003	B	128.29	16.15	C+ / 6.0	4.15%	B / 8.4

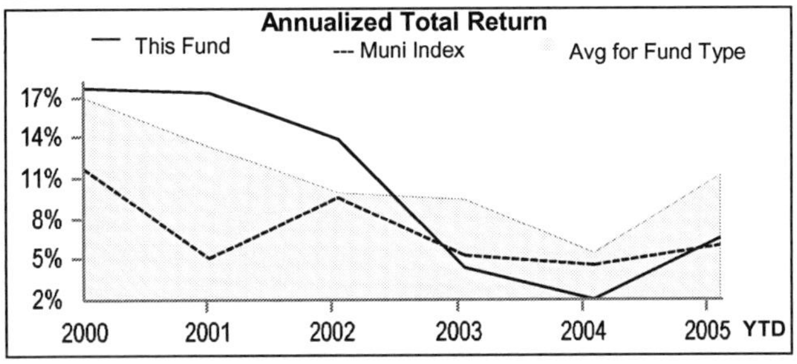

Van Kampen Value Muni Inc Trust (VKV) — C Fair

Fund Family: Van Kampen Asset Management
Fund Type: Municipal - National
Inception Date: March 26, 1993

Major Rating Factors:
Middle of the road best describes Van Kampen Value Muni Inc Trust whose Weiss Investment Rating is currently a C (Fair). The fund currently has a performance rating of C- (Fair) based on an annualized return of 4.70% over the last three years and a total return of 2.61% year to date 2005. Factored into the performance evaluation is an expense ratio of 1.17% (low).

The fund's risk rating is currently B- (Good). It carries a beta of 2.10, meaning it is expected to move 21.0% for every 10% move in the market. Volatility, as measured by both the semi-deviation and a drawdown factor, is considered low. As of June 30, 2005, Van Kampen Value Muni Inc Trust traded at a discount of 13.86% below its net asset value, which is better than its one-year historical average discount of 10.86%.

Tim Haney has been running the fund for 12 years and currently receives a manager quality ranking of 11 (0=worst, 99=best). If you desire an average level of risk, then this fund may be an option.

Data Date	Weiss Investment Rating	Net Assets ($Mil)	Price	Performance Rating/Pts	Total Return Y-T-D	Risk Rating/Pts
6-05	C	370.26	13.73	C- / 3.1	2.61%	B- / 7.6
2004	C+	357.91	13.81	C- / 4.2	-0.57%	B- / 7.9
2003	B	366.88	14.84	C+ / 6.7	10.04%	B / 8.1

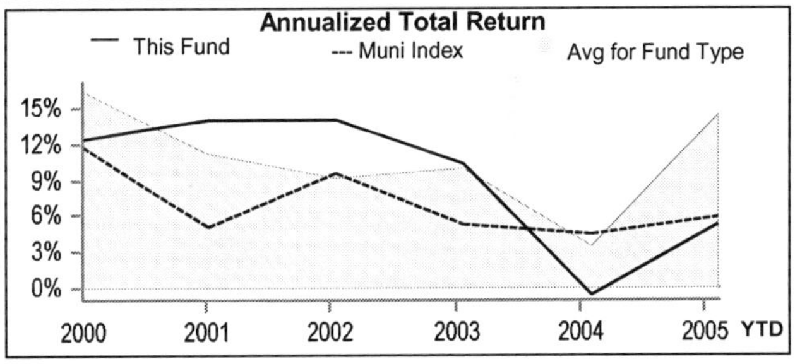

Vanguard Extended Market VIPERs (VXF) — C Fair

Fund Family: Vanguard Quantity Equity Group, Inc
Fund Type: Income
Inception Date: December 27, 2001

Major Rating Factors:
Middle of the road best describes Vanguard Extended Market VIPERs whose Weiss Investment Rating is currently a C (Fair). The fund currently has a performance rating of C (Fair) based on an annualized return of 14.96% over the last three years and a total return of 0.34% year to date 2005. Factored into the performance evaluation is an expense ratio of 0.20% (very low).

The fund's risk rating is currently C+ (Fair). It carries a beta of 0.99, meaning that its performance tracks fairly well with that of the overall stock market. Volatility, as measured by standard deviation, is considered low for equity funds at 15.70. As of June 30, 2005, Vanguard Extended Market VIPERs traded at a discount of .36% below its net asset value, which is better than its one-year historical average discount of .02%.

George U.Sauter has been running the fund for 4 years and currently receives a manager quality ranking of 86 (0=worst, 99=best). If you desire an average level of risk, then this fund may be an option.

Data Date	Weiss Investment Rating	Net Assets ($Mil)	Price	Performance Rating/Pts	Total Return Y-T-D	Risk Rating/Pts
6-05	C	231.41	83.10	C / 5.2	0.34%	C+ / 6.2

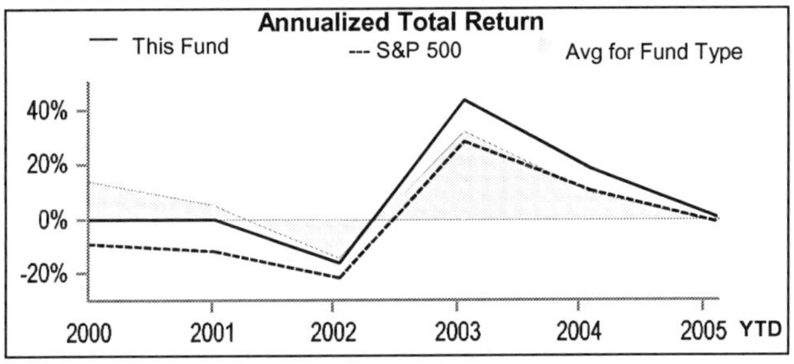

Vanguard Total Stock Market VIPERs (VTI) D+ Weak

Fund Family: Vanguard Quantity Equity Group, Inc
Fund Type: Income
Inception Date: May 24, 2001

Major Rating Factors:
Disappointing performance is the major factor driving the D+ (Weak) Weiss Investment Rating for Vanguard Total Stock Market VIPERs. The fund currently has a performance rating of D+ (Weak) based on an annualized return of 9.64% over the last three years and a total return of -0.47% year to date 2005. Factored into the performance evaluation is an expense ratio of 0.13% (very low).

The fund's risk rating is currently C+ (Fair). It carries a beta of 0.98, meaning that its performance tracks fairly well with that of the overall stock market. Volatility, as measured by standard deviation, is considered low for equity funds at 14.01. As of June 30, 2005, Vanguard Total Stock Market VIPERs traded at a discount of .13% below its net asset value, which is better than its one-year historical average premium of .01%.

George U. Sauter has been running the fund for 4 years and currently receives a manager quality ranking of 71 (0=worst, 99=best). This fund offers only a moderate level of risk but investors looking for strong performance are still waiting.

Data Date	Weiss Investment Rating	Net Assets ($Mil)	Price	Performance Rating/Pts	Total Return Y-T-D	Risk Rating/Pts
6-05	D+	4259.18	117.05	D+ / 2.4	-0.47%	C+ / 6.8
2004	D+	3544.92	118.05	D+ / 2.9	12.78%	C+ / 6.5

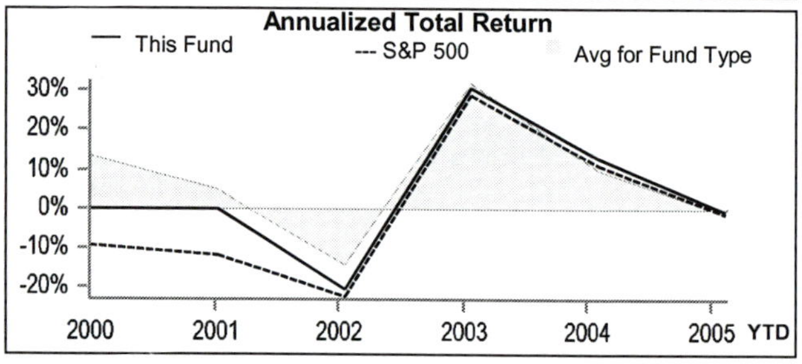

Western Asset Income Fund (PAI) C- Fair

Fund Family: LMM, LLC
Fund Type: General - Investment Grade
Inception Date: March 22, 1973

Major Rating Factors:
Disappointing performance is the major factor driving the C- (Fair) Weiss Investment Rating for Western Asset Income Fund. The fund currently has a performance rating of D+ (Weak) based on an annualized return of 8.48% over the last three years and a total return of -0.06% year to date 2005. Factored into the performance evaluation is an expense ratio of 0.76% (very low).

The fund's risk rating is currently B- (Good). It carries a beta of 1.37, meaning it is expected to move 13.7% for every 10% move in the market. Volatility, as measured by both the semi-deviation and a drawdown factor, is considered low. As of June 30, 2005, Western Asset Income Fund traded at a discount of 8.07% below its net asset value, which is worse than its one-year historical average discount of 8.51%.

Western Asset Management has been running the fund for 32 years and currently receives a manager quality ranking of 71 (0=worst, 99=best). This fund offers only a moderate level of risk but investors looking for strong performance are still waiting.

Data Date	Weiss Investment Rating	Net Assets ($Mil)	Price	Performance Rating/Pts	Total Return Y-T-D	Risk Rating/Pts
6-05	C-	153.29	14.81	D+ / 2.9	-0.06%	B- / 7.6
2004	C+	150.59	15.44	C / 5.0	10.60%	B- / 7.6
2003	C	155.28	15.16	C- / 3.5	12.73%	B / 8.6

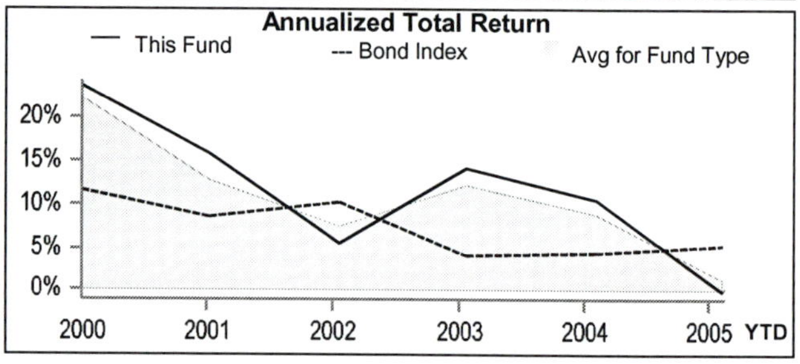

Western Asset Premier Bond Fund (WEA) C- Fair

Fund Family: Western Asset Management Co
Fund Type: General - Investment Grade
Inception Date: March 28, 2002

Major Rating Factors:
Middle of the road best describes Western Asset Premier Bond Fund whose Weiss Investment Rating is currently a C- (Fair). The fund currently has a performance rating of C- (Fair) based on an annualized return of 10.15% over the last three years and a total return of -4.95% year to date 2005. Factored into the performance evaluation is an expense ratio of 1.17% (low).

The fund's risk rating is currently B- (Good). It carries a beta of 1.47, meaning it is expected to move 14.7% for every 10% move in the market. Volatility, as measured by both the semi-deviation and a drawdown factor, is considered low. As of June 30, 2005, Western Asset Premier Bond Fund traded at a discount of 3.26% below its net asset value, which is better than its one-year historical average discount of .94%.

Western Asset's Inv Strategy G has been running the fund for 3 years and currently receives a manager quality ranking of 77 (0=worst, 99=best). If you desire an average level of risk, then this fund may be an option.

Data Date	Weiss Investment Rating	Net Assets ($Mil)	Price	Performance Rating/Pts	Total Return Y-T-D	Risk Rating/Pts
6-05	C-	177.29	14.85	C- / 3.2	-4.95%	B- / 7.2

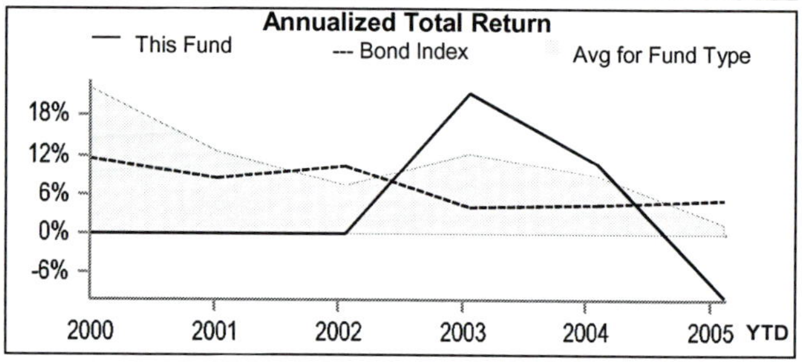

Z-Seven Fund (ZSEV) E Very Weak

Fund Family: Top Fund Management
Fund Type: Global
Inception Date: December 29, 1983

Major Rating Factors:
Very poor performance is the major factor driving the E (Very Weak) Weiss Investment Rating for Z-Seven Fund. The fund currently has a performance rating of E- (Very Weak) based on an annualized return of 0.39% over the last three years and a total return of 0.00% year to date 2005. Factored into the performance evaluation is an expense ratio of 3.80% (high).

The fund's risk rating is currently C- (Fair). It carries a beta of 0.58, meaning the fund's expected move will be 5.8% for every 10% move in the market. Volatility, as measured by both the semi-deviation and a drawdown factor, is considered average. As of June 30, 2005, Z-Seven Fund traded at a discount of 21.20% below its net asset value, which is better than its one-year historical average discount of 17.66%.

Barry Ziskin has been running the fund for 21 years and currently receives a manager quality ranking of 16 (0=worst, 99=best). This fund offers an average level of risk but investors looking for strong performance will be frustrated.

Data Date	Weiss Investment Rating	Net Assets ($Mil)	Price	Performance Rating/Pts	Total Return Y-T-D	Risk Rating/Pts
6-05	E	10.43	4.35	E- / 0.0	0.00%	C- / 3.1
2004	E+	9.55	4.35	E / 0.3	-8.61%	C- / 3.8
2003	E+	8.67	4.76	E+ / 0.6	46.01%	C- / 3.3

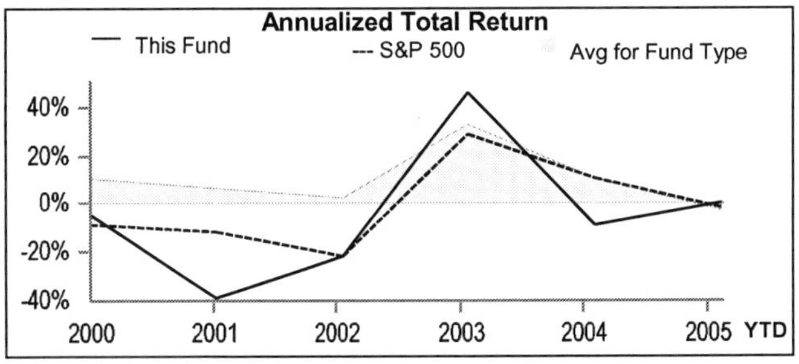

Zenix Income Fund (ZIF) D+ Weak

Fund Family: Smith Barney Mutual Funds Mgmt. Inc
Fund Type: Corporate - High Yield
Inception Date: April 29, 1988

Major Rating Factors:
Zenix Income Fund receives a Weiss Investment Rating of D+ (Weak). The fund currently has a performance rating of C (Fair) based on an annualized return of 16.07% over the last three years and a total return of -1.08% year to date 2005. Factored into the performance evaluation is an expense ratio of 2.14% (high).

The fund's risk rating is currently C (Fair). It carries a beta of 1.86, meaning it is expected to move 18.6% for every 10% move in the market. Volatility, as measured by both the semi-deviation and a drawdown factor, is considered average. As of June 30, 2005, Zenix Income Fund traded at a premium of 6.93% above its net asset value, which is better than its one-year historical average premium of 15.41%.

Beth Semmel has been running the fund for 17 years and currently receives a manager quality ranking of 6 (0=worst, 99=best). If you desire an average level of risk, then this fund may be an option.

Data Date	Weiss Investment Rating	Net Assets ($Mil)	Price	Performance Rating/Pts	Total Return Y-T-D	Risk Rating/Pts
6-05	D+	56.56	3.24	C / 4.3	-1.08%	C / 4.8
2004	D-	57.48	3.45	C- / 3.7	-2.92%	C- / 3.9
2003	C-	53.78	3.93	B- / 7.0	45.85%	C- / 3.3

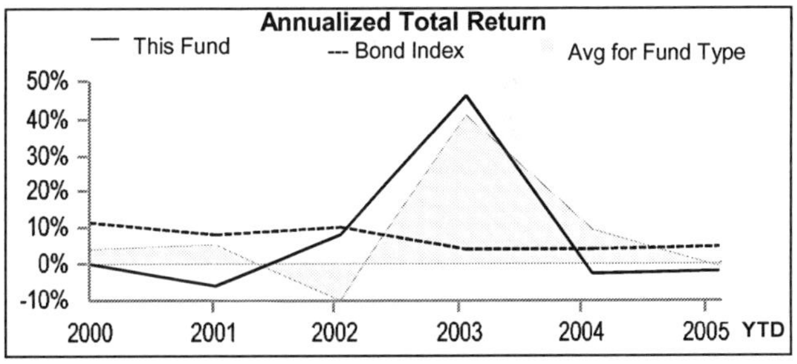

Zweig Fund (ZF) D- Weak

Fund Family: Altman Group
Fund Type: Growth
Inception Date: October 3, 1986

Major Rating Factors:
Disappointing performance is the major factor driving the D- (Weak) Weiss Investment Rating for Zweig Fund. The fund currently has a performance rating of D- (Weak) based on an annualized return of 3.20% over the last three years and a total return of 2.42% year to date 2005. Factored into the performance evaluation is an expense ratio of 1.38% (average).

The fund's risk rating is currently C (Fair). It carries a beta of 0.74, meaning the fund's expected move will be 7.4% for every 10% move in the market. Volatility, as measured by both the semi-deviation and a drawdown factor, is considered average. As of June 30, 2005, Zweig Fund traded at a discount of 6.76% below its net asset value, which is worse than its one-year historical average discount of 8.42%.

Martin Zweig has been running the fund for 19 years and currently receives a manager quality ranking of 29 (0=worst, 99=best). This fund offers an average level of risk but investors looking for strong performance will be frustrated.

Data Date	Weiss Investment Rating	Net Assets ($Mil)	Price	Performance Rating/Pts	Total Return Y-T-D	Risk Rating/Pts
6-05	D-	440.64	5.38	D- / 1.1	2.42%	C / 5.5
2004	E	420.10	5.55	E / 0.4	18.16%	D+ / 2.8
2003	D-	403.71	4.84	E- / 0.1	8.19%	C / 4.9

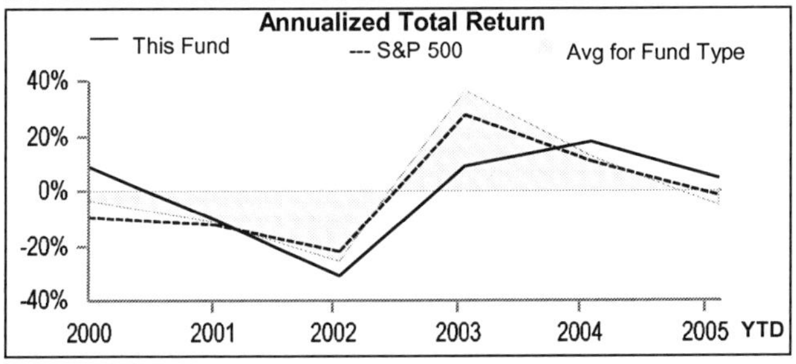

Zweig Total Return Fund (ZTR) E+ Very Weak

Fund Family: Altman Group
Fund Type: Growth and Income
Inception Date: September 22, 1988

Data Date	Weiss Investment Rating	Net Assets ($Mil)	Price	Perfor-mance Rating/Pts	Total Return Y-T-D	Risk Rating/Pts
6-05	E+	522.10	5.12	E / 0.4	0.88%	C+ / 5.8
2004	D-	519.14	5.35	E / 0.5	13.38%	C / 5.5
2003	D	529.90	4.98	E+ / 0.7	-0.98%	C+ / 6.1

Major Rating Factors:

Very poor performance is the major factor driving the E+ (Very Weak) Weiss Investment Rating for Zweig Total Return Fund. The fund currently has a performance rating of E (Very Weak) based on an annualized return of 2.21% over the last three years and a total return of 0.88% year to date 2005. Factored into the performance evaluation is an expense ratio of 1.28% (average).

The fund's risk rating is currently C+ (Fair). It carries a beta of 0.21, meaning the fund's expected move will be 2.1% for every 10% move in the market. Volatility, as measured by both the semi-deviation and a drawdown factor, is considered low. As of June 30, 2005, Zweig Total Return Fund traded at a discount of 5.88% below its net asset value, which is worse than its one-year historical average discount of 6.10%.

Chris Capano has been running the fund for 17 years and currently receives a manager quality ranking of 58 (0=worst, 99=best). This fund offers only a moderate level of risk but investors looking for strong performance are still waiting.

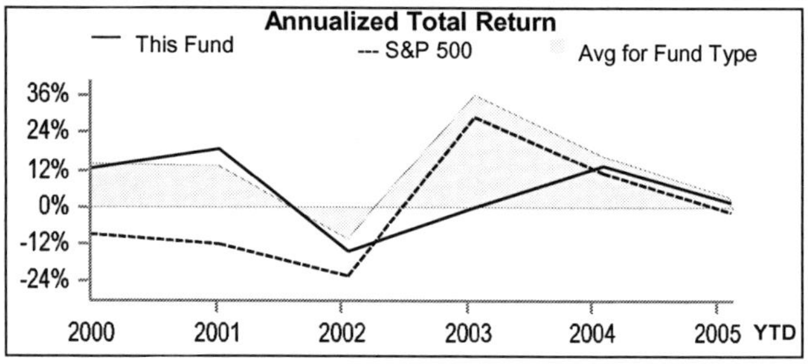

Section III

Top 200 Closed-End Mutual Funds

A compilation of those

Closed-End Mutual Funds

receiving the highest Weiss Investment Ratings.

Funds are listed in order by Overall Weiss Investment Rating.

Section III Contents

This section contains a summary analysis of each of the top 200 closed-end mutual funds as determined by their overall Weiss Investment Rating. You can use this section to identify those mutual funds that have achieved the best possible combination of total return on investment and reduced volatility over the past three years. Consult each fund's individual Performance Rating and Risk Rating to find the fund that best matches your investing style.

1. Fund Type

The mutual fund's peer category based on an analysis of its investment portfolio.

COH	Corporate – High Yield	HL	Health
COI	Corporate – Inv. Grade	IN	Income
EM	Emerging Market	LP	Loan Participation
EN	Energy/Natural Resources	MTG	Mortgage
FS	Financial Services	MUH	Municipal – High Yield
FO	Foreign	MUN	Municipal – National
GEI	General – Inv. Grade	MUS	Municipal – Single State
GEN	General Bond	PM	Precious Metals
GL	Global	USA	U.S. Gov. – Agency
GR	Growth	UT	Utilities
GI	Growth and Income		

A blank fund type means that the mutual fund has not yet been categorized.

2. Fund Name

The name of the mutual fund as stated in its prospectus, which can sometimes differ slightly from the name that the company uses for advertising. If you cannot find the particular mutual fund you are interested in, or if you have any doubts regarding the precise name, verify the information with your broker or on your account statement. Also, use the fund's ticker symbol for confirmation. (See column 3.)

3. Ticker Symbol

The unique alphabetic symbol used for identifying and trading a specific mutual fund. No two funds can have the same ticker symbol.

A handful of funds currently show no associated ticker symbol. This means that the fund is either small or new since the NASD only assigns a ticker symbol to funds with at least $25 million in assets or 1,000 shareholders.

4. Overall Weiss Investment Rating

Our overall rating is measured on a scale from A to E based on each fund's risk-adjusted performance. Please see page 10 for specific descriptions of each letter grade. Also, refer to page 7 for information on how our ratings are derived. Most important, when using this rating, please be sure to consider the warnings beginning on page 11 regarding the ratings' limitations and the underlying assumptions.

5.	**Price**	Closing price of the fund on the date shown.
6.	**Performance Rating/Points**	A letter grade rating based solely on the mutual fund's financial performance over the trailing three years, without any consideration for the amount of risk the fund poses. Like the overall Weiss Investment Rating, the Performance Rating is measured on a scale from A to E for ease of interpretation. The points score indicates where the Performance Rating falls on a scale of 0 to 10.
7.	**1-Year Total Return**	The total return the fund has provided investors over the preceeding 52 weeks. This total return figure is computed based on the fund's dividend distributions and share price appreciation/depreciation during the period, net of the expenses and fees it imposes on its shareholders.
8.	**1-Year Total Return Percentile**	The fund's percentile rank based on its one-year performance compared to that of all other closed-end funds in existence for at least one year. A score of 99 is the best possible, indicating that the fund outperformed 99% of the closed-end mutual funds. Zero is the worst possible percentile score.
9.	**3-Year Total Return**	The total annual return the fund has provided investors over the preceeding 156 weeks.
10.	**3-Year Total Return Percentile**	The fund's percentile rank based on its three-year performance compared to that of all other closed-end funds in existence for at least three years. A score of 99 is the best possible, indicating that the fund outperformed 99% of the closed-end mutual funds. Zero is the worst possible percentile score.
11.	**5-Year Total Return**	The total annual return the fund has provided investors over the preceeding 260 weeks.
12.	**5-Year Total Return Percentile**	The fund's percentile rank based on its five-year performance compared to that of all other closed-end funds in existence for at least five years. A score of 99 is the best possible, indicating that the fund outperformed 99% of the closed-end mutual funds. Zero is the worst possible percentile score.
13.	**Dividend Yield**	Most recent quarterly dividend to fund investors annualized, expressed as a percent of the fund's current share price. The dividend yield of a fund can have little correlation to the amount of dividends the fund has received from its underlying investments. Rather, dividend distributions are based on a fund's need to pass earnings from both dividends and gains on the sale of investments along to shareholders. Thus, these dividend distributions are included as a part of the fund's total return. Keep in mind that dividend income may be taxed at a different rate than capital gains depending on your income tax bracket.

14. Risk Rating/Points A letter grade rating based solely on the mutual fund's risk as determined by its monthly performance volatility over the trailing three years. The risk rating does not take into consideration the overall financial performance the fund has achieved or the total return it has provided to its shareholders. Like the overall Weiss Investment Rating, the Risk Rating is measured on a scale from A to E for ease of interpretation. The points score indicates where the Risk Rating falls on a scale of 0 to 10.

15. Premium/ Discount A comparison of the fund's price to its NAV as of the date indicated. The premium (+) or discount (-) indicates the percentage the shares are trading above or below the fund's NAV per share.

If the price is above the fund's NAV, the fund is said to be trading at a premium. If the price is lower than the fund's NAV, the fund is trading at a discount.

16. 1-Year Average Premium/ Discount The average of the fund's premium/discount over the preceeding year.

It can be useful to compare the fund's current premium/discount to its one-year average. If the fund is currently trading at a premium/discount that is lower/higher than its one-year average, then there has been less demand for the fund in more recent times than over the past year. Conversely, if the fund is currently trading at a premium/discount that is higher/lower than its one-year average, this indicates that there has been greater demand for the fund in more recent times than over the past year.

99 Pct = Best
0 Pct = Worst

Fund Type	Fund Name	Ticker Symbol	Overall Weiss Investment Rating	Price As of 6/30/05	PERFORMANCE: Performance Rating/Pts	PERFORMANCE: Annualized Total Return Through 6/30/05 1Yr/Pct	PERFORMANCE: Annualized Total Return Through 6/30/05 3Yr/Pct	PERFORMANCE: Annualized Total Return Through 6/30/05 5Yr/Pct	PERFORMANCE: Dividend Yield %	RISK: Risk Rating/Pts	VALUATION: Premium/Discount As of 6/30/05	VALUATION: Premium/Discount 1 Year Average
FO	Canadian General Investments Ltd	T.CGI	**A+**	18.40	**A+ / 9.7**	47.72 / 98	29.43 / 97	18.56 / 90	1.30	**C+ / 6.7**	-17.23	-25.05
MUN	BlackRock Investment Qual Muni Tr	BKN	**A+**	16.61	**A+ / 9.6**	28.68 / 97	13.47 / 90	12.60 / 92	5.43	**C+ / 6.5**	4.07	-3.77
MUN	MuniHoldings Fund II	MUH	**A+**	15.32	**A+ / 9.6**	27.08 / 95	14.47 / 93	13.96 / 96	6.85	**C+ / 6.9**	1.26	-1.61
MUN	Scudder Strategic Municipal Inc Tr	KSM	**A+**	13.66	**A+ / 9.6**	26.81 / 95	13.43 / 90	12.44 / 91	6.47	**B- / 7.1**	9.11	2.56
MUN	BlackRock Municipal Bond Trust	BBK	**A+**	16.09	**A / 9.5**	28.64 / 97	12.44 / 87	--	6.38	**C+ / 6.5**	-0.12	-3.63
MUN	MuniHoldings Fund	MHD	**A+**	16.71	**A / 9.5**	25.09 / 92	14.87 / 94	12.17 / 90	6.87	**B- / 7.2**	1.21	-1.27
MUN	MuniVest Fund II	MVT	**A+**	16.20	**A / 9.5**	24.93 / 91	14.19 / 92	14.72 / 97	6.81	**C+ / 6.8**	3.85	0.13
HL	HOLDRS Biotech	BBH	**A+**	167.30	**A / 9.4**	16.87 / 41	27.32 / 96	-0.69 / 11	0.00	**C+ / 6.6**	0.00	N/A
MUN	Eaton Vance Municipal Inc Tr	EVN	**A+**	16.67	**A / 9.3**	20.87 / 79	14.78 / 93	17.28 / 99	6.77	**C+ / 6.9**	14.26	14.05
MUN	MuniAssets Fund	MUA	**A+**	13.45	**A / 9.3**	28.55 / 97	11.50 / 83	10.73 / 80	6.08	**B- / 7.2**	-0.30	-3.95
MUN	MuniYield Fund	MYD	**A+**	14.99	**A- / 9.2**	29.19 / 97	11.30 / 81	11.40 / 86	6.66	**B- / 7.4**	0.54	-3.62
MUN	MuniVest Fund	MVF	**A+**	9.94	**A- / 9.1**	26.19 / 94	11.34 / 82	12.89 / 93	6.68	**B- / 7.1**	-2.83	-6.26
MUS	BlackRock NY Muni Bond Trust	BQH	**A+**	15.21	**B+ / 8.9**	24.76 / 91	10.54 / 78	--	6.04	**B- / 7.0**	-5.06	-8.31
MUN	MuniYield Quality Fund II	MQT	**A+**	13.37	**B+ / 8.9**	24.18 / 89	11.04 / 80	10.17 / 75	6.41	**B- / 7.2**	-3.33	-7.60
FO	iShares MSCI Pacific ex-Japan Idx	EPP	**A+**	94.11	**B+ / 8.8**	34.03 / 83	21.35 / 91	--	3.20	**B- / 7.0**	-0.14	0.31
MUN	Nuveen Dividend Advantage Muni 2	NXZ	**A+**	16.00	**B+ / 8.8**	23.48 / 87	11.25 / 81	--	6.43	**B- / 7.3**	-0.99	-2.92
MUN	Apex Municipal Fund	APX	**A+**	9.36	**B+ / 8.6**	21.50 / 81	10.92 / 80	7.95 / 55	6.08	**B- / 7.6**	-4.49	-6.68
MUN	PIMCO Municipal Income Fund	PMF	**A+**	15.54	**B+ / 8.6**	27.28 / 95	9.08 / 68	--	6.18	**B- / 7.6**	2.85	0.04
MUN	Alliance Nat Municipal Income Fund	AFB	**A+**	14.90	**B+ / 8.5**	22.30 / 84	10.26 / 76	--	6.09	**B- / 7.6**	-5.99	-8.51
MUS	Alliance CA Municipal Income Fund	AKP	**A+**	14.87	**B / 8.1**	21.46 / 81	9.61 / 72	--	5.87	**B- / 7.8**	-4.74	-6.59
MUN	BlackRock Municipal 2018 Income Tr	BPK	**A+**	15.70	**B / 8.0**	17.99 / 69	10.98 / 80	--	4.92	**B- / 7.9**	-1.32	-4.38
MUN	Nuveen Div Adv Muni 3	NZF	**A+**	14.92	**B / 7.9**	21.16 / 80	8.90 / 67	--	6.44	**B- / 7.7**	-5.33	-6.75
MUN	BlackRock Strategic Municipal Tr	BSD	**A**	16.40	**A+ / 9.6**	31.70 / 98	12.40 / 87	12.47 / 91	5.89	**C+ / 5.8**	3.34	-6.42
FO	iShares MSCI Australia Index	EWA	**A**	17.66	**A / 9.3**	36.87 / 89	24.75 / 95	13.56 / 63	3.25	**C+ / 6.2**	-0.23	0.25
MUN	BlackRock Municipal Income Trust	BFK	**A**	15.15	**A- / 9.2**	28.30 / 96	11.60 / 84	--	6.32	**C+ / 6.4**	1.07	-1.81
MUS	BlackRock VA Muni Bond Trust	BHV	**A**	17.27	**A- / 9.2**	25.93 / 93	11.16 / 81	--	5.11	**C+ / 6.4**	6.54	1.21
MUS	Eaton Vance NY Muni Inc Tr	EVY	**A**	16.70	**A- / 9.2**	27.07 / 95	11.14 / 81	16.66 / 99	5.91	**C+ / 6.2**	3.28	-2.01
MUN	Scudder Municipal Income Trust	KTF	**A**	12.74	**A- / 9.1**	22.60 / 85	11.54 / 83	9.64 / 70	6.28	**C+ / 6.5**	1.43	-3.63
MUS	MuniYield FL Fund	MYF	**A**	15.06	**A- / 9.0**	26.38 / 94	10.66 / 79	13.21 / 94	6.13	**C+ / 6.3**	-2.40	-7.33
MUS	PIMCO NY Muni Income Fund	PNF	**A**	14.89	**B+ / 8.8**	25.83 / 93	8.40 / 63	--	6.00	**C+ / 6.3**	6.81	0.17
MUS	BlackRock NJ Muni Bond Trust	BLJ	**A**	15.55	**B+ / 8.7**	27.66 / 96	8.99 / 67	--	5.98	**C+ / 6.5**	-3.05	-4.85
MUS	MuniHoldings NJ Insured Fund	MUJ	**A**	15.59	**B+ / 8.6**	21.69 / 82	10.87 / 79	13.40 / 95	6.04	**B- / 7.0**	-1.45	-4.36
MUS	BlackRock CA Municipal Income Trust	BFZ	**A**	14.55	**B+ / 8.4**	22.97 / 86	9.62 / 72	--	6.19	**B- / 7.1**	-5.58	-7.79
MUS	Nuveen PA Div Adv Muni	NXM	**A**	16.10	**B+ / 8.4**	22.85 / 85	10.62 / 78	--	5.76	**C+ / 6.7**	0.94	-0.84
MUS	Nuveen NY Div Adv Muni 2	NXK	**A**	15.54	**B / 8.2**	20.88 / 79	10.06 / 75	--	6.04	**C+ / 6.9**	-2.02	-4.71
MUS	BlackRock NJ Municipal Income Trust	BNJ	**A**	15.39	**B / 8.1**	21.66 / 81	8.85 / 66	--	5.74	**B- / 7.1**	-4.29	-6.65
MUS	Nuveen CA Div Adv Muni	NAC	**A**	15.59	**B / 8.0**	20.04 / 77	9.58 / 72	10.24 / 76	6.35	**B- / 7.2**	-2.44	-4.95
MUN	MuniYield Insured Fund	MYI	**A**	15.14	**B / 7.9**	22.18 / 83	8.40 / 62	11.03 / 83	6.30	**B- / 7.7**	-5.02	-7.28
EN	Petroleum and Resources Corp.	PEO	**A**	30.01	**B / 7.8**	30.76 / 77	15.59 / 76	10.32 / 44	1.74	**B- / 7.3**	-7.94	-7.42
GI	iShares Cohen&Steers Realty Major	ICF	**A-**	70.50	**A- / 9.0**	33.54 / 82	21.41 / 92	--	5.10	**C+ / 5.9**	0.09	N/A
MUN	Dreyfus Strategic Muni Bond Fund	DSM	**A-**	9.25	**B+ / 8.8**	24.27 / 90	9.07 / 67	10.01 / 73	6.52	**C+ / 6.1**	1.87	-3.64
MUS	Alliance NY Municipal Income Fund	AYN	**A-**	14.85	**B+ / 8.6**	24.47 / 90	9.44 / 71	--	5.61	**C+ / 6.4**	-4.32	-7.89
MUS	MuniHoldings FL Insured Fund	MFL	**A-**	15.57	**B+ / 8.5**	22.65 / 85	10.65 / 79	14.53 / 97	6.34	**C+ / 6.5**	0.97	-2.25
MUS	MuniYield AZ Fund	MZA	**A-**	15.76	**B+ / 8.5**	25.61 / 92	9.35 / 70	14.67 / 97	5.85	**C+ / 6.3**	4.72	1.03
MUS	BlackRock NY Municipal Income Trust	BNY	**A-**	15.13	**B+ / 8.4**	22.85 / 85	9.68 / 72	--	6.00	**C+ / 6.5**	-3.51	-7.26
MUH	MFS Municipal Income Trust	MFM	**A-**	8.26	**B+ / 8.4**	21.69 / 82	9.08 / 67	9.35 / 67	6.63	**C+ / 6.5**	3.12	-1.25
MUS	Nuveen VA Div Adv Muni 2	NNB	**A-**	17.00	**B+ / 8.4**	22.45 / 84	11.14 / 81	--	4.93	**C+ / 6.5**	7.80	4.97
MUS	Nuveen NC Div Adv Muni	NRB	**A-**	17.33	**B / 8.2**	24.75 / 91	10.47 / 78	--	5.33	**C+ / 6.7**	11.73	7.96
MUS	Delaware Inv CO Ins Muni Inc	VCF	**A-**	17.64	**B / 8.0**	23.63 / 87	11.27 / 81	13.19 / 94	5.42	**C+ / 6.9**	10.53	8.79
MUN	MuniHoldings Insured Fund	MUS	**A-**	14.29	**B / 8.0**	22.46 / 84	10.10 / 75	11.14 / 84	6.35	**B- / 7.0**	-1.65	-5.00
MUS	MuniHoldings NY Insured Fund	MHN	**A-**	14.96	**B / 8.0**	19.68 / 75	9.24 / 69	12.21 / 90	6.28	**B- / 7.0**	-4.10	-8.13
MUS	BlackRock FL Muni Bond Trust	BIE	**A-**	15.62	**B / 7.9**	25.96 / 93	8.10 / 59	--	5.88	**B- / 7.1**	-3.76	-6.55

N/A denotes number is not available

Fund Type	Fund Name (99 Pct = Best, 0 Pct = Worst)	Ticker Symbol	Overall Weiss Investment Rating	Price As of 6/30/05	PERFORMANCE: Performance Rating/Pts	Annualized Total Return Through 6/30/05: 1Yr/Pct	3Yr/Pct	5Yr/Pct	Dividend Yield %	RISK: Risk Rating/Pts	VALUATION: Premium/Discount As of 6/30/05	1 Year Average
MUS	Nuveen Insured NY Div Adv Muni Fund	NKO	A-	15.14	B / 7.7	22.46 / 84	7.32 / 49	--	5.45	B- / 7.2	-5.02	-7.46
MUS	BlackRock CA Muni 2018 Income Trust	BJZ	A-	14.99	B- / 7.4	17.26 / 65	8.83 / 65	--	4.92	B- / 7.6	-2.15	-5.03
MUS	MuniYield CA Insured Fund	MCA	A-	14.22	B- / 7.3	19.95 / 77	8.19 / 61	7.80 / 53	6.14	B- / 7.6	-7.54	-9.95
FO	Chile Fund	CH	B+	15.03	A+ / 9.7	46.55 / 98	33.72 / 98	17.78 / 87	5.42	C / 4.3	-11.59	-10.68
GL	Scudder Multi-Market Income Trust	KMM	B+	10.21	A- / 9.2	42.62 / 96	21.05 / 91	14.63 / 69	7.72	C / 4.9	5.48	-1.71
FO	The New Ireland Fund	IRL	B+	21.20	A- / 9.2	36.97 / 89	25.91 / 96	14.24 / 66	0.14	C / 5.1	-13.96	-13.38
MUS	BlackRock NJ Inv Qual Muni Tr	RNJ	B+	15.56	B+ / 8.6	25.00 / 92	8.71 / 64	10.64 / 80	5.18	C+ / 5.7	4.92	-1.54
EM	Morgan Stanley Emerging Mkts Debt	MSD	B+	9.97	B+ / 8.6	28.11 / 70	21.23 / 91	18.01 / 88	7.24	C / 5.4	-7.69	-8.26
GI	iShares Dow Jones US Real Estate	IYR	B+	62.82	B+ / 8.5	29.40 / 74	19.09 / 87	18.47 / 89	4.04	C+ / 5.9	-0.49	-0.11
MUN	MuniYield Quality Fund	MQY	B+	15.27	B+ / 8.4	24.12 / 89	9.36 / 71	11.96 / 89	6.31	C+ / 6.3	-1.93	-5.60
MUS	Delaware Inv FL Insured Muni Inc	VFL	B+	16.70	B+ / 8.3	21.90 / 82	10.32 / 76	13.81 / 96	5.73	C+ / 6.1	7.33	2.95
GI	Franklin Multi-Income Trust	FMI	B+	9.35	B+ / 8.3	40.29 / 94	14.65 / 71	11.24 / 48	4.48	C+ / 5.8	-1.89	-9.77
MUS	MuniYield FL Insured Fund	MFT	B+	15.45	B+ / 8.3	24.04 / 89	9.32 / 70	11.93 / 89	5.80	C+ / 6.4	1.11	-3.13
MUS	Nuveen VA Div Adv Muni Fund	NGB	B+	17.47	B+ / 8.3	23.72 / 88	12.22 / 86	--	5.26	C+ / 6.3	12.35	12.71
MUS	Nuveen Insured FL Prem Inc Muni	NFL	B+	16.47	B / 8.2	24.22 / 90	8.28 / 61	11.40 / 86	5.23	C+ / 5.9	1.29	-1.96
MUS	Nuveen GA Div Adv Muni	NZX	B+	16.00	B / 8.1	23.82 / 88	9.83 / 74	--	5.18	C+ / 6.3	4.17	0.74
MUS	Eaton Vance FL Muni Inc Tr	FEV	B+	15.55	B / 7.9	19.22 / 74	10.60 / 78	15.49 / 98	5.72	C+ / 6.6	1.63	-0.20
MUN	Putnam Managed Muni Inc Tr	PMM	B+	7.88	B / 7.9	21.46 / 81	6.88 / 43	4.23 / 27	5.24	C+ / 6.9	-5.40	-11.22
MUS	BlackRock FL Municipal Income Trust	BBF	B+	15.29	B / 7.8	26.78 / 95	7.72 / 55	--	5.95	B- / 7.0	-2.80	-6.57
MUN	Morgan Stanley Muni Inc Op	OIA	B+	8.10	B / 7.8	26.34 / 94	6.96 / 44	6.49 / 41	6.26	C+ / 6.9	1.00	-4.20
MUN	MuniEnhanced Fund	MEN	B+	11.43	B / 7.6	22.35 / 84	8.36 / 62	10.40 / 78	6.34	B- / 7.1	-3.63	-6.84
MUS	Nuveen Insured NY Prem Inc Muni	NNF	B+	15.80	B / 7.6	23.43 / 87	7.28 / 48	10.34 / 77	5.38	C+ / 6.7	-1.99	-6.13
MUS	Nuveen TX Quality Inc Muni	NTX	B+	15.96	B / 7.6	21.62 / 81	7.88 / 57	11.52 / 87	5.43	C+ / 6.4	2.05	-1.26
MUN	Nuveen Insured Quality Muni	NQI	B+	16.22	B- / 7.5	21.36 / 80	8.10 / 59	11.34 / 86	5.79	C+ / 6.7	2.14	-0.31
MUS	BlackRock CA Muni Bond Trust	BZA	B+	14.92	B- / 7.4	23.34 / 87	7.46 / 51	--	6.38	B- / 7.3	-6.57	-6.56
MUN	MuniHoldings Insured Fund II	MUE	B+	13.70	B- / 7.4	20.27 / 78	8.60 / 64	12.63 / 92	6.38	B- / 7.2	-5.58	-8.38
MUS	MuniYield MI Insured Fund II	MYM	B+	14.70	B- / 7.3	17.41 / 66	9.35 / 70	11.75 / 88	6.03	B- / 7.0	-3.10	-5.16
MUS	Nuveen NY Div Adv Muni	NAN	B+	15.93	B- / 7.3	19.11 / 74	9.16 / 68	11.15 / 84	6.13	C+ / 6.7	-0.93	-3.11
MUS	MuniYield NJ Fund	MYJ	B+	15.31	B- / 7.2	18.63 / 71	7.88 / 57	10.77 / 80	6.07	B- / 7.3	-3.83	-5.91
MUS	Nuveen CA Div Adv Muni 2	NVX	B+	14.59	B- / 7.1	18.51 / 71	7.87 / 57	--	6.20	B- / 7.3	-6.29	-8.09
MUS	Nuveen CA Prem Inc Muni	NCU	B+	14.16	B- / 7.1	20.44 / 78	7.41 / 50	8.60 / 61	5.94	B- / 7.1	-6.04	-7.07
MUN	Nuveen Muni Advantage	NMA	B+	15.59	B- / 7.0	18.96 / 73	8.25 / 61	11.81 / 88	6.36	B- / 7.3	-3.47	-4.09
MUS	Morgan Stanley CA Qual Muni Sec	IQC	B+	14.30	C+ / 5.6	13.78 / 52	8.77 / 65	8.39 / 58	5.87	B+ / 9.1	-9.49	-8.13
FS	First Financial Fund	FF	B	18.10	A- / 9.1	29.71 / 74	28.34 / 96	35.77 / 99	2.10	C / 4.6	2.20	2.97
GI	Cohen&Steers Adv Inc Realty Fund	RLF	B	21.87	A- / 9.0	37.42 / 90	20.42 / 90	--	8.11	C / 4.7	-6.58	-6.41
EM	Scudder Global High Income Fund	LBF	B	7.91	B+ / 8.9	34.74 / 85	20.30 / 89	21.16 / 96	7.22	C / 4.9	-10.11	-9.99
MUS	BlackRock MD Muni Bond Trust	BZM	B	16.69	B+ / 8.7	26.28 / 94	9.81 / 73	--	5.26	C / 5.1	4.31	-2.24
GL	Scudder Strategic Income Fund	KST	B	14.01	B+ / 8.7	32.08 / 79	20.89 / 91	8.78 / 34	7.63	C / 5.0	0.79	-1.85
MUS	Eaton Vance PA Muni Inc Tr	EVP	B	15.85	B+ / 8.3	25.40 / 92	12.24 / 86	15.20 / 98	5.97	C+ / 5.6	5.04	2.76
UT	Gabelli Utility Trust	GUT	B	10.00	B / 8.2	26.20 / 65	17.94 / 84	18.56 / 90	7.29	C / 5.5	36.24	37.15
GI	Nuveen Real Estate Inc Fund	JRS	B	20.11	B / 8.1	31.77 / 78	17.42 / 82	--	8.00	C+ / 5.6	-10.26	-7.44
MUS	BlackRock FL Inv Qual Muni Tr	RFA	B	15.38	B / 7.8	24.21 / 89	7.54 / 52	10.15 / 75	5.59	C+ / 5.7	4.13	-3.36
COH	40/86 Strategic Income Fund	CFD	B	10.16	B- / 7.5	15.27 / 38	19.85 / 88	10.39 / 44	10.02	C+ / 6.0	-9.69	-10.31
MUS	Nuveen NJ Div Adv Muni Fund 2	NUJ	B	15.64	B- / 7.5	19.90 / 76	8.07 / 59	--	5.77	C+ / 6.2	-1.01	-2.92
MUS	MuniYield NJ Insured Fund	MJI	B	15.65	B- / 7.3	21.68 / 81	7.65 / 54	10.09 / 74	5.92	C+ / 6.6	-0.38	-2.97
MUS	MuniYield PA Insured Fund	MPA	B	15.99	B- / 7.3	21.01 / 80	8.72 / 64	12.29 / 91	5.96	C+ / 6.6	-1.84	-3.71
MUS	Nuveen OH Div Adv Muni 2	NBJ	B	16.06	B- / 7.3	23.90 / 89	9.69 / 73	--	5.41	C+ / 6.5	2.95	2.01
MUS	Nuveen GA Prem Inc Muni	NPG	B	16.95	B- / 7.2	23.09 / 86	6.95 / 44	11.08 / 84	4.94	C+ / 6.5	11.15	7.63
UT	iShares Dow Jones US Utilities	IDU	B	76.12	B- / 7.1	33.36 / 82	12.74 / 62	6.38 / 26	2.80	C+ / 6.5	-0.05	-0.02
FO	iShares MSCI Singapore Index	EWS	B	7.61	B- / 7.1	29.85 / 75	15.90 / 77	3.08 / 17	3.64	C+ / 6.4	0.26	0.27
MUS	Nuveen NY Performance Plus Muni	NNP	B	16.02	B- / 7.1	19.22 / 74	7.85 / 56	10.84 / 81	6.06	C+ / 6.7	-4.30	-5.65
MUS	Minnesota Municipal Inc Portfolio	MXA	B	16.07	B- / 7.0	21.20 / 80	7.54 / 52	11.58 / 88	5.57	C+ / 6.6	3.81	0.81

N/A denotes number is not available

Fund Type	Fund Name (99 Pct = Best, 0 Pct = Worst)	Ticker Symbol	Overall Weiss Investment Rating	Price As of 6/30/05	PERFORMANCE: Performance Rating/Pts	Annualized Total Return Through 6/30/05: 1Yr/Pct	3Yr/Pct	5Yr/Pct	Dividend Yield %	RISK: Risk Rating/Pts	VALUATION: Premium/Discount As of 6/30/05	1 Year Average
MUS	Nuveen NC Div Adv Muni 2	NNO	**B**	16.60	**B- / 7.0**	11.25 / 43	10.12 / 75	--	5.32	**C+ / 6.7**	6.34	2.80
MUS	BlackRock NY Muni 2018 Income Trust	BLH	**B**	15.29	**C+ / 6.5**	13.88 / 53	9.75 / 73	--	4.77	**B / 8.4**	-5.91	-5.29
MUN	Morgan Stanley Muni Inc Op II	OIB	**B**	8.14	**C+ / 6.1**	15.00 / 57	7.08 / 46	9.22 / 65	5.84	**B / 8.5**	-9.05	-9.83
MUN	Morgan Stanley Qual Muni Sec	IQM	**B**	14.40	**C+ / 6.0**	14.65 / 56	7.81 / 56	9.93 / 72	5.85	**B / 8.7**	-12.09	-11.77
MUN	Morgan Stanley Insured Muni Inc Tr	IIM	**B**	14.23	**C / 5.4**	12.77 / 49	7.30 / 48	8.24 / 57	5.66	**B / 8.3**	-11.06	-10.70
MUN	Morgan Stanley Qual Muni Inc Tr	IQI	**B**	13.93	**C / 5.2**	12.92 / 50	7.04 / 45	8.46 / 59	5.80	**B / 8.4**	-11.89	-11.31
MUN	Nuveen Muni Value	NUV	**B**	9.57	**C / 5.0**	15.95 / 61	6.06 / 33	8.68 / 62	4.87	**B / 8.8**	-7.71	-8.65
GL	Salomon Br 2008 Wldwide $ Gov Tm Tr	SBG	**B**	11.19	**C- / 3.8**	11.46 / 28	12.18 / 58	14.77 / 70	7.72	**B+ / 9.7**	-2.95	-0.42
FO	India Fund	IFN	**B-**	30.50	**A+ / 9.9**	50.84 / 99	50.94 / 99	18.32 / 89	5.09	**C- / 3.5**	1.63	0.14
EN	SPDR Energy	XLE	**B-**	44.94	**A / 9.5**	44.57 / 97	21.81 / 92	10.07 / 42	1.27	**C- / 3.8**	0.02	0.01
EN	iShares Dow Jones US Energy Sector	IYE	**B-**	77.92	**A / 9.3**	40.78 / 95	20.88 / 90	11.30 / 49	1.28	**C- / 3.9**	0.14	0.05
GI	Cohen&Steers Quality Income Realty	RQI	**B-**	20.52	**A- / 9.1**	36.48 / 88	20.68 / 90	--	7.93	**C / 4.3**	-10.67	-8.82
GL	Herzfeld Caribbean Basin Fund	CUBA	**B-**	6.30	**B+ / 8.9**	28.05 / 70	22.86 / 94	5.93 / 25	0.00	**C / 4.4**	-12.98	-13.44
EN	iShares S&P Global Energy Sector	IXC	**B-**	86.99	**B+ / 8.9**	36.75 / 88	19.50 / 88	--	1.47	**C / 4.5**	0.06	0.22
COH	Scudder High Income Trust	KHI	**B-**	7.31	**B+ / 8.5**	26.71 / 66	18.53 / 85	9.20 / 37	9.21	**C / 4.7**	22.86	17.41
FO	Scudder New Asia Fund	SAF	**B-**	15.82	**B+ / 8.3**	26.66 / 65	20.06 / 89	5.53 / 23	0.44	**C / 5.1**	-11.92	-12.98
COH	Corporate High Yield Fund	COY	**B-**	8.74	**B / 7.8**	18.39 / 46	19.44 / 88	9.52 / 38	9.60	**C / 5.3**	1.16	-1.08
FO	Singapore Fund	SGF	**B-**	8.91	**B / 7.8**	24.29 / 60	20.77 / 90	6.10 / 25	2.48	**C / 5.5**	-13.24	-14.23
GI	Cohen&Steers Total Return Realty	RFI	**B-**	19.80	**B / 7.7**	27.56 / 69	17.60 / 82	19.31 / 92	6.56	**C+ / 5.7**	-0.25	0.51
EM	Global High Income Dollar Fund	GHI	**B-**	16.94	**B / 7.7**	30.31 / 76	19.70 / 88	19.21 / 92	8.30	**C / 5.3**	8.66	12.51
GL	Alliance World Dollar Govt Fund II	AWF	**B-**	12.29	**B- / 7.5**	19.98 / 50	18.93 / 86	16.59 / 80	7.20	**C+ / 5.8**	-12.78	-11.59
COH	Pioneer High Income Trust	PHT	**B-**	16.20	**B- / 7.5**	19.09 / 48	18.29 / 84	--	10.02	**C / 5.5**	0.31	-0.81
COH	Corporate High Yield Fund V	HYV	**B-**	14.63	**B- / 7.2**	19.62 / 49	19.28 / 87	--	9.80	**C+ / 6.1**	-1.81	-3.52
COH	Senior High Income Portfolio	ARK	**B-**	5.93	**B- / 7.0**	16.61 / 41	17.79 / 83	9.09 / 35	9.46	**C+ / 6.4**	-1.00	-3.11
MUS	MuniYield MI Insured Fund	MIY	**B-**	15.49	**C+ / 6.9**	17.48 / 66	9.16 / 68	12.54 / 92	6.18	**B- / 7.5**	-3.25	-3.95
MUS	Nuveen CA Div Adv Muni 3	NZH	**B-**	13.96	**C+ / 6.9**	19.43 / 75	7.62 / 53	--	6.16	**B- / 7.7**	-8.82	-9.70
MUN	Nuveen Select Quality Muni	NQS	**B-**	15.12	**C+ / 6.9**	16.52 / 64	8.12 / 59	10.45 / 78	6.29	**B- / 7.5**	-4.91	-5.91
MUS	PIMCO CA Municipal Income Fund	PCQ	**B-**	14.75	**C+ / 6.9**	22.28 / 83	6.62 / 39	--	6.20	**B- / 7.2**	-0.27	-2.31
MUN	Salomon Br Municipal Partners	MNP	**B-**	13.88	**C+ / 6.9**	15.43 / 59	8.34 / 62	9.85 / 71	6.03	**B- / 7.1**	-9.40	-11.98
MUS	Nuveen MA Div Adv Muni	NMB	**B-**	16.80	**C+ / 6.8**	22.16 / 83	6.64 / 39	--	5.20	**B- / 7.1**	7.21	5.48
MUS	Nuveen NJ Div Adv Muni	NXJ	**B-**	15.07	**C+ / 6.8**	18.49 / 71	8.73 / 64	--	5.58	**B- / 7.2**	-3.64	-2.45
MUN	American Municipal Income Portfolio	XAA	**B-**	14.82	**C+ / 6.7**	16.50 / 63	8.60 / 64	11.29 / 85	6.10	**B- / 7.8**	-6.68	-7.07
MUS	Nuveen NY Quality Inc Muni	NUN	**B-**	15.00	**C+ / 6.7**	17.82 / 68	7.74 / 56	9.29 / 67	5.59	**B- / 7.2**	-6.25	-7.47
MUN	Nuveen Premium Income Muni 2	NPM	**B-**	14.66	**C+ / 6.7**	18.74 / 72	7.36 / 50	9.58 / 69	6.05	**B- / 7.5**	-6.51	-7.46
MUS	MuniHoldings CA Insured Fund II	MUC	**B-**	14.77	**C+ / 6.6**	18.82 / 73	8.14 / 60	10.53 / 79	6.33	**B- / 7.3**	-4.09	-5.50
MUN	Nuveen Investment Quality Muni	NQM	**B-**	15.15	**C+ / 6.6**	17.73 / 67	7.26 / 48	10.82 / 81	6.07	**B- / 7.1**	-5.61	-6.39
GR	iShares Russell Midcap Value Index	IWS	**B-**	116.86	**C+ / 6.5**	21.09 / 52	16.11 / 77	--	1.44	**B- / 7.0**	-0.09	0.03
MUN	Nuveen Muni Market Opportunity	NMO	**B-**	14.68	**C+ / 6.4**	16.47 / 63	6.94 / 44	9.48 / 68	6.11	**B- / 7.1**	-6.08	-7.81
MUS	MuniYield NY Insured Fund	MYN	**B-**	13.57	**C+ / 6.3**	17.64 / 67	6.66 / 40	10.19 / 75	6.18	**B- / 7.7**	-8.93	-11.36
MUN	Nuveen Div Adv Muni	NAD	**B-**	15.20	**C+ / 6.3**	15.17 / 58	7.25 / 48	11.45 / 87	6.42	**B- / 7.0**	-3.31	-4.47
MUS	BlackRock NY Inv Qual Muni Tr	RNY	**B-**	14.79	**C+ / 6.2**	19.92 / 76	6.58 / 38	9.39 / 68	5.90	**B- / 7.1**	-4.21	-7.45
MUS	Nuveen CA Muni Value	NCA	**B-**	9.90	**C+ / 6.2**	19.66 / 75	6.21 / 35	7.88 / 54	4.69	**B- / 7.1**	-4.07	-8.09
MUN	Salomon Br Municipal Partners II	MPT	**B-**	13.50	**C+ / 6.2**	14.56 / 55	7.69 / 55	9.65 / 70	6.00	**B- / 7.7**	-9.70	-12.28
MUS	Nuveen MI Div Adv Muni	NZW	**B-**	15.57	**C+ / 6.1**	22.12 / 83	7.40 / 50	--	5.50	**B- / 7.7**	-0.32	0.10
MUS	Nuveen NY Investment Quality Muni	NQN	**B-**	15.50	**C+ / 6.1**	18.01 / 70	7.69 / 55	9.84 / 71	5.76	**B- / 7.2**	-4.38	-5.37
MUN	Nuveen Performance Plus Muni	NPP	**B-**	14.79	**C+ / 6.1**	16.40 / 63	6.92 / 44	11.25 / 85	6.25	**B- / 7.4**	-7.97	-8.12
MUS	Eaton Vance CA Muni Inc Tr	CEV	**B-**	14.99	**C+ / 6.0**	12.91 / 50	8.86 / 66	13.67 / 95	5.90	**B- / 7.6**	-5.13	-2.72
MUS	Nuveen CA Inv Quality Muni	NQC	**B-**	15.06	**C+ / 6.0**	19.04 / 74	6.43 / 37	7.27 / 48	5.75	**B- / 7.6**	-5.22	-6.20
MUS	Nuveen CA Muni Market Opportunity	NCO	**B-**	14.99	**C+ / 6.0**	18.54 / 71	6.70 / 40	6.56 / 43	6.06	**B- / 7.3**	-7.13	-7.76
MUN	Nuveen Insured Div Adv Muni Fund	NVG	**B-**	14.70	**C+ / 6.0**	17.38 / 66	6.50 / 38	--	5.74	**B- / 7.5**	-6.96	-7.52
MUS	Nuveen NJ Prem Inc Muni	NNJ	**B-**	15.62	**C+ / 6.0**	19.48 / 75	7.18 / 47	9.80 / 71	5.41	**B- / 7.3**	-2.68	-2.83
MUN	Morgan Stanley Muni Inc Op III	OIC	**B-**	8.86	**C+ / 5.9**	15.95 / 62	6.35 / 36	8.56 / 60	5.73	**B- / 7.8**	-8.57	-10.16

N/A denotes number is not available

Fund Type	Fund Name (99 Pct = Best, 0 Pct = Worst)	Ticker Symbol	Overall Weiss Investment Rating	Price As of 6/30/05	PERFORMANCE: Perform-ance Rating/Pts	Annualized Total Return Through 6/30/05: 1Yr/Pct	3Yr/Pct	5Yr/Pct	Dividend Yield %	RISK: Risk Rating/ Pts	VALUATION: Premium/Discount As of 6/30/05	1 Year Average
MUN	Nuveen Insured Muni Opportunity	NIO	B-	15.65	C+ / 5.9	16.42 / 63	7.08 / 46	10.67 / 80	5.69	B- / 7.0	-2.86	-3.59
MUS	Nuveen NY Muni Value	NNY	B-	9.68	C+ / 5.9	17.01 / 65	6.70 / 41	7.80 / 53	4.40	B- / 7.8	-4.72	-7.98
MUN	Putnam Municipal Bond Fund	PMG	B-	12.74	C+ / 5.8	15.85 / 61	7.35 / 49	10.20 / 76	6.13	B- / 7.5	-9.19	-8.55
MUN	Nuveen Quality Inc Muni	NQU	B-	14.45	C+ / 5.6	16.54 / 64	6.70 / 40	8.84 / 63	6.10	B- / 7.7	-8.14	-7.85
MUS	Van Kampen FL Qual Muni	VFM	B-	14.99	C+ / 5.6	16.25 / 62	7.90 / 57	10.07 / 74	5.27	B- / 7.8	-11.25	-10.86
FO	Morgan Stanley India Inv Fund	IIF	C+	33.42	A+ / 9.9	65.14 / 99	54.11 / 99	29.60 / 99	0.47	D+ / 2.3	6.74	2.57
FO	Central Europe & Russia Fund	CEE	C+	31.40	A+ / 9.8	46.25 / 98	34.81 / 98	18.50 / 90	0.55	D+ / 2.4	-6.91	-10.15
FO	Latin American Discovery Fund	LDF	C+	20.01	A+ / 9.8	63.53 / 99	34.65 / 98	16.12 / 79	0.22	D+ / 2.6	-12.81	-13.21
FO	Morgan Stanley Eastern Europe	RNE	C+	29.85	A+ / 9.8	31.07 / 77	38.86 / 99	23.47 / 98	0.00	D+ / 2.3	-5.72	-8.93
FO	Templeton Russia&East European Fund	TRF	C+	40.02	A+ / 9.8	28.90 / 72	38.99 / 99	28.72 / 99	0.00	D / 2.2	4.87	2.42
FO	iShares MSCI Austria Index	EWO	C+	23.33	A+ / 9.7	39.40 / 92	37.92 / 99	25.33 / 98	0.36	D+ / 2.8	-0.34	0.14
FO	Latin America Equity Fund	LAQ	C+	23.00	A+ / 9.7	64.53 / 99	29.30 / 97	14.45 / 67	1.97	D+ / 2.6	-13.63	-13.99
GL	Aberdeen Australia Equity Fund	IAF	C+	12.20	A+ / 9.6	51.75 / 99	31.89 / 97	20.13 / 93	8.55	D+ / 2.8	4.18	-2.98
FO	China Fund	CHN	C+	28.73	A+ / 9.6	16.58 / 40	35.45 / 98	29.04 / 99	0.69	D+ / 2.3	11.70	17.54
FO	Templeton Dragon Fund	TDF	C+	17.99	A / 9.5	32.87 / 80	28.90 / 96	23.12 / 97	0.78	D+ / 2.5	-9.37	-10.70
FO	Mexico Equity & Income Fund	MXE	C+	17.16	A / 9.4	42.76 / 96	26.45 / 96	11.88 / 52	0.00	C- / 3.2	-13.68	-11.42
EM	Morgan Stanley Emerging Markets	MSF	C+	18.11	A / 9.3	39.60 / 93	24.43 / 95	8.67 / 34	0.37	D+ / 2.7	-11.62	-9.89
FO	Mexico Fund	MXF	C+	23.65	A- / 9.0	30.29 / 75	22.24 / 93	18.97 / 91	0.17	D+ / 2.8	-12.70	-12.52
GI	streetTRACKS Wilshire REIT	RWR	C+	194.85	B+ / 8.8	31.89 / 79	19.98 / 89	--	4.19	C- / 3.9	-0.02	0.01
EN	iShares Goldman Sachs Nat Res Index	IGE	C+	76.30	B+ / 8.7	34.36 / 84	18.73 / 85	--	1.15	C- / 3.8	-0.05	0.04
FO	iShares MSCI Canada Index	EWC	C+	18.29	B+ / 8.7	30.76 / 77	21.01 / 91	4.82 / 20	1.09	C- / 4.1	0.27	0.22
GR	HOLDRS Wireless	WMH	C+	55.80	B / 8.1	11.50 / 28	23.25 / 95	--	0.59	C- / 4.1	0.00	N/A
UT	HOLDRS Utilities	UTH	C+	109.69	B / 8.0	38.97 / 92	14.25 / 69	7.62 / 29	2.39	C- / 4.2	0.00	N/A
FO	Asia Tigers Fund	GRR	C+	12.19	B / 7.6	31.78 / 79	17.04 / 80	7.22 / 28	0.00	C / 4.4	-6.45	-7.75
COH	Corporate High Yield Fund III	CYE	C+	8.45	B / 7.6	18.67 / 46	19.40 / 88	8.00 / 32	9.33	C / 5.3	-1.29	-2.13
EM	Templeton Emerging Markets Income	TEI	C+	13.93	B / 7.6	26.81 / 66	17.45 / 82	17.31 / 85	7.20	C / 4.8	-0.50	-2.58
MUS	BlackRock PA Strategic Muni Tr	BPS	C+	15.36	C+ / 6.8	15.08 / 58	9.89 / 74	8.56 / 60	5.82	C+ / 6.7	-0.90	-4.16
MUS	Nuveen MD Div Adv Muni 2	NZR	C+	15.93	C+ / 6.8	19.80 / 76	7.84 / 56	--	5.51	C+ / 6.6	2.71	-0.17
MUS	Nuveen NY Select Quality Muni	NVN	C+	15.48	C+ / 6.8	17.88 / 68	8.06 / 58	10.00 / 73	5.62	C+ / 6.7	-4.68	-6.34
COH	Debt Strategies Fund I Inc	DSU	C+	6.52	C+ / 6.7	13.26 / 32	18.03 / 84	10.59 / 46	9.61	C+ / 6.0	-2.10	-2.23
MUS	Nuveen MD Div Adv Muni	NFM	C+	16.29	C+ / 6.7	20.18 / 77	7.67 / 54	--	5.34	C+ / 6.0	7.24	5.10
MUN	Nuveen Muni Income	NMI	C+	10.68	C+ / 6.7	17.81 / 67	6.81 / 42	4.50 / 28	4.99	C+ / 6.9	-3.26	-6.62
MUS	MA Health & Education Tax-Exempt Tr	MHE	C+	15.06	C+ / 6.6	22.24 / 83	8.17 / 61	10.53 / 79	5.31	C+ / 6.8	6.81	7.66
MUS	Nuveen OH Div Adv Muni	NXI	C+	16.24	C+ / 6.6	18.51 / 71	8.83 / 65	--	5.78	C+ / 6.2	3.18	3.60
IN	J Hancock Patriot Prem Div Fd II	PDT	C+	12.07	C+ / 6.5	27.68 / 69	13.59 / 65	13.66 / 64	6.46	C+ / 6.7	-3.44	-3.61
MUS	Nuveen AZ Div Adv Muni	NFZ	C+	16.27	C+ / 6.4	23.87 / 88	6.99 / 45	--	5.35	C+ / 6.6	4.16	2.85
MUS	Nuveen PA Div Adv Muni Fund 2	NVY	C+	14.98	C+ / 6.4	17.92 / 69	7.35 / 50	--	5.40	C+ / 6.8	-5.79	-5.32
MUN	Nuveen Premier Insured Muni Inc	NIF	C+	15.69	C+ / 6.4	17.90 / 68	6.79 / 41	10.99 / 83	5.70	C+ / 6.7	-1.69	-3.44
COI	PIMCO Corporate Income Fund	PCN	C+	15.40	C+ / 6.4	24.49 / 61	13.06 / 63	--	9.24	C+ / 6.1	1.32	-1.26
FS	J Hancock Bank & Thrift Oppty Fd	BTO	C+	9.77	C+ / 6.2	18.38 / 45	16.97 / 80	20.51 / 94	1.16	C+ / 6.2	-6.86	-7.88
GI	AIM Select Real Estate Income Fund	RRE	C+	16.84	C+ / 6.1	23.32 / 58	13.59 / 65	--	7.26	C+ / 5.8	-15.38	-13.62
MUN	DTF Tax Free Income	DTF	C+	15.90	C+ / 5.9	17.01 / 64	7.45 / 51	10.93 / 82	5.45	C+ / 6.8	-6.36	-7.71
GI	Delaware Inv Glob Div & Inc	DGF	C+	13.07	C+ / 5.8	27.51 / 68	11.10 / 48	12.97 / 59	7.43	C+ / 6.0	-2.90	-7.40
COH	High Yield Income Fund	HYI	C+	5.42	C+ / 5.8	10.42 / 25	16.53 / 79	10.61 / 46	8.79	C+ / 6.1	-3.04	1.18

N/A denotes number is not available

Section IV

Bottom 200 Closed-End Mutual Funds

A compilation of those

Closed-End Mutual Funds

receiving the lowest Weiss Investment Ratings.

Funds are listed in order by Overall Weiss Investment Rating.

Section IV Contents

This section contains a summary analysis of each of the bottom 200 closed-end mutual funds as determined by their overall Weiss Investment Rating. Typically, these funds have invested in securities that are currently out of favor, presenting a risky investment proposition. As such, these are the funds that you should generally avoid since they have historically underperformed most other mutual funds given the level of risk in their underlying investments.

1. Fund Type

The mutual fund's peer category based on an analysis of its investment portfolio.

COH	Corporate – High Yield	HL	Health
COI	Corporate – Inv. Grade	IN	Income
EM	Emerging Market	LP	Loan Participation
EN	Energy/Natural Resources	MTG	Mortgage
FS	Financial Services	MUH	Municipal – High Yield
FO	Foreign	MUN	Municipal – National
GEI	General – Inv. Grade	MUS	Municipal – Single State
GEN	General Bond	PM	Precious Metals
GL	Global	USA	U.S. Gov. – Agency
GR	Growth	UT	Utilities
GI	Growth and Income		

A blank fund type means that the mutual fund has not yet been categorized.

2. Fund Name

The name of the mutual fund as stated in its prospectus, which can sometimes differ slightly from the name that the company uses for advertising. If you cannot find the particular mutual fund you are interested in, or if you have any doubts regarding the precise name, verify the information with your broker or on your account statement. Also, use the fund's ticker symbol for confirmation. (See column 3.)

3. Ticker Symbol

The unique alphabetic symbol used for identifying and trading a specific mutual fund. No two funds can have the same ticker symbol.

A handful of funds currently show no associated ticker symbol. This means that the fund is either small or new since the NASD only assigns a ticker symbol to funds with at least $25 million in assets or 1,000 shareholders.

4. Overall Weiss Investment Rating

Our overall rating is measured on a scale from A to E based on each fund's risk-adjusted performance. Please see page 10 for specific descriptions of each letter grade. Also, refer to page 7 for information on how our ratings are derived. Most important, when using this rating, please be sure to consider the warnings beginning on page 11 regarding the ratings' limitations and the underlying assumptions.

5. Price Closing price of the fund on the date shown.

6. Performance Rating/Points A letter grade rating based solely on the mutual fund's financial performance over the trailing three years, without any consideration for the amount of risk the fund poses. Like the overall Weiss Investment Rating, the Performance Rating is measured on a scale from A to E for ease of interpretation. The points score indicates where the Performance Rating falls on a scale of 0 to 10.

7. 1-Year Total Return The total return the fund has provided investors over the preceeding 52 weeks. This total return figure is computed based on the fund's dividend distributions and share price appreciation/depreciation during the period, net of the expenses and fees it imposes on its shareholders.

8. 1-Year Total Return Percentile The fund's percentile rank based on its one-year performance compared to that of all other closed-end funds in existence for at least one year. A score of 99 is the best possible, indicating that the fund outperformed 99% of the closed-end mutual funds. Zero is the worst possible percentile score.

9. 3-Year Total Return The total annual return the fund has provided investors over the preceeding 156 weeks.

10. 3-Year Total Return Percentile The fund's percentile rank based on its three-year performance compared to that of all other closed-end funds in existence for at least three years. A score of 99 is the best possible, indicating that the fund outperformed 99% of the closed-end mutual funds. Zero is the worst possible percentile score.

11. 5-Year Total Return The total annual return the fund has provided investors over the preceeding 260 weeks.

12. 5-Year Total Return Percentile The fund's percentile rank based on its five-year performance compared to that of all other closed-end funds in existence for at least five years. A score of 99 is the best possible, indicating that the fund outperformed 99% of the closed-end mutual funds. Zero is the worst possible percentile score.

13. Dividend Yield Most recent quarterly dividend to fund investors annualized, expressed as a percent of the fund's current share price. The dividend yield of a fund can have little correlation to the amount of dividends the fund has received from its underlying investments. Rather, dividend distributions are based on a fund's need to pass earnings from both dividends and gains on the sale of investments along to shareholders. Thus, these dividend distributions are included as a part of the fund's total return.

Keep in mind that dividend income may be taxed at a different rate than capital gains depending on your income tax bracket.

14. Risk Rating/Points

A letter grade rating based solely on the mutual fund's risk as determined by its monthly performance volatility over the trailing three years. The risk rating does not take into consideration the overall financial performance the fund has achieved or the total return it has provided to its shareholders. Like the overall Weiss Investment Rating, the Risk Rating is measured on a scale from A to E for ease of interpretation. The points score indicates where the Risk Rating falls on a scale of 0 to 10.

15. Premium/ Discount

A comparison of the fund's price to its NAV as of the date indicated. The premium (+) or discount (-) indicates the percentage the shares are trading above or below the fund's NAV per share.

If the price is above the fund's NAV, the fund is said to be trading at a premium. If the price is lower than the fund's NAV, the fund is trading at a discount.

16. 1-Year Average Premium/ Discount

The average of the fund's premium/discount over the preceeding year.

It can be useful to compare the fund's current premium/discount to its one-year average. If the fund is currently trading at a premium/discount that is lower/higher than its one-year average, then there has been less demand for the fund in more recent times than over the past year. Conversely, if the fund is currently trading at a premium/discount that is higher/lower than its one-year average, this indicates that there has been greater demand for the fund in more recent times than over the past year.

Fund Type	Fund Name (99 Pct = Best, 0 Pct = Worst)	Ticker Symbol	Overall Weiss Investment Rating	Price As of 6/30/05	PERFORMANCE: Performance Rating/Pts	Annualized Total Return Through 6/30/05: 1Yr/Pct	3Yr/Pct	5Yr/Pct	Dividend Yield %	RISK: Risk Rating/Pts	VALUATION: Premium/Discount As of 6/30/05	1 Year Average
GR	HOLDRS B2B Internet	BHH	**E-**	2.00	**E- / 0.0**	-9.46 / 1	-8.09 / 0	-43.03 / 0	14.73	**E- / 0.0**	0.00	N/A
GR	NAIC Growth Fund	GRF	**E-**	8.55	**E- / 0.0**	-3.56 / 4	-3.63 / 0	-1.25 / 10	3.57	**D / 1.6**	-10.66	-14.29
GR	Tuxis Corporation	TUX	**E-**	0.00	**E- / 0.1**	13.14 / 31	-3.52 / 0	2.02 / 15	0.00	**D- / 1.4**		-18.64
GR	iShares Goldman Sachs Semicon Index	IGW	**E-**	53.60	**E- / 0.2**	-8.12 / 1	3.81 / 5	--	0.00	**D / 1.6**	0.00	N/A
GR	HOLDRS Semiconductor	SMH	**E-**	34.10	**E / 0.3**	-8.22 / 1	4.07 / 6	-18.30 / 1	0.09	**E- / 0.0**	0.00	N/A
FO	Germany Fund	GER	**E-**	7.77	**E+ / 0.6**	15.30 / 38	4.42 / 6	-6.71 / 5	0.32	**D / 1.7**	-12.30	-12.99
FO	iShares MSCI Netherlands Index	EWN	**E-**	18.40	**E+ / 0.6**	13.65 / 34	3.75 / 5	-4.35 / 6	1.40	**E- / 0.0**	-0.33	0.16
HL	iShares Biotechnology Index Fund	IBB	**E-**	67.57	**D- / 1.1**	-8.95 / 1	9.83 / 37	--	0.00	**D / 1.6**	0.04	-0.02
GL	iShares S&P Global Technology Sect	IXN	**E-**	48.77	**D- / 1.1**	-2.82 / 4	8.50 / 25	--	1.29	**D- / 1.4**	0.06	0.36
GR	iShares Goldman Sachs Technology	IGM	**E-**	43.46	**D- / 1.2**	-4.23 / 3	9.23 / 33	--	0.04	**D- / 1.3**	0.12	0.04
GR	iShares Dow Jones US Technology	IYW	**E-**	46.09	**D- / 1.4**	-2.13 / 5	9.11 / 32	-18.16 / 1	0.23	**D- / 1.4**	0.11	0.03
FO	iShares MSCI Germany Index	EWG	**E-**	17.65	**D- / 1.4**	13.16 / 32	7.91 / 22	-3.03 / 7	1.10	**E- / 0.0**	-0.23	-0.01
COH	Prospect Street High Inc Portfolio	PHY	**E-**	3.40	**D- / 1.5**	23.31 / 58	3.40 / 4	2.95 / 17	8.72	**D- / 1.2**	-5.03	0.64
GR	SPDR Technology	XLK	**E-**	19.99	**D- / 1.5**	-0.49 / 5	9.20 / 32	-17.59 / 2	0.56	**D- / 1.5**	0.15	-0.01
PM	ASA Limited	ASA	**E-**	38.59	**D / 1.8**	8.40 / 20	8.77 / 28	22.47 / 97	1.55	**E- / 0.0**	-11.14	-12.48
FO	iShares MSCI Taiwan Index	EWT	**E-**	12.34	**D+ / 2.4**	15.89 / 39	6.27 / 14	-6.91 / 5	0.66	**E- / 0.0**	-1.52	-0.08
GR	iShares Goldman Sachs Software Indx	IGV	**E-**	38.38	**D+ / 2.6**	3.02 / 9	12.04 / 56	--	0.20	**E- / 0.0**	0.08	-0.05
GI	TCW Convertible Securities Fund	CVT	**E**	5.09	**E- / 0.0**	9.29 / 22	-0.90 / 1	-3.58 / 7	8.06	**C- / 3.1**	-7.62	-9.26
GL	Z-Seven Fund	ZSEV	**E**	4.35	**E- / 0.0**	7.94 / 18	0.39 / 1	-10.13 / 3	0.00	**C- / 3.1**	-21.20	-17.66
GR	HOLDRS Telecom	TTH	**E**	27.02	**E- / 0.1**	7.27 / 16	2.01 / 2	-15.79 / 2	0.21	**C- / 3.6**	0.00	N/A
FO	Japan Equity Fund	JEQ	**E**	6.08	**E- / 0.2**	-6.17 / 2	4.68 / 8	-4.58 / 6	0.00	**C- / 4.0**	-7.60	-4.08
GR	iShares Dow Jones US Basic Mtrls	IYM	**E**	46.50	**E / 0.3**	6.10 / 13	6.05 / 13	7.82 / 31	1.75	**C- / 3.0**	-0.13	0.02
FO	iShares S&P/Topix 150 Index Fund	ITF	**E**	88.09	**E+ / 0.6**	-2.85 / 4	6.76 / 15	--	0.39	**C- / 3.6**	-0.22	0.14
FO	Japan Smaller Cap Fund Inc.	JOF	**E**	10.78	**E+ / 0.7**	-18.40 / 0	10.50 / 42	5.36 / 22	0.00	**D+ / 2.4**	-7.94	5.57
GR	SPDR Consumer Discretionary	XLY	**E**	32.84	**E+ / 0.9**	3.83 / 10	6.86 / 16	5.95 / 25	0.60	**C- / 3.3**	-0.06	0.02
GR	SPDR Materials	XLB	**E**	27.34	**D- / 1.0**	5.89 / 13	7.84 / 22	9.58 / 39	2.08	**C- / 3.2**	0.00	N/A
GR	HOLDRS Internet Architecture	IAH	**E**	34.23	**D / 1.6**	-1.73 / 5	10.35 / 41	-17.65 / 2	0.18	**D+ / 2.6**	0.00	N/A
GR	Gabelli Equity Trust	GAB	**E**	8.93	**D / 1.9**	17.44 / 43	6.27 / 14	6.72 / 27	8.04	**D+ / 2.8**	7.20	6.22
GR	HOLDRS Software	SWH	**E**	34.96	**D / 2.0**	3.03 / 9	10.27 / 40	--	0.05	**D+ / 2.6**	0.00	N/A
GR	iShares Russell 2000 Growth	IWO	**E**	63.50	**D / 2.1**	2.99 / 9	10.47 / 42	--	0.47	**D+ / 2.6**	-0.66	-0.06
GR	iShares Dow Jones US Telecom	IYZ	**E**	23.19	**D+ / 2.5**	12.77 / 31	9.88 / 37	-15.69 / 3	2.27	**D / 1.8**	0.17	0.02
FO	iShares MSCI France Index	EWQ	**E**	23.82	**D+ / 2.8**	14.84 / 37	10.58 / 43	-2.06 / 9	1.25	**D- / 1.3**	0.13	0.11
GR	streetTRACKS MS Technology Index	MTK	**E**	47.33	**D+ / 2.8**	-1.87 / 5	12.52 / 60	--	0.05	**E+ / 0.7**	-0.17	-0.02
FO	iShares MSCI EMU Index	EZU	**E**	70.36	**C- / 3.0**	16.78 / 41	11.67 / 52	--	1.83	**D- / 1.0**	-0.61	0.17
GR	Foxby Corp	FXX	**E+**	2.18	**E- / 0.0**	1.40 / 7	-1.77 / 1	-23.58 / 1	0.00	**C / 5.5**	-12.80	-12.76
IN	Boulder Total Return Fund	BTF	**E+**	17.11	**E- / 0.1**	7.47 / 17	2.45 / 3	10.56 / 45	0.00	**C+ / 5.9**	-16.50	-13.34
MTG	BlackRock Income Trust	BKT	**E+**	6.70	**E / 0.4**	6.60 / 15	4.95 / 8	10.70 / 46	9.04	**C+ / 5.8**	0.45	6.47
GI	Zweig Total Return Fund	ZTR	**E+**	5.12	**E / 0.4**	11.70 / 28	2.21 / 2	4.00 / 19	10.53	**C+ / 5.8**	-5.88	-6.10
GR	HOLDRS Retail	RTH	**E+**	94.62	**E / 0.5**	6.58 / 15	3.89 / 5	--	0.09	**C / 4.7**	0.00	N/A
GEN	ACM Managed Income Fund	AMF	**E+**	3.67	**E+ / 0.6**	-4.63 / 3	5.77 / 12	0.45 / 13	5.83	**C / 5.2**	-12.20	-6.00
FO	iShares MSCI Japan Index	EWJ	**E+**	10.22	**E+ / 0.6**	-2.37 / 4	6.78 / 16	-6.95 / 4	0.42	**C / 4.7**	-0.68	0.01
GR	Alliance All-Market Advantage Fd	AMO	**E+**	14.49	**E+ / 0.7**	5.74 / 13	4.49 / 7	-8.56 / 3	8.94	**C / 4.7**	7.97	8.86
IN	Boulder Growth&Income Fund	BIF	**E+**	6.63	**E+ / 0.7**	9.77 / 23	6.20 / 13	2.78 / 16	0.00	**C / 4.3**	-14.34	-12.27
GR	Liberty All-Star Growth Fund	ASG	**E+**	5.89	**E+ / 0.9**	2.12 / 8	7.10 / 18	-2.46 / 8	9.52	**C / 4.3**	2.43	5.53
GI	Gabelli Convertible&Income Sec Fund	GCV	**E+**	9.50	**D- / 1.4**	4.22 / 10	6.82 / 16	9.99 / 42	8.06	**C / 4.9**	18.75	17.05
FO	iShares MSCI Malaysia Index	EWM	**E+**	6.99	**D / 2.0**	10.78 / 26	8.95 / 30	4.00 / 19	2.28	**C- / 3.0**	0.00	0.23
FO	Europe Fund	EF	**E+**	10.54	**D+ / 2.4**	8.79 / 21	10.62 / 43	-0.21 / 12	7.34	**D+ / 2.7**	-10.68	-7.75
FS	iShares S&P Global Financials Sect	IXG	**E+**	65.00	**D+ / 2.4**	11.20 / 27	10.18 / 39	--	1.37	**C- / 3.8**	0.32	0.23
FO	Malaysia Fund	MF	**E+**	5.64	**D+ / 2.6**	8.35 / 20	11.95 / 56	5.02 / 21	0.69	**D / 2.2**	-2.25	-1.64
GR	Nasdaq 100 Trust Series I	QQQQ	**E+**	36.97	**D+ / 2.8**	0.07 / 6	12.71 / 61	-16.75 / 2	0.19	**D / 2.1**	0.03	0.01
FO	iShares S&P Europe 350 Index Fund	IEV	**E+**	74.40	**C- / 3.1**	14.75 / 37	11.71 / 53	--	1.81	**C- / 3.4**	-0.32	0.35
GL	Canadian World Fund Limited	T.CWF	**E+**	4.10	**C- / 3.2**	19.88 / 50	12.24 / 58	-3.89 / 6	0.00	**D / 1.7**	-25.86	-24.04

N/A denotes number is not available

99 Pct = Best
0 Pct = Worst

Fund Type	Fund Name	Ticker Symbol	Overall Weiss Investment Rating	Price As of 6/30/05	PERFORMANCE: Performance Rating/Pts	PERFORMANCE: Annualized Total Return Through 6/30/05: 1Yr/Pct	PERFORMANCE: Annualized Total Return Through 6/30/05: 3Yr/Pct	PERFORMANCE: Annualized Total Return Through 6/30/05: 5Yr/Pct	Dividend Yield %	RISK: Risk Rating/Pts	VALUATION: Premium/Discount As of 6/30/05	VALUATION: Premium/Discount 1 Year Average
GR	streetTRACKS DJ US Small Cap Growth	DSG	**E+**	74.74	**C- / 3.2**	8.80 / 21	11.91 / 55	--	0.42	**C- / 3.3**	-0.07	0.04
FO	Taiwan Fund	TWN	**E+**	13.69	**C- / 3.5**	23.73 / 59	7.32 / 19	-6.06 / 5	0.22	**D+ / 2.6**	-12.13	-11.53
GI	Renaissance Cap Growth & Inc III	RENN	**E+**	11.25	**C / 4.3**	-2.37 / 4	16.31 / 78	4.82 / 20	3.46	**E+ / 0.8**	-17.40	-16.91
GL	Morgan Stanley Global Opp Bond Fund	MGB	**E+**	7.80	**C / 4.4**	13.93 / 35	15.54 / 75	7.85 / 31	7.10	**D / 1.6**	-4.06	8.79
FO	HOLDRS TeleBras	TBH	**E+**	30.45	**C+ / 6.3**	16.96 / 42	14.75 / 72	-17.92 / 2	0.87	**E- / 0.0**	0.00	N/A
HL	HOLDRS Pharmaceutical	PPH	**D-**	74.03	**E- / 0.1**	-3.62 / 3	0.37 / 1	-5.35 / 5	2.23	**C+ / 6.5**	0.00	N/A
GL	Global Income Fund	GIF	**D-**	4.35	**E / 0.4**	10.14 / 24	4.08 / 6	8.11 / 32	6.44	**C+ / 6.9**	-5.23	-6.13
GR	HOLDRS Market 2000 +	MKH	**D-**	53.59	**E / 0.4**	1.89 / 7	4.75 / 8	--	1.38	**B- / 7.1**	0.00	N/A
GL	Transamerica Income Shares	TAI	**D-**	22.19	**E / 0.4**	9.64 / 23	1.44 / 2	7.71 / 30	7.09	**B- / 7.2**	-5.37	-5.79
GR	Diamond Series Trust I	DIA	**D-**	102.86	**E / 0.5**	1.06 / 6	5.80 / 12	1.63 / 14	1.33	**B- / 7.2**	-0.05	0.02
GR	streetTRACKS DJ US Lg Cap Growth	ELG	**D-**	46.51	**E / 0.5**	-0.47 / 6	5.47 / 11	--	0.81	**C+ / 6.6**	0.45	0.03
USA	ACM Government Opportunity Fund	AOF	**D-**	7.89	**E+ / 0.6**	4.51 / 11	3.98 / 5	11.13 / 47	5.90	**B- / 7.2**	-8.26	-5.93
IN	Tri-Continental Corporation	TY	**D-**	17.83	**E+ / 0.7**	7.98 / 18	4.84 / 8	-2.11 / 9	1.35	**C+ / 6.5**	-16.80	-16.42
GR	iShares Dow Jones US Cns Sv Sct Idx	IYC	**D-**	58.97	**E+ / 0.8**	5.72 / 13	6.05 / 13	0.09 / 12	0.16	**C+ / 6.3**	-0.10	N/A
COI	Lincoln National Income Fund	LND	**D-**	11.80	**D- / 1.0**	3.28 / 9	6.99 / 17	12.16 / 54	5.28	**C+ / 6.6**	-12.20	-6.38
FO	iShares MSCI Switzerland Index	EWL	**D-**	16.60	**D- / 1.1**	9.26 / 22	7.41 / 20	1.40 / 14	0.52	**C+ / 5.7**	-0.18	0.51
GR	Zweig Fund	ZF	**D-**	5.38	**D- / 1.1**	21.65 / 53	3.20 / 4	-3.12 / 7	11.14	**C / 5.5**	-6.76	-8.42
COH	Van Kampen High Income Trust	VIT	**D-**	3.68	**D- / 1.2**	7.78 / 17	6.94 / 16	4.98 / 21	9.47	**C / 5.4**	2.79	9.34
COH	Salomon Br High Income Fund	HIF	**D-**	9.43	**D- / 1.4**	-8.33 / 1	9.45 / 34	4.60 / 20	7.56	**C+ / 5.7**	-10.10	-2.51
PM	Central Fund of Canada	CEF	**D-**	5.40	**D- / 1.5**	2.07 / 8	8.37 / 24	9.34 / 37	0.19	**C+ / 5.8**	0.00	6.46
GL	Prospect Street Income Shares	CNN	**D-**	5.99	**D / 2.0**	13.61 / 33	7.49 / 20	3.71 / 18	7.85	**C / 4.8**	-9.65	-6.87
FO	HOLDRS Europe 2001	EKH	**D-**	63.10	**D / 2.1**	7.82 / 18	9.17 / 32	--	2.05	**C / 4.5**	0.00	N/A
GI	Blue Chip Value Fund	BLU	**D-**	6.24	**D+ / 2.5**	6.19 / 14	10.84 / 45	4.58 / 20	8.75	**C / 4.7**	10.44	16.76
FO	Taiwan Greater China Fund	TFC	**D-**	5.17	**D+ / 2.7**	19.42 / 49	6.02 / 13	-8.49 / 4	0.20	**C / 4.8**	-7.18	-8.91
COH	BlackRock High Yield Trust	BHY	**D-**	9.40	**D+ / 2.9**	10.97 / 26	10.13 / 38	6.60 / 27	8.66	**C / 4.3**	22.88	20.89
GI	Franklin Universal Trust	FT	**D-**	6.14	**C- / 3.0**	22.71 / 56	7.22 / 18	5.16 / 22	6.81	**C / 4.6**	-12.03	-12.55
COH	Van Kampen High Income Trust II	VLT	**D-**	4.75	**C- / 3.1**	20.65 / 51	8.74 / 27	3.95 / 19	9.25	**C- / 4.1**	5.32	4.42
GR	iShares S&P SmallCap 600/BarraValue	IJS	**D-**	60.43	**C- / 3.2**	13.24 / 32	11.52 / 51	--	0.70	**C- / 3.8**	-0.21	-0.05
IN	Liberty All-Star Equity Fund	USA	**D-**	8.92	**C- / 3.3**	7.70 / 17	12.10 / 57	4.28 / 20	9.33	**C- / 3.9**	2.76	3.69
GR	iShares Russell 2000	IWM	**D-**	62.21	**C- / 3.4**	8.03 / 19	12.43 / 59	5.00 / 21	0.92	**C- / 3.4**	-0.70	-0.05
GL	iShares S&P Global Telecomm Sect	IXP	**D-**	49.24	**C- / 3.6**	11.92 / 29	13.07 / 63	--	1.35	**C- / 3.3**	0.29	0.32
COH	New America High Income Fund	HYB	**D-**	2.13	**C / 4.7**	22.92 / 57	11.22 / 48	3.86 / 18	9.91	**C- / 3.0**	-0.93	-4.00
FO	iShares MSCI Italy Index	EWI	**D-**	24.22	**C / 4.9**	17.78 / 44	16.79 / 79	2.46 / 15	2.61	**D+ / 2.5**	-0.49	0.08
GR	Royce Micro-Cap Trust	RMT	**D-**	13.59	**C / 5.3**	14.30 / 35	16.09 / 77	20.17 / 93	8.93	**D / 2.2**	1.87	1.45
FO	iShares MSCI Belgium Index	EWK	**D-**	17.81	**C+ / 6.5**	27.44 / 68	18.44 / 85	9.05 / 35	1.59	**E / 0.4**	-1.17	0.38
GR	HOLDRS Broadband	BDH	**D-**	15.33	**B- / 7.2**	-4.47 / 3	22.85 / 94	-29.76 / 0	0.01	**E- / 0.0**	0.00	N/A
GR	HOLDRS Internet Infrastructure	IIH	**D-**	4.05	**B- / 7.4**	10.36 / 25	21.65 / 92	-41.59 / 0	0.00	**E- / 0.0**	0.00	N/A
FO	iShares MSCI South Korea Index	EWY	**D-**	32.68	**B / 7.7**	36.30 / 87	14.78 / 72	9.70 / 39	0.31	**E- / 0.0**	0.25	0.18
FO	iShares MSCI Sweden Index	EWD	**D-**	20.25	**B / 7.7**	17.74 / 43	21.38 / 92	-3.70 / 7	0.73	**E- / 0.0**	-1.79	0.21
GI	Bancroft Convertible Fund	BCV	**D**	17.32	**E- / 0.0**	-2.20 / 5	0.65 / 1	2.79 / 16	3.89	**B / 8.3**	-15.10	-11.94
GI	Castle Convertible Fund	CVF	**D**	22.15	**E- / 0.1**	2.58 / 8	1.97 / 2	5.72 / 24	3.07	**B / 8.2**	-15.52	-12.55
GI	Ellsworth Convertible Growth & Inc	ECF	**D**	7.49	**E- / 0.1**	1.70 / 7	1.05 / 2	3.45 / 17	3.62	**B- / 7.8**	-14.20	-11.70
MTG	American Select Portfolio	SLA	**D**	11.88	**E- / 0.2**	2.99 / 9	2.81 / 4	9.58 / 39	7.02	**B / 8.1**	-9.31	-3.70
MTG	BlackRock Advantage Term Trust	BAT	**D**	10.26	**E- / 0.2**	1.64 / 7	2.64 / 3	9.38 / 38	5.85	**B / 8.3**	-0.68	-0.76
GR	SPDR Consumer Staples	XLP	**D**	22.74	**E- / 0.2**	0.90 / 6	2.56 / 3	-0.49 / 11	1.97	**B / 8.2**	0.13	0.02
MTG	American Strat Inc Portfolio II	BSP	**D**	11.64	**E / 0.3**	-0.84 / 5	3.61 / 5	10.21 / 43	8.22	**B- / 7.7**	-5.67	-1.74
LP	Citigroup Investments Corp Loan	TLI	**D**	13.11	**E / 0.3**	-7.60 / 2	5.84 / 12	5.60 / 23	5.53	**B / 8.2**	-8.45	-2.02
LP	Eaton Vance Senior Income Trust	EVF	**D**	7.93	**E / 0.3**	-12.01 / 0	6.65 / 15	3.76 / 18	6.12	**B- / 7.9**	-9.27	0.99
MTG	American Strat Inc Portfolio	ASP	**D**	11.40	**E / 0.4**	0.41 / 6	4.58 / 7	9.19 / 36	6.83	**B- / 7.5**	-8.65	-3.59
GR	iShares S&P 500/Barra Growth	IVW	**D**	56.50	**E+ / 0.7**	1.99 / 8	5.94 / 13	-7.72 / 4	0.89	**B- / 7.3**	0.02	0.06
MUN	Colonial Insured Muni	CFX	**D**	14.15	**E+ / 0.8**	6.02 / 22	2.08 / 4	8.24 / 58	5.92	**B- / 7.4**	-5.48	-3.16
GL	streetTRACKS DJ Global Titan	DGT	**D**	63.21	**E+ / 0.9**	4.68 / 11	6.18 / 13	--	2.14	**B- / 7.0**	-0.09	0.10

N/A denotes number is not available

99 Pct = Best
0 Pct = Worst

Fund Type	Fund Name	Ticker Symbol	Overall Weiss Investment Rating	Price As of 6/30/05	PERFORMANCE: Performance Rating/Pts	Annualized Total Return Through 6/30/05: 1Yr/Pct	3Yr/Pct	5Yr/Pct	Dividend Yield %	RISK: Risk Rating/Pts	VALUATION: Premium/Discount As of 6/30/05	1 Year Average
MUN	ACM Municipal Securities Income Fd	AMU	D	10.73	D- / 1.0	3.13 / 11	2.83 / 6	5.95 / 36	5.89	B- / 7.2	-7.66	-1.62
GR	iShares Russell 1000 Growth	IWF	D	47.82	D- / 1.0	1.51 / 7	6.98 / 17	-10.50 / 3	0.68	B- / 7.1	-0.04	0.04
GR	iShares Russell 3000 Growth	IWZ	D	38.78	D- / 1.0	1.32 / 7	6.96 / 17	--	0.43	C+ / 6.8	0.05	0.02
FS	HOLDRS Regional Bank	RKH	D	134.50	D- / 1.2	5.62 / 12	7.19 / 18	10.29 / 44	0.78	C+ / 6.7	0.00	N/A
GR	iShares Dow Jones US Industrial	IYJ	D	53.39	D- / 1.2	3.58 / 10	8.46 / 25	-1.07 / 11	0.48	C+ / 6.7	-0.07	0.02
MUN	Putnam Investment Grade Muni Tr	PGM	D	9.67	D- / 1.3	9.86 / 38	1.12 / 2	6.05 / 37	5.06	C+ / 6.8	-12.88	-10.50
FS	SPDR Financial	XLF	D	29.31	D- / 1.3	4.88 / 11	7.50 / 20	6.20 / 26	2.38	C+ / 6.8	0.07	N/A
GR	SPDR Industrial	XLI	D	29.29	D- / 1.3	4.40 / 11	8.67 / 27	2.04 / 15	1.02	B- / 7.0	0.03	-0.01
IN	iShares S&P Global 100	IOO	D	60.30	D- / 1.4	6.33 / 14	7.89 / 22	--	1.70	C+ / 6.8	0.08	0.11
GR	Salomon Br Fund	SBF	D	12.88	D / 1.6	6.44 / 14	7.79 / 22	-2.76 / 8	0.92	C+ / 6.3	-13.27	-14.33
COI	1838 Bond Debenture Fund	BDF	D	18.74	D / 1.7	14.36 / 35	5.88 / 12	8.95 / 34	6.05	C+ / 6.7	-11.06	-10.88
GR	SPDR 500	SPY	D	118.98	D / 1.8	6.62 / 15	8.20 / 23	-2.42 / 8	1.64	C+ / 6.8	-0.09	0.01
MUS	Van Kampen Adv PA Muni	VAP	D	14.70	D / 1.8	10.22 / 39	3.03 / 7	8.40 / 58	5.09	C+ / 6.7	-14.29	-11.21
MUS	Colonial CA Insured Muni	CCA	D	14.53	D / 2.1	14.49 / 55	0.07 / 1	6.88 / 45	5.77	C+ / 6.4	-5.09	-7.86
IN	Flaherty&Crumrine Preferred Income	PFD	D	16.75	D+ / 2.6	2.53 / 8	10.76 / 45	14.73 / 69	6.39	C / 5.2	4.56	11.08
MUS	BlackRock CA Inv Qual Muni Tr	RAA	D	14.26	D+ / 2.8	17.87 / 68	3.54 / 10	7.36 / 50	5.94	C+ / 5.7	-1.86	-3.03
FS	J Hancock Financial Trends Fund	JHFT	D	15.72	D+ / 2.9	10.88 / 26	11.35 / 50	15.30 / 72	1.25	C / 5.4	-15.48	-13.08
GI	Delaware Inv Div & Inc	DDF	D	12.51	C- / 3.7	23.30 / 58	6.71 / 15	12.60 / 57	7.67	C / 4.5	-3.62	-7.59
IN	Source Capital	SOR	D	69.45	C- / 3.7	16.17 / 40	11.71 / 53	16.12 / 78	5.71	C / 4.9	11.41	12.27
GR	iShares S&P SmallCap 600	IJR	D	53.70	C- / 4.0	11.96 / 29	12.95 / 63	9.84 / 40	0.76	C / 4.4	-0.44	-0.05
HL	H&Q Healthcare Investors	HQH	D	17.65	C / 4.3	12.32 / 30	12.46 / 59	2.83 / 16	7.95	C- / 3.7	-2.00	-2.06
GR	iShares Russell 2000 Value	IWN	D	63.10	C / 4.4	13.25 / 32	13.52 / 65	--	1.33	C- / 3.9	-0.39	-0.04
COH	Dreyfus High Yield Strategies Fund	DHF	D	4.37	C / 4.5	8.61 / 20	15.11 / 74	-1.31 / 10	8.92	C- / 3.7	-6.02	-1.41
IN	Cornerstone Strategic Value Fund	CLM	D	7.17	C / 5.5	-3.77 / 3	18.63 / 85	-1.50 / 10	14.52	C- / 3.0	22.77	27.68
IN	Cornerstone Total Return Fund	CRF	D	15.48	C+ / 6.5	5.10 / 12	18.82 / 86	13.29 / 61	13.45	D- / 1.3	35.79	35.33
GR	iShares Goldman Sachs Ntwr Index Fd	IGN	D	27.70	B- / 7.0	-10.27 / 0	22.96 / 94	--	0.00	D- / 1.4	-0.14	-0.06
MTG	Hyperion 2005 Inv Gr Opp Tm Tr	HTO	D+	9.78	E / 0.3	3.95 / 10	2.65 / 3	8.55 / 33	0.12	B / 8.9	-1.11	-1.39
GL	MFS Intermediate Income Trust	MIN	D+	6.51	E / 0.5	7.31 / 16	2.48 / 3	7.04 / 28	5.51	B / 8.3	-9.83	-10.27
MTG	American Strat Inc Portfolio III	CSP	D+	11.34	E+ / 0.7	5.52 / 12	5.57 / 11	10.67 / 46	8.58	B / 8.2	-5.81	-1.38
IN	iShares S&P 100 Index Fund	OEF	D+	55.77	E+ / 0.8	2.86 / 9	6.35 / 14	--	1.65	B- / 7.8	-0.13	N/A
GR	SPDR Health Care	XLV	D+	31.10	E+ / 0.8	3.46 / 10	5.24 / 9	1.86 / 14	1.24	B- / 7.9	0.03	0.02
GR	iShares Dow Jones US Cns Gd Sct Idx	IYK	D+	52.30	E+ / 0.9	2.41 / 8	6.42 / 14	6.51 / 27	1.61	B- / 7.8	0.02	N/A
GEI	Montgomery Street Inc. Sec.	MTS	D+	18.11	D- / 1.2	10.92 / 26	5.47 / 10	9.89 / 41	6.38	B- / 7.4	-8.67	-6.70
LP	ING Prime Rate Trust	PPR	D+	6.99	D- / 1.3	-7.80 / 2	10.17 / 39	2.53 / 15	6.47	B- / 7.9	-5.03	2.56
MUS	Nuveen AZ Prem Inc Muni	NAZ	D+	15.41	D- / 1.3	12.39 / 48	2.39 / 5	7.59 / 51	5.00	B- / 7.5	4.69	8.71
MUS	Van Kampen PA Qual Muni	VPQ	D+	14.91	D- / 1.3	9.48 / 36	2.24 / 4	7.59 / 51	5.43	B- / 7.5	-12.45	-9.57
UT	J Hancock Patriot Select Div Tr	DIV	D+	13.65	D / 1.6	5.68 / 12	7.95 / 22	10.17 / 43	6.53	B- / 7.1	-9.36	-2.10
GR	streetTRACKS Total Market ETF	TMW	D+	85.14	D / 1.6	7.68 / 17	7.69 / 21	--	1.70	B- / 7.2	0.12	0.01
GR	General American Investors	GAM	D+	31.72	D / 1.7	8.89 / 21	7.17 / 18	2.89 / 17	0.01	B- / 7.6	-14.39	-11.80
IN	Adams Express Company	ADX	D+	12.91	D / 1.8	8.64 / 20	8.51 / 26	-5.05 / 6	1.55	B- / 7.0	-13.99	-12.92
GR	iShares S&P 500	IVV	D+	119.00	D / 1.8	6.72 / 15	8.23 / 23	-2.45 / 8	1.30	B- / 7.3	-0.07	0.02
FS	iShares Dow Jones US Financial Srv	IYG	D+	107.64	D / 2.0	6.42 / 14	9.01 / 31	7.99 / 32	1.17	C+ / 6.9	-0.05	0.01
MTG	Hyperion Total Return Fund	HTR	D+	9.26	D / 2.1	13.50 / 33	9.20 / 33	14.28 / 66	9.43	C+ / 6.7	1.76	9.12
FS	iShares Dow Jones US Financial Sct	IYF	D+	94.37	D / 2.1	7.17 / 16	8.92 / 29	7.75 / 30	1.77	C+ / 6.9	0.15	N/A
GEI	J Hancock Investors Trust	JHI	D+	19.98	D / 2.1	8.88 / 21	9.56 / 35	11.00 / 47	7.28	B- / 7.1	-3.38	1.51
GR	iShares Dow Jones US Total Mkt	IYY	D+	57.37	D / 2.2	7.93 / 18	9.35 / 34	-1.84 / 9	1.39	B- / 7.1	-0.03	0.02
GR	iShares Russell 3000	IWV	D+	68.35	D / 2.2	8.03 / 19	9.33 / 34	-1.43 / 10	1.19	B- / 7.1	0.00	0.03
MUN	Van Kampen Trust for Ins Muni	VIM	D+	14.80	D / 2.2	11.22 / 42	3.50 / 10	7.87 / 53	5.46	C+ / 6.6	-11.11	-9.22
IN	Vanguard Total Stock Market VIPERs	VTI	D+	117.05	D+ / 2.4	8.04 / 19	9.64 / 36	--	1.38	C+ / 6.8	-0.13	0.01
IN	Flaherty&Crumrine Preferred Inc Opp	PFO	D+	12.77	D+ / 2.5	7.89 / 18	9.57 / 35	14.46 / 68	6.57	C+ / 6.5	0.24	5.43
GR	iShares S&P 500/Barra Value	IVE	D+	62.17	D+ / 2.6	11.00 / 26	9.91 / 37	3.02 / 17	1.47	C+ / 6.7	-0.06	0.03
COH	Putnam Managed High Yield Trust	PTM	D+	8.16	D+ / 2.7	12.56 / 30	8.62 / 27	4.28 / 19	7.16	C+ / 5.9	-10.33	-10.42

N/A denotes number is not available

Fund Type	Fund Name (99 Pct = Best, 0 Pct = Worst)	Ticker Symbol	Overall Weiss Investment Rating	Price As of 6/30/05	PERFORMANCE: Performance Rating/Pts	Annualized Total Return Through 6/30/05: 1Yr/Pct	3Yr/Pct	5Yr/Pct	Dividend Yield %	RISK: Risk Rating/Pts	VALUATION: Premium/Discount As of 6/30/05	1 Year Average
GR	Central Securities	CET	D+	23.78	C- / 3.4	10.58 / 25	11.08 / 47	-0.06 / 12	0.25	C+ / 5.6	-15.49	-14.30
FO	Swiss Helvetia Fund	SWZ	D+	13.69	C- / 3.5	13.56 / 33	13.40 / 64	5.05 / 22	0.15	C+ / 5.6	-14.70	-14.86
COH	Managed High Income Portfolio	MHY	D+	6.35	C- / 3.6	9.34 / 23	11.80 / 54	4.07 / 19	8.16	C+ / 5.7	-8.63	-8.35
EM	Salomon Br Emerging Mkts Income II	EDF	D+	13.35	C- / 3.6	2.54 / 8	15.88 / 76	16.63 / 81	7.84	C+ / 5.8	-8.81	8.62
GL	Templeton Global Income Fd	GIM	D+	8.87	C- / 3.7	20.04 / 50	12.51 / 60	15.69 / 76	5.41	C / 5.3	-2.42	-1.46
COH	CIM High Yield Securities	CIM	D+	4.00	C- / 4.0	4.27 / 10	14.08 / 68	5.14 / 22	9.01	C / 4.8	-8.05	-5.27
GL	Gabelli Global Multimedia Trust	GGT	D+	10.03	C- / 4.2	13.24 / 32	13.63 / 66	-2.94 / 7	2.38	C / 5.0	-13.61	-14.19
COH	Zenix Income Fund	ZIF	D+	3.24	C / 4.3	-1.26 / 5	16.07 / 77	5.57 / 23	9.97	C / 4.8	6.93	15.41
GR	Royce Value Trust	RVT	D+	18.70	C / 4.9	19.03 / 47	15.67 / 76	18.25 / 88	8.47	C- / 3.7	7.35	6.58
COH	Credit Suisse Asset Mgmt Income	CIK	D+	4.65	C / 5.4	24.21 / 60	10.32 / 41	5.52 / 23	9.91	C- / 3.4	7.89	0.80
FO	iShares MSCI Hong Kong Index	EWH	D+	12.32	C+ / 6.1	27.66 / 69	13.61 / 66	1.88 / 14	2.19	D+ / 2.9	-0.81	0.12
FO	iShares MSCI Spain Index	EWP	D+	33.76	B- / 7.2	21.92 / 54	21.56 / 92	7.09 / 28	1.79	D / 1.8	-0.27	0.09
FO	Greater China Fund	GCH	D+	16.20	B- / 7.5	20.92 / 51	19.96 / 89	14.29 / 66	1.28	D- / 1.2	-12.24	-9.26
EN	HOLDRS Oil Services	OIH	D+	102.90	A / 9.3	44.01 / 97	19.31 / 87	--	0.88	E- / 0.0	0.00	N/A
MUN	BlackRock Muni Target Tm Tr	BMN	C-	10.18	E / 0.5	-1.13 / 5	3.38 / 9	5.70 / 34	4.72	B+ / 9.0	-1.26	-0.67
HL	iShares S&P Global Healthcare Sect	IXJ	C-	50.15	E+ / 0.8	4.84 / 11	5.35 / 9	--	0.73	B / 8.9	0.06	0.34
GL	MFS Government Markets Income Trust	MGF	C-	6.62	E+ / 0.9	8.14 / 19	4.54 / 7	7.59 / 29	4.59	B+ / 9.2	-11.62	-11.36
USA	Morgan Stanley Govt Inc Tr	GVT	C-	8.92	E+ / 0.9	7.74 / 17	4.45 / 7	7.25 / 29	4.67	B+ / 9.5	-10.17	-9.50
LP	Van Kampen Senior Inc Tr	VVR	C-	7.90	D- / 1.0	-5.58 / 2	9.13 / 32	5.70 / 24	6.28	B / 8.6	-8.56	-1.17
GR	MVC Capital	MVC	C-	0.00	D- / 1.1	6.17 / 14	5.35 / 9	-7.09 / 4	1.20	B / 8.9		-1.17
GEN	Van Kampen Income Trust	VIN	C-	5.81	D- / 1.2	13.30 / 32	4.66 / 7	4.84 / 21	5.70	B / 8.4	-10.62	-11.68
GEN	Allmerica Securities Trust	ALM	C-	9.42	D- / 1.5	13.07 / 31	4.99 / 8	6.29 / 26	5.79	B / 8.0	-10.54	-11.75
HL	iShares Dow Jones US Healthcare	IYH	C-	61.20	D- / 1.5	5.63 / 12	7.07 / 17	-0.49 / 12	0.78	B- / 7.9	-0.03	N/A
MUN	Municipal High Income Fund	MHF	C-	7.21	D- / 1.5	8.67 / 32	2.59 / 6	5.85 / 35	5.63	B / 8.4	-8.73	-7.64
GEI	BlackRock Broad Inv Gr 2009 Tm Tr	BCT	C-	15.81	D / 1.6	9.13 / 22	7.10 / 18	13.19 / 60	5.70	B / 8.1	4.01	1.56
LP	Nuveen Sr Inc	NSL	C-	8.57	D / 1.6	-5.91 / 2	10.90 / 47	6.03 / 25	7.03	B- / 7.8	1.30	10.89
MTG	American Income Fund	MRF	C-	8.28	D / 1.7	8.70 / 21	6.77 / 16	9.64 / 39	6.60	B / 8.4	-7.90	-7.96
GEI	Pioneer Interest Shares	MUO	C-	11.43	D / 1.7	13.67 / 34	5.06 / 9	8.30 / 32	5.59	B / 8.3	-9.29	-10.25
COI	Van Kampen Bond	VBF	C-	17.71	D / 1.7	12.46 / 30	5.47 / 10	8.38 / 33	5.61	B- / 7.9	-9.92	-10.28
GEI	Fort Dearborn Inc. Secs.	FDI	C-	14.90	D / 1.8	15.35 / 39	5.46 / 10	9.13 / 36	5.32	B / 8.6	-10.72	-10.57
MUS	BlackRock FL Insured Muni 2008 Term	BRF	C-	15.46	D / 1.9	6.05 / 23	5.33 / 23	6.22 / 39	4.85	B / 8.5	-0.39	-0.60
GEI	J Hancock Income Securities Tr	JHS	C-	14.98	D / 1.9	11.02 / 26	7.76 / 21	9.97 / 41	6.88	B- / 7.6	-5.25	-4.67
IN	J Hancock Patriot Prem Div Fd I	PDF	C-	9.30	D / 1.9	11.70 / 28	7.55 / 20	10.01 / 42	5.94	B- / 7.8	-6.16	-0.61
COI	Morgan Stanley Income Sec	ICB	C-	15.88	D / 1.9	13.03 / 31	5.66 / 11	6.52 / 27	6.12	B / 8.4	-10.03	-9.53
MUS	BlackRock NY Insured Muni 2008 Term	BLN	C-	15.83	D / 2.0	4.98 / 17	5.32 / 23	6.96 / 46	4.73	B / 8.5	-2.22	-3.02
GEN	MFS Charter Income Trust	MCR	C-	8.70	D / 2.0	11.97 / 29	7.28 / 19	7.33 / 29	5.71	B / 8.5	-10.95	-9.88
GR	iShares Russell 1000	IWB	C-	64.40	D / 2.2	8.28 / 20	9.18 / 32	-1.97 / 9	1.10	B- / 7.3	-0.02	0.03
MUS	Van Kampen PA Val Muni Inc	VPV	C-	15.00	D / 2.2	11.81 / 45	4.65 / 18	10.25 / 77	5.32	B- / 7.5	-9.09	-5.19
MUS	Delaware Inv MN Muni Income	VMN	C-	14.93	D+ / 2.3	7.93 / 29	7.69 / 55	10.03 / 74	5.22	B- / 7.3	-1.26	5.38
MUN	Investment Grade Municipal Income	PPM	C-	13.67	D+ / 2.3	11.78 / 45	3.14 / 8	8.16 / 56	5.45	B- / 7.8	-13.97	-12.93
GEN	Putnam Master Intermediate Inc Tr	PIM	C-	6.50	D+ / 2.3	8.26 / 19	8.97 / 30	9.20 / 37	6.49	B- / 7.2	-8.96	-8.65
MUN	Putnam Muni Opp Tr	PMO	C-	12.03	D+ / 2.3	6.39 / 24	4.83 / 20	7.14 / 47	5.61	B / 8.1	-9.82	-5.74
GR	streetTRACKS DJ US Lg Cap Value	ELV	C-	136.14	D+ / 2.3	11.00 / 26	8.87 / 28	--	2.18	B- / 7.1	0.17	N/A
MUS	MuniYield CA Fund	MYC	C-	13.91	D+ / 2.4	11.36 / 43	4.40 / 16	7.95 / 55	5.85	B / 8.1	-8.61	-6.89

N/A denotes number is not available

Section V

Performance:
100 Best and Worst Closed-End Mutual Funds

A compilation of those

Closed-End Mutual Funds

receiving the highest and lowest Performance Ratings.

Funds are listed in order by Performance Rating.

Section V Contents

This section contains a summary analysis of each of the top 100 and bottom 100 closed-end mutual funds as determined by their Weiss Performance Rating. Since the Performance Rating does not take into consideration the amount of risk a fund poses, the selection of funds presented here is based solely on each fund's financial performance over the past three years.

You can use this section to identify those funds that have historically given shareholders the highest returns on their investments. A word of caution though: past performance is not necessarily indicative of future results. While these funds have provided the highest returns, some of them may be currently overvalued and due for a correction.

1. Fund Type

The mutual fund's peer category based on an analysis of its investment portfolio.

COH	Corporate – High Yield	HL	Health
COI	Corporate – Inv. Grade	IN	Income
EM	Emerging Market	LP	Loan Participation
EN	Energy/Natural Resources	MTG	Mortgage
FS	Financial Services	MUH	Municipal – High Yield
FO	Foreign	MUN	Municipal – National
GEI	General – Inv. Grade	MUS	Municipal – Single State
GEN	General Bond	PM	Precious Metals
GL	Global	USA	U.S. Gov. – Agency
GR	Growth	UT	Utilities
GI	Growth and Income		

A blank fund type means that the mutual fund has not yet been categorized.

2. Fund Name

The name of the mutual fund as stated in its prospectus, which can sometimes differ slightly from the name that the company uses for advertising. If you cannot find the particular mutual fund you are interested in, or if you have any doubts regarding the precise name, verify the information with your broker or on your account statement. Also, use the fund's ticker symbol for confirmation. (See column 3.)

3. Ticker Symbol

The unique alphabetic symbol used for identifying and trading a specific mutual fund. No two funds can have the same ticker symbol.

A handful of funds currently show no associated ticker symbol. This means that the fund is either small or new since the NASD only assigns a ticker symbol to funds with at least $25 million in assets or 1,000 shareholders.

4. Overall Weiss Investment Rating

Our overall rating is measured on a scale from A to E based on each fund's risk-adjusted performance. Please see page 10 for specific descriptions of each letter grade. Also, refer to page 7 for information on how our ratings are derived. Most important, when using this rating, please be sure to consider the warnings beginning on page 11 regarding the ratings' limitations and the underlying assumptions.

5.	**Price**	Closing price of the fund on the date shown.
6.	**Performance Rating/Points**	A letter grade rating based solely on the mutual fund's financial performance over the trailing three years, without any consideration for the amount of risk the fund poses. Like the overall Weiss Investment Rating, the Performance Rating is measured on a scale from A to E for ease of interpretation. The points score indicates where the Performance Rating falls on a scale of 0 to 10.
7.	**1-Year Total Return**	The total return the fund has provided investors over the preceeding 52 weeks. This total return figure is computed based on the fund's dividend distributions and share price appreciation/depreciation during the period, net of the expenses and fees it imposes on its shareholders.
8.	**1-Year Total Return Percentile**	The fund's percentile rank based on its one-year performance compared to that of all other closed-end funds in existence for at least one year. A score of 99 is the best possible, indicating that the fund outperformed 99% of the closed-end mutual funds. Zero is the worst possible percentile score.
9.	**3-Year Total Return**	The total annual return the fund has provided investors over the preceeding 156 weeks.
10.	**3-Year Total Return Percentile**	The fund's percentile rank based on its three-year performance compared to that of all other closed-end funds in existence for at least three years. A score of 99 is the best possible, indicating that the fund outperformed 99% of the closed-end mutual funds. Zero is the worst possible percentile score.
11.	**5-Year Total Return**	The total annual return the fund has provided investors over the preceeding 260 weeks.
12.	**5-Year Total Return Percentile**	The fund's percentile rank based on its five-year performance compared to that of all other closed-end funds in existence for at least five years. A score of 99 is the best possible, indicating that the fund outperformed 99% of the closed-end mutual funds. Zero is the worst possible percentile score.
13.	**Dividend Yield**	Most recent quarterly dividend to fund investors annualized, expressed as a percent of the fund's current share price. The dividend yield of a fund can have little correlation to the amount of dividends the fund has received from its underlying investments. Rather, dividend distributions are based on a fund's need to pass earnings from both dividends and gains on the sale of investments along to shareholders. Thus, these dividend distributions are included as a part of the fund's total return. Keep in mind that dividend income may be taxed at a different rate than capital gains depending on your income tax bracket.

14. Risk Rating/Points	A letter grade rating based solely on the mutual fund's risk as determined by its monthly performance volatility over the trailing three years. The risk rating does not take into consideration the overall financial performance the fund has achieved or the total return it has provided to its shareholders. Like the overall Weiss Investment Rating, the Risk Rating is measured on a scale from A to E for ease of interpretation. The points score indicates where the Risk Rating falls on a scale of 0 to 10.
15. Premium/ Discount	A comparison of the fund's price to its NAV as of the date indicated. The premium (+) or discount (-) indicates the percentage the shares are trading above or below the fund's NAV per share. If the price is above the fund's NAV, the fund is said to be trading at a premium. If the price is lower than the fund's NAV, the fund is trading at a discount.
16. 1-Year Average Premium/ Discount	The average of the fund's premium/discount over the preceeding year. It can be useful to compare the fund's current premium/discount to its one-year average. If the fund is currently trading at a premium/discount that is lower/higher than its one-year average, then there has been less demand for the fund in more recent times than over the past year. Conversely, if the fund is currently trading at a premium/discount that is higher/lower than its one-year average, this indicates that there has been greater demand for the fund in more recent times than over the past year.

Fund Type	Fund Name (99 Pct = Best, 0 Pct = Worst)	Ticker Symbol	Overall Weiss Investment Rating	Price As of 6/30/05	PERFORMANCE: Performance Rating/Pts	Annualized Total Return Through 6/30/05: 1Yr/Pct	3Yr/Pct	5Yr/Pct	Dividend Yield %	RISK: Risk Rating/Pts	VALUATION: Premium/Discount As of 6/30/05	1 Year Average
FO	India Fund	IFN	B-	30.50	A+ / 9.9	50.84 / 99	50.94 / 99	18.32 / 89	5.09	C- / 3.5	1.63	0.14
FO	Morgan Stanley India Inv Fund	IIF	C+	33.42	A+ / 9.9	65.14 / 99	54.11 / 99	29.60 / 99	0.47	D+ / 2.3	6.74	2.57
FO	Turkish Investment Fund	TKF	C	15.89	A+ / 9.9	74.90 / 99	55.92 / 99	7.67 / 29	0.49	E+ / 0.8	8.61	11.87
FO	iShares MSCI Brazil Index	EWZ	C-	23.94	A+ / 9.9	68.67 / 99	37.41 / 98	--	1.86	E- / 0.0	-0.42	N/A
FO	Brazil Fund	BZF	C-	37.10	A+ / 9.9	80.66 / 99	46.52 / 99	21.10 / 96	2.06	E+ / 0.6	-5.50	-9.82
FO	Central Europe & Russia Fund	CEE	C+	31.40	A+ / 9.8	46.25 / 98	34.81 / 98	18.50 / 90	0.55	D+ / 2.4	-6.91	-10.15
FO	Latin American Discovery Fund	LDF	C+	20.01	A+ / 9.8	63.53 / 99	34.65 / 98	16.12 / 79	0.22	D+ / 2.6	-12.81	-13.21
FO	Morgan Stanley Eastern Europe	RNE	C+	29.85	A+ / 9.8	31.07 / 77	38.86 / 99	23.47 / 98	0.00	D+ / 2.3	-5.72	-8.93
FO	Templeton Russia&East European Fund	TRF	C+	40.02	A+ / 9.8	28.90 / 72	38.99 / 99	28.72 / 99	0.00	D / 2.2	4.87	2.42
FO	Indonesia Fund	IF	C	5.75	A+ / 9.8	56.91 / 99	40.95 / 99	11.75 / 52	3.08	D- / 1.2	-5.12	-1.13
FO	iShares S&P Latin American 40 Idx	ILF	C-	90.69	A+ / 9.8	58.53 / 99	32.02 / 97	--	1.01	E- / 0.0	0.49	0.58
FO	Canadian General Investments Ltd	T.CGI	A+	18.40	A+ / 9.7	47.72 / 98	29.43 / 97	18.56 / 90	1.30	C+ / 6.7	-17.23	-25.05
FO	Chile Fund	CH	B+	15.03	A+ / 9.7	46.55 / 98	33.72 / 98	17.78 / 87	5.42	C / 4.3	-11.59	-10.68
FO	iShares MSCI Austria Index	EWO	C+	23.33	A+ / 9.7	39.40 / 92	37.92 / 99	25.33 / 98	0.36	D+ / 2.8	-0.34	0.14
FO	Latin America Equity Fund	LAQ	C+	23.00	A+ / 9.7	64.53 / 99	29.30 / 97	14.45 / 67	1.97	D+ / 2.6	-13.63	-13.99
FO	Thai Capital Fund	TF	C-	9.52	A+ / 9.7	40.61 / 94	34.72 / 98	7.77 / 30	0.45	E / 0.3	9.68	-1.69
MUN	BlackRock Investment Qual Muni Tr	BKN	A+	16.61	A+ / 9.6	28.68 / 97	13.47 / 90	12.60 / 92	5.43	C+ / 6.5	4.07	-3.77
MUN	Scudder Strategic Municipal Inc Tr	KSM	A+	13.66	A+ / 9.6	26.81 / 95	13.43 / 90	12.44 / 91	6.47	B- / 7.1	9.11	2.56
MUN	MuniHoldings Fund II	MUH	A+	15.32	A+ / 9.6	27.08 / 95	14.47 / 93	13.96 / 96	6.85	C+ / 6.9	1.26	-1.61
MUN	BlackRock Strategic Municipal Tr	BSD	A	16.40	A+ / 9.6	31.70 / 98	12.40 / 87	12.47 / 91	5.89	C+ / 5.8	3.34	-6.42
FO	China Fund	CHN	C+	28.73	A+ / 9.6	16.58 / 40	35.45 / 98	29.04 / 99	0.69	D+ / 2.3	11.70	17.54
GL	Aberdeen Australia Equity Fund	IAF	C+	12.20	A+ / 9.6	51.75 / 99	31.89 / 97	20.13 / 93	8.55	D+ / 2.8	4.18	-2.98
MUN	BlackRock Municipal Bond Trust	BBK	A+	16.09	A / 9.5	28.64 / 97	12.44 / 87	--	6.38	C+ / 6.5	-0.12	-3.63
MUN	MuniVest Fund II	MVT	A+	16.20	A / 9.5	24.93 / 91	14.19 / 92	14.72 / 97	6.81	C+ / 6.8	3.85	0.13
MUN	MuniHoldings Fund	MHD	A+	16.71	A / 9.5	25.09 / 92	14.87 / 94	12.17 / 90	6.87	B- / 7.2	1.21	-1.27
EN	SPDR Energy	XLE	B-	44.94	A / 9.5	44.57 / 97	21.81 / 92	10.07 / 42	1.27	C- / 3.8	0.02	0.01
FO	Templeton Dragon Fund	TDF	C+	17.99	A / 9.5	32.87 / 80	28.90 / 96	23.12 / 97	0.78	D+ / 2.5	-9.37	-10.70
FO	Korea Fund	KF	C	27.28	A / 9.5	49.47 / 98	22.48 / 93	20.11 / 93	1.65	D- / 1.1	-6.35	-7.95
HL	HOLDRS Biotech	BBH	A+	167.30	A / 9.4	16.87 / 41	27.32 / 96	-0.69 / 11	0.00	C+ / 6.6	0.00	N/A
FO	Mexico Equity & Income Fund	MXE	C+	17.16	A / 9.4	42.76 / 96	26.45 / 96	11.88 / 52	0.00	C- / 3.2	-13.68	-11.42
EM	Templeton Emerging Markets Fd	EMF	C	17.48	A / 9.4	45.84 / 98	24.37 / 95	14.27 / 66	1.06	D- / 1.3	1.92	0.88
FO	iShares MSCI Mexico Index	EWW	C	26.57	A / 9.4	37.42 / 90	24.74 / 95	12.44 / 56	1.02	D / 1.7	-0.30	0.05
FO	Thai Fund	TTF	C-	9.69	A / 9.4	22.58 / 56	28.98 / 96	14.23 / 66	1.31	E+ / 0.7	16.89	11.36
MUN	Eaton Vance Municipal Inc Tr	EVN	A+	16.67	A / 9.3	20.87 / 79	14.78 / 93	17.28 / 99	6.77	C+ / 6.9	14.26	14.05
MUN	MuniAssets Fund	MUA	A+	13.45	A / 9.3	28.55 / 97	11.50 / 83	10.73 / 80	6.08	B- / 7.2	-0.30	-3.95
FO	iShares MSCI Australia Index	EWA	A	17.66	A / 9.3	36.87 / 89	24.75 / 95	13.56 / 63	3.25	C+ / 6.2	-0.23	0.25
EN	iShares Dow Jones US Energy Sector	IYE	B-	77.92	A / 9.3	40.78 / 95	20.88 / 90	11.30 / 49	1.28	C- / 3.9	0.14	0.05
EM	Morgan Stanley Emerging Markets	MSF	C+	18.11	A / 9.3	39.60 / 93	24.43 / 95	8.67 / 34	0.37	D+ / 2.7	-11.62	-9.89
EN	HOLDRS Oil Services	OIH	D+	102.90	A / 9.3	44.01 / 97	19.31 / 87	--	0.88	E- / 0.0	0.00	N/A
MUN	MuniYield Fund	MYD	A+	14.99	A- / 9.2	29.19 / 97	11.30 / 81	11.40 / 86	6.66	B- / 7.4	0.54	-3.62
MUN	BlackRock Municipal Income Trust	BFK	A	15.15	A- / 9.2	28.30 / 96	11.60 / 84	--	6.32	C+ / 6.4	1.07	-1.81
MUS	BlackRock VA Muni Bond Trust	BHV	A	17.27	A- / 9.2	25.93 / 93	11.16 / 81	--	5.11	C+ / 6.4	6.54	1.21
MUS	Eaton Vance NY Muni Inc Tr	EVY	A	16.70	A- / 9.2	27.07 / 95	11.14 / 81	16.66 / 99	5.91	C+ / 6.2	3.28	-2.01
FO	The New Ireland Fund	IRL	B+	21.20	A- / 9.2	36.97 / 89	25.91 / 96	14.24 / 66	0.14	C / 5.1	-13.96	-13.38
GL	Scudder Multi-Market Income Trust	KMM	B+	10.21	A- / 9.2	42.62 / 96	21.05 / 91	14.00 / 09	7.72	C / 4.9	5.48	-1.71
MUN	MuniVest Fund	MVF	A+	9.94	A- / 9.1	26.19 / 94	11.34 / 82	12.89 / 93	6.68	B- / 7.1	-2.83	-6.26
MUN	Scudder Municipal Income Trust	KTF	A	12.74	A- / 9.1	22.60 / 85	11.54 / 83	9.64 / 70	6.28	C+ / 6.5	1.43	-3.63
FS	First Financial Fund	FF	B	18.10	A- / 9.1	29.71 / 74	28.34 / 96	35.77 / 99	2.10	C / 4.6	2.20	2.97
GI	Cohen&Steers Quality Income Realty	RQI	B-	20.52	A- / 9.1	36.48 / 88	20.68 / 90	--	7.93	C / 4.3	-10.67	-8.82
FO	Third Canadian General Invst Tr	T.THD	C-	28.95	A- / 9.1	37.81 / 91	22.53 / 93	19.75 / 93	1.03	D- / 1.1	-21.67	-15.44
MUS	MuniYield FL Fund	MYF	A	15.06	A- / 9.0	26.38 / 94	10.66 / 79	13.21 / 94	6.13	C+ / 6.3	-2.40	-7.33
GI	iShares Cohen&Steers Realty Major	ICF	A-	70.50	A- / 9.0	33.54 / 82	21.41 / 92	--	5.10	C+ / 5.9	0.09	N/A

N/A denotes number is not available

	99 Pct = Best *0 Pct = Worst*				PERFORMANCE					RISK	VALUATION	
						Annualized Total Return Through 6/30/05					Premium/Discount	
Fund Type	Fund Name	Ticker Symbol	**Overall Weiss Investment Rating**	Price As of 6/30/05	**Perform-ance Rating/Pts**	1Yr/Pct	3Yr/Pct	5Yr/Pct	Dividend Yield %	**Risk Rating/ Pts**	As of 6/30/05	1 Year Average
GI	Cohen&Steers Adv Inc Realty Fund	RLF	B	21.87	A- / 9.0	37.42 / 90	20.42 / 90	--	8.11	C / 4.7	-6.58	-6.41
FO	Mexico Fund	MXF	C+	23.65	A- / 9.0	30.29 / 75	22.24 / 93	18.97 / 91	0.17	D+ / 2.8	-12.70	-12.52
FO	Korea Equity Fund	KEF	C	6.99	A- / 9.0	46.54 / 98	18.70 / 85	13.26 / 61	0.00	D / 2.1	-5.67	-8.49
GR	HOLDRS Internet	HHH	C	55.94	A- / 9.0	-10.32 / 0	32.31 / 97	-12.11 / 3	0.00	D+ / 2.7	0.00	N/A
MUN	MuniYield Quality Fund II	MQT	A+	13.37	B+ / 8.9	24.18 / 89	11.04 / 80	10.17 / 75	6.41	B- / 7.2	-3.33	-7.60
MUS	BlackRock NY Muni Bond Trust	BQH	A+	15.21	B+ / 8.9	24.76 / 91	10.54 / 78	--	6.04	B- / 7.0	-5.06	-8.31
EM	Scudder Global High Income Fund	LBF	B	7.91	B+ / 8.9	34.74 / 85	20.30 / 89	21.16 / 96	7.22	C / 4.9	-10.11	-9.99
EN	iShares S&P Global Energy Sector	IXC	B-	86.99	B+ / 8.9	36.75 / 88	19.50 / 88	--	1.47	C / 4.5	0.06	0.22
GL	Herzfeld Caribbean Basin Fund	CUBA	B-	6.30	B+ / 8.9	28.05 / 70	22.86 / 94	5.93 / 25	0.00	C / 4.4	-12.98	-13.44
FO	New Germany Fund	GF	C	9.18	B+ / 8.9	27.62 / 69	24.15 / 95	-6.33 / 5	3.00	D / 1.8	-14.37	-15.27
FO	iShares MSCI Pacific ex-Japan Idx	EPP	A+	94.11	B+ / 8.8	34.03 / 83	21.35 / 91	--	3.20	B- / 7.0	-0.14	0.31
MUN	Nuveen Dividend Advantage Muni 2	NXZ	A+	16.00	B+ / 8.8	23.48 / 87	11.25 / 81	--	6.43	B- / 7.3	-0.99	-2.92
MUS	PIMCO NY Muni Income Fund	PNF	A	14.89	B+ / 8.8	25.83 / 93	8.40 / 63	--	6.00	C+ / 6.3	6.81	0.17
MUN	Dreyfus Strategic Muni Bond Fund	DSM	A-	9.25	B+ / 8.8	24.27 / 90	9.07 / 67	10.01 / 73	6.52	C+ / 6.1	1.87	-3.64
GI	streetTRACKS Wilshire REIT	RWR	C+	194.85	B+ / 8.8	31.89 / 79	19.98 / 89	--	4.19	C- / 3.9	-0.02	0.01
MUS	BlackRock NJ Muni Bond Trust	BLJ	A	15.55	B+ / 8.7	27.66 / 96	8.99 / 67	--	5.98	C+ / 6.5	-3.05	-4.85
GL	Scudder Strategic Income Fund	KST	B	14.01	B+ / 8.7	32.08 / 79	20.89 / 91	8.78 / 34	7.63	C / 5.0	0.79	-1.85
MUS	BlackRock MD Muni Bond Trust	BZM	B	16.69	B+ / 8.7	26.28 / 94	9.81 / 73	--	5.26	C / 5.1	4.31	-2.24
EN	iShares Goldman Sachs Nat Res Index	IGE	C+	76.30	B+ / 8.7	34.36 / 84	18.73 / 85	--	1.15	C- / 3.8	-0.05	0.04
FO	iShares MSCI Canada Index	EWC	C+	18.29	B+ / 8.7	30.76 / 77	21.01 / 91	4.82 / 20	1.09	C- / 4.1	0.27	0.22
FO	Spain Fund	SNF	C	12.45	B+ / 8.7	27.50 / 68	22.65 / 93	9.16 / 36	8.24	D / 2.0	26.14	22.87
MUN	Apex Municipal Fund	APX	A+	9.36	B+ / 8.6	21.50 / 81	10.92 / 80	7.95 / 55	6.08	B- / 7.6	-4.49	-6.68
MUN	PIMCO Municipal Income Fund	PMF	A+	15.54	B+ / 8.6	27.28 / 95	9.08 / 68	--	6.18	B- / 7.6	2.85	0.04
MUS	MuniHoldings NJ Insured Fund	MUJ	A	15.59	B+ / 8.6	21.69 / 82	10.87 / 79	13.40 / 95	6.04	B- / 7.0	-1.45	-4.36
MUS	Alliance NY Municipal Income Fund	AYN	A-	14.85	B+ / 8.6	24.47 / 90	9.44 / 71	--	5.61	C+ / 6.4	-4.32	-7.89
EM	Morgan Stanley Emerging Mkts Debt	MSD	B+	9.97	B+ / 8.6	28.11 / 70	21.23 / 91	18.01 / 88	7.24	C / 5.4	-7.69	-8.26
MUS	BlackRock NJ Inv Qual Muni Tr	RNJ	B+	15.56	B+ / 8.6	25.00 / 92	8.71 / 64	10.64 / 80	5.18	C+ / 5.7	4.92	-1.54
MUN	Alliance Nat Municipal Income Fund	AFB	A+	14.90	B+ / 8.5	22.30 / 84	10.26 / 76	--	6.09	B- / 7.6	-5.99	-8.51
MUS	MuniYield AZ Fund	MZA	A-	15.76	B+ / 8.5	25.61 / 92	9.35 / 70	14.67 / 97	5.85	C+ / 6.3	4.72	1.03
MUS	MuniHoldings FL Insured Fund	MFL	A-	15.57	B+ / 8.5	22.65 / 85	10.65 / 79	14.53 / 97	6.34	C+ / 6.5	0.97	-2.25
GI	iShares Dow Jones US Real Estate	IYR	B+	62.82	B+ / 8.5	29.40 / 74	19.09 / 87	18.47 / 89	4.04	C+ / 5.9	-0.49	-0.11
COH	Scudder High Income Trust	KHI	B-	7.31	B+ / 8.5	26.71 / 66	18.53 / 85	9.20 / 37	9.21	C / 4.7	22.86	17.41
MUS	BlackRock CA Municipal Income Trust	BFZ	A	14.55	B+ / 8.4	22.97 / 86	9.62 / 72	--	6.19	B- / 7.1	-5.58	-7.79
MUS	Nuveen PA Div Adv Muni	NXM	A	16.10	B+ / 8.4	22.85 / 85	10.62 / 78	--	5.76	C+ / 6.7	0.94	-0.84
MUH	MFS Municipal Income Trust	MFM	A-	8.26	B+ / 8.4	21.69 / 82	9.08 / 67	9.35 / 67	6.63	C+ / 6.5	3.12	-1.25
MUS	BlackRock NY Municipal Income Trust	BNY	A-	15.13	B+ / 8.4	22.85 / 85	9.68 / 72	--	6.00	C+ / 6.5	-3.51	-7.26
MUS	Nuveen VA Div Adv Muni 2	NNB	A-	17.00	B+ / 8.4	22.45 / 84	11.14 / 81	--	4.93	C+ / 6.5	7.80	4.97
MUN	MuniYield Quality Fund	MQY	B+	15.27	B+ / 8.4	24.12 / 89	9.36 / 71	11.96 / 89	6.31	C+ / 6.3	-1.93	-5.60
GI	Franklin Multi-Income Trust	FMI	B+	9.35	B+ / 8.3	40.29 / 94	14.65 / 71	11.24 / 48	4.48	C+ / 5.8	-1.89	-9.77
MUS	Delaware Inv FL Insured Muni Inc	VFL	B+	16.70	B+ / 8.3	21.90 / 82	10.32 / 76	13.81 / 96	5.73	C+ / 6.1	7.33	2.95
MUS	MuniYield FL Insured Fund	MFT	B+	15.45	B+ / 8.3	24.04 / 89	9.32 / 70	11.93 / 89	5.80	C+ / 6.4	1.11	-3.13
MUS	Nuveen VA Div Adv Muni Fund	NGB	B+	17.47	B+ / 8.3	23.72 / 88	12.22 / 86	--	5.26	C+ / 6.3	12.35	12.71
MUS	Eaton Vance PA Muni Inc Tr	EVP	B	15.85	B+ / 8.3	25.40 / 92	12.24 / 86	15.20 / 98	5.97	C+ / 5.6	5.04	2.76
FO	Scudder New Asia Fund	SAF	B-	15.82	B+ / 8.3	26.66 / 65	20.06 / 89	5.53 / 23	0.44	C / 5.1	-11.92	-12.98
MUS	Nuveen NY Div Adv Muni 2	NXK	A	15.54	B / 8.2	20.88 / 79	10.06 / 75	--	6.04	C+ / 6.9	-2.02	-4.71
MUS	Nuveen NC Div Adv Muni	NRB	A-	17.33	B / 8.2	24.75 / 91	10.47 / 78	--	5.33	C+ / 6.7	11.73	7.96
MUS	Nuveen Insured FL Prem Inc Muni	NFL	B+	16.47	B / 8.2	24.22 / 90	8.28 / 61	11.40 / 86	5.23	C+ / 5.9	1.29	-1.96
UT	Gabelli Utility Trust	GUT	B	10.00	B / 8.2	26.20 / 65	17.94 / 84	18.56 / 90	7.29	C / 5.5	36.24	37.15

N/A denotes number is not available

Fund Type	Fund Name (99 Pct = Best, 0 Pct = Worst)	Ticker Symbol	Overall Weiss Investment Rating	Price As of 6/30/05	PERFORMANCE: Performance Rating/Pts	Annualized Total Return Through 6/30/05: 1Yr/Pct	3Yr/Pct	5Yr/Pct	Dividend Yield %	RISK: Risk Rating/Pts	VALUATION: Premium/Discount As of 6/30/05	1 Year Average
GR	NAIC Growth Fund	GRF	E-	8.55	E- / 0.0	-3.56 / 4	-3.63 / 0	-1.25 / 10	3.57	D / 1.6	-10.66	-14.29
GR	HOLDRS B2B Internet	BHH	E-	2.00	E- / 0.0	-9.46 / 1	-8.09 / 0	-43.03 / 0	14.73	E- / 0.0	0.00	N/A
GI	TCW Convertible Securities Fund	CVT	E	5.09	E- / 0.0	9.29 / 22	-0.90 / 1	-3.58 / 7	8.06	C- / 3.1	-7.62	-9.26
GL	Z-Seven Fund	ZSEV	E	4.35	E- / 0.0	7.94 / 18	0.39 / 1	-10.13 / 3	0.00	C- / 3.1	-21.20	-17.66
GR	Foxby Corp	FXX	E+	2.18	E- / 0.0	1.40 / 7	-1.77 / 1	-23.58 / 1	0.00	C / 5.5	-12.80	-12.76
GI	Bancroft Convertible Fund	BCV	D	17.32	E- / 0.0	-2.20 / 5	0.65 / 1	2.79 / 16	3.89	B / 8.3	-15.10	-11.94
GR	Tuxis Corporation	TUX	E-	0.00	E- / 0.1	13.14 / 31	-3.52 / 0	2.02 / 15	0.00	D- / 1.4		-18.64
GR	HOLDRS Telecom	TTH	E	27.02	E- / 0.1	7.27 / 16	2.01 / 2	-15.79 / 2	0.21	C- / 3.6	0.00	N/A
IN	Boulder Total Return Fund	BTF	E+	17.11	E- / 0.1	7.47 / 17	2.45 / 3	10.56 / 45	0.00	C+ / 5.9	-16.50	-13.34
HL	HOLDRS Pharmaceutical	PPH	D-	74.03	E- / 0.1	-3.62 / 3	0.37 / 1	-5.35 / 5	2.23	C+ / 6.5	0.00	N/A
GI	Ellsworth Convertible Growth & Inc	ECF	D	7.49	E- / 0.1	1.70 / 7	1.05 / 2	3.45 / 17	3.62	B- / 7.8	-14.20	-11.70
GI	Castle Convertible Fund	CVF	D	22.15	E- / 0.1	2.58 / 8	1.97 / 2	5.72 / 24	3.07	B / 8.2	-15.52	-12.55
GR	iShares Goldman Sachs Semicon Index	IGW	E-	53.60	E- / 0.2	-8.12 / 1	3.81 / 5	--	0.00	D / 1.6	0.00	N/A
FO	Japan Equity Fund	JEQ	E	6.08	E- / 0.2	-6.17 / 2	4.68 / 8	-4.58 / 6	0.00	C- / 4.0	-7.60	-4.08
GR	SPDR Consumer Staples	XLP	D	22.74	E- / 0.2	0.90 / 6	2.56 / 3	-0.49 / 11	1.97	B / 8.2	0.13	0.02
MTG	BlackRock Advantage Term Trust	BAT	D	10.26	E- / 0.2	1.64 / 7	2.64 / 3	9.38 / 38	5.85	B / 8.3	-0.68	-0.76
MTG	American Select Portfolio	SLA	D	11.88	E- / 0.2	2.99 / 9	2.81 / 4	9.58 / 39	7.02	B / 8.1	-9.31	-3.70
GR	HOLDRS Semiconductor	SMH	E-	34.10	E / 0.3	-8.22 / 1	4.07 / 6	-18.30 / 1	0.09	E- / 0.0	0.00	N/A
GR	iShares Dow Jones US Basic Mtrls	IYM	E	46.50	E / 0.3	6.10 / 13	6.05 / 13	7.82 / 31	1.75	C- / 3.0	-0.13	0.02
LP	Eaton Vance Senior Income Trust	EVF	D	7.93	E / 0.3	-12.01 / 0	6.65 / 15	3.76 / 18	6.12	B- / 7.9	-9.27	0.99
LP	Citigroup Investments Corp Loan	TLI	D	13.11	E / 0.3	-7.60 / 2	5.84 / 12	5.60 / 23	5.53	B / 8.2	-8.45	-2.02
MTG	American Strat Inc Portfolio II	BSP	D	11.64	E / 0.3	-0.84 / 5	3.61 / 5	10.21 / 43	8.22	B- / 7.7	-5.67	-1.74
MTG	Hyperion 2005 Inv Gr Opp Tm Tr	HTO	D+	9.78	E / 0.3	3.95 / 10	2.65 / 3	8.55 / 33	0.12	B / 8.9	-1.11	-1.39
GI	Zweig Total Return Fund	ZTR	E+	5.12	E / 0.4	11.70 / 28	2.21 / 2	4.00 / 19	10.53	C+ / 5.8	-5.88	-6.10
MTG	BlackRock Income Trust	BKT	E+	6.70	E / 0.4	6.60 / 15	4.95 / 8	10.70 / 46	9.04	C+ / 5.8	0.45	6.47
GL	Global Income Fund	GIF	D-	4.35	E / 0.4	10.14 / 24	4.08 / 6	8.11 / 32	6.44	C+ / 6.9	-5.23	-6.13
GL	Transamerica Income Shares	TAI	D-	22.19	E / 0.4	9.64 / 23	1.44 / 2	7.71 / 30	7.09	B- / 7.2	-5.37	-5.79
GR	HOLDRS Market 2000 +	MKH	D-	53.59	E / 0.4	1.89 / 7	4.75 / 8	--	1.38	B- / 7.1	0.00	N/A
MTG	American Strat Inc Portfolio	ASP	D	11.40	E / 0.4	0.41 / 6	4.58 / 7	9.19 / 36	6.83	B- / 7.5	-8.65	-3.59
GR	HOLDRS Retail	RTH	E+	94.62	E / 0.5	6.58 / 15	3.89 / 5	--	0.09	C / 4.7	0.00	N/A
GR	Diamond Series Trust I	DIA	D-	102.86	E / 0.5	1.06 / 6	5.80 / 12	1.63 / 14	1.33	B- / 7.2	-0.05	0.02
GR	streetTRACKS DJ US Lg Cap Growth	ELG	D-	46.51	E / 0.5	-0.47 / 6	5.47 / 11	--	0.81	C+ / 6.6	0.45	0.03
GL	MFS Intermediate Income Trust	MIN	D+	6.51	E / 0.5	7.31 / 16	2.48 / 3	7.04 / 28	5.51	B / 8.3	-9.83	-10.27
MUN	BlackRock Muni Target Tm Tr	BMN	C-	10.18	E / 0.5	-1.13 / 5	3.38 / 9	5.70 / 34	4.72	B+ / 9.0	-1.26	-0.67
FO	iShares MSCI Netherlands Index	EWN	E-	18.40	E+ / 0.6	13.65 / 34	3.75 / 5	-4.35 / 6	1.40	E- / 0.0	-0.33	0.16
FO	Germany Fund	GER	E-	7.77	E+ / 0.6	15.30 / 38	4.42 / 6	-6.71 / 5	0.32	D / 1.7	-12.30	-12.99
FO	iShares S&P/Topix 150 Index Fund	ITF	E	88.09	E+ / 0.6	-2.85 / 4	6.76 / 15	--	0.39	C- / 3.6	-0.22	0.14
FO	iShares MSCI Japan Index	EWJ	E+	10.22	E+ / 0.6	-2.37 / 4	6.78 / 16	-6.95 / 4	0.42	C / 4.7	-0.68	0.01
GEN	ACM Managed Income Fund	AMF	E+	3.67	E+ / 0.6	-4.63 / 3	5.77 / 12	0.45 / 13	5.83	C / 5.2	-12.20	-6.00
USA	ACM Government Opportunity Fund	AOF	D-	7.89	E+ / 0.6	4.61 / 11	3.98 / 5	11.13 / 47	5.90	B- / 7.2	-8.26	-5.93
FO	Japan Smaller Cap Fund Inc.	JOF	E	10.78	E+ / 0.7	-18.40 / 0	10.50 / 42	5.36 / 22	0.00	D+ / 2.4	-7.94	5.57
GR	Alliance All-Market Advantage Fd	AMO	E+	14.49	E+ / 0.7	5.74 / 13	4.49 / 7	-8.56 / 3	8.94	C / 4.7	7.97	8.86
IN	Boulder Growth&Income Fund	BIF	E+	6.63	E+ / 0.7	9.77 / 23	6.20 / 13	2.78 / 16	0.00	C / 4.3	-14.34	-12.27
IN	Tri-Continental Corporation	TY	D-	17.83	E+ / 0.7	7.98 / 18	4.84 / 8	-2.11 / 9	1.35	C+ / 6.5	-16.80	-16.43
GR	iShares S&P 500/Barra Growth	IVW	D	56.50	E+ / 0.7	1.00 / 8	5.94 / 13	-7.72 / 4	0.89	B- / 7.3	0.02	0.06
MTG	American Strat Inc Portfolio III	CSP	D+	11.34	E+ / 0.7	5.52 / 12	5.57 / 11	10.67 / 46	8.58	B / 8.2	-5.81	-1.38
GR	iShares Dow Jones US Cns Sv Sct Idx	IYC	D-	58.97	E+ / 0.8	5.72 / 13	6.05 / 13	0.09 / 12	0.16	C+ / 6.3	-0.10	N/A
MUN	Colonial Insured Muni	CFX	D	14.15	E+ / 0.8	6.02 / 22	2.08 / 4	8.24 / 58	5.92	B- / 7.4	-5.48	-3.16
GR	SPDR Health Care	XLV	D+	31.10	E+ / 0.8	3.46 / 10	5.24 / 9	1.86 / 14	1.24	B- / 7.9	0.03	0.02
IN	iShares S&P 100 Index Fund	OEF	D+	55.77	E+ / 0.8	2.86 / 9	6.35 / 14	--	1.65	B- / 7.8	-0.13	N/A
HL	iShares S&P Global Healthcare Sect	IXJ	C-	50.15	E+ / 0.8	4.84 / 11	5.35 / 9	--	0.73	B / 8.9	0.06	0.34
GR	SPDR Consumer Discretionary	XLY	E	32.84	E+ / 0.9	3.83 / 10	6.86 / 16	5.95 / 25	0.60	C- / 3.3	-0.06	0.02

N/A denotes number is not available

99 Pct = Best
0 Pct = Worst

Fund Type	Fund Name	Ticker Symbol	Overall Weiss Investment Rating	Price As of 6/30/05	PERFORMANCE: Performance Rating/Pts	Annualized Total Return Through 6/30/05: 1Yr/Pct	3Yr/Pct	5Yr/Pct	Dividend Yield %	RISK: Risk Rating/Pts	VALUATION: Premium/Discount As of 6/30/05	1 Year Average
GR	Liberty All-Star Growth Fund	ASG	**E+**	5.89	**E+ / 0.9**	2.12 / 8	7.10 / 18	-2.46 / 8	9.52	**C / 4.3**	2.43	5.53
GL	streetTRACKS DJ Global Titan	DGT	**D**	63.21	**E+ / 0.9**	4.68 / 11	6.18 / 13	--	2.14	**B- / 7.0**	-0.09	0.10
GR	iShares Dow Jones US Cns Gd Sct Idx	IYK	**D+**	52.30	**E+ / 0.9**	2.41 / 8	6.42 / 14	6.51 / 27	1.61	**B- / 7.8**	0.02	N/A
GL	MFS Government Markets Income Trust	MGF	**C-**	6.62	**E+ / 0.9**	8.14 / 19	4.54 / 7	7.59 / 29	4.59	**B+ / 9.2**	-11.62	-11.36
USA	Morgan Stanley Govt Inc Tr	GVT	**C-**	8.92	**E+ / 0.9**	7.74 / 17	4.45 / 7	7.25 / 29	4.67	**B+ / 9.5**	-10.17	-9.50
GR	SPDR Materials	XLB	**E**	27.34	**D- / 1.0**	5.89 / 13	7.84 / 22	9.58 / 39	2.08	**C- / 3.2**	0.00	N/A
COI	Lincoln National Income Fund	LND	**D-**	11.80	**D- / 1.0**	3.28 / 9	6.99 / 17	12.16 / 54	5.28	**C+ / 6.6**	-12.20	-6.38
GR	iShares Russell 1000 Growth	IWF	**D**	47.82	**D- / 1.0**	1.51 / 7	6.98 / 17	-10.50 / 3	0.68	**B- / 7.1**	-0.04	0.04
GR	iShares Russell 3000 Growth	IWZ	**D**	38.78	**D- / 1.0**	1.32 / 7	6.96 / 17	--	0.43	**C+ / 6.8**	0.05	0.02
MUN	ACM Municipal Securities Income Fd	AMU	**D**	10.73	**D- / 1.0**	3.13 / 11	2.83 / 6	5.95 / 36	5.89	**B- / 7.2**	-7.66	-1.62
LP	Van Kampen Senior Inc Tr	VVR	**C-**	7.90	**D- / 1.0**	-5.58 / 2	9.13 / 32	5.70 / 24	6.28	**B / 8.6**	-8.56	-1.17
GL	iShares S&P Global Technology Sect	IXN	**E-**	48.77	**D- / 1.1**	-2.82 / 4	8.50 / 25	--	1.29	**D- / 1.4**	0.06	0.36
HL	iShares Biotechnology Index Fund	IBB	**E-**	67.57	**D- / 1.1**	-8.95 / 1	9.83 / 37	--	0.00	**D / 1.6**	0.04	-0.02
FO	iShares MSCI Switzerland Index	EWL	**D-**	16.60	**D- / 1.1**	9.26 / 22	7.41 / 20	1.40 / 14	0.52	**C+ / 5.7**	-0.18	0.51
GR	Zweig Fund	ZF	**D-**	5.38	**D- / 1.1**	21.65 / 53	3.20 / 4	-3.12 / 7	11.14	**C / 5.5**	-6.76	-8.42
GR	MVC Capital	MVC	**C-**	0.00	**D- / 1.1**	6.17 / 14	5.35 / 9	-7.09 / 4	1.20	**B / 8.9**		-1.17
GR	iShares Goldman Sachs Technology	IGM	**E-**	43.46	**D- / 1.2**	-4.23 / 3	9.23 / 33	--	0.04	**D- / 1.3**	0.12	0.04
COH	Van Kampen High Income Trust	VIT	**D-**	3.68	**D- / 1.2**	7.78 / 17	6.94 / 16	4.98 / 21	9.47	**C / 5.4**	2.79	9.34
FS	HOLDRS Regional Bank	RKH	**D**	134.50	**D- / 1.2**	5.62 / 12	7.19 / 18	10.29 / 44	0.78	**C+ / 6.7**	0.00	N/A
GR	iShares Dow Jones US Industrial	IYJ	**D**	53.39	**D- / 1.2**	3.58 / 10	8.46 / 25	-1.07 / 11	0.48	**C+ / 6.7**	-0.07	0.02
GEI	Montgomery Street Inc. Sec.	MTS	**D+**	18.11	**D- / 1.2**	10.92 / 26	5.47 / 10	9.89 / 41	6.38	**B- / 7.4**	-8.67	-6.70
GEN	Van Kampen Income Trust	VIN	**C-**	5.81	**D- / 1.2**	13.30 / 32	4.66 / 7	4.84 / 21	5.70	**B / 8.4**	-10.62	-11.68
FS	SPDR Financial	XLF	**D**	29.31	**D- / 1.3**	4.88 / 11	7.50 / 20	6.20 / 26	2.38	**C+ / 6.8**	0.07	N/A
GR	SPDR Industrial	XLI	**D**	29.29	**D- / 1.3**	4.40 / 11	8.67 / 27	2.04 / 15	1.02	**B- / 7.0**	0.03	-0.01
MUN	Putnam Investment Grade Muni Tr	PGM	**D**	9.67	**D- / 1.3**	9.86 / 38	1.12 / 2	6.05 / 37	5.06	**C+ / 6.8**	-12.88	-10.50
LP	ING Prime Rate Trust	PPR	**D+**	6.99	**D- / 1.3**	-7.80 / 2	10.17 / 39	2.53 / 15	6.47	**B- / 7.9**	-5.03	2.56
MUS	Nuveen AZ Prem Inc Muni	NAZ	**D+**	15.41	**D- / 1.3**	12.39 / 48	2.39 / 5	7.59 / 51	5.00	**B- / 7.5**	4.69	8.71
MUS	Van Kampen PA Qual Muni	VPQ	**D+**	14.91	**D- / 1.3**	9.48 / 36	2.24 / 4	7.59 / 51	5.43	**B- / 7.5**	-12.45	-9.57
FO	iShares MSCI Germany Index	EWG	**E-**	17.65	**D- / 1.4**	13.16 / 32	7.91 / 22	-3.03 / 7	1.10	**E- / 0.0**	-0.23	-0.01
GR	iShares Dow Jones US Technology	IYW	**E-**	46.09	**D- / 1.4**	-2.13 / 5	9.11 / 32	-18.16 / 1	0.23	**D- / 1.4**	0.11	0.03
GI	Gabelli Convertible&Income Sec Fund	GCV	**E+**	9.50	**D- / 1.4**	4.22 / 10	6.82 / 16	9.99 / 42	8.06	**C / 4.9**	18.75	17.05
COH	Salomon Br High Income Fund	HIF	**D-**	9.43	**D- / 1.4**	-8.33 / 1	9.45 / 34	4.60 / 20	7.56	**C+ / 5.7**	-10.10	-2.51
IN	iShares S&P Global 100	IOO	**D**	60.30	**D- / 1.4**	6.33 / 14	7.89 / 22	--	1.70	**C+ / 6.8**	0.08	0.11
COH	Prospect Street High Inc Portfolio	PHY	**E-**	3.40	**D- / 1.5**	23.31 / 58	3.40 / 4	2.95 / 17	8.72	**D- / 1.2**	-5.03	0.64
GR	SPDR Technology	XLK	**E-**	19.99	**D- / 1.5**	-0.49 / 5	9.20 / 32	-17.59 / 2	0.56	**D- / 1.5**	0.15	-0.01
PM	Central Fund of Canada	CEF	**D-**	5.40	**D- / 1.5**	2.07 / 8	8.37 / 24	9.34 / 37	0.19	**C+ / 5.8**	0.00	6.46
GEN	Allmerica Securities Trust	ALM	**C-**	9.42	**D- / 1.5**	13.07 / 31	4.99 / 8	6.29 / 26	5.79	**B / 8.0**	-10.54	-11.75
HL	iShares Dow Jones US Healthcare	IYH	**C-**	61.20	**D- / 1.5**	5.63 / 12	7.07 / 17	-0.49 / 12	0.78	**B- / 7.9**	-0.03	N/A
MUN	Municipal High Income Fund	MHF	**C-**	7.21	**D- / 1.5**	8.67 / 32	2.59 / 6	5.85 / 35	5.63	**B / 8.4**	-8.73	-7.64
GR	HOLDRS Internet Architecture	IAH	**E**	34.23	**D / 1.6**	-1.73 / 5	10.35 / 41	-17.65 / 2	0.18	**D+ / 2.6**	0.00	N/A
GR	Salomon Br Fund	SBF	**D**	12.88	**D / 1.6**	6.44 / 14	7.79 / 22	-2.76 / 8	0.92	**C+ / 6.3**	-13.27	-14.33
GR	streetTRACKS Total Market ETF	TMW	**D+**	85.14	**D / 1.6**	7.68 / 17	7.69 / 21	--	1.70	**B- / 7.2**	0.12	0.01
UT	J Hancock Patriot Select Div Tr	DIV	**D+**	13.65	**D / 1.6**	5.68 / 12	7.95 / 22	10.17 / 43	6.53	**B- / 7.1**	-9.36	-2.10
GEI	BlackRock Broad Inv Gr 2009 Tm Tr	BCT	**C-**	15.81	**D / 1.6**	9.13 / 22	7.10 / 18	13.19 / 60	5.70	**B / 8.1**	4.01	1.56
LP	Nuveen Sr Inc	NSL	**C-**	8.57	**D / 1.6**	-5.91 / 2	10.90 / 47	6.03 / 25	7.03	**B- / 7.8**	1.30	10.89
COI	1838 Bond Debenture Fund	BDF	**D**	18.74	**D / 1.7**	14.36 / 35	5.88 / 12	8.95 / 34	6.05	**C+ / 6.7**	-11.06	-10.88
GR	General American Investors	GAM	**D+**	31.72	**D / 1.7**	8.89 / 21	7.17 / 18	2.89 / 17	0.01	**B- / 7.6**	-14.39	-11.80
COI	Van Kampen Bond	VBF	**C-**	17.71	**D / 1.7**	12.46 / 30	5.47 / 10	8.38 / 33	5.61	**B- / 7.9**	-9.92	-10.28

N/A denotes number is not available

Section VI

Risk: 100 Best and Worst Closed-End Mutual Funds

A compilation of those

Closed-End Mutual Funds

receiving the highest and lowest Risk Ratings.

Funds are listed in order by Risk Rating.

Section VI Contents

This section contains a summary analysis of each of the top 100 and bottom 100 mutual funds as determined by their Weiss Risk Rating. Since the Risk Rating does not take into consideration a fund's overall financial performance, the selection of funds presented here is based solely on each fund's performance volatility over the past three years.

You can use this section to identify those funds that have historically given shareholders the most consistent returns on their investments. A word of caution though: consistency in the past is not necessarily indicative of future results. While these funds have provided the most stable returns, it is possible for a fund manager – especially a newly appointed fund manager – to suddenly shift the fund's investment focus which could lead to greater volatility.

1. Fund Type The mutual fund's peer category based on an analysis of its investment portfolio.

COH	Corporate – High Yield	HL	Health
COI	Corporate – Inv. Grade	IN	Income
EM	Emerging Market	LP	Loan Participation
EN	Energy/Natural Resources	MTG	Mortgage
FS	Financial Services	MUH	Municipal – High Yield
FO	Foreign	MUN	Municipal – National
GEI	General – Inv. Grade	MUS	Municipal – Single State
GEN	General Bond	PM	Precious Metals
GL	Global	USA	U.S. Gov. – Agency
GR	Growth	UT	Utilities
GI	Growth and Income		

A blank fund type means that the mutual fund has not yet been categorized.

2. Fund Name The name of the mutual fund as stated in its prospectus, which can sometimes differ slightly from the name that the company uses for advertising. If you cannot find the particular mutual fund you are interested in, or if you have any doubts regarding the precise name, verify the information with your broker or on your account statement. Also, use the fund's ticker symbol for confirmation. (See column 3.)

3. Ticker Symbol The unique alphabetic symbol used for identifying and trading a specific mutual fund. No two funds can have the same ticker symbol.

A handful of funds currently show no associated ticker symbol. This means that the fund is either small or new since the NASD only assigns a ticker symbol to funds with at least $25 million in assets or 1,000 shareholders.

4. Overall Weiss Investment Rating Our overall rating is measured on a scale from A to E based on each fund's risk-adjusted performance. Please see page 10 for specific descriptions of each letter grade. Also, refer to page 7 for information on how our ratings are derived. Most important, when using this rating, please be sure to consider the warnings beginning on page 11 regarding the ratings' limitations and the underlying assumptions.

5. **Price** Closing price of the fund on the date shown.

6. **Performance Rating/Points** A letter grade rating based solely on the mutual fund's financial performance over the trailing three years, without any consideration for the amount of risk the fund poses. Like the overall Weiss Investment Rating, the Performance Rating is measured on a scale from A to E for ease of interpretation. The points score indicates where the Performance Rating falls on a scale of 0 to 10.

7. **1-Year Total Return** The total return the fund has provided investors over the preceeding 52 weeks. This total return figure is computed based on the fund's dividend distributions and share price appreciation/depreciation during the period, net of the expenses and fees it imposes on its shareholders.

8. **1-Year Total Return Percentile** The fund's percentile rank based on its one-year performance compared to that of all other closed-end funds in existence for at least one year. A score of 99 is the best possible, indicating that the fund outperformed 99% of the closed-end mutual funds. Zero is the worst possible percentile score.

9. **3-Year Total Return** The total annual return the fund has provided investors over the preceeding 156 weeks.

10. **3-Year Total Return Percentile** The fund's percentile rank based on its three-year performance compared to that of all other closed-end funds in existence for at least three years. A score of 99 is the best possible, indicating that the fund outperformed 99% of the closed-end mutual funds. Zero is the worst possible percentile score.

11. **5-Year Total Return** The total annual return the fund has provided investors over the preceeding 260 weeks.

12. **5-Year Total Return Percentile** The fund's percentile rank based on its five-year performance compared to that of all other closed-end funds in existence for at least five years. A score of 99 is the best possible, indicating that the fund outperformed 99% of the closed-end mutual funds. Zero is the worst possible percentile score.

13. **Dividend Yield** Most recent quarterly dividend to fund investors annualized, expressed as a percent of the fund's current share price. The dividend yield of a fund can have little correlation to the amount of dividends the fund has received from its underlying investments. Rather, dividend distributions are based on a fund's need to pass earnings from both dividends and gains on the sale of investments along to shareholders. Thus, these dividend distributions are included as a part of the fund's total return.

    Keep in mind that dividend income may be taxed at a different rate than capital gains depending on your income tax bracket.

14. Risk Rating/Points

A letter grade rating based solely on the mutual fund's risk as determined by its monthly performance volatility over the trailing three years. The risk rating does not take into consideration the overall financial performance the fund has achieved or the total return it has provided to its shareholders. Like the overall Weiss Investment Rating, the Risk Rating is measured on a scale from A to E for ease of interpretation. The points score indicates where the Risk Rating falls on a scale of 0 to 10.

15. Premium/ Discount

A comparison of the fund's price to its NAV as of the date indicated. The premium (+) or discount (-) indicates the percentage the shares are trading above or below the fund's NAV per share.

If the price is above the fund's NAV, the fund is said to be trading at a premium. If the price is lower than the fund's NAV, the fund is trading at a discount.

16. 1-Year Average Premium/ Discount

The average of the fund's premium/discount over the preceeding year.

It can be useful to compare the fund's current premium/discount to its one-year average. If the fund is currently trading at a premium/discount that is lower/higher than its one-year average, then there has been less demand for the fund in more recent times than over the past year. Conversely, if the fund is currently trading at a premium/discount that is higher/lower than its one-year average, this indicates that there has been greater demand for the fund in more recent times than over the past year.

Fund Type	Fund Name (99 Pct = Best, 0 Pct = Worst)	Ticker Symbol	Overall Weiss Investment Rating	Price As of 6/30/05	PERFORMANCE: Performance Rating/Pts	Annualized Total Return Through 6/30/05: 1Yr/Pct	3Yr/Pct	5Yr/Pct	Dividend Yield %	RISK: Risk Rating/Pts	VALUATION: Premium/Discount As of 6/30/05	1 Year Average
GL	Salomon Br 2008 Wldwide $ Gov Tm Tr	SBG	B	11.19	C- / 3.8	11.46 / 28	12.18 / 58	14.77 / 70	7.72	B+ / 9.7	-2.95	-0.42
USA	Morgan Stanley Govt Inc Tr	GVT	C-	8.92	E+ / 0.9	7.74 / 17	4.45 / 7	7.25 / 29	4.67	B+ / 9.5	-10.17	-9.50
MUN	Putnam Tax-Free Health Care Fund	PMH	C+	12.25	C- / 3.3	9.36 / 36	5.71 / 28	6.34 / 40	4.49	B+ / 9.2	-13.67	-13.84
GL	MFS Government Markets Income Trust	MGF	C-	6.62	E+ / 0.9	8.14 / 19	4.54 / 7	7.59 / 29	4.59	B+ / 9.2	-11.62	-11.36
MUS	Morgan Stanley CA Qual Muni Sec	IQC	B+	14.30	C+ / 5.6	13.78 / 52	8.77 / 65	8.39 / 58	5.87	B+ / 9.1	-9.49	-8.13
MUS	Morgan Stanley CA Muni Sec	ICS	C+	14.09	C- / 3.4	14.23 / 54	5.45 / 25	7.02 / 47	4.66	B+ / 9.1	-8.92	-9.56
MUN	BlackRock Muni Target Tm Tr	BMN	C-	10.18	E / 0.5	-1.13 / 5	3.38 / 9	5.70 / 34	4.72	B+ / 9.0	-1.26	-0.67
GR	MVC Capital	MVC	C-	0.00	D- / 1.1	6.17 / 14	5.35 / 9	-7.09 / 4	1.20	B / 8.9		-1.17
HL	iShares S&P Global Healthcare Sect	IXJ	C-	50.15	E+ / 0.8	4.84 / 11	5.35 / 9	--	0.73	B / 8.9	0.06	0.34
MTG	Hyperion 2005 Inv Gr Opp Tm Tr	HTO	D+	9.78	E / 0.3	3.95 / 10	2.65 / 3	8.55 / 33	0.12	B / 8.9	-1.11	-1.39
MUN	Nuveen Muni Value	NUV	B	9.57	C / 5.0	15.95 / 61	6.06 / 33	8.68 / 62	4.87	B / 8.8	-7.71	-8.65
MUN	Morgan Stanley Qual Muni Sec	IQM	B	14.40	C+ / 6.0	14.65 / 56	7.81 / 56	9.93 / 72	5.85	B / 8.7	-12.09	-11.77
MUS	BlackRock CA Insured Muni 2008 Term	BFC	C	16.06	D+ / 2.5	6.45 / 24	6.01 / 33	7.78 / 53	4.78	B / 8.7	-2.37	-2.57
MUN	Seligman Quality Municipal Fund	SQF	C	12.27	D+ / 2.7	9.32 / 35	4.94 / 21	7.29 / 48	4.64	B / 8.6	-14.67	-13.78
GEI	Fort Dearborn Inc. Secs.	FDI	C-	14.90	D / 1.8	15.35 / 39	5.46 / 10	9.13 / 36	5.32	B / 8.6	-10.72	-10.57
LP	Van Kampen Senior Inc Tr	VVR	C-	7.90	D- / 1.0	-5.58 / 2	9.13 / 32	5.70 / 24	6.28	B / 8.6	-8.56	-1.17
MUN	Morgan Stanley Muni Inc Op II	OIB	B	8.14	C+ / 6.1	15.00 / 57	7.08 / 46	9.22 / 65	5.84	B / 8.5	-9.05	-9.83
MUN	BlackRock Insured Muni 2008 Tm Tr	BRM	C	16.10	D+ / 2.3	5.99 / 22	5.54 / 26	8.51 / 59	4.94	B / 8.5	-1.47	-2.56
MUN	Seligman Select Municipal Fund	SEL	C	10.34	D+ / 2.7	8.84 / 33	5.45 / 24	8.67 / 62	5.52	B / 8.5	-12.67	-11.35
GEN	MFS Charter Income Trust	MCR	C-	8.70	D / 2.0	11.97 / 29	7.28 / 19	7.33 / 29	5.71	B / 8.5	-10.95	-9.88
MUS	BlackRock NY Insured Muni 2008 Term	BLN	C-	15.83	D / 2.0	4.98 / 17	5.32 / 23	6.96 / 46	4.73	B / 8.5	-2.22	-3.02
MUS	BlackRock FL Insured Muni 2008 Term	BRF	C-	15.46	D / 1.9	6.05 / 23	5.33 / 23	6.22 / 39	4.85	B / 8.5	-0.39	-0.60
MUN	Morgan Stanley Qual Muni Inc Tr	IQI	B	13.93	C / 5.2	12.92 / 50	7.04 / 45	8.46 / 59	5.80	B / 8.4	-11.89	-11.31
MUS	BlackRock NY Muni 2018 Income Trust	BLH	B	15.29	C+ / 6.5	13.88 / 53	9.75 / 73	--	4.77	B / 8.4	-5.91	-5.29
MUN	Morgan Stanley Insured Muni Tr	IMT	C+	13.93	C / 4.4	13.18 / 51	5.89 / 31	7.31 / 49	5.81	B / 8.4	-11.10	-11.00
MUN	Nuveen Select Maturities Muni	NIM	C	9.72	D+ / 2.7	11.28 / 43	3.83 / 12	3.80 / 24	4.82	B / 8.4	-6.18	-7.27
MUN	Insured Municipal Income Fund	PIF	C	13.18	D+ / 2.7	11.64 / 44	4.04 / 14	8.41 / 59	5.00	B / 8.4	-14.02	-13.36
COI	Morgan Stanley Income Sec	ICB	C-	15.88	D / 1.9	13.03 / 31	5.66 / 11	6.52 / 27	6.12	B / 8.4	-10.03	-9.53
GEN	Van Kampen Income Trust	VIN	C-	5.81	D- / 1.2	13.30 / 32	4.66 / 7	4.84 / 21	5.70	B / 8.4	-10.62	-11.68
MTG	American Income Fund	MRF	C-	8.28	D / 1.7	8.70 / 21	6.77 / 16	9.64 / 39	6.60	B / 8.4	-7.90	-7.96
MUN	Municipal High Income Fund	MHF	C-	7.21	D- / 1.5	8.67 / 32	2.59 / 6	5.85 / 35	5.63	B / 8.4	-8.73	-7.64
MUN	Morgan Stanley Insured Muni Inc Tr	IIM	B	14.23	C / 5.4	12.77 / 49	7.30 / 48	8.24 / 57	5.66	B / 8.3	-11.06	-10.70
MUN	Nuveen Select Tax-Free Inc 3	NXR	C+	13.44	C- / 4.2	11.63 / 44	5.82 / 30	5.95 / 36	4.81	B / 8.3	-7.69	-9.01
MUS	Putnam CA Inv Grade Muni	PCA	C+	13.65	C- / 3.9	14.97 / 57	5.46 / 25	5.86 / 35	4.79	B / 8.3	-11.76	-11.13
MUS	Putnam NY Inv Gr Muni Tr	PMN	C+	12.17	C- / 3.6	13.45 / 51	4.75 / 19	5.53 / 33	4.32	B / 8.3	-12.51	-12.89
MUN	Managed Municipals Portfolio	MMU	C	10.76	C- / 3.0	6.10 / 23	6.80 / 41	7.99 / 55	5.14	B / 8.3	-7.96	-7.43
GEI	Pioneer Interest Shares	MUO	C-	11.43	D / 1.7	13.67 / 34	5.06 / 9	8.30 / 32	5.59	B / 8.3	-9.29	-10.25
GL	MFS Intermediate Income Trust	MIN	D+	6.51	E / 0.5	7.31 / 16	2.48 / 3	7.04 / 28	5.51	B / 8.3	-9.83	-10.27
GI	Bancroft Convertible Fund	BCV	D	17.32	E- / 0.0	-2.20 / 5	0.65 / 1	2.79 / 16	3.89	B / 8.3	-15.10	-11.94
MTG	BlackRock Advantage Term Trust	BAT	D	10.26	E- / 0.2	1.64 / 7	2.64 / 3	9.38 / 38	5.85	B / 8.3	-0.68	0.76
MUN	Morgan Stanley Muni Prem Inc Tr	PIA	C+	9.12	C / 4.8	12.22 / 47	6.97 / 45	9.74 / 70	5.87	B / 8.2	-13.14	-11.76
MUN	Van Kampen Muni Trust	VKQ	C+	14.41	C- / 3.8	12.54 / 48	5.85 / 30	8.17 / 56	5.75	B / 8.2	-13.76	-12.06
MUS	Eaton Vance MI Muni Inc Tr	EMI	C+	15.46	C / 4.5	7.95 / 29	10.36 / 77	15.07 / 98	5.48	B / 8.2	1.31	7.75
GEN	Putnam Premier Income Trust	PPT	C	6.51	C- / 3.3	15.88 / 39	9.50 / 34	9.38 / 38	5.57	B / 8.2	-9.21	-9.96
MUN	Nuveen Select T-F Inc Portf 2	NXQ	C	13.51	C- / 3.1	11.01 / 42	4.69 / 19	5.57 / 33	4.87	B / 8.2	-8.03	-8.99
MTG	American Strat Inc Portfolio III	CSP	D+	11.34	E+ / 0.7	5.52 / 12	5.57 / 11	10.67 / 46	8.58	B / 8.2	-5.81	-1.38
GI	Castle Convertible Fund	CVF	D	22.15	E- / 0.1	2.58 / 8	1.97 / 2	5.72 / 24	3.07	B / 8.2	-15.52	-12.55
GR	SPDR Consumer Staples	XLP	D	22.74	E- / 0.2	0.90 / 6	2.56 / 3	-0.49 / 11	1.97	B / 8.2	0.13	0.02
LP	Citigroup Investments Corp Loan	TLI	D	13.11	E / 0.3	-7.60 / 2	5.84 / 12	5.60 / 23	5.53	B / 8.2	-8.45	-2.02
MUN	BlackRock Insured Muni Tm Tr	BMT	C+	11.17	C / 4.3	10.26 / 39	7.45 / 51	8.31 / 58	5.14	B / 8.1	2.67	1.36
MUN	Nuveen Select T-F Inc Portf	NXP	C+	14.00	C- / 3.7	11.70 / 44	5.44 / 24	5.80 / 34	4.87	B / 8.1	-6.35	-6.80
MUN	Van Kampen Invmt Grade Muni	VIG	C+	9.06	C / 4.6	13.66 / 51	6.44 / 38	6.54 / 42	5.44	B / 8.1	-13.55	-13.41

N/A denotes number is not available

99 Pct = Best
0 Pct = Worst

Fund Type	Fund Name	Ticker Symbol	Overall Weiss Investment Rating	Price As of 6/30/05	PERFORMANCE: Performance Rating/Pts	Annualized Total Return Through 6/30/05: 1Yr/Pct	3Yr/Pct	5Yr/Pct	Dividend Yield %	RISK: Risk Rating/Pts	VALUATION: Premium/Discount As of 6/30/05	1 Year Average
MUS	Morgan Stanley NY Qual Muni Sec	IQN	C+	13.77	C / 4.9	14.43 / 55	6.87 / 43	7.89 / 54	5.42	B / 8.1	-12.18	-11.54
GEI	BlackRock Broad Inv Gr 2009 Tm Tr	BCT	C-	15.81	D / 1.6	9.13 / 22	7.10 / 18	13.19 / 60	5.70	B / 8.1	4.01	1.56
MUN	Putnam Muni Opp Tr	PMO	C-	12.03	D+ / 2.3	6.39 / 24	4.83 / 20	7.14 / 47	5.61	B / 8.1	-9.82	-5.74
MUS	MuniYield CA Fund	MYC	C-	13.91	D+ / 2.4	11.36 / 43	4.40 / 16	7.95 / 55	5.85	B / 8.1	-8.61	-6.89
MTG	American Select Portfolio	SLA	D	11.88	E- / 0.2	2.99 / 9	2.81 / 4	9.58 / 39	7.02	B / 8.1	-9.31	-3.70
MUN	Van Kampen Sel Sector Muni	VKL	C	12.62	C- / 3.1	12.72 / 49	4.81 / 19	10.18 / 75	5.81	B / 8.0	-13.92	-12.70
GEN	Allmerica Securities Trust	ALM	C-	9.42	D- / 1.5	13.07 / 31	4.99 / 8	6.29 / 26	5.79	B / 8.0	-10.54	-11.75
MUH	Colonial High Inc Muni Tr	CXE	C-	6.29	D+ / 2.6	12.16 / 46	4.91 / 21	7.88 / 53	6.53	B / 8.0	-4.70	-1.16
MUN	BlackRock Municipal 2018 Income Tr	BPK	A+	15.70	B / 8.0	17.99 / 69	10.98 / 80	--	4.92	B- / 7.9	-1.32	-4.38
MUN	Morgan Stanley Muni Inv Tr	IQT	C+	13.91	C / 4.8	13.86 / 52	6.24 / 36	7.50 / 51	5.80	B- / 7.9	-11.96	-11.68
COI	Van Kampen Bond	VBF	C-	17.71	D / 1.7	12.46 / 30	5.47 / 10	8.38 / 33	5.61	B- / 7.9	-9.92	-10.28
HL	iShares Dow Jones US Healthcare	IYH	C-	61.20	D- / 1.5	5.63 / 12	7.07 / 17	-0.49 / 12	0.78	B- / 7.9	-0.03	N/A
GR	SPDR Health Care	XLV	D+	31.10	E+ / 0.8	3.46 / 10	5.24 / 9	1.86 / 14	1.24	B- / 7.9	0.03	0.02
LP	ING Prime Rate Trust	PPR	D+	6.99	D- / 1.3	-7.80 / 2	10.17 / 39	2.53 / 15	6.47	B- / 7.9	-5.03	2.56
LP	Eaton Vance Senior Income Trust	EVF	D	7.93	E / 0.3	-12.01 / 0	6.65 / 15	3.76 / 18	6.12	B- / 7.9	-9.27	0.99
MUS	Alliance CA Municipal Income Fund	AKP	A+	14.87	B / 8.1	21.46 / 81	9.61 / 72	--	5.87	B- / 7.8	-4.74	-6.59
MUN	Morgan Stanley Muni Inc Op III	OIC	B-	8.86	C+ / 5.9	15.95 / 62	6.35 / 36	8.56 / 60	5.73	B- / 7.8	-8.57	-10.16
MUN	American Municipal Income Portfolio	XAA	B-	14.82	C+ / 6.7	16.50 / 63	8.60 / 64	11.29 / 85	6.10	B- / 7.8	-6.68	-7.07
MUS	Nuveen NY Muni Value	NNY	B-	9.68	C+ / 5.9	17.01 / 65	6.70 / 41	7.80 / 53	4.40	B- / 7.8	-4.72	-7.98
MUS	Van Kampen FL Qual Muni	VFM	B-	14.99	C+ / 5.6	16.25 / 62	7.90 / 57	10.07 / 74	5.27	B- / 7.8	-11.25	-10.86
MUN	Van Kampen Trust for Inv Muni	VGM	C+	15.01	C- / 3.9	12.12 / 46	6.18 / 35	9.97 / 73	5.75	B- / 7.8	-13.83	-12.70
MUS	Van Kampen NY Val Muni Inc	VNV	C+	14.83	C- / 4.0	13.99 / 53	5.90 / 31	8.98 / 64	5.34	B- / 7.8	-12.25	-11.03
GEN	MFS Multimarket Income Trust	MMT	C	6.29	D+ / 2.9	14.29 / 35	9.09 / 32	7.77 / 31	6.05	B- / 7.8	-8.97	-9.56
GL	Colonial InterMkt Inc Tr I	CMK	C	8.82	C- / 3.9	19.92 / 50	10.48 / 42	9.82 / 40	7.32	B- / 7.8	-6.96	-8.81
IN	J Hancock Patriot Prem Div Fd I	PDF	C-	9.30	D / 1.9	11.70 / 28	7.55 / 20	10.01 / 42	5.94	B- / 7.8	-6.16	-0.61
LP	Nuveen Sr Inc	NSL	C-	8.57	D / 1.6	-5.91 / 2	10.90 / 47	6.03 / 25	7.03	B- / 7.8	1.30	10.89
MUN	Investment Grade Municipal Income	PPM	C-	13.67	D+ / 2.3	11.78 / 45	3.14 / 8	8.16 / 56	5.45	B- / 7.8	-13.97	-12.93
GR	iShares Dow Jones US Cns Gd Sct Idx	IYK	D+	52.30	E+ / 0.9	2.41 / 8	6.42 / 14	6.51 / 27	1.61	B- / 7.8	0.02	N/A
IN	iShares S&P 100 Index Fund	OEF	D+	55.77	E+ / 0.8	2.86 / 9	6.35 / 14	--	1.65	B- / 7.8	-0.13	N/A
GI	Ellsworth Convertible Growth & Inc	ECF	D	7.49	E- / 0.1	1.70 / 7	1.05 / 2	3.45 / 17	3.62	B- / 7.8	-14.20	-11.70
MUN	Nuveen Div Adv Muni 3	NZF	A+	14.92	B / 7.9	21.16 / 80	8.90 / 67	--	6.44	B- / 7.7	-5.33	-6.75
MUN	MuniYield Insured Fund	MYI	A	15.14	B / 7.9	22.18 / 83	8.40 / 62	11.03 / 83	6.30	B- / 7.7	-5.02	-7.28
MUN	Nuveen Quality Inc Muni	NQU	B-	14.45	C+ / 5.6	16.54 / 64	6.70 / 40	8.84 / 63	6.10	B- / 7.7	-8.14	-7.85
MUN	Salomon Br Municipal Partners II	MPT	B-	13.50	C+ / 6.2	14.56 / 55	7.69 / 55	9.65 / 70	6.00	B- / 7.7	-9.70	-12.28
MUS	MuniYield NY Insured Fund	MYN	B-	13.57	C+ / 6.3	17.64 / 67	6.66 / 40	10.19 / 75	6.18	B- / 7.7	-8.93	-11.36
MUS	Nuveen CA Div Adv Muni 3	NZH	B-	13.96	C+ / 6.9	19.43 / 75	7.62 / 53	--	6.16	B- / 7.7	-8.82	-9.70
MUS	Nuveen MI Div Adv Muni	NZW	B-	15.57	C+ / 6.1	22.12 / 83	7.40 / 50	--	5.50	B- / 7.7	-0.32	0.10
MUN	Morgan Stanley Insured Muni Sec	IMS	C+	14.48	C / 4.5	14.43 / 55	5.70 / 28	8.24 / 57	4.34	B- / 7.7	-6.70	-8.91
MUN	Van Kampen Muni Income	VMT	C+	9.09	C / 4.8	11.59 / 44	7.62 / 53	7.48 / 50	5.74	B- / 7.7	-13.84	-12.55
MUN	Van Kampen Muni Opp II	VOT	C+	13.60	C- / 4.0	13.83 / 52	5.45 / 24	10.86 / 81	6.05	B- / 7.7	-11.75	-9.23
MUS	Eaton Vance NJ Muni Inc Tr	EVJ	C+	14.87	C- / 4.2	8.92 / 34	7.56 / 52	13.67 / 95	5.63	B- / 7.7	-3.25	0.56
MUS	Nuveen NY Select Tax-Free Inc Port	NXN	C+	14.15	C / 5.0	16.48 / 63	6.15 / 34	7.32 / 49	4.28	B- / 7.7	-3.08	-5.55
MUS	Van Kampen CA Qual Muni	VQC	C+	16.40	C / 4.7	15.83 / 61	6.36 / 37	8.86 / 63	5.91	B- / 7.7	-5.15	-4.95
MUS	Van Kampen CA Val Muni Inc	VCV	C+	15.26	C / 4.5	13.47 / 51	6.19 / 35	8.91 / 64	5.79	B- / 7.7	-10.76	-9.62
MUN	Morgan Stanley Insured Muni Bond	IMB	C	13.98	C- / 3.5	11.69 / 44	5.27 / 23	7.41 / 50	5.45	B- / 7.7	-11.57	-11.02
MUN	Municipal Advantage Fund	MAF	C	12.95	C- / 4.0	12.57 / 48	6.30 / 36	10.05 / 74	5.57	B- / 7.7	-13.32	-12.68
MUS	Nuveen MI Quality Inc Muni	NUM	C	15.86	C- / 3.7	15.80 / 60	5.98 / 33	9.50 / 69	5.37	B- / 7.7	-1.73	0.12
MTG	American Strat Inc Portfolio II	BSP	D	11.64	E / 0.3	-0.84 / 5	3.61 / 5	10.21 / 43	8.22	B- / 7.7	-5.67	-1.74

N/A denotes number is not available

99 Pct = Best
0 Pct = Worst

Fund Type	Fund Name	Ticker Symbol	Overall Weiss Investment Rating	Price As of 6/30/05	PERFORMANCE: Performance Rating/Pts	Annualized Total Return Through 6/30/05: 1Yr/Pct	3Yr/Pct	5Yr/Pct	Dividend Yield %	RISK: Risk Rating/Pts	VALUATION: Premium/Discount As of 6/30/05	1 Year Average
FO	iShares MSCI Germany Index	EWG	**E-**	17.65	**D- / 1.4**	13.16 / 32	7.91 / 22	-3.03 / 7	1.10	**E- / 0.0**	-0.23	-0.01
FO	iShares MSCI Netherlands Index	EWN	**E-**	18.40	**E+ / 0.6**	13.65 / 34	3.75 / 5	-4.35 / 6	1.40	**E- / 0.0**	-0.33	0.16
FO	iShares MSCI Taiwan Index	EWT	**E-**	12.34	**D+ / 2.4**	15.89 / 39	6.27 / 14	-6.91 / 5	0.66	**E- / 0.0**	-1.52	-0.08
GR	iShares Goldman Sachs Software Indx	IGV	**E-**	38.38	**D+ / 2.6**	3.02 / 9	12.04 / 56	--	0.20	**E- / 0.0**	0.08	-0.05
GR	HOLDRS B2B Internet	BHH	**E-**	2.00	**E- / 0.0**	-9.46 / 1	-8.09 / 0	-43.03 / 0	14.73	**E- / 0.0**	0.00	N/A
GR	HOLDRS Semiconductor	SMH	**E-**	34.10	**E / 0.3**	-8.22 / 1	4.07 / 6	-18.30 / 1	0.09	**E- / 0.0**	0.00	N/A
PM	ASA Limited	ASA	**E-**	38.59	**D / 1.8**	8.40 / 20	8.77 / 28	22.47 / 97	1.55	**E- / 0.0**	-11.14	-12.48
FO	HOLDRS TeleBras	TBH	**E+**	30.45	**C+ / 6.3**	16.96 / 42	14.75 / 72	-17.92 / 2	0.87	**E- / 0.0**	0.00	N/A
FO	iShares MSCI Sweden Index	EWD	**D-**	20.25	**B / 7.7**	17.74 / 43	21.38 / 92	-3.70 / 7	0.73	**E- / 0.0**	-1.79	0.21
FO	iShares MSCI South Korea Index	EWY	**D-**	32.68	**B / 7.7**	36.30 / 87	14.78 / 72	9.70 / 39	0.31	**E- / 0.0**	0.25	0.18
GR	HOLDRS Broadband	BDH	**D-**	15.33	**B- / 7.2**	-4.47 / 3	22.85 / 94	-29.76 / 0	0.01	**E- / 0.0**	0.00	N/A
GR	HOLDRS Internet Infrastructure	IIH	**D-**	4.05	**B- / 7.4**	10.36 / 25	21.65 / 92	-41.59 / 0	0.00	**E- / 0.0**	0.00	N/A
EN	HOLDRS Oil Services	OIH	**D+**	102.90	**A / 9.3**	44.01 / 97	19.31 / 87	--	0.88	**E- / 0.0**	0.00	N/A
FO	iShares MSCI Brazil Index	EWZ	**C-**	23.94	**A+ / 9.9**	68.67 / 99	37.41 / 98	--	1.86	**E- / 0.0**	-0.42	N/A
FO	iShares S&P Latin American 40 Idx	ILF	**C-**	90.69	**A+ / 9.8**	58.53 / 99	32.02 / 97	--	1.01	**E- / 0.0**	0.49	0.58
FO	Thai Capital Fund	TF	**C-**	9.52	**A+ / 9.7**	40.61 / 94	34.72 / 98	7.77 / 30	0.45	**E / 0.3**	9.68	-1.69
FO	iShares MSCI Belgium Index	EWK	**D-**	17.81	**C+ / 6.5**	27.44 / 68	18.44 / 85	9.05 / 35	1.59	**E / 0.4**	-1.17	0.38
FO	Brazil Fund	BZF	**C-**	37.10	**A+ / 9.9**	80.66 / 99	46.52 / 99	21.10 / 96	2.06	**E+ / 0.6**	-5.50	-9.82
GR	streetTRACKS MS Technology Index	MTK	**E**	47.33	**D+ / 2.8**	-1.87 / 5	12.52 / 60	--	0.05	**E+ / 0.7**	-0.17	-0.02
FO	Thai Fund	TTF	**C-**	9.69	**A / 9.4**	22.58 / 56	28.98 / 96	14.23 / 66	1.31	**E+ / 0.7**	16.89	11.36
GI	Renaissance Cap Growth & Inc III	RENN	**E+**	11.25	**C / 4.3**	-2.37 / 4	16.31 / 78	4.82 / 20	3.46	**E+ / 0.8**	-17.40	-16.91
FO	Turkish Investment Fund	TKF	**C**	15.89	**A+ / 9.9**	74.90 / 99	55.92 / 99	7.67 / 29	0.49	**E+ / 0.8**	8.61	11.87
FO	iShares MSCI EMU Index	EZU	**E**	70.36	**C- / 3.0**	16.78 / 41	11.67 / 52	--	1.83	**D- / 1.0**	-0.61	0.17
FO	Third Canadian General Invst Tr	T.THD	**C-**	28.95	**A- / 9.1**	37.81 / 91	22.53 / 93	19.75 / 93	1.03	**D- / 1.1**	-21.67	-15.44
FO	Korea Fund	KF	**C**	27.28	**A / 9.5**	49.47 / 98	22.48 / 93	20.11 / 93	1.65	**D- / 1.1**	-6.35	-7.95
COH	Prospect Street High Inc Portfolio	PHY	**E-**	3.40	**D- / 1.5**	23.31 / 58	3.40 / 4	2.95 / 17	8.72	**D- / 1.2**	-5.03	0.64
FO	Greater China Fund	GCH	**D+**	16.20	**B- / 7.5**	20.92 / 51	19.96 / 89	14.29 / 66	1.28	**D- / 1.2**	-12.24	-9.26
FO	Indonesia Fund	IF	**C**	5.75	**A+ / 9.8**	56.91 / 99	40.95 / 99	11.75 / 52	3.08	**D- / 1.2**	-5.12	-1.13
GR	iShares Goldman Sachs Technology	IGM	**E-**	43.46	**D- / 1.2**	-4.23 / 3	9.23 / 33	--	0.04	**D- / 1.3**	0.12	0.04
FO	iShares MSCI France Index	EWQ	**E**	23.82	**D+ / 2.8**	14.84 / 37	10.58 / 43	-2.06 / 9	1.25	**D- / 1.3**	0.13	0.11
IN	Cornerstone Total Return Fund	CRF	**D**	15.48	**C+ / 6.5**	5.10 / 12	18.82 / 86	13.29 / 61	13.45	**D- / 1.3**	35.79	35.33
FO	JF China Region Fund	JFC	**C-**	12.82	**B / 8.2**	13.35 / 33	22.94 / 94	10.41 / 44	0.00	**D- / 1.3**	-13.79	-9.84
EM	Templeton Emerging Markets Fd	EMF	**C**	17.48	**A / 9.4**	45.84 / 98	24.37 / 95	14.27 / 66	1.06	**D- / 1.3**	1.92	0.88
GL	iShares S&P Global Technology Sect	IXN	**E-**	48.77	**D- / 1.1**	-2.82 / 4	8.50 / 25	--	1.29	**D- / 1.4**	0.06	0.36
GR	iShares Dow Jones US Technology	IYW	**E-**	46.09	**D- / 1.4**	-2.13 / 5	9.11 / 32	-18.16 / 1	0.23	**D- / 1.4**	0.11	0.03
GR	Tuxis Corporation	TUX	**E-**	0.00	**E- / 0.1**	13.14 / 31	-3.52 / 0	2.02 / 15	0.00	**D- / 1.4**		-18.64
GR	iShares Goldman Sachs Ntwr Index Fd	IGN	**D**	27.70	**B- / 7.0**	-10.27 / 0	22.96 / 94	--	0.00	**D- / 1.4**	-0.14	-0.06
GR	SPDR Technology	XLK	**E-**	19.99	**D- / 1.5**	-0.49 / 5	9.20 / 32	-17.59 / 2	0.56	**D- / 1.5**	0.15	-0.01
GR	iShares Goldman Sachs Semicon Index	IGW	**E-**	53.60	**E- / 0.2**	-8.12 / 1	3.81 / 5	--	0.00	**D / 1.6**	0.00	N/A
GR	NAIC Growth Fund	GRF	**E-**	8.55	**E- / 0.0**	-3.56 / 4	-3.63 / 0	-1.25 / 10	3.57	**D / 1.6**	-10.66	-14.29
HL	iShares Biotechnology Index Fund	IBB	**E-**	67.57	**D- / 1.1**	-8.95 / 1	9.83 / 37	--	0.00	**D / 1.6**	0.04	-0.02
GL	Morgan Stanley Global Opp Bond Fund	MGB	**E+**	7.80	**C / 4.4**	13.93 / 35	15.54 / 75	7.85 / 31	7.10	**D / 1.6**	-4.06	8.79
FO	Germany Fund	GER	**E-**	7.77	**E+ / 0.6**	15.30 / 38	4.42 / 6	6.71 / 5	0.32	**D / 1.7**	-12.30	-12.99
GI	Canadian World Fund Limited	T.CWF	**E+**	4.10	**C- / 3.2**	19.88 / 50	12.24 / 58	-3.89 / 6	0.00	**D / 1.7**	-25.86	-24.04
FO	iShares MSCI Mexico Index	EWW	**C**	26.57	**A / 9.4**	37.42 / 90	24.74 / 95	12.44 / 56	1.02	**D / 1.7**	-0.30	0.05
GR	iShares Dow Jones US Telecom	IYZ	**E**	23.19	**D+ / 2.5**	12.77 / 31	9.88 / 37	-15.69 / 3	2.27	**D / 1.8**	0.17	0.02
FO	iShares MSCI Spain Index	EWP	**D+**	33.76	**B- / 7.2**	21.92 / 54	21.56 / 92	7.09 / 28	1.79	**D / 1.8**	-0.27	0.09
FO	New Germany Fund	GF	**C**	9.18	**B+ / 8.9**	27.62 / 69	24.15 / 95	-6.33 / 5	3.00	**D / 1.8**	-14.37	-15.27
FO	Spain Fund	SNF	**C**	12.45	**B+ / 8.7**	27.50 / 68	22.65 / 93	9.16 / 36	8.24	**D / 2.0**	26.14	22.87
GR	Nasdaq 100 Trust Series I	QQQQ	**E+**	36.97	**D+ / 2.8**	0.07 / 6	12.71 / 61	-16.75 / 2	0.19	**D / 2.1**	0.03	0.01
FO	Korea Equity Fund	KEF	**C**	6.99	**A- / 9.0**	46.54 / 98	18.70 / 85	13.26 / 61	0.00	**D / 2.1**	-5.67	-8.49
FO	Malaysia Fund	MF	**E+**	5.64	**D+ / 2.6**	8.35 / 20	11.95 / 56	5.02 / 21	0.69	**D / 2.2**	-2.25	-1.64

N/A denotes number is not available

99 Pct = Best
0 Pct = Worst

					PERFORMANCE					RISK	VALUATION	
						Annualized Total Return Through 6/30/05					Premium/Discount	
Fund Type	Fund Name	Ticker Symbol	Overall Weiss Investment Rating	Price As of 6/30/05	Performance Rating/Pts	1Yr/Pct	3Yr/Pct	5Yr/Pct	Dividend Yield %	Risk Rating/ Pts	As of 6/30/05	1 Year Average
GR	Royce Micro-Cap Trust	RMT	**D-**	13.59	**C / 5.3**	14.30 / 35	16.09 / 77	20.17 / 93	8.93	**D / 2.2**	1.87	1.45
FO	Templeton Russia&East European Fund	TRF	**C+**	40.02	**A+ / 9.8**	28.90 / 72	38.99 / 99	28.72 / 99	0.00	**D / 2.2**	4.87	2.42
FO	China Fund	CHN	**C+**	28.73	**A+ / 9.6**	16.58 / 40	35.45 / 98	29.04 / 99	0.69	**D+ / 2.3**	11.70	17.54
FO	Morgan Stanley India Inv Fund	IIF	**C+**	33.42	**A+ / 9.9**	65.14 / 99	54.11 / 99	29.60 / 99	0.47	**D+ / 2.3**	6.74	2.57
FO	Morgan Stanley Eastern Europe	RNE	**C+**	29.85	**A+ / 9.8**	31.07 / 77	38.86 / 99	23.47 / 98	0.00	**D+ / 2.3**	-5.72	-8.93
FO	Japan Smaller Cap Fund Inc.	JOF	**E**	10.78	**E+ / 0.7**	-18.40 / 0	10.50 / 42	5.36 / 22	0.00	**D+ / 2.4**	-7.94	5.57
FO	Central Europe & Russia Fund	CEE	**C+**	31.40	**A+ / 9.8**	46.25 / 98	34.81 / 98	18.50 / 90	0.55	**D+ / 2.4**	-6.91	-10.15
FO	iShares MSCI Italy Index	EWI	**D-**	24.22	**C / 4.9**	17.78 / 44	16.79 / 79	2.46 / 15	2.61	**D+ / 2.5**	-0.49	0.08
FO	Templeton Dragon Fund	TDF	**C+**	17.99	**A / 9.5**	32.87 / 80	28.90 / 96	23.12 / 97	0.78	**D+ / 2.5**	-9.37	-10.70
GR	iShares Russell 2000 Growth	IWO	**E**	63.50	**D / 2.1**	2.99 / 9	10.47 / 42	--	0.47	**D+ / 2.6**	-0.66	-0.06
GR	HOLDRS Internet Architecture	IAH	**E**	34.23	**D / 1.6**	-1.73 / 5	10.35 / 41	-17.65 / 2	0.18	**D+ / 2.6**	0.00	N/A
GR	HOLDRS Software	SWH	**E**	34.96	**D / 2.0**	3.03 / 9	10.27 / 40	--	0.05	**D+ / 2.6**	0.00	N/A
FO	Taiwan Fund	TWN	**E+**	13.69	**C- / 3.5**	23.73 / 59	7.32 / 19	-6.06 / 5	0.22	**D+ / 2.6**	-12.13	-11.53
FO	Latin America Equity Fund	LAQ	**C+**	23.00	**A+ / 9.7**	64.53 / 99	29.30 / 97	14.45 / 67	1.97	**D+ / 2.6**	-13.63	-13.99
FO	Latin American Discovery Fund	LDF	**C+**	20.01	**A+ / 9.8**	63.53 / 99	34.65 / 98	16.12 / 79	0.22	**D+ / 2.6**	-12.81	-13.21
FO	Europe Fund	EF	**E+**	10.54	**D+ / 2.4**	8.79 / 21	10.62 / 43	-0.21 / 12	7.34	**D+ / 2.7**	-10.68	-7.75
GR	HOLDRS Internet	HHH	**C**	55.94	**A- / 9.0**	-10.32 / 0	32.31 / 97	-12.11 / 3	0.00	**D+ / 2.7**	0.00	N/A
EM	Morgan Stanley Emerging Markets	MSF	**C+**	18.11	**A / 9.3**	39.60 / 93	24.43 / 95	8.67 / 34	0.37	**D+ / 2.7**	-11.62	-9.89
GR	Gabelli Equity Trust	GAB	**E**	8.93	**D / 1.9**	17.44 / 43	6.27 / 14	6.72 / 27	8.04	**D+ / 2.8**	7.20	6.22
FO	iShares MSCI Austria Index	EWO	**C+**	23.33	**A+ / 9.7**	39.40 / 92	37.92 / 99	25.33 / 98	0.36	**D+ / 2.8**	-0.34	0.14
FO	Mexico Fund	MXF	**C+**	23.65	**A- / 9.0**	30.29 / 75	22.24 / 93	18.97 / 91	0.17	**D+ / 2.8**	-12.70	-12.52
GL	Aberdeen Australia Equity Fund	IAF	**C+**	12.20	**A+ / 9.6**	51.75 / 99	31.89 / 97	20.13 / 93	8.55	**D+ / 2.8**	4.18	-2.98
FO	iShares MSCI Hong Kong Index	EWH	**D+**	12.32	**C+ / 6.1**	27.66 / 69	13.61 / 66	1.88 / 14	2.19	**D+ / 2.9**	-0.81	0.12
GR	iShares Dow Jones US Basic Mtrls	IYM	**E**	46.50	**E / 0.3**	6.10 / 13	6.05 / 13	7.82 / 31	1.75	**C- / 3.0**	-0.13	0.02
FO	iShares MSCI Malaysia Index	EWM	**E+**	6.99	**D / 2.0**	10.78 / 26	8.95 / 30	4.00 / 19	2.28	**C- / 3.0**	0.00	0.23
COH	New America High Income Fund	HYB	**D-**	2.13	**C / 4.7**	22.92 / 57	11.22 / 48	3.86 / 18	9.91	**C- / 3.0**	-0.93	-4.00
IN	Cornerstone Strategic Value Fund	CLM	**D**	7.17	**C / 5.5**	-3.77 / 3	18.63 / 85	-1.50 / 10	14.52	**C- / 3.0**	22.77	27.68
GI	TCW Convertible Securities Fund	CVT	**E**	5.09	**E- / 0.0**	9.29 / 22	-0.90 / 1	-3.58 / 7	8.06	**C- / 3.1**	-7.62	-9.26
GL	Z-Seven Fund	ZSEV	**E**	4.35	**E- / 0.0**	7.94 / 18	0.39 / 1	-10.13 / 3	0.00	**C- / 3.1**	-21.20	-17.66
GR	SPDR Materials	XLB	**E**	27.34	**D- / 1.0**	5.89 / 13	7.84 / 22	9.58 / 39	2.08	**C- / 3.2**	0.00	N/A
FO	Mexico Equity & Income Fund	MXE	**C+**	17.16	**A / 9.4**	42.76 / 96	26.45 / 96	11.88 / 52	0.00	**C- / 3.2**	-13.68	-11.42
GR	SPDR Consumer Discretionary	XLY	**E**	32.84	**E+ / 0.9**	3.83 / 10	6.86 / 16	5.95 / 25	0.60	**C- / 3.3**	-0.06	0.02
GR	streetTRACKS DJ US Small Cap Growth	DSG	**E+**	74.74	**C- / 3.2**	8.80 / 21	11.91 / 55	--	0.42	**C- / 3.3**	-0.07	0.04
GL	iShares S&P Global Telecomm Sect	IXP	**D-**	49.24	**C- / 3.6**	11.92 / 29	13.07 / 63	--	1.35	**C- / 3.3**	0.29	0.32
COH	Pacholder High Yield Fund	PHF	**C**	9.68	**B / 8.1**	20.22 / 50	19.28 / 87	9.93 / 41	9.50	**C- / 3.3**	6.37	3.23
FO	iShares S&P Europe 350 Index Fund	IEV	**E+**	74.40	**C- / 3.1**	14.75 / 37	11.71 / 53	--	1.81	**C- / 3.4**	-0.32	0.35
GR	iShares Russell 2000	IWM	**D-**	62.21	**C- / 3.4**	8.03 / 19	12.43 / 59	5.00 / 21	0.92	**C- / 3.4**	-0.70	-0.05
COH	Credit Suisse Asset Mgmt Income	CIK	**D+**	4.65	**C / 5.4**	24.21 / 60	10.32 / 41	5.52 / 23	9.91	**C- / 3.4**	7.89	0.80
COH	Blackrock High Income Shares	HIS	**C-**	2.84	**C+ / 6.3**	22.34 / 55	14.92 / 73	-1.37 / 10	9.89	**C- / 3.4**	5.97	0.81
FO	India Fund	IFN	**B-**	30.50	**A+ / 9.9**	50.84 / 99	50.94 / 99	18.32 / 89	5.09	**C- / 3.5**	1.63	0.14
FO	iShares S&P/Topix 150 Index Fund	ITF	**E**	88.09	**E+ / 0.6**	-2.85 / 4	6.76 / 15	--	0.39	**C- / 3.6**	-0.22	0.14
GR	HOLDRS Telecom	TTH	**E**	27.02	**E- / 0.1**	7.27 / 16	2.01 / 2	-15.79 / 2	0.21	**C- / 3.6**	0.00	N/A
GL	PIMCO Strategic Glob Gov Fund	RCS	**C-**	12.67	**C+ / 6.6**	31.45 / 78	12.24 / 58	17.00 / 84	7.28	**C- / 3.6**	16.45	7.98
COH	Dreyfus High Yield Strategies Fund	DHF	**D**	4.37	**C / 4.5**	8.61 / 20	15.11 / 74	-1.31 / 10	8.92	**C- / 3.7**	-6.02	-1.41
HL	H&Q Healthcare Investors	HQH	**D**	17.65	**C / 4.3**	12.32 / 30	12.46 / 59	2.83 / 16	7.95	**C- / 3.7**	-2.00	-2.06
GR	Royce Value Trust	RVT	**D+**	18.70	**C / 4.9**	19.03 / 47	15.67 / 76	18.25 / 88	8.47	**C- / 3.7**	7.35	6.58
FS	iShares S&P Global Financials Sect	IXG	**E+**	65.00	**D+ / 2.4**	11.20 / 27	10.18 / 39	--	1.37	**C- / 3.8**	0.32	0.23
GR	iShares S&P SmallCap 600/BarraValue	IJS	**D-**	60.43	**C- / 3.2**	13.24 / 32	11.52 / 51	--	0.70	**C- / 3.8**	-0.21	-0.05

N/A denotes number is not available

Section VII

Top-Rated Closed-End Mutual Funds by Risk Category

A compilation of those

Closed-End Mutual Funds

receiving the highest Weiss Investment Ratings

within each risk grade.

Funds are listed in order by Overall Weiss Investment Rating.

Section VII Contents

This section contains a summary analysis of the top 100 rated closed-end mutual funds within each risk grade. Based on your personal risk tolerance, each page shows those funds that have achieved the best financial performance over the past three years.

Take the Investor Profile Quiz on page 333 of the Appendix for assistance in determining your own risk tolerance level. Then you can use this section to identify those funds that are most appropriate for your investing style.

Note that increased risk does not always mean increased performance. Most of the riskiest mutual funds in the E (Very Weak) Risk Rating category have also provided very poor returns to their shareholders. Funds in the D and E Risk Rating categories generally represent speculative ventures that should not be entered into lightly.

1. Fund Type The mutual fund's peer category based on an analysis of its investment portfolio.

COH	Corporate – High Yield	HL	Health
COI	Corporate – Inv. Grade	IN	Income
EM	Emerging Market	LP	Loan Participation
EN	Energy/Natural Resources	MTG	Mortgage
FS	Financial Services	MUH	Municipal – High Yield
FO	Foreign	MUN	Municipal – National
GEI	General – Inv. Grade	MUS	Municipal – Single State
GEN	General Bond	PM	Precious Metals
GL	Global	USA	U.S. Gov. – Agency
GR	Growth	UT	Utilities
GI	Growth and Income		

A blank fund type means that the mutual fund has not yet been categorized.

2. Fund Name The name of the mutual fund as stated in its prospectus, which can sometimes differ slightly from the name that the company uses for advertising. If you cannot find the particular mutual fund you are interested in, or if you have any doubts regarding the precise name, verify the information with your broker or on your account statement. Also, use the fund's ticker symbol for confirmation. (See column 3.)

3. Ticker Symbol The unique alphabetic symbol used for identifying and trading a specific mutual fund. No two funds can have the same ticker symbol.

A handful of funds currently show no associated ticker symbol. This means that the fund is either small or new since the NASD only assigns a ticker symbol to funds with at least $25 million in assets or 1,000 shareholders.

4.	**Overall Weiss Investment Rating**	Our overall rating is measured on a scale from A to E based on each fund's risk-adjusted performance. Please see page 10 for specific descriptions of each letter grade. Also, refer to page 7 for information on how our ratings are derived. Most important, when using this rating, please be sure to consider the warnings beginning on page 11 regarding the ratings' limitations and the underlying assumptions.
5.	**Price**	Closing price of the fund on the date shown.
6.	**Performance Rating/Points**	A letter grade rating based solely on the mutual fund's financial performance over the trailing three years, without any consideration for the amount of risk the fund poses. Like the overall Weiss Investment Rating, the Performance Rating is measured on a scale from A to E for ease of interpretation. The points score indicates where the Performance Rating falls on a scale of 0 to 10.
7.	**1-Year Total Return**	The total return the fund has provided investors over the preceeding 52 weeks. This total return figure is computed based on the fund's dividend distributions and share price appreciation/depreciation during the period, net of the expenses and fees it imposes on its shareholders.
8.	**1-Year Total Return Percentile**	The fund's percentile rank based on its one-year performance compared to that of all other closed-end funds in existence for at least one year. A score of 99 is the best possible, indicating that the fund outperformed 99% of the closed-end mutual funds. Zero is the worst possible percentile score.
9.	**3-Year Total Return**	The total annual return the fund has provided investors over the preceeding 156 weeks.
10.	**3-Year Total Return Percentile**	The fund's percentile rank based on its three-year performance compared to that of all other closed-end funds in existence for at least three years. A score of 99 is the best possible, indicating that the fund outperformed 99% of the closed-end mutual funds. Zero is the worst possible percentile score.
11.	**5-Year Total Return**	The total annual return the fund has provided investors over the preceeding 260 weeks.
12.	**5-Year Total Return Percentile**	The fund's percentile rank based on its five-year performance compared to that of all other closed-end funds in existence for at least five years. A score of 99 is the best possible, indicating that the fund outperformed 99% of the closed-end mutual funds. Zero is the worst possible percentile score.

13. Dividend Yield

Most recent quarterly dividend to fund investors annualized, expressed as a percent of the fund's current share price. The dividend yield of a fund can have little correlation to the amount of dividends the fund has received from its underlying investments. Rather, dividend distributions are based on a fund's need to pass earnings from both dividends and gains on the sale of investments along to shareholders. Thus, these dividend distributions are included as a part of the fund's total return.

Keep in mind that dividend income may be taxed at a different rate than capital gains depending on your income tax bracket.

14. Risk Rating/Points

A letter grade rating based solely on the mutual fund's risk as determined by its monthly performance volatility over the trailing three years. The risk rating does not take into consideration the overall financial performance the fund has achieved or the total return it has provided to its shareholders. Like the overall Weiss Investment Rating, the Risk Rating is measured on a scale from A to E for ease of interpretation. The points score indicates where the Risk Rating falls on a scale of 0 to 10.

15. Premium/ Discount

A comparison of the fund's price to its NAV as of the date indicated. The premium (+) or discount (-) indicates the percentage the shares are trading above or below the fund's NAV per share.

If the price is above the fund's NAV, the fund is said to be trading at a premium. If the price is lower than the fund's NAV, the fund is trading at a discount.

16. 1-Year Average Premium/ Discount

The average of the fund's premium/discount over the preceeding year.

It can be useful to compare the fund's current premium/discount to its one-year average. If the fund is currently trading at a premium/discount that is lower/higher than its one-year average, then there has been less demand for the fund in more recent times than over the past year. Conversely, if the fund is currently trading at a premium/discount that is higher/lower than its one-year average, this indicates that there has been greater demand for the fund in more recent times than over the past year.

99 Pct = Best
0 Pct = Worst

Fund Type	Fund Name	Ticker Symbol	Overall Weiss Investment Rating	Price As of 6/30/05	PERFORMANCE: Performance Rating/Pts	Annualized Total Return Through 6/30/05: 1Yr/Pct	3Yr/Pct	5Yr/Pct	Dividend Yield %	RISK: Risk Rating/Pts	VALUATION: Premium/Discount As of 6/30/05	1 Year Average
MUN	Scudder Strategic Municipal Inc Tr	KSM	**A+**	13.66	**A+ / 9.6**	26.81 / 95	13.43 / 90	12.44 / 91	6.47	**B- / 7.1**	9.11	2.56
MUN	MuniHoldings Fund	MHD	**A+**	16.71	**A / 9.5**	25.09 / 92	14.87 / 94	12.17 / 90	6.87	**B- / 7.2**	1.21	-1.27
MUN	MuniAssets Fund	MUA	**A+**	13.45	**A / 9.3**	28.55 / 97	11.50 / 83	10.73 / 80	6.08	**B- / 7.2**	-0.30	-3.95
MUN	MuniYield Fund	MYD	**A+**	14.99	**A- / 9.2**	29.19 / 97	11.30 / 81	11.40 / 86	6.66	**B- / 7.4**	0.54	-3.62
MUN	MuniVest Fund	MVF	**A+**	9.94	**A- / 9.1**	26.19 / 94	11.34 / 82	12.89 / 93	6.68	**B- / 7.1**	-2.83	-6.26
MUS	BlackRock NY Muni Bond Trust	BQH	**A+**	15.21	**B+ / 8.9**	24.76 / 91	10.54 / 78	--	6.04	**B- / 7.0**	-5.06	-8.31
MUN	MuniYield Quality Fund II	MQT	**A+**	13.37	**B+ / 8.9**	24.18 / 89	11.04 / 80	10.17 / 75	6.41	**B- / 7.2**	-3.33	-7.60
FO	iShares MSCI Pacific ex-Japan Idx	EPP	**A+**	94.11	**B+ / 8.8**	34.03 / 83	21.35 / 91	--	3.20	**B- / 7.0**	-0.14	0.31
MUN	Nuveen Dividend Advantage Muni 2	NXZ	**A+**	16.00	**B+ / 8.8**	23.48 / 87	11.25 / 81	--	6.43	**B- / 7.3**	-0.99	-2.92
MUN	Apex Municipal Fund	APX	**A+**	9.36	**B+ / 8.6**	21.50 / 81	10.92 / 80	7.95 / 55	6.08	**B- / 7.6**	-4.49	-6.68
MUN	PIMCO Municipal Income Fund	PMF	**A+**	15.54	**B+ / 8.6**	27.28 / 95	9.08 / 68	--	6.18	**B- / 7.6**	2.85	0.04
MUN	Alliance Nat Municipal Income Fund	AFB	**A+**	14.90	**B+ / 8.5**	22.30 / 84	10.26 / 76	--	6.09	**B- / 7.6**	-5.99	-8.51
MUS	Alliance CA Municipal Income Fund	AKP	**A+**	14.87	**B / 8.1**	21.46 / 81	9.61 / 72	--	5.87	**B- / 7.8**	-4.74	-6.59
MUN	BlackRock Municipal 2018 Income Tr	BPK	**A+**	15.70	**B / 8.0**	17.99 / 69	10.98 / 80	--	4.92	**B- / 7.9**	-1.32	-4.38
MUN	Nuveen Div Adv Muni 3	NZF	**A+**	14.92	**B / 7.9**	21.16 / 80	8.90 / 67	--	6.44	**B- / 7.7**	-5.33	-6.75
MUS	MuniHoldings NJ Insured Fund	MUJ	**A**	15.59	**B+ / 8.6**	21.69 / 82	10.87 / 79	13.40 / 95	6.04	**B- / 7.0**	-1.45	-4.36
MUS	BlackRock CA Municipal Income Trust	BFZ	**A**	14.55	**B+ / 8.4**	22.97 / 86	9.62 / 72	--	6.19	**B- / 7.1**	-5.58	-7.79
MUS	BlackRock NJ Municipal Income Trust	BNJ	**A**	15.39	**B / 8.1**	21.66 / 81	8.85 / 66	--	5.74	**B- / 7.1**	-4.29	-6.65
MUS	Nuveen CA Div Adv Muni	NAC	**A**	15.59	**B / 8.0**	20.04 / 77	9.58 / 72	10.24 / 76	6.35	**B- / 7.2**	-2.44	-4.95
MUN	MuniYield Insured Fund	MYI	**A**	15.14	**B / 7.9**	22.18 / 83	8.40 / 62	11.03 / 83	6.30	**B- / 7.7**	-5.02	-7.28
EN	Petroleum and Resources Corp.	PEO	**A**	30.01	**B / 7.8**	30.76 / 77	15.59 / 76	10.32 / 44	1.74	**B- / 7.3**	-7.94	-7.42
MUN	MuniHoldings Insured Fund	MUS	**A-**	14.29	**B / 8.0**	22.46 / 84	10.10 / 75	11.14 / 84	6.35	**B- / 7.0**	-1.65	-5.00
MUS	MuniHoldings NY Insured Fund	MHN	**A-**	14.96	**B / 8.0**	19.68 / 75	9.24 / 69	12.21 / 90	6.28	**B- / 7.0**	-4.10	-8.13
MUS	BlackRock FL Muni Bond Trust	BIE	**A-**	15.62	**B / 7.9**	25.96 / 93	8.10 / 59	--	5.88	**B- / 7.1**	-3.76	-6.55
MUS	Nuveen Insured NY Div Adv Muni Fund	NKO	**A-**	15.14	**B / 7.7**	22.46 / 84	7.32 / 49	--	5.45	**B- / 7.2**	-5.02	-7.46
MUS	BlackRock CA Muni 2018 Income Trust	BJZ	**A-**	14.99	**B- / 7.4**	17.26 / 65	8.83 / 65	--	4.92	**B- / 7.6**	-2.15	-5.03
MUS	MuniYield CA Insured Fund	MCA	**A-**	14.22	**B- / 7.3**	19.95 / 77	8.19 / 61	7.80 / 53	6.14	**B- / 7.6**	-7.54	-9.95
MUS	BlackRock FL Municipal Income Trust	BBF	**B+**	15.29	**B / 7.8**	26.78 / 95	7.72 / 55	--	5.95	**B- / 7.0**	-2.80	-6.57
MUN	MuniEnhanced Fund	MEN	**B+**	11.43	**B / 7.6**	22.35 / 84	8.36 / 62	10.40 / 78	6.34	**B- / 7.1**	-3.63	-6.84
MUS	BlackRock CA Muni Bond Trust	BZA	**B+**	14.92	**B- / 7.4**	23.34 / 87	7.46 / 51	--	6.38	**B- / 7.3**	-6.57	-6.56
MUN	MuniHoldings Insured Fund II	MUE	**B+**	13.70	**B- / 7.4**	20.27 / 78	8.60 / 64	12.63 / 92	6.38	**B- / 7.2**	-5.58	-8.38
MUS	MuniYield MI Insured Fund II	MYM	**B+**	14.70	**B- / 7.3**	17.41 / 66	9.35 / 70	11.75 / 88	6.03	**B- / 7.0**	-3.10	-5.16
MUS	MuniYield NJ Fund	MYJ	**B+**	15.31	**B- / 7.2**	18.63 / 71	7.88 / 57	10.77 / 80	6.07	**B- / 7.3**	-3.83	-5.91
MUS	Nuveen CA Div Adv Muni 2	NVX	**B+**	14.59	**B- / 7.1**	18.51 / 71	7.87 / 57	--	6.20	**B- / 7.3**	-6.29	-8.09
MUS	Nuveen CA Prem Inc Muni	NCU	**B+**	14.16	**B- / 7.1**	20.44 / 78	7.41 / 50	8.60 / 61	5.94	**B- / 7.1**	-6.04	-7.07
MUN	Nuveen Muni Advantage	NMA	**B+**	15.59	**B- / 7.0**	18.96 / 73	8.25 / 61	11.81 / 88	6.36	**B- / 7.3**	-3.47	-4.09
MUS	Morgan Stanley CA Qual Muni Sec	IQC	**B+**	14.30	**C+ / 5.6**	13.78 / 52	8.77 / 65	8.39 / 58	5.87	**B+ / 9.1**	-9.49	-8.13
MUS	BlackRock NY Muni 2018 Income Trust	BLH	**B**	15.29	**C+ / 6.5**	13.88 / 53	9.75 / 73	--	4.77	**B / 8.4**	-5.91	-5.29
MUN	Morgan Stanley Muni Inc Op II	OIB	**B**	8.14	**C+ / 6.1**	15.00 / 57	7.08 / 46	9.22 / 65	5.84	**B / 8.5**	-9.05	-9.83
MUN	Morgan Stanley Qual Muni Sec	IQM	**B**	14.40	**C+ / 6.0**	14.65 / 56	7.81 / 56	9.93 / 72	5.85	**B / 8.7**	-12.09	-11.77
MUN	Morgan Stanley Insured Muni Inc Tr	IIM	**B**	14.23	**C / 5.4**	12.77 / 49	7.30 / 48	8.24 / 57	5.66	**B / 8.3**	-11.06	-10.70
MUN	Morgan Stanley Qual Muni Inc Tr	IQI	**B**	13.93	**C / 5.2**	12.92 / 50	7.04 / 45	8.46 / 59	5.80	**B / 8.4**	-11.89	-11.31
MUN	Nuveen Muni Value	NUV	**B**	9.57	**C / 5.0**	15.95 / 61	6.06 / 33	8.68 / 62	4.87	**B / 8.8**	-7.71	-8.65
GL	Salomon Br 2008 Wldwide $ Gov Tm Tr	SBG	**B**	11.19	**C- / 3.8**	11.46 / 28	12.18 / 58	14.77 / 70	7.72	**B+ / 9.7**	-2.95	-0.42
MUS	MuniYield MI Insured Fund	MIY	**B-**	15.49	**C+ / 6.9**	17.48 / 66	9.16 / 68	12.54 / 92	6.18	**B- / 7.5**	-3.25	-3.95
MUS	Nuveen CA Div Adv Muni 3	NZH	**B-**	13.96	**C+ / 6.9**	19.43 / 75	7.62 / 53	--	6.16	**B- / 7.7**	-8.82	-9.70
MUN	Nuveen Select Quality Muni	NQS	**B-**	15.12	**C+ / 6.9**	16.52 / 64	8.12 / 59	10.45 / 78	6.29	**B- / 7.5**	-4.91	-5.91
MUS	PIMCO CA Municipal Income Fund	PCQ	**B-**	14.75	**C+ / 6.9**	22.28 / 83	6.62 / 39	--	6.20	**B- / 7.2**	-0.27	-2.31
MUN	Salomon Br Municipal Partners	MNP	**B-**	13.88	**C+ / 6.9**	15.43 / 59	8.34 / 62	9.85 / 71	6.03	**B- / 7.1**	-9.40	-11.98
MUS	Nuveen MA Div Adv Muni	NMB	**B-**	16.80	**C+ / 6.8**	22.16 / 83	6.64 / 39	--	5.20	**B- / 7.1**	7.21	5.48
MUS	Nuveen NJ Div Adv Muni	NXJ	**B-**	15.07	**C+ / 6.8**	18.49 / 71	8.73 / 64	--	5.58	**B- / 7.2**	-3.64	-2.45
MUN	American Municipal Income Portfolio	XAA	**B-**	14.82	**C+ / 6.7**	16.50 / 63	8.60 / 64	11.29 / 85	6.10	**B- / 7.8**	-6.68	-7.07

N/A denotes number is not available

99 Pct = Best
0 Pct = Worst

Fund Type	Fund Name	Ticker Symbol	Overall Weiss Investment Rating	Price As of 6/30/05	PERFORMANCE: Performance Rating/Pts	Annualized Total Return Through 6/30/05: 1Yr/Pct	3Yr/Pct	5Yr/Pct	Dividend Yield %	RISK: Risk Rating/Pts	VALUATION: Premium/Discount As of 6/30/05	1 Year Average
MUS	Nuveen NY Quality Inc Muni	NUN	**B-**	15.00	**C+ / 6.7**	17.82 / 68	7.74 / 56	9.29 / 67	5.59	**B- / 7.2**	-6.25	-7.47
MUN	Nuveen Premium Income Muni 2	NPM	**B-**	14.66	**C+ / 6.7**	18.74 / 72	7.36 / 50	9.58 / 69	6.05	**B- / 7.5**	-6.51	-7.46
MUS	MuniHoldings CA Insured Fund II	MUC	**B-**	14.77	**C+ / 6.6**	18.82 / 73	8.14 / 60	10.53 / 79	6.33	**B- / 7.3**	-4.09	-5.50
MUN	Nuveen Investment Quality Muni	NQM	**B-**	15.15	**C+ / 6.6**	17.73 / 67	7.26 / 48	10.82 / 81	6.07	**B- / 7.1**	-5.61	-6.39
GR	iShares Russell Midcap Value Index	IWS	**B-**	116.86	**C+ / 6.5**	21.09 / 52	16.11 / 77	--	1.44	**B- / 7.0**	-0.09	0.03
MUN	Nuveen Muni Market Opportunity	NMO	**B-**	14.68	**C+ / 6.4**	16.47 / 63	6.94 / 44	9.48 / 68	6.11	**B- / 7.1**	-6.08	-7.81
MUS	MuniYield NY Insured Fund	MYN	**B-**	13.57	**C+ / 6.3**	17.64 / 67	6.66 / 40	10.19 / 75	6.18	**B- / 7.7**	-8.93	-11.36
MUN	Nuveen Div Adv Muni	NAD	**B-**	15.20	**C+ / 6.3**	15.17 / 58	7.25 / 48	11.45 / 87	6.42	**B- / 7.0**	-3.31	-4.47
MUS	BlackRock NY Inv Qual Muni Tr	RNY	**B-**	14.79	**C+ / 6.2**	19.92 / 76	6.58 / 38	9.39 / 68	5.90	**B- / 7.1**	-4.21	-7.45
MUS	Nuveen CA Muni Value	NCA	**B-**	9.90	**C+ / 6.2**	19.66 / 75	6.21 / 35	7.88 / 54	4.69	**B- / 7.1**	-4.07	-8.09
MUN	Salomon Br Municipal Partners II	MPT	**B-**	13.50	**C+ / 6.2**	14.56 / 55	7.69 / 55	9.65 / 70	6.00	**B- / 7.7**	-9.70	-12.28
MUS	Nuveen MI Div Adv Muni	NZW	**B-**	15.57	**C+ / 6.1**	22.12 / 83	7.40 / 50	--	5.50	**B- / 7.7**	-0.32	0.10
MUS	Nuveen NY Investment Quality Muni	NQN	**B-**	15.50	**C+ / 6.1**	18.01 / 70	7.69 / 55	9.84 / 71	5.76	**B- / 7.2**	-4.38	-5.37
MUN	Nuveen Performance Plus Muni	NPP	**B-**	14.79	**C+ / 6.1**	16.40 / 63	6.92 / 44	11.25 / 85	6.25	**B- / 7.4**	-7.97	-8.12
MUS	Eaton Vance CA Muni Inc Tr	CEV	**B-**	14.99	**C+ / 6.0**	12.91 / 50	8.86 / 66	13.67 / 95	5.90	**B- / 7.6**	-5.13	-2.72
MUS	Nuveen CA Inv Quality Muni	NQC	**B-**	15.06	**C+ / 6.0**	19.04 / 74	6.43 / 37	7.27 / 48	5.75	**B- / 7.6**	-5.22	-6.20
MUS	Nuveen CA Muni Market Opportunity	NCO	**B-**	14.99	**C+ / 6.0**	18.54 / 71	6.70 / 40	6.56 / 43	6.06	**B- / 7.3**	-7.13	-7.76
MUN	Nuveen Insured Div Adv Muni Fund	NVG	**B-**	14.70	**C+ / 6.0**	17.38 / 66	6.50 / 38	--	5.74	**B- / 7.5**	-6.96	-7.52
MUS	Nuveen NJ Prem Inc Muni	NNJ	**B-**	15.62	**C+ / 6.0**	19.48 / 75	7.18 / 47	9.80 / 71	5.41	**B- / 7.3**	-2.68	-2.83
MUN	Morgan Stanley Muni Inc Op III	OIC	**B-**	8.86	**C+ / 5.9**	15.95 / 62	6.35 / 36	8.56 / 60	5.73	**B- / 7.8**	-8.57	-10.16
MUN	Nuveen Insured Muni Opportunity	NIO	**B-**	15.65	**C+ / 5.9**	16.42 / 63	7.08 / 46	10.67 / 80	5.69	**B- / 7.0**	-2.86	-3.59
MUS	Nuveen NY Muni Value	NNY	**B-**	9.68	**C+ / 5.9**	17.01 / 65	6.70 / 41	7.80 / 53	4.40	**B- / 7.8**	-4.72	-7.98
MUN	Putnam Municipal Bond Fund	PMG	**B-**	12.74	**C+ / 5.8**	15.85 / 61	7.35 / 49	10.20 / 76	6.13	**B- / 7.5**	-9.19	-8.55
MUN	Nuveen Quality Inc Muni	NQU	**B-**	14.45	**C+ / 5.6**	16.54 / 64	6.70 / 40	8.84 / 63	6.10	**B- / 7.7**	-8.14	-7.85
MUS	Van Kampen FL Qual Muni	VFM	**B-**	14.99	**C+ / 5.6**	16.25 / 62	7.90 / 57	10.07 / 74	5.27	**B- / 7.8**	-11.25	-10.86
MUS	Nuveen CA Select Quality Muni	NVC	**C+**	15.04	**C+ / 5.7**	18.23 / 70	6.82 / 42	7.74 / 52	6.09	**B- / 7.2**	-5.82	-5.83
MUS	Nuveen MI Prem Inc Muni	NMP	**C+**	15.44	**C+ / 5.7**	18.94 / 73	6.94 / 44	10.90 / 82	5.45	**B- / 7.0**	-2.15	-1.91
GEI	BlackRock Core Bond Trust	BHK	**C+**	14.32	**C+ / 5.6**	21.19 / 52	11.45 / 50	--	7.35	**B- / 7.2**	-5.10	-8.09
COH	Colonial Interm High Inc	CIF	**C+**	3.44	**C / 5.5**	15.69 / 39	15.56 / 75	0.76 / 13	9.12	**B- / 7.0**	-7.03	-7.92
MUS	Nuveen CA Performance Plus Muni	NCP	**C+**	14.55	**C / 5.5**	18.17 / 70	6.59 / 39	6.50 / 42	5.82	**B- / 7.4**	-7.79	-7.77
MUN	Colonial Invst Gr Muni Tr	CXH	**C+**	10.49	**C / 5.3**	17.63 / 67	6.19 / 35	9.96 / 73	5.69	**B- / 7.3**	-7.98	-9.78
UT	DNP Select Income Fund Inc	DNP	**C+**	11.70	**C / 5.3**	18.21 / 45	12.65 / 61	11.71 / 51	6.75	**B- / 7.3**	28.29	33.55
MUN	Nuveen Prem Inc Muni	NPI	**C+**	14.33	**C / 5.3**	17.27 / 65	6.47 / 38	10.61 / 79	6.09	**B- / 7.5**	-7.25	-6.83
MUS	Nuveen Insured CA Div Adv Muni Fund	NKL	**C+**	14.77	**C / 5.2**	18.99 / 73	6.44 / 38	--	5.81	**B- / 7.4**	-6.52	-6.09
MUS	Van Kampen NY Qual Muni	VNM	**C+**	14.86	**C / 5.2**	15.48 / 59	6.78 / 41	9.79 / 71	5.38	**B- / 7.4**	-12.95	-11.54
MUS	Nuveen NJ Investment Quality Muni	NQJ	**C+**	15.20	**C / 5.0**	16.02 / 62	7.19 / 47	8.51 / 59	5.74	**B- / 7.6**	-2.63	-0.53
MUS	Nuveen NY Select Tax-Free Inc Port	NXN	**C+**	14.15	**C / 5.0**	16.48 / 63	6.15 / 34	7.32 / 49	4.28	**B- / 7.7**	-3.08	-5.55
MUS	Morgan Stanley NY Qual Muni Sec	IQN	**C+**	13.77	**C / 4.9**	14.43 / 55	6.87 / 43	7.89 / 54	5.42	**B / 8.1**	-12.18	-11.54
MUN	Morgan Stanley Muni Inv Tr	IQT	**C+**	13.91	**C / 4.8**	13.86 / 52	6.24 / 36	7.50 / 51	5.80	**B- / 7.9**	-11.96	-11.68
MUN	Morgan Stanley Muni Prem Inc Tr	PIA	**C+**	9.12	**C / 4.8**	12.22 / 47	6.97 / 45	9.74 / 70	5.87	**B / 8.2**	-13.14	-11.76
MUN	Van Kampen Muni Income	VMT	**C+**	9.09	**C / 4.8**	11.59 / 44	7.62 / 53	7.48 / 50	5.74	**B- / 7.7**	-13.84	-12.55
MUS	Van Kampen CA Qual Muni	VQC	**C+**	16.40	**C / 4.7**	15.83 / 61	6.36 / 37	8.86 / 63	5.91	**B- / 7.7**	-5.15	-4.95
MUN	Van Kampen Invmt Grade Muni	VIG	**C+**	9.06	**C / 4.6**	13.66 / 51	6.44 / 38	6.54 / 42	5.44	**B / 8.1**	-13.55	-13.41
MUS	Eaton Vance MI Muni Inc Tr	EMI	**C+**	15.46	**C / 4.5**	7.95 / 29	10.36 / 77	15.07 / 98	5.48	**B / 8.2**	1.31	7.75
MUN	Morgan Stanley Insured Muni Tr	IMT	**C+**	13.93	**C / 4.4**	13.18 / 51	5.89 / 31	7.31 / 49	5.81	**B / 8.4**	-11.10	-11.00
MUN	Nuveen Select Tax-Free Inc 3	NXR	**C+**	13.44	**C- / 4.2**	11.63 / 44	5.82 / 30	5.95 / 36	4.81	**B / 8.3**	-7.69	-9.01
MUS	Morgan Stanley CA Muni Sec	ICS	**C+**	14.09	**C- / 3.4**	14.23 / 54	5.45 / 25	7.02 / 47	4.66	**B+ / 9.1**	-8.92	-9.56
MUN	Putnam Tax-Free Health Care Fund	PMH	**C+**	12.25	**C- / 3.3**	9.36 / 36	5.71 / 28	6.34 / 40	4.49	**B+ / 9.2**	-13.67	-13.84

N/A denotes number is not available

Fund Type	Fund Name (99 Pct = Best; 0 Pct = Worst)	Ticker Symbol	Overall Weiss Investment Rating	Price As of 6/30/05	PERFORMANCE: Performance Rating/Pts	Annualized Total Return Through 6/30/05: 1Yr/Pct	3Yr/Pct	5Yr/Pct	Dividend Yield %	RISK: Risk Rating/Pts	VALUATION: Premium/Discount As of 6/30/05	1 Year Average
FO	Canadian General Investments Ltd	T.CGI	A+	18.40	A+ / 9.7	47.72 / 98	29.43 / 97	18.56 / 90	1.30	C+ / 6.7	-17.23	-25.05
MUN	BlackRock Investment Qual Muni Tr	BKN	A+	16.61	A+ / 9.6	28.68 / 97	13.47 / 90	12.60 / 92	5.43	C+ / 6.5	4.07	-3.77
MUN	MuniHoldings Fund II	MUH	A+	15.32	A+ / 9.6	27.08 / 95	14.47 / 93	13.96 / 96	6.85	C+ / 6.9	1.26	-1.61
MUN	BlackRock Municipal Bond Trust	BBK	A+	16.09	A / 9.5	28.64 / 97	12.44 / 87	--	6.38	C+ / 6.5	-0.12	-3.63
MUN	MuniVest Fund II	MVT	A+	16.20	A / 9.5	24.93 / 91	14.19 / 92	14.72 / 97	6.81	C+ / 6.8	3.85	0.13
HL	HOLDRS Biotech	BBH	A+	167.30	A / 9.4	16.87 / 41	27.32 / 96	-0.69 / 11	0.00	C+ / 6.6	0.00	N/A
MUN	Eaton Vance Municipal Inc Tr	EVN	A+	16.67	A / 9.3	20.87 / 79	14.78 / 93	17.28 / 99	6.77	C+ / 6.9	14.26	14.05
MUN	BlackRock Strategic Municipal Tr	BSD	A	16.40	A+ / 9.6	31.70 / 98	12.40 / 87	12.47 / 91	5.89	C+ / 5.8	3.34	-6.42
FO	iShares MSCI Australia Index	EWA	A	17.66	A / 9.3	36.87 / 89	24.75 / 95	13.56 / 63	3.25	C+ / 6.2	-0.23	0.25
MUN	BlackRock Municipal Income Trust	BFK	A	15.15	A- / 9.2	28.30 / 96	11.60 / 84	--	6.32	C+ / 6.4	1.07	-1.81
MUS	BlackRock VA Muni Bond Trust	BHV	A	17.27	A- / 9.2	25.93 / 93	11.16 / 81	--	5.11	C+ / 6.4	6.54	1.21
MUS	Eaton Vance NY Muni Inc Tr	EVY	A	16.70	A- / 9.2	27.07 / 95	11.14 / 81	16.66 / 99	5.91	C+ / 6.2	3.28	-2.01
MUN	Scudder Municipal Income Trust	KTF	A	12.74	A- / 9.1	22.60 / 85	11.54 / 83	9.64 / 70	6.28	C+ / 6.5	1.43	-3.63
MUS	MuniYield FL Fund	MYF	A	15.06	A- / 9.0	26.38 / 94	10.66 / 79	13.21 / 94	6.13	C+ / 6.3	-2.40	-7.33
MUS	PIMCO NY Muni Income Fund	PNF	A	14.89	B+ / 8.8	25.83 / 93	8.40 / 63	--	6.00	C+ / 6.3	6.81	0.17
MUS	BlackRock NJ Muni Bond Trust	BLJ	A	15.55	B+ / 8.7	27.66 / 96	8.99 / 67	--	5.98	C+ / 6.5	-3.05	-4.85
MUS	Nuveen PA Div Adv Muni	NXM	A	16.10	B+ / 8.4	22.85 / 85	10.62 / 78	--	5.76	C+ / 6.7	0.94	-0.84
MUS	Nuveen NY Div Adv Muni 2	NXK	A	15.54	B / 8.2	20.88 / 79	10.06 / 75	--	6.04	C+ / 6.9	-2.02	-4.71
GI	iShares Cohen&Steers Realty Major	ICF	A-	70.50	A- / 9.0	33.54 / 82	21.41 / 92	--	5.10	C+ / 5.9	0.09	N/A
MUN	Dreyfus Strategic Muni Bond Fund	DSM	A-	9.25	B+ / 8.8	24.27 / 90	9.07 / 67	10.01 / 73	6.52	C+ / 6.1	1.87	-3.64
MUS	Alliance NY Municipal Income Fund	AYN	A-	14.85	B+ / 8.6	24.47 / 90	9.44 / 71	--	5.61	C+ / 6.4	-4.32	-7.89
MUS	MuniHoldings FL Insured Fund	MFL	A-	15.57	B+ / 8.5	22.65 / 85	10.65 / 79	14.53 / 97	6.34	C+ / 6.5	0.97	-2.25
MUS	MuniYield AZ Fund	MZA	A-	15.76	B+ / 8.5	25.61 / 92	9.35 / 70	14.67 / 97	5.85	C+ / 6.3	4.72	1.03
MUS	BlackRock NY Municipal Income Trust	BNY	A-	15.13	B+ / 8.4	22.85 / 85	9.68 / 72	--	6.00	C+ / 6.5	-3.51	-7.26
MUH	MFS Municipal Income Trust	MFM	A-	8.26	B+ / 8.4	21.69 / 82	9.08 / 67	9.35 / 67	6.63	C+ / 6.5	3.12	-1.25
MUS	Nuveen VA Div Adv Muni 2	NNB	A-	17.00	B+ / 8.4	22.45 / 84	11.14 / 81	--	4.93	C+ / 6.5	7.80	4.97
MUS	Nuveen NC Div Adv Muni	NRB	A-	17.33	B / 8.2	24.75 / 91	10.47 / 78	--	5.33	C+ / 6.7	11.73	7.96
MUS	Delaware Inv CO Ins Muni Inc	VCF	A-	17.64	B / 8.0	23.63 / 87	11.27 / 81	13.19 / 94	5.42	C+ / 6.9	10.53	8.79
FO	Chile Fund	CH	B+	15.03	A+ / 9.7	46.55 / 98	33.72 / 98	17.78 / 87	5.42	C / 4.3	-11.59	-10.68
GL	Scudder Multi-Market Income Trust	KMM	B+	10.21	A- / 9.2	42.62 / 96	21.05 / 91	14.63 / 69	7.72	C / 4.9	5.48	-1.71
FO	The New Ireland Fund	IRL	B+	21.20	A- / 9.2	36.97 / 89	25.91 / 96	14.24 / 66	0.14	C / 5.1	-13.96	-13.38
MUS	BlackRock NJ Inv Qual Muni Tr	RNJ	B+	15.56	B+ / 8.6	25.00 / 92	8.71 / 64	10.64 / 80	5.18	C+ / 5.7	4.92	-1.54
EM	Morgan Stanley Emerging Mkts Debt	MSD	B+	9.97	B+ / 8.6	28.11 / 70	21.23 / 91	18.01 / 88	7.24	C / 5.4	-7.69	-8.26
GI	iShares Dow Jones US Real Estate	IYR	B+	62.82	B+ / 8.5	29.40 / 74	19.09 / 87	18.47 / 89	4.04	C+ / 5.9	-0.49	-0.11
MUN	MuniYield Quality Fund	MQY	B+	15.27	B+ / 8.4	24.12 / 89	9.36 / 71	11.96 / 89	6.31	C+ / 6.3	-1.93	-5.60
MUS	Delaware Inv FL Insured Muni Inc	VFL	B+	16.70	B+ / 8.3	21.90 / 82	10.32 / 76	13.81 / 96	5.73	C+ / 6.1	7.33	2.95
GI	Franklin Multi-Income Trust	FMI	B+	9.35	B+ / 8.3	40.29 / 94	14.65 / 71	11.24 / 48	4.48	C+ / 5.8	-1.89	-9.77
MUS	MuniYield FL Insured Fund	MFT	B+	15.45	B+ / 8.3	24.04 / 89	9.32 / 70	11.93 / 89	5.80	C+ / 6.4	1.11	-3.13
MUS	Nuveen VA Div Adv Muni Fund	NGB	B+	17.47	B+ / 8.3	23.72 / 88	12.22 / 86	--	5.26	C+ / 6.3	12.35	12.71
MUS	Nuveen Insured FL Prem Inc Muni	NFL	B+	16.47	B / 8.2	24.22 / 90	8.28 / 61	11.40 / 86	5.23	C+ / 5.9	1.29	-1.96
MUS	Nuveen GA Div Adv Muni	NZX	B+	16.00	B / 8.1	23.82 / 88	9.83 / 74	--	5.18	C+ / 6.3	4.17	0.74
MUS	Eaton Vance FL Muni Inc Tr	FEV	B+	15.55	B / 7.9	19.22 / 74	10.60 / 78	15.49 / 98	5.72	C+ / 6.6	1.63	-0.20
MUN	Putnam Managed Muni Inc Tr	PMM	B+	7.88	B / 7.9	21.46 / 81	6.88 / 43	4.23 / 27	5.24	C+ / 6.0	-5.40	-11.22
MUN	Morgan Stanley Muni Inc Op	OIA	B+	8.10	B / 7.8	26.34 / 94	6.96 / 44	6.49 / 41	6.26	C+ / 6.9	1.00	-4.20
MUS	Nuveen Insured NY Prem Inc Muni	NNF	B+	15.80	B / 7.6	23.43 / 87	7.28 / 48	10.34 / 77	5.38	C+ / 6.7	-1.99	-6.13
MUS	Nuveen TX Quality Inc Muni	NTX	B+	15.90	B / 7.6	21.62 / 81	7.88 / 57	11.52 / 87	5.43	C+ / 6.4	2.05	-1.26
MUN	Nuveen Insured Quality Muni	NQI	B+	16.22	B- / 7.5	21.36 / 80	8.10 / 59	11.34 / 86	5.79	C+ / 6.7	2.14	-0.31
MUS	Nuveen NY Div Adv Muni	NAN	B+	15.93	B- / 7.3	19.11 / 74	9.16 / 68	11.15 / 84	6.13	C+ / 6.7	-0.93	-3.11
FS	First Financial Fund	FF	B	18.10	A- / 9.1	29.71 / 74	28.34 / 96	35.77 / 99	2.10	C / 4.6	2.20	2.97
GI	Cohen&Steers Adv Inc Realty Fund	RLF	B	21.87	A- / 9.0	37.42 / 90	20.42 / 90	--	8.11	C / 4.7	-6.58	-6.41
EM	Scudder Global High Income Fund	LBF	B	7.91	B+ / 8.9	34.74 / 85	20.30 / 89	21.16 / 96	7.22	C / 4.9	-10.11	-9.99
MUS	BlackRock MD Muni Bond Trust	BZM	B	16.69	B+ / 8.7	26.28 / 94	9.81 / 73	--	5.26	C / 5.1	4.31	-2.24

N/A denotes number is not available

Fund Type	Fund Name (99 Pct = Best, 0 Pct = Worst)	Ticker Symbol	Overall Weiss Investment Rating	Price As of 6/30/05	PERFORMANCE: Performance Rating/Pts	Annualized Total Return Through 6/30/05: 1Yr/Pct	3Yr/Pct	5Yr/Pct	Dividend Yield %	RISK: Risk Rating/Pts	VALUATION: Premium/Discount As of 6/30/05	1 Year Average
GL	Scudder Strategic Income Fund	KST	B	14.01	B+ / 8.7	32.08 / 79	20.89 / 91	8.78 / 34	7.63	C / 5.0	0.79	-1.85
MUS	Eaton Vance PA Muni Inc Tr	EVP	B	15.85	B+ / 8.3	25.40 / 92	12.24 / 86	15.20 / 98	5.97	C+ / 5.6	5.04	2.76
UT	Gabelli Utility Trust	GUT	B	10.00	B / 8.2	26.20 / 65	17.94 / 84	18.56 / 90	7.29	C / 5.5	36.24	37.15
GI	Nuveen Real Estate Inc Fund	JRS	B	20.11	B / 8.1	31.77 / 78	17.42 / 82	--	8.00	C+ / 5.6	-10.26	-7.44
MUS	BlackRock FL Inv Qual Muni Tr	RFA	B	15.38	B / 7.8	24.21 / 89	7.54 / 52	10.15 / 75	5.59	C+ / 5.7	4.13	-3.36
COH	40/86 Strategic Income Fund	CFD	B	10.16	B- / 7.5	15.27 / 38	19.85 / 88	10.39 / 44	10.02	C+ / 6.0	-9.69	-10.31
MUS	Nuveen NJ Div Adv Muni Fund 2	NUJ	B	15.64	B- / 7.5	19.90 / 76	8.07 / 59	--	5.77	C+ / 6.2	-1.01	-2.92
MUS	MuniYield NJ Insured Fund	MJI	B	15.65	B- / 7.3	21.68 / 81	7.65 / 54	10.09 / 74	5.92	C+ / 6.6	-0.38	-2.97
MUS	MuniYield PA Insured Fund	MPA	B	15.99	B- / 7.3	21.01 / 80	8.72 / 64	12.29 / 91	5.96	C+ / 6.6	-1.84	-3.71
MUS	Nuveen OH Div Adv Muni 2	NBJ	B	16.06	B- / 7.3	23.90 / 89	9.69 / 73	--	5.41	C+ / 6.5	2.95	2.01
MUS	Nuveen GA Prem Inc Muni	NPG	B	16.95	B- / 7.2	23.09 / 86	6.95 / 44	11.08 / 84	4.94	C+ / 6.5	11.15	7.63
UT	iShares Dow Jones US Utilities	IDU	B	76.12	B- / 7.1	33.36 / 82	12.74 / 62	6.38 / 26	2.80	C+ / 6.5	-0.05	-0.02
FO	iShares MSCI Singapore Index	EWS	B	7.61	B- / 7.1	29.85 / 75	15.90 / 77	3.08 / 17	3.64	C+ / 6.4	0.26	0.27
MUS	Nuveen NY Performance Plus Muni	NNP	B	16.02	B- / 7.1	19.22 / 74	7.85 / 56	10.84 / 81	6.06	C+ / 6.7	-4.30	-5.65
MUS	Minnesota Municipal Inc Portfolio	MXA	B	16.07	B- / 7.0	21.20 / 80	7.54 / 52	11.58 / 88	5.57	C+ / 6.6	3.81	0.81
MUS	Nuveen NC Div Adv Muni 2	NNO	B	16.60	B- / 7.0	11.25 / 43	10.12 / 75	--	5.32	C+ / 6.7	6.34	2.80
FO	India Fund	IFN	B-	30.50	A+ / 9.9	50.84 / 99	50.94 / 99	18.32 / 89	5.09	C- / 3.5	1.63	0.14
EN	SPDR Energy	XLE	B-	44.94	A / 9.5	44.57 / 97	21.81 / 92	10.07 / 42	1.27	C- / 3.8	0.02	0.01
EN	iShares Dow Jones US Energy Sector	IYE	B-	77.92	A / 9.3	40.78 / 95	20.88 / 90	11.30 / 49	1.28	C- / 3.9	0.14	0.05
GI	Cohen&Steers Quality Income Realty	RQI	B-	20.52	A- / 9.1	36.48 / 88	20.68 / 90	--	7.93	C / 4.3	-10.67	-8.82
GL	Herzfeld Caribbean Basin Fund	CUBA	B-	6.30	B+ / 8.9	28.05 / 70	22.86 / 94	5.93 / 25	0.00	C / 4.4	-12.98	-13.44
EN	iShares S&P Global Energy Sector	IXC	B-	86.99	B+ / 8.9	36.75 / 88	19.50 / 88	--	1.47	C / 4.5	0.06	0.22
COH	Scudder High Income Trust	KHI	B-	7.31	B+ / 8.5	26.71 / 66	18.53 / 85	9.20 / 37	9.21	C / 4.7	22.86	17.41
FO	Scudder New Asia Fund	SAF	B-	15.82	B+ / 8.3	26.66 / 65	20.06 / 89	5.53 / 23	0.44	C / 5.1	-11.92	-12.98
COH	Corporate High Yield Fund	COY	B-	8.74	B / 7.8	18.39 / 46	19.44 / 88	9.52 / 38	9.60	C / 5.3	1.16	-1.08
FO	Singapore Fund	SGF	B-	8.91	B / 7.8	24.29 / 60	20.77 / 90	6.10 / 25	2.48	C / 5.5	-13.24	-14.23
GI	Cohen&Steers Total Return Realty	RFI	B-	19.80	B / 7.7	27.56 / 69	17.60 / 82	19.31 / 92	6.56	C+ / 5.7	-0.25	0.51
EM	Global High Income Dollar Fund	GHI	B-	16.94	B / 7.7	30.31 / 76	19.70 / 88	19.21 / 92	8.30	C / 5.3	8.66	12.51
GL	Alliance World Dollar Govt Fund II	AWF	B-	12.29	B- / 7.5	19.98 / 50	18.93 / 86	16.59 / 80	7.20	C+ / 5.8	-12.78	-11.59
COH	Pioneer High Income Trust	PHT	B-	16.20	B- / 7.5	19.09 / 48	18.29 / 84	--	10.02	C / 5.5	0.31	-0.81
COH	Corporate High Yield Fund V	HYV	B-	14.63	B- / 7.2	19.62 / 49	19.28 / 87	--	9.80	C+ / 6.1	-1.81	-3.52
COH	Senior High Income Portfolio	ARK	B-	5.93	B- / 7.0	16.61 / 41	17.79 / 83	9.09 / 35	9.46	C+ / 6.4	-1.00	-3.11
FO	Mexico Equity & Income Fund	MXE	C+	17.16	A / 9.4	42.76 / 96	26.45 / 96	11.88 / 52	0.00	C- / 3.2	-13.68	-11.42
GI	streetTRACKS Wilshire REIT	RWR	C+	194.85	B+ / 8.8	31.89 / 79	19.98 / 89	--	4.19	C- / 3.9	-0.02	0.01
EN	iShares Goldman Sachs Nat Res Index	IGE	C+	76.30	B+ / 8.7	34.36 / 84	18.73 / 85	--	1.15	C- / 3.8	-0.05	0.04
FO	iShares MSCI Canada Index	EWC	C+	18.29	B+ / 8.7	30.76 / 77	21.01 / 91	4.82 / 20	1.09	C- / 4.1	0.27	0.22
GR	HOLDRS Wireless	WMH	C+	55.80	B / 8.1	11.50 / 28	23.25 / 95	--	0.59	C- / 4.1	0.00	N/A
UT	HOLDRS Utilities	UTH	C+	109.69	B / 8.0	38.97 / 92	14.25 / 69	7.62 / 29	2.39	C- / 4.2	0.00	N/A
FO	Asia Tigers Fund	GRR	C+	12.19	B / 7.6	31.78 / 79	17.04 / 80	7.22 / 28	0.00	C / 4.4	-6.45	-7.75
COH	Corporate High Yield Fund III	CYE	C+	8.45	B / 7.6	18.67 / 46	19.40 / 88	8.00 / 32	9.33	C / 5.3	-1.29	-2.13
EM	Templeton Emerging Markets Income	TEI	C+	13.93	B / 7.6	26.81 / 66	17.45 / 82	17.31 / 85	7.20	C / 4.8	-0.50	-2.58
COH	Debt Strategies Fund I Inc	DSU	C+	6.52	C+ / 6.7	13.26 / 32	18.03 / 84	10.59 / 46	9.61	C+ / 6.0	-2.10	-2.23
MUS	Nuveen MD Div Adv Muni	NFM	C+	16.29	C+ / 6.7	20.18 / 77	7.67 / 54	--	5.34	C+ / 6.0	7.24	5.10
COI	PIMCO Corporate Income Fund	PCN	C+	15.40	C+ / 6.4	24.49 / 61	13.06 / 63	--	9.24	C+ / 6.1	1.32	-1.26
MUN	DTF Tax Free Income	DTF	C+	15.90	C+ / 5.9	17.01 / 64	7.45 / 51	10.93 / 82	5.45	C+ / 6.8	-6.36	-7.71
GI	Putnam High Income Bond Fund	PCF	C+	7.80	C+ / 5.8	16.90 / 41	15.29 / 74	9.53 / 38	7.18	C+ / 6.9	-8.24	-9.66
GR	iShares Russell Midcap Index	IWR	C+	81.12	C+ / 5.7	16.41 / 40	15.47 / 75	--	0.98	C+ / 6.9	-0.04	0.03
MUS	Nuveen AZ Div Adv Muni Fund 2	NKR	C+	15.70	C / 5.1	18.68 / 72	5.85 / 30	--	5.42	C+ / 6.9	-0.63	-0.93

N/A denotes number is not available

99 Pct = Best
0 Pct = Worst

Fund Type	Fund Name	Ticker Symbol	Overall Weiss Investment Rating	Price As of 6/30/05	PERFORMANCE: Performance Rating/Pts	Annualized Total Return Through 6/30/05: 1Yr/Pct	3Yr/Pct	5Yr/Pct	Dividend Yield %	RISK: Risk Rating/Pts	VALUATION: Premium/Discount As of 6/30/05	1 Year Average
FO	Morgan Stanley India Inv Fund	IIF	C+	33.42	A+ / 9.9	65.14 / 99	54.11 / 99	29.60 / 99	0.47	D+ / 2.3	6.74	2.57
FO	Central Europe & Russia Fund	CEE	C+	31.40	A+ / 9.8	46.25 / 98	34.81 / 98	18.50 / 90	0.55	D+ / 2.4	-6.91	-10.15
FO	Latin American Discovery Fund	LDF	C+	20.01	A+ / 9.8	63.53 / 99	34.65 / 98	16.12 / 79	0.22	D+ / 2.6	-12.81	-13.21
FO	Morgan Stanley Eastern Europe	RNE	C+	29.85	A+ / 9.8	31.07 / 77	38.86 / 99	23.47 / 98	0.00	D+ / 2.3	-5.72	-8.93
FO	Templeton Russia&East European Fund	TRF	C+	40.02	A+ / 9.8	28.90 / 72	38.99 / 99	28.72 / 99	0.00	D / 2.2	4.87	2.42
FO	iShares MSCI Austria Index	EWO	C+	23.33	A+ / 9.7	39.40 / 92	37.92 / 99	25.33 / 98	0.36	D+ / 2.8	-0.34	0.14
FO	Latin America Equity Fund	LAQ	C+	23.00	A+ / 9.7	64.53 / 99	29.30 / 97	14.45 / 67	1.97	D+ / 2.6	-13.63	-13.99
GL	Aberdeen Australia Equity Fund	IAF	C+	12.20	A+ / 9.6	51.75 / 99	31.89 / 97	20.13 / 93	8.55	D+ / 2.8	4.18	-2.98
FO	China Fund	CHN	C+	28.73	A+ / 9.6	16.58 / 40	35.45 / 98	29.04 / 99	0.69	D+ / 2.3	11.70	17.54
FO	Templeton Dragon Fund	TDF	C+	17.99	A / 9.5	32.87 / 80	28.90 / 96	23.12 / 97	0.78	D+ / 2.5	-9.37	-10.70
EM	Morgan Stanley Emerging Markets	MSF	C+	18.11	A / 9.3	39.60 / 93	24.43 / 95	8.67 / 34	0.37	D+ / 2.7	-11.62	-9.89
FO	Mexico Fund	MXF	C+	23.65	A- / 9.0	30.29 / 75	22.24 / 93	18.97 / 91	0.17	D+ / 2.8	-12.70	-12.52
FO	Indonesia Fund	IF	C	5.75	A+ / 9.8	56.91 / 99	40.95 / 99	11.75 / 52	3.08	D- / 1.2	-5.12	-1.13
FO	Korea Fund	KF	C	27.28	A / 9.5	49.47 / 98	22.48 / 93	20.11 / 93	1.65	D- / 1.1	-6.35	-7.95
FO	iShares MSCI Mexico Index	EWW	C	26.57	A / 9.4	37.42 / 90	24.74 / 95	12.44 / 56	1.02	D / 1.7	-0.30	0.05
EM	Templeton Emerging Markets Fd	EMF	C	17.48	A / 9.4	45.84 / 98	24.37 / 95	14.27 / 66	1.06	D- / 1.3	1.92	0.88
GR	HOLDRS Internet	HHH	C	55.94	A- / 9.0	-10.32 / 0	32.31 / 97	-12.11 / 3	0.00	D+ / 2.7	0.00	N/A
FO	Korea Equity Fund	KEF	C	6.99	A- / 9.0	46.54 / 98	18.70 / 85	13.26 / 61	0.00	D / 2.1	-5.67	-8.49
FO	New Germany Fund	GF	C	9.18	B+ / 8.9	27.62 / 69	24.15 / 95	-6.33 / 5	3.00	D / 1.8	-14.37	-15.27
FO	Spain Fund	SNF	C	12.45	B+ / 8.7	27.50 / 68	22.65 / 93	9.16 / 36	8.24	D / 2.0	26.14	22.87
FO	Third Canadian General Invst Tr	T.THD	C-	28.95	A- / 9.1	37.81 / 91	22.53 / 93	19.75 / 93	1.03	D- / 1.1	-21.67	-15.44
FO	JF China Region Fund	JFC	C-	12.82	B / 8.2	13.35 / 33	22.94 / 94	10.41 / 44	0.00	D- / 1.3	-13.79	-9.84
FO	Greater China Fund	GCH	D+	16.20	B- / 7.5	20.92 / 51	19.96 / 89	14.29 / 66	1.28	D- / 1.2	-12.24	-9.26
FO	iShares MSCI Spain Index	EWP	D+	33.76	B- / 7.2	21.92 / 54	21.56 / 92	7.09 / 28	1.79	D / 1.8	-0.27	0.09
FO	iShares MSCI Hong Kong Index	EWH	D+	12.32	C+ / 6.1	27.66 / 69	13.61 / 66	1.88 / 14	2.19	D+ / 2.9	-0.81	0.12
GR	iShares Goldman Sachs Ntwr Index Fd	IGN	D	27.70	B- / 7.0	-10.27 / 0	22.96 / 94	--	0.00	D- / 1.4	-0.14	-0.06
IN	Cornerstone Total Return Fund	CRF	D	15.48	C+ / 6.5	5.10 / 12	18.82 / 86	13.29 / 61	13.45	D- / 1.3	35.79	35.33
GR	Royce Micro-Cap Trust	RMT	D-	13.59	C / 5.3	14.30 / 35	16.09 / 77	20.17 / 93	8.93	D / 2.2	1.87	1.45
FO	iShares MSCI Italy Index	EWI	D-	24.22	C / 4.9	17.78 / 44	16.79 / 79	2.46 / 15	2.61	D+ / 2.5	-0.49	0.08
GL	Morgan Stanley Global Opp Bond Fund	MGB	E+	7.80	C / 4.4	13.93 / 35	15.54 / 75	7.85 / 31	7.10	D / 1.6	-4.06	8.79
FO	Taiwan Fund	TWN	E+	13.69	C- / 3.5	23.73 / 59	7.32 / 19	-6.06 / 5	0.22	D+ / 2.6	-12.13	-11.53
GL	Canadian World Fund Limited	T.CWF	E+	4.10	C- / 3.2	19.88 / 50	12.24 / 58	-3.89 / 6	0.00	D / 1.7	-25.86	-24.04
GR	Nasdaq 100 Trust Series I	QQQQ	E+	36.97	D+ / 2.8	0.07 / 6	12.71 / 61	-16.75 / 2	0.19	D / 2.1	0.03	0.01
FO	Malaysia Fund	MF	E+	5.64	D+ / 2.6	8.35 / 20	11.95 / 56	5.02 / 21	0.69	D / 2.2	-2.25	-1.64
FO	Europe Fund	EF	E+	10.54	D+ / 2.4	8.79 / 21	10.62 / 43	-0.21 / 12	7.34	D+ / 2.7	-10.68	-7.75
FO	iShares MSCI EMU Index	EZU	E	70.36	C- / 3.0	16.78 / 41	11.67 / 52	--	1.83	D- / 1.0	-0.61	0.17
FO	iShares MSCI France Index	EWQ	E	23.82	D+ / 2.8	14.84 / 37	10.58 / 43	-2.06 / 9	1.25	D- / 1.3	0.13	0.11
GR	iShares Dow Jones US Telecom	IYZ	E	23.19	D+ / 2.5	12.77 / 31	9.88 / 37	-15.69 / 3	2.27	D / 1.8	0.17	0.02
GR	iShares Russell 2000 Growth	IWO	E	63.50	D / 2.1	2.99 / 9	10.47 / 42	--	0.47	D+ / 2.6	-0.66	-0.06
GR	HOLDRS Software	SWH	E	34.96	D / 2.0	3.03 / 9	10.27 / 40	--	0.05	D+ / 2.6	0.00	N/A
GR	Gabelli Equity Trust	GAB	E	8.93	D / 1.9	17.44 / 43	6.27 / 14	6.72 / 27	8.04	D+ / 2.8	7.20	6.22
GR	HOLDRS Internet Architecture	IAH	E	34.23	D / 1.6	-1.73 / 5	10.35 / 41	-17.65 / 2	0.18	D+ / 2.6	0.00	N/A
FO	Japan Smaller Cap Fund Inc.	JOF	E	10.78	E+ / 0.7	-18.40 / 0	10.50 / 42	5.36 / 22	0.00	D+ / 2.4	-7.94	5.57
COH	Prospect Street High Inc Portfolio	PHY	E-	3.40	D- / 1.5	23.31 / 58	3.40 / 4	2.95 / 17	8.72	D- / 1.2	-5.03	0.64
GR	SPDR Technology	XLK	E-	19.99	D- / 1.5	-0.49 / 5	9.20 / 32	-17.59 / 2	0.56	D- / 1.5	0.15	-0.01
GR	iShares Dow Jones US Technology	IYW	E-	46.09	D- / 1.4	-2.13 / 5	9.11 / 32	-18.16 / 1	0.23	D- / 1.4	0.11	0.03
GR	iShares Goldman Sachs Technology	IGM	E-	43.46	D- / 1.2	-4.23 / 3	9.23 / 33	--	0.04	D- / 1.3	0.12	0.04
HL	iShares Biotechnology Index Fund	IBB	E-	67.57	D- / 1.1	-8.95 / 1	9.83 / 37	--	0.00	D / 1.6	0.04	-0.02
GL	iShares S&P Global Technology Sect	IXN	E-	48.77	D- / 1.1	-2.82 / 4	8.50 / 25	--	1.29	D- / 1.4	0.06	0.36
FO	Germany Fund	GER	E-	7.77	E+ / 0.6	15.30 / 38	4.42 / 6	-6.71 / 5	0.32	D / 1.7	-12.30	-12.99
GR	iShares Goldman Sachs Semicon Index	IGW	E-	53.60	E- / 0.2	-8.12 / 1	3.81 / 5	--	0.00	D / 1.6	0.00	N/A
GR	Tuxis Corporation	TUX	E-	0.00	E- / 0.1	13.14 / 31	-3.52 / 0	2.02 / 15	0.00	D- / 1.4		-18.64

N/A denotes number is not available

Fund Type	Fund Name (99 Pct = Best, 0 Pct = Worst)	Ticker Symbol	Overall Weiss Investment Rating	Price As of 6/30/05	PERFORMANCE: Performance Rating/Pts	Annualized Total Return Through 6/30/05: 1Yr/Pct	3Yr/Pct	5Yr/Pct	Dividend Yield %	RISK: Risk Rating/Pts	VALUATION: Premium/Discount As of 6/30/05	1 Year Average
GR	NAIC Growth Fund	GRF	**E-**	8.55	**E-** / **0.0**	-3.56 / 4	-3.63 / 0	-1.25 / 10	3.57	**D** / **1.6**	-10.66	-14.29

N/A denotes number is not available

Fund Type	Fund Name (99 Pct = Best, 0 Pct = Worst)	Ticker Symbol	Overall Weiss Investment Rating	Price As of 6/30/05	PERFORMANCE: Performance Rating/Pts	Annualized Total Return Through 6/30/05: 1Yr/Pct	3Yr/Pct	5Yr/Pct	Dividend Yield %	RISK: Risk Rating/Pts	VALUATION: Premium/Discount As of 6/30/05	1 Year Average
FO	Turkish Investment Fund	TKF	**C**	15.89	**A+ / 9.9**	74.90 / 99	55.92 / 99	7.67 / 29	0.49	**E+ / 0.8**	8.61	11.87
FO	Brazil Fund	BZF	**C-**	37.10	**A+ / 9.9**	80.66 / 99	46.52 / 99	21.10 / 96	2.06	**E+ / 0.6**	-5.50	-9.82
FO	iShares MSCI Brazil Index	EWZ	**C-**	23.94	**A+ / 9.9**	68.67 / 99	37.41 / 98	--	1.86	**E- / 0.0**	-0.42	N/A
FO	iShares S&P Latin American 40 Idx	ILF	**C-**	90.69	**A+ / 9.8**	58.53 / 99	32.02 / 97	--	1.01	**E- / 0.0**	0.49	0.58
FO	Thai Capital Fund	TF	**C-**	9.52	**A+ / 9.7**	40.61 / 94	34.72 / 98	7.77 / 30	0.45	**E / 0.3**	9.68	-1.69
FO	Thai Fund	TTF	**C-**	9.69	**A / 9.4**	22.58 / 56	28.98 / 96	14.23 / 66	1.31	**E+ / 0.7**	16.89	11.36
EN	HOLDRS Oil Services	OIH	**D+**	102.90	**A / 9.3**	44.01 / 97	19.31 / 87	--	0.88	**E- / 0.0**	0.00	N/A
FO	iShares MSCI South Korea Index	EWY	**D-**	32.68	**B / 7.7**	36.30 / 87	14.78 / 72	9.70 / 39	0.31	**E- / 0.0**	0.25	0.18
FO	iShares MSCI Sweden Index	EWD	**D-**	20.25	**B / 7.7**	17.74 / 43	21.38 / 92	-3.70 / 7	0.73	**E- / 0.0**	-1.79	0.21
GR	HOLDRS Internet Infrastructure	IIH	**D-**	4.05	**B- / 7.4**	10.36 / 25	21.65 / 92	-41.59 / 0	0.00	**E- / 0.0**	0.00	N/A
GR	HOLDRS Broadband	BDH	**D-**	15.33	**B- / 7.2**	-4.47 / 3	22.85 / 94	-29.76 / 0	0.01	**E- / 0.0**	0.00	N/A
FO	iShares MSCI Belgium Index	EWK	**D-**	17.81	**C+ / 6.5**	27.44 / 68	18.44 / 85	9.05 / 35	1.59	**E / 0.4**	-1.17	0.38
FO	HOLDRS TeleBras	TBH	**E+**	30.45	**C+ / 6.3**	16.96 / 42	14.75 / 72	-17.92 / 2	0.87	**E- / 0.0**	0.00	N/A
GI	Renaissance Cap Growth & Inc III	RENN	**E+**	11.25	**C / 4.3**	-2.37 / 4	16.31 / 78	4.82 / 20	3.46	**E+ / 0.8**	-17.40	-16.91
GR	streetTRACKS MS Technology Index	MTK	**E**	47.33	**D+ / 2.8**	-1.87 / 5	12.52 / 60	--	0.05	**E+ / 0.7**	-0.17	-0.02
GR	iShares Goldman Sachs Software Indx	IGV	**E-**	38.38	**D+ / 2.6**	3.02 / 9	12.04 / 56	--	0.20	**E- / 0.0**	0.08	-0.05
FO	iShares MSCI Taiwan Index	EWT	**E-**	12.34	**D+ / 2.4**	15.89 / 39	6.27 / 14	-6.91 / 5	0.66	**E- / 0.0**	-1.52	-0.08
PM	ASA Limited	ASA	**E-**	38.59	**D / 1.8**	8.40 / 20	8.77 / 28	22.47 / 97	1.55	**E- / 0.0**	-11.14	-12.48
FO	iShares MSCI Germany Index	EWG	**E-**	17.65	**D- / 1.4**	13.16 / 32	7.91 / 22	-3.03 / 7	1.10	**E- / 0.0**	-0.23	-0.01
FO	iShares MSCI Netherlands Index	EWN	**E-**	18.40	**E+ / 0.6**	13.65 / 34	3.75 / 5	-4.35 / 6	1.40	**E- / 0.0**	-0.33	0.16
GR	HOLDRS Semiconductor	SMH	**E-**	34.10	**E / 0.3**	-8.22 / 1	4.07 / 6	-18.30 / 1	0.09	**E- / 0.0**	0.00	N/A
GR	HOLDRS B2B Internet	BHH	**E-**	2.00	**E- / 0.0**	-9.46 / 1	-8.09 / 0	-43.03 / 0	14.73	**E- / 0.0**	0.00	N/A

N/A denotes number is not available

Section VIII

Top-Rated Closed-End Mutual Funds by Fund Type

A compilation of those

Closed-End Mutual Funds

receiving the highest Weiss Investment Rating

within each type of fund.

Funds are listed in order by Overall Weiss Investment Rating.

Section VIII Contents

This section contains a summary analysis of the top 100 rated mutual funds within each fund type. If you are looking for a particular type of mutual fund, these pages show those funds that have achieved the best combination of risk and financial performance over the past three years.

1. Fund Type

The mutual fund's peer category based on an analysis of its investment portfolio.

COH	Corporate – High Yield	HL	Health
COI	Corporate – Inv. Grade	IN	Income
EM	Emerging Market	LP	Loan Participation
EN	Energy/Natural Resources	MTG	Mortgage
FS	Financial Services	MUH	Municipal – High Yield
FO	Foreign	MUN	Municipal – National
GEI	General – Inv. Grade	MUS	Municipal – Single State
GEN	General Bond	PM	Precious Metals
GL	Global	USA	U.S. Gov. – Agency
GR	Growth	UT	Utilities
GI	Growth and Income		

A blank fund type means that the mutual fund has not yet been categorized.

2. Fund Name

The name of the mutual fund as stated in its prospectus, which can sometimes differ slightly from the name that the company uses for advertising. If you cannot find the particular mutual fund you are interested in, or if you have any doubts regarding the precise name, verify the information with your broker or on your account statement. Also, use the fund's ticker symbol for confirmation. (See column 3.)

3. Ticker Symbol

The unique alphabetic symbol used for identifying and trading a specific mutual fund. No two funds can have the same ticker symbol.

A handful of funds currently show no associated ticker symbol. This means that the fund is either small or new since the NASD only assigns a ticker symbol to funds with at least $25 million in assets or 1,000 shareholders.

4. Overall Weiss Investment Rating

Our overall rating is measured on a scale from A to E based on each fund's risk-adjusted performance. Please see page 10 for specific descriptions of each letter grade. Also, refer to page 7 for information on how our ratings are derived. Most important, when using this rating, please be sure to consider the warnings beginning on page 11 regarding the ratings' limitations and the underlying assumptions.

5. Price

Closing price of the fund on the date shown.

6. **Performance Rating/Points** — A letter grade rating based solely on the mutual fund's financial performance over the trailing three years, without any consideration for the amount of risk the fund poses. Like the overall Weiss Investment Rating, the Performance Rating is measured on a scale from A to E for ease of interpretation. The points score indicates where the Performance Rating falls on a scale of 0 to 10.

7. **1-Year Total Return** — The total return the fund has provided investors over the preceeding 52 weeks. This total return figure is computed based on the fund's dividend distributions and share price appreciation/depreciation during the period, net of the expenses and fees it imposes on its shareholders.

8. **1-Year Total Return Percentile** — The fund's percentile rank based on its one-year performance compared to that of all other closed-end funds in existence for at least one year. A score of 99 is the best possible, indicating that the fund outperformed 99% of the closed-end mutual funds. Zero is the worst possible percentile score.

9. **3-Year Total Return** — The total annual return the fund has provided investors over the preceeding 156 weeks.

10. **3-Year Total Return Percentile** — The fund's percentile rank based on its three-year performance compared to that of all other closed-end funds in existence for at least three years. A score of 99 is the best possible, indicating that the fund outperformed 99% of the closed-end mutual funds. Zero is the worst possible percentile score.

11. **5-Year Total Return** — The total annual return the fund has provided investors over the preceeding 260 weeks.

12. **5-Year Total Return Percentile** — The fund's percentile rank based on its five-year performance compared to that of all other closed-end funds in existence for at least five years. A score of 99 is the best possible, indicating that the fund outperformed 99% of the closed-end mutual funds. Zero is the worst possible percentile score.

13. **Dividend Yield** — Most recent quarterly dividend to fund investors annualized, expressed as a percent of the fund's current share price. The dividend yield of a fund can have little correlation to the amount of dividends the fund has received from its underlying investments. Rather, dividend distributions are based on a fund's need to pass earnings from both dividends and gains on the sale of investments along to shareholders. Thus, these dividend distributions are included as a part of the fund's total return.

    Keep in mind that dividend income may be taxed at a different rate than capital gains depending on your income tax bracket.

14. Risk Rating/Points

A letter grade rating based solely on the mutual fund's risk as determined by its monthly performance volatility over the trailing three years. The risk rating does not take into consideration the overall financial performance the fund has achieved or the total return it has provided to its shareholders. Like the overall Weiss Investment Rating, the Risk Rating is measured on a scale from A to E for ease of interpretation. The points score indicates where the Risk Rating falls on a scale of 0 to 10.

15. Premium/ Discount

A comparison of the fund's price to its NAV as of the date indicated. The premium (+) or discount (-) indicates the percentage the shares are trading above or below the fund's NAV per share.

If the price is above the fund's NAV, the fund is said to be trading at a premium. If the price is lower than the fund's NAV, the fund is trading at a discount.

16. 1-Year Average Premium/ Discount

The average of the fund's premium/discount over the preceeding year.

It can be useful to compare the fund's current premium/discount to its one-year average. If the fund is currently trading at a premium/discount that is lower/higher than its one-year average, then there has been less demand for the fund in more recent times than over the past year. Conversely, if the fund is currently trading at a premium/discount that is higher/lower than its one-year average, this indicates that there has been greater demand for the fund in more recent times than over the past year.

	99 Pct = Best 0 Pct = Worst				PERFORMANCE					RISK	VALUATION	
						Annualized Total Return Through 6/30/05					Premium/Discount	
Fund Type	Fund Name	Ticker Symbol	Overall Weiss Investment Rating	Price As of 6/30/05	Performance Rating/Pts	1Yr/Pct	3Yr/Pct	5Yr/Pct	Dividend Yield %	Risk Rating/ Pts	As of 6/30/05	1 Year Average
COH	40/86 Strategic Income Fund	CFD	**B**	10.16	**B- / 7.5**	15.27 / 38	19.85 / 88	10.39 / 44	10.02	**C+ / 6.0**	-9.69	-10.31
COH	Scudder High Income Trust	KHI	**B-**	7.31	**B+ / 8.5**	26.71 / 66	18.53 / 85	9.20 / 37	9.21	**C / 4.7**	22.86	17.41
COH	Corporate High Yield Fund	COY	**B-**	8.74	**B / 7.8**	18.39 / 46	19.44 / 88	9.52 / 38	9.60	**C / 5.3**	1.16	-1.08
COH	Pioneer High Income Trust	PHT	**B-**	16.20	**B- / 7.5**	19.09 / 48	18.29 / 84	--	10.02	**C / 5.5**	0.31	-0.81
COH	Corporate High Yield Fund V	HYV	**B-**	14.63	**B- / 7.2**	19.62 / 49	19.28 / 87	--	9.80	**C+ / 6.1**	-1.81	-3.52
COH	Senior High Income Portfolio	ARK	**B-**	5.93	**B- / 7.0**	16.61 / 41	17.79 / 83	9.09 / 35	9.46	**C+ / 6.4**	-1.00	-3.11
COH	Corporate High Yield Fund III	CYE	**C+**	8.45	**B / 7.6**	18.67 / 46	19.40 / 88	8.00 / 32	9.33	**C / 5.3**	-1.29	-2.13
COH	Debt Strategies Fund I Inc	DSU	**C+**	6.52	**C+ / 6.7**	13.26 / 32	18.03 / 84	10.59 / 46	9.61	**C+ / 6.0**	-2.10	-2.23
COH	High Yield Income Fund	HYI	**C+**	5.42	**C+ / 5.8**	10.42 / 25	16.53 / 79	10.61 / 46	8.79	**C+ / 6.1**	-3.04	1.18
COH	Colonial Interm High Inc	CIF	**C+**	3.44	**C / 5.5**	15.69 / 39	15.56 / 75	0.76 / 13	9.12	**B- / 7.0**	-7.03	-7.92
COH	Pacholder High Yield Fund	PHF	**C**	9.68	**B / 8.1**	20.22 / 50	19.28 / 87	9.93 / 41	9.50	**C- / 3.3**	6.37	3.23
COH	Credit Suisse High Yield Bond Fund	DHY	**C**	4.81	**C+ / 6.6**	11.15 / 27	17.95 / 84	5.90 / 24	10.37	**C- / 4.0**	12.91	12.69
COH	Blackrock High Income Shares	HIS	**C-**	2.84	**C+ / 6.3**	22.34 / 55	14.92 / 73	-1.37 / 10	9.89	**C- / 3.4**	5.97	0.81
COH	High Yield Plus Fund	HYP	**C-**	4.00	**C+ / 5.7**	9.03 / 22	17.45 / 82	2.54 / 16	8.98	**C / 4.8**	3.36	9.08
COH	BlackRock Strategic Bond Trust	BHD	**C-**	15.10	**C / 4.9**	13.99 / 35	14.27 / 70	--	9.12	**C / 5.1**	5.59	7.77
COH	Morgan Stanley High Yield Fund	MSY	**C-**	6.31	**C- / 4.1**	18.17 / 45	11.26 / 49	-1.24 / 11	8.60	**C+ / 5.6**	-7.61	-9.53
COH	High Income Opportunity Fund Inc.	HIO	**C-**	6.46	**C- / 3.2**	6.45 / 14	11.57 / 51	3.65 / 18	8.36	**C+ / 6.1**	-9.78	-8.74
COH	Credit Suisse Asset Mgmt Income	CIK	**D+**	4.65	**C / 5.4**	24.21 / 60	10.32 / 41	5.52 / 23	9.91	**C- / 3.4**	7.89	0.80
COH	Zenix Income Fund	ZIF	**D+**	3.24	**C / 4.3**	-1.26 / 5	16.07 / 77	5.57 / 23	9.97	**C / 4.8**	6.93	15.41
COH	CIM High Yield Securities	CIM	**D+**	4.00	**C- / 4.0**	4.27 / 10	14.08 / 68	5.14 / 22	9.01	**C / 4.8**	-8.05	-5.27
COH	Managed High Income Portfolio	MHY	**D+**	6.35	**C- / 3.6**	9.34 / 23	11.80 / 54	4.07 / 19	8.16	**C+ / 5.7**	-8.63	-8.35
COH	Putnam Managed High Yield Trust	PTM	**D+**	8.16	**D+ / 2.7**	12.56 / 30	8.62 / 27	4.28 / 19	7.16	**C+ / 5.9**	-10.33	-10.42
COH	Dreyfus High Yield Strategies Fund	DHF	**D**	4.37	**C / 4.5**	8.61 / 20	15.11 / 74	-1.31 / 10	8.92	**C- / 3.7**	-6.02	-1.41
COH	New America High Income Fund	HYB	**D-**	2.13	**C / 4.7**	22.92 / 57	11.22 / 48	3.86 / 18	9.91	**C- / 3.0**	-0.93	-4.00
COH	Van Kampen High Income Trust II	VLT	**D-**	4.75	**C- / 3.1**	20.65 / 51	8.74 / 27	3.95 / 19	9.25	**C- / 4.1**	5.32	4.42
COH	BlackRock High Yield Trust	BHY	**D-**	9.40	**D+ / 2.9**	10.97 / 26	10.13 / 38	6.60 / 27	8.66	**C / 4.3**	22.88	20.89
COH	Salomon Br High Income Fund	HIF	**D-**	9.43	**D- / 1.4**	-8.33 / 1	9.45 / 34	4.60 / 20	7.56	**C+ / 5.7**	-10.10	-2.51
COH	Van Kampen High Income Trust	VIT	**D-**	3.68	**D- / 1.2**	7.78 / 17	6.94 / 16	4.98 / 21	9.47	**C / 5.4**	2.79	9.34
COH	Prospect Street High Inc Portfolio	PHY	**E-**	3.40	**D- / 1.5**	23.31 / 58	3.40 / 4	2.95 / 17	8.72	**D- / 1.2**	-5.03	0.64

N/A denotes number is not available

	99 Pct = Best 0 Pct = Worst				PERFORMANCE					RISK	VALUATION	
						Annualized Total Return Through 6/30/05					Premium/Discount	
Fund Type	Fund Name	Ticker Symbol	Overall Weiss Investment Rating	Price As of 6/30/05	Perform-ance Rating/Pts	1Yr/Pct	3Yr/Pct	5Yr/Pct	Dividend Yield %	Risk Rating/ Pts	As of 6/30/05	1 Year Average
COI	PIMCO Corporate Income Fund	PCN	**C+**	15.40	**C+ / 6.4**	24.49 / 61	13.06 / 63	--	9.24	**C+ / 6.1**	1.32	-1.26
COI	Morgan Stanley Income Sec	ICB	**C-**	15.88	**D / 1.9**	13.03 / 31	5.66 / 11	6.52 / 27	6.12	**B / 8.4**	-10.03	-9.53
COI	Van Kampen Bond	VBF	**C-**	17.71	**D / 1.7**	12.46 / 30	5.47 / 10	8.38 / 33	5.61	**B- / 7.9**	-9.92	-10.28
COI	1838 Bond Debenture Fund	BDF	**D**	18.74	**D / 1.7**	14.36 / 35	5.88 / 12	8.95 / 34	6.05	**C+ / 6.7**	-11.06	-10.88
COI	Lincoln National Income Fund	LND	**D-**	11.80	**D- / 1.0**	3.28 / 9	6.99 / 17	12.16 / 54	5.28	**C+ / 6.6**	-12.20	-6.38

N/A denotes number is not available

99 Pct = Best
0 Pct = Worst

Fund Type	Fund Name	Ticker Symbol	Overall Weiss Investment Rating	Price As of 6/30/05	PERFORMANCE: Performance Rating/Pts	PERFORMANCE: Annualized Total Return Through 6/30/05: 1Yr/Pct	3Yr/Pct	5Yr/Pct	Dividend Yield %	RISK: Risk Rating/Pts	VALUATION: Premium/Discount As of 6/30/05	1 Year Average
EM	Morgan Stanley Emerging Mkts Debt	MSD	**B+**	9.97	**B+ / 8.6**	28.11 / 70	21.23 / 91	18.01 / 88	7.24	**C / 5.4**	-7.69	-8.26
EM	Scudder Global High Income Fund	LBF	**B**	7.91	**B+ / 8.9**	34.74 / 85	20.30 / 89	21.16 / 96	7.22	**C / 4.9**	-10.11	-9.99
EM	Global High Income Dollar Fund	GHI	**B-**	16.94	**B / 7.7**	30.31 / 76	19.70 / 88	19.21 / 92	8.30	**C / 5.3**	8.66	12.51
EM	Morgan Stanley Emerging Markets	MSF	**C+**	18.11	**A / 9.3**	39.60 / 93	24.43 / 95	8.67 / 34	0.37	**D+ / 2.7**	-11.62	-9.89
EM	Templeton Emerging Markets Income	TEI	**C+**	13.93	**B / 7.6**	26.81 / 66	17.45 / 82	17.31 / 85	7.20	**C / 4.8**	-0.50	-2.58
EM	Templeton Emerging Markets Fd	EMF	**C**	17.48	**A / 9.4**	45.84 / 98	24.37 / 95	14.27 / 66	1.06	**D- / 1.3**	1.92	0.88
EM	Emerging Market Telecom Fund	ETF	**C**	10.10	**C+ / 6.3**	30.32 / 76	14.26 / 69	-2.71 / 8	0.00	**C / 4.6**	-13.16	-13.58
EM	Salomon Br Emerging Mkts Floating	EFL	**C**	12.54	**C- / 4.1**	7.96 / 18	14.42 / 71	10.31 / 44	5.74	**C+ / 6.7**	-10.17	-4.04
EM	Salomon Br Emerging Markets Income	EMD	**C-**	16.38	**C / 5.2**	10.08 / 24	17.72 / 83	16.97 / 83	7.63	**C / 5.1**	-3.19	9.10
EM	Salomon Br Emerging Mkts Income II	EDF	**D+**	13.35	**C- / 3.6**	2.54 / 8	15.88 / 76	16.63 / 81	7.84	**C+ / 5.8**	-8.81	8.62

N/A denotes number is not available

Fund Type	Fund Name (99 Pct = Best, 0 Pct = Worst)	Ticker Symbol	Overall Weiss Investment Rating	Price As of 6/30/05	PERFORMANCE: Performance Rating/Pts	Annualized Total Return Through 6/30/05: 1Yr/Pct	3Yr/Pct	5Yr/Pct	Dividend Yield %	RISK: Risk Rating/Pts	VALUATION: Premium/Discount As of 6/30/05	1 Year Average
EN	Petroleum and Resources Corp.	PEO	**A**	30.01	**B / 7.8**	30.76 / 77	15.59 / 76	10.32 / 44	1.74	**B- / 7.3**	-7.94	-7.42
EN	SPDR Energy	XLE	**B-**	44.94	**A / 9.5**	44.57 / 97	21.81 / 92	10.07 / 42	1.27	**C- / 3.8**	0.02	0.01
EN	iShares Dow Jones US Energy Sector	IYE	**B-**	77.92	**A / 9.3**	40.78 / 95	20.88 / 90	11.30 / 49	1.28	**C- / 3.9**	0.14	0.05
EN	iShares S&P Global Energy Sector	IXC	**B-**	86.99	**B+ / 8.9**	36.75 / 88	19.50 / 88	--	1.47	**C / 4.5**	0.06	0.22
EN	iShares Goldman Sachs Nat Res Index	IGE	**C+**	76.30	**B+ / 8.7**	34.36 / 84	18.73 / 85	--	1.15	**C- / 3.8**	-0.05	0.04
EN	HOLDRS Oil Services	OIH	**D+**	102.90	**A / 9.3**	44.01 / 97	19.31 / 87	--	0.88	**E- / 0.0**	0.00	N/A

N/A denotes number is not available

Fund Type	Fund Name (99 Pct = Best, 0 Pct = Worst)	Ticker Symbol	Overall Weiss Investment Rating	Price As of 6/30/05	PERFORMANCE: Performance Rating/Pts	Annualized Total Return Through 6/30/05: 1Yr/Pct	3Yr/Pct	5Yr/Pct	Dividend Yield %	RISK: Risk Rating/Pts	VALUATION: Premium/Discount As of 6/30/05	1 Year Average
FS	First Financial Fund	FF	**B**	18.10	**A-** / **9.1**	29.71 / 74	28.34 / 96	35.77 / 99	2.10	**C** / **4.6**	2.20	2.97
FS	J Hancock Bank & Thrift Oppty Fd	BTO	**C+**	9.77	**C+** / **6.2**	18.38 / 45	16.97 / 80	20.51 / 94	1.16	**C+** / **6.2**	-6.86	-7.88
FS	iShares Dow Jones US Financial Sct	IYF	**D+**	94.37	**D** / **2.1**	7.17 / 16	8.92 / 29	7.75 / 30	1.77	**C+** / **6.9**	0.15	N/A
FS	iShares Dow Jones US Financial Srv	IYG	**D+**	107.64	**D** / **2.0**	6.42 / 14	9.01 / 31	7.99 / 32	1.17	**C+** / **6.9**	-0.05	0.01
FS	J Hancock Financial Trends Fund	JHFT	**D**	15.72	**D+** / **2.9**	10.88 / 26	11.35 / 50	15.30 / 72	1.25	**C** / **5.4**	-15.48	-13.08
FS	SPDR Financial	XLF	**D**	29.31	**D-** / **1.3**	4.88 / 11	7.50 / 20	6.20 / 26	2.38	**C+** / **6.8**	0.07	N/A
FS	HOLDRS Regional Bank	RKH	**D**	134.50	**D-** / **1.2**	5.62 / 12	7.19 / 18	10.29 / 44	0.78	**C+** / **6.7**	0.00	N/A
FS	iShares S&P Global Financials Sect	IXG	**E+**	65.00	**D+** / **2.4**	11.20 / 27	10.18 / 39	--	1.37	**C-** / **3.8**	0.32	0.23

N/A denotes number is not available

	99 Pct = Best 0 Pct = Worst				PERFORMANCE					RISK	VALUATION	
						Annualized Total Return Through 6/30/05					Premium/Discount	
Fund Type	Fund Name	Ticker Symbol	Overall Weiss Investment Rating	Price As of 6/30/05	Performance Rating/Pts	1Yr/Pct	3Yr/Pct	5Yr/Pct	Dividend Yield %	Risk Rating/Pts	As of 6/30/05	1 Year Average
FO	Canadian General Investments Ltd	T.CGI	**A+**	18.40	**A+ / 9.7**	47.72 / 98	29.43 / 97	18.56 / 90	1.30	**C+ / 6.7**	-17.23	-25.05
FO	iShares MSCI Pacific ex-Japan Idx	EPP	**A+**	94.11	**B+ / 8.8**	34.03 / 83	21.35 / 91	--	3.20	**B- / 7.0**	-0.14	0.31
FO	iShares MSCI Australia Index	EWA	**A**	17.66	**A / 9.3**	36.87 / 89	24.75 / 95	13.56 / 63	3.25	**C+ / 6.2**	-0.23	0.25
FO	Chile Fund	CH	**B+**	15.03	**A+ / 9.7**	46.55 / 98	33.72 / 98	17.78 / 87	5.42	**C / 4.3**	-11.59	-10.68
FO	The New Ireland Fund	IRL	**B+**	21.20	**A- / 9.2**	36.97 / 89	25.91 / 96	14.24 / 66	0.14	**C / 5.1**	-13.96	-13.38
FO	iShares MSCI Singapore Index	EWS	**B**	7.61	**B- / 7.1**	29.85 / 75	15.90 / 77	3.08 / 17	3.64	**C+ / 6.4**	0.26	0.27
FO	India Fund	IFN	**B-**	30.50	**A+ / 9.9**	50.84 / 99	50.94 / 99	18.32 / 89	5.09	**C- / 3.5**	1.63	0.14
FO	Scudder New Asia Fund	SAF	**B-**	15.82	**B+ / 8.3**	26.66 / 65	20.06 / 89	5.53 / 23	0.44	**C / 5.1**	-11.92	-12.98
FO	Singapore Fund	SGF	**B-**	8.91	**B / 7.8**	24.29 / 60	20.77 / 90	6.10 / 25	2.48	**C / 5.5**	-13.24	-14.23
FO	Morgan Stanley India Inv Fund	IIF	**C+**	33.42	**A+ / 9.9**	65.14 / 99	54.11 / 99	29.60 / 99	0.47	**D+ / 2.3**	6.74	2.57
FO	Latin American Discovery Fund	LDF	**C+**	20.01	**A+ / 9.8**	63.53 / 99	34.65 / 98	16.12 / 79	0.22	**D+ / 2.6**	-12.81	-13.21
FO	Central Europe & Russia Fund	CEE	**C+**	31.40	**A+ / 9.8**	46.25 / 98	34.81 / 98	18.50 / 90	0.55	**D+ / 2.4**	-6.91	-10.15
FO	Morgan Stanley Eastern Europe	RNE	**C+**	29.85	**A+ / 9.8**	31.07 / 77	38.86 / 99	23.47 / 98	0.00	**D+ / 2.3**	-5.72	-8.93
FO	Templeton Russia&East European Fund	TRF	**C+**	40.02	**A+ / 9.8**	28.90 / 72	38.99 / 99	28.72 / 99	0.00	**D / 2.2**	4.87	2.42
FO	Latin America Equity Fund	LAQ	**C+**	23.00	**A+ / 9.7**	64.53 / 99	29.30 / 97	14.45 / 67	1.97	**D+ / 2.6**	-13.63	-13.99
FO	iShares MSCI Austria Index	EWO	**C+**	23.33	**A+ / 9.7**	39.40 / 92	37.92 / 99	25.33 / 98	0.36	**D+ / 2.8**	-0.34	0.14
FO	China Fund	CHN	**C+**	28.73	**A+ / 9.6**	16.58 / 40	35.45 / 98	29.04 / 99	0.69	**D+ / 2.3**	11.70	17.54
FO	Templeton Dragon Fund	TDF	**C+**	17.99	**A / 9.5**	32.87 / 80	28.90 / 96	23.12 / 97	0.78	**D+ / 2.5**	-9.37	-10.70
FO	Mexico Equity & Income Fund	MXE	**C+**	17.16	**A / 9.4**	42.76 / 96	26.45 / 96	11.88 / 52	0.00	**C- / 3.2**	-13.68	-11.42
FO	Mexico Fund	MXF	**C+**	23.65	**A- / 9.0**	30.29 / 75	22.24 / 93	18.97 / 91	0.17	**D+ / 2.8**	-12.70	-12.52
FO	iShares MSCI Canada Index	EWC	**C+**	18.29	**B+ / 8.7**	30.76 / 77	21.01 / 91	4.82 / 20	1.09	**C- / 4.1**	0.27	0.22
FO	Asia Tigers Fund	GRR	**C+**	12.19	**B / 7.6**	31.78 / 79	17.04 / 80	7.22 / 28	0.00	**C / 4.4**	-6.45	-7.75
FO	Turkish Investment Fund	TKF	**C**	15.89	**A+ / 9.9**	74.90 / 99	55.92 / 99	7.67 / 29	0.49	**E+ / 0.8**	8.61	11.87
FO	Indonesia Fund	IF	**C**	5.75	**A+ / 9.8**	56.91 / 99	40.95 / 99	11.75 / 52	3.08	**D- / 1.2**	-5.12	-1.13
FO	Korea Fund	KF	**C**	27.28	**A / 9.5**	49.47 / 98	22.48 / 93	20.11 / 93	1.65	**D- / 1.1**	-6.35	-7.95
FO	iShares MSCI Mexico Index	EWW	**C**	26.57	**A / 9.4**	37.42 / 90	24.74 / 95	12.44 / 56	1.02	**D / 1.7**	-0.30	0.05
FO	Korea Equity Fund	KEF	**C**	6.99	**A- / 9.0**	46.54 / 98	18.70 / 85	13.26 / 61	0.00	**D / 2.1**	-5.67	-8.49
FO	New Germany Fund	GF	**C**	9.18	**B+ / 8.9**	27.62 / 69	24.15 / 95	-6.33 / 5	3.00	**D / 1.8**	-14.37	-15.27
FO	Spain Fund	SNF	**C**	12.45	**B+ / 8.7**	27.50 / 68	22.65 / 93	9.16 / 36	8.24	**D / 2.0**	26.14	22.87
FO	First Israel Fund	ISL	**C**	14.38	**C+ / 6.3**	8.61 / 20	20.12 / 89	0.23 / 12	0.00	**C / 4.8**	-12.53	-10.83
FO	Brazil Fund	BZF	**C-**	37.10	**A+ / 9.9**	80.66 / 99	46.52 / 99	21.10 / 96	2.06	**E+ / 0.6**	-5.50	-9.82
FO	iShares MSCI Brazil Index	EWZ	**C-**	23.94	**A+ / 9.9**	68.67 / 99	37.41 / 98	--	1.86	**E- / 0.0**	-0.42	N/A
FO	iShares S&P Latin American 40 Idx	ILF	**C-**	90.69	**A+ / 9.8**	58.53 / 99	32.02 / 97	--	1.01	**E- / 0.0**	0.49	0.58
FO	Thai Capital Fund	TF	**C-**	9.52	**A+ / 9.7**	40.61 / 94	34.72 / 98	7.77 / 30	0.45	**E / 0.3**	9.68	-1.69
FO	Thai Fund	TTF	**C-**	9.69	**A / 9.4**	22.58 / 56	28.98 / 96	14.23 / 66	1.31	**E+ / 0.7**	16.89	11.36
FO	Third Canadian General Invst Tr	T.THD	**C-**	28.95	**A- / 9.1**	37.81 / 91	22.53 / 93	19.75 / 93	1.03	**D- / 1.1**	-21.67	-15.44
FO	JF China Region Fund	JFC	**C-**	12.82	**B / 8.2**	13.35 / 33	22.94 / 94	10.41 / 44	0.00	**D- / 1.3**	-13.79	-9.84
FO	Asia Pacific Fund	APB	**C-**	15.21	**C+ / 6.2**	29.18 / 73	14.25 / 69	9.95 / 41	0.98	**C- / 4.2**	-10.58	-10.74
FO	Morgan Stanley Asia Pacific Fund	APF	**C-**	13.05	**C / 5.5**	19.66 / 49	15.59 / 76	5.90 / 24	0.05	**C / 4.7**	-11.41	-11.89
FO	iShares MSCI UK Index	EWU	**C-**	18.07	**C- / 3.3**	13.69 / 34	11.80 / 54	2.08 / 15	1.92	**C+ / 6.6**	-0.50	0.45
FO	iShares MSCI EAFE Index Fund	EFA	**C-**	52.50	**D+ / 2.9**	12.97 / 31	11.61 / 52	--	1.53	**C+ / 6.8**	-0.06	0.31
FO	Greater China Fund	GCH	**D+**	16.20	**B- / 7.5**	20.92 / 51	19.96 / 89	14.29 / 66	1.28	**D- / 1.2**	-12.24	-9.26
FO	iShares MSCI Spain Index	EWP	**D+**	33.76	**B- / 7.2**	21.92 / 54	21.56 / 92	7.09 / 28	1.79	**D / 1.8**	-0.27	0.09
FO	iShares MSCI Hong Kong Index	EWH	**D+**	12.32	**C+ / 6.1**	27.66 / 69	13.61 / 66	1.88 / 14	2.19	**D+ / 2.9**	-0.81	0.12
FO	Swiss Helvetia Fund	SWZ	**D+**	13.69	**C- / 3.5**	13.56 / 33	13.40 / 64	5.05 / 22	0.15	**C+ / 5.6**	-14.70	-14.86
FO	iShares MSCI South Korea Index	EWY	**D-**	32.68	**B / 7.7**	36.30 / 87	14.78 / 72	9.70 / 39	0.31	**E- / 0.0**	0.25	0.18
FO	iShares MSCI Sweden Index	EWD	**D-**	20.25	**B / 7.7**	17.74 / 43	21.38 / 92	-3.70 / 7	0.73	**E- / 0.0**	-1.79	0.21
FO	iShares MSCI Belgium Index	EWK	**D-**	17.81	**C+ / 6.5**	27.44 / 68	18.44 / 85	9.05 / 35	1.59	**E / 0.4**	-1.17	0.38
FO	iShares MSCI Italy Index	EWI	**D-**	24.22	**C / 4.9**	17.78 / 44	16.79 / 79	2.46 / 15	2.61	**D+ / 2.5**	-0.49	0.08
FO	Taiwan Greater China Fund	TFC	**D-**	5.17	**D+ / 2.7**	19.42 / 49	6.02 / 13	-8.49 / 4	0.20	**C / 4.8**	-7.18	-8.91
FO	HOLDRS Europe 2001	EKH	**D-**	63.10	**D / 2.1**	7.82 / 18	9.17 / 32	--	2.05	**C / 4.5**	0.00	N/A
FO	iShares MSCI Switzerland Index	EWL	**D-**	16.60	**D- / 1.1**	9.26 / 22	7.41 / 20	1.40 / 14	0.52	**C+ / 5.7**	-0.18	0.51

N/A denotes number is not available

Fund Type	Fund Name (99 Pct = Best, 0 Pct = Worst)	Ticker Symbol	Overall Weiss Investment Rating	Price As of 6/30/05	PERFORMANCE: Performance Rating/Pts	Annualized Total Return Through 6/30/05: 1Yr/Pct	3Yr/Pct	5Yr/Pct	Dividend Yield %	RISK: Risk Rating/Pts	VALUATION: Premium/Discount As of 6/30/05	1 Year Average
GEI	BlackRock Core Bond Trust	BHK	**C+**	14.32	**C+ / 5.6**	21.19 / 52	11.45 / 50	--	7.35	**B- / 7.2**	-5.10	-8.09
GEI	Duff & Phelps Utilities & Crp Bd Tr	DUC	**C**	14.57	**C / 5.4**	24.22 / 60	11.26 / 49	13.48 / 62	7.00	**C+ / 6.0**	10.30	5.81
GEI	Western Asset Premier Bond Fund	WEA	**C-**	14.85	**C- / 3.2**	16.72 / 41	10.15 / 39	--	7.32	**B- / 7.2**	-3.26	-0.94
GEI	Western Asset Income Fund	PAI	**C-**	14.81	**D+ / 2.9**	17.08 / 42	8.48 / 25	11.36 / 50	5.73	**B- / 7.6**	-8.07	-8.51
GEI	J Hancock Income Securities Tr	JHS	**C-**	14.98	**D / 1.9**	11.02 / 26	7.76 / 21	9.97 / 41	6.88	**B- / 7.6**	-5.25	-4.67
GEI	Fort Dearborn Inc. Secs.	FDI	**C-**	14.90	**D / 1.8**	15.35 / 39	5.46 / 10	9.13 / 36	5.32	**B / 8.6**	-10.72	-10.57
GEI	Pioneer Interest Shares	MUO	**C-**	11.43	**D / 1.7**	13.67 / 34	5.06 / 9	8.30 / 32	5.59	**B / 8.3**	-9.29	-10.25
GEI	BlackRock Broad Inv Gr 2009 Tm Tr	BCT	**C-**	15.81	**D / 1.6**	9.13 / 22	7.10 / 18	13.19 / 60	5.70	**B / 8.1**	4.01	1.56
GEI	J Hancock Investors Trust	JHI	**D+**	19.98	**D / 2.1**	8.88 / 21	9.56 / 35	11.00 / 47	7.28	**B- / 7.1**	-3.38	1.51
GEI	Montgomery Street Inc. Sec.	MTS	**D+**	18.11	**D- / 1.2**	10.92 / 26	5.47 / 10	9.89 / 41	6.38	**B- / 7.4**	-8.67	-6.70

N/A denotes number is not available

Fund Type	Fund Name (99 Pct = Best, 0 Pct = Worst)	Ticker Symbol	Overall Weiss Investment Rating	Price As of 6/30/05	PERFORMANCE: Performance Rating/Pts	Annualized Total Return Through 6/30/05: 1Yr/Pct	3Yr/Pct	5Yr/Pct	Dividend Yield %	RISK: Risk Rating/Pts	VALUATION: Premium/Discount As of 6/30/05	1 Year Average
GEN	Putnam Premier Income Trust	PPT	**C**	6.51	**C- / 3.3**	15.88 / 39	9.50 / 34	9.38 / 38	5.57	**B / 8.2**	-9.21	-9.96
GEN	MFS Multimarket Income Trust	MMT	**C**	6.29	**D+ / 2.9**	14.29 / 35	9.09 / 32	7.77 / 31	6.05	**B- / 7.8**	-8.97	-9.56
GEN	Putnam Master Intermediate Inc Tr	PIM	**C-**	6.50	**D+ / 2.3**	8.26 / 19	8.97 / 30	9.20 / 37	6.49	**B- / 7.2**	-8.96	-8.65
GEN	MFS Charter Income Trust	MCR	**C-**	8.70	**D / 2.0**	11.97 / 29	7.28 / 19	7.33 / 29	5.71	**B / 8.5**	-10.95	-9.88
GEN	Allmerica Securities Trust	ALM	**C-**	9.42	**D- / 1.5**	13.07 / 31	4.99 / 8	6.29 / 26	5.79	**B / 8.0**	-10.54	-11.75
GEN	Van Kampen Income Trust	VIN	**C-**	5.81	**D- / 1.2**	13.30 / 32	4.66 / 7	4.84 / 21	5.70	**B / 8.4**	-10.62	-11.68
GEN	ACM Managed Income Fund	AMF	**E+**	3.67	**E+ / 0.6**	-4.63 / 3	5.77 / 12	0.45 / 13	5.83	**C / 5.2**	-12.20	-6.00

N/A denotes number is not available

99 Pct = Best
0 Pct = Worst

Fund Type	Fund Name	Ticker Symbol	Overall Weiss Investment Rating	Price As of 6/30/05	PERFORMANCE: Performance Rating/Pts	Annualized Total Return Through 6/30/05: 1Yr/Pct	3Yr/Pct	5Yr/Pct	Dividend Yield %	RISK: Risk Rating/Pts	VALUATION: Premium/Discount As of 6/30/05	1 Year Average
GL	Scudder Multi-Market Income Trust	KMM	**B+**	10.21	**A- / 9.2**	42.62 / 96	21.05 / 91	14.63 / 69	7.72	**C / 4.9**	5.48	-1.71
GL	Scudder Strategic Income Fund	KST	**B**	14.01	**B+ / 8.7**	32.08 / 79	20.89 / 91	8.78 / 34	7.63	**C / 5.0**	0.79	-1.85
GL	Salomon Br 2008 Wldwide $ Gov Tm Tr	SBG	**B**	11.19	**C- / 3.8**	11.46 / 28	12.18 / 58	14.77 / 70	7.72	**B+ / 9.7**	-2.95	-0.42
GL	Herzfeld Caribbean Basin Fund	CUBA	**B-**	6.30	**B+ / 8.9**	28.05 / 70	22.86 / 94	5.93 / 25	0.00	**C / 4.4**	-12.98	-13.44
GL	Alliance World Dollar Govt Fund II	AWF	**B-**	12.29	**B- / 7.5**	19.98 / 50	18.93 / 86	16.59 / 80	7.20	**C+ / 5.8**	-12.78	-11.59
GL	Aberdeen Australia Equity Fund	IAF	**C+**	12.20	**A+ / 9.6**	51.75 / 99	31.89 / 97	20.13 / 93	8.55	**D+ / 2.8**	4.18	-2.98
GL	BlackRock Income Opportunity Trust	BNA	**C+**	11.25	**C / 4.6**	18.77 / 46	10.80 / 45	11.97 / 52	7.41	**B- / 7.6**	-7.02	-7.95
GL	Managed High Yield Plus Fund	HYF	**C**	5.16	**B- / 7.0**	14.44 / 36	19.64 / 88	0.77 / 13	11.07	**C- / 4.2**	4.45	9.86
GL	Aberdeen Asia-Pacific Income Fund	FAX	**C**	6.35	**C+ / 6.9**	19.05 / 47	18.33 / 85	16.92 / 83	6.67	**C- / 4.2**	-4.65	-3.03
GL	ACM Managed Dollar Income Fund	ADF	**C**	7.80	**C+ / 5.9**	6.13 / 13	16.77 / 79	10.55 / 45	7.93	**C+ / 5.7**	-4.29	-1.26
GL	Alliance World Dollar Govt Fund	AWG	**C**	12.39	**C+ / 5.8**	21.56 / 53	13.61 / 66	13.98 / 65	6.08	**C / 5.5**	-12.25	-11.51
GL	Salomon Br Worldwide Inc Fd	SBW	**C**	15.16	**C+ / 5.8**	13.82 / 34	17.43 / 82	17.57 / 86	7.66	**C+ / 5.9**	-7.67	3.53
GL	Aberdeen Global Income Fund	FCO	**C**	13.76	**C / 5.5**	21.35 / 53	16.34 / 78	16.65 / 81	5.37	**C+ / 5.7**	-2.89	-0.39
GL	Salomon Br Global Partners Income	GDF	**C**	12.87	**C / 5.1**	2.30 / 8	17.73 / 83	15.99 / 78	8.04	**C+ / 5.8**	0.39	11.43
GL	Hartford Income Shares Fund Inc	HSF	**C**	7.75	**C / 4.7**	14.73 / 37	11.71 / 53	9.30 / 37	7.14	**C+ / 6.9**	-5.02	-6.85
GL	J Hancock Patriot Global Div Fd	PGD	**C**	13.20	**C- / 4.2**	19.71 / 49	11.83 / 55	12.59 / 56	6.25	**B- / 7.3**	-8.01	-2.60
GL	Colonial InterMkt Inc Tr I	CMK	**C**	8.82	**C- / 3.9**	19.92 / 50	10.48 / 42	9.82 / 40	7.32	**B- / 7.8**	-6.96	-8.81
GL	PIMCO Strategic Glob Gov Fund	RCS	**C-**	12.67	**C+ / 6.6**	31.45 / 78	12.24 / 58	17.00 / 84	7.28	**C- / 3.6**	16.45	7.98
GL	Strategic Global Income Fund	SGL	**C-**	13.25	**C / 4.9**	24.92 / 62	14.58 / 71	16.85 / 82	7.44	**C / 4.6**	11.44	11.43
GL	Salomon Br High Inc Fd II	HIX	**C-**	10.81	**C- / 3.9**	-0.39 / 6	15.17 / 74	11.24 / 49	8.93	**C+ / 5.7**	-6.33	2.60
GL	MFS Government Markets Income Trust	MGF	**C-**	6.62	**E+ / 0.9**	8.14 / 19	4.54 / 7	7.59 / 29	4.59	**B+ / 9.2**	-11.62	-11.36
GL	Gabelli Global Multimedia Trust	GGT	**D+**	10.03	**C- / 4.2**	13.24 / 32	13.63 / 66	-2.94 / 7	2.38	**C / 5.0**	-13.61	-14.19
GL	Templeton Global Income Fd	GIM	**D+**	8.87	**C- / 3.7**	20.04 / 50	12.51 / 60	15.69 / 76	5.41	**C / 5.3**	-2.42	-1.46
GL	MFS Intermediate Income Trust	MIN	**D+**	6.51	**E / 0.5**	7.31 / 16	2.48 / 3	7.04 / 28	5.51	**B / 8.3**	-9.83	-10.27
GL	streetTRACKS DJ Global Titan	DGT	**D**	63.21	**E+ / 0.9**	4.68 / 11	6.18 / 13	--	2.14	**B- / 7.0**	-0.09	0.10
GL	iShares S&P Global Telecomm Sect	IXP	**D-**	49.24	**C- / 3.6**	11.92 / 29	13.07 / 63	--	1.35	**C- / 3.3**	0.29	0.32
GL	Prospect Street Income Shares	CNN	**D-**	5.99	**D / 2.0**	13.61 / 33	7.49 / 20	3.71 / 18	7.85	**C / 4.8**	-9.65	-6.87
GL	Global Income Fund	GIF	**D-**	4.35	**E / 0.4**	10.14 / 24	4.08 / 6	8.11 / 32	6.44	**C+ / 6.9**	-5.23	-6.13
GL	Transamerica Income Shares	TAI	**D-**	22.19	**E / 0.4**	9.64 / 23	1.44 / 2	7.71 / 30	7.09	**B- / 7.2**	-5.37	-5.79
GL	Morgan Stanley Global Opp Bond Fund	MGB	**E+**	7.80	**C / 4.4**	13.93 / 35	15.54 / 75	7.85 / 31	7.10	**D / 1.6**	-4.06	8.79
GL	Canadian World Fund Limited	T.CWF	**E+**	4.10	**C- / 3.2**	19.88 / 50	12.24 / 58	-3.89 / 6	0.00	**D / 1.7**	-25.86	-24.04
GL	Z-Seven Fund	ZSEV	**E**	4.35	**E- / 0.0**	7.94 / 18	0.39 / 1	-10.13 / 3	0.00	**C- / 3.1**	-21.20	-17.66
GL	iShares S&P Global Technology Sect	IXN	**E-**	48.77	**D- / 1.1**	-2.82 / 4	8.50 / 25	--	1.29	**D- / 1.4**	0.06	0.36

N/A denotes number is not available

	99 Pct = Best 0 Pct = Worst				PERFORMANCE					RISK	VALUATION	
						Annualized Total Return Through 6/30/05					Premium/Discount	
Fund Type	Fund Name	Ticker Symbol	Overall Weiss Investment Rating	Price As of 6/30/05	Performance Rating/Pts	1Yr/Pct	3Yr/Pct	5Yr/Pct	Dividend Yield %	Risk Rating/Pts	As of 6/30/05	1 Year Average
GR	iShares Russell Midcap Value Index	IWS	**B-**	116.86	**C+ / 6.5**	21.09 / 52	16.11 / 77	--	1.44	**B- / 7.0**	-0.09	0.03
GR	HOLDRS Wireless	WMH	**C+**	55.80	**B / 8.1**	11.50 / 28	23.25 / 95	--	0.59	**C- / 4.1**	0.00	N/A
GR	iShares Russell Midcap Index	IWR	**C+**	81.12	**C+ / 5.7**	16.41 / 40	15.47 / 75	--	0.98	**C+ / 6.9**	-0.04	0.03
GR	HOLDRS Internet	HHH	**C**	55.94	**A- / 9.0**	-10.32 / 0	32.31 / 97	-12.11 / 3	0.00	**D+ / 2.7**	0.00	N/A
GR	iShares S&P MidCap 400/Barra Value	IJJ	**C**	65.64	**C / 4.8**	14.77 / 37	13.82 / 67	--	1.58	**C+ / 6.6**	-0.11	-0.01
GR	iShares Russell Midcap Growth Index	IWP	**C**	84.87	**C / 4.6**	9.65 / 23	14.36 / 70	--	0.27	**C+ / 6.4**	0.07	0.04
GR	iShares S&P SmallCap 600/Barra Gwth	IJT	**C**	106.60	**C / 4.4**	11.07 / 27	14.19 / 68	--	0.82	**C+ / 6.3**	-0.20	-0.01
GR	iShares S&P MidCap 400	IJH	**C**	67.60	**C- / 4.1**	13.34 / 32	12.50 / 60	7.90 / 31	0.91	**C+ / 6.9**	-0.12	N/A
GR	Equus II	EQS	**C**	8.38	**C- / 3.8**	16.91 / 42	9.67 / 36	0.73 / 13	6.91	**B- / 7.0**	-27.82	-26.32
GR	SPDR Mid Cap 400	MDY	**C**	123.21	**C- / 3.8**	12.57 / 30	12.32 / 58	7.75 / 30	0.89	**C+ / 6.9**	-0.29	-0.02
GR	Royce Focus Trust	FUND	**C-**	8.47	**C / 5.4**	16.85 / 41	18.29 / 84	20.20 / 94	2.81	**C / 4.8**	-3.86	1.19
GR	streetTRACKS DJ US Small Cap Value	DSV	**C-**	174.03	**C / 5.0**	14.29 / 35	15.03 / 73	--	2.16	**C / 4.4**	-0.51	-0.09
GR	iShares Russell 3000 Value	IWW	**C-**	86.82	**C- / 3.0**	14.05 / 35	10.71 / 44	--	1.14	**B- / 7.1**	-0.08	0.03
GR	iShares S&P MidCap 400/Barra Growth	IJK	**C-**	68.46	**C- / 3.0**	11.08 / 27	10.95 / 47	--	0.57	**B- / 7.2**	-0.09	-0.01
GR	streetTRACKS DJ US Lg Cap Value	ELV	**C-**	136.14	**D+ / 2.3**	11.00 / 26	8.87 / 28	--	2.18	**B- / 7.1**	0.17	N/A
GR	iShares Russell 1000	IWB	**C-**	64.40	**D / 2.2**	8.28 / 20	9.18 / 32	-1.97 / 9	1.10	**B- / 7.3**	-0.02	0.03
GR	MVC Capital	MVC	**C-**	0.00	**D- / 1.1**	6.17 / 14	5.35 / 9	-7.09 / 4	1.20	**B / 8.9**		-1.17
GR	Royce Value Trust	RVT	**D+**	18.70	**C / 4.9**	19.03 / 47	15.67 / 76	18.25 / 88	8.47	**C- / 3.7**	7.35	6.58
GR	Central Securities	CET	**D+**	23.78	**C- / 3.4**	10.58 / 25	11.08 / 47	-0.06 / 12	0.25	**C+ / 5.6**	-15.49	-14.30
GR	iShares S&P 500/Barra Value	IVE	**D+**	62.17	**D+ / 2.6**	11.00 / 26	9.91 / 37	3.02 / 17	1.47	**C+ / 6.7**	-0.06	0.03
GR	iShares Russell 3000	IWV	**D+**	68.35	**D / 2.2**	8.03 / 19	9.33 / 34	-1.43 / 10	1.19	**B- / 7.1**	0.00	0.03
GR	iShares Dow Jones US Total Mkt	IYY	**D+**	57.37	**D / 2.2**	7.93 / 18	9.35 / 34	-1.84 / 9	1.39	**B- / 7.1**	-0.03	0.02
GR	iShares S&P 500	IVV	**D+**	119.00	**D / 1.8**	6.72 / 15	8.23 / 23	-2.45 / 8	1.30	**B- / 7.3**	-0.07	0.02
GR	General American Investors	GAM	**D+**	31.72	**D / 1.7**	8.89 / 21	7.17 / 18	2.89 / 17	0.01	**B- / 7.6**	-14.39	-11.80
GR	streetTRACKS Total Market ETF	TMW	**D+**	85.14	**D / 1.6**	7.68 / 17	7.69 / 21	--	1.70	**B- / 7.2**	0.12	0.01
GR	iShares Dow Jones US Cns Gd Sct Idx	IYK	**D+**	52.30	**E+ / 0.9**	2.41 / 8	6.42 / 14	6.51 / 27	1.61	**B- / 7.8**	0.02	N/A
GR	SPDR Health Care	XLV	**D+**	31.10	**E+ / 0.8**	3.46 / 10	5.24 / 9	1.86 / 14	1.24	**B- / 7.9**	0.03	0.02
GR	iShares Goldman Sachs Ntwr Index Fd	IGN	**D**	27.70	**B- / 7.0**	-10.27 / 0	22.96 / 94	--	0.00	**D- / 1.4**	-0.14	-0.06
GR	iShares Russell 2000 Value	IWN	**D**	63.10	**C / 4.4**	13.25 / 32	13.52 / 65	--	1.33	**C- / 3.9**	-0.39	-0.04
GR	iShares S&P SmallCap 600	IJR	**D**	53.70	**C- / 4.0**	11.96 / 29	12.95 / 63	9.84 / 40	0.76	**C / 4.4**	-0.44	-0.05
GR	SPDR 500	SPY	**D**	118.98	**D / 1.8**	6.62 / 15	8.20 / 23	-2.42 / 8	1.64	**C+ / 6.8**	-0.09	0.01
GR	Salomon Br Fund	SBF	**D**	12.88	**D / 1.6**	6.44 / 14	7.79 / 22	-2.76 / 8	0.92	**C+ / 6.3**	-13.27	-14.33
GR	SPDR Industrial	XLI	**D**	29.29	**D- / 1.3**	4.40 / 11	8.67 / 27	2.04 / 15	1.02	**B- / 7.0**	0.03	-0.01
GR	iShares Dow Jones US Industrial	IYJ	**D**	53.39	**D- / 1.2**	3.58 / 10	8.46 / 25	-1.07 / 11	0.48	**C+ / 6.7**	-0.07	0.02
GR	iShares Russell 1000 Growth	IWF	**D**	47.82	**D- / 1.0**	1.51 / 7	6.98 / 17	-10.50 / 3	0.68	**B- / 7.1**	-0.04	0.04
GR	iShares Russell 3000 Growth	IWZ	**D**	38.78	**D- / 1.0**	1.32 / 7	6.96 / 17	--	0.43	**C+ / 6.8**	0.05	0.02
GR	iShares S&P 500/Barra Growth	IVW	**D**	56.50	**E+ / 0.7**	1.99 / 8	5.94 / 13	-7.72 / 4	0.89	**B- / 7.3**	0.02	0.06
GR	SPDR Consumer Staples	XLP	**D**	22.74	**E- / 0.2**	0.90 / 6	2.56 / 3	-0.49 / 11	1.97	**B / 8.2**	0.13	0.02
GR	HOLDRS Internet Infrastructure	IIH	**D-**	4.05	**B- / 7.4**	10.36 / 25	21.65 / 92	-41.59 / 0	0.00	**E- / 0.0**	0.00	N/A
GR	HOLDRS Broadband	BDH	**D-**	15.33	**B- / 7.2**	-4.47 / 3	22.85 / 94	-29.76 / 0	0.01	**E- / 0.0**	0.00	N/A
GR	Royce Micro-Cap Trust	RMT	**D-**	13.59	**C / 5.3**	14.30 / 35	16.09 / 77	20.17 / 93	8.93	**D / 2.2**	1.87	1.45
GR	iShares Russell 2000	IWM	**D-**	62.21	**C- / 3.4**	8.03 / 19	12.43 / 59	5.00 / 21	0.92	**C- / 3.4**	-0.70	-0.05
GR	iShares S&P SmallCap 600/BarraValue	IJS	**D-**	60.43	**C- / 3.2**	13.24 / 32	11.52 / 51	--	0.70	**C- / 3.8**	-0.21	-0.05
GR	Zweig Fund	ZF	**D-**	5.38	**D- / 1.1**	21.65 / 53	3.20 / 4	-3.12 / 7	11.14	**C / 5.5**	-6.76	-8.42
GR	iShares Dow Jones US Cns Sv Sct Idx	IYC	**D-**	58.97	**E+ / 0.8**	5.72 / 13	6.05 / 13	0.09 / 12	0.16	**C+ / 6.3**	-0.10	N/A
GR	Diamond Series Trust I	DIA	**D-**	102.86	**E / 0.5**	1.06 / 6	5.80 / 12	1.63 / 14	1.33	**B- / 7.2**	-0.05	0.02
GR	streetTRACKS DJ US Lg Cap Growth	ELG	**D-**	46.51	**E / 0.5**	-0.47 / 6	5.47 / 11	--	0.81	**C+ / 6.6**	0.45	0.03
GR	HOLDRS Market 2000 +	MKH	**D-**	53.59	**E / 0.4**	1.89 / 7	4.75 / 8	--	1.38	**B- / 7.1**	0.00	N/A
GR	streetTRACKS DJ US Small Cap Growth	DSG	**E+**	74.74	**C- / 3.2**	8.80 / 21	11.91 / 55	--	0.42	**C- / 3.3**	-0.07	0.04
GR	Alliance All-Market Advantage Fd	AMO	**E+**	14.49	**E+ / 0.7**	5.74 / 13	4.49 / 7	-8.56 / 3	8.94	**C / 4.7**	7.97	8.86
GR	HOLDRS Retail	RTH	**E+**	94.62	**E / 0.5**	6.58 / 15	3.89 / 5	--	0.09	**C / 4.7**	0.00	N/A
GR	Foxby Corp	FXX	**E+**	2.18	**E- / 0.0**	1.40 / 7	-1.77 / 1	-23.58 / 1	0.00	**C / 5.5**	-12.80	-12.76

N/A denotes number is not available

					PERFORMANCE					RISK	VALUATION	
	99 Pct = Best *0 Pct = Worst*					Annualized Total Return Through 6/30/05					Premium/Discount	
Fund Type	Fund Name	Ticker Symbol	Overall Weiss Investment Rating	Price As of 6/30/05	Perform-ance Rating/Pts	1Yr/Pct	3Yr/Pct	5Yr/Pct	Dividend Yield %	Risk Rating/ Pts	As of 6/30/05	1 Year Average
GI	iShares Cohen&Steers Realty Major	ICF	A-	70.50	A- / 9.0	33.54 / 82	21.41 / 92	--	5.10	C+ / 5.9	0.09	N/A
GI	iShares Dow Jones US Real Estate	IYR	B+	62.82	B+ / 8.5	29.40 / 74	19.09 / 87	18.47 / 89	4.04	C+ / 5.9	-0.49	-0.11
GI	Franklin Multi-Income Trust	FMI	B+	9.35	B+ / 8.3	40.29 / 94	14.65 / 71	11.24 / 48	4.48	C+ / 5.8	-1.89	-9.77
GI	Cohen&Steers Adv Inc Realty Fund	RLF	B	21.87	A- / 9.0	37.42 / 90	20.42 / 90	--	8.11	C / 4.7	-6.58	-6.41
GI	Nuveen Real Estate Inc Fund	JRS	B	20.11	B / 8.1	31.77 / 78	17.42 / 82	--	8.00	C+ / 5.6	-10.26	-7.44
GI	Cohen&Steers Quality Income Realty	RQI	B-	20.52	A- / 9.1	36.48 / 88	20.68 / 90	--	7.93	C / 4.3	-10.67	-8.82
GI	Cohen&Steers Total Return Realty	RFI	B-	19.80	B / 7.7	27.56 / 69	17.60 / 82	19.31 / 92	6.56	C+ / 5.7	-0.25	0.51
GI	streetTRACKS Wilshire REIT	RWR	C+	194.85	B+ / 8.8	31.89 / 79	19.98 / 89	--	4.19	C- / 3.9	-0.02	0.01
GI	AIM Select Real Estate Income Fund	RRE	C+	16.84	C+ / 6.1	23.32 / 58	13.59 / 65	--	7.26	C+ / 5.8	-15.38	-13.62
GI	Delaware Inv Glob Div & Inc	DGF	C+	13.07	C+ / 5.8	27.51 / 68	11.10 / 48	12.97 / 59	7.43	C+ / 6.0	-2.90	-7.40
GI	Putnam High Income Bond Fund	PCF	C+	7.80	C+ / 5.8	16.90 / 41	15.29 / 74	9.53 / 38	7.18	C+ / 6.9	-8.24	-9.66
GI	Chartwell Dividend and Income Fund	CWF	C	10.59	B- / 7.4	31.72 / 78	13.99 / 68	11.15 / 48	9.44	C- / 3.9	21.86	14.27
GI	MFS Special Value Trust	MFV	C	10.77	C+ / 6.4	10.42 / 25	18.96 / 86	5.18 / 22	8.95	C / 4.9	7.70	12.72
GI	Delaware Inv Div & Inc	DDF	D	12.51	C- / 3.7	23.30 / 58	6.71 / 15	12.60 / 57	7.67	C / 4.5	-3.62	-7.59
GI	Castle Convertible Fund	CVF	D	22.15	E- / 0.1	2.58 / 8	1.97 / 2	5.72 / 24	3.07	B / 8.2	-15.52	-12.55
GI	Ellsworth Convertible Growth & Inc	ECF	D	7.49	E- / 0.1	1.70 / 7	1.05 / 2	3.45 / 17	3.62	B- / 7.8	-14.20	-11.70
GI	Bancroft Convertible Fund	BCV	D	17.32	E- / 0.0	-2.20 / 5	0.65 / 1	2.79 / 16	3.89	B / 8.3	-15.10	-11.94
GI	Franklin Universal Trust	FT	D-	6.14	C- / 3.0	22.71 / 56	7.22 / 18	5.16 / 22	6.81	C / 4.6	-12.03	-12.55
GI	Blue Chip Value Fund	BLU	D-	6.24	D+ / 2.5	6.19 / 14	10.84 / 45	4.58 / 20	8.75	C / 4.7	10.44	16.76
GI	Renaissance Cap Growth & Inc III	RENN	E+	11.25	C / 4.3	-2.37 / 4	16.31 / 78	4.82 / 20	3.46	E+ / 0.8	-17.40	-16.91
GI	Gabelli Convertible&Income Sec Fund	GCV	E+	9.50	D- / 1.4	4.22 / 10	6.82 / 16	9.99 / 42	8.06	C / 4.9	18.75	17.05
GI	Zweig Total Return Fund	ZTR	E+	5.12	E / 0.4	11.70 / 28	2.21 / 2	4.00 / 19	10.53	C+ / 5.8	-5.88	-6.10
GI	TCW Convertible Securities Fund	CVT	E	5.09	E- / 0.0	9.29 / 22	-0.90 / 1	-3.58 / 7	8.06	C- / 3.1	-7.62	-9.26

N/A denotes number is not available

Fund Type	Fund Name (99 Pct = Best, 0 Pct = Worst)	Ticker Symbol	Overall Weiss Investment Rating	Price As of 6/30/05	PERFORMANCE: Performance Rating/Pts	Annualized Total Return Through 6/30/05: 1Yr/Pct	3Yr/Pct	5Yr/Pct	Dividend Yield %	RISK: Risk Rating/Pts	VALUATION: Premium/Discount As of 6/30/05	1 Year Average
HL	HOLDRS Biotech	BBH	**A+**	167.30	**A / 9.4**	16.87 / 41	27.32 / 96	-0.69 / 11	0.00	**C+ / 6.6**	0.00	N/A
HL	H&Q Life Sciences Investors	HQL	**C-**	15.89	**C / 5.3**	12.12 / 29	14.23 / 69	0.99 / 14	7.81	**C- / 4.2**	-1.85	-1.84
HL	iShares Dow Jones US Healthcare	IYH	**C-**	61.20	**D- / 1.5**	5.63 / 12	7.07 / 17	-0.49 / 12	0.78	**B- / 7.9**	-0.03	N/A
HL	iShares S&P Global Healthcare Sect	IXJ	**C-**	50.15	**E+ / 0.8**	4.84 / 11	5.35 / 9	--	0.73	**B / 8.9**	0.06	0.34
HL	H&Q Healthcare Investors	HQH	**D**	17.65	**C / 4.3**	12.32 / 30	12.46 / 59	2.83 / 16	7.95	**C- / 3.7**	-2.00	-2.06
HL	HOLDRS Pharmaceutical	PPH	**D-**	74.03	**E- / 0.1**	-3.62 / 3	0.37 / 1	-5.35 / 5	2.23	**C+ / 6.5**	0.00	N/A
HL	iShares Biotechnology Index Fund	IBB	**E-**	67.57	**D- / 1.1**	-8.95 / 1	9.83 / 37	--	0.00	**D / 1.6**	0.04	-0.02

N/A denotes number is not available

	99 Pct = Best 0 Pct = Worst				PERFORMANCE					RISK	VALUATION	
Fund Type	Fund Name	Ticker Symbol	Overall Weiss Investment Rating	Price As of 6/30/05	Performance Rating/Pts	Annualized Total Return Through 6/30/05 1Yr/Pct	3Yr/Pct	5Yr/Pct	Dividend Yield %	Risk Rating/Pts	Premium/Discount As of 6/30/05	1 Year Average
IN	J Hancock Patriot Prem Div Fd II	PDT	C+	12.07	C+ / 6.5	27.68 / 69	13.59 / 65	13.66 / 64	6.46	C+ / 6.7	-3.44	-3.61
IN	J Hancock Patriot Pref Div Fd	PPF	C	13.76	C / 5.5	18.84 / 47	12.91 / 62	14.05 / 65	6.28	C+ / 6.1	-4.24	-5.09
IN	Vanguard Extended Market VIPERs	VXF	C	83.10	C / 5.2	13.63 / 33	14.96 / 73	--	0.96	C+ / 6.2	-0.36	-0.02
IN	iShares Russell 1000 Value	IWD	C-	66.58	C- / 3.2	14.46 / 36	10.90 / 47	6.00 / 25	1.69	B- / 7.1	-0.15	0.02
IN	J Hancock Patriot Prem Div Fd I	PDF	C-	9.30	D / 1.9	11.70 / 28	7.55 / 20	10.01 / 42	5.94	B- / 7.8	-6.16	-0.61
IN	Flaherty&Crumrine Preferred Inc Opp	PFO	D+	12.77	D+ / 2.5	7.89 / 18	9.57 / 35	14.46 / 68	6.57	C+ / 6.5	0.24	5.43
IN	Vanguard Total Stock Market VIPERs	VTI	D+	117.05	D+ / 2.4	8.04 / 19	9.64 / 36	--	1.38	C+ / 6.8	-0.13	0.01
IN	Adams Express Company	ADX	D+	12.91	D / 1.8	8.64 / 20	8.51 / 26	-5.05 / 6	1.55	B- / 7.0	-13.99	-12.92
IN	iShares S&P 100 Index Fund	OEF	D+	55.77	E+ / 0.8	2.86 / 9	6.35 / 14	--	1.65	B- / 7.8	-0.13	N/A
IN	Cornerstone Total Return Fund	CRF	D	15.48	C+ / 6.5	5.10 / 12	18.82 / 86	13.29 / 61	13.45	D- / 1.3	35.79	35.33
IN	Cornerstone Strategic Value Fund	CLM	D	7.17	C / 5.5	-3.77 / 3	18.63 / 85	-1.50 / 10	14.52	C- / 3.0	22.77	27.68
IN	Source Capital	SOR	D	69.45	C- / 3.7	16.17 / 40	11.71 / 53	16.12 / 78	5.71	C / 4.9	11.41	12.27
IN	Flaherty&Crumrine Preferred Income	PFD	D	16.75	D+ / 2.6	2.53 / 8	10.76 / 45	14.73 / 69	6.39	C / 5.2	4.56	11.08
IN	iShares S&P Global 100	IOO	D	60.30	D- / 1.4	6.33 / 14	7.89 / 22	--	1.70	C+ / 6.8	0.08	0.11
IN	Liberty All-Star Equity Fund	USA	D-	8.92	C- / 3.3	7.70 / 17	12.10 / 57	4.28 / 20	9.33	C- / 3.9	2.76	3.69
IN	Tri-Continental Corporation	TY	D-	17.83	E+ / 0.7	7.98 / 18	4.84 / 8	-2.11 / 9	1.35	C+ / 6.5	-16.80	-16.42
IN	Boulder Growth&Income Fund	BIF	E+	6.63	E+ / 0.7	9.77 / 23	6.20 / 13	2.78 / 16	0.00	C / 4.3	-14.34	-12.27
IN	Boulder Total Return Fund	BTF	E+	17.11	E- / 0.1	7.47 / 17	2.45 / 3	10.56 / 45	0.00	C+ / 5.9	-16.50	-13.34

N/A denotes number is not available

Fund Type	Fund Name (99 Pct = Best, 0 Pct = Worst)	Ticker Symbol	Overall Weiss Investment Rating	Price As of 6/30/05	PERFORMANCE: Performance Rating/Pts	Annualized Total Return Through 6/30/05: 1Yr/Pct	3Yr/Pct	5Yr/Pct	Dividend Yield %	RISK: Risk Rating/Pts	VALUATION: Premium/Discount As of 6/30/05	1 Year Average
LP	Nuveen Sr Inc	NSL	**C-**	8.57	**D / 1.6**	-5.91 / 2	10.90 / 47	6.03 / 25	7.03	**B- / 7.8**	1.30	10.89
LP	Van Kampen Senior Inc Tr	VVR	**C-**	7.90	**D- / 1.0**	-5.58 / 2	9.13 / 32	5.70 / 24	6.28	**B / 8.6**	-8.56	-1.17
LP	ING Prime Rate Trust	PPR	**D+**	6.99	**D- / 1.3**	-7.80 / 2	10.17 / 39	2.53 / 15	6.47	**B- / 7.9**	-5.03	2.56
LP	Citigroup Investments Corp Loan	TLI	**D**	13.11	**E / 0.3**	-7.60 / 2	5.84 / 12	5.60 / 23	5.53	**B / 8.2**	-8.45	-2.02
LP	Eaton Vance Senior Income Trust	EVF	**D**	7.93	**E / 0.3**	-12.01 / 0	6.65 / 15	3.76 / 18	6.12	**B- / 7.9**	-9.27	0.99

N/A denotes number is not available

Fund Type	Fund Name (99 Pct = Best, 0 Pct = Worst)	Ticker Symbol	Overall Weiss Investment Rating	Price As of 6/30/05	PERFORMANCE: Performance Rating/Pts	Annualized Total Return Through 6/30/05: 1Yr/Pct	3Yr/Pct	5Yr/Pct	Dividend Yield %	RISK: Risk Rating/Pts	VALUATION: Premium/Discount As of 6/30/05	1 Year Average
MTG	PIMCO Commercial Mortgage Trust	PCM	C-	14.34	C / 4.3	18.56 / 46	8.86 / 28	13.31 / 61	8.04	C / 5.3	14.72	10.52
MTG	American Income Fund	MRF	C-	8.28	D / 1.7	8.70 / 21	6.77 / 16	9.64 / 39	6.60	B / 8.4	-7.90	-7.96
MTG	Hyperion Total Return Fund	HTR	D+	9.26	D / 2.1	13.50 / 33	9.20 / 33	14.28 / 66	9.43	C+ / 6.7	1.76	9.12
MTG	American Strat Inc Portfolio III	CSP	D+	11.34	E+ / 0.7	5.52 / 12	5.57 / 11	10.67 / 46	8.58	B / 8.2	-5.81	-1.38
MTG	Hyperion 2005 Inv Gr Opp Tm Tr	HTO	D+	9.78	E / 0.3	3.95 / 10	2.65 / 3	8.55 / 33	0.12	B / 8.9	-1.11	-1.39
MTG	American Strat Inc Portfolio	ASP	D	11.40	E / 0.4	0.41 / 6	4.58 / 7	9.19 / 36	6.83	B- / 7.5	-8.65	-3.59
MTG	American Strat Inc Portfolio II	BSP	D	11.64	E / 0.3	-0.84 / 5	3.61 / 5	10.21 / 43	8.22	B- / 7.7	-5.67	-1.74
MTG	American Select Portfolio	SLA	D	11.88	E- / 0.2	2.99 / 9	2.81 / 4	9.58 / 39	7.02	B / 8.1	-9.31	-3.70
MTG	BlackRock Advantage Term Trust	BAT	D	10.26	E- / 0.2	1.64 / 7	2.64 / 3	9.38 / 38	5.85	B / 8.3	-0.68	-0.76
MTG	BlackRock Income Trust	BKT	E+	6.70	E / 0.4	6.60 / 15	4.95 / 8	10.70 / 46	9.04	C+ / 5.8	0.45	6.47

N/A denotes number is not available

Fund Type	Fund Name (99 Pct = Best, 0 Pct = Worst)	Ticker Symbol	Overall Weiss Investment Rating	Price As of 6/30/05	PERFORMANCE: Performance Rating/Pts	Annualized Total Return Through 6/30/05: 1Yr/Pct	3Yr/Pct	5Yr/Pct	Dividend Yield %	RISK: Risk Rating/Pts	VALUATION: Premium/Discount As of 6/30/05	1 Year Average
MUH	MFS Municipal Income Trust	MFM	**A-**	8.26	**B+ / 8.4**	21.69 / 82	9.08 / 67	9.35 / 67	6.63	**C+ / 6.5**	3.12	-1.25
MUH	Putnam High Yield Municipal Trust	PYM	**C**	7.17	**C / 4.9**	18.80 / 73	3.63 / 11	5.41 / 32	5.28	**C+ / 6.7**	-8.78	-13.05
MUH	Colonial Muni Inc Trust	CMU	**C-**	5.57	**D+ / 2.8**	12.20 / 47	5.47 / 25	6.42 / 40	6.26	**B- / 7.6**	-5.11	-1.44
MUH	Colonial High Inc Muni Tr	CXE	**C-**	6.29	**D+ / 2.6**	12.16 / 46	4.91 / 21	7.88 / 53	6.53	**B / 8.0**	-4.70	-1.16

N/A denotes number is not available

Fund Type	Fund Name (99 Pct = Best, 0 Pct = Worst)	Ticker Symbol	Overall Weiss Investment Rating	Price As of 6/30/05	PERFORMANCE: Performance Rating/Pts	Annualized Total Return Through 6/30/05: 1Yr/Pct	3Yr/Pct	5Yr/Pct	Dividend Yield %	RISK: Risk Rating/Pts	VALUATION: Premium/Discount As of 6/30/05	1 Year Average
MUN	BlackRock Investment Qual Muni Tr	BKN	**A+**	16.61	**A+ / 9.6**	28.68 / 97	13.47 / 90	12.60 / 92	5.43	**C+ / 6.5**	4.07	-3.77
MUN	MuniHoldings Fund II	MUH	**A+**	15.32	**A+ / 9.6**	27.08 / 95	14.47 / 93	13.96 / 96	6.85	**C+ / 6.9**	1.26	-1.61
MUN	Scudder Strategic Municipal Inc Tr	KSM	**A+**	13.66	**A+ / 9.6**	26.81 / 95	13.43 / 90	12.44 / 91	6.47	**B- / 7.1**	9.11	2.56
MUN	BlackRock Municipal Bond Trust	BBK	**A+**	16.09	**A / 9.5**	28.64 / 97	12.44 / 87	--	6.38	**C+ / 6.5**	-0.12	-3.63
MUN	MuniHoldings Fund	MHD	**A+**	16.71	**A / 9.5**	25.09 / 92	14.87 / 94	12.17 / 90	6.87	**B- / 7.2**	1.21	-1.27
MUN	MuniVest Fund II	MVT	**A+**	16.20	**A / 9.5**	24.93 / 91	14.19 / 92	14.72 / 97	6.81	**C+ / 6.8**	3.85	0.13
MUN	MuniAssets Fund	MUA	**A+**	13.45	**A / 9.3**	28.55 / 97	11.50 / 83	10.73 / 80	6.08	**B- / 7.2**	-0.30	-3.95
MUN	Eaton Vance Municipal Inc Tr	EVN	**A+**	16.67	**A / 9.3**	20.87 / 79	14.78 / 93	17.28 / 99	6.77	**C+ / 6.9**	14.26	14.05
MUN	MuniYield Fund	MYD	**A+**	14.99	**A- / 9.2**	29.19 / 97	11.30 / 81	11.40 / 86	6.66	**B- / 7.4**	0.54	-3.62
MUN	MuniVest Fund	MVF	**A+**	9.94	**A- / 9.1**	26.19 / 94	11.34 / 82	12.89 / 93	6.68	**B- / 7.1**	-2.83	-6.26
MUN	MuniYield Quality Fund II	MQT	**A+**	13.37	**B+ / 8.9**	24.18 / 89	11.04 / 80	10.17 / 75	6.41	**B- / 7.2**	-3.33	-7.60
MUN	Nuveen Dividend Advantage Muni 2	NXZ	**A+**	16.00	**B+ / 8.8**	23.48 / 87	11.25 / 81	--	6.43	**B- / 7.3**	-0.99	-2.92
MUN	PIMCO Municipal Income Fund	PMF	**A+**	15.54	**B+ / 8.6**	27.28 / 95	9.08 / 68	--	6.18	**B- / 7.6**	2.85	0.04
MUN	Apex Municipal Fund	APX	**A+**	9.36	**B+ / 8.6**	21.50 / 81	10.92 / 80	7.95 / 55	6.08	**B- / 7.6**	-4.49	-6.68
MUN	Alliance Nat Municipal Income Fund	AFB	**A+**	14.90	**B+ / 8.5**	22.30 / 84	10.26 / 76	--	6.09	**B- / 7.6**	-5.99	-8.51
MUN	BlackRock Municipal 2018 Income Tr	BPK	**A+**	15.70	**B / 8.0**	17.99 / 69	10.98 / 80	--	4.92	**B- / 7.9**	-1.32	-4.38
MUN	Nuveen Div Adv Muni 3	NZF	**A+**	14.92	**B / 7.9**	21.16 / 80	8.90 / 67	--	6.44	**B- / 7.7**	-5.33	-6.75
MUN	BlackRock Strategic Municipal Tr	BSD	**A**	16.40	**A+ / 9.6**	31.70 / 98	12.40 / 87	12.47 / 91	5.89	**C+ / 5.8**	3.34	-6.42
MUN	BlackRock Municipal Income Trust	BFK	**A**	15.15	**A- / 9.2**	28.30 / 96	11.60 / 84	--	6.32	**C+ / 6.4**	1.07	-1.81
MUN	Scudder Municipal Income Trust	KTF	**A**	12.74	**A- / 9.1**	22.60 / 85	11.54 / 83	9.64 / 70	6.28	**C+ / 6.5**	1.43	-3.63
MUN	MuniYield Insured Fund	MYI	**A**	15.14	**B / 7.9**	22.18 / 83	8.40 / 62	11.03 / 83	6.30	**B- / 7.7**	-5.02	-7.28
MUN	Dreyfus Strategic Muni Bond Fund	DSM	**A-**	9.25	**B+ / 8.8**	24.27 / 90	9.07 / 67	10.01 / 73	6.52	**C+ / 6.1**	1.87	-3.64
MUN	MuniHoldings Insured Fund	MUS	**A-**	14.29	**B / 8.0**	22.46 / 84	10.10 / 75	11.14 / 84	6.35	**B- / 7.0**	-1.65	-5.00
MUN	MuniYield Quality Fund	MQY	**B+**	15.27	**B+ / 8.4**	24.12 / 89	9.36 / 71	11.96 / 89	6.31	**C+ / 6.3**	-1.93	-5.60
MUN	Putnam Managed Muni Inc Tr	PMM	**B+**	7.88	**B / 7.9**	21.46 / 81	6.88 / 43	4.23 / 27	5.24	**C+ / 6.9**	-5.40	-11.22
MUN	Morgan Stanley Muni Inc Op	OIA	**B+**	8.10	**B / 7.8**	26.34 / 94	6.96 / 44	6.49 / 41	6.26	**C+ / 6.9**	1.00	-4.20
MUN	MuniEnhanced Fund	MEN	**B+**	11.43	**B / 7.6**	22.35 / 84	8.36 / 62	10.40 / 78	6.34	**B- / 7.1**	-3.63	-6.84
MUN	Nuveen Insured Quality Muni	NQI	**B+**	16.22	**B- / 7.5**	21.36 / 80	8.10 / 59	11.34 / 86	5.79	**C+ / 6.7**	2.14	-0.31
MUN	MuniHoldings Insured Fund II	MUE	**B+**	13.70	**B- / 7.4**	20.27 / 78	8.60 / 64	12.63 / 92	6.38	**B- / 7.2**	-5.58	-8.38
MUN	Nuveen Muni Advantage	NMA	**B+**	15.59	**B- / 7.0**	18.96 / 73	8.25 / 61	11.81 / 88	6.36	**B- / 7.3**	-3.47	-4.09
MUN	Morgan Stanley Muni Inc Op II	OIB	**B**	8.14	**C+ / 6.1**	15.00 / 57	7.08 / 46	9.22 / 65	5.84	**B / 8.5**	-9.05	-9.83
MUN	Morgan Stanley Qual Muni Sec	IQM	**B**	14.40	**C+ / 6.0**	14.65 / 56	7.81 / 56	9.93 / 72	5.85	**B / 8.7**	-12.09	-11.77
MUN	Morgan Stanley Insured Muni Inc Tr	IIM	**B**	14.23	**C / 5.4**	12.77 / 49	7.30 / 48	8.24 / 57	5.66	**B / 8.3**	-11.06	-10.70
MUN	Morgan Stanley Qual Muni Inc Tr	IQI	**B**	13.93	**C / 5.2**	12.92 / 50	7.04 / 45	8.46 / 59	5.80	**B / 8.4**	-11.89	-11.31
MUN	Nuveen Muni Value	NUV	**B**	9.57	**C / 5.0**	15.95 / 61	6.06 / 33	8.68 / 62	4.87	**B / 8.8**	-7.71	-8.65
MUN	Nuveen Select Quality Muni	NQS	**B-**	15.12	**C+ / 6.9**	16.52 / 64	8.12 / 59	10.45 / 78	6.29	**B- / 7.5**	-4.91	-5.91
MUN	Salomon Br Municipal Partners	MNP	**B-**	13.88	**C+ / 6.9**	15.43 / 59	8.34 / 62	9.85 / 71	6.03	**B- / 7.1**	-9.40	-11.98
MUN	Nuveen Premium Income Muni 2	NPM	**B-**	14.66	**C+ / 6.7**	18.74 / 72	7.36 / 50	9.58 / 69	6.05	**B- / 7.5**	-6.51	-7.46
MUN	American Municipal Income Portfolio	XAA	**B-**	14.82	**C+ / 6.7**	16.50 / 63	8.60 / 64	11.29 / 85	6.10	**B- / 7.8**	-6.68	-7.07
MUN	Nuveen Investment Quality Muni	NQM	**B-**	15.15	**C+ / 6.6**	17.73 / 67	7.26 / 48	10.82 / 81	6.07	**B- / 7.1**	-5.61	-6.39
MUN	Nuveen Muni Market Opportunity	NMO	**B-**	14.68	**C+ / 6.4**	16.47 / 63	6.94 / 44	9.48 / 68	6.11	**B- / 7.1**	-6.08	-7.81
MUN	Nuveen Div Adv Muni	NAD	**B-**	15.20	**C+ / 6.3**	15.17 / 58	7.25 / 48	11.45 / 87	6.42	**B- / 7.0**	-3.31	-4.47
MUN	Salomon Br Municipal Partners II	MPT	**B-**	13.50	**C+ / 6.2**	14.56 / 55	7.69 / 55	9.65 / 70	6.00	**B- / 7.7**	-9.70	-12.28
MUN	Nuveen Performance Plus Muni	NPP	**B-**	14.79	**C+ / 6.1**	16.40 / 63	6.92 / 44	11.25 / 85	6.25	**B- / 7.4**	-7.97	-8.12
MUN	Nuveen Insured Div Adv Muni Fund	NVG	**B-**	14.70	**C+ / 6.0**	17.38 / 66	6.50 / 38	--	5.74	**B- / 7.5**	-6.96	-7.52
MUN	Nuveen Insured Muni Opportunity	NIO	**B-**	15.65	**C+ / 5.9**	16.42 / 63	7.08 / 46	10.67 / 80	5.69	**B- / 7.0**	-2.86	-3.59
MUN	Morgan Stanley Muni Inc Op III	OIC	**B-**	8.86	**C+ / 5.9**	15.95 / 62	6.35 / 36	8.56 / 60	5.73	**B- / 7.8**	-8.57	-10.16
MUN	Putnam Municipal Bond Fund	PMG	**B-**	12.74	**C+ / 5.8**	15.85 / 61	7.35 / 49	10.20 / 76	6.13	**B- / 7.5**	-9.19	-8.55
MUN	Nuveen Quality Inc Muni	NQU	**B-**	14.45	**C+ / 5.6**	16.54 / 64	6.70 / 40	8.84 / 63	6.10	**B- / 7.7**	-8.14	-7.85
MUN	Nuveen Prem Inc Muni	NPI	**C+**	14.33	**C / 5.3**	17.27 / 65	6.47 / 38	10.61 / 79	6.09	**B- / 7.5**	-7.25	-6.83
MUN	Morgan Stanley Muni Prem Inc Tr	PIA	**C+**	9.12	**C / 4.8**	12.22 / 47	6.97 / 45	9.74 / 70	5.87	**B / 8.2**	-13.14	-11.76
MUN	Morgan Stanley Insured Muni Tr	IMT	**C+**	13.93	**C / 4.4**	13.18 / 51	5.89 / 31	7.31 / 49	5.81	**B / 8.4**	-11.10	-11.00

N/A denotes number is not available

99 Pct = Best
0 Pct = Worst

					PERFORMANCE					RISK	VALUATION	
						Annualized Total Return Through 6/30/05					Premium/Discount	
Fund Type	Fund Name	Ticker Symbol	Overall Weiss Investment Rating	Price As of 6/30/05	Performance Rating/Pts	1Yr/Pct	3Yr/Pct	5Yr/Pct	Dividend Yield %	Risk Rating/Pts	As of 6/30/05	1 Year Average
MUS	BlackRock NY Muni Bond Trust	BQH	A+	15.21	B+ / 8.9	24.76 / 91	10.54 / 78	--	6.04	B- / 7.0	-5.06	-8.31
MUS	Alliance CA Municipal Income Fund	AKP	A+	14.87	B / 8.1	21.46 / 81	9.61 / 72	--	5.87	B- / 7.8	-4.74	-6.59
MUS	Eaton Vance NY Muni Inc Tr	EVY	A	16.70	A- / 9.2	27.07 / 95	11.14 / 81	16.66 / 99	5.91	C+ / 6.2	3.28	-2.01
MUS	BlackRock VA Muni Bond Trust	BHV	A	17.27	A- / 9.2	25.93 / 93	11.16 / 81	--	5.11	C+ / 6.4	6.54	1.21
MUS	MuniYield FL Fund	MYF	A	15.06	A- / 9.0	26.38 / 94	10.66 / 79	13.21 / 94	6.13	C+ / 6.3	-2.40	-7.33
MUS	PIMCO NY Muni Income Fund	PNF	A	14.89	B+ / 8.8	25.83 / 93	8.40 / 63	--	6.00	C+ / 6.3	6.81	0.17
MUS	BlackRock NJ Muni Bond Trust	BLJ	A	15.55	B+ / 8.7	27.66 / 96	8.99 / 67	--	5.98	C+ / 6.5	-3.05	-4.85
MUS	MuniHoldings NJ Insured Fund	MUJ	A	15.59	B+ / 8.6	21.69 / 82	10.87 / 79	13.40 / 95	6.04	B- / 7.0	-1.45	-4.36
MUS	BlackRock CA Municipal Income Trust	BFZ	A	14.55	B+ / 8.4	22.97 / 86	9.62 / 72	--	6.19	B- / 7.1	-5.58	-7.79
MUS	Nuveen PA Div Adv Muni	NXM	A	16.10	B+ / 8.4	22.85 / 85	10.62 / 78	--	5.76	C+ / 6.7	0.94	-0.84
MUS	Nuveen NY Div Adv Muni 2	NXK	A	15.54	B / 8.2	20.88 / 79	10.06 / 75	--	6.04	C+ / 6.9	-2.02	-4.71
MUS	BlackRock NJ Municipal Income Trust	BNJ	A	15.39	B / 8.1	21.66 / 81	8.85 / 66	--	5.74	B- / 7.1	-4.29	-6.65
MUS	Nuveen CA Div Adv Muni	NAC	A	15.59	B / 8.0	20.04 / 77	9.58 / 72	10.24 / 76	6.35	B- / 7.2	-2.44	-4.95
MUS	Alliance NY Municipal Income Fund	AYN	A-	14.85	B+ / 8.6	24.47 / 90	9.44 / 71	--	5.61	C+ / 6.4	-4.32	-7.89
MUS	MuniYield AZ Fund	MZA	A-	15.76	B+ / 8.5	25.61 / 92	9.35 / 70	14.67 / 97	5.85	C+ / 6.3	4.72	1.03
MUS	MuniHoldings FL Insured Fund	MFL	A-	15.57	B+ / 8.5	22.65 / 85	10.65 / 79	14.53 / 97	6.34	C+ / 6.5	0.97	-2.25
MUS	BlackRock NY Municipal Income Trust	BNY	A-	15.13	B+ / 8.4	22.85 / 85	9.68 / 72	--	6.00	C+ / 6.5	-3.51	-7.26
MUS	Nuveen VA Div Adv Muni 2	NNB	A-	17.00	B+ / 8.4	22.45 / 84	11.14 / 81	--	4.93	C+ / 6.5	7.80	4.97
MUS	Nuveen NC Div Adv Muni	NRB	A-	17.33	B / 8.2	24.75 / 91	10.47 / 78	--	5.33	C+ / 6.7	11.73	7.96
MUS	Delaware Inv CO Ins Muni Inc	VCF	A-	17.64	B / 8.0	23.63 / 87	11.27 / 81	13.19 / 94	5.42	C+ / 6.9	10.53	8.79
MUS	MuniHoldings NY Insured Fund	MHN	A-	14.96	B / 8.0	19.68 / 75	9.24 / 69	12.21 / 90	6.28	B- / 7.0	-4.10	-8.13
MUS	BlackRock FL Muni Bond Trust	BIE	A-	15.62	B / 7.9	25.96 / 93	8.10 / 59	--	5.88	B- / 7.1	-3.76	-6.55
MUS	Nuveen Insured NY Div Adv Muni Fund	NKO	A-	15.14	B / 7.7	22.46 / 84	7.32 / 49	--	5.45	B- / 7.2	-5.02	-7.46
MUS	BlackRock CA Muni 2018 Income Trust	BJZ	A-	14.99	B- / 7.4	17.26 / 65	8.83 / 65	--	4.92	B- / 7.6	-2.15	-5.03
MUS	MuniYield CA Insured Fund	MCA	A-	14.22	B- / 7.3	19.95 / 77	8.19 / 61	7.80 / 53	6.14	B- / 7.6	-7.54	-9.95
MUS	BlackRock NJ Inv Qual Muni Tr	RNJ	B+	15.56	B+ / 8.6	25.00 / 92	8.71 / 64	10.64 / 80	5.18	C+ / 5.7	4.92	-1.54
MUS	MuniYield FL Insured Fund	MFT	B+	15.45	B+ / 8.3	24.04 / 89	9.32 / 70	11.93 / 89	5.80	C+ / 6.4	1.11	-3.13
MUS	Nuveen VA Div Adv Muni Fund	NGB	B+	17.47	B+ / 8.3	23.72 / 88	12.22 / 86	--	5.26	C+ / 6.3	12.35	12.71
MUS	Delaware Inv FL Insured Muni Inc	VFL	B+	16.70	B+ / 8.3	21.90 / 82	10.32 / 76	13.81 / 96	5.73	C+ / 6.1	7.33	2.95
MUS	Nuveen Insured FL Prem Inc Muni	NFL	B+	16.47	B / 8.2	24.22 / 90	8.28 / 61	11.40 / 86	5.23	C+ / 5.9	1.29	-1.96
MUS	Nuveen GA Div Adv Muni	NZX	B+	16.00	B / 8.1	23.82 / 88	9.83 / 74	--	5.18	C+ / 6.3	4.17	0.74
MUS	Eaton Vance FL Muni Inc Tr	FEV	B+	15.55	B / 7.9	19.22 / 74	10.60 / 78	15.49 / 98	5.72	C+ / 6.6	1.63	-0.20
MUS	BlackRock FL Municipal Income Trust	BBF	B+	15.29	B / 7.8	26.78 / 95	7.72 / 55	--	5.95	B- / 7.0	-2.80	-6.57
MUS	Nuveen Insured NY Prem Inc Muni	NNF	B+	15.80	B / 7.6	23.43 / 87	7.28 / 48	10.34 / 77	5.38	C+ / 6.7	-1.99	-6.13
MUS	Nuveen TX Quality Inc Muni	NTX	B+	15.96	B / 7.6	21.62 / 81	7.88 / 57	11.52 / 87	5.43	C+ / 6.4	2.05	-1.26
MUS	BlackRock CA Muni Bond Trust	BZA	B+	14.92	B- / 7.4	23.34 / 87	7.46 / 51	--	6.38	B- / 7.3	-6.57	-6.56
MUS	Nuveen NY Div Adv Muni	NAN	B+	15.93	B- / 7.3	19.11 / 74	9.16 / 68	11.15 / 84	6.13	C+ / 6.7	-0.93	-3.11
MUS	MuniYield MI Insured Fund II	MYM	B+	14.70	B- / 7.3	17.41 / 66	9.35 / 70	11.75 / 88	6.03	B- / 7.0	-3.10	-5.16
MUS	MuniYield NJ Fund	MYJ	B+	15.31	B- / 7.2	18.63 / 71	7.88 / 57	10.77 / 80	6.07	B- / 7.3	-3.83	-5.91
MUS	Nuveen CA Prem Inc Muni	NCU	B+	14.16	B- / 7.1	20.44 / 78	7.41 / 50	8.60 / 61	5.94	B- / 7.1	-6.04	-7.07
MUS	Nuveen CA Div Adv Muni 2	NVX	B+	14.59	B- / 7.1	18.51 / 71	7.87 / 57	--	6.20	B- / 7.3	-6.29	-8.09
MUS	Morgan Stanley CA Qual Muni Sec	IQC	B+	14.30	C+ / 5.6	13.78 / 52	8.77 / 65	8.39 / 58	5.87	B+ / 9.1	-9.49	-8.13
MUS	BlackRock MD Muni Bond Trust	BZM	B	16.69	B+ / 8.7	26.28 / 94	9.81 / 73	--	5.26	C / 5.1	4.31	-2.24
MUS	Eaton Vance PA Muni Inc Tr	EVP	B	15.85	B+ / 8.3	25.40 / 92	12.24 / 86	15.20 / 98	5.97	C+ / 5.6	5.04	2.76
MUS	Nuveen NJ Div Adv Muni Fund 2	NUJ	B	15.64	B- / 7.5	19.90 / 76	8.07 / 59	--	5.77	C+ / 6.2	-1.01	-2.92
MUS	Nuveen OH Div Adv Muni 2	NBJ	B	16.06	B- / 7.3	23.90 / 89	9.69 / 73	--	5.41	C+ / 6.5	2.95	2.01
MUS	MuniYield NJ Insured Fund	MJI	B	15.65	B- / 7.3	21.68 / 81	7.65 / 54	10.09 / 74	5.92	C+ / 6.6	-0.38	-2.97
MUS	MuniYield PA Insured Fund	MPA	B	15.99	B- / 7.3	21.01 / 80	8.72 / 64	12.29 / 91	5.96	C+ / 6.6	-1.84	-3.71
MUS	Nuveen GA Prem Inc Muni	NPG	B	16.95	B- / 7.2	23.09 / 86	6.95 / 44	11.08 / 84	4.94	C+ / 6.5	11.15	7.63
MUS	Nuveen NY Performance Plus Muni	NNP	B	16.02	B- / 7.1	19.22 / 74	7.85 / 56	10.84 / 81	6.06	C+ / 6.7	-4.30	-5.65
MUS	Minnesota Municipal Inc Portfolio	MXA	B	16.07	B- / 7.0	21.20 / 80	7.54 / 52	11.58 / 88	5.57	C+ / 6.6	3.81	0.81
MUS	Nuveen NC Div Adv Muni 2	NNO	B	16.60	B- / 7.0	11.25 / 43	10.12 / 75	--	5.32	C+ / 6.7	6.34	2.80

N/A denotes number is not available

99 Pct = Best
0 Pct = Worst

					PERFORMANCE					RISK	VALUATION	
						Annualized Total Return Through 6/30/05					Premium/Discount	
Fund Type	Fund Name	Ticker Symbol	Overall Weiss Investment Rating	Price As of 6/30/05	Performance Rating/Pts	1Yr/Pct	3Yr/Pct	5Yr/Pct	Dividend Yield %	Risk Rating/ Pts	As of 6/30/05	1 Year Average
PM	Central Fund of Canada	CEF	**D-**	5.40	**D-** / **1.5**	2.07 / 8	8.37 / 24	9.34 / 37	0.19	**C+** / **5.8**	0.00	6.46
PM	ASA Limited	ASA	**E-**	38.59	**D** / **1.8**	8.40 / 20	8.77 / 28	22.47 / 97	1.55	**E-** / **0.0**	-11.14	-12.48

N/A denotes number is not available

Fund Type	Fund Name (99 Pct = Best, 0 Pct = Worst)	Ticker Symbol	Overall Weiss Investment Rating	Price As of 6/30/05	PERFORMANCE: Performance Rating/Pts	Annualized Total Return Through 6/30/05: 1Yr/Pct	3Yr/Pct	5Yr/Pct	Dividend Yield %	RISK: Risk Rating/Pts	VALUATION: Premium/Discount As of 6/30/05	1 Year Average
USA	ACM Income Fund	ACG	**C-**	8.29	**C / 4.4**	15.12 / 38	12.16 / 58	15.30 / 72	7.28	**C+ / 5.8**	-0.72	0.42
USA	Morgan Stanley Govt Inc Tr	GVT	**C-**	8.92	**E+ / 0.9**	7.74 / 17	4.45 / 7	7.25 / 29	4.67	**B+ / 9.5**	-10.17	-9.50
USA	ACM Government Opportunity Fund	AOF	**D-**	7.89	**E+ / 0.6**	4.51 / 11	3.98 / 5	11.13 / 47	5.90	**B- / 7.2**	-8.26	-5.93

N/A denotes number is not available

Fund Type	Fund Name (99 Pct = Best, 0 Pct = Worst)	Ticker Symbol	Overall Weiss Investment Rating	Price As of 6/30/05	PERFORMANCE: Performance Rating/Pts	Annualized Total Return Through 6/30/05: 1Yr/Pct	3Yr/Pct	5Yr/Pct	Dividend Yield %	RISK: Risk Rating/Pts	VALUATION: Premium/Discount As of 6/30/05	1 Year Average
UT	Gabelli Utility Trust	GUT	**B**	10.00	**B / 8.2**	26.20 / 65	17.94 / 84	18.56 / 90	7.29	**C / 5.5**	36.24	37.15
UT	iShares Dow Jones US Utilities	IDU	**B**	76.12	**B- / 7.1**	33.36 / 82	12.74 / 62	6.38 / 26	2.80	**C+ / 6.5**	-0.05	-0.02
UT	HOLDRS Utilities	UTH	**C+**	109.69	**B / 8.0**	38.97 / 92	14.25 / 69	7.62 / 29	2.39	**C- / 4.2**	0.00	N/A
UT	DNP Select Income Fund Inc	DNP	**C+**	11.70	**C / 5.3**	18.21 / 45	12.65 / 61	11.71 / 51	6.75	**B- / 7.3**	28.29	33.55
UT	SPDR Utilities	XLU	**C**	31.12	**B- / 7.2**	35.48 / 86	12.77 / 62	6.35 / 26	3.16	**C / 4.4**	0.10	N/A
UT	J Hancock Patriot Select Div Tr	DIV	**D+**	13.65	**D / 1.6**	5.68 / 12	7.95 / 22	10.17 / 43	6.53	**B- / 7.1**	-9.36	-2.10

N/A denotes number is not available

Appendix

What is a Mutual Fund?

Picking individual stocks is difficult and buying individual bonds can be expensive. Mutual funds were introduced to allow the small investor to participate in the stock and bond market for just a small initial investment. Mutual funds are pools of stocks or bonds that are managed by investment professionals. First, an investment company organizes the fund and collects the money from investors. The company then takes that money and pays a portfolio manager to invest it in stocks, bonds, money market instruments and other types of securities.

Most funds fit within one of two main categories, open-end funds or closed-end funds. Open-end funds issue new shares when investors put in money and redeem shares when investors withdraw money. The price of a share is determined by dividing the total net assets of the fund by the number of shares outstanding.

On the other hand, closed-end funds issue a fixed number of shares in an initial public offering, trading thereafter in the open market like a stock. Thus by their very nature, closed-end funds are unique in that they do not always trade at their net asset value (NAV). Unlike their open-end counterparts, closed-end funds trade on an exchange at market prices that are independent of their NAV. If the price is above the fund's NAV, the fund is said to be trading at a premium. If the price is lower than the fund's NAV, the fund trades at a discount. Investing in either class of funds means you own a share of the portfolio, so you participate in the fund's gains and losses.

There are more than 11,000 different mutual funds, each with a stated investment objective. Here are descriptions for five of the most popular types of funds:

Stock funds: A mutual fund which invests mainly in stocks. These funds are more actively traded than other more conservative funds. The stocks chosen may vary widely according to the fund's investment strategy.

Bond funds: A mutual fund which invests in bonds, in an effort to provide stable income while preserving principal as much as possible. These funds invest in medium- to long-term bonds issued by corporations and governments.

Index funds: A mutual fund that aims to match the performance of a specific index, such as the S&P 500. Index funds tend to have fewer expenses than other funds because portfolio decisions are automatic and transactions are infrequent.

Balanced funds: A mutual fund that buys a combination of stocks and bonds, in order to supply both income and capital growth while ensuring a minimal amount of risk for investors.

Money market funds: An open-end mutual fund which invests only in stable, short-term securities. The fund's value remains at a constant $1 per share, but only those administered by banks are government insured.

Investing in a mutual fund has several advantages over owning a single stock or bond. For example, funds offer instant portfolio diversification by giving you ownership of many stocks or bonds simultaneously. This diversification protects you in case a part of your investment takes a sudden downturn. You also get the benefit of having a professional handling your investment, though a management fee is charged for these services, typically 1% or 2% a year. You should be aware that the fund may also levy other fees and that you will likely have to pay a commission to purchase the fund through a brokerage firm.

The fund manager's strategy is laid out in the fund's prospectus, which is the official name for the legal document that contains financial information about the fund, including its history, its officers and its performance. Mutual fund investments are fully liquid so you can easily get in or out by just placing an order through a broker.

How Do Open-End and Closed-End Funds Differ?

Similarities:

Both open-end and closed-end mutual funds…

- employ a fund manager or management team to invest assets in various types of securities according to the fund's stated objectives and policies.
- may be invested in stocks, bonds, or a combination of both.
- provide benefits of diversification by holding a basket of stocks and/or bonds.

Differences:

Open-End	**Closed-End**
• The mutual fund company issues and redeems shares on demand, whenever investors put money into the fund or take it out.	• The mutual fund company issues a set number of shares in an initial public offering and the shares then trade on an exchange.
• There is no limit to the number of shares the fund can issue.	• The fund offers a fixed number of shares.
• The share price is determined by the total value of the assets it holds.	• The share price is determined by investor demand for the fund.
• Fund shares trade at net asset value (NAV).	• Fund shares generally trade at a premium (above NAV) or discount (below NAV).
• Open-end funds are more popular. There are more than 13,000 open-end funds available. The general term "mutual funds" typically refers to the much more common, open-end mutual funds.	• Closed-end funds are lesser known, and there are much fewer in existence.
• Fund companies may require an initial minimum amount that must be invested.	• There is no minimum initial investment required.
• Investors cannot utilize limit and stop orders.	• Investors may utilize limit and stop orders.
• 12b-1 fees are used to pay for marketing the fund.	• 12b-1 fees are not charged.
• All transactions occur at the end of each business day based upon the movement in the value of the fund's portfolio of securities.	• Shares are traded on an exchange throughout the day.

Investor Profile Quiz

We recognize that each person approaches his or her investment decisions from a unique perspective. A mutual fund that is perfect for someone else may be totally inappropriate for you due to factors such as:

- How much risk you are comfortable taking
- Your age and the number of years you have before retirement
- Your income level and tax rate
- Your other existing investments and personal net worth
- Preconceived expectations about investment performance

The following quiz will help you quantify your tolerance for risk based on your own personal life situation. As you read through each question, circle the letter next to the single answer that you feel most accurately describes your current position. Keep in mind that there are no "correct" answers to this quiz, only answers that are helpful in assessing your investment style. So don't worry about how your answer might be perceived by others; just try to be as honest and accurate as possible.

Then at the end of the quiz, use the point totals listed on the right side of the page to compute your test score. Once you've added up your total points, refer to the corresponding investor profile for an evaluation of your personal risk tolerance. Each profile also lists the page number where you will find the top performing mutual funds matching your risk profile.

	Points	Your Score
1. I am currently investing to pay for:		
a. Retirement	0 pts	
b. College	0 pts	
c. A house	0 pts	
2. I expect I will need to liquidate some or all of this investment in:		
a. 2 years or less	0 pts	
b. 2 to 5 years	5 pts	
c. 5 to 10 years	8 pts	
d. 10 years or more	10 pts	
3. My age group is		
a. Under 30	10 pts	
b. 30 to 44	9 pts	
c. 45 to 60	7 pts	
d. 60 to 74	5 pts	
e. 75 and older	1 pts	
4. I am currently looking to invest money through:		
a. An IRA or other tax-deferred account	0 pts	
b. A fully taxable account	0 pts	

5.	I have a cash reserve equal to 3 to 6 months expenses. a. Yes b. No	 10 pts 1 pts	
6.	My primary source of income is: a. Salary and other earnings from my primary occupation b. Earnings from my investment portfolio c. Retirement pension and/or Social Security	 7 pts 5 pts 3 pts	
7.	I will need regular income from this investment now or in the near future. a. Yes b. No	 6 pts 10 pts	
8.	Over the long run, I expect this investment to average returns of: a. 8% annually or less b. 8% to 12% annually c. 12% to 15% annually d. 15% to 20% annually e. Over 20% annually	 0 pts 6 pts 8 pts 10 pts 18 pts	
9.	The worst loss I would be comfortable accepting on my investment is: a. Less than 5%. Stability of principal is very important to me. b. 5% to 10%. Modest periodic declines are acceptable. c. 10% to 15%. I understand that there may be losses in the short run but over the long term, higher risk investments will offer highest returns. d. Over 15%. You don't get high returns without taking risk. I'm looking for maximum capital gains and understand that my funds can substantially decline.	 1 pts 3 pts 8 pts 15 pts	
10.	If the stock market were to suddenly decline by 15%, which of the following would most likely be your reaction? a. I should have left the market long ago, at the first sign of trouble. b. I should have substantially exited the stock market by now to limit my exposure. c. I'm still in the stock market but I've got my finger on the trigger. d. I'm staying fully invested so I'll be ready for the next bull market.	 3 pts 5 pts 7 pts 10 pts	
11.	The best defense against a bear market is: a. A defensive market timing system that avoids large losses. b. A potent offense that will make big gains in the next bull market.	 4 pts 10 pts	
12.	The best strategy to employ during bear markets is: a. Move to cash. It's the only safe hiding place. b. Short the market and try to make a profit as it declines. c. Wait it out because the market will eventually recover.	 5 pts 10 pts 8 pts	

13. I would classify myself as:				
a. A buy-and-hold investor who rides out all the peaks and valleys.			10 pts	
b. A market timer who wants to capture the major bull markets.			7 pts	
c. A market timer who wants to avoid the major bear markets.			5 pts	
14. My attitude regarding trading activity is:				
a. Active trading is costly and unproductive.			0 pts	
b. I don't mind frequent trades as long as I'm making money			2 pts	
c. Occasional trading is okay but too much activity is not good.			1 pts	
15. If the S&P 500 advanced strongly over the last 12 months, my investment should have:				
a. Grown even more than the market.			10 pts	
b. Approximated the performance of the broad market.			5 pts	
c. Focused on reducing the risk of loss in a bear market, even if it meant giving up some upside potential in the bull market.			2 pts	
16. I have experience (extensive, some, or none) with the following types of investments.	Exten-sive	Some	None	
a. U.S. stocks or stock mutual funds	2 pts	1 pts	0 pts	
b. International stock funds	2 pts	1 pts	0 pts	
c. Bonds or bond funds	1 pts	0 pts	0 pts	
d. Futures and/or options	5 pts	3 pts	0 pts	
e. Managed futures or funds	3 pts	1 pts	0 pts	
f. Real estate	2 pts	1 pts	0 pts	
g. Private hedge funds	3 pts	1 pts	0 pts	
h. Privately managed accounts	2 pts	1 pts	0 pts	
17. Excluding my primary residence, this investment represents ___% of my investment holdings.				
a. Less than 5%			10 pts	
b. 5% to 10%			7 pts	
c. 10% to 20%			5 pts	
d. 20% to 30%			3 pts	
e. 30% or more			1 pts	
			TOTAL	

Under 58 pts	**Very Conservative.** You appear to be very risk averse with capital preservation as your primary goal. As such, most closed-end mutual funds may be a little too risky for your taste, especially in a turbulent market environment. We recommend you stick to the safest open-end bond and money market mutual funds where your income stream is predictable and more secure. Those funds are not covered in this publication, but you can easily find them in Section VII of *Weiss Ratings' Guide to Bond and Money Market Mutual Funds.*
58 to 77 pts	**Conservative.** Based on your responses, it appears that you are more concerned about minimizing the risk to your principal than you are about maximizing your returns. Don't worry, there are plenty of good mutual funds that offer strong returns with very little volatility. As a starting point, we recommend you turn to page 294 where you will find a list of the top-rated funds receiving the best risk rating we issue to closed-end mutual funds (B– or better, meaning Good).
78 to 108 pts	**Moderate.** You are prepared to take on a little added risk in order to enhance your investment returns. This is probably the most common approach to mutual fund investing. To select a mutual fund matching your style, we recommend you turn to page 296. There you can easily pick from the top-rated mutual funds receiving a risk rating in the C (Fair) range.
109 to 129 pts	**Aggressive.** You appear to be ready to ride out almost any financial storm on your way toward maximizing your investment returns. You understand that the only way to make large returns on your investments is by taking on added risk, and your personal situation seems to allow for that approach. We recommend you use pages 296 - 299 as a starting point for selecting a top-rated mutual fund with a risk rating in the C (Fair) or D (Weak) range.
Over 129 pts	**Very Aggressive.** Based on your responses, you appear to be leaning heavily toward speculation. Your primary concern is maximizing your investment growth, and you are prepared to take on as much risk as necessary in order to do so. To this end, turn to page 300 where you'll find the top-rated mutual funds with a risk rating in the E (Very Weak) range. These investments have historically been extremely volatile, oftentimes investing in securities that are currently out of favor. As such, they are highly speculative investments that could provide superior results if you can stomach the volatility and uncertainty. For a list of the top performing closed-end mutual funds regardless of risk category, turn to page 274. Also see section VII in *Weiss Ratings' Guide to Stock Mutual Funds* and section VI in *Weiss Ratings' Guide to Common Stocks.*

Performance Benchmarks

The following benchmarks represent the average performance for all mutual funds within each closed-end fund type category. Comparing an individual mutual fund's returns to these benchmarks is yet another way to assess its performance. For the top performing funds within each of the following categories, turn to Section VIII, Top-Rated Closed-End Mutual Funds By Fund Type, beginning on page 306. You can also use this information to compare the average performance of one category of funds to another (updated through June 30, 2005).

		3 Month Total Return %	1 Year Total Return %	Refer to page:
COH	Corporate – High Yield	8.47%	15.31%	306
COI	Corporate – Investment Grade	5.49%	12.77%	307
EM	Emerging Market	4.41%	26.96%	308
EN	Energy/Natural Resources	5.68%	38.54%	309
FS	Financial Services	4.02%	11.36%	310
FO	Foreign	2.19%	27.50%	311
GEI	General – Investment Grade	6.39%	13.51%	312
GEN	General Bond	4.63%	10.33%	313
GL	Global	2.67%	16.59%	314
GR	Growth	1.67%	6.51%	315
GI	Growth & Income	8.13%	20.59%	316
HL	Health	7.34%	5.60%	317
IN	Income	4.10%	11.90%	318
LP	Loan Participation	-5.81%	-7.01%	319
MTG	Mortgage	2.37%	6.80%	320
MUH	Municipal – High Yield	7.07%	19.25%	321
MUN	Municipal – National	8.34%	16.90%	322
MUS	Municipal – Single State	7.01%	18.94%	323
PM	Precious Metals	1.98%	5.24%	324
USA	U.S. Government/Agency	3.93%	9.65%	325
UT	Utilities	9.50%	27.76%	326

Fund Type Descriptions

COH - Corporate - High Yield - Seeks high current income by investing a minimum of 65% of its assets in generally low-quality corporate debt issues.

COI - Corporate - Investment Grade - Seeks current income by investing a minimum of 65% in investment grade corporate debt issues. Investment grade securities must be BBB or higher, as rated by Standard & Poor's.

EM - Emerging Market - Seeks long term capital appreciation and/or income by investing primarily in emerging market equity and/or income producing securities.

EN - Energy/Natural Resources - Invests primarily in equity securities of companies involved in the exploration, distribution, or processing of natural resources.

FS - Financial - Seeks capital appreciation by investing in equity securities of companies engaged in providing financial services. Typically, securities are from commercial banks, S&Ls, finance companies, securities brokerages, investment managers, insurance companies, and leasing companies.

FO - Foreign - Invests primarily in non-U.S. equity securities of any market capitalization. Income is usually incidental.

GEI - General - Investment Grade - Seeks income by investing in investment grade domestic or foreign corporate debt, government debt and preferred securities.

GEN - General Bond - Seeks income by investing without geographic boundary in corporate debt, government debt or preferred securities. Investments are not tied to any specific maturity or duration.

GL - Global - Invests primarily in domestic and foreign equity securities of any market capitalization and/or fixed income securities issued by domestic and/or foreign governments.

GR - Growth - Seeks long term capital appreciation by investing primarily in equity securities of any market capitalization. Income is usually incidental.

GI - Growth and Income - Seeks both capital appreciation and income primarily by investing in equities with a level or rising dividend stream.

HL - Health - Seeks capital appreciation by investing primarily in equities of companies engaged in the design, manufacture, or sale of products or services connected with health care or medicine.

IN - Income - Seeks current income by investing a minimum of 65% of its assets in income-producing equity securities.

LP - Loan Participation - Invests a minimum of 65% of its assets in loan interests.

MTG - Mortgage - Invests a minimum of 65% of its assets in a broad range of mortgage or mortgage-related securities, including those issued by the U.S. government and by government related and private organizations.

MUH - Municipal - High Yield - Seeks tax-free income by investing a minimum of 65% of its assets in generally low-quality issues from any state municipality.

MUN - Municipal - National - Seeks federally tax-free income by investing at least 65% in issues from any state municipality.

MUS - Municipal - Single State - Seeks tax-free income by investing in issues which are exempt from federal and the taxation of a specified state.

PM - Precious Metals - Seeks capital appreciation by investing primarily in equity securities of companies involved in mining, distribution, processing, or dealing in gold, silver, platinum, diamonds, or other precious metals and minerals.

USA - U.S. Government - Agency - Invests a minimum of 65% in securities issued or guaranteed by the Government, its agencies or instrumentalities. Investments are not tied to any specific maturity or duration.

UT - Utilities - Seeks a high level of current income by investing primarily in the equity securities of utility companies.

Weiss Ratings'

PRODUCTS

WEISS RATINGS' RISK GUIDES

Weiss Ratings' comprehensive industry-wide guides provide the most accurate, complete source of risk ratings on more than 15,000 financial institutions including banks and insurance companies.

Issued Quarterly. Price: $499 + $19.95 s/h for 4 quarterly issues, or $249 + $8.95 s/h for a single edition.

Guide to Life, Health, and Annuity Insurers covers more than 1,500 U.S. life, health and annuity insurers.

Guide to Property and Casualty Insurers covers more than 2,500 property and casualty insurers in the U.S.

Guide to HMOs and Health Insurers is the only source covering more than 1,200 U.S. health insurers including all Blue Cross/Blue Shield plans and over 500 HMOs.

Guide to Banks and Thrifts covers more than 9,000 banks and thrifts in the U.S.

WEISS RATINGS' INVESTMENT GUIDES

Weiss Ratings' comprehensive investment guides provide the most accurate, complete information for more than 20,000 investment choices.

Issued Quarterly. Price: $499 + $19.95 s/h for 4 quarterly issues, or $249 + $8.95 s/h for a single edition.

Ultimate Guided Tour of Stock Investing is a must-have, easy-to-understand guide presented in a friendly, fun format complete with our "Wise Guide" who leads you on an informative safari through the stock market jungle. Complete with how-to information on stock investing, useful worksheets, examples on common topics such as diversification, the Weiss Performance and Risk Ratings, and much more! This guide will help you learn to invest and successfully manage your stock portfolio. Covers every stock on the American Stock Exchange, New York Stock Exchange, and the NASDAQ.

Guide to Stock Mutual Funds covers more than 7,000 equity mutual funds, including balanced funds, international funds, and individual sector funds.

Guide to Bond and Money Market Mutual Funds covers more than 4,200 fixed-income mutual funds, including government bond funds, municipal bond funds, and corporate bond funds.

Guide to Closed-End Mutual Funds covers more than 600 closed-end mutual funds, including growth funds, sector funds, international funds, municipal bond funds and other closed-end funds.

Guide to Common Stocks covers stocks on the American Stock Exchange, New York Stock Exchange, and the NASDAQ, plus more.

WEISS RATINGS' SHOPPER'S GUIDES

Weiss Ratings' Shopper's Guides come packed with customized information needed to make sound purchasing decisions.

Fully Customized Reports. Price: $49 + $4.95 s/h

Shopper's Guide to Medicare Supplement Insurance has price comparisons for Medigap insurance based on your age, gender, and zip code. Insurance companies are listed by Weiss rating to provide price and financial safety comparisons.

Shopper's Guide to Term Life Insurance has price comparisons for term life insurance based on your age, gender, zip code and other unique information. You'll find the insurers who are currently offering the best rates.

WEISS RATINGS' CONSUMER GUIDES

Weiss Ratings' Consumer Guides provide the critical information needed to make sound financial decisions including step-by-step instructions, worksheets, sample rates and more.

Price: $119 + $7.95 s/h for 4 quarterly issues, or $49 + $4.95 s/h for a single edition.
Consumer Guide Box Set Price: $399 + $19.95 s/h includes one full year of updates.

Consumer Guide to Variable Annuities leads you step by step through understanding when variable annuities make sense and how they actually work. This easy-to-use guide looks at the 20 best and worst variable annuities on the market today, all the costs to look for, and the advantages and disadvantages of variable annuities versus other investments.

Consumer Guide to Elder Care Choices is designed to educate you on the many care options available and to provide you with the necessary tools to make informed decisions on Continuing Care Retirement Communities, Assisted Living Facilities, Home Health Care Agencies, Adult Day Care, Nursing Homes, and more.

Consumer Guide to Long-Term Care Insurance gives you how-to information on how to select the right long-term care policy for you, with worksheets, definitions and sample policy information.

Consumer Guide to Medicare Supplement Insurance is a must have for anyone considering the purchase of Medigap insurance. This how-to guide leads you through the process showing where the gaps are, how to fill them, and how you determine what type of policy is best for you.

Consumer Guide to Auto Insurance can help you save hundreds of dollars on auto insurance. The guide can help you understand the coverage required in your state, get the right insurance for your vehicle, save money on your premiums, and so much more.

Consumer Guide to Homeowners Insurance provides a complete how-to guide on purchasing homeowner's insurance including types of coverage, how to save money, choosing the right company, and more.

For a consumer-friendly guide on Stock Investing, see the "Weiss Ratings' Investment Guides" category on the previous page for our ***Ultimate Guided Tour of Stock Investing***.

WEISS RATINGS' BOOKS

Price: $19.95 + $4.95 s/h

Stock Investing Made Simple: Your Guided Tour to Getting Started is an easy-to-understand informative book that leads you through the stock market jungle in a friendly, fun format. The book includes information on stock investing, useful worksheets and examples of common topics such as diversification to help you learn to invest.

WEISS RATINGS' REPORTS AND SERVICES

See pricing below for each report and service.

Ratings Online — An on-line summary covering an individual company's Weiss Risk Rating or an investment's unique Weiss Investment Rating with the factors contributing to that rating; available 24 hours a day by visiting www.WeissRatings.com. Price: $14.99 each.

Ratings Over the Phone — Call our customer hotline at 1-800-289-9222 to receive a rating over the telephone. Price: $19 each.

Unlimited Ratings Research — The ultimate research tool providing fast, easy online access to the very latest Weiss Risk Ratings and Weiss Investment Ratings (includes 4 quarterly editions of one guide). Price: $559 per industry, + $19.95 s/h.

WEISS RATINGS' REPORTS AND SERVICES continued

See pricing below for each report and service.

Rating Analysis Report — A detailed report on an individual company or investment including the rating and an in-depth analysis of each of the factors contributing to the rating. Price: $49 + $4.95 s/h.

Weiss Watchdog Service — An immediate notification service announcing any changes in a company's rating, plus a quarterly rating update. Price: $59 for first company, and $49 for each additional company.

WEISS RATINGS' CUSTOM REPORTS

Weiss Ratings is pleased to offer two customized options for receiving our data. Each taps into our vast data repositories and is designed to provide exactly the data you need. Choose from a variety of industries, companies, data variables, and delivery formats including print, Excel, SQL, Text or Access.

Call 1-800-289-9222 today for pricing.

Customized Reports - get right to the heart of your company's research and data needs with a report customized with just the data you need.

Complete Database Download - we design and deliver the database; you're then free to sort it, recalculate it, and format your results to suit your specific needs.

2 EASY WAYS TO ORDER

1. Call our Customer Hotline at 1-800-289-9222
2. Order Online at www.WeissRatings.com